FUNDAMENTALS OF INTERNATIONAL TAXATION

U.S. Taxation of Foreign Income and Foreign Taxpayers

1998-1999 EDITION

BORIS I. BITTKER
Sterling Professor of Law Emeritus, Yale University

LAWRENCE LOKKEN
High Culverhouse Eminent Scholar in Taxation,
University of Florida

Warren,
Gorham &
Lamont
RIA GROUP

For Claudia Anne

Preface

This volume consists of the nine chapters on international income taxation from the five volume treatise *Federal Taxation of Income, Estates and Gifts*. It is intended for use in a law or accounting course on the international income tax rules of the United States. It contains a Table of Cases, a Table of IRC Sections, and an Index covering only these nine chapters. Readers needing more complete tables should refer to the end matter for the entire treatise.

In my work on these chapters over the last 12 years, I have grappled with a problem that has also played a prominent role in my teaching of the international tax rules: how to deal with an explosive growth in detail in the statutes and regulations on U.S. international taxation.

Some of this growth has consisted of additional elaboration, sometimes reflecting new or revised policies, in rules dealing with familiar topics. Examples of this are the set of regulations issued in 1984 defining the phrase "income, war profits, and excess profits taxes" for purposes of the foreign tax credit (discussed in ¶ 69.4), the 1995 regulations on transfer pricing (chapter 79), and the 1997 regulations on withholding tax on U.S.-source payments to foreign persons (¶ 66.2B). The statutes and regulations governing transfers of property by U.S. persons to foreign corporations and vice versa (§ 367, discussed in ¶¶ 68.6, 68.7) have undergone repeated revisions, which sometimes increase complexity and sometimes decrease complexity but never operate on a level that could be described as anything but complex. The enactment in 1986 of statutory rules on foreign currencies, supplemented over the following 10 years by extensive regulations, brought this once-obscure subject to a prominent place in international tax practice.

Further proliferation of detail has consisted of full-scale development of some approaches found in the law in embryonic form when the first edition of this treatise was published in 1981. An example is the separate basket mechanism of § 904(d), which was adopted in 1986 but whose antecedents go back to the enactment in 1958 of a provision separately limiting the credit for foreign taxes on interest income. Also, the continuing debate over when and how the United States should tax foreign income beneficially owned by U.S. persons through foreign corporations was brought to a new plateau during the 1980s: Subpart F and related provisions, which were regarded for at least 20 years after their enactment in 1962 as the apex of complexity (¶ 68.2), were supplemented in 1986 with a complex and surprisingly far reaching set of rules for passive foreign investment companies (PFICs), which virtually compel U.S. shareholders of foreign corporations caught in this web to elect pass-through treatment for all corporate income (¶ 68.5). The interrelationships of the separate basket rules, subpart F, and the rules on PFICs continually surprise the most experienced scholars and practitioners of this area.

The last two decades have also seen the enactment of rules with little precedent in U.S. law. Until 1980, it was axiomatic that nonresident aliens and foreign corporations were not taxed by the United States on U.S.-source capital gains, but Congress cut a large hole in this exemption in 1980 by the enactment of § 897, which taxes foreign persons on gains on dispositions of interests in real property located in the United States (¶ 66.4). In 1984, the effectively connected income tax on foreign corporations doing business in the United States (¶ 66.4) was augmented by two additional taxes on these corporations that were previously unknown in this country: a branch profits tax intended to mimic the taxes that foreign shareholders of U.S. corporations pay on dividends and a branch-level interest tax designed to ensure that interest deducted by a foreign corporation in determining effectively connected income does not escape U.S. tax unless an equivalent interest payment by a domestic corporation would not be taxed (¶ 66.5). Tax minimization opportunities arising from the use of hybrid entities (entities classified as separately taxable corporations in one jurisdiction and as pass-through entities in another) were facilitated by the adoption in 1996 of check-the-box regulations allowing free taxpayer choice of classification for many types of entities, but these opportunities were attacked in 1997 by the enactment of a new statutory provision (§ 894(c)) and the promulgation of detailed regulations (¶ 66.2A.1).

Teaching an effective course in international taxation in the face of the bulk and complexity of these developments is a real challenge, and the challenge is surely even greater for students. Some respond to this challenge by searching for ways to teach and study the basic principles without bothering with the details. This approach, I fear, may leave students without a practical command over the material because few international tax problems can be addressed realistically with basic principles alone. Even when the answer to a problem depends on basic principles, it is usually necessary to place the problem in the context of a welter of detail in order to understand the role of the basic principles. The opposite approach, plowing through as much detail as time permits without spending much time thinking about whether it all adds up to anything, is likely to be equally futile. The volume of the material is overwhelming and students' retention of a mass of disconnected detail is likely to be minimal.

My approach to this dilemma is to push students into the details where real life problems tend to occur, but only after laying a foundation by identifying the policies and principles underlying those details. Also, as the details unfold through the course, students are urged to consider how they relate to the underlying policies and principles. This is not to say that all of the international tax rules can be justified as a rational working out of some overarching idea. However, identifying when the rules are out of tune with basic policies and principles is important to understanding the rules and how they might be applied by a court. Also, a sensitive student learns to treat dissonance as a signal to check on whether she is playing the right notes.

In addition to posing a daunting challenge, the complexity of the international tax rules offers a special opportunity to teachers and students. This complexity is an example (perhaps a preeminent example) of a phenomenon that pervades federal taxation today, and the course thus presents a valuable opportunity to explore the question, "Why is it so complicated?" Frustration with complexity in the tax laws has given currency to several conspiracy theories. Taxpayers sometimes believe that complexity was invented by tax practitioners to increase their incomes, and a few tax practitioners suspect dark conspiracies by staffers in Congress and the Treasury and IRS. Classroom discussion of conspiracy theories is not likely to be productive, but several alternative possibilities merit closer inspection.

For example, is complexity a necessary consequence of policy choices Congress has made, or does it arise from techniques employed to effectuate these policies? The tension between simplicity and equity has often been noted, as has the inherent complexity of an income tax. Is complexity in the international rules a necessary consequence of Congress searching for ways to effectuate an income tax fairly and rationally through the entirety of our economy, including those aspects that interface with the economies of other countries?

On the other hand, if complexity results from the way in which policy is effectuated, rather than the policies themselves, it is necessary to ask, "What is it in our political and bureaucratic culture that leads people to do things in such complicated ways?" Given the long history of complexity in U.S. tax laws, it is difficult to accept simple explanations attributing complexity to some group of people not knowing how to do their jobs or purposefully mucking things up. A phenomenon of such pervasiveness does not exist without reasons. The reasons for simplicity may be even more compelling, but no one will ever know unless the reasons for complexity are identified and analyzed.

Such an unwieldy subject as the underlying causes of complexity can hardly be a primary focus of a crowded course such as international taxation. It would be a shame, however, to let the opportunity pass without some meaningful consideration.

Lawrence Lokken

March 1998

Summary of Contents

Table of Contents

TABLE OF CONTENTS

Chapter 66

NONRESIDENT ALIENS, FOREIGN CORPORATIONS, AND OTHER FOREIGN PERSONS

TABLE OF CONTENTS

TABLE OF CONTENTS

Chapter 67

U.S. POSSESSIONS

Chapter 68

SPECIAL TAXPAYERS AND PROBLEMS

TABLE OF CONTENTS

TABLE OF CONTENTS

TABLE OF CONTENTS

Chapter 69

FOREIGN TAX CREDIT

TABLE OF CONTENTS

Chapter 70

SOURCES OF INCOME

TABLE OF CONTENTS

Chapter 71

FOREIGN CURRENCIES

Chapter 79

REALLOCATION OF INCOME AND
DEDUCTIONS AMONG RELATED TAXPAYERS

TABLE OF CONTENTS

TABLE OF CONTENTS

Chapter 134

SPECIALLY TREATED TAXPAYERS

CHAPTER
65

Introduction, Classification of Individuals and Entities, and Special Rules for U.S. Persons

¶65.1 SUMMARY OF U.S. INTERNATIONAL TAX RULES

¶65.1.1 Introductory

There are two bases on which countries typically exercise income tax jurisdiction—connections between the taxpayer and the taxing country and connections between the taxpayer's income and that country.[1] Under U.S. law,

---

[1] The international tax provisions of the Code have been the subject of an extensive study by the American Law Institute, which culminated in numerous proposals for reform, some of which were enacted in 1986. ALI, United States Taxation of Foreign Persons and of the Foreign Income of United States Persons (1987).

Other general works covering the taxation of foreign income and foreign taxpayers include Doernberg, International Taxation in a Nutshell (West 3d ed. 1997); Isenbergh, International Taxation: U.S. Taxation of Foreign Taxpayers and Foreign Income (Little, Brown, 2d Ed. 1995); Kuntz & Peroni, U.S. International Taxation (Warren Gorham Lamont 1992); McIntyre, International Income Tax Rules of the United States (Butterworths 1989); Roberts & Warren, U.S. Income Taxation of Foreign Corporations and Nonresident Aliens (PLI 1966); Krause & Dam, Federal Tax Treatment of Foreign Income (Brookings 1964) (policy issues); Choate, Hurok & Klein, Federal Tax Policy for Foreign Income and Foreign Taxpayers, 44 Temp. LQ 441 (1971); Dale, Tax Accounting for Foreign Persons, 37 Tax L. Rev. 275 (1982); Frisch, The Economics of International Tax Policy: Some Old and New Approaches, 47 Tax Notes 581 (May 2, 1990); Graetz & O'Hear, The "Original Intent" of U.S. International Taxation, 46 Duke LJ 1021 (1997); Ross, U.S. International Tax Policy: Where Are We? Where Should We Be Going? 47 Tax Notes 331 (Apr. 18, 1990); Ross, National Versus International Approaches to Cross-Border Tax Issues, 54 Tax Notes 589 (Feb. 3, 1992). See also Bruce, IRS International Tax Training Materials: What International Examiners Are Taught, 14 Tax Notes Int'l 1003 (Mar. 24, 1997); Kay, European Tax Harmonization and the Implications for U.S. Tax Policy, 19 BC Int'l & Comp. L Rev. 109 (1996); Owens & Hovemeyer, Bibliography on Taxation of Foreign Operations and Foreigners, 1976-1982 and 1968-1975 (Harvard Law School International Tax Program 1975 and 1983).

taxpayer connections are the basis for taxing U.S. citizens and residents and domestic corporations, and income connections are the basis on which all other taxpayers are taxed. The application of this approach, and various extensions of and deviations from the approach, are described briefly below and are elaborated upon throughout this and the following five chapters.

¶65.1.2 U.S. Persons

1. *Generally.* U.S. citizens, alien individuals residing in the United States, and corporations organized under the laws of the United States or one of the states (domestic corporations) are taxed by the United States on all of their income, regardless of geographic origin—that is, on worldwide income.[2] Many (perhaps most) countries tax residents and domestic corporations on worldwide income, but the United States is virtually unique in taxing its citizens on worldwide income, even if they have resided outside the United States for years for reasons wholly unrelated to taxes.

The rule on taxing U.S. persons on worldwide income arises more by indirection than by explicit statutory command: Since §61 does not distinguish between domestic and foreign income, foreign income is taxable unless expressly excluded from gross income. Foreign income of nonresident aliens and foreign corporations is ordinarily excluded.[3] No similar exclusion is allowed to citizens, resident aliens, and domestic corporations, and they are accordingly taxed on worldwide income except in special circumstances described below.[4]

For challenges to international tax systems posed by widening business uses of advanced electronic systems, see U.S. Treasury, Selected Tax Policy Implications of Global Electronic Commerce (1996); Dunahoo & Carlisle, Cybertax 1.0: The U.S. Treasury Paper on Electronic Commerce, 74 Tax Notes 1321 (Mar. 10, 1997).

[2] For the distinction between resident and nonresident aliens, see infra ¶65.2. For the distinction between domestic and foreign corporations, partnerships, trusts, and estates, see infra ¶65.3.

There are relatively few tax cases on the occasionally troublesome issue of an individual's citizenship, which may rest on complex naturalization laws with constitutional overtones. See US v. Rexach, 558 F2d 37 (1st Cir. 1977) (naturalized citizen who lost citizenship under law later held unconstitutional was taxable as citizen for part of prior period); Rev. Rul. 70-506, 1970-2 CB 1 (similar result); Rev. Rul. 75-357, 1975-2 CB 5 (individual who lost citizenship under statute that Supreme Court would now hold unconstitutional is and always has been citizen); Rev. Rul. 75-82, 1975-1 CB 5 (foreign-born individual obtaining U.S. citizenship as a minor when parents were naturalized remains a citizen despite residence in country of birth, in absence of acts to abandon nationality). As to the status of persons renouncing U.S. citizenship, see Dillin v. CIR, 56 TC 228 (1971) (acq.) (taxpayer abandoned citizenship and became nonresident alien); US v. Matheson, 532 F2d 809 (2d Cir.), cert. denied, 429 US 823 (1976) (renunciation of U.S. citizenship ineffective); see also infra ¶65.4 (regarding tax-motivated expatriation).

[3] IRC §§872(a), 882(b).

[4] See Rev. Rul. 74-351, 1974-2 CB 144 (election to defer U.S. taxation of "blocked foreign income," defined as income that cannot readily be converted into U.S. dollars

In *Cook v. Tait*, the Supreme Court held that neither the U.S. Constitution nor international law is violated by U.S. taxation of the worldwide income of citizens who reside and are permanently domiciled in a foreign country and who receive their income from property located there. In response to the taxpayer's charge that the United States acted beyond its territorial jurisdiction in taxing a nonresident citizen on income derived from property situated in Mexico, the Court stated:

> [The taxing power] is based on the presumption that government by its very nature benefits the citizen and his property wherever found. ... Or to express it another way, the basis of the power to tax was not and cannot be made dependent upon the situs of the property in all cases, it being in or out of the United States, and was not and cannot be made dependent upon the domicile of the citizen, that being in or out of the United States, but upon his relation as citizen to the United States and the relation of the latter to him as citizen. The consequence of the relations is that the native citizen who is taxed may have domicile, and the property from which his income is derived may have situs, in a foreign country and the tax be legal—the government having power to impose the tax.[5]

The Court might have added that a U.S. citizen's worldwide income is a better measure of his ability to pay taxes—or, at least, that Congress could properly have so believed—than income from domestic sources alone. Although *Cook v. Tait* involved a U.S. citizen, the benefit rationale of the decision clearly encompasses domestic corporations as well as resident aliens.[6]

It is not clear why the Court did not refer in *Cook v. Tait* to the sixteenth amendment, which confers on Congress the power to tax income "from whatever source derived." Perhaps, it did not wish to rely on language whose purpose has no relationship to *geographical* sources.[7] Another possibility is that construing the sixteenth amendment to obliterate any distinction between foreign and domestic income would imply that Congress could tax the worldwide income of persons with minimal or even accidental contacts with the United States, such as passengers on a foreign aircraft landing in the United States while on a flight

---

because of monetary or exchange restrictions imposed by foreign government); Berman v. CIR, 45 TCM (CCH) 1357 (1983) (where taxpayer did not follow deferral procedures of Rev. Rul. 74-351, gain on sale of condominium in Spain was taxable in year of sale, notwithstanding exchange restrictions, because taxpayer could have spent sale proceeds locally).

[5] Cook v. Tait, 265 US 47, 56 (1924). See Skiriotes v. Florida, 313 US 69, 73 (1941) (sustaining constitutionality of Florida statute governing conduct of American citizens in Gulf of Mexico beyond territorial limits of Florida; "the United States is not debarred by any rule of international law from governing the conduct of its own citizens upon the high seas or even in foreign countries when the rights of other nations or other nationals are not infringed").

[6] See National Paper & Type Co. v. Bowers, 266 US 373 (1924) (New Jersey corporations not denied due process by subjection to tax from which foreign corporations are exempt).

[7] For the background of the sixteenth amendment, see supra ¶1.1.3.

from Canada to Mexico because of adverse weather conditions. Despite the unqualified reference in the sixteenth amendment to income "from whatever source derived," it was surely not intended to transcend limitations imposed by the due process clause of the fifth amendment or by international law on the power of Congress to tax persons with no significant American ties, although these limitations are concerned with such extreme circumstances that they are inconsequential for practical purposes.[8]

Although the taxpayer in *Cook v. Tait* did not allege that his Mexican income was taxed where earned, it is quite clear that the taxpayer would have lost even if the result were double taxation of the foreign income. To mitigate or eliminate international double taxation, however, the United States relies on two important devices. First, bilateral income tax treaties with many countries exempt American nationals from foreign taxes on some types of income (e.g., interest and royalties) and reduce the rate on other receipts (e.g., dividends), in exchange for parallel concessions by the United States to the other country's nationals.[9] Second, foreign income taxes paid by citizens, resident aliens, and domestic corporations usually qualify for a credit against the U.S. tax on foreign income, subject to limitations discussed below.[10]

2. *Credit for foreign income taxes.* The rules on taxing U.S. citizens and residents and domestic corporations are importantly modified by §901, which allows a credit against U.S. tax for income taxes paid to foreign countries.[11] The credit is an expression of a consensus generally observed by all countries—that the country of source has the first crack at taxing income and that the country of the taxpayer's residence has only a residual right to tax the income. If income were fully taxed both in the source country and the country of the taxpayer's residence, the resulting double taxation would put cross-border investments and transactions at a disadvantage in comparison with investments and transactions confined to the taxpayer's home country—a disadvantage frequently substantial enough to make international investments and business infeasible. Most countries, including the United States, have entered into numerous bilateral income tax treaties that limit taxation in the source country, but the international consensus is that to the extent taxation at the source is not eliminated by treaty, the burden of eliminating double taxation rests with the residence country.

Many foreign countries effectuate this consensus by exempting residents from tax on certain classes of foreign source income that are likely to be taxed in the country of origin—primarily, income from the active conduct of business in a foreign country. The United States (like most other English-speaking countries) instead uses a credit system under which foreign income taxes are credited

---

[8] See DeGanay v. Lederer, 250 US 376 (1919) (nonresident alien taxable on property with U.S. situs); Norr, Jurisdiction to Tax and International Income, 17 Tax L. Rev. 431 (1962).

[9] See infra ¶66.2.

[10] See infra ¶69.1.

[11] See infra ¶69.1.

against U.S. tax.[12] Thus, if foreign income of a U.S. corporation is taxed at 25 percent in the country of source and the U.S. tax rate is 35 percent, the U.S. tax is 10 percent (precredit U.S. tax of 35 percent less credit for the 25 percent foreign tax).

Generally, the credit may not exceed the precredit U.S. tax on foreign source income.[13] Assume a domestic corporation's taxable income is $1,000, including foreign source income of $100 on which foreign income taxes of $40 are imposed, and the corporation's precredit U.S. tax is $350. The credit is limited to $35—the foreign source income (before taxes), multiplied by the ratio of the precredit U.S. tax to entire taxable income:

$$(\$100)(\$350/\$1,000) = \$35$$

After credit, the U.S. tax on the foreign income is zero (35 percent of $100 less $35), and the foreign tax of $40 is the only tax on the income. The $5 by which the foreign tax exceeds the credit is carried to other years, but will never be creditable unless the limitation for a carryover year is less than the taxes paid for that year.[14] Generally, the total after-credit tax on foreign source income is at the U.S. rate or the foreign rate, whichever is higher.

When a domestic corporation receives dividends from a foreign corporation in which it has a 10 percent or greater voting interest, it is treated as having paid a ratable share of the foreign income taxes imposed on the foreign corporation.[15] The deemed paid taxes are treated as additional dividend income and are also allowed as a foreign tax credit, subject to the same limitations that apply to taxes actually paid by the domestic corporation. Assume domestic corporation D owns all of the stock of foreign corporation F, which has earnings and profits of $600, has paid foreign income taxes of $400, and distributes a dividend of $120 to D. D is treated as having paid foreign income taxes actually imposed on F as follows:

$$(\$400)(\$120/\$600) = \$80$$

The $80 is treated as additional dividend income to D, giving it total dividends of $200 (sum of $120 and $80). If this comprises all of D's foreign income and foreign income taxes, D is allowed a foreign tax credit of $70—the lesser of the foreign income taxes deemed paid ($80) or the precredit U.S. tax on the foreign income (35 percent of $200).

3. *Exemption for foreign earned income.* The United States uses an exemption system in one context. Section 911 allows a U.S. citizen residing in a foreign country to exclude from gross income up to $70,000 annually of earned income

---

[12] For the term "foreign income tax," see infra ¶69.4.

[13] See infra ¶69.5.

[14] See infra ¶69.5.4.

[15] See infra ¶69.8.

from sources outside the United States.[16] The exclusion is also allowed to a U.S. citizen or resident who is present in a foreign country for at least 330 days during a 12-month period. Foreign taxes on the excluded income do not qualify for the foreign tax credit. The exclusion thus is valuable only for individuals working in countries that tax their wages and salaries at rates lower than the U.S. rates. Because U.S. tax rates are relatively low by world standards, §911 is principally advantageous to U.S. citizens and residents who work in countries without developed income tax systems or who qualify for exemption or some other special treatment in the countries in which they work.

¶65.1.3 Foreign Persons

1. *Generally.* Foreign persons—aliens who do not reside in the United States and foreign corporations (corporations organized under the laws of a foreign country or U.S. possession)—are only taxed by the United States on income originating in the United States. U.S. law contains two systems for taxing foreign persons on U.S. income. If a nonresident alien individual or foreign corporation carries on a trade or business in the United States, the person is taxed at the regular rates of §1 or §11 on taxable income that is effectively connected with the U.S. business.[17] If a foreign person has U.S. source income that is not effectively connected with a U.S. business (either because the person has no such business or because the income is not related to the business), the income may be taxed at a flat rate of 30 percent (or lower rate provided by bilateral treaty).[18] The effectively connected income tax and the 30 percent tax differ most radically in the allowability of deductions. Effectively connected taxable income is determined on a net basis with deductions for all otherwise deductible items that are directly connected with the effectively connected income. The 30 percent tax is a gross income tax; no deductions are allowed.

There is an important reason for this distinction in the allowability of deductions. At an early date in the history of the income tax laws, Congress concluded that because the conduct of a trade or business in the United States usually entails a physical presence in the country, it is feasible for tax on the income of such a business to be computed, imposed, and collected in essentially the same ways as for citizens, residents, and domestic corporations. The self-assessment system for domestic taxpayers thus applies to the effectively connected income of nonresident aliens and foreign corporations. Congress recognized, however, that self-assessment is not a feasible means of taxing income of foreign persons not engaged in business in the United States. For example, if a nonresident alien author has a book published in the United States under a

---

[16] See infra ¶65.5.
[17] See infra ¶66.3.
[18] See infra ¶66.2.

contract requiring the publisher to pay royalties to the author, there is little chance of the United States ever collecting tax on the royalties once they leave the country. The tax on nonbusiness income of foreigners thus is enforced by requiring that it be withheld by the U.S. persons who pay the income to the foreign recipients. In the example, the U.S. publisher must withhold and remit to the IRS 30 percent of the royalties payable to the nonresident alien author. This withholding tax is unlike the system for withholding tax from wages because it is not expected that the foreign taxpayer will file a return at the end of the year. It thus is necessary that the amount withheld be precisely equal to the tax. Because the U.S. payor has no way of knowing what deductions the foreign taxpayer has, the amount withheld and the tax can be made equal only if deductions are not allowed in either the withholding system or the tax computation.

The lack of deductions in determining U.S. tax on nonbusiness income of nonresident aliens and foreign corporations creates considerable pressure for the U.S. to mitigate or waive the tax. Assume a foreign bank buys a bond issued by a U.S. corporation. The bond is purchased largely with depositors' money, and the bank's net income from the bond investment is thus reduced by interest on depositors' funds. For example, if the bank receives 10 percent interest on the bond, it may have interest expense allocable to the bond of 8 percent. If so, a 30 percent tax on gross interest income is 150 percent of net interest income. In 1984, Congress responded to this problem by exempting from the 30 percent tax all "portfolio interest," defined to include all interest from U.S. sources, excepting interest on some unregistered obligations and interest on bank loans and on obligations held by 10 percent or greater owners of the debtor.[19]

However, the 30 percent tax can also have a very high percentage of net income in other situations (e.g., royalties on a U.S. license of property developed by a foreign corporation at a substantial cost), and the only possible defense against the tax in these cases is a tax treaty. The United States has bilateral income tax treaties with about 50 countries (including substantially all of the economically developed countries of the world and many developing countries), and the 30 percent tax is one of the principal subjects of these treaties. Most of them follow a pattern established by a Model Treaty promulgated by the Organisation for Economic Cooperation and Development (OECD), an organization of the developed countries. The U.S. Treasury has had its own model, which essentially serves as the United States' opening offer in treaty negotiations, but the U.S. model follows the OECD in most particulars. Typically, an income tax treaty reduces the 30 percent tax on dividends to 15 percent (5 percent on dividends from subsidiary to parent), and the treaties either exempt U.S. source interest and royalties from the tax or reduce the tax on this income (often to 10 percent).

2. *Gains on sales of property.* Congress decided more than 50 years ago to exempt foreign persons from U.S. tax on most nonbusiness capital gains. Because

---

[19] See infra ¶66.2.2.

a buyer generally has no way of knowing a foreign seller's basis, tax on such gains could feasibly be collected only by withholding at source on the gross sales proceeds, but a tax on gross sales proceeds would often bite so hard as to discourage foreign investment in the United States.

In 1980, however, Congress enacted the Foreign Investors Real Property Tax Act (FIRPTA), which withdraws this exemption for gains on sales of U.S. real property.[20] In formulating FIRPTA, Congress realized that if the tax extended only to gains on direct sales of real property, foreign investors would avoid the tax by holding U.S. real property through domestic corporations and selling their stock, rather than the real property. FIRPTA therefore treats as effectively connected income any gain on the sale of a U.S. real property interest, defined to include real property located in the United States and stock of a domestic corporation if U.S. real property constitutes at least 50 percent, by value, of the corporation's assets. A buyer of a U.S. real property interest from a foreign person is required to withhold 10 percent of the selling price to cover the tax, but the withholding is only tentative, subject to adjustment on the filing of a return by the foreign taxpayer; also, by an advance ruling procedure, the amount withheld can be tailored more closely to the ultimate tax liability.

3. *Branch taxes.* In 1986, Congress enacted a branch profits tax and a branch-level interest tax applicable only to foreign corporations carrying on business through unincorporated branches in the United States.[21] If a foreign corporation does business in the United States through a U.S. subsidiary, profits of the subsidiary distributed to the shareholder as dividends are subject to two U.S. taxes—the corporate income tax and the 30 percent tax on the dividends. The branch profits tax—a tax on profits earned in the United States through an unincorporated branch and repatriated by the foreign owner of the branch—is intended to be comparable to the 30 percent tax that would apply if the branch were incorporated as a U.S. subsidiary. If a U.S. subsidiary borrows from abroad, interest on the debt is generally deductible by the corporation, but it is U.S. source income to the creditor, which may be subject to the 30 percent tax. The branch-level interest tax is intended to be a comparable levy on interest deducted by an unincorporated U.S. branch of a foreign corporation.

¶65.1.4 Foreign Corporations With U.S. Owners

A foreign corporation is not subject to U.S. tax on any income that is neither from U.S. sources nor effectively connected with a U.S. business. This exemption is unquestionably appropriate for foreign corporations that are owned by foreigners, but it is the root of endless controversy in its application to foreign corporations owned by U.S. persons (e.g., a foreign subsidiary of a domestic corporation). Normally, when a U.S. person is a shareholder of a U.S. corpora-

---

[20] See infra ¶66.4.
[21] See infra ¶66.5.

tion, the shareholder is taxed only on dividends and gains on sales of stock, not on the corporation's undistributed earnings, but because the corporation is itself taxed on its worldwide income, none of the income beneficially owned by the shareholder escapes current taxation. In contrast, if a U.S. person is a shareholder of a foreign corporation whose property and business activities are located wholly outside the United States, the corporation pays no U.S. tax, and under the normal rules, the shareholder pays no U.S. tax on the corporation's earnings until they are distributed as dividends. By the mere expedient of putting foreign operations or investments in a foreign corporation, the U.S. person thus avoids current U.S. taxation of income beneficially owned by the U.S. person.

1. *Foreign personal holding companies.* Congress has repeatedly narrowed, but never wholly eliminated, this opportunity to defer tax. In 1937, it adopted the rules on foreign personal holding companies, under which a foreign corporation is treated as a pass-through entity (like a partnership) if (1) more than 50 percent of its stock is owned by five or fewer U.S. citizens or residents and (2) most of its income consists of dividends, interest, royalties, gains from stocks, securities, and commodities trading, and a few other designated sources.[22] The principal target of these rules is the foreign incorporated pocketbook of U.S. individuals, and the rules have no application to a foreign corporation that is a subsidiary of a widely held domestic corporation.

2. *Controlled foreign corporations.* In 1962, Congress adopted subpart F of subchapter N of chapter 1 of subtitle A of the Code, which uses a somewhat different pass-through technique.[23] The subpart F rules apply only if a foreign corporation is a controlled foreign corporation—that is, if at least 50 percent of a foreign corporation's stock, by vote or by value, is owned by U.S. persons (both individual and corporate), counting only persons owning more than 10 percent of the voting stock. When applicable, the subpart F rules tax U.S. shareholders on their ratable shares of several categories of corporate income, whether distributed or not, including (1) dividends, interest, royalties, and other passive income, (2) income from sales of goods where the foreign corporation either buys from or sells to or on behalf of a related person, (3) income from services performed for or on behalf of related persons, and (4) income from shipping operations. Also, if the foreign corporation invests substantial accumulated earnings in passive assets, these earnings are taxed to the U.S. shareholders, regardless of the source of the earnings.

A principal purpose of subpart F is to tax U.S. shareholders on income of their foreign corporations from tax haven investments and activities—that is, investments and activities organized or carried on in a way likely to avoid substantial foreign taxation, as well as U.S. tax. Assume a domestic corporation organizes a subsidiary corporation in a country that taxes local corporations only on income from business conducted within that country; the domestic parent

---

[22] See infra ¶68.3.
[23] See infra ¶68.2.

sells goods it manufactures to the foreign subsidiary, and the subsidiary resells the goods to foreign distributors. The subsidiary buys and resells the goods under continuing contracts arranged by the efforts of employees of the parent, and the goods are shipped directly from the domestic corporation's plants in the United States to the foreign distributors. The subsidiary has no full-time employees, and its only presence in the country of its incorporation is through a law office in that country. Because the subsidiary effectuates its transactions with very little activity, it easily arranges not to be subject to tax in either the United States or the foreign countries in which the goods are sold to consumers, and the country of incorporation does not tax the income because the subsidiary is not engaged in business in that country. The subsidiary thus pays no income taxes to any country. Until 1962, the subsidiary's income was taxed only when it was distributed to the parent as dividends. Subpart F, however, includes the subsidiary's income in the parent's U.S. gross income as it is earned, effectively treating the subsidiary as a pass-through entity.

In contrast, assume a domestic corporation has a foreign subsidiary that manufactures goods in a foreign country. The subsidiary's undistributed income is not taxed to the shareholders under the primary rules of subpart F because manufacturing is not a tax haven activity. Income from manufacturing is normally taxed as local source income by the country in which the manufacturing occurs. Even if the country of the manufacturing operations does not tax the income from these operations (e.g., under a tax holiday given to encourage foreign investment), the pass-through rules do not apply because the principal purpose of subpart F is to curb tax avoidance schemes, not to attack the carrying on of substantial business activities in low-tax countries.

Another purpose of subpart F is to ensure that U.S. shareholders are taxed when foreign earnings are repatriated to the United States, whether this is done directly or indirectly. Assume the manufacturing subsidiary in the last example makes a loan to its domestic parent from funds accumulated from earnings of the manufacturing operations. The parent has the use of the funds earned abroad, essentially as it would if the funds had been distributed as a dividend. The same would be true if the subsidiary purchased newly issued stock of the parent. Congress decided that because such investments have essentially the same economic effect as dividends, they should be taxed as dividends.

A provision related to subpart F (although found elsewhere in the Code) characterizes gain on a sale of stock of a controlled foreign corporation as dividend income to the extent of the corporate earnings that are ratably attributable to the stock and were accumulated while the selling shareholder owned the stock (exclusive of earnings already taxed to the shareholder under the pass-through mechanism described above).[24] The original purpose of this provision was to block U.S. shareholders of foreign corporations from cashing in their investments at the sole U.S. tax cost of a capital gains tax. However, if the shareholder is a

---

[24] IRC §1248, discussed infra ¶68.2.15.

domestic corporation, a principal effect of the dividend characterization is to allow the shareholder credit for foreign income taxes paid by the foreign corporation, thereby usually reducing the tax on the gain below that which would be imposed if the gain were treated as capital gain.

3. *Passive foreign investment companies.* Subpart F applies only if more than 50 percent of a foreign corporation's stock is owned by "U.S. shareholders" (U.S. persons owning at least 10 percent of the voting stock), and when it applies, subpart F taxes U.S. shareholders only on their ratable shares of the corporation's tax haven income and income indirectly repatriated to the United States. A separate set of rules for passive foreign investment companies (PFICs) is designed to curb tax avoidance through minority ownership in foreign corporations.[25]

A foreign corporation is a PFIC if 75 percent or more of its income is passive (e.g., dividends, interest, and gains from sales of securities) or if 50 percent or more of its assets are productive of passive income. The proportion of the corporation's stock that is held by U.S. persons is not relevant. A PFIC can make an election under which U.S. persons owning shares treat the PFIC as a pass-through entity under rules similar to those applicable to U.S. mutual funds. If the election is made, a U.S. shareholder is taxed on a ratable share of all corporate income, passive and nonpassive. If the election is not made, the PFIC and U.S. persons owning shares are governed by the general rules; the PFIC is taxed only on U.S. source income and income effectively connected with U.S. businesses, and shareholders are taxed only on dividends and gains on sales of shares. U.S. shareholders of a nonelecting PFIC, however, are subject to an interest charge on the U.S. tax on a gain on a sale of stock or a large dividend. The interest charge is generally computed as though the shareholder had been taxed on a ratable portion of the gain or dividend for each year the stock was held and these taxes had been loaned back to the shareholders. The interest computation contains many approximations, most of which are disadvantageous to taxpayers and therefore tend to discourage U.S. persons from owning shares of nonelecting PFICs.

4. *Foreign Sales Corporations.* Congress went radically in the opposite direction with a set of rules for Foreign Sales Corporations (FSCs), which are closely held foreign corporations (usually owned by U.S. persons) that meet several requirements, most of which are relatively formalistic.[26] Income of an FSC from exports of goods and services produced in the United States is generally treated as foreign source income, not effectively connected with a U.S. trade or business, and is therefore generally exempt from U.S. taxation until it is distributed as dividends to U.S. shareholders. Economically, FSC income often derives largely from activities in the United States, and the FSC rules are intended to create an incentive for export sales without providing a subsidy for such sales that would violate international trade agreements.

---

[25] See infra ¶68.5.
[26] IRC §§921-927, discussed infra ¶68.1.4.

5. *Transfers to and from foreign corporations.* Gain on a U.S. person's transfer of property to a foreign corporation, partnership, estate, or trust is sometimes taxed even though the transfer is encompassed by a nonrecognition rule.[27] Also, U.S. shareholders of foreign corporations are sometimes taxed on their shares of accumulated corporate earnings when the corporations liquidate or are absorbed into other corporations in reorganizations, even though the transactions would normally yield capital gains or losses or fall within nonrecognition rules.[28]

These rules were adopted to recognize the special status of foreign corporations owned by U.S. persons. Because a U.S. person is taxed on gains and losses on sales and exchanges of property, but foreign corporations usually are not, Congress decided that nonrecognition rules for transfers to foreign corporations had to be modified in order to block U.S. persons from utilizing foreign corporations to make tax-free roll-overs from investment to investment. Because the earnings of domestic corporations are normally taxed as realized, while the earnings of foreign corporations (even foreign corporations owned by U.S. persons) are subject to U.S. tax only if they originate in the United States, Congress wanted to make sure that foreign earnings beneficially owned by U.S. shareholders were ultimately subjected to an ordinary income tax, not cashed out as capital gains or avoided by nonrecognition transactions.

¶65.1.5 U.S. Possessions

The term "United States" is defined to include only the states and the District of Colombia.[29] Puerto Rico and the U.S. possessions are generally treated as foreign countries for U.S. income tax purposes, and corporations organized under their laws are generally treated as foreign corporations.[30]

Individuals who reside in a U.S. possession but are not U.S. citizens are treated as nonresident aliens for U.S. tax purposes, but citizens of the United States residing in the possessions are generally subject to U.S. tax on worldwide income, just like citizens residing in the United States proper. However, worldwide income taxation is mitigated under a series of special rules, which exempt residents of the possessions from U.S. taxation, in whole or in part.[31]

---

[27] IRC §367(a), discussed infra ¶68.6.

[28] IRC §367(b), discussed infra ¶68.7.

[29] IRC §7701(a)(9).

[30] See infra ¶67.1.

[31] IRC §931 (for residents of Guam, American Samoa, or Northern Mariana Islands, U.S. gross income does not include income from sources within that possession or income effectively connected with conduct of trade or business in possession), discussed infra ¶67.5; §932 (bona fide resident of Virgin Islands computes tax on worldwide income under U.S. Internal Revenue Code, but files return with and pays tax to Virgin Islands), discussed infra ¶67.4; §933 (for bona fide resident of Puerto Rico, income from sources in Puerto Rico is excluded from U.S. gross income), discussed infra ¶67.3.

Also, a controversial provision largely exempts from U.S. taxation the income of a domestic corporation that is actively engaged in business in a U.S. possession (including Puerto Rico) and meets various other qualification criteria.[32] This exemption generally applies only to income from businesses carried on in the possessions, but when applicable, it exempts both the corporation from U.S. tax on the income as it is earned and the corporation's shareholders from tax on dividends distributed from the income.

¶65.1.6   Bilateral Income Tax Treaties

The United States has entered into numerous bilateral income tax treaties, which affect in various ways the U.S. taxation of residents of the countries with which the treaties were made and also have some effects on the U.S. taxation of U.S. citizens, residents, and corporations.[33] For example, treaties usually bar the United States from taxing the business profits of a resident of a treaty country unless the person has a permanent establishment in the United States, and if the taxpayer has a U.S. permanent establishment, only profits attributable to the permanent establishment may be taxed by the United States.[34]

The U.S. Treasury Department issued a model income tax treaty in 1981, which it uses in formulating its initial position in treaty negotiations, and it extensively revised this model in 1996.[35] The Treasury model closely resembles a

---

[32] IRC §936, discussed infra ¶67.2.

[33] For a list of tax treaties in force as of March 31, 1998, and other information about treaties, international tax agreements, and negotiations in progress, see Fogarasi, Gordon, Venuti & Renfroe, Current Status of U.S. Tax Treaties, 27 Tax Mgmt. Int'l J. 252 (1998). For an index as of October 1, 1995, of all tax treaties to which the United States is a party and of various documents relating to these treaties, see Worldwide Tax Treaty Index 195, 205 (Tax Analysts 1995). For a list of treaties as of November 1992 and a summary of tax exemptions provided by treaties for individuals working or otherwise present in the United States, see IRS Pub. No. 901, U.S. Tax Treaties (Rev. Nov. 1992).

See generally ABA Section of Taxation Committee on U.S. Activities of Foreigners and Tax Treaties, Issues Paper on the Tax Treaty Making Process, 46 Tax Lawyer 477 (1993) (discussing lack of public participation in treaty-making process and congressional overrides of income tax treaties); Berman, Covering the World: The Expanding U.S. Tax Treaty Network, 74 Taxes 1064 (1996); Roin, Rethinking Tax Treaties in a Strategic World With Disparate Tax Systems, 81 Va. L. Rev. 1753 (1995) (discussing implications for treaty policy of foreign corporate tax integration systems and lower U.S. corporate tax rates) Tillinghast, Tax Treaty Issues, 50 U. Miami L. Rev. 455 (1996).

See also Notice 97-40, 1997-28 IRB 6 (Hong Kong is not covered by U.S.-China tax convention because Chinese tax laws do not apply there); Brewer, Unilateral Speculation on the Question of Hong Kong, 76 Tax Notes 1355 (Sept. 8, 1997); Cohen, Pollack & Scherer, Analysis of the New U.S.-Switzerland Income Tax Treaty, 26 Tax Mgmt. Int'l J. 47 (1997).

[34] See infra ¶66.3.9.

[35] United States Model Income Tax Convention of September 20, 1996. See Majure & Lindholm, New U.S. Model Treaty Broadens Scope of Residence and Increases Avail-

model treaty promulgated by the Organisation for Economic Co-operation and Development (OECD),[36] an organization of the industrialized countries of the world (who make up a majority of the United States' income tax treaty partners). Most income tax treaties made in recent decades conform in large part to the models. The model treaty rules are described in succeeding sections of this and succeeding Chapters in the discussions of the various statutory provisions that are affected by treaty rules. The Treasury's model also contains an overarching denial of treaty benefits to entities deemed to be treaty shopping.[37]

In rejecting an IRS contention that, in determining U.S. tax consequences, a court should interpret a treaty "consistently with [U.S.] expectations and intentions" in making the treaty, the Tax Court offered the following comments on treaty interpretation:

> Courts liberally construe treaties to give effect to their purpose. ... Tax treaties are purposive, and, accordingly, we should consider the perceived underlying intent or purpose of the treaty provision. ... While the meaning attributed to treaty provisions by Government agencies charged with their negotiation and enforcement can be very helpful to us, and we give great weight to that meaning, ... deference is not ... blind acceptance. ... The deference afforded depends upon the degree to which the interpretation proffered by respondent, as the official U.S. position, is reasonable, unbiased, and consistent with what appear to be the circumstances surrounding the convention.[38]

Article VI, clause 2 of the U.S. Constitution states: "Laws of the United States which shall be made in Pursuance thereof; and all Treaties made, or which

---

ability of Benefits to "Fiscally Transparent Entities" and Their Members, 8 J. Int'l Tax'n 164 (1997); Majure & Lindholm, New U.S. Model Treaty Revises Business Profits, Residence Rules, 7 J. Int'l Tax'n 532 (1996); Ruchelman, Highlights of Revised Model Income Tax Treaty Issued by U.S. Treasury Department, 25 Tax Mgmt. Int'l J. 803 (1996). The model treaty and an accompanying technical explanation are reproduced in Berman, Covering the World: The Expanding U.S. Tax Treaty Network, 74 Taxes 1064 (1996).

[36] OECD Comm. on Fiscal Affairs, Model Tax Convention on Income and on Capital (OECD 1995). The OECD Model, which was issued in 1977, was updated in 1992, 1994, and 1995, and the updating is expected to continue. See Owens, A Report on the Current Work Program of the OECD Committee on Fiscal Affairs, 9 Tax Notes Int'l 993 (Sept. 26, 1994). See also Tax Treaties: Linkages Between OECD Member Countries and Dynamic Non-Member Economies (Vann ed. OECD 1996).

The United Nations has promulgated a model treaty, designed for use in treaty negotiations between developed and developing countries. United Nations Model Double Taxation Convention Between Developed and Developing Counties (1981). The United Nations model also follows the OECD Model in most particulars, but it differs in several aspects of special interest to developing countries.

[37] See infra ¶66.2.11.

[38] North West Life Assurance Co. v. CIR, 107 TC No. 19 (1997). See Madole, U.S.-Canada Treaty Overrides Section 842(b): North West Life Assurance, 26 Tax Mgmt. Int'l J. 151 (1997); Smith, Tax Treaty Interpretation by the Judiciary, 49 Tax Lawyer 845 (1996).

shall be made, under the Authority of the United States, shall be the supreme Law of the Land." This provision has been construed to put statutes and treaties on a common footing.[39] When a statute and treaty conflict, the statute does not take precedence merely because it is a statute, but neither does the treaty prevail merely because it is a treaty. Instead, the conflict is generally resolved by applying an ancient common law rule, originally formulated for conflicts between statutes, that the one adopted last controls.[40] The courts, however, try to harmonize treaties and statutes, regardless of the order of adoption, under the same rules as are applied to seemingly conflicting statutes.[41] According to the Supreme Court, "a treaty will not be deemed to have been abrogated or modified by a later statute unless such purpose on the part of Congress has been clearly expressed."[42]

Traditionally, Congress has generally allowed income tax treaties to take precedence over income statutes. Until 1988, §894(a) stated, "Income of any kind, to the extent required by any treaty obligation of the United States, shall not be included in gross income and shall be exempt from [U.S. income] taxation," and §7852(d) stated, "No provision of this title shall apply in any case where its application would be contrary to any treaty obligation of the United States in effect on the date of enactment of this title."

In recent years, however, Congress has become less deferential to income tax treaties. Tax planners have utilized treaties to accomplish results that many in Congress have found abusive. The Treasury has responded by insisting that new treaties have an antishopping article,[43] but treaty shopping and other abuses have provoked congressional responses as well. Congress has often found that income tax treaties are an inconvenient restraint on the development of U.S. international tax policy. Because all income tax treaties are bilateral, the renegotiation of treaties is a complex process, and it takes decades to reflect a policy change in all of our treaties. For example, although the inclusion of an antishopping article has been Treasury policy for more than 15 years, some treaties do not yet contain such an article.

Congressional impatience with treaties also has a political aspect. The House of Representatives, which jealously guards its prerogatives in tax legislation, plays no role in the ratification of treaties. In the Senate, treaties come under the jurisdiction of the Foreign Affairs Committee, not the Finance Committee. That the Senate's responsibility is to ratify treaties already fully developed and agreed upon between governments contrasts sharply with the usual legislative process,

---

[39] Reid v. Covert, 354 US 1 (1957).

[40] See Sachs, Is the 19th Century Doctrine of Treaty Override Good Law for Modern Day Tax Treaties? 47 Tax Lawyer 867 (1994).

[41] See Whitney v. Robertson, 124 US 190 (1888).

[42] Cook v. US, 288 US 102, 120 (1933). But see S. Rep. No. 445, 100th Cong., 2d Sess. 325 (1988) (Cook does not require that "Congress must specifically advert to the treaties to have later statutes given effect," but mention of conflict in statute or legislative history is "dispositive" in favor of later statute).

[43] See infra ¶66.2.11.

where Congress need not wait for recommendations from the executive and may rework any recommendations it receives in any way it sees fit.

On several occasions, Congress has enacted provisions intended to override inconsistent treaties.[44] Also, in 1988, it revised §894(a) and enacted a battery of companion provisions. Section 894(a) now states, "The provisions of this title shall be applied to any taxpayer with due regard to any treaty obligation of the United States which applies to such taxpayer." Due regard is determined under §7852(d)(1), which states, "For purposes of determining the relationship between a provision of a treaty and any law of the United States affecting revenue, neither the treaty nor the law shall have preferential status by reason of its being a treaty or law."[45] The Senate Finance Committee described these provisions as follows:

> [T]he committee intends to permanently codify (with respect to tax-related provisions) present law to the effect that canons of construction applied by the courts to the interaction of two statutes enacted at different times apply also in construing the interactions of revenue statutes and treaties enacted and entered into at different times. The committee does not intend this modification to alter the initial presumption of harmony between, for example, earlier treaties and later statutes. Thus, for example, the bill continues to allow an earlier ratified treaty provision to continue in effect where there is not an actual conflict between that treaty provision and a subsequent revenue statute (i.e., where it is consistent with the intent of each provision to interpret them in a way that gives effect to both). Nor does the committee intend that this codification blunt in any way the superiority of the latest expression of the sovereign will in cases involving actual conflicts, whether that expression appears in a treaty or a statute.[46]

In response to those exclaiming in horror, "a deal's a deal, even between countries," the Committee stated:

> [W]hen a treaty partner's internal tax laws and policies change, treaty provisions designed and bargained to coordinate the predecessor laws and policies must be reviewed for purposes of determining how those provisions apply under the changed circumstances . . . . In some cases the continued effect of the existing treaty provision would be to give an unbargained-for benefit to taxpayers or one of the treaty partners. At that point, the treaty provision in question may no longer eliminate double taxation or prevent fiscal evasion; if not, its intended purpose would no longer be served.
>
> The committee recognizes that some would prefer that existing treaties be conformed to changing U.S. tax policy solely by treaty renegotiation.

---

[44] For an early example, see Pub. L. No. 87-834, §31, 76 Stat. 960 (1962); HR Rep. No. 1447, 87th Cong., 2d Sess. 96 (1962) (Revenue Act of 1962 expressly overrode inconsistent treaties "in the interest of forestalling any possible litigation").

[45] See HR Rep. No. 1104, 100th Cong., 2d Sess. 12 (Conf. Rep. 1988) ("in determining what regard is due to a treaty, reference must be made to the principle that neither the treaty nor any relevant law shall have preferential status by reason of its being a treaty or law").

[46] S. Rep. No. 445, supra note 42, at 321-322.

However, . . . in recent years, U.S. tax laws have been constantly changing. Moreover, once U.S. tax policy has changed, the existence of an unbargained-for benefit created by the change would have the effect of making renegotiation to reflect current U.S. tax policy extremely difficult, because the other country may have little or no incentive to remove an unbargained-for benefit whose cost is borne by the United States.[47]

Section 6114(a), also enacted in 1988, requires that a taxpayer who "takes the position that a treaty of the United States overrules (or otherwise modifies) an internal revenue law of the United States" must disclose this position on a statement attached to the taxpayer's return.[48] This rule requires disclosure, for example, whenever "the taxpayer takes a position in reliance on a treaty and that position is contrary to the result that a later-enacted statute would have dictated had the treaty not existed."[49] Section 6712 imposes a penalty on any taxpayer failing to disclose a treaty position as required by §6114(a). According to the Senate Finance Committee, these provisions were enacted "in the interest of bringing issues to light expeditiously and apprising the IRS in a timely manner of treaty claims whose merit is not now known."[50]

The disclosure rule applies whether the treaty believed to override a statutory tax rule is an income tax treaty, an estate and gift tax treaty, a friendship, commerce, and navigation treaty, or any other form of treaty obligation to which the United States is a party.[51] An override requiring disclosure occurs if (1) the taxpayer's tax for the taxable year, computed under the statutes without regard to any treaty, exceeds the tax reported on the taxpayer's return in reliance on a treaty rule, or (2) a carryback or carryover from the year is reported in an amount that exceeds the carryback or carryover allowable in the absence of all treaties.[52] The disclosure rule applies to an assertion that a treaty is consistent with but "alter[s] the scope of the Code provision."[53]

The regulations give several examples of return positions that must be disclosed under §6114, including a contention that (1) a Code provision violates a nondiscrimination rule in a treaty, (2) a treaty exempts a foreign corporation

---

[47] Id. at 378–379.

[48] For the contents of the statement, see Reg. §301.6114-1(d). The IRS has developed a form, Form 8833, for making the statement.

Section 6114 applies to a return if its due date (without extensions) is after 1988. See Reg. §301.6114-1(e).

[49] S. Rep. No. 445, supra note 42, at 377. See H.R. Rep. No. 1104, supra note 45, at 12.

[50] S. Rep. No. 445, supra note 42, at 322.

[51] Reg. §301.6114-1(a)(1)(i).

[52] Reg. §301.6114-1(a)(2)(i). See Reg. §301.6114-1(a)(3) Ex. 1 (disclosure required if treaty does not affect current tax but increases net operating loss carryback).

[53] Reg. §301.6114-1(a)(2)(ii).

from the branch profits tax or the branch-level interest tax,[54] (3) a foreign person's income effectively connected with a U.S. trade or business is exempt from U.S. taxation because it is not attributable to a permanent establishment,[55] (4) a treaty permits a foreign tax credit for a tax that is not creditable under the statutes, or (5) an alien individual's residence for U.S. tax purposes is determined under a treaty rather than under §7701(b).[56]

Moreover, a taxpayer's assertion that the disclosure rule is inapplicable must itself be disclosed unless this assertion "has a substantial probability of successful defense if challenged."[57] If the taxpayer's construction of a treaty obviates the need for the filing of a return, a return nevertheless must be filed in order to disclose the treaty position.[58]

However, the regulations also exempt several treaty-based positions from disclosure. For example, disclosure is excused if the otherwise reportable payments or income do not exceed $10,000 ($100,000 if the issue is determination of the taxpayer's residence).[59] Also, disclosure is not required where withholding tax on a foreign person's U.S. source dividends, interest, or other fixed or determinable annual or periodical income is reduced or eliminated by treaty unless the payment to the taxpayer is not properly disclosed by the payor to the IRS on a Form 1042S.[60] If a partnership, trust, or estate discloses a treaty-based position on its return in accordance with §6114, the partners or beneficiaries are not required to disclose the position on their individual returns even if their taxes are reduced by the entity's use of the treaty.[61]

When disclosure is not made as required by §6114, §6712 normally imposes a penalty of $10,000 if the taxpayer is a C corporation or $1,000 if the taxpayer is an individual, S corporation, partnership, trust, or estate. The penalty is separately imposed for each treaty-based position that is not disclosed.[62] More than one penalty can thus be incurred by a taxpayer in filing one return. No penalty is imposed, however, if the taxpayer's failure is not "material." Also, the IRS may waive the penalty on a showing that the failure to disclose was "not due to willful neglect."[63]

---

[54] For the branch taxes, see infra ¶66.5.

[55] For treaty limitations on the effectively connected income tax, see ¶66.3.9.

[56] Reg. §301.6114-1(b). The rule for residence determinations applies to returns due after December 15, 1997. Reg. §301.6114-1(b)(8). The form of disclosure is provided by the regulations under §7701(b). Reg. §301.7701(b)-7(b), discussed infra ¶65.2.8 note 89.

[57] Reg. §301.6114-1(a)(2)(iii).

[58] Reg. §301.6114-1(a)(1)(ii).

[59] Reg. §301.6114-1(c)(2).

[60] Reg. §301.6114-1(b)(4)(ii)(A).

[61] Reg. §301.6114-1(c)(4).

[62] Reg. §301.6712-1(a).

[63] Reg. §301.6712-1(b).

¶65.2   RESIDENT AND NONRESIDENT ALIENS

¶65.2.1   Introductory

Because resident aliens are taxed on worldwide income while nonresident aliens are taxed only on income that originates in the United States,[1] it is frequently necessary to distinguish between these two categories of taxpayers. Neither status is uniformly preferable to the other. Resident status has the disadvantage of requiring the alien to report worldwide income, but nonresident aliens cannot take certain deductions that are allowed to citizens and resident aliens.[2] Resident versus nonresident status is also important for many ancillary issues. For example, a nonresident alien spouse can join in a joint return only in the limited circumstances described in §§6013(g) and (h), and under §152(b)(3), some nonresident aliens cannot qualify as dependents.[3] Whether one set of disadvantages outweighs the other depends on the facts of each case and may vary from year to year with respect to any individual.

Until 1984, the statutes did not define the terms "resident" and "nonresident," and the concept of residence was "elusive."[4] The regulations stated:

> An alien actually present in the United States who is not a mere transient or sojourner is a resident of the United States for purposes of the income tax. Whether he is a transient is determined by his intentions with regard to the length and nature of his stay. A mere floating intention, indefinite as to time, to return to another country is not sufficient to constitute him a transient. If he lives in the United States and has no definite intention as to his stay, he is a resident. One who comes to the United States for a definite purpose which in its nature may be promptly accomplished is a transient; but, if his purpose is of such a nature that an extended stay may be necessary for its accomplishment, and to that end the alien makes his home temporarily in the United States, he becomes a resident, though it may be his intention at all times to return to his domicile abroad when the purpose for which he came has been consummated or abandoned.[5]

In 1984, Congress superseded this vague test by adopting §7701(b), which was intended to provide "a more objective definition of residence for income tax

---

[1] See supra ¶¶65.1.2, 65.1.3.

[2] See infra ¶66.3.1.

[3] See infra ¶111.3.2 for joint returns and supra ¶30.3.1 note 1 for §152(b)(3). See also IRC §879, discussed infra ¶76.3 (taxation of community income when one spouse is a nonresident alien); Gutierrez v. CIR, 53 TC 394 (1969), aff'd per curiam, 72-1 USTC ¶9121 (DC Cir. 1971) (not officially reported) (foreign personal holding company status).

[4] Brittingham v. CIR, 66 TC 373, 412 (1976), aff'd on other grounds, 598 F2d 1375 (5th Cir. 1979).

[5] Reg. §1.871-2(b). See generally Langer, When Does a Nonresident Alien Become a Resident for U.S. Tax Purposes? 44 J. Tax'n 220 (1976); Packman & Rosenberg, How Foreigners (Unintentionally) Become U.S. Residents, 57 Taxes 85 (1979).

purposes."[6] Under §7701(b), an individual who is not a citizen of the United States is treated as a resident for all federal tax purposes (excepting the gift and estate taxes) if he is a "lawful permanent resident" at some time during the taxable year or meets a "substantial presence test" for the year.[7] Also, a person who establishes residence under the substantial presence test is sometimes allowed to elect to be treated as a resident for the year preceding the year in which the test is first met.[8] An alien individual who is not a resident under the lawful permanent resident or substantial presence test is classified as a nonresident.[9] According to the Staff of the Joint Committee on Taxation:

> Congress believed that aliens who have entered the United States as permanent residents and who have not officially lost or surrendered the right to permanent U.S. residence should be taxable as U.S. residents. These persons have rights in the United States that are similar to those afforded U.S. citizens (including the right to enter the United States at will); equity demands that they contribute to the cost of running the government on the same basis as citizens.

> Congress similarly decided that it was appropriate to treat as residents individuals who spend significant time in the United States. Recognizing that there is no single system that is perfect, Congress believed that a regime that depends on length of stay meets the criteria of objectivity and establishing nexus with the United States and is appropriate. Almost all individuals present in the United States for more than half a year should be taxable as U.S. residents. Moreover, individuals who repeatedly spend significant amounts of time in the United States should have to note their presence with the Internal Revenue Service; if they do not have a closer connection with a foreign country than with the United States and a tax home in that foreign country, they, too, should be taxable as U.S. residents.

> Congress believed that an average of 122 days of presence over a three-year period is a significant amount of time for the purpose of imposing U.S.

---

[6] Staff of Joint Comm. on Tax'n, 98th Cong., 2d Sess, General Explanation of the Revenue Provisions of the Deficit Reduction Act of 1984 at 464–465 (Comm. Print 1984) [hereinafter 1984 Bluebook].

Section 7701(b) generally applies for 1985 and subsequent years. See Reg. §301.7701(b)-9.

[7] For the residence test applied for estate and gift tax purposes, see infra ¶134.2.1. For regulations under §7701(b), see TD 8411, 1992-1 CB 254. See Rev. Proc. 98-7, 1998-1 CB __, §4.01(24) (IRS ordinarily will not rule on residence of alien "in situations where the determination depends on facts that cannot be confirmed until the close of the taxable year (including, for example, the length of the alien's stay or the nature of the alien's activities)").

See generally Lederman & Hirsh, U.S. Tax Residency Rules Broadened in Final Regulations, 77 J. Tax'n 152 (1992); Williams, Back to the Future: A Time for Rethinking the Test for Resident Alien Status Under the Income Tax Laws, 21 Vand. J. Transnational L. 965 (1988).

[8] IRC §7701(b)(4).

[9] IRC §7701(b)(1)(B).

tax in such circumstances, but that an individual who is present for fewer than 31 days in a year should not be subject to this rule for that year . . . .

Congress believed that [§7701(b)'s] definition of residence imposes U.S. tax on aliens only when their relationship with the United States is so close that U.S. inclusion of worldwide income in the tax base is appropriate.[10]

¶65.2.2 Lawful Permanent Resident (Greencard) Test

A "lawful permanent resident" of the United States is considered a U.S. resident under §7701(b). An individual becomes a lawful permanent resident of the United States by being "lawfully accorded the privilege of residing permanently in the United States as an immigrant in accordance with the immigration laws."[11] An alien holding a green card, in other words, is a resident.

Once permanent residence is obtained, an individual continues to be a lawful permanent resident until this status is either revoked or administratively or judicially determined to have been abandoned.[12] In the absence of such a revocation or determination, a holder of a green card is a resident even if the person "comes to the United States so infrequently that, on scrutiny, he or she is no longer legally entitled to permanent resident status."[13] Congress required a revocation or formal determination of abandonment to terminate residence in order to "prevent aliens from attempting to retain an apparent right to enter or remain in the United States while attempting to avoid the tax responsibility that accompanies that right."

¶65.2.3 Substantial Presence Test

Under the substantial presence test, an alien individual who is present in the United States for at least 183 days during the taxable year is usually a resident for tax purposes, and an alien present in the country for less than 183 days during the current year is usually a resident if he is present for at least 31 days during the year, spends substantial portions of his time in the country during the three-year period ending with the taxable year, and has a closer connection to the United States than to any foreign country. Exceptions are provided, however, for

---

[10] 1984 Bluebook, supra note 6, at 464.

[11] IRC §7701(b)(6). See generally Mailman, How Immigration Law Concepts Clarify, Mesh With the Code's "Resident Alien" Definition, 65 J. Tax'n 26 (1986).

[12] Permanent residency is revoked only by "a final administrative or judicial order of exclusion or deportation." Reg. §301.7701(b)-1(b)(2). A taxpayer may abandon permanent residency by filing an "application for abandonment (INS Form I-407) or a letter . . . with the INS or a consular officer" or by mailing the Alien Registration Receipt Card to the INS or a consular officer, together with a letter expressing the individual's intention .andon resident status. Reg. §301.7701(b)-1(b)(3).

[13] 1984 Bluebook, supra note 6, at 467–468.

teachers, students, commuters from Canada and Mexico, and a few others. These rules are described in more detail below.

Normally, the substantial presence test is met for a particular calendar year if the taxpayer is present in the United States on at least 31 days during the year and meets a 183-day test.[14] The 183-day test is satisfied only if the sum of the days present in the United States during the taxable year, one third of the days present during the immediately preceding calendar year, and one sixth of the days present during the second preceding year is at least 183. The 183-day test is met, for example, if the taxpayer has been present for 122 or more days during each of these three calendar years (122 plus one third of 122 plus one sixth of 122 equals 183).[15]

An alien individual who meets both the 31-day test and the 183-day test is nevertheless a nonresident if he (1) is present in the United States for fewer than 183 days during the current year, (2) has a tax home in a foreign country during the year, and (3) has a closer connection to that country than to the United States.[16] An individual has a "tax home" at a particular place if he would be allowed a deduction under §162(a)(2) for expenses incurred in traveling away from that place on business.[17] According to the regulations, this means that an individual's tax home is at his regular place of business or, if there is more than one regular place, at the principal place of business.[18] An individual has the closest connection with the country with which he "has maintained more significant contacts," including the location of his permanent home, family, personal belongings, and personal bank accounts, the location of the social, political, cultural, and religious organizations "with which the individual has a current relationship," where he obtained his driver's license, where he votes, and the

---

[14] IRC §7701(b)(3)(A).

[15] See Reg. §301.7701(b)-1e) Ex. 1. The Bluebook states that "an average of 122 days of presence over three years will trigger the test." 1984 Bluebook, supra note 6, at 466 n.53. This is not necessarily so. For example, if the taxpayer is present for 100 days during the current year, 120 days during the preceding year, and 150 days during the second preceding year, the average over the three years is 123 days, but the 183-day test is not met (100 plus one third of 120 plus one sixth of 150 is only 165).

[16] IRC §7701(b)(3)(B). See Reg. §301.7701(b)-2(b) ("foreign country" includes Puerto Rico and U.S. possessions).

However, the exemption is allowed only if an annual statement is filed explaining the basis of the taxpayer's claim. Reg. §§301.7701(b)-8(a)(1), 301.7701(b)-8(b)(1), 301.7701(b)-8(c), 301.7701(b)-8(d).

[17] IRC §911(d)(3). For §162(a)(2), see supra ¶21.1.

Generally, the closer connection exception is inapplicable unless the tax home is in one location for the entire year, but the regulations recognize some circumstances in which the test may be met by a taxpayer whose tax home changes from one foreign country to another during the taxable year. Reg. §§301.7701(b)-2(c)(2), 301.7701(b)-2(e).

[18] Reg. §301.7701(b)-2(c)(1) ("if the individual has no regular or principal place of business because of the nature of the business, ... then [tax home is] at the individual's regular place of abode in a real and substantial sense"; tax home is regular place of abode if alien individual has no trade or business within meaning of §162).

country of residence designated on documents filed by the individual.[19] The closer connection exception is not available, however, if the taxpayer has applied to become a permanent resident and this application is pending at any time during the taxable year.[20]

In applying the substantial presence test, an individual is considered present in the country for a particular day if he "is physically present in the United States at any time during such day."[21] For example, if an individual arrives in the United States one evening and leaves the country early the next day, she is present for two days. The "United States" includes the states and the District of Columbia, but not Puerto Rico or the U.S. possessions.[22]

Presence in the country is ignored, however, in the circumstances described below:

1. *Commuters from Canada and Mexico.* An individual who "regularly commutes to" work in the United States "from a place of residence in Canada or Mexico" is deemed not present in the United States on any day "during which he so commutes."[23] The individual's work may be as either an employee or a self-employed person.

The regulations construe "commutes" to require that the person return home at least once during each 24-hour period.[24] An individual who, for example, travels to the United States once each week, staying for two or more days on each trip, thus is not protected by this rule.

Also, the person must commute to a U.S. place of employment or self-employment "on more than 75% of the workdays during the working period."[25] The "working period" begins with the first day during the calendar year when the individual is physically present in the United States for employment or self-employment and ends with the last day during the calendar year when the

---

[19] Reg. §301.7701(b)-2(d) (that individual carries on business activities at particular place is also evidence of connection with that place, even if it is not principal place of business).

[20] IRC §7701(b)(3)(C). See Reg. §301.7701(b)-2(f) (alien who has applied for permanent residency or "taken other affirmative steps" to become permanent resident cannot meet closer connection test; various "affirmative steps" described); 1984 Bluebook, supra note 6, at 466 (only filing by individual counts; filings by family members on individual's behalf not relevant).

[21] IRC §7701(b)(7)(A). See Reg. §301.7701(b)-1(c)(1) (fractional days of presence are counted as whole days).

[22] IRC §7701(a)(9). See Reg. §301.7701(b)-1(c)(2)(ii) ("United States" also includes "the territorial waters of the United States and the seabed and subsoil of those submarine areas which are adjacent to the territorial waters of the United States and over which the United States has exclusive rights, in accordance with international law, with respect to the exploration and exploitation of natural resources").

[23] IRC §7701(b)(7)(B).

[24] Reg. §301.7701(b)-3(e)(2)(i).

[25] Reg. §301.7701(b)-3(e)(1).

individual is so present.[26] It is therefore possible for "seasonal and cyclical employees, as well as those who begin employment in the United States in mid-year, to exclude the days of presence on which they commute to the United States."[27] However, a seasonal employee who commutes daily to the United States from, say, September through April each year and works in Canada or Mexico for the remainder of the year is out of luck because the working period for each calendar year begins in January and ends in December and the May through August hiatus includes more than 25 percent of the working days of the year.

2. *Short stopovers.* Presence while in transit between two points outside the United States is ignored if the person is in the United States for less than 24 hours.[28] For example, a Canadian who passes through an airport in the United States en route to South America is deemed not present in the United States at all for purposes of the substantial presence test. This exemption is lost, however, if the individual conducts business while on a stopover in the United States, even a meeting in an airport.[29]

This rule is usually important only to persons who are also present in the country for other reasons during the year. It is unlikely that an individual would pass through the United States in transit often enough to be caught by the substantial presence test, even in the absence of this rule. However, for a person who becomes or ceases to be a resident by reason of a more sustained stay in the country, this rule can play an important role in determining when residence begins or ends. For example, if an alien leaves the United States in July, concluding a lengthy period of domicile in the country, but passes through the country in transit during November of the same year, the person may rely on this rule to establish that residence ends in July, not November.

3. *Medical emergency.* A day of presence in the United States is disregarded if the taxpayer is "unable to leave the United States on such day because of a medical condition which arose while such individual was present in the United States."[30] The exception applies only if "the individual intends to leave and is unable to leave the United States because of a medical condition . . . that arose while the individual was present in the United States."[31]

---

[26] Reg. §301.7701(b)-3(e)(2)(iii).

[27] TD 8411, supra note 7, at 256.

[28] IRC §7701(b)(7)(C).

[29] Reg. §301.7701(b)-3(d).

[30] IRC §7701(b)(3)(D)(ii). An individual claiming this exemption must annually file a statement stating the basis of the claim. Reg. §§301.7701(b)-8(a)(2), 301.7701(b)-8(b)(2), 301.7701(b)-8(c). The exemption is denied if the statement is not filed. Reg. §301.7701(b)-8(d).

[31] Reg. §301.7701(b)-3(c)(1). In response to complaints that the intent test contradicts the congressional objective of eliminating subjective inquiries in residence cases, the Treasury commented:

The exception applies to persons who are unable to leave the United States. The exception hinges on the involuntariness of the stay; the individual would leave but is

It does not apply if the "condition or problem existed prior to the individual's arrival in the United States [and] the individual was aware of the condition or problem, regardless of whether the individual required treatment for the condition or problem when the individual entered the United States."[32] Congress expected that "few individuals would be physically unable to leave the United States."[33] The exemption might apply, for example, to a person who is "in a serious automobile accident shortly before a planned departure date." Also, even if an individual initially qualifies for the exemption, the §7701(b) clock starts running if, on becoming well enough to travel, the individual "remains in the United States beyond a reasonable period for making arrangements to leave."[34]

The medical exception does not apply to "aliens who come to the United States for medical treatment and stay for extended periods of time."[35] Because the federal government "has contributed to the creation of medical facilities in the United States that are second to none in the world," Congress decided that a person who comes here for medical care should be taxable as a resident if his stay in the country brings him within the substantial presence test.

4. *Diplomats, employees of international organizations, and their families.* An additional exemption is provided for a "foreign government-related individual," defined as an individual temporarily present in the United States as a diplomat, a full-time employee of an international organization, or a member of the immediate family of a diplomat or full-time employee of an international organization.[36] Such a person is "temporarily present" even if the individual's assignment in the United States is of indefinite duration and is not subject to termination by a foreign government.[37] For example, an alien admitted to the

---

unable to do so because of the medical condition. If the individual did not intend to leave, there is no element of involuntariness; the individual would be in the United States regardless of the medical condition . . . .[E]ven though, in general, Congress intended to eliminate the "subjective" tests that existed under old law, the proper application of the medical exception requires an "intent test" in order to determine whether the individual's stay is voluntary or involuntary.

TD 8411, supra note 7, at 255. See Reg. §301.7701(b)-3(c)(2) (describing facts evidencing intent to leave United States).

[32] Reg. §301.7701(b)-3(c)(3).

[33] 1984 Bluebook, supra note 6, at 466.

[34] Reg. §301.7701(b)-3(c)(1).

[35] 1984 Bluebook, supra note 6, at 465.

[36] IRC §7701(b)(5)(B). For the term "diplomat," see Reg. §301.7701(b)-3(b)(2)(iii). For the term "international organization," see §7701(a)(18), discussed infra ¶66.7.3. See also Reg. §301.7701(b)-3(b)(8) (immediate family includes spouse and children under age 21, but not "attendants, servants, and personal employees").

An individual claiming this exemption must annually file a statement stating the basis of the claim. Reg. §§301.7701(b)-8(a)(2), 301.7701(b)-8(b)(2), 301.7701(b)-8(c). The exemption is denied if the statement is not filed. Reg. §301.7701(b)-8(d).

[37] TD 8411, supra note 7, at 255 ("the days of presence of all these individuals should be excluded indefinitely").

United States to serve as an employee of the United Nations in New York is a foreign government-related individual, and therefore not a U.S. resident, even if the employment is indefinite in duration and has continued for many years.

5. *Participants in charitable sports events.* A professional athlete's presence in the United States is disregarded if the person is temporarily present in the country to compete in a "charitable sports event," defined as an event organized primarily to benefit an organization exempt from tax under §501(c)(3), where all of the net proceeds of the event go to that organization and "substantially all of the work performed in carrying out" the event is done by volunteers.[38] The exemption only applies to days on which the "athlete actually competes," not days "on which the individual is present to practice for the event, [or] to perform promotional or other activities related to the event."[39]

6. *Teachers, trainees, and students.* Exemptions are also provided for teachers, trainees, and students in order to "help the United States to maintain its paramount position in the field of education."[40] The exemptions, however, are intended to cover only aliens who "come to the United States to teach or to learn rather than for employment, business, economic opportunity, pleasure, personal or family reasons, political stability, or other reasons."

To qualify for exemption as a teacher or trainee, a person must be temporarily present in the United States under a so-called J visa (other than as a student) and must "substantially" comply with all visa limitations.[41] Moreover, the exemption for a teacher or trainee is lost if the individual has been present in the United States as a teacher, trainee, or student for two or more of the preceding six years.[42] For example, if an alien spends several years in the United States obtaining a graduate degree and returns for a year as a visiting professor soon after finishing her studies, she might become a resident during the visiting year even though she is present under a J visa.

The student exemption applies only if the taxpayer is temporarily present in this country under an F, J, or M visa and substantially complies with visa limitations.[43] The student exemption is denied after an individual has been exempted as a student, trainee, or teacher for five calendar years (which need not be consecutive) unless the taxpayer establishes that he "does not intend to per-

---

[38] IRC §§274(*l*)(1)(B), 7701(b)(3)(D)(i), 7701(b)(5)(A)(iv). See infra ¶100.2 for §501(c)(3).

[39] Reg. §301.7701(b)-3(b)(5).

[40] 1984 Bluebook, supra note 6, at 464. Individuals claiming these exemptions must annually file statements of the bases of their claims. Reg. §§301.7701(b)-8(a)(2), 301.7701(b)-8(b)(2), 301.7701(b)-8(c).

[41] IRC §7701(b)(5)(C).

[42] IRC §7701(b)(5)(E)(i). If the taxpayer is being paid by a foreign employer while a teacher or trainee in this country, the exemption is lost only if the taxpayer has been a teacher or trainee in the United States for four or more of the preceding six years.

[43] IRC §7701(b)(5)(D). The Treasury can require individuals claiming the student exemption to file annual reports on their status. IRC §7701(b)(8).

manently reside in the United States" and continues to comply substantially with visa limitations.[44] A lack of intent to permanently reside in this country can be shown by demonstrating that the taxpayer maintains a closer connection with a foreign country than with the United States and has not applied for permanent residence.[45]

A person claiming exemption as a teacher, trainee, or student substantially complies with visa requirements by refraining from "activities that are prohibited by the Immigration and Nationality Act and the regulations thereunder and could result in the loss of F, J or M visa status."[46] A person with a student visa is not in substantial compliance, for example, if she accepts unauthorized employment or is not a full-time student. Whether a person has substantially complied with visa limitations is independently determined for tax purposes and is not established by showing merely that the visa has not been revoked.[47]

If a person qualifies for exemption as a teacher, trainee, or student, the exemption also applies to the individual's immediate family, including spouse and unmarried children under the age of 21 who reside regularly in the individual's household and are not part of another household.[48]

7. *Crew members of foreign vessels.* A nonresident alien is deemed not present in the United States on any day when the person is "temporarily present" in the United States "as a regular member of the crew of a foreign vessel engaged in transportation between the United States and a foreign country" or U.S. possession unless the person is "otherwise engaged in any trade or business in the United States on such day."[49]

¶65.2.4 Election Rule

An alien can sometimes elect to be treated as a resident for a portion of the year that immediately precedes the year in which the substantial presence test is first met. The purpose of the election is to allow an individual to elect to have U.S. residence begin when he moves to this country even though the substantial presence test is not met until the next year. Although the election accelerates the time when the alien becomes subject to U.S. tax on worldwide income, it may reduce tax if most of the alien's income is from U.S. sources (e.g., because some of the income would otherwise be taxed the 30 percent rate often applied to nonbusiness income of nonresident aliens). Assume an alien comes to the United States on November 1, 1996, intending to stay for two years. The substantial

---

[44] IRC §7701(b)(5)(E)(ii).

[45] Reg. §301.7701(b)-3(b)(7)(iii). For the closer connection test, see Reg. §301.7701(b)-2(d), discussed supra note 19 and accompanying text.

[46] Reg. §301.7701(b)-3(b)(6).

[47] Id.; 1984 Bluebook, supra note 6, at 467.

[48] Reg. §301.7701(b)-3(b)(8).

[49] IRC §7701(b)(7)(D).

presence test is not met until 1997 because the 61 days of presence in 1996 do not satisfy the 183-day prong of the test. The election, however, allows the taxpayer to be treated as a resident starting on her arrival in the country on November 1, 1996. The election is advantageous if the taxpayer's income for the last two months of 1996 is taxed by the United States in any event (e.g., is salary for U.S. services) because some tax benefits (e.g., dependency exemptions) are not available to nonresident aliens.

To qualify for the election, the following requirements must be met:[50] The individual must not be a U.S. resident for the year preceding the election year and must not satisfy the lawful permanent resident or substantial presence test for the election year. The substantial presence test, however, must be met during the year following the election year. The taxpayer must be present in the United States for a continuous period of at least 31 days during the election year. Moreover, for the period beginning at the start of these 31 days and continuing until the end of the year, the taxpayer must be in the country on at least 75 percent of the days. In applying the latter rule (but not the 31-day rule) up to five days on which the taxpayer is actually elsewhere may be treated as days of presence in the United States. For purposes of both rules, periods during which the taxpayer is present in the country as a diplomat, employee of an international organization, teacher, trainee, or student are not counted if the days are disregarded in applying the substantial presence test.[51]

When a qualifying individual makes the election, U.S. residence commences on the first day of the 31-day period used in applying the 31-day and 75 percent rules described in the preceding paragraph.[52] The election is made on the taxpayer's return for the election year.[53] The election may not be made until the taxpayer satisfies the substantial presence test during the following year, which requires that the taxpayer either obtain an extension of the filing date for the election year or file as a nonresident and make the election by an amended return.[54] Once made, the election is revocable only with IRS consent.[55]

---

[50] IRC §7701(b)(4)(A).

[51] IRC §7701(b)(4)(D). See supra ¶65.2.3 text accompanying notes 36-48 for the exclusions for diplomats, employees of international organizations, teachers, trainees, and students.

[52] IRC §7701(b)(4)(C). If the taxpayer is in and out of the country during the year and more than one 31-day period of continuous presence satisfies the 31-day and 75 percent rules, U.S. residence begins for an electing taxpayer at the beginning of the earliest of these 31-day periods.

[53] IRC §7701(b)(4)(E); Reg. §301.7701(b)-4(c)(3)(v). A taxpayer can make the election for a dependent child who is not required to file an income tax return for the year and who qualifies to elect. See Reg. §301.7701(b)-4(c)(3)(vi) (alien failing to comply with election procedures must file as nonresident alien unless there is "clear and convincing evidence" of "reasonable" effort to comply).

[54] Reg. §301.7701(b)-4(c)(3)(v)(A).

[55] IRC §7701(b)(4)(F).

¶65.2.5   Continuity of Residence

Normally, an alien individual who satisfies the lawful permanent resident or substantial presence test for a calendar year is considered a resident for the entire year, including the portions of the year during which he is absent from the United States. According to the Staff of the Joint Committee on Taxation, Congress "believed that aliens should not be able to switch back and forth between resident status and nonresident status for short periods, and that there should be no gap in resident status when an alien is a resident for part of two consecutive years."[56]

> For example, an alien who is present in the United States from January 1 to August 1 in 1985 and from June 1 to December 31 in 1986 is a U.S. resident [under the substantial presence test] for all of 1985 and 1986. Similarly, an alien who is present in the United States from January 1 to August 1 in 1985, who first arrives in the United States in 1986 on December 1, and who becomes a lawful permanent U.S. resident on December 1, 1986, is a U.S. resident for all of 1985 [under the substantial presence test] and 1986 [under the lawful permanent resident test].[57]

The regulations state this more generally:[58] If the taxpayer is a U.S. resident for the preceding year and the current year, the current year's residence begins on the first day of the year. If the taxpayer is a resident for the current year and the succeeding year, the current year's residence ends on the last day of the year. If the taxpayer is a resident for the preceding, current, and succeeding years, the current year's residence extends throughout the year.

¶65.2.6   Year in Which Residence Changes

The year in which an individual establishes or terminates residence is sometimes split between periods of residence and nonresidence under rules described below.[59]

1. *Year in which residence is established.* If an individual meets one of the residence tests for the current year but was not a resident for the preceding calendar year, the current year may be divided between a period of nonresidence and a period of residence.[60] If residence is established by the taxpayer becoming a lawful permanent resident, the period of residence usually begins on the first day the taxpayer is present in the country with a green card.[61] If residence is

---

[56] 1984 Bluebook, supra note 6, at 465.

[57] Id. at 469.

[58] Reg. §301.7701(b)-4(e).

[59] Residence can be established and terminated within a single year, in which case periods of nonresidence begin and end the year and a period of residence is sandwiched between them. See Reg. §301.7701(b)-4(d) Ex. 1.

[60] IRC §7701(b)(2)(A)(i).

[61] IRC §7701(b)(2)(A)(ii).

established under the substantial presence test, the period of residence usually begins with the first day during the year that the taxpayer is present in the United States, excluding days disregarded for purposes of the substantial presence rule.[62] "For example, an alien (who has never before been a U.S. resident for tax purposes) who lives in Spain until May 15, who moves to the United States on May 15 and who remains in the United States through the end of the year . . . begin[s] to be a U.S. resident . . . on May 15."[63] If the taxpayer satisfies both the lawful permanent resident test and the substantial presence test, residence begins on the first day he is present as a lawful permanent resident or, if earlier, the first day the individual is present for purposes of the substantial presence test.

In determining the first day of presence for purposes of the substantial presence test, presence in the United States for up to 10 days is ignored if, while present in the United States, the taxpayer had "a closer connection to a foreign country than to the United States."[64] According to the Staff of the Joint Committee on Taxation, "the purpose of this nominal presence exception is to allow brief presence in the United States (for example, for business or for house-hunting) before moving to the United States without triggering residence status."[65] Assume "an alien (who has never before been a U.S. resident for tax purposes) . . . comes to a business meeting in the United States on February 2 through 8, . . . otherwise lives in Spain until May 15, . . . moves to the United States on May 15 and . . . remains in the United States through the end of the year." Because the February visit consists of only seven days, the individual's U.S. residence begins on May 15 if a closer connection to Spain than to the United States is shown to have existed during the period of U.S. presence in February. The nominal presence rule, however, is wholly inapplicable to a period of presence exceeding 10 days.[66] For example, if the February business meeting in the example continues from February 2 through February 12 (11 days), the individual's U.S. residence begins on February 2, not on the eleventh day of presence (February 12), because the exception is not available.

Presence as a commuter from Canada or Mexico and presence for less than 24 hours while in transit between two foreign points are also ignored in determining the residence starting date under the substantial presence rule.[67]

---

[62] IRC §7701(b)(2)(A)(iii).

[63] 1984 Bluebook, supra note 6, at 470.

[64] IRC §7701(b)(2)(C)(i). Days of presence in the United States are disregarded under the 10-day rule only for purposes of determining the residency starting and termination dates, not for purposes of applying the substantial presence test. TD 8411, supra note 7, at 262.

[65] 1984 Bluebook, supra note 6, at 470.

[66] Reg. §301.7701(b)-4(c)(1) ("days that occur in a period of consecutive days of presence [may not be disregarded unless] all the days that occur during that period [can] be excluded").

[67] See supra ¶65.2.3 text accompanying notes 23–29 for the commuter and presence-in-transit rules.

The foregoing rules do not apply if the taxpayer has elected to be treated as a resident for the previous calendar year. An electing taxpayer's U.S. residence begins in the election year, and for the succeeding calendar year, residence begins on the first day.[68]

2. *Final year of residence.* If an alien meets the lawful permanent resident or substantial presence test for the current year but is not a resident for the immediately following calendar year, the current year may be divided between a period of residence and a period of nonresidence.[69] When this division occurs, the taxpayer is treated as a nonresident for the portion of the year after he ceases to be a lawful permanent resident (if residence is based on the lawful permanent resident test) or after the last day during the year on which the taxpayer is present in the United States (if residence is based on the substantial presence test). If the taxpayer meets both the lawful permanent resident test and the substantial presence test for the year, residence ceases on the later of these two days.[70]

Moreover, U.S. residence terminates before the end of the year only if the taxpayer "has a closer connection to a foreign country than to the United States" for the portion of the year that the foregoing rules would treat as a period of nonresidence.[71] "For example, an alien (who is not during the following year a U.S. resident for tax purposes) who lives in the United States until September 15, who moves to Brazil on September 15, and who does not return to the United States during the year . . . cease[s] to be a U.S. resident for tax purposes on September 15" because the move to Brazil establishes a closer connection to that country than to the United States for the period after September 15.[72]

In determining the last day on which the taxpayer is present in the United States for purposes of the substantial presence rule, presence for up to 10 days is ignored if, while in the United States, the taxpayer has "a closer connection to a foreign country than to the United States."[73] The purpose of this nominal presence rule is "to allow brief presence in the United States (for example, for business or for disposing of a U.S. residence) without extending residence status."[74] Presence as a commuter from Canada or Mexico and presence for less than 24 hours while in transit between two foreign points are also ignored.[75]

3. *Tax computations for partial years of residence.* If an alien individual is a U.S. resident for only a portion of a taxable year, the individual is taxed on

---

[68] IRC §7701(b)(2)(A)(iv).

[69] IRC §7701(b)(2)(B).

[70] 1984 Bluebook, supra note 6, at 471.

[71] IRC §7701(b)(2)(B)(ii). See Reg. §301.7701(b)-4(b)(2) (alien must have tax home in country with which closer connection is claimed).

[72] 1984 Bluebook, supra note 6, at 471.

[73] IRC §7701(b)(2)(C), discussed supra text accompanying notes 16–20. See Reg. §301.7701(b)-4(c)(1) (alien must have tax home in country of closer connection).

[74] 1984 Bluebook, supra note 6, at 471.

[75] For the commuter and in transit rules, see supra ¶65.2.3 text accompanying notes 23-29.

worldwide income for only that portion of the year, and the rules for nonresident aliens apply for the remainder of the year.[76] Nonbusiness income for the period of nonresidence is taxed, if at all, under §871(a), which imposes a 30 percent tax (often reduced or eliminated by treaty) on income from U.S. sources.[77] Business income for the period of nonresidence is subject to U.S. tax only if it is effectively connected with a trade or business carried on in the United States.[78] If the individual has such a business, however, gross income effectively connected with the business and deductions allocable to this income are included in the taxable income taxed under §1. Since §1 also applies to worldwide taxable income for the period of residence, the taxable income subject to §1 consists of the sum of the effectively connected taxable income for the period of nonresidence and taxable income from all sources for the period of residence.[79]

Personal and dependency exemptions are allowed in determining the taxable income subject to §1.[80] The exemptions are not prorated to reflect the taxpayer's residence for only part of the year, but the exemptions for the taxpayer's spouse and dependents may not exceed taxable income for the period of residence.

For an individual who becomes a resident during the year, the day on which residence begins is included in the period of residence; for an individual who sheds residence during the year, the day on which residence ends is included in the period of nonresidence.[81]

¶65.2.7 Fiscal Year Taxpayers

Section 7701(b) is always applied on a calendar year basis. Aliens are generally required to use the calendar year as their taxable year.[82] For the rare individual who has a taxable year other than the calendar year, §7701(b) is applied on the basis of calendar years, and the individual's residence status for a particular calendar year applies to the portions of the individual's taxable years that fall within the calendar year.[83]

¶65.2.8 Treaty Residence Rules

Section 7701(b) does not override residence rules of bilateral treaties to which the United States is a party.[84] Generally, an individual who is a U.S.

---

[76] Reg. §1.871-13(a)(1). See Nico v. CIR, 565 F2d 1234 (2d Cir. 1977); Steur v. CIR, 7 TC 1075 (1946).

[77] See infra ¶66.2.

[78] See infra ¶66.3.

[79] Reg. §1.871-13(a)(1).

[80] Reg. §1.871-13(d)(2). For the personal and dependency exemptions, see ¶30.1.

[81] Reg. §1.871-13(a)(2).

[82] IRC §7701(b)(9)(A).

[83] IRC §7701(b)(9)(B).

[84] 1984 Bluebook, supra note 6, at 468; Reg. §301.7701(b)-7(a).

resident under U.S. tax law is also a U.S. resident for purposes of treaties. More specifically, under most treaties, an individual is considered a resident of a treaty country if, "under the laws of that State, [the person] is liable to tax therein by reason of his domicile, residence, citizenship, ... or any other criterion of a similar nature."[85]

Most treaties provide that when an individual is a resident under the internal laws of both countries, residence for purposes of the treaty is assigned to one of the countries under a series of tie-breaking rules.[86] Assume A, a citizen of country X, is a resident but not a citizen of the United States. Absent treaty modification, A is taxed by the United States on worldwide income. If country X also subjects A to income taxes not imposed on nonresident aliens, tie-breaking rules under a U.S.-country X treaty apply. In contrast, assume that under country X law, nonresident citizens are taxed like nonresident aliens, and A is classified as a nonresident of country X. In this case, the tie breaking rules do not apply because only one of the countries (the United States) taxes A on the basis of residence or citizenship.

Under the tie-breaking rules of the Model Income Tax Treaty promulgated by the U.S. Treasury Department, if an individual is claimed as a resident by both countries, residence for purposes of the treaty is determined as follows:

1. Normally, the individual is a resident of the country in which he has "a permanent home available to him."
2. If the individual has a permanent home in both or neither of the countries, his residence is in the country "with which his personal and economic relations are closer (center of vital interests)."
3. If the center of vital interests cannot be determined, residence is in the country of the taxpayer's "habitual abode."
4. If the individual has a habitual abode in both or neither of the countries, he is a resident of the country of which he is a citizen or national.
5. If all of the foregoing rules fail, the individual's residence is determined by agreement between the competent authorities of the two countries.[87]

Treaties are never applied to increase the taxes imposed by statute.[88] An individual who is a U.S. resident under §7701(b) and a foreign resident under a treaty thus pays the lesser of (1) the tax computed under the statutes treating the taxpayer as a resident or (2) the tax computed giving effect to all treaty rules, including the rule classifying the taxpayer as a nonresident.

---

[85] See, e.g., U.S. Treasury Dep't, Model Income Tax Treaty, art. 4(1)(a) (1981) [hereinafter U.S. Model Treaty].

[86] See Rev. Proc. 97-7, 1997-1 CB 608, at §4.01(14) (IRS ordinarily will not rule on whether taxpayer is resident of treaty country).

[87] U.S. Model Treaty art. 4(2).

[88] See id. at art. 1(2)(a) (treaty "shall not restrict in any manner any exclusion, exemption, deduction, credit, or other allowance now or hereafter accorded by the laws of either Contracting State").

Moreover, such an individual is treated as a U.S. resident in applying all provisions of U.S. law other than those determining how the individual is taxed.

For example, if the alien owns more than 50 percent of the voting power of a foreign corporation, the foreign corporation [is] a controlled corporation [because a U.S. resident is deemed to be majority shareholder]. The U.S. income tax treaty with the alien's country may prevent U.S. taxation of the alien's share of the undistributed earnings of the controlled foreign corporation. However, the United States will apply its regular rules in determining the U.S. tax of a U.S. citizen who is a minority 10-percent shareholder in that controlled foreign corporation.[89]

An alien who is a U.S. resident under §7701(b) but claims nonresident status under an income tax treaty must file Form 1040NR, together with a statement in which the treaty claim and the legal and factual basis for it are described.[90] The regulations warn: "The filing of a Form 1040NR . . . may affect the determination by the Immigration and Naturalization Service as to whether the individual qualifies to maintain a residency permit."[91]

¶65.3 CLASSIFICATION OF ENTITIES AS DOMESTIC OR FOREIGN

¶65.3.1 Introductory

Domestic corporations, trusts, and estates, like U.S. citizens and residents, are taxed on worldwide income, while foreign corporations, trusts, and estates, like nonresident aliens, are only taxed on U.S. source income and income effectively connected with the conduct of business in the United States.[1] Although partnerships are not subject to the income tax, the distinction between domestic and foreign partnerships is occasionally relevant.

Generally, a corporation or partnership is domestic if it is organized under the laws of the United States or one of the states,[2] a trust is domestic if it is subject to primary supervision by a U.S. court and is controlled by U.S. trustees,[3] and an

---

[89] 1984 Bluebook, supra note 6, at 468. See Reg. §301.7701(b)-7(e) Ex. 1.

[90] Reg. §§301.7701(b)-7(b), 301.7701(b)-7(c)(1) (statement should be headed "TREATY-BASED RETURN POSITION DISCLOSURE UNDER §301.7701(b)-7(b) AND SECTION 6114").

[91] Reg. §301.7701(b)-7(b).

[1] See Tuerff & Moreland, U.S. Multinationals and International Joint Ventures, 78 Tax Notes 725 (Feb. 9, 1998); Sharp, Establishing a Multinational Operating Structure: Hybrid and Other "Outbound" Planning Considerations, 16 Tax Notes Int'l 689 (Mar. 2, 1998).

[2] See infra ¶65.3.2.

[3] See infra ¶65.3.3.

estate is domestic if it has a substantial presence in the United States;[4] all other entities are foreign. Entities organized under foreign laws equivalent to the corporation laws of the states of the United States are classified as corporations, but many other types of foreign entities may elect to be treated as corporations or as partnerships for U.S. tax purposes.[5]

¶65.3.2 Corporations and Partnerships

A corporation or partnership is considered domestic if it is created or organized under the laws of the United States or one of the states.[6] A foreign corporation or partnership is one that is created or organized under the laws of a foreign country or a political subdivision of a foreign country or under the laws of a possession of the United States.[7]

A corporation is entitled to the benefits of a bilateral income tax treaty if it is a resident of one of the countries joining in the treaty. Under the Model Income Tax Convention of the U.S. Treasury Department, a corporation is a resident of a treaty country if, under that country's laws, it is taxed as a domestic company because of its "place of management, place of incorporation, or any other criterion of a similar nature."[8] It is possible for a corporation to be a resident of both countries under this definition because the laws of many countries base corporate residence on the place of management, whereas the touchstone under U.S. law is the place of incorporation. The model treaty resolves this conflict by assigning priority to the place of incorporation.[9] Thus, a corporation organized under the laws of the United States, the District of Columbia, or one of the states is a U.S.

---

[4] See infra ¶65.3.4.

[5] See infra ¶65.3.5.

[6] IRC §7701(a)(4). See also IRC §1504(d) (domestic corporation may elect to have wholly owned Canadian or Mexican subsidiary treated as domestic corporation for all U.S. income tax purposes if subsidiary is organized and "maintained solely for the purpose of complying with the laws of [Canada or Mexico] as to the title and operation of property").

[7] IRC §7701(a)(5). Although the terms "resident" and "nonresident" are rarely applied to corporations or partnerships, the regulations state that (1) all domestic corporations are U.S. residents, (2) a foreign corporation is a resident if it is engaged in a trade or business in this country, and (3) a partnership, whether domestic or foreign, is a resident if it has a U.S. business. Reg. §301.7701-5. For an instance where the residence of a partnership is apparently relevant, see §861(a)(1) (interest is from U.S. sources if paid on obligation of "noncorporate residents or domestic corporations").

[8] U.S. Treasury Dep't, Model Income Tax Convention, art. 4(1) (1996) [hereinafter U.S. Model]. The OECD model is the same, except that it does not refer to the place of incorporation. Organisation for Economic Co-operation and Development, Model Tax Convention on Income and on Capital art. 4(1) (1992) [hereinafter OECD Model].

[9] U.S. Model, supra note 8, art. 4(3). The OECD model provides instead that such a corporation is a resident of the country "in which its place of effective management is situated." OECD Model, supra note 8, art. 4(3).

resident under a treaty following the Treasury model, regardless of the classification of the entity under the laws of the other country.

The same treaty rules apply to a partnership, but since a partnership is a pass-through entity, entitlement to treaty benefits must usually be established by the partners, not the partnership. Treaty analysis can be quite confusing if an entity is a partnership under the tax laws of one country and a corporation in the other country. The IRS has apparently historically taken the position that, in determining eligibility for treaty reductions of U.S. tax, only classification under U.S. law is relevant, but it is reported to be considering changing its position to give controlling effect to the characterization under the tax laws of the treaty country.[10]

Assume a limited liability company (*LLC*) is organized under the laws of a state of the United States and does business and is managed in this country, but its owners are residents of country X, a foreign country that has an income tax treaty with the United States; *LLC* is a partnership for U.S. tax purposes, but it is classified as a corporation under the laws of country X. If the U.S. characterization determines eligibility for treaty benefits, these benefits are allowed to each member of *LLC* that is a resident of country X. On the other hand, if the country X characterization is determinative, treaty benefits are denied with respect to *LLC*'s income because *LLC* is not a country X resident.

Under §269B(a)(1), a foreign corporation is reclassified as a domestic corporation for all federal tax purposes if it and a domestic corporation are "stapled entities."[11] A foreign corporation and a domestic corporation are stapled entities if more than 50 percent in value of the stock of each corporation consists of "stapled interests."[12] Stock is a stapled interest if a transfer of the stock must

---

[10] See Cooper, Interpretation of "Beneficial Owner" Under U.S. Tax Treaties, 13 Tax Notes Int'l 1319 (Oct. 14, 1996).

[11] See Notice 89-94, 1989-2 CB 416 (even if §269B(a)(1) treats it as domestic, foreign corporation cannot join in consolidated return).

If an existing foreign corporation becomes a stapled entity, the recharacterization of the corporation as a domestic corporation is treated as a reorganization under §368(a)(1)(F) (reincorporations), and the reorganization is subject to §367(b) because it consists of the transformation of a foreign corporation into a domestic corporation. Staff of Joint Comm. on Tax'n, 98th Cong., 2d Sess., General Explanation of the Tax Reform Act of 1984 at 456 (Comm. Print 1984) [hereinafter 1984 Bluebook]; Rev. Rul. 89-103, 1989-2 CB 65. See infra ¶¶68.6, 68.7 for §367.

The unstapling of two previously stapled entities is also a §368(a)(1)(F) reorganization. This reorganization is subject to §367(a) because it consists of the transformation of domestic corporation into a foreign corporation. 1984 Bluebook, supra, at 457.

If a foreign corporation and a domestic corporation were stapled entities on June 30, 1983, the foreign corporation is treated as a foreign subsidiary of the domestic corporation if this treatment was elected before January 15, 1985. 1984 Bluebook, supra, at 457; Notice 89-94, supra. The usual effect of this election is that the domestic corporation is subject to tax on the foreign corporation's subpart F income, but other foreign income is not subject to U.S. tax until distributed as dividends.

[12] IRC §269B(c)(2).

include a transfer of stock of the other corporation.[13] This coupling of the stocks of the two corporations can occur "by reason of form of ownership, restrictions on transfer, or other terms or conditions."[14] Parent and subsidiary corporations are not stapled entities because, although stock of the parent includes a beneficial interest in the subsidiary, shareholders of the parent are not shareholders of the subsidiary.[15] Also, stock is not stapled where two corporations are owned by the same persons and shareholders' agreements provide for the survivors to buy the stock of any shareholder who dies and give the shareholders a right of first refusal on the stock of any living shareholder wishing to sell.

The stapled entity rules were adopted in 1984 to prevent the pairing of entities from being used as a device for avoiding U.S. tax.[16] A foreign subsidiary of a domestic corporation is a controlled foreign corporation, and its tax haven income is taxable to the domestic parent, whether or not distributed, as subpart F income.[17] If the foreign corporation's stock is held by a large group of unrelated U.S. investors, in contrast, subpart F is inapplicable because it only applies to income of a "controlled foreign corporation," defined as a corporation more than 50 percent owned by U.S. persons, each of whom owns at least 10 percent of the voting stock. The stapling of foreign corporations to domestic corporations was utilized as a device to avoid classification of the foreign corporation as a controlled foreign corporation, while at the same time preserving essentially the same ownership and management structure as would exist in a parent-subsidiary relationship. By requiring that any transfer of stock of the domestic corporation also include a transfer of stock of the foreign corporation, and vice versa, it was possible to ensure that the two corporations would be owned and managed by the same persons, just as though the foreign corporation were a subsidiary of the domestic corporation. In the absence of §269B(a)(1), stapling could also be used to avoid the U.S. corporate tax on foreign income that is not subpart F income. If a domestic corporation has a foreign subsidiary whose income is from foreign business operations but is not subpart F income, dividends paid by the subsidiary are taxable to the domestic parent without the benefit of the deduction for dividends received.[18] If the foreign corporation is stapled to the domestic corporation, in contrast, the dividends bypass the domestic corporation and thereby the U.S. corporate tax. Section 269B(a)(1) frustrates both of these schemes by reclassifying the stapled foreign corporation as domestic, thus causing it to be subject to U.S. tax currently on its worldwide income.

---

[13] IRC §269B(c)(3).

[14] Id. See Rev. Rul. 89-103, 1989-2 CB 65 (stock of two corporations is stapled by "an agreement prohibiting the conveyance of shares of either stock without a coincidental transfer of an equal number of shares of the companion stock").

[15] 1984 Bluebook, supra note 11, at 458.

[16] See 1984 Bluebook, supra note 11, at 454-456.

[17] See infra ¶68.2 for subpart F.

[18] For the dividends-received deduction, see infra ¶90.2.3.

The stapled entities rule does not apply if the IRS is satisfied that both corporations are "foreign owned."[19] A corporation is foreign owned if U.S. persons own less than 50 percent of its stock.[20] For this purpose, ownership is measured by voting power or value, whichever produces the highest percentage of U.S. ownership. Also, stock owned by a foreign entity is attributed to its shareholders, partners, or beneficiaries—successively through a chain of foreign entities, if necessary, until the stock is attributed to an individual or U.S. entity. Moreover, stock subject to an option held by a U.S. person is treated as owned by the optionee.

If a foreign corporation treated as domestic under the stapled entities rule is also a resident of a foreign country under the terms of an income tax treaty between the United States and that country, §269B(a)(1) overrides the treaty, and the corporation is classified as domestic for U.S. tax purposes, notwithstanding the treaty.[21]

¶65.3.3 Trusts

A trust is a U.S. person (domestic trust) if a "court within the United States is able to exercise primary supervision over [its] administration" and it has a U.S. trustee with "authority to control all substantial decisions of the trust"; if both of these requirements are not met, it is a "foreign trust."[22] The proposed regu-

---

[19] IRC §269B(e)(1).

[20] IRC §269B(e)(2).

[21] IRC §269B(d). However, a treaty is not overridden if, on June 30, 1983, the corporations were stapled and the foreign corporation was a resident of the treaty country. 1984 Bluebook, supra note 11, at 457; Notice 89-94, 1989-2 CB 416. Assume that on June 30, 1983, a stapled foreign corporation was a resident of a foreign country having an income tax treaty that precludes the United States from taxing business profits of a corporate resident of the treaty country unless the profits are attributable to a permanent establishment in the United States. Notwithstanding §269B(a)(1), the corporation is exempt from U.S. taxes on foreign business profits until the treaty is amended to disqualify stapled entities from claiming treaty benefits.

[22] IRC §§7701(a)(30)(E), 7701(a)(31)(B), as amended by Pub. L. No. 104-188, §1907, 110 Stat. 1755 (1996) (applicable for taxable years beginning after 1996 or, at trustee's election, for taxable years ending after August 20, 1996). See Notice 96-65, 1996-52 IRB 28, 29 (procedure for electing to apply change for taxable years ending after August 20, 1996). Regulations have been proposed under these rules (REG-251703-96, 1997-25 IRB 5), which apply to all taxable years governed by the statutory rules. Prop. Reg. §301.7701-5(f). See Levine & Weintraub, Further Guidance on the Taxation of Foreign Trusts: Many Questions Remain, 26 Tax Mgmt. Int'l J. 435 (1997).

If a trust was domestic under prior law but became a foreign trust as a result of the 1996 amendments, it is treated as transferring all of its assets to a new foreign trust when it becomes foreign unless some person is then treated as owner of the trust under the grantor trust rules. Notice 96-65, supra, at 29-30. For the grantor trust rules, see infra ¶80.1.1. This deemed transfer may be taxable under §1491, which applies when a U.S. person transfers appreciated property to a foreign trust. For §1491, see infra ¶68.6.7.

lations refer to the first of these requirements as the "court test" and the second as the "control test."[23] The application of both tests depends on the "terms of the trust instrument and applicable law."[24] Although the taxable income of a foreign trust is computed under the rules for nonresident alien individuals, §7701(b), which determines whether an alien individual is a U.S. resident, does not apply to a foreign trust.[25] The court and control tests were enacted in 1996 in order to have "an objective test for determining whether a trust is foreign or domestic."[26]

1. *Court test.* For purposes of the court test, the "court" may be a "federal, state, or local court," and the "United States" includes only the states and the District of Columbia, not Puerto Rico or a U.S. possession.[27] A court is "able to exercise . . . supervision" if it has "the authority under applicable law to render orders or judgments resolving issues concerning administration of the trust," and this supervision is primary if the court has authority to determine "substantially all issues regarding the administration of the entire trust." This authority may derive from the trust instrument or governing law.[28] "Simply having jurisdiction over the trustee, a beneficiary, or trust property is not primary supervision."[29]

"[A]dministration" means "the carrying out of the duties imposed on a fiduciary by the terms of the trust instrument and applicable law."[30] Administration includes "maintaining the books and records of the trust, filing tax returns, defending the trust from suits by creditors, and determining the amount and timing of distributions." Primary supervision over trust administration may

---

A trust classified as domestic under prior law may continue to file tax post-1996 returns as a domestic trust, even if it is foreign under the rule described in the text, if (1) the trustee "initiate[s] modification of the trust to conform with the domestic trust criteria by the due date (including extensions) for filing the trust's income tax returns for its first taxable year beginning after . . . 1996," (2) the modification is effected within two years thereafter, and (3) the trust's returns contain a statement specifying that this procedure is being used and stating various other information. Notice 96-65, supra, at 28–29. The procedure might be used if, for example, a trust is subject to the jurisdiction of a U.S. court but, at the beginning of its first post-1986 year, it has only a foreign trustee, which resigns effective with the appointment of a U.S. trustee. The two-year deadline for the modification may be extended on a showing of "reasonable cause." However, if the modification is not accomplished within these two years (as extended), the trust is retroactively treated as foreign for all post-1986 years.

Moreover, a 1997 amendment allows a trust that was domestic under prior law to elect to continue its status as a U.S. person indefinitely, without any modifications to conform to the new regime, unless, on August 20, 1996, all of the trust was considered owned by its grantor. Pub. L. No. 105-34, §1161, 111 Stat. 788 (1997); Notice 98-25, 1998-18 IRB 11.

[23] Prop. Reg. §301.7701-5(a).

[24] Prop. Reg. §301.7701-5(b).

[25] Prop. Reg. §301.7701-5(a)(2).

[26] REG-251703-96, supra note 22, at 5.

[27] Prop. Reg. §301.7701-5(d)(1).

[28] Prop. Reg. §301.7701-5(d)(3) Ex. 2.

[29] REG-251703-96, supra note 22, at 6.

[30] Prop. Reg. §301.7701-5(d)(1)(v).

rest with a U.S. court even if a foreign court has authority over a trustee or beneficiary or trust property. The court test is satisfied if both a U.S. court and a foreign court are able to exercise primary supervision over trust administration.[31] However, if a foreign court has the primary supervisory power, the test is not met, even if the trust instrument requires the court to apply the laws of one of the U.S. states.[32]

A trust meets the court test if it is "registered by an authorized fiduciary" in a U.S. court under a statute "substantially similar" to the trust article of the Uniform Probate Code.[33] Also, a testamentary trust satisfies the test if the will is probated in the United States, the U.S. probate is not an ancillary probate, and "all fiduciaries of the trust have been qualified as trustees of the trust by a [U.S.] court." An inter vivos trust meets the test if the fiduciaries or beneficiaries "take steps with a court within the United States that cause the administration of the trust to be subject to the primary supervision of the court."

However, the test is not satisfied if the trust instrument contains a "flee clause"—a provision that "a United States court's attempt to assert jurisdiction or otherwise supervise the administration of the trust directly or indirectly would cause the trust to migrate from the United States."[34] For example, a trust cannot be domestic, even if it is administered by a U.S. trustee under the primary jurisdiction of a U.S. court, if the trust instrument provides that in the event that a creditor sues the trustee in a U.S. court, the U.S. court's powers over the trust will terminate and the trust will thereafter be subject to the exclusive jurisdiction of the courts of foreign country X.[35]

2. *Control test.* Under the control test, a trust can be domestic only if U.S. persons have authority to control all substantial decisions to be made for the trust.[36] "U.S. persons" includes individual citizens and residents of the United States and domestic corporations, partnerships, and trusts. A domestic corporation is a U.S. person even if its shareholders are foreign.

A "substantial decision" is a decision made under the trust instrument and applicable law that is not "ministerial."[37] Decisions as to the timing or amount of a distribution, choice of beneficiary, investments, allocation of receipts to income or principal, and resolution of claims against the trust are all substantial. Ministerial decisions include bookkeeping, collection of rents, and the execution of investment decisions made by others. Decisions by a grantor or by a beneficiary affecting only the portion of the trust in which the beneficiary has an

---

[31] Prop. Reg. §301.7701-5(d)(2)(iv).

[32] Prop. Reg. §301.7701-5(d)(3) Ex. 1.

[33] Prop. Reg. §301.7701-5(d)(2).

[34] Prop. Reg. §301.7701-5(d)(2)(v).

[35] Prop. Reg. §301.7701-5(d)(3) Ex. 3.

[36] As originally enacted, §7701(a)(30)(E) required that U.S. "fiduciaries" have control. The statute was amended in 1997 to substitute "persons" for "fiduciaries," retroactively to the effective date of the 1996 enactment.

[37] Prop. Reg. §301.7701-5(e)(1)(ii).

interest are not substantial decisions unless, in making the decisions, the grantor or beneficiary acts as fiduciary. For example, a trust may be domestic even if a nonresident alien beneficiary has a power of appointment over the beneficiary's share of the trust.[38]

"Control means having the power, by vote or otherwise, to make all of the substantial decisions of the trust, with no other person having the power to veto the substantial decision," except that a grantor's or beneficiary's power to veto a decision does not take control away from the fiduciary making the decision unless that power is exercised as a fiduciary.[39] For example, if a nonresident alien grantor has power to revoke the trust, this power is ignored in determining whether U.S. fiduciaries control all substantial decisions,[40] as is an exclusive power over withdrawals and investment choices held by a nonresident alien owner of an individual retirement account (IRA).[41]

If a trust has U.S. and foreign fiduciaries, the control test can be met only if the U.S. fiduciaries can control all substantial decisions. If decisions must be by unanimous consent of the trustees, the presence of a single foreign trustee precludes the control test from being met,[42] although the test can be met if the trustees may act by majority vote and more than one half of the trustees are U.S. persons.[43] A U.S. fiduciary's power to veto decisions made by a foreign fiduciary is not sufficient to vest control in a U.S. fiduciary because the U.S. person has no power to initiate action.[44] On the other hand, a trust can be domestic even if U.S. fiduciaries are required to consider the advice of a foreign person, so long as the U.S. fiduciaries may act contrary to the advice and may act when no advice has been received.[45] Also, U.S. fiduciaries can delegate powers to foreign persons if they remain responsible for all substantial decisions.

If "an inadvertent change in fiduciaries" would otherwise cause a domestic trust to become foreign or vice versa, the trust can avoid any change in its status by, within six months after the inadvertent change, changing fiduciaries or the residence of the fiduciaries in a manner consistent with its historical status.[46] A change in fiduciary is "inadvertent" if, for example, it results from the death or "abrupt resignation" of a fiduciary. Assume a trust has three trustees, two being U.S. citizens and a third a nonresident alien, who may act by majority vote, and the trust instrument designates a nonresident alien as successor to any trustee who dies or resigns; the trust is domestic so long as the original trustees remain

---

[38] Prop. Reg. §301.7701-5(e)(4) Ex. 7.

[39] Prop. Reg. §301.7701-5(e)(1)(iii).

[40] Prop. Reg. §301.7701-5(e)(4) Ex. 2.

[41] Prop. Reg. §301.7701-5(e)(4) Ex. 1.

[42] Prop. Reg. §301.7701-5(e)(4) Ex. 5.

[43] Prop. Reg. §301.7701-5(e)(4) Ex. 6.

[44] Prop. Reg. §301.7701-5(e)(4) Ex. 3.

[45] Prop. Reg. §301.7701-5(e)(4) Ex. 4.

[46] Prop. Reg. §301.7701-5(e)(2).

in office.[47] If one of the U.S. trustees dies, the control test is no longer met because a majority of the trustees are not U.S. persons. However, the trust's status as a domestic trust can continue unbroken if one of the foreign trustees is replaced by a U.S. person within six months.

However, substantial decisions are considered not controlled by U.S. fiduciaries "if an attempt by any governmental agency or creditor to collect information from or assert a claim against the trust would cause one or more substantial decisions of the trust to no longer be controlled by United States fiduciaries."[48]

3. *Safe harbor.* Under a safe harbor rule, a trust is considered domestic if it has only U.S. fiduciaries, is "administered exclusively in the United States pursuant to the terms of a trust instrument," and "is not subject to an automatic migration provision."[49] An automatic migration provision, sometimes known as a "flee clause," is a provision of the trust instrument purporting to divest U.S. courts of supervisory powers in the event a U.S. court asserts jurisdiction over the trust or divest U.S. fiduciaries of their control over substantial decisions if a government agency or creditor asserts a claim against or attempts to obtain information from the trust.[50] The safe harbor rule is intended to settle a trust's status before it has come before any court and is "based upon the principle that when the administration of a trust is conducted entirely within a particular locality, the local courts will exercise primary supervision over the trust."[51]

¶65.3.4 Estates

An estate is a "foreign estate" if it is not subject to U.S. tax on income that is neither from U.S. sources nor effectively connected with a U.S. trade or business.[52] Such an exclusion is provided by §872(a) for nonresident alien individuals and by §882(b) for foreign corporations. Since estates are not corporations, they are considered foreign whenever they can realistically be classified as nonresident aliens.[53] The statutory rules distinguishing resident from nonresident aliens apply only to natural persons.[54] Whether a estate is a nonresident alien is thus determined by regulations predating the statutory rules, which state:

---

[47] Prop. Reg. §301.7701-5(e)(4) Ex. 6.

[48] Prop. Reg. §301.7701-5(e)(3).

[49] Prop. Reg. §301.7701-5(c)(1).

[50] Prop. Reg. §§301.7701-5(d)(2)(v),(e)(3).

[51] REG-251703-96, supra note 22, at 5.

[52] IRC §7701(a)(31). See Rev. Proc. 97-7, 1997-1 CB 608, at §4.01(25) (IRS ordinarily will not rule in advance on whether trust or estate is foreign or domestic).

[53] Reg. §301.7701-5.

[54] 1984 Bluebook, supra note 11, at 469. See supra ¶65.2 for the statutory rules on residence.

An alien actually present in the United States who is not a mere transient or sojourner is a resident of the United States for purposes of the income tax. Whether he is a transient is determined by his intentions with regard to the length and nature of his stay. A mere floating intention, indefinite as to time, to return to another country is not sufficient to constitute him a transient. If he lives in the United States and has no definite intention as to his stay, he is a resident. One who comes to the United States for a definite purpose which in its nature may be promptly accomplished is a transient; but, if his purpose is of such a nature that an extended stay may be necessary for its accomplishment, and to that end the alien makes his home temporarily in the United States, he becomes a resident, though it may be his intention at all times to return to his domicile abroad when the purpose for which he came has been consummated or abandoned.[55]

Unfortunately, this test, which until 1996 also applied to trusts, refers exclusively to physical presence, a factor that is ambiguous as applied to an artificial entity such as a trust or estate. The leading case applying the test to trusts is *B.W. Jones Trust v. CIR*, which involved five trusts created in England by an English settlor.[56] During the years before the court, approximately 90 percent of the trusts' assets consisted of stocks and securities issued by U.S. corporations. The trusts had four trustees, of whom three were English and one was a U.S. citizen. The trusts maintained an office in New York, from which the American trustee managed the day-to-day investment activities of the trusts. Major investment decisions were made by the American trustee and one of the English trustees, who made semiannual trips to New York for this purpose. The trusts, having been created in a foreign country and apparently being governed by foreign law, were held to be aliens, but also to be residents of the United States. The Board of Tax Appeals stated: "That there was an intention to keep the securities in this country is evident . . . . That there was not even a 'floating intention' to take the securities out of the United States is apparent . . . . [T]he trustees . . . maintain[ed] a permanent establishment in the United States under the control of a trustee."[57] In affirming, the Court of Appeals said:

> What is nonresidence on the part of a trust . . . is a question which in some instances may be difficult of determination; but we feel no hesitation in saying that it cannot be predicated of a trust 90% of whose property consists of stocks and bonds of domestic corporations, held in this country in the possession of a trustee who is a citizen of the country, traded by that trustee on the exchange of the country, and returning income which is collected by such trustee in the country and handled from an office maintained in the

---

[55] Reg. §1.871-2(b).
[56] B.W. Jones Trust v. CIR, 132 F2d 914 (4th Cir. 1943).
[57] B.W. Jones Trust v. CIR, 46 BTA 531, 536 (1942).

country for that purpose. No individual who was present and operating within the country as were these trusts could claim to be a nonresident.[58]

The suggestion of the last sentence—that a trust is a resident if its activities in the United States are of such magnitude that an alien could not carry them on without becoming a resident—is probably not a good test. Assume 90 percent of the assets and activities of a trust are in England, but the trust is so large that the remaining assets and activities, all located in the United States, require the full-time service of one of the trustees. Because the effect of classifying a trust as resident is to subject it to U.S. tax on worldwide income, it would not be reasonable to so classify this trust, even though the U.S. trustee, if an alien, could not discharge her duties in this country without becoming a resident.

The analogy to individual residence should rather be as follows: Under the test of the regulations, an individual is a resident if his physical presence in the United States sufficiently predominates over his presence in foreign countries that it is reasonable to say that, at least for the time being, he has made his home in this country. Similarly, a trust should be classified as a resident only if its physical connections with the United States predominate over those to foreign countries.

Notwithstanding the vagueness of the *B.W. Jones* approach, the IRS has adopted it[59] and has extended it to estates.[60]

---

[58] B.W. Jones Trust v. CIR, 132 F2d 914, 916 (4th Cir. 1943). See also Maximov v. US, 373 US 49 (1963) (trust established in United States, governed by Connecticut law and having resident trustee, was not U.K. resident under U.S.-U.K. income tax treaty even though all beneficiaries were U.K. subjects and residents).

[59] Rev. Rul. 60-181, 1960-1 CB 257 ("where the property of a trust, established under the laws of a foreign jurisdiction, consists principally of securities of United States corporations and such securities are held, controlled, and traded in the United States on a domestic exchange by a trustee who is a citizen and resident of this country, the trust is deemed to be a resident alien entity of the United States"). See Rev. Rul. 87-61, 1987-2 CB 219 (trust was nonresident where settlor was U.S. resident but trust was established and administered under foreign law, trustee was foreign entity, and trust corpus was kept outside United States); Rev. Rul. 73-521, 1973-2 CB 209 (trust established by nonresident alien with U.S. trustee was resident even though all beneficiaries were nonresident aliens and all assets were foreign); Rev. Rul. 70-242, 1970-1 CB 89 (Canadian trust with Canadian and U.S. trustees was U.S. resident because it invested solely in U.S. assets and its activities were largely in United States).

[60] Rev. Rul. 81-112, 1981-1 CB 598, 599 (estate of U.S. citizen who resided in foreign country for 20 years before death was nonresident alien because estate assets and administrators were located in foreign countries; that decedent was U.S. citizen and decedent's children, who were estate beneficiaries, were citizens and residents of United States "weigh against alien status for the estate [but] these factors by themselves ... do not prevent the estate from being considered an alien entity"); Rev. Rul. 64-307, 1964-2 CB 163 (estate of decedent who was citizen and resident of United States held to be U.S. resident even though 80 percent of assets were foreign and foreign assets were disposed of by separate will that was probated in foreign country by foreign executor; although not

Under most income tax treaties, a trust or estate is treated as a resident of a particular country if, under the country's laws, the entity is taxed as a resident.[61] For example, if a country taxes residents on worldwide income but exempts nonresidents from tax on foreign source income, a trust or estate taxed on worldwide income is a resident of the country under the treaty definition. If both countries claim residence, treaty residence is usually determined by agreement between the competent authorities of the two countries.[62]

¶65.3.5 Classification of Foreign Entities

Under regulations issued in 1996, entities organized under laws analogous to the corporation laws of the U.S. states would be classified as corporations for U.S. tax purposes and all other entities organized under foreign law would be allowed to elect to be classified as either corporations or partnerships.[63]

Under prior law, whether a foreign entity was classified as a corporation, partnership, or trust for U.S. tax purposes was determined by a resemblance test.[64] For example, an organization whose objective is to carry on business for

---

conclusive, "the decedent's residence is one of the most important facts"); Rev. Rul. 62-154, 1962-2 CB 148 (estate of nonresident alien may be U.S. resident).

[61] U.S. Model, supra note 8, art. 4(1)(b). The OECD model is the same on this point. OECD Model, supra note 8, art. 4(1).

[62] U.S. Model, supra note 8, art. 4(4). The OECD model provides instead that such an entity is a resident of the country "in which its place of effective management is situated." OECD Model, supra note 8, art. 4(3).

[63] See infra ¶90.1.2. See generally Davis, Check-the-Box Entity Classification Regulations, 25 Tax Mgmt. Int'l J. 498 (1996); Magee, Farmer & Katcher, Branching Out—Reexamining Branch Rules in the Context of Check-the-Box, 15 Tax Notes Int'l 1951 (Dec. 15, 1997); Walser & Culbertson, Encore Une Fois: Check-the-Box on the International Stage, 76 Tax Notes 403 (July 21, 1997). See also Benson, Rollinson, O'Connor & Baik, "Hybrid" Entities: Practical Application under the Check-the-Box Regime, 26 Tax Mgmt. Int'l J. 363 (1997).

[64] Rev. Rul. 73-254, 1973-1 CB 613. The corporate resemblance test is stated in Reg. §301.7701-2(a), discussed infra ¶90.1. See Rev. Proc. 95-10, 1995-1 CB 501 (conditions under which IRS will consider ruling request relating to classification of entity, whether or not "incorporated," that is organized under foreign law providing limited liability for any member), discussed infra ¶90.1.4; Rev. Proc. 96-7, 1996-1 CB 559, at §§3.01(3), (4), 4.01(23), (24) (additional no-rulings policies on classification of foreign entities).

See generally Ball & Siegel, U.S. Issues Foreign Entity Classification Ruling Procedure Guidelines: The Insanity Continues, 10 Tax Notes Int'l 315 (Jan. 23, 1995); Davis, Foreign Entity Classification After Rev. Proc. 95-10, 24 Tax Mgmt. Int'l J. 136 (1995); NY State Bar Ass'n Tax Section, Report on Foreign Entity Characterization for Federal Income Tax Purposes, 35 Tax L. Rev. 167 (1980); Spudis, Lemein & Waimon, Using Partnerships in International Tax Planning, 73 Taxes 834 (1995).

For planning strategies using entities that are classified in one way for U.S. tax purposes (e.g., as partnerships) and in other ways for foreign tax purposes (e.g., as corporate entities), see Davis, U.S. Tax Treatment of "Reverse Hybrid" Foreign Entities, 24

the profit of its owners was classified as an association (taxable as a corporation) if it possessed at least three of the corporate characteristics of continuity of life, centralized management, limited liability, and free transferability of interests; it was classified as a partnership if it possessed fewer than three of these characteristics.[65]

In a 1993 ruling, the IRS applied the corporate resemblance test to a German Gesellschaft mit beschrankter Haftung (GmbH).[66] According to the ruling, a GmbH has the corporate characteristics of limited liability and centralization of management, and it may or may not have the characteristics of continuity of life and free transferability of interests, depending on how the parties utilize various alternatives available under German law. The memorandum of association of the GmbH in the ruling, which was owned by two subsidiaries of a domestic corporation, provided that the GmbH would dissolve on the bankruptcy of either owner and that neither owner could transfer its interest, except with the consent of the other. The ruling holds that the GmbH lacked continuity of life because of the provision for dissolution on the bankruptcy of an owner of an interest.[67] However, the ruling holds that the GmbH possessed the characteristic of free transferability of interests because the parent controlled any transfer decision by either subsidiary; "to lack free transferability, the possibility of an impediment to transfer must exist." Since the entity possessed three of the four corporate characteristics, it was classified as an association taxable as a corporation.

Under German law, a GmbH's memorandum of association may prohibit the transfer of any interest and deny effect to an attempted transfer, or it may provide that the GmbH will dissolve in the event of a transfer of an interest. According to the ruling, a GmbH lacks free transferability if its memorandum of association utilizes either of these alternatives. However, neither alternative imposes a real "impediment to transfer" in the factual context of the ruling, and the ruling thus allows a GmbH wholly owned by a controlled group of corporations to be treated as a partnership or as an association, as the group chooses.

Tax Mgmt. Int'l J. 593 (1995) (associations taxable as corporations for U.S. purposes and partnerships for foreign purposes); Harvey, Burke & Shapiro, Uses of Hybrid Entities in the International Arena, 11 Tax Notes Int'l 1609 (Dec. 11, 1995).

[65] See Rev. Rul. 88-8, 1988-1 CB 403 (entity's characteristics are determined by governing foreign law). See also Rev. Proc. 98-3, 1998-1 CB —, §4.01(46) (IRS ordinarily will not rule in advance on whether foreign partnership is association for U.S. tax purposes "if the taxpayer requests classification as an association").

[66] Rev. Rul. 93-4, 1993-1 CB 225. The ruling, which supersedes Rev. Rul. 77-214, 1977-1 CB 408, is effective as of January 22, 1993, but preexisting organizations that relied on the 1977 ruling in determining classification need not change classification.

[67] Rev. Rul. 77-214, which involved the same facts, held that the GmbH had continuity of life, notwithstanding the possibility of dissolution on the bankruptcy of a member, because the two members were controlled by a common parent.

¶65.4 FORMER CITIZENS AND FORMER RESIDENT ALIENS

¶65.4.1 Introductory

Normally, nonresident aliens who were formerly citizens or residents of the United States are taxed like all other nonresident aliens; only specified types of income originating in this country are taxed, and much of this income is taxed at a flat rate without deductions.[1] However, if citizenship was renounced in order to avoid U.S. taxes, a special regime—an alternative tax under §877(b) that is imposed on net income at the normal individual rates of §1 but with an exemption for income originating outside the United States[2] —applies for 10 years after citizenship was lost. The alternative tax also applies to an alien who (1) was a permanent resident of the United States for at least eight of 15 taxable years and, in order to avoid U.S. tax, either ceases being a U.S. resident or takes up residence in a country with which the United States has a tax treaty or (2) was a U.S. resident for at least three consecutive calendar years and resumes residence in this country before completing three full calendar years of nonresidence.[3]

---

[1] See infra ¶66.2.

[2] See generally Abreu, Taxing Exits, 29 UC Davis L. Rev. 1087 (1996); Zimble, Expatriate Games: The U.S. Taxation of Former Citizens, 61 Tax Notes 617 (Nov. 3, 1993). See also Tilevitz & Czapiewska, Getting the Tax-Free Boot: Tax-Motivated Expatriation May Preclude U.S. Visa, 74 Tax Notes 1715 (Mar. 31, 1997) (discussing 1996 amendment to immigration laws making tax-motivated expatriates excludable aliens).

For 1996 amendments to these rules, see Pub. L. No. 104-191, §511 (1996); Notice 97-19, 1997-1 CB 394 (guidance on 1996 amendments to §§2107 and 2501); Staff of Joint Comm. on Tax'n, 98th Cong., 2d Sess., General Explanation of the Revenue Provisions of the Deficit Reduction Act of 1984 at 465 (Comm. Print 1984) [hereinafter 1984 Bluebook] ("Congress believed that [§877] should be reexamined in the future (especially to the extent that [it] allow[s] the subsequent disposition of foreign assets held during U.S. citizenship or residence free of U.S. tax)"); Brewer, Reining in the Terror of Section 1491, 74 Tax Notes 1725 (Mar. 31, 1997); Conlon, IRS Provides Detailed Guidance for Tax-Motivated Expats Following 1996 Amendments, 8 J. Int'l Tax'n 202 (1997); Lederman & Hirsh, New Reporting Rules for Departing U.S. Persons and Property after IRS Guidance and TRA '97, 87 J. Tax'n 149 (1997); Siegler, The Increased Cost of Expatriation: Notice 97-19, 26 Tax Mgmt. Int'l J. 272 (1997). For alternative solutions to problems presented by expatriates, see generally Abreu, Taxing Exits, 29 U.C. Davis L. Rev. 1087 (1996), digested at 73 Tax Notes 359 (Oct. 21, 1996); Ass'n of Bar of City of NY Comm. on Tax'n of Int'l Transactions, The Effect of Changes in the Type of United States Tax Jurisdiction Over Individuals and Corporations: Residence, Source and Doing Business, 46 Record 914 (1991).

The 1996 amendments generally apply to persons losing U.S. citizenship or relinquishing U.S. residence after February 5, 1995, but a special rule is provided for persons who lost citizenship as a result of an expatriating act before February 6, 1995 but who did not, until after February 5, 1995, furnish to the State Department a statement confirming that act. Pub. L. No. 104-191, §511(g)(3) (1996); Notice 97-19, supra, X.

[3] For return requirements for former citizens and residents who are subject to §877(b), see Notice 97-19, 1997-1 CB 394, VII.

Section 877 does not explicitly deny to former citizens or resident aliens the benefits provided by tax treaties between the United States and the countries to which they move. Most treaties reserve to the United States the right to tax its citizens without regard to the treaty, and many treaties define "citizen" to include former citizens who lost citizenship for tax avoidance purposes.[4] Treaties not containing this explicit deference to §877 may raise the possibility of §877 being only a paper tiger for former citizens residing in treaty countries, since treaties sharply reduce the U.S. rate (sometimes to zero) on much of the income intended to be caught by §877. The IRS ruled in 1979 that §877 overrides these treaty provisions in the case of expatriates becoming residents of treaty countries to avoid U.S. taxation,[5] but the Tax Court, in the only case addressing the issue, has declined to follow the ruling.[6] In reporting on 1996 amendments to §877, the Conference Committee stated:

> While it is believed that the expatriation tax provisions, as amended by the bill, are generally consistent with the underlying principles of income tax treaties to the extent the bill provides a foreign tax credit for items taxed by another country, it is intended that the purpose of the expatriation tax provisions as amended, not be defeated by any treaty provision.[7]

However, the Committee's report indicates that any conflicting treaty provision remaining in effect on August 21, 2006 will thereafter take precedence over §877. The IRS' construction of this history is as follows:

> In accordance with Congressional intent, Treasury and the Service will interpret section 877 as consistent with U.S. income tax treaties. To the extent that there is a conflict, however, all provisions of section 877, as amended, prevail over treaty provisions in effect on August 21, 1996. This coordination rule is effective until August 21, 2006, and applies to those provisions of section 877 that were amended [in 1996] as well as those that were not amended . . . . In addition, Treasury and the Service will interpret all treaties, whether or not in force on August 21, 1996, that preserve U.S. taxing jurisdiction with respect to former U.S. citizens or former U.S. long-

---

Section 877 affects a former citizen's or resident's tax liability but does not restore citizenship. Its discrimination against a nonresident alien solely because of former citizenship or residence possibly raises a constitutional issue.

[4] E.g., U.S.–Australia Income Tax Convention, art. 1(3).

[5] Rev. Rul. 79-152, 1979-1 CB 237 (§877 applies even if treaty between United States and country of expatriate's residence does not preserve U.S. right to tax under §877). See generally Ness, Federal Tax Treatment of Expatriates Entitled to Treaty Protection, 21 Tax Lawyer 393 (1968); Roberts, Is Revenue Ruling 79-152, Which Taxes an Expatriate's Gain, Consistent With the Code? 51 J. Tax'n 204 (1979).

[6] Crow v. CIR, 85 TC 376 (1985) (declining to follow Rev. Rul 79-152 under pre-1984 U.S.–Canada treaty).

[7] HR Rep. No. 496, 104th Cong., 2d Sess. 329 (Conf. Rep. 1996).

term residents who expatriate with a principal purpose to avoid U.S. taxes as consistent with the provisions of section 877, as amended.[8]

A person losing U.S. citizenship must file a statement with the State Department or a federal court providing information regarding the person's residence, citizenship, net worth, and various other matters, and the office or court receiving this statement must furnish a copy to the IRS.[9] This statement must be given when the person renounces citizenship before a diplomatic or consular representative, files with the State Department a statement of voluntary relinquishment of citizenship, is issued a certificate of loss of citizenship, or loses citizenship as a result of a court's cancellation of a certificate of naturalization, whichever occurs first. A long-term resident who relinquishes residence under circumstances subjecting the person to §877(b) must also furnish such a statement, but the statement must be filed with the person's return for the year residence is relinquished. Failure to provide this statement is subject to a penalty of $1,000 or, if greater, 5 percent of the tax under §877 for the year.

¶65.4.2   Former Citizens

The §877(b) alternative tax applies to a former citizen for each taxable year ending within 10 years after citizenship was lost unless the loss of citizenship "did not have for one of its principal purposes the avoidance of [federal income, estate, gift, or generation-skipping transfer] taxes."[10] A parallel estate and gift tax regime is provided for such individuals and their estates.[11] However, the §877(b) tax applies even if the purpose of the expatriation was to avoid only gift or estate taxes, and the special gift and estate taxes apply even if income tax avoidance was the sole reason for the loss of citizenship.

Some former citizens are "treated as having a principal purpose to avoid such taxes," regardless of actual motivation.[12] This irrebuttable presumption generally applies if (1) the individual's average annual U.S. income tax for the five taxable years preceding the loss of citizenship exceeded $100,000 or (2) the person's net worth was at least $500,000 when citizenship was lost.[13] Net worth

---

[8] Notice 97-19, 1997-1 CB 394, VIII.

[9] IRC §6039F (applicable to any loss of citizenship after February 5, 1995); Notice 97-19, 1997-1 CB 394, IX.

[10] IRC §877(a)(1). See cases and rulings cited supra ¶65.1 note 2 for problems in determining whether citizenship has been renounced or otherwise lost.

[11] See infra ¶134.4.

[12] IRC §877(a)(2) (applicable to persons losing citizenship after February 5, 1996).

[13] The U.S. income tax for each year is the sum of the regular tax liability and the alternative minimum tax, less all allowable credits. IRC §§38(c)(1), 877(a)(2). If a joint return was filed for any of these years, the relevant amount is the tax on the joint return. Notice 97-19, 1997-1 CB 394, III.

The $100,000 and $500,000 figures are adjusted for inflation since 1994. See Rev. Proc. 97-57, 1997-2 CB — (inflation adjusted amounts are $543,000 and $109,000 for 1998); Rev. Proc. 96-59, 1996-2 CB 392 ($528,000 and $106,000 for 1997).

includes "any interest in property that would be taxable as a gift" if transferred by the person immediately before the loss of citizenship.[14] A beneficial interest in a trust is included, even if the person's rights in the trust are subject to the discretion of trustees or others. Property is valued for this purpose using the principles and approaches applicable for gift tax purposes.[15]

The presumption can be avoided by a few categories of former citizens, including (1) a person who, at birth, became a citizen of the United States and another country and continues to be a citizen of the other country, (2) a taxpayer who, within a "reasonable period" after losing U.S. citizenship, becomes a citizen of the country of birth of the taxpayer, the taxpayer's spouse, or both of the taxpayer's parents, (3) a person who was not present in the United States for more than 30 days during any year over the 10-year period preceding the loss of U.S. citizenship, and (4) a person who loses U.S. citizenship before reaching the age of $18^1/_2$.[16] However, an individual who meets the tax liability or net worth test, but is within one of these categories, is subject to the irrebuttable presumption unless, within one year after losing citizenship, the individual requests an IRS ruling that avoidance of U.S. taxes was not a principal purpose for the loss of citizenship.[17] Section 877 generally applies to such an individual unless the IRS ultimately rules favorably on the request, but a negative ruling can be challenged by paying the tax computed under §877 and filing a refund claim.[18]

In any case not subject to the irrebuttable presumption, the burden of negating a tax-avoidance purpose is on the taxpayer if the IRS establishes it was

---

[14] Notice 97-19, 1997-1 CB 394, III. Net worth includes any "interest in the right to use property," such as "a nonexclusive license to use property."

[15] See id. ("prohibitions or restrictions on [any] interest" in property are disregarded). The Notice also provides rules for valuing interests in trusts.

[16] IRC §877(c) (applicable to taxpayers who lost citizenship after February 5, 1996). The Treasury may, by regulations, add additional categories of taxpayers eligible for this exemption. It has indicated that in a variety of circumstances, it will provide such relief to long-term residents who are subjected to §877 by §877(e). Notice 97-19, 1997-1 CB 394, IV.

Under a similar provision of prior law, §877 does not apply to persons who lost citizenship before February 6, 1996, in specified circumstances that Congress believed not to be tax-motivated, including renunciation of U.S. citizenship by a person who acquired dual citizenship at birth. IRC §877(d) (before amendment in 1996).

[17] For procedures for obtaining such a ruling, see Notice 97-19, 1997-1 CB 394, IV. The request may be filed before expatriation if the taxpayer "has formed a definite intention to expatriate."

The IRS will consider such requests by "former long-term residents and former citizens who narrowly fail to satisfy the criteria of an enumerated category." Id. See id. Ex. 3 (ruling request considered from former citizen who met 10-year, 30-day test, except that she had vacationed in Hawaii for 35 days during one of relevant 10 years), Ex. 4 (same for former long-term resident who would have met country of birth test, except that parents were naturalized citizens of that country and taxpayer was born while parents were temporarily away from country).

[18] Notice 97-19, 1997-1 CB 394, IV. If no ruling has been issued by the due date of the taxpayer's return, the taxpayer must file as though §877 applies and make an amended return if a favorable ruling is issued.

reasonable to believe that, but for §877, the loss of citizenship would result in a substantial reduction in taxes on the taxpayer's probable income for the taxable year.[19]

¶65.4.3 Aliens Who Formerly Resided in the United States

Some long-time alien residents are treated as citizens in applying §877. This occurs if an alien (1) ceases to be a lawful permanent resident of the United States and (2) was a lawful permanent resident of the United States during at least eight years of the 15-year period ending with the year when the alien ceases to be a U.S. resident.[20] An alien is also treated as a citizen for this purpose if, without ceasing to be a lawful U.S. resident, the individual (1) becomes a resident of another country with which the United States has an income tax treaty, (2) does not waive treaty benefits available as a resident of that country, and (3) was a lawful permanent resident of the United States during at least eight years of the 15-year period ending with the year that residence in the treaty country begins.[21]

An alien caught by this rule is treated as having lost citizenship when lawful permanent residence in the U.S. ends or residence in the treaty country begins. Whether avoiding U.S. taxes was a principal purpose of this constructive loss of citizenship is determined by the same rules that apply to actual losses of citizenship. For example, if an alien's average annual U.S. tax liability exceeded $100,000 over the preceding five years or the alien's net worth is at least $500,000 when citizenship is constructively lost, the loss is deemed tax motivated, regardless of actual purpose.[22] If the constructive loss of citizenship is or is deemed tax motivated, U.S. tax is the greater of the tax under the usual rules for nonresident aliens or the tax determined under §877(b). However, in computing the §877(b) tax, the basis of property held when the alien became a U.S. resident is not less than its fair market value at that time.[23]

---

[19] IRC §877(f).

[20] IRC §877(e)(1) (applicable to aliens who, after February 5, 1996, cease being U.S. residents or acquire residence in a treaty country). For this purpose, an alien ceases being a lawful permanent resident of the United States only if the right of permanent residence is revoked or is administratively or judicially determined to be abandoned. IRC §§877(e)(1), 7701(b)(6)(B).

[21] Whether the alien loses U.S. residence or assumes residence in a treaty country, the alien is not, for purposes of the eight of 15 test, treated as a lawful U.S. resident for any year for which he or she is entitled to treaty benefits as a resident of a treaty country.

[22] IRC §877(a)(2). In a few cases, the taxpayer may attempt to rebut this presumption by a ruling request. Notice 97-19, 1997-1 CB 394, IV. This relief is allowed if (1) the taxpayer is, at the time of expatriation, a citizen of the country of birth of the taxpayer, the taxpayer's spouse, or either of the taxpayer's parents, (2) the taxpayer was not present in the United States for more than 30 years during any of the 10 years preceding expatriation, or (3) expatriation occurs before age 18^{1}/$_{2}$. For the effect of such a request and 3t procedures, see supra ¶65.4.2 text accompanying notes 16–18.

[23] IRC §877(e)(3)(B). The taxpayer can elect not to apply this rule.

Section 7701(b)(10) also sometimes subjects former resident aliens to the alternative tax of §877(b).[24] This provision was enacted in 1984 so that "long-time U.S. residents [would] not be able to leave the United States for a short period, dispose of assets free of U.S. tax, and then resume U.S. residence."[25] It applies if an alien (1) was a U.S. resident during at least three consecutive calendar years, (2) is not a resident for all or a portion of the taxable year, and (3) subsequently resumes U.S. residence before three complete calendar years of nonresidence have elapsed. It can apply whether the taxpayer was a lawful permanent resident or had U.S. residence under the substantial presence test of §7701(b).[26] The taxpayer's motivation for losing or regaining residence is not relevant.

Section 7701(b)(10) can apply even if the taxpayer was not a U.S. resident for portions of the first and last of the three consecutive calendar years in the residence period, although, according to the regulations, it is applicable only if the individual was present in the United States for at least 183 days during each of three consecutive calendar years.[27] Assume B, an alien individual, entered the United States on April 1, 1994, as a lawful permanent resident, abandoned permanent residence and left the United States on August 1, 1996, and resumes lawful permanent residence on October 5, 1999.[28] Section 877(b) applies because B (1) was a resident for more than 183 days during each of three consecutive calendar years (1994, 1995, and 1996) and (2) again becomes a resident before the end of 1999, which is the third calendar year following the year (1996) during which the initial period of residence terminated. That B's absence from the United States exceeds three years (from August of 1996 through October of 1999) is not relevant.

When the conditions of §7701(b)(10) are met, the taxpayer is subject to the §877(b) tax for each year or portion of a year in the period of nonresidence. Section 877(b) can apply in as many as four taxable years. In the example, B is subject to the alternative tax for a portion of 1996 (from August 2, 1996, the day after residence was abandoned, until the end of the year), all of 1997 and 1998, and a portion of 1999 (from the beginning of the year until the taxpayer's reentry on October 4).

Section 7701(b)(10) differs from the rules for former citizens in two important respects. Section 7701(b)(10) never subjects a former resident alien to the §877(b) tax in more than four taxable years, whereas a former citizen may be burdened by the tax for 10 years. Also, §7701(b)(10), unlike §877(a), contains no purpose test.[29] Although §7701(b)(10) was enacted to catch aliens who abandon

---

[24] For the application of this provision, see Notice 97-19, 1997-1 CB 394, XI.

[25] 1984 Bluebook, supra note 2, at 465.

[26] For §7701(b), see supra ¶65.2.3.

[27] Reg. §301.7701(b)-5(a)(2).

[28] See Reg. §301.7701(b)-5(c) Ex.

[29] See Reg. §301.7701(b)-5(a).

U.S. residence for short periods in order to avoid U.S. tax on income recognized during the period of nonresidence, it operates wholly mechanically. If an alien is a U.S. resident during at least three consecutive years, abandons residence, and becomes a resident again after fewer than three complete calendar years of nonresidence, §877(b) applies in the intervening period, regardless of the taxpayer's purpose in abandoning residence and even if the resumption of residence was not planned when residence was abandoned.

¶65.4.4 Computation of §877(b) Tax

For each year or portion of a year to which §877(b) applies, a former citizen or former resident alien pays the greater of the tax imposed under the general rules for nonresident aliens or a tax computed under §877(b). For purposes of the §877(b) tax, gross income includes only income from sources within the United States and income effectively connected with the conduct of a U.S. trade or business, regardless of source, and deductions are generally allowed only for items connected with this gross income. The §877(b) tax is at the rates prescribed by §§1 and 55. Assume a former citizen subject to §877(b) has gross income for a year consisting of dividends from U.S. sources of $100,000 and portfolio interest from U.S. sources of $50,000.[30] In the absence of treaty, the tax under the rules normally applicable to nonresident aliens is $30,000 (30 percent of the dividends); the portfolio interest is exempt from tax under these rules. For purposes of the §877(b) tax, the dividends and interest are both included in gross income. If the §1 tax on this gross income, reduced by allowable deductions, is $40,000, the §877(b) tax is $40,000, and because it is the larger of the two alternatives, it is the taxpayer's liability for the year.

For purposes of §877(b), source and gain recognition rules are modified in some significant ways, which are described below together with the rules for deductions, tax rates, and other matters.

1. *Source.* Under the usual rules, a nonresident alien's gain on a sale of property is usually foreign source income.[31] However, for purposes of §877(b), gain on a sale or exchange is from U.S. sources if the property sold or exchanged is (1) stock of a domestic corporation, (2) a debt instrument issued by a U.S. person, the U.S. government, a state or a political subdivision thereof, or the District of Columbia, or (3) any other property "located in the United States."[32] The latter category encompasses, for example, a valuable painting kept in the taxpayer's home in the United States.

---

[30] See Notice 97-19, 1997-1 CB 394, II.

[31] IRC §865(a) (gains on sales of property are from sources within taxpayer's country of residence).

[32] IRC §877(d)(1). Gains on sales of tangible personal property are covered by this only if the taxpayer lost U.S. citizenship after February 5, 1996.

Dividends from a foreign corporation, and gain on a sale or exchange of the taxpayer's stock in the corporation, are also from U.S. sources if, when citizenship was lost or sometime during the preceding two years, the taxpayer owned more than 50 percent of the corporation's stock, by vote or by value.[33] The income or gain reached by this rule may not, however, exceed the earnings and profits attributable to the stock that were accumulated before the loss of citizenship and while the taxpayer satisfied the ownership condition.

2. *Gain recognition.* A special gain recognition rule applies if, during the 15 years beginning five years before expatriation, the taxpayer exchanges property that generated U.S. source income for property that will generate foreign source income.[34] Under this rule, gain is recognized on the exchange, even if the transaction fully satisfies a nonrecognition provision of the Code.[35] The gain is computed as though the taxpayer had sold the property for cash equal to its fair market value.

Removal of appreciated tangible personal property from the United States is treated as an exchange for purposes of this rule if the aggregate amount of such property removed from the United States during the 15-year period exceeds $250,000.[36] For example, if an individual expatriating for tax-avoidance reasons takes a $5 million painting with her when she moves her residence from the United States to a foreign country, she is deemed to make a taxable sale of the painting for its fair market value on the date it is removed from this country.[37]

Any other "occurrence" that changes the source of future income from U.S. to foreign is also treated as an exchange for purposes of this rule.[38] Assume a U.S. citizen and resident enters into a notional principal contract (e.g., a swap), thereafter moves her residence and principal place of business to a foreign country, and, during the following year, renounces U.S. citizenship principally to avoid U.S. taxes.[39] Income from a notional principal contract is from sources in the country of the taxpayer's tax home.[40] The change in the individual's tax home

---

[33] IRC §877(d)(1)(C) (applicable to taxpayers losing citizenship after February 5, 1996). Stock ownership is determined with the constructive ownership rules of §958(b), which are described in ¶68.2.2.

[34] IRC §877(d)(2) (applicable to taxpayers losing U.S. citizenship or residence after February 5, 1995); Notice 97-19, 1997-1 CB 394, V. The source rules of §877(d)(1) apply in determining the sources of income from the property exchanged and the property received in the exchange.

[35] If the exchange occurred during the five years preceding expatriation, it is recognized in the taxable year of the expatriation. Notice 97-19, 1997-1 CB 394, V.

[36] Only the portion of the gain ratably allocable to the value in excess of $250,000 is recognized. Property removed from the United States before February 6, 1995, is ignored in applying this rule.

[37] Notice 97-19, 1997-1 CB 394, V Ex. 7.

[38] This rule does not apply if the occurrence happened before February 24, 1997, and before the taxpayer expatriated.

[39] Notice 97-19, 1997-1 CB 394, V Ex. 5.

[40] Reg. §1.863-7(b)(1), discussed infra ¶70.9.

is thus an occurrence during the 15-year period that changes the source of income from the contract, and she is deemed to have sold the contract for an amount equal to its fair market value on the date of the change of tax home. Similarly, if, during the 15-year period, the individual sells her home in the United States and purchases a home in the country of her new residence, she is denied the benefit of the nonrecognition rule of §1034.[41] Because gain on the sale of the old residence is from U.S. sources, whereas gain on a sale of the new residence would be from foreign sources, the sale and repurchase are an occurrence that changes the source of future income, and this occurrence is treated as a taxable exchange.

In lieu of recognizing gain on an exchange or deemed exchange under the foregoing rules, the taxpayer may make an agreement with the IRS to report income or gain from the property received as U.S. source income for the remainder of the 15-year period.[42] Assume individual A, soon after expatriating principally to avoid U.S. taxes, transfers stock of a domestic corporation to a foreign trust for the benefit of herself and her spouse and children.[43] The transfer is treated as an exchange because it potentially changes the source of gain on a sale of the stock; if A had sold the stock, gain would be from U.S. sources under §877(d)(1), whereas gain on a sale by the trust would be from foreign sources under §865(a) because the trust is not a U.S. person. A thus recognizes gain on the transfer to the trust, computed as though she had sold the stock for a price equal to its fair market value at the time of the transfer in trust, unless she files a gain recognition agreement, which would obligate her to recognize as U.S. source income any income or gain from her beneficial interest in the trust during the 10 years following her expatriation.

3. *Transfers to controlled foreign corporations.* If a former citizen or resident contributes property to a foreign corporation during the 15-year period beginning five years before expatriation, he or she is sometimes taxed on income or gain from the property as though the taxpayer continued to own it.[44] This rule applies only if, but for the taxpayer's expatriation, the corporation would be a

---

[41] Notice 97-19, 1997-1 CB 394, V Ex. 6.

[42] IRC §877(d)(2)(C). For the terms of the agreement, which must be filed with the taxpayer's return for the year of the exchange (or for the year of expatriation if the exchange occurred during the preceding five years), see Notice 97-19, 1997-1 CB 394, V. Among other things, the taxpayer must agree to file a return for each year during the 10 years following expatriation and to include with each return a certificate describing income or gain from the property during the year.

[43] See Notice 97-19, 1997-1 CB 394, V Ex. 9.

[44] IRC §877(d)(4) (applicable to taxpayers losing citizenship or residence after February 5, 1995); Notice 97-19, 1997-1 CB 394, VI (transfers before February 24, 1997 are subject to this rule only if they occur after taxpayer's expatriation). An individual making a transfer subject to this rule must attach to his or her return for the year of the transfer (or, if later, the year of expatriation) a statement describing the transfer and including various other information. Notice 97-19, supra, VI.

controlled foreign corporation (CFC) at the time of the contribution and the taxpayer would then be a U.S. shareholder.[45] Moreover, a sale of the taxpayer's stock in the corporation is treated as a sale by the corporation of the contributed property, and a sale of any portion of this stock is treated as a sale of a ratable share of the property.

4. *Extension of 10-year period where risk of loss is diminished.* If the taxpayer's "risk of loss with respect to . . . property is substantially diminished by" any transaction during the 10 years following expatriation, the "running" of the 10-year period of §877(b)'s applicability is "suspended" for as long as the risk is so diminished, but only for the purpose of determining the taxability under §877 of gain on a sale of the property.[46] The transactions that may substantially diminish risk of loss include a short sale of the property, the holding of a put option with respect to the property or "similar property," or "the holding by another person of a right to acquire the property."

Assume an individual renounces U.S. citizenship for a tax avoidance reason on December 1, 1996, makes a short sale of stock of a domestic corporation during 2001, and closes the short sale in January 1997. Gain recognized on the closing is taxable under §877(b), even though more than 10 years has elapsed since the loss of citizenship, because, for this limited purpose, the 10 years of §877(b)'s application stops running in 2001, only five years after the loss of citizenship, and does not start running again until the short sale is closed.

5. *Deductions.* Deductions are allowed in determining the §877(b) tax but generally only for items that are connected with gross income taken into account.[47] However, casualty losses to property located in the United States, the charitable deduction, and one personal exemption are allowed, even though not connected with this gross income.[48] Also, loss in a transaction entered into for profit is deductible if income or gain from the transaction would have been included in determining the §877(b) tax. No capital loss carryover is allowed.

6. *Tax calculation.* The §877(b) tax is usually imposed at the rates of §1. The §1 tax, however, may be increased by an alternative minimum tax under §55.[49] If a lump sum distribution from a qualified pension, profit sharing, or stock bonus plan is included in the §877(b) tax base, tax on the distribution may be computed under the five-year averaging rule of §402(e)(1).[50]

---

[45] A foreign corporation is a CFC if more than one half of its stock, by vote or value, is owned by U.S. shareholders, and a U.S. shareholder is a U.S. person owning, actually or constructively, at least 10 percent of the corporation's voting stock. IRC §§957(a), 958, discussed infra ¶68.2.2.

[46] IRC §877(d)(3) (applicable to taxpayers losing citizenship after February 5, 1995).

[47] IRC §877(b)(2).

[48] IRC §§873(b), 877(b)(2). If the taxpayer resides in Canada or Mexico, dependency exemptions are also allowed.

[49] For the alternative minimum tax, see infra ¶111.4.

[50] See infra ¶61.13.4 for the five-year averaging rule.

Credit is allowed against the §877(b) tax for foreign taxes on income subjected to U.S. tax solely because of §877.[51]

¶65.4.5　Retroactive Restoration of Citizenship; Erroneous Understanding of Citizenship

Citizenship is relinquished by performing one of several acts specified in the Immigration and Nationality Act, but only if the act is voluntary and is performed with the intention of relinquishing citizenship and a certificate of loss of nationality is issued.[52] The requirement that the act of expatriation be with the intention of relinquishing citizenship was not explicit in the statutes until 1986. In amending the statutes to make the requirement explicit, Congress provided that an individual who lost citizenship before November 14, 1986 could have citizenship restored by demonstrating to the State Department that he or she did not intend to relinquish citizenship. The restoration, if allowed, is retroactive to the date of the expatriating act. If citizenship was restored under this procedure before 1993, the IRS treats the individual as an alien for income and gift tax purposes from the date of the expatriating act until the date of restoration.[53] If citizenship is restored after 1992, the individual is taxed as an alien from the date of the expatriating act through 1992, but because the restoration is retroactive, the individual is treated as a citizen beginning with 1993, even if the restoration occurs thereafter.

If a U.S. citizen performs an expatriating act but the State Department does not determine that citizenship has been lost and does not issue a certificate of loss of nationality, citizenship is not lost, and the individual continues to be taxable as a citizen. However, because the immigration statutes were not explicit on this point until 1986, an individual who performed an expatriating act before November 14, 1986 thus might have believed, reasonably and in good faith, that she was no longer a citizen and therefore was not obligated to file U.S. tax returns as a citizen. Because the 1986 legislation clarified that such a person never lost citizenship, she is liable for income and gift taxes on the basis of citizenship for all years. Under a 1992 ruling, however, the IRS may grant relief similar to that described in the preceding paragraph for persons who actually lost citizenship but have citizenship restored retroactively.[54] Whether relief is given to a particular individual depends primarily on whether the person "acted in a manner consistent with a good faith belief that [the person] had lost United States citizenship by, among other things, not affirmatively exercising any rights of United

---

[51] IRC §877(b) (applicable for persons losing citizenship after February 5, 1995).
[52] 8 USC §1501 (1988).
[53] Rev. Rul. 92-109, 1992-2 CB 3.
[54] Id.

States citizenship in the period when he did not file federal tax returns as [a] United States citizen."[55]

¶65.5 CITIZENS AND RESIDENT ALIENS WITH FOREIGN EARNED INCOME

¶65.5.1 Introductory

Normally, a citizen or resident alien of the United States is taxed on worldwide income even if he is not present in the country during the taxable year. However, §§911 and 912 provide several exclusions from gross income for U.S. citizens and residents living abroad. The principal exclusion, provided by §911(a)(1), permits up to $80,000 in earned income from services performed in foreign countries to be omitted from gross income if the taxpayer's tax home is in a foreign country and the taxpayer is either a bona fide resident of a foreign country or is present in a foreign country for at least 330 days over a 12-month period. Under a subsidiary rule, housing allowances received by employees qualifying for the earned income exclusion are partially excluded from gross income. A variation on the housing exclusion allows self-employed persons to deduct portions of their foreign housing costs. Employees of the U.S. government and agencies thereof do not qualify for the §911 exclusions and deduction. However, §912 allows federal employees stationed abroad to exclude various allowances for overseas employees and also permits Peace Corps volunteers to exclude some allowances.

Section 911, which was enacted in 1951, originally allowed citizens satisfying the bona fide foreign residence test or a physical presence test to exclude all foreign earned income, regardless of amount—a bonanza for movie stars and successful novelists in the days when it was cheap to live on the French Riviera and foreign tax collectors seldom asked embarrassing questions. In the ensuing years, Congress chipped away at the exclusion by imposing dollar limits and other restrictions, the most drastic of which was a 1978 amendment that limited the exclusion to taxpayers residing in camps in hardship areas. For taxpayers living in countries where the cost of living was markedly higher than in the United States, an elective deduction was provided by §913, also enacted in 1978, for excess foreign living expenses.

The 1978 innovations were short lived. In 1981, the §911 exclusions were substantially liberalized, taking on a garb closely resembling the pre-1978 exclusions, and §913 was repealed. The Senate Finance Committee explained the reasons for the liberalization as follows:

---

[55] Id. at 8.

The committee believes that American business faces increasing competitive pressures abroad, and that, in view of the nation's continuing trade deficits, it is important to allow Americans working overseas to contribute to the effort to keep American business competitive. The tax burdens imposed on these individuals . . . have made it difficult for U.S. businesses to utilize American employees abroad. In many cases, the policy of these businesses is to make their employees whole for any extra tax expenses the employees incur because of overseas transfers. Thus, an extra tax cost to the employees becomes a cost to the business, which cost often must be passed through to customers in the form of higher prices. In intensely competitive industries, such as construction, this leads to higher, and thus often noncompetitive bids for work by American firms. . . . As a result, some U.S. companies either have cut back their foreign operations or have replaced American citizens in key executive positions with foreign nationals. In many cases, these foreign nationals may purchase goods and services for their companies from their home countries, rather than from the United States because they often are more familiar with those goods and services.[1]

In 1997, in connection with another liberalization of §911, the House Ways and Means Committee reiterated the reasons for the provision:

The Committee recognizes that for U.S. businesses to be effective competitors overseas it is necessary to dispatch U.S. citizens or residents to sites of foreign operations. Being stationed abroad typically imposes additional financial burdens on the employee and his family. These burdens may arise from maintaining two homes (one in the United States and one abroad), additional personal travel to maintain family ties, or the added expenses of living in a foreign location that has a high cost of living. Businesses often remunerate their employees for these additional burdens by paying higher wages. Because the increased remuneration is offset by larger burdens, the remuneration does not truly reflect an increase in economic well being. The Committee, therefore, believes that the exclusion of section 911 is a simple way to prevent taxpayers from facing an increased tax burden when there has been no increase in economic well being by accepting an overseas assignment.[2]

---

[1] S. Rep. No. 144, 97th Cong., 1st Sess. 35–36 (1981), reprinted in 1981-2 CB 412, 419-420. See generally Maiers, The Foreign Earned Income Exclusion: Reinventing the Wheel, 34 Tax Lawyer 691 (1981); Kingson, A Somewhat Different View, 34 Tax Lawyer 737 (1981); Sobel, United States Taxation of its Citizens Abroad: Incentive or Equity, 38 Vand. L. Rev. 101 (1985).

[2] HR Rep. No. 148, 105th Cong., 1st Sess. — (1997).

As amended in 1981, §911 applies only at the taxpayer's election.[3] An election applies to the year for which made and all subsequent years until revoked.[4] IRS consent is not required for a revocation, but a taxpayer revoking without IRS consent is barred from renewing the election until the sixth year after the first year affected by the revocation.

¶65.5.2 Foreign Residence or Physical Presence

Section 911(a) applies to a "qualified individual," defined as a citizen or resident alien whose tax home is in a foreign country and who meets at least one of two foreign presence tests—a bona fide residence test or a 330-day test.[5] A person's tax home is at a particular place if costs of travel away from that place on business are deductible as business expenses.[6]

1. *Bona fide residence test.* A U.S. citizen[7] with a foreign tax home qualifies for the §911 allowances if he is a "bona fide resident of a foreign country or

---

[3] IRC §911(a). See Reg. §1.911-7(a)(1) (election made separately for earned income exclusion of §911(a)(1) and housing exclusion of §911(a)(2)); §1.911-7(a)(2)(D) (election may be made (1) by timely original return, timely amendment of timely return, or late original return filed not more than one year after due date, determined without extensions, (2) at any time if tax liability, taking the §911 exclusion into account, is zero, or (3) at any time before IRS "discovers that the taxpayer failed to elect the exclusion" if tax liability, computed with exclusion, exceeds zero). See also Brewster v. CIR, 67 TC 352 (1976), aff'd per curiam, 607 F2d 1369 (D.C. Cir.), cert. denied, 444 US 991 (1979) (under earlier nonelective version of §911, taxpayer operating farm in Ireland at loss was required to exclude portion of gross farm income along with same proportion of expenses, thereby effectively making loss partially nondeductible).

[4] IRC §911(e); Reg. §1.911-7(b). See Rev. Rul. 90-77, 1990-2 CB 183 (election is revoked by filing return reporting excludable amounts as gross income and claiming credit for foreign taxes on these amounts).

[5] IRC §911(d)(1). The term "foreign country" includes the territorial waters of and airspace over a foreign country. Reg. §1.911-2(h). However, Puerto Rico and the U.S. possessions are treated as parts of the United States for this purpose.

[6] IRC §911(d)(3), discussed infra text accompanying notes 25–28.

[7] By statute, the bona fide residence test is restricted to U.S. citizens and is not available to resident aliens, who can be qualified individuals only by satisfying the 330-day test. Congress may have assumed that U.S. residence is inconsistent with bona fide residence in a foreign country. The residence tests, however, are not the same; an alien becomes a U.S. resident by satisfying one or more of the mechanical tests of §7701(b), whereas a more flexible test—dependent on all the facts and circumstances—is used in applying the bona fide residence test. See supra ¶65.2 for §7701(b).

Most income tax treaties made by the United States contain nondiscrimination articles, and the IRS construes most of these articles to require that nationals of the foreign countries that are parties to the treaties must be allowed to qualify under §911(d)(1) by satisfying the bona fide residence test. Rev. Rul. 91-58, 1991-2 CB 340 (identifying 39 treaties with such nondiscrimination articles).

countries for an uninterrupted period which includes an entire taxable year."[8] According to the regulations, "whether an individual is a bona fide resident of a foreign country shall be determined by applying to the extent practical, the principles of section 871 and the regulations thereunder, relating to the determination of the residence of aliens."[9] The term "bona fide" seems to add nothing to the inherent meaning of the term "resident."

In *Sochurek v. CIR*, the Court of Appeals for the Seventh Circuit listed some of the factors to be weighed in determining a taxpayer's residence:

a. The taxpayer's intention.
b. Establishment of a home temporarily in the foreign country for an indefinite period.
c. Participation in the activities of the community on social and cultural levels, identification with the daily lives of the people, and, in general, assimilation into the foreign environment.
d. Physical presence in the foreign country consistent with the taxpayer's employment.
e. The nature, extent, and reasons for temporary absences from the foreign home.
f. Assumption of economic burdens and payment of taxes to the foreign country.
g. Status of a resident of the foreign country as contrasted to that of a transient or sojourner.
h. The treatment of the taxpayer's income tax status by his employer.
i. Marital status and residence of the taxpayer's family.
j. Nature and duration of his employment; whether his assignment abroad could be promptly accomplished within a definite or specified time.

---

[8] IRC §911(d)(1)(A). The statute says the taxpayer must establish bona fide foreign residence "to the satisfaction of" the IRS. Although this language does not make the IRS determination conclusive, "strong proof" is needed to overcome that determination. Schoneberger v. CIR, 74 TC 1016, 1024 (1980).

[9] Reg. §1.911-2(c). The meaning of the quoted language is not clear because, since 1984, the residence of aliens has been determined under §7701(b) and the regulations thereunder, not §871 and accompanying regulations. The intended meaning seems to be to refer to the pre-1984 regulations defining residence. Reg. §1.871-2(b). See Schoneberger v. CIR, 74 TC 1016, 1027 (1980) (immigration laws of foreign country are not conclusive, and nominal restrictions on duration of residence "are of little weight"); Rev. Rul. 71-565, 1971-2 CB 266. See also Downs v. CIR, 166 F2d 504 (9th Cir.), cert. denied, 334 US 832 (1948) (presence on a ship of foreign registry in New York Harbor insufficient to establish foreign residence); Ferrer v. CIR, 50 TC 177 (1968), aff'd per curiam, 409 F2d 1359 (2d Cir. 1969) (actor did not become bona fide resident of foreign countries by presence for limited periods on specific projects); Stierhout v. CIR, 24 TC 483 (1955) (exclusion allowed because mode of living indicated intention to become foreign resident for indefinite period).

k. Whether the taxpayer's purpose in establishing a foreign home is tax evasion.[10]

Once foreign resident status is acquired, it is not broken by temporary visits to the United States or elsewhere on vacation or business,[11] but continues until the taxpayer "abandons the same and actually departs from" the foreign country.[12] An intention to change residence does not terminate foreign residence.

To meet the bona fide residence test, the taxpayer's residence in a foreign country or countries must encompass an uninterrupted period that includes an entire taxable year.[13] If this requirement is met, however, the test may also be met for portions of years preceding and following this taxable year. Assume an individual resides in a foreign country from November 1, 1996, through March 31, 1998.[14] The bona fide residence test is met because the uninterrupted period of foreign residence includes all of one taxable year (1997). The test is therefore met for the entire uninterrupted period, including the last two months of 1996 and the first three months of 1996.

To qualify for the §911 exclusions, an individual need not be taxed as a resident by any foreign country, but a person who avoids foreign taxation by disclaiming residence may be disqualified. Specifically, an individual cannot qualify as a bona fide resident of a foreign country if (1) he submits a statement to "the authorities of that country" denying residence in the country and (2) his earned income from sources within the country is not subject to the country's income tax because he is determined to be a nonresident of the country.[15]

2. *330-day test.* A U.S. citizen who fails to meet the bona fide residence test may qualify for the §911(a) exclusions if, during a period of 12 consecutive

---

[10] Sochurek v. CIR, 300 F2d 34 (7th Cir. 1962), citing numerous earlier cases. See Jones v. CIR, 927 F2d 849, 853 (5th Cir. 1991) (applying *Sochurek* factors to find airline pilot for Japanese airline was resident of Japan, even though pilot's wife remained in couple's historic home in Alaska and pilot did not speak Japanese and was little integrated into Japanese community; residence must be determined "in light of congressional intent, which was to encourage foreign trade by encouraging foreign employment for citizens of the United States, and to place them in an equal position with citizens of other countries going abroad who are not taxed by their own countries").

[11] Reg. §1.911-2(c). See Wood v. Glenn, 92 F. Supp. 1 (WD Ky. 1950) (30-day vacation in United States did not end foreign residence).

[12] Reg. §1.871-5. See Carpenter v. US, 495 F2d 175, 182 (5th Cir. 1974) ("twofold test" for determining whether U.S. citizen's return to United States terminates bona fide residence in foreign country); Craig v. CIR, 73 TC 1034 (1980) (acq. in result) (residence in Switzerland abandoned when taxpayer and family moved back to United States, not earlier date when taxpayer came to United States to begin employment of indefinite duration that later ripened into permanent job).

[13] IRC §911(d)(1)(A).

[14] Reg. §1.911-3(d)(3).

[15] IRC §911(d)(5); Reg. §1.911-2(c). See Riley v. CIR, 74 TC 414 (1980) (taxpayer's claim for exemption from Canadian tax under article of U.S.-Canada treaty exempting visiting teachers was not statement of nonresidence).

months, the individual is present in one or more foreign countries for at least 330 full days.[16] Also, the 330-day test, unlike the bona fide residence test, may be met by a resident alien of the United States.[17]

The 12-month period may begin on any day of any month.[18] The period may begin before or after the taxpayer actually arrives in the country, and may end before or after the taxpayer's departure from the country. The required 330 days of presence during the 12-month period need not be consecutive.[19] A series of foreign stays, including vacation trips abroad,[20] can therefore be pieced together to make up the requisite 330 days. Since 330 days is more than 90 percent of the days in the 12-month period, however, occasional foreign travel does not come near to satisfying the test. Moreover, a day is counted toward the 330 only if the taxpayer is present in one or more foreign countries from midnight to midnight, except that periods of travel between foreign countries are counted even if the taxpayer is not in any country for portions of the trip. Even presence in the United States for no more than 24 hours while in transit between two foreign locations is treated as a period of foreign presence. Ships' crews who spend most of their time on the high seas, in contrast, generally cannot satisfy the 330-day rule for lack of sufficient presence in foreign countries.[21]

Assume a U.S. citizen arrives in Venezuela from New York at noon on April 24, 1996, and remains there until leaving for New York at noon on March 21, 1997.[22] The taxpayer is present in a foreign country on the days April 25, 1996, through March 20, 1997. The 330-day test is met for the 12-month period March 21, 1996, through March 20, 1997. It is also met for the period April 25, 1996, through April 24, 1997. If the taxpayer is in the United States at all times while not in Venezuela, it makes no difference which of these 12-month periods is used. If the taxpayer is present and has her tax home in another foreign country before

---

[16] IRC §911(d)(1)(B). If the taxpayer comes to a foreign country during the last eight months of a taxable year, the return for the year might fall due before the taxpayer has been there long enough to satisfy the 330-day test. When this happens, the taxpayer can (1) file the return without the §911 exclusions and claim a refund once the test is met or (2) apply for an extension of the filing date. Reg. §1.911-7(c). The regulations do not allow the return to be filed on or before the due date with exclusions determined on the assumption that the test will eventually be met, although there is apparently no penalty for doing so if the test is ultimately satisfied. See Reg. §1.911-7(d) (estimated tax payments may be computed with exclusions taxpayer "reasonably believes" will be allowable).

[17] See Reg. §1.911-2(e) (nonresident alien who joins with citizen or resident spouse in filing joint return under §6013(g) or (h) is treated as resident alien for this purpose).

[18] Reg. §1.911-2(d)(1).

[19] Reg. §1.911-2(d)(2).

[20] Rev. Rul. 57-590, 1957-2 CB 458.

[21] See Plaisance v. US, 433 F. Supp. 936 (ED La. 1977) (exclusion denied tugboat captain who worked on boat in North Sea). See also Reg. §1.911-2(d)(2).

[22] See Reg. §1.911-2(d)(3) Ex. 1. For a more complex example involving a taxpayer making repeated trips between foreign countries and the United States, see Reg. §1.911-2(d)(3) Ex. 2.

coming to Venezuela or after leaving Venezuela, however, the choice of 12-month period can bring time spent in the other country within the period for which the taxpayer qualifies for the §911 exclusions.

Although compensation received as an employee of the U.S. government cannot qualify for the §911(a) exclusions,[23] days of presence in a foreign country while a federal employee may be counted toward the required 330 days and therefore aid in establishing a right to the exclusions with respect to compensation received from nongovernmental employers.[24]

3. *Tax home requirement.* Regardless of the taxpayer's other connections with foreign countries, the §911(a) exclusions are allowed only for periods when the taxpayer's "tax home" is in a foreign country. For example, in determining whether the taxpayer is a foreign resident for an uninterrupted period satisfying the bona fide residence test, times when the taxpayer's tax home is in the United States are excluded. Also, a day of presence in a foreign country is not counted in applying the 330-day test if the taxpayer's tax home is in the United States on that day.

Generally, an individual has a tax home in a particular country if expenses in traveling away from the country on business would be deductible under §162(a).[25] According to the regulations, "an individual's tax home is considered to be located at his regular or principal (if more than one regular) place of business or, if the individual has no regular or principal place of business because of the nature of the business, then at his regular place of abode in a real and substantial sense."[26]

However, an individual whose "abode" is in the United States is deemed to have his tax home in this country, regardless of the application of §162(a)(2).[27] A dwelling maintained by an individual in the United States is not necessarily the individual's abode, even if the dwelling is the principal residence of his spouse or dependents.[28]

---

[23] See infra ¶65.5.3 notes 45–46 and accompanying text.

[24] Reg. §1.911-2(e).

[25] IRC §911(d)(3).

[26] Reg. §1.911-2(b).

[27] IRC §911(d)(3). See Jones v. CIR, 927 F2d 849, 856 (5th Cir. 1991) (legislative history "seems to indicate that the congressional purpose in adding the abode limitation was to make these tax benefits available only to those individuals who actually incurred increased living expenses while living abroad"; "abode" refers to where taxpayer lives, not where taxpayer works); Harrington v. CIR, 93 TC 297, 307–308 (1989) (whether taxpayer has U.S. abode is determined by comparing "the taxpayer's domestic ties (i.e., his familial, economic, and personal ties) to the United States with his ties to the foreign country in which he claims a tax home").

[28] Reg. §1.911-2(b). But see Lemay v. CIR, 837 F2d 681, 684 (5th Cir. 1988) (taxpayer's abode was in United States where he maintained a house in Louisiana occupied by his wife and children and had "strong economic, familial, and personal ties to [this] residence").

4. *Exception for war or civil unrest.* An individual who leaves a foreign country because of war or civil unrest may be exempted from some of the requirements of the foreign presence tests. The exemption, which was enacted in 1980 in response to the plight of many Americans forced to leave Iran in 1978 and 1979 because of civil unrest there,[29] applies if all of the following requirements are satisfied:[30]

  a. The taxpayer was a bona fide resident of or present in a foreign country.
  b. The taxpayer left the country before satisfying the bona fide residence or 330-day test.
  c. The IRS, in consultation with the State Department, determines that at the time of the taxpayer's departure from the country, "individuals were required to leave [it] because of war, civil unrest, or similar adverse conditions . . . which precluded the normal conduct of business by such individuals."[31]
  d. The IRS is satisfied that the taxpayer would have met one of the foreign presence tests in the absence of the adverse conditions.

When these conditions are met, the taxpayer qualifies for the §911 allowances for the period he was a bona fide resident of or present in the foreign country.

¶65.5.3 Foreign Earned Income Exclusion

Section 911(a)(1) excludes all or a portion of a qualifying individual's "foreign earned income" from gross income. The exclusion may not exceed a fixed dollar amount, which was $70,000 for 1997 and prior years, increases by $2,000 annually over the period 1998–2001, and is $80,000 for 2002 and subsequent years. The terms "earned income" and "foreign earned income" and the application of the dollar ceiling are discussed below.

1. *Earned income.* The term "earned income" includes wages, salaries, professional fees, and other "compensation for personal services actually rendered."[32] It includes the fair market value of any such compensation paid in a

---

[29] S. Rep. No. 1031, 96th Cong., 2d Sess., reprinted in 1980-2 CB 730, 732.

[30] IRC §911(d)(4).

[31] See S. Rep. No. 1031, supra note 29, at 732 ("it is anticipated, for example, that such determinations ordinarily would be made in situations where the State Department issues a travel advisory recommending that U.S. citizens avoid travel to a country because of unsettled conditions there"); Reg. §1.911-2(f) (IRS publishes names of countries qualifying for this treatment and times when adverse conditions existed; exemption inapplicable in absence of such publication); Rev. Proc. 97-51, 1997-45 IRB 9 (listing countries where and times when conditions justified premature departures qualifying for relief under §911(d)(4) for taxable year 1996); for lists of countries where such conditions existed but ended before 1996, see Rev. Proc. 96-33, 1996-2 CB 720; Rev. Proc. 95-45, 1995-2 CB 421; Rev. Proc. 94-31, 1994-1 CB 625; Rev. Proc. 94-15, 1994-1 CB 575.

[32] IRC §911(d)(2)(A).

form other than cash.[33] Compensation paid by a corporation is disqualified to the extent that it represents a distribution of earnings or profits. On the other hand, professional fees are earned income even if the taxpayer "employs assistants to perform part or all of the services, provided the patients or clients are those of the [taxpayer] and look to the [taxpayer] as the person responsible for the services rendered."[34]

Generally, gains on sales of property are not earned income, even if the taxpayer exercises the wiles of a salesman in pursuing buyers. However, amounts received on sales of property created by the taxpayer, such as works of art sold by the artist, are earned income even if the work was not commissioned by the buyer and was created before the artist had a customer to whom services could be "rendered" in the layman's sense.[35] An author's royalties are also earned income whether the royalty agreement is a license or sale of the author's work.[36]

If the taxpayer carries on a trade or business in which both personal services and capital are "material income-producing factors" or is a partner in a partnership engaged in such a business, a "reasonable allowance" for the taxpayer's personal services in the business is treated as earned income, but this reasonable allowance may not exceed 30 percent of the taxpayer's share of the "net profits" of the trade or business.[37] The 30 percent ceiling has been held to apply only if the business produces a net profit.[38] Under this construction, the taxpayer's earned income equals the value of the services rendered if the enterprise operates at a loss but drops abruptly if the business manages to rise above the break-even level.

Whether capital is a material income-producing factor, so as to bring the 30 percent limit into play, is a factual question. The applicable standards have been summarized by the Tax Court as follows:

---

[33] Reg. §1.911-3(b)(1).

[34] Reg. §1.911-3(b)(3).

[35] Cook v. US, 599 F2d 400 (Ct. Cl. 1979); Tobey v. CIR, 60 TC 227 (1973) (acq.); Rev. Rul. 79-85, 1979-1 CB 246. See Robida v. CIR, 460 F2d 1172 (9th Cir. 1972) ("key element is the presence or absence of capital as the income-producing factor, not the existence or nonexistence of an independent recipient for the personal services rendered by the taxpayer"; held, taxpayer who "manipulated" slot machines for personal profit realized earned income); Vanderpool, *Robida* and *Tobey*: The New Test for Section 911 "Earned Income," 27 Tax Lawyer 493 (1974).

[36] Rev. Rul. 80-254, 1980-2 CB 222.

[37] IRC §911(d)(2)(B).

[38] Brewster v. CIR, 55 TC 251 (1970) (divided court), aff'd per curiam, 473 F2d 160 (DC Cir. 1972); Brewster v. CIR, 67 TC 352 (1976), aff'd per curiam, 607 F2d 1369 (DC Cir.), cert. denied, 444 US 991 (1979) (same taxpayer, same issue, different tax year). This holding is less significant than it once was because the effect of §911 in a loss situation is to make part of the loss nondeductible, and the present §911, unlike the statutes involved in the *Brewster* cases, is elective, thus allowing this adverse consequence to be avoided by simply not exercising the election.

Capital is a material income-producing factor if a substantial portion of the gross income of the business is attributable to the employment of capital in the business conducted by the enterprise. Moreover, capital is ordinarily a material income-producing factor if the operation of the business requires substantial inventories or substantial investments in plant, machinery, or other equipment. On the other hand, capital is not a material income-producing factor where the gross income of the enterprise consists principally of fees, commissions, or other compensation for personal services. . . . If capital is "utilized merely to pay the cost of salaries, wages, office space, and general business expenses, it is not a material income-producing factor but is only incidental to the production of the income."[39]

The cases hold that property contributing to the production of income must be taken into account, even if it is leased rather than owned by the taxpayer.[40]

If all members of a partnership are active in a business in which capital and labor are both material income-producing factors, each partner reports a pro rata share of the partnership's earned income after applying the 30 percent ceiling at the partnership level. Complications arise, however, if there are inactive partners, special allocations of partnership items, or guaranteed payments to one or more of the partners.[41]

2. *Foreign earned income.* Earned income is "foreign earned income" if it is attributable to services performed by the taxpayer in one or more foreign countries during periods while the bona fide residence or 330-day test is satis-

---

[39] Rousku v. CIR, 56 TC 548, 550-551 (1971) (citations omitted). See Parker v. CIR, 822 F2d 905 (9th Cir. 1987) (capital was material in business of renting and servicing slot machines); Van Kalker v. CIR, 804 F2d 967, 970 (7th Cir. 1984) (capital not material in business of fabricating and installing custom-made iron railings; "the test is whether the capital is income-producing in its own right or whether its worth depends on the application of the taxpayer's personal skills"); US v. Van Dyke, 696 F2d 957, 962 (Fed. Cir. 1982) (where "the value added by personal skills is so substantial that the capital investment, by comparison, is relatively small, capital will not be deemed a material income producing factor"); Bruno v. CIR, 71 TC 191 (1978) (capital not material in taxpayer's bail bond business); infra ¶85.2 (capital as a material income-producing factor in applying §704(e)(4), relating to family partnerships). See generally Asimow, Section 1348: The Death of Mickey Mouse? 58 Cal. L. Rev. 801, 836-842 (1970).

[40] Rousku v. CIR, 56 TC 548 (1971), and cases there cited; Rev. Rul. 74-597, 1974-2 CB 272 (farmland leased by taxpayer taken into account in determining that capital was material income-producing factor in operation of truck farm); Rev. Rul. 66-326, 1966-2 CB 281 (same).

[41] See Reg. §1.702-1(a)(8)(ii); Vogt v. US, 537 F2d 405 (Ct. Cl. 1976) (partner's earned income based on partnership net profit, not gross income; extensive analysis); Zahler v. CIR, 684 F2d 356 (6th Cir. 1982) (30 percent ceiling inapplicable to commissions received by partner from brokerage partnership because commissions not part of partnership profits); Rev. Rul. 78-306, 1978-2 CB 218 (30 percent ceiling applied where partnership maintained capital to facilitate its investment banking and broker-dealer activities); infra ¶¶86.2, 87.2.2 (partners' distributive shares and guaranteed payments).

Similar problems arise in allocating the partnership's foreign source income among the partners.

fied.[42] The place at which the taxpayer receives the income is not relevant.[43] For example, an employee working abroad for a U.S. employer does not lose the exclusions by having her compensation paid into a bank account in the United States.

Deferred compensation generally is not foreign earned income, regardless of its source. This disqualification extends to social security benefits, pensions (including amounts received from nonexempt employee's trusts), annuities (including benefits under nonqualified employee's annuities), and any amount "received after the close of the taxable year following the taxable year in which the services . . . are performed."[44] For example, salary for services performed in 1996 may be foreign earned income if received in 1997, but not if received in 1998 or later.

Also, compensation received as an employee of the U.S. government or an agency thereof cannot be foreign earned income.[45] Generally, salaries and wages received from the federal government or a federal agency are disqualified even if the government or agency is reimbursed for the salaries and wages by another person and even if compensation received directly from that other person could qualify for exclusion under §911.[46]

3. *Dollar ceiling.* The annual exclusion under §911(a)(1) is limited to a fixed dollar amount, which was $70,000 for 1997, increases by $2,000 for each of the succeeding five years, and is $80,000 for 2002 and succeeding years.[47] The purpose of the ceiling is to prevent "abuse of the exclusion by, for example, highly paid entertainers or athletes who might otherwise move abroad to escape large amounts of U.S. tax on their income."[48] The ceiling was reduced to $70,000

---

[42] IRC §911(b)(1)(A). See supra ¶65.5.2 for the bona fide residence and 330-day tests.

[43] Reg. §1.911-3(a).

[44] IRC §911(b)(1)(B).

[45] IRC §911(b)(1)(B)(ii). See Chin v. US, 57 F3d 722 (9th Cir. 1995) (physician working under contract with U.S. Agency for International Development (AID) qualified for §911 exclusion because he was independent contractor, not U.S. employee); Payne v. US, 980 F2d 148 (2d Cir. 1992) (Panama Canal Commission is U.S. agency for purposes of §911); McCain v. CIR, 81 TC 918 (1983) (same); Mathews v. CIR, 907 F2d 1173 (DC Cir. 1990) ("nonappropriated fund instrumentalities," which are "partially self supporting, quasi-governmental organizations that provide services to military personnel," are U.S. agencies); Adair v. CIR, 70 TCM (CCH) 998 (1995) (acq.) (employee of U.S. Army was transferred to NATO; held, during NATO service, taxpayer was not U.S. employee).

[46] See Smith v. CIR, 701 F2d 807 (9th Cir. 1983) (overtime pay of Customs Inspector stationed abroad is not foreign earned income even though government was reimbursed by airlines that requested overtime work to accommodate passengers); Soboleski v. CIR, 88 TC 1024 (1987), aff'd without opinion, 842 F2d 1292 (4th Cir. 1988) (salary from U.S. Army Corps of Engineers not foreign earned income even though taxpayer worked on project undertaken by the Corps for foreign government and taxpayer's salary was paid from funds supplied by that government); Rev. Rul. 85-29, 1985-1 223 (same).

[47] IRC §§911(b)(2)(A), 911(b)(2)(D). The $80,000 figure will be indexed for inflation for years after 2007.

[48] S. Rep. No. 144, supra note 1, at 420.

in 1986 from somewhat higher levels adopted in 1981.[49] The reduction was made because "in connection with the lowering of tax rates for U.S. individuals, [the 1986 Act] repealed or restricted a great number of tax preferences."[50] The $70,000 figure was not indexed for inflation, and in 1997, Congress decided to raise the ceiling gradually and eventually to index it for inflation because "the extra costs from working abroad have increased with worldwide inflation."[51] The ceiling only applies to the exclusion under §911(a)(1), which equals the lesser of the ceiling or the portion of the taxpayer's foreign earned income that is not excluded by the housing exclusion of §911(a)(2).[52]

If the taxpayer does not qualify for the §911(a)(1) exclusion for the entire year, the ceiling is prorated, and the maximum exclusion is the ceiling amount for the year, multiplied by a fraction whose numerator is the number of qualifying days in the taxable year and whose denominator is the number of days in the year.[53] A qualifying day is a day on which the taxpayer has his tax home in a foreign country and meets either the bona fide residence or 330-day test.[54] Assume an individual is a resident of a foreign country from November 1, 1997, through March 31, 1999, and has her tax home in that country during all of this period. The bona fide residence test is satisfied because the period of foreign residence includes all of one taxable year (1998). For 1997, the taxpayer has 61 qualifying days (all of the days of November and December), and the ceiling is $11,699 ($70,000 × 61 ÷ 365). Because all days in 1998 are qualifying days, the ceiling for that year is $72,000. For 1999, there are 90 qualifying days (all of the days of January, February, and March), and the ceiling is $18,247 ($74,000 × 90 ÷ 365).

Foreign earned income is counted against the ceiling for the year in which the services are performed.[55] For example, salary that is earned in one year and received in the next is lumped with the remainder of the salary for the former year in determining the portion of it that is excludable under §911(a). Also, if a tax equalization payment reimbursing the taxpayer for foreign income taxes is received in the year following the year in which the taxpayer earned the income

---

[49] Pub. L. No. 99-514, §1233(c), 100 Stat. 2085 (1986). The limitation was $75,000 for 1982 and $80,000 for 1983 through 1987. IRC §911(b)(2)(A) (before amendment in 1986).

[50] Staff of Joint Comm. on Tax'n, 99th Cong., 2d Sess., General Explanation of the Tax Reform Act of 1986 at 1009 (Comm. Print 1987) [hereinafter 1986 Bluebook].

[51] Staff of Joint Comm. on Tax'n, 105th Cong., 1st Sess., General Explanation of Tax Legislation Enacted in 1997, at 325 (Comm. Print 1997).

[52] For the housing exclusion, see infra ¶65.5.4.

[53] Reg. §1.911-3(d)(2).

[54] Reg. §1.911-3(d)(3).

[55] IRC §911(b)(2)(B); Reg. §1.911-3(e)(1). But see Reg. §1.911-3(e)(3) (first paycheck received during year is attributable entirely to that year, even if payroll period includes days from preceding year, providing that payroll period is not longer than 16 days). See Reg. §1.911-3(e)(4) (rules for determining year to which bonus or nonvested property is attributable).

subject to the foreign taxes, the payment relates back to the preceding year. However, if foreign earned income for a particular year exceeds the ceiling, the excludable amount consists first of income received during that year.[56] Assume an individual's foreign earned income for work done during 1998 consists of an advance bonus of $10,000 received in 1997, salary of $80,000 received in 1998, and a performance bonus of $10,000 received in 1999. The exclusion for all of these amounts is limited by the $72,000 ceiling for 1998. Since $80,000 is received in 1998, $72,000 of the 1998 receipts are excluded, and the 1997 and 1999 bonuses are included in gross income.

Section 911(a)(1) excludes up to the ceiling amount of *gross* income. If the taxpayer has deductions allocable to the excluded gross income, they are disallowed under a rule described below,[57] and the exclusion thus has the effect of reducing taxable income by something less than the ceiling amount.[58] Assume a qualifying individual carries on a professional practice in a foreign country; for 1999, fee income is $296,000, and expenses are $160,000. Section 911(a)(1) excludes $74,000 of the fees from gross income, but since one fourth of the gross income is excluded, one fourth of the deductions ($40,000) are disallowed. The exclusion thus reduces taxable income by only $34,000 ($74,000 exclusion less $40,000 of disallowed deductions).

If a husband and wife both qualify for the §911 exclusion, the ceiling amount is excludable by each of them.[59] Earned income that is community income is treated as income of the spouse performing the services.[60]

¶65.5.4 Exclusion or Deduction for Excess Foreign Housing Expenses

An employee qualifying for the foreign earned income exclusion of §911(a)(1) is also eligible for a second exclusion under §911(a)(2) if housing costs are high. The exclusion may consist of portions of a housing allowance provided by the employer, or it might consist of an amount of salary equal to a portion of the taxpayer's housing expenses. Self-employed persons are allowed an equivalent deduction. The exclusion or deduction is allowed only for periods when the taxpayer's tax home is in a foreign country and the taxpayer satisfies the bona fide residence or 330-day test. The exclusion or deduction equals the "housing cost amount," which is the excess of the taxpayer's "housing expenses" over a stipulated amount that is apparently intended to approximate the typical housing costs of an individual living in the United States.

---

[56] Reg. §1.911-3(e)(2).

[57] See infra ¶65.5.5 text accompanying notes 75–81.

[58] Cook v. US, 599 F2d 400 (Ct. Cl. 1979). But see Vogt v. US, 537 F2d 405 (1976) (for partners, §911(a) excludes up to the ceiling amount of each partner's distributive share of partnership's net profits).

[59] S. Rep. No. 144, supra note 1, at 37, reprinted in 1981-2 CB at 420; Reg. §1.911-5(a).

[60] IRC §911(b)(2)(C).

The term "housing expenses" refers to the costs of housing in a foreign country for the taxpayer and the taxpayer's spouse and dependents, including rent, the fair rental value of housing provided in kind by the taxpayer's employer, utilities (except telephone charges), insurance on real and personal property, household repairs, residential parking, and other "expenses attributable to the housing."[61] Several costs associated with housing, however, are excluded, including the costs of purchasing a house or apartment, capital improvements, or furniture, payments of principal and interest on a home mortgage, real property taxes, moving expenses deductible under §217, cable or pay television charges, and wages and salaries of maids, gardeners, and other domestic labor.[62] A cost qualifies only if "reasonable," not "lavish or extravagant under the circumstances."[63] Moreover, qualifying expenses are limited to those incurred while the taxpayer has a foreign tax home and satisfies either the bona fide residence or 330-day test.[64]

Normally, the taxpayer's "housing expenses" can include only the costs of one foreign home, and the exclusion is wholly lost if the employer provides housing in kind whose value is excluded from the taxpayer's gross income by §119.[65] If the taxpayer has more than one dwelling and does not receive housing excluded by §119, only the costs of the foreign "abode" that "bears the closest relationship to the [taxpayer's] tax home" qualify.[66] However, if a separate foreign abode is maintained for the taxpayer's spouse or dependents because of "dangerous, unhealthful, or otherwise adverse" living conditions where the taxpayer resides, costs of both the taxpayer's abode and that of the spouse or children are included in the taxpayer's housing expenses, and the expenses of the residence for the spouse or children qualify even if the value of the housing occupied by the taxpayer is excludable under §119.[67]

The "housing cost amount"—the amount of the §911(a)(2) exclusion or deduction—is the excess of the taxpayer's housing expenses for the taxable year over the following amount: (1) 16 percent of the daily salary of an employee of the federal government who is in the first step of grade GS-14, multiplied by (2) the number of days during the year on which the taxpayer has a foreign tax home

---

[61] IRC §911(c)(2)(A); Reg. §1.911-4(b)(1).

[62] Reg. §1.911-4(b)(2). Interest and real property taxes are excluded because they are separately deductible under §§163 and 164. S. Rep. No. 144, supra note 1, at 37, reprinted in 1981-2 CB at 420.

[63] IRC §911(c)(2)(A).

[64] Reg. §1.911-4(b)(3).

[65] Id. See supra ¶14.5 for §119.

[66] IRC §911(c)(2)(B)(i). See Reg. §1.911-4(b)(3) (closest relationship is "not necessarily geographic").

[67] See Reg. §1.911-4(b)(5)(ii) ("adverse conditions" exist if taxpayer resides on employer's business premises and nature of employer's business makes it not feasible for spouse or dependents to live there).

and meets the bona fide residence or 330-day test.[68] When these rules were enacted in 1981, the annual salary in the first step of grade GS-14 was $37,871, and the housing cost amount for a taxpayer qualifying for the entire year was the excess of the taxpayer's housing expenses over $6,059 (16 percent of $37,871).[69]

The housing allowance is usually an exclusion from gross income of "employer provided amounts," defined as amounts that are paid or incurred to or on the taxpayer's behalf by the taxpayer's employer and are part of the taxpayer's foreign earned income.[70] Salary, wages, an employer's reimbursement of the taxpayer, and employer payments on the taxpayer's behalf are employer provided amounts, whether or not the payments or reimbursements are related to housing.[71] In other words, §911(a)(2) simply provides an exclusion for a portion of the taxpayer's foreign earned income equal to the housing cost amount, and this portion need not be tied in any economic way to the taxpayer's housing expenses.

A self-employed person, however, has no employer provided amounts, and therefore is usually allowed a deduction in computing adjusted gross income in lieu of the exclusion.[72] The deduction may not exceed the taxpayer's foreign earned income, less the amount excluded from gross income by §911(a)(1).[73] When the latter rule reduces the deduction, the amount made nondeductible is carried to the next year, where it is deductible to the extent current unreimbursed housing expenses are less than the deduction ceiling for the carryover year.[74] If foreign earned income comes both from employment and self-employment, compensation received as employee is first excluded, and the deduction is allowed for only the excess of the housing cost amount over the excluded foreign earned income received as employee.[75]

¶65.5.5 Special Rules and Limitations for §911 Exclusions

1. *Disallowance of deductions and credits allocable to excluded income.* Under §911(d)(6), an otherwise allowable exclusion, deduction, or credit is denied to the extent it is allocable to gross income excluded by §911(a).[76] For example, all or a portion of a taxpayer's business expenses are nondeductible if gross

---

[68] IRC §911(c)(1). For the computation of the housing cost amount where a joint return is filed by spouses, both of whom qualify for the §911 exclusions, see Reg. §1.911-5(a)(3).

[69] Reg. §1.911-4(c)(2) (GS-14 salary in effect on January 1 of taxable year governs).

[70] IRC §911(c)(3)(D).

[71] Reg. §1.911-4(d)(2).

[72] IRC §911(c)(3)(A).

[73] IRC §911(c)(3)(B).

[74] IRC §911(c)(3)(C).

[75] Reg. §1.911-4(d)(3).

[76] The deductions and credits allocable to excludable amounts are determined under Reg. §1.861-8, discussed infra ¶70.10. Reg. §1.911-6(a).

income of the business is excluded by §911.[77] Deductions not definitely related to any class of gross income are not allocated in any part to excludable income and thus are exempted from the disallowance rule.[78] For example, the rule does not affect deductions for medical costs, IRA contributions, real property taxes and mortgage interest on a personal residence, charitable contributions, alimony, and personal and dependency exemptions.

Assume an individual qualifying for the §911(a) exclusions practices as an architect in a foreign country.[79] For a particular year, fee receipts, all of which are foreign earned income, are $1 million, and otherwise deductible business expenses of the practice are $500,000. If the §911(a) exclusion for the year is $70,000, $35,000 of the expenses ($500,000 times $70,000/$1,000,000) are nondeductible. Taxable income from the practice is $465,000 (gross income of $1 million less $70,000 and deductions of $500,000 less $35,000). Because of §911(d)(6), the $70,000 of exclusions from gross income under §911(a) have the effect of reducing taxable income by $35,000 (profits of $500,000 as against taxable income of $465,000).

A major consequence of §911(d)(6) is that an individual electing the §911(a) exclusion cannot deduct or take a credit for foreign income taxes on the excluded amount.[80] If less than all of the taxpayer's foreign earned income is excluded under §911(a), the nondeductible and noncreditable amount equals the foreign income taxes multiplied by a fraction. The numerator of the fraction is the sum of the §911(a) exclusions for the year, reduced by the deductions denied by §911(d)(6) (other than for foreign income taxes). The denominator is the sum of the taxpayer's foreign earned income for the year (less all otherwise deductible expenses allocated to this income) and any income included in the foreign tax base that is not foreign earned income. Also, if the taxpayer is self employed and is allowed a deduction in lieu of the housing exclusion of §911(a)(2), the denominator is reduced by the amount of the deduction.

Assume an individual is a bona fide resident of foreign country X for all of a taxable year and maintains her tax home in that country throughout the year.[81] Her foreign earned income for the year consists of professional fees of $140,000, business expenses allocable to this income are $40,000, and a $15,000 deduction is allowed for the year under §911 for housing expenses. The individual pays income taxes to country X of $30,000, which are imposed on a base consisting of the professional income and interest income of $10,000; the ceiling amount for

---

[77] See Brewster v. CIR, 67 TC 352 (1976), aff'd per curiam, 607 F2d 1369 (DC Cir.), cert. denied, 444 US 991 (1979) (denied business expenses computed as total expenses multiplied by fraction whose numerator is gross income of business excluded by §911 and denominator is entire gross income of business).

[78] Reg. §1.911-6(a).

[79] Reg. §1.911-6(d) Ex. 1.

[80] Reg. §1.911-6(c)(1). See S. Rep. No. 144, supra note 1, at 37, reprinted in 1981-2 CB at 420.

[81] See Reg. §1.911-6(d) Ex. 5.

the year is $70,000. Since the taxpayer qualifies under §911 for the entire year, the §911(a)(1) exclusion is allowed for $70,000 of the gross professional income of $140,000, and the business expenses made nondeductible by §911(d)(6) are $20,000 (total expenses of $40,000 multiplied by $70,000/$140,000). The numerator of the fraction determining the nondeductible, noncreditable portion of the foreign income taxes is $50,000 ($70,000 exclusion less $20,000 of nondeductible expenses). The denominator is $95,000 ($140,000 of foreign earned income, less $40,000 of business expenses, less $15,000 deduction for housing costs, plus $10,000 of income in foreign tax base other than foreign earned income). The nondeductible, noncreditable portion of the foreign income taxes is thus $15,789 (tax of $30,000 multiplied by $50,000/$95,000).

2. *Moving expenses and moving expense reimbursements.* Normally, reimbursements to employees for moving expenses are treated as compensation for future services.[82] Thus, a reimbursement for expenses incurred in moving to a foreign country is usually foreign earned income, and a reimbursement for expenses of moving back to the United States is usually compensation for services to be performed in the United States. However, if an employee is transferred to a foreign country and the employer has a written policy of reimbursing for the expenses of both moving to the foreign location and moving back to the United States, both reimbursements are foreign earned income. The same rule applies where the employer has no policy but makes a written agreement with the employee before the move to the foreign country requiring reimbursements for the expenses of both moves.

For purposes of the rule denying deductions allocable to excluded income,[83] moving expenses are usually matched against income earned at the new place of work.[84] Expenses incurred in moving to a new principal place of work in a foreign country thus are allocable to foreign earned income, and the expenses of moving back to the United States are usually allocable to U.S. income. Expenses incurred in moving back to the United States, however, are matched with foreign earned income if a reimbursement for the expenses is foreign earned income under the rules described in the preceding paragraph. Moving expenses allocable to foreign

---

[82] Reg. §1.911-3(e)(5)(i). See IRC §82 (moving expense reimbursements included in gross income as compensation for services).

The rules described here generally apply for moves beginning after 1983. For earlier moves, the rules are similar but not identical. See Reg. §1.911-3(e)(5)(ii)(B); Hughes v. CIR, 65 TC 566 (1975) (where taxpayer is transferred by employer from United States to foreign location, moving expense reimbursement is attributable to future services and thus qualifies for exclusion); Dammers v. CIR, 76 TC 835 (1981) (where, before taxpayer's transfer to foreign location, employer agrees to reimburse for expenses of eventual move back to United States, reimbursement for move back is allocable to past services in foreign country for purposes of foreign tax credit); Redding v. CIR, 43 TCM (CCH) 719 (1982) (*Dammers* followed in applying §911).

[83] See supra text accompanying notes 76–81.

[84] Reg. §1.911-6(b)(1). The rules discussed here apply for moves after 1983. For earlier moves, see Reg. §1.911-6(b)(5); Butka v. CIR, 91 TC 110 (1988).

earnings are matched with income earned in the year of the move if the taxpayer qualifies for the §911 exclusions for at least 120 days in that year. If this 120-day requirement is not met, the expenses are allocable to foreign earned income for the year of the move and the next year (in the case of a move abroad) or foreign income for the year of the move and the preceding year (where expenses of a move back to the United States are matched with foreign earned income).[85]

Whenever otherwise deductible moving expenses are allocated to foreign earned income, the deduction is disallowed for an amount equal to the expenses multiplied by a fraction whose numerator is the sum of the exclusions under §911(a) and whose denominator is the taxpayer's foreign earned income for the year or years to which the moving expenses are allocated.[86]

Assume an individual becomes a bona fide resident of a foreign country on July 1, 1996, and qualifies for the §911(a) exclusions for 219 days in 1996 (July 1 through December 31).[87] She incurs otherwise deductible expenses of $6,000 in moving to her new residence, all of which are paid during 1996. Her foreign earned income for the year is $60,000, including a $5,000 reimbursement for moving expenses. The maximum §911(a)(1) exclusion for 1995 is $42,000 ($70,000 × 219÷365); assume the exclusion under §911(a)(2) for housing costs is $3,000. The deduction for moving expenses is $1,500—the otherwise deductible expenses of $6,000, less the nondeductible amount of $4,500 ($6,000 × $45,000÷$60,000).

3. *Naughty country exception.* The benefits of §911 are barred for a taxpayer residing in or having earned income from sources within a country to which travel by U.S. citizens and residents is prohibited by regulations issued under the Trading With the Enemy Act or the International Emergency Economic Powers Act.[88] According to the IRS' most recent listing, the countries

---

[85] Reg. §1.911-6(b)(2). The moving expense deduction is allowable only for the year in which the expenses are paid or incurred, even if the expenses are allocable to foreign income for two years. Where expenses are allocable to foreign earned income for the year of move and the following year, the taxpayer may follow either of two procedural alternatives. First, a filing extension can be obtained allowing the return for the year of the move to be filed after the end of the succeeding year. Second, the taxpayer may file a timely return for the year of the move, deducting moving expenses except to extent allocable to foreign earned income for that year, and when foreign earned income for next year is ascertained, either file an amended return for the year of the move or report income for the succeeding year equal to the portion of the expenses allocable to foreign earned income for the succeeding year. Reg. §§1.911-6(b)(4), 1.911-7(c)(2). See Reg. §1.911-6(d) Ex. 4.

[86] Reg. §1.911-6(b)(3).

[87] Reg. §1.911-6(d) Ex. 3.

[88] IRC §911(d)(8) (applicable for taxable years after 1986). Technically, these statutes and regulations do not forbid travel in the proscribed countries, but instead impose criminal penalties on transactions related to the travel.

covered by this limitation are Cuba, Libya, and Iraq.[89] A resident of a proscribed country is not considered a bona fide resident of a foreign country, time spent in the country is not counted as days present in a foreign country, income from sources within the country cannot qualify as foreign earned income, and for purposes of the housing exclusion, the taxpayer's housing expenses do not include cost of housing in a proscribed country or housing for the taxpayer's spouse or dependents in another country while the taxpayer is present in the proscribed country.

These restrictions are lifted if, although citizens are generally prohibited from traveling to the country, the taxpayer's travel falls within an exception to the prohibition. For example, although travel to Cuba is generally forbidden, "American individuals may be present in Cuba to visit close family members, to engage in journalistic activity, or to perform research."[90]

¶65.5.6 Exempt Allowances for Federal Employees and Peace Corps Volunteers

Salaries and wages of employees of the federal government do not qualify for the §911(a) exclusions,[91] but §912 excludes a few types of compensation received by federal employees. Several allowances for Peace Corps volunteers are also excluded by §912.

1. *Foreign areas allowances.* A civilian officer or employee of the U.S. government may exclude allowances received under the following statutory provisions:[92]

    a. Chapter 9 of title I of the Foreign Service Act of 1980.[93]

       Section 4 of the Central Intelligence Agency Act of 1949.[94]

    b. Title II of the Overseas Differentials and Allowances Act.[95]

    c. Section 1(e), 1(f), or 22 of the Administrative Expenses Act of 1946.

These statutes authorize payments to employees stationed outside the United

---

[89] Rev. Rul. 92-63, 1992-2 CB 195 (as of August 17, 1992). See Rev. Rul. 87-35, 1987-1 CB 182 (preceding list, including Cambodia, Cuba, Libya, North Korea, and Vietnam).

[90] 1986 Bluebook, supra note 50, at 1010.

[91] See supra ¶65.5.3 text accompanying notes 44-45.

[92] IRC §912(1). See Pub. L. 99-514, §1232(b), 100 Stat. 2085 (1986) (although Panama Canal Act is not mentioned in §912(1), allowances under Act are excludable if comparable to excludable allowances paid to State Department employees in Panama); Rev. Rul. 89-131, 1989-2 CB 133 (overseas tropical differential not excludable because it is "essentially a recruitment or retention allowance" and State Department employees receive nothing comparable).

[93] 22 USC §§4081-4085.

[94] 50 USC §403(e).

[95] 5 USC §§5922-5925.

States for travel expenses, moving expenses, storage expenses for items that cannot be taken along, temporary housing, cost of living adjustments, and a few other costs. The exclusion, however, does not apply to "post differentials," which are incentive pay to induce employees to accept assignments in "an environment which differs substantially from the United States."[96]

2. *Cost of living allowances.* Civilian officers and employees of the U.S. government may also exclude cost of living allowances from gross income for periods they are "stationed outside the continental United States" if the allowances are paid under regulations approved by the President.[97] The requirement of being stationed outside the continental United States is satisfied by those stationed in Alaska, Hawaii, Puerto Rico, and the U.S. possessions, as well as those stationed in foreign countries.[98]

3. *Peace Corps allowances.* Allowances under sections 5 and 6 of the Peace Corps Act for volunteers, volunteer leaders, and members of their families are generally excluded from gross income.[99] However, the exclusion does not apply to living allowances to the extent they are "basic compensation" or to leave allowances, termination payments, and allowances to family members of volunteer leaders while training in the United States.

¶65.6 EFFECT OF TREATIES ON U.S. CITIZENS AND RESIDENTS

The United States is a party to many bilateral tax treaties under which the contracting states extend tax concessions to each other's residents.[1] For U.S. citizens, this means that income derived from sources in the other contracting state is often subject to reduced foreign tax rates or entirely exempted from tax. These allowances are usually extended to aliens resident in the United States unless they are also residents of the other treaty country.[2] Conversely, the normal U.S. tax rates applicable to the income of nonresident aliens and foreign corporations are mitigated by reductions or exemptions for residents of the other treaty country.

---

[96] 5 USC §5925.

[97] IRC §912(2). Also, for "judicial officers or employees," the allowances must be paid under rules "similar to" the presidential regulations under which cost of living allowances are paid to nonjudicial officers and employees.

[98] Reg. §1.912-1(b). See Sjoroos v. CIR, 81 TC 971 (1983) (exclusion of cost of living allowances for federal employees stationed in Alaska does not violate constitutional right of nongovernmental employees in Alaska to equal protection of the laws).

[99] IRC §912(3).

[1] See supra ¶65.1.6.

[2] More completely, a person is entitled to treaty benefits, regardless of citizenship, if the person is a resident of the United States under the treaty definition of "residence," which is discussed supra ¶65.2.8.

1. *Savings clauses.* In general, U.S. citizens and resident aliens may not enforce treaty concessions against the United States, even if they have some connection with the other contracting party. A U.S. citizen resident in France, for example, is not entitled to the reduced rate of tax on dividends allowed by the United States to residents of France. This disqualification is often embodied in a "saving clause," under which the United States reserves the right to tax its citizens and residents "as if this convention had not come into effect."[3]

Saving clauses, in turn, may be subject to exceptions for a few treaty provisions. Under the U.S. Model Income Tax Treaty, which was promulgated as a starting point for treaty negotiations with other countries, U.S. citizens may benefit from a few provisions as against their own government, including an exemption for social security benefits paid by the other treaty country and a mutual agreement procedure under which the countries agree to resolve complaints about the construction of the treaty by either country.[4] Moreover, by designating particular foreign taxes as qualifying for the foreign tax credit, treaties can relieve U.S. citizens of the necessity of proving that the taxes are "foreign income taxes" qualifying for the credit under §901.[5]

2. *Competent authority proceedings.* Nearly all tax treaties provide mutual agreement procedures under which a tax official of either country, known as the competent authority, or the taxpayer can request that the competent authorities of the two countries try to agree on a consistent way of taxing particular transactions in accordance with the treaty's terms.[6] A taxpayer's request for competent authority proceedings must be addressed to the competent authority of the

---

[3] See U.S. Treasury Dep't, Model Income Tax Treaty art. 1(3) (1996) [hereinafter U.S. Model Treaty]; Crerar v. CIR, 26 TC 702 (1956) (U.S. citizen resident in Canada barred by saving clause from claiming reduced rate granted by United States to "individuals residing in" Canada); Rev. Rul. 59-56, 1959-1 CB 737 (same result under treaty with United Kingdom, despite absence of saving clause); Doernberg & van Raad, The Forthcoming U.S. Model Income Tax Treaty and the Savings Clause, 5 Tax Notes Int'l 775 (Oct. 12, 1992) (advocating that savings clause be restated to provide that all U.S. citizens, wherever actually residing, are U.S. residents for treaty purposes).

See also O'Connor v. US, 479 US 27 (1986) (provision of Implementation Agreement to Panama Canal Treaty that U.S. citizen employees shall be "exempt from any taxes" on compensation from Panama Canal Commission refers to Panamanian taxes and confers no exemption from U.S income tax); Pub. L. No. 99-514, §1232, 100 Stat. 2085 (1986) (same).

[4] U.S. Model Treaty, supra note 3, art. 25(3). For more limited exceptions to the model saving clause for resident aliens, see U.S. Model Treaty, supra, arts. 24(1), 24(2)(b), 25(3)(b).

[5] See infra ¶69.4 (foreign taxes qualifying for credit).

[6] See Rev. Proc. 96-13, 1996-1 CB 366 (procedures for taxpayer requests for competent authority assistance, applicable to extent not in conflict with procedural provisions of particular treaty); Rev. Proc. 98-21, 1998-8 IRB 27 (competent authority requests under U.S.-Canada treaty); Halphen & Bordeaux, International Issue Resolution Through the Competent Authority Process, 64 Tax Notes 657 (Aug. 4, 1994); Skaar, The Legal Nature of Mutual Agreements Under Tax Treaties, 5 Tax Notes Int'l 1441 (Dec. 21, 1992).

taxpayer's country of residence, even if the tax complained of is imposed by the other country.

In *Yamaha Motor Corp. v. United States*, the taxpayers requested that the IRS commence competent authority negotiations under the U.S.-Japan treaty on a transfer pricing issue.[7] The taxpayers were U.S. subsidiaries of a Japanese parent, and the IRS was apparently proposing in audit to decrease the prices paid to the parent or other affiliated Japanese entities for goods that the taxpayers resold in the United States. The taxpayers claimed that this adjustment would result in the same profits being taxed by both the United States and Japan, and they requested that the IRS commence negotiations with the Japanese competent authority to eliminate this double taxation. The Assistant Commissioner (International), who serves as competent authority, denied the request because the Chief Counsel declined to relinquish the case to the competent authority.[8] The taxpayer was advised:

> After a decision is entered by the Tax Court that disposes of your case, either by settlement or after trial, you may wish to resubmit your request to us if there is still a potential double tax result. At that time, of course, our flexibility in negotiations will be limited by whatever the Tax Court has decided.[9]

The IRS promptly issued a notice of deficiency. The taxpayer sued in federal district court for a declaratory judgment that the IRS had violated the competent authority article of the treaty and for an order compelling the IRS to review the request for competent authority proceedings on the merits. The court dismissed the suit, holding that it was barred by the Anti-Injunction Act and a parallel provision of the Declaratory Judgment Act.[10]

The taxpayers in *Yamaha* contended that competent authority negotiations, when requested by taxpayers, are mandatory, not discretionary with the tax authorities. The general competent authority provisions of the OECD and U.S. Treasury Department model treaties state in Article 25(1) and (2):

> Where a person considers that the actions of one or both of the Contracting States result or will result for him in taxation not in accordance with the provisions of this Convention, he may, irrespective of the remedies provided by the domestic law of those States, present his case to the com-

---

[7] Yamaha Motor Corp. v. US, 779 F. Supp. 610 (DDC 1991).

[8] Under IRS procedures, "the U.S. competent authority will not, without the consent of the Chief Counsel, accept (or continue to consider) a taxpayer's request for assistance if the request involves a taxable period pending in a U.S. court or involves a matter pending in a U.S. court or designated for litigation for any taxable period." Rev. Proc. 96-13, 1996-1 CB 366, §7.03. Although still in audit, the *Yamaha* case was apparently designated for litigation before the competent authority request was made.

[9] Plaintiffs' Memorandum of Points and Authorities in Opposition to Defendants' Motion to Dismiss at 4.

[10] See infra ¶115.9.

petent authority of the Contracting State of which he is a resident or national.

The competent authority shall endeavor, if the objection appears to it to be justified and if it is not itself able to arrive at a satisfactory solution, to resolve the case by mutual agreement with the competent authority of the other Contracting State, with a view to the avoidance of taxation which is not in accordance with the Convention.[11]

The *Yamaha* taxpayers' claim that competent authority negotiations are mandatory finds support in the treaties' command that the competent authority "shall endeavor" to reach agreement with the competent authority of the other country whenever a taxpayer's complaint of double taxation appears well grounded.

The most obvious difficulty with the taxpayers' claim is that the IRS did not deny that competent authority negotiations might eventually become appropriate in the case; the dispute was only over the timing of the negotiations. The taxpayers wanted them to occur before the issue was litigated, while the IRS wanted to proceed to a final determination under U.S. law (probably, a Tax Court decision) and then utilize competent authority negotiations to alleviate any double taxation resulting from this determination. The issue in the case was therefore whether the taxpayer or the IRS had the right to decide when competent authority negotiations should commence.[12]

Yamaha had persuasive reasons for wanting competent authority negotiations to precede litigation. The taxpayers wanted to avoid the great expense of a trial on complex transfer pricing issues. Moreover, the IRS, in competent au-

---

[11] Article 25(1) of the U.S.-Japan treaty is essentially the same, although stated in somewhat different language. For example, the second paragraph is stated in the U.S.-Japan treaty as follows: "Should the resident's claim be considered to have merit by the competent authority of the Contracting State to which the claim is made, it shall endeavor to come to an agreement with the competent authority of the other Contracting State with a view to the avoidance of taxation contrary to the provisions of this Convention." The U.S. Model contains a sentence not found in the OECD Model or the U.S.-Japan treaty: "In particular the competent authorities of the Contracting States may agree . . . to the same allocation of income, deductions, credits, or allowances between persons." U.S. Model Treaty, supra note 3, art. 25(3)(b).

[12] IRS procedures assume the timing lies within IRS discretion. Taxpayers may request competent authority assistance "as soon as practical after the amount of the proposed adjustment is determined and communicated in writing to the taxpayer." Rev. Proc. 96-13, 1996-1 CB 366, §4.01. However, if the case is pending in court or "has been designated for litigation," the request may be granted only with consent of the Chief Counsel. Id. at §7.03. If the case is in the Tax Court, "the taxpayer may, in appropriate cases, be asked to join" in motions to the court to facilitate competent authority negotiations. If the case is in a federal district court or the Court of Federal Claims, "the Chief Counsel will consult with the Department of Justice about appropriate action." A competent authority request "does not . . . relieve the taxpayer from taking any action that may be necessary or required with respect to litigation."

thority negotiations after litigation, would not relinquish any victory won in litigation. IRS procedures state:

> Once a taxpayer's tax liability ... has been determined by a U.S. court (including settlement of the proceedings before or during trial), the U.S. competent authority ... will endeavor only to obtain a correlative adjustment from the treaty country and will not undertake any action that would otherwise reduce the taxpayer's federal tax liability for the taxable years in issue as determined by a U.S. court.[13]

---

[13] Rev. Proc. 96-13, 1996-1 CB 366, §7.05.

CHAPTER

66

Nonresident Aliens, Foreign Corporations, and Other Foreign Persons

¶66.1 INTRODUCTORY

¶66.1.1 Generally

Two very different taxing schemes are provided for foreign persons (nonresident aliens and foreign corporations).[1] If a foreign person carries on a trade or business in the United States, U.S. tax is imposed on all taxable income that is effectively connected with the trade or business.[2] This taxable income is generally computed under the same rules that apply to U.S. persons, except that gross income not effectively connected with the U.S. trade or business is excluded and deductions are limited to those that are connected with effectively connected income. The tax on effectively connected income is imposed under §1 or §11 at the same rates that apply to a similarly situated U.S. person.

In contrast, income of a foreign person that is not effectively connected with a U.S. trade or business is exempt from U.S. tax unless it is from sources within the United States and falls within certain designated classes, which include dividends, interest, rents, and royalties but generally not capital gains and other income realized on sales of property.[3] When noneffectively connected income is subject to U.S. tax, the tax rate is a flat 30 percent (except as reduced by treaty) and is applied to the gross amount of the income, without any deductions or personal exemptions.

The rules for noneffectively connected income reflect the difficulty of collecting taxes from foreigners who are neither physically present in the United

---

[1] For the terms "nonresident alien" and "foreign corporation," see supra ¶¶65.2 and 65.3. See Avi-Yonah, Virtual Taxation: Source-Based Taxation in the Age of Derivatives, in Nat'l Tax Ass'n, Proceedings of 89th Annual Conf. on Tax'n 269 (1997); Brumbaugh, Federal Taxes and Foreign Investment in the United States: An Assessment, 4 Tax Notes Int'l 229 (Feb. 3, 1992) (arguing that income from equity investments of foreign persons may be subject to U.S. tax at near optimal rates but that effective rates of U.S. tax on income from foreign investments in form of debt are generally negative); Hobbs, Foreign-Controlled Domestic Corporations, 1993, 16 Stat. Income Bull. 127 (Fall 1996) (for 1993, these corporations accounted for 10.2 percent of receipts reported on all corporate income tax returns, 6.4 percent of taxable income, and 6.8 percent of income tax after credits); Holik & Nutter, Transactions Between Large Foreign-Owned Domestic Corporations and Related Foreign Persons, 1992, 16 Stat. Income Bull. 154 (Fall 1996).

[2] See infra ¶66.3.

[3] See infra ¶66.2.9. For a proposal to tax capital gains realized by foreign shareholders of domestic corporations, see Renfroe, Fogarasi, Gordon & Venuti, 1989 Tax Bill: Taxing Foreign Investors on Capital Gains, 44 Tax Notes 1415 (Sept. 18, 1989).

States nor tied to this country by residence or business operations.[4] Congress concluded that the only feasible way to tax U.S. income of foreign persons not engaged in business in the United States is to require the U.S. persons who remit the income abroad to withhold the tax from the income. A withholding tax is feasible only if it is imposed at a flat rate on gross income because it is usually impractical to require U.S. payors to obtain and verify the information necessary to administer a withholding tax based on the obligee's domestic or worldwide net income. The inherent unfairness of a tax on gross income is minimized if the tax is confined to items like dividends, interest, and royalties, which are often earned without substantial expense by ordinary investors. For example, a tax on the gross proceeds of a sale of property would often be confiscatory because the net gain may be only a small fraction of the sales price or a loss may be incurred, and a tax on net gain would require the person charged with withholding to ascertain the taxpayer's adjusted basis. Net gain could be taxed, subject to a rule requiring buyers, brokers, and other U.S. agents to withhold a stipulated percentage of the gross sales price unless the foreign seller establishes the amount of the gain, but such a rule might drive foreign investors to more hospitable financial centers.[5]

The withholding scheme for noneffectively connected income often comes in conflict with a broader policy to tax foreign persons fairly without opening avenues for evasion. For example, although interest, dividends, rents, and royalties are often earned without substantial expense, this is not always the case, and a 30 percent tax on the gross amount of these items sometimes exceeds 100 percent of the taxpayer's net income. For example, whenever an investment is financed with borrowed money, the lack of a deduction for interest expense can cause a gross income tax to be confiscatory. The net income of banks and other financial institutions is usually far less than 30 percent of gross interest receipts. Also, the lack of a deduction for depreciation often causes the 30 percent tax on gross rents and royalties to be greatly in excess of 30 percent of net income.

The exemption of gains on sales of property introduces a further element of arbitrariness. For example, a foreign investor in a domestic corporation that distributes all of its profits is subject to substantial U.S. taxes, while a foreign investor in a domestic corporation that accumulates all of its income realizes income solely in the form of tax-free capital gains.

Caught on the horns of a dilemma between feasibility, on the one hand, and rationality and fairness, on the other, Congress has adopted or acquiesced in

---

[4] For problems in enforcing the tax liabilities of recalcitrant nonresident aliens and foreign corporations, see infra ¶112.1.8.

[5] Such a scheme has been adopted for gains on dispositions of U.S. real property and has not noticeably affected foreigners' appetite for owning U.S. realty. See infra ¶66.4.10. However, the withholding mechanism for real property would not work well for stocks and bonds, for example, because the market for stocks and bonds is much more dependent on investors' ability to trade quickly and with minimal expense. Moreover, foreigners can easily buy and sell U.S. securities in transactions solely between foreign persons that have no physical connection with the United States.

several deviations from the general scheme for taxing nonbusiness income of foreign persons, including:

1. The United States is a party to numerous bilateral income tax treaties under which residents of our treaty partners are typically exempted from U.S. tax on nonbusiness interest and royalty income and are usually taxed on nonbusiness dividend income at rates less than 30 percent.[6]

2. By statute, most interest income is exempt from the 30 percent withholding tax unless the taxpayer is a bank or the interest is received from an entity in which the taxpayer has a 10 percent or greater equity stake.[7]

3. Passive foreign lessors of U.S. real property are allowed to elect to treat the property as a business, thus permitting deductions to be taken for interest, depreciation, and other expenses connected with the property.[8]

4. A nonresident alien or foreign corporation holding an interest in U.S. real property, either directly or indirectly through ownership of stock of a domestic corporation, is taxed on gain on a disposition of the interest.[9]

When a foreign person holds stock in a domestic corporation, the shareholder's share of corporate earnings can be taxed twice—once as the earnings are realized by the corporation and again as they are distributed to the shareholder as dividends. Congress decided in 1986 that the same potential for double taxation should exist when a foreign corporation conducts business in the United States through an unincorporated branch. This is accomplished by a branch profits tax, imposed in addition to the regular corporate tax on effectively connected taxable income whenever branch profits are deemed withdrawn from the U.S. business.[10] The branch profits tax is computed in a way designed to mimic how the withholding tax would have applied if the branch were separately incorporated as domestic subsidiary. The 1986 legislation also imposes a branch-level interest tax to ensure that interest deducted in determining effectively connected taxable income is, if paid to a foreign person, subject to the withholding tax essentially as the tax would have applied if the branch were incorporated as a domestic corporation.[11]

Normally, a foreign person is subject to the same rules for choosing accounting periods and methods as a U.S. person. However, an alien individual's taxable year must be the calendar year unless the person adopted a fiscal year as his taxable year before he first became subject to U.S. taxes. An alien can estab-

---

[6] See infra ¶66.2.2 (interest), ¶66.2.3 (dividends), ¶66.2.7 (royalties). For a table showing withholding rates for 1992 on all types of income under all treaties, see IRS Pub. No. 515, Withholding of Tax On Nonresident Aliens and Foreign Corporations (Rev. Nov. 1994).

[7] IRC §871(h), discussed infra ¶66.2.2 text accompanying notes 21–56.

[8] IRC §§871(d), 882(d), discussed infra ¶66.3.6.

[9] IRC §897, discussed infra ¶66.4.

[10] IRC §884(a), discussed infra ¶66.5.

[11] IRC §884(f), discussed infra ¶66.5.3.

lish a fiscal year as his taxable year by keeping his books on a fiscal year basis or by using the fiscal year in filing returns under a foreign income tax law.[12]

¶66.1.2 Income Tax Treaties

The United States has entered into numerous bilateral income tax treaties, which affect in various ways the U.S. taxation of residents of the countries with which the treaties were made.[13] For example, treaties usually bar the United States from taxing the business profits of a resident of a treaty country unless the person has a permanent establishment in the United States, and if the taxpayer has a U.S. permanent establishment, only profits attributable to the permanent establishment may be taxed by the United States.[14] Also, the treaties typically reduce the 30 percent withholding tax rate for some types of income and exempt other items from the tax. For example, the rate on dividends is frequently reduced by treaty to 15 percent (5 percent if the recipient is a corporation owning a significant portion of the payor's stock), and interest and royalties are commonly exempted. These provisions are discussed in more detail throughout this Chapter in the discussions of the statutory rules that are modified by the treaties.

Most treaties contain provisions barring either country from discriminating against nationals of the other. For example, Article 24(1) of the OECD and Treasury model treaties provide that "nationals" of one country "shall not be subjected in the other [country] to any taxation or any requirement connected therewith which is other or more burdensome than the taxation and connected requirements to which nationals of that other State in the same circumstances are or may be subjected."[15] Moreover, under article 24(4), the taxation of a permanent establishment maintained by "an enterprise" of one of the countries in the other country "shall not be less favorably levied in that other State than the taxation levied on enterprises of that other State carrying on the same activities." Whereas tax treaties generally apply only to federal taxes specifically designated in the treaty, the nondiscrimination articles apply to all taxes imposed by all governments, federal, state, and local.

---

[12] IRC §7701(b)(9)(A). See Reg. §301.7701(b)-6(a) (without obtaining consent to change of accounting period, alien individual may adopt calendar year for U.S. tax purposes, even if fiscal year was established as taxable year under foreign income tax law before individual was first subject to U.S. tax).

[13] See supra ¶65.1.6.

[14] See infra ¶66.3.9.

[15] See Goldberg & Glicklich, Treaty-Based Nondiscrimination: Now You See It Now You Don't, 1 Fla. Tax Rev. 51 (1992).

¶66.2 NONBUSINESS INCOME FROM U.S. SOURCES

¶66.2.1 Introductory

Under §§871(a)(1) and 881(a), nonresident aliens and foreign corporations are subject to a 30 percent tax on several types of nonbusiness income from U.S. sources.[1] Because the tax is collected by requiring U.S. payors to withhold tax from remittances to the foreign taxpayers, it is often referred to as a withholding tax.[2] In addition, §871(a)(2), a provision with very limited application, imposes a tax of 30 percent on the net capital gain of a nonresident alien who is present in the United States for more than 182 days during the taxable year.[3]

The withholding tax is imposed at a flat 30 percent, without any deduction or other allowance for costs incurred in earning or collecting the income. The tax applies to interest, dividends, rents, royalties, and other "fixed or determinable annual or periodical" income, but only if the income is (1) an "amount received," (2) included in gross income, (3) from sources within the United States, and (4) not effectively connected with the conduct of a U.S. business. As a result of the first of these requirements, the withholding tax is imposed on a cash basis, regardless of the taxpayer's regular method of accounting.[4] The second require-

---

[1] For whether an alien is a resident or a nonresident, see supra ¶65.2.

For the application of these taxes to income from derivatives and innovative financial instruments, see Avi-Yonah & Swartz, U.S. International Tax Treatment of Financial Derivatives, 13 Tax Notes Int'l 787 (Mar. 3, 1996); May, Flying on Instruments: Synthetic Investment and the Avoidance of Withholding Tax, 13 Tax Notes 1625 (Nov. 11, 1996); Neigbour, Innovative Financial Instruments Challenge the Global Tax System, 14 Tax Notes Int'l 931 (Mar. 17, 1997). See also Korge, Debt or Equity Financing of Foreign Investments in the United States, 12 Tax Notes Int'l 753 (March 4, 1996); Schneider, U.S. Tax Rules Affecting Foreign Investors in REITs, 24 J. Real Est. Tax'n 40 (1996).

[2] For the withholding obligation, see IRC §§1441-1443, discussed infra ¶66.2B.

The gross income subject to tax under §871(a)(1) or 882(a) is the pretax amount of the income, and the amount withheld is allowed as a credit against the beneficial owner's tax liability. IRC §1462; Reg. §1.1462-1(a). If the payee is not the person "ultimately liable for the tax," the credit is allowed to that person. Reg. §1.1462-1(b). For example, if tax is withheld from income of a foreign partnership, the credit is allowed to the partners.

A foreign person is usually relieved of the burden of filing a U.S. tax return if it is not engaged in a trade or business in the United States and "its tax liability for the taxable year is fully satisfied by the withholding of tax at source." Reg. §§1.6012-1(b)(1), -2(g)(2).

[3] See infra ¶66.2.9.

[4] However, the Tax Court has held that an item can be subject to the tax even if there is no payment of the item from which the tax can be withheld. Central de Gas de Chihuahua, S.A. v. CIR, 102 TC 515 (1994) (taxpayer foreign corporation leased equipment to related foreign corporation for use in United States but collected no rent; held, rents imputed under §482 are taxable under §881(a)). See also Climaco v. IRS, 96-1 USTC ¶50,153 (EDNY 1996) (not officially reported) (borrower under interest-free loan required to withhold tax from interest imputed under §7872). See generally Benson & Leary, Taxation of Foreign Corporation Based on Section 482 Allocation Upheld, 23 Tax Mgmt. Int'l J. 393 (Aug. 12, 1994); Levey, Gordon & Grauer, Chihuahua: Tax Court Accepts

ment exempts interest on state and municipal obligations and other amounts excludable from gross income under general statutory provisions.[5] The third exempts amounts derived from foreign sources.[6] The fourth offers no exemption, but merely transfers certain types of income from the jurisdiction of §§871(a)(1) and 881(a) to §§871(b) and 882(a), under which taxable income effectively connected with a U.S. trade or business is taxed at graduated rates.[7]

When a domestic partnership has income of one of the described types, the partnership is not subject to the withholding tax, but the tax applies to any portion of the income that is includable in the distributive share of a foreign partner.[8] The withholding tax rules, in other words, follow the general tax scheme for partnerships and partners, under which a partnership is not a taxpaying entity, but its income is instead allocated among the partners, who must treat their distributive shares of partnership income as their own. Tax must be withheld from a taxable item paid to a foreign partnership,[9] but even in this circumstance, the taxpayers are the partners, not the partnership.

Trusts and estates, unlike partnerships, are taxable entities. A foreign trust or estate is therefore subject to the withholding tax on its U.S. source dividends, interest, and other fixed or determinable annual or periodical income.[10] A beneficiary of a trust or estate, however, must include in gross income any amount distributed or distributable to the beneficiary from the distributable net income of the trust or estate, and this amount has the same character in the beneficiary's hands as it had to the trust or estate.[11] These rules have been construed to impose the withholding tax when income of a trust or estate of a type subject to the tax is includable in the gross income of a foreign beneficiary.[12]

IRS Withholding on Deemed Payments, 6 J. Int'l Tax'n 148 (1995); Stark & Baillif, Do Section 482 Allocations to Foreign Entities Trigger a Withholding Obligation? 82 J. Tax'n 178 (1995).

[5] For the exclusion for interest on obligations of state and local governments, see §103, discussed in Ch. 15.

[6] For the source rules, see §§861–865, discussed in Ch. 70.

[7] For the effectively connected income tax, see infra ¶66.3.

[8] For the term "distributive share," see infra ¶86.2.1. For the possibility of allocating disproportionately low amounts of domestic source income (and correspondingly large amounts of foreign source income) to a firm's foreign partners, see §704(b), discussed infra ¶86.2.1.

[9] IRC §1441(a). For more on withholding from partnership items, see infra ¶66.2.12 text accompanying notes 226–28.

[10] For whether a trust or estate is domestic or foreign, see supra ¶¶65.3.3, 65.3.4.

[11] See IRC §652(b) (simple trusts) and §662(b) (estates and complex trusts), discussed infra ¶¶81.4.2 and 81.4.3.

[12] Reg. §1.652(b)-1 (last two sentences), §1.662(b)-1; Reg. §1.1441-2(a)(2) (beneficiary's share of estate's or trust's fixed or determinable annual or periodical income from U.S. sources retains its character as fixed or determinable income when distributed). See Rev. Rul. 86-76, 1986-1 CB 284, discussed infra ¶66.2.2 note 57.

¶66.2.2 Interest

The term "interest," which comes first in the statutory list of items subject to the withholding tax, is defined broadly to include unstated interest and original issue discount (OID).[13] The withholding tax, however, is not often imposed on interest. Portfolio interest, defined to include most interest received from unrelated borrowers by taxpayers other than banks, is exempted from the tax by statute.[14] Also, treaties commonly exempt residents of treaty countries from U.S. tax on nonbusiness interest income.[15]

1. *Original issue discount and unstated interest.* For purposes of §§871(a)(1) and 881(a), "interest" includes "unstated interest," which is the portion of a deferred payment under a contract for the sale of property that is recharacterized as interest by §483.[16] Original issue discount (OID) is also taxed, but is subject to special rules that adapt the accrual system for taxing OID to the cash basis system of §§871(a)(1) and 881(a).

Normally, OID (the excess of a debt instrument's face amount over the price for which the instrument was originally issued) is allocated over the instrument's term, and the holder is required to recognize the amount allocated to each year as gross income for that year.[17] However, if no payments are made to the holder in a particular year, there is nothing from which tax under §§871(a)(1) or 881(a) could be withheld. Since withholding is basic to the policies underlying the tax, OID is not recognized for purposes of §§871(a)(1) and 881(a) until the holder receives payment under the obligation or sells or exchanges it.[18] When a payment of interest or principal is received by a foreign holder of a discount obligation, the withholding tax is usually imposed on all OID that has accrued while the taxpayer held the obligation and has not been recognized on the receipt of prior payments. The taxable amount is limited so that the tax does not exceed the payment. When the obligation is sold or exchanged, tax is imposed on all OID

---

[13] If a foreign person transfers a debt instrument or shares of stock in a securities lending or "sale-repurchase" transaction, payments received by that person in substitution for interest or dividends on the transferred security are, for purposes of the withholding tax and treaties, treated as interest or dividends on the transferred security. Reg. §§1.871-7(b)(2), 1.881-2(b)(2), 1.894-1(c), 1.1441-2(b)(4) (these payments are, to the extent from U.S. sources, subject to withholding); see §§1.871-7(f), 1.881-2(e), 1.894-1(d) (this rule applies to payments made after November 13, 1997). See generally Solomon, Eurobond Transactions, in Taxation of Financial Instruments (Avi-Yonah, Newman & Ring, eds. Clark Boardman Callaghan 1996); Tuckner & Cohen, Final Regulations on the Source and Gross-Basis Taxation of Substitute Dividend and Interest Payments: A Work in Progress on Transparency, Translucency, and Opacity, 27 Tax Mgmt. Int'l J. 3 (1998).

[14] See infra text accompanying notes 21–56.

[15] See infra text accompanying notes 58–60.

[16] For §483, which applies for "for purposes of this title," see supra ¶57.1.

[17] IRC §1272(a), discussed supra ¶56.1.

[18] IRC §§871(a)(1)(C), 881(a)(3).

that accrued during the taxpayer's holding period, excepting OID already recognized on the receipt of payments under the obligation.

Although obligations maturing within one year of original issue are usually exempted from the OID accrual rules, the foregoing rules apply to all obligations of nongovernmental issuers that are payable more than 183 days after original issue.[19] OID is exempt from the withholding tax if interest on the obligation is excluded from gross income by §103, relating to obligations of state and local governments.[20] Also, the rules for strippers (of bonds, that is) apply in determining OID under §§871(a)(1) and 881(a).[21]

2. *Portfolio interest.* An exemption from the withholding tax is provided for "portfolio interest," including both interest (explicit and unstated) and OID on most debt instruments not connected with a U.S. trade or business of the holder.[22] This exemption was adopted in 1984 to permit U.S. companies to participate directly in the Eurobond market, which was described as follows:

> A major capital market outside the United States is the Eurobond market. It is not an organized exchange, but rather a network of underwriters and financial institutions that market bonds issued by private corporations, . . . foreign governments and government agencies, and other borrowers. . . . Although a majority of the bond issues in the Eurobond market are denominated in dollars (whether or not the issuer is a U.S. corporation), bonds issued in the Eurobond market are also frequently denominated in other currencies (even at times when issued by U.S. multinationals).
>
> In general, debt securities in the Eurobond market are free of taxes withheld at source, and the issuer is generally required to pay interest, premiums, and principal net of any tax which might be withheld at source

---

[19] IRC §§871(g)(1)(B)(i), 1272(a)(2)(C). See Rev. Proc. 98-7, 1998-1 CB —, §3.01(1) (IRS will not rule on whether instrument has OID if it is payable less than 184 days from date of original issue).

[20] IRC §871(g)(1)(B)(ii). See supra ¶15.2.1 for §103.

[21] IRC §871(g)(4). For the rules on stripped bonds and stripped coupons, see supra ¶59.5.

[22] IRC §§871(h), 881(c); Reg. §1.871-14(a) (exemption inapplicable if interest is effectively connected with U.S. business). The exemption generally applies only to interest on obligations issued after July 18, 1984. Pub. L. No. 98-369, §127(g)(1), 98 Stat. 494, 652 (1984). See Staff of Joint Comm. on Tax'n, 98th Cong., 2d Sess., General Explanation of the Revenue Provisions of the Deficit Reduction Act of 1984 at 396 (Comm. Print 1984) [hereinafter 1984 Bluebook] ("Congress intended that interest (and original issue discount) on publicly traded mortgage pass-through securities be eligible for the exemption from the 30-percent tax").

If a foreign person transfers a debt instrument or shares of stock in a securities lending or "sale-repurchase" transaction, payments received by that person in substitution for interest or dividends on the transferred security are, for purposes of the withholding tax and treaties, treated as interest or dividends on the transferred security. Reg. §§1.871-7(b)(2), 1.881-2(b)(2), 1.894-1(c), 1.1441-2(b)(4) (these payments are, to the extent from U.S. sources, subject to withholding); see §§1.871-7(f), 1.881-2(e), 1.894-1(d) (this rule applies to payments made after November 13, 1997).

... Thus, an issuer's borrowing cost is higher to the extent that payments must be grossed up to cover withholding tax.[23]

Before the adoption of the exemption for portfolio interest, U.S. companies borrowed in the Eurobond market through finance subsidiaries organized in the Netherlands Antilles. Such a subsidiary issued Eurobonds and reloaned the proceeds to its parent and other U.S. affiliates. The subsidiary sometimes had few assets beyond the notes evidencing its loans to the U.S. affiliates, and the bonds issued by the subsidiary were either guaranteed by the U.S. parent or secured by pledges of the notes held by the subsidiary. The Netherlands Antilles imposed no taxes on interest paid by the subsidiary, and the interest was assumed to be exempt from U.S. withholding tax as foreign source income. Interest paid by the U.S. parent and its affiliates to the Netherlands Antilles subsidiary was exempt from U.S. tax under an income tax treaty with the Netherlands, as extended to the Netherlands Antilles.

The indirectness of transactions effected through finance subsidiaries probably increased borrowing costs and "in many cases, provided incomplete access to the Eurobond market."[24] Moreover, some borrowings through finance subsidiaries were challenged in audit by the IRS on the theory that the U.S. parents were liable for withholding tax on interest paid by the finance subsidiaries because the subsidiaries were lacking in substance and the U.S. parents therefore were the real issuers of the bonds.[25] These challenges "made it difficult to trade U.S. obligations in international bond markets, since holders of international obligations desire assurance that there will be no withholding tax on any interest income."[26] In order to avoid a collapse of the economy of the Netherlands Antilles, the portfolio interest exemption was made applicable only to interest on obligations issued after the exemption's enactment.

The exemption covers much more than interest on Eurobonds. It makes the withholding tax inapplicable to substantially all interest on obligations issued after 1984, with the exception of interest received from related persons and interest received by banks and other financial institutions.

The scope of the exemption is described more fully below.

   a. *Registration; notice to withholding agent.* If the instrument is in registered form,[27] the portfolio interest exemption applies only if a statement is given

---

[23] 1984 Bluebook, supra note 22, at 388–89.

[24] Id. at 392.

[25] See infra ¶66.2.10.

[26] 1984 Bluebook, supra note 22, at 392.

[27] An obligation is in registered form only if (1) it is registered as to both principal and stated interest and may be transferred only by surrendering the instrument for reissuance to the transferee or (2) rights to principal and stated interest can be transferred only through a book entry system maintained by the issuer or an agent that identifies the owner. Reg. §1.871-14(c)(1)(i).

declaring that the beneficial owner of the instrument is not a U.S. person.[28] The statement must be filed with the U.S. person who would otherwise be required to withhold tax from the interest (typically, the issuer or an agent of the issuer) and must be filed by the beneficial owner of the obligation (the taxpayer) or by a financial institution or securities clearing organization "that holds customers' securities in the ordinary course of its trade or business."[29]

The statement requirement is met if the withholding agent or its "authorized foreign agent . . . can reliably associate the payment with" one of the following:

(1) "[D]ocumentation upon which it can rely to treat the payment as made to a foreign beneficial owner."

(2) A withholding certificate "from a foreign person claiming to be withholding foreign partnership and the foreign partnership can reliably associate the payment with documentation upon which it can rely to treat the payment made to a foreign beneficial owner."

(3) A withholding statement "from a person representing to be a qualified intermediary that has assumed primary withholding responsibility . . . and the qualified intermediary can reliably associate the payment with documentation upon which it can rely to treat the payment as made to a foreign beneficial owner in accordance with" an agreement with the IRS.

(4) A withholding certificate "from a person claiming to be a U.S. branch of a foreign bank or of a foreign insurance company . . . and the U.S. branch can reliably associate the payment with documentation upon which it can rely to treat the payment as made to a foreign beneficial owner."[30]

The statement requirement is also met if the withholding agent

(5) Receives a statement from a securities clearing organization, bank, or

---

[28] IRC §§871(h)(2)(B), 881(c)(2)(B). The statement is not required for interest on registered obligations if (1) the obligations were issued under procedures targeting them to foreign markets, (2) the interest is paid by a U.S. person, a withholding foreign partnership, or a U.S. branch to a securities clearing organization bank, or other financial institution holding customers' securities in the ordinary course of business, (3) the recipient is "registered owner" of the obligations and receives the interest at an address outside the United States, and (3) the payor receives a certificate from the beneficial owner. Reg. §1.871-14(e).

The regulations on the statement requirement (Reg. §1.871-14) generally apply to interest payments made after 1998. Reg. §1.871-14(h). See Notice 97-66, 1997-2 CB — (for period November 14, 1997 through December 31, 1998, statement requirement is met for substitute interest payment in securities lending transaction "if any written, electronic, or oral statement that reasonably establishes that the payee is a foreign person is given or made to the payor prior to, or within a reasonable period of time after, the payment").

[29] IRC §871(h)(5); Reg. §1.871-14(c)(1)(ii)(C).

[30] Reg. §§1.871-14(c)(2)(i)–(iv). For the application of the statement requirement for interest on pass-through certificates, see Reg. §1.871-14(d).

other financial institution that holds customers' securities in the ordinary course of business stating "under penalties of perjury" that the institution has received from the beneficial owner a Form W-8 or an acceptable substitute or has received such a statement from another institution or

(6) Complies with procedures established by the competent authorities of the United States and another country under the mutual agreement procedures of an income tax treaty.[31]

In each of these six situations, the statement requirement is not met, even if the withholding agent has the required documentation, if the withholding agent has "actual knowledge or reason to know that the beneficial owner is a U.S. person."[32] Absent such knowledge or reason to know, interest qualifies as portfolio interest if the withholding agent receives the statement or documentation at any time before the statute of limitations runs on a claim by the beneficial owner for refund of the withheld tax, although the withholding agent risks personal liability for the tax if the interest is paid without withholding before the agent receives the needed documents.[33]

b. *Unregistered instruments.* If the instrument is not in registered form, no statement to the withholding agent is required, but the exemption is denied unless the instrument was issued under guidelines designed to prevent it coming into the hands of U.S. persons.[34] The guidelines require, for example, that interest must be payable only outside the United States and that the instrument must state on its face that a U.S. holder is subject to U.S. tax laws.

These requirements are odd because they cause interest income to be subject to the withholding tax, which normally applies only to foreign taxpayers, unless assurance is given that the recipient is not a U.S. person. Their purpose, however, is to ensure that the exemption of portfolio interest from the withholding tax is not used by U.S. persons as a means of avoiding the regular income tax.

c. *Banks.* Interest income of a foreign corporation that is a bank cannot qualify for the exemption for portfolio interest if the interest is "received . . . on an extension of credit made pursuant to a loan agreement entered into in the ordinary course of its trade or business."[35] This disqualification is lifted, however, for interest on loans to the U.S. government. The Staff of the Joint Committee on Taxation provided the following comments on the disqualification.

Interest on any obligation that performs the function of a loan entered into in the ordinary course of banking business [is] ineligible for the exemption. Interest on an obligation that does not perform that function—for example,

---

[31] Reg. §§1.871-14(c)(2)(v), (vi).

[32] Reg. §1.871-14(c)(2).

[33] Reg. §1.871-14(c)(3).

[34] IRC §§163(f)(2)(B), 871(h)(2)(A), 881(c)(2)(A); Reg. §§163-12(c); 1.871-14(b). For these guidelines, see supra ¶31.9 text accompanying notes 7–8.

[35] IRC §881(c)(3)(A).

a Eurobond held by a foreign bank as an investment asset—may be eligible for the exemption . . . . [T]he foreign bank exception was intended to prevent U.S. banks, which are subject to U.S. tax on interest income, from suffering a competitive disadvantage vis-à-vis foreign banks that make loans to U.S. persons.[36]

d. *Interest received by 10 percent shareholders and partners.* The exemption for portfolio interest is not allowed for interest (including unstated interest or OID) on an instrument issued by a corporation if the taxpayer owns stock of the issuer carrying 10 percent or more of the total combined voting power of all classes of the corporation's stock.[37] Also, the exemption is denied to interest on an obligation of a partnership if the taxpayer owns a 10 percent or greater interest in the partnership's profits or capital. Congress adopted this limitation on the exemption because the combination of the payor's U.S. deduction for the interest and an exemption of the foreign payee from tax would create a preference for interest over dividends and other forms of profit distributions.[38]

The limitation can apply whether the loan between the domestic corporation or partnership and its foreign shareholder or partner is direct or is made indirectly through an intermediary. According to the Staff of the Joint Committee on Taxation:

> Congress was concerned that taxpayers might attempt to circumvent the 10-percent shareholder . . . exclusion by entering into "back to back" loans, wherein a foreign affiliate of a U.S. taxpayer . . . lends money to an unrelated foreign party that relends that money at discount to the U.S. taxpayer. Congress intended that the IRS, when appropriate, use means at its disposal to determine whether back to back loans exist.[39]

Broad attribution rules are provided for determining whether the 10 percent threshold is reached or exceeded.[40] These rules are borrowed from §318(a), under which (1) an individual is constructive owner of stock owned by members of his family, (2) shareholders, partners, and beneficiaries are sometimes treated as owners of stock owned by corporations, partnerships, trusts, and estates, and (3) entities are sometimes treated as owners of stock owned by their shareholders, partners, and beneficiaries.[41] For this purpose, the §318(a) rules are broadened in two respects and narrowed in one.

---

[36] 1984 Bluebook, supra note 22, at 395 (bank rule applies if "a foreign bank lends money to an unrelated foreign party that relends that money at discount to" a U.S. borrower and the loans are "back to back"). For back to back arrangements, see infra ¶66.2.10. See NY State Bar Ass'n, The "Bank Loan" Exception to the "Portfolio" Interest Rules, summarized in 57 Tax Notes 123 (Sept. 17, 1992).

[37] IRC §§871(h)(3)(A), (B); 881(c)(3)(B).

[38] 1984 Bluebook, supra note 22, at 393–94.

[39] Id. at 395. For back-to-back arrangements generally, see infra ¶66.2.10.

[40] IRC §871(h)(3)(C).

[41] See infra ¶93.1.7.

Under §318, a shareholder is usually deemed to own a ratable portion of any stock owned by the corporation, but only if the shareholder is the direct or indirect owner of at least 50 percent, by value, of the corporation's stock.[42] The 50 percent limitation is lifted in this context.[43] Assume a nonresident alien owns 10 percent of the stock of X Corp., and X owns 100 percent of the stock of Y Corp., a domestic corporation that is the issuer of a bond held by the nonresident alien. The nonresident alien is constructive owner of 10 percent of the Y stock held by X, and since this constructively owned stock includes 10 percent of Y's voting stock, the interest on the Y bond held by the nonresident alien is not portfolio interest.

The rule for attributing stock from shareholder to corporation is also modified. Normally, shareholder to corporation attribution does not occur under §318(a) unless the shareholder is a 50 percent or greater shareholder, but when this threshold is reached, the corporation is constructive owner of all of the shareholder's stockholdings.[44] For purposes of the portfolio interest rules, the 50 percent limitation is eliminated, but only a ratable portion of the shareholder's stock is attributed to the corporation if the shareholder's interest is less than 50 percent.[45] Assume A owns 20 percent of the stock of domestic corporation X and also is a shareholder of foreign corporation Y, which owns a bond issued by X. If the value of A's Y stock is 50 percent or more of the aggregate value of all Y stock, Y is constructive owner of all of A's X stock, and because this stock includes more than 10 percent of X's voting stock, the interest received by Y on the X bond is not portfolio interest. In contrast, if A owns only 45 percent of the Y stock, Y is constructive owner of only 45 percent of A's 20 percent of the X stock (9 percent), and the interest received by Y on the X bond may be portfolio interest.

Finally, for this purpose, a foreign person is constructive owner of any stock that is subject to an option held by the person, but stock attributed to a foreign optionee under the option rule is not reattributed from the optionee to other persons by the entity to owner or owner to entity attribution rule.[46] For example, if A, a nonresident alien, has an option to purchase 10 percent of the stock of Y Corp., interest on an obligation of Y held by A cannot be portfolio interest. But assume A owns all of the stock of X Corp., which holds an option to purchase 10 percent of the stock of Y. X is constructive owner of the stock subject to the option, but the stock is not reattributed to A.

The §318(a) attribution rules speak of attributions of stock only, but the Treasury is directed to adapt the §318(a) rules for the attribution of partnership interests.

---

[42] IRC §318(a)(2)(C).
[43] IRC §871(h)(3)(C)(i).
[44] IRC §318(a)(3)(C).
[45] IRC §871(h)(3)(C)(ii).
[46] IRC §§871(h)(3)(C)(iii), 318(a)(4).

e. *CFC exception.* Interest received by a controlled foreign corporation cannot be portfolio interest if it is received from a related person.[47]

f. *Residents of countries refusing to supply tax information to United States.* If the exchange of information between the United States and a foreign country is not adequate "to prevent evasion of the United States income tax by United States persons," the Treasury may deny the exemption for portfolio interest payable to persons "within" that country, including interest "payments addressed to, or for the account of, persons within such foreign country."[48] This power is meant to provide the Treasury with a club—a threat to tax a foreign country's residents on U.S. source interest unless the country provides mechanisms for the IRS to obtain information on income earned by U.S. persons in that country.

g. *Contingent interest.* Generally, contingent interest received after 1993 cannot be portfolio interest unless it is paid under an instrument issued before April 8, 1993.[49] More specifically, post-1993 interest income is not portfolio interest if it is "determined by reference to" (1) receipts, sales, other cash flow, income, or profits of the debtor or a related person, (2) a change in the value of property owned by the debtor or a related person, or (3) dividends, partnership distributions, or similar payments made by the debtor or a related person.[50] The Treasury may, by regulation, deny the portfolio interest exemption to "any other type of contingent interest" if it finds the denial "necessary or appropriate to prevent avoidance of Federal income tax."[51]

If both contingent and noncontingent interest is payable on an instrument, this rule does not preclude the noncontingent amounts from being portfolio interest.[52] Moreover, a minimum noncontingent amount is exempted from the rule, regardless of how it is expressed. For example, if the annual interest on an instrument is the greater of 6 percent of the principal amount or 10 percent of the

---

[47] IRC §881(c)(3)(C). For the terms "controlled foreign corporation" and "related person," see infra ¶¶68.2.2 and 68.2.5 text accompanying notes 111–14.

[48] IRC §§871(h)(6)(A), 881(c)(6).

[49] IRC §§871(h)(4), 881(c)(4), enacted by Pub. L. No. 103-66, §13237(a), 107 Stat. 312 (1993). See Royse, RRA '93 Limits Application of Portfolio Interest Exemption, 79 J. Tax'n 360 (1993).

[50] IRC §871(h)(4)(A)(i). See Notice 94-39, 1994-1 CB 350 ("a payment on a shared appreciation mortgage that is otherwise treated for U.S. tax purposes as interest will not qualify for the portfolio interest exemption if the payment is contingent on the appreciation of the financed real property").

The definitions of "related person" found in §§267(b) and 707(b)(1) are borrowed for this purpose, but an otherwise unrelated person is considered related if the person is "a party to any arrangement undertaken for a purpose of avoiding the application of" the rules on contingent interest. IRC §871(h)(4)(B). For §§267(b) and 707(b)(1), see infra ¶¶78.3 and 87.2.4.

[51] IRC §871(h)(4)(A)(ii).

[52] H.R. Rep. No. 213, 103d Cong., 1st Sess. 652 (Conf. Rep. 1993).

issuer's profits, only the excess of the interest for a year over 6 percent of principal is contingent.[53]

The foregoing rules on contingent interest apply only for purposes of the portfolio interest exemption and do not override treaties exempting interest income from U.S. tax or providing reduced rates of tax.[54] Also, portfolio-interest status is not lost under the statutory rule "solely by reason of the fact" that

(1) The "timing of any interest or principal payment is subject to a contingency,"[55]

(2) The indebtedness is without recourse or recourse is limited,[56] or

(3) The debtor or a related person "enters into a hedging transaction to reduce the risk of interest rate or currency fluctuations with respect to such interest."[57]

Also, interest is not contingent if "substantially all" of it is "determined by reference to any other amount of [noncontingent] interest" or by reference to the principal on which such other interest is paid.[58] Moreover, interest "determined by reference to" any one of the following factors is not contingent:

(1) Changes in the value of actively traded property (other than a U.S. real property interest) or "changes in any index of the value of" such property.[59]

(2) The yield on any such property or "changes in any index of" such a yield.[60]

Finally, the portfolio interest exemption is not denied to contingent interest on an instrument with a "fixed term" that was issued before April 8, 1993 or pursuant to a written binding contract that was in effect on April 7, 1993 and continuously thereafter until the instrument was issued.[61]

3. *Interest on deposits.* An exemption from the withholding tax is provided for interest income on bank deposits, deposits with domestic savings and loan associations, and "amounts held by an insurance company under an agreement

---

[53] Id. at 653.

[54] Id.

[55] IRC §871(h)(4)(C)(i).

[56] IRC §871(h)(4)(C)(ii).

[57] IRC §871(h)(4)(C)(iv).

[58] IRC §871(h)(4)(C)(iii).

[59] IRC §§871(h)(4)(C)(v)(I), (III). The term "actively traded" was borrowed from §1092(d). See supra ¶45.3.2. For the term "U.S. real property interest," see §897(c), discussed infra ¶¶66.4.2–66.4.4.

[60] IRC §§871(h)(4)(C)(v)(II), (III). However, the portfolio interest exemption does not apply to interest determined with regard to the yield on a debt instrument with contingent interest or "stock or other property that represents a beneficial interest in the debtor or a related person."

[61] IRC §871(h)(4)(D).

to pay interest thereon."[62] The exemption only applies for purposes of §§871(a)(1) and 881(a) and is denied if the interest is effectively connected with a U.S. business of the recipient.

Most interest exempted by the deposit rule is also exempted as portfolio interest. However, the deposit exemption has independent significance if, for example, the depositor owns 10 percent or more of the stock of the bank, savings and loan, or insurance company holding the deposit.

4. *Treaty modifications.* The Treasury's model treaty, following the lead of many U.S. income tax treaties in force, generally bars the United States from taxing interest income paid to residents of treaty countries.[63] The OECD model, and some U.S. income tax treaties, do not exempt interest, but reduce the statutory tax rate (e.g., to 10 percent).[64] A treaty exemption or rate reduction does not apply if the taxpayer (1) carries on business through a permanent establishment in the United States and the interest income is attributable to the permanent establishment or (2) performs independent personal services through a fixed base in the United States to which the interest is attributable.[65] Interest attributable to such a permanent establishment or fixed base is taxable by the United States as part of the taxpayer's U.S. business income.

---

[62] IRC §§871(i)(2)(A), (3); 881(d). In this form, the exemption is effective for interest paid after 1986 on deposits made after 1985. Pub. L. No. 99-514, §§1214(d)(1), (2)(A), 100 Stat. 2085, 2543 (1986). The 1986 amendments, however, were merely a rearrangement of earlier provisions that indirectly exempted interest on such deposits by characterizing it as foreign source income. IRC §861(a)(1)(A), (c) (before amendment in 1986). See Isidro Martin-Montis Trust v. CIR, 75 TC 381 (1980) (acq.) (under statutory predecessor of §871(i), nonresident alien beneficiary of domestic estate qualified for exemption where estate received interest on bank deposit and distributed it to beneficiary during same year); Rev. Rul. 86-76, 1986-1 CB 284 (same; but if interest is not distributed in year received, it is taxable to domestic estate even if nonresident alien is its beneficial owner); Rev. Rul. 81-244, 1981-2 CB 151 (same). See also Reg. §§1.6049-4(b)(5), 1.6049-8 (if depositor is resident of Canada and deposit is "maintained at an office in the United States," bank must report interest on Form 1042-S); TD 8664, 1996-20 IRB 7 (reporting required by U.S.-Canada income tax treaty).

[63] U.S. Treasury Dep't, Model Income Tax Convention of September 20, 1996, art. 11(1) [hereinafter Treasury Model]. The Model is accompanied by a Technical Explanation issued on the same date. See Spencer, Interest Clauses in Recent U.S. Income Tax Treaties Are More (Or Less) Complex, 8 J. Int'l Tax'n 250 (1997). For tables listing maximum tax rates on interest under all treaties, see IRS Pub. No. 515, Withholding of Tax on Nonresident Aliens and Foreign Corporations (Rev. Nov. 1997); IRS Pub. No. 901, U.S. Tax Treaties 26 (Rev. Nov. 1997); Notice 97-29, 1997-14 IRB 16 (updating tables to reflect new treaties or protocols with Kazakstan and Indonesia).

[64] Organisation for Economic Co-operation and Development, Model Tax Convention on Income and Capital art. 11(2) (1992) [hereinafter OECD Model].

[65] Treasury Model, supra note 63, art. 11(3). See OECD Model, supra note 64, art. 11(4).

¶66.2.3 Dividends

U.S. source dividends are generally subject to the withholding tax. A limited exception is provided for dividends from domestic corporations that derive at least 80 percent of their incomes from businesses carried on in foreign countries. A much broader exception is provided for dividends from foreign corporations. Also, treaties usually reduce the rate of the withholding tax on dividends.

1. *"Dividends."* The term "dividends" generally includes only distributions by corporations from their current or accumulated earnings and profits.[66]

However, if a foreign person transfers shares of stock in a securities lending or "sale-repurchase" transaction, payments received by that person in substitution for dividends on the transferred shares are, for purposes of the withholding tax and treaties, treated as or dividends on the transferred shares.[67] A substitute payment is deemed to be from U.S. sources if the underlying dividends are from U.S. sources.

A substitute payment is treated as a dividend because the actual dividend might otherwise escape U.S. tax. Assume a U.S. person borrows stock of a U.S. company from a foreign person, receives dividends on the borrowed stock, and makes an equal substitute payment to the lender. The dividend is gross income to the borrower, but the substitute payment is allowed as a deduction, resulting in no net income. Thus, if the substitute payment were not taxed to the foreign person, a dividend paid by a U.S. company would pass to a foreign beneficial owner without withholding tax. Since the lender has the economic benefits and burdens of stock ownership, treating the substitute payment as a U.S. source dividend is the most effective and realistic means of avoiding this result.

The substitute payment rule generally applies whether the person making the substitute payment is a U.S. person or a foreigner. However, the rule can result in double taxation where the borrower and lender are both foreign. Assume a foreign person borrows stock of a U.S. company from another foreign person, receives a dividend on the borrowed stock, and makes an equal substitute payment to the lender. If the dividend is subject to a U.S. withholding tax on payment to the borrower, the borrower has no U.S. deduction for the substitute payment, and a U.S. withholding tax on the substitute payment would be a second tax.

On the other hand, if the rule for substitute payments only applied to payments by U.S. persons to foreign persons, such payments could effectively be used to make treaty benefits available to residents of nontreaty countries. Assume

---

[66] IRC §316(a), discussed in Ch. 92.

[67] Reg. §§1.871-7(b)(2), 1.881-2(b)(2), 1.894-1(c), 1.1441-2(b)(4) (these payments are, to the extent from U.S. sources, subject to withholding); see §§1.871-7(f), 1.881-2(e), 1.894-1(d) (this rule applies to payments made after November 13, 1997). See Tuckner & Cohen, Final Regulations on the Source and Gross-Basis Taxation of Substitute Dividend and Interest Payments: A Work in Progress on Transparency, Translucency, and Opacity, 27 Tax Mgmt. Int'l J. 3 (1998).

a foreign person residing in a country with an income tax treaty with the United States borrows stock of a U.S. company from a foreign person residing in a country with no such treaty; the borrower receives dividends on the borrowed stock, from which a U.S. tax is withheld at the treaty rate of 15 percent, and makes an equal substitute payment to the lender. If the substitute payment were not taxed, the lender, who does not reside in a treaty country, would effectively benefit by the treaty reduction of withholding tax.

The IRS has thus provided a special rule for "foreign-to-foreign" substitute dividend payments. The U.S. withholding tax on such a payment is

> the amount of the underlying dividend multiplied by a rate equal to the excess of the rate of U.S. withholding tax that would be applicable to U.S. source dividends paid by a U.S. person directly to the recipient of the substitute payment over the rate of U.S. withholding tax that would be applicable to U.S. source dividends paid by a U.S. person directly to the payor of the substitute payment.[68]

Thus, if both parties are residents of nontreaty countries or the same treaty country, the withholding rate is zero (e.g., 30 percent, less 30 percent, or 15 percent, less 15 percent). On the other hand, if the borrower resides in a country with a treaty providing a 15 percent dividend rate and the lender resides in a nontreaty country, the substitute payment is subject to a U.S. withholding tax of 15 percent (30 percent, less 15 percent). If withholding on the dividend exceeds the borrower's liability (e.g., if U.S. tax is withheld at the statutory 30 percent, rather than the treaty 15 percent), the excess withholding on the dividend may be applied against the withholding tax on the substitute payment.

However, the withholding tax on the substitute payment may not be less than zero. Assume the borrower does not reside in a treaty country, and U.S. tax is thus withheld from the dividends at 30 percent, but the lender (recipient of the substitute payment) resides in a country having a treaty with the United States prescribing a 15 percent rate for dividends. No U.S. tax is due on the substitute payment, but the lender is not allowed a refund of one half of the tax withheld from the dividend.

2. *Domestic corporations.* Generally, dividends from domestic corporations are from U.S. sources,[69] and thus are subject to the withholding tax when paid to a foreign investor. However, a dividend from a domestic corporation is wholly or partially exempted from the withholding tax if at least 80 percent of the payor's gross income during a test period was foreign source income derived in the active conduct of business in a foreign country or a U.S. possession.[70] The test period usually consists of the three years preceding the beginning of the taxable year of

---

[68] Notice 97-66, 1997-48 IRB 8, §3.

[69] IRC §861(a)(2)(A), discussed infra ¶70.3.

[70] IRC §§861(c)(1), 871(i)(2)(B), 881(d). The exemption is effective for dividends received after 1986. Pub. L. No. 99-514, §1214(d)(1), 100 Stat. 2085, 2543 (1986). Pre-1987 dividends from a domestic corporation that derived at least 80 percent of its gross income from foreign sources over the preceding three years were characterized as foreign

the payor corporation in which the dividend is paid or, if shorter, the period of the corporation's existence prior to that taxable year.[71] If the dividend is paid during the payor's first taxable year, that year is the test period. When the exemption applies, the exempted amount is the dividend multiplied by a fraction whose numerator is the gross income of the payor for the test period from sources outside the United States (including passive as well as active business income) and whose denominator is the total of the payor's gross income for this period.[72]

Assume a nonresident alien receives a dividend from a domestic corporation whose gross income over the preceding three years, in the aggregate, consists of $85 of foreign source income derived in the active conduct of a business in a foreign country, $10 of passive interest income from foreign sources, and $5 of U.S. source income. The exemption applies because at least 80 percent of the payor's gross income for the test period was active business income from foreign sources ($85 of $100). The exempted amount is 95 percent of the dividend because 95 percent of the payor's gross income for the test period was foreign source income ($85 of business income and $10 of interest). The withholding tax thus applies only to the five percent of the dividend that is traceable to the payor's U.S. source income. However, if the foreign source income of the payor had consisted of $75 of active business income and $20 of passive interest income, the exemption would be unavailable because the corporation would not meet the requirement that at least 80 percent of its gross income come from the active conduct of a foreign business; the dividend would be from U.S. sources since the payor is a domestic corporation, and the withholding tax would apply to the entire dividend.

Generally, the foreign source income in the numerator of the test and exclusion fractions is identified using the source rules of general application.[73] However, if the payor has subsidiaries, the sources of dividends from the subsidiaries are apparently determined by a pass-through principle rather than the usual source rules for dividends.[74] Assume domestic corporation P receives a dividend from domestic corporation S, in which it is a 50 percent shareholder. Over the three years preceding the taxable year of S in which the dividend is paid, S's gross income consisted of $450 of foreign source income from the active conduct of a business in a foreign country and $50 of U.S. source income. Under the usual rules, the dividend is U.S. source income because dividends received by a domestic corporation from another domestic corporation are from U.S.

---

source income, and therefore were wholly exempt from the §§871(a)(1) and 881(a) taxes. IRC §861(a)(2)(A) (before amendment in 1986).

The foreign business requirement is described more fully in ¶70.2 text accompanying notes 7–15.

[71] IRC §861(c)(1)(C).

[72] IRC §861(c)(2)(A).

[73] IRC §861(c)(2)(A)(i). For the source rules, see Ch. 70.

[74] H.R. Rep. No. 841, 99th Cong., 2d Sess., II-603 (Conf. Rep. 1986), reprinted in 1986-3 CB (vol. 4) 602–03.

sources, with only one limited exception not relevant here.[75] The legislative history indicates, however, that in applying the 80-20 exclusion to a dividend received by a nonresident alien or foreign corporation from *P*, 90 percent of *P*'s dividend income is from foreign sources (and derived from the active conduct of a foreign business) because that percentage of *S*'s gross income for the three preceding years is foreign source, active business income. Fifty percent or greater stock ownership is needed to establish a parent-subsidiary relationship for this purpose.[76]

3. *Foreign corporations.* At least a portion of a dividend from a foreign corporation is from U.S. sources, and thus is potentially subject to the withholding tax, if 25 percent or more of the corporation's gross income during the preceding three years was effectively connected with the conduct of business in the United States.[77] However, a foreign corporation's withdrawal of profits from a U.S. trade or business is subject to a branch profits tax, which is generally imposed at 30 percent and is intended to take the place of the withholding tax that would be imposed on dividends if the U.S. business were separately incorporated as a domestic subsidiary.[78] Because the withholding tax on dividends is a shareholder-level tax and because the basic theory of the corporate tax system requires only one shareholder-level tax on any given increment of corporate profit, dividends from foreign corporations subject to the branch profits tax are usually exempted from the withholding tax.

Specifically, if a foreign corporation is subject to the branch profits tax for a particular year and does not qualify for an exemption from the tax under an income tax treaty, a dividend from earnings and profits of that year is not subject to the withholding tax.[79] Since all foreign corporations engaged in business in the United States are subject to the branch profits tax unless exempted by treaty, the foregoing rule exempts all dividends from foreign corporations from the withholding tax unless the dividends are paid from earnings and profits accumulated before 1987 (the first year the branch profits tax was imposed) or during a year the corporation qualifies for a treaty exemption.

4. *Treaty modifications.* Income tax treaties typically allow U.S. tax to be imposed on dividends paid by corporate residents of the United States to residents of the treaty country.[80] Generally, for treaty purposes, domestic corpora-

---

[75] See infra ¶70.3.

[76] H.R. Rep. No. 841, supra note 74, at II-602.

[77] IRC §861(a)(2)(B), discussed infra ¶70.3 text accompanying notes 6–14.

[78] IRC §884(a), discussed infra ¶66.5.2.

[79] IRC §884(e)(3)(A).

[80] See Treasury Model, supra note 63, art. 10(2); OECD Model, supra note 64, art. 10(2). For a table listing maximum tax rates on dividends under all treaties, see IRS Pub. No. 901, U.S. Tax Treaties 26 (Rev. Nov. 1994). See also Merrill, Patrick & Belanger, Tax Treaties in a Global Economy: The Case for Zero Withholding on Direct Dividends, 5 Tax Notes Int'l 1387 (1992).

tions are considered U.S. residents, and foreign corporations are nonresidents.[81] The tax rate is usually reduced to 15 percent, but a 5 percent ceiling applies if the "beneficial owner" of the dividends is a corporation that owns at least 10 percent of the payor corporation's stock. Neither ceiling applies, however, if the dividends are attributable to a permanent establishment of the recipient in the United States.

Under the Treasury's model treaty, the United States is generally barred from taxing dividends paid by a corporate resident of the other country, except in two situations.[82] U.S. residents can be taxed on such dividends, and the United States may also tax the dividends, even though received by a resident of another country, if they are attributable to a permanent establishment or fixed base of the dividend recipient in the United States. The model treaty also allows the United States to impose its branch profits tax, a type of surrogate dividend tax, on the profits of a permanent establishment maintained by the distributing corporation in the United States.[83]

Congress has imposed three statutory restrictions on treaty benefits otherwise allowed for a dividend received by one foreign corporation from another foreign corporation, where the dividend is from U.S. sources and from corporate earnings for a year that the distributing corporation was not subject to the branch profits tax.[84] First, no claim of exemption or rate reduction may be based on a treaty other than an income tax treaty. The second restriction applies if an income tax treaty between the United States and the country of residence of the payor of the dividend contains a provision barring the United States from taxing dividends paid by residents of the treaty country. A corporate recipient of a dividend is denied this treaty exemption unless the payor is a "qualified resident" of the treaty country, a term defined to require that the corporation be predominantly owned by individual residents of the treaty country and not function as a conduit for channeling interest, royalties, or insurance premiums from the United States to ultimate recipients in third countries.[85] The third restriction applies if the recipient resides in a country having a treaty with the United States that reduces the tax rate or provides an exemption for U.S. source dividends received by residents of the treaty country. A foreign corporation receiving a

---

See Reg. §1.894-1(c) (treaty provisions on dividends generally apply to substitute payments received by lender of stock in securities lending transaction).

[81] See Treasury Model, supra note 63, art. 4(1); OECD Model, supra note 64, art. 4(1).

[82] Treasury Model, supra note 63, art. 10(7). The OECD Model contains a very similar provision. OECD Model, supra note 64, art. 10(5).

[83] Treasury Model, supra note 63, art. 10(8). For the branch profits tax, see §884, discussed infra ¶66.5.2.

[84] IRC §§884(e)(3)(B), (f)(3). See supra text accompanying note 78 for the branch profits rule.

[85] IRC §§884(e)(3)(B), (f)(3)(A). For the definition of "qualified resident," see IRC §884(e)(4), discussed infra ¶66.5.4 text accompanying notes 90-107.

dividend from another foreign corporation is allowed the benefits of such a rate reduction or exemption only if it is a qualified resident of the treaty country.[86]

5. *Constructive dividends under §304.* A 1992 ruling illustrates the application of the foregoing rules in conjunction with §304.[87] In the ruling, *FP*, a foreign corporation organized under the laws of foreign country *A*, is sole shareholder of domestic corporation *DX* and foreign corporation *FX*, which is organized under the laws of foreign country *Z*. *FX* also owned the stock of another country *Z* corporation, *FY*, but sells this stock to *DX* for $200, its fair market value. Under §304(a), the price is treated as a distribution in redemption of stock of the acquiring corporation (*DX*) because one person (*FP*) controls both the seller (*FX*) and the buyer (*DX*); under §302(d), this deemed distribution is considered equivalent to a dividend because the seller (*FX*) actually or constructively owns all *FY* stock both before and after the sale. The distribution (the selling price of $200) is treated as coming first from the earnings and profits of the acquiring corporation (*DX*), which are assumed to be $90, and then from the earnings and profits of the corporation that issued the stock being sold (*FY*), which are assumed to be $110.[88] These earnings cover the entire $200 received by *FX*, and this amount is thus a dividend.

The $110 dividend from *FY* is not subject to U.S. tax because the taxpayer (*FX*) and the distributing corporation (*FY*) are foreign corporations, it is assumed that neither of them has ever been engaged in business in the United States, and the dividend is therefore from foreign sources and not effectively connected with U.S. business. In contrast, the $90 dividend deemed received by *FX* from *DX* is taxable under §882(a) because *DX* is a domestic corporation and dividends from *DX* are therefore from U.S. sources.

If the United States has a treaty with country *Z* (the country of *FX*'s incorporation) and if *FX* is a resident of country *Z* for purposes of the treaty, the 30 percent withholding tax rate may be reduced by the treaty's dividend article. According to the ruling, the deemed dividend under §304(a) is "income from shares" within the meaning of the dividend definition of the OECD and Treasury model treaties. Most treaties provide one maximum rate for source-country taxation of dividends generally (often 15 percent) and a lower ceiling (often 5 percent) for dividends received by a corporation owning at least 10 percent of the stock of the corporation distributing the dividend. Although the taxpayer (*FX*) actually owns no stock of the distributing corporation (*DX*), the ruling holds that the lower rate is applicable because, for purposes of §304, the *DX* stock is attributed to *FX* by the constructive ownership rules.

The ruling warns, however, that the benefits of the *Z* treaty may be denied if *FX* is utilized in the transaction as a conduit. Assume the *FY* stock was

---

[86] IRC §§884(e)(3)(B), (f)(3)(B).

[87] Rev. Rul. 92-85, 1992-2 CB 69. See Birnkrant & Croker, IRS Clarifies Redemptions Through Related Corporations in Cross-Border Transactions, 78 J. Tax'n 38 (1993); Staffaroni, The International Boundaries of Section 304, 46 Tax Lawyer 125 (1992).

[88] IRC §304(b)(2).

originally held by the parent corporation (*FP*), and the United States either has no income tax treaty with *FP*'s home country (country *A*) or has a treaty permitting source taxation of dividends at higher rates than under the country *Z* treaty; *FP* transfers the *FY* stock to *FX* as a capital contribution, *FX* sells the stock to *DX*, and the selling price is quickly distributed by *FX* to *FP* as a dividend. In this case, the IRS will likely contend that *FP*, not *FX*, is the true recipient of the dividend and that the favorable provisions of the treaty with country *Z* are therefore unavailable.[89]

¶66.2.4 Rents

Rents are listed among the items subject to the withholding tax,[90] and rents are from U.S. sources whenever paid for the use of property, real or personal, that is located in the United States.[91] However, rents are seldom subject to this tax. The activities of managing real property, whether carried on by the owner or by agents of the owner, often constitute a trade or business.[92] When this is so, U.S. source income from the property is subject to the effectively connected income tax and is exempted from the withholding tax. When the investment is so passive as not to be a trade or business, the taxpayer may elect to treat it as a business.[93] This election is often irresistible because the denial of deductions in determining the withholding tax usually makes the tax confiscatory when applied to rents. The harshness of the tax is not even avoidable by making a net lease requiring the lessee to pay taxes, mortgage interest, and repair costs on the property because the term "rents" includes all payments by the lessee that satisfy obligations of the lessor.[94]

¶66.2.5 Compensation for Services

Salaries and wages are listed in §871(a)(1) among the items subject to the withholding tax if from U.S. sources, and compensation for services is usually income from U.S. sources if it is paid for services performed in the United States.[95] Compensation for U.S. services, if in a form other than wages or salaries, is within the catch-all phrase of §§871(a)(1) and 881(a)—fixed or determinable

---

[89] For whether this contention will succeed, see infra ¶66.2.10.

[90] See generally Klein, Investments by Foreign Persons in United States Real Estate, 2 J. Real Est. Tax'n 265 (1975).

[91] IRC §861(a)(4), discussed infra ¶70.5.

[92] See infra ¶66.3.2.

[93] IRC §§871(d), 882(d), discussed infra ¶66.3.6.

[94] Reg. §1.1.1441-2(a)(2); Rev. Rul. 73-522, 1973-2 CB 226.

[95] IRC §861(a)(3), discussed infra ¶70.4.

annual or periodical income.[96] However, because the performance of services in the United States generally constitutes a U.S. trade or business,[97] salaries, wages, and other compensation for U.S. services, if taxed at all, are almost always subject to the effectively connected income tax, not the withholding tax. Even if compensation is paid before the year in which the services are performed, or deferred until a later year, and even if the taxpayer is not present in the United States when the compensation is paid, it is effectively connected income if payments for the services received contemporaneously with the performance of the services would be so characterized.[98]

Compensation for services performed in the United States by a nonresident alien is treated as foreign source income if (1) the compensation is earned while the taxpayer is temporarily present in the United States, (2) the taxpayer is not present in the United States for more than 90 days during the taxable year, (3) the compensation does not exceed $3,000, and (4) the employer is either a foreign person not engaged in business in the United States or a foreign office of a U.S. person.[99] Also, when these conditions are met, the performer of the services is deemed not engaged in business in the United States by reason of this employment.[100] The principal effect of these rules is to exempt such compensation from both the withholding tax and the effectively connected income tax. For example, if an employee of a foreign company spends several days in the United States negotiating a deal for her employer with a U.S. company, no U.S. tax is imposed on the employee's salary for this period unless it exceeds $3,000.

Income tax treaties generally allow the United States to tax compensation for services rendered in this country by residents of the other treaty country, but they typically contain a somewhat more generous exemption for compensation received by those who are present in the United States for short periods of time. Employee compensation for U.S. services is usually exempted from U.S. tax if (1) the treaty-country resident is present in the United States for not more than 183 days during the taxable year, (2) the employer is not a resident of the United States, and (3) the compensation is not borne by a permanent establishment or fixed base of the employer in the United States.[101] Fees and other compensation

---

[96] But see Miller v. CIR, 73 TCM (CCH) 2319, 2323 (1997) (compensation not FDAP where "it was unascertainable during the year of payment what portion of the contract would be performed in the United States").

[97] IRC §864(b), discussed infra ¶66.3.2.

[98] IRC §864(c)(6) (effective for taxable years beginning after 1986). Under prior law, income recognized for a particular year could be effectively connected income only if the taxpayer was engaged in a trade or business in the United States during that year, and advance and deferred payments for U.S. services were often subject to the withholding tax. IRC §864(c)(1)(B); Reg. §1.871-8(c)(1) Ex. 2.

[99] IRC §861(a)(3).

[100] IRC §864(b)(1), discussed infra ¶66.3.2 text accompanying notes 15–22.

[101] See Treasury Model, supra note 63, art. 15; OECD Model, supra note 64, art. 15. For descriptions of treaty provisions affecting U.S. taxation of personal services income, see IRS Pub. No. 515, Withholding of Tax on Nonresident Aliens and Foreign Corpo-

for services performed by independent contractors resident in the treaty country are usually taxable by the United States only if the taxpayer has a fixed base in the United States.[102]

Although pensions and other distributions from retirement plans can be subject to the withholding tax,[103] the statutes provide a broad exemption for annuity distributions received by nonresident aliens from qualified pension, profit sharing, stock bonus, and annuity plans.[104] In order for the exemption to apply, all of the taxpayer's entitlement under the plan must have accrued on account of services that were performed (1) outside the United States while the taxpayer was a nonresident alien or (2) within the United States while the taxpayer was temporarily present and earning salary or wages that were foreign source income under the 90-day rule described in the second preceding paragraph. Also, if fewer than 90 percent of the participants in the qualified plan are citizens or residents of the United States when the taxpayer's annuity begins, the exemption is denied unless the taxpayer's country of residence either (1) allows a "substantially equivalent exclusion" to citizens and residents of the United States or (2) is a beneficiary developing country under the Trade Act of 1974.

A partial exemption is provided for pensions received by former employees of the U.S. government and their beneficiaries.[105] A nonresident alien receiving such a pension is required to include in gross income no more than an amount equal to the amounts received during the taxable year multiplied by a fraction whose numerator is the U.S. source compensation received by the employee for services performed for the federal government and whose denominator is the sum of the U.S. and foreign source compensation for these services. A federal pension received by a nonresident alien who worked for the U.S. government only in foreign countries (or by beneficiaries of the employee) thus is wholly free of U.S. tax.

Income tax treaties typically bar the United States from taxing pensions and other deferred compensation received from U.S. sources by residents of the treaty country.[106]

---

rations (Rev. Nov. 1997); IRS Pub. No. 901, U.S. Tax Treaties 26 (Rev. Nov. 1997); Notice 97-29, 1997-1 CB 415 (updating tables to reflect new treaties or protocols with Kazakstan and Indonesia).

[102] See Treasury Model, supra note 63, art. 14; OECD Model, supra note 64, art. 14.

[103] Until 1987, lump sum distributions from qualified pension, profit sharing, stock bonus, and annuity plans were sometimes taxed as though they were gains on sales and exchanges of capital assets. IRC §§402(a)(2), 403(a)(2) (repealed in 1986). Such distributions, however, were subject to the withholding tax. IRC §871(a)(1)(B) (before amendment in 1986).

[104] IRC §871(f).

[105] IRC §402(e)(2).

[106] See Treasury Model, supra note 63, art. 18(1); OECD Model, supra note 64, art. 18. See Clayton v. US, 33 Ct. Fed. Cl. 628, 95-2 USTC ¶50,391 (1995), aff'd without published opinion, 96-1 USTC ¶50,314 (Fed. Cir. 1996) (exemption for pensions and

Under §871(c), taxable scholarships and grants received by nonresident alien students, researchers, and visiting teachers temporarily present in the United States under nonimmigrant visas under §§101(a)(15)(F), (J), (M), or (Q) of the Immigration and Nationality Act are deemed to be effectively connected with a U.S. trade or business, whether or not the recipient actually has such a trade or business, and this income is subject to withholding at source at the rate of 14 percent.[107] If such an individual receives a scholarship from U.S. sources that is only partially excluded from gross income under §117(a), the 14 percent withholding tax applies to the taxable portion of the scholarship.[108] Very generally, scholarships are excludable from gross income only to the extent of the student's tuition and related expenses, not including living expenses.[109] If a student receives a scholarship that covers living expenses as well as tuition and incidental expenses, the amount for living expenses thus is taxable. If the student is a nonresident alien present in the United States under a student visa, the taxable amount is subject to the 14 percent withholding tax.

Also, if a nonresident alien present in the United States on an F, J, M, or Q visa is not a candidate for a degree at an educational institution, §871(c) applies to grants received from (1) an educational or charitable organization that is exempt from tax under §501(c)(3), (2) the government of a foreign country, the United States, or one of the U.S. states, (3) an agency or instrumentality of the federal or a state or local government, or (4) an international organization.[110]

The tax on scholarships and grants is often waived by treaty.[111] The Treasury's model treaty exempts a student, apprentice, or business trainee from U.S. tax on any payment received for maintenance, education, or training if (1) the payments come from a foreign country, (2) the recipient was a resident of the treaty country immediately before coming to the United States, and (3) the recipient is present in the United States for full-time education or training.[112]

---

annuities under U.S.-Canada treaty does not cover lump sum distribution from employee stock ownership plan (ESOP) because distribution is not pension or annuity).

[107] IRC §§871(c), 1441(b). See Rev. Proc. 88-24, 1988-1 CB 800 (withholding procedures for scholarships and grants paid to foreign students and grantees). See Harding, Making Scholarship and Fellowship Payments to Foreign Students: An Overview of Tax Issues and Problems, 55 Tax Notes 533 (April 27, 1992).

In lieu of withholding at 14 percent, the withholding agent may choose to withhold as though the income were wages subject to wage withholding. Reg. §1.1441-4(c)(2).

[108] IRC §1441(b)(1). For the application of the source rules to scholarships and fellowships, see infra ¶70.9 text accompanying notes 4-7.

[109] See supra ¶11.2.

[110] IRC §1441(b)(2).

[111] A claim for this treaty benefit must usually be made by Form W-8. Reg. §1.1441-4(c)(1).

[112] U.S. Treasury Dep't, Model Income Tax Convention of September 20, 1996, art. 20 [hereinafter Treasury Model]. The OECD Model is the same. Organisation for Economic Co-operation and Development, Model Tax Convention on Income and Capital art. 20 (1992).

¶66.2.6 Social Security Benefits

The withholding tax applies to 85 percent of any monthly old age, survivors, and disability benefits (OASDI) received by a nonresident alien under title II of the Social Security Act.[113] The tax also applies to 85 percent of a nonresident alien's tier I railroad retirement benefits, which usually equal the OASDI benefits the retiree would receive if he were covered by social security rather than the railroad retirement system.[114] The Treasury's Model Income Tax Treaty preserves to the United States the right to tax these benefits,[115] but they are exempted by some treaties in force.[116]

¶66.2.7 Royalties

Royalties are not among the statutory listing of items subject to the withholding tax, but royalties under licenses of patents, copyrights, secret processes, and similar property (intellectual property) are caught by the catchall phrase "other fixed or determinable annual or periodical gains, profits and income."[117] Contrary to the implication of the phrase "annual or periodical," royalties are taxable whether received in installments over time or as a lump sum. Gains on sales and exchanges of intellectual property are also subject to the withholding tax if they are recognized on the receipt of payments contingent on the property's productivity, use, or disposition.[118] Gain on a sale or exchange of intellectual property is not subject to the tax if the price is not contingent on the property's productivity, use, or disposition, but the courts have shown an inclination to

---

The United Nations Model provides further that with respect to grants, scholarships, and employee compensation not covered by this exemption, the host country must allow "the same exemptions, reliefs or reductions" as are extended to residents of that country. United Nations Model Double Taxation Convention Between Developed and Developing Counties art. 20(2) (1981). The United States has made a few treaties containing the United Nations provision. See Rev. Proc. 93-20, 1993-1 CB 528 (applying United States-India treaty; "exemptions, reliefs or reductions" include standard deduction and spousal and dependency exemptions, but not right to file joint return).

[113] IRC §871(a)(3).

[114] See S. Rep. No. 23, 98th Cong., 1st Sess. 26, reprinted in 1983-2 CB 326.

[115] Treasury Model, supra note 63, art. 18(2). See S. Rep. No. 23, supra note 114, at 25, 28, reprinted in 1983-2 CB 327-28, 329.

[116] The OECD model contains no provision on social security benefits, which therefore fall under the article on Other Income and are taxable only by the country of the taxpayer's residence. OECD Model, supra note 64, art. 21(1).

[117] Reg. §1.871-7(b). Royalties are from U.S. sources if they are paid for the use of the licensed property in the United States. IRC §861(a)(4), discussed infra ¶70.5.

[118] IRC §871(a)(1)(D). This provision only applies to sales and exchanges after October 4, 1966. Gains on earlier sales by nonresident aliens were subject to the withholding tax if capital gains treatment was allowed under §1235. IRC §871(a)(1)(B). See supra ¶54.4 for §1235. For the background of §871(a)(1)(D), see S. Rep. No. 1707, 89th Cong., 2d Sess., reprinted in 1966-2 CB 1059, 1075.

classify a transfer as a license rather than a sale if it conveys less than the taxpayer's entire interest in the property.[119]

Royalties received by owners of tangible property (e.g., mineral royalties) are also covered by the catchall phrase. Under §§631(b) and (c), gain on a disposition of timber, coal, or domestic iron ore is treated as gain on a sale even though the taxpayer retains an economic interest in the timber, coal, or iron ore.[120] Nevertheless, if received by a nonresident alien or foreign corporation from sources within the United States,[121] such a gain is subject to the withholding tax unless it is effectively connected with a U.S. trade or business.[122]

---

[119] See CIR v. Wodehouse, 337 US 369 (1949).

The IRS has proposed regulations on the classification of transactions in computer programs. REG-251520-96, 1996-48 IRB 15; Sprague, Proposed Regulations on Computer Software Revenue Characterization, 26 Tax Mgmt. Int'l J. 128 (1997). See Prop. Reg. §1.861-18(a)(3) (defining "computer program"). Under the proposed regulations, a transaction relating to a computer program is classified as (1) a transfer of a "copyright right," (2) a transfer of a copy of the program, (3) a provision of "services for the development or modification" of the program, or (4) a provision of know-how. Prop. Reg. §1.861-18(b)(1). A transaction is treated as a transfer of a "copyright right" if the transferee acquires the right to (1) make copies of the computer program and sell, rent, or lend them "to the public," (2) "prepare derivative computer programs," (3) "make a public performance" of the program, or (4) "publicly display" the program. Prop. Reg. §1.861-18(c)(2). Whether the transaction is a provision of services depends on the facts and circumstances, including the parties' intentions and the allocations of financial risks. Prop. Reg. §1.861-18(d). A transaction is a provision of "know-how" only if the information relates to "programming techniques," cannot be copyrighted, and enjoys legal protection as a trade secret. Prop. Reg. §1.861-18(e). A transaction may have aspects falling into two or more of the four categories, in which case it is separated into its various aspects unless one or more of the aspects is "de minimis." Prop. Reg. §1.861-18(b)(2).

A transfer of a copyright right is classified as a sale or exchange if "all substantial rights" are transferred; if less than all substantial rights are transferred, the transaction is a license producing royalty income. Prop. Reg. §1.861-18(f)(1). A transfer of a copy of the program is a sale or exchange if "the benefits and burdens of ownership" are transferred; otherwise, it is a lease producing rents. Prop. Reg. §1.861-18(f)(2). The "special characteristics of computer programs" must be considered in applying these rules. Prop. Reg. §1.861-18(f)(3). For example, a requirement that a disk containing the program be destroyed at a particular time is equivalent to a requirement that the disk be returned, as is a transfer of a copy that automatically deactivates at a particular time. Prop. Reg. §1.861-18(f)(3).

"Neither the form adopted by the parties to a transaction, nor the classification of the transaction under copyright law, shall be determinative," and the nature of "the physical or electronic medium used to effectuate a transfer of" the program is also not determinative. Prop. Reg. §1.861-18(g).

The proposed regulations contain many examples illustrating the application of the foregoing rules. Prop. Reg. §1.861-18(h).

[120] See supra ¶54.2 for §§631(b) and (c).

[121] Gain on a sale of any interest in real property located in the United States is from U.S. sources. IRC §861(a)(5), discussed infra ¶70.6.2.

[122] IRC §§871(a)(1)(B), 881(a)(2).

The Treasury's model treaty generally bars each country from taxing royalties paid to residents of the other country.[123] The United States thus cannot tax royalties paid to residents of the many countries that have made treaties with the United States following the Treasury model on this point.[124] In other treaties, royalties can be taxed by the country of source, but the withholding tax rate is reduced (often to 10 percent).[125] The exemption or rate reduction usually covers royalties from licensees of copyrights, patents, know-how, trademarks, and other forms of intellectual property.[126] Under the Treasury model, gain on a sale of such property is also covered if it is recognized on the receipt of a payment that is contingent on the property's productivity, use, or disposition, and the treaty exemption is denied to royalties from "cinematographic films" and films and tapes licensed for television or radio broadcast.[127] Under virtually all treaties, the exemption or rate reduction for royalties is not available to a resident of the treaty country who is engaged in business through a permanent establishment in the United States or performs independent personal services through a fixed base in this country if the royalties are attributable to the U.S. establishment or fixed base.[128] Royalties attributable to a permanent establishment or fixed base in the United States are instead taxable as part of the taxpayer's U.S. business profits.

The royalties articles of treaties usually apply only to intangible property, and under the articles on real property, royalties received by owners of natural

---

[123] Treasury Model, supra note 63, art. 12(1).

[124] For tables listing maximum tax rates on royalties under U.S. income tax treaties, see IRS Pub. No. 515, Withholding of Tax on Nonresident Aliens and Foreign Corporations (Rev. Nov. 1997); IRS Pub. No. 901, U.S. Tax Treaties 26 (Rev. Nov. 1997); Notice 97-29, 1997-14 IRB 16 (updating tables to reflect new treaties or protocols with Kazakstan and Indonesia).

[125] See, e.g., Convention between the United States of America and Japan for the Avoidance of Double Taxation and the Prevention of Fiscal Evasion with Respect to Taxes on Income, Mar. 8, 1971, art. 14(2). See also Hershberger & Siegel, Services, Know-How Create Withholding Dilemmas Under U.S.-Mexico Treaty, 6 J. Int'l Tax'n 338 (1995).

[126] See Treasury Model, supra note 63, art. 12(2)(a); OECD Model, supra note 64, art. 12(2). See also Doernberg, The U.S.-India Income Tax Treaty: Breaking New Ground in Taxing Services Income from Licensing Technology, 44 Tax Lawyer 735 (1991) (discussing royalty article of U.S.-India treaty, which allows source country to tax "royalties and fees for included services" at 15 or 20 percent and defines "included services" as services ancillary to license of intellectual property and services that "make available technical knowledge, experience, skill, know-how, or processes, or consist of the development and transfer of a technical plan or technical design").

[127] Treasury Model, supra note 63, art. 12(2)(b). The royalties article of the OECD model makes no mention of gains on sales of intellectual property, but it applies to "cinematograph films, or films or tapes used for radio or television broadcasting." OECD Model, supra note 64, art. 12(3).

[128] See Treasury Model, supra note 63, art. 12(3); OECD Model, supra note 64, art. 12(3).

resources deposits are usually taxable by the country in which the deposits are located.[129]

¶66.2.8 Other Fixed or Determinable Annual or Periodical Income

In addition to the items discussed above, the withholding tax applies to "other fixed or determinable annual or periodical gains, profits and income" from U.S. sources.[130] According to the regulations, the term "fixed or determinable annual or periodical income" includes all items of gross income, except gains on sales of property (including market discount on bonds and option premiums) and insurance premiums paid to a foreign insurer or reinsurer.[131] Moreover,

> The term *fixed or determinable annual or periodical* income is merely descriptive of the character of a class of income. If an item of income falls within the class of income contemplated by the statute . . . , it is immaterial whether payment of that item is made in a series of repeated payments or in a single lump sum . . . . Further, the income need not be paid annually if it is paid periodically; that is to say, from time to time, whether or not at regular intervals. The fact that a payment is not made annually or periodically does not, however, prevent its being fixed or determinable annual or periodical income (e.g., a lump sum payment). In addition, the fact that the length of time during which the payments are to be made may be increased or diminished in accordance with someone's will or with the happening of an event does not disqualify the payment as determinable or periodical. . . .
>
> An item of income is fixed when it is to be paid in amounts definitely pre-determined. An item of income is determinable if the amount to be paid is not known but there is a basis of calculation by which the amount may be ascertained. . . . [A]n amount of income does not have to be determined at the time that the payment is made in order to be determinable.[132]

However, "a payment which may be income in the future based upon events that are not anticipated at the time the payment is made is not determinable."[133] For example, although loan proceeds may ultimately be taxed to the recipient as debt discharge income in the event the loan is not repaid, they are not fixed or determinable annual or periodical income if default is not "anticipated at the time of disbursement."

---

[129] See Treasury Model, supra note 63, art. 6; OECD Model, supra note 64, art. 6.

[130] IRC §§871(a)(1)(A), 881(a)(1).

[131] Reg. §§1.1441-2(b)(1)(i), (2). However, gain on a sale or exchange of §306 stock of a domestic corporation is fixed or determinable annual or periodical income to the extent §306(a) treats it as ordinary income. Reg. §1.306-3(h). For §306, see infra ¶95.3.

[132] Reg. §§1.1441-2(b)(1)(ii), (iii) (withholding rules), incorporated by reference by Reg. §1.871-7(b).

[133] Reg. §1.1441-2(b)(1)(iii).

The fixed or determinable category has been held to embrace alimony,[134] commissions, prizes, gambling winnings,[135] and income on the surrender of a life insurance policy.[136] Income of a kind usually paid annually or periodically is included even if paid in a lump sum.[137] In other words, "fixed or determinable annual or periodical" income need not be annual or periodical. Moreover, the words "fixed or determinable" are meaningless because income cannot be taxed if it is not quantifiable. However, gain on the sale of property is not included in this category even if the selling price is received in installments.[138]

Income tax treaties frequently eliminate the withholding tax on many items picked up by the catchall phrase. Under most treaties, a resident of a treaty country may not be taxed by the other country on any item of income of a type that is not explicitly dealt with in the treaty.[139]

---

[134] See Howkins v. CIR, 49 TC 689 (1968). See Manning v. CIR, 614 F2d 815 (1st Cir. 1980) (alimony paid by U.S. resident is from sources within United States). But see U.S. Treasury Dep't, Model Income Tax Convention of September 20, 1996, art. 18(4) (United States may not tax alimony received by resident of country having treaty with United States based on Treasury model).

[135] See Barba v. US, 2 Cl. Ct. 674, 83-1 USTC ¶9,404 (1983) (gambling winnings; no deduction or offset for gambling losses); Rev. Rul. 58-479, 1958-2 CB 60 (commissions, prizes, gambling winnings).

However, Congress has exempted from the withholding tax "the proceeds from a wager placed in any of the following games: blackjack, baccarat, craps, roulette, or big-6 wheel." IRC §871(j). The exemption was enacted in 1988 to conform the statute to the prior administrative practice of not collecting the tax from casino operators, who might reasonably complain if they were required to determine the citizenship and residence of every person throwing the dice or spinning the wheel. H.R. Rep. No. 1104, 100th Cong., 2d Sess. 196–97 (Conf. Rep. 1988). The exemption is inapplicable in situations where the Treasury has determined "by regulations" that "collection of the tax is administratively feasible." IRC §871(j). The Treasury has not yet exercised this power.

[136] See Rev. Rul. 64-51, 1964-1 (Part 1) CB 322 (surrender of insurance policy). But see Rev. Rul. 89-91, 1989-2 CB 129 (insurance premiums received by foreign casualty insurance company not taxable under §881(a) because subject to excise tax under §4371 that Congress intended to be substitute for income tax); Rev. Proc. 92-39, 1992-1 CB 860 (procedures for establishing exemption from §4371 tax under income tax treaties with Germany, Finland, India, and Spain; also applicable under treaties becoming effective after May 18, 1992 that contain "similar limitations on benefits and excise tax exemption provisions"). See also US v. International Business Machines Corp., 116 S. Ct. 1793 (1996) (§4371 tax, as applied to premiums on insurance covering risks associated with goods in export transit from United States, violates Export Clause, Art. I, §9, cl. 5, of U.S. constitution); Notice 96-37, 1996-31 IRB 29 (procedures for obtaining refunds pursuant to *IBM*).

[137] See CIR v. Wodehouse, 337 US 369 (1949); Reg. §1.1441-2(a)(1) (lump sum royalties); Rev. Rul. 64-51, 1964-1 (Part 1) CB 322 (lump sum payment of insurance contract at maturity).

[138] Reg. §1.1441-2(a)(3).

[139] Treasury Model, supra note 63, art. 21(1); OECD Model, supra note 64, art. 21(1).

¶66.2.9 Capital Gains and Losses

Capital gains are generally exempted from the withholding tax, although a few particular types of gains are subject to the tax (e.g., gains on sales of intellectual property where the price is contingent on the property's productivity, use, or disposition).

Under §871(a)(2), a nonresident alien who is physically present in the United States for 183 or more days during the taxable year is subject to a 30 percent tax on the excess of U.S. source gains on sales and exchanges of capital assets over capital losses allocable to U.S. sources, except for gains and losses taken into account under §871(a)(1) (fixed or determinable income) or §871(b) (effectively connected income). Two or more periods can be aggregated to make up the requisite 183 days of physical presence.[140] This tax is not enforced by withholding.

A cryptic statement in §871(a)(2), providing that gains and losses shall be taken into account only if they would be recognized in determining effectively connected income, presumably incorporates by reference the normal rules governing the computation and recognition of gain or loss and the taxable year in which the recognized amount is reported or deducted. However, capital loss carryovers are not allowed. In applying §871(a)(2), no distinction is drawn between sales while the nonresident alien is present in the United States and those effected during the alien's absence.

Section 871(a)(2) is a relic of the past with an extremely limited scope under current law, and Congress probably would have repealed the provision if it had squarely addressed the question. Normally, an alien who is present in the United States for 183 days or more during a calendar year is a resident for the year under the substantial presence test of §7701(b).[141] Thus, an alien whose taxable year is the calendar year usually cannot be taxable under §871(a)(2) because the 183 days of presence needed to trigger the §871(a)(2) tax makes the alien a resident and thereby taxable under §1 rather than §871. Since the residence test is always applied on a calendar year basis, an alien using a taxable year other than the calendar year can be present in the United States for 183 days during a taxable year without being present for that many days during any calendar year, but the situation is extremely rare.[142]

Under various circumstances, days of presence in the United States are ignored in applying the substantial presence test. For example, visiting teachers and students, diplomats, and daily commuters from Canada and Mexico are usually not classified as U.S. residents, even if they are present in this country for most of the year.[143] These exclusions do not apply for purposes of the 183-day test

---

[140] For complications in computing the 183-day period, see Reg. §1.871-7(d)(3).

[141] For the substantial presence test, see supra ¶65.2.3.

[142] See IRC §7701(b)(9) (most alien individuals required to use calendar year as taxable year).

[143] IRC §§7701(b)(5), (7).

of §871(a)(2). Thus, a person who is present in the United States for at least 183 days during a taxable year, but whose presence is not counted in applying the substantial presence test, is subject to the 30 percent tax on capital gains from U.S. sources. But, even for these persons, the reach of the tax is quite limited because, with only a few exceptions, capital gains have their source in the United States only if the taxpayer is a U.S. resident[144] and an alien whose presence in the United States is not counted in applying the substantial presence test is usually not a U.S. resident.

However, if an alien's tax home (usually, principal place of business) is in the United States, the person is treated as a U.S. resident for purposes of the source rule, even if the person is classified as a nonresident for other tax purposes.[145] Thus, the principal application of the §871(a)(2) tax is probably to nonresident aliens who are present in the United States for at least 183 days during the taxable year (at least some of which are not counted for purposes of the substantial presence test) and whose principal places of business are located in this country.

Even in the few cases in which it applies, the §871(a)(2) tax may be barred by treaty.[146]

¶66.2A NONBUSINESS INCOME FROM U.S. SOURCES: TREATY LIMITATIONS AND ANTIABUSE RULES

¶66.2A.1 Treaty Benefits for Payments to Fiscally Transparent Entities

The rate at which U.S. withholding tax is imposed on a dividend, interest, royalty, or other payment may be reduced by an income tax treaty only if the taxpayer is a resident of the foreign country with which the United States concluded the treaty (the treaty country). Application of the residence requirement is often complicated when the item is paid to an entity that is treated as a pass-through entity (e.g., partnership) under the tax laws of either the United States or the treaty country. For example, if a U.S.-source dividend is received by a country Y entity owned by residents of country X, what treaty benefits, if any, are allowed if the entity is classified as a partnership under U.S. law? Under the laws of country Y? The laws of country X? The problems are most vexing if an

---

[144] IRC §865(a), discussed infra ¶70.6. One of the principal exceptions from this rule is that gains on sales of U.S. real property interests are from U.S. sources. IRC §861(a)(5). However, these gains are subject to the effectively connected income tax under §897(a), and effectively connected income is exempted from tax under §871(a)(2). For U.S. real property interests, see infra ¶66.4.

[145] IRC §865(g)(1))(A)(i)(II).

[146] See Treasury Model, supra note 63, art. 13(5); OECD Model, supra note 64, art. 13(4).

entity is classified as a corporation for U.S. tax purposes and as a partnership (fiscally transparent entity) under the laws of the treaty country or vice versa.

Under §894(c)(1),[1] enacted in 1997, a withholding tax reduction provided by a tax treaty with respect to any item is denied to a foreign person if the item is "derived through an entity" that, under U.S. tax law, is "treated as a partnership (or is otherwise treated as fiscally transparent)" and if all of the following are true:

1. The item is not, under the tax laws of the treaty country, considered income of the foreign person (e.g., partner),
2. The treaty does not contain a provision on "the applicability of the treaty in the case of an item of income derived through a partnership," and
3. The treaty country "does not impose tax on a distribution of such item of income from such entity to such person."[2]

This provision was enacted, according to the House Ways and Means Committee, because:

> The Committee is concerned about the potential tax-avoidance opportunities available for foreign persons that invest in the United States through hybrid entities. In particular, the Committee understands that the interaction of the tax laws and the applicable tax treaty may provide a business structuring opportunity that would allow Canadian corporations with U.S. subsidiaries to avoid both U.S. and Canadian income taxes with respect to those U.S. operations. . . . Through the use of a U.S. limited liability company, which is treated as a partnership for U.S. tax purposes but as a corporation for Canadian tax purposes, a payment of interest (which is deductible for U.S. tax purposes) may be converted into a dividend (which is excludable for Canadian tax purposes). . . . The Committee believes that such tax-avoidance opportunities should be eliminated.[3]

Section 894(c)(1) is quite narrow in scope. However, §894(c)(2) authorizes the Treasury to issue regulations limiting "the extent to which a taxpayer" not

---

[1] Section 894(c) is effective as of August 5, 1997. Pub. L. No. 105-34, §1054(a) (1997). According to the House Ways and Means Committee, "the provision generally is consistent with U.S. treaty obligations, including the U.S.-Canada treaty. The United States has recognized authority to implement its tax treaties so as to avoid abuses." H.R. Rep. No. 105-148, 105th Cong., 1st Sess. __ (1997). See generally Hess, TRA '97 Toughens Rules for Foreign Partnerships, 8 J. Int'l Tax'n 534 (1997); Postlewaite, Tax Treaty Benefits and Partnership Classification, 88 J. Tax'n 31 (1998).

[2] See H.R. Rep. No. 148, 105th Cong., 1st Sess. __ (1997) ("the foreign country will be considered to impose tax on a distribution even though such tax may be reduced or eliminated by reason of deductions or credits otherwise available to the taxpayer"); Rev. Proc. 98-7, 1998-1 CB __, §4.01(15) (IRS ordinarily will not rule on whether foreign jurisdiction treats entity as fiscally transparent).

[3] H.R. Rep. No. 148, supra note 2, at __. For the structure referred to by the Committee, see Klein & Renfroe, Section 894: Payments to Flow-Through Entities, 26 Tax Mgmt. Int'l J. 547 (1997).

subject to §894(c)(1) may enjoy treaty benefits "with respect to any payment received by, or income attributable to any activities of, an entity organized in any jurisdiction (including the United States) that is treated as a partnership or is otherwise treated as fiscally transparent for [U.S. tax] purposes . . . and is treated as fiscally nontransparent for purposes of the tax laws of the [taxpayer's country of residence]." The Treasury issued such regulations in 1997, essentially contemporaneously with the enactment of §894(c).[4]

To deal with these "hybrid entities," the regulations

> rely on the basic principle that income tax treaties are designed to relieve double taxation or excessive taxation. This objective is generally achieved with provisions in treaties that limit the tax that a country may impose on income arising from sources within its borders to the extent that the income is derived by a resident of a jurisdiction with which the source country has an income tax treaty in effect. . . . However, the agreement by the source country to cede part of all of its taxation rights to the treaty partner is predicated on a mutual understanding that the treaty partner is asserting tax jurisdiction over the income. Stated simply, tax treaties contemplate that income relieved from taxation in the source country will be subject to tax in the treaty country. This principle is central to the interpretation of treaty provisions in determining the extent to which payments received by a hybrid entity are eligible for benefits under tax treaties. Some treaties have specific rules reflecting this principle that are helpful in deciding how the treaties should be applied in such cases. However, the lack of specific rules in a treaty does not suggest that this principle does not apply under that treaty.[5]

Under the regulations, a payment received by an entity qualifies for a reduced withholding tax rate under a treaty only to the extent that the payment is "subject to tax in the hands of a resident" of the treaty country, that resident is the beneficial owner of the payment, and all other requirements of the treaty are satisfied.[6] The term "entity" means a person (other than a natural person) that is recognized under the laws of the United States or the treaty country.[7] Residence is determined under the tax treaty.[8]

1. *Subject to tax in treaty country.* If the entity is "fiscally transparent" under the laws of the treaty country, the payment is considered taxable to residents of that country only to the extent that it is allocable to "interest holders," exclusive of interest holders that are themselves fiscally transparent, who

---

[4] TD 8722, 1997-29 IRB 4. The Treasury believes that the regulations "are consistent with U.S. tax treaty obligations and basic tax treaty obligations." See generally Tax Section of NY State Bar Ass'n, Withholding on U.S.-Source Investment Income Paid to "Fiscally Transparent" Entities, 76 Tax Notes 609 (Nov. 3, 1997).

The regulations apply to amounts paid after 1997. Reg. §1.894-1T(d)(7).

[5] TD 8722, supra note 4, at 4-5.

[6] Reg. §1.894-1T(d)(1).

[7] Reg. §1.894-1T(d)(4)(i).

[8] Reg. §1.894-1T(d)(4)(iv).

are residents of the country.[9] An entity is "fiscally transparent" under the laws of a country to the extent that those laws require "interest holders in the entity to take into account separately on a current basis their respective shares of the items of income paid to the entity and to determine the character of such items as if such items were realized directly from the source from which realized by the entity . . . ."[10] The fiscally transparent entities under U.S. law are partnerships, proprietorships, common trust funds, simple trusts, grantor trusts, and other entities that are treated as partnerships or are disregarded for U.S. tax purposes.

Assume entity A, which is a partnership for U.S. tax purposes, is organized under the laws of country Z, which has no tax treaty with the United States, and is owned by two interest holders—G, a resident of country X (which has a tax treaty with the United States), and H, a resident of country Y (with which the United States also has a treaty).[11] Unless A is taxed on a residence basis by country X or Y, it is entitled to no treaty benefits because it is not a resident of a treaty country. Since A is a partnership for U.S. tax purposes, G's and H's distributive shares of U.S.-source dividends, royalties, and other items received by A may be subject to U.S. withholding taxes. However, if country X (G's residence country) treats A as a nontransparent entity, G is denied the benefits of the U.S.-country X treaty with respect to these items, even if A immediately distributes G's share of the income to her or G is immediately taxed on this share under the country X analogue to subpart F.[12] In contrast, if country Y (H's residence country) treats A as fiscally transparent and immediately taxes H on her share of such items, U.S. withholding taxes on H's distributive share of the items may be reduced by the U.S.-country Y treaty. It is not relevant whether the treaty refers to income of entities treated as partnerships under the laws of either of the countries.

This approach applies even if the entity is classified as a corporation for U.S. tax purposes, as long as it is not organized under the laws of the United States or one of its states.[13] Assume entity C, which is organized under the laws of country

---

[9] Reg. §1.894-1T(d)(1). The entity is not eligible for treaty benefits because a person is a resident of a treaty country only if it is taxed on a residence basis by that country. This is so even if the entity is not fiscally transparent under U.S. law. TD 8722, supra note 4, at 5.

[10] Reg. §1.894-1T(d)(4)(ii).

[11] Reg. §1.894-1T(d)(6) Ex. 4. The results would be the same if A were organized under the laws of one of the states of the United States or if it were a "dual organized entity," organized under both U.S. and country Z law. Reg. §1.894-1T(d)(6) Exs. 5, 6.

[12] Reg. §1.894-1T(d)(6) Exs. 7, 8.

[13] The question in this case is

whether the source country's laws or the laws of each owner's jurisdiction of residence should govern the determination of who is the person deriving the income for tax treaty purposes. Making that determination under the tax laws of the applicable treaty jurisdiction where the owners are resident leads to results consistent with the principle . . . that the source country cedes its tax jurisdiction to the treaty partner based on the understanding that the treaty partner asserts tax jurisdiction over the

X and is wholly owned by a country X corporation, is fiscally transparent under X law but elects to be treated as a corporation for U.S. tax purposes.[14] U.S. source income received by C is treated for withholding tax purposes as income of C's owner and qualifies for any applicable reduced rate of withholding tax under the U.S.-country X treaty because C is fiscally transparent under X law and its owner is a resident of country X.

However, a corporation classified as a domestic corporation for U.S. tax purposes may not qualify for a reduced treaty rate, even if it is fiscally transparent under the laws of a treaty country and its shareholders are residents of that country.[15] For example, if C in the last example were organized under the laws of one of the U.S. states, neither C nor its owner would be allowed treaty benefits with respect to U.S. source income received by C.[16]

If the entity is not fiscally transparent under the laws of the treaty country, a reduced treaty rate applies only if the entity is a resident of the treaty country.[17] This rule applies whether or not the entity is fiscally transparent under U.S. law. Assume entity B is classified as a partnership under U.S. law but is taxable as an entity and as a resident under the laws of country X, which has a treaty with the United States providing a reduced withholding rate for royalties.[18] B is an X resident under the treaty because country X taxes it as a resident; if it receives and is beneficial owner of royalties from U.S. sources, the U.S. withholding tax rate on the royalties is reduced by the treaty because the income is beneficially owned by a resident of the treaty country. The residence of B's owners is not relevant, even though the owners are the U.S. taxpayers.[19]

---

income by insuring that it is taxable in the hands of a resident.

TD 8722, supra note 4, at 5.

[14] Reg. §1.894-1T(d)(6) Ex. 9.

[15] Reg. §1.894-1T(d)(3). This rule derives from the savings clauses contained in all U.S. tax treaties, which preserve to the United States the right to tax its residents in accordance with U.S. law. TD 8722, supra note 4, at 7.

[16] Reg. §1.894-1T(d)(6) Ex. 10.

[17] Reg. §1.894-1T(d)(1).

[18] Reg. §1.894-1T(d)(6) Exs. 1, 2.

[19] According to the Treasury:

Applying the tax laws of the source country to determine the person deriving the income for treaty purposes would not only be inconsistent with the basic principle that income should be treated as derived by the person in the treaty country who is liable to tax on that income, it also potentially leads to tax avoidance under tax conventions, including an inappropriate double exemption. For example, if the entity does not fall within the taxing jurisdiction of the applicable treaty jurisdiction (e.g., because the entity is organized in a third country or as a fiscally transparent entity in the source country), the income could be eligible for a treaty-reduced tax rate in the source country and yet not be subject to tax in the jurisdiction where the owners are resident.

TD 8722, supra note 4, at 6.

2. *Beneficial ownership.* An entity that is fiscally transparent under U.S. law is treated as beneficial owner of a payment if it would be considered beneficial owner were it not fiscally transparent.[20] A treaty-country resident who is taxed by that country on any portion of a payment received by a fiscally transparent entity is also treated as beneficial owner of that portion unless (1) the person would not have been considered beneficial owner if he or she had received the payment directly or (2) the entity is not the beneficial owner of the payment.[21] Assume residents of country X hold interests in a country Y entity that is fiscally transparent under country X law. The interest holders are beneficial owners of any U.S.-source payment beneficially owned by the entity unless they would not have been beneficial owners if the payments had been made directly to them (e.g., because their interests in the entity are held as conduits or nominees for other persons). However, the interest holders cannot be beneficial owners if the entity does not beneficially own the payment (e.g., because it receives the payment as conduit or nominee).

3. *Application of regulations.* The foregoing rules generally apply under all income tax treaties to which the United States is a party, except treaties that "explicitly" provide otherwise.[22] However, treaty benefits otherwise allowed by the rules are denied "to the extent that the [treaty country] would not grant a reduced rate under the tax treaty to a U.S. resident in similar circumstances." This reciprocity may be evidenced by an agreement between the competent authorities of the United States and the treaty country or by "a published notice of the treaty partner."

¶66.2A.2   Disregard of Conduit Entities

If the form of transactions is respected, liability for the withholding tax can often be reduced or eliminated by routing a U.S. investment through one or more conduit entities. Assume a foreign corporation (*FP*) decides to make a loan to a U.S. subsidiary (*DS*). If *FP*'s country of residence does not have an income tax treaty with the United States, interest paid by *DS* to *FP* on this loan would be taxed at 30 percent under §881. But, suppose *FP* organizes a subsidiary corporation in country Y, which has an income tax treaty with the United States that exempts from U.S. tax all interest paid by U.S. persons to country Y residents, and *FP* makes the loan to this subsidiary (*FS*), which loans an identical amount to *DS*. If the form of these transactions is honored, no U.S. tax is due because the treaty exempts the only interest paid by a U.S. person (*DS*'s payments to *FS*). Alternatively, suppose *FP* deposits the funds with an unrelated foreign bank on the condition that a foreign nonbanking subsidiary of the bank make a loan to *DS*. If the form is honored in this case, U.S. tax is again avoided because the

---

[20] Reg. §1.894-1T(d)(2)(i).
[21] Reg. §1.894-1T(d)(2)(ii).
[22] Reg. §1.894-1T(d)(5).

interest paid by the U.S. borrower (*DS*)—not being paid to a person related to the borrower or to a bank—is portfolio interest.[23] A foreign conduit corporation might be equally effective in avoiding U.S. tax if *FP* wanted to license a patent or other intellectual property to *DS* in exchange for periodic royalty payments.

The IRS has had some success in attacking conduit schemes in litigation. In the leading case, *Aiken Industries, Inc. v. CIR*, a Honduran corporation was sandwiched between a U.S. obligor and a Bahamian creditor in order to obtain the benefit of a U.S.-Honduras treaty that exempted residents of Honduras from U.S. tax on interest from U.S. sources.[24] The Tax Court denied the exemption, finding that the corporation was merely a conduit through which the interest passed to the Bahamian corporation, which was not eligible for any treaty benefit.[25] In another case, it was held that a Swedish prizefighter, who organized and purportedly worked for a "paper Swiss corporation," was not entitled to the benefit of the U.S. tax treaty with Switzerland, which exempted compensation received by employees of Swiss corporations for services performed while temporarily present in the United States for not more than half of the taxable year.[26]

---

[23] For portfolio interest, see §871(h), discussed supra ¶66.2.2 text accompanying notes 21-56.

[24] Aiken Indus., Inc. v. CIR, 56 TC 925 (1971). In Northern Ind. Pub. Serv. Co. v. CIR, 105 TC 341 (1995), aff'd, 115 F3d 506 (7th Cir. 1997), the taxpayer's Netherlands Antilles subsidiary issued "Euronotes" to foreign investors and loaned the proceeds to the taxpayer. The court held that the taxpayer was not required to withhold tax from interest paid to the subsidiary. *Aiken* was distinguished on the grounds that (1) in *Aiken*, all parties to the transactions were related, whereas the subsidiary's debt in *Northern Ind. Pub. Serv.* was owed to unrelated persons and (2) the subsidiary in *Northern* realized significant earnings from the transactions because the interest rate on the Euronotes was one percentage point less than the interest paid by the taxpayer to the subsidiary, whereas the transactions in *Aiken* were a wash.

[25] See Rev. Rul. 84-152, 1984-2 CB 381, declared obsolete, Rev. Rul. 95-56, 1995-2 CB 322 (following *Aiken Indus.* where foreign parent loaned funds to Netherlands Antilles subsidiary at 10 percent interest and subsidiary reloaned funds to domestic sister subsidiary at 11 percent interest); Rev. Rul. 84-153, 1984-2 CB 383, declared obsolete, Rev. Rul. 95-56, 1995-2 CB 322 (following *Aiken Indus.* where Netherlands Antilles subsidiary of domestic corporation issued bonds to foreign investors, and subsidiary loaned bond proceeds to domestic subsidiary of same parent at interest rate one percentage point higher than bond rate); Rev. Rul. 89-110, 1989-2 CB 275 (explaining effect of partial termination of Netherlands Antilles treaty on Rev. Ruls. 84-152 and 84-153). See also Rev. Rul. 87-89, 1987-2 CB 195, declared obsolete, Rev. Rul. 95-56, 1995-2 CB 322 (where foreign parent corporation organized in nontreaty country makes deposit in bank in treaty country and bank makes loan to parent's U.S. subsidiary, parent is treated as loaning directly to subsidiary unless loan would have been made on same terms without deposit; right of bank to offset deposit against subsidiary's obligation is "presumptive evidence" that loan would not have been made but for deposit).

[26] Johansson v. US, 336 F2d 809 (5th Cir. 1964). See Rev. Rul. 74-330, 1974-2 CB 278 ("single loan-out" arrangements between foreign entertainers and foreign corporations treated as employment contracts in applying tax treaty with United Kingdom); Rev. Rul. 74-331, 1974-2 CB 281 (same as to "double loan-out" arrangements involving two foreign corporations).

In 1993, Congress, wanting to strengthen the IRS' position in such cases, enacted §7701(*l*), which authorizes the issuance of regulations "recharacterizing any multiple-party financing transaction [as] appropriate to prevent avoidance of any tax." The regulations under §7701(*l*), issued in 1995,[27] allow the IRS to "disregard . . . the participation of one or more intermediate entities in a financing arrangement" for purposes of §§871, 881, 1441, and 1442 (the withholding taxes).[28]

1. *Definitions.* The regulations rest on their definitions of five crucial terms—"financing arrangement," "financing transaction," "conduit entity," "conduit financing arrangement," and "related."[29]

A *"financing arrangement"* is

> a series of transactions by which one person (the financing entity) advances money or other property, or grants rights to use property, and another person (the financed entity) receives money or other property, or rights to use property, if the advance and receipt are effected through one or more other persons (intermediate entities) and . . . there are financing transactions linking the financing entity, each of the intermediate entities, and the financed entity.[30]

The "order in which the transactions are entered into" is not relevant, but a

---

[27] TD 8611, 1995-2 CB 286. See Dolan, DuPuy & Walsh, Final Conduit Regulations, 24 Tax Mgmt. Int'l J. 522 (1995); Glicklich, Final Regulations on Conduit Financing Arrangements Empower the IRS, 84 J. Tax'n 5 (1996); Hirshfeld, Final Regs. Refine Rules on Abusive Conduit Financing, 6 J. Int'l Tax'n 484 (1995); North & French, Final Conduit Financing Regs Examined, 11 Tax Notes Int'l 726 (Sept. 11, 1995).

For the proposed regulations, see INTL-64-93, 1994-2 CB 880; Amico, Stemming the Flow of Conduit Financing, 11 Tax Notes Int'l 97 (July 3, 1995); Bennett, Cacciatore, Morrison, Rohleder, O'Donnell & Penn, The Proposed Anti-Conduit Regulations Under Section 7701(*l*), 24 Tax Mgmt. Int'l J. 3 (1995); Brenneman, Conduit Regulations Address Multi-Party Financing Arrangements, 22 J. Real Est. Tax'n 238 (1995); Lederman & Hirsh, Conduit Proposed Regulations Are Potent in Effect, but Limited in Scope, 82 J. Tax'n 116 (1995); Schler, A Handy Guide to the Conduit Financing Regulations, 65 Tax Notes 627 (Oct. 31, 1994); Spector & Stearns, Proposed Conduit Rules Focus on U.S. Withholding Tax, 9 Tax Notes Int'l 1623 (Nov. 21, 1994).

[28] Reg. §1.881-3(a)(1). The regulations generally apply to payments made by financed entities after September 10, 1995, including payments under loans and other financing transactions made before that date, but not to interest under obligations issued before October 15, 1984. Reg. §1.881-3(g).

The regulations generally refer only to §881, but this reference "includes, except as otherwise provided and as the context may require," §§871, 884(f)(1)(A), 1441, and 1442. Reg. §1.881-3(a)(1).

[29] See Rev. Proc. 98-7, 1998-1 CB __, §4.01(27) (IRS ordinarily will not rule on whether intermediate entity is conduit entity, whether transaction is financing transaction, whether intermediate entity's participation is pursuant to tax avoidance plan, whether intermediate entity performs significant financing activities, or whether unrelated intermediate entity would not have participated on substantially same terms).

[30] Reg. §1.881-3(a)(2)(i)(A). See TD 8611, supra note 27, at 289 (this test is applied by "tak[ing] a 'snapshot' after all the transactions are in place").

financing arrangement "exists only for the period during which all of the financing transactions coexist."

The IRS generally has discretion to determine whether an advance from a financing entity to an intermediate entity should be matched with a particular advance from the intermediate entity to a financed entity.[31] For example, if an entity borrows $100 from a related foreign person and $100 from an unrelated person and loans $100 to a related U.S. person, the IRS "may determine[,] based on the facts," that the U.S. borrower, the intermediate entity, and the related foreign person are parties to a financing arrangement or that the arrangement is among the U.S. borrower, the intermediate entity, and the unrelated person.[32]

The advances need not be made at the same time or be on identical terms. Assume foreign corporation *FP* loans $100 to its foreign subsidiary *FS* under a 10-year note requiring no periodic interest payments but a single payment at maturity of $240; one year later *FS* loans $100 to *FP*'s U.S. subsidiary under a 10-year note bearing interest at 10 percent payable annually and a principal payment of $100 at maturity.[33] The two loans are a financing arrangement.

The financing and financed entities need not be related persons. Assume *FP* organizes *FS* with a capital contribution of $1,000, and *FS* borrows $10,000 from an unrelated foreign bank (*BK*); *DS*, *FP*'s domestic subsidiary, makes installment sales of automobiles to U.S. customers; *DS* sells the installment notes to *FS* for $10,000 (their fair market value), but continues to service the notes as *FS*'s agent.[34] The financing arrangement in this case consists of *FS*'s borrowing from *BK* (the financing entity) and the installment notes of *DS*'s U.S. customers (the financed entities). Depending on the circumstances, the regulations might have the effect of requiring *FS* to be disregarded as a conduit and determining withholding taxes as though interest paid by the U.S. customers were paid to *BK*, rather than *FS*.

There may be more than one intermediate entity in a financing arrangement, but a chain of financing transactions must link the intermediate entities. Assume *FP*·deposits funds with an unrelated foreign bank (*BK*), *BK* makes a loan to its foreign subsidiary (*BK2*), *BK2* makes a loan to *FS*, and *FS* makes a loan to *DS*.[35] *BK*, *BK2*, and *FS* are intermediate entities, and all of the loans comprise a single financing arrangement.

Moreover, the IRS may treat two or more related persons as a single intermediate entity, notwithstanding the absence of any linking transaction between them, if "one of the principal purposes for the structure of the financing trans-

---

[31] See TD 8611, supra note 27, at 289 ("Among other things, the district director may determine the composition of the financing arrangements and the number of parties to the financing arrangement").

[32] INTL-64-93, supra note 27, at 882.

[33] Reg. §1.881-3(e) Ex. 16. See Reg. §1.881-3(e) Ex. 5 (financing arrangement consisting of 10-year, 8 percent loan and 8-year, 10 percent note issued one year later).

[34] Reg. §1.881-3(e) Ex. 3.

[35] Reg. §1.881-3(e) Ex. 8.

actions is to prevent the characterization of such arrangement as a financing arrangement."[36] Assume *FP* deposits $100 with *BK*, and a nonbanking corporation owned by *BK*'s sole shareholder loans $100 to *DS*.[37] Because *BK* and the nonbanking lender are related persons, they are treated as one intermediate entity, even if there are no transactions between them, if these entities are utilized in order to prevent the deposit by *FP* and the loan to *DS* from being linked together as a financing arrangement.[38]

The term *"financing transaction"* includes a debt instrument, lease, or license.[39] Assume foreign corporation *FP* loans $100 to its U.S. subsidiary, *DS*; sometime later, *FP* transfers *DS*'s note to *FP*'s foreign subsidiary, *FS*, in exchange for *FS*'s note to *FP*.[40] *DS*'s note and *FS*'s note are both financing transactions; together, they are a financing arrangement. These conclusions also obtain if, for example, *FP* licenses a patent to *FS* and *FS* sublicenses the patent to *DS*. The term "financing transaction" also includes any other transaction by which "a person makes an advance of money or other property or grants rights to use property to a transferee who is obligated to repay or return a substantial portion of the money or other property advanced or the equivalent in value."[41]

A guarantee is not a financing transaction. Assume *DS* borrows $100 from *BK*, a foreign bank that is not related to *DS* or *FP*, and *FP* guarantees *DS*' obligation to *BK*.[42] *BK*'s loan to *DS* is a financing transaction, but *FP*'s guarantee is not. The transactions thus are not a financing arrangement because there is no series of financing transactions connecting *DS* and *FP*.

Corporate stock or an interest in a partnership or trust is a financing transaction only if one of the following circumstances exists:

    a. The corporation, partnership, or trust (the issuer) is required to redeem the stock or interest at a particular time.

    b. The issuer has a right to redeem the stock or interest and "based on all

---

[36] Reg. §1.881-3(a)(2)(i)(B). See Reg. §1.881-3(a)(4)(ii)(B), discussed infra text accompanying note 56.

[37] Reg. §1.881-3(e) Ex. 4.

[38] See Reg. §1.881-3(e) Ex. 5 (*FP* loans to *FS*; *FS* transfers loan proceeds to newly organized subsidiary (*FS2*) in exchange for stock; *FS2* loans same amount to *DS*; *FS2* pays dividends to *FS* from interest received from *DS*, and *FS* uses these funds to pay interest to *FP*; held, if avoiding conduit regulations is principal purpose of having no financing transaction between *FS* and *FS2*, *FS* and *FS2* are treated as one, and financing arrangement consists of *FP*'s loan to *FS* and *FS2*'s loan to *DS*), §1.881-3(e) Ex. 7 (same, except that 99 percent of funds borrowed from *FP* are transferred by *FS* to *FS2* as equity and one percent is loaned to *FS2*).

[39] Reg. §1.881-3(a)(2)(ii)(A).

[40] Reg. §1.881-3(e) Ex. 2.

[41] Reg. §1.881-3(a)(2)(ii)(A)(4). This rule does not include a transfer of property as collateral for a loan unless the collateral is cash or the person holding the collateral may "reduce [it] to cash" before any default on the underlying obligation.

[42] Reg. §1.881-3(e) Ex. 1.

of the facts and circumstances as of the issue date, redemption pursuant to that right is more likely than not to occur."

    c. The holder has a right to require the issuer to redeem or "to make any other payment with respect to the stock or similar interest."

    d. The holder has a right to require that the stock or interest be acquired by a person related to the issuer or by a "person who is acting pursuant to a plan or arrangement with the issuer."[43]

For example, "common stock or ordinary perpetual preferred stock" is usually not a financing transaction, but "perpetual subordinated debt" usually is, even if the instrument is treated as equity for U.S. tax purposes, because the holder has the right to require the issuer to make payments (nominal interest).[44] Also, "the right to elect the majority of the board of directors will not, in and of itself, cause an equity instrument to be a financing arrangement."[45]

For purposes of the foregoing rules, a holder is considered to have a right to require a redemption or payment if the person may "enforce the payment through a legal proceeding or . . . cause the issuer to be liquidated if it fails to redeem the interest or to make a payment."[46] Such a right is taken into account if it exists when the stock or interest is issued or if, "as of the issue date, it is more likely than not that the person will receive such a right" (e.g., on the occurrence of a contingency that is likely to occur). It is not relevant whether the issuer has funds legally available to make the redemption or that payment in the designated currency might be blocked at the time of payment.[47] However, a right to enforce a corporation's payment of a declared dividend (or analogous right in a partnership or trust context) is not treated as a payment right. Also, power deriving from ownership of a controlling issuer is disregarded unless control "arise[s] from a default or similar contingency under the instrument."[48]

The term *"conduit entity"* refers to "an intermediate entity whose participation in a financing arrangement may be disregarded in whole or in part" under the regulations.[49] A *"conduit financing arrangement"* is a financing arrangement effectuated through one or more conduit entities.[50]

---

[43] Reg. §1.881-3(a)(2)(ii)(B)(*1*). See Reg. §1.881-3(e) Ex. 14 (instrument designated as preferred stock, issued by foreign entity classified as partnership for U.S. tax purposes, is financing transaction where entity is required to redeem instrument in seven years).

[44] INTL-64-93, supra note 27, at 881. See Reg. §1.881-3(e) Ex. 15 (perpetual subordinated debt, issued by foreign partnership to partner and treated for U.S. tax purposes as partnership interest, is financing transaction where partner has right to require partnership liquidation if partnership misses interest payment on instrument).

[45] TD 8611, supra note 27, at 290.

[46] Reg. §1.881-3(a)(2)(ii)(B)(2)(i).

[47] Reg. §1.881-3(a)(2)(ii)(B)(2)(ii).

[48] Reg. §1.881-3(a)(2)(ii)(B)(2)(i).

[49] Reg. §1.881-3(a)(2)(iii).

[50] Reg. §1.881-3(a)(2)(iv).

The many aspects of the regulations depend on whether two or more entities are *"related."* Persons are "related" for this purpose if they are related under §267(b) or §707(b)(1) or if they are considered commonly controlled for purposes of §482.[51] The constructive ownership rules of §318 apply in determining whether persons are related,[52] and the attribution rules of §267(c) also apply when their effects are broader than the §318 rules.[53]

2. *Intermediate entities as conduits.* The regulations allow the IRS to disregard the participation of an intermediate entity in a financing arrangement if the entity is a "conduit."[54] Generally, an intermediate entity is a conduit if its participation in the financing arrangement reduces tax under §881 and is "pursuant to a tax avoidance plan."[55] However, if the intermediate entity is not related to either the financing entity or the financed entity, it is a conduit only it meets these conditions and one other: Its participation in the financing arrangement must be on terms that it would not have agreed to in the absence of the financing entity's transaction with the intermediate entity.

If more than one intermediate entity participates in a financing arrangement, two or more of them can be disregarded as conduits.[56] Also, the IRS may treat two or more related intermediate entities as a single entity if "one of the principal purposes for the involvement of multiple intermediate entities in the financing arrangement is to . . . circumvent the" conduit rules by, for example, "prevent[ing] the characterization of an intermediate entity as a conduit" or "reduc[ing] the portion of a payment that is subject to withholding tax."[57] If two or more related entities are treated as one, transactions between them are disregarded in applying the conduit rules.

a. *Tax reduction.* As noted above, an intermediate entity is a conduit only if its participation in the financing arrangement, if given effect, would reduce U.S. withholding tax.

An intermediate entity does not reduce tax where the withholding tax resulting from giving effect to the role of the intermediate entity is no less than it would be if the financed entity had directly made the transaction between the intermediate and financing entities. Assume *FP*, a resident of a treaty country, issues bonds in a public offering; the buyers of the bonds include many persons

---

[51] Reg. §1.881-3(a)(2)(v). For §§267(b) and 707(b)(1), see infra ¶¶78.3 and 87.2.4. For control under §482, see infra ¶79.2.

[52] For §318, see infra ¶93.1.7.

[53] For §267(c), see infra ¶78.3 text accompanying notes 16–18.

[54] Reg. §1.881-3(a)(3)(i). The conduit rule is an antiabuse rule available only to the IRS; a taxpayer may not reduce tax liability by "disregarding the form of its financing transactions . . . or by compelling the [IRS] to do so." Reg. §1.881-3(a)(3)(iii).

[55] Reg. §1.881-3(a)(4)(ii). The IRS believes that its application of this rule "generally will be reviewed by the court under an abuse of discretion standard." TD 8611, supra note 27, at 290.

[56] Reg. §1.881-3(a)(4)(ii)(A). See Reg. §1.881-3(e) Ex. 8.

[57] Reg. §1.881-3(a)(4)(ii)(B).

who are not residents of treaty countries; *FP* loans the issue proceeds to its U.S. subsidiary (*DS*).[58] *FP* is an intermediate entity in a financing arrangement. However, if the bonds were issued in a way that would have qualified interest on them as portfolio interest, were *FP* a domestic corporation, *FP* is not a conduit; the arrangement does not reduce withholding tax because the interest would be exempt portfolio interest if the bonds had been issued by *DS*.[59]

As another illustration of this principle, assume *FP*, in this instance not a resident of a treaty country, licenses a U.S. patent to a subsidiary organized in a treaty country (*FS*), which sublicenses the patent to *DS*.[60] Since a U.S. patent can only be used in the United States, the royalties paid by *FS* to *FP* are from U.S. sources and therefore subject to U.S. withholding tax at the statutory rate. Because the transaction between *FP* and *FS* results in the same withholding tax obligation as would have resulted if this license had been between *FP* and *DS*, the insertion of *FS* as an intermediate entity does not reduce withholding tax.

b. *Tax avoidance plan.* As noted above, the conduit rule applies only if an intermediate entity's participation in the financing arrangement is pursuant to a tax avoidance plan. The tax avoidance condition is intended to restrict the rule's application to "transactions that are related to each other through the taxpayer's intention to secure, in an artificial manner, exemptions or reductions of withholding tax that would not otherwise be available given the economic substance of its transactions."[61]

"A tax avoidance plan is a plan one of the principal purposes of which is the avoidance of [withholding] tax."[62] The plan may be "formal or informal, written or oral," and "it may be inferred from the facts and circumstances." Not all parties to the financing arrangement need be parties to the plan, but the plan must exist at the time of the last of the transactions comprising the financing arrangement.

Avoidance of withholding tax may be a principal purpose, even if other purposes also underlie the plan and even if the "other purposes (taken together or separately)" outweigh the purpose to avoid withholding tax.[63] The relevant purposes include only those that relate to the participation of the intermediate entity or entities. Assume foreign corporation *FS* makes a 10-year, 8 percent loan to domestic corporation *DS*; *FS* and *DS* are subsidiaries of foreign corporation *FP*.[64] Six months after *FS*'s loan but pursuant to intentions formulated before that loan was made, *FP* makes an interest-free demand loan to *FS* in a principal

---

[58] Reg. §1.881-3(e) Ex. 9.

[59] See Reg. §1.881-3(e) Ex. 18 (no avoidance purpose where interest on debt issued by *FP* could, but would not necessarily, have been portfolio interest if debt had been issued by *DS*).

[60] Reg. §1.881-3(e) Ex. 10.

[61] INTL-64-93, supra note 27, at 882.

[62] Reg. §1.881-3(b)(1).

[63] Id.

[64] Reg. §1.881-3(e) Ex. 11. See also Reg. §1.881-3(e) Ex. 12.

amount equal to that loaned by *FS* to *DS*. One principal purpose of *FS*'s participation in these and similar transactions is to have *FS* coordinate financing for all of *FP*'s subsidiaries. Another principal purpose is to gain the advantage of the zero withholding rate provided under the treaty between *FS*'s home country and the United States for interest payments by U.S. persons to residents of that country. *FS*'s participation is pursuant to a tax avoidance plan.

If the intermediate entity's participation in the arrangement "significantly reduces" U.S. withholding tax, that fact is evidence of a tax avoidance plan.[65] The significance of a reduction is weighed by comparing the withholding taxes on payments by the financed entity to the intermediate entity (assuming the form of the transactions is respected) with the taxes that would result from disregarding the intermediate entity as a conduit. The determining factor is the amount of tax, not the rate of tax. A tax reduction may be significant if it is large either "in absolute terms or in relative terms." A significant reduction may result from the application of a treaty,[66] but the fact that a treaty reduces the taxes on the financed entity's payments to the intermediate entity is not conclusive of the issue.

Assume *FP*, a foreign corporation that is not a resident of a treaty country, owns a 10 percent interest in a foreign partnership whose other partner resides in a country that has a treaty with the United States exempting U.S. source interest paid to residents of that country; *FP* loans $100 to the partnership, which reloans this amount to *FP*'s domestic subsidiary (*DS*).[67] If the form of the transaction is honored, 90 percent of the interest paid by *DS* to the partnership is exempt under the treaty because it is allocated to the distributive share of the treaty partner. If the partnership is disregarded as a conduit and *FP* is treated as making the loan directly to *DS*, none of the interest is protected by treaty. The participation of the partnership in the financing arrangement thus reduces tax significantly, and the significant reduction is evidence of a tax avoidance purpose for this participation.

However, this evidence may be rebutted by other circumstances. Assume *FP* has historically maintained an interest-bearing account with *BK*, a U.S. bank, for use in connection with sales made by *FP* in the United States; *BK* makes a loan to *DS*.[68] *FP*'s deposit with *BK* and *BK*'s loan to *DS* comprise a financing arrangement. *BK*'s role as intermediary in this financing arrangement reduces tax because interest paid by *BK* on *FP*'s account is exempted by statute from the withholding tax,[69] whereas interest on a loan from *FP* to *BK* would be subject to that tax. However, this evidence of tax avoidance purpose may be rebutted by showing that the balance in *FP*'s account is "reasonably related to its dollar-

---

[65] Reg. §1.881-3(b)(2)(i).

[66] See Reg. §1.881-3(e) Ex. 8.

[67] Reg. §1.881-3(e) Ex. 15. See Reg. §1.881-3(e) Exs. 13, 14.

[68] Reg. §1.881-3(e) Ex. 19.

[69] IRC §§871(i)(2), 881(d) (exempting interest on accounts with U.S. banks).

denominated working capital needs" and is not larger during the term of the loan to *DS* than at other times.[70]

A tax avoidance plan may also be evidenced by the intermediate entity's lack of "sufficient available money or other property of its own to have made the advance to the financed entity without the advance of money or other property to it by the financing entity."[71] If there is more than one intermediate entity, the implication of tax avoidance is dispelled only if each of the intermediate entities could have made its advance without money or property provided by the financing entity or another intermediate entity.

Although a substantial interval may elapse between the several financing transactions of a conduit financing arrangement, a "short period of time" between the financing entity's advance to the intermediate entity and the latter's advance to the financed entity is evidence of a tax avoidance plan.[72] Twelve months is considered a "short period of time."[73]

In contrast, if the parties to a financing transaction are related, a lack of a tax avoidance plan is evidenced by the fact that "the financing transaction occurs in the ordinary course of the active conduct of complementary or integrated trades or businesses engaged in by these entities."[74] Assume a foreign holding company (*FP*) loans $100 million to a foreign subsidiary (*FS*) for use in *FS*'s manufacturing operations; a U.S. subsidiary (*DS*) manufactures goods using a component manufactured by *FS*; *FS* ships $30 million of components to *DS* and sets up in its books a $30 million, interest-bearing receivable from *DS* for the price of the components.[75] A lack of tax avoidance purpose is evidenced by the fact that the obligation of *DS* (the financed entity) arises in the ordinary course of a business that is complementary with a business of *FS* (the intermediate entity). For this purpose, a loan is not considered to have been made in the ordinary course of a complementary business unless the business is a banking, insurance, financing, or similar business that consists "predominantly of transactions with customers who are not related persons."[76] For example, if *FS* had loaned $30 million to *DS*, rather than making a $30 million credit sale, the complementary natures of the businesses of *FS* and *DS* would not be relevant to whether the loans from *FP* to *FS* and from *FS* to *DS* are parts of a tax avoidance plan.

---

[70] See Reg. §1.881-3(e) Ex. 20 (tax avoidance purpose probably exists if *FP*'s account balance "substantially exceeds" working capital needs while *BK*'s loan to *DS* is outstanding and *BK* has right of offset against *FP*'s account if *DS* defaults, but "other facts relevant to the presence of such a plan must also be taken into account").

[71] Reg. §1.881-3(b)(2)(ii).

[72] Reg. §1.881-3(b)(2)(iii).

[73] Reg. §1.881-3(e) Ex. 16.

[74] Reg. §1.881-3(b)(2)(iv).

[75] Reg. §1.881-3(e) Ex. 17.

[76] Reg. §1.881-3(b)(2)(iv).

Also, an intermediate entity's participation in a financing arrangement is rebuttably presumed not to be pursuant to a tax avoidance plan if the entity (1) is related to either the financed entity or the financing entity and (2) carries on "significant financing activities" with respect to its transactions in the financing arrangement.[77] The intermediate entity's financing activities are considered significant only if it meets either of two tests. First, if the financing transaction is a lease or license, the intermediate entity meets the significant activities requirement if its rental or royalty income from the transaction is "derived in the active conduct of a trade or business."[78] Second, regardless of the character of the intermediate entity's income from the transaction, the entity satisfies the significant activities requirement if

(1) Its officers and employees "participate actively and materially in arranging the intermediate entity's participation in such financing transactions" and perform business and risk management activities and

(2) The entity's participation in the financing transactions "produces (or reasonably can be expected to produce) efficiency savings, by reducing transaction costs and overhead and other fixed costs."[79]

The business and risk management requirement of (1) is satisfied only if the officers and employees perform various functions in the country in which the intermediate entity is organized or, if different, the country of which it claims to be a resident for treaty purposes.[80] These functions must include actively conducting and managing the entity's day-to-day operations, which must include "a

---

[77] Reg. §1.881-3(b)(3)(i).

[78] Reg. §1.881-3(b)(3)(ii)(A). The quoted words are given the same meaning here as under §954(c)(2)(A), which is discussed infra ¶68.2.4 text accompanying note 67.

[79] Reg. §1.881-3(b)(3)(ii)(B)(*1*). See Reg. §1.881-3(e) Ex. 23 (*FP* lends Deutschmarks to *FS*, which lends U.S. dollars to *DS* and "manages the interest rate and currency risk arising from the transactions on a daily, weekly or quarterly basis by entering into forward currency contracts"; however, presumption of no tax avoidance purpose may be rebutted if *FS* lacked ability to make loan to *DS* without loan from *FP*).

If the intermediate entity's activities consist of "cash management" for a controlled group of corporations of which it is a member, its officers and employees need not participate in arranging the entity's participation in financing transactions with the financed or financing entity if those transactions arise in the ordinary course of a "substantial trade or business" of the latter entity. Reg. §1.881-3(b)(3)(ii)(B)(*3*). The term "cash management" includes "the operation of a sweep account whereby the intermediate entity nets intercompany trade payables and receivables arising from transactions among the other members of the controlled group and between members of the controlled group and unrelated persons." However, in this situation, the officers and employees of the intermediate entity must have "participated actively and materially in arranging the trade receivable or trade payable." See Reg. §1.881-3(e) Ex. 21.

[80] Reg. §1.881-3(b)(3)(ii)(B)(*2*). For purposes of these rules, activities of the intermediate entity's officers and employees are disregarded if any officer or employee of a related person participated materially in the activities, other than to approve a guarantee or to exercise general supervision and control over the intermediate entity. Reg. §1.881-3(b)(3)(ii)(B)(*4*).

substantial trade or business or the supervision, administration and financing for a substantial group of related persons." The functions must also include "actively manag[ing], on an ongoing basis, material market risks arising from such financing transactions as an integral part of the management of the intermediate entity's financial and capital requirements . . . and . . . short-term investments of working capital."[81] The risk management activities must consist of transactions with unrelated persons.

　　　c. *Unrelated intermediate entities.* As noted above, if the intermediate entity is not related to either the financing entity or the financed entity, it is not a conduit unless it would not have entered into the financing arrangement "on substantially the same terms" without the financing entity's participation.[82] Whether the intermediate entity would have participated in the transaction on substantially the same terms is generally an issue of fact.[83]

　　　However, the IRS "may presume" that this condition is met if the obligation of the financed entity to the intermediate entity is guaranteed or, in the case of multiple intermediate entities, if the obligation to any intermediate entity is guaranteed.[84] A "guarantee" is an "arrangement under which a person, directly or indirectly, assures, on a conditional or unconditional basis, the payment of another person's obligation."[85] A guarantee is taken into account for this purpose only if it existed or was "contemplated" at the time of the last of the transactions making up the financing arrangement.[86] When the presumption applies, the taxpayer can rebut it only by "clear and convincing evidence" that the intermediate entity would have entered into the transaction on substantially the same terms without the participation of the financing entity.

　　　3. *Effects of disregarding conduit entities.* If a conduit entity is disregarded, the financing arrangement is recharacterized as occurring directly between the remaining parties (usually, the financing and financed entities).[87] Any payments made or received by a disregarded conduit entity are deemed made or received as agent for the financing entity. These recharacterizations apply for all purposes of the withholding tax, including any treaty provisions relevant to withholding taxes.[88] Thus, no exemption from or reduction of the rate of withholding tax is allowed under a treaty between the United States and the residence country of

---

[81] See Reg. §1.881-3(e) Ex. 22 (currency risks).

[82] Reg. §1.881-3(a)(4)(i)(C)(2).

[83] Reg. §1.881-3(c)(1).

[84] Reg. §1.881-3(c)(2)(i).

[85] Reg. §1.881-3(c)(2)(ii). See Reg. §1.881-3(e) Ex. 8 (pledge of bank deposit is "guarantee"; *FP* deposits funds with *BK*, which makes loan to its foreign subsidiary (*BK2*), which makes loan to *FP*'s subsidiary *FS*; *FP* pledges its deposit with *BK* to secure *FS*'s obligation to *BK2*; held, although only *BK2* receives guarantee, presumption applies to both *BK* and *BK2*).

[86] Reg. §1.881-3(c)(2)(i).

[87] Reg. §1.881-3(a)(3)(ii)(A).

[88] Reg. §1.881-3(a)(3)(ii)(C). According to the Treasury:

the disregarded conduit entity, although treaty benefits may be allowed under any treaty that might exist between the United States and the residence country of the financing entity.

The financed entity, as withholding agent, must withhold tax as though all payments were actually made to the financing entity.[89] The withholding agent is generally liable for the tax and any interest and penalties thereon, whether or not tax is actually withheld.[90]

However, the withholding agent is relieved of liability if it neither knew nor had reason to know that the financing arrangement is a conduit financing arrangement.[91] That is, the withholding agent is liable only if it knew or had reason to know "facts sufficient to establish that the participation of the intermediate entity in the financing arrangement is pursuant to a tax avoidance plan." Mere knowledge of the transactions constituting the financing arrangement is not necessarily enough. Assume *FP* makes a loan to a foreign subsidiary organized in a treaty country (*FS*), which uses the loan proceeds to purchase from *DS* installment notes resulting from installment sales made in the United States by *DS*.[92] The financing arrangement consists of *FP*'s loan to *FS* and *FS*' ownership of the installment notes; the installment purchasers (the obligors under the notes) are the financed entity. However, installment purchasers who are unrelated to *DS* generally do not know or have reason to know that the financing arrangement is a conduit arrangement.[93] They are therefore relieved of any obligation to withhold, but if *DS* services the notes as agent for *FS*, it must withhold tax from the amounts collected from the installment purchasers on *FS*'s behalf. On the other hand, a financed entity that participates in the formulation of all of the financing

---

[T]hese regulations supplement, but do not conflict with, the limitation on benefits articles in tax treaties. They do so by determining which person is the beneficial owner of income with respect to a particular financing arrangement. Because the financing entity is the beneficial owner of the income, . . . [t]he conduit entity, as an agent of the financing entity, cannot claim the benefits of a treaty to reduce the amount of [withholding] tax . . . with respect to payments made pursuant to the financing arrangement.

TD 8611, supra note 27, at 289. See Doernberg, Treaty Override by Administrative Regulation: The Multiparty Financing Regulations, 2 Fla. Tax Rev. 521 (1995); Guenther, Tax Treaties and Overrides: The Multiple-Party Financing Dilemma, 16 Va. Tax Rev. 645 (1997).

Whether the conduit entity is disregarded for purposes other than the withholding tax depends on general substance-over-form principles. See supra ¶4.3.3.

[89] Reg. §1.1441-3(g)(1). The rules described here are effective for all payments made after September 10, 1995, except payments under instruments issued before October 15, 1984. Reg. §§1.1441-3(g)(2), 1.1441-7(f)(3).

[90] Reg. §1.1441-7(f)(1).

[91] Reg. §1.1441-7(f)(2)(i).

[92] Reg. §1.1441-7(f)(2)(ii) Ex. 1.

[93] See Reg. §1.1441-7(f)(2)(ii) Ex. 2 (installment purchaser's receipt of payment booklet indicating that *DS* will thereafter act as agent for *FS*, as owner of the note, does not give installment purchaser reason to know of conduit nature of arrangement).

transactions comprising the financing arrangement generally has knowledge or reason to know that the arrangement is a conduit.[94]

When a financing arrangement is a conduit arrangement, the recharacterization of payments as made to the financing entity applies to the full amount paid by the financed entity if the principal amount of the transaction or transactions to which the financed entity is a party does not exceed the principal amount of the transaction or transactions of the financing entity or any intermediate entity.[95] However, if the principal amount of the financed entity's transactions exceeds that of the transactions of the financing entity or any intermediate entity in the chain of linked transactions, payments made by the financed entity are recharacterized only in part. The recharacterized portion is the entire payment, multiplied by a fraction whose numerator is the lowest principal amount of any transaction or transactions in the chain linking the financed and financing entities and whose denominator is the principal amount of the financed entity's transactions.

Payments made by a financed entity to a disregarded conduit entity take the character of the payments received by the financing entity.[96] Assume *FP* makes a loan to *FS*, and *FS* uses the loan proceeds to purchase property that it leases to *DS*. If these transactions are treated as a conduit financing arrangement, withholding tax is determined by treating *DS* as paying interest, not rent, to *FP*. Thus, no withholding tax is imposed if *FP* is a resident of a country having a treaty with the United States that exempts U.S. source interest paid to residents of that country from U.S. withholding tax, even though the treaty provides no comparable exemption for U.S. source rents.

However, any recharacterization under this rule of the payments made by the financed entity may not have the effect of bringing the payments within an

---

[94] See Reg. §1.1441-7(f)(2)(ii) Ex. 3.

[95] Reg. §1.881-3(d)(1)(i). For purposes of these rules, the principal amount is usually the amount of money or the fair market value of the property advanced in the financing transaction. Reg. §1.881-3(d)(1)(ii)(A). However, this general rule is superseded for most transactions by the following more specific rules:

a. If the financing transaction is a debt instrument, the principal amount is usually the instrument's issue price, reduced by principal repayments and increased by accruals of original issue discount, but the instrument's fair market value on the issue date is substituted for the issue price if these two amounts differ "materially." Reg. §1.881-3(d)(1)(ii)(B). See Reg. §1.881-3(e) Ex. 24 (adjustments for principal repayments), §1.881-3(e) Ex. 25 (foreign currency amounts are translated into dollars by exchange rate as of date of last transaction in financing arrangement).

b. If the transaction is a lease or license, the principal amount is the fair market value of the property when the lease or license is made, "adjusted for depreciation or amortization, calculated on a basis that accurately reflects the anticipated decline in the value of the property over its life." Reg. §1.881-3(d)(1)(ii)(D).

c. The principal amount of stock is usually the stock's issue price. Reg. §1.881-3(d)(1)(ii)(B). The principal amount of a partnership interest or interest in a trust is amount of money or the fair market value of the property transferred to the partnership or trust in exchange for the issuance of the interest. Reg. §1.881-3(d)(1)(ii)(C).

[96] Reg. §1.881-3(a)(3)(ii)(B).

exemption from withholding tax, either under statute or treaty, if the exemption depends on terms, facts, and circumstances relating to the financing entity's transaction that do not apply to the financed entity's transaction. For example, if the financing arrangement consists of *FP*'s deposit of funds with an unrelated bank (*BK*) and *BK*'s loan to *DS* and if *BK* is disregarded as a conduit entity, the statutory exemption for interest paid on bank deposits does not apply to *DS*'s payment unless *DS* is a bank.[97] Also, if the financing transaction to which the financing entity is a party is corporate stock or an interest in a partnership or trust and the payments received by the financing entity (if made by the financed entity) would not be deductible, the character of the payments made by the financed entity to the disregarded entity generally governs.

Although the recharacterization generally applies for all purposes under the withholding tax, a financing entity is not liable for a withholding tax resulting from the recharacterization if (1) it is not related to either the financed entity or the disregarded conduit and (2) it neither knows nor has reason to know that its transaction is part of a conduit financing arrangement.[98] A financing entity has reason to know of the conduit aspect of the arrangement if it "knows or has reason to know of facts sufficient to establish that the financing arrangement is a conduit financing arrangement, including facts sufficient to establish that the participation of the intermediate entity in the financing arrangement is pursuant to a tax avoidance plan."[99] The financed entity is presumed not to have reason to know of the conduit aspect if it is unrelated to all other participants in the financing arrangement and the intermediate entity with which it dealt is "actively engaged in a substantial trade or business."[100] However, the rule described in this paragraph protects only an innocent financing entity and does not relieve the financed entity of its liability for the withholding tax as withholding agent.[101]

Assume *FP*, which is a resident of a country having a treaty with the United States exempting residents of that country from U.S. tax on interest from U.S. sources, has borrowed $100 million for use in its manufacturing business under a credit facility arranged with a syndicate of unrelated banks that are residents of nontreaty countries; *FP* makes a $100 million stock offering, uses $90 million of the proceeds to pay down the bank loan, and loans the remaining $10 million to its domestic subsidiary *DS*.[102] *FP*'s loan to *DS* and *FP*'s remaining obligation to the banks constitute a financing arrangement. The arrangement is a conduit financing arrangement, and *FP* is disregarded as a conduit, if a principal reason for *FP* making the loan to *DS*, rather than having *DS* borrow directly from the banks, is to avoid the withholding taxes that would be imposed on interest

---

[97] For the bank deposits rule, see IRC §§871(i), 881(d), discussed supra ¶66.2.2 text accompanying note 57.

[98] Reg. §1.881-3(a)(3)(ii)(E)(*1*).

[99] Reg. §1.881-3(a)(3)(ii)(E)(2)(i).

[100] Reg. §1.881-3(a)(3)(ii)(E)(2)(ii).

[101] Reg. §1.1441-3(g)(1).

[102] Reg. §1.881-3(e) Ex. 6.

payments by *DS* to the banks. If the arrangement is a conduit arrangement, *DS* must withhold tax from its interest payments to *FP* because they are deemed made to the banks and therefore are not within any statutory or treaty exemption from the tax. However, the banks are not liable for the tax unless they had known or had reason to know of the conduit nature of the arrangement, and the banks are presumed not to know or have reason to know because they are not related to *FP* or *DS* and made their loans to an entity (*FP*) that is actively engaged in a substantial trade or business.

4. *Reporting and record keeping.* Every taxpayer and every person responsible for the collection of withholding tax must maintain records on financing transactions to which the person is a party, including any records "that may be relevant to" whether the transaction is part of a financing arrangement and whether the financing arrangement is a conduit financing arrangement.[103] This record keeping obligation is also imposed on any financed entity that is (1) a domestic corporation at least 25 percent of the stock of which (by vote or by value) is owned by a foreign person or (2) a U.S. person in control of a foreign corporation.[104] The regulations describe in detail the information that must be contained in the records and the documents to be kept in support of these records.[105]

¶66.2A.3 Limitations on Treaty Benefits

Since about 1980, the United States has insisted on including in new income tax treaties provisions denying treaty benefits in situations where they are likely to flow primarily to residents of third countries.[106] A model treaty promulgated by the Treasury in 1981 contained a limitation of benefits article that denied

---

[103] Reg. §1.881-4(b)(1). The record keeping requirements apply to payments made after September 10, 1995, excepting payments on obligations issued before October 15, 1984. Reg. §1.881-4(d).

[104] Reg. §1.881-4(b)(2). In this situation, the records are deemed required by §§6038 or 6038A, and the penalties accompanying those provisions may therefore apply.

[105] Reg. §§1.881-4(c)(1), (2). See Reg. §1.881-4(c)(3) (these rules "generally" do not "require the original creation of records that are ordinarily not created by affected entities," but any described document that is actually created must be retained even if it is not of a type ordinarily retained).

[106] See Amico, Planning Under Article 26 of the 1992 U.S.-Netherlands Tax Treaty, 6 Tax Notes Int'l 1333 (May 31, 1993); Kim, The U.S.-West German Income Tax Treaty: Can Article 28's Limitation on Benefits Serve as a Model for the Treasury's Anti-Treaty Shopping Policy? 43 Tax Lawyer 983 (1990); Morrison & Bennett, The New U.S.-Netherlands Treaty: Part I—Limitation on Benefits and Related Issues, 6 Tax Notes Int'l 331, 601 (Feb. 8, 1993); Overman, Note, The U.S.-Netherlands Tax Treaty: Important Changes, Practitioners' Response, and Primary Effects, 48 Tax Lawyer 207 (1994); Schinabeck, The Limitation on Benefits Article of the U.S.-France Tax Treaty, 25 Tax Mgmt. Int'l J. 26 (1996); Streng, "Treaty Shopping": Tax Treaty "Limitation of Benefits" Issues, 15 Houston J. of Int'l Law 4 (1992).

treaty benefits to an entity resident in a treaty country unless more than 75 percent of the beneficial interests in the entity were owned by individual residents of that country and no substantial part of its income was paid out as interest, royalties, or other deductible items to residents of other countries.[107] This provision proved to be too blunt an instrument, and it was increasingly refined in treaties made during the late 1980s and early 1990s. Article 22 of the present U.S. model treaty, reflecting the Treasury's views on the matter as of 1996, is described below.[108] According to the Treasury's Technical Explanation of this article:

> The United States views an income tax treaty as a vehicle for providing treaty benefits to residents of the two Contracting States . . . . The United States holds strongly to the view that tax treaties should include provisions that specifically prevent misuse of treaties by residents of third countries . . .

> A treaty that provides treaty benefits to any resident of a Contracting State permits "treaty shopping": the use, by residents of third states, of legal entities established in a Contracting State with a principal purpose to obtain the benefits of a tax treaty between the United States and the other Contracting State . . . . [T]he fundamental problem presented by this [definition] is that it is based on the taxpayer's intent, which a tax administration is normally ill-equipped to identify. In order to avoid the necessity of making this subjective determination, Article 22 sets forth a series of objective tests. The assumption underlying each of these tests is that a taxpayer that satisfies the requirements of any of the tests probably has a real business purpose for the structure it has adopted, or has a sufficiently strong nexus to the other Contracting State . . . . to warrant benefits even in the absence of a business connection, and that this business purpose or connection outweighs any purpose to obtain the benefits of the Treaty.

Other countries have not rushed to imitate this initiative,[109] but the need for a limitation of benefits provision may derive from two aspects of U.S. law that are relatively unique. First, for U.S. tax purposes, an entity is generally considered

---

[107] The provision, Article 16 of that model, also denied treaty benefits if, under the laws of the treaty country, the income bore "significantly lower tax than similar income arising within [the treaty country] derived by [treaty country] residents."

[108] See Rev. Proc. 98-7, 1998-1 CB —, §3.01(2) (IRS will rule on "the legal interpretation of a particular [limitation of benefits] provision," but not on whether provision disqualifies particular foreign person from treaty benefits). The competent authorities of the United States and the Netherlands have developed a "pilot certification procedure" under which a corporate resident of the Netherlands can, on an adequate showing, obtain a certificate from the Dutch tax authorities that the limitation of benefits article of the U.S.-Netherlands treaty does not deny treaty benefits to the taxpayer. Notice 94-85, 1994-2 CB 511.

[109] The OECD Model contains no analogue. See RSM Int'l Tax Comm., Will the World Follow the U.S. Lead on Limitation of Treaty Benefits? 7 J. Int'l Tax'n 124 (1996) ("as yet no wholesale shift in favor of the U.S. strong-arm approach to LOB").

resident in the country in which it is organized, regardless of the sources of its income or the location of its business activities or management. In the absence of a limitation of benefits article, this rule makes it quite easy for individuals residing in countries having no income tax treaty with the United States to obtain the benefits of a treaty by investing in the United States through a corporation organized under the laws of a treaty country. Second, although the U.S. treaty network has steadily expanded over the years, the United States still does not have treaties with many nations from which it draws capital, and the suppliers of this capital, being denied direct access to treaty benefits, can be expected to exploit any indirect routes to these benefits that may be open to them.

Article 22 does not restrict treaty benefits for individuals.[110] However, if an individual resident of a treaty country is used as a conduit to obtain treaty benefits for income beneficially owned by a resident of a third country, the benefits are denied on the ground that the true taxpayer is not a resident of the treaty country.[111]

Under Article 22, an entity resident in a treaty country is entitled to treaty benefits only if it falls within one of the following categories.[112]

1. *Publicly traded companies.* A "company" is allowed treaty benefits if all shares of one or more classes of its stock "are regularly traded on a recognized stock exchange" and these classes represent "more than 50 percent of the voting power and value of the company."[113] The recognized stock exchanges in the United States are the NASDAQ System and all exchanges registered with the Securities Exchange Commission as national exchanges.[114] The recognized exchanges of the treaty country are designated in the treaty. The term "regularly traded" is not defined by the treaty and therefore takes its meaning from the domestic law of the taxing country.[115]

Subsidiaries of publicly traded companies are also eligible for treaty benefits. Specifically, "at least 50 percent of each class of shares in the company [must be] owned directly or indirectly by [publicly traded] companies," and "in the case of indirect ownership, each intermediate owner is a person entitled to benefits of the

---

[110] Treasury Model, art. 22(2)(a).

[111] Technical Explanation ¶290.

[112] Treasury Model, art. 22(1). The treaty benefits limited by Article 22 include only those based on the taxpayer's residence; benefits allowed to residents and nonresidents alike (e.g., some aspects of the nondiscrimination article) are not restricted. Technical Explanation ¶288.

[113] Treasury Model, art. 22(2)(c)(i).

[114] Id. art. 22(5).

[115] According to the Technical Explanation, the relevant U.S. domestic law is Reg. §1.884-5(d)(4)(i)(B), under which a class of shares is "regularly traded" if (1) trades in the shares are made in more than de minimis quantities on at least 60 days during the taxable year and (2) the aggregate number of shares in the class traded during the year is at least 10 percent of the average number of shares outstanding during the year. Technical Explanation ¶294. "Trading on one or more recognized stock exchanges may be aggregated for purposes of this requirement." Id. ¶295.

Convention," either as a publicly traded company or a subsidiary of a publicly traded company.[116]

2. *Tax-exempt entities.* An entity organized under the laws of the treaty country is entitled to treaty benefits if it is "generally exempt from tax in that State and is established and maintained in that State . . . exclusively for a religious, charitable, educational, scientific, or other similar purpose."[117] The residence or location of the organization's beneficiaries is not relevant.[118]

3. *Pension trusts and funds.* A pension trust or fund organized under the laws of the treaty country is entitled to treaty benefits if it is "generally exempt from tax in that State and is established and maintained in that State . . . to provide pensions or other similar benefits to employees pursuant to a plan" and "more than 50 percent of the person's beneficiaries, members or participants are individuals resident in either Contracting State."[119]

4. *Qualified governmental entities.* A qualified governmental entity is eligible for treaty benefits.[120] The term "qualified governmental entity" includes (1) "a governing body" of the treaty country, (2) "a political subdivision or local authority" of that country, (3) various entities that are wholly owned by the treaty country, a political subdivision, or a local authority and do not "carry on commercial activities," and (4) governmental pension trusts and funds.[121]

5. *Entities meeting ownership and base erosion tests.* An entity is allowed treaty benefits if it meets both an ownership test and a base erosion test. The ownership test requires that, "on at least half the days of the taxable year," 50 percent or more of each class of the entity's shares or other beneficial interests must be owned by individual residents of the treaty country and entities allowed treaty benefits by one or more of the rules described above.[122] This ownership may be direct or indirect "through a chain of ownership in which each person is entitled to benefits of the Convention under this paragraph."

The base erosion test is failed if 50 percent or more of the entity's "gross income for the taxable year is paid or accrued, directly or indirectly, to persons who are not residents of either Contracting State . . . in the form of payments that are deductible for income tax purposes in the person's State of residence."[123] For

---

[116] Treasury Model, art. 22(2)(c)(ii).

[117] Id. arts. 4(b)(i), 22(2)(d).

[118] Technical Explanation ¶299.

[119] Treasury Model, arts. 4(b)(ii), 22(2)(e).

[120] Id. art. 22(2)(b).

[121] Id. art. 3(1)(i).

[122] Id. art. 22(2)(f)(i). In applying the ownership test to a trust, "the beneficial interests in a trust will be considered to be owned by its beneficiaries in proportion to each beneficiary's actuarial interest in the trust[, and t]he interest of a remainder beneficiary will be equal to 100 percent less the aggregate percentages held by income beneficiaries." Technical Explanation ¶303. A trust cannot satisfy this test if the beneficiaries' actuarial interests are unascertainable.

[123] Treasury Model, art. 22(2)(f)(ii).

this purpose, a payment attributable to a permanent establishment of the recipient in either country is deemed to be a payment to a resident of that country. The base erosion test is intended to determine "whether the income derived from the source State is in fact subject to the tax regime of that other State."[124] Since the term "gross income" is not defined in the treaty, the definition of U.S. domestic law applies for U.S. tax purposes.[125]

6. *Benefits allowed for particular income items.* Even if it does not qualify for treaty benefits under any of the foregoing rules, an entity resident in the treaty country is entitled to these benefits "with respect to an item of income derived from the" United States if (1) it is "engaged in the active conduct of a trade or business" in the treaty country, (2) the U.S. income "is connected with or incidental to the trade or business," and (3) "the trade or business is substantial in relation to the activity in the [United States] generating the income."[126] According to the Technical Explanation of this provision:

[T]he assumption underlying [this] test . . . is that a third country resident that establishes a "substantial" operation in the other State [the treaty country] and that derives income from a similar activity in the United States would not do so primarily to avail itself of the benefits of the Treaty; it is presumed in such a case that the investor had a valid business purpose for investing in the other State, and that the link between that trade or business and the U.S. activity that generates the treaty-benefited income manifests a business purpose for placing the U.S. investments in the entity in the other State. It is considered unlikely that the investor would incur the expense of establishing a substantial trade or business in the other State simply to obtain the benefits of the Convention.[127]

For purposes of the first of these requirements, the "making or managing [of] investments" is not an active trade or business "unless the activity is banking, insurance or securities activity conducted by a bank, insurance company or registered securities dealer."[128] "Because a headquarters operation is in the business of managing investments, a company that functions solely as a headquarter[s] company will not be considered to be engaged in an active trade or business."[129] Since the treaty does not otherwise define "trade or business," local law definitions prevail. According to the Technical Explanation, under U.S. law,

a trade or business [is] a specific unified group of activities that constitute or could constitute an independent economic enterprise carried on for profit. Furthermore, a corporation generally will be considered to carry on a trade or

---

[124] Technical Explanation ¶304.
[125] Id. ¶305.
[126] Treasury Model, art. 22(3)(a).
[127] Technical Explanation ¶284.
[128] Treasury Model, art. 22(3)(b).
[129] Technical Explanation ¶311.

business only if the officers and employees of the corporation conduct substantial managerial and operational activities.[130]

For purposes of the second requirement, U.S. income is connected with a trade or business in the treaty country "if the activity in the [United States] generating the income is a line of business that forms a part of or is complementary to the trade or business."[131] A U.S. activity is "a part of" a business activity in the treaty country "if the two activities involve the design, manufacture or sale of the same products or type of products, or the provision of similar services."[132] For example, if a U.S. corporation has a subsidiary in the treaty country that distributes in that country goods produced by the parent in the United States, the subsidiary's trade or business is part of the trade or business of the parent. Businesses are "complementary" if they are "part of the same overall industry and [are] related in the sense that the success or failure of one activity will tend to result in success or failure for the other." Assume a U.S. airline has a subsidiary in the treaty country that owns and operates hotels in that country, and the airline sells tour packages consisting of air travel to the treaty country and a stay in one of the subsidiary's hotels. Although the subsidiary's business is not part of the parent's business, the two businesses are complementary.

For purposes of the alternative prong of the second requirement, which is satisfied if the U.S. income is "incidental" to the trade or business in the treaty country, "[i]ncome is incidental to a trade or business if it facilitates the conduct of the trade or business in the other State."[133] "An example of incidental income is the temporary investment of working capital derived from a trade or business."[134]

Whether the trade or business in the treaty country is substantial (third requirement) generally depends "on all the facts and circumstances,"[135] including "the relative scale of the activities conducted in the two States and the relative contributions made to the conduct of the trade or businesses in the two States."[136] A safe harbor rule is provided: A trade or business is deemed substantial if "the asset value, the gross income, and the payroll expense that are related to the trade or business in the [treaty country is] at least 7.5 percent of the [entity's] (and any related parties') proportionate share of the asset value, gross income and payroll expense, respectively, that are related to the activity that generated the income in the [United States], and the average of the three ratios exceeds 10 percent."[137] The business is within the safe harbor if this test is met either "for the preceding taxable year, or for the average of the three preceding taxable years."

---

[130] Id. ¶309.

[131] Treasury Model, art. 22(3)(d).

[132] Technical Explanation ¶312.

[133] Treasury Model, art. 22(3)(d).

[134] Technical Explanation ¶319.

[135] Treasury Model, art. 22(3)(c).

[136] Technical Explanation ¶319.

[137] Treasury Model, art. 22(3)(c). Asset value is generally the value used for financial accounting purposes. Technical Explanation ¶321.

7. *Discretionary grant of treaty benefits.* An entity not entitled to treaty benefits under any of the foregoing rules "may be granted" treaty benefits in the United States if the U.S. competent authority "so determines."[138] The purpose of Article 22 is to deny treaty benefits to treaty shoppers, but Article 22 effectuates this purpose through a series of mechanical tests designed as "surrogates for identifying actual intent."[139] The discretionary authority to allow treaty benefits is provided because "these mechanical tests cannot account for every case in which the taxpayer was not treaty shopping."[140] It should be exercised only for "investors whose residence in the [treaty country] can be justified by factors other than a purpose to derive treaty benefits." The discretion may be exercised by allowing all or any portion of the benefits of the treaty.[141]

8. *Relationship to nontreaty doctrines.* According to the Technical Explanation of Article 22:

> Article 22 and the anti-abuse provisions of domestic law complement each other, as Article 22 effectively determines whether an entity has a sufficient nexus to the Contracting State to be treated as a resident for treaty purposes, while domestic anti-abuse provisions (e.g., business purpose, substance-over-form, step transaction or conduit principles) determine whether a particular transaction should be recast in accordance with its substance. Thus, internal law principles of the source State may be applied to identify the beneficial owner of an item of income, and Article 22 then will be applied to the beneficial owner to determine if that person is entitled to the benefits of the Convention with respect to such income.[142]

¶66.2B NONBUSINESS INCOME FROM U.S. SOURCES: WITHHOLDING OF TAX AT SOURCE

¶66.2B.1 Introductory

The 30 percent tax imposed by §§871(a)(1) and 881(a) is almost entirely enforced by the withholding of tax at the source.[1] Under §§1441(a) and 1442(a),

---

[138] Treasury Model, art. 22(4).

[139] Technical Explanation ¶285.

[140] See id. ¶324 ("This discretionary provision is included in recognition of the fact that, with the increasing scope and diversity of international economic relations, there may be cases where significant participation by third country residents in an enterprise of a Contracting State is warranted by sound business practice or long-standing business structures and does not necessarily indicate a motive of attempting to derive unintended Convention benefits").

[141] Id. ¶326.

[142] Technical Explanation ¶286. For contrasting views, see Doernberg, Treaty Override by Administrative Regulation: The Multiparty Financing Regulations, 2 Fla. Tax Rev. 521 (1995).

[1] See generally Dale, Withholding Tax on Payments to Foreign Persons, 36 Tax L. Rev. 49 (1980).

tax must be withheld and remitted to the IRS by any person, including a lessee, mortgagee, employer, or fiduciary, having "the control, receipt, custody, disposal, or payment" of income subject to the 30 percent tax. A person obligated to withhold is called a withholding agent. The withholding agent is usually the last person in the United States who handles the item before it is remitted to the taxpayer or a foreign agent of the taxpayer. Assume a nonresident alien is beneficial owner of shares of stock. If the taxpayer's foreign address is listed on the corporation's stock records, the corporation must withhold tax from dividends paid on the stock. If the stock is held in street name by a U.S. broker, the corporation usually has no way of knowing the beneficial owner is foreign and does not withhold, but the broker must withhold tax from any dividends received on the shares.

The withholding obligation is worked out in great detail in the regulations,[2] which were promulgated in 1997 and generally apply to all payments made after 1998.[3] The regulations on withholding tax from foreign persons are integrated with information reporting and backup withholding rules applied to similar payments to U.S. persons.[4] For example, a payor of dividends must determine whether the beneficial owner of the dividends is a U.S. person or a foreign person, relying either on documents supplied by the payee or a presumption applied in the absence of documentation. If the beneficial owner is foreign, tax must be withheld from the dividends under §1441 or §1442. If the beneficial owner is a U.S. person, the corporation may be required to report the dividends on a Form 1099 and, if the payee does not disclose his or her taxpayer identification number, the dividends may be subject to backup withholding under §3406.[5] Because the taxpayer's status is determined once for purposes of both of these systems, one or the other of the systems necessarily applies to the dividends.

According to the regulations, a withholding agent must withhold tax at 30 percent from any payment of "an amount subject to withholding" to a "payee" that is a "foreign person," unless (1) the withholding agent "can reliably asso-

---

[2] See Bennett, New Withholding Regs: Implications for Claiming U.S. Treaty Benefits, 78 Tax Notes 465 (Jan. 26, 1998), reprinted in 16 Tax Notes Int'l 133 (Jan. 12, 1998); Klein & Renfroe, The Final Withholding Regulations: A Rube Goldberg Contraption—Will it Work? 27 Tax Mgmt. Int'l J. 67 (1998); Lederman & Hirsh, Final Regs. Revamp Withholding on Foreign Persons—Will the New Burdens Backfire? 88 J. Tax'n 112 (1998); Shapiro & Lorence, New Regs. on Securities Lending, Withholding on Payments to Foreign Persons: Will One Year's Preparation Be Enough? 9 J. Int'l Tax'n 14 (1998). See also ABA Tax Section Comm. on U.S. Activities of Foreigners and Tax Treaties, Report on Consolidating and Simplifying the Withholding Rules and Procedures Under Sections 1441 Through 1446, 47 Tax Lawyer 425 (1994).

[3] Reg. §§1.1441-1(f), -2(f), -3(h), -4(g), -5(g), -6(g), 7(g), -8(f), -9(d); 1.1461-1(i). Withholding certificates and other documentation valid under the prior regulations usually remain effective after 1998 for as long as they could have been relied upon under those regulations. For the prior regulations, see infra ¶66.2C.

[4] See TD 8734, 1997-44 IRB 5, 6.

[5] For §3406, see infra ¶111.5.3.

ciate the payment with documentation upon which it can rely to treat the payment as made to a beneficial owner that is a U.S. person or . . . a foreign person entitled to a reduced rate of withholding" or (2) the foreign person assumes responsibility for withholding as a "qualified intermediary," U.S. branch of a foreign bank or insurance company, "withholding foreign partnership," or "authorized foreign agent."[6] The meanings of some of the terms quoted in the preceding sentence are discussed immediately below, and the remaining terms are discussed later in this section.[7]

1. *Withholding agent.* A withholding agent is a person having "control, receipt, custody, disposal, or payment" of an income item of a foreign person subject to withholding.[8] A withholding agent may be a U.S. person or a foreign person, but the withholding obligation nearly always falls on a U.S. person or on a foreign person acting within the United States

If a withholding agent delegates some or all of its responsibilities to an agent, the agent's acts "are imputed to the withholding agent on whose behalf it is acting."[9] A U.S. withholding agent may use a foreign agent, but it must have a written agreement with the foreign agent, the IRS must be notified of the agency, and the withholding agent is liable for the foreign agent's acts and is deemed to know anything that the foreign agent knows or has reason to know.

2. *Payee.* Generally, the "payee" is the person to whom a payment is made, regardless of whether that person beneficially owns the payment.[10] However, if a withholding agent has actual knowledge that a U.S. payee receives a payment "as agent of a foreign person," it must treat the payment as made to the foreign person unless the payee is a bank, securities firm, or other financial institution and the withholding agent "has no reason to believe that the financial institution will not comply with its obligation to withhold."[11] For example, if a corporation

---

[6] Reg. §1.1441-1(b)(1). See Reg. §1.1441-1(c)(1) ("withholding" means to deduct tax from payment at applicable rate).

[7] See infra ¶66.2B.2 for "an amount subject to withholding."

[8] Reg. §1.1441-7(a). If a corporation's obligations are assumed in connection with a sale of the corporation's "property," the assuming party succeeds to the corporation's obligations as withholding agent. Reg. §1.1441-7(e).

[9] Reg. §1.1441-7(c).

[10] Reg. §1.1441-1(b)(2)(i).
If an entity with one owner is disregarded for U.S. tax purposes, a withholding agent must treat payments to the entity as made to the owner. Reg. §1.1441-1(b)(2)(iii). For example, a payment to a one-owner limited liability company must be treated as a payment to the owner unless the entity has elected to be treated as a corporation for U.S. tax purposes. Thus, if the entity is domestic and the owner is a foreign person, the entity may not file a Form W-9 representing that it is a U.S. person, but it must instead file a Form W-8 identifying its foreign owner. Conversely, if the entity is foreign and its owner is a U.S. person, the entity may not claim the benefits of an income tax treaty as a resident of the treaty country.

[11] Reg. §1.1441-1(b)(2)(ii). The term "financial institution" includes persons engaged in the conduct of a banking, financing, or similar businesses, brokers and dealers in securities, insurance companies, persons whose primary business is rendering investment

pays dividends to a reputable U.S. securities firm on shares held in street name, it need not withhold because the obligation to withhold tax from any portion of the dividends allocable to foreign beneficial owners rests with the securities firm.

A payment to a U.S. branch of a foreign person is normally treated as a payment to the foreign person, but a withholding agent may make an agreement to treat a U.S. branch of a foreign bank or insurance company as a U.S. person for purposes of "specified payments to the U.S. branch."[12] The payor need not withhold tax from a payment to the U.S. branch if it can reliably associate the payment with a withholding certificate furnished by the U.S. branch under the agreement. If the U.S. branch forwards to the withholding agent a withholding certificate made by another person and the withholding agent can reliably associate a payment with the certificate, the withholding agent must withhold or not withhold as though the payment were to the person or persons identified in the withholding certificate. If a payment to the branch is not covered by any withholding certificate, it is treated as a payment to a foreign person of income effectively connected with a U.S. trade or business, and this characterization also relieves the payor of any obligation to withhold. The U.S. branch is the withholding agent with respect to items covered by the agreement and items treated as effectively connected income under the rule of the preceding sentence.

Whether a payee is U.S. or foreign and other aspects of status are usually determined by the withholding agent from withholding certificates on Form W-8 or 8233 (indicating foreign status) or Form W-9 (indicating U.S. status).[13]

3. *Foreign persons.* The term "foreign person" includes (1) nonresident alien individuals, (2) foreign corporations, partnerships, trusts, and estates, (3) government of foreign countries, including their political subdivisions, agencies, and instrumentalities, and (2) foreign branches of U.S. persons furnishing "intermediary withholding certificates."[14]

---

advice, and finance corporations whose business consists in substantial part of making loans, acquiring accounts receivable or notes or installment obligations arising in sales of tangible personal property or the performance of services, and servicing debt obligations. Reg. §§1.165-12(c)(1)(v), 1.1441-1(c)(5).

[12] Reg. §1.1441-1(b)(2)(iv). The branch must be subject to banking or insurance regulation in the United States. A payment is considered made to a U.S. branch if it is credited to a U.S. account in the name of the U.S. branch or if it is made to an address in the United States where the branch is located and the branch's name appears on the relevant documents (e.g., check or covering letter).

The IRS may extend this procedure to a U.S. branch of a foreign entity other than a bank or insurance company if it is satisfied that "its situation is analogous."

[13] Reg. §1.1441-1(b)(2)(i). For withholding certificates, see infra ¶66.2B.6.

[14] Reg. §1.1441-1(c)(2). A nonresident alien individual is a natural person who is not a U.S. citizen and is not a resident of the United States under §7701(b). Reg. §1.1441-1(c)(3). For §7701(b), see supra ¶65.2.

Generally, a foreign corporation is one organized under the laws of any jurisdiction other than the United States, one of its states, or the District of Columbia, but some corporations organized in Guam, the Commonwealth of Northern Mariana Islands, the

4. *Beneficial owner.* The beneficial owner of a payment is the person who, under "U.S. tax principles," is required to recognize the payment as gross income.[15] A person who receives income as a nominee, agent, or custodian is not the beneficial owner, and neither is a conduit disregarded under the regulations promulgated under §7701(*l*).[16] A person making a payment to a disregarded conduit entity must withhold as if the payment were made to the person identified as the recipient under the conduit rules.[17]

5. *Reliably associating payments with documentation.* According to the regulations:

> Generally, a withholding agent can reliably associate a payment with documentation if, for that payment, it holds valid documentation to which the payment relates, it can reliably determine how much of the payment relates to the valid documentation . . . , and it has no actual knowledge or reason to know that any of the information or certifications stated in the documentation are incorrect.[18]

6. *U.S. persons.* Tax need not be withheld under §1441 or §1442 from payments to U.S. persons. U.S. status is generally established by furnishing to the withholding agent a Form W-9, which is the form for reporting a U.S. payee's taxpayer identification number (TIN). Specifically, a withholding agent may consider a payee to be a U.S. person if the payee must furnish a Form W-9 in order to avoid backup withholding and does as required.[19] The backup withholding rules apply to dividends, interest, royalties, compensation for services performed as independent contractor, and a few other items.[20] A withholding agent may also rely on a Form W-9 certifying U.S. status filed by a payee not subject to the backup withholding rules if the form is signed by the payee under penalties of perjury and a few other requirements are observed.[21] Also, a payment is deemed beneficially owned by a U.S. person if the withholding agent can reliably

---

U.S. Virgin Islands, and American Samoa are not foreign corporations for this purpose. IRC §881(b), Reg. §1.1441-1(c)(4).

Payments to foreign governments and international organizations are treated as made to foreign corporations for purposes of the withholding rules. Reg. §1.1441-1(c)(4).

For intermediary withholding certificates, see infra ¶66.2B.6.

[15] Reg. §1.1441-1(c)(6)(i) (beneficial owner is "the person who is the owner of the income for tax purposes and who beneficially owns that income"). Beneficial ownership of a payment not included in gross income is determined "as if the amount was income." For example, a scholarship is beneficially owned by the student, even if it is excluded from gross income by §117.

[16] For the conduit regulations, see supra ¶66.2A.2.

[17] Reg. §1.1441-3(g) (generally applicable to payments made after September 10, 1995).

[18] Reg. §1.1441-1(b)(2)(vii).

[19] Reg. §1.1441-1(d)(2).

[20] IRC §§3406(b), (g). Backup withholding does not apply to any such item if withholding is required under any other regime (e.g., §§1441 and 1442).

[21] Reg. §1.1441-1(d)(3).

associate it with a Form W-9 attached to a valid intermediary, flow-through, or U.S. branch withholding certificate.[22] However, in all of the foregoing cases, a withholding agent may not treat a payee or beneficial owner as a U.S. person if the agent has "actual knowledge or reason to know" that the person is foreign.[23]

¶66.2B.2   Amounts Subject to Withholding

A payment is subject to withholding if it is (1) fixed or determinable annual or periodical income from sources within the United States, (2) U.S. source gain on a disposition of standing timber or a coal or iron ore deposit in which the seller retains an economic interest, or (3) gain on a contingent-price sale of a U.S. patent, copyright, or similar intangible property.[24] Fixed or determinable annual or periodical income includes all items of gross income, except gains on sales of property (including market discount on bonds and option premiums) and insurance premiums paid to a foreign insurer or reinsurer.

Generally, an item is not subject to withholding if it is excluded from gross income (e.g., interest on obligations of the U.S. states and their political subdivisions),[25] but in some situations described below, amounts exceeding gross income may be subject to withholding because the amount of gross income cannot be determined at the time of withholding.

1. *Payment.* Withholding occurs only on payment of an item subject to withholding. An amount is deemed paid when it is included in the beneficial owner's gross income under the cash method of accounting, "whether or not such income results from an actual transfer of cash or other property."[26] For example, forgiveness of a debt results in cancellation of indebtedness income to the debtor, and this income is deemed paid to the debtor at the time of the cancellation.[27] Dividends are considered paid on the payment date, not the record

---

[22] Reg. §1.1441-1(d)(4).

[23] Reg. §1.1441-1(d)(1).

[24] IRC §§871(a)(1), 882(a), 1441, 1442; Reg. §§1.1441-2(a), (c). See Reg. §1.1441-2(a) (income is not considered to be from U.S. sources "merely because the source of the amount cannot be determined at the time of payment").

The withholding agent must withhold 30 percent of the gross proceeds of the transactions described in (2) and (3) in text unless the withholding certificate states the beneficial owner's basis for the property. Reg. §1.1441-3(d)(2). The withholding agent may accept the basis amount given in the withholding certificate unless it has "actual knowledge or reason to know otherwise."

[25] Reg. §1.1441-2(b)(1)(i).

[26] Reg. §1.1441-2(e)(1). If a payment is blocked under executive authority (e.g., the President's emergency power under the Trading with the Enemy Act), it is considered paid only when the restrictions are lifted. Reg. §1.1441-2(e)(3).

[27] However, this income is not subject to withholding unless the creditor has money or property of the debtor from which tax can be withheld. Reg. §1.1441-2(d)(1), discussed text accompanying notes 53–55. For cancellation of indebtedness income, see supra

date.[28] A payment to an agent or other intermediary is deemed made to the beneficial owner, as is a payment made to a creditor in satisfaction of a liability of the beneficial owner. It does not matter whether the payment is in U.S. dollars or some other medium.[29]

Reallocations among related persons under §482 may result in income subject to withholding.[30] For example, if a foreign corporation loans funds to a U.S. subsidiary at a below-market rate, additional interest income may be imputed to the parent under §482. Income resulting from a §482 allocation is deemed paid on the last day of the taxable year during which the relevant transactions occur.

2. *Measurement of amounts subject to withholding.* The amount subject to withholding is usually the amount of the gross income, not reduced by any deductions.[31] However, in several situations described below, tax may be withheld from amounts exceeding the beneficial owner's gross income. Also, rules are provided for measuring the amount subject to withholding where payment is not in U.S. dollars.

3. *Interest and original issue discount (OID).* The gross amount of interest paid on an obligation is subject to withholding (absent an exception such as the portfolio interest rule), even though, for some holders, portions of the interest may be returns of capital.[32] For example, if the holder purchased the obligation at a premium, a portion of each interest payment is a recovery of the premium, and if the holder purchased between interest payment dates, a portion of the first interest payment received by the holder is a recovery of the portion of the purchase price allocable to accrued interest. The excess withholding from such a holder can be corrected by a refund or adjustment.[33]

OID is subject to withholding if stated interest on the same obligation would be subject to withholding. Accrued OID is taxed only when a discount obligation is sold or exchanged or a payment of interest or principal is made on the obligation.[34] In either situation, the taxable amount is usually the OID accrued under the instrument from the date of the taxpayer's purchase to the date of the taxable event, less any amount taxed on an earlier receipt of payment.[35] However, if a

---

[28] Reg. §1.1441-2(e)(4).

[29] Reg. §1.1441-2(e)(6).

[30] Reg. §1.1441-2(e)(2). See Central de Gas de Chihuahua, S.A. v. CIR, 102 TC 515 (1994) (taxpayer foreign corporation leased equipment to related foreign corporation for use in United States but collected no rent; held, rents imputed under §482 are taxable under §881(a)).

If a secondary adjustment results in additional income, this income is also deemed paid. For secondary adjustments, see infra ¶79.11.

[31] Reg. §1.1441-3(a).

[32] Reg. §1.1441-3(b)(1).

[33] Reg. §§1.1441-1(b)(8), 1.1461-2(b), discussed infra ¶66.2B.8.

[34] Reg. §1.1441-2(b)(3)(i). The withholding rules for OID apply only to obligations with terms exceeding 183 days issued after 1998. Reg. §1.1441-2(b)(3)(iv).

[35] OID accruals may often be determined from an IRS publication, List of Original Issue Discount Instruments (IRS Publication No. 1212).

payment consists of or includes interest, the tax on accrued OID may not exceed the excess of the payment over the tax on the interest.

A person having control or custody of a payment on a discount obligation or the proceeds of a sale or exchange of the obligation must withhold tax on OID if "it has actual knowledge of" the amount taxable to the beneficial owner as OID.[36] A withholding agent has this knowledge if it knows, or from "reasonably available information" could know, how long the beneficial owner has held the obligation, the obligation's terms, and the amount of any premium the holder may have paid on acquisition. This information is considered reasonably available if the withholding agent has a "direct account relationship with the beneficial owner." For example, if a discount obligation is held in a brokerage account, the brokerage firm must obtain from its customer whatever information it needs to determine the withholding tax on OID triggered by an interest payment or a sale of the instrument. The information is considered not reasonably available if the withholding agent has no such customer relationship and "has no access to [the] information in the ordinary course of its business due to the manner in which the obligation is held (e.g., in street name or through intermediaries)." However, regardless of what it knows, a withholding agent must withhold from the full amount of accrued interest and OID if this income would, with proper documentation, be portfolio interest, but no documentation is provided and the beneficial owner is, in the absence of documentation, presumed to be foreign.[37]

When a debt instrument is sold between interest payment dates, the portion of the selling price representing accrued interest is interest income to the seller,[38] but this interest income is not subject to withholding unless the sale is "part of a plan," known to the withholding agent, "the principal purpose of which is to avoid tax by selling and repurchasing securities."[39]

4. *Corporate distributions.* Generally, the entire amount of a corporate distribution to shareholders is subject to withholding,[40] even though any amount by which the distribution exceeds corporate earnings and profits is excluded from gross income as a recovery of basis or is treated as gain on a sale of the shares, rather than as a dividend.[41] Because a distribution is a dividend to the extent of current earnings and profits, which are determined as of the end of the year of distribution, it may not be possible to know at the time of distribution just what portion of a corporation distribution may be a dividend; because withholding

---

[36] Reg. §1.1441-2(b)(3)(ii).

[37] Reg. §1.1441-2(b)(3)(iii). For portfolio interest, see supra ¶66.2.2.

[38] Reg. §1.61-7(d).

[39] Reg. §1.1441-3(b)(2). The IRS has proposed amending this regulation to require withholding with respect to interest accrued on the date of sale if "the withholding agent has knowledge of the amount paid as interest." Prop. Reg. §1.1441-3(b)(2). The knowledge rules of the OID provisions would be applied for this purpose.

[40] Reg. §1.1441-3(c)(1). For special rules for distributions by mutual funds and other regulated investment companies, see Reg. §1.1441-3(c)(3).

[41] See infra ¶92.1.

must usually occur, if at all, before the withholding agent disburses the funds, the regulations generally subject the entire amount of a corporate distribution to withholding.

However, a withholding agent may elect not to withhold tax from a distribution to the extent it exceeds a "reasonable estimate" of earnings and profits.[42] This reasonable estimate must be made by the distributing corporation "at a time reasonably close to the date of payment."[43] It must include accumulated earnings and profits to the date of distribution and estimated earnings and profits for all of the current year, taking into account prior distributions and "all other relevant facts and circumstances." If estimated earnings and profits turn out to be less than actual earnings and profits, a withholding agent relying on the estimate, whether it be the distributing corporation or an intermediary, is usually liable for any resulting underwithholding.[44] However, the corporation, rather than an intermediary relying on the corporation's estimate, is liable for underwithholding resulting from the corporation's failure to estimate reasonably or "to properly communicate the information to the withholding agent."[45] Also, a withholding agent other than the distributing corporation need not accept the corporation's estimate and may withhold from the entire distribution even if the corporation, for shareholders for which it acts as withholding agent, withholds only from the estimated dividend.[46]

A withholding agent may elect not to withhold from (1) a nontaxable distribution of stock or stock rights, (2) a distribution "in part or full payment in exchange for stock," (3) a capital gains or exempt interest dividend by a mutual fund or other regulated investment company, and (4) a distribution subject to withholding under §1445, which applies to dispositions of interests in U.S. real property holding corporations.[47]

5. *Taxable amount undetermined.* In any other situation where the withholding agent cannot determine the amount subject to withholding because the source or amount of the gross income "depends on facts not known at the time of payment," the withholding agent may withhold an amount, not greater than 30 percent of the payment, that will "assure" against underwithholding.[48] Alter-

---

[42] Reg. §1.1441-3(c)(2)(i).

[43] Reg. §1.1441-3(c)(2)(ii)(A).

[44] Reg. §1.1441-3(c)(2)(ii)(B). However, the payment of the tax is not additional income subject to withholding unless the withholding agent agreed to bear the shareholder's entire withholding tax liability. Also, no penalties are imposed on the underwithholding if the corporation's estimate was reasonable and the tax is fully paid by the due date of the withholding tax return or, if later, within 60 days after the close of the taxable year of the distribution.

[45] Reg. §1.1441-3(c)(2)(ii)(C).

[46] Reg. §1.1441-3(c)(2)(ii)(A).

[47] Reg. §1.1441-3(c)(2)(i). For rules coordinating withholding under §§1441 and 1442 with withholding under §1445, see Reg. §1.1441-3(c)(4). For §1445, see infra ¶66.4.10.

[48] Reg. §1.1441-3(d)(1).

natively, the withholding agent may withhold based on a "reasonable estimate" of the taxable amount and hold an additional amount "in escrow" until the taxable amount is finally determined. Uncertainty as to the amount subject to withholding does not relieve the withholding agent from personal liability for the amount of tax ultimately determined.

6. *Payment not in U.S. dollars.* If a taxable item is paid in a medium other than U.S. dollars, the amount subject to withholding is the fair market value of the transferred property or services.[49] If the item is paid in a currency other than the U.S. dollar, the amount paid is translated into dollars at the spot rate on the date of payment.[50] Because the withholding tax must always be paid in U.S. dollars, the withholding agent may "liquidate the property" before making payment.[51] However, the withholding obligation "is not deferred even if no alternative source can be located." If the withholding agent pays the tax from its own funds, this payment may be additional income subject to withholding.[52]

7. *Withholding agent without access to funds or knowledge.* A withholding agent is usually obligated to withhold only if it has (1) "control over or custody of money or property owned by the recipient or beneficial owner from which to withhold" and (2) "knowledge of the facts that give rise to the payment."[53] For example, a creditor forgiving a debt is not obligated to withhold tax on the resulting cancellation of indebtedness income of the debtor unless it has custody or control over some money or property of the debtor.[54] This control or custody and knowledge must exist when the obligation to withhold otherwise accrues or at some subsequent time not later than the due date (with extensions) of the withholding tax return for the year.

However, the withholding obligation attaches, notwithstanding the withholding agent's lack of control, custody, or knowledge, (1) "to distributions with respect to stock," (2) if the withholding agent is related to the payee or beneficial owner, or (3) if the lack of control or custody "is part of a pre-arranged plan

---

[49] Reg. §1.1441-3(e)(1).

[50] Reg. §1.1441-3(e)(2) ("A withholding agent making regular or frequent payments in foreign currency may use a month-end spot rate or a monthly average spot rate," but any such convention must be used consistently and may be changed only with IRS consent). See Reg. §1.988-1(d)(1) ("spot rate" is "a fair market rate of exchange available to the public for currency under a spot contract in a free market" in which "representative amounts" are traded; quotation sources include International Financial Statistics of International Monetary Fund, newspapers, financial journals, and electronic financial news services).

[51] Reg. §1.1441-3(e)(1).

[52] Reg. §1.1441-3(f), discussed infra text accompanying notes 53–55.

[53] Reg. §1.1441-2(d)(1).

[54] Reg. §1.1441-2(d)(2). A partial payment by the borrower is not considered property of the borrower.

known to the withholding agent to avoid withholding."[55] As an example of (2), income allocated among related persons under §482 may be subject to withholding, whether or not the withholding agent has custody or control of money or property of the payee.

8. *Withholding agent's payment of tax from its own funds.* If a withholding agent fails to withhold and pays the withholding tax from its own funds, the payment is either additional income to the beneficial owner or an advance of funds, depending on the contractual arrangement between the parties and "applicable laws governing the transaction."[56] For example, if the contract between the parties requires the withholding agent to make specified income payments to the beneficial owner without deduction and to absorb any withholding tax that may be imposed on the payments, the withholding agent's tax payments are additional income to the beneficial owner, which are also subject to withholding. Whenever a withholding agent's tax payment is additional income, the total amount subject to withholding is the amount of the payment before withholding, divided by the excess of one over the tax rate (expressed as a decimal).[57] Assume a U.S. college grants a scholarship to a foreign student, of which $8,600 (amounts covering room and board and travel costs) is taxable and subject to withholding at 14 percent under §1441(b). If the college agrees to pay the tax, the amount subject to withholding is $10,000 (the pretax amount of $8,600, divided by (1 −.14)), and the tax is $1,400.[58]

If the withholding agent's payment is an advance to the beneficial owner, no tax consequence normally follows from the withholding agent's payment of the tax or the beneficial owner's reimbursement of the withholding agent. However, if the beneficial owner fails to repay the advance, the beneficial owner may have cancellation of indebtedness income, which is subject to withholding if the withholding agent then has any money or property of the beneficial owner from which the withholding tax can be paid.[59]

¶66.2B.3 **Amounts Not Subject to Withholding or Subject to Withholding at Reduced Rates**

If a withholding agent determines that an item is of a type that is normally subject to withholding and that the payee is a foreign person, it must determine whether the payee is entitled to an exemption from withholding or to a reduced

---

[55] Reg. §1.1441-2(d)(1). The withholding agent is related to the recipient or beneficial owner if transactions between them would be subject to adjustment under §482. For §482, see infra ¶79.1.

[56] Reg. §1.1441-2(d)(3).

[57] Reg. §1.1441-3(f)(1).

[58] Reg. §1.1441-3(f)(2) Ex.

[59] Reg. §1.1441-2(d)(3).

rate of withholding tax.[60] Statutory exemptions and reduced rates are described below. Exemptions and reduced rates under treaties are discussed in the next section.

Several statutory exemptions from withholding under §§1441 and 1442 may be allowed by a withholding agent, even if it has no documentation on the identity or status of the beneficial owner:[61]

1. Income from sources outside the United States.
2. Interest on deposits with banks, insurance companies, and some other financial institutions.[62]
3. Interest and original issue discount on instruments issued for terms not exceeding 183 days.[63]
4. Dividends from a domestic corporation deriving at least 80 percent of its gross income from businesses actively carried on outside the United States, but only to the extent the dividends are ratably allocable to the gross income of those businesses.[64]
5. Dividends paid by a foreign corporation out of earnings and profits for any year the corporation was subject to the branch profits tax.[65]
6. Payments under notional principal contracts.[66]

Other exemptions from withholding under §§1441 and 1442 and rate reductions may be allowed only with documentation:[67]

1. *Portfolio interest.* Portfolio interest is exempt from the taxes imposed by §§871(a) and 881(a) and thus is not subject to withholding under §1441 or §1442.[68] A withholding agent may honor the exemption for interest on registered instruments if it has documents allowing it to treat the payee as a foreign person

---

[60] Reg. §1.1441-1(b)(4).

[61] Reg. §§1.1441-1(b)(4)(ii)-(vii). However, without documents establishing foreign status or providing a taxpayer identification number, the items may be subject to information reporting and backup withholding. For a list of items that may be exempted from information reporting and backup withholding on a showing that the payee is a foreign person, see Reg. §1.1441-1(b)(5).

[62] IRC §§871(i), 881(d), discussed supra ¶66.2.2.

[63] IRC §871(g)(1)(B)(i); Reg. §1.1441-2(a).

[64] IRC §§861(c), 871(i)(2)(B), 871(d), discussed ¶70.2.

[65] IRC §884(e)(3). For the branch profits tax, see infra ¶66.5.2.

[66] Reg. §1.1441-4(a)(3). For notional principal contracts, see supra ¶45.7.

[67] If withholding on a payment to joint owners can be only reduced with documentation, the withholding agent must usually withhold at 30 percent unless it has documents covering all of the joint owners. Reg. §1.1441-1(b)(9). However, such a payment is exempt from withholding under §§1441 and 1442 if any one of the joint owners provides a Form W-9 certifying that it is a U.S. person or the withholding agent has a withholding certificate allowing it to treat the payment as beneficially owned by U.S. persons.

[68] For portfolio interest, see supra ¶66.2.2.

If a foreign person transfers a debt instrument in a securities lending or "sale-repurchase" transaction, payments received by that person in substitution for interest on the transferred instrument may also be portfolio interest. See supra ¶66.2.2 note 13.

and does not have actual knowledge or reason to know that the beneficial owner is a U.S. person.[69] No documentation is required for portfolio interest on bearer instruments or for interest on foreign-targeted registered obligation if the registered owner is a financial institution that certifies the beneficial owners to be foreign.[70]

2. *Effectively connected income.* Income that is or is deemed to be effectively connected with a foreign person's conduct of a trade or business in the United States is not subject to withholding if it is currently included in the beneficial owner's gross income.[71] Effectively connected income is not gross income to the beneficial owner if, for example, the beneficial owner claims a treaty exemption from the effectively connected income tax on the ground that it does not have a permanent establishment in the United States. Generally, a withholding agent may recognize the exemption for effectively connected income only if, at the time of payment, it has a withholding certificate by which the beneficial owner claims that it is foreign and that the income is effectively connected income included in gross income.[72] However, a payment to a U.S. branch of a foreign bank, insurance company, or other financial institution is deemed to be effectively connected income unless the branch provides a withholding certificate representing otherwise.[73]

3. *Compensation for personal services.* Compensation for an individual's personal services is often subject to wage withholding, rather than withholding under §1441 or §1442.[74] Such compensation is also exempted from withholding

---

[69] Reg. §§1.871-14(c)(2), 1.1441-1(b)(4)(i). This documentation must usually be (1) a withholding certificate from the beneficial owner, a qualified intermediary that has assumed primary withholding responsibility, a withholding foreign partnership, or a U.S. branch of a foreign financial institution, or (2) a statement from a securities clearing organization or financial institution that holds customers' securities in the ordinary course of business stating that the institution or another intermediary has received such a beneficial owner withholding certificate. Reg. §1.871-14(c)(2).

[70] Reg. §§1.871-14(e), 1.1441-2(a). Documents establishing foreign status may be necessary to avoid backup withholding.
For the requirements for foreign-targeted registered obligations, see Reg. §1.871-14(e)(2).

[71] IRC §1441(c)(1); Reg. §1.1441-4(a)(1).

[72] Reg. §§1.1441-1(b)(4)(viii); 1.1441-4(a)(2). The withholding certificate must be on Form W-8, include the taxpayer's taxpayer identification number (usually, its employer identification number), and specify the payments claimed to be effectively connected income.

[73] Reg. §1.1441-4(a)(2)(ii). If the branch furnishes no withholding certificate but a payment is not effectively connected income, the branch must withhold from the payment whether the item is beneficially owned by the recipient or collected on behalf of another person.

[74] IRC §1441(c)(4); Reg. §§1.1441-1(b)(4)(ix), 1.1441-4(b). Documentation is required under the wage withholding rules.
When an individual's services income is subject to withholding under §1441, the withholding agent may reduce the amount subject to withholding by $1/365$ of one personal

under §1441 or §1442, whether the services are performed as employee or independent contractor, if (1) it would be subject to wage withholding, except for an exemption in the wage withholding rules, (2) the taxpayer is a resident of Canada or Mexico "who enters and leaves the United States at frequent intervals," or (3) the compensation is exempt from U.S. tax by statute or treaty.[75] A withholding agent may recognize a treaty exemption only if the employee or other services performer claims the exemption on a Form 8233 filed with the employer, the withholding agent has no knowledge or reason to know that any facts stated in the Form are false, the Form is submitted to the IRS, and the IRS registers no objection to the Form within 10 days of its submission.[76]

The IRS may make an agreement with a nonresident alien individual exempting U.S.-source nonemployee compensation from withholding or specifying amounts to be withheld from the compensation.[77] Also, the last payment of nonemployee compensation during a year is exempt from withholding, in whole or in part, if the services performer applies to the local IRS district office for this exemption and the IRS issues a letter to the withholding agent specifying the final payment amount that can be exempted.[78]

4. *Qualified plan distributions.* Annuities under qualified pension, profit sharing, stock bonus, and annuity plans are exempt the tax imposed by §871(a)(1) and therefore from withholding.[79] This exemption is allowed only if the beneficial owner submits a withholding certificate on Form W-8 claiming foreign status and providing the taxpayer's taxpayer identification number.[80]

5. *Military allowances.* Per diem subsistence allowances paid by the U.S. government to nonresident aliens "engaged in any program of training in the United States under the Mutual Security Act of 1954" are exempt from withholding, even if they are taxable under §871(a)(1).[81] This exemption may be

---

exemption for each day the individual is present in the United States for the performance of the services. Reg. §1.1441-4(b)(6). If the individual resides in Canada or Mexico, more than one exemption may be allowed, but the exemption or exemptions are apportioned on the same daily basis.

[75] Reg. §1.1441-4(b)(1).

[76] Reg. §1.1441-4(b)(2). If the IRS does not object, the withholding agent is liable for tax that should have been withheld only if "the withholding agent knew or had reason to know [facts] regarding the payment and eligibility for a reduced rate . . . that were not disclosed to the IRS."

[77] Reg. §1.1441-4(b)(3).

[78] Reg. §1.1441-4(b)(4). The tax determination made by the IRS is only tentative; the services performer must file a return making a final settlement of tax liability for the year. Reg. §1.1441-4(b)(5).

[79] IRC §§871(f), 1441(c)(7); Reg. §1.1441-4(d).

[80] Reg. §§1.1441-1(b)(4)(x), 1.1441-4(d). If the beneficial owner has never been a U.S. citizen or resident, the taxpayer identification number may be an individual taxpayer identification number (ITIN), which is a number issued by the IRS to nonresident alien individuals who are not eligible for social security numbers. Reg. §§301.6109-1(d)(3), (g), (h)(1).

[81] Reg. §§1.1441-1(b)(4)(xviii); 1.1441-4(e).

recognized whether or not the withholding agent has documentation from the beneficial owner, but documentation establishing foreign status may be required to avoid information reporting and backup withholding.

6. *Scholarships and grants to foreign students and researchers.* Section 1441(b) reduces the withholding tax rate to 14 percent for taxable scholarships and grants received by nonresident aliens who are temporarily present in the United States under nonimmigrant visas under §§101(a)(15)(F), (J), (M), or (Q) of the Immigration and Nationality Act, which are issued to students, researchers, and visiting teachers.[82] If such an individual receives a scholarship from U.S. sources that is only partially excluded from gross income under §117(a), the 14 percent withholding tax applies to the taxable portion of the scholarship.[83] Very generally, scholarships are excludable from gross income only to the extent of the student's tuition and related expenses, not including living expenses.[84] If a student receives a scholarship that covers living expenses as well as tuition and incidental expenses, the amount for living expenses thus is taxable. If the student is a nonresident alien present in the United States under a student visa, the taxable amount is subject to the 14 percent withholding tax.

Also, if a nonresident alien present in the United States on an F, J, M, or Q visa is not a candidate for a degree at an educational institution, the 14 percent withholding tax applies to grants received from (1) an educational or charitable organization that is exempt from tax under §501(c)(3), (2) the government of a foreign country, the United States, or one of the U.S. states, (3) an agency or instrumentality of the federal or a state or local government, or (4) an international organization.[85]

A withholding agent may allow the 14 percent rate only if it has documentation that the payee is a nonresident alien.[86] Any portion of the scholarship or grant that is compensation for services is subject to wage withholding, not 14 percent withholding under §1441(b).

7. *Foreign governments, central banks of issue, and international organizations.* The exemption under §892(a) for payments to foreign governments may be allowed only with a Form W-8 that represents the beneficial owner to be a foreign government, indicates whether it is an integral part of a foreign govern-

---

[82] IRC §1441(b). This income is deemed to be effectively connected with a U.S. trade or business, whether or not the recipient actually has such a trade or business. IRC §871(c). See Rev. Proc. 88-24, 1988-1 CB 800 (withholding procedures for scholarships and grants paid to foreign students and grantees). See Harding, Making Scholarship and Fellowship Payments to Foreign Students: An Overview of Tax Issues and Problems, 55 Tax Notes 533 (April 27, 1992).

In lieu of withholding at 14 percent, the withholding agent may choose to withhold as though the income were wages subject to wage withholding. Reg. §1.1441-4(c)(2).

[83] IRC §1441(b)(1). For the application of the source rules to scholarships and fellowships, see infra ¶70.9 text accompanying notes 4-7.

[84] See supra ¶11.2.

[85] IRC §1441(b)(2).

[86] Reg. §§1.1441-1(b)(4)(xvi), 1.1441-4(c)(1).

ment or a controlled entity, and certifies that the income is exempt under §892.[87] Similarly, the exemption under §895 for interest paid to a foreign central bank of issue or the Bank for International Settlements must be established by a Form W-8 certifying that the beneficial owner is a bank entitled to the exemption and that it will not hold obligations or bank deposits covered by the Form in connection with the conduct of a commercial banking function or other commercial activity.[88] The exemption under §892(b) for U.S.-source investment income of international organizations may be allowed without documentation if "the name of the payee and other facts surrounding the payment reasonably indicate" that the payment is beneficially owned by an international organization.[89]

8. *Foreign tax-exempt organizations.* A foreign tax-exempt organization is usually exempt from withholding with respect to income not included in the organization's taxable income from an unrelated trade or business.[90] An organization establishes its entitlement to this exemption by providing to the withholding agent a Form W-8 stating the organization's taxpayer identification number and certifying that it has obtained an IRS ruling recognizing its exemption under §501(c).[91] Amounts included in determining unrelated business taxable income are subject to withholding to the same extent as they would be if the organization were not exempt.[92] Typically, with appropriate documentation, such amounts may be exempted from withholding as effectively connected income.

If a foreign tax-exempt organization is or is treated as a private foundation, a 4 percent tax, withheld at source, is imposed on U.S.-source interest, dividends, rents, payments with respect to securities loans, and royalties.[93]

9. *Gambling winnings.* Gambling winnings are exempt from withholding under §1441 if they are exempt from the 30 percent tax under §871(j), which

---

[87] Reg. §§1.1441-1(b)(4)(xi), 1.1441-8(b). These payments are also exempt from information reporting.

[88] Reg. §§1.1441-1(b)(4)(xii), 1.1441-8(c)(1). No withholding certificate is required for bankers' acceptances "if the name of the payee and other facts surrounding the payment reasonably indicate that the payee or beneficial owner is a foreign central bank of issue." Reg. §1.1441-8(c)(2).

[89] Reg. §§1.1441-1(b)(4)(xiv), 1.1441-8(d). These payments are also exempt from information reporting.

[90] Reg. §1.1441-9(a). All payments to foreign tax-exempt organizations are exempt from information reporting. Reg. §1.1441-1(b)(4)(xvii).

[91] Reg. §§1.1441-1(b)(4)(xvii), 1.1441-9(b)(2). An opinion of a U.S. lawyer that the organization is exempt may be substituted for the certification of IRS recognition of exemption. The certificate must also identify any portion of the amounts paid to be included in determining unrelated business taxable income and indicate whether the organization is a private foundation. If the certification on unrelated business income or private foundation status is missing or not reliable, the withholding agent may accept the certificate and treat all payments as includable in unrelated business taxable income or treat the organization as a private foundation. Reg. §1.1441-9(b)(3).

[92] IRC §1443(a); Reg. §§1.1441-1(b)(4)(xvii), 1.1443-1(a).

[93] IRC §§1443(b), 4948(a); Reg. §1.1443-1(b). Any such item is not subject to the 4 percent tax if it is included in unrelated business taxable income.

applies to winnings from "blackjack, baccarat, craps, roulette, and big-6 wheel."[94] Foreign status need not be documented to establish entitlement to this exemption, but documentation may be needed to exempt the winnings from information reporting and backup withholding.[95]

¶66.2B.4 Treaty Benefits

Withholding may be reduced or eliminated by an income tax treaty, which must usually be a treaty between the United States and the country of the beneficial owner's residence.[96]

1. *Documentation requirements.* Documentation is required to establish entitlement to any exemption from or lesser rate of withholding tax under an income tax treaty.[97] A withholding agent may "rely" on a beneficial owner's claim of a treaty benefit if (1) the claim is made on a withholding certificate or other documentation sufficient to establish foreign status, (2) the withholding agent, at the time of payment, does not know or have reason to know that the claim is false and can reliably associate the payment with the certificate, and (3) the withholding agent has not received notice from the IRS that the withholding certificate cannot be relied upon.[98] These requirements are modified for a few types of income, including compensation for services[99] and payments to indi-

---

[94] IRC §1441(c)(11); Reg. §1.1441-2(a). See supra ¶66.2.8 note 135 for §871(j).

[95] Reg. §1.1441-1(b)(4)(xx).

[96] Reg. §1.1441-6(a). See Bennett, New Withholding Regs: Implications for Claiming U.S. Treaty Benefits, 78 Tax Notes 465 (Jan. 26, 1998), reprinted in 16 Tax Notes Int'l 133 (Jan. 12, 1998).

[97] Reg. §1.1441-1(b)(4)(xv). This documentation also establishes foreign status for purposes of information reporting and backup withholding.

On the rare occasions where U.S. persons benefit by treaty provisions reducing U.S. withholding rates, the treaty benefit may be claimed by a Form W-9. Reg. §1.1441-6(b)(5).

The procedures for withholding agents to recognize the benefits of any treaty may be altered by agreement between the competent authorities of the United States and the treaty country. Reg. §1.1441-6(b)(3).

[98] Reg. §1.1441-6(b)(1). For withholding certificates, see infra ¶66.2B.6.

If the payee is an entity that is fiscally transparent under the laws of the treaty country, the withholding certificate requirements for partnerships apply, regardless of how the entity is classified for U.S. tax purposes. Reg. §1.1441-6(b)(4)(ii)(A). For these requirements, see Reg. §1.1441-5, discussed infra ¶66.2B.5. Similarly, if an entity is not transparent under the laws of the treaty country, the withholding certificate requirements are applied as though it were a corporation, even if it is classified as a partnership under U.S. tax laws.

[99] A claim of treaty exemption of compensation for personal services may be accepted only if the employee or other services performer makes the claim on a Form 8233, the withholding agent has no knowledge or reason to know that any facts stated in the Form are false, the Form is submitted to the IRS district office, and the IRS registers no objection to the Form within 10 days of its submission. Reg. §1.1441-4(b)(2). If the IRS

vidual beneficial owners made outside the United States with respect to an offshore account.[100] If a payment is made to joint owners, documentation must be received from all of the owners.[101]

The beneficial owner's taxpayer identification number (TIN) need not appear on a withholding certificate claiming treaty benefits for dividends and interest on actively traded securities.[102] In other cases, a withholding agent may recognize a claim of treaty benefits only if the withholding certificate includes the beneficial owner's TIN, which must have been certified by the IRS.[103] The IRS will normally certify a TIN only if the taxpayer presents a certificate of residence, which is a document, issued by the competent authority or other "appropriate tax official" of the treaty country, certifying that "the taxpayer has filed its most recent income tax return as a resident of that country (within the meaning of the applicable tax treaty)."[104] A certificate of residence is valid for three years or such longer period as the IRS may prescribe. The IRS' certification of the TIN is normally indicated on the certificate of residence.

A taxpayer seeking IRS certification of a TIN may show residence by other official documents if the residence country does not have a procedure for "routinely" issuing certificates of residence or if "obtaining such certificate would require an unreasonable amount of time or costs relative to the taxpayer's circumstances."[105] For an individual, this alternative documentation must be an "official document issued by an authorized governmental body" that includes the

---

does not object, the withholding agent is liable for tax that should have been, but was not, withheld only if "the withholding agent knew or had reason to know [facts] regarding the payment and eligibility for a reduced rate . . . that were not disclosed to the IRS."

[100] In this situation, a certificate of residence or other documentary evidence of an individual's residence may be substituted for the withholding certificate. Reg. §1.1441-6(b)(2)(i). For certificates of residence, see infra ¶66.2B.4.

[101] Reg. §1.1441-6(d).

[102] Reg. §1.1441-6(b)(2). This rule also applies to (1) dividends on redeemable securities of investment companies registered under the Investment Company Act of 1940, (2) dividends, interest, and royalties on publicly offered units of beneficial interest in a unit investment trust if the offering was registered under the Securities Act of 1933, and (3) amounts received by a lender of publicly traded securities in substitution for dividends or interest on the securities.

[103] Reg. §1.1441-6(b)(1). A qualified intermediary may act for the beneficial owner in obtaining IRS certification of the TIN. Reg. §1.1441-6(c)(2)(iii).

An entity's request for certification of its TIN must include a sworn affidavit showing that it is not denied treaty benefits under the treaty's limitation of benefits article. Reg. §1.1441-6(c)(5).

The IRS may confirm residence through information exchanges with the competent authority of the treaty country, and it may request that the beneficial owner confirm residence in that country. Reg. §1.1441-6(c)(2)(ii).

[104] Reg. §1.1441-6(c)(3). The competent authorities of the United States and the treaty country may agree upon a different procedures for certifying residence.

A beneficial owner whose TIN has been certified must notify the IRS within 30 days of any change in "tax residence." Reg. §1.1441-6(c)(2)(ii).

[105] Reg. §1.1441-6(c)(2)(ii).

individual's name, address, and photograph.[106] The alternative documentation required of an entity is a document issued by an authorized governmental body that includes the entity's name and the address of its principal office in the treaty country.[107] Regardless of the availability of certificates of residence, a "corporate body" organized in the treaty country may establish residence by furnishing a certificate or articles of incorporation or some "other official document reflecting the taxpayer's status as a corporate body in that jurisdiction."[108]

A withholding agent may accept the representations made in a withholding certificate claiming treaty benefits and need not "inquire into the truthfulness of these representations or . . . research foreign law."[109] The withholding agent need not ask whether a TIN has been certified if the TIN "appears correct on its face and the permanent residence address on the certificate is in the country whose tax treaty with the United States is invoked."[110]

2. *Payments to entities.* A payment to an entity is considered income of a resident of a treaty country only "to the extent that the payment is subject to tax in the hands of a resident of that jurisdiction."[111] Such a payment thus qualifies for treaty benefits if the treaty country taxes the entity on the item as a resident.[112] If the entity is fiscally transparent (a pass-through entity) under the tax laws of the treaty country, treaty benefits are allowed only to the extent that the payment is allocable to "interest holders in the entity [that] are residents of the jurisdiction."[113] If an owner of an interest in a fiscally transparent entity is also a fiscally transparent entity, the latter entity is looked through, and treaty benefits are restricted to amounts ultimately allocable to interest holders that are not fiscally transparent and are resident of the treaty country.

Assume U.S.-source royalty income is paid to *DP*, an entity classified as (1) a domestic partnership for U.S. tax purposes, (2) a separately taxable entity under the tax laws of country *Z*, the residence country of one of *DP*'s two owners, and (3) a pass-through entity under the tax laws of country *X*, the residence

---

[106] Reg. §1.1441-6(c)(4)(i). The document must usually have been issued within three years before it is presented to the IRS, but an older document may suffice if it is "accompanied by additional evidence of the person's residence in the treaty country (e.g., a bank statement, utility bills, or medical bills)."

The original or a certified copy of the document must be presented, and it must be accompanied by a sworn affidavit that the document is "true and complete."

[107] Reg. §1.1441-6(c)(4)(ii).

[108] Reg. §1.1441-6(c)(2)(ii).

[109] Reg. §1.1441-6(b)(4)(ii)(A).

[110] Reg. §1.1441-6(b)(1).

[111] Reg. §1.1441-6(b)(4)(i).

[112] An entity's request for IRS certification of its TIN must include an affidavit certifying that the income for which it intends to claim treaty benefits "will properly be treated as derived by itself as a resident of the applicable treaty jurisdiction." Reg. §1.1441-6(c)(5).

[113] The application of treaties to payments to fiscally transparent entities is developed further by §894(c) and §1.894-1T(d), discussed supra ¶66.2A.1.

country of *DP*'s other owner.[114] Because *DP* is a domestic partnership under U.S. law, the two owners are subject to U.S. tax on their distributive shares of the royalty income, and *DP* must withhold the tax imposed on its foreign partners.[115] If the income is not effectively connected with a U.S. business of *DP*, the tax rate is 30 percent under §871(a) or §881(a) unless it is reduced by treaty. The U.S.-country *Z* treaty cannot apply to the distributive share of *DP*'s country *Z* owner because, under country *Z* law, *DP* is a separately taxable foreign entity and the country *Z* owner is thus not subject to country *Z* tax on its distributive share of the royalties. However, the royalty rate under the U.S.-country *X* treaty applies to the distributive share of *DP*'s country *X* owner because country *X* treats *DP* as fiscally transparent and taxes the country *X* owner on its distributive share of the royalty income.

A withholding agent making a payment to a foreign entity may, but need not, accept claims with respect to one payment under more than one treaty.[116] Assume royalties are paid to a country *Y* entity that claims (1) a 5 percent withholding rate for one half of the royalties under the U.S.-country *Y* treaty and (2) withholding exemption under the U.S.-country *Z* treaty for the one half of the royalties allocable to *T*, who holds an interest in the entity and resides in country *Z*.[117] The claims may be warranted if, for example, the entity is taxed as a resident corporation under the laws of country *Y* but is fiscally transparent under the laws of country *Z*. The withholding agent may therefore honor the two treaty claims, but it may instead withhold on the entire payment at the 5 percent rate of the U.S.-country *Y* treaty.

¶66.2B.5　Payments to Partnerships and Other Fiscally Transparent Entities

Partnership income is considered beneficially owned by the partners.[118] In a tiered structure, the ultimate, nonflow-through taxpayers are the beneficial owners. For example, if a partnership is a partner in another partnership, the former's distributive share of the income of the latter is beneficially owned by its partners. The same approach applies to any entity that is disregarded for U.S. tax purposes (e.g., a single-owner limited liability company that has not elected to be treated as a corporation).

1. *Domestic partnerships.* A payment to a domestic partnership is considered made to a U.S. payee, and tax need not be withheld from it under §§1441

---

[114] Reg. §1.1441-6(b)(4)(iv) Ex. 3.

[115] See infra ¶66.2A.5.

[116] Reg. §1.1441-6(b)(4)(iii).

[117] Reg. §1.1441-6(b)(4)(iv) Ex. 2.

[118] Reg. §1.1441-1(c)(6)(ii). For the treatment of trusts and estates, see Reg. §1.1441-3(f), (g) (before restatement in 1997); Reg. §1.1441-1(c)(6)(B).

or 1442.[119] However, if the partnership receives income subject to withholding, it must withhold tax from any portion of the item that is included in the distributive share of a foreign partner.[120] The withholding obligation normally attaches when the partnership supplies Forms K-1 reporting the distributive shares to its partners (or, if earlier, on the due date of the K-1s), but if the income is distributed before then, withholding must occur at the time of distribution. If the income is effectively connected with a U.S. trade or business of the partnership, withholding occurs under §1446, not §1441 or §1442.[121]

2. *Foreign partnerships.* A foreign partnership's partners are considered the payees of a payment to the partnership unless the partnership's withholding certificate represents that it is a foreign withholding partnership or that the payment is effectively connected income.[122] A foreign withholding partnership is a foreign partnership that has made an agreement with the IRS to withhold tax from its partners and satisfy various reporting requirements, essentially as though it were a domestic partnership.[123] A payment is treated as effectively connected income if the partnership's withholding certificate identifies it as such and is presumed to be effectively connected income in a few other situations.[124] In the two cases where the partnership is considered payee, the payor need not withhold tax under §1441 or §1442, but the partnership must withhold from foreign partners' distributive shares.

In all other cases, a payment to a foreign partnership is treated as a payment to the partners, and withholding certificates for all of the partners should therefore be attached to the partnership's withholding certificate.[125] If the withholding agent can reliably associate a partner's distributive share of the payment with documentation establishing the partner's status, the withholding agent may withhold from that portion consistently with that status.[126] If the partner has given an intermediary withholding certificate, withholding from the partner's distributive share is determined as though the distributive share were paid directly to the

---

[119] Reg. §§1.1441-5(a)(7), (b)(1).

[120] Reg. §1.1441-5(b)(2). Any such item must be separately stated on the partnership's returns and in the allocations to the partners.

[121] For §1446, see infra ¶66.3.8. When withholding occurs under §1446, the partners are not required to provide withholding certificates claiming exemption from withholding under §1441 or §1442.

[122] Reg. §1.1441-5(c)(1)(ii).

[123] Reg. §§1.1441-5(a)(6), (c)(2). The agreement may also designate the partnership as an "acceptance agent" for obtaining taxpayer identification numbers for the partners.

[124] Reg. §§1.1441-4(a)(2)(ii), (3), discussed supra ¶66.2B.3 text accompanying notes 71-73.

[125] Reg. §1.1441-5(c)(3)(iii). If the partnership furnishes the requisite documents, it is relieved of any withholding obligation it would otherwise have. Reg. §1.1441-5(c)(3)(v).

[126] Reg. §1.1441-5(c)(1)(i)(A). The withholding agent may rely on a partner's claim of reduced withholding if, at the time of payment, it has the partner's withholding certificate making this claim and does not know or have reason to know that the claim is not valid. Reg. §1.1441-5(c)(3)(ii).

intermediary, which means that the intermediary certificate must be accompanied by beneficial owner withholding certificates.[127] The partnership must "furnish information sufficient for the withholding agent to determine each partner's distributive share . . . ."[128]

If the withholding agent cannot reliably associate a partner's distributive share with appropriate documentation, withholding status is determined by presumption.[129] If the withholding agent does not have a reliable withholding certificate for a partner, the partner is presumed to be a foreign person, and tax is withheld under §1441 at 30 percent. Tax is withheld at 30 percent from the entire payment if the withholding agent cannot reliably determine how much of the payment is allocable to each partner. If a payment can reliably be associated with a group of partners, but the withholding agent lacks reliable information on the separate share of each of these partners, tax is withheld at the highest rate applicable to any member of the group.

The foregoing rules are applied "looking through partners that are foreign flow-through entities."[130] Assume foreign partnership P has two partners: foreign corporation X and foreign partnership $P-1$, which has three partners, a foreign pension fund, domestic partnership $P-2$, and foreign partnership $P-3$.[131] If the status of all of these persons is established by appropriate documentation, the payees of a payment to P are X (one half), the foreign pension fund (one sixth), $P-2$ (one sixth), and the partners of $P-3$ (one sixth).

3. *Classification.* A payment is considered made to a partnership if the withholding agent has received a withholding certificate from the payee representing it to be a partnership.[132] In the absence of documentation, a payee is presumed to be a partnership if there are no "reliable indications that the payee is an individual, estate, or trust" and the payee is not presumed to be a corporation or other type or organization (e.g., because of an indication of corporate status in its name).[133]

A partnership is considered domestic if it has furnished a Form W-9 to the withholding agent and the withholding agent can reliably associate the particular payment with that Form; it is deemed foreign if the payment can reliably be associated with a withholding certificate on Form W-8.[134] In the absence of a withholding certificate, a partnership is presumed to be a foreign partnership and

---

[127] Reg. §1.1441-5(c)(1)(i)(B).

[128] Reg. §1.1441-5(c)(3)(iv) ("The sum of all partners' distributive shares, expressed as a percentage, must equal . . . 100 percent").

[129] Reg. §§1.1441-5(c)(1)(i)(E), (d)(3).

[130] Reg. §1.1441-5(c)(1)(i).

[131] Reg. §1.1441-5(c)(1)(iv) Ex.

[132] Reg. §1.1441-5(a)(4).

[133] Reg. §1.1441-1(b)(3)(ii).

[134] Reg. §§1.1441-5(a)(4), (b)(1). If a foreign partnership's Form W-8 lacks some or all of the required documents from its partners, it is nevertheless effective to establish that the payee is a foreign partnership. Reg. §1.1441-5(c)(3)(i).

its partners are presumed to be foreign persons in three situations: (1) the partnership's employer identification number is known to the withholding agent and begins with "98," (2) the withholding agent's communications with the partnership are mailed to an address in a foreign country, or (3) payment is made outside the United States.[135] In other undocumented cases, partnerships are apparently classified as domestic.

¶66.2B.6 Withholding Certificates and Other Documentation of Foreign Beneficial Ownership

A withholding agent "may rely on information or certifications contained in, or attached to, a withholding certificate or other document furnished by or for a beneficial owner or payee unless the withholding agent has actual knowledge or reason to know that the information or certifications are not correct" and the facts that the withholding agent knows or has reason to know indicate a withholding tax liability greater than the tax based on the withholding certificate.[136] A foreign person's withholding certificate should be on Form 8233 (compensation for personal services) or Form W-8 (all other income).[137]

1. *Withholding certificates from beneficial owners.* "Absent actual knowledge or reason to know otherwise, a withholding agent may consider a payment to be beneficially owned by a foreign person if the withholding agent can reliably associate the payment with a beneficial owner withholding certificate furnished by the person identified in the certificate.[138] A beneficial owner withholding certificate is a statement by which a beneficial owner represents that it is a foreign person; it may also claim a withholding exemption or reduced rate.[139] The certificate must be on Form W-8, signed by the beneficial owner under penalties of perjury, and contain all of the information required by the Form (e.g., name, permanent address in the beneficial owner's country of residence, and, for entities, place of organization and entity classification).[140] The Form's "validity period" must not have expired.

A beneficial owner withholding certificate must state the beneficial owner's U.S. taxpayer identification number (TIN) if the certificate claims a reduced rate

---

[135] Reg. §1.1441-5(d)(2).

[136] Reg. §1.1441-7(b)(1).

[137] Withholding agents may substitute their own forms for Forms W-8 and 8233. Reg. §1.1441-1(e)(4)(vi).

[138] Reg. §§1.1441-1(e)(1)(i), (ii)(A)(*1*).

[139] Reg. §1.1441-1(e)(2)(i). A separate certificate is required for each withholding agent, and separate certificates may be required for various payments from one withholding agent (e.g., because the beneficial owner asserts that some, but not all of the items paid by the withholding agent are effectively connected income).

[140] Reg. §1.1441-1(e)(2)(ii). The address may not be a post office box or other address used only for mailing purposes and may not be that of a financial institution with which the beneficial owner has an account.

or exemption under an income tax treaty or claims that the income is effectively connected with a U.S. business or that the beneficial owner is a tax-exempt organization or private foundation.[141]

2. *Beneficial owner withholding certificates from intermediaries.* "Absent actual knowledge or reason to know" that it is not reliable, a withholding agent may rely on a beneficial owner withholding certificate attached to a valid foreign intermediary certificate,[142] which is a Form W-8 by which a payee represents that it is a foreign person and is not the beneficial owner of the payment.[143] An intermediary withholding certificate is used by a custodian, broker, nominee, or other agent.[144] The intermediary must attach to the certificate copies of all needed documentation for all persons covered by the certificate (e.g., beneficial owner withholding certificates or other intermediary withholding certificates with attached beneficial owner certificates), or it must separately identify amounts allocable to beneficial owners for whom the intermediary lacks reliable documentation.[145] Assume a U.S. person (W) pays dividends to foreign intermediary X, who remits the dividends to foreign intermediary Y, who collects the dividends for foreign beneficial owners A and B, who provide beneficial owner withholding certificates to Y.[146] Y must provide an intermediary withholding certificate on Form W-8 to X, with the originals or copies of the certificates received from A and B, and X must deliver to W a certificate on Form W-8 with the original or a copy of Y's certificate (with attachments) attached.

The intermediary must inform the withholding agent of portion of each payment allocable to each person covered by the certificate, and the withholding agent may rely on this information.[147] The intermediary need not disclose the name of any beneficial owner unless it has "actual knowledge" that a beneficial owner is a U.S. person and is not tax-exempt.[148]

---

[141] Reg. §1.1441-1(e)(4)(vii). A TIN is an individual taxpayer identification number (ITIN), employer identification number, or social security number. ITINs are issued by the IRS to nonresident alien individuals who are not eligible to obtain social security numbers. Reg. §§301.6109-1(d)(3), (g), (h)(1).

[142] Reg. §§1.1441-1(e)(1)(i), (ii)(A)(*I*).

[143] Reg. §1.1441-1(e)(3)(i). An intermediary must update the information on an intermediary withholding certificate whenever necessary to enable the withholding agent to withhold at the proper rates and to make its withholding tax returns. Reg. §1.1441-1(e)(3)(iv)(B).

[144] The certificate must be signed by a person authorized to act for the intermediary, must contain a variety of information, statements, and certifications, and must not have expired. Reg. §1.1441-1(e)(3)(ii).

[145] All attached documentation may be copies, but the intermediary privy to the beneficial owner must have and retain the original documents. See Reg. §1.1441-1(e)(3)(iv)(C) Ex. 2.

[146] Reg. §1.1441-1(e)(3)(iv)(C) Ex. 1.

[147] Reg. §1.1441-1(e)(3)(iv)(A). See Reg. §1.1441-1(e)(3)(iv)(C) Ex. 2.

[148] See Reg. §1.1441-1(e)(3)(iv)(C) Ex. 3.

If a withholding agent can reliably associate a payment with a intermediary withholding certificate, the payment is usually deemed made to the persons for whom the intermediary acts in receiving the payment, even if some of the withholding certificates or other documentation establishing beneficial ownership are missing or "unreliable."[149] If the withholding agent cannot reliably associate any portion of the payment with a beneficial owner, that portion is considered beneficially owned by an unidentified foreign person, subject to withholding at 30 percent.[150] The withholding tax is 30 percent of the entire payment if the withholding agent "cannot reliably determine how much of the payment is allocable to" each person for whom the withholding agent has a withholding certificate.[151] If the withholding agent can reliably associate a payment with a group of beneficial owners but does not have reliable information on how much of the payment is allocable to one or more of the group, the amount allocable to these beneficial owners is subject to withholding at the highest rate applicable to any of them.[152]

3. *Withholding certificates from qualified intermediaries.* A withholding agent's responsibilities are reduced with respect to payments to a "qualified intermediary." Qualified intermediaries sometimes take on "primary withholding responsibility," in which case U.S. persons making payments to them need not withhold tax or collect information about the beneficial owners of the payments. In other instances, a qualified intermediary does not withhold, in which case U.S. payors to the intermediary must withhold but can rely on representations made in the intermediary withholding certificate, which is based on beneficial owner and intermediary certificates that are held by the qualified intermediaries but not transmitted to the payors.[153]

A qualified intermediary is a foreign financial institution or clearing organization that has made a withholding agreement with the IRS.[154] The agreement subjects the qualified intermediary to all withholding and reporting provisions of the Code, except as the agreement limits these responsibilities.[155] It specifies the certification and documentation upon which the qualified intermediary can rely to determine the nationality, residence, and treaty eligibility of beneficial owners

---

[149] Reg. §§1.1441-1(b)(2)(v)(A), (3)(v)(A).

[150] Reg. §1.1441-1(b)(3)(v)(B).

[151] Reg. §1.1441-1(b)(3)(v)(D).

[152] Reg. §1.1441-1(b)(3)(v)(C).

[153] Reg. §1.1441-1(e)(5)(i).

[154] Reg. §1.1441-1(e)(5)(ii). A foreign branch of a U.S. financial institution or clearing organization or foreign corporation claiming treaty benefits on behalf of its shareholders can also be a qualified intermediary.

[155] Reg. §1.1441-1(e)(5)(iii)(A). A withholding agreement may apply to the entity as a whole or to particular branches. It may allow the intermediary to adjust for underwithholding and overwithholding and to obtain refunds on behalf of its customers.

and U.S. payees for whom the qualified intermediary collects payments.[156] It can allow the intermediary to satisfy U.S. reporting requirements without disclosing the identity of its customers, but the IRS may require the intermediary to provide the names and addresses of customers claiming treaty benefits, particularly if the treaty contains a limitation of benefits clause.[157] The qualified intermediary may agree to act as an "acceptance agent"—a person who obtains individual taxpayer identification numbers (ITINs) from the IRS on behalf of nonresident alien individuals.[158]

A qualified intermediary may assume primary responsibility to withhold tax under §§1441 and 1442 only if its agreement with the IRS allows it to do so.[159] If the agreement authorizes primary withholding responsibility, it must delineate procedures for the qualified intermediary to deposit withheld taxes and provide for the assessment and collection of any tax that the intermediary fails to withhold or remit to the IRS. A withholding agent need not withhold tax from a payment if a qualified intermediary assumes primary withholding responsibility. If the intermediary does not assume primary responsibility for a particular payment, the withholding agent has "full withholding responsibility for that payment."

A qualified intermediary withholding certificate must be on Form W-8, state the intermediary's TIN, be signed by an officer authorized to act for it, and contain a variety of information, statements, and certifications (including a certification that the intermediary has all documentation from beneficial owners that is required by its agreement with the IRS).[160] The intermediary must provide the withholding agent with a breakdown into three categories of the assets generating income subject to withholding and a few other "reportable amounts."[161]

---

[156] Reg. §1.1441-1(e)(5)(iii)(B). The agreement must also spell out how the IRS will verify compliance, which may take the form of reliance on the intermediary's independent auditor (possibly coupled with IRS audits of the auditor's records).

[157] For limitation of benefits clauses, see supra ¶66.2A.3.

[158] For ITINs, see Reg. §§301.6109-1(d)(3), (g), (h)(1).

[159] Reg. §1.1441-1(e)(5)(iv).

[160] Reg. §§1.1441-1(e)(3)(iii), (e)(4)(vii). An entity's TIN must be an employer identification number issued by the IRS. Reg. §1.1441-1(e)(4)(viii).

[161] The "reportable amounts" are all amounts subject to withholding under §1441 or §1442, interest on deposits with U.S. banks and insurance companies, and interest and original issue discount on obligations maturing within 183 days from issue. Reg. §1.1441-1(e)(3)(vi). The three categories are:

a. Assets covered by the intermediary withholding certificate that are "associated with" non-U.S. payees. If amounts paid with respect to these assets are subject to more than one withholding rate, the breakdown must further divide the assets among rate categories. It must also specify any assets for which the qualified intermediary assumes primary withholding responsibility.

b. Covered assets "associated with" U.S. payees. For each such payee required to provide a Form W-9, the intermediary must furnish to the withholding agent either a Form W-9 or the payee's name and address.

A withholding agent may consider a payment made to foreign persons if it can reliably associate the payment with assets that a qualified intermediary has represented as being allocable to foreign persons for whom the qualified intermediary holds valid documentation.[162]

4. *Beneficial owner withholding certificates from U.S. branches.* "Absent actual knowledge or reason to know otherwise," a withholding agent may treat a payment as beneficially owned by a foreign person if the withholding agent can reliably associate the payment with a beneficial owner withholding certificate attached to a valid U.S. branch certificate.[163] A U.S. branch certificate is a Form W-8 filed by a U.S. branch of a foreign bank or insurance company that is subject to U.S. banking or insurance regulations.[164] The certificate must represent that the payment is not effectively connected with the branch's U.S. business and that it is filed either to transmit documentation for persons the branch represents as intermediary or to evidence its agreement with the withholding agent to be treated as a U.S. person for withholding tax purposes.[165] A U.S. branch withholding certificate must be signed by an authorized person under penalties of perjury, must not have expired, and must contain a variety of information, statements, and certifications, including the branch's taxpayer identification number.[166] If a withholding agent can reliably associate a payment with a U.S. branch certificate, the payment is usually deemed made to the persons for whom the branch acts in receiving the payment, even if some of the withholding certificates or other documentation establishing beneficial ownership are missing or "unreliable."[167]

5. *Others recognized as foreign beneficial owners.* "Absent actual knowledge or reason to know otherwise," a withholding agent may treat a payment as beneficially owned by a foreign person in each of the following cases:

a. The payment is made outside the United States with respect to an offshore account and the withholding agent can reliably associate the payment with specified documents.[168]

---

c. Assets associated with payees for whom the intermediary lacks reliable documentation. If the intermediary has assumed primary withholding responsibility, it need not provide the withholding agent with information about this category.

Reg. §1.1441-1(e)(5)(v)(B). The required information on each category of assets must be presented in a way that allows the withholding agent to determine its withholding responsibilities and must be updated as necessary for this purpose. Reg. §1.1441-1(e)(5)(v)(C). All of this information is considered part of the intermediary withholding certificate.

[162] Reg. §1.1441-1(e)(1)(ii)(A)(*3*).
[163] Reg. §§1.1441-1(e)(1)(i), (ii)(A)(*1*).
[164] Reg. §1.1441-1(e)(3)(i).
[165] Reg. §1.1441-1(e)(3)(v).
[166] Reg. §1.1441-1(e)(4)(vii).
[167] Reg. §§1.1441-1(b)(2)(v)(A), (3)(v)(A).
[168] Reg. §1.1441-1(e)(1)(ii)(A)(*2*).

b. The payee is an international organization identified as such by executive order or a wholly-owned agency of such an organization.[169]

c. The income is interest from bankers' acceptances and the payee is a foreign central bank of issue.[170]

6. *Documentation requirements.* Documentation required by these rules must usually be held when the payment is made, and the withholding agent must not have been notified by the IRS that any of the information in the documents is "incorrect or unreliable."[171] The documentation must be retained "for as long as it may be relevant to the determination of the withholding agent's tax liability."[172]

A financial institution, including a bank, mutual fund, or broker, must usually obtain a separate withholding certificate for each account of each customer, but aggregations are allowed in various circumstances.[173] For example, if the institution has a "universal account system that uses a customer identifier that can be used to retrieve systematically all of the accounts of the customer," a customer need provide only one withholding certificate.

Generally, a withholding certificate or other document furnished under these rules expires at the end of the third calendar year following the year in which it is signed or created.[174] However, several types of withholding certificates are valid as long as the status of the person providing the certificate remains unchanged, including the following:

a. A beneficial owner withholding certificate containing the beneficial owner's taxpayer identification number (TIN), but only with respect to income subject to withholding under §§1441 and 1442 and not income claimed to be effectively connected with a U.S. business.[175]

b. A certificate from a qualified intermediary or from a withholding foreign partnership.[176]

---

[169] Reg. §1.1441-1(e)(1)(ii)(A)(6). See IRC §7701(a)(18) ("international organization" is public organization entitled to privileges, exemptions, and immunities provided by International Organizations Immunities Act).

[170] Reg. §1.1441-1(e)(1)(ii)(A)(7).

[171] Reg. §1.1441-1(e)(1)(ii)(B). The IRS has proposed regulations that would allow withholding agents to receive and transmit Forms W-8 electronically. REG-107872-97, 1997-47 IRB 11.

[172] Reg. §1.1441-1(e)(4)(iii).

[173] Reg. §1.1441-1(e)(4)(ix).

[174] Reg. §§1.1441-1(e)(4)(ii)(A), (D). A change in address is a change in circumstances only if it alters withholding status. For example, if a beneficial owner does not claim treaty benefits, a new address is a changed circumstance only if it is in the United States, and for a beneficial owner claiming treaty benefits, a new address within the same treaty country is not a changed circumstance.

[175] Reg. §§1.1441-1(e)(4)(ii)(B)(*1*), (C); 1.1461-1(c)(2)(i).

[176] Reg. §§1.1441-1(e)(4)(ii)(B)(2), (5). For foreign withholding partnerships, see §1.1441-5(c)(2)(iv), discussed supra ¶66.2B.5 text accompanying note 123.

c. A certificate from a nonqualified intermediary, U.S. branch of a foreign financial institution, or a foreign partnership other than a withholding foreign partnership, but certificates and other documents attached to the intermediary's or branch's certificate are governed by the general rule unless another exception applies.[177]

d. A certificate from a person claiming to be an integral part of a foreign government or foreign central bank of issue.[178]

A change in circumstances invalidates a certificate with respect to information affected by the change.[179] A person supplying a certificate or document is required to inform the withholding agent of any such change in circumstances, and an intermediary must pass along any information it receives about changed circumstances affecting beneficial owners or other intermediaries whose withholding certificates are attached to its own intermediary withholding certificate. A withholding agent is not required to make any inquiry about changed circumstances "unless in knows or has reason to know that circumstances have changed," but it may demand a new certificate from any payee even if it has no reason to know of changed circumstances.[180]

Generally, a withholding agent is protected in relying on information and certifications stated in an unexpired withholding certificates and need not "inquire into the truthfulness of this information or certification" unless "it has actual knowledge or reason to know that [particular information or certifications are] untrue."[181] For example, if a foreign financial institution submits a beneficial owner certificate, the withholding agent may treat the institution as beneficial owner, not as an intermediary, unless it has contradictory information in its records or "the certificate contains information that is not consistent with beneficial owner status (e.g., sub-account numbers or names)."[182] However, if an entity's name "indicates" that it is of a type always classified for U.S. tax purposes as a corporation, a withholding agent may accept a claim that the entity is not a corporation only if its certificate represents that the entity is exempted from corporate status by a grandfather rule in the entity classification rules.[183]

7. *Actual knowledge and reason to know.* Generally, a withholding agent has reason to know that a withholding certificate or other document is unreliable

---

[177] Reg. §§1.1441-1(e)(4)(ii)(B)(3), (4), (6).

[178] Reg. §1.1441-1(e)(4)(ii)(B)(7).

[179] On acquiring knowledge of a change of circumstances, the withholding agent may, instead of immediately considering the certificate invalid as to the changed information, continue to honor the certificate for 90 days "while awaiting a new certificate or documentation or while seeking information regarding changes, or suspected changes, in the person's circumstances." Any underwithholding during the 90-day grace period must eventually be made up. Reg. §1.1441-1(b)(3)(iv).

[180] Reg. §1.1441-1(e)(4)(ii)(D).

[181] Reg. §1.1441-1(e)(4)(viii).

[182] Reg. §1.1441-1(e)(4)(viii)(B).

[183] Reg. §1.1441-1(e)(4)(viii)(A). For the entity classification rules, see infra ¶90.1.3.

"if its knowledge of relevant facts or statements contained in the withholding certificate or other documentation is such that a reasonably prudent person in the position of the withholding agent would question the claims made."[184]

However, a financial institution (including a mutual fund) paying dividends or interest on publicly traded securities has reason to know that a beneficial owner withholding certificate is not reliable only in five specified circumstances:

a. The beneficial owner's permanent address is in the United States.
b. "The payment is directed to a P.O. Box, an in-care-of address, or a U.S. address."
c. The withholding certificate claims a reduction of the withholding tax under a treaty but shows an address outside the treaty country.
d. The address in the withholding certificate is in the United States or a country other than the treaty country.
e. The beneficial owner is an entity claiming a status inconsistent with its name (e.g., an entity with a corporate name claims to be a partnership).[185]

In each of these circumstances, the withholding agent must either have additional supporting information or make additional inquiries. For example, for an individual, trust, or estate with a U.S. address, the withholding agent "may rely on information in its files" to support the claim of foreign status if this information is not more than three years old. In the absence of such supporting information, the withholding agent must obtain from the beneficial owner or a U.S. agent a written statement of facts supporting the claimed foreign status. If the beneficial owner is not an individual, trust, or estate, the withholding agent must ask whether the taxpayer identified on the withholding certificate is organized or created under the laws of a foreign country. An individual's claim of foreign status may be supported by a certificate of residence or other official identity document.

If a withholding agent receives IRS notice that a claim of rate reduction, withholding exemption, or U.S. status is not correct, it has "actual knowledge" of this fact beginning 30 calendar days after it receives the notice.[186]

---

[184] Reg. §1.1441-7(b)(2)(i). If a financial institution uses a "coordinated account information system" under which it obtains one withholding certificate from each foreign customer, applicable to all of the customer's accounts with the institution, it is deemed to know all "facts recorded in the system." Reg. §1.1441-7(b)(3).

[185] Reg. §1.1441-7(b)(2)(ii). This rule also applies to (1) dividends on redeemable securities of investment companies registered under the Investment Company Act of 1940, (2) dividends, interest, and royalties on publicly offered units of beneficial interest in a unit investment trust if the offering was registered under the Securities Act of 1933, and (3) amounts received by a lender of publicly traded securities in substitution for dividends or interest on the securities.

[186] Reg. §1.1441-7(b)(1).

¶66.2B.7 Withholding in the Absence of Documentation

1. *Classifying payees without documentation.* If a withholding agent cannot associate a payment with documents establishing the payee's status, it may rely on the following presumptions:[187]

a. A payee is presumed to be an individual, trust, or estate if, from "the payee's name or other indications," the payee "appears to be" an individual, trust, or estate.[188]

b. A payee is presumed to be a corporation if its name "contains an unambiguous expression of corporate status" (e.g., "Incorporated, Inc., Corporation, Corp., P.C., but not Company or Co.)" or if its name indicates that it is a foreign organization of a type that the regulations always classify as corporations (per se foreign corporations).[189]

c. A payee is presumed to be a tax-exempt organization, government, or any one of several other categories of organizations if the regulations permit this status to be recognized without documentation.[190] For example, an entity is presumed to be a tax-exempt organization if its name is included in the IRS' list of charitable organizations, and a payee is presumed to be a foreign government if "its name reasonably indicates that it is a foreign government."[191]

d. A payee is presumed to be a partnership if there are no "reliable indications that the payee is an individual, estate, or trust" and the payee is not presumed to be a corporation or other type or organization.[192]

e. An entity presumed to be a corporation, partnership, tax-exempt organization, government, or other specified type is presumed to be a foreign person in four situations:

   (1) The payee's employer identification number is known to the withholding agent and begins with "98";

   (2) The withholding agent's communications with the payee are mailed to an address in a foreign country;

   (3) The payee's name indicates that it is a foreign entity of a type per se classified as a corporation; or

   (4) Payment is made outside the United States.[193]

f. The recipient of a taxable scholarship or fellowship grant is presumed to

---

[187] Reg. §1.1441-1(b)(3)(i).

[188] Reg. §1.1441-1(b)(3)(ii).

[189] Reg. §§1.1441-1(b)(3)(ii), 1.6049-4(c)(1)(ii)(A)(*1*). The types of foreign entities that are always corporations are listed in §301.7701-2(b)(8)(i), discussed infra ¶90.1.3.

[190] Reg. §§1.1441-1(b)(3)(ii), 1.6049-4(c)(1)(ii)(B)-(Q).

[191] Reg. §§1.6049-4(c)(1)(ii)(B), (F).

[192] Reg. §1.1441-1(b)(3)(ii).

[193] Reg. §§1.1441-1(b)(3)(iii)(A), 1.1441-5(d).

be a nonresident alien if "the withholding agent has a record that the payee has a U.S. visa that is not an immigrant visa."[194]

g. A recipient of payments from a qualified pension, profit sharing, stock bonus, or annuity plan or a tax-deferred annuity is presumed to be a nonresident alien unless (1) the withholding agent has the payee's social security number and (2) the payee's address used by the withholding agent for tax reporting purposes is located in the United States or a country with which the United States has an income tax treaty that exempts such payments from tax.[195]

h. A payment to an offshore account is presumed made to a foreign person if it is not subject to backup withholding under §3406.[196]

i. Joint payees are presumed to be U.S. persons if the withholding agent cannot reliably associate the payment with documentation covering all of them.[197]

j. All other payees are presumed to be U.S. persons.[198]

In each of these cases, a payee or beneficial owner may rebut the presumption by providing reliable documentation to the withholding agent or (in connection with a refund claim) the IRS.[199]

Also, a withholding agent may not rely on a presumption if (1) it has actual knowledge or reason to know that the presumption contradicts the payee's or beneficial owner's actual status and (2) withholding based on the actual status is greater than that resulting from the presumption.[200] In these cases, withholding must be based on the actual knowledge or reason to know.[201]

In any other case, a withholding agent acting on actual knowledge, rather than an applicable presumption, is liable for withholding tax based on the presumption, and interest and penalties thereon, unless it can establish the correctness of the actual knowledge.[202] Assume a dividend paid to X, Inc. at a foreign address.[203] Because of its name and foreign address, X is presumed to be a foreign

---

[194] Reg. §1.1441-1(b)(3)(iii)(B).

[195] Reg. §1.1441-1(b)(3)(iii)(C).

[196] Reg. §1.1441-1(b)(3)(iii)(D).

[197] Reg. §1.1441-1(b)(3)(vii). This rule does not apply to a payment to an offshore account subject to the rule described in the text accompanying the previous note.

[198] Reg. §1.1441-1(b)(3)(iii).

[199] Reg. §1.1441-1(b)(3)(viii).

[200] Reg. §1.1441-1(b)(3)(ix)(B).

[201] See Reg. §1.1441-1(b)(3)(x) Ex. 3 (withholding agent has actual knowledge that X, Inc., presumed to be domestic, is foreign; withholding agent must withhold under §1442, based on actual knowledge, because U.S. status results in no withholding).

[202] Reg. §1.1441-1(b)(3)(ix)(A).

[203] Reg. §1.1441-1(b)(3)(x) Ex. 1. See Reg. §1.1441-1(b)(3)(x) Ex. 2 (withholding agent acts on actual knowledge that individual, presumed to be U.S. person, is nonresident alien).

corporation. If, relying on actual knowledge that X is domestic corporation, the withholding agent does not withhold, it is liable for withholding tax under §1442 unless it can prove that X is a domestic corporation.

2. *Payees presumed to be U.S. persons.* A presumption that a payee is a U.S. person is not necessarily advantageous because it may subject the payee to wage withholding (§3402), withholding from pension payments (§3405), or backup withholding on interest and dividends (§3406).[204] If, in reliance on a presumption that a payee is a U.S. person, tax is withheld under §3402, §3405, or §3406, the withholding agent is generally not liable for withholding under §1441 or §1442, even if it is ultimately established that the beneficial owner is a foreign person.[205]

During a grace period of up to 90 days, a withholding agent may (but need not) treat a payee as a foreign person, even if payee is presumed to be a U.S. person, if (1) the payee's address is in a foreign country or (2) the payee has submitted a withholding certificate that claims foreign status but is invalid because it was transmitted by a nonqualified electronic means (e.g., by fax) or "is no longer reliable."[206] During the grace period, the withholding agent may withhold under §1441 or §1442, rather than §3406, and may allow reduced withholding at any rate justified by a faxed, but complete, withholding certificate. The grace period begins when the withholding agent credits any amount to a new account or first credits an amount after an existing certificate is no longer reliable. It ends 90 days later or, if earlier, at the end of the calendar year or when the account balance falls to less than 31 percent of the amounts credited during the grace period. If documentation establishing foreign status is not submitted during the grace period, the presumption of U.S. status again takes effect at the end of the grace period, and backup withholding may apply to all amounts credited during the grace period.

3. *Payees presumed foreign.* If a payee is presumed to be a foreign person, tax must usually be withheld at 30 percent from the payment, without reduction under any treaty provision or under any statutory provision other than one reducing the rate or exempting the item for all foreign payees.[207] More completely, a withholding agent is liable for a tax of 30 percent of a payment, even if the agent did not withhold or withheld at a lesser rate, unless (1) a withholding agent can reliably associate the payment with documentation, (2) the withholding agent may presume the payee to be a U.S. person or the payment to be effectively connected income of the payee, or (3) the payment qualifies for a

---

[204] For §3406, see infra ¶111.5.3.

[205] Reg. §1.1441-1(b)(3)(ix)(A).

[206] Reg. §§1.1441-1(b)(3)(iv), 1.6049-5(d)(2)(ii). The grace period is available for joint payees only if one of these conditions holds for each of the payees. Reg. §1.1441-1(b)(3)(vii).

[207] Reg. §1.1441-1(b)(3)(i).

reduced rate of withholding without documentation.[208] The withholding agent bears the burden of demonstrating that this tax has been paid.

A withholding certificate or other documentation received after a payment is made may be used to establish that the correct amount has been withheld.[209] However, if a reduced rate or withholding exemption is not justified by documents in hand at the time of payment or by a presumption, the withholding agent is liable for interest and penalties on the amount that should have been withheld, even if the underlying tax liability is not greater than the amount withheld.[210] Interest accrues from the due date of the withholding tax return until the withholding tax is paid or the withholding agent receives documentation justifying the amount withheld.

Assume domestic corporation D, which pays interest on a post-1984 obligation to a foreign corporation on June 15 of year 1, treats the interest as portfolio interest and withholds no tax, even though it has no Form W-8 or other documentation on the payment; it receives a valid Form W-8 on September 30 of year 3.[211] The Form W-8 relieves D of liability for withholding tax, but D owes the IRS interest on 30 percent of the payment from March 15 of year 2 (the due date for the withholding tax return covering the year 1 payment) to September 30 of year 3 (when D receives the needed documentation).[212]

Generally, if a withholding agent withholds tax under §1441 or §1442 in reliance on a presumption that a payee is a foreign person, the withholding agent is not liable for withholding under the rules for wage withholding (§3402), withholding from pension payments (§3405), or backup withholding on interest and dividends (§3406), even if it is ultimately established that the beneficial owner is a U.S. person.[213]

---

[208] Reg. §1.1441-1(b)(7)(i). Although the regulations generally apply to payment made after 1998, a withholding agent may elect to apply §1.1441-1(b)(7) for all open tax years. Reg. §1.1441-1(f)(2)(ii).

[209] Reg. §1.1441-1(b)(7)(ii). However, the IRS "may require additional proof" if it determines that the delays in obtaining documentation "affect its reliability."

[210] Reg. §1.1441-1(b)(7)(iii). However, if the IRS collects interest from the beneficial owner of the payment, that interest is credited against the withholding agent's interest obligation.

[211] Reg. §1.1441-1(b)(7)(v) Ex. 1.

[212] If the payment were instead a dividend qualifying for reduced withholding at 15 percent under an income tax treaty, D would be liable for (1) the 15 percent tax, (2) interest on that tax from March 15 of year 2 until it is paid, and (3) interest on the remaining 15 percent that should have been withheld from March 15 of year 2 until D receives the justifying documentation on September 30 of year 3. Reg. §1.1441-1(b)(7)(v) Ex. 2.

[213] Reg. §1.1441-1(b)(3)(ix)(A).

¶66.2B.8 Payments and Returns

A withholding agent is personally liable for any amount required to be withheld under §§1441–1443, whether or not the tax is actually withheld.[214] If the tax is paid by the beneficial owner, the withholding agent is relieved of liability for the tax, but it remains liable for interest and penalties.[215] A withholding agent is "indemnified against the claims and demands of any person for the amount of" tax withheld under §§1441–1443 if it withholds "based on a reasonable belief" that withholding is required.[216]

A withholding agent must deposit tax withheld under §§1441–1443 with a federal reserve bank or other authorized financial institution.[217] For each calendar year, the withholding agent must prepare a Form 1042-S reporting the amounts subject to withholding paid to or for each beneficial owner and, not later than March 15 of the following year, it must file these forms with a return on Form 1042.[218] The Form 1042 is due even if no tax was required to be withheld from the items paid during the year (e.g., because of treaty exemptions).

If a withholding agent withholds and deposits more than the amount required, it may pay the amount overwithheld to the beneficial owner or other payee and recoup this amount by reducing a subsequent deposit of tax withheld.[219] Alternatively, the withholding agent may credit the amount overwithheld against the amount required to be withheld from a subsequent payment to or for the same beneficial owner if that payment is made not later than the due date of the Form 1042-S for the year of the overwithholding.[220] Assume tax is withheld at 30 percent from a U.S.-source dividend of $100 and deposited in due course,

---

[214] IRC §1461. See Casa De La Jolla Park, Inc. v. CIR, 94 TC 384 (1990) (bank collected proceeds of sales made by taxpayer and used portions of proceeds to pay interest owed by taxpayer to nonresident alien; held, taxpayer liable for withholding tax because bank received and disbursed funds at taxpayer's direction); Fitzgerald v. CIR, 4 TC 494, 503 (1944) (nonacq.) (grantor of alimony trust not subject to withholding, even though income was taxable to him, because he lacked ownership rights under local law; in using withholding as medium of collection, IRS "must be viewed purely as any other creditor"). See also Northern Ind. Pub. Serv. Co. v. CIR, 101 TC 294 (1993) (taxpayer filed Form 1042, reporting withholding under §1441, but omitted amounts subject to withholding in excess of 25 percent of amounts reported; held, deficiency subject to six-year statute of limitations under §6501(e)(1), which applies if return improperly "omits from gross income" amounts exceeding 25 percent of reported gross income; not relevant that omitted amounts were gross income of payees, not taxpayer).

[215] IRC §1463; Reg. §1.1463-1(a). See Krebs, IRS Reverses Its Position and Decides to Penalize Withholding Agents for Understatements on Form 1042, 24 Tax Mgmt. Int'l J. 380 (1995).

[216] Reg. §1.1461-1(e).

[217] Reg. §1.1461-1(a).

[218] Reg. §1.1461-1(b). For extensions of the filing deadlines, see Reg. §1.1461-1(g).

[219] Reg. §1.1461-2(a)(2). The deposit offset must usually occur within the same calendar year, but an offset may be made during next calendar year if proper disclosure is made on a timely filed Form 1042-S for the year of the overwithholding.

[220] Reg. §1.1461-2(a)(3).

but the beneficial owner *(BO)* subsequently provides a Form W–8 establishing a right to a treaty reduction of the withholding rate to 15 percent.[221] Within the time limits described above, the withholding agent may either reimburse *BO* for the $15 of excess withholding and recoup the $15 from a subsequent deposit, or it may reduce by $15 the amount withheld from a subsequent payment to *BO*.

If a withholding agent withholds too little, it may recoup the underwithholding by withholding more from a subsequent payment to or for the beneficial owner or it may satisfy the withholding obligation from property of the beneficial owner held by the withholding agent.[222]

¶66.2C   WITHHOLDING OF TAX AT SOURCE: PRE-1999 RULES

¶66.2C.1   Generally

The 30 percent tax imposed by §§871(a)(1) and 881(a) is almost entirely enforced by the withholding of tax at the source.[1] Under §§1441(a) and 1442(a), tax must be withheld and remitted to the IRS by any person, including a lessee, mortgagee, employer, or fiduciary, having "the control, receipt, custody, disposal, or payment" of income subject to the 30 percent tax.[2] A person obligated to withhold is called a withholding agent.[3] The withholding agent is usually the

---

[221] Reg. §1.1461-2(a)(4) Exs.

[222] Reg. §1.1461-2(b).

[1] See generally ABA Tax Section Comm. on U.S. Activities of Foreigners and Tax Treaties, Report on Consolidating and Simplifying the Withholding Rules and Procedures Under Sections 1441 Through 1446, 47 Tax Lawyer 425 (1994); Dale, Withholding Tax on Payments to Foreign Persons, 36 Tax L. Rev. 49 (1980); Krebs, IRS Reverses Its Position and Decides to Penalize Withholding Agents for Understatements on Form 1042, 24 Tax Mgmt. Int'l J. 380 (1995).

[2] See Casa De La Jolla Park, Inc. v. CIR, 94 TC 384 (1990) (bank collected proceeds of sales made by taxpayer and used portions of proceeds to pay interest owed by taxpayer to nonresident alien; held, taxpayer liable for withholding tax because bank received and disbursed funds at taxpayer's direction); Fitzgerald v. CIR, 4 TC 494, 503 (1944) (nonacq.) (grantor of alimony trust not subject to withholding, even though income was taxable to him, because he lacked ownership rights under local law; in using withholding as medium of collection, IRS "must be viewed purely as any other creditor").

[3] Reg. §1.1441-7(a)(1). For return requirements for withholding agents, see Reg. §1.1461-2. For the payment of taxes withheld, see Reg. §1.1461-3. See also Reg. §1.1441-7(a)(2) (U.S. government is withholding agent with respect to interest on its obligations); §1.1441-7(b) (withholding agent may designate agent to carry out its withholding responsibilities, but must give notice to IRS of designation and remains liable if designated agent fails to pay); Northern Ind. Pub. Serv. Co. v. CIR, 101 TC 294 (1993) (taxpayer filed Form 1042, reporting withholding under §1441, but omitted amounts subject to withholding in excess of 25 percent of amounts reported; held, deficiency subject to six-year

last person in the United States who handles the item before it is remitted to the taxpayer or a foreign agent of the taxpayer. Assume a nonresident alien is beneficial owner of shares of stock. If the taxpayer's foreign address is listed on the corporation's stock records, the corporation must withhold tax from dividends paid on the stock. If the stock is held in street name by a U.S. broker, the corporation usually has no way of knowing the beneficial owner is foreign and does not withhold, but the broker must withhold tax from any dividends received on the shares.

Withholding agents are personally liable for the amount required to be withheld, whether or not the tax is actually withheld from the amount paid to the foreign taxpayer.[4] The withholding tax rate is 30 percent of each taxable item unless a lower rate is prescribed by treaty.

Amounts withheld under §§1441 and 1442 are included in the payee's gross income and credited against the tax otherwise due.[5] For example, if $100 of dividends is payable by a domestic corporation to a nonresident alien shareholder, the shareholder's gross income is $100, but $30 of this amount is withheld and remitted to the IRS, and the shareholder receives only $70.

Because the withholding tax is determined on a cash basis, the withholding agent usually has cash in hand from which tax can be withheld. However, the tax occasionally applies to noncash income.[6] For example, a taxable stock dividend is subject to withholding if the shareholder is a foreign person. Since the IRS does not accept payment in any medium other than money, the regulations instruct withholding agents to retain possession of noncash items "until the property has been converted into funds sufficient to enable the withholding agent to pay over in money the tax required to be withheld."[7] For example, the withholding agent might inform the taxpayer that the income item will not be delivered to him until he makes a cash payment to the withholding agent equal to the withholding tax.

1. *Withholding from income of foreign partners.* Because partnerships are not taxpayers, the withholding tax on interest, dividends, and other fixed or determinable annual or periodical income of a partnership is imposed on foreign partners' distributive shares of the items, not on the partnership itself. The tax is

---

statute of limitations under §6501(e)(1), which applies if return improperly "omits from gross income" amounts exceeding 25 percent of reported gross income; not relevant that omitted amounts were gross income of payees, not taxpayer).

[4] IRC §1461. But see IRC §1463 (withholding agent cannot be required to pay if income recipient pays).

[5] IRC §§1462, 1463; Reg. §1.1462-1(a).

[6] See Central de Gas de Chihuahua, S.A. v. CIR, 102 TC 515 (1994) (withholding tax applies to income allocated to foreign person under §482, even though item was never paid), discussed supra ¶66.2.1 note 3.

[7] Reg. §1.1441-7(c). See R.T. French Co. v. CIR, 60 TC 836, 856 (1973) (unnecessary to answer "tantalizing question" whether constructive distributions are subject to withholding).

enforced by requiring the partnership to withhold if it is domestic or by withholding on payments to the partnership if it is foreign.[8]

2. *Domestic partnerships.* A domestic partnership is required to withhold under §1441 or §1442 if it has an item of U.S. source income of a type that is subject to the withholding tax and some portion of the item is included in the distributive share of a partner who is a nonresident alien or a foreign corporation, partnership, trust, or estate.[9] The term "distributive share" refers to the portion of the item that is allocated to the partner's capital account, not the amounts actually distributed to the partner.[10] Because a partner's distributive share often cannot be determined until the end of the year, a domestic partnership is required to withhold from a distribution to a foreign partner if it is traceable to partnership income of a type subject to the withholding tax. Amounts withheld from distributions are credited against the amount required to be withheld from the partner's distributive share.

3. *Foreign partnerships.* Although withholding obligations under §§1441 and 1442 usually parallel the taxes imposed by §§871(a) and 881(a), both in the items subject to tax and the amounts of tax, §1441(a) requires that tax be withheld from amounts paid to foreign partnerships even though they are not taxpayers. Underlying this rule is a supposition that all partners of foreign partnerships are themselves foreign persons and that it is therefore appropriate to withhold from payments to the partnerships as a means of collecting the withholding tax on the partners. Congress indulged in this supposition because collecting withholding tax from a foreign partnership is likely to be as difficult as collecting tax directly from the partners. Amounts withheld from payments to foreign partnerships are presumably credits against the withholding tax on foreign partners, and a domestic partner should be entitled to a refund of his share or to credit the withheld amount against the regular income tax.

The Treasury sometimes excuses withholding on payments to a foreign partnership if the partnership is engaged in business in the United States, withholding imposes an undue administrative burden, and the collection of tax imposed on foreign partners is not jeopardized by exempting the payments from withholding.[11]

4. *Withholding from income of trusts and estates.* A trust or estate is itself a taxable entity, but it is allowed a deduction for income currently distributed or distributable to beneficiaries.[12] Distributed income is taxable to the beneficiaries, in whose returns the income has the same character as it does to the trust or

---

[8] For the terms "domestic partnership" and "foreign partnership," see supra ¶65.3 text accompanying notes 1-2. See Comm. on Tax'n of Int'l Trans., Tax Treatment of Partnerships and Partners Under United States Income Tax Treaties, 50 Rec. Ass'n of Bar of City of NY 773 (1995).

[9] Reg. §1.1441-3(f).

[10] See infra ¶86.1.

[11] IRC §1441(d); Reg. §1.1441-4(f).

[12] See infra ¶81.1.1.

estate. A beneficiary of a trust or estate is subject to the withholding tax if trust income of a kind subject to this tax is included in a distribution. The mechanism for collecting this tax depends on whether the trust or estate is foreign or domestic.[13]

Because a foreign trust or estate is itself subject to the withholding tax, tax is withheld from payments to the trust or estate. The amount withheld is treated as a payment of the trust's or estate's tax if the income is not distributed or as payment of the beneficiary's tax if it is distributed.[14] In contrast, if the trust or estate is domestic, payments to the entity are not subject to withholding, but the trust or estate must withhold tax if income of a taxable variety is included in the gross income of a foreign beneficiary.[15]

However, if a trust created by a nonresident alien is treated as owned by the grantor under the grantor trust rules, tax must be withheld from payments to the trust whether the trust, viewed as an independent entity, would be classified as domestic or foreign.[16]

5. *Scholarships and grants to foreign students and researchers.* The withholding rate is reduced to 14 percent for certain scholarships and grants received by nonresident aliens who are temporarily present in the United States under nonimmigrant visas under §§101(a)(15)(F), (J), (M), or (Q) of the Immigration and Nationality Act, which are issued to students, researchers, and visiting teachers.[17] If such an individual receives a scholarship from U.S. sources that is only partially excluded from gross income under §117(a), the 14 percent withholding tax applies to the taxable portion of the scholarship.[18] Very generally, scholarships are excludable from gross income only to the extent of the student's tuition and related expenses, not including living expenses.[19] If a student receives a scholarship that covers living expenses as well as tuition and incidental expenses, the amount for living expenses thus is taxable. If the student is a nonresident alien present in the United States under a student visa, the taxable amount is subject to the 14 percent withholding tax.

---

[13] For rules classifying a trust or estate as domestic or foreign, see supra ¶65.3 text accompanying notes 16-26.

[14] Reg. §1.1462-1(b). Applied literally, the statutes would impose the 30 percent tax on both the trust or estate and the beneficiary because both are foreign persons and the trust's normal deduction for distributions is not allowed in determining the 30 percent tax. IRC §873(a).

[15] Reg. §1.1441-3(f).

[16] Reg. §1.1441-3(g). For the grantor trust rules, see infra ¶80.1.

[17] IRC §1441(b); Reg. §1.1441-2(c). See Rev. Proc. 88-24, 1988-1 CB 800 (withholding procedures for scholarships and grants paid to foreign students and grantees). See Harding, Making Scholarship and Fellowship Payments to Foreign Students: An Overview of Tax Issues and Problems, 55 Tax Notes 533 (April 27, 1992).

[18] IRC §1441(b)(1). For the application of the source rules to scholarships and fellowships, see infra ¶70.9 text accompanying notes 4-7.

[19] See supra ¶11.2.

Also, if a nonresident alien present in the United States on an F, J, M, or Q visa is not a candidate for a degree at an educational institution, the 14 percent withholding tax applies to grants received from (1) an educational or charitable organization that is exempt from tax under §501(c)(3), (2) the government of a foreign country, the United States, or one of the states, (3) an agency or instrumentality of the federal or a state or local government, or (4) an international organization.[20]

The 14 percent tax is often waived by treaty. The Treasury's model treaty exempts a student, apprentice, or business trainee from U.S. tax on any payment received for maintenance, education, or training if (1) the payments come from a foreign country, (2) the recipient was a resident of the treaty country immediately before coming to the United States, and (3) the recipient is present in the United States for full-time education or training.[21]

6. *Withholding when taxable amount not known.* Tax need only be withheld from amounts of the described types that are "gross income."[22] However, when a payment is made, a withholding agent may not be able to determine whether it is of one of the described types or determine the portion of it that is gross income because the item's characterization may depend on the payee's individual circumstances or on future events. The regulations usually require that tax be withheld on the entire payment in such a situation, thereby leaving it to the payee to straighten matters out by applying for a refund.[23]

For example, tax must be withheld on all amounts paid to a foreign investor as interest unless the amounts are covered by the exemption for portfolio interest, the exemption for interest on deposits, or a treaty exemption.[24] If a foreign person purchases a bond on a secondary market between interest payment dates, the first interest payment to the bondholder is fully subject to withholding even though the amount that accrued before the purchase is a return of capital that is excluded

---

[20] IRC §1441(b)(2).

[21] U.S. Treasury Dep't, Model Income Tax Convention of September 20, 1996 art. 20 [hereinafter Treasury Model]. See Organisation for Economic Co-operation and Development, Model Tax Convention on Income and Capital art. 20 (1992) [hereinafter OECD Model].

The United Nations Model provides further that with respect to grants, scholarships, and employee compensation not covered by this exemption, the host country must allow "the same exemptions, reliefs or reductions" as are extended to residents of that country. United Nations Model Double Taxation Convention Between Developed and Developing Counties art. 20(2) (1981). The United States has made a few treaties containing the United Nations provision. See Rev. Proc. 93-20, 1993-1 CB 528 (applying United States-India treaty; "exemptions, reliefs or reductions" include standard deduction and spousal and dependency exemptions, but not right to file joint return).

[22] IRC §§1441(a), 1442(a).

[23] For refunds of withholding taxes, see Reg. §1.1464-1.

[24] Reg. §1.1441-3(c)(3). The statutes also require that tax be withheld from original issue discount accruing while a foreign person holds a discount bond, but the Treasury has never unscrambled the many problems raised by this requirement. See Prop. Reg. §1.1441-3(c)(6) (proposed in 1976).

from gross income.[25] The bondholder, however, is entitled to a refund of the tax withheld from the capital recovery.

Also, a domestic corporation must usually withhold from a distribution to a foreign shareholder, whether the distribution is a dividend from earnings and profits or is a nontaxable recovery of capital or capital gain, because the amount that is a dividend depends on earnings and profits for the entire year and therefore cannot be known with certainty when the distribution is made.[26] Exceptions are made only for kinds of distributions that cannot be taxable dividends, such as a stock dividend qualifying for exclusion from gross income or a distribution in redemption or liquidation that is treated as an exchange of the shareholder's stock.

A contingent payment to a seller of intellectual property presents a similar situation. Gain on a foreign person's sale of a U.S. patent, copyright, or other intellectual property is taxed under §871(a)(1) or §881(a) if it is realized on the receipt of a payment that is contingent on the productivity, use, or disposition of the property.[27] Gain, however, is determined with a subtraction for the seller's adjusted basis for the property, which usually is not known to the buyer or other person in the role of withholding agent. The regulations thus allow the withholding agent either to withhold 30 percent from the entire amount of the contingent payment or to obtain a statement from the seller showing the amount of gain.[28]

7. *Proof that recipient is U.S. person.* Although tax need not be withheld from a payment to a U.S. person, personal liability for withholding tax on a payment to a foreign person generally cannot be avoided by showing the withholding agent believed the recipient was a U.S. person. The regulations, however, specify various forms of evidence that may be relied upon in determining whether the recipient of particular amounts is a nonresident alien or foreign corporation.

8. *Payee's statement.* A withholding agent can generally rely on an individual's statement that he is a U.S. citizen or resident or the statement of a corporation or partnership that it is domestic.[29] The withholding agent must provide the IRS with a copy of a statement accepted under this rule.

9. *Dividends.* A payor of dividends may generally rely on the address shown for the shareholder in the payor's records.[30] If an address outside the United States is given, tax must be withheld unless the payor has "definite knowledge" that the shareholder is a U.S. person. An address within the United States, in contrast, may be accepted as proof that the shareholder is a U.S. person

---

[25] Rev. Rul. 85-193, 1985-2 CB 191.

[26] Reg. §1.1441-3(b); Rev. Rul. 72-87, 1972-1 CB 274.

[27] IRC §§871(a)(1)(D), 881(a)(4).

[28] Reg. §1.1441-3(d). The statement may be relied upon unless the withholding agent "has reason to believe" that it is not correct. See Voce, Basis of Foreign Property That Becomes Subject to U.S. Taxation, 49 Tax Lawyer 341 (1996).

[29] Reg. §1.1441-5.

[30] Reg. §1.1441-3(b)(3).

not subject to withholding. An address in care of another person in the United States does not trigger the withholding obligation unless the circumstances "indicate clearly" that the shareholder is a foreign person. Once a foreign address has been designated for a shareholder, withholding must continue, even after a U.S. address is substituted, until the shareholder furnishes proof that he is a U.S. person.

10. *Interest.* Tax must be withheld from all interest payments to debt holders whose status is not known to the payor.[31] A debt holder makes his status known by filing an ownership certificate with the withholding agent.[32]

11. *Reduction of withholding tax rate under treaty.* When the withholding tax rate is reduced by treaty for a particular item or when an item is exempted by treaty, the treaty reduction or exemption may be reflected in the amount withheld from the item.[33] The withholding agent must determine a dividend recipient's eligibility for a rate reduction under a treaty, usually on the basis of the address shown for the taxpayer in the withholding agent's records.[34] For other income, the statutory rate is reduced to reflect a treaty only if a certificate (Form 1001) is filed with the withholding agent asserting the recipient's entitlement to the reduction.[35] The withholding agent, however, is entitled to rely on the statement without inquiry or verification.

¶66.2C.2 Exemptions

Several exemptions from withholding are allowed, most of them paralleling exemptions from the taxes imposed by §§871(a)(1) and 881(a).

1. *Effectively connected income.* Income effectively connected with a U.S. trade or business of the recipient is usually exempted from withholding because tax on this income is determined and collected in much the same way as it is for U.S. persons.[36] The exemption is unqualified for effectively connected income other than compensation received by individuals for personal services performed in the United States.[37] To obtain the benefit of the withholding exemption for noncompensation income, a foreign person engaged in business in the United States need only file a statement with the withholding agent indicating that the income is or is expected to be effectively connected income and providing a few other items of information.[38] Compensation income of nonresident alien indi-

---

[31] Reg. §1.1441-3(c)(4).
[32] Reg. §1.1461-1.
[33] Reg. §§1.1441-1, 1.1441-6(a).
[34] Reg. §1.1441-6(a).
[35] Reg. §§1.1441-6(b), (c).
[36] For the effectively connected income tax, see infra ¶66.3.
[37] IRC §1441(c)(1); Reg. §1.1441-4(a)(1).
[38] Reg. §1.1441-4(a)(2).

viduals is also exempted from §1441 withholding in many situations, but usually only if the compensation is subject to wage withholding.[39]

2. *Portfolio interest.* Portfolio interest is exempted from withholding because it is exempted from the taxes imposed by §871(a)(1) and 881(a).[40] Interest does not qualify as portfolio interest if the payor is a corporation or partnership and the recipient owns 10 percent or more of the stock or partnership interests.[41] Withholding agents do not always have access to the facts needed to apply the 10 percent test. Because ownership is determined with attribution rules, the issuer of the obligation may not know whether a debt holder is a 10 percent or greater shareholder or partner. Moreover, the withholding obligation can fall on trustees, brokers, and others who have no access to the debtor's shareholder or partner list. The statutes therefore provide that if interest satisfies all aspects of the definition of portfolio interest other than the 10 percent test, the interest is exempt from withholding unless the withholding agent "knows, or has reason to know," that the 10 percent test is failed.[42]

3. *Interest on bank and similar deposits.* Interest on a deposit with a bank or insurance company and dividends on a deposit with a savings and loan association are exempt from withholding if they are exempt from the 30 percent tax under §871(i).[43]

4. *Gambling winnings.* Gambling winnings are exempt from withholding if they are exempt from the 30 percent tax under §871(j).[44]

5. *Income of foreign governments.* Section 892 generally exempts foreign governments from U.S. taxation.[45] An item exempt under §892 is also exempt from withholding if the foreign government furnishes the withholding agent with a statement documenting its claim for exemption.[46]

¶66.3 INCOME EFFECTIVELY CONNECTED WITH U.S. BUSINESS

¶66.3.1 Introductory

In contrast with the 30 percent tax ordinarily imposed by §§871(a)(1) and 881(a) on interest, dividends, and other fixed or determinable income, nonresi-

---

[39] IRC §1441(c)(4); Reg. §1.1441-4(b)(1). See Rev. Proc. 89-47, 1989-2 CB 598 (procedures for making agreement with IRS that a central withholding agent will withhold at rates less than 30 percent on income of a group of nonresident alien entertainers, athletes, and "similarly situated individuals" from athletic events in United States).

[40] IRC §1441(c)(9). For portfolio interest, see supra ¶66.2.2 text accompanying notes 21-56.

[41] IRC §§871(h)(3), 881(c)(3)(B).

[42] IRC §1441(c)(9).

[43] IRC §1441(c)(10). For §871(i), see supra ¶66.2.2 text accompanying note 57.

[44] IRC §1441(c)(11). See supra ¶66.2.8 note 120 for §871(j).

[45] See infra ¶66.7.

[46] Reg. §1.1441-8T(b).

dent aliens and foreign corporations are taxed by §§871(b) and 882(a) at graduated rates on taxable income effectively connected with a U.S. trade or business.[1] Although most effectively connected income is derived from domestic sources, the effectively connected income tax also reaches a few items of foreign source income connected with U.S. business.

Enacted in 1966, the effectively connected principle broadens prior law, under which foreign persons were never taxed on foreign source income, even when earned by a U.S. business. It also narrows prior law by supplanting a force of attraction principle under which foreign persons engaged in business in the United States were taxed at graduated rates on all domestic income, including interest, dividends, and other income normally subject to the withholding tax, even if the income was not connected with the U.S. business.[2]

If a true and accurate return is filed, a nonresident alien or foreign corporation with a U.S. trade or business can deduct all expenses incurred in earning effectively connected income, as well as casualty and theft losses attributable to

---

[1] See generally Finlayson, U.S. Source Income Earned By Foreign Branches and Affiliates, 47 Tax Lawyer 349 (1994). See Hobbs, Foreign Corporations With Income Effectively Connected With a U.S. Business, 1988, 11 Statistics of Income Bull. 39 (Spring 1992) (for 1988, banks accounted for 66 percent of receipts reported by U.S. businesses of foreign persons; insurance and other finance businesses accounted for another 15 percent); Nutter, Statistics of Income Studies of International Income and Taxes, 13 Statistics of Income Bull. 10 (Winter 1993-1994) (for 1989, 9,321 returns reported effectively connected income, showing total receipts of $102.9 billion, effectively connected taxable income of $2.9 billion, and $997 million of U.S. tax liability).

For the application of the effectively connected income tax and foreign equivalents to income from electronic commerce, see U.S. Treasury Dep't, Selected Tax Policy Implications of Global Electronic Commerce (1996); Benjamin & Nathanson, Conducting Business Using the Internet: Gauging the Threat of Foreign Taxation, 9 J. Int'l Tax'n 29 (1998); O'Donnell & DiSangro, United States Tax Policy on Electronic Commerce, 24 Intertax 429 (1996).

See also Masek, Foreign Investors: Using a U.S. Grantor Trust, 45 Bus. Lawyer 539 (1990) (discussing plan for avoiding tax on U.S. business income by conducting U.S. business through grantor trust that borrows most of its capital from foreign corporation owned by grantor); Reich, U.S. Federal Income Taxation of U.S. Branches of Foreign Banks: Selected Issues and Perspectives, 2 Fla. Tax Rev. 1 (1994); Royse & Rashkin, Effectively Connected Income in a Global Economy, 6 Tax Notes Int'l 925 (Apr. 12, 1993) (discussing possibility that U.S. activities of U.S. parent in managing businesses of foreign subsidiaries might cause subsidiaries' income to be subject to effectively connected income tax).

If a foreign corporation engaged in business in the United States has transactions with related persons in the course of this business, it is subject to various reporting and enforcement rules found in §6038A, discussed infra ¶112.4.4.

[2] See generally Roberts, The Force of Attraction Doctrine in the United States Tax Law Today, 21 Bull. for Int'l Fiscal Documentation 487 (1967); Ross, United States Taxation of Aliens and Foreign Corporations: The Foreign Investors Tax Act of 1966and Related Developments, 22 Tax L. Rev. 277 (1967).

property located here, charitable contributions, and personal exemptions.[3] The resulting tax base is taxed at the rates given by §1 if the taxpayer is an individual, trust, or estate or §11 if the taxpayer is a corporation. Although the foreign tax credit is not ordinarily allowed to foreign persons, they are entitled to a credit under §906 for taxes imposed by foreign countries other than their home countries on their effectively connected income from foreign sources.[4]

A foreign person engaged in U.S. activities that might or might not be a trade or business could be advantaged or disadvantaged by a determination that these activities are a trade or business, depending on the interplay of four factors: (1) Effectively connected taxable income includes some income that is not otherwise taxable to nonresident aliens or foreign corporations; (2) deductions are allowed if the activities are a U.S. trade or business, but not otherwise; (3) the §1 or §11 rates apply to effectively connected taxable income instead of the 30 percent flat rate on the different tax base prescribed by §§871(a)(1) and 881(a); and (4) the 30 percent tax is often reduced or eliminated by treaty, whereas income tax treaties generally allow the United States to tax at the statutory rates all income that is attributable to U.S. permanent establishments of residents of treaty countries. Depending on how these elements are mixed in a particular case, a graduated tax on the effectively connected taxable income plus a 30 percent tax on any residual §871(a)(1) or §881(a) items can be greater or less than a 30 percent tax on all §871(a)(1) or §881(a) items.

¶66.3.2   U.S. Trade or Business

Neither the Code nor the regulations fully define the term "trade or business within the United States."[5] The cases hold that profit-oriented activities in the United States, whether carried on by the taxpayer directly or through agents, are a trade or business if they are regular, substantial, and continuous.[6] The line of

---

[3] IRC §§873(a), (b); 882(c). Residents of Canada and Mexico may deduct all personal and dependency exemptions allowed by §151; other aliens are limited to a single exemption. See infra ¶66.6 (returns).

A foreign income tax on income from U.S. sources is usually not deductible in determining effectively connected taxable income, even if the income taxed by the foreign country is included in effectively connected taxable income. IRC §906(b)(1), discussed infra ¶69.9 text accompanying note 13.

[4] See infra ¶69.9.

[5] See Rev. Proc. 98-7, 1998-1 CB —, §4.01(3) (IRS ordinarily will not rule on whether taxpayer is engaged in trade or business in United States).

[6] See CIR v. Spermacet Whaling & Shipping Co., 281 F2d 646 (6th Cir. 1960) (taxpayer conducting whaling expedition on high seas and selling sperm oil for resale to U.S. refiner not engaged in U.S. business, despite close financial links); Amalgamated Dental Co. v CIR, 6 TC 1009 (1964) (foreign corporation purchasing merchandise in United States not engaged in trade or business here even though U.S. vendors, because of wartime conditions, shipped directly to taxpayer's customers and remitted part of sales price to taxpayer); Pasquel v. CIR, 12 TCM (CCH) 1431 (1953) (purchase and sale of two

demarcation is similar to the distinction drawn by §162 (business expenses) and §212 (expenses of producing nonbusiness income).[7] Sometimes, however, a non-resident alien or foreign corporation is clearly engaged in a business, but the U.S. activities are too incidental or sporadic to constitute a U.S. business, even though they feed the foreign business.[8] In effect, the U.S. activities must be judged in isolation, a task straining the imagination if the activities would not have been undertaken absent the foreign business to which they are subservient.

Special statutory rules, described below, are provided for activities associated with trading in securities and commodities, the performance of services, and U.S. businesses operated by partnerships.

1. *Securities and commodities trading.* The usual rule that a U.S. trade or business can be carried on through agents is modified for trading in stocks, securities, and commodities. Trading "through a resident broker, commission agent, custodian, or other independent agent" is not a trade or business if the

---

ships in three-month period not a trade or business). For the attribution of agents' activities to the taxpayer, see Zaffaroni v. CIR, 65 TC 982 (1976) (nonresident aliens with community property earned in United States by active spouse; held, agent for other spouse); Lewenhaupt v. CIR, 20 TC 151 (1953), aff'd per curiam, 221 F2d 227 (9th Cir. 1955) (agent with power of attorney); Rev. Rul. 70-424, 1970-2 CB 150 (U.S. sales agent). But see Reg. §1.864-3(b) Ex. 2 (foreign corporation not engaged in U.S. trade or business merely because one of its officers is also chief executive officer of corporation's U.S. subsidiary and spends substantial time in United States in latter capacity). Compare Handfield v. CIR, 23 TC 633 (1955) (nonresident alien held to be engaged in business in United States through a consignee found to be taxpayer's agent), with Rev. Rul. 76-322, 1976-2 CB 487 (consignor-consignee relationship assimilated to seller-buyer, not principal-agent, under treaty with Australia).

[7] For §§162 and 212, see supra ¶20.5. For authorities holding investment activities not to be a trade or business, see Reg. §1.864-3(b) Ex. 2 (officer of foreign corporation present in United States to supervise corporation's investment in domestic subsidiaries); Continental Trading, Inc. v. CIR, 265 F2d 40 (9th Cir.), cert. denied, 361 US 827 (1959) (management of investments and collection of investment income); Abegg v. CIR, 50 TC 145 (1968), aff'd on other issues, 429 F2d 1209 (2d Cir. 1970), cert. denied, 400 US 1008 (1971) (management of investments, including buying and selling, and investigations of business opportunities); Scottish Am. Inv. Co. v. CIR, 12 TC 49 (1949) (management of portfolio investments, where decisions to buy and sell were made abroad); Rev. Rul. 73-522, 1973-2 CB 226 (receipt of rent, payment of expenses, and sporadic activities in negotiating new leases). See also deKrause v. CIR, 33 TCM (CCH) 1362 (1974) (trust's management of stock held for investment was not trade or business; hence nonresident alien beneficiary, whose status under §875(2) depended on trust's status, was not engaged in business and was taxable on flat basis without deductions). But see InverWorld, Inc. v. CIR, 71 TCM (CCH) 3231 (1996), reconsideration denied, 73 TCM (CCH) 2777 (1997) (financial services activities through U.S. office of subsidiary, which was found to be acting as taxpayer's agent, were U.S. trade or business); Brown, Note, Cayman Islands Corporation Engaged in U.S. Trade or Business: *InverWorld v. Commissioner*, 50 Tax Lawyer 659 (1997); Toan, Gold, Connors & Patton, Foreign Broker Was Engaged in U.S. Trade or Business Through the Activities of an Agent: *InverWorld, Inc. v. Cmr.*, 25 Tax Mgmt. Int'l J. 655 (1996).

[8] See CIR v. Spermacet Whaling & Shipping Co., 281 F2d 646 (6th Cir. 1960); Amalgamated Dental Co. v CIR, 6 TC 1009 (1964).

taxpayer does not have an office in the United States through which the trades are directed or effected.[9] The foregoing rule applies to brokers and dealers in securities and commodities, as well as to casual investors, and the volume of the taxpayer's securities and commodities transactions in the United States is irrelevant to its application.[10]

Also, trading in stocks, securities, or commodities for the taxpayer's own account is not a U.S. trade or business, whether the trading activities are carried on directly by the taxpayer while present in the United States or through employees, brokers, custodians, or other agents.[11] When employees or agents are used, this rule can apply even if the employees have discretionary authority. The rule covers trading (including margin transactions) in stocks, securities, and options to buy or sell stocks or securities.[12] It also covers activities "closely related" to the taxpayer's securities trading, including the obtaining of credit for the transactions. The volume of the taxpayer's transactions is ignored in applying the rule. The rule, however, is not available to a dealer in securities or commodities.[13]

2. *Personal services.* Generally, the performance of personal services within the United States at any time during the taxable year is a U.S. trade or business.[14] This draconic pronouncement has been applied to a single performance by a

---

[9] IRC §§864(b)(2)(A)(i), (B)(i), (C). The term "commodities" includes only commodities "of a kind customarily dealt in on an organized commodity exchange" and the rules for commodities trading apply only to transactions "of a kind customarily consummated" on an organized commodity exchange. IRC §864(b)(2)(B)(iii). See Reg. §1.864-2(d)(3) ("commodities" does not include "goods or merchandise in the ordinary channels of commerce").

[10] Reg. §§1.864-2(c)(1), (d)(1).

[11] IRC §§864(b)(2)(A)(ii), (B)(ii).

[12] Reg. §§1.864-2(c)(2)(i), (d)(2)(i).

[13] IRC §§864(b)(2)(A)(ii), (B)(ii). For the term "dealer in stocks or securities," see Reg. §1.864-2(c)(2)(iv).

Also, for taxable years beginning before 1998, the exception could not apply to securities trading by a foreign corporation whose principal business was trading in securities for its own account and whose principal office was in the United States. IRC §864(b)(2)(A)(ii) (before amendment in 1997). For the location of a corporation's principal office, see Reg. §1.864-2(c)(2)(iii). See H.R. Rep. No. 148, 105th Cong., 1st Sess. — (1997) ("the principal office rule operates simply to shift certain administrative functions with respect to securities trading and the associated jobs offshore . . . . [E]limination of this rule would facilitate the foreign investment in U.S. markets that the safe harbor was designed to promote").

Under an exception to the pre-1997 rule, a foreign corporation engaged principally in securities trading through a U.S. office could qualify for the trading-for-its-own-account exemption if it was a personal holding company or would have been a personal holding company but for exceptions covering foreign corporations owned exclusively by nonresident aliens and passive foreign investment companies. IRC §864(b)(2)(A)(ii) (before amendment in 1997). See infra ¶95.2 for personal holding companies.

[14] IRC §864(b); Reg. §1.864-2(a). But see Rev. Rul. 79-388, 1979-2 CB 270 (pension received in year when nonresident alien was not engaged in U.S. business is not effectively

visiting entertainer or athlete.[15] It contrasts sharply with the cases and rulings allowing foreign persons engaged in other kinds of pursuits to exploit U.S. markets to a considerable extent without acquiring a local trade or business.

A limited exception is provided for some services performed by nonresident aliens while present in the United States for short periods.[16] The exception applies if (1) the services are performed while the taxpayer is temporarily present in the United States, (2) the taxpayer is present in the United States for no more than 90 days during the taxable year,[17] (3) the compensation for the services in this country does not exceed $3,000,[18] and (4) the employer is either a nonresident alien, foreign partnership, or foreign corporation not engaged in business in the United States or a foreign office of a U.S. person.[19] When these requirements are met, the exception applies whether the services are performed as an employee or an independent contractor.[20] Treaties typically contain rules exempting foreign employees of foreign employers from U.S. tax on wages and salaries earned during even longer periods of service in the United States.[21]

3. *Partnerships.* Under §875(1), a nonresident alien or foreign corporation that is a member of a partnership, domestic or foreign, is deemed engaged in any U.S. trade or business carried on by the partnership.[22] The principal effect of this rule is that the partner's distributive share of the partnership's effectively connected income is subject to the effectively connected income tax in the partner's

---

connected income but is instead subject to 30 percent rate to extent attributable to employer's contributions for services rendered in United States).

[15] Rev. Rul. 70-543, 1970-2 CB 172. See also Rev. Rul. 85-4, 1985-1 CB 294 (race-horse owners); Rev. Rul. 73-107, 1973-1 CB 376 (freelance journalist).

[16] IRC §864(b)(1).

[17] A day is counted against the 90-day ceiling if the taxpayer is present in the United States during any portion of the day. Reg. §1.864-2(b)(2)(i).

[18] See Reg. §1.864-2(b)(3) Ex. 2 ($3,000 ceiling applies to entire compensation for period of temporary presence in United States, not merely portion received during current year or compensation for services performed during current year); §1.864-2(b)(2)(iv) (travel advances or reimbursements not counted against $3,000 ceiling if taxpayer is required to and does account to employer for expenses; pensions also ignored).

[19] An office in Puerto Rico or a U.S. possession counts as a foreign office. See Reg. §1.864-2(b)(2)(ii) (taxpayer's services in United States ignored in determining whether employer is engaged in U.S. business).

[20] Reg. §1.864-2(b)(2)(iii).

[21] See infra ¶66.3.9 text accompanying note 135–140.

[22] The same approach has been applied to the corresponding inquiry under income tax treaties—whether a resident of a treaty country has a permanent establishment in the United States. See Unger v. CIR, 936 F2d 1316 (DC Cir. 1991) (under 1942 treaty with Canada, limited partnership's permanent establishment in United States is considered permanent establishment of each limited partner); Donroy, Ltd. v. US, 301 F2d 200 (9th Cir. 1962) (same); Rev. Rul. 90-80, 1990-2 CB 170 (same under U.S. Model Treaty). See generally Comm. on Tax'n of Int'l Trans., Tax Treatment of Partnerships and Partners Under United States Income Tax Treaties, 50 Rec. Ass'n of Bar of City of NY 773 (1995).

hands.[23] The converse issue—whether a partnership is engaged in a U.S. business by virtue of a partner's activities—depends on whether the partner is acting as agent for the firm or on his own behalf.[24]

The IRS has ruled that if a foreign partner sells or exchanges an interest in a partnership that carries on a U.S. trade or business through an office or other fixed place of business in this country, at least part of the gain or loss on the disposition is effectively connected income or loss.[25] The amount so treated is the lesser of the gain or loss or the partner's distributive share of the gain or loss that the partnership would realize if it sold all of the assets of the U.S. business. This amount is considered U.S. source income effectively connected with a U.S. trade or business of the partner.[26] If the office or other fixed place of business in the United States is a permanent establishment under an applicable treaty, the gain or loss is considered attributable to the permanent establishment.

4. *Trusts and estates.* Under §875(2), nonresident aliens and foreign corporations are treated as engaged in a U.S. trade or business if they are beneficiaries of a trust or estate that is so engaged.[27] A trust or estate, unlike a partnership, is itself a taxable entity that is subject to the effectively connected income tax if it is engaged in a U.S. business.[28] The taxable income of a trust or estate,

---

[23] For the term "distributive share," see infra ¶86.2.1. For the possibility of allocating disproportionately low amounts of domestic source income (and correspondingly large amounts of foreign source income) to a firm's foreign partners, see §704(b), discussed infra ¶86.2.1.

[24] See Reg. §1.875-1 (last sentence); US v. Balanovski, 236 F2d 298 (2d Cir. 1956), cert. denied, 352 US 968, reh'g denied, 352 US 1019 (1957) (partnership engaged in U.S. trade or business by virtue of acts of partner in buying and selling goods for the firm); Handfield v. CIR, 23 TC 633 (1955); Lewenhaupt v. CIR, 20 TC 151 (1953), aff'd per curiam, 221 F2d 227 (9th Cir. 1955); Rev. Rul. 70-424, 1970-2 CB 150.

[25] Rev. Rul. 91-32, 1991-1 CB 107. See Blanchard, Rev. Rul. 91-32: Extrastatutory Attribution of Partnership Activities to Partners, 76 Tax Notes 1331 (Sept. 8, 1997), reprinted in 14 Tax Notes Int'l 859 (Sept. 15, 1997); Hollander, Is a Sale of a Partnership Interest "Attributable" to the Partnership's Place of Business? The Missing Analysis in Rev. Rul. 91-32, 52 Tax Notes 1321 (Sept. 9, 1991); Reavey & Elliott, Sales of U.S. Partnership Interests by Foreign Partners: New Rules after Rev. Rul. 91-32, 3 Tax Notes Int'l 1295 (Dec. 11, 1991).

[26] IRC §§864(c)(2), 865(e). For §865(e)(2), under which income on a foreign person's sale of personal property is from U.S. sources if the sale is attributable to a U.S. office of the taxpayer, see infra ¶70.6.4 text accompanying notes 89-90. For §864(c), dealing with the effective connection of capital gains, see infra ¶66.3.3.

[27] See Rev. Rul. 85-60, 1985-1 CB 187 (where nonresident alien is beneficiary of foreign trust and foreign trust is partner of domestic partnership, beneficiary is deemed engaged in any U.S. business of partnership under §§875(1) and (2)).

See IRC §679 (transferors to certain foreign trusts treated as owners of the transferred property), discussed infra ¶80.1.7; §1491 (excise tax on certain transfers to foreign trusts) and §1057 (election to treat certain transfers to foreign trusts as taxable events), discussed infra ¶68.6.7.

[28] See infra ¶81.1.1.

however, is determined with a deduction for amounts distributed to beneficiaries, and the deductible amounts are taxed to the beneficiaries, who must treat them as having the same character as they did to the trust or estate.[29] Section 875(2), together with the general rules for taxing beneficiaries of trusts and estates, imposes the effectively connected income tax on amounts distributed to a beneficiary from the effectively connected income of a trust or estate.

¶66.3.3　Effectively Connected Income From U.S. Sources

The effective connection of a foreign person's income, gain, and losses from U.S. sources is tested by segregating these items into two categories. One category consists of income that would otherwise be subject to the 30 percent tax of §871(a)(1) or §881(a), portfolio interest, interest on bank deposits, and capital gains and losses, which are here collectively referred to as FDAP items. The second category consists of all other income, gain, and loss from sources within the United States. An FDAP item is effectively connected with a U.S. trade or business only if an actual connection exists. All items in the second category are effectively connected income, whether or not there is an actual connection.

1. *FDAP items.* An FDAP item from sources within the United States may be effectively connected income under either an asset use test or a business activities test.[30] The asset use test is met if the income is "derived from assets used in or held for use in the conduct of" a U.S. business.[31] The business activities test applies if activities of the U.S. business were "a material factor in the realization of the income, gain, or loss."[32] These two tests are often applied together. For example, although the effective connection of passive income is determined primarily by the asset use test, any activities of the U.S. business that materially contribute to the realization of the income are also taken into account.[33]

The regulations identify three situations where the asset use test is met. First, an asset is used in or held for use in a U.S. business if it is "held for the principal purpose of promoting the present conduct of" the U.S. business.[34] This rule covers plant and equipment used in the daily conduct of business in the United States. Second, property "acquired and held in the ordinary course of" the U.S. business is effectively connected with the business.[35] Examples are accounts and notes receivable for goods sold or services performed in the business.

---

[29] See IRC §652(b) (simple trusts) and §662(b) (estates and complex trusts), discussed supra ¶¶81.4.2 and 81.4.3.

[30] IRC §864(c)(2). Special rules are provided for banking and financing businesses. Reg. §1.864-4(c)(5).

[31] IRC §864(c)(2)(A).

[32] IRC §864(c)(2)(B).

[33] Reg. §1.864-4(c)(2)(i).

[34] Reg. §1.864-4(c)(2)(ii)(*a*).

[35] Reg. §1.864-4(c)(2)(ii)(*b*).

Third, bank accounts, securities, and other investments are used in a U.S. business if they are "held to meet the present needs" of the business, as distinguished from "its anticipated future needs."[36] The third test is presumed met if the asset was acquired with funds generated in the U.S. business, income from the asset is retained by that business, and employees or other personnel present in the United States and actively involved in the business "exercise significant management and control over the . . . asset."[37] Stock of a corporation is deemed not used or held for use in a U.S. trade or business.[38]

Assume a foreign corporation has a branch in the United States that acts as importer and distributor of goods produced by the corporation in a foreign country.[39] The branch operations require substantial amounts of cash during some portions of each year, but much of this cash is invested in U.S. Treasury bills during other parts of the year. Because the cash is held to meet present needs of the U.S. business, the Treasury bills are used in the business, and interest on the bills is effectively connected income.

The business activities test is met if income, gain, or loss, "even though generally of the passive type, arises directly from the active conduct of the taxpayer's trade or business in the United States."[40] Examples are dividends and interest received by a dealer in securities, royalties derived in a business of licensing patents or other intellectual property,[41] and income from services. An investment company's gains and losses on sales of capital assets in the ordinary course of its business are caught by the business activities test, but activities relating to management of the taxpayer's own investments are not treated as activities of a U.S. business unless the business consists principally of investing.[42]

The business activities test picks up all salaries and wages earned by nonresident alien employees while working in the United States, as well as U.S. source pensions and other compensation for these services.[43] Income from property (including capital gains) is generally not covered by the asset use or business

---

[36] Reg. §1.864-4(c)(2)(iv)(a).

[37] Reg. §1.864-4(c)(2)(iv)(b). See Reg. §1.864-4(c)(2)(v) Ex. 5 (presumption, although applicable to portfolio of securities, was rebutted by evidence that securities were investments of funds held by U.S. branch to finance future expansion).

[38] Reg. §1.864-4(c)(2)(iii)(a). This rule is effective for taxable years beginning after June 5, 1996. Reg. §1.864-4(c)(7).

[39] Reg. §1.864-4(c)(2)(v) Ex. 1.

[40] Reg. §1.864-4(c)(3)(i).

[41] See Reg. §1.864-4(c)(3)(ii) Ex. 2 (royalties not effectively connected with U.S. business where negotiations and other activities relating to license agreements were carried on by foreign employees not connected with taxpayer's U.S. branch). See Lokken, The Sources of Income From International Uses and Dispositions of Intellectual Property, 36 Tax L. Rev. 233, 298-339 (1981).

[42] See Reg. §1.864-4(c)(3)(ii) Ex. 1.

[43] Reg. §1.864-4(c)(6)(ii). But see IRC §864(b) (under narrowly defined circumstances, employee temporarily present in United States is not engaged in U.S. trade or business), discussed supra ¶66.3.2 text accompanying notes 17-22.

activities test if a nonresident alien's only business activity in the United States is the performance of personal services. An exception from the latter rule, however, is made where there is a "direct economic relationship" between particular property and the performance of personal services.[44] An example is stock of a domestic corporation held by a nonresident alien "to assure the opportunity of performing personal services in the United States for [the] corporation."

In applying the asset use and business activities test, "due regard shall be given to whether or not such asset or such income, gain, or loss was accounted for through [the taxpayer's U.S.] business."[45] Neither the statutes nor the regulations, however, elaborate on the phrase "due regard," and one might reasonably conclude that in most situations, due regard is complete disregard.[46]

2. *U.S. source income other than FDAP items.* Income, gain, or loss that is not an FDAP item is effectively connected income if it is from sources within the United States, whether or not it is connected in fact with the taxpayer's U.S. business.[47] The principal type of income subject to this rule is income and gain on sales of inventory and other property held for sale to customers in the ordinary course of business.

The rule for non-FDAP items is a holdover from the pre-1966 force of attraction regime.[48] Assume a foreign corporation has an office in the United States from which it sells electronic equipment.[49] From an office in a foreign country, the corporation also sells wines. Advertisements for the wines are placed in magazines sold in the United States, and customers in this country often place mail orders for wines from the foreign office. U.S. source income from wine sales (i.e., income from sales in which title passes to the purchasers in this country) is effectively connected with the U.S. business, even if all of the taxpayer's activities in connection with these sales is outside the United States and the taxpayer's U.S. office is not involved in any way with the sales.

¶66.3.4 Effectively Connected Income From Foreign Sources

Income from sources without the United States is generally not effectively connected with U.S. business.[50] However, foreign source rents, royalties, dividends, interest, and income on sales of goods in the ordinary course of business are sometimes included in effectively connected income in order to cover a few

---

[44] Reg. §1.864-4(c)(6)(i).

[45] IRC §864(c)(2).

[46] Until 1984, interest on loans made by a bank or other financing business was not usually effectively connected with U.S. business unless the loans were recorded on the books of a U.S. branch of the taxpayer. This booking rule was, however, eliminated in 1984. Reg. §1.864-4(c)(5)(ii).

[47] IRC §864(c)(3).

[48] Reg. §1.864-4(b).

[49] Reg. §1.864-4(b) Ex. 3.

[50] IRC §864(c)(4)(A).

situations where income earned principally by business activities in the United States is labeled foreign by the source rules.

1. *U.S. office requirement.* No foreign source income is effectively connected with a U.S. business unless the taxpayer has an office or other "fixed place of business" within the United States and the income is "attributable" to that office.[51]

2. *Office within the United States.* Whether a nonresident alien or foreign corporation has a U.S. office depends on the facts and circumstances, "particularly . . . the nature of the taxpayer's trade or business and the physical facilities actually required by the taxpayer in the ordinary course of the conduct of his trade or business."[52] Any "fixed facility," including a sales outlet, factory, or mine, may be an office, whether or not used continuously by the taxpayer.[53]

The taxpayer's use of facilities of another person (e.g., an affiliated corporation) can make those facilities an office of the taxpayer, but this does not occur if the taxpayer's use is "relatively sporadic or infrequent, taking into account the overall needs and conduct of [the taxpayer's] business."[54] Also, a foreign person is not considered to have an office in the United States merely because a related person has such an office.[55] For example, a foreign subsidiary of a domestic corporation is not treated as having a U.S. office merely because of the parent's activities and facilities in the United States. Moreover, U.S. offices of a domestic parent of a foreign corporation are not considered an office of the latter merely because the parent generally supervises and controls the subsidiary from those offices or merely because the subsidiary's employees regularly confer with officers of the parent and occasionally visit the parent's U.S. office.[56] However, a U.S. office of the parent is an office of the foreign subsidiary if normal operating activities of the subsidiary are regularly conducted from the office. Generally, in order to avoid an imputation of the parent's office to the subsidiary, the subsidiary must have a chief executive officer who conducts the day-to-day business of the foreign corporation from a foreign office.[57]

A U.S. office of an agent of the taxpayer is not treated as an office of the taxpayer if the agent is "a general commission agent, broker, or other agent of independent status acting in the ordinary course of his business."[58] An agent is independent, for example, if, "in pursuance of his usual trade or business, and for compensation, [the agent] sell[s] goods . . . entrusted [by the taxpayer] to his

---

[51] IRC §864(c)(4)(B). See Reg. §1.864-5(a) (office must exist at some time during year item is realized, but not necessarily when it is realized).

[52] Reg. §1.864-7(a)(2).

[53] Reg. §1.864-7(b)(1).

[54] Reg. §1.864-7(b)(2).

[55] Reg. §1.864-7(f).

[56] Reg. §1.864-7(c).

[57] See Reg. §1.864-7(g) Exs. 1-3.

[58] IRC §864(c)(5)(A).

possession, management, and control for that purpose."[59] A person related to the taxpayer (e.g., the taxpayer's parent or subsidiary) may be an independent agent.[60] A person whose sole business is acting as the taxpayer's agent may also be an independent agent.[61]

The statutes say that a U.S. office of an agent who is not independent (e.g., an employee) is considered an office of the taxpayer only if the agent has and regularly exercises authority to make contracts on the taxpayer's behalf or regularly fills orders from a stock of the taxpayer's merchandise in the agent's possession.[62] This rule, however, is deceptive. If a nonresident alien or foreign corporation maintains an office in the United States and staffs the office with employees who have neither authority to contract nor a stock of goods, the office is a U.S. office of the taxpayer, not because an agent's office is attributed to the taxpayer but because the taxpayer maintains the office directly.[63] The statutory rule thus applies only if the dependent agent in the United States does not operate from a fixed place of business, operates from a foreign office, or maintains an office at his own expense (e.g., an office in his home).

A U.S. office of a person purchasing goods from the taxpayer is not attributed to the taxpayer, even if the person is related to the taxpayer.[64] For example, a foreign corporation is not considered to have a U.S. office merely because it regularly sells goods to a related domestic corporation for resale through offices maintained by the latter in the United States.[65]

3. *Items attributable to U.S. office.* An item of foreign source income, gain, or loss is "attributable" to a U.S. office of the taxpayer if the office is a "material factor in the production of" the item and "regularly carries on activities of the type from which [the item] is derived."[66] Activities of an office are a material factor if "they provide a significant contribution to, by being an essential economic element in, the realization of the income, gain, or loss."[67] An office can be a material factor without being a "major factor" in the item's realization. The activities of each of two or more offices (e.g., a U.S. office and a foreign office) can be material factors. The application of the material factor test to particular types of foreign source income is discussed further below.

4. *Royalties and rents.* Royalties or rents received for the use outside the United States of intangible personal property, including patents, copyrights, and trademarks, are effectively connected income if they are derived in the active conduct of business in the United States and are attributable to a U.S. office of

---

[59] Reg. §1.864-7(d)(3)(i).

[60] Reg. §1.864-7(d)(3)(ii).

[61] Reg. §1.864-7(d)(3)(iii).

[62] IRC §864(c)(5)(A).

[63] Reg. §1.864-7(e).

[64] Reg. §1.864-7(d)(1)(i).

[65] See Reg. §1.864-7(g) Exs. 4-6.

[66] IRC §864(c)(5)(B).

[67] Reg. §1.864-6(b)(1).

the taxpayer.[68] Rents from lessees of tangible property, in contrast, are never effectively connected income under the rules for foreign source income.

Whether a foreign person is actively engaged in a licensing or rental business depends on all of the facts and circumstances, not merely the frequency with which licenses or leases are made.[69] Even if the taxpayer has an active U.S. licensing or leasing business, however, foreign source royalties and rents are not effectively connected income unless a U.S. office of the taxpayer is a material factor in the realization of the income. A U.S. office is a material factor if the office "either actively participates in soliciting, negotiating, or performing other activities required to arrange the lease [or] license . . . or performs significant services incident to such lease [or] license."[70] Personnel of the U.S. office must directly participate in such activities or perform such services; "general supervision" of the persons engaged in the activities or services is not enough. Also, a royalty or rent is not attributable to a U.S. office merely because the office (1) created, developed, or purchased the licensed property, (2) collects or accounts for the royalties or rents, (3) performs "merely clerical functions," or (4) "exercises final approval over the execution" of the license or lease.[71]

Even if the taxpayer has an active U.S. licensing or rental business and a foreign source royalty or rent is attributable to a U.S. office, however, this item is not effectively connected income if it is received from a foreign corporation and the taxpayer actually or constructively owns stock of the corporation carrying more than 50 percent of the voting power of the corporation's outstanding stock.[72]

Also, this rule does not encompass foreign source gains on sales of intangibles, but gain on a sale of personal property held for use in a U.S. trade or business is usually from U.S. sources[73] and thus is generally effectively connected income under one of the rules for U.S. source income.

5. *Dividends and interest.* Dividends and interest from foreign sources can be effectively connected with a U.S. business only if the taxpayer is a bank or similar institution or is a foreign corporation whose principal business is trading in stocks and securities for its own account.

---

[68] IRC §864(c)(4)(B)(i). See generally McCollom, Limitations Upon the Use of "Shadow" Foreign Subsidiaries as a Tax Shield for Intangible Property Under the Foreign Investors Tax Act of 1966, 21 Tax Lawyer 383 (1968).

[69] Reg. §1.864-5(b)(1)(iii).

[70] Reg. §1.864-6(b)(2)(i).

[71] See Reg. §1.864-6(b)(2)(i) Ex. 1 (royalties not attributable to U.S. office where licenses were negotiated by foreign employees "subject to approval by an officer [of taxpayer] in the U.S. office"), Ex. 2 (film rents not attributable to U.S. office where U.S. office acquires foreign distribution rights, collects rents, maintains records, and supervises activities of foreign offices, but film rentals solicited and negotiated by employees of foreign offices).

[72] IRC §864(c)(4)(D)(i).

[73] IRC §865(e)(2), discussed infra ¶70.6.4.

First, foreign source dividends and interest are effectively connected income if they are attributable to a U.S. office of the taxpayer and are derived in the active conduct of a U.S. banking, financing, or similar business.[74] Dividends and interest are attributable to a U.S. office if the office "either actively participates in soliciting, negotiating, or performing other activities required to arrange the issue [or] acquisition [of the stock or interest bearing obligation] or performs significant services incident to such issue [or] acquisition."[75] Generally, dividends and interest are considered derived in the active conduct of a banking or financing business if the stock or interest bearing obligation (1) was acquired in the course of making loans to the public or distributing stocks or securities to the public, (2) is held to meet reserve requirements imposed by banking regulators, (3) is an obligation payable on demand or within one year of the taxpayer's acquisition of it, or (4) is an obligation of the U.S. government or an agency thereof.[76] A limited amount of interest on other obligations may also be included. On the other hand, foreign source dividends and interest are not effectively connected income merely because the taxpayer maintains a U.S. office that (1) collects or accounts for dividends or interest, (2) "exercises general supervision" over employees engaged in acquiring securities or making loans, (3) "performs merely clerical functions," or (4) "exercises final approval" over the acquisition of stocks and interest bearing obligations.[77]

Second, foreign source dividends and interest are effectively connected income if the taxpayer is a corporation whose principal business is trading in stocks or securities for its own account through an office in the United States and the dividends and interest are attributable to that office.[78] The latter requirement is met if the office actively participates in the acquisition of the stocks and securities on which the dividends and interest are paid or performs significant services in connection with the acquisition transactions. Collection, accounting, and supervisory activities are not sufficient to meet this test.[79]

Even if foreign source dividend or interest income is covered by one of the foregoing rules, it is not effectively connected income if it is received from a

---

[74] IRC §864(c)(4)(B)(ii). See Reg. §1.864-5(b)(2)(ii) (foreign holding company "owning significant percentages" of stocks and securities of other foreign corporations is not primarily engaged in trading even if it makes "sporadic purchases or sales of stocks or securities to adjust its portfolio").

[75] Reg. §1.864-6(b)(2)(ii)(a).

[76] Reg. §§1.864-4(c)(5)(ii), 1.864-6(b)(2)(ii)(b).

[77] Reg. §1.864-6(b)(2)(ii)(a).

[78] IRC §864(c)(4)(B)(ii). See Reg. §1.864-5(b)(2)(ii) (foreign holding company "owning significant percentages" of stocks and securities of other foreign corporations is not primarily engaged in trading even if it makes "sporadic purchases or sales of stocks or securities to adjust its portfolio").

[79] Reg. §1.864-6(b)(2)(ii)(d).

foreign corporation and the taxpayer actually or constructively owns stock of the corporation carrying more than 50 percent of the voting power of all stock.[80]

Also, the rules discussed here do not reach foreign source gains on sales of stocks and debt obligations. Gain on a sale of personal property held for use in a U.S. trade or business, however, is usually from U.S. sources, regardless of the place of sale.[81] Gains and losses thus are typically effectively connected income under one of the rules for U.S. source income if dividends and interest on the stocks and securities are effectively connected with a U.S. business under the rules discussed here.

6. *Income on sales in ordinary course of business.* Foreign source income on a sale of personal property is usually effectively connected income if the taxpayer holds the property for sale to customers in the ordinary course of business and the sale is made through the taxpayer's U.S. office.[82] Even if these requirements are met, however, the income is not effectively connected if the property is sold for "use, consumption, or disposition" outside the United States and an office of the taxpayer in a foreign country participates materially in the sale. Moreover, even if all of the foregoing requirements are satisfied, income on a sale of goods manufactured by the taxpayer outside the United States is divided between effectively connected and noneffectively connected portions under the source rule that would have applied if the sale had occurred in the United States.[83]

Since 1986, it has been virtually impossible for a foreign person to have income within this category because a source rule enacted in 1986 uses almost identical language in making income from such sales U.S. source income[84] and sales income from sources within the United States is covered by the force of attraction rule described earlier, not the rule described here.[85]

---

[80] IRC §864(c)(4)(D)(i).

[81] IRC §865(e)(2), discussed infra ¶70.6.4.

[82] IRC §864(c)(4)(B)(iii).

[83] IRC §864(c)(5)(C).

[84] IRC §865(e)(2), discussed infra ¶70.6.4.

[85] The rule can apply in at least one situation. The effectively connected income tax applies to alien individuals who are nonresidents within the meaning of §7701(b), discussed supra ¶65.2. The source rule, §865(e)(2), applies to individuals who are nonresidents within the meaning of §865(g)(1). An alien who is a nonresident under §7701(b) is a U.S. resident under §865(g)(1) if the person's principal place of business ("tax home") is in the United States. Income on inventory sales by U.S. residents usually has its source at the place where title passes in the sale. IRC §865(b); Reg. §1.861-7(b). Thus, if an alien individual who is a nonresident under §7701(b), but a U.S. resident under §865(g)(1), sells inventory property in a transaction in which title passes to the buyer outside the United States, income on the sale is from foreign sources, but it is effectively connected income under §864(c)(4) if the taxpayer carries on business through an office in the United States and the sale is attributable to the office. An example might be a citizen and resident of Mexico whose business, carried on exclusively through an office in Texas, consists of exporting goods from Mexico to the United States and who makes sales to U.S. customers

7. *Insurance companies.* Foreign source income of a foreign insurance company is effectively connected income if it is "attributable to its United States business."[86]

8. *Exception for subpart F income.* A foreign source item that would be effectively connected with a U.S. trade or business under any of the rules for foreign source income is excluded if the taxpayer is a controlled foreign corporation (CFC) and the item is subpart F income.[87] Although a foreign corporation is not a CFC unless more than 50 percent of its stock is owned by U.S. shareholders, a CFC may have foreign shareholders. The exception for subpart F income applies to the entirety of the income, including the portion of it that would go to foreign shareholders if the income were distributed as dividends.

¶66.3.5　Effectively Connected Income for Years When Taxpayer Is Not Engaged in U.S. Business

Normally, income, gain, or loss cannot be effectively connected with a U.S. business if the taxpayer is not engaged in business in the United States at any time during the taxable year in which the item is recognized, regardless of how closely the item might be connected with business done in the United States during an earlier or later year.[88] The policy underlying this rule is that the effectively connected income tax should be imposed only in circumstances where the IRS is likely to be able to collect it and that the factor usually making collection feasible—the taxpayer's physical presence in this country—disappears when business operations in the United States are discontinued.

In 1986, however, Congress modified this rule and policy in two respects. First, if the taxpayer engages in a transaction in one year but recognizes income or gain from the transaction in an earlier or later year, the effective connection of the income or gain is determined as though it was recognized when the transaction occurred.[89] This rule applies whether the transaction is a sale or exchange of property, the performance of services, or a transaction of another

---

under contracts by which title passes to the customers when the goods are shipped to them from locations in Mexico.

In contrast, all foreign corporations are nonresidents under §865(g)(1), and the U.S. office rule thus applies to all inventory sales by all foreign corporations.

[86] IRC §864(c)(4)(C); Reg. §1.864-5(c).

[87] IRC §864(c)(4)(D)(ii); Reg. §1.864-5(d)(2). See infra ¶68.2 for subpart F.

[88] IRC §864(c)(1)(B); Reg. §1.864-3(a).

[89] IRC §864(c)(6). This rule applies only if both the transaction and the recognition of the income or gain occur in a taxable year beginning after 1986. Staff of Joint Comm. on Tax'n, 99th Cong., 2d Sess., General Explanation of the Tax Reform Act of 1986 at 1049 (Comm. Print 1987) [hereinafter 1986 Bluebook]. See S. Rep. No. 445, 100th Cong., 2d Sess. 320 (1988) (provision does not conflict with permanent establishment articles of treaties because these articles "do not prevent imposition of U.S. tax on income that was, when realized attributable to a permanent establishment, even though that income is recognized after the permanent establishment no longer exists").

kind. The staff of the Joint Committee on Taxation explained the reasons for the rule as follows:

> Under prior law, foreign taxpayers could avoid U.S. tax by receiving income that was earned by a U.S. trade or business in a year after the trade or business had ceased to exist. For example, the business could sell property and accept an installment obligation as payment. By recognizing the gain on the installment basis, the taxpayer could defer the income to a later taxable year. If the taxpayer had no U.S. trade or business in that year, then the income recognized in that year was not treated as effectively connected with a U.S. trade or business. Congress believed that income earned by a foreign person's U.S. trade or business should be taxed as such, regardless of whether recognition of that income is deferred until a later taxable year. Similarly, Congress believed that foreign persons should not be able to avoid U.S. tax on their income from the performance of services in the United States where payment of the income is deferred until a subsequent year in which the individual is not present in the United States.[90]

Although the rule usually applies to income or gain recognized after U.S. business operations cease, it can also apply when income is recognized before the taxpayer begins business in the United States. For example, if a nonresident alien is paid in one year for personal services to be performed in the United States during the following year, the payment is effectively connected income when received even if the taxpayer is not actually engaged in a trade or business in the United States during the year of receipt.

The second modification made in 1986 applies where property used by the taxpayer in a U.S. trade or business is transferred to another use and income or gain is recognized on a disposition of the property within 10 years thereafter. Income or gain on such a disposition is effectively connected income if it would have been so characterized had the disposition occurred immediately before the change in use.[91] This rule was enacted because

> Congress believed that gains accrued by a foreign person's U.S. trade or business should be subject to U.S. tax, and that such tax should not be avoidable through the simple expedient of removing property from the country prior to its disposition. . . . U.S. persons that transfer assets out of U.S. tax jurisdiction may be subject to tax on unrealized appreciation (sec.

---

[90] Id. at 1048. For prior law, see Reg. §1.864-3(b) Ex. 1 (where installment sales were made in ordinary course of U.S. business, no effectively connected income recognized on receipt of installment payments in year after U.S. business operations ceased), Ex. 3 (salary for services performed in United States not effectively connected income when received during year taxpayer not present in United States).

[91] IRC §864(c)(7). This rule applies only if the property was used in a U.S. trade or business during a taxable year beginning after 1986. 1986 Bluebook, supra note 89, at 1049.

367). Congress believed a similar rule is appropriate for foreign persons as well.[92]

Although the income or gain is characterized as though the disposition occurred immediately before the change in use, it is measured by the terms of the actual disposition. Assume a foreign corporation owns equipment used in a U.S. business, but U.S. business activities are terminated and the equipment is removed from this country when the equipment is worth $100 and has an adjusted basis of $70. Two years later, when the adjusted basis is still $70, the equipment is sold for $150. The gain on the sale is effectively connected income because gain on a disposition of the property immediately before U.S. business operations ceased would have been effectively connected with this business. The entire gain of $80 (amount realized of $150 less adjusted basis of $70) is effectively connected income even though the effectively connected income on a sale immediately before U.S. operations ceased would only have been $30 (fair market value of $100 less adjusted basis of $70).

When either of the foregoing rules applies, the taxpayer is deemed engaged in a trade or business in the United States during the year the income or gain is recognized, and the income or gain is considered attributable to a U.S. office of the U.S. trade or business.[93]

¶66.3.6 Election to Treat Real Property Income as Effectively Connected Income

Under §871(d), a nonresident alien owning U.S. real property may elect to treat income from the property as effectively connected income even if the taxpayer's operation and management of the property is not a U.S. trade or business under the general rules.[94] Section 881(d) allows the same election to a foreign

---

[92] 1986 Bluebook, supra note 89, at 1048.

[93] Id. at 1049.

[94] For election procedures, see Reg. §1.871-10(d). See Rev. Rul. 91-7, 1991-1 CB 110 (election under §871(d) or §881(d) may not be made for year in which taxpayer has no income from U.S. real property; real estate taxes, mortgage interest, and other expenses incurred by nonresident alien or foreign corporation in carrying unimproved real property thus are not deductible if property produces no income and taxpayer has no income-producing U.S. real property).

Where U.S. real property is held by a partnership, the election must be made by the partners, not the partnership. Reg. §1.871-10(d)(3). Where such property is held by a foreign trust or estate, an election may made by the entity, but it only applies in determining the trust's or estate's tax. An election made by a nonresident alien beneficiary of a trust or estate, domestic or foreign, applies to any U.S. real property income of the entity that is taxed to the beneficiary under §652 or §653. Reg. §1.871-10(b)(1). See infra ¶81.1. for §§652 and 662.

For a survey of the rules affecting foreign investors in U.S. real property, see Austrian & Schneider, Tax Aspects of Foreign Investment in U.S. Real Estate, 45 Tax Lawyer 385 (1992).

corporation. The election is most often made by lessors of U.S. realty in order to avoid the 30 percent tax on gross rents.

Once made for any taxable year, the election remains in force for subsequent years unless the IRS consents to its revocation.[95] Moreover, the election applies to all income from nonbusiness real property in the United States, including rents, gains from sales or exchanges, royalties from mines, wells, and other natural deposits, and gain on sales of timber, coal, and iron ore where the taxpayer retains an economic interest in the property.[96] The election does not apply to interest received on mortgage notes secured by U.S. realty, dividends from corporations whose assets include real property, or rents or royalties from lessees or licensees of personal property.[97] Also, for nonresident aliens, the election's effect is restricted to property held for the production of income, thus excluding gains on sales of personal residences.

Deductions connected with income covered by the election are allowed to an electing taxpayer.[98] Typically, the principal reason for making the election is to obtain the benefit of deductions for depreciation, interest, real property taxes, and operating expenses. If the taxpayer is actually engaged in a trade or business in the United States, the election only applies to U.S. real property income that would not otherwise be effectively connected with the U.S. trade or business, but this income is aggregated with other effectively connected income of the taxpayer in computing the tax under §871(b) or §882(a). Also, deductions connected with real property income covered by the election are aggregated with deductions connected with other effectively connected income.

Until 1980, the election usually had costs as well as benefits because several of the categories of income covered by the election (most importantly, gains on sales) were exempt from U.S. tax in the absence of the election. In 1980, however, Congress enacted §897, which subjects foreigners' gains on sales of U.S. real property to the effectively connected income tax whether or not the gains are actually connected with a U.S. business or the taxpayer elects to treat real property income as effectively connected income.[99] After the enactment of §897, a foreign person usually gives up no advantage by making the election, and the

---

[95] The election may be revoked without IRS consent for the first year to which it applies if the revocation is made before the expiration of the statute of limitations on assessments for that year. Reg. §1.871-10(d)(1). Consent is thus required only to revoke for years after the year for which the election is made. If the election applies for one or more years and is then revoked with IRS consent, the revocation disqualifies the taxpayer from electing again until the revocation has been in effect for five taxable years or the IRS consents to a new election. IRC §§871(d)(2), 882(d)(2); Reg. §1.871-10(d)(2).

[96] See Reg. §1.871-10(b)(1) ("the election may not be made with respect to only one class of such income").

[97] Reg. §1.871-10(b)(2). When a lease covers both real and personal property, rents are allocated between the two classes of property in proportion to their fair market values unless the lease expressly provides a different allocation. Reg. §1.871-10(b)(3).

[98] Reg. §1.871-10(c)(1).

[99] See infra ¶66.4 for §897.

election usually has the sole effect of avoiding the harshness of the 30 percent tax on gross rents.

The election does not cause the taxpayer to be treated as engaged in a U.S. trade or business for any other purpose.[100] For example, in determining the character of gain on a sale or exchange of U.S. realty covered by the election, the property is treated as a capital asset, not property used in a trade or business.[101] Also, because there is no trade or business in fact, the net operating loss deduction of §172 is not allowed to a noncorporate taxpayer.[102] Moreover, if a foreign person is actually engaged in business in the United States, a force of attraction rule described above treats income from U.S. sources other than FDAP items as effectively connected income whether or not an actual connection to the U.S. business exists.[103] Because the election affects only U.S. real property income, the force of attraction rule does not apply to an electing taxpayer who is not actually engaged in business in the United States.

¶66.3.7 Transportation Income

If a nonresident alien or foreign corporation has U.S. source income from air or water transportation activities or from the leasing or hiring out of a vessel or aircraft,[104] the income, unless exempted under a reciprocal exemption rule, is subject either to the effectively connected income tax or to a special 4 percent tax on gross income.

The effectively connected income tax applies if two tests are met. First, the taxpayer must carry on a trade or business in the United States and have "a fixed place of business in the United States involved in the earning of . . . transportation income."[105] Second, "substantially all" of the taxpayer's U.S. source transportation income must either be "attributable to regularly scheduled transportation" or, if the income consists of rents, be "attributable" to the taxpayer's fixed place of business in this country.[106] A foreign airline that operates regularly scheduled flights from an airport in the United States, for example, is subject to the effectively connected income tax if it has a fixed place of business here. A foreign corporation that operates tramp steamers, in contrast, is not subject to this tax, regardless of the extent of its operations in the United States.

If a foreign person has "United States source gross transportation income" that is not subject to the effectively connected income tax, a special 4 percent

---

[100] Reg. §1.871-10(c)(1).

[101] Reg. §1.871-10(c)(2).

[102] Id. See supra ¶25.11 for §172.

[103] See supra ¶66.3.3 text accompanying notes 47–49 for the force of attraction rule.

[104] For more on the income subject to these rules (collectively called "transportation income") and the source rules for this income, see infra ¶70.4.

[105] IRC §§887(b)(4)(A), (c).

[106] IRC §§887(b)(4)(B), (c).

gross income tax is imposed on the income.[107] The term "United States source gross transportation income" includes all gross income from transportation by sea or air that is from sources within the United States.[108] No deductions are allowed in computing this tax. If a foreign person has $100 of United States source gross transportation income and the income is not subject to the effectively connected income tax, the tax is $4 whether the taxpayer's transportation business produces net profit or loss. Income subject to the 4 percent tax is exempted from the 30 percent taxes of §§871(a)(1) and 881(a). A taxpayer subject to the 4 percent tax must file returns and pay the tax in the normal way because no withholding mechanism applies.[109] This tax was adopted in 1986 because "Congress believed that a tax based on gross U.S. source [transportation] income derived by foreign persons was the most practical way to collect U.S. tax on such income, unless the foreign person has a substantial and regular presence in the United States."[110]

A reciprocal exemption from these taxes is allowed. Income of a nonresident alien or foreign corporation from the operation of ships or aircraft is exempted from U.S. tax if an equivalent exemption is provided for citizens and corporations of the United States by the country in which taxpayer resides (in the case of an individual) or is organized (in the case of a corporation).[111] An exemption is also allowed for "income which is derived from the rental on a full or bareboat basis of a ship or ships or aircraft" if the taxpayer's home country provides an equivalent exemption.[112]

To prevent flag shopping, the exemption is generally denied to a foreign corporation if 50 percent or more of its stock (by value) is held (directly or by attribution through entities) by individuals who do not reside in the country in which the corporation is organized.[113] This bar is lifted, however, in three situations: (1) where at least 50 percent of the stock is held by persons who reside in some other foreign country granting an equivalent exemption to U.S. citizens and corporations, (2) where more than 50 percent of the stock is held by U.S. shareholders, and (3) where the taxpayer's stock or the stock of its parent "is primarily and regularly traded on an established securities market in [the] foreign country in which [the taxpayer] is organized."[114]

---

[107] IRC §887(a). See generally Rev. Proc. 91-12, 1991-1 CB 473.

[108] IRC §887(b)(1).

[109] See 1986 Bluebook, supra note 89, at 930 ("Congress was concerned that this method of collecting the tax would not yield adequate compliance" and therefore directed its committee staffs to study whether more effective methods are feasible).

[110] 1986 Bluebook, supra note 89, at 927 ("Congress further anticipated that increased U.S. taxation of persons from foreign countries that have not entered into reciprocal exemptions with the United States will encourage those countries to do so").

[111] IRC §§872(b)(1), (2); 883(a)(1), (2).

[112] IRC §§872(b)(5), 883(a)(4).

[113] IRC §883(c)(1). See 1986 Bluebook, supra note 89, at 927-28, 930-32.

[114] IRC §§883(c)(1), (2), (3).

Income tax treaties commonly contain provisions exempting residents of the treaty country from U.S. tax on income from shipping and air transportation "in international traffic," including income from the rental of ships, aircraft, and containers for international use.[115]

¶66.3.8 Withholding

Effectively connected income is not usually subject to withholding.[116] Rather, a nonresident alien or foreign corporation engaged in a trade or business in the United States is required to file a return and pay tax under the same rules that apply to U.S. citizens and residents and domestic corporations. There are a few exceptions, however, to the general rule of no withholding. Salaries and wages paid to nonresident alien employees working in the United States are subject to either withholding at 30 percent under §1441 or wage withholding on the same basis as U.S. employees.[117] Also, the withholding tax imposed by §1441 applies to a few items received by foreign students, researchers, and teachers.[118]

Moreover, under §1446, a partnership engaged in a trade or business in the United States must withhold from the distributive share of any "foreign partner," defined to include any partner who is a nonresident alien or a foreign corporation, partnership, trust, or estate.[119] The amount withheld is meant to cover the partner's liability for tax on the partnership's income effectively connected with U.S. business. A foreign partner is deemed engaged in any business in the United States carried on by the partnership, and is thus subject to the effectively connected income tax on his distributive share of the partnership's effectively con-

---

[115] See U.S. Treasury Dep't, Model Income Tax Treaty, art. 8 (1996) [hereinafter Model Treaty]. See also Organisation for Economic Co-operation and Development, Model Tax Convention on Income and on Capital, art. 8 (1992) [hereinafter OECD Model] (allowing international shipping and air profits to be taxed only by country in which is located taxpayer's "place of effective management"). See Rev. Rul. 97-31, 1997-32 IRB 4 (summarizing treaty provisions and agreements on shipping and aircraft operations); Rev. Proc. 91-12, 1991-1 CB 473, at §8 (procedures for claiming exemption under §872(b), §883, or income tax convention).

The United States has also made special agreements with several countries for reciprocal exemptions of shipping profits. See 1991-1 CB 304 (Chile); 1989-2 CB 332–338 (Cyprus, Finland, Peru, St. Vincent and the Grenadines, West Indies, and Taiwan);1991-1 CB 304 (Norway); 1991-1 CB 305 (Pakistan).

[116] IRC §§1441(c)(1), 1442(b), discussed supra ¶66.2B.

[117] See supra ¶66.2.12.

[118] See supra ¶66.2B.3 text accompanying notes 82–86.

[119] IRC §§1446(e), 7701(a)(30). Section 1446 applies for taxable years beginning after 1987. Pub. L. No. 100-647, §1012(s)(1)(A), 102 Stat. 3342, 3526–27 (1988). See S. Rep. No. 445, 100th Cong. 2d Sess. 320 (1988) (because §1446 is only a "reasonable collection mechanism," it does not conflict with nondiscrimination articles in treaties). See generally Onsager, The Tax Treatment of Real Estate Partnerships With Foreign Partners, 17 J. Real Est. Tax'n 126 (1990).

nected taxable income.[120] According to the Staff of the Joint Committee on Taxation, commenting on the enactment in 1986 of the statutory predecessor of §1446:

> Congress was concerned that the prior structure of the withholding rules applicable to foreign persons who invested in the United States through partnerships may have permitted passive investors to escape U.S. taxation on their income. Foreign persons who acquired U.S. partnership interests have frequently done so as portfolio investments, representing the functional equivalent of stock investments. In fact, interests in a number of U.S. partnerships have been publicly traded on stock markets in a manner indistinguishable from corporate stock. These types of partnership investments ordinarily do not represent the type of substantial and continuing U.S. presence that justifies the absence of a withholding requirement. Moreover, Congress did not believe that a partnership's conduct of a U.S. trade or business provided adequate assurance that its foreign partners would comply with U.S. tax laws even where the partnership is not publicly traded. In these cases, the investors were required to file U.S. tax returns and pay U.S. tax, but if they failed to do so the IRS was likely to find it nearly impossible to locate them and collect the tax. Therefore, Congress believed that all effectively connected income earned by foreign persons through U.S. partnerships should be subjected to U.S. withholding.[121]

Section 1446 applies to a partnership, domestic or foreign, if, for a particular year, (1) it is engaged in a trade or business in the United States, (2) it has at least one foreign partner, and (3) some portion of its effectively connected taxable income for the year is included in the distributive share of a foreign partner.[122] The term "effectively connected taxable income" includes taxable income of the partnership that is in fact effectively connected with a U.S. trade or business or is treated as effectively connected income under, for example, §897, pertaining to gains on dispositions of U.S. real property interests.[123] Taxable income is computed in the usual manner except that depletion allowances are allowed only on a cost basis and deductions allocable to U.S. partners are ignored.

---

[120] IRC §875(1), discussed supra ¶66.3.2.

[121] 1986 Bluebook, supra note 89, at 1055.

[122] Establishing which partners are foreign may not be a simple matter for many partnerships. A partnership can accomplish this by withholding under §1446 from the distributive shares of all partners, except those furnishing certificates of nonforeign status. Rev. Proc. 89-31, 1989-1 CB 895, §5.02. See id. §5.04 (sample certifications). The partnership may use other means of determining whether partners are U.S. or foreign, but it is liable for tax required to be withheld from any foreign partner that it mistakenly classifies as not foreign. Id. §5.03.

[123] IRC §1446(c). See infra ¶66.4 for §897. See Rev. Proc. 89-31, 1989-1 CB 895, §6.01 (determination of effectively connected taxable income).

The withholding rate is 39.6 percent if the foreign partner is an individual, partnership, trust, or estate or 35 percent if the partner is a foreign corporation.[124] The withholding rate is applied to the foreign partner's distributive share of the partnership's effectively connected taxable income for the year.[125] The term "distributive share" refers to the portion of the partnership's income that is credited to the partner's capital account; it has no relation to the distributions actually made by the partnership. The withholding tax thus is the same whether the partnership currently distributes all of its income or none of it. The reference to the partner's distributive share, rather than to distributions received by the partner, is appropriate because it is the distributive share of effectively connected taxable income that is included in the partner's return and subjected to the effectively connected income tax.[126]

Withholding under §1446 does not relieve a foreign partner of the obligation to file a return, but the amount withheld is allowed as a credit against the tax shown on the partner's return.[127] Also, the amount withheld is treated as though it were distributed in cash to the partner on the last day of the partnership's taxable year, which causes the amount to be subtracted from the partner's adjusted basis for his partnership interest and requires the recognition of gain by the partner to the extent the basis is not sufficient to absorb the reduction.[128]

¶66.3.9 Treaty Modifications

Under a typical income tax treaty, business profits of a resident of the other country joining in the treaty (the treaty country) may be taxed by the United

---

[124] See Rev. Proc. 89-31, 1989-1 CB 895, §7.01 (withholding tax must usually be paid in installments on fifteenth days of fourth, sixth, ninth, and twelfth months of partnership taxable year; safe harbor rule allows installments to be based on effectively connected income for preceding year); id. §7.02 (coordination with withholding under §§1441 and 1442). See also Rev. Proc. 92-66, 1992-2 CB 428, §3.03 (tax withheld by partnership under §1445 on U.S. real property gains allocated to foreign partners may be credited against amount required to be withheld under §1446).

[125] See Rev. Proc. 89-31, 1989-1 CB 895, §6.02 (determination of effectively connected taxable income).

[126] However, a publicly traded partnership must withhold from distributions unless it elects to withhold instead from distributive shares under the rules for nonpublicly traded partnerships. See Rev. Proc. 89-31, 1989-1 CB 895, §10. See also Rev. Proc. 92-66, 1992-2 CB 428, §3.02 (publicly traded partnership can obtain refund if it overpays withholding tax).

[127] IRC §§33, 1446(d)(1). See Rev. Proc. 89-31, 1989-1 CB 895, §9. The credit is allowed for the taxable year of the partner that includes the last day of the partnership's taxable year. The partner's distributive share must be reported on the return for the same year. IRC §706(a).

[128] IRC §§731(a)(1), 733, discussed infra ¶87.1.1.

States only if the taxpayer has a permanent establishment in the United States and the profits are attributable to the permanent establishment.[129]

The Treasury's model treaty defines the term "permanent establishment" as "a fixed place of business through which the business of an enterprise is wholly or partly carried on" and gives as examples an office, factory, mine, and place of management.[130] The site of a construction, installation, or natural resource exploration project is a permanent establishment only if the project continues in that location for at least 12 months, but the idea of permanence is not otherwise defined. A facility is not a permanent establishment if it is used solely for purchasing, storing, displaying, or delivering goods, collecting information, or carrying on any other activity of a "preparatory or auxiliary character." Also, a person is not deemed to have a permanent establishment in the United States merely because the person maintains a stock of goods in this country for processing by another person.

A fixed place of business of an independent agent of the taxpayer is not attributed to the taxpayer if the agent acts for the taxpayer in the ordinary course of the agent's business.[131] In contrast, a foreign taxpayer with a dependent agent in the United States is deemed to have a permanent establishment in the country if the agent has and "habitually exercises" authority to make contracts for the principal and the agent's activities go beyond purchasing and other preparatory

---

[129] For the concept of residence under treaties, see supra ¶65.2.8 (re individuals) and ¶65.3 (re entities). For income tax treaties generally, see supra ¶65.1.6.

[130] United States Model Income Tax Convention of September 20, 1996, art. 5 [hereinafter Treasury Model]. The model treaty of the Organisation for Economic Co-operation and Development is identical. Organisation for Economic Co-operation and Development, Model Double Taxation Convention on Income and on Capital art. 5 (1992) [herein OECD Model]. See generally Skaar, Permanent Establishment: Erosion of a Tax Treaty Principle (Kluwer 1991); Hershberger & Siegel, PE or No PE—That Is the Question, 9 Tax Notes Int'l 1993 (Dec. 26, 1994) (emphasis on U.S.-Mexico treaty); Peschcke-Koedt, A Practical Approach to Permanent Establishment Issues in a Multinational Enterprise, 16 Tax Notes Int'l 1601 (May 18, 1998).
See also Unger v. CIR, 936 F2d 1316 (DC Cir. 1991) (under 1942 treaty with Canada, limited partnership's permanent establishment in United States is considered permanent establishment of each limited partner); Donroy, Ltd. v. US, 301 F2d 200 (9th Cir. 1962) (same); Rev. Proc. 98-7, 1998-1 CB __, §4.01(9) (IRS will not rule on whether taxpayer has permanent establishment in United States).

[131] Treasury Model, supra note 130, art. 5(6); OECD Model, supra note 130, art. 5(6). See Taisei Fire & Marine Ins. Co. v. CIR, 104 TC 535 (1995) (acq.) (U.S. agent of Japanese insurance companies, through which companies wrote reinsurance coverage, was agent of independent status because it "had complete discretion over the details of its work" and bore "entrepreneurial risk"); Madole, The Importance of Being Independent: The Taisei Case, 24 Tax Mgmt. Int'l J. 371 (1995); Reynolds & Stretch, First Tax Court Test of New IRS Approach to Agency Permanent Establishment: Service Loses, 83 J. Tax'n 169 (1995); Schwartz, Taisei: U.S. Agent Did Not Create Permanent Establishment, 6 J. Int'l Tax'n 292 (1995). See generally Madole, Agents as Permanent Establishments Under U.S. Income Tax Treaties, 23 Tax Mgmt. Int'l J. 281 (1994).

or auxiliary activities.[132] A foreign corporation is not deemed to have a permanent establishment in the United States merely because it is owned or controlled by a domestic corporation or a corporation engaged in business in the United States.[133]

If a resident of a treaty country carries on business in the United States through a permanent establishment, U.S. tax may be imposed at the statutory rates on any business profits that are attributable to the permanent establishment.[134] The term "business profits" includes income of any trade or business, including the rental of tangible personal property, the rental of films and video tapes, and the licensing of films and tapes for use in radio or television broadcasts.[135] The profits attributable to a permanent establishment are those that "it might be expected to make if it were a distinct and independent enterprise engaged in the same or similar activities under the same or similar conditions."[136] For example, if a foreign corporation residing in a treaty country maintains a branch in the United States that sells goods produced by the corporation in a foreign country, the profits attributable to the branch are computed as though the branch purchased the goods at an arm's length price from the foreign factory.[137] No business profits are attributed to a permanent establishment "by reason of the mere purchase" of goods.[138]

The business profits of a permanent establishment are determined with deductions for all expenses "incurred for the purposes of the permanent estab-

---

[132] Treasury Model, supra note 130, art. 5(5); OECD Model, supra note 130, art. 5(5).

[133] Treasury Model, supra note 130, art. 5(7); OECD Model, supra note 130, art. 5(7).

[134] Treasury Model, supra note 130, art. 7(1); OECD Model, supra note 130, art. 7(1).

[135] Treasury Model, supra note 130, art. 7(7). The OECD model uses the term "profits of an enterprise" rather than business profits and does not define the term.

[136] Treasury Model, supra note 130, art. 7(2). The OECD model uses very similar language, but adds the words "and dealing wholly independently with the enterprise of which it is a permanent establishment." OECD Model, supra note 130, art. 7(2). See North West Life Assurance Co. v. CIR, 107 TC No. 19 (1997) (under corresponding article of U.S.-Canada treaty, profits of permanent establishment are "based on the facts as they relate to [the] permanent establishment, by reference to the establishment's separate accounts," and article therefore overrides §842(b), which imputes minimum amount of effectively connected income to U.S. trade or business of foreign insurance company); Rev. Rul. 81-78, 1981-1 CB 604 (rules defining statutory term "effectively connected" used to construe term "attributable to" under treaty provision on permanent establishments).

[137] The OECD model allows the profits of a permanent establishment to be determined by apportionment if the results are "in accordance with the principles" of the treaty. OECD Model, supra note 130, art. 7(4). The OECD model also requires the profits of a permanent establishment to be "determined by the same method year by year unless there is good and sufficient reason to the contrary." Id. art. 7(6).

[138] Treasury Model, supra note 130, art. 7(4); OECD Model, supra note 130, art. 7(5).

lishment," including "a reasonable allocation" of executive and general administrative expenses, interest, research and development costs, whether incurred in the United States or a foreign country.[139]

The rules for business profits do not apply to any type of income for which the treaty makes special provision.[140] Some of specially treated types of income are described below.

1. *Real property.* Treaties typically do not restrict U.S. taxation of income from real property in this country.[141] Some treaties allow residents of treaty countries owning U.S. real property to elect to treat the property as a permanent establishment subject to the business profits rules.[142]

2. *Shipping and air transport.* A resident of a treaty country is usually exempted from U.S. tax on income from shipping and air transportation "in international traffic," including income from the rental of ships, aircraft, and containers for international use.[143]

3. *Personal services.* Treaties often contain several provisions affecting U.S. taxation of income of residents of treaty countries from personal services performed in the United States.[144] Under the Treasury's model treaty, income of an individual from "the performance of personal services in an independent capacity" is taxable by the United States if the services are performed in this country and the income is attributable to a fixed base maintained by the individual in the United States.[145] Services are apparently rendered in an "independent capacity" unless the individual is an employee.

Compensation for services performed in the United States as an employee is generally subject to U.S. taxation, but treaties commonly allow two exemptions.[146] The broadest applies if (1) the employee is present in the United States for no more than 183 days during the taxable year, (2) the employer is not a resident of the United States, and (3) the compensation is not "borne" by a permanent establishment of the employer in this country. The second exemption applies to "a member of the regular complement of a ship or aircraft operated in international traffic."

---

[139] Treasury Model, supra note 130, art. 7(3); OECD Model, supra note 130, art. 7(3).

[140] Treasury Model, supra note 130, art. 7(6); OECD Model, supra note 130, art. 7(7).

[141] Treasury Model, supra note 130, art. 6; OECD Model, supra note 130, art. 6.

[142] Treasury Model, supra note 130, art. 6(5). The election resembles an election allowed by statute, which is discussed above in ¶66.3.6. The OECD model does not provide this election.

[143] Treasury Model, supra note 130, art. 8; OECD Model, supra note 130, art. 8.

[144] See also Treasury Model, supra note 130, art. 18(1) (U.S. may not tax pensions received by residents of treaty country); OECD Model, supra note 130, art. 18 (same).

[145] Treasury Model, supra note 130, art. 14. See OECD Model, supra note 130, art. 14 (same rule provided for "professional services or other activities of an independent character").

[146] Treasury Model, supra note 130, art. 15; OECD Model, supra note 130, art. 15.

The foregoing rules, however, do not apply to an entertainer, musician, or athlete residing in a country having a treaty with the United States based on the Treasury model.[147] Such an individual (hereinafter "entertainer") is subject to U.S. tax on amounts earned in the United States unless these earnings are less than $20,000 for the taxable year. If the entertainer is independent, this rule applies whether or not he has a fixed base in the United States. If he is an employee, it applies regardless of the amount of time he is present in the United States during the taxable year.

Also, an agent or employer of an entertainer deriving income from U.S. activities of the entertainer is subject to U.S. tax on the income, even if it falls within an exempting rule of the treaty, unless the agent or employer is shown not to be a front for the entertainer.[148] This rule applies whenever income accrues to a person other than an entertainer from U.S. activities of the entertainer. When the rule applies, the person is subject to U.S. tax on the income, even if it would normally be exempt under the treaty rules for business profits or independent personal services, unless it is shown that no portion of the income will flow to the entertainer or a related person through deferred compensation, bonuses, fees, dividends, partnership distributions, or any other means. If this showing is made, the regular rules for business profits or independent personal services apply.

An additional exemption is provided for government workers. Under the Treasury's model treaty, the United States may not tax compensation received by an employee of the government of a treaty country or an employee of a political subdivision of that country unless the employee works in a business carried on in the United States by the treaty country or a political subdivision.[149]

Most income tax treaties also have exemptions for some personal-services income of students, teachers, and researchers. For example, under article 20 of the U.S.-Germany treaty, a "professor or teacher" who is a resident of Germany is exempt from U.S. tax on amounts received for teaching, advanced study, or research in the United States for a period not exceeding two years, and a German resident present in the United States as a full-time student or "business trainee" for a period not exceeding four years is exempt from U.S. tax on up to $5,000 annually in personal services income from U.S. sources.[150]

4. *Treaty shopping rules.* Under the Treasury's model, an entity is denied all treaty benefits, even if it is a resident of the treaty country, if it is owned by

---

[147] Treasury Model, supra note 130, art. 17(1). The OECD model is the same except that it does not contain the $20,000 floor. OECD Model, supra note 130, art. 17(1).

[148] Treasury Model, supra note 130, art. 17(2). The OECD model states the rule even more broadly. OECD Model, supra note 130, art. 17(2).

[149] Treasury Model, supra note 130, art. 19. See OECD Model, supra note 130, art. 19.

[150] See Rev. Proc. 87-9, 1987-1 CB 368 (procedures for claiming teacher and researcher exemptions under 28 designated treaties); Rev. Proc. 87-8, 1987-1 CB 366 (procedures for claiming student exemption under 17 designated treaties); Rev. Proc. 93-22, 1993-2 CB 535 (revising foregoing procedures for residents of Cyprus, Germany, Finland, Indonesia, India, Spain, Indonesia, Tunisia, and former Soviet republics).

nonresidents or functions as a conduit for transmitting income from U.S. sources to persons who are not residents of the treaty country.[151]

¶66.4 GAINS ON DISPOSITIONS OF U.S. REAL PROPERTY INTERESTS

¶66.4.1 Introductory

The United States generally does not tax foreign persons' gains on sales and exchanges of property unless the gains are effectively connected with business done in this country.[1] The principal reason for this is that Congress has traditionally believed that tax on nonbusiness income of foreign persons can feasibly be collected only by withholding and that withholding on gains on sales of property is not feasible. A significant inroad into the exemption of nonbusiness capital gains was made by the enactment in 1980 of §897.[2] Under §897(a)(1), gain or loss of a nonresident alien or foreign corporation on a disposition of a U.S. real property interest is deemed to be effectively connected with a trade or business carried on in the United States, even if the property was a wholly passive investment of the taxpayer. The gain or loss is combined with income, gain, or loss for the taxable year from any business actually carried on by the taxpayer in this country and, if the taxpayer so elects, with other nonbusiness income from real property in the United States.[3] Under §871(b) or §882(a), the taxpayer's effectively connected taxable income (including the §897(a)(1) gain or loss) is taxed at the rates provided by §1 or §11.

---

[151] Treasury Model, supra note 130, art. 16, discussed supra ¶66.2.11. The OECD model does not contain this provision.

[1] See infra ¶66.2.8 text accompanying note 123, ¶66.2.9.

[2] See generally Foreign Investment in U.S. Real Estate (Powers, Ed.; ABA Section of Real Prop., Prob. & Tr. Law 1990); Austrian & Schneider, Tax Aspects of Foreign Investment in U.S. Real Estate, 45 Tax Lawyer 385 (1992); Feder & Parker, The Foreign Investment in Real Property Tax Act of 1980, 34 Tax Lawyer 545 (1981); Feingold & Alpert, Observations on the Foreign Investment in Real Property Tax Act of 1980, 1 Va. Tax Rev. 105 (1981); Frechter, Alien Land Ownership in the United States: A Matter of State Control, XIV Brooklyn J. Int'l L. 147 (1988); Kaplan, Creeping Xenophobia and the Taxation of Foreign-Owned Real Estate, 71 Geo. LJ 1091 (1983); Maiers, Foreign-Owned United States Real Estate: Post FIRPTA Tax Planning, 37 Tax Lawyer 577 (1984); Richards, Reporting and Disclosure Requirements for the Foreign Investor in U.S. Real Estate, 25 Real Prop., Prob & Tr. J. 217 (1990); Rubin, New Audit Guidelines in the IRS Manual Target FIRPTA Transactions, 80 J. Tax'n 170 (1994). See also Nutter, Statistics of Income Studies of International Income and Taxes, 13 Statistics of Income Bull. 10, 24 (Winter 1993-1994) (for 1992, 10,097 withholding tax returns were filed reporting sales subject to §897, showing total amount realized of $1.5 billion and tax withheld of $120 million); Rudnick, Taxing Foreign Investment in Real Property, 13 BU Int'l LJ 395 (1995) (surveying approaches for taxing such investments under income and other taxes).

[3] For the election to treat U.S. real property as a trade or business, see supra ¶66.3.6.

Section 897 was enacted in 1980 because Congress believed it

> essential to establish equity of tax treatment in U.S. real property between foreign and domestic investors .... [T]he United States should not ... provide an inducement through the tax laws for foreign investment in U.S. real property which afford the foreign investor ... mechanisms to minimize or eliminate his tax on income from the property while at the same time effectively exempting himself from U.S. tax on the gain realized on disposition of the property.[4]

Section 897 applies to gain or loss on a disposition of a "United States real property interest" (USRP interest), defined to include a direct interest in real property in the United States and stock in a domestic corporation whose assets consist principally of U.S. real property interests.[5] Also, a disposition of an interest in a partnership or trust holding a USRP interest is treated as including a disposition of the taxpayer's ratable share of the USRP interest, and gain or loss on this disposition within a disposition is subject to §897. The rules for dispositions of interests in entities holding U.S. real property were included because "otherwise, a foreign investor could ... avoid tax on the gain by holding the real estate through a corporation, partnership, or trust and disposing of his interest in that entity rather than having the entity itself sell the real estate."[6]

Originally, the §897 tax was not enforced by withholding, but an elaborate reporting system was provided to give the Treasury information on all foreign interests in real property in this country. In 1984, Congress abandoned the reporting system, and established a separate withholding mechanism for the collection of tax imposed by §897.[7]

The Treasury's Model Income Tax Treaty reserves to the United States the right to tax residents of treaty countries on gains "from the alienation of real property ... situated" in this country.[8] It also allows a U.S. tax on gain from a sale of stock of a corporation whose assets consist principally of U.S. real property and on gain on a sale of an interest in a partnership, trust, or estate to the extent the gain is attributable to the entity's U.S. real property holdings.[9] Other

---

[4] H.R. Rep. No. 1167, 96th Cong., 2d Sess. 511, reprinted in 1980-2 CB 530, 571.

[5] See infra ¶¶66.4.2, 66.4.3.

[6] H.R. Rep. No. 1167, supra note 4, at 511, reprinted in 1980-2 CB 571.

[7] See infra ¶66.4.10.

[8] U.S. Treasury Dep't, Model Income Tax Treaty, art. 13(1) (1981) [hereinafter Treasury Model]. The OECD Model is the same, except that it uses the term "immovable property," instead of "real property." Organisation for Economic Co-operation and Development, Model Tax Convention on Income and on Capital, art. 13(1) (1992).

See Rev. Rul. 90-37, 1990-1 CB 141 (agreement between United States and Argentina exempting residents of each country from other country's taxes on income from international operations of ships and aircraft does not exempt Argentine enterprise from §897 tax on gain from sale of U.S. real property used in shipping or airline business).

[9] Treasury Model, supra note 8, at 13(2). The OECD Model does not contain this provision.

treaties are less generous in the grant of U.S. taxing authority. Also, Congress foresaw that the §897 tax on a foreign corporation's distribution of U.S. real property to shareholders might conflict with nondiscrimination articles of treaties, and it provided an election as the exclusive remedy for this discrimination.[10]

¶66.4.2 USRP Interests—Direct Ownership

Section 897 applies to all interests in real property located in the United States or the Virgin Islands.[11] The term "real property" includes "land and unsevered natural products of the land," buildings, other "inherently permanent" structures, and the structural components of buildings and structures.[12] The unsevered natural products of land include growing crops, timber, and mineral deposits.[13]

The term "real property" also includes "personal property associated with the use of the real property."[14] The regulations identify six types of personal property that are considered associated with the use of real property: (1) movable walls and furnishings; (2) mining equipment; (3) farm machinery and other equipment used to "cultivate the soil and harvest its products"; (4) equipment used predominantly to construct real property improvements; (5) beds and other furniture owned by the owner or operator of a lodging facility and used predominantly in the operation of the facility; (6) office furniture and equipment provided by a lessor for the use of lessees of furnished office space.[15] Personal property not within any of these categories is considered not associated with the use of real property. Associated personal property is usually treated as a USRP interest even if it is disposed of separately from the real property, except that the link with the real property is sometimes considered broken where the personal property is disposed of a substantial period of time before or after the real property.[16]

All forms of ownership of real property may be USRP interests, including leasehold interests and options to buy or lease real property.[17] Partial interests,

---

[10] See infra ¶66.4.7.

[11] IRC §897(c)(1)(A)(i).

[12] Reg. §1.897-1(b)(3).

[13] Reg. §§1.897-1(b)(1), (2). However, the severance of crops or timber or the extraction of minerals is not a disposition of a USRP interest. Reg. §1.897-1(g). Thus, operating revenues of a farm, timber property, mine, or well are not taxable under §897, and the §897 gain or loss on a disposition of farm or timber land or a mine or well is computed by excluding from the amount realized any portion of the price attributable to severed crops, timber, or mineral deposits.

[14] IRC §897(c)(6)(B).

[15] Reg. §1.897-1(b)(4)(i).

[16] Reg. §1.897-1(b)(4)(ii).

[17] IRC §897(c)(6)(A).

including mineral royalties, life estates, remainders, reversions, and "rights of refusal in real property," can also be USRP interests.[18]

In contrast, an interest in real property solely as creditor may not be a USRP interest.[19] An interest is not solely as creditor, however, if it includes "any direct or indirect right to share in the appreciation in the value of, or in the gross or net proceeds or profits generated by, the real property."[20] For example, under a shared appreciation mortgage, the mortgagee's right to a portion of the proceeds on the sale of the mortgaged property is an interest in the property that goes beyond a mere creditor's interest. Also, a production payment is more than a creditor's interest if the holder's rights are not limited to fixed dollar amounts. A secured creditor's right to repossess or foreclose, however, does not elevate his rights above those of a mere creditor.[21]

¶66.4.3 USRP Interests—Stock of Domestic Corporations

An interest in a domestic corporation, "other than an interest solely as a creditor," is a USRP interest if the corporation was "a United States real property holding corporation" (USRP holding corporation) at any time during the five years preceding the taxpayer's disposition of the interest.[22] Although this rule most frequently applies to corporate stock, it is phrased in a way intended to cover any equity interest in the corporation, whether or not formally labeled stock. For example, debt convertible into stock is an interest not "solely as creditor" and thus may be a USRP interest.[23] In the ensuing discussion, the word "stock" is used to include all such interests.

Stock of a foreign corporation is never a USRP interest. When a foreign person owns stock in a domestic corporation, the assets of which are predomi-

---

[18] H.R. Rep. No. 1167, supra note 4, at 513, reprinted in 1980-2 CB 571-72.

[19] Reg. §1.897-1(c)(1). In some cases, interests held solely as creditor are aggregated with equity interests, and the aggregate is treated as an equity interest. Reg. §1.897-1(d)(4).

[20] Reg. §1.897-1(d)(2). See Reg. §§1.897-1(d)(2)(ii)(D), (E), (F) (no right to share in appreciation where taxpayer holds obligation bearing interest at indexed rates, is entitled to commission or fee for arranging purchase, sale, lease, or financing of real property, or is a fiduciary whose fee is measured as a percentage of assets).

[21] Reg. §1.897-1(d)(2)(ii)(C).

[22] IRC §897(c)(1)(A)(ii). In determining the taxability of gains and losses on dispositions before June 19, 1985, §897 only applies if the corporation was a USRP holding corporation after June 18, 1980.

If an interest in a partnership or trust is regularly traded on an established securities market, it is treated as corporate stock for this purpose, whether or not the entity is classified as a corporation for other tax purposes. Reg. §1.897-1(c)(2)(iv). For special rules for interests in REITs, see §897(h); Reg. §1.897-1(c)(2)(I).

[23] H.R. Rep. No. 1167, supra note 4, at 514, reprinted in 1980-2 CB 572. See Reg. §1.897-1(d)(3). For cases where an interest held solely as creditor may be aggregated with an equity interest and the aggregate treated as an equity interest, see Reg. §1.897-1(d)(4).

nantly USRP interests, appreciation in the value of the interests is taxed indirectly by taxing the foreign shareholder's gain on a disposition of stock in the corporation. In contrast, when a foreign person owns stock in a foreign corporation, the appreciation is taxed when the corporation disposes of its USRP interests, not when the shareholder sells his stock.

1. *USRP holding corporation.* A domestic corporation is a USRP holding corporation whenever it holds USRP interests having an aggregate fair market value that equals or exceeds 50 percent of the fair market value of the corporation's real property and business assets, including its USRP interests, its interests in real property located outside the United States, and all other assets used in a trade or business, wherever located.[24] A corporation that holds a USRP interest as its principal asset, for example, is a USRP holding corporation. A corporation that holds a USRP interest and a portfolio of securities is also a USRP holding corporation, even if the securities predominate the corporate assets, because the securities are not counted in applying the 50 percent test.

2. *Valuations.* For purposes of the 50 percent test, corporate assets are valued at the price at which they would change hands between a willing buyer and seller, neither being under compulsion to buy or sell and both having a reasonable knowledge of the facts.[25] An asset's gross value is reduced by purchase money mortgages and secured debt incurred in refinancing purchase money obligations. Also, if business assets or foreign real property is purchased for the purpose of reducing the testing percentage below 50, the values of these assets are reduced by any amounts owing on loans obtained to finance the purchases. Otherwise, asset values are not diminished by liabilities.

The regulations provide a presumption that sometimes obviates the need for determining the fair market value of corporate assets. A domestic corporation is presumed not to be a USRP holding corporation as of any date on which the book values of its USRP interests do not exceed 25 percent of the book values of the corporation's USRP interests, foreign real property, and business assets.[26] "Book value" is the amount at which an asset is carried on financial accounting records kept consistently with generally accepted accounting principles as applied in the United States. Unless the corporation has "reason to believe" that it does not pass the 50 percent test on the basis of asset value, the book value presumption is effectively conclusive until the corporation receives written notice from the IRS that it may not rely on the presumption.[27]

3. *Determination dates—generally.* If the statutes were applied literally, a nonresident alien or foreign corporation selling or exchanging stock of a domestic

---

[24] IRC §897(c)(2). For the term "asset used or held for use in a trade or business," see Reg. §1.897-1(f).

[25] Reg. §1.897-1(o)(2). See Reg. §1.897-1(o)(3) (fair market value of leases and options), §1.897-1(o)(4) (fair market value of other intangibles).

[26] Reg. §1.897-2(b)(2).

[27] See Reg. §1.897-2(b)(2)(iv) Ex. 2 (corporation has "reason to know" where it receives offer to purchase USRP interest at price exceeding likely value of all other assets).

corporation would have to apply the definition of USRP interest minute by minute over the entire time the stock was held (or if shorter, the preceding five years) in order to determine whether the corporation was a USRP holding corporation at any time during that period. The regulations soften the rigor of the statute by providing that the definition need only be applied on specified determination dates.[28] Generally, during each taxable year of the corporation, the determination dates are (1) the last day of the year, (2) any day on which the corporation acquires a USRP interest, and (3) any day on which the corporation disposes of foreign real property or a business asset. Also, if the corporation's assets are deemed to include its ratable share of the assets of another entity under one of the look-through rules described below, a determination date occurs whenever the other entity acquires a USRP interest or disposes of foreign real property or a business asset.

The foregoing rules are modified by several exceptions for routine business transactions and for acquisitions and dispositions that do not mark major shifts in corporate assets. Determination dates are not triggered by dispositions of inventory or livestock or by cash payments to meet regular operating needs of a business.[29] Also, acquisitions of USRP interests and dispositions of business assets are disregarded until the acquisitions and dispositions since the last determination date exceed prescribed ceilings. If the corporation's USRP interests accounted for less than 25 percent of the relevant asset pool on the most recent determination date, the ceiling on USRP interest acquisitions is 10 percent of the fair market value of the USRP interests on the most recent determination date, and the ceiling on business asset dispositions is 10 percent of the fair market value of the business assets on that date. If the USRP interests comprised at least 35 percent of the asset pool on the most recent valuation date, the ceiling is 2 percent. A 5 percent ceiling is provided for intermediate cases.

Assume a domestic corporation's assets on a particular determination date consist of USRP interests worth $50 and business assets worth $160.[30] Since the value of the USRP interests makes up less than 25 percent of the total ($50/$210 is 23.8 percent), the 10 percent ceiling applies, and the corporation can, without triggering another determination date, acquire up to $5 of additional USRP interests and dispose of up to $16 of business assets.

Moreover, even if a corporation has several determination dates within a year, property need not be valued more often than annually. For determination dates other than at year-end, each asset may be assigned a value equal to its fair market value on the last day of the preceding year or, if later, when the asset was acquired.[31] Determinations within a year are made only to account for acquisitions and dispositions.

---

[28] Reg. §1.897-2(c).

[29] Reg. §1.897-2(c)(2).

[30] Reg. §1.897-2(c)(2) Ex. 1.

[31] Reg. §1.897-2(c)(4).

4. *Determination dates—monthly alternative.* An elective alternative is provided to the foregoing rules under which a domestic corporation generally determines whether it is a USRP holding corporation as of the end of each calendar month.[32] A corporation choosing this alternative must, however, make a determination within a month if it acquires USRP interests or disposes of business assets or foreign realty for a price exceeding 5 percent of the aggregate value of the corporation's USRP interests, foreign real property, and business assets as of the end of the preceding month. In each determination other than the one at year-end, each asset may be valued at its fair market value as of the end of the preceding year or, if later, the date of the asset's acquisition.[33] The election might be advantageous for a corporation that makes frequent purchases of USRP interests or sales of foreign real property or business assets because it avoids the need for reapplying the 50 percent tests at the time of each such purchase or sale unless the transactions affect more than 5 percent of the property in the relevant class.

5. *Look-through rule where domestic corporation controls foreign corporation.* If a corporation (the parent) owns 50 percent or more of the fair market value of all classes of the stock of another corporation (the subsidiary), the definition of USRP holding corporation is applied by treating the parent as owner of a proportionate share of each asset of the subsidiary.[34] Also, the parent's shareholdings in the subsidiary are excluded from the parent's assets, and the parent's share of the subsidiary's business assets are treated as business assets of the parent.[35] Assume domestic corporation *P* owns 90 percent of the stock of *S* Corp., which might be domestic or foreign. *S* owns farm land in Minnesota and carries on a business in New York. The issue of whether *P* is a USRP holding corporation is determined by aggregating *P*'s directly owned assets together with 90 percent of the value of *S*'s Minnesota land and 90 percent of the value of the assets of *S*'s New York business. The rule applies successively. For example, if *S* owns 90 percent of the stock of *S1* Corp., the rule attributes 90 percent of *S1*'s assets to *S*, and then reattributes 90 percent of this 90 percent to *P*.

6. *Domestic corporation with noncontrolling interest in another corporation.* If a domestic corporation owns less than 50 percent of the stock of another

---

[32] Reg. §1.897-2(c)(3).

[33] Reg. §1.897-2(c)(4).

[34] IRC §897(c)(5). With a few modifications, the constructive ownership rules of §318(a) are used in determining whether the parent's ownership of the subsidiary is at least 50 percent. IRC §897(c)(6)(C); Reg. §1.897-2(e)(3). According to the regulations, (1) the parent's proportionate share of the subsidiary's assets is its "percentage ownership interest" multiplied by the fair market value of the assets, (2) the percentage ownership interest at any particular time is the ratio of the amount the parent would receive if the subsidiary then liquidated to the amounts distributable to all shareholders in this liquidation, and (3) the hypothetical liquidation distributions are determined as though all options to acquire stock from the subsidiary were exercised immediately before liquidation. Reg. §1.897-1(e)(2).

[35] Reg. §1.897-2(e)(3).

corporation and the latter is a USRP holding corporation, the former's stock-holdings in the latter are treated as a USRP interest in determining whether it is a USRP holding corporation. Assume domestic corporation P owns 10 percent of the stock of domestic corporation S. S's sole asset is a tract of land located in the United States. S is a USRP holding corporation, and the S stock held by P is thus a USRP interest. If the value of the S stock, when added to the value of any other USRP interests P holds, amounts to at least 50 percent of the aggregate value of P's real property interests and business assets, P is also a USRP holding corporation, and any stock of P held by a foreign person is a USRP interest. The same procedure would be followed through successive tiers if, for example, S held stock of another corporation.

Moreover, for the limited purpose of applying this rule, a foreign corporation may be a USRP holding corporation.[36] Assume a foreign corporation, whose sole asset is Minnesota farmland, has two shareholders, a domestic corporation and a nonresident alien individual. For purposes of determining whether the domestic corporation is a USRP holding corporation, the foreign corporation is treated as a USRP holding corporation, and the domestic corporation's share-holdings are thus a USRP interest. The stock of the foreign corporation held by the nonresident alien, however, is not a USRP interest.

7. *Partners and beneficiaries of trusts and estates.* In applying the USRP holding corporation definition, assets held by partnerships, trusts, and estates are considered owned ratably by their partners and beneficiaries.[37] For example, if domestic corporation P is a 50 percent partner in a partnership owning Minnesota farmland, P is treated as owning one half of the land in determining whether P is a USRP holding corporation. An asset owned by a partnership, trust, or estate and used in the entity's trade or business is treated as a business asset when attributed to the partners or beneficiaries. Also, the attribution rule is applied successively to tiered arrangements. Assume a domestic corporation is a partner of partnership $P1$, which is a partner of partnership $P2$, which is a partner of partnership $P3$. The USRP holding corporation definition is applied to the corporation by treating it as owner of a ratable portion of all of the assets of $P1$, $P2$, or $P3$ (exclusive of the partnership interests held by $P1$ and $P2$).

8. *Five-year rule.* If a domestic corporation is a USRP holding corporation at any moment in time, stock of the corporation held by a foreign shareholder is

---

[36] IRC §897(c)(4)(A); Reg. §1.897-2(e)(1).

[37] IRC §897(c)(4)(B); Reg. §1.897-2(e)(2). The regulations provide that (1) a partner's ratable share of a partnership asset is the partner's "percentage ownership interest" in the partnership multiplied by the asset's fair market value, (2) the percentage ownership interest at any particular time is the ratio of the amount the partner would receive if the partnership then liquidated to the amounts distributable to all partners in this liquidation, and (3) the hypothetical liquidation distributions are determined as though all options to acquire partnership interests from the partnership were exercised immediately before liquidation. Reg. §1.897-1(e)(2). For a beneficiary's proportionate share of the assets of a trust or estate, see Reg. §1.897-1(e)(3).

usually a USRP interest for five years thereafter, regardless of whether the corporation meets the definition of USRP holding corporation at any time during those five years.[38] Assume a domestic corporation owns farm land in Minnesota worth $100, which is initially the corporation's only asset. On January 1, 1996, the corporation purchases beach property in the Bahamas for $400. The corporation ceases to be a USRP holding corporation on January 1, 1996, but under the general rule, its stock continues to be a USRP interest until at least January 1, 2001. For example, if stock in the corporation is sold by a nonresident alien or foreign corporation during 1999, any gain on the sale is taxed under §897(a)(1).

However, if the selling shareholder held the stock for less than five years, the stock is not a USRP interest unless the corporation was a USRP holding corporation at some time while the taxpayer owned the stock. If the shareholder in the example bought her stock in 1997 and sold it in 1999, gain or loss on the sale would not be caught by §897 because, although the corporation was a USRP holding corporation during the five-year period ending with the sale, it never had this status while the taxpayer held the stock.

Moreover, the taint disappears immediately if the corporation disposes of all of its USRP interests in taxable transactions.[39] The object of §897 is to tax appreciation in the value of U.S. realty that is attributable to the interest of a foreign person. Stock of a USRP holding corporation is tainted for five years to make it difficult for taxpayers to frustrate this policy by diluting corporate assets to fall below the 50 percent mark. The exception is provided because the policy to collect a tax on the appreciation is satisfied once the corporation has disposed of all of its assets in taxable transactions.

Assume a nonresident alien individual is sole shareholder of a domestic corporation whose only asset is Minnesota farmland.[40] The corporation liquidates by distributing the land to the shareholder, and §336(a) requires the corporation to recognize gain on the distribution as though the property had been sold for a price equal to its fair market value. Because the distribution is a taxable disposition, the stock ceases to be a USRP interest at the instant of the distribution, and the shareholder's gain or loss on the liquidation is not subject to §897.

---

[38] IRC §897(c)(1)(A)(ii). For dispositions occurring before June 19, 1985, stock of a domestic corporation is a USRP interest only if the corporation was a USRP holding corporation at some time after June 18, 1980 while the taxpayer held the interest disposed of.

[39] IRC §897(c)(1)(B); Reg. §1.897-2(f)(2). A USRP interest is deemed disposed of for this purpose if it consists of stock of another domestic corporation and this stock ceased to be a USRP interest by reason of the application of the rule described in the text to the issuer of the stock. Assume domestic corporation P owns a minority shareholding in S, which is initially a USRP holding corporation but loses this taint by reason of a sale of all of its USRP interests. P is deemed to dispose of its S stock in a taxable transaction at the time of S's sale of its USRP interests.

[40] See Reg. §1.897-5T(b)(5) Ex. 1.

This rule applies, however, only if the corporation holds no USRP interests at the time of the stock sale and all USRP interests held by the corporation at any time during the preceding five years (or if less, during the period when the shareholder held the stock) were disposed of in transactions in which all gain was recognized. Assume a USRP holding corporation sells all of its USRP interests and reinvests the proceeds in a business, a minority of whose assets consists of real property located in the United States. A nonresident alien or foreign corporation selling stock of the corporation during the interval between the sale and the reinvestment qualifies for the exception. Once the reinvestment is made, the normal five-year taint reappears, even though the corporation's USRP interests then account for less than 50 percent of its business and real property assets.

9. *Publicly traded stock.* Some publicly traded stock is excepted from §897. If stock of a domestic corporation is regularly traded on an established securities market, it usually is not a USRP interest, regardless of the makeup of the corporate assets.[41] If the corporation has more than one class of stock, the exception applies to stock of a particular class only if shares of that class are publicly traded. Also, the benefit of the exception is lost if the taxpayer owned more than 5 percent of the stock of the publicly traded class at any time during the five years preceding the disposition in which the gain or loss is recognized.[42]

10. *Establishing that stock is not USRP interest.* Generally, a noncreditor interest in a domestic corporation is a USRP interest unless the taxpayer establishes that the corporation was not a USRP holding corporation at any time during the five years preceding the disposition (or if less, the period during which the taxpayer owned stock).[43] The taxpayer can meet this burden by getting a statement from the corporation or obtaining a determination by the Director of the Foreign Operations District of the IRS.[44]

A statement by the corporation that its stock is not a USRP interest meets the shareholder's burden of proof only if the corporation has observed a notice procedure.[45] Under this procedure, the corporation must, within a reasonable period of time, respond to a foreign shareholder's request that he be informed of whether the corporation's stock is a USRP interest. The corporation's response need not be in any particular form, but it must be signed by a corporate officer under penalties of perjury. Generally, the corporation must provide the same

---

[41] IRC §897(c)(3); Reg. §1.897-9T. See Reg. §1.897-1(m) ("established securities market" includes domestic or foreign national securities exchange or over-the-counter market). This exclusion can also apply to an interest in a trust or partnership. Reg. §1.897-1(c)(2)(iv), discussed supra note 22.

[42] The constructive ownership rules of §318(a) apply in determining whether a foreign person holds more than five percent of the stock of a particular class. IRC §897(c)(6)(C).

[43] IRC §897(c)(1)(A)(ii).

[44] Reg. §1.897-2(g).

[45] Reg. §1.897-2(h).

information to the IRS no later than 30 days after the statement is mailed to the shareholder. In lieu of notifying the IRS of statements to particular shareholders, however, the corporation may include a statement of its status with its tax returns.

If the taxpayer makes a request to the corporation more than 90 days before the due date of the taxpayer's return for the year of the disposition and the corporation fails to respond within 30 days, the taxpayer can request that the IRS determine from records available to it whether the stock is a USRP interest. The taxpayer can furnish information to the IRS to aid this determination.

¶66.4.4 USRP Interests Held Through Partnerships, Trusts, and Estates

If a foreign person sells or exchanges an interest in a partnership, trust, or estate, the transaction is treated for purposes of §897 as a disposition of the partner's or beneficiary's proportionate interest in the assets of the entity.[46] If the entity owns a USRP interest, a portion of the amount realized in the sale or exchange is considered received for a USRP interest, and gain or loss is computed separately for this indirect disposition. The separately computed gain or loss is subject to §897. Whether a partnership, trust, or estate is domestic or foreign is not relevant to the application of this rule.

Assume a partnership owns land in Minnesota and a portfolio of securities. A nonresident alien partner of the partnership sells her interest. A portion of the amount realized and a portion of the partner's basis for the partnership interest is allocated to the partner's indirect interest in the land. The difference between these two figures is gain or loss on a disposition of a USRP interest.

---

[46] IRC §897(g). According to the regulations, (1) a partner's ratable share of a partnership asset is the partner's "percentage ownership interest" in the partnership multiplied by the asset's fair market value, (2) the percentage ownership interest at any particular time is the ratio of the amount the partner would receive if the partnership then liquidated to the amounts distributable to all partners in this liquidation, and (3) the hypothetical liquidation distributions are determined as though all options to acquire partnership interests from the partnership were exercised immediately before liquidation. Reg. §1.897-1(e)(2). For a beneficiary's proportionate share of the assets of a trust or estate, see Reg. §1.897-1(e)(3).

The rule described in the text does not apply to an interest in a partnership or trust if the interest is of a class that is regularly traded on an established securities market. Rather, the interest is treated as corporate stock, even if the entity is not classified as a corporation for other tax purposes, and may be a USRP interest under the rules for stock. Reg. §1.897-1(c)(2)(iv).

See generally Milani & Wrappe, Dispositions of U.S. Real Property Interests by Foreign Partners—Tax Provisions, Pitfalls, and Planning Possibilities, 20 J. Real Est. Tax'n 149 (1993).

¶66.4.5 Modifications of Nonrecognition Rules

Section 897 makes three modifications of nonrecognition rules in order to reduce opportunities for avoiding the §897 tax on appreciation in the value of a USRP interest accruing while a foreign person is the direct or indirect owner of the interest.

First, under §897(e)(1), a nonrecognition rule can apply to a foreign person's disposition of a USRP interest only if the transaction is an exchange and the taxpayer would be subject to U.S. tax on any gain recognized on a sale of the property received in the exchange.[47] For example, an exchange of a USRP interest for another USRP interest can qualify for nonrecognition unless gain on a sale of the property received in the exchange would be exempt from U.S. tax under a treaty.[48] Assume a nonresident alien transfers land located in the United States to a domestic corporation in exchange for stock of the corporation. If the domestic corporation is a USRP holding corporation immediately after the exchange, the nonrecognition provided by §351(a) is not overridden by §897(e)(1) because both the property exchanged and the property received are USRP interests.[49] In contrast, gain or loss on an exchange of a USRP interest for property that is not a USRP interest is normally recognized even if the exchange fully satisfies the conditions of a nonrecognition rule. Assume a foreign person exchanges Minnesota farmland for land in the Bahamas. The exchange is of like kind property, and gain or loss on the exchange would normally not be recognized under §1031(a).[50] However, because the property given in the exchange is a USRP interest while the property received is not, gain or loss is recognized for purposes of §897.

Second, §897(j) requires that gain be recognized when a foreign person contributes an appreciated USRP interest to the capital of a foreign corporation. The recognized gain equals the excess of the property's fair market value over the sum of the transferor's adjusted basis for the property and any gain recognized by the transferor on the transfer apart from §897(j). Under §897(e)(1), described above, a foreign person transferring a USRP interest in exchange for stock or securities of a foreign corporation must recognize any gain realized in the exchange, notwithstanding the nonrecognition rule of §351, because the stock or securities received in the exchange are not USRP interests. Section 897(j) merely requires the same result when the transferor is an existing shareholder and receives no additional stock or securities in exchange for the transfer of the USRP interest.

---

[47] See Reg. §1.897-5T(d). For the application of this rule to exchanges in corporate reorganizations, see Reg. §1.897-6T. For the rule's application to the liquidation of a USRP holding corporation into a foreign parent corporation, see Reg. §1.897-5T(b)(3).

[48] H.R. Rep. No. 1167, supra note 4, at 512, reprinted in 1980-2 CB 571.

[49] Rev. Rul. 84-160, 1984-2 CB 125.

[50] See supra ¶44.2 for §1031.

Third, under §897(d)(1), a nonrecognition rule that would otherwise protect a foreign corporation from recognizing gain on a distribution of appreciated property to shareholders is inapplicable if the distributed property is a USRP interest.[51] Because gains on sales of stock of foreign corporations are never taxable under §897, the tax on the corporation itself is the only means by which §897 reaches USRP interests held by a foreign corporation, and Congress decided that the corporation should not be able to avoid this tax through nonrecognition rules.

However, most of the nonrecognition rules attacked by §897(d)(1) were repealed in 1986. Assume a foreign corporation owning farmland in Minnesota distributes the land in complete liquidation to its shareholders, all of whom are nonresident aliens. Section 336(a), before amendment in 1986, provided that a corporation recognized no gain or loss on the distribution of its property to shareholders in complete liquidation.[52] In the example, §897(d)(1) overrode §336(a), requiring the corporation to recognize gain (but not loss) as though the property distributed to shareholders had been sold for a price equal to its fair market value. As amended in 1986, however, §336(a) requires gain or loss to be recognized with respect to all property distributed in complete liquidation. Also, §311(b)(1), as amended in 1986, requires a corporation to recognize gain on a distribution of appreciated property to shareholders as a dividend or in a nonliquidating redemption of stock. When the amended §§311(b)(1) and 336(a) apply, §897(d)(1) merely duplicates those provisions.

Moreover, most of the cases excepted from the amended §§311(b)(1) and 336(a) are also excepted from §897(d)(1). Under §897(d)(2)(A), a foreign corporation is allowed the benefit of a nonrecognition provision applicable to a distribution of a USRP interest to a shareholder if (1) the distributee's adjusted basis for the property is no higher than the corporation's basis for it and (2) the distributee would be taxed on gain realized on a sale of the interest immediately after its distribution.[53] Assume a domestic corporation, whose only asset is Minnesota farmland, distributes the land in complete liquidation to its sole shareholder, a foreign corporation. Under §§332 and 337, neither corporation recognizes gain or loss on the liquidation, and §334(b) requires that the parent take the subsidiary's adjusted basis for its property.[54] Section 897(d) does not disturb these results because (1) the parent's adjusted basis for the land is not higher than the subsidiary's basis and (2) the parent would be taxed under §897 on gain realized on a sale of the land immediately after the liquidation.[55]

---

[51] IRC §897(d)(1); Reg. §1.897-5T(c).

[52] See infra ¶93.7.

[53] IRC §897(d)(2)(A).

[54] See infra ¶93.6 for subsidiary to parent liquidations.

[55] Notwithstanding §§332 and 337, a foreign corporation must usually recognize gain on a liquidating distribution of a USRP interest if (1) the corporation's parent is a domestic corporation, (2) the foreign corporation has not elected to be treated as a domestic corporation under §897(i), (3) gain on a foreign person's sale of stock of the

¶66.4.6   Special Basis Rule for Property Received in Distributions

Under §897(f), if a foreign shareholder of a domestic corporation receives a USRP interest in a distribution from the corporation, the shareholder's adjusted basis for the property immediately after the distribution may not exceed the sum of (1) the corporation's adjusted basis immediately before the distribution, (2) gain recognized by the corporation on the distribution, and (3) any tax paid by the shareholder on income or gain recognized on the receipt of the property. The significance of this rule was largely eliminated by the 1986 amendments to the corporate tax rules.

Assume a domestic corporation makes a dividend distribution to a foreign shareholder consisting of a USRP interest that is worth $500 and has an adjusted basis to the corporation of $100. Under §311, as it existed before the 1986 amendments, the distributing corporation might have recognized no gain or loss on the distribution.[56] Assume the distribution is a dividend to the shareholder, but the shareholder resides in a foreign country that has a tax treaty with the United States limiting the U.S. tax on the dividend to 5 percent. Under §301(d), a shareholder's basis for property received in a dividend distribution equals its fair market value when received. If the corporation qualified for nonrecognition under the pre-1986 §311, the fair market value basis under §301(d) would effectively make the 5 percent dividend tax the only tax on the $400 of appreciation in the USRP interest that accrued up to the time of the distribution. Section 897(f) preserved the potential for a future tax on most of this appreciation by limiting the shareholder's basis to $125—the sum of $100 (the corporation's basis), zero (gain recognized by the corporation on the distribution), and $25 (the shareholder's tax on the dividend (5 percent of $500 or $25)).

Under the 1986 amendments, §897(f) has no effect, but the results to the taxpayers are even less advantageous. Under the amended §311(b), the corporation recognizes the $400 of appreciation in the property's value when the distribution is made. The shareholder takes a basis equal to the property's value of $500 under §301(d). The §897(f) ceiling is $525—the sum of the corporation's basis of $100, the corporation's gain on the distribution of $400, and the shareholder's tax of $25—and has no application because it is higher than the basis otherwise allowed to the shareholder. While the pre-1986 statutes merely kept alive the possibility of taxing the shareholder on $375 in the future, the 1986 amendments substitute an immediate corporate tax on $400.

---

foreign corporation's stock on the date of the liquidation would be subject to §897 if a §897(i) election were in effect, and (4) during the five years preceding the liquidation, at least one sale of the foreign corporation's stock was made under circumstances that would have caused gain to be taxed under §897 if a §897(i) election had been in effect. Reg. § 1.897-5T(c)(2)(ii)(B).

[56] See infra ¶92.3.2.

¶66.4.7 Election by Foreign Corporation to be Treated as Domestic Corporation

Congress feared that the certain aspects of §897 would lead foreign corporations to claim discrimination in violation of nondiscrimination articles of treaties.[57] For example, the pre-1986 nonrecognition rules that applied to many corporate distributions to shareholders were made inapplicable to a foreign corporation's distribution of a USRP interest.[58] Although the benefit of these nonrecognition rules was denied to ensure that a foreign corporation holding USRP interests and its shareholders fared no better than a domestic corporation and its shareholders would have in similar circumstances, a foreign corporation, viewed in isolation from its shareholders, was subject to taxes not imposed on domestic corporations.

To forestall the discrimination claim, a foreign corporation is allowed to elect to be treated as a domestic corporation for purposes of §897 if it holds a USRP interest, directly or through another entity, and is entitled to the benefits of a nondiscrimination article of a treaty with respect to its USRP interests.[59] Although the pre-1986 corporate nonrecognition rules provided the primary impetus for the enactment of the election rule, the election remains available after the repeal of those rules. It is the exclusive remedy for any person claiming to be discriminated against in the application of §897.[60]

The election must include a waiver of all treaty benefits with respect to gains and losses on dispositions by the electing corporation of USRP interests, and it must also include the corporation's consent to be treated as a domestic corporation in determining its tax on these gains and losses.[61] Also, the corporation's shareholders must join in the election and agree to be taxed on dispositions of their shares under the rules of §897 that would apply if the corporation were domestic.[62] The persons joining in the election must include "all of the owners of all classes of interests (other than interests solely as a creditor)," excepting holders of less than 5 percent of any class that is regularly traded on an established securities exchange. The election is revocable only with IRS consent.[63]

Normally, the §897(i) election must be made before any shareholder disposes of stock in a transaction that would have been taxable under §897 if the

---

[57] See Treasury Model, supra note 8, art. 24.

[58] See supra ¶66.4.5.

[59] IRC §897(i); Reg. §1.897-3(b). For the application of §897(i) to Netherlands Antilles corporations, see Notice 88-1, 1988-1 CB 471; Notice 88-53, 1988-1 CB 538.

[60] IRC §897(i)(4).

[61] Reg. §1.897-3(c).

[62] IRC §897(i)(3). The corporation normally must file the shareholder's consents with the corporation's election. However, in lieu of filing these consents, the corporation may include a legend on stock certificates warning shareholders of the §897(i) election. Reg. §1.897-3(c)(4)(ii).

[63] IRC §897(i)(2); Reg. §1.897-3(f).

corporation had always been domestic.[64] However, a stock disposition in a non-recognition transaction does not disqualify the corporation from later electing if the transferee in the transaction took the transferor's basis. Also, an earlier stock disposition in a transaction that would have been taxable under §897 does not disqualify the corporation if it either (1) makes the election retroactive to a date before the disposition and includes with the election an agreement by the shareholder to pay the §897 tax or (2) pays to the IRS an amount equal to the §897 tax the shareholder would have been paid if the election had always been in effect.[65] An antiabuse rule is provided to prevent the shareholder-level tax from being avoided by a combination of sales and nonrecognition transactions before the effective date of a §897(i) election.[66]

An electing foreign corporation is treated as a domestic corporation only for purposes of §897 and the withholding, reporting, and return requirements that accompany §897.[67] The corporation is taxed as a domestic corporation on any gain or loss on a disposition of a USRP interest or of property received in a nonrecognition exchange for a USRP interest. It is not, however, treated as a domestic corporation for any other purpose. For example, if the corporation has income or gain of other types, the rules for foreign corporations determine how the income or gain is taxed, and deductions for items other than losses on dispositions of USRP interest are only allowable under the rules for foreign corporations.

¶66.4.8   Computation of §897 Tax

Under §897(a)(1), gain or loss of a nonresident alien or foreign corporation on a disposition of a USRP interest is treated for purposes of the effectively connected income tax as though the taxpayer were engaged in business in the United States and the gain or loss were effectively connected with the business. This rule applies whether the taxpayer's ownership and operation of real property investments in the United States is actually a business or the taxpayer is a wholly passive investor having no business in this country.

Rules of general application determine the character of the gain or loss (e.g., as capital gain or loss or as ordinary income or loss), and determine the deductibility of any loss. Loss on a nonresident alien's disposition of a USRP interest is deductible only under §165(c), which allows an individual to deduct a loss only if it is incurred in a trade or business or a transaction entered into for profit or is a casualty loss.[68] For example, loss on a sale of a house or apartment used for

---

[64] Reg. §1.897-3(d)(1).

[65] For the application of this rule under the U.S.-Canada income tax treaty, see Notice 89-85, 1989-2 CB 403.

[66] Reg. §1.897-3(e).

[67] IRC §897(i)(1); Reg. §1.897-3(a).

[68] See supra ¶25.3 for §165(c).

personal purposes is not deductible because §165(c) does not allow losses on dispositions of property held for personal use.[69]

The gains and allowable losses on dispositions of USRP interests are combined with the income and deductions for the taxable year of any business that the taxpayer may actually carry on in this country. If the taxpayer has elected under §871(d) or 881(d) to treat income from U.S. real property as effectively connected income, the income and deductions covered by this election are also aggregated with the §897 gains and losses.[70] For example, if operating income or loss from the real property prior to its sale is effectively connected income, either because the taxpayer's operation of the property is a U.S. trade or business or because the taxpayer elected to treat it as such, the operating income or loss is aggregated with the §897 gain or loss. The aggregate is taxable income effectively connected with the conduct of business in the United States.

This taxable income is taxed under the rules that apply generally to effectively connected income.[71] The alternative minimum tax rules, however, are modified to ensure that the amount subject to the alternative minimum tax for a year in which §897 gains are realized is not less than the net gain on dispositions of USRP interests.[72] Generally, the policy of §897 is to tax nonresident aliens on §897 gains in the same way as a citizen or resident would be taxed on the gain. The special floor on the alternative minimum tax base was thought justified, even though no such floor applies to a citizen or resident, because nonresident aliens, whose taxable incomes include no items of foreign derivation, tend for this reason to be in lower tax brackets than their domestic equivalents.

¶66.4.9 Annual Filing Requirement

A nonresident alien or foreign corporation "holding direct investments" in USRP interests must file an annual return describing the interests and providing other information that the IRS might require.[73] A foreign person is a holder of direct investments in USRP interests if (1) the individual or corporation is not engaged in a trade or business in the United States and (2) the fair market value of the person's USRP interests equals or exceeds $50,000 at any time during the year.[74] For purposes of the $50,000 floor, only interests "held directly by such person" are counted, but this restriction has little consequence because stock of a domestic corporation can be a directly owned USRP interest and USRP interests held by partnerships, trusts, and estates are treated as owned proportion-

---

[69] H.R. Rep. No. 1167, supra note 4, at 512, reprinted in 1980-2 CB 571.
[70] See supra ¶66.3.6 for this election.
[71] See supra ¶66.3.
[72] IRC §§55(b)(1)(A); 897(a)(2).
[73] IRC §6039C(a).
[74] IRC §6039C(b).

ately by their partners and beneficiaries.[75] Moreover, in determining whether the $50,000 floor is reached or exceeded, an individual's USRP interests are aggregated with those of his spouse and minor children.

¶66.4.10   Withholding

Under §1445, a buyer of a USRP interest from a foreign seller must withhold amounts from the purchase price to cover any §897 tax on the seller's gain. More broadly, the withholding requirement applies to any transferee receiving a USRP interest from a foreign person in a transaction that is a disposition of the interest for purposes of §897.[76] The obligation usually arises when the transferee receives the USRP interest, whether the consideration for the transfer is cash or property of another kind and whether it is delivered to the transferor at the time of the disposition or at a later time.[77] When the requirement applies, 10 percent of the amount realized by the transferor must usually be withheld and remitted to the IRS, but procedures are provided for tailoring the amount withheld more closely to the transferor's tax under §897. A person who fails to withhold when obligated to do so is personally liable for the amount required to be withheld unless the transferor's tax on gain recognized on the transfer is fully paid or established to be zero.[78]

When §897 was enacted in 1980, Congress relied on an elaborate reporting system as the primary enforcement mechanism for the tax. Section 1445 was enacted in 1984, after experience had shown the reporting system to be difficult to implement and ineffective. As the staff of the Joint Committee on Taxation reported in 1984:

> A major problem with [§897] under prior law was that it could often be easily evaded. Since the tax was not due until a tax return was filed after the end of the year, a foreign person could sell his or her U.S. real estate, take the proceeds out of the United States, and since he or she was beyond the jurisdiction of the United States, not pay any tax to the United States on the sale. Moreover, through nominees and foreign corporations established in tax havens, he or she could reinvest these untaxed proceeds back in the United States with impunity.[79]

Although the Joint Committee staff believed that §1445 was "designed so that complication of real estate transactions and uncertainty regarding withholding

---

[75] IRC §6039C(c)(3).

[76] IRC §1445(a); Reg. §1.1445-2(a). See ABA Sec. of Tax'n Comm. on Sales, Exchanges and Basis, Report on the Application of Sections 1031 and 1445 to Exchanges of U.S. Real Property by Foreign Persons, 48 Tax Lawyer 471 (1995).

[77] Reg. §1.1445-1(b)(1).

[78] Reg. §1.1445-1(e).

[79] Staff of Joint Comm. on Tax'n, 98th Cong., 2d Sess., General Explanation of the Revenue Provisions of the Deficit Reduction Act of 1984 at 406 (Comm. Print 1984).

liability should be minimal,"[80] the statute and regulation issued thereunder contain a plethora of rules elaborating on and modifying the withholding obligation imposed by §1445, including

1. An affidavit procedure for protecting a transferee from liability for the withholding tax where the transferor claims that he is not a foreign person or that corporate stock involved in the transfer is not a USRP interest.[81]
2. Exemptions from withholding for transactions covered by nonrecognition rules and treaty exemptions,[82] gifts,[83] transfers of property that the transferees intend to use as their personal residences,[84] and sales of publicly traded stock.[85]
3. A rule exempting the U.S. government and state and local governments from withholding.[86]
4. A requirement that a domestic partnership, trust, or estate with foreign partners or beneficiaries must pay the withholding tax when it sells a USRP interest.[87]
5. Rules requiring that a foreign corporation pay the withholding tax on a distribution of a USRP interest to a shareholder and that a domestic corporation pay the tax on a liquidating or redemption distribution to a foreign shareholder whose stock is a USRP interest.[88]
6. Special rules on options and the exercise of options.[89]
7. Procedures for obtaining certificates from the IRS reducing the withholding tax where the tax on the transferor's gain on the transfer is certain to be less than 10 percent of the amount realized.[90]
8. Reporting and payment rules for transferees subject to the withholding tax, including special rules on the timing of the tax payments on installment sales.[91]

1. *Affidavit procedure for establishing transferor is not foreign or stock is not a USRP interest.* Withholding is not required if the transferor is not a foreign person or the property is not a USRP interest. However, a transferee who fails to withhold usually is personally liable for any amount required to be withheld,

---

[80] Id. at 407.
[81] See infra text accompanying notes 92–101.
[82] See infra text accompanying note 102.
[83] See infra text accompanying notes 103–04.
[84] See infra text accompanying notes 105–07.
[85] See infra text accompanying notes 108–11.
[86] See infra text accompanying notes 112–13.
[87] See infra text accompanying note 114.
[88] See infra text accompanying notes 115–18.
[89] See infra text accompanying note 119.
[90] See infra text accompanying notes 122–30.
[91] See infra text accompanying notes 133–34.

even if the transferee acted on a good faith but mistaken belief that the transferor or the property was outside §897's ambit.

This liability can be avoided by utilizing an affidavit procedure. If the transferor makes an affidavit, "under penalty of perjury," that states he is not a foreign person[92] and gives his U.S. taxpayer identification number, the transferee is usually relieved of the obligation to withhold.[93] If a transferor refuses the transferee's request for such an affidavit, the transferee may withhold under §1445 even if the transferee has no knowledge of facts suggesting the transferor is foreign.[94]

Also, if the transaction is a disposition of stock of a domestic corporation, the transferee can rely on an affidavit of the corporation that it is not and during the preceding five years has not been a USRP holding corporation.[95] The transferee is also protected in relying on an affidavit of the corporation that it presently has no USRP interests and made taxable dispositions of any such interests it had during the preceding five years. The transferee is left to his own devices in determining whether property other than corporate stock is a USRP interest.

The protection usually provided by an affidavit is lost if the transferee has actual knowledge that the affidavit is false or if the transferee fails to comply with the IRS' request for a copy of it.[96] Also, an affidavit of the transferor or a corporation is nullified if an agent of the transferor or the transferee gives the transferee notice that the affidavit is false.[97] An agent is required to notify the transferee if the agent has "actual knowledge" that the affidavit contains a false statement.[98] An agent who has such knowledge but fails to notify the transferee is liable for the withholding tax up to the amount of the agent's compensation in the transaction.[99] Also, regardless of actual knowledge, this penalty falls on an agent for a corporate transferor that falsely swears to be a domestic corporation unless the agent ascertains the true facts and reports them to the transferee. The

---

[92] Reg. §1.1445-2(b)(2) (foreign persons include nonresident aliens and foreign corporations, partnerships, trusts, and estates, except that foreign corporation electing under §897(i) is not foreign for this purpose). But see Reg. §1.1445-2(b)(4)(ii) (if transferee knows transferor is foreign corporation, affidavit based on §897(i) election is not valid unless copy of IRS' acknowledgment of election is attached).

[93] IRC §1445(b)(2). See Reg. §1.1445-2(b)(3) (transferee must retain affidavit until end of fifth taxable year after year in which transfer occurs). For a sample affidavit, see Reg. §1.1445-2(b)(2)(iii).

[94] Reg. §1.1445-2(b)(1).

[95] IRC §1445(b)(3). See Reg. §1.1445-2(c)(3)(I) (corporation's affidavit must not be dated more than 30 days before date of transfer).

[96] IRC §1445(b)(7).

[97] IRC §1445(b)(7). But see Reg. §§1.1445-2(b)(4)(iv), (c)(3)(iii) (if transferee has no knowledge of affidavit's falsity until agent's notice is received, withholding obligation only applies to consideration delivered to transferor after notice is received).

[98] IRC §1445(d)(1); Reg. §1.1445-4.

[99] IRC §1445(d)(2).

term "agent" includes any person who represents the transferor or transferee in negotiations with the other party or the other party's agent or in settling the transaction.[100] A person is not considered an agent of either party, however, if he does no more than receiving and disbursing the sales proceeds, recording documents, typing or other clerical tasks, obtaining reports on the property, or delivering documents.[101]

2. *Transactions covered by nonrecognition rules and treaty exemptions.* A transferee is not obligated to withhold in some cases where the transferor claims that gain or loss qualifies for nonrecognition or is exempted from tax by treaty. This exemption applies if (1) the transferor provides a statement to the transferee that the transferor's gain or loss on the transaction is wholly nontaxable under a statutory nonrecognition rule or treaty provision and (2) the transferee provides a copy of the statement to the IRS within 20 days after the transfer.[102] The exemption applies even if the transferor's gain or loss is in fact taxable unless the transferee "knows or has reason to know" that the transferor does not qualify for nonrecognition or exemption under treaty.

3. *Gifts.* Since the withholding obligation is measured with reference to the amount realized by the transferor, nothing need be withheld when property is received by gift or in another transaction where the transferor's amount realized is zero.[103] However, the "amount realized" includes the amount of any liability that the transferee assumes or takes subject to.[104] A gift of encumbered property is therefore treated as part sale and part gift, and the withholding obligation applies to the sale portion of the transaction, although it is unclear what the donee withholds from when the donor makes no cash payment to the donor.

4. *Transferee's residence.* A transferee is exempt from the withholding requirement if the transferee is an individual who intends to use the property as his residence and the price does not exceed $300,000.[105] To satisfy the requirement that the property be used as the transferee's residence, the transferee must have "definite plans to reside" at the property for at least one half of the 24 months following the purchase, exclusive of periods when the property is expected to be vacant.[106] If the transferee rents the property out or puts it to some other nonresidential use for more than one half of this 24-month period, he is liable for the withholding tax unless his failure to use it for residential purposes at least one

---

[100] IRC §§1445(d)(3), (4).

[101] IRC §1445(d)(5); Reg. §1.1445-4(f)(3).

[102] Reg. §1.1445-2(d)(2). For the statement required where the transferor claims nonrecognition under §1034, see Reg. §1.1445-9T(b). For §1034, which allows nonrecognition of gain on a sale of a personal residence if another residence is acquired within two years before or after the sale, see supra ¶44.5.

[103] Reg. §1.1445-1(b)(1).

[104] Reg. §1.1445-1(g)(5)(iii).

[105] IRC §1445(b)(5).

[106] Reg. §1.1445-2(d)(1).

half of the time resulted from "a change in circumstances that could not reasonably have been anticipated at the time of the transfer."[107]

The foregoing rule looks solely to the transferee's use of the property. The withholding tax applies to property used by the transferor as a personal residence if the transferee intends to hold it for investment or for resale to customers.

5. *Publicly traded stock.* A transferee of stock of a class that is regularly traded on an established securities market need not withhold.[108] Also, no withholding is required by the purchaser of a publicly traded interest in a partnership or trust.[109] These exemptions can apply even if the transferor is taxed under §897 because he holds or has held more than 5 percent of the stock in the class.[110] Withholding is required, however, if the transferee acquires 5 percent or more of the publicly traded stock or partnership or trust interests in a single transaction from one foreign person.[111]

6. *Governmental transferees.* The U.S. government, the states and possessions of the United States and their political subdivisions, and the District of Columbia are exempted from withholding.[112] The withholding rules apply, however, to a foreign government acquiring a USRP interest.[113]

7. *Dispositions by domestic partnerships, trusts, and estates.* When a domestic partnership, trust, or estate recognizes gain on a disposition of a USRP interest, it must pay the withholding tax on any portion of the gain that is allocable to a foreign partner or beneficiary or, if the trust is a grantor trust, the gain allocable to any portion of the trust considered owned by a foreign person.[114] The amount to be withheld is usually 35 percent of the gain allocable to foreign partners, beneficiaries, or grantors. Assume a domestic partnership recognizes gain of $300 on a sale of a USRP interest; $100 of the gain is included in the distributive share of a partner who is a nonresident alien, and the remainder of the gain is allocable to partners who are U.S. persons. The partnership must pay a withholding tax of $35 on the gain.

If the partnership's or trust's disposition consists of a distribution of the USRP interest to a foreign partner or beneficiary, the distributing entity is not required to withhold unless the distribution triggers a tax under §897. Moreover,

---

[107] Id.

[108] IRC §1445(b)(6).

[109] Reg. §1.1445-2(c)(2).

[110] See supra ¶66.4.3 text accompanying notes 41–42 for the 5 percent rule.

[111] Reg. §1.1445-2(c)(2) (transactions within 90-day period and transactions pursuant to "prearranged plan" are treated as one transaction; acquisitions from transferors related under §267(b) or 707(b) are deemed made from one transferor).

[112] Reg. §1.1445-2(d)(5).

[113] Reg. §1.1445-10T(b)(2).

[114] IRC §1445(e)(1); Reg. §1.1445-5(c). See Reg. §1.1445-8 (if interests in partnership or trust are publicly traded, entity's withholding obligation arises only when proceeds of entity's sale of USRP interest are distributed to foreign partners or beneficiaries). See infra ¶80.1 for grantor trusts.

if the distribution is taxable, the amount to be withheld is determined under the general rule of §1445(a) and is usually 10 percent of the property's fair market value.

8. *Distributions by foreign corporations.* A foreign corporation recognizes gain, taxable under §897, on any distribution of a USRP interest to its shareholders.[115] Because the transferee-shareholders give no consideration from which tax could be withheld under §1445, the corporation must pay a withholding tax equal to 35 percent of its gain on the distribution.[116]

9. *Liquidating and redemption distributions by domestic corporations.* Section 897 usually applies to gain recognized by a foreign shareholder on the receipt of a distribution in liquidation or redemption of stock if the corporation has been a USRP holding corporation at any time during the five years preceding the distribution.[117] There is no transferee in such a transaction, however, because the stock retired in the liquidation or redemption simply ceases to exist. The statutes overcome this technical obstacle by requiring the corporation to withhold from the distribution as though it were the shareholder's transferee.[118]

10. *Options.* The grantee of an option to purchase a USRP interest from a foreign optionor need not withhold from the amount paid for the option, either when the option is granted or when it lapses.[119] If the option is exercised, the withholding rules apply to the resulting sale, and the amount paid for the option is then included in the optionor-seller's amount realized in computing the amount required to be withheld. Assume an individual pays $10 for an option to purchase Minnesota farmland from a foreign corporation for $100. The individual has no obligation to withhold when the option is purchased. If the option lapses unexercised, there is never an obligation to withhold. If the individual exercises the option, she must withhold when she acquires the property pursuant to the exercise. The amount required to be withheld under the general rule is $11, 10 percent of the sum of the $10 paid for the option and the additional $100 paid on exercise of the option.

Also, if an option to acquire a USRP interest is issued (sold) by a foreign owner of the interest, the buyer of the option must withhold from the purchase price.

11. *Amount required to be withheld—generally.* Normally, when §1445 applies, the transferee must withhold 10 percent of the amount realized by the transferor on the disposition.[120] The amount realized consists of the sum of (1) the

---

[115] See supra ¶66.4.5 text accompanying note 51.

[116] IRC §1445(e)(2); Reg. §1.1445-5(d). See Reg. §1.1445-7(c) (rule inapplicable to foreign corporation electing to be treated as domestic under §897(i)).

[117] See supra ¶66.4.1.

[118] IRC §1445(e)(3); Reg. §1.1445-5(e). See Reg. §1.1445-7(c) (rule applies to foreign corporation electing to be treated as domestic under §897(i)).

[119] Reg. §1.1445-1(b)(3).

[120] IRC §1445(a). See Reg. §1.1445-1(b)(2) (where transfer is made by joint owners and some but not all of them are foreign persons, amount realized is allocated among

cash paid or to be paid by the transferee, (2) the fair market value of property other than cash received or to be received by the transferor, and (3) the principal amount of any liability that the transferee assumes or that encumbers the property both before and after the transfer.[121] Assume a foreign corporation exchanges Blackacre, a USRP interest, for Whiteacre. The corporation's amount realized in the exchange equals the fair market value of Whiteacre, and the corporation's transferee (the former owner of Whiteacre) is therefore liable for withholding tax, payable in cash, equal to 10 percent of Whiteacre's value. Similarly, if a foreign person sells a USRP interest for $5 in cash plus the buyer's agreement to take the property subject to a $95 mortgage, the buyer's withholding obligation under the general rule is $10.

The 10 percent rule is modified by a procedure for tailoring the amount withheld more closely to the transferor's tax liability. At the request of the transferor or the transferee, the IRS must issue a withholding certificate specifying the transferor's "maximum tax liability."[122] The maximum tax liability is usually the largest amount of tax that could be imposed under §871(b) or 882(a) on the transferor's gain on the disposition.[123] The IRS normally computes this amount as the gain multiplied by the highest individual or corporate rate on long-term capital gain, but modifies the computation for reduced rates under treaties, statutory nonrecognition rules, losses recognized on dispositions of other USRP interests during the same taxable year, and ordinary income treatment under recapture or other rules.[124] Also, if the transferor acquired the property from another foreign person and failed to pay the entire amount required to be withheld under §1445 in the acquisition transaction, the unpaid amount is added to the maximum tax liability on the disposition.[125]

The IRS issues a certificate wholly excusing the transferee from withholding if the certificate application establishes that any gain realized by the transferor in the transaction is exempt from U.S. tax under a treaty or under §892, which exempts foreign governments and their controlled entities from tax on income not derived from commercial activities.[126] An exempting certificate is not issued, however, if the transferor incurred a withholding tax liability on acquiring the property and has not fully paid this tax.

---

transferors, one half to each where transferors are husband and wife and in proportion to capital contributions in other cases).

[121] Reg. §1.1445-1(g)(5).

[122] IRC §1445(c)(1)(B). For procedures for applying for withholding certificate and amendments of applications, see Reg. §§1.1445-3(b), (f); Rev. Proc. 88-23, 1988-1 CB 787. The IRS must respond to the application within 90 days. IRC §1445(c)(3)(B). See Reg. §1.1445-3(a) (request deemed received when all necessary information has been provided).

[123] IRC §1445(f)(4).

[124] Reg. §1.1445-3(c)(2).

[125] See Reg. §1.1445-3(c)(3) (application for withholding certificate must include evidence that any withholding obligation on transferor's acquisition was satisfied).

[126] Reg. §1.1445-3(d). For §892, see infra ¶66.7.

A withholding certificate either reducing or eliminating the withholding tax may also be issued to reflect an agreement between the transferor and the IRS on the payment of the transferor's tax on the gain.[127] Such an agreement must include provisions for security for the transferor's obligation to pay the tax and any interest on it accruing between the date the transferee would normally pay the withholding tax and the date the transferor will pay tax under the agreement. The security usually consists of a bond or letter of credit.

If a withholding certificate is issued before the disposition transaction, the transferee must withhold the lesser of the maximum tax liability specified in the certificate or 10 percent of the amount realized.[128] If the transfer is completed before the certificate is issued, the transferor may obtain a refund of any excess of the amount withheld over the maximum tax liability.[129]

Also, the IRS may, at the request of the transferor or transferee, reduce the withholding tax if it determines that the reduction does not "jeopardize the collection" of the §871(b) or §882(a) tax.[130] Such a reduction may be made without determining the transferor's maximum tax liability. If the maximum tax liability is determined, the reduced amount may be less than the maximum.

12. *Foreclosures.* A foreclosure or a transfer to a mortgagee in lieu of foreclosure is treated as a sale by the mortgagor for the amount of the mortgage,[131] and §897 and the accompanying withholding obligation under §1445 can apply to a foreign mortgagor's gain in such a transaction. The withholding obligation can often be a monkey wrench in the gears because, once the mortgage is foreclosed or the property is taken by the mortgagee in lieu of foreclosure, the mortgagor-transferor's equity is usually minimal. The regulations therefore often limit the amount required to be withheld in such a transaction to the amount received by the mortgagor.

Under the rule for foreclosures, the withholding obligation of the purchaser in a foreclosure sale usually may not exceed 100 percent of the amount the mortgagor is entitled to receive from the proceeds of the sale.[132] Assume Minnesota farmland held by a foreign person is sold in foreclosure for $410 in order to satisfy a $400 mortgage. Although the general rule of §1445 would require the buyer in the sale to withhold $41 (10 percent of $410), only $10—100 percent of the portion of the proceeds going to the mortgagor—need be withheld under the

---

[127] IRC §1445(b)(4); Reg. §1.1445-3(e). See Rev. Proc. 88-23, 1988-1 CB 787 (elaborating on the procedures described in the regulations and providing a procedure for obtaining a blanket exemption from withholding for all transactions occurring during a period as long as 12 months).

[128] IRC §1445(c)(1)(A).

[129] IRC §1445(c)(1)(C); Reg. §1.1445-3(g). See Reg. §1.1445-3(a) (application for refund may be made with request for withholding certificate).

[130] IRC §1445(c)(2). The IRS must respond within 90 days after such a request is received. IRC §1445(c)(3)(B).

[131] See supra ¶40.8.4.

[132] Reg. §1.1445-2(d)(3).

foreclosure rule. The companion rule for conveyances in lieu of foreclosure wholly relieves a transferee-mortgagee of the obligation to withhold if (1) the mortgagor receives no consideration other than the satisfaction of the mortgage, (2) the mortgagee pays nothing other than incidental fees to any person in connection with the transfer, and (3) the mortgagee is the only person having a security interest in the property.

However, the rule for foreclosures applies only if the mortgagor's interest in the sale proceeds is determined by a court or trustee having jurisdiction over the foreclosure. Moreover, various notice requirements must be satisfied in order for the rules for foreclosures and conveyances in lieu of foreclosure to be applicable. Also, the full rigors of the withholding requirement apply to a mortgagee who receives a conveyance in lieu of foreclosure as part of a scheme for avoiding withholding.

13. *Reporting and payment requirements.* Generally, an amount required to be withheld under §1445 must be paid to the IRS within 20 days after the transfer.[133] However, if application is made to the IRS for a withholding certificate no later than the date of the transfer and the application is not made principally to delay payment, the due date for payment is deferred until the twentieth day after the IRS mails to the transferee either a withholding certificate or a notice of denial of the certificate.

The transferee's payment of the withholding tax does not relieve the transferor of the obligation to file a return reporting the gain or loss on the transfer.[134] The IRS supplies to the transferor a copy of the withholding return filed by the transferee, and the transferor is entitled to credit for the withholding tax paid.

14. *Installment sales.* In an installment sale, the withholding tax on the entire purchase price is usually due at the time of the sale, although the IRS has provided a procedure for paying the withholding tax in installments as the purchase price is received.[135] Moreover, the withholding obligation is measured with reference to the face amounts of installment payments, not the fair market value of the installment note.[136] Deferred payments of stated or unstated interest or original issue discount, however, are not included in the amount realized.[137]

---

[133] See Reg. §1.1445-1(c)(1) (payment must be accompanied by Forms 8288 and 8288-A), §1.1445-1(g)(8) (transfer occurs when transferee first pays consideration, including assumption of liability but excluding earnest money or deposit).

[134] Reg. §1.1445-1(f).

[135] Reg. §1.1445-2(d)(4); Rev. Proc. 88-23, 1988-1 CB 787. The procedures for paying the withholding tax in installments are part of the withholding certificate procedures described above in note 127 and accompanying text.

[136] Reg. §1.1445-1(g)(5).

[137] For unstated interest and original issue discount, see supra Ch. 57.

¶66.5 BRANCH PROFITS TAX AND BRANCH-LEVEL INTEREST TAX

¶66.5.1 Introductory

Section 884, enacted in 1986, subjects foreign corporations engaged in business in the United States to a branch profits tax and a branch-level interest tax in addition to the regular tax on income effectively connected with the conduct of a trade or business in the United States.[1] Also, interest received from a U.S. trade or business of a foreign corporation is treated as income from U.S. sources and is therefore subject to the withholding tax of §871(a) or §881(a) if the recipient is a foreign person and the interest is of a type that is reached by that tax.[2]

The object of the branch profits tax is to burden a foreign corporation's U.S. business profits with roughly the same taxes whether the business is done through a domestic subsidiary or an unincorporated branch in the United States.[3] Income of a domestic subsidiary is potentially taxable twice. The subsidiary is subject to the regular corporate tax, and dividends from the subsidiary to the foreign parent are taxed by §881(a). If a foreign corporation's U.S. business is not separately incorporated but is operated as a branch, income effectively connected

---

[1] See IRC §884(e)(5) (international organizations exempted from branch taxes); H.R. Rep. No. 841, 99th Cong., 2d Sess. II-647 (Conf. Rep. 1986) (taxes apply to foreign corporations that have elected to be treated as a domestic corporation under §897(i)); Reg. §1.884-1(h) (foreign corporation treated as foreign corporation for purposes of branch taxes even if generally treated as domestic under §269B, relating to stapled entities). See supra ¶65.3 text accompanying notes 5–15 for stapled entities.

See generally Blessing, The Branch Tax, 40 Tax Lawyer 587 (1987); Brown, Federal Income Taxation of U.S. Branches of Foreign Corporations: Separate Entity or Separate Rules? 49 Tax L. Rev. 133 (1993); Feingold & Rozen, New Regime of Branch Level Taxation Now Imposed on Certain Foreign Corporations, 66 J. Tax'n 2 (1987); Lederman & Hirsh, Final Branch Regulations Fail to Clear the Thicket of Complexity, 78 J. Tax'n 110 (1993); Musher, Coping With the Branch Tax Temporary Regulations, 71 J. Tax'n 110, 186 (1989); N.Y. State Bar Ass'n Tax Section, The Branch Profits Tax: Issues to Be Addressed in the Regulations, 34 Tax Notes 607 (Feb. 9, 1987); N.Y. State Bar Ass'n Tax Section, More on the Branch Profits Tax, 37 Tax Notes 191 (Oct. 12, 1987); Reich, U.S. Federal Income Taxation of U.S. Branches of Foreign Banks: Selected Issues and Perspectives, 2 Fla. Tax Rev. 1 (1994).

[2] See supra ¶66.2 for the withholding tax.

[3] The Treasury first proposed the branch profits tax as a means of "plac[ing] the branch of a foreign corporation on a more comparable footing with a U.S. subsidiary of a foreign corporation." 2 Dep't of Treasury, Tax Reform for Fairness, Simplicity, and Economic Growth 369 (1984) [hereinafter cited as Treasury I]. The Conference Report on the 1986 legislation says the branch profits tax was enacted "to achieve greater parity between the remittance of branch profits and the distribution of subsidiary earnings." H.R. Rep. No. 841, supra note 1, at II-647. See also Staff of Joint Comm. on Tax'n, 99th Cong., 2d Sess., General Explanation of the Tax Reform Act of 1986 at 1036-38 (Comm. Print 1987) [hereinafter 1986 Bluebook].

with the U.S. business is taxed by §882(a).[4] The effectively connected income tax is imposed at the normal corporate tax rates and is generally equivalent to the tax a separate domestic subsidiary would pay. However, the profits of the U.S. branch are not subject to the withholding tax of §881(a) when the profits are repatriated to the corporation's head office because the repatriation is merely a transfer within the corporation, not a dividend. Moreover, these profits often escape the withholding tax when they are distributed to the foreign corporation's shareholders.[5] The branch profits tax of §884(a)—essentially, a withholding tax on withdrawals from a U.S. branch—generally substitutes for the withholding tax that would be imposed on dividends if the branch were incorporated as a domestic subsidiary.

The branch-level interest tax is intended to provide a similar parity for interest paid by foreign corporations engaged in business in the United States, either directly or through domestic subsidiaries.[6] When interest is paid by a domestic subsidiary engaged in business in the United States, the recipient's interest income is from sources within the United States, and if the recipient is a foreign person, it might be subject to the withholding tax under §871(a)(1) or §881(a).[7] In contrast, until the branch-level interest tax was adopted in 1986, interest received by a foreign debt holder from a foreign corporation with an unincorporated U.S. branch was wholly exempted from withholding taxes unless more than 50 percent of the corporation's worldwide income was effectively connected with business done in the United States.[8] Congress decided that regardless of the size of a U.S. branch in relation to a foreign corporation's worldwide operations, the withholding tax should apply to all interest deducted in determining effectively connected taxable income, except to the extent that the

---

[4] See supra ¶66.3.

[5] Under §861(a)(2), if 25 percent or more of a foreign corporation's gross income is effectively connected with U.S. businesses, a ratable portion of a dividend from the corporation is from U.S. sources, and this portion can be subject to the withholding tax if the shareholder is a foreign person. Many, perhaps most, foreign corporations with U.S. branches do not reach the 25 percent threshold. The Staff of the Joint Committee on Taxation concluded that before 1986, when the threshold was 50 percent, "nearly all foreign corporations with branches in the United States avoided liability for the withholding taxes . . . because their U.S. income was kept beneath the 50-percent threshold." 1986 Bluebook, supra note 3, at 1036-37. "Congress did not believe that U.S. jurisdiction over outbound payments should depend only on whether the amount of business conducted in the United States rose to some predetermined level." Id. at 1037.

When §884 was enacted, Congress exempted foreign persons from the withholding tax on dividends from a foreign corporation, except where the corporation is exempted from the branch profits tax by treaty. IRC §884(e)(3)(A).

[6] See H.R. Rep. No. 841, supra note 1, at II-648 to II-649.

[7] See supra ¶66.2.2.

[8] IRC §§861(a)(1)(C), (D); 871(a)(1)(A), 881(a)(1) (before amendment in 1986). When the withholding taxes applied, the taxable amount was a portion of the interest commensurate with proportion of the corporation's gross income that was effectively connected with U.S. business. IRC §861(a)(1)(D) (before amendment in 1986).

interest would be exempt if paid by a domestic corporation, because "a deduction allowed against gross U.S. effectively connected income generally should give rise to an inclusion subject to U.S. tax."[9] The interest expense of a U.S. branch, in other words, should be treated as nearly as possible in the same way as interest paid by a separately incorporated domestic subsidiary.

The branch taxes may be reduced or eliminated by income tax treaties, more or less in the same way the treaties apply to dividends and interest paid by domestic subsidiaries.[10] The rules, however, contain a prohibition on treaty shopping that disqualifies a foreign corporation from a treaty reduction of the branch taxes unless it is genuinely rooted in the treaty country and is not a vehicle for funneling treaty benefits to residents of third countries.

¶66.5.2 Branch Profits Tax

Generally, the branch profits tax is an annual tax equal to 30 percent of the "dividend equivalent amount."[11] The tax is payable with the corporation's return for the year, but it is not included in its estimated tax.[12] Because the branch profits tax is a substitute for the tax on dividends that would be imposed under §881(a) if a U.S. branch were a separately incorporated domestic subsidiary, the rate and the tax base are intended to replicate those of the dividend tax. Also, the branch profits tax may be reduced or eliminated by treaty, more or less in the same way as the §881(a) tax on dividends is affected by treaties.[13]

Normally, dividends are measured by looking to what the shareholder receives.[14] The branch profits tax base could be measured equivalently as the amount received by the head office as remittances from the U.S. branch. Congress concluded, however, that it is not feasible to measure what the head office receives. A tax on head office receipts might effectively be limited to cases where the U.S. branch is kept segregated from other assets and activities of the corporation. Also, Congress decided that the branch profits tax should apply when profits are withdrawn from a U.S. business and invested in passive assets, even if the passive assets are held in the United States.

Congress therefore looked instead to withdrawals from U.S. business activities, but concluded that even withdrawals cannot feasibly be measured directly. The amount deemed distributed from the branch's current earnings is measured indirectly as branch earnings less the portions of these earnings that are reinvested in branch operations. For a year in which the investment in the branch does not increase, all current earnings are deemed distributed, and the branch is

---

[9] 1986 Bluebook, supra note 3, at 1037.
[10] See infra ¶66.5.4.
[11] IRC §884(a).
[12] IRC §6655(g)(1).
[13] For the treaty rules, see infra ¶66.5.4.
[14] IRC §301(b), discussed infra ¶92.1.1.

deemed to have made a further distribution from accumulated profits equal to the amount of any decline in investment in the branch. The "dividend equivalent amount"—the branch profits tax base—thus is current branch earnings, decreased by any increase in the corporation's investment in the branch and increased (to the extent of previously reinvested earnings) by any decrease in that investment.

1. *Effectively connected earnings and profits.* A U.S. branch's current profits are called "effectively connected earnings and profits" (ECE&P).[15] This figure is computed by the rules used in determining the earnings and profits of a domestic corporation, except that only items effectively connected with the U.S. business are included and distributions are disregarded.[16] The effectively connected items taken into account include income and deductions actually connected with a U.S. business and items that are treated as effectively connected income and deductions because, for example, the corporation elects to treat income from U.S. real property as effectively connected income or has gains from dispositions of U.S. real property interests.[17] Also, if a foreign corporation is a partner of a partnership that is engaged in business in the United States, ECE&P includes the corporation's distributive share of the partnership's effectively connected income.[18]

Economic income that is excluded from gross income but included in earnings and profits (e.g., interest on obligations of state and local governments) is included in ECE&P if the income would be effectively connected with U.S. business but for the gross income exclusion.[19] Similarly, an item that is not deductible but reduces earnings and profits is subtracted out in determining ECE&P if it is connected with effectively connected income.[20] For example, income taxes on effectively connected income, including U.S. taxes, reduce ECE&P.[21]

Exclusions are provided for a few items. For example, gain recognized by a foreign corporation on a disposition of stock of a U.S. real property holding corporation, though taxed by §897 as effectively connected income, is not in-

---

[15] IRC §884(b).

[16] IRC §884(d)(1). See Reg. §1.884-1(f)(1) (to be included in ECE&P, item need not be recognized for earnings and profits purposes in the same year it is included in effectively connected taxable income). For the definition of "earnings and profits," see infra ¶92.1.3.

[17] For the election to treat real property income as effectively connected income, see supra ¶66.3.6. For gains on dispositions of U.S. real property interests, see supra ¶66.4. See 1986 Bluebook, supra note 3, at 1039 n.2 (branch profits tax applies to foreign corporation electing to be treated as domestic corporation under §897(i) because election only applies for purposes of §897 and related provisions).

[18] 1986 Bluebook, supra note 3, at 1040. See IRC §875(1) (foreign partner deemed engaged in any U.S. trade or business carried on by partnership), discussed supra ¶66.3.2 text accompanying notes 23–27.

[19] H.R. Rep. No. 841, supra note 1, at II-647; 1986 Bluebook, supra note 3, at 1040.

[20] See IRC §882(c)(1)(A).

[21] See 2 Treasury I, supra note 3, at 370.

cluded in ECE&P because the §897 tax is a shareholder-level tax in this instance and a branch profits tax on the gain would often be a third tax.[22]

2. *U.S. net equity.* The increase or decrease in investment in a U.S. business is measured as the change in the corporation's "United States net equity." U.S. net equity is (1) the sum of the money and the adjusted basis of the assets connected with the U.S. business, reduced by (2) the liabilities of the taxpayer connected with this business.[23] U.S. net equity can be less than zero.

The statute does not provide a rule for identifying the assets and liabilities "connected" with a U.S. business, but it directs the Treasury to promulgate regulations on the subject that are "consistent with the allocation of deductions" under the effectively connected income tax.[24] Generally, U.S. net equity includes "only those assets that generate income taxable by the United States on a net basis and those liabilities that generate expenses which are allocable to income taxable by the United States on a net basis."[25] According to the regulations,[26] a foreign corporation's U.S. assets include:

a. Cash balances needed in the present conduct of a U.S. trade or business.
b. Inventory if it is taken into account in determining the cost of goods sold by a U.S. business.
c. Depreciable property if depreciation on the property is allocable to effectively connected income.
d. An account receivable if income on the sale, services, or leasing transaction generating the receivable is effectively connected income and if the receivable does not bear interest and matures within six months.
e. An installment obligation if both gain on the installment sale and interest on the obligation are effectively connected income.[27]
f. An interest in a partnership engaged in business in the United States.[28]
g. Any other asset if income from its use and gain on its disposition would

---

[22] IRC §884(d)(2) (also excluding income from operations of ships and aircraft and effectively connected income of FSCs, certain captive insurance companies, foreign governments, and international organizations).

[23] IRC §884(c).

[24] IRC §884(c)(2)(C).

[25] 1986 Bluebook, supra note 3, at 1040.

[26] Reg. §1.884-1(d).

[27] Reg. §1.884-1(d)(2)(iii). If the gain, but not the interest, is effectively connected, the corporation may elect to treat the interest as effectively connected income in order to prevent the sale from causing an immediate decline in U.S. assets. If effectively connected gain is realized on an installment sale of the entire business, the corporation might pass up the election so that the U.S. business terminates at the time of the sale and the rule of §1.884(a), exempting a corporation from the branch profits tax for the year of the complete termination of the U.S. business, applies for the year of sale.

[28] Extensive rules are provided for determining the portion of a partnership interest to be treated as a U.S. asset where the partnership has businesses or property in addition to its U.S. business. Reg. §1.884-1(d)(3). The rules allow this determination to be based, at the taxpayer's election, on the relative adjusted bases of the partnership's assets or on

be effectively connected income.[29]

If the income or gain generated by an asset includes both effectively connected income and other income, only a proportionate part of it is treated as a U.S. asset.

An asset is excluded from U.S. net equity if one of the corporation's principal purposes for acquiring the property or using it in a U.S. business is to increase U.S. net equity "artificially."[30] Factors indicative of the corporation's purposes include "the length of time during which the asset was used in a U.S. trade or business, whether the asset was acquired from, or disposed of to, a related person, and whether the aggregate value of the U.S. assets of the foreign corporation increased temporarily on the determination date."

If a U.S. asset has a separate adjusted basis for earnings and profits purposes under §312, that basis is used in determining U.S. net equity.[31] For example, although depreciation on tangible personal property is usually determined by an accelerated method, depreciation must be taken on a straight line basis in computing earnings and profits.[32] Since the adjusted basis of depreciable property is reduced by depreciation, corporate property depreciated on an accelerated method has two adjusted bases—one for regular tax purposes and another for earnings and profits purposes. The property is included in U.S. net equity at the latter amount.[33] If property is a U.S. asset only in part, the earnings and profits basis is apportioned.[34]

Rather than tracing particular liabilities to a U.S. trade or business, the regulations require that a ratable share of all of a foreign corporation's liabilities be treated as U.S. liabilities. Specifically, the U.S. liabilities equal the corporation's worldwide liabilities, multiplied by the ratio of its U.S. assets to its worldwide assets.[35] A liability that has been repaid is included in the corporation's worldwide liabilities if one of the corporation's principal purposes in repaying the liability is to "decrease artificially" the corporation's U.S. liabilities.[36] The regulations allow a corporation to reduce its U.S. liabilities from the amount deter-

---

the relative amounts of effectively connected and other income for the partnership taxable year ending with or within the taxpayer's taxable year.

[29] If the corporation is a beneficiary of a trust, this beneficial interest is not a U.S. asset, even if the trust is engaged in business in the United States. Reg. §1.884-1(d)(4)(i). However, if, under the grantor trust rules, the corporation is treated as the owner of a trust, an asset of the trust so treated as owned by the corporation may be a U.S. asset. Reg. §1.884-1(d)(4)(ii). These rules are effective for taxable years beginning after June 5, 1996. Reg. §1.884-1(i)(4).

[30] Reg. §1.884-1(d)(5)(ii) (a principal purpose is one that is "important" although not necessarily the "primary purpose" for the acquisition or use of the property).

[31] IRC §884(c)(2)(A); Reg. §1.884-1(d)(6)(i).

[32] IRC §312(k), discussed infra ¶92.1.3.

[33] H.R. Rep. No. 841, supra note 1, at II-648; 1986 Bluebook, supra note 3, at 1040.

[34] Reg. §1.884-1(c)(2)(i).

[35] Reg. §1.884-1(e)(1).

[36] Reg. §1.884-1(e)(4).

mined under the apportionment procedure, so long as the reduced amount is not less than the liabilities shown on the books of the U.S. business.[37]

3. *Dividend equivalent amount.* Under the statutes, the branch profits tax is 30 percent of the dividend equivalent amount, which generally equals the foreign corporation's ECE&P for the year, reduced or increased by the change in U.S. net equity. If U.S. net equity at the end of the taxable year exceeds U.S. net equity at the close of the preceding year, the dividend equivalent amount is the excess of ECE&P over the increase in U.S. net equity.[38] The increase in U.S. net equity reduces the dividend equivalent amount because, to this extent, earnings have been reinvested in the U.S. business, rather than repatriated to the head office or diverted to some other use. The reduction, however, cannot diminish the dividend equivalent amount to less than zero. Assume foreign corporation X has $100 of ECE&P for year 1, and its U.S. net equity increases from $1,000 at the beginning of the year to $1,100 at year-end.[39] The dividend equivalent amount for the year is zero, the ECE&P of $100 less the $100 increase in U.S. net equity.

Conversely, if U.S. net equity declines over the year, the dividend equivalent amount is usually the sum of ECE&P and the amount of the decline because the amounts effectively repatriated exceed current U.S. earnings in this case.[40] However, the addition for the decrease in U.S. net equity may not exceed the corporation's "accumulated effectively connected earnings and profits" (accumulated ECE&P), which is the excess of (1) the sum of the ECE&P for all prior years (excepting years beginning before 1987), over (2) the sum of the dividend equivalent amounts for all prior years.[41] In other words, the amount deemed repatriated from accumulated earnings cannot exceed (1) the U.S. earnings for earlier years that were accumulated in the U.S. business rather than repatriated, less (2) the amounts deemed repatriated in earlier years from these accumulated earnings.

Assume X, the foreign corporation in the example, has ECE&P of zero for year 2, and its U.S. net equity declines from $1,100 at the end of year 1 to $1,060 at the end of year 2.[42] The dividend equivalent amount is $40, computed as the

---

[37] Reg. §1.884-1(e)(3). This election can be utilized to exempt from the branch profits tax amounts of U.S. earnings that are accumulated for future use in the U.S. business. "For example, if a foreign corporation has $50 of ECE&P, it can retain $50 for expansion of its U.S. trade or business without triggering a $50 dividend equivalent amount if it elects to reduce its U.S. liabilities by $50, thereby increasing its U.S. net equity by $50." TD 8432, 1992-2 CB 157, 160. The principal cost of the election is that interest on the debt removed from U.S. liabilities cannot be deducted in determining effectively connected taxable income. Also, because interest paid on U.S. liabilities is subjected to the branch interest tax, a corporation with an effectively connected loss might utilize the election, thereby foregoing an interest deduction producing no immediate tax savings in exchange for an elimination of the branch interest tax.

[38] IRC §884(b)(1).

[39] Reg. §1.884-1(b)(4) Ex. 1.

[40] IRC §884(b)(2)(A).

[41] IRC §884(b)(2)(B).

[42] Reg. §1.884-1(b)(4) Ex. 3.

sum of current ECE&P (zero) and the decline during the year in U.S. net equity ($40). The decline in U.S. net equity thus causes $40 of ECE&P accumulated in year 1 to be subject to the branch profits tax in year 2. In contrast, if U.S. net equity had declined by $125 during year 2, the dividend equivalent amount would have been $100 because only $100 of ECE&P was accumulated during year 1.[43]

The branch profits tax can apply for a year in which a foreign corporation has a deficit in ECE&P if the decline in U.S. net equity exceeds the deficit. Assume a foreign corporation has an ECE&P deficit of $90 for 1991; its U.S. net equity is $450 at the beginning of the year and $350 at year-end.[44] If the corporation has at least $10 of accumulated ECE&P from prior years, the dividend equivalent amount for 1991 is $10, computed as current ECE&P (minus $90) increased by the decline in U.S. net equity ($100).[45]

The foregoing rules embody a nimble dividend rule similar to that found in the general dividend rules.[46] Assume a foreign corporation has a deficit of $200 in accumulated ECE&P at the beginning of a particular year; for the year, it has ECE&P of $90, and U.S. net equity remains unchanged.[47] The dividend equivalent amount is $90—current ECE&P ($90) plus or minus the change in U.S. net equity (zero)—even though current ECE&P is not sufficient to restore the accumulated deficit.

4. *Special rules for terminations, suspensions, liquidations, reorganizations, and incorporations.* Several rules alter the computation of the branch profits tax for a year in which a foreign corporation terminates U.S. business operations or participates in a liquidation, reorganization, or incorporation transaction affecting a U.S. business. Very generally, these rules (1) exempt a foreign corporation from the branch profits tax for the year it terminates all business activity in the United States,[48] (2) provide a mechanism for preventing accumulated ECE&P from being taxed when U.S. business operations are temporarily suspended,[49] (3) allow the potential tax on accumulated ECE&P to be shifted over to another corporation when a foreign corporation transfers its U.S. business assets to another corporation in a subsidiary to parent liquidation or a reorganization,[50] and

---

[43] See Reg. §1.884-1(b)(4) Ex. 4.

[44] Reg. §1.884-1(b)(4) Ex. 5.

[45] In a deficit case, the statute fails to carry out the policy to parallel the results that would have obtained if the branch had been incorporated as a domestic subsidiary. If a domestic subsidiary with a current deficit of $90 distributed $100, the dividend would be the lesser of $100 or the corporation's accumulated earnings and profits on the date of the distribution.

[46] See infra ¶92.1.1.

[47] Reg. §1.884-1(b)(4) Ex. 6.

[48] See infra text accompanying notes 49–52.

[49] See infra text accompanying note 53.

[50] See infra text accompanying note 54.

(4) permit the assets of a U.S. business to be transferred to a domestic subsidiary without triggering a tax on accumulated ECE&P.[51]

a. *Terminations.* A foreign corporation is usually exempt from the branch profits tax for the year during which it completely terminates its business in the United States, and the termination extinguishes the corporation's accumulated ECE&P.[52] By the usual definition, the dividend equivalent amount for a termination year would be the sum of all current and accumulated ECE&P because U.S. net equity is zero at the end of the year. However, this result is inconsistent with the policy to parallel the treatment of domestic subsidiaries because (1) the termination of a branch is analogous to the liquidation of a subsidiary and (2) a distribution in liquidation of a domestic subsidiary into a foreign parent is not taxed as a dividend to the parent. The complete termination rule is intended to restore the desired equivalence.

The complete termination rule applies for a particular year only if:

i. At the end of the year, the corporation either has no U.S. assets or has adopted an irrevocable plan of complete liquidation, pursuant to which all U.S. assets are either sold, distributed, or cease to be U.S. assets by the end of the following year.

ii. During the succeeding three years, the U.S. assets of the terminated business are not used by the foreign corporation or a related corporation in a trade or business carried on in the United States.

iii. The corporation has no effectively connected taxable income during the succeeding three years.[53]

iv. The corporation files an extension of the statute of limitations enabling additional tax to be assessed for the year of termination if any of the foregoing limitations is not satisfied.[54]

If a foreign corporation's stock is acquired by another corporation that makes an election under §338, the foreign corporation is deemed to have liqui-

---

[51] See infra text accompanying notes 55-58.

[52] Reg. §1.884-2T(a)(1).

[53] This rule is not violated by the corporation's subsequent recognition of effectively connected income under §864(c)(6) on the collection of an account receivable or installment obligation that was received in a sale of property or services in the course of the terminated business. Neither is it violated if gain on a subsequent sale or exchange of property is characterized as effectively connected income under §864(c)(7) because of the property's earlier use in the terminated business. See supra ¶66.3.5 for §§864(c)(6) and (7). Subsequently recognized effectively connected income under §§864(c)(6) and (7) is subject to the effectively connected income tax, but it is exempted from the branch profits tax if the foreign corporation has no other effectively connected income in the year it is recognized and the corporation has no U.S. assets in that year. Reg. §1.884-2T(a)(4). The exemption is justified on the ground that the income would not have been subject to the branch profits tax if it had been recognized in the year of the termination.

[54] Reg. §§1.884-2T(a)(2), 1.884-2(a)(2)(ii).

dated on the acquisition date.[55] This constructive liquidation allows the complete termination rule to apply unless the proceeds of the stock sale are used to carry on a U.S. business through a related corporation.

b. *Suspensions.* If a foreign corporation terminates its U.S. business but reenters business in the United States within three years thereafter, the rules described above would tax all current and accumulated ECE&P for the year of termination because (1) the corporation's U.S. net equity drops to zero at the end of the termination year and (2) the corporation's failure to stay out of business in the United States for three years makes the complete termination exception unavailable. The regulations allow this result to be avoided by making an election (when the old business is terminated) to treat designated marketable securities as U.S. assets during the period the corporation is not engaged in business in the United States.[56] The election is available only if the winding up of the old business would qualify as a complete termination but for the prohibition against reinvesting in a U.S. business during the succeeding three years. The effect of the election is to keep U.S. net equity during the interregnum at a level equal to the lesser of (1) corporation's cost for the designated securities or (2) its adjusted basis for the property that ceases to be U.S. assets when the old business is terminated.

Assume an electing foreign corporation sells the assets of its U.S. business for $1,000 and invests the proceeds in marketable securities that are designated as substitutes for the business assets under the election rule; the corporation's U.S. net equity is $700 at the beginning of the year, the adjusted basis of the assets sold is $800, and ECE&P for the year of termination, including the gain of $200 on the asset sale, are $325. Since gain on the sale of the assets is fully recognized, U.S. net equity at year-end should be $1,000—the lesser of the adjusted basis of the assets removed from U.S. business use ($1,000 of sale proceeds) or the adjusted basis of the designated securities ($1,000). The dividend equivalent amount for the year of the termination thus is $25, computed as current ECE&P of $325 less the increase in U.S. net equity during the year of $300 (excess of $1,000 over $700).

c. *Reorganizations and subsidiary to parent liquidations.* If a foreign corporation transfers a U.S. business to another corporation in a reorganization or a tax-free liquidation of subsidiary into parent, the transferee generally succeeds to the tax characteristics of the business.[57] For the taxable year of the transferor that ends with the reorganization or liquidation, U.S. net equity is measured immediately before the assets are transferred. The dividend equivalent amount for the transferor's last taxable year thus equals current ECE&P, increased or decreased to reflect any change in U.S. net equity occurring during the year before the reorganization or liquidation. That the U.S. net equity falls to zero as a result of the reorganization or liquidation is ignored. The transferor's accumu-

---

[55] Reg. §1.884-2T(a)(3). For the §338 election, see infra ¶93.8.2.

[56] Reg. §1.884-2T(b).

[57] Reg. §§1.884-2T(c), 1.884-2(c)(2)(iii).

lated ECE&P, including any untaxed portion of the ECE&P for the final year, is added to the transferee's accumulated ECE&P.

d. *Incorporation.* Under the general rules, a foreign corporation's transfer of assets of a U.S. trade or business to a subsidiary corporation usually triggers a branch profits tax on accumulated ECE&P because the transfer reduces the corporation's U.S. net equity—to zero if all U.S. assets are included in the transfer. Under an elective rule, this result may be avoided if (1) the subsidiary is a domestic corporation, (2) the incorporation exchange qualifies for nonrecognition of gain or loss under §351, and (3) the foreign corporation holds at least 80 percent of the domestic corporation's stock immediately after the exchange.[58]

When the election is made, the transferred assets are included in U.S. net equity at the end of the year of the incorporation exchange, even though the foreign corporation no longer owns them. They are included at an amount equal to their adjusted basis immediately before the transfer, increased by any gain recognized on the transfer in the §351 exchange and decreased by any additional income taxes incurred because of the recognition of the gain. The amounts of the increase and decrease are also included in ECE&P for the year unless the gain is excluded or reduced by the general rules on measuring earnings and profits. The effect of these rules is that ECE&P repatriated to the head office in the year of the incorporation are subject to the branch profits tax, but reinvested profits transferred over to the new subsidiary are not.

The election is subject to two conditions. First, the transferee domestic corporation must agree to increase its earnings and profits by all or a portion of the transferor's untaxed ECE&P.[59] The increase equals 100 percent of the transferor's untaxed ECE&P if the transferee receives all of the transferor's U.S. assets. If the transferee receives less than all of these assets, a ratable portion of the untaxed ECE&P, determined with reference to the adjusted bases of the transferred and untransferred assets, is added to the transferee's earnings and profits. The untaxed ECE&P consist of the sum of the foreign corporation's current and accumulated ECE&P immediately before the transfer to the domestic corporation, unreduced by the transferor's dividend equivalent amount for the year. To prevent double counting, a ceiling is placed on the dividend equivalent amount for the year equal to the current and accumulated ECE&P computed at year-end, reduced by the earnings and profits allocated to the transferee.[60] Also, as of the close of the year, the transferor's accumulated ECE&P are reduced by the amount of the addition to the transferee's earnings and profits.

Second, the transferor must agree to pay the branch profits tax when any portion of the stock or securities received in the §351 exchange is disposed of in

---

[58] Reg. §1.884-2T(d). For §351, see infra ¶91.1.

[59] Reg. §1.884-2T(d)(4). The transferee must attach a statement to its return for the year of the transfer identifying the amount of this earnings and profits increase.

[60] Reg. §1.884-2T(d)(3)(iii).

a taxable transaction.[61] This requirement is imposed because the assets and liabilities transferred to the domestic subsidiary are removed from the corporation's U.S. net equity at the end of the year of the transfer but the removal is ignored in determining the dividend equivalent amount for the year. Under the agreement required by this rule, the transferor must usually recognize a dividend equivalent amount for a year in which such a disposition is made equal to the lesser of (1) the amount realized in the disposition or (2) the ECE&P transferred to the transferee under the rule described in the preceding paragraph. If dispositions occur in more than one year, the ECE&P amount for later years is reduced by the amounts taxed under this rule in earlier years. The constructive dividend equivalent amount is subject to the branch profits tax unless an exception applies. For example, if a disposition of tainted stock and securities terminates the foreign corporation's interest in the domestic corporation and the foreign corporation has no U.S. assets at the end of the year, the branch profits tax might be avoided under the rule for complete terminations.

e. *Liquidations and reorganizations of domestic subsidiaries.* Additional rules are provided for cases where ECE&P of a foreign corporation have been added to the earnings and profits of a domestic subsidiary as a result of an incorporation exchange or reorganization and the domestic corporation subsequently liquidates into the foreign parent or transfers its assets to another foreign corporation in a reorganization.[62] In such a case, the foreign corporation receiving the assets in the subsequent transfer must increase its accumulated ECE&P by the lesser of (1) the ECE&P added to the domestic corporation's earnings and profits as a result of the earlier transfer or (2) the domestic corporation's post-1986 earnings and profits. Similarly, an adjustment is made to the change in the foreign corporation's U.S. net equity for the year of the subsequent transaction, essentially treating the assets received in the transaction as though the foreign corporation held them at the beginning of the year.

¶66.5.3   Branch-Level Interest Tax

The branch-level interest tax applies in two contexts. First, if a U.S. branch of a foreign corporation pays interest to a foreign person, the withholding tax of §871(a)(1) or §881(a) can apply to the recipient's interest income. Second, if the interest deduction allowed to a foreign corporation exceeds the interest paid by the corporation's U.S. branch, the corporation is subject to the withholding tax on the excess as though it were interest received from a domestic subsidiary. For purposes of both rules, the term "interest" includes original issue discount.[63]

1. *Tax on actual interest payments.* According to the statutes, "any interest paid by [a] trade or business [of a foreign corporation] in the United States shall

---

[61] Reg. §1.884-2T(d)(5).

[62] Reg. §1.884-2T(e).

[63] Reg. §1.884-4(a)(3). See supra Ch. 56 for original issue discount.

be treated as if it were paid by a domestic corporation."[64] This rule applies if the foreign corporation has effectively connected income for the year of the interest payment or is engaged in business in the United States at any time during the year.[65] Interest received from the hypothetical domestic corporation is from sources within the United States.[66] As a consequence, the interest is subject to the withholding tax if the recipient is a foreign person and the interest is of a kind within the ambit of this tax.[67] The interest, however, may be exempted from the withholding tax under any rule that would apply to interest received from an actual domestic corporation. If the recipient is neither a bank nor a person related to the payor, the interest may be exempted as portfolio interest.[68] If the payor is a bank, the exemption for interest on bank deposits may apply.[69] Treaty rules on interest payments can also apply.

The characterization of the interest as domestic source income also applies for purposes of any other statutory provision under which the source of income is relevant. For example, if the recipient is a foreign person engaged in a trade or business in the United States, the interest is classified as U.S. income in determining whether it is effectively connected with that business. Also, if received by a U.S. person, the interest is treated as domestic source income in computing the recipient's maximum foreign tax credit.[70]

2. *Tax on "excess interest" constructively paid to head office.* Congress recognized that interest expense attributable to branch operations is not always paid by the branch. It therefore provided a further rule for the case where the sum of a branch's interest payments is less than its "allocable interest," which is the interest expense of the corporation that is allocated to the branch's income under the regulations for allocating and apportioning deductions.[71]

Under this rule, the excess of the allocable interest over the branch's interest payments (the "excess interest") is treated as though it were paid to the foreign

---

[64] IRC §884(f)(1)(A).

[65] Reg. §1.884-4(a)(1). The corporation is deemed engaged in business in the United States during the taxable year if it has property that is treated as a U.S. asset in determining its interest deduction for the year. For the interest deduction allowed in computing effectively connected taxable income, see infra ¶70.10.3.

[66] See Reg. §1.884-4(a)(1) (hypothetical domestic corporation not described in §861(c)(1), relating to domestic corporations whose foreign business income accounts for at least 80 percent of worldwide gross income and whose interest payments are thus foreign source income).

[67] For the application of the withholding tax to interest, see supra ¶66.2.2.

[68] See supra ¶66.2.2 text accompanying notes 21–56 for the exemption of portfolio interest.

[69] See supra ¶66.2.2 text accompanying note 57 for the exemption for interest on bank deposits.

[70] See IRC §904, discussed infra ¶69.5.1.

[71] IRC §884(f)(2). The Tax Court has held that interest expense may be "allocable interest" even if the corporation's deduction for the interest is denied by §267(a)(3). Taiyo Hawaii Co. v. CIR, 108 TC No. 27 (1997). According to the legislative history of a 1996 amendment, retroactive to 1986, that introduced the term "allocable interest":

corporation by its branch, which is treated for this purpose as a domestic corporation.[72] This constructive payment is deemed made on the last day of the corporation's taxable year. Under §881(a)(1), the corporation is taxed at 30 percent on the constructive payment unless it qualifies for exemption or a reduced rate under an income tax treaty.[73]

The tax is reported on the foreign corporation's income tax return for the year that the excess interest is deducted.[74] It is payable as part of the corporation's estimated tax payments, and to the extent not so paid, payment is due on the due date for the return (without extensions).

3. *Interest paid by U.S. business.* Although the foregoing rules generally cover all interest deducted in determining effectively connected taxable income, the amount of the branch-level interest tax often depends on whether this interest is paid by the U.S. branch (in which case the recipient is the taxpayer) or by the head office (in which case the foreign corporation is itself the taxpayer). Assume a foreign corporation issues bonds to foreign investors. If interest on the bonds is paid by a U.S. branch of the corporation, the bondholders' interest income is likely to be exempted as portfolio interest. If the U.S. branch is not the payor but a deduction for the interest is nevertheless allocated to effectively connected income, the interest is constructively paid by the branch (treated for this purpose as a domestic corporation) to the head office, which cannot claim the exemption for portfolio interest because it is related to the payor.

Thus, where an interest expense of a foreign corporation is allocable to U.S. effectively connected income, but that interest expense would not have been fully deductible for tax purposes under another Code provision had it been paid by a U.S. corporation, the [amendment] clarifies that such interest is nonetheless treated for branch level interest tax purposes like a payment by a U.S. corporation to a foreign corporate parent.

Staff of Joint Comm. on Tax'n, 104th Cong., 2d Sess., General Explanation of Tax Legislation Enacted in the 104th Congress (Comm. Print 1996).

[72] IRC §884(f)(1)(B). See Reg. §1.884-4(a)(1) (hypothetical domestic corporation not described in §861(c)(1), relating to domestic corporations whose foreign business income accounts for at least 80 percent of their gross income and whose interest payments are thus foreign source income).

[73] See Reg. §1.884-4(a)(2)(iii) (if branch is engaged in banking business and substantial portion of corporation's worldwide business is receiving deposits and making loans, at least 85 percent of constructive interest payment is exempt under §871(i) as interest on bank deposits), §1.884-4(c)(3) (treaty rules on interest received can apply to tax on constructive payments, but tax is not affected by treaty rules on interest paid by foreign corporation because payments are deemed made by domestic corporation); TD 8432, supra note 34, at 160 ("The Treasury Department has concluded that the tax on excess interest is not prohibited by the nondiscrimination provision or any other provision in any income tax treaty to which the United States is a party"). For treaty rules, see infra ¶66.5.4.

[74] Reg. §1.884-4(a)(2)(iv). See H.R. Rep. No. 841, supra note 1, at II-648; 1986 Bluebook, supra note 3, at 1041.

The application of treaty exemptions and rate reductions are also affected by whether the branch is the payor of the interest.[75] Assume a foreign corporation borrows money from a foreign bank, and interest on the loan is treated as an expense of a U.S. business of the corporation. Under the statutes, the interest is taxable whether the branch is treated as paying it to the bank or the head office because neither a bank nor a related person is eligible to receive portfolio interest. However, a treaty exemption or rate reduction for interest may turn on who is deemed to receive the interest because the bank may be a resident of a treaty country while the foreign corporation is not, or vice versa.

Neither the statute nor the legislative history defines the crucial phrase "interest paid by [a U.S.] trade or business." The regulations, however, identify three situations where a U.S. business is considered a payor of interest. Contrary to the implication of the statutory phrase, the regulations look principally to the relationship between the U.S. business and the underlying liability, not to the physical act of paying the interest.

First, interest on indebtedness carried on books and records maintained by the corporation for a U.S. business is treated as paid by that business if it is classified as a U.S. booked liability under the rules determining the corporation's interest deduction.[76] Generally, a liability is a U.S. booked liability if it is predominantly secured by a U.S. asset or is recorded on the books of the U.S. business "reasonably contemporaneous[ly]" with the incurring of the liability.[77]

Second, for a corporation other than a bank, interest is usually deemed paid by the U.S. business if the underlying liability is "specifically identified" as a liability of the business not later than the date on which interest is first paid on the liability or, if earlier, the due date (including extensions) of the corporation's return for the taxable year.[78] A liability can be specifically identified by being shown in the records of the U.S. business or being identified as a liability of the U.S. business in other records of the corporation or on a schedule identifying the liabilities of that business.[79] However, this rule cannot apply to interest exceeding 85 percent of what would otherwise be the corporation's excess interest for the taxable year.[80] Also, it can apply only if the corporation either files an information return with the IRS reporting the interest payments or sends a notice to the

---

[75] See infra ¶66.5.4 for the application of treaties to the branch taxes.

[76] Reg. §1.884-4(b)(1)(i)(A). For purposes of the interest deduction, partnership liabilities are generally attributed to the partner, but this attribution does not apply in this context. For a special rule for insurance businesses, see Reg. §§1.884-1(e)(2), 1.884-4(b)(1)(i)(B).

[77] Reg. §1.882-5(d)(2), discussed infra ¶70.10.3 text accompanying notes 137–39.

[78] Reg. §1.884-4(b)(1)(ii).

[79] Reg. §1.884-4(b)(3)(i). The identification must be sufficiently detailed so that the branch interest on the liability and the name and address of the recipient can "readily" be determined.

[80] Reg. §1.884-4(b)(1)(ii)(A).

recipient that the interest is from U.S. sources.[81] Moreover, the rule cannot apply if the liability is incurred in the ordinary course of a business carried on outside the United States or is predominantly secured by property that is not a U.S. asset.[82]

Third, if a foreign corporation's U.S. assets account for at least 80 percent of its property at the close of the taxable year, the U.S. business is treated as paying all of the corporation's interest expense, excepting only interest on liabilities directly incurred in the course of a trade or business carried on outside the United States and liabilities predominantly secured by property not located in the United States.[83]

The sum of the interest treated as paid by a U.S. business under these three rules may not exceed the interest deduction allowed to the corporation in determining effectively connected taxable income. If this ceiling would otherwise be exceeded, the interest payments deemed made by the U.S. business reduced.[84] The reduction is taken first from interest described in the immediately preceding paragraph, then, to the extent necessary, from interest covered by the rule described in the second preceding paragraph, and finally from interest described in the third preceding paragraph. Within each category, the excluded amounts consist of interest on the most recently incurred liabilities unless the corporation elects a different ordering.

This ceiling sometimes raises a practical dilemma for foreign corporations. Interest paid by a U.S. business to a foreign debt holder is sometimes subject to the withholding tax, and this tax is collected by withholding. Interest not paid by the U.S. business, in contrast, is not subject to withholding. The corporation usually must decide whether to withhold when interest is paid, but the rule described in the preceding paragraph turns on the amount of the corporation's interest deduction for the year, which may not be calculable until after the close of the year. The regulations indicate that this dilemma may be resolved by ignoring the rule in deciding whether to withhold and applying for a refund if the corporation later determines that the rule exempts the interest from withholding.[85]

Generally, the interest payment rules operate on a cash basis even if the foreign corporation uses the accrual method of accounting. Assume a foreign corporation's only liability associated with a U.S. business is a mortgage held by a U.S. lender that is secured by property used in the business. For a particular year, an interest deduction of $100 is allowed for interest accrued on the mortgage, but only $80 of this interest is paid. Under the general rules, the $80, having

---

[81] Reg. §§1.884-4(b)(1)(ii)(B), (3)(ii).

[82] Reg. §1.884-4(b)(3)(iii)(A).

[83] Reg. §1.884-4(b)(5). For purposes of the 80 percent test, each asset is taken into account at an amount equal to its adjusted basis for earnings and profits purposes. See supra ¶66.5.2 text accompanying notes 30–32.

[84] Reg. §1.884-4(b)(6).

[85] Reg. §1.884-4(b)(6)(iv) Ex. 1.

been paid by the U.S. business, is U.S. source income to the recipient but is not subject to a withholding tax because the recipient is a U.S. person. The remaining $20 of the deduction is treated as paid to the foreign corporation itself and is therefore taxed under §881(a), even if the lender uses the accrual method and also pays U.S. tax on this amount for the same year. When paid, the $20 will be treated as paid by the U.S. business, but it will be matched with interest accrued during the year of payment. Even though all of the interest accrues to a U.S. person and may be currently taxable to that person, the §881(a) tax paid by the foreign corporation on the $20 will be not be refunded until a year when interest payments exceed the interest deduction.

The regulations permit a foreign corporation using the accrual method of accounting to make an election that avoids this mismatch.[86] For purposes of computing the interest constructively paid to itself, an electing corporation treats accrued interest as paid in the year of accrual. In the example, the foreign corporation is treated as paying the interest of $100 as it accrues even though $20 is in fact not paid until later. The constructive payment subject to the §881(a) tax is thus reduced to zero. Withholding obligations, however, are still determined on the cash basis. If the lender in the example were a foreign bank, the corporation would withhold tax from the $80 paid currently at the time of payment and would withhold tax from the $20 when it is subsequently paid.

¶66.5.4 Treaty Modifications

The branch taxes can be reduced or eliminated by an income tax treaty, more or less in the same way as the withholding taxes on dividends or interest from a domestic subsidiary can be reduced by treaty.[87] Income tax treaties typically provide that dividends from subsidiary to parent can be taxed by the subsidiary's home country, but at a rate not to exceed 5 percent. The source country tax on interest is frequently reduced to zero by treaty.

The branch profits tax can also be barred by nondiscrimination provisions of treaties. According to the staff of the Joint Committee on Taxation:

> Although Congress generally believed that a branch profits tax does not unfairly discriminate against foreign corporations because it treats foreign corporations and their shareholders together no worse than U.S. corporations and their shareholders, it understood that most treaty nondiscrimination articles relating to permanent establishments arguably operate to consider corporations and their shareholders separately in determining whether discriminatory tax rules exist. Congress generally did not intend to override

---

[86] Reg. §1.884-4(b)(7). The election also applies when interest is paid before it accrues. Once made, the election remains in effect indefinitely until revoked with IRS consent.

[87] See IRC §§884(e)(1)(A), (f)(3)(A)(i) (no treaty other than an income tax treaty may be applied to reduce or eliminate branch tax).

U.S. income tax treaty obligations that arguably prohibit imposition of the branch profits tax even though as later-enacted legislation the . . . branch tax provisions normally would do so. Congress adopted this position, however, only on the understanding that the Treasury Department will renegotiate outstanding treaties that prohibit imposition of the tax.[88]

Treaty benefits, however, are limited by a provision directed against treaty shopping. The reasons for this limitation were described as follows:

> Congress was . . . concerned that foreign investors resident in one country would attempt to use another country's tax treaty with the United States to avoid the branch profits tax and branch-level interest tax (i.e., they would treaty shop). In these cases, Congress believed such use of treaties to be improper. [Generally, this is so] whether or not a third-country investor would have been entitled to treaty benefits had the investor made a direct U.S. investment since the United States is not certain, when an intervening entity in a second country is used to make an investment, if a residence country tax will be imposed on U.S. source income from the investment. The United States has particular reason to believe that there will be no residence country tax when a third-country investor routes U.S. investments through a low-tax jurisdiction. It was Congress' view that the United States should generally forego source basis taxation of dividends and interest only when residents of the treaty partner are taxed in the treaty country on this income. In cases of treaty shopping, then, Congress intended [§884] to override conflicting provisions in U.S. treaties.[89]

Under the antishopping rule, a branch tax imposed on a foreign corporation usually may not be reduced or eliminated under a treaty between the United States and a particular foreign country unless the taxpayer is a "qualified resident" of that foreign country (the treaty country).[90]

1. *Qualified resident.* A foreign corporation is a qualified resident of a foreign country having an income tax treaty with the United States if the corporation meets at least one of three tests—an ownership/base erosion test, a public ownership test, or an active business test.

a. *Ownership/base erosion test.* The first of the three tests is met if (1) the foreign corporation satisfies the treaty's conception of residence in the treaty country, (2) at least 50 percent of the corporation's stock is held by individuals who are either residents of that country or citizens or residents of the United States, and (3) less than 50 percent of the corporation's income is used to "meet

---

[88] 1986 Bluebook, supra note 3, at 1038. See id. at 1043 (branch profits tax is prohibited by nondiscrimination article of Treasury's 1981 Model Income Tax Treaty).
[89] Id. at 1038.
[90] IRC §884(e)(1)(B).

liabilities" owing to persons who are not residents of the treaty country or the United States.[91]

The stock ownership test is applied by comparing the value of the stock held by qualifying individuals with the value of all of the corporation's outstanding stock. Stock held by a corporation, partnership, trust, or estate is attributed ratably to its owners and, if necessary, reattributed from entity to entity until an individual owner is reached.[92] Also, stock of the foreign corporation that is held directly or by attribution by another foreign corporation is considered held by an individual resident of the treaty country if the shareholder corporation is a resident of that country under the terms of the treaty and its stock is "primarily and regularly traded" on an established securities market in the treaty country.[93] Similarly, stock of the foreign corporation held by a domestic corporation is treated as owned by a U.S. resident if stock of the shareholder corporation is so traded on an established securities market in the United States. In order to be a qualified resident for a particular year, a foreign corporation must, before the due date of its return for the year, assemble documents showing that the stock ownership test is met, and it must retain the documents until the expiration of the statute of limitations on assessments of tax for the year.[94]

The income requirement is called "base erosion" test because its purpose is to deny treaty benefits where a foreign corporation functions as a conduit for persons who do not reside in the treaty country.[95] Assume a country X corporation is wholly owned by individuals residing in country X, but its gross income consists primary of interest on loans to U.S. persons made by the corporation from funds borrowed from individuals who are not residents of country X or the United States. Because the corporation functions a conduit between the U.S. borrowers and the nonresident lenders, the latter would be the principal beneficiaries if the corporation were allowed an exemption or reduced tax rate for U.S. source interest under a U.S.-country X treaty. Because these lenders do not reside in either of the countries signatory to the treaty, Congress concluded that the

---

[91] IRC §884(e)(4)(A). See 1986 Bluebook, supra note 3, at 1044 (taxpayer has burden of proving foreign corporation is qualified resident of treaty country).

[92] IRC §884(e)(4)(A)(i); Reg. §§1.884-5(b)(1)(i), (2).

[93] Reg. §1.884-5(b)(1)(i)(C). For the term "primarily and regularly traded on an established securities market," see infra text accompanying notes 96–103. See also Reg. §1.884-5(b)(1)(i)(B) (stock held by foreign government treated as held by individual resident of that country, and stock held by U.S. government or government of state of United States deemed held by U.S. citizen or resident).

[94] Reg. §§1.884-5(b)(3), (9). See Reg. §1.884-5(b)(3)(iii) (if corporation has at least 250 shareholders, residence of less-than-one-percent shareholders may be determined from addresses shown on corporation's records), §1.884-5(b)(3)(v) (on showing of good cause, deadline for obtaining documentation may be extended beyond due date of return).

[95] H.R. Rep. No. 841, supra note 5, at II-649. See 1986 Bluebook, supra note 3, at 1043 (base erosion rule needed "to prevent nonresidents of a treaty country from gaining treaty benefits").

branch taxes should not be eliminated or reduced by treaty in such a case. The base erosion rule is the instrument for effecting this policy.

The base erosion test is failed for a taxable year unless the foreign corporation establishes that interest, rents, royalties, reinsurance premiums, and other obligations paid or accrued during the year to persons not residing in the treaty country or the United States amount to less than 50 percent of the corporation's gross income for the year.[96] Such an item is taken into account in applying the 50 percent test for the year in which it is deductible or added to the basis of corporate property or yields some other tax benefit. For example, if the foreign corporation uses the accrual method of accounting, an item is accounted for in the year in which it accrues, not the year in which it is paid. Generally, an item counts against the 50 percent ceiling only if it is deductible or is added to the basis of corporate property. Principal payments on loans, for example, are ignored.

b. *Public ownership test.* Under this test, a foreign corporation that is a resident of a foreign country under a treaty between that country and the United States is a qualified resident if the corporation's stock is "primarily and regularly traded on an established securities market" in the treaty country or the United States.[97] The public ownership test is also met if at least 90 percent of the corporation's stock is directly or indirectly owned by another corporation that is organized in the treaty country and whose stock is so traded there or in the United States.[98] Further, consistent with the policy of allowing treaty benefits to corporations owned by U.S. persons, a foreign subsidiary of a publicly held domestic corporation can qualify. Specifically, a foreign corporation is a qualified resident of a treaty country if (1) it is a resident of that country under the treaty and (2) at least 90 percent of its stock is owned by a domestic corporation whose shares are primarily and regularly traded on an established securities market in the United States.[99]

Generally, a foreign securities exchange is an "established securities market" only if it is officially recognized or supervised by the government of its home country, is the principal exchange in that country, and executes trades aggregating more than $1 billion annually.[100] The IRS, however, may designate other

---

[96] Reg. §1.884-5(c). For this purpose, a foreign corporation receiving one of the described items is treated as a resident of the treaty country only if it is a qualified resident under §884, and a domestic corporation must be a qualified resident of the United States to be treated as a U.S. resident. See TD 8432, supra note 34, at 161 (regulations' definition of base eroding payments does not exclude "bona fide payments at arms' length to unrelated persons . . . because of the difficulty in administering a rule that would exclude such payments"; however, "payments by a foreign corporation included in its cost of goods sold are not considered base eroding payments since such payments are excluded from gross income").

[97] IRC §884(e)(4)(B); Reg. §1.884-5(d).

[98] See Reg. §1.884-5(d)(1) (90 percent test must be met with respect to both voting power and value of outstanding shares).

[99] IRC §884(e)(4)(C).

[100] Reg. §1.884-5(d)(2).

foreign exchanges as qualifying. The established securities markets in the United States include all national securities exchanges and over-the-counter markets. An over-the-counter market in a foreign country does not qualify.

A foreign corporation's stock is "primarily" traded on established securities markets in the treaty country and the United States if the following requirements are met.[101] The class or classes of stock that are traded on such markets must carry at least 80 percent of the voting power of all classes of the corporation's stock and must have an aggregate value more than 80 percent of the value of all of the corporation's outstanding stock. A class of stock is counted toward the required 80 percent only if (1) the stock is listed and regularly traded on the market and (2) the number of shares of the class that are traded during the taxable year on established markets in the treaty country and the United States exceeds the number traded during the year on established securities markets in any other country.

A particular class is "regularly" traded on established securities markets in the treaty country or the United States if trades occur on at least 60 days during the taxable year and the aggregate number of shares of the class traded during the year is at least 10 percent of the average number of shares in the class outstanding during the year.[102]

Even if the 60-day and floor requirements are satisfied, stock of a particular class is not considered regularly traded during a taxable year if 50 percent or more of the class is held by one or more persons, each of whom is a 5 percent or greater shareholder and is not a resident of the treaty country.[103] On the other hand, stock traded on a national exchange or over-the-counter market in the United States is considered regularly traded if it is "regularly quoted by brokers or dealers making a market in the stock," whether or not the 60-day test and floor requirement are satisfied.[104]

c. *Active business test.* Under this test, a foreign corporation that is a resident of a foreign country under a treaty between that country and the United States is a qualified resident of the treaty country for purposes of §884 if it (1) is actively engaged in business in the treaty country, (2) has a substantial presence there, and (3) the U.S. income for which a treaty exemption is claimed derives from activities in the United States that are an integral part of the corporation's active business in the treaty country.[105] Whether the corporation is actively engaged in business in the treaty country is a factual inquiry, but the test is not

---

[101] Reg. §1.884-5(d)(3).

[102] Reg. §1.884-5(d)(4). Days on which the stock trades only in de minimis quantities are not counted toward the required 60 trading days.

[103] Reg. §1.884-5(d)(4)(iii). See Reg. §1.884-5(d)(5) (foreign corporation claiming to be qualified resident under public trading rule must keep shareholder lists showing it is not disqualified by this requirement and must make lists available to IRS on request).

[104] Reg. §1.884-5(d)(4)(ii).

[105] Reg. §1.884-5(e). For the Treasury's authority to establish this rule, see §884(e)(4)(D); 1986 Bluebook, supra note 3, at 1044.

met unless its officers and employees "carry out substantial managerial and operational activities" in that country.[106]

To determine whether the corporation has a substantial presence in the treaty country, three ratios are computed: (1) the ratio of assets used in the active conduct of business in the treaty country to the corporation's worldwide assets, (2) the ratio of its active business income in the treaty country to its worldwide gross income, and (3) the ratio of its payroll in the treaty country to the worldwide payroll. The corporation has a substantial presence in the treaty country only if each of the three ratios is at least 20 percent and the average of the ratios exceeds 25 percent.[107]

The corporation's U.S. activities are considered to be an integral part of an active business in the treaty country if the activities in the two countries are, "in principal part, complementary and mutually interdependent steps ... in the production and sale or lease of goods or in the provision of services."[108] If the U.S. business consists of selling goods, this test is generally not met unless the corporation produces the goods in the treaty country or takes physical possession of and stores the goods in that country pending sale. Alternatively, the integral-part test can be met by showing that (1) at least 50 percent of the corporation's gross income from all sources comes from sales or leases of goods or services for use, consumption, or resale in the treaty country and (2) the U.S. income derives from sales or leases of goods or services of the same type.

2. *Treaty reductions of branch profits tax for qualified residents.* If a foreign corporation subject to the branch profits tax is a qualified resident of a country that has an income tax treaty with the United States, the branch profits tax can be reduced under either of two types of treaty provisions.[109] First, if the treaty specifies a maximum rate for branch profits taxes, the §884(a) tax is imposed at that rate if it is less than the statutory rate of 30 percent; if the treaty prohibits a branch profits tax, the §884(a) rate is zero. Moreover, if the treaty allows a branch profits tax but alters the tax base or adds limitations not stated in the

---

The active business test may be applied to the affiliated group to which the corporation belongs, rather than to the corporation alone. Reg. §1.884-5(e)(1). This option might, for example, be utilized by a group carrying on business in the United States through a subsidiary that is organized under the laws of the home country but is engaged in business only in the United States.

[106] Reg. §§1.884-5(e)(2), 1.367(a)-2T(b)(3).

[107] Reg. §1.884-5(e)(3). A corporation engaged primarily in selling, manufacturing, or otherwise producing tangible property may substitute a ratio based on direct materials costs for the gross income ratio. Reg. §1.884-5(e)(3)(iii).

[108] Reg. §1.884-5(e)(4)(i).

[109] IRC §884(e)(2)(A). See Reg. §1.884-1(g)(3) (list of treaties existing on January 1, 1987 that barred branch profits tax), §1.884-1(g)(4)(i) (list of treaties existing on January 1, 1987 that provided reduced rates for branch profits tax), §1.884-1(g)(4)(iv) (special rules under U.S.-Canada treaty).

statute, the treaty rule governs the computation of the tax unless the statutory computation yields a smaller tax.[110]

Second, if the treaty makes no reference to branch profits taxes or bars the imposition of the tax, the maximum rate is the rate that would apply under the treaty to a dividend received by a corporate resident of the treaty country from a wholly owned U.S. corporation. For example, the branch profits tax rate is 5 percent if a foreign corporation is a qualified resident of country X and an income tax treaty between the United States and country X limits to 5 percent the tax the U.S. can impose on dividends received by a country X corporation from a U.S. subsidiary.

Permanent establishment rules in income tax treaties also affect the application of the branch profits tax.[111] A foreign corporation engaged in business in the United States is exempted from the tax if the corporation has no permanent establishment in the United States and the lack of a permanent establishment bars the United States from imposing the regular corporate tax on income effectively connected with the corporation's U.S. business. If a foreign corporation has a permanent establishment in the United States, ECE&P includes only profits attributable to the permanent establishment, and U.S. net equity includes only the assets and liabilities connected with the permanent establishment.

If a foreign corporation is a qualified resident of a treaty country for the taxable year but has not always been a qualified resident, it may be necessary to distinguish between the portions of the dividend equivalent amount traceable to current and accumulated ECE&P, respectively. If the corporation has been a qualified resident for all of the 36-month period ending with the taxable year, all of the dividend equivalent amount is eligible for treaty relief, regardless of the corporation's status when the ECE&P was earned. However, if the corporation fails to meet this 36-month test, the dividend equivalent amount is taxable at 30 percent, without reduction under the treaty, to the extent it is traced to ECE&P accumulated while the corporation was not a qualified resident.[112]

3. *Treaty reductions of branch-level interest tax.*

a. *Actual payments by U.S. business.* When the branch-level interest tax applies to a branch payment of interest, the tax (which falls on the payee) may be reduced or eliminated by a treaty between the United States and the recipient's country of residence or the payor's country of residence, subject to the qualifications described below.[113]

If the recipient is not a corporation, an income tax treaty between the United States and the recipient's country of residence is applied by its terms, without

---

[110] 1986 Bluebook, supra note 3, at 1041 (U.S.-Canada treaty allows branch profits tax to be computed differently from statutory computation).

[111] H.R. Rep. No. 841, supra note 5, at II-650.

[112] Reg. §1.884-1(g)(2) (dividend equivalent amount traced to particular ECE&P on last-in-first-out basis).

[113] IRC §884(e)(3)(B). See H.R. Rep. No. 841, supra note 1, at II-649.

modification under §884. However, if the recipient is a foreign corporation, a rate reduction or zero rate provided by a treaty with the recipient's country of residence is inapplicable unless (1) the recipient is a qualified resident of that country or (2) the treaty entered into force after 1986 and the antishopping provisions of the treaty are satisfied.[114] Assume a U.S. branch pays interest to a bank that is a resident of country X, a country with which the United States has an income tax treaty. If the treaty became effective before 1987, the interest rules of the U.S.-country X treaty apply in determining the bank's tax on the interest if the bank is a resident of country X under the terms of the treaty and is a qualified resident of that country under §884. The treaty rules apply by their terms, without modification by §884, if the treaty became effective after 1986.

Analogous rules apply if the foreign corporation paying the interest is a resident of a foreign country that has an income tax treaty with the United States barring a U.S. tax on interest paid by residents of the country.[115] Generally, such a treaty rule applies only if the payor is a qualified resident of the treaty country. Satisfaction of an antishopping provision of the treaty itself is sufficient, however, if the treaty entered into force after 1986.

b. *Constructive interest payments.* When the branch-level interest tax applies to a constructive interest payment from a U.S. branch to its foreign head office, a treaty reduction or elimination of the tax is available if the foreign corporation owning the branch (1) is a resident of a foreign country under the terms of a treaty between that country and the United States and (2) is a qualified resident of that country for purposes of §884.[116] Assume a country X corporation is allowed an interest deduction in determining effectively connected taxable income that exceeds the interest paid by the corporation's U.S. business. The excess is taxed as interest paid by a hypothetical U.S. corporation to the country X corporation. The tax is limited by the interest rules of the U.S.-country X income tax treaty if the corporation qualifies as a country X resident both under the treaty and under the qualified residence rules of §884.

The interaction between the actual and constructive payment rules may be illustrated as follows: Assume a foreign corporation organized in country X is allowed an interest deduction of $100 in determining taxable income effectively connected with the corporation's U.S. business; $80 of this interest is paid by the U.S. branch to an unrelated corporation organized in country Y, and the remaining $20 is paid by the corporation's head office in country X.[117] The $80 can be exempted from the withholding tax under an exempting article of a U.S.-country Y treaty, but only if the recipient is a qualified resident of country Y. The $20 is subject to the withholding tax unless it is exempted or taxed at a lesser rate

---

[114] Reg. §1.884-4(b)(8)(ii).

[115] Reg. §1.884-4(b)(8).

[116] IRC §884(f)(3)(B).

[117] See 1986 Bluebook, supra note 3, at 1045.

under a U.S.-country X treaty and the foreign corporation is a qualified resident of country X.

4. *Treaty reduction of branch profits tax where corporation is not qualified resident.* Generally, the treaty shopping rules preclude any reduction of the branch taxes on a foreign corporation unless the corporation is a qualified resident of a treaty country. The statutes, however, recognize one exception to this principle. For purposes of the branch profits tax, a foreign corporation that is not a qualified resident is entitled to the benefits of a dividend rule under a treaty with the corporation's country of residence if the treaty allows the United States to tax dividends paid by the corporation to the extent these dividends are from U.S. sources under §861(a)(2)(B).[118] Under §861(a)(2)(B), if 25 percent or more of a foreign corporation's gross income for the preceding three years was effectively connected with U.S. businesses of the corporation, a portion of any dividends received from the corporation (commensurate with the proportion of the corporation's income that has been effectively connected income) is from U.S. sources. Most treaties that are popular with treaty shoppers either deny or sharply limit the United States' ability to tax dividends paid by corporations resident of the treaty countries. Congress thus concluded that its purpose to limit treaty shopping did not require any limitation on the operation of treaties that allow the United States to tax all §861(a)(2)(B) dividends.

¶66.6 RETURNS AND SAILING PERMITS

1. *Returns required.* Nonresident aliens and foreign corporations not engaged in a trade or business in the United States at any time during the taxable year are not required to file tax returns if their tax liabilities are fully satisfied by withholding at source.[1] If engaged in a U.S. business, however, nonresident aliens and foreign corporations must file returns even if no effectively connected income or domestic source income is recognized or the income is exempt by statute or treaty.[2] If the return is not "true and accurate," deductions and credits otherwise allowable to the taxpayer are disallowed.[3]

According to the regulations, the true and accurate return rule requires that a return be filed "on a timely basis."[4] If the taxpayer filed a return for the

---

[118] IRC §884(e)(3)(B). For §861(a)(2)(B), see infra ¶70.3.

[1] Reg. §1.6012-1(b)(2)(i) (nonresident aliens), §1.6012-2(g)(2)(i) (foreign corporations).

[2] Reg. §1.6012-1(b)(1)(i) (nonresident aliens), §1.6012-2(g)(1)(i) (foreign corporations).

[3] IRC §§874(a), 882(c)(2); Reg. §1.874-1(a). See Brittingham v. CIR, 66 TC 373, 408-09 (1976), aff'd on other issues, 598 F2d 1375 (5th Cir. 1979) (return must contain "sufficient information upon which the claimed deductions and credits can be evaluated").

[4] Reg. §1.874-1(b)(1), 1.882-4(a)(3)(i). See Reg. §1.882-4(a)(3)(v) (timely filing also required to preserve foreign corporation's right to deductions and credits in determining

immediately preceding year or is not required to file a return for that year, the timely basis requirement is met by filing the current year's return within 16 months after the due date if the taxpayer is a nonresident alien or foreign trust or 18 months if the taxpayer is a foreign corporation.[5] If a return is required for the preceding year but has not been filed, the current year's return must be filed within the 16- or 18-month grace period and before the IRS mails the taxpayer a notice that deductions and credits are disallowed for failure to file timely. Meeting the applicable one of these deadlines merely prevents the disallowance of deductions and credits and does not relieve the taxpayer of any other penalties for late filing. The applicable deadline may be waived by the IRS "in rare and unusual circumstances" on a showing of "good cause."[6]

The application of the true and accurate return rule could be quite harsh if a taxpayer files no return in the good faith belief that he is not engaged in a trade or business or that all of effectively connected income is exempted from U.S. tax by treaty and this belief is determined to be wrong only after the 16- or 18-month period has expired. The regulations alleviate this harshness by providing that if such a taxpayer has only "limited activities" in the United States, the rule can be avoided by filing a protective return that reports no gross income and is accompanied with a statement identifying it as a protective return.[7]

2. *Joint returns.* Spouses are generally not allowed to file a joint return if either spouse is a nonresident alien at any time during the year,[8] but two exceptions are made from this rule. First, if a nonresident alien is married to a U.S. citizen or resident, a joint return may be filed if the spouses elect to treat the nonresident spouse as a resident for all income and withholding tax purposes.[9] Once made for any year, such an election remains in effect for all subsequent years until it is terminated or both spouses become nonresident aliens. The taxpayers can revoke the election for any year, but only at the cost of forfeiting the right to elect for any subsequent year. The election is automatically terminated if one spouse dies or the spouses are divorced or legally separated. The IRS can terminate the election if it is denied access to the spouses' books and records or other information it might request.

---

accumulated earnings tax); Espinosa v. CIR, 107 TC 146 (1997) (no deductions allowed where taxpayer filed returns after IRS had prepared returns for taxpayer, but before notice of deficiency was issued). See generally Schickli, New House Rules for Foreign Taxpayers That Play the U.S. Audit Lottery, 43 Tax Lawyer 915 (1990).

[5] This rule applies only for years ending after July 1990.

[6] Reg. §§1.874-1(b)(2), 1.882-4(a)(3)(ii).

[7] Reg. §§1.874-1(b)(4), 1.882-4(a)(3)(iv).

[8] IRC §6013(a)(1). See also infra ¶76.3 (taxation of community income when one spouse is a nonresident alien).

[9] IRC §6013(g). See Reg. §1.6013-6(a)(2)(v) (when election is made, nonresident spouse is ineligible for benefits extended by treaty to residents of foreign countries).

Second, an election may be made to treat a nonresident alien spouse as a resident for the entirety of the year in which the spouse becomes a resident.[10] The election is available only if the spouse (1) is a nonresident alien at the beginning of the year but is a resident at year-end and (2) is married to a U.S. citizen or resident at the end of the year. Both spouses might qualify for the election for a year in which they jointly take up residence in the United States. When the election is made, the spouse affected by the election is treated as a resident throughout the year for all income and withholding tax purposes. Both spouses must join in the election, and the making of the election disqualifies them from electing in any subsequent year.

3. *Sailing permits.* Under §6851(d)(1), an alien, whether resident or nonresident, may not depart from the United States without procuring a certificate of compliance with federal income tax laws.[11] This requirement does not apply to diplomats and their families and servants, employees of foreign governments and international organizations, and various students, trainees, and exchange visitors.[12] When a sailing permit is requested, the IRS usually responds by terminating the alien's taxable year, thus permitting assessment and collection of the resulting tax liability. This procedure is not employed, however, if the IRS finds that the alien's departure will not jeopardize collection of his tax liability, as in the case of a resident alien planning to return to the United States.[13]

¶66.7 FOREIGN GOVERNMENTS, INTERNATIONAL ORGANIZATIONS, AND THEIR EMPLOYEES

¶66.7.1 Foreign Governments

Under §892, a foreign government is exempt from U.S. taxation on interest and dividend income, gains on sales of securities, and a few other types of income.[1] The term "foreign government" includes "the integral parts [and] con-

---

[10] IRC §6013(h). See Reg. §§1.6013-6(a)(2)(v), 1.6013-7(a)(2) (for year of election, both spouses are ineligible for benefits extended by treaty to residents of foreign countries).

[11] See generally Guttman, The Sailing Permit: Tax Compliance and Departing Aliens, 63 Tax Notes 24 (Apr. 14, 1994).

[12] Reg. §1.6851-2(a)(2).

[13] Reg. §1.6851-2(b). See Hofstetter v. CIR, 98 TC 695 (1992) (issuance of certificate of compliance under §6851(d) does not preclude IRS from later asserting deficiency; no estoppel in absence of showing of detrimental reliance).

[1] IRC §892(a)(1). See Reg. §§1.892-7T(d), (e) (earnings and profits attributable to income exempt under §892 are exempt from branch profits tax; items exempt under §892 are also exempt from withholding). See supra ¶66.5 for the branch profits tax and ¶66.2.12 for withholding. See generally Bergquist, U.S. Taxation of Foreign Governments and Their Controlled Entities, 39 Tax Notes 115 (Apr. 4, 1988); Levine & Shajnfeld, U.S. Tax

trolled entities of a foreign sovereign."[2] A government's integral parts include agencies and instrumentalities that are governing authorities, but not property whose income inures to the benefit of private persons.[3] A "controlled" entity is an entity that is separate in form from the foreign government but is wholly owned and controlled by the government, either directly or through other controlled entities, provided that (1) it is organized under the laws of that government, (2) no part of its earnings inures to any private person, and (3) the foreign government is entitled to its assets on liquidation.[4] A pension trust for government employees can qualify as a controlled entity.[5] For purposes of the foregoing rules, income inures to the benefit of a private person if a governmental agency or controlled entity is used as a conduit for investment by individuals for their personal benefit or if individuals divert income from its intended use by "means explicitly or implicitly approved of by the foreign sovereign."[6]

The §892 exclusion is also allowed to political subdivisions of a foreign country and "transnational entities," defined as "an organization created by more than one foreign sovereign that has broad powers over external and domestic affairs of all participating foreign countries stretching beyond economic subjects to those concerning legal relations and transcending state or political boundaries."[7] This definition seems designed to cover the European Union and may have no other application. An entity controlled by two or more foreign governments cannot qualify as a controlled entity unless it is a transnational entity.[8]

The §892 exemption covers income from stocks, bonds and other securities, and bank deposits. The term "other securities" is construed to include any "evidence of indebtedness,"[9] thereby extending the exclusion to all interest in-

---

Exemption for Foreign Governments and Controlled Entities after TRA, 66 J. Tax'n 222 (1987); Forouhar, Section 892 Revisited, 70 Tax Notes 1013 (Feb. 19, 1996).

In the version described here, §892 applies to amounts received after July 1, 1986. Pub. L. No. 99-514, §1247(b), 100 Stat. 2085, 2584 (1986); Reg. §1.892-1T(b). The present statute, however, is quite similar to regulations under the pre-1986 version of §892. Reg. §1.892-1T. See Qantas Airways Ltd. v. US, 62 F3d 385 (Fed. Cir. 1995), cert. denied, 116 S. Ct. 910 (1996) (regulations under pre-1986 §892, denying §892 exemption to "integral parts" and "controlled entities" of foreign government to extent they were "engaged in commercial activities in the United States," were valid).

[2] Reg. §1.892-2T(a)(1). See H.R. Rep. No. 841, 99th Cong., 2d Sess., at II-655 (Conf. Rep.), reprinted in 1986-3 CB (vol. 4) 655; Rev. Rul. 69-361, 1969-1 CB 193 (quasi-governmental foreign hospital, with separate assets, not exempt).

[3] Reg. §1.892-2T(a)(2).

[4] Reg. §1.892-2T(a)(3).

[5] Reg. §1.892-2T(c). See Rev. Rul. 88-7, 1988-1 CB 269 (where foreign local government holds employee retirement funds directly, income is that of government itself, not controlled entity).

[6] Reg. §1.892-2T(b).

[7] Reg. §1.892-2T(d).

[8] Reg. §1.892-2T(a)(3).

[9] Reg. §1.892-3T(a)(3).

come, possibly excepting interest on an open account indebtedness not evidenced in writing. The exempted income also includes gains on sales of stocks and debt instruments and income received under agreements to loan securities to brokers for use in short sales.

The exemption also extends to income from "financial instruments held in the execution of governmental financial or monetary policy."[10] The term "financial instruments" includes forward, futures, and option contracts in any currency and currency swap agreements, but not currency itself unless it is held by a foreign central bank of issue.[11] Income from a financial instrument is exempt under this rule only if the implementation of governmental financial or monetary policy is the primary purpose for holding the instrument.[12]

The exemption does not cover income from real property in the United States, including gain on a sale of a U.S. real property interest.[13] For example, if a foreign government owns an office building in New York City that it holds for rental, its rental income is not exempt under §892. However, gain on a sale of stock of a corporation is normally exempt, even if the corporation's assets consist primarily of U.S. real property, unless the foreign government holds a controlling interest.[14] Other types of income not qualifying for the exemption are (1) income and gains from commodities trading (except financial instruments held to implement financial or monetary policy),[15] (2) gains on spot sales of currencies other than the government's own currency,[16] (3) gain on a disposition of an interest in a partnership or trust,[17] and (4) income from a foreign government's sponsorship of a tour in the United States of a ballet troupe.[18]

The exemption is also denied to income "derived from the conduct of any commercial activity" whether the commercial activity is located within or outside the United States.[19] The term "commercial activities" includes activities that "are ordinarily conducted . . . with a view towards the current or future production of income."[20] The term does not include "governmental functions," defined as "activities performed for the general public with respect to the common

---

[10] IRC §892(a)(1).

[11] Reg. §1.892-3T(a)(4).

[12] Reg. §1.892-3T(a)(5).

[13] Reg. §1.892-3T(a).

[14] See infra text accompanying notes 23–30 for controlled commercial entities.

[15] Reg. §1.892-3T(a)(3).

[16] Reg. §1.892-3T(b) Ex. 1.

[17] Reg. §1.892-3T(a)(2).

[18] Reg. §1.892-3T(b) Ex. 3.

[19] IRC §892(a)(2)(A)(i). See Rev. Proc. 98-7, 1998-1 CB —, §4.01(7) (IRS will not rule in advance on whether particular activity is commercial or particular income derives from commercial activities). For the application of the commercial activities rule to a foreign central bank of issue, see infra ¶66.7.2.

[20] Reg. §1.892-4T(b).

welfare or which relate to the administration of some phase of government."[21] It also excludes (1) the holding of stocks, bonds, and financial instruments, (2) the holding of real property that produces no current income, (3) trading in stocks, securities, or commodities for the foreign government's own account, (4) athletic events and arts performances and exhibitions, and (5) the purchasing of goods for the government's use.[22]

Moreover, the exemption is denied to a "controlled commercial entity" and to a foreign government's income from such an entity, including gain on a disposition of the government's interest in the entity.[23] An entity is a "controlled commercial entity" if it engages in "commercial activities" anywhere in the world and the foreign government owns either (1) 50 percent or more (by value or voting power) of the shares or other interests in the entity or (2) any interest that permits it to exercise "effective control" over the entity.[24] In applying the ownership tests, the foreign government is treated as owner of all interests held by its integral parts and controlled entities.[25] A foreign government may have effective control even if it owns only a small equity interest in the entity.[26] For example, if a foreign government is a minority shareholder of a corporation but also is a substantial creditor and controls a natural resource exploited by the corporation, the corporation may be a controlled commercial entity.

Whether a corporation is engaged in a commercial activity is determined under the definition of that term described above. A corporation is deemed engaged in commercial activities, however, if it is a U.S. real property holding corporation or would be but for the fact it is a foreign corporation.[27] A pension trust for the benefit of government employees is a controlled commercial entity if it has income that in the hands of a pension trust of a private U.S. employer, would be taxed as unrelated business income.[28] Commercial activities of one controlled corporation are not usually attributed to other controlled entities of the foreign government, even if a parent-subsidiary or brother-sister relationship exists between the controlled entities,[29] but commercial activities of partnerships are attributed to their partners.

Income of a controlled entity engaged in commercial activity "is treated like income of a privately owned entity."[30]

---

[21] Reg. §1.892-4T(c)(4).

[22] Reg. §1.892-4T(c).

[23] IRC §892(a)(2)(A)(ii).

[24] IRC §892(a)(2)(B).

[25] Reg. §1.892-5T(c)(1).

[26] Reg. §1.892-5T(c)(2).

[27] Reg. §1.892-5T(b)(1). For the term "U.S. real property holding corporation," see supra ¶¶66.4.2, 66.4.3.

[28] Reg. §1.892-5T(b)(3).

[29] Reg. §1.892-5T(d).

[30] H.R. Rep. No. 841, 99th Cong., 2d Sess. II-655 (1986).

A foreign government is treated as a corporate resident of its country.[31] The principal importance of this rule is to qualify the government for benefits afforded its residents under an income tax treaty with the United States if the government similarly treats the U.S. government.

If a foreign government has income that is not exempt under §892, the tax treatment of the income is apparently determined by the rules for foreign corporations.[32]

¶66.7.2 Foreign Central Banks of Issue

Income derived by foreign central banks of issue from U.S. government obligations and bank deposits is exempt from U.S. tax under §895 unless the securities or deposits are held for use in "commercial banking functions or other commercial activities."[33] "A foreign central bank of issue is a bank which is by law or government sanction the principal authority, other than the government itself, issuing instruments intended to circulate as currency."[34]

Section 895 stands in the shadow of §892, which usually provides a broader exemption.[35] A central bank of issue is a "controlled commercial entity" for purposes of §892 only if it engages in commercial activities in the United States.[36] If the bank eschews such activities, it qualifies for the §892 exemption, and the foreign government's income from the bank is also exempt. Although gains on a foreign government's spot sales of currency other than its own currency are not exempt under §892, such gains qualify for exemption under §895 when realized by a central bank of issue if the holding of the currency is "an essential part" of the country's reserve policy.[37]

¶66.7.3 International Organizations

International organizations enjoy a blanket exemption from U.S. income taxation that covers income from stocks, bonds and other securities, interest on

---

[31] IRC §892(a)(3). See Reg. §1.884-0(a) (because §892(a)(3) treats foreign government as "corporate resident of its country," it may be subject to branch taxes under §884 for taxable years ending after September 10, 1992).

[32] See supra ¶66.3.

[33] For purposes of §895, the Bank for International Settlements is treated as a foreign central bank of issue. See Reg. §1.895-1(c) (exemption inapplicable to obligations and deposits held by central bank as agent, custodian, or trustee).

[34] Reg. §1.895-1(b)(1) (such a bank is generally custodian of country's banking reserves).

[35] Section 895 applies to some central banks that are not entitled to exemption under §892 because, for example, they are not wholly owned by a foreign government. Reg. §§1.892-7T(b), 1.895-1(b)(2).

[36] IRC §892(a)(2)(B). For the application of the pre-1986 version of §892 to central banks of issue, see Rev. Rul. 75-298, 1975-2 CB 290.

[37] Reg. §1.892-3T(b) Exs. 1, 2.

bank deposits, as well as income "from any other source within the United States."[38] The term "international organization" includes any public international organization entitled to the benefits of the International Organizations Immunities Act.[39] An organization enjoys these benefits only if designated as a qualifying organization pursuant to an Executive Order, but the exemption is sometimes allowed for periods before such an order is entered.[40]

¶66.7.4   Employees

Under §893, salaries and wages received by an employee of an international organization for "official services" are excluded from gross income unless the employee is a U.S. citizen.[41] This exclusion is also available to an employee of a foreign government if (1) the employee's services are similar to services performed by employees of the U.S. government in foreign countries, (2) the services are not "primarily in connection with a commercial activity," and (3) the foreign government allows a similar exemption to U.S. employees performing similar services in that government's home country.[42] The exclusion for employees of a foreign government encompasses officials of the government, consular officers, and nondiplomatic representatives. Subject to the same limitations, the exclusion is allowed to an employee of an entity controlled by a foreign government unless the entity is a "controlled commercial entity."

An alien employee of an international organization or foreign government usually loses the §893 exclusion on applying for permanent residence in the United States.[43] In *Ying v. CIR*, the taxpayers, who were employed in the United States by UNICEF and the United Nations, applied for permanent residence, and as part of their application, filed a standard INS form by which they "waive[d] all rights, privileges, exemptions and immunities which would otherwise accrue to them under any law or executive order by reason of such occu-

---

[38] IRC §892(b); Reg. §1.892-6T. See Rev. Rul. 72-183, 1972-1 CB 213 (international organization's staff benefit fund is exempt).

[39] IRC §7701(a)(18).

[40] Reg. §1.892-6T(b).

[41] IRC §893. A citizen of the Republic of the Philippines is entitled to this exclusion even if also a citizen of the United States. IRC §893(a)(1).

[42] The Secretary of State certifies to the IRS the countries granting the required reciprocal exemption. IRC §893(b). See Reg. §1.892-7T(a) ("foreign government" has same meaning here as under §892); Reg. §1.893-1(a)(4), (5) (employees filing waivers to maintain immigrant status under Immigration and Nationality Act lose exemption under §893); Rev. Rul. 75-425, 1975-2 CB 291 (same but treaty benefits not waived); Rev. Rul. 72-54, 1972-1 CB 213 (compensation paid to employee of foreign municipality qualifies); Rev. Rul. 56-44, 1956-1 CB 319 (former employee's pension not exempt). See generally Tillinghast, Sovereign Immunity From the Tax Collector: United States Income Taxation of Foreign Governments and International Organizations, 10 Law & Pol'y Int'l Bus. 495 (1978).

[43] Reg. §§1.893-1(a)(4), (5), (b)(4).

pational status" as employee of an international organization.[44] The court held that the waiver disqualified them from the exclusion.[45]

¶66.8 RETALIATORY AUTHORITY

Section 891, enacted in 1938 but never invoked, authorizes a doubling of the tax rates applicable to citizens and corporations of a foreign country if the President finds that the foreign country subjects United States citizens or corporations to "discriminatory or extraterritorial taxes."

A less drastic presidential power is granted by §896, permitting (1) restoration of the pre-1967 tax rules for residents and corporations of a foreign country if U.S. citizens are subject to "more burdensome taxes" on income derived from sources within that country than the United States imposes on that country's residents or corporations and (2) adjustments to the effective rate of tax on residents or corporations of a foreign country that subject their U.S. counterparts to "discriminatory taxes," provided the foreign country does not mend its ways on request and certain other conditions are satisfied. These powers were vested in the President by §896 when the U.S. tax rules applicable to foreign investors were liberalized in 1966.[1] The big stick was intended more as a prod to be used in treaty negotiations seeking reciprocal concessions than as a weapon for unilateral use.[2] Since the President has not invoked his authority under §896, one can conclude either that the implied threats worked or that following them up with action was deemed counterproductive.

---

[44] Ying v. CIR, 25 F3d 84 (2d Cir. 1994).

[45] One of the taxpayers was a citizen of the Philippines, and the statute allows the exclusion for Philippine citizens who are also citizens of United States. See supra note 41. From this, the Tax Court inferred that, for Philippine citizens, the exclusion is not "inconsistent with an assumption of the responsibilities of [U.S.] citizenship." The Court of Appeals disagreed, noting that the immigration laws require renunciation of foreign citizenship as a condition to naturalization in the United States.

[1] For the 1966 legislation, see S. Rep. No. 1707, 89th Cong., 2d Sess., reprinted in 1966-2 CB 1059, 1087.

[2] See S. Rep. No. 1707, supra note 1, at 1087.

For a similar tit-for-tat approach in taxing foreign nationals, see §901(c) (permitting the President to suspend the foreign tax credit in the case of resident aliens whose country does not provide a reciprocal credit for U.S. citizens resident there).

CHAPTER
67

U.S. Possessions

¶67.1 INTRODUCTORY

When used in a geographical sense, the term "United States" includes only the states and the District of Columbia.[1] As a consequence, income derived from U.S. possessions or from Puerto Rico (which is treated as a possession for federal

---

[1] IRC §7701(a)(9). The statute leaves open the meaning of the term United States when used in senses other than "the geographical sense"—for example, to denote sovereignty as in the phrase "law of the United States." See the reference to "geographical and governmental sense" in Reg. §1.935-1(c)(1)(i)(A).

See generally Hoff, U.S. Federal Tax Policy Towards the Territories: Past, Present and Future, 37 Tax L. Rev. 51 (1981).

income tax purposes)[2] is ordinarily foreign source income. The possessions of the United States are American Samoa, Guam, the Northern Mariana Islands, and the Virgin Islands.[3] Statutory provisions referring to "foreign countries," however, usually make specific reference to U.S. possessions if they are intended to be covered. For example, §§901(b)(1) and 901(b)(2) state that income taxes imposed by U.S. possessions qualify for the foreign tax credit. Corporations organized under the laws of U.S. possessions are foreign corporations by virtue of §§7701(a)(4) and 7701(a)(5) and can therefore be controlled foreign corporations within the meaning of subpart F.[4]

These general principles are qualified, however, by several special rules applicable only to citizens and residents of and persons doing business in U.S. possessions. Some of the special rules have the effect of dividing taxing authority between the federal and possessions governments, and others are designed to prevent federal law from negating tax incentives used by possessions to attract investors. In applying these rules, it is often necessary to determine the amount of the taxpayer's gross or taxable income from sources within and outside a U.S. possession. The rules for determining U.S. source income are used for this purpose, substituting the name of the possession for "the United States."[5]

¶67.2 POSSESSIONS CORPORATIONS

¶67.2.1 Generally

Domestic corporations often derive no benefit from foreign tax holidays because a reduction in the foreign tax may simply result in an equal reduction in the foreign tax credit allowed against their U.S. taxes. To avoid nullifying tax incentives granted by U.S. possessions, §936 permits domestic corporations deriving most of their income from a U.S. possession (including Puerto Rico) to elect a special credit that effectively exempts possessions income from U.S. taxa-

---

[2] IRC §7701(d).

[3] For an obsolete listing, see Reg. §1.931-1(a)(1) (excluding Virgin Islands, for reasons peculiar to §931 as in effect when regulation was promulgated, and Northern Mariana Islands, whose relationship with United States was established after regulation's adoption).

[4] For controlled foreign corporations, see infra ¶68.2. See also IRC §957(c) (certain corporations of possessions and Puerto Rico excluded from controlled foreign corporation classification).

[5] See Reg. §1.863-6. See also Reg. §§1.861-8(f)(1)(vi)(E), 1.861-8(f)(1)(vi)(F), 1.861-8(f)(1)(vi)(G), 1.861-8(f)(1)(vi)(H) (allocation and apportionment of deductions). Section 863(b)(3) requires income from the purchase of property within a possession and its sale within the United States to be allocated between possessions and U.S. sources, instead of being allocated wholly to domestic sources under §861(a)(6). For permissible methods of allocation, see Reg. §1.863-3(c).

tion.[1] This benefit has been repealed for possessions businesses begun after 1995.[2] However, under complex rules described below, it is preserved over as long as 10 years for corporations that claimed the benefit for 1995.

The exempted income is subject only to the possession's income tax, and the corporation therefore reaps the benefit of local tax exemptions or rate reductions. The §936 credit has been described as follows:

> [I]n lieu of the ordinary foreign tax credit (for income taxes paid to foreign governments) a tax credit was enacted (the possession tax credit) for the full amount of U.S. tax liability on possessions source income. This is referred to as "tax sparing" since a credit is granted whether or not foreign taxes are paid.[3]

Most corporations claiming the §936 credit operate in Puerto Rico. The staff of the Joint Committee on Taxation reported in 1982:

> Puerto Rico generally has matched the United States' tax incentives with incentives of its own. Puerto Rico grants tax exemptions of up to 90 percent for income of certain approved enterprises for specified periods of time (generally 10 to 25 years). In addition Puerto Rico exempts from income taxation certain passive income, such as interest on fixed-term deposits in qualifying banks, in the hands of certain companies to which it has granted investment incentives.[4]

The statutory predecessor of §936 was enacted in 1921, "primarily to help U.S. corporations compete with foreign firms in the Philippines (then a U.S. possession)."[5] The present purpose of the credit is to "assist the U.S. possessions

---

[1] See IRC §936(d)(1) ("possession" includes Puerto Rico). See also IRC §936(f) (§936 credit not allowed to DISC, former DISC, or corporation owning stock in a DISC, former DISC, FSC, or former FSC). See generally Griggs, Operating in Puerto Rico in the Section 936 Era, 32 Tax L. Rev. 239 (1977). See also Godoy, U.S. and Local Taxation of Individuals and Businesses in Puerto Rico, 12 Tax Notes Int'l 597 (Feb. 19, 1996); Griggs, Puerto Rico Enacts New Tax Incentives Law to Counteract Section 936 Phase-Down, 9 J. Int'l Tax'n 35 (1998); Hexner & Jenkins, Puerto Rico and Section 936: A Costly Dependence, 10 Tax Notes Int'l 235 (Jan. 16, 1995); Nutter, U.S. Possessions Corporations, 1993, 17 Stat. Income Bull. 144 (Fall 1997) (for 1993, 474 possessions corporations claimed possessions tax credits of $4.6 billion).

[2] IRC §936(j)(1), as enacted by Pub. L. No. 104-188, §1601 (1996). See Griggs, Congress Votes Partial 936 Repeal to Pay for Small Business Tax Relief, 7 J. Int'l Tax'n 377 (1996).

[3] Staff of Joint Comm. on Tax'n, 99th Cong., 2d Sess., General Explanation of the Tax Reform Act of 1986 at 1000 (Comm. Print 1987) [hereinafter 1986 Bluebook].

[4] Staff of Joint Comm. on Tax'n, 97th Cong., 2d Sess., General Explanation of the Revenue Provisions of the Tax Equity and Fiscal Responsibility Act of 1982 at 80-81 (Comm. Print 1982) [hereinafter 1982 Bluebook]. See 1986 Bluebook, supra note 3, at 999 ("since the Puerto Rican Industrial Incentives Act of 1948, most possessions subsidiaries have operated under a complete or partial exemption from Puerto Rican taxes").

[5] 1986 Bluebook, supra note 3, at 999. From 1921 until 1976, a domestic corporation was wholly exempt from U.S. tax if it derived at least 80 percent of its income from

in obtaining employment producing investments by U.S. corporations."[6] "The need for special tax incentives [has been] attributed, in part, to the additional costs imposed by the possessions status, such as the U.S. minimum wage standards and the requirement to use U.S. flag ships."[7]

To qualify for the credit, a domestic corporation must elect under §936 and must derive at least 80 percent of its gross income from possessions sources and at least 75 percent of its gross income from the active conduct of a trade or business in a possession. Very few independent corporations meet these requirements. Most commonly, a corporation with business operations in a possession segregates these operations into a separate subsidiary whose activities and investments are restricted to those generating income qualifying for the credit. Corporations qualifying for the §936 credit are sometimes called §936 corporations, possessions corporations, or island affiliates.[8]

¶67.2.2   Qualification for Credit

The §936 credit is only available to domestic corporations that elect it.[9] The election can be made only for a year in which the corporation satisfies both of the gross income tests described below.[10] Once effectively made, the election applies for the year of the election and all subsequent years until it is revoked. Although no credit is allowed for taxable years in which the gross income tests are not met, failure to satisfy the tests does not terminate the election; rather, it continues in effect and results in a credit in later years for which the tests are satisfied. During the first nine years it is in effect, the election may be revoked only with IRS

---

sources within a possession and at least 50 percent of its income was from the active conduct of a business. The credit mechanism was adopted in 1976 to limit the exemption to income from possessions sources. Id. at 1000.

[6] See S. Rep. No. 938, 95th Cong., 2d Sess. 279 (1976). The efficiency and effectiveness of §936 in boosting employment in the possessions is often questioned. During 1987, approximately 122,000 persons were employed in manufacturing industries in Puerto Rico, of whom approximately 101,000 were employees of §936 companies. The tax benefits allowed to these companies, however, amounted to 94.5 percent of the total compensation paid to their workers. In the pharmaceuticals industry, which accounted for more than one half of the §936 credits claimed, the tax benefits were 267.4 percent of the total compensation paid. Bradford, U.S. Possessions Corporation Returns, 1987, 11 Statistics of Income Bull. 51 (Summer 1991). See U.S. Possessions Corporation Returns, 1989, 12 Statistics of Income Bull. 97 (Fall 1992); Nutter, Statistics of Income Studies of International Income and Taxes, 13 Statistics of Income Bull. 10 (Winter 1994) (from 1985 to 1989, number of possessions corporations declined from 594 to 513, but §936 credits increased from $2.5 billion to $2.8 billion). See also Salzarulo, An Analysis of the Section 936 Disclosures of a Major Drug Company, 62 Tax Notes 1451 (Mar. 14, 1994) (analyzing income tax disclosures by Eli Lilly for 1988–1992).

[7] 1986 Bluebook, supra note 3, at 999–1000.

[8] See 1982 Bluebook, supra note 4, at 87.

[9] For election procedures, see Reg. §1.936-1(a).

[10] IRC §936(e)(1). See infra ¶67.2.2 text accompanying note 12 for the gross income tests.

consent.[11] It is freely revocable thereafter. A corporation that has revoked a §936 election is eligible to elect again for any subsequent year in which it meets the gross income tests.

A domestic corporation qualifies for the §936 credit for a particular taxable year only if, during a test period, it derived at least 80 percent of its gross income from sources within a possession and at least 75 percent of its gross income from the active conduct of a business in a possession.[12] The test period usually consists of the three taxable years preceding the taxable year. If the corporation was organized less than three years before the start of the year, the test period is the period of the corporation's existence prior to the current year. For the first year of the corporation's operations, the current year is apparently the test period.

For a taxable year beginning after 1995, the credit may be elected only if the taxpayer is an "existing credit claimant," defined as a corporation that (1) was actively engaged in a trade or business in a possession on October 13, 1995, and made the §936 election for the taxable year including that date or (2) acquired all of the assets of a trade or business of a corporation meeting the foregoing requirements.[13] An existing credit claimant loses this privileged status if, after October 13, 1995, it adds a new line of business (other than by acquisition of a trade or business of another existing credit claimant).[14]

¶67.2.3 Computation of Credit

The §936 credit generally equals the electing corporation's precredit tax on two types of income: (1) income from sources without the United States that is earned in the active conduct of a trade or business in a possession and (2) foreign

---

[11] IRC §936(e)(2). See Rev. Rul. 85-124, 1985-2 CB 179 (where one §936 corporation absorbs another in statutory merger, neither corporation's election is terminated by merger); Rev. Rul. 80-138, 1980-1 CB 178 (election not terminated by corporation's reincorporation in another state in transaction qualifying as a reorganization under §368(a)(1)(F)).

[12] IRC §§30A(a)(1), 936(a)(2). For purposes of the 80 percent rule, source is determined without regard to §904(f), which sometimes recharacterizes foreign source income as domestic income after the taxpayer has had an overall foreign loss. See infra ¶69.8 for §904(f).

The floor on active business income from a possession, presently 75 percent, was 65 percent for 1985, 60 percent for 1984, 55 percent for 1983, and 50 percent for earlier years. See 1986 Bluebook, supra note 3, at 1003 ("Congress believed that requiring possessions corporations to derive a larger fraction of their income directly from the conduct of an active trade or business would better achieve the objectives of creating employment-producing investment in the possessions").

[13] IRC §936(j)(9)(A). A trade or business commenced as late as December 31, 1995, qualifies if, on October 13 of that year, the corporation had a binding contract to acquire assets to be used in the business or to sell goods to be produced in the business. IRC §936(j)(9)(C).

Whether a corporation is an existing credit claimant is determined separately with respect to operations in each U.S. possession. IRC §936(j)(10).

[14] IRC §936(j)(9)(B).

source income on a sale or exchange of substantially all assets of an active business in a possession.[15]

For taxable years beginning before 1996 (and for the portion of the succeeding year preceding July 1, 1996), the credit also includes the precredit tax on a third category of income: qualified possession source investment income. To be "qualified possession source investment income," an item must meet three requirements.[16] First, it must be from sources within a possession in which the taxpayer is actively engaged in business. Second, the property producing the income must be located in the possession or held "for use therein." A deposit in a possessions bank normally meets this test only if the bank reloans the funds in a possession in which the corporation carries on an active business.[17] Funds deposited with or otherwise invested in a financial institution are deemed used in Puerto Rico, however, if they are reloaned to borrowers who invest them in active business assets or development projects in a Caribbean Basin country or the Virgin Islands.[18] Third, the invested funds either must be derived from the

---

[15] IRC §§30A(a)(1), 936(a)(1).

If an electing corporation's adjusted basis for property is determined with reference to the basis of another person for the property, gain on a sale or exchange of the property is excluded in computing the credit unless the prior owner qualified for the §936 credit throughout the period it held the property. IRC §936(d)(3)(A). For example, if a domestic corporation engaged primarily in business in the United States transfers property to a newly organized domestic subsidiary that elects under §936, gain recognized by the subsidiary on a subsequent sale of the property is not eligible for the §936 credit because the subsidiary inherits the parent's basis for the property incident to the rules providing for nonrecognition of the parent's gain on the incorporation transaction. See IRC §§351, 362(a), discussed infra ¶91.1. On the other hand, if the assets of one §936 corporation are transferred to another such corporation in a reorganization, this disqualification is inapplicable unless the transferor failed to qualify for the §936 credit for a portion of the period it held the property.

[16] IRC §936(d)(2).

[17] According to the staff of the Joint Committee on Taxation:

The Government of Puerto Rico has established rules ... which apply to financial institutions that accept deposits from possessions corporations. The purpose of these rules is to require that such deposits be invested only in specified assets located in Puerto Rico including: loans for commercial, agricultural, and industrial purposes; business and residential mortgage loans; loans and investments in securities of the government of Puerto Rico and its instrumentalities; student loans; and automobile loans. In addition, financial institutions are required to invest 30 percent of possessions corporation deposits in Puerto Rico Government obligations, including 10 percent in obligations of the Government Development Bank for Puerto Rico ("GDB").

1986 Bluebook, supra note 3, at 1000. See id. at 1003 ("deposits of possessions corporations constitute over one third of commercial bank liabilities" in Puerto Rico).

[18] IRC §936(d)(4) (loans may be made by financial institution holding taxpayer's deposits, the Government Development Bank for Puerto Rico, or the Puerto Rico Economic Development Bank); Reg. §1.936-10(c). See 1986 Bluebook, supra note 3, at 1005 ("active business assets generally mean plant, equipment, and inventory associated with a

active business in the possession or must consist of a reinvestment of qualified possessions source investment income or the proceeds of a sale of property producing such income.[19]

For years beginning after 1993, the credit is usually limited by a ceiling computed with reference to the payroll and depreciation expenses of the corporation's activities in a possession, but the corporation may instead elect to take a fixed percentage of the credit otherwise allowable.[20] According to the House Ways and Means Committee, which recommended a ceiling based solely on wages paid:

> Although the section 936 tax credit was enacted to foster economic development in the U.S. possessions, past studies have indicated that a disproportionate share of the tax benefits attributable to section 936 is realized by certain industries that create relatively few jobs in the possessions. These industries tend to be those for which a large portion of taxable income is derived from the use of intangible assets (e.g., exploitation of patents, tradenames, or secret formulas). The committee is concerned, moreover, that a disproportionate share of the cost that all U.S. taxpayers bear in order to provide the section 936 credit may have inured to the benefit of the stockholders of the possession corporations, as compared to the U.S. citizens residing in the possessions. To address this concern without hurting the people for whose benefit the credit was adopted, the committee believes that a better approach would be to place a limit on the tax benefit available to a possession corporation, and to base that limit on a measure of the employment created by the corporation in the possession.[21]

1. *Economic activity limitation.* Under the general rule, the §936 credit with respect to active possession income—foreign source income from the active conduct of a trade or business in a U.S. possession and from the sale of substantially all of the assets of the trade or business—may not exceed the sum of the four amounts.[22] These amounts, described more fully below, are 60 percent of the corporation's "qualified possession wages," 60 percent of the employee fringe benefit expense allocable to these wages, varying percentages of the depreciation

---

manufacturing operation"; "a development project generally means an infrastructure investment, such as a road or water treatment facility, that directly supports industrial development").

An investment in a Caribbean Basin country does not qualify, however, unless the country has entered into an agreement under §274(h)(6) to exchange tax information with the United States. IRC §936(d)(4)(B). For §274(h)(6), see supra ¶21.1.9.

See Lederman, Obtaining Tax-Advantaged Financing for Investments in the Caribbean Basin, 72 J. Tax'n 104 (1990).

[19] See Prop. Reg. §1.936-3A.

[20] Pub. L. No. 103-66, §13227, 107 Stat. 312 (1993). See Salzarulo, One Company's Efforts to Ameliorate the Loss of Tax Benefits Under Section 936, 11 Tax Notes Int'l 670 (Sept. 4, 1995).

[21] HR Rep. No. 111, 103d Cong., 1st Sess. 676 (1993). See supra note 6.

[22] IRC §936(a)(4)(A).

allowances for tangible property used in a possession business, and possessions income taxes on the income no longer sheltered from U.S. tax by the §936 credit.

The first amount is 60 percent of the "qualified possession wages" paid or incurred by the corporation during the taxable year.[23] Generally, wages are qualified possession wages only if they are (1) paid or incurred "in connection with" the active conduct of business in a U.S. possession (2) for services performed in the possession (3) while the employee's "principal place of employment" is in the possession.[24] However, the qualified possession wages for a particular employee may not exceed 85 percent of the contribution and benefit base under the Social Security Act for the calendar year during which the taxable year begins.[25] For 1996, this base—the maximum earnings subject to tax under the OASDI portion of Social Security—is $62,700, and the 85 percent ceiling for that year is $53,295. The ceiling is proportionately reduced if the employee is not employed "on a substantially full-time basis" throughout the taxable year or if the principal place of the employee's employment is in the possession for less than all of the year.[26] Wages paid to an employee "assigned by the employer to perform services for another person" are not qualified possession wages unless the corporation's principal business is "to make employees available for temporary periods to other persons in return for compensation."[27]

The second amount is 60 percent of the corporation's "allocable employee fringe benefit expenses" for the year.[28] The employee fringe benefit expenses taken into account are the amounts deductible for the year for employer contributions to qualified pension, profit sharing, stock bonus, and annuity plans, employer-provided medical benefits, and life and disability insurance provided to employees.[29] The "allocable employee fringe benefit expenses" are usually the employee fringe benefit expenses, multiplied by a fraction whose numerator is the corporation's qualified possession wages for the year and whose denominator is the aggregate of all wages paid or incurred during the year.[30] However, the allocable expenses may not exceed 15 percent of the qualified possession wages.

The third amount is the sum of 15 percent of the current depreciation allowances for "short-life qualified tangible property," 40 percent of the depreciation allowances for "medium-life qualified tangible property," and 65 percent

---

[23] IRC §936(a)(4)(A)(i).

[24] IRC §936(i)(1)(A). The term "wages" has the same meaning here as for purposes of the federal unemployment tax. IRC §936(i)(1)(D).

[25] IRC §936(i)(1)(B)(i).

[26] IRC §936(i)(1)(B)(ii).

[27] IRC §936(i)(1)(C).

[28] IRC §936(a)(4)(A)(i).

[29] IRC §936(i)(2)(B). Amounts treated as wages in determining qualified possession wages may not also be treated as employee fringe benefit expenses.

[30] IRC §936(i)(2)(A).

of the allowances for "long-life qualified tangible property."[31] Tangible property is "qualified" if (1) it is used by the corporation in a U.S. possession in the active conduct of a trade or business in the possession and (2) depreciation is determined under §168.[32] Qualified tangible property is "short-life" if it is classified under §168 as 3-year property or 5-year property, is "mid-life" if it is 7-year or 10-year property, or is "long-life" if it is not short-life or mid-life property.[33]

The fourth amount is the "qualified possession income taxes for the taxable year allocable to nonsheltered income."[34] The effect of this aspect of the ceiling is to give the corporation a credit, equivalent to a foreign tax credit, for possessions income taxes on the portion of the corporation's income that is also taxed by the federal government. The creditable amount is the "possession income taxes" for the year, multiplied by a fraction whose numerator is the increase in federal taxes resulting from the economic activity ceiling on the §936 credit and whose denominator is the corporation's federal tax liability, determined without the §936 credit.[35] The "possession income taxes" are the income taxes imposed by U.S. possessions on the taxable income "taken into account in computing" the §936 credit,[36] but if these taxes exceed 9 percent of the corporation's taxable income, the excess is disregarded. In determining the increase in tax resulting from the economic activity ceiling, the inclusion of qualified possession income taxes in the ceiling is disregarded.

Qualified possession income taxes are included in the ceiling only if the corporation does not elect to use the profit split method provided by §936(h)(5)(C)(ii).[37] An electing corporation is instead allowed a deduction (equivalent to the deduction for state income taxes) for the amount of possession income taxes that would be included in the ceiling if the election were not in effect.[38] However, this deduction is not allowed either in determining the §936 credit or in computing the amount of the deduction.

The credit, subject to the economic activity limitation, is generally allowable only for taxable years beginning before 2002.[39] The credit is also allowable for years beginning during the period 2002 through 2005, except that for active businesses in Puerto Rico and the Virgin Islands, the income taken into account in computing the credit is restricted to the corporation's "adjusted base period

---

[31] IRC §936(a)(4)(A)(ii). See IRC §936(i)(4)(A) ("depreciation allowances" are amounts allowable as depreciation under §167).

[32] IRC §936(i)(4)(B)(i). For §168, see supra ¶23.3.

[33] IRC §§936(i)(4)(B)(ii)–936(i)(4)(B)(iv).

[34] IRC §936(a)(4)(A)(iii).

[35] IRC §936(i)(3)(A).

[36] IRC §§936(c), 936(i)(3)(C).

[37] IRC §936(a)(4)(A)(iii). For the profit split method, see infra ¶67.2.4 text accompanying notes 121–127.

[38] IRC §936(i)(3)(B).

[39] IRC §§30A(a)(1), 936(j)(2)(A).

income,"[40] which is the average of the corporation's "inflation-adjusted posses-sion incomes" for three "base year[s]" preceding 1996.[41]

Possession income for a year is foreign source taxable income from the active conduct of a trade or business in a possession and from the sale or ex-change of substantially all of the assets of such a business.[42] The inflation-adjusted possession income for a base year is the possession income for the year, multiplied by one plus the "inflation adjustment percentage" for the year.[43] The inflation adjustment percentage is the sum of (1) the amount by which the consumer price index for 1995 exceeds the index for the calendar year during which the base period year ends and (2) an arbitrary percentage, which is five for a taxable year ending during the 12 months ending October 13, 1995, 10.25 for the preceding 12 months (1994), 15.76 for 1993, 21.55 for 1992, and 27.63 for 1991. The base period consists of the three of these five years that remain after excluding the year for which inflation-adjusted possession income is highest and the year for which that income is lowest.[44] Alternatively, the corporation can elect to have only one base year, which may be either the taxable year ending during 1992 or the first 10 months of 1995.[45] If the latter is chosen, base-year possession income (before inflation adjustment) is six fifths of the income for these 10 months.

2. *Percentage limitation.* In lieu of applying the economic activity ceiling, a possession corporation may elect a credit with respect to active possessions in-come equal to a prescribed percentage of the credit otherwise allowable.[46] The percentage is 60 percent for taxable years beginning in 1994, 55 percent for 1995, 50 percent for 1996, 45 percent for 1997, and 40 percent for 1998 and subsequent years. An electing corporation is allowed a deduction for income taxes paid or incurred to a possession on the portion of the corporation's income that is not sheltered from tax by the §936 credit.[47]

The election must be made for the first taxable year beginning after 1993 for which the corporation is a possession corporation.[48] Thus, a possession corpora-

---

[40] IRC §§30A(a)(1), 936(j)(3)(A). This restriction does not apply if the corporation's active trade or business is located in Guam, American Samoa, or the Commonwealth of the Northern Mariana Islands. IRC §936(j)(8).

[41] IRC §936(j)(4)(A).

[42] IRC §936(j)(6).

[43] IRC §936(j)(4)(B).

[44] IRC §936(j)(5). If the corporation does not have significant possession income for all five of these years, the base period consists of the years (not exceeding three) for which the income is significant. Possession income for a year is not significant if it is 2 percent or less of the largest amount of possession income for any year of the six-year period consisting of the five years described in the text and the succeeding year.

[45] IRC §936(j)(5)(C). The election must be made for the taxable year beginning during 1996.

[46] IRC §936(a)(4)(B).

[47] IRC §§936(a)(4)(B)(i), 936(i)(3)(B).

[48] IRC §936(a)(4)(B)(iii).

tion existing during 1994 must have made the election for the taxable year beginning in 1994, and a corporation organized or becoming a possession corporation thereafter must elect for its first taxable year. The election applies for all subsequent years until it is revoked. It is automatically revoked for a taxable year if the corporation is a member of an affiliated group that includes a possession corporation that does not have an election in effect for the year. "If, for example, a possession corporation that uses the percentage limitation becomes a member of an affiliated group that contains a second possession corporation that uses the economic-activity limitation, then the first corporation will be deemed to have revoked its election to use the percentage limitation."[49] However, the election cannot be revoked later than the taxable year beginning in 1997.[50] A corporation whose election has been revoked may not elect again.

For taxable years beginning after 1995, the credit, subject to the percentage limitation, is allowed only to existing credit claimants (generally, corporations that validly elected §936 credit for the taxable year including October 13, 1995). For such a corporation, the credit is computed as described above for the taxable years beginning in 1996 and 1997.[51] The credit is also allowed for years beginning in the period 1998 through 2005, but for active possessions businesses in Puerto Rico and the Virgin Islands, the income taken into account in computing the credit (before applying the percentage limitation) may not exceed adjusted base period income.[52]

3. *Aggregation election for affiliated groups.* An affiliated group may elect to apply §936 treating as one corporation all possession corporations that would be members of the group, but for the rule of §§1504(b)(3) and 1504(b)(4) excluding possession corporations and foreign corporations from affiliated groups.[53] The §936 credit determined for the aggregate is allocated among the possession corporations included in the affiliated group. The election applies for the year for which it is made and all subsequent years until it is revoked with IRS consent.

4. *Other limitations.* The §936 credit is allowed against the corporation's regular income tax, but not against the environmental tax imposed by §59A, the personal holding company tax imposed by §541, or the tax imposed by §1351 on recoveries of foreign expropriation losses.[54] Although the credit is not allowed against the accumulated earnings tax imposed by §531, income qualifying for the §936 credit is excluded from accumulated taxable income, and assets producing

---

[49] HR Rep. No. 213, 103d Cong., 1st Sess. 627 (Conf. Rep. 1993).

[50] IRC §936(j)(2)(B)(ii).

[51] IRC §936(j)(2)(B)(i).

[52] IRC §936(j)(3)(A).

[53] IRC §936(i)(5). For election procedures, see Rev. Proc. 95-37, 1995-2 CB 395.

[54] IRC §936(a)(3). See infra ¶111.3.12 for the environmental tax and ¶95.2 for the personal holding company tax.

income eligible for the credit are deemed held for the reasonable needs of the business, rather than as unreasonable accumulations of earnings.[55]

A §936 corporation may not take the foreign tax credit or a deduction for taxes imposed by a possession or foreign country on any income that is effectively exempted from U.S. taxation by the §936 credit.[56] The credit and deduction for foreign income taxes (including income taxes imposed by possessions) are allowed to alleviate double taxation. Since the §936 credit eliminates U.S. tax on possessions income, no antidote to double taxation is needed.[57]

5. *Source rules.* Several of the rules in §936, including the 80 percent gross income test and the rules for computing the credit, refer to the corporation's income from sources within the possessions. The source of an item of gross income is determined for these purposes under the rules identifying income from sources within the United States, except that the name of the possession is substituted for the United States in each of these rules.[58]

Generally, the place where the taxpayer receives income is not relevant to the determination of its source. However, gross income usually cannot qualify as possessions source income, regardless of its characterization under the regular source rules, if the corporation receives it in the United States.[59] This disqualification is lifted for income from the active conduct of business in a possession if the income is received from a person not related to the corporation. The exception was added in 1986 "because, in certain situations, where payment must be received in the United States (e.g., certain defense contracts), the rule [forbidding U.S. receipt] may discourage production in the possessions."[60]

6. *Consolidated returns.* To prevent losses incurred in possessions from being used to reduce income from other sources, a §936 corporation cannot join with affiliated corporations in filing a consolidated return while the election is in force, even if it does not currently qualify for a credit under §936.[61]

7. *Taxation of shareholders.* Dividends distributed by a §936 corporation are taxable in the usual manner to its shareholders. If the shareholder is another domestic corporation, the dividends qualify for the dividends received deduction of §243. If a corporate shareholder is a member of the same affiliated group as the distributing corporation, the dividends received deduction is 100 percent.[62] In the common situation where a §936 corporation is a wholly owned subsidiary of a domestic corporation and arranges its affairs so that all of its income qualifies

---

[55] IRC §936(g). See infra ¶95.1 for the accumulated earnings tax.

[56] IRC §936(d). For the foreign tax credit, see infra ¶69.1.

[57] See 1982 Bluebook, supra note 4, at 80.

[58] Reg. §1.863-6. See Prop. Reg. §1.936-2.

[59] IRC §936(b). See Rev. Rul. 79-268, 1979-2 CB 283 (checks received at corporation's office in Puerto Rico qualify even if deposited in U.S. bank account).

[60] 1986 Bluebook, supra note 3, at 1003.

[61] IRC §1504(b)(4).

[62] IRC §§243(a)(3), 243(b). For this purpose, the term "affiliated group" does not exclude possessions corporations.

for the §936 credit, the combined effect of the credit and the dividends received deduction is to exempt the possessions income from U.S. tax at both the subsidiary and parent level. If dividends from a §936 corporation are taxed by a possession or foreign country, however, a shareholder qualifying for a dividends received deduction is not entitled to a foreign tax credit or deduction for the tax.[63]

¶67.2.4 Intangible Property Income

Section 936(h) limits the §936 credit with respect to income from intangibles. The staff of the Joint Committee on Taxation explained the reasons for the enactment of the limitation in 1982 as follows:

> Under prior law, some taxpayers [took] the position that they could make tax-free transfers of intangible assets created or acquired in the United States (such as patents, secret processes, and trademarks) to an electing section 936 corporation, and that no allocation of income generated by those intangibles to the U.S. parent was required . . . .
>
> For instance, a U.S. pharmaceutical company could spend (and deduct or amortize and take a research and development tax credit for) large sums on research and development of new drugs. When it developed an effective drug, it could transfer the patent on the drug and the know-how to manufacture the drug to a section 936 subsidiary in a purportedly tax-free exchange. Thereafter, the 936 company could manufacture the drug and claim for itself the extremely high profits which typically result from the sale of pharmaceutical products. It was Congress' understanding that high profits on certain pharmaceutical products must be realized because, according to the industry, the profits from the relatively few successful drugs must, in effect, amortize the development costs of all the unsuccessful products and finance the necessary research and development for future products. This results in the creation of extremely valuable intangibles (e.g., patents and trademarks) in the drug industry. If there is no allocation of income from the intangibles to their developer (the U.S. parent), a distortion of income results, with the parent obtaining deductions for its efforts while the 936 company realizes tax-free income.[64]

Congress responded to this problem by providing in §936(h) that income of a §936 corporation from the use of patents, copyrights, and other intellectual property must be reallocated to the corporation's shareholders. The reallocated amount is included in the shareholders' gross income and is removed from the corporation's gross income, thereby reducing the income qualifying for the §936 credit. Generally, the reallocated amount includes all income of the corporation that is attributable to its use of intellectual property, excepting only an amount equal to the corporation's production costs and a profit representing a reasonable

---

[63] IRC §901(g).

[64] 1982 Bluebook, supra note 4, at 83.

return on these costs. The purpose of §936(h) "is generally to subject to U.S. tax income attributable to intangibles that add value to the products produced by a section 936 corporation."[65]

Many §936 corporations can avoid the reallocation scheme by electing to compute taxable income under a cost sharing or profit splitting method. Under the cost sharing method, the corporation makes annual payments to affiliated entities engaged in research and development activities in amounts intended to reimburse these entities for the costs of research and development that will ultimately benefit the §936 corporation. The payments are deductible by the corporation and therefore reduce the income qualifying for the credit to amounts intended to represent a fair return on the costs incurred by the corporation itself. Under the profit split method, the combined taxable income of the §936 corporation and all affiliated businesses from sales of goods and services produced by the corporation in a possession is split equally between the corporation and its affiliates.

1. *Intangible property income.* The reallocation rules apply to a §936 corporation's "intangible property income," which generally includes all gross income of a §936 corporation that is attributable to a patent, formula, process, copyright, trademark, franchise, customer list, technical data, or similar item of intangible property.[66] Intangible property generates intangible property income, however, only if the property "has substantial value independent of the services of any individual."[67]

When covered intangible property is used in producing goods or services in a possession, at least a portion of the gross income on a sale of the goods or services is intangible property income if the property's "value is reflected in the price received by the . . . corporation."[68] The amount attributable to the intangible property is the excess of the price over "the reasonable direct and indirect costs [the corporation] incurs in manufacturing the product . . . plus a reasonable profit" on the working capital used to carry these costs.[69] The qualifying costs, however, do not include interest expense, royalties, or other amounts incurred in connection with intangibles.

2. *Treatment of intangible property income.* A §936 corporation's intangible property income is usually included ratably in the gross income of its shareholders, based on the stockholdings at the close of the corporation's taxable year.[70] Each shareholder must treat its ratable share of this income as U.S. source

---

[65] Id. at 85.

[66] IRC §§936(h)(3)(A), 936(h)(3)(B). An exception is allowed for intangible property that has been licensed to the corporation since 1947 and was used by it on September 3, 1982. The significance of the 1947 date is that "Puerto Rico's 'Operation Bootstrap' tax incentive program" began in 1948. 1982 Bluebook, supra note 4, at 86.

[67] IRC §936(h)(3)(B).

[68] 1982 Bluebook, supra note 4, at 86.

[69] Id. See IRC §936(h)(3)(C); Reg. §1.936-4.

[70] IRC §936(h)(1)(A).

income, and the income must be reported on the shareholder's return for its taxable year that includes the last day of the corporation's taxable year. Because the income is taxed to the shareholder whether or not the corporation distributes it, later distributions are excluded from the shareholder's gross income to the extent traceable to the previously taxed amounts.[71] The intangible property income taxed to the shareholders is excluded from the §936 corporation's gross income.[72]

If the corporation's shareholders include a nonresident alien or a foreign corporation, trust, or estate, this shareholder's portion of the intangible property income is taxable to the §936 corporation rather than to the shareholder unless the shareholder carries on a trade or business in the United States and the shareholder's share of the intangible property income is effectively connected with the U.S. business.[73] The corporation is also taxed on the portion of the income that is allocated to stock held by a tax-exempt organization or other shareholder who would be exempt from tax on the income. The intangible property income allocated to shares held by foreign and tax-exempt shareholders is included in the §936 corporation's return as gross income from U.S. sources, and it therefore cannot qualify for credit under §936.

Assume a §936 corporation has $1,000 of Puerto Rican source gross income from an active business in Puerto Rico, of which $600 is intangible property income; 80 percent of the corporation's stock is held by a domestic corporation, 10 percent is held by a foreign corporation not engaged in business in the United States, and 10 percent is held by a U.S. pension fund.[74] The domestic corporation is taxed on $480 (80 percent) of the §936 corporation's intangible property income of $600. The dividends received deduction is not allowed to the domestic corporation with respect to this amount because the $480 is intangible property income, not a dividend. The §936 corporation is taxed on the $120 of its intangible property income because this amount is allocable to the shares held by the foreign corporation and the pension fund, which is tax exempt. Because the $120 is from U.S. sources, no §936 credit is allowed with respect to it, and the tax on it may not be offset by the foreign tax credit.

Whether intangible property income is taxed to the shareholders or to the §936 corporation, it is ignored in applying the gross income tests.[75] When the shareholders are taxed, the income is excluded from the corporation's gross income. When the corporation is taxed, a special rule requires that it be ignored in applying the gross income tests.[76] Assume the taxable year in the example in the preceding paragraph is the corporation's first year. For purposes of the 75

---

[71] 1982 Bluebook, supra note 4, at 87.

[72] IRC §936(h)(1)(B).

[73] IRC §936(h)(2). For income effectively connected with U.S. business, see supra ¶66.3.1.

[74] See 1982 Bluebook, supra note 4, at 85–86.

[75] See supra ¶67.2.2 text accompanying note 12 for the gross income tests.

[76] IRC §936(h)(2)(B)(ii).

percent test, the corporation's active business income from a possession is $400—the $1,000 initially reported less the $600 reallocated to shareholders or specially taxed under the surrogate rule. The 75 percent test is met unless the corporation's gross income exceeds $533 ($400 is 75 percent of $533). If the $400 represents all of the corporation's gross income from sources within possessions, however, the 80 percent test is failed unless gross income is $500 or less ($400 is 80 percent of $500).

3. *Distributions to save qualification.* Since, in the absence of §936(h), intangible property income would often be possessions source income from the active conduct of business in a possession, the exclusion of this income from the corporation's gross income might cause the corporation to fail one or both of the gross income tests.[77] When this happens, qualification under §936 can be preserved by making a distribution to shareholders after the close of the taxable year.[78]

If the exclusion of intangible property income causes the corporation to fail the 80 percent test (income from possessions sources must make up at least 80 percent of the corporation's gross income for the test period consisting of the preceding three years), the distribution must equal the amount by which the corporation's income from nonpossessions sources during the test period exceeds 25 percent of the income from possessions sources during this period. If the 75 percent test is failed (income from the active conduct of business in a possession must account for at least 75 percent of the corporation's gross income), the distribution must equal the amount by which the corporation's income from all sources other than the active conduct of business in possessions exceeds one third of the income from the active conduct of a possessions business during this period. If both tests are failed, the distribution must be large enough so that both tests are met when the amount of the distribution is subtracted from the corporation's income from sources outside possessions and income from sources other than the active conduct of a possessions business.

The distribution must be made pro rata to the corporation's shareholders and must be designated when made as a distribution intended to preserve qualification under this rule. The distribution is usually included in the shareholder's gross income under the rules generally applied to dividends, but two special rules are provided to ensure that the dividends are taxed. First, if the shareholder is a domestic corporation, it is denied the dividends received deduction that is normally allowed for dividends from the §936 corporation.[79] Second, if a shareholder is a nonresident alien or a foreign corporation, estate, or trust, the distribution must be reported as income that is both effectively connected with a U.S. business

---

[77] See supra ¶67.2.2 note 12 and accompanying text for the gross income tests.
[78] IRC §936(h)(4)(A).
[79] IRC §246(e).

and attributable to a permanent establishment of the shareholder in the United States.[80]

The right to preserve §936 qualification by making a distribution under the foregoing rules is lost if the corporation's failure to satisfy the gross income tests without the distributions resulted from "fraud with intent to evade tax or willful neglect."[81]

4. *Election of cost sharing or profit splitting.* In lieu of reallocating intangible property income to their domestic affiliates under §936(h), some §936 corporations may elect to compute possessions income under either a cost sharing method or a profit split method.[82] The cost sharing and profit split methods are intended to strip income from intangible property out of the corporation's taxable income unless the corporation developed the intangible. The cost sharing method does this by giving the corporation a deduction for a share of the research and development costs incurred by all members of its affiliated group. The profit split method does so by limiting the corporation's taxable income to one half of the income of the affiliated group as a whole on sales of goods and services produced by the corporation in a possession.

A corporation is eligible to elect the cost sharing or profit split method with respect to a particular product[83] or service only if it has "a significant business presence in a possession with respect to such product or type of service" during each year the election is in effect.[84] The election thus is limited to corporations that have "real and significant business activity in the possessions."[85] The election is automatically revoked as of the beginning of any year during which this presence is lacking, thus causing the general rules on intangible property income to apply for the year.

A corporation has the required presence in a possession with respect to a product or service if at least one of three alternative tests is met.[86] Also, if the corporation engages in any production activities, the product or service must be "manufactured or produced" by the corporation in a possession. The corporation meets the latter requirement if its possessions operations (1) substantially transform direct materials inputs, (2) are of a type generally considered to be manu-

---

[80] IRC §936(h)(4)(B). For the taxation of effectively connected income, see supra ¶66.3.1. The reference to a permanent establishment is intended to subject the distribution to the effectively connected income tax even if the shareholder is a resident of a country having an income tax treaty with the United States. See supra ¶66.3.9.

[81] IRC §936(h)(4)(C).

[82] IRC §936(h)(5)(A).

[83] For the term "product," see Reg. §1.936-5(a); Notice 86-9, 1986-2 CB 376.

[84] IRC §936(h)(5)(B)(i).

[85] 1982 Bluebook, supra note 4, at 89.

[86] IRC §936(h)(5)(B)(ii). These tests are sometimes relaxed during a corporation's startup period. Reg. §1.936-5(b)(7).

facturing, or (3) incur conversion costs accounting for at least 20 percent of the cost of goods sold.[87] The three alternative tests are described below.

a. *Value added test.* This test is satisfied if the "total production costs" incurred by the corporation in a possession in manufacturing the product are at least 25 percent of the excess of the gross receipts on sales of the product over the direct materials costs for the product.[88] For example, if $150 is realized in selling a product and materials costs for the product are $50, this test is met if the corporation's total production costs in a possession are at least $25 (25 percent of excess of $150 over $50). Very generally, the latter test is met when "at least 25 percent of the value added by the affiliated group to the product is added by the island affiliate in a possession."[89]

The production costs, gross receipts, and direct materials costs of the §936 corporation and other members of its affiliated group are aggregated, and intercompany transactions are ignored.[90] Assume a §936 corporation acquires materials for $50, incurs production costs of $25, and sells the goods for $100 to its parent corporation, which further processes them and resells them for $150. The relevant figures are possessions production costs of $25, materials costs of $50, and gross receipts of $150, the amount received by the parent on selling the goods to unrelated buyers. Similarly, if the §936 corporation receives materials from another member of its affiliated group, only costs incurred in purchasing materials from buyers outside the affiliated group are included in the direct materials costs.

However, only costs and receipts relating to units of the product produced in whole or in part by the §936 corporation in a possession are included. For example, if an affiliated group includes two corporations that produce a particular product and if only one of these corporations qualifies for the §936 credit, only the costs and receipts pertaining to the goods produced by the §936 corporation are taken into account.

The term "total production costs" includes direct labor and overhead costs, but not direct materials costs.[91] The Treasury has the power to promulgate regulations excluding interest expense. The production costs taken into account for a particular taxable year are those incurred in producing the goods sold during the year. If the corporation sells or otherwise transfers goods to another member of the same affiliated group of corporations, the goods are considered sold only when they are sold to a buyer who is not a member of the group. Also, if the §936 corporation or another member of its affiliated group contracts to have manufacturing done for it by an unrelated person, the contract price is

---

[87] Reg. §1.936-5(b)(6), which borrows the tests of §1.954-3(a)(4), discussed infra ¶68.2.5.

[88] IRC §936(h)(5)(B)(ii)(I). For the terms "gross receipts" and "direct materials cost," see Reg. §§1.936-5(b)(3), 1.936-5(b)(5).

[89] 1982 Bluebook, supra note 4, at 89.

[90] Reg. §1.936-5(b)(1).

[91] IRC §936(h)(5)(B)(ii)(I); Reg. §1.936-5(b)(4).

treated as a production cost incurred by a member of the affiliated group other than the §936 corporation.[92]

Assume corporation P purchases materials for $100, performs certain manufacturing processes on the materials at a cost of $25, and sells them to its subsidiary S, a §936 corporation, for $130. S incurs $50 of additional costs in further manufacturing operations located exclusively in a possession, and sells finished goods back to P for $200. P sells the finished goods to unrelated persons for $250. The total production costs incurred in the possession are $50. The excess of gross receipts over direct material costs is $150—the amount realized by P in selling the goods ($250) over the amount paid by P for the direct materials incorporated into the goods ($100). Since total production costs are at least 25 percent of the excess of gross receipts over direct material costs ($50/$150 is 33 percent), S has a substantial business presence in a possession with respect to this product.

b. *Direct labor test.* A §936 corporation has a substantial business presence in a possession with respect to a product or type of services if at least 65 percent of the direct labor costs incurred in producing the goods or services consist of amounts incurred by the corporation as compensation for services performed for it in a possession.[93] The term "direct labor costs" includes costs incurred by other corporations in the same affiliated group, but only with respect to goods or services produced in part by the §936 corporation in a possession.[94] If the §936 corporation or another member of its affiliated group contracts to have manufacturing done for it by an unrelated person, the contract price is treated as a direct labor cost incurred outside the possession.[95]

Assume corporation P incurs direct labor costs of $25 in the United States in manufacturing a product and transfers partially completed goods to its subsidiary S, a §936 corporation, which incurs $50 in additional labor costs in completing the goods in a possession. Because the labor costs incurred by S in a possession ($50) comprise two thirds of the direct labor costs incurred by S and all other members of its affiliated group in producing the goods ($25 plus $50), the 65 percent test is satisfied, and S has a substantial business presence in a possession with respect to these goods.

c. *Test for purchases and sales.* If §936 corporation's business consists of purchasing and selling goods that are produced by and sold to unrelated persons, the corporation has a substantial presence in a possession if at least 65 percent of its direct labor costs consists of compensation paid by the corporation for services performed in a possession.[96] The term "direct labor costs" includes only costs relating to the purchase and sale of these goods. If the corporation is a member

---

[92] IRC §936(h)(5)(B)(iii)(II). See Reg. §1.936-5(c).

[93] IRC §936(h)(5)(B)(ii)(II).

[94] For more on the term "direct labor costs," see Reg. §1.936-5(b)(2).

[95] IRC §936(h)(5)(B)(iii)(II). See Reg. §1.936-5(c).

[96] IRC §936(h)(5)(B)(ii)(III).

of an affiliated group of corporations, however, all such costs incurred by all members of the group in connection with the goods are included in the base against which the corporation's direct labor costs in the possession are compared. Also, if the §936 corporation or another member of its affiliated group contracts to have manufacturing done for it by an unrelated person, the goods are treated as produced by the affiliated group rather than acquired by purchase.[97]

d. *Election procedures.* The election of the cost sharing or profit split method must be made for the §936 corporation's first taxable year.[98] If an affiliated group contains more than one §936 corporation producing goods or services within a single product area, all of them must elect in order for any election to be valid.[99] The election generally applies for all taxable years unless revoked with IRS consent.[100]

5. *Cost sharing method.* A §936 corporation that has a substantial business presence in a possession with respect to a product or service may elect to determine its taxable income from the product or service by the cost sharing or profit split method. If the cost sharing method is elected, the corporation must bear a portion of the costs of the "product area research" done by all members of the affiliated group to which it belongs.[101]

The term "product area" includes all goods and services within a "three-digit classification of the Standard Industrial Classification code,"[102] which is issued by the Office of Management and Budget of the Executive Office of the President. The Treasury may aggregate classifications and utilize classifications other than those of the code.[103]

The term "product area research" refers to research, development, and experimentation in "the same product area as that in which the electing corpo-

---

[97] IRC §936(h)(5)(B)(iii)(II).

[98] IRC §936(h)(5)(F)(i); Reg. §1.936-7(a). The election must be made no later than the due date (as extended) of the corporation's return for the year. The election, in other words, cannot be made by a delinquent or amended return. If the corporation existed during 1982, the election must be made for the first year beginning after 1982. For an election to switch from cost sharing to the profit split method or other method permitted under §936(h), see Rev. Proc. 92-68, 1992-2 CB 433; Rev. Proc. 94-70, 1994-2 CB 806 (change must be made by amended returns filed not later than December 31, 1994).

[99] IRC §936(h)(5)(F)(iv)(I). For the term "product area," see §936(h)(5)(C)(i)(I)(e), discussed infra text accompanying notes 102-103.

[100] IRC §936(h)(5)(F)(iii). Once the election is revoked, the corporation cannot elect again except with IRS consent. IRC §936(h)(5)(F)(i).

[101] IRC §936(h)(5)(C)(i)(I). See Reg. §1.936-7(a) (cost sharing may be elected even if affiliated group has no research costs in product area, in which case cost sharing payment is zero); Altama Delta Corp. v. CIR, 104 TC 424 (1995) (applying cost sharing rules).

[102] IRC §936(h)(5)(C)(i)(I)(e).

[103] See Reg. §1.936-7(a) (corporation may not "elect to define product area more narrowly than the 3-digit code").

ration conducts its activities."[104] The costs of product area research include (1) amounts paid or incurred under contracts by which the §936 corporation or an affiliated entity hires an unrelated person to do research work, (2) royalties and similar amounts paid for the right to use a patent, invention, formula, process, design, pattern, or know-how (manufacturing intangible), (3) depreciation on a manufacturing intangible acquired by purchase, and (4) costs qualifying for the research credit under §41.[105] The costs of product area research, however, include only (1) "costs, losses, expenses and other related deductions [that] are properly apportioned or allocated to" research in the particular product area and (2) a ratable portion of the research, development, and experimentation expenses that "cannot definitely be allocated to a particular product area."[106]

A §936 corporation's share of the product area research costs incurred by its affiliated group must be no less than an amount determined by multiplying the total amount of the costs by 110 percent of the ratio of "possession sales" to "total sales."[107] The "possession sales" are the revenues of the affiliated group on sales during the taxable year to buyers outside the group of goods produced in a possession by the §936 corporation.[108] For example, if a §936 corporation manufactures goods and sells them for $100 to its parent corporation, which resells them to unrelated buyers for $125, possession sales are $125. The entire selling price is included even if the goods are only partially manufactured in a possession. For example, if a §936 corporation receives $100 on a sale to its parent of unfinished goods that the parent completes and resells to unrelated buyers for $200, possession sales are $200. If the affiliated group performs a service and any portion of the service is performed by a §936 affiliate in a possession, the entire amount received for the service is included in possession sales. The "total sales" are the revenues on all sales by members of the affiliated group to buyers outside the group of goods and services within the product area.[109] If the corporation produces goods or services in more than one product area, only sales within a particular product area are included as possession sales and total sales in computing the corporation's share of research costs within that product area.

A §936 corporation's share of product area research costs must usually be paid by the corporation to the members of the affiliated group who incur these costs. If the corporation incurs research costs directly, however, these costs are counted in satisfaction of its share unless they are paid to or for the benefit of a related person.[110] If the affiliated group includes both domestic and foreign mem-

---

[104] IRC §936(h)(5)(C)(i)(I)(a). See Reg. §1.936-6(a)(1).

[105] See supra ¶27.4.2 for the research credit.

[106] IRC §936(h)(5)(C)(i)(I)(a).

[107] IRC §936(h)(5)(C)(i)(I). For examples, see Reg. §1.936-6(a)(4).

[108] IRC §936(h)(5)(C)(i)(I)(c); Reg. §1.936-6(a)(2).

[109] IRC §936(h)(5)(C)(i)(I)(e); Reg. §1.936-6(a)(2).

[110] IRC §936(h)(5)(C)(i)(I). See Reg. §1.936-6(a)(3). For the term "related person," see IRC §936(h)(3)(D).

bers, the payments to affiliates must be made to domestic members.[111]

The payments must be made no later than the due date (as extended) of the corporation's return for the year.[112] If a payment is late as a result of "fraud or willful neglect," the election of the cost sharing method is terminated as of the beginning of the taxable year.[113] If lateness does not cause a termination of the election, the cost sharing payment must be increased by interest at the rates for underpayments of tax, and the interest is not deductible as a cost sharing payment or as interest.[114] In the absence of fraud or willful neglect, the interest rule applies when the IRS determines on audit that a timely cost sharing payment was too small.[115]

The recipients of cost sharing payments treat them as reductions of their deductible costs, not as gross income.[116] If a foreign country imposes an income tax on the receipt of a cost sharing payment, neither the foreign tax credit nor the deduction for income taxes is allowed for the tax.[117] The payments are deductible by the §936 corporation, but the only effect of the deductions is to reduce the taxable income qualifying for the §936 credit.

A §936 corporation electing cost sharing is generally treated as owner of the intangibles it uses in its manufacturing processes.[118] As a consequence, it may include a return on this asset in the prices it charges in sales to related corporations.[119] Also, if goods or services produced with the use of intangible property are sold by the corporation to unrelated buyers, the IRS may not reallocate a portion of the profit on the sale to an affiliate on the ground that an intangible owned or created by the affiliate contributed to the profit.

These rules, however, only apply to patents, inventions, formulas, processes, designs, patterns, and know-how, collectively called manufacturing intangibles. They generally do not apply to nonmanufacturing intangibles, including copyrights, trademarks, trade names, and brand names, even if the corporation ac-

---

[111] IRC §936(h)(5)(C)(i)(IV)(a).

[112] IRC §936(h)(5)(C)(i)(III)(a).

[113] See Altama Delta Corp. v. CIR, 104 TC 424 (1995) (failure to make cost sharing payment found not to be due to fraud or willful neglect and therefore did not terminate election).

[114] If the due date for the corporation's return is extended but the payment is not made by the due date as extended, interest on the cost sharing payment accrues from the original due date. For the interest rate on underpayments, see §6621, discussed infra ¶114.1.

[115] 1982 Bluebook, supra note 4, at 91.

[116] Reg. §1.936-6(a)(5). The §41 credit for research costs, however, is not reduced. IRC §936(h)(5)(C)(i)(IV)(c).

[117] IRC §936(h)(5)(C)(i)(III)(b).

[118] IRC §936(h)(5)(C)(i)(II). See Reg. §1.936-6(a)(5); 1982 Bluebook, supra note 4, at 90 ("it is not necessary that the intangibles be transferred to the island affiliate").

[119] For intercompany pricing, see generally §482, discussed infra ¶79.1.

tually owns the intangible.[120] For example, if a §936 corporation sells goods to unrelated buyers in the United States under a trademark, the portion of the profit on the sale that is attributable to the trademark is removed from the §936 corporation's gross income and is reallocated to a domestic affiliate of the corporation. A §936 corporation is entitled to keep a profit attributable to a non-manufacturing intangible only if (1) the corporation developed the intangible and owns it or (2) the profit is realized in a sale for ultimate use or consumption in a possession.

6. *Profit split method.* Under the profit split method, a §936 corporation's income from the active conduct of business in a possession includes 50 percent of the combined taxable income of the corporation and all other members of the affiliated group of which it is a member from "covered sales."[121] The term "covered sales" includes sales by domestic members of the affiliated group to persons who are not members of the group or to foreign members of the group.[122] A sale is included, however, only if it is a sale of goods produced or services performed, in whole or in part, by the §936 corporation in a possession.

Combined taxable income is computed separately for each product produced or type of service performed by the corporation in a possession.[123] The combined taxable income for each product or type of service includes the selling prices received in sales of the goods and services by domestic members of the affiliated group to nonmembers or to foreign members. These receipts are reduced by (1) the costs of all domestic group members that are properly apportioned or allocated to the sales and (2) a ratable portion of the group's costs that "cannot definitely be allocated" to particular items or classes of gross income. Marketing expenses are included.[124] However, only costs incurred to persons outside the group or to foreign affiliates are included; intercompany payments are ignored.[125]

Assume a §936 corporation incurs costs of $75 in producing goods and sells the goods to its domestic parent for $100, and the parent incurs $35 of additional costs and sells the goods to an unrelated person for $150. Combined taxable income is $40 ($150 received in the final sale, less the §936 corporation's costs of $75 and the parent's costs of $35). The $100 price in the intercompany sale is not

---

[120] See Reg. §1.936-6(a)(5). For more on the distinction between manufacturing and nonmanufacturing intangibles, see 1982 Bluebook, supra note 4, at 90–91.

[121] IRC §936(h)(5)(C)(ii)(I). If the affiliated group includes foreign members, however, the taxable income of the foreign members is excluded.

[122] IRC §936(h)(5)(C)(ii)(IV).

[123] IRC §936(h)(5)(C)(ii)(II). For regulations on the computation of combined taxable income, see TD 8669, 1996-1 CB 172, amending Reg. §1.936-6(b)(1); Swanick, IRS Issues Final Section 936 Profit Split Rules, 25 Tax Mgmt. Int'l J. 434 (1996).

[124] 1982 Bluebook, supra note 4, at 92. See Reg. §1.936-6(b)(1); Coca-Cola Co. v. CIR, 106 TC No. 1 (1996) (applying regulations on computation of combined taxable income).

[125] Id. at 89.

included in the computation as either gross income of the subsidiary or a cost of the parent.

The research, development, and experimental costs deducted in computing combined taxable income for a particular product or type of services must equal or exceed a prescribed floor.[126] The minimum allocation to goods and services within a product area[127] equals the research costs of the affiliated group for that product area multiplied by 120 percent of the ratio of (1) the group's sales of goods and services within the product area that are produced in whole or in part by the §936 corporation to (2) the group's sales within the product area, including goods and services not produced by the §936 corporation. If the corporation produces more than one product or type of services within the product area, the minimum allocation under the foregoing rule is divided among the several products or services in proportion to the amounts received by the affiliated group in sales during the year of these goods and services.

7. *Affiliated group.* Many of the rules on intangible property income use the term "affiliated group," which is defined to include all organizations, trades, or businesses—whether domestic or foreign, incorporated or unincorporated—that are owned or controlled by the same interests as the §936 corporation.[128]

¶67.3 RESIDENTS OF PUERTO RICO

Aliens residing in Puerto Rico are taxed on their worldwide income, like aliens resident in the United States.[1] Under §933, however, individuals, whether

---

[126] IRC §936(h)(5)(C)(ii)(II).

[127] For the term "product area," see §936(h)(5)(C)(i)(I)(e), discussed supra text accompanying note 102-103.

[128] IRC §936(h)(5)(C)(i)(I)(b). This definition is borrowed from §482. See infra ¶79.2.

[1] IRC §876(a). For many other purposes, however, an alien resident of Puerto Rico is considered a nonresident alien. Reg. §1.876-1(b). For example, a dependency exemption is not allowed for a child or other dependent of the taxpayer who is an alien resident of Puerto Rico even though an alien residing in the United States can qualify as a dependent. IRC §152(b)(3). Also, an alien resident of Puerto Rico cannot file a joint return with his spouse. IRC §6013(a)(1).

The United States and Puerto Rico have entered into an agreement for the exchange of information and mutual assistance in the enforcement of their respective tax Laws. Tax Coordination Agreement Between the United States of America and the Commonwealth of Puerto Rico, 1990-1 CB 199.

See generally Godoy, U.S. and Local Taxation of Individuals and Businesses in Puerto Rico, 12 Tax Notes Int'l 597 (Feb. 19, 1996). See Bergersen v. CIR, 109 F3d 56 (1st Cir. 1997) (claim of bona fide residence in Puerto Rico not sustained); Maestre v. CIR, 73 TC 337 (1979) (disqualification of compensation from agencies of U.S. government does not violate compact between Puerto Rico and United States); Rev. Proc. 89-8, 1989-1 CB 778 (procedures for resolving inconsistent tax treatment by IRS and Puerto Rican tax authorities).

citizens or aliens, who are bona fide residents of Puerto Rico for the entire taxable year can exclude income from sources within Puerto Rico from gross income unless it is received for services performed as an employee of the United States or an agency thereof.[2] Residence is determined by the rules that determine whether an alien is a resident of the United States.[3] Income from sources within Puerto Rico is identified under the normal source rules, applied by substituting "Puerto Rico" for "the United States" in the rules defining the term "income from sources within the United States."[4] Except for personal exemptions, deductions and credits allocable to excludable amounts are disallowed.[5]

Normally, the §933 exclusion applies only if the taxpayer is a bona fide resident of Puerto Rico for the entire taxable year. It is never allowed for the year in which an individual becomes a resident of Puerto Rico unless this residence is established on the first day of the year.[6] It is also disallowed for the year Puerto Rican residence is abandoned unless the taxpayer is a citizen of the United States and was a bona fide resident of Puerto Rico for at least two years before the residence change. In the latter case, the exclusion applies to income from sources within Puerto Rico that is attributable to the part of the year when the taxpayer was a bona fide Puerto Rican resident.[7] As under the general rule, deductions and

---

[2] IRC §933(1).

[3] Reg. §1.933-1(a). For these rules, see supra ¶65.2. See Rev. Rul. 61-2, 1961-1 CB 393 (although Puerto Rican residence was retained during temporary period of study in United States, salary received from Puerto Rican employer for this period was U.S. source income not qualifying for §933 exclusion).

[4] Reg. §1.863-6. For the source rules, see infra ¶70.1. See also Manning v. CIR, 614 F2d 815 (1st Cir. 1980) (§933 exclusion not allowed for alimony received by Puerto Rican resident from former husband residing in New York because alimony has its source where payor resides); Pledger v. CIR, 71 TC 618 (1979), aff'd on another issue, 641 F2d 287 (5th Cir.), cert. denied, 454 US 964 (1981) (exclusion allowed for income on exercise of employee stock option, even though employer was domestic corporation, because taxpayer's employment was exclusively in Puerto Rico when option was granted and exercised); Rev. Rul. 77-86, 1977-1 CB 241 (dividends from domestic corporation were from Puerto Rican sources where corporation derived 96 percent of its gross income from Puerto Rican sources).

[5] Reg. §1.933-1(c). See Christensen v. CIR, 601 F2d 75 (2d Cir. 1979) (no deduction for legal and accounting expenses in tax audit of Puerto Rican income); Rinehart v. US, 429 F2d 1286 (10th Cir. 1970) (no deduction for Puerto Rican tax on income excluded by §933 even though tax was paid while taxpayer resided in United States); Rev. Rul. 56-585, 1956-2 CB 166 (resident of Puerto Rico employed by U.S. government allowed deduction for alimony because salary income not excluded by §933; not relevant that former spouse, also a Puerto Rican resident, excluded it from her gross income under §933). For the allocation of moving expenses to excludable income, see Roque v. CIR, 65 TC 920 (1976) (expenses of moving to Puerto Rico disallowed); Rev. Rul. 76-162, 1976-1 CB 197.

[6] Reg. §1.933-1(a).

[7] IRC §933(2); Reg. §1.933-1(b). See Rev. Rul. 68-7, 1968-1 CB 345 (salary for Puerto Rican employment prior to residence change is attributable to period before change if received in same year, but not if received during next year).

credits "properly allocable to and chargeable against" the excluded income are disallowed.

The exemption of residents of Puerto Rico from tax on income from sources within Puerto Rico was explained as follows by the Senate Finance Committee in 1950, when recommending enactment of the statutory predecessor of §933:

> Puerto Rican residents are singled out in this fashion because Puerto Rico is in a unique position. It is neither a foreign country nor an integral part of the United States. Moreover, it differs from all other possessions in that it has its own income tax law which takes the place of the Federal income tax law. For these reasons your committee believes it is desirable in the case of Puerto Rican residents to apply the United States tax only to income derived from sources outside of Puerto Rico; for income from sources within Puerto Rico the Puerto Rican income tax takes the place of the United States income tax.
>
> Since Puerto Rico allows a credit for income taxes paid to the United States, the Puerto Rican tax would in effect apply only to income derived from Puerto Rico except when the Puerto Rican tax is higher than the United States tax. In such a case Puerto Rico would collect a tax equal to the difference between the Puerto Rican rates and the United States rates applicable to income derived from sources outside Puerto Rico.[8]

¶67.4 VIRGIN ISLANDS

¶67.4.1 Introductory

By a statute enacted in 1921, Congress made the Internal Revenue Code part of the internal law of the Virgin Islands. Specifically, the income tax laws of the United States are treated as though adopted by the legislature of the Virgin Islands.[1] One court described the results as follows:

> Congress neither passed a separate income tax law for the Virgin Islands nor permitted its legislature to do so. Instead, congress provided that the provisions of United States income tax law should be used in the tax code of the Virgin Islands with necessary nomenclature changes to make them effective, that is, "Virgin Islands" should be substituted for "United States" whenever appropriate. The United States and the Virgin Islands are two separate and distinct taxing authorities, and the revenue due the Virgin Islands is paid

---

[8] S. Rep. No. 2375, 81st Cong., 2d Sess., reprinted in 1950-2 CB 483, 519.

[1] 48 USC §1397; Naval Service Appropriation Act of 1921, §1, 42 Stat. 123. See Erwin, The U.S. Virgin Islands Mirror Code and S Corporations, 77 Tax Notes 1161 (Dec. 8, 1997); Roberts, Owning a Piece of Paradise: Tax Rules Governing U.S. Investors' Acquisition, Ownership, and Sale of Virgin Islands Real Property, 23 J. Real Est. Tax'n 47 (1995); Schneider & Bozzuto, Tax Structure of the U.S. Virgin Islands, 12 Tax Notes Int'l 1897 (June 10, 1996).

into its treasury. This resulted in what has been called the "mirror system" of taxation.[2]

Persons incurring income tax obligations to both the United States and the Virgin Islands are required to file tax returns and pay income tax to both jurisdictions.[3] The Virgin Islands may also impose "nondiscriminatory local income taxes" in addition to the taxes imposed by the mirror Code.[4]

Section 932, enacted in 1986, largely supersedes the mirror system for individuals. If an individual is a U.S. citizen or is an alien residing in the United States or the Virgin Islands, only one tax is computed under the Code. If the individual is a bona fide resident of the Virgin Islands, this tax is payable to the Virgin Islands, and no U.S. tax is imposed.[5] In contrast, if a citizen or resident of the United States has income from sources within the Virgin Islands but does not reside there, the tax is apportioned; the portion that is ratably attributable to Virgin Islands income is payable to the Virgin Islands and the remainder is payable to the United States.

The mirror system is applied somewhat more literally to corporations. If a corporation is an "inhabitant" of the Virgin Islands, it is classified as a domestic corporation for Virgin Islands tax purposes and a foreign corporation for U.S. tax purposes. Such a corporation is subject to U.S. tax only on income from U.S. sources and income effectively connected with the conduct of business in the United States; it is taxed by the Virgin Islands on its worldwide income but is allowed a foreign tax credit against Virgin Islands tax for tax imposed by the United States as well as taxes imposed by foreign countries and other possessions. A domestic corporation that is not an inhabitant of the Virgin Islands is domestic for U.S. tax purposes and foreign under the mirror Code. It is therefore taxed by the Virgin Islands only on income from Virgin Islands sources and income effectively connected with a trade or business in the Virgin Islands; the U.S. taxes the corporation on worldwide income, but allows the foreign tax credit for Virgin Islands tax.

---

[2] Vitco, Inc. v. Virgin Islands, 560 F2d 180, 181-82 (3d Cir. 1977), cert. denied, 435 US 980 (1978).

[3] See Tax Implementation Agreement Between the United States of America and the Virgin Islands, 1989-1 CB 347 (agreement for information exchanges, competent authority negotiations to resolve inconsistent positions, and other enforcement procedures); Rev. Proc. 89-8, 1989-1 CB 778 (procedures for resolving inconsistent tax treatment by IRS and Virgin Island tax authorities).

[4] Pub. L. No. 99-514, §1274(b), 100 Stat. 2598 (1986).

[5] Section 932 applies for taxable years beginning after 1986. Pub. L. No. 99-514, supra note 4, at §1277(a). Until 1987, inhabitants of the Virgin Islands were required to file only a Virgin Islands return, and payment of their territorial tax on income from all sources satisfied their obligations to both jurisdictions. 48 USC §§1642, 1397.

¶67.4.2 Individuals

The reasons for the enactment of §932 (and the changes simultaneously made in the taxation of residents of Guam) were explained as follows:

> The Internal Revenue Code, with all its complexities, is designed primarily to tax income in the highly developed U.S. economy. The mirror system, which entails imposing the Code in its entirety as local law, may be wholly inappropriate for the island economies of the U.S. possessions. The possessions need the option to devise tax systems that permit them to pursue their own development policies and to exercise greater control over their own economic welfare.

> The frequency and extent of revisions to the Code in recent years have highlighted the problems inherent in the mirror systems. For example, in the possessions, a large portion of the revenue was collected from individuals in the lower tax brackets . . . .Thus, revisions to the Code that lower the tax rates on individuals . . . could have a substantial adverse effect on the possessions. In addition, revenue-neutral legislation that compensates for lowering tax rates by broadening the tax base may well not be revenue neutral in a possession where relatively little tax is collected from corporations or higher-income individuals.[6]

1. *Bona fide residents of the Virgin Islands.* For an individual who is a bona fide resident of the Virgin Islands at the close of the taxable year, taxable income is computed under the Internal Revenue Code as though the Virgin Islands were part of the United States.[7] Taxable income, in other words, is computed on a worldwide basis even if the individual is not a citizen or resident of the United States.[8]

With respect to income of a bona fide resident of the Virgin Islands from sources within the Virgin Islands and income effectively connected with the conduct of business in the Virgin Islands, the Virgin Islands is free to impose tax at whatever rates it chooses (including zero).[9] Other income must be taxed at the rates prescribed by the U.S. Internal Revenue Code, and the tax on this income may not be "reduced or remitted in any way, directly or indirectly, whether by grant, subsidy, or other similar payment."[10] Withholding or estimated taxes paid to the U.S. Treasury by or for the individual are allowed as a credit against the Virgin Islands tax.[11]

The U.S. Treasury has the power to prescribe special source rules to prevent abuse of any rate reductions allowed by the Virgin Islands.

---

[6] Staff of Joint Comm. on Tax'n, 99th Cong., 2d Sess., General Explanation of the Tax Reform Act of 1986 at 1118 (Comm. Print 1987) [hereinafter 1986 Bluebook].

[7] IRC §932(c).

[8] See IRC §§7701(a)(9), 7701(b), discussed supra ¶65.2.

[9] IRC §934(b)(1).

[10] IRC §934(a).

[11] 1986 Bluebook, supra note 6, at 1123. Under §7654, these taxes are paid over to the Virgin Islands Treasury.

For example, Congress did not believe that a mainland resident who moves to the Virgin Islands while owning appreciated personal property such as corporate stock or precious metals and who sells that property in the Virgin Islands should escape all tax, both in the United States and the Virgin Islands, on that appreciation. Similarly, Congress did not believe that a resident of the Virgin Islands who owns financial assets such as stocks or debt of companies organized in, but the underlying value of which is primarily attributable to activities performed outside, the Virgin Islands should escape tax on the income from those assets. The Secretary should treat such income as sourced outside the Virgin Islands.[12]

The Treasury also has power to prescribe regulations on when an individual may be considered a bona fide resident of the Virgin Islands.[13]

A bona fide resident of the Virgin Islands must file income tax returns with the Virgin Islands Bureau of Internal Revenue, and the tax shown on the return is payable to the Virgin Islands. The information shown on the return is transmitted to the IRS "to facilitate enforcement assistance."[14]

A bona fide resident of the Virgin Islands is excused from U.S. income taxation if (1) a return is filed with the Virgin Islands reporting all of the individual's gross income (including foreign income and income from U.S. sources), (2) the source of each item of gross income is identified on the return, and (3) the tax on this income is fully paid to the Virgin Islands.[15] The exemption from U.S. tax is accomplished by excluding all income reported on the Virgin Islands return from U.S. gross income. If the foregoing conditions are not satisfied, the individual owes tax to the United States as well as to the Virgin Islands, but tax collected by the U.S. Treasury is covered over to the Treasury of the Virgin Islands.[16] By conditioning the exemption from U.S. tax on the filing of a complete Virgin Islands return, Congress enabled the IRS to pursue nonfilers without fear of learning after the statute of limitations runs that the Virgin Islands Internal Revenue Bureau is the proper agency.

If a bona fide resident of the Virgin Islands is married to a U.S. citizen or resident who does not reside in the Virgin Islands and a joint return is filed, the foregoing rules apply to both spouses or to neither of them.[17] If the spouse residing in the Virgin Islands has adjusted gross income exceeding that of the other spouse, both spouses are classified as bona fide residents of the Virgin Islands. If the spouse not residing in the Virgin Islands has the larger adjusted gross income, both spouses are considered nonresidents of the Virgin Islands.

---

[12] 1986 Bluebook, supra note 6, at 1124–1125.

[13] Pub. L. No. 99-514, supra note 4, at §1274(c). See 1986 Bluebook, supra note 6, at 1125.

[14] See 1986 Bluebook, supra note 6, at 1125.

[15] IRC §932(c)(4).

[16] IRC §7654.

[17] IRC §§932(c)(1), 932(d).

2. *U.S. citizens and residents not residing in the Virgin Islands.* A U.S. citizen or resident who is not a bona fide resident of the Virgin Islands must pay a ratable portion of his tax to the Virgin Islands if he has income from sources within the Virgin Islands or has income effectively connected with the conduct of a trade or business in the Virgin Islands.[18] Such an individual's tax is computed in the normal way, except that the Code is applied treating the Virgin Islands as part of the United States.[19] For example, although income from sources within a possession is usually considered foreign source income in determining the limitation under §904 on the credit for foreign income taxes, Virgin Islands income of an individual subject to these rules is treated as U.S. income.[20]

The individual makes one return for the year, but must file it with both the IRS and the Virgin Islands.[21] The tax shown on this return is paid partly to the IRS and partly to the Virgin Islands.[22] The Virgin Islands' share equals the entire tax multiplied by a fraction whose numerator is the individual's Virgin Islands adjusted gross income and whose denominator is the entire adjusted gross income. "Virgin Islands adjusted gross income" is the individual's gross income from sources within the Virgin Islands, reduced by deductions allowable in determining adjusted gross income, to the extent allocated or apportioned to Virgin Islands income.[23] The Virgin Islands may not reduce or remit this tax "in any way, directly or indirectly, whether by grant, subsidy, or other similar payment."[24]

The portion of the tax payable to the U.S. Treasury is the excess of the total tax over the Virgin Islands' share.[25] Taxes paid to the Virgin Islands in addition to the Virgin Islands' share of the U.S. tax are treated as state and local taxes; they may be deductible under §164(a) but do not qualify for the foreign tax credit.[26]

When spouses file a joint return, the foregoing rules are applied to the income of both spouses and the entire tax shown on the return even if only one of the spouses has Virgin Islands income.[27]

---

[18] IRC §932(a)(1).

[19] IRC §932(a)(3).

[20] For the §904 limitation, see infra ¶69.5.

[21] IRC §932(a)(2).

[22] IRC §932(b).

[23] Income from sources within the Virgin Islands is determined under the rules defining the term "income from sources within the United States" except that "the Virgin Islands" is substituted for "the United States." Reg. §1.863-6.

[24] IRC §934(a).

[25] IRC §932(b)(3). See 1986 Bluebook, supra note 6, at 1123 (credit for Virgin Islands tax not allowed unless paid).

[26] Pub. L. No. 99-514, supra note 4, at §1274(b).

[27] IRC §932(a)(1)(B).

¶67.4.3 Corporations

Section 28(a) of the Revised Organic Act of the Virgin Islands—the statute making the Internal Revenue Code part of the internal law of the Virgin Islands—imposes Virgin Islands tax on the worldwide income of any corporation that is an "inhabitant" of the Virgin Islands. The term "inhabitant" includes corporations incorporated in the Virgin Islands and other corporations, including corporations organized under the laws of the states of the United States, that have sufficient contacts with the Virgin Islands to be classified as residents of the Virgin Islands.[28]

Until 1987, the Virgin Islands tax imposed on a Virgin Islands inhabitant by the mirror Code satisfied the inhabitant's entire income tax liability to the United States and the Virgin Islands. The Virgin Islands was sharply constrained in its ability to reduce or waive the tax so imposed. In 1986, however, Congress restated the mirror system for corporations as follows:

Section 7651(5)(B) was added, stating that §28(a) of the Revised Organic Act of the Virgin Islands is to be applied as though it had been enacted before the Internal Revenue Code. The intended effect of §7651(5)(B) is that "in cases of conflict, the Code controls."[29] The Code provides no exemption from U.S. tax for corporations taxed by the Virgin Islands. A corporation subject to Virgin Islands tax therefore is also subject to U.S. tax under the normal application of the Code. A domestic corporation is allowed the foreign tax credit, subject to the usual limitations, for income taxes imposed by the Virgin Islands, which like all other possessions is treated as a foreign country in determining the credit for foreign income taxes. Virgin Islands corporations are subject to U.S. tax under the rules for foreign corporations.[30] Because §7651(5)(B) was enacted to close a potentially gaping loophole, Congress made it applicable to all taxable years, including years before 1986, unless, on October 22, 1986, the IRS was barred by the statute of limitations or some other rule of law from assessing a deficiency for the year.[31]

---

[28] Vitco, Inc. v. Virgin Islands, 560 F2d 180 (3d Cir. 1977), cert. denied, 435 US 980 (1978) (corporation organized in Virgin Islands is inhabitant thereof, regardless of location of business or property); Condor Int'l, Inc. v. CIR, 98 TC 203 (1992), aff'd on other issues, 78 F3d 1355 (9th Cir. 1996) (Delaware corporation was inhabitant of Virgin Islands; although it had no trade or business there, its mailing address, officer and director, bank account, stockholder's meetings, and corporate records were in Virgin Islands, and these things were corporation's "only material presence" anywhere); Rev. Rul. 80-40, 1980-1 CB 175 (domestic corporation is inhabitant of Virgin Islands where all significant business operations, shareholder meetings, and board of directors meetings are conducted in Virgin Islands).

[29] 1986 Bluebook, supra note 6, at 1124.

[30] See supra ¶66.1.

[31] Pub. L. No. 99-514, supra note 4, at §1277(c)(2). For the loophole, see Danbury, Inc. v. Olive, 820 F2d 618 (3d Cir.), cert. denied, 484 US 964 (1987) (reversing District Court decision that domestic corporation inhabitant of Virgin Islands was not taxable by either United States or Virgin Islands on U.S. source income). The courts have found no

As before 1987, Virgin Islands tax on any corporation, including a Virgin Islands or U.S. corporation, is determined under the mirrored version of the Internal Revenue Code. In computing Virgin Islands tax under the mirrored Code, Virgin Islands corporations and other corporations classified as Virgin Islands inhabitants are treated as domestic corporations, taxable by the Virgin Islands on worldwide income with credit for foreign income taxes—including U.S. taxes.[32] All other corporations, including domestic corporations that are not Virgin Islands inhabitants, are treated as foreign corporations, taxable by the Virgin Islands only on income from sources within the Virgin Islands and income effectively connected with a trade or business in the Virgin Islands. Normally, the mirrored Code both defines the tax base and provides tax rates. The Virgin Islands, however, is free to reduce or eliminate the tax on any income from sources within the Virgin Islands and all income effectively connected with the conduct of a trade or business in the Virgin Islands.[33] The mirror tax must be imposed at the normal rates on all other income of (1) a domestic corporation (i.e., a corporation organized under federal law or the laws of one of the states) or (2) a Virgin Islands or other foreign corporation 10 percent or more of the stock of which is held by U.S. persons. For Virgin Islands or other foreign corporations that are less than 10 percent owned by U.S. persons, the Virgin Islands may reduce or eliminate the mirror tax on any income except income from U.S. sources and income effectively connected with a trade or business in the United States.[34]

If the Virgin Islands grants a tax concession to a domestic corporation doing business in the Virgin Islands, the reduction in Virgin Islands tax is typically matched by an increase in U.S. tax because the foreign tax credit is the only mechanism for reducing a domestic corporation's U.S. tax to reflect Virgin Islands tax and it is only allowed for tax actually imposed by the Virgin Islands. To facilitate efforts by the Virgin Islands to attract investment through tax incentive programs, the 1986 amendments extended the §936 credit to domestic corporations operating in the Virgin Islands. The §936 credit effectively exempts a

---

constitutional infirmity in the retroactive application of the rule. Island Acres, Inc. v. Olive, 893 F2d 647 (3d Cir. 1990); Business Ventures Int'l v. Olive, 893 F.2d 641 (3d Cir. 1990); Condor Int'l, Inc. v. CIR, 98 TC 203 (1992), aff'd on other issues, 78 F3d 1355 (9th Cir. 1996).

[32] See Abramson Enters., Inc. v. Government of Virgin Islands, 994 F2d 140 (3d Cir. 1993), cert. denied, 510 US 965 (1993) (Virgin Islands tax is not deductible in determining Virgin Islands tax, even though §§164(a)(3) and 164(b)(2) allow deduction for income taxes of "a possession of the United States"); Johnson v. Quinn, 821 F2d 212 (3d Cir. 1987) (under pre-1987 law, Virgin Islands resident was not allowed foreign tax credit against Virgin Islands tax for income taxes imposed by states of United States).

[33] IRC §934(b)(1).

[34] IRC §934(b)(3). See Blum, The Tax-Free Entity Under the U.S. Flag: A U.S. Virgin Islands Exempt Company, 20 J. Corp. Tax'n 250 (1993); Roberts, U.S. Virgin Islands Exempt Companies Offer Complete Tax Exemption With U.S. Flag Protection, 23 Tax Mgmt. Int'l J. 441 (1994).

domestic corporation from U.S. tax on income from sources within a possession if the corporation's income derives predominantly from the active conduct of business in a possession.[35] The §936 credit, unlike the foreign tax credit, does not depend on the amount of tax imposed by the possession.

¶67.4.4 Withholding

Since the Virgin Islands is not considered part of the United States for U.S. tax purposes, the withholding tax rules of §§1441 and 1442 apply to payments to Virgin Islands residents who are not citizens or residents of the United States and to Virgin Islands corporations.[36] For example, if a Virgin Islands corporation owns stock of a domestic corporation, the latter must withhold tax at 30 percent from any dividends paid on the stock. However, if the taxpayer is an individual who is a bona fide resident of the Virgin Islands, the tax withheld is "covered over" (paid) to the Virgin Islands Treasury and is credited against the individual's Virgin Islands tax liability.[37]

The mirrored Code in force in the Virgin Islands also contains the withholding tax rules of §§1441 and 1442. For example, if a U.S. citizen owns stock of a Virgin Islands corporation, the latter must withhold tax for the Virgin Islands Treasury on any dividends on the stock. The Virgin Islands may change the 30 percent withholding rate, but the withholding tax on income of a U.S. citizen or resident or domestic corporation may not exceed 30 percent.[38]

¶67.5 GUAM, AMERICAN SAMOA, NORTHERN MARIANA ISLANDS

1. *Guam for years after 1990.* Guam may impose whatever taxes it chooses on all income of residents of Guam and on income of nonresidents of Guam that is from sources within Guam or is effectively connected with the conduct of a trade or business in Guam.[1] This regime, which will also apply for American Samoa and the Northern Mariana Islands once the governments of these possessions enter into implementation agreements with the U.S. Treasury, was

---

[35] See supra ¶67.2.

[36] For §§1441 and 1442, see supra ¶66.2.11.

[37] 1986 Bluebook, supra note 6, at 1123 (commenting on §7654).

[38] IRC §1444.

[1] Pub. L. No. 99-514, §1271(a), 100 Stat. 2592 (1986). The prior statutory rules, found in §935, were repealed by the Tax Reform Act of 1986, but the repeal and the substitution of the rules described here took effect only as of the effective date of an implementation agreement between the federal government and Guam, January 1, 1991. Pub. L. 99-514, supra, at §1277(b); Tax Implementation Agreement Between the United States of America and Guam, 1989-1 CB 342.

adopted principally to give these possessions greater control over their tax systems.[2]

Although Guam generally has "full authority over [its] own local income tax systems,"[3] Guam tax laws may not discriminate against any U.S. person or any corporate or individual resident of another possession.[4]

For purposes of the U.S. income tax, an individual who is a bona fide resident of Guam may exclude from gross income all income from sources within Guam and all income effectively connected with the conduct of a trade or business in Guam.[5] With respect to these taxpayers, in other words, the federal government cedes to Guam exclusive tax jurisdiction over income from Guam. In determining U.S. tax, a taxpayer eligible for this exclusion is allowed no deduction or credit for any item (other than the personal exemptions) that is "properly allocable or chargeable against" amounts covered by the exclusion.[6] Also, the exclusion does not apply to compensation received as an employee of the federal government or any federal agency.[7]

The Treasury may prescribe special source and residence rules to prevent abuse of the exclusion.[8] According to the Staff of the Joint Committee on Taxation:

> For example, Congress did not believe that a mainland resident who moves to [Guam] while owning appreciated personal property such as corporate stock or precious metals and who sells that property in the possession should escape all tax, both in the United States and [Guam], on that appreciation. Similarly, Congress did not believe that a resident of a possession who owns financial assets such as stocks or debt of companies organized in, but the underlying value of which is primarily attributable to activities performed outside, the possession should escape tax on the income from those assets. The Secretary should treat such income as sourced outside the possession where the taxpayer resides.[9]

---

[2] See supra ¶67.4.2 text accompanying note 6.

[3] Staff of Joint Comm. on Tax'n, 99th Cong., 2d Sess., General Explanation of the Tax Reform Act of 1986 at 1119 (Comm. Print 1987) [hereinafter 1986 Bluebook].

[4] Pub. L. No. 99-514, supra note 1, at §1271(d). The pre-1991 mirror system will go back into effect if the Secretary of the Treasury determines that Guam violates this nondiscrimination rule and the government of Guam fails to remedy the problem within 90 days after notice given by the Treasury Secretary. Id. at §1271(e).

For the years 1991 through 1995, Guam was required to impose taxes that raised at least as much revenue as it received for 1990 under the old system (adjusted for inflation). Pub. L. No. 99-514, supra, at §1271(c). Failure to satisfy this requirement would also have revived the old mirror system.

[5] IRC §931(a).

[6] IRC §931(b).

[7] IRC §931(d)(1).

[8] IRC §§931(d)(2), 931(d)(3).

[9] 1986 Bluebook, supra note 3, at 1122–1123.

An individual resident of Guam who is also a citizen or resident of the United States is subject to U.S. taxes on all income that is neither from sources within Guam nor effectively connected with business carried on in Guam.[10] A resident of Guam with income from sources within a foreign country, for example, is subject to U.S. tax on the income. Guam may also tax all income of its residents, regardless of source. A taxpayer must resort to the foreign tax credit for relief from any resulting double taxation.

2. *Guam for years before 1991.* To coordinate the individual income taxes of the United States and Guam, §935, which was repealed in 1986 but applied until 1991, provided special filing requirements for (1) residents of Guam, (2) citizens of Guam who were not otherwise citizens of the United States, (3) citizens and residents of the United States deriving income from Guam, and (4) persons filing joint returns with any of the foregoing.[11] Residents of the United States filed their income tax returns with the United States; residents of Guam filed with Guam.[12] Any other individual filed with the United States unless he was a citizen of Guam and not otherwise a citizen of the United States, in which event he filed with Guam. In case of conflict, persons filing joint returns determined the place of filing by reference to the residence and citizenship of the spouse with the greater adjusted gross income, determined without regard to community property laws.[13] Taxpayers filing as required by §935 were relieved of liability to the other jurisdiction.[14]

In determining the U.S. taxes of persons subject to §935, the United States was treated as including Guam; conversely, for purposes of the Guam territorial income tax, Guam was treated as including the United States.[15] Thus, in com-

---

[10] See IRC §876 (individual who is not a U.S. citizen but is a bona fide resident of Guam for entire taxable year is taxed under §1, not rules for nonresident aliens). Taxes collected by the IRS from residents of Guam are paid over to the government of Guam, which also gets taxes paid to the IRS by federal employees in Guam and by military personnel stationed in Guam who are exempted from Guam income taxes. IRC §7654. See 1986 Bluebook, supra note 3, at 1121 ("Congress did not intend that [Guam] grant any taxpayer a tax rebate or other benefit based upon . . . covered-over taxes that are attributable to non-possessions income").

[11] For "residence" and "citizenship," see Reg. §1.935-1(a)(3). See generally U.S. Dep't of Treasury, Territorial Income Tax Systems: Income Taxation in the Virgin Islands, Guam, the Northern Mariana Islands, and American Samoa (1979); Leiserowitz, Coordination of Taxation Between the United States and Guam, 1 Int'l Tax & Bus. Lawyer 218 (1983).

[12] See Holmes v. Director of Revenue, 87-1 USTC ¶9242 (9th Cir. 1987) (not officially reported) (eligibility of Guam resident to claim losses of S corporation), in further proceedings, 937 F2d 481 (9th Cir. 1991) (statute of limitations on deficiency based on adjustments to S corporation's losses is same as in domestic context).

[13] IRC §935(b)(3) (before repeal in 1986).

[14] IRC §935(c)(3) (before repeal in 1986).

[15] IRC §§935(c)(1), 935(c)(2) (before repeal in 1986). For qualifications on these statutory principles, see Reg. §1.935-1(c)(1)(ii)(A) (not applicable where manifestly inap-

puting a U.S. person's foreign tax credit, income from sources within Guam was not treated as foreign source income.

3. *Northern Mariana Islands.* The mirror system applicable in Guam for years before 1991 also applies to the Commonwealth of the Northern Mariana Islands for years after 1985.[16] Once a tax implementation agreement is made between the United States and the government of the Northern Mariana Islands, the post-1990 scheme for Guam will apply to the Northern Mariana Islands.

4. *American Samoa.* American Samoa has long had autonomy over its income tax system. In 1963, however, American Samoa adopted a mirror version of the U.S. Internal Revenue Code as its local income tax.[17] Citizens of American Samoa are taxed by the United States as nonresident aliens unless they reside in the United States or are U.S. citizens apart from their citizenship in the possession.[18]

Under the pre-1986 version of §931, which continues to apply for this purpose, a citizen of the United States can exclude gross income from sources within American Samoa and foreign countries if (1) 80 percent or more of his gross income for the preceding two years was derived from sources within American Samoa and (2) 50 percent or more of his gross income for the same period was derived from the active conduct of a trade or business within American Samoa. This exclusion does not embrace amounts received within the United States, regardless of source.[19] A qualifying individual's deductions and foreign tax credit are ratably reduced or disallowed.[20]

The mirror rules and the pre-1986 §931 will cease to apply when the United States and American Samoa enter into a tax implementation agreement. Once this occurs, the post-1990 rules for Guam will also apply to American Samoa.

---

propriate, as in determining source of dividends and interest paid by domestic corporations).

[16] 1986 Bluebook, supra note 3, at 1116. See Preece v. CIR, 95 TC 594 (1990) (whether U.S. citizen is resident of Northern Mariana Islands depends on all facts and circumstances, not mechanical rules of §7701(b), discussed supra ¶65.2, which apply only to aliens).

[17] 1986 Bluebook, supra note 3, at 1117.

[18] IRC §932 (before amendment in 1986). See generally Reg. §1.932-1.

[19] IRC §931(b); Reg. §1.931-1(c). See Pacific Basin Manufacturing & Trade Co. v. CIR, 44 TCM (CCH) 314, aff'd per curiam, 716 F2d 638 (9th Cir. 1983) (income from taxpayer's sale of goods to its parent was received in the United States where parent deposited purchase price in taxpayer's U.S. bank account).

[20] IRC §931(d) (deductions), §931(e) (exemptions), §931(g) (foreign tax credit).

CHAPTER

68

Special Taxpayers and Problems

¶68.1 EXPORT SUBSIDIARIES

¶68.1.1 Introductory

Since 1942, tax reductions or exemptions have been provided for special classes of corporations organized to export goods and services from the United States. The earliest of these regimes was for Western Hemisphere Trade Corporations (WHTCs), which were domestic corporations that, until their privilege was phased out beginning in 1976, enjoyed a 14 percentage point reduction in the normal corporate tax rate.[1] In enacting the WHTC provisions in 1942, Congress probably hoped that the rate reduction would spur American direct investment throughout the Western hemisphere, but most WHTCs were export arms of domestic manufacturers.

Beginning in 1971, a more explicit stimulus to exports was provided by the rules for domestic international sales corporations (DISCs).[2] In order to qualify as a DISC, a corporation usually had to confine its activities to exporting goods produced by others in the United States. A DISC was a tax-exempt entity. Portions of its income were immediately taxed to its shareholders, whether or not distributed, but the remainder was insulated from U.S. taxes until distributed as dividends. Moreover, because the tax-deferred earnings could be loaned to the producer of the goods sold by the DISC (typically, its parent corporation) and invested in other assets relating to its export activities, the distribution of these earnings could frequently be put off indefinitely.

The DISC regime evoked complaints from other countries that it provided an export subsidy in violation of the General Agreement on Tariffs and Trade (GATT). In 1984, Congress responded to the complaints by largely replacing the DISC rules with provisions creating a new class of entity—foreign sales corporations (FSCs).[3] A FSC is a foreign corporation, typically a subsidiary of a domestic corporation, that elects to be subject to the FSC rules. Portions of a FSC's income from exporting goods produced in the United States is exempt from U.S. taxation, even if it is effectively connected with a trade or business carried on by the FSC in the United States. Moreover, domestic corporations owning stock of a FSC are allowed a 100 percent dividends received deduction for dividends paid out of the FSC's foreign trade income. As a result, neither the FSC nor its domestic corporate shareholders pay any U.S. tax on the exempt portion of the foreign trade income, and the nonexempt portion of this income is taxed only once.

---

[1] See infra ¶68.1.2.

[2] See infra ¶68.1.3.

[3] See infra ¶68.1.4.

¶68.1.2   Western Hemisphere Trade Corporations

From 1942 until 1980, the corporate income tax rate was reduced for a WHTC. A corporation qualified as a WHTC if (1) it was a domestic corporation, (2) all of its business, except for incidental purchases, was done in North, Central, or South America or the West Indies, (3) 95 percent or more of its gross income for a specified three-year period was from foreign sources, and (4) 90 percent or more was derived from the active conduct of a trade or business.[4] As applied to corporations engaged in exporting goods produced by their parent corporations in the United States, these requirements led to two developments that cause WHTCs to linger in the memory of tax lawyers.

First, in order to comply with the requirement that at least 95 percent of their incomes be from foreign sources, export WHTCs typically retained title to the exported goods until arrival at their destination rather than selling them F.O.B. the U.S. port of shipment. The IRS persistently tried to disregard these formalities and ascribe the income to domestic sources, on the theory that this conformed to the substance of the transactions. This argument, however, was rejected by the courts, and the IRS eventually acceded.[5] This concession is now significant for other purposes, especially in applying the limitation imposed by §904 on the foreign tax credit, which depends on the ratio of the claimant's taxable income from foreign sources to its entire taxable income.[6] It is possible, however, that the IRS might seek to limit its concession in the WHTC cases to that area because several of the cases stressed the legislative intent underlying the WHTC rules.

Second, the IRS was also unsuccessful in denying WHTC status to export corporations that were merely paper subsidiaries of domestic manufacturers, with no assets of their own. Mindful of the requirement that 90 percent or more of a WHTC's gross income must be derived "from the active conduct of a trade or business," cautious tax advisers often recommended economic penetration of the foreign market by the establishment of foreign offices, employees, and facilities. The courts, however, did not insist on activities of this type, holding instead that an export subsidiary could be engaged in the active conduct of a business even if it was a virtual shell whose parent supplied all necessary services and

---

[4] IRC §921 (before amendment in 1984). See Otis Elevator Corp. v. US, 618 F2d 712 (Ct. Cl. 1980) (purchases amounting to 15 percent and 15.7 percent of gross receipts did not violate incidental purchases test). See generally Raskind, The Western Hemisphere Trade Corporation: A Functional Perspective, 16 Vand. L. Rev. 1 (1962); Surrey, Current Issues in the Taxation of Corporate Foreign Investment, 56 Colum. L. Rev. 815, 830–38 (1956); Tillinghast, The Western Hemisphere Trade Corporation: Comparison With Locally Incorporated Entities: Its Utility; Its Future, 28 NYU Inst. on Fed. Tax'n 437 (1970).

[5] Rev. Rul. 64-198, 1964-2 CB 189. For the cases, see infra ¶70.6.3 text accompanying notes 37–39.

[6] See infra ¶69.5.1.

facilities on a reimbursable basis.[7] Although these decisions do not necessarily govern in construing other provisions of the Code, they are echoed by the IRS's concession that a corporation could qualify as a DISC even if it had no employees and owned nothing more than a bank account and its books and records.

¶68.1.3 Domestic International Sales Corporations

In 1971, to stimulate the export of goods manufactured in the United States and encourage exporting through U.S. rather than foreign affiliates, Congress enacted §§991-997, granting special tax benefits to DISCs.[8] Departing from the American practice of taxing domestic corporations currently on worldwide income, these provisions tax the income of a DISC solely to its shareholders—part as a constructive dividend when earned and the balance only when actually distributed, when the corporation's DISC status terminates, or when the shareholders dispose of their stock.

In the beginning, the deferral privilege usually applied to approximately 50 percent of DISC earnings. In 1976, however, Congress concluded that "the DISC program could become more efficient and less costly while still providing the same incentive for increased exports and jobs by granting DISC benefits only to the extent that a company increases its exports over a base period amount."[9] Under the resulting legislation, the deferral privilege applied, roughly speaking, to 50 percent of the amount by which current earnings exceeded 67 percent of the DISC's earnings during a four-year base period. For taxable years beginning in 1980, the base period was 1973-1976, and it moved forward one year at a time thereafter. Income failing to qualify for deferral under this incremental test was taxed to the shareholders when earned, along with illegal bribes, kickbacks, and similar payments to foreign officials, income attributable to participation in international boycotts, and a few other items.

In 1984, Congress largely terminated the DISC rules, substituting the rules on FSCs. For years after 1984, the constructive dividend to DISC shareholders includes all taxable income attributable to gross receipts in excess of $10 million and at least one half of the remainder of the DISC's taxable income. Also, DISC shareholders must pay an interest charge on the post-1984 taxes they defer with respect to the portion of DISC taxable income that is not included in the constructive dividend. Moreover, a controlled group of corporations may not have both a DISC and a FSC. For years after 1984, the DISC rules thus amount to no more than a right, available only to those who forgo the FSC rules, to obtain an

---

[7] See, e.g., Frank v. International Canadian Corp., 308 F2d 520 (9th Cir. 1962).

[8] S. Rep. No. 437, 92d Cong., 1st Sess., reprinted in 1972-1 CB 559, 609.

[9] Staff of Joint Comm. on Tax'n, 94th Cong., 2d Sess., General Explanation of the Revenue Act of 1976, reprinted in 1976-3 CB (Vol. 2) 302. See also U.S. Dep't of Treasury, The Operation and Effect of the Domestic International Sales Corporation Legislation (issued annually until 1984).

annual interest-bearing loan from the government. A post-1984 DISC is called an interest charge DISC. Congress retained provisions for the interest charge DISC, rather than repealing the DISC rules altogether, because it believed that smaller businesses might have difficulty meeting certain foreign presence requirements of the FSC rules.[10]

The 1984 curtailment of the DISC rules was a response to the contention that the rules provided an export subsidy in violation of GATT.[11] The inconsistency with GATT arose, it was argued, because the rules allowed an indefinite deferral of tax on income from activities located in the United States and no interest was charged on the deferred tax. The argument was supported by a GATT panel of experts and a majority of the members of the GATT council. The European Community requested authority from the council to take retaliatory action. When it appeared that the DISC debate threatened "a breakdown in the GATT dispute-settlement process" and that the United States stood wholly alone on the issue, the Treasury agreed to propose legislation on the issue.[12] Although "Congress did not find the GATT arguments against DISC persuasive and believed the EC had made no credible showing of any injury resulting from DISC exports," it acquiesced "in the interest of resolving the GATT dispute over DISC and assisting the Administration in fulfilling its commitment to the GATT Council."[13]

1. *DISC qualification.* To qualify as a DISC, a corporation must meet these conditions:

  a. It must be incorporated under the laws of one of the states of the United States or the District of Columbia.[14]
  b. At least 95 percent its gross receipts for the taxable year must be "qualified export receipts."[15] These receipts consist principally of revenues on sales and leases of "export property"—goods manufactured, produced, grown, or extracted in the United States by persons other than the DISC and sold for use, consumption, or disposition outside the United States,

---

[10] The FSC provisions, however, waive these rules for a "small FSC," thus providing a second alternative for those seeking less costly means of capturing congressional largess. See infra ¶68.1.4 text accompanying notes 103–05. See also Holik, Interest-Charge Domestic International Sales Corporations, 1991, 15 Stat. Income Bull. 46 (Summer 1995) (for 1991, 980 interest-charge DISCs filed returns, reporting assets of $972 million and receipts of $1,688 million).

[11] Staff of Joint Comm. on Tax'n, 98th Cong., 2d Sess., General Explanation of the Revenue Provisions of the Deficit Reduction Act of 1984 at 1041 (1984) [hereinafter 1984 Bluebook].

[12] Id.

[13] Id. at 1042.

[14] IRC §§992(a)(1), 7701(a)(10).

[15] IRC §992(a)(1)(A).

provided not more than 50 percent of the property's value is attributable to articles imported into the United States.[16]

c. At least 95 percent of the adjusted basis of its assets must be basis of "qualified export assets" (primarily export property, facilities used to sell, store, package, assemble, or service export property, receivables owed by customers, producer's loans, working capital, and related assets).[17]

d. The corporation must have only one class of stock, whose par or stated value is at least $2,500 on each day of the taxable year.[18]

e. A DISC election, made with the consent of all shareholders, must be in force for the taxable year.[19]

If a corporation fails to satisfy the gross export receipts or export assets conditions in a particular year, but it has reasonable cause for this failure, it can remedy the deficiency by making a qualifying distribution of the disqualifying amounts to their shareholders within the time specified by §992(c).[20] Personal

---

[16] IRC §§993(a), (c). See IRC §993(f) (if DISC is agent for seller or lessor, gross receipts include seller's or lessor's gross receipts, not DISC's commission). See General Dynamics Corp. v. CIR, 108 TC No. 9 (1997) (Reg. §1.994-1(c)(6), requiring that purchaser directly use export property outside United States within one year of sale, is valid and applies even if such use is prevented by unforeseen circumstances); FMC Corp. v. CIR, 100 TC 595 (1993) (in determining qualification of sales of cranes used on oil drilling platforms, "United States" includes Outer Continental Shelf, as provided by §638); Hughes Int'l Sales Corp. v. CIR, 100 TC 293 (1993) (Reg. §1.993-6(e)(1), which requires qualified export receipts to be determined using related supplier's method of accounting, is invalid); Sim-Air, USA, Ltd. v. CIR, 98 TC 187 (1992) (price received on sale was not qualified export receipts where buyer was U.S. person and did not use or resell outside United States within one year thereafter).

[17] IRC §§992(a)(1)(B), 993(b). See L&F Int'l Sales Corp. v. US, 912 F2d 377 (9th Cir. 1990) (Reg. §1.993-2(d), which requires that trade receivables representing commissions due DISC from related supplier be paid within 60 days after end of taxable year, is valid); Gibbons Int'l v. CIR, 89 TC 1156 (1987) (same). See also TSI, Inc. v. US, 977 F2 424 (8th Cir. 1992) (not officially reported) (commissions receivable were not "paid" by eliminating entries made in accountants' work papers); Stokely-Van Camp, Inc. v. US, 21 Cl. Ct. 731, 90-2 USTC ¶50,561 (1990), aff'd, 974 F2d 1319 (Fed. Cir. 1992) (trade receivables as qualified export assets).

Qualified export assets include a "producer's loan," defined as a loan by a DISC to a person who manufactures, produces, grows, or extracts export property in the United States if the aggregate of such loans does not exceed accumulated DISC income and the loan is payable in five years or less. IRC §993(d). The producer/borrower is often the DISC's parent or a related corporation. See Garnac Grain Co. v. CIR, 95 TC 7 (1990) (grain elevator's activities of drying, cleaning, aerating, blending, and fumigating grain were not production); Webb Export Corp. v. CIR, 91 TC 131 (1988) (cutting standing timber, cleaning branches off trees, and cutting trees into veneer logs was production).

[18] IRC §992(a)(1)(C). See Reg. §1.992-1(d)(2)(ii) (safe harbor protecting purported debt from being treated as equity).

[19] IRC §§992(a)(1)(D), 992(b).

[20] For reasonable cause, see Reg. §1.992-3(c)(2).

holding companies, S corporations, and a few other special classes are ineligible.[21]

A DISC need not have its own employees, equipment, or office. For example, the export arm of a manufacturer can qualify if it has its own bank account throughout the taxable year and is maintained as a separate accounting entity with its own books and records.[22] Separate incorporation is required only to facilitate keeping an accurate record of the income subject to DISC treatment, a limited function that warrants "a relaxation of the general rules of corporate substance otherwise applicable under the Code."[23]

2. *Intercompany prices.* Given the parasitic character and meager corporate substance of the typical DISC, the arm's length pricing requirement of §482 would reallocate substantially all the DISC's export profits to the parent corporation because the parent is the source from which the DISC's blessings flow.[24] Recognizing that the goals of the DISC provisions would be defeated if the lion's share of the profits were reallocated from export subsidiary to parent, Congress enacted the intercompany pricing rules of §994 to shield DISCs against §482.[25]

Under §994(a), transfer prices on a related supplier's sales of export property to a DISC are fixed at amounts enabling the DISC to obtain a specified share of the combined profit of the corporate group on the manufacture and sale of the goods, regardless of the sales prices actually charged. The DISC's share is the greatest of (1) 4 percent of the DISC's qualified export receipts from the resale of the property, plus 10 percent of its export promotion expenses, (2) 50 percent of the combined taxable income of the supplier and the DISC, plus 10 percent of the export promotion expenses, or (3) the DISC's taxable income based on the actual sales price, subject to adjustments under §482.[26] Each of these methods

---

[21] IRC §992(d).

[22] See Reg. §§1.992-1(a)(6), (7). See Dresser Indus., Inc. v. CIR, 911 F2d 1128 (5th Cir. 1990) ("typically, a DISC is a paper company without facilities, employees, or inventory of its own").

[23] Reg. §1.992-1(a)(6). See Rev. Rul. 72-166, 1972-1 CB 220 (minimal DISC requirements illustrated).

[24] For §482, see infra ¶79.1.

[25] See S. Rep. No. 437, supra note 8, at 618.

[26] For agreements allowing the DISC to earn the maximum allowable amounts, see Rev. Rul. 72-166, 1972-1 CB 220. See also Reg. §§1.994-1(e)(5),(6) (procedure for adjustment and payment of transfer prices). See Dow Corning Corp. v. US, 984 F2d 416 (Fed. Cir. 1993) (Reg. §1.994-2(b)(3), under which combined taxable income is limited by overall profit percentage based on all sales (domestic and foreign) with full costing, is valid); Brown-Forman Corp. v. CIR, 955 F2d 1037 (6th Cir. 1992), cert. denied, 506 US 827 (1992) (regulations allow combined taxable income to be determined by marginal cost method if DISC is seeking to establish or maintain foreign market, but provide that taxable income allocable to export sales under this method may not exceed gross receipts multiplied by "overall profit percentage," which is ratio of worldwide taxable income of DISC and related supplier to worldwide gross receipts; held, gross receipts are determined without reduction for excise taxes paid on domestic sales of liquor); Dresser Indus., Inc. v. CIR, 911 F2d 1128 (5th Cir. 1990) (in determining combined taxable income, interest expense may be netted against interest income, so that only net interest expense is allo-

can also be used in determining the DISC's commissions if it acts as a sales agent for the related supplier.[27] Neither the gross receipts method nor the combined taxable income method can be used to create or increase a loss for the related supplier, but this rule is not violated if there is a combined loss and the transfer prices are fixed at amounts permitting the DISC to recover its costs.[28]

3. *Taxation of DISC income.* Since a DISC is not taxed, tax on its income is deferred to the extent that it exceeds the amount currently taxed to the shareholders. Each year, a DISC shareholder is taxed on a constructive dividend, and if actual dividends exceed amounts taxed currently and in previous years as constructive distributions, the excess is also taxed. A shareholder's constructive dividend is a pro rata share of the components described by §995(b) or, if less, the DISC's current earnings and profits. Several items are included in the shareholders' constructive dividends in their entirety and hence do not qualify for deferral to any extent. These fully taxable amounts include interest on producer's loans, certain gains on dispositions of property previously received by the DISC in tax-free transactions, income attributable to participation in international boycotts,[29] and illegal bribes, kickbacks, or similar payments paid by or on behalf of the DISC to foreign officials. In addition, for years after 1984, the shareholders' constructive dividends include 100 percent of the DISC's taxable income attributable to qualified export receipts for the year in excess of $10 million. Finally, one seventeenth of the remainder of DISC taxable income is taxed to the shareholders.

Since constructive dividends are taxed to the shareholders but not actually received by them, they increase the shareholder's basis for the stock, substantially as though the distribution had been received and reinvested as a contribution to

---

cated among noninterest income; Reg. §1.994-1(c)(6)(v), relating to effect on combined taxable income of sales of accounts receivable to DISC at discount, is valid); Bowater Inc. v. CIR, 108 F3d 12 (2d Cir. 1997) (contra to *Dresser* on interest allocation issue; Reg. §1.861-8(e)(2) "requires a taxpayer to allocate interest expense ratably to *all* income producing activities"); General Dynamics Corp. v. CIR, 108 TC 107 (1997) (under Reg. §1.994-1(c)(6), combined taxable income is reduced by related period costs, even if related supplier properly elected to deduct them for prior years); Computervision Corp. v. CIR, 96 TC 652 (1991) (where commission DISC purchases parent's receivables at discount, gross receipts figures used in computing combined taxable income is discounted amount paid by DISC for receivables; Reg. §1.994-1(c)(6)(v) applied).

For the inclusion of 10 percent of export promotion expenses in a DISC's profits under the 4 percent or combined taxable income method, see Computervision Corp. v. CIR, supra ("export promotion expenses must be incurred by the DISC in carrying on a trade or business"; if DISC is mere paper company, it has no export promotion expenses; not sufficient that DISC reimburse parent for such expenses).

[27] For the inclusion of sales commissions in "qualified export receipts," see IRC §993(a)(1)(C); Reg. §1.993-1(d); Rev. Rul. 74-551, 1974-2 CB 238; Rev. Rul. 72-166, 1972-1 CB 220.

[28] Reg. §1.994-1(e)(1). See Archer-Daniels-Midland Co. v. US, 37 F3d 321 (7th Cir. 1994), cert. denied, 115 Sup. Ct. 1724 (1995) (regulation is valid).

[29] For the international boycott penalty, see §999, discussed infra ¶68.8.

the DISC's capital.[30] This previously taxed income, when actually distributed, is excluded from gross income by the shareholders, whose basis for the stock is then correspondingly reduced.[31] Actual distributions are considered made first from previously taxed income, then from accumulated tax-deferred DISC income, and finally from earnings and profits accumulated in non-DISC years.[32] Since the DISC itself is exempted from the income tax, its shareholders are not subjected to double taxation on either actual or constructive dividends, and hence they are not entitled to a dividends received deduction for these amounts.[33]

To ensure that tax-deferred DISC income is eventually reported as ordinary income by the shareholders, gain recognized on a disposition of DISC stock is ordinary income to the extent of the shareholder's share of tax-deferred income.[34] A similar result is triggered by transactions terminating a DISC's corporate existence (except a mere change in place of organization) and certain other transactions that are ordinarily tax free.[35] Moreover, if the corporation's DISC status terminates by revocation of its DISC election or a failure to satisfy the conditions of §992(a)(1) (requisite percentage of export receipts and assets, etc.), the tax-deferred DISC income is deemed distributed to the shareholders in equal annual installments over a 10-year period prescribed by §995(b)(2).

4. *Interest charge.* A DISC shareholder is required to pay interest on "DISC-related deferred tax liability,"[36] which generally consists of the additional tax the shareholder would pay for the taxable year if its gross income included a ratable share of all DISC income that was accumulated after 1984 and was not taxed to the shareholders as constructive or actual dividends. The interest rate equals that on Treasury bills with 52-week terms.[37]

5. *Pre-1985 accumulations.* The 1984 legislation contained a major gift for shareholders of existing DISCs. The taxable years and DISC elections of all

---

[30] IRC §996(e)(1).

[31] IRC §§996(a)(3), (e)(2).

[32] IRC §996.

[33] IRC §246(d).

[34] IRC §995(c)(1)(A).

[35] IRC §995(c)(1)(B).

[36] IRC §995(f)(1).

[37] Under §995(f)(4), the average yield on 52-week Treasury bills auctioned during the 12 months ending September 30 is the T-bill rate for any shareholder taxable year ending on the last day of that calendar year or at any time during the following year before the last day of that year. Thus, the average yield for the 12 months ending September 30 of year 1 is the T-bill rate for shareholder taxable years ending during the period December 31 of year 1 through December 30 of year 2. See Rev. Rul. 97-49, 1997-48 IRB 4 (T-bill rate is 5.68 percent for shareholder taxable years ending December 31, 1997 and during 1998 before December 31); Rev. Rul. 96-55, 1996-2 CB 57 (5.51 percent for 1996-1997); Rev. Rul. 95-77, 1995-2 CB 122 (6.3 percent for 1995-1996); Rev. Rul. 94-68, 1994-2 CB 177 (4.55 percent for 1994-1995); Rev. Rul. 93-77, 1993-2 CB 253 (3.47 percent for 1993-1994); Rev. Rul. 92-98, 1992-2 CB 210 (4.23 percent for 1992-1993); Rev. Rul. 91-59 1991-2 CB 347 (6.42 percent for 1991-1992); Rev. Rul. 90-96, 1990-2 CB 188 (8.02 percent for 1990-1991).

DISCs terminated as of December 31, 1984.[38] Tax deferred income accumulated by a DISC during 1984 and all earlier years was given a permanent tax exemption by being included in previously taxed income, thereby qualifying it to be distributed tax-free to the shareholders.[39]

¶68.1.4 Foreign Sales Corporations

Under §§921-927, portions of the foreign trade income of a foreign sales corporation (FSC) are exempted from tax.[40] Also, a domestic corporation holding stock in a FSC is allowed a 100 percent dividends received deduction for FSC distributions of earnings and profits derived from qualifying foreign trade income. In the usual case where the FSC is a subsidiary of a domestic corporation, the income that is nontaxable to the FSC is therefore wholly exempted from the U.S. corporate income tax.

The FSC provisions are successors to the DISC rules, which were largely retired at the end of 1984. The substitution of FSCs for DISCs was made principally to satisfy complaints of U.S. trading partners that the DISC rules violated a GATT provision prohibiting export subsidies.

> Under the GATT rules, a country need not tax income from economic processes occurring outside its territory. Accordingly, Congress believed that certain income attributable to economic activities occurring outside the United States should be exempt from U.S. tax in order to afford U.S. exporters treatment comparable to what exporters customarily obtain under territorial systems of taxation. Congress intended that certain activities and economic processes related to that income would be undertaken by a foreign sales corporation outside the U.S. customs territory. . . .
>
> Congress recognized that the Act would affect prior law DISCs in different ways, and that some DISCs could have difficulty meeting the foreign presence requirements of foreign sales corporations. . . . Nonetheless, Congress considered the foreign presence requirements of the legislation to be essential in responding to the GATT rules which formed the background of this legislation.[41]

---

[38] Pub. L. No. 98-369, §805(b)(1), 98 Stat. 494, 1001 (1984).

[39] Id. §805(b)(2).

[40] See Holik, Foreign Sales Corporations, 1992, 17 Stat. Income Bull. 114 (Summer 1997) (for 1992, 3,073 FSCs filed returns, reporting total income of $15.6 billion and net exempt income of $4.1 billion; most FSCs were incorporated in U.S. possessions, but significant numbers of FSCs were organized in Barbados, Bermuda, Jamaica, and the Netherlands).

[41] 1984 Bluebook, supra note 11, at 1042. See generally Note, The Making of a Subsidy, 1984: The Tax and Trade Implications of the Foreign Sales Corporation Legislation, 38 Stan. L. Rev. 1327 (1986); Sharp, Steele & Jacobson, Foreign Sales Corporations: Export Analysis and Planning, 63 Taxes 163 (1985). See also Erwin, Issues in Using a FSC in the Export of Computer Software, 86 J. Tax'n 147 (1997); Zukowski, Tax Benefits for Internet Export Sales, 13 Tax Notes Int'l 529 (Aug. 12, 1996).

A FSC is a foreign corporation that elects to be governed by the FSC rules and satisfies various organizational requirements.[42] It is exempt from tax on portions of its income from "foreign trading gross receipts," which include (1) receipts on sales and leases of goods produced in the United States and exported to foreign countries and (2) compensation for various services in connection with these exports and also some architectural, engineering, and managerial services.[43] The FSC may be the seller or lessor or the performer of the services, or it may act as commission agent in sales, leasing, or services transactions of others. The FSC's receipts from a particular transaction qualify as foreign trading gross receipts, however, only if it carries on activities outside the United States that include solicitations, negotiations, or the making of the contract for the transaction.[44] Also, none of a FSC's receipts qualify unless certain activities relating to its management are located outside the United States.[45]

When a FSC deals in goods or services produced by its parent or some other related corporation, the normal arm's length pricing rule of §482 is sometimes relaxed by two administrative pricing rules. One of these rules allows the FSC to capture at least 23 percent of the combined taxable income of the FSC and the related supplier, and the other sometimes allocates taxable income to the FSC equal to 1.83 percent of the gross receipts from the transaction.[46]

Foreign trading gross receipts, reduced by the cost of goods sold, is foreign trade income. When foreign trade income is determined with one of the administrative pricing rules, the FSC is exempted from U.S. tax on $15/23$ of the income, but the remainder is taxable as income effectively connected with a U.S. trade or business, whether or not actually connected with such a business.[47] In contrast, 32 percent is exempt when foreign trade income is based on actual intercompany prices, as they may be adjusted under §482, and the FSC is taxed on the remainder only if the income is actually connected with a trade or business of the FSC in the United States.

In the typical case where the FSC is a subsidiary of a domestic corporation, the shareholder is allowed the deduction for intercorporate dividends received in amounts calculated to relieve the shareholder from tax on income that is exempt to the FSC and ensure that the remainder of the foreign trade income is taxed only once, either to the FSC or the shareholder.[48] Foreign shareholders of a FSC are taxed on FSC dividends as though the dividends were effectively connected

---

[42] Infra text accompanying notes 48-58. See Zukowski, Tax Benefits For Internet Export Sales, 13 Tax Notes Int'l 529 (Aug. 12, 1996).

[43] Infra text accompanying notes 59-79.

[44] Infra text accompanying notes 80-99.

[45] Infra text accompanying notes 100-101.

[46] Infra text accompanying notes 105-13.

[47] Infra text accompanying notes 127-34.

[48] Infra text accompanying notes 135-43.

with a U.S. trade or business. Domestic noncorporate shareholders are taxed under the general rules for dividend income.

1. *FSC defined.* In order to qualify as a FSC, a corporation must satisfy all of the following requirements:[49]

    a. It must be organized under the laws of a foreign country or a U.S. possession other than Puerto Rico.[50]

    b. If the corporation is organized in a foreign country, that country must have an agreement with the United States for the sharing of tax information or must be a party to a tax treaty with the United States under which tax information is shared.[51]

    c. The corporation may not have more than 25 shareholders.[52]

    d. While multiple classes of common stock are permitted, a FSC may not have any preferred stock outstanding.[53]

    e. A FSC must have an office in a foreign country that has an adequate tax information sharing arrangement with the United States, or it must have an office in a U.S. possession other than Puerto Rico.[54]

    f. At this office, which need not be in the jurisdiction in which the FSC is organized, the corporation must keep a set of "permanent books of ac-

---

[49] IRC §922(a). See Notice 95-60, 1995-2 CB 338 (some FSC requirements suspended because of "major disruptions in the United States Virgin Islands caused by Hurricane Marilyn on September 16 and 17, 1995").

[50] See IRC §927(d)(5) (for purposes of FSC rules, possessions include Guam, American Samoa, Northern Mariana Islands, and the U.S. Virgin Islands). See 1984 Bluebook, supra note 11, at 1043 ("in other words, the corporation must be formed under the laws of a jurisdiction outside U.S. customs territory"). See also Larkins, Recent Changes Enhance Barbados as FSC Domicile, 7 J. Int'l Tax'n 58 (1996). For Virgin Islands taxation of FSCs incorporated in that possession, see Polychrome Int'l Corp. v. Krigger, 5 F3d 1522 (3d Cir. 1993).

[51] IRC §927(e)(3). For information exchange agreements under §274(h)(6), see supra ¶21.1.9. See 1984 Bluebook, supra note 11, at 1043 ("the country of organization must be authorized to exchange information with respect to the FSC (whether or not the FSC is a resident of that country)").

[52] See 1984 Bluebook, supra note 11, at 1044 ("a member of the corporation's board of directors that holds qualifying shares required to be owned by a resident of the country under whose laws the FSC is organized will not count as a shareholder for this purpose"); Reg. §1.922-1(f) (when FSC stock is owned by trust or partnership, each beneficiary or partner is counted as one shareholder).

[53] See Reg. §1.922-1(g); 1984 Bluebook, supra note 11, at 1044 ("dividend rights may not be used to direct dividends from exempt foreign trade income to shareholders that have taxable income and to direct other dividends to shareholders that have net operating loss carryovers").

[54] For the term "office," see Reg. §1.922-1(h); 1984 Bluebook, supra note 11, at 1044 ("Congress intended that the office conduct activities comparable to those of a 'permanent establishment' under income tax treaty concepts").

count" including, at a minimum, invoices, quarterly income statements, and year-end balance sheets.[55]

g. Records sufficient to substantiate U.S. tax returns must be kept within the United States.

h. The corporation must have a board of directors, and at least one of the directors must be a nonresident of the United States (but may be a U.S. citizen).[56]

i. A FSC may not be a member of a controlled group of corporations that includes an interest charge DISC.[57]

j. The corporation must elect to be a FSC.

The election must be made during the 90 days preceding the first taxable year to which it applies, and all persons holding shares of the FSC's stock at the beginning of the first year must consent to the election.[58] An effective election applies for all subsequent years until it is revoked or is terminated by the corporation's failure to qualify as a FSC for five successive years.[59]

2. *Foreign trading gross receipts.* A FSC's exempt foreign trade income is some portion of the taxable income inherent in its "foreign trading gross receipts," which include gross receipts from the certain sales and leasing transactions and from the performance of some types of services.[60] In these transactions, the FSC may be the seller, lessor, or services performer, or it may act as commission agent in arranging for a sale, lease, or service to be made or performed by another person.[61]

a. *Export property.* A sale or lease yields foreign trading gross receipts only if the property sold or leased is "export property," which includes goods that are (1) manufactured, produced, grown, or extracted in the United States by a person other than a FSC,[62] (2) held primarily for sale or lease in the ordinary course of the FSC's business, and (3) sold or leased for direct consumption, use, or dispo-

---

[55] 1984 Bluebook, supra note 11, at 1044; Reg. §1.922-1(i).

[56] See Reg. §1.922-1(j).

[57] The term "controlled group of corporations" includes corporations joined together by parent-subsidiary or brother-sister relationships, or a combination of both, where each link consists of shareholdings of 50 percent or more, by voting power or value. IRC §§927(d)(4), 1563(a); Reg. §1.924(a)-1T(h).

[58] IRC §927(f)(1); Reg. §1.927(f)-1.

[59] IRC §§927(f)(2), (3). A revocation is effective for the taxable year during which it is filed if the filing occurs during the first 90 days of the year; in any other case, it is effective for the following year.

[60] IRC §924(a). See Park, Note, Cross-Border Equipment Leasing: Recent Developments Relating to Section 168(g), 16 Va. Tax Rev. 299 (1996).

[61] Reg. §§1.924(a)-1T(b), (c).

[62] See Reg. §1.927(a)-1T(c); Delap & Zukowski, Impact of the "U.S.-Manufactured" Requirement on FSC Tax Savings, 87 J. Tax'n 38 (1997).

sition outside the United States.[63] No more than 50 percent of the value of export property may be attributable to materials or components imported into the United States.[64] The requirement that export property be sold or leased for consumption, use, or disposition outside the United States is reinforced by a rule excluding receipts from foreign trading gross receipts if the property is "for ultimate use in the United States."[65] Also, the foreign economic processes requirement described below demands that the FSC participate in the making of a foreign sale, not merely sell to someone in the United States who later resells the goods in an export transaction.

Patents, copyrights, and similar intangibles may not be export property, but films, tapes, records, and computer software can be whether they are sold for commercial or home use.[66] Oil and gas and the primary products of oil and gas are excluded, as are items whose export is prohibited by statute.[67] Also, an item that could otherwise qualify is not export property if it is leased for use by another member of a controlled group of corporations that includes the FSC.[68]

b. *Qualifying services.* If a FSC performs services that are "related and subsidiary" to a sale or lease of export property by the FSC, any compensation received for the services is a foreign trading gross receipt.[69] Foreign trading gross

---

[63] IRC §927(a)(1). According to the Staff of the Joint Committee on Taxation:

Congress intended that the destination test (whether "use, consumption, or disposition occurs outside the United States") will be considered satisfied if the FSC delivers the property to a carrier or freight forwarder for ultimate delivery, use, or consumption outside of the United States. This rule will apply without regard to (1) the F.O.B. point or place of passage of title, (2) whether the purchaser is a United States or foreign purchaser, or (3) whether the property is for use of the purchaser or for resale.

1984 Bluebook, supra note 11, at 1060. For more on the destination test, see Reg. §1.927(a)-1T(d).

[64] IRC §927(a)(1)(C); Reg. §1.927(a)-1T(e). The fair market value of an imported item is its appraised value for customs purposes at the time of importation.

[65] IRC §924(f)(1)(A)(i).

[66] IRC §927(a)(2)(B). See Reg. §1.927(a)-1T(f)(3) (goods produced under patents and copyrights, including books, may be export property if sale does not convey right to reproduce).

Computer software was added to the statutory enumeration in 1997 (effective for periods after 1997). For periods covered by this addition, software may be export property, even in transactions by which the buyer or licensee acquires a right to reproduce the software abroad. See Staff of Joint Comm. on Tax'n, 105th Cong., 1st Sess., General Explanation of Tax Legislation Enacted in 1997, at 323 (Comm. Print 1997) ("No inference is intended regarding the qualification as export property of computer software licensed for reproduction abroad under [prior] law").

[67] IRC §§927(a)(2)(C), (D); Reg. §§1.927(a)-1T(g), (h).

[68] IRC §927(a)(2)(A); Reg. §1.927(a)-1T(f)(2). For the term "controlled group of corporations," see §927(d)(4), discussed supra note 57.

[69] IRC §924(a)(3).

receipts can also take the form of commissions received by the FSC in selling a related and subsidiary service to be performed by another. Examples of related services are warranty, maintenance, repair, and installation.[70] A service is not subsidiary to a sale or lease unless, at the time of the sale or lease, it is reasonably expected that the compensation for the services will not exceed the gross receipts from the sale. A FSC performing (or receiving a commission for) a related and subsidiary service must also play a role in the sale or leasing transaction, but this role may be either as seller or lessor or as commission agent. The related and subsidiary services may be performed within or outside the United States.

A FSC may also earn foreign trading gross receipts from engineering or architectural services for construction projects.[71] Although the construction projects must be located outside the United States, the services may be performed in this country. Also, the services may be performed by the FSC's employees, an independent contractor hired by the FSC, or some other person for whom the FSC acts as commission agent.

Income from managerial services performed for an unrelated FSC or DISC are also foreign trading gross receipts if (1) the services are "in furtherance of the production of foreign trading gross receipts" of the managed corporation and (2) at least 50 percent of the FSC's gross receipts comes from other transactions in which it sells or leases export property or performs related and subsidiary services in connection with such sales or leases.[72] Examples of qualifying managerial services are export marketing studies, making shipping arrangements, and contacting foreign purchasers. The services, however, may not be legal, accounting, scientific, or technical services. The services may be performed by the FSC, directly or through an independent contract, or by another person for whom the FSC is a commission agent.

c. *Excluded receipts.* Receipts from a sale, lease, or performance of services for use by the U.S. government or an "instrumentality thereof" cannot be foreign trading gross receipts if the government or instrumentality is required by law or regulation to purchase domestically produced goods or services.[73] Gross receipts from a transaction "accomplished by a subsidy granted by the United States or any instrumentality thereof" are also excluded.[74] The idea underlying these exclusions is apparently that the FSC stimulus for exports is not needed if the buyer is required by statute to buy U.S. goods or services or if some other subsidy program applies to the transaction.

---

[70] Reg. §1.924(a)-1T(d).

[71] IRC §924(a)(4); Reg. §1.924(a)-1T(e).

[72] IRC §924(a)(5); Reg. §1.924(a)-1T(f).

[73] IRC §924(f)(1)(A)(ii); Reg. §1.924(a)-1T(g)(4).

[74] IRC §924(f)(1)(B). For a list of subsidies covered by this rule, see Reg. §1.924(a)-1T(g)(3).

Receipts from services performed for another FSC are usually excluded if the two FSCs belong to the same controlled group of corporations.[75] Also, receipts from a sale or lease of goods to another FSC in the same controlled group (and from the performance of related and subsidiary services) can qualify only if neither the taxpayer nor any other FSC in the controlled group determines its income from a transaction in the goods with either of the administrative pricing rules described below.[76] Receipts in transactions between unrelated FSCs may qualify under the general rules.[77]

A FSC's foreign trading gross receipts include no "investment income," such as dividends, interest, royalties, rents under leases of property not qualifying as export property, gains on sales and exchanges of securities, and gains in futures transactions not arising "out of a bona fide hedging transaction reasonably necessary to conduct the business of the FSC in the manner in which such business is customarily conducted by others."[78] Also, "carrying charges" do not qualify even if received with respect to accounts receivable from transactions generating qualifying receipts.[79] Carrying charges include "any amount in excess of the price for an immediate cash sale and any other unstated interest."[80]

d. *Foreign economic processes.* The gross receipts from a transaction are foreign trading gross receipts only if "economic processes with respect to such transaction take place outside the United States."[81] This requirement consists of two subsidiary requirements.

First, by activities located outside the United States, the FSC must participate in solicitations or negotiations leading to the sale or in the making of the contract of sale.[82] For this purpose, solicitation is "a communication (either by telephone, telegraph, mail, or in person) [with] a specific, targeted, potential customer."[83] Negotiation is a "communication . . . to a customer or potential customer of the terms of sale, such as the price, credit, delivery, or other specification."[84] The making of a contract includes "any of the elements necessary to complete a sale such as making an offer or accepting the offer"; it also includes a "written confirmation . . . to the customer of an oral agreement which confirms

---

[75] IRC §924(f)(1)(C). For the term "controlled group of corporations," see §927(d)(4), discussed supra note 57.

[76] IRC §924(f)(1). For the administrative pricing rules, see infra text accompanying notes 106-18.

[77] 1984 Bluebook, supra note 11, at 1053.

[78] IRC §§924(f)(2), 927(c).

[79] IRC §924(f)(2).

[80] IRC §927(d)(1); 1984 Bluebook, supra note 11, at 1053. See Reg. §1.927(d)-1(a) (carrying charge normally imputed if price paid more than 60 days after sale).

[81] IRC §924(b)(1)(B); Reg. §1.924(d)-1(a).

[82] IRC §924(d)(1)(A); Reg. §1.924(d)-1(c)(1).

[83] 1984 Bluebook, supra note 11, at 1048-49. See Reg. §1.994(d)-1(c)(2).

[84] 1984 Bluebook, supra note 11, at 1049. See Reg. §1.994(d)-1(c)(3).

variable contract terms or specifies . . . additional contract terms."[85] An act of solicitation, negotiation, or contract making occurs outside the United States if it is "initiated" there.[86] The requisite foreign activities may be carried on directly by the FSC or by another person (including the FSC's parent) acting as the FSC's agent, but they must be more than advertising.[87] Where the FSC acts as commission agent, it "may act upon standing instructions from its principal."[88]

The solicitation, negotiation, or contract making requirement is generally applied transaction by transaction. However, the regulations allow an annual election to group transactions, by combining all sales of a particular product or product line, by grouping all transactions with a particular customer or all transactions under a particular contract, or by combining sales of a particular product or product line to a particular customer or under a particular contract.[89]

Second, a specified portion of the FSC's direct costs for the transaction must be incurred outside the United States.[90] For this purpose, direct costs include only the costs of (1) advertising[91] and sales promotions,[92] (2) processing customer orders[93] and arranging for delivery,[94] (3) transporting the goods,[95] (4) invoicing

---

[85] 1984 Bluebook, supra note 11, at 1048–49. See Reg. §1.994(d)-1(c)(4).

[86] 1984 Bluebook, supra note 11, at 1049.

[87] For activities of other persons, see Reg. §1.994(d)-1(b).

[88] 1984 Bluebook, supra note 11, at 1049.

[89] Reg. §1.994(d)-1(c)(5). Compare 1984 Bluebook, supra note 11, at 1048 (suggesting that grouping be allowed if (1) the sales are made under a single contract that specifies the material terms of each sale and extends for no longer than one year, (2) the sales are of fungible commodities or products that are substantially similar, and (3) the FSC engages in solicitation, negotiation, or contract making at least once with respect to this customer).

[90] See Reg. §1.924(d)-1(d).

[91] See Reg. §1.924(e)-1(a)(1); 1984 Bluebook, supra note 11, at 1050 (advertising is "an appeal, related to a specific product or product line made through any medium and directed at all or a part of the general population of potential export customers"; advertising cost is incurred where advertising is "aired, displayed, published, or otherwise presented to the potential customer").

[92] See Reg. §1.924(e)-1(a)(2); 1984 Bluebook, supra note 11, at 1050 (sales promotion is "an appeal made in person to a potential export customer for the sale of a specific product or product line made in the context of trade shows or annual customer meetings"; costs of sales promotion include salaries of persons hired for trade shows or annual customer meetings, but not salaries and commissions of "direct sales people"; costs deemed incurred at location of trade show or customer meeting).

[93] See Reg. §1.924(e)-1(b); 1984 Bluebook, supra note 11, at 1050 (processing customer orders "means notifying the related supplier of the order and of the requirements for delivery").

[94] See Reg. §1.924(e)-1(b)(2); 1984 Bluebook, supra note 11, at 1050 (costs of arranging for delivery include "the cost of salaries for clerks, telephone, telegraph, and documentation," but not shipping expenses; delivery may be within or outside United States).

[95] See Reg. §1.924(e)-1(c); 1984 Bluebook, supra note 11, at 1051 (transportation costs are zero "if the customer pays the cost of transportation directly"; if FSC pays

the customer and collecting the price, and (5) the assumption of credit risk.[96] Direct costs include both costs incurred directly by the FSC and amounts paid to independent contractors acting on its behalf.[97] The foreign share of the direct costs is the portion "attributable to activities performed outside the United States."[98] Generally, the foreign share must be at least 50 percent.[99] Under an alternative test, however, a FSC meets the direct cost requirement if at least 85 percent of the costs in each of two of the five categories are foreign.[100]

e. *Foreign management requirement.* Normally, if a FSC is not managed outside the United States during a taxable year, foreign trading gross receipts for the year are zero, even if the corporation meets all of the qualification and transactional requirements described above.[101] This requirement, however, is more formal than substantive because it is met if (1) all meetings of shareholders and directors occur outside the United States, (2) the corporation's principal bank account is maintained outside the United States throughout the year, and (3) all dividends, legal and accounting fees, and salaries of officers and directors are disbursed from foreign bank accounts.[102]

f. *Small FSCs.* A FSC need not satisfy the foreign management and foreign economic process requirements if it elects to be a "small FSC."[103] This election can be made regardless of the size of the assets or business of the FSC or its parent, but it has the effect of sharply limiting the amount of the FSC exclusion. The foreign trading gross receipts of a small FSC may not exceed $5 million for any taxable year. As described below, a FSC's exempt foreign trade income is a fraction of the taxable income from the transactions yielding foreign trading gross receipts. A small FSC, however, may freely allocate the $5 million ceiling among gross receipts that would otherwise qualify, thus allowing the qualifying amount to be assigned to the receipts with the highest taxable income content.

---

transportation cost, foreign share is determined by "ratio of mileage outside the U.S. customs territory to total transportation mileage"; for fungible goods, direct costs include only costs of transportation after goods are identified to contract).

[96] IRC §§924(d)(3)(A), (e). See Reg. §§1.924(e)-1(d), (e) (invoicing, payment, and assumption of credit risk). See 1984 Bluebook, supra note 11, at 1050 (in connection with foreign military sales that must be made through U.S. government, expenses incurred in negotiating with government are excluded).

[97] 1984 Bluebook, supra note 11, at 1049.

[98] IRC §924(d)(3)(B).

[99] IRC §924(d)(1)(B).

[100] IRC §924(d)(2).

[101] IRC §§924(b)(1)(A), 927(d)(3); Reg. §1.924(c)-1. For this purpose, the United States includes Puerto Rico, but not the U.S. possessions. IRC §§927(d)(3), (5).

[102] IRC §924(c). To meet the second of these requirements, the corporation must, at all times during the taxable year, maintain its principal bank account in a foreign country that exchanges tax information with the United States pursuant to agreement or treaty or in a possession of the United States other than Puerto Rico.

[103] IRC §924(b)(2); Reg. §1.924(a)-1T(j). For the possibility of switching from small FSC status to regular FSC status, see Rev. Rul. 90-108, 1990-2 CB 185.

Only a single $5 million ceiling, however, is allowed to a controlled group of corporations, and it is therefore allocated among FSCs if the group includes more than one small FSC.[104]

The purpose of the small FSC rule is to make the FSC exemption available to smaller businesses that cannot afford the expense of complying with the foreign economic processes and management requirements. The statutes provide two additional alternatives—interest charge DISCs and shared FSCs. The latter, described below, allows several otherwise unrelated domestic corporations to join in organizing a single FSC that keeps a separate account for dealings in the goods of each shareholder.[105]

3. *Transfer pricing rules.* Special pricing rules may apply if a FSC sells or leases goods purchased from a person or trade or business under common control with the FSC, sells export property to a commonly controlled person or trade or business, or acts as commission agent in sales, leases, or services transactions of a commonly controlled person or trade or business. Normally, the FSC's income from such a transaction is determined with one of three intercompany pricing regimes—a combined taxable income method, a gross receipts method, or the arm's length pricing rule of §482—whichever produces the most taxable income for the FSC.[106] The combined taxable income and gross receipts methods are called "administrative pricing rules."[107]

Under the combined taxable income method, the FSC's taxable income is 23 percent of the combined taxable income of the FSC and the related person from the transaction.[108] Combined taxable income is determined without any exclusion ultimately allowable under the FSC rules.[109] Marginal costing rules may be used in determining combined taxable income if the FSC is seeking to establish or maintain a foreign market for the product.[110]

Under the gross receipts method, FSC taxable income is 1.83 percent of the gross receipts on the sale or lease or, if less, 46 percent of the combined taxable

---

[104] For the term "controlled group of corporations," see §927(d)(4), discussed supra note 57.

[105] Infra text accompanying notes 145-47.

[106] IRC §925(a); Reg. §1.925(a)-1T. See Joranko, A FSCful of Dollars: Maximizing FSC Benefits Through Transaction-Level Pricing, 13 Tax Notes Int'l 197 (July 15, 1996).

[107] See 1984 Bluebook, supra note 11, at 1043, 1054, 1057 (these methods "are intended to approximate arm's-length pricing [and thereby] comply with GATT's requirement of arm's-length prices"; they may not be used, however, for transactions not involving FSCs).

[108] IRC §925(a)(2).

[109] IRC §925(e). Also, if the related supplier is a qualified cooperative, deductions allowable to the cooperative for patronage dividends, per-unit retain allocations, and nonpatronage distributions are ignored. IRC §925(f). See IRC §927(a)(4) (cooperative is qualified if subject to §§1381-1383 and "engaged in the marketing of agricultural or horticultural products"); 1984 Bluebook, supra note 11, at 1060-61.

[110] Reg. §1.925(b)-1T.

income of the FSC and related person.[111] Gross receipts consist of "total receipts" from a sale or lease of property held for sale to customers in the ordinary course of business, and the gross income from any other transaction.[112] If the FSC acts as a commission agent, the principal's gross receipts, not the FSC's commission, are used.[113]

Whenever one of the administrative pricing methods applies, gross income is determined by working backward from the taxable income figure produced by the applicable pricing method, and it does not depend on the intercompany price actually charged. FSC taxable income is zero under both methods, however, if the combined taxable income of the FSC and the related supplier is negative.[114]

Under the third alternative, FSC taxable income is based on the intercompany price actually charged, subject to adjustment under §482. Very generally, an adjustment is made under §482 if the price paid or received by the FSC or the commission it received differs from the amount that would have been paid or received if the transaction had been between unrelated persons dealing at arm's length.[115]

Assume (1) a FSC receives $1,000 on sales of goods that its parent produced for $550 and sold to the FSC for $625 and (2) the FSC incurs expenses of $350 in selling the goods. Combined taxable income is $100 ($1,000 less sum of $550 and $350). Under the combined taxable income method, FSC taxable income is $23 (23 percent of $100). Under the gross receipts method, taxable income is $18.3 (lesser of 1.83 percent of FSC gross receipts of $1,000 or 46 percent of combined taxable income of $100). Using the actual price paid by the FSC, taxable income is $25 ($1,000 selling price less $625 cost of goods sold and $350 of selling expenses). If the actual intercompany price withstands scrutiny under §482, the FSC's taxable income from the transaction is $25—the amount determined with the actual price—because it is larger than the amounts determined under the combined taxable income method ($23) and the gross receipts method ($18.3).

In contrast, assume the arm's length price for the sale from parent to FSC is $635. In this case, FSC taxable income is $23—the amount determined with the combined taxable income method—because it is larger than the amount determined with the actual price adjusted under §482 ($1,000 selling price less $635 cost of goods sold and $350 of selling expenses, or $15) and also exceeds the amount under the gross receipts method ($18.3). In this situation, the FSC's gross income is determined as though it had purchased the goods from the parent for $627 ($1,000 sales revenues less $627 cost of goods sold and less $350 selling expenses yields taxable income of $23).

---

[111] IRC §§925(a)(1),(d).

[112] IRC §927(b)(1).

[113] IRC §927(b)(2).

[114] Reg. §1.925(a)-1T(e)(1).

[115] See infra ¶79.1.

The results would be the same as in the original example if the parent made the sale for $1,000 and the FSC received a commission of $375 for acting as the parent's agent in arranging the sale.[116] Combined taxable income is $100 ($1,000 selling price received by parent less parent's costs of $550 and the FSC's costs of $350), and FSC taxable income under the combined taxable income method is $23 (23 percent of $100). Since the parent's gross receipts are treated as the FSC's receipts in this situation, FSC taxable income under the gross receipts method is $18.3 (lesser of 1.83 of the gross receipts of $1,000 or twice the amount under the combined taxable income method). If the $375 commission is an arm's length price, it determines FSC taxable income because the resulting taxable income figure ($375 of gross income less expenses of $350, or $25) is larger than amounts under the other two methods. If the commission is reduced to $365 under §482, in contrast, the resulting figure ($365 less $350 or $15) is less than the amount under the combined taxable income method ($23), and the latter governs.

The administrative pricing rules, however, may not be used unless the FSC or a person acting under a contract with the FSC carries on all of the following activities with respect to the transaction: (1) solicitation, negotiation, and the making of the contract of sale; (2) advertising and sales promotion; (3) transporting of the goods while the FSC owns them or is acting as commission agent; (4) invoicing the customer and collecting the price; and (5) assumption of any credit risk.[117] This requirement can be met whether the activities are performed by the FSC's employees or by independent contractors acting on its behalf and whether the activities occur within or outside the United States.[118] For example, if a FSC sells goods manufactured by its parent in the United States pursuant to a contract solicited and negotiated by the parent, the requirement that the FSC do the solicitation and negotiation is satisfied if the parent acted as the FSC's agent in arranging the sale.[119]

4. *Exempt foreign trade income.* The exempt income is a portion of the FSC's foreign trade income, which is the gross income from transactions yielding foreign trading gross receipts.[120] The exempt portion of the foreign trade income from a transaction is:

a. 100 percent if (1) taxable income from the transaction is determined by one of the administrative pricing rules, (2) the income "is properly allocable to the marketing of agricultural or horticultural products (or the providing of related services)," (3) the FSC's shareholders are coopera-

---

[116] See 1984 Bluebook, supra note 11, at 1057 ("the same intercompany allocation to the FSC [occurs] whether the FSC takes title as principal or acts as a commission agent").

[117] IRC §925(c); Reg. §1.925(a)-1T(b).

[118] Reg. §1.925(a)-1T(b)(2)(ii); 1984 Bluebook, supra note 11, at 1054.

[119] 1984 Bluebook, supra note 11, at 1054–55.

[120] IRC §923(b); Reg. §1.923-1T(a).

tives, and (4) the FSC currently distributes at least $7/23$ (approximately 30 percent) of the income to shareholders.[121]

b. $15/23$ (approximately 65 percent) in other cases where taxable income from the transaction is determined by one of the administrative pricing rules.[122]

c. 30 percent if the FSC does not deal with a related person in the transaction or if a related person is involved but the transfer price is determined under §482 rather than one of the administrative pricing rules.[123]

d. One half of the otherwise applicable percentage if the transaction involves military property.[124]

e. Zero for income from a sale or license of a patent, copyright, or similar property.[125]

The exemption of exempt foreign trade income is accomplished by treating the income as foreign source income that is not effectively connected with the conduct of a trade or business in the United States.[126] Because a FSC must be a foreign corporation, §882(b) excludes from its gross income any item that is neither from U.S. sources nor effectively connected with U.S. business.

Foreign trade income is gross income. Deductions allocated and apportioned to foreign trade income are prorated between the exempt and nonexempt portions of the income, and the amounts assigned to the exempt portion are disallowed.[127]

5. *Taxation of FSCs.* The nonexempt portion of the foreign trade income (less the deductions prorated to it) is usually taxed by the United States. When FSC taxable income from a transaction is determined with one of the administrative pricing rules, the nonexempt portion is characterized as income effectively connected with a trade or business carried on in the United States through a permanent establishment and therefore is subject to U.S. tax whether or not

---

[121] IRC §923(a)(4); Reg. §1.923-1T(b)(2).

[122] IRC §§291(a)(4), 923(a)(3); Reg. §1.923-1T(b)(1)(i). The exclusion fraction is $16/23$ if none of the FSC's shareholders are C corporations. If only a portion of the stock is held by C corporations, the $15/23$ exclusion applies to C corporations' ratable share of the income, and the remainder is subject to the $16/23$ exclusion.

[123] IRC §§291(a)(4), 923(a)(2); Reg. §1.923-1T(b)(1)(ii). The exclusion is 32 percent if none of the FSC's shareholders are C corporations. If only a portion of the stock is held by C corporations, the 30 percent exclusion applies to the C corporations' ratable share of the income, and the remainder is subject to the 32 percent exclusion.

[124] IRC §923(a)(5). See IRC §995(b)(3)(B) (military property includes arms, ammunition, and any other "implement of war" on munitions list published under Military Security Act of 1954).

[125] IRC §§923(a)(2), 927(a)(2)(B). Films, tapes, and records are not considered copyrights for this purpose.

[126] IRC §921(a).

[127] IRC §921(b); 1984 Bluebook, supra note 11, at 1046.

actually connected with a U.S. business or permanent establishment.[128] Interest, carrying charges, dividends, royalties, and other investment income are also automatically taxable as effectively connected, permanent establishment income. The taxability of other income, including the nonexempt portion of foreign trade income that is determined without either of the administrative pricing rules, depends on the regular rules for foreign corporations.[129] A FSC, however, is denied the benefits of income tax treaties, including any treaty between the United States and the country in which the FSC is incorporated.[130]

A FSC is allowed the foreign tax credit.[131] Foreign income taxes on foreign trade income, however, are neither creditable nor deductible,[132] and the credit for other foreign income taxes is subject to the restrictive credit rules for foreign corporations.[133] Moreover, if taxable income from a transaction is determined with one of the administrative pricing rules, the nonexempt portion of foreign trade income is deemed to be from U.S. sources, which has the effect of precluding the credit for foreign taxes on other income from offsetting the precredit tax on this income.[134]

A FSC is also allowed the credits for taxes withheld and for gasoline taxes on fuels used in off-road vehicles, but it is denied all other credits.[135]

6. *Taxation of FSC shareholders.* Although the dividends received deduction for intercorporate dividends is not usually allowed for dividends from foreign corporations, a 100 percent deduction is available to a domestic corporation with respect to dividends received from a FSC if the dividend is distributed from earnings and profits attributable to foreign trade income accumulated while the distributing corporation was a FSC.[136] The deduction is usually allowed whether the distributed earnings and profits were exempt or nonexempt to the FSC. As a consequence, the exempt portion of foreign trade income is wholly exempted from the U.S. corporate tax, and the nonexempt portion is taxable only at the FSC level.

The deduction, however, is denied for dividends from the nonexempt portion of foreign trade income if (1) the income was determined with the arm's length pricing rule of §482 rather than the administrative pricing rules and (2) the earnings were not subjected to U.S. taxation as effectively connected in-

---

[128] IRC §921(d).

[129] See supra ¶66.1.

[130] IRC §927(e)(4).

[131] IRC §921(c); Reg. §§1.921-3T(d)(2),(3).

[132] IRC §§275(a)(4)(B), 906(b)(5).

[133] See IRC §906, discussed infra ¶69.9.

[134] See infra ¶69.5.1 for the foreign tax credit limitation.

[135] IRC §921(c).

[136] IRC §245(c)(1)(A). For the effects of net operating and capital losses on a FSC's earnings and profits, see Reg. §1.921-3T(c).

come.[137] Since the nonexempt portion is automatically taxable as effectively connected income only when the administrative pricing rules apply, this rule serves to ensure that all nonexempt FSC income is taxed at least once, to the shareholder if not to the FSC.

In contrast, a partial doubling of U.S. corporate taxation occurs if (1) a FSC distributes dividends to a domestic corporation from earnings and profits attributable to FSC income other than foreign trade income and (2) this income was taxed to the FSC as effectively connected income.[138] A dividends received deduction is allowed for these dividends, but for only 80 percent of the dividends if the recipient owns 20 percent or more of the FSC's stock or 70 percent in any other case. Assume a FSC collects interest on accounts receivable. Interest income cannot qualify as foreign trading gross receipts but is automatically taxable to the FSC as effectively connected income.[139] A 70 or 80 percent dividends received deduction is therefore allowed on a distribution of earnings and profits attributable to this income if the shareholder is a domestic corporation.

No dividends received deduction is allowed for FSC dividends from earnings and profits attributable to income other than foreign trade income that was not taxed to the FSC as effectively connected income.[140] The tax on these dividends, however, is usually the first U.S. tax on the income.

A tracing rule generally ensures that nontaxable earnings and profits are received before taxable earnings.[141] A FSC dividend is deemed to come from earnings and profits attributable to the following classes of income, in the order given: (1) exempt foreign trade income (qualifying for 100 percent dividends received deduction); (2) nonexempt foreign trade income determined with the administrative pricing rules (also qualifying for 100 percent deduction); (3) nonexempt foreign trade income determined under §482 and not taxed to the FSC as effectively connected income (no dividends received deduction); and (4) all other income (70 or 80 percent deduction if the FSC paid effectively connected income tax).

A nonresident alien or foreign corporation owning stock of a FSC is taxed on FSC dividends as effectively connected income and is allowed no dividends received deduction.[142] Domestic noncorporate shareholders are taxed on FSC dividends under the general rules for dividend income.

If a FSC shareholder is required to pay a foreign income tax on a dividend from the FSC, no foreign tax credit is allowable for this tax.[143] Also, FSC divi-

---

[137] IRC §245(c)(2). The deduction is also denied for dividends from earnings and profits attributable to income from engineering or architectural services for foreign construction projects.

[138] IRC §245(c)(1)(B).

[139] IRC §921(d), discussed supra text accompanying note 128.

[140] IRC §245(c)(3).

[141] IRC §926(a); Reg. §1.926(a)-1T(b).

[142] IRC §926(b).

[143] IRC §901(h); 1984 Bluebook, supra note 11, at 1059.

dends comprise a separate basket for purposes of the foreign tax credit limitation, which precludes foreign taxes on other income from offsetting U.S. tax on the FSC dividends.[144]

7. *Shared FSCs.* Special rules are provided for a "shared FSC," defined as a corporation that "maintains a separate account for transactions with each shareholder (and persons related to such shareholder)" and makes distributions to shareholders based on the amounts in their separate accounts.[145] Generally, each account maintained by a shared FSC is treated as a separate corporation.[146] A shared FSC, however, must qualify for and elect FSC status as a unitary whole.[147] For example, a shared FSC may not have more than 25 shareholders even if a separate account is maintained for each shareholder. Also, the corporation is treated as a unitary whole in determining whether it satisfies the requirements that it be managed in a foreign country and participate in economic processes outside the United States. The principal advantage of a shared FSC is that the expense of foreign management is effectively shared by the participating shareholders.

¶68.2　CONTROLLED FOREIGN CORPORATIONS

¶68.2.1　Introductory

Under §§951–964, commonly known as subpart F,[1] a U.S. shareholder of a controlled foreign corporation (CFC) is taxed directly on portions of the earnings

---

[144] IRC §904(d)(1)(H). See infra ¶69.5.1 for the foreign tax credit limitation.

[145] IRC §927(g)(3).

[146] IRC §927(g)(1).

[147] IRC §927(g)(2).

[1] The provisions are subpart F of part III of subchapter N of chapter 1 of subtitle A of the Code. See Data Release, Controlled Foreign Corporations, 1992, 15 Stat. Income Bull. 93 (Winter 1996); Dolan & Walsh, Use of Holding Companies in International Tax Planning, 73 Taxes 873 (1995); Friedman, U.S. Tax Considerations in Choosing an Entity to Hold Foreign Business Operations, 45 Tax Lawyer 15 (1991); Skaletsky & Shackelford, U.S. Tax Deferral Considerations and Strategies, 12 Tax Notes Int'l 125 (Jan. 8, 1996); Spudis, Lemein & Waimon, Using Partnerships in International Tax Planning, 73 Taxes 834 (1995); Yoder & McGill, Subpart F: New Foreign Currency Hedging Exception, 74 Taxes 147 (1996). For legislative proposals to expand the categories of income of foreign corporations taxed to U.S. shareholders, see Gravelle, Foreign Tax Provisions of the American Jobs Act of 1996, 72 Tax Notes 1165 (Aug. 26, 1996); Oosterhuis & Cutrone, The Cost of Deferral's Repeal: If Done Properly, It Loses Billions, 58 Tax Notes 765 (Feb. 9, 1993); Shay, Revisiting U.S. Anti-Deferral Rules, 74 Taxes 1042 (1996); Weiner, Real World Approaches to Taxing International Income: The View from Washington, in Nat'l Tax Ass'n, Proceedings of 89th Annual Conf. on Tax'n 229 (1997). See also Avi-Yonah, To End Deferral as We Know It: Simplification Potential of Check-the-Box, 74 Tax Notes 219 (Jan. 13, 1997).

For foreign analogues to subpart F, see Thill & Milhac, French CFC Regime Examined, 14 Tax Notes Int'l 779 (Mar. 3, 1997).

of the corporation, even if the corporation does not distribute them. A U.S. shareholder is a U.S. person who owns at least 10 percent of the foreign corporation's voting stock. A foreign corporation is a CFC if more than 50 percent of its stock, by voting power or value, is owned by U.S. shareholders.[2]

Three categories of CFC earnings are taxed directly to U.S. shareholders: subpart F income, earnings invested in U.S. property, and earnings invested in excess passive assets. Subpart F income is a collection of types of income that Congress found subject to tax haven manipulation,[3] including income from insuring risks outside the CFC's country of incorporation,[4] passive investment income,[5] income from sales of goods purchased from or sold to a related person,[6] income from services performed for or on behalf of a related person,[7] income from shipping operations in foreign commerce,[8] and income from processing, transporting, or distributing oil or gas.[9] Also, income of any character may be included in subpart F income if the CFC engages in activities proscribed by Congress, such as paying illegal bribes or kickbacks, participating in an international boycott, or doing business in a country on bad terms with the United States.[10] Subpart F income is the sum of all of the foregoing or, if less, the CFC's earnings and profits for the year.

CFC earnings other than subpart F income are taxed directly to the shareholders if they are invested in assets located in the United States or (for the years 1994–1996) in excess passive assets.[11] Moreover, if a CFC accumulates earnings that are not taxed to the shareholders as subpart F income or as earnings invested in U.S. property or excess passive assets, a U.S. shareholder is usually taxed on his share of the accumulated earnings as a dividend when he sells his stock.[12]

The Senate Finance Committee, commenting on the 1962 bill by which subpart F was enacted, said:

> Under [pre-1962] law foreign corporations, even though they may be American controlled, are not subject to U.S. tax laws on foreign source income. As a result no U.S. tax is imposed with respect to the foreign source

---

[2] See infra ¶68.2.2.

[3] See Reg. §1.952-2(a)(1) (subpart F income consists of items of gross income, determined under §61 as though CFC was domestic corporation); Reg. §1.954-1(e) (character of each item of income determined by substance of transaction; single transaction may generate income in more than one category (e.g., sales income and interest on account receivable)).

[4] See infra ¶68.2.3.

[5] See infra ¶68.2.4.

[6] See infra ¶68.2.5.

[7] See infra ¶68.2.6.

[8] See infra ¶68.2.7.

[9] See infra ¶68.2.8.

[10] See infra ¶68.2.10.

[11] See infra ¶¶68.2.11, 68.2.12.

[12] See infra ¶68.2.13.

earnings of these corporations . . . until dividends paid by the foreign corporations are received by their American parent corporations or their other American shareholders. The tax at that time is imposed on the American shareholder with respect to the dividend income received, and if this shareholder is a corporation it is eligible for a foreign tax credit with respect to the taxes paid by the foreign subsidiary. . . . [T]his means that foreign income taxes are paid currently, to the extent of the applicable foreign income tax, and not until distributions are made will an additional U.S. tax be imposed, to the extent the U.S. rate is above that applicable in the foreign country. This latter tax effect has been referred to as "tax deferral. . . . "

The House bill . . . did not eliminate tax deferral generally, but instead was concerned primarily with what had been referred to as "tax haven" devices. To accomplish this result the House bill in general sought to end tax deferral for income derived by U.S. controlled foreign corporations from insurance abroad of U.S. risks; for certain foreign investment income of these corporations; for their income from foreign sales subsidiaries which are separately incorporated from their manufacturing operations; and . . . earnings . . . indirectly brought back to the United States without full payment of U.S. tax.[13]

---

[13] S. Rep. No. 1881, 87th Cong., 2d Sess., reprinted at 1962-3 CB 703, 784-85. Senator Eugene J. McCarthy objected:

[T]he controlled foreign corporations provision erects a barrier to the achievement of vital national objectives, namely the expansion of trade and an improvement in our balance-of-payments position. We cannot promote either of these related objectives through a restrictive policy which, in the hope of correcting tax abuses, slashes with a broad sword at America's overseas subsidiaries. . . .

There are controlled corporations which have been established in foreign countries primarily, if not solely, for purposes of tax avoidance here in the United States. It is also true that some of these subsidiaries probably serve no real purpose as far as the interests of the United States are concerned. We should not throw the baby out with the bath water but should reconsider the means by which we undertake to correct abuses. [Subpart F's] approach to overseas income is far too complex in its administration, far too selective in its application, and far too uncertain in its effects.

Id. at 1057. Senators Carlson, Bennett, Butler, Curtis, and Morton found subpart F "truly amazing" and predicted that "normal trade relations will be seriously disturbed." Id. at 1059. On the other hand, Senators Douglas and Gore argued:

The best and indeed the only sure way to achieve substantial equity, guard against the untoward weakening of American industry and assist in the solution of the balance-of-payments problem through taxation is to tax American taxpayers annually on income and profits earned anywhere in the world. . . . This entire section [of the bill containing subpart F], embodying as it does the tax haven approach, ought to be deleted and have substituted therefor the complete removal of the deferral privilege.

Id. at 1126-27. See generally IRS, Tax Havens and Their Use by United States Taxpayers—An Overview (1981); Irish, Tax Havens, 15 Vand. J. Transnat'l L. 449 (1982).

In these broad outlines, the House bill was accepted by the Senate and enacted into law.

Twenty-four years later, the Staff of the Joint Committee on Taxation summarized the policies underlying subpart F as follows:

> It has long been the policy of the United States to impose current tax when a significant purpose of earnings income through a foreign corporation is the avoidance of tax. Such a policy serves to limit the role that tax considerations play in the structuring of U.S. persons' operations and investments. Because movable income earned through a foreign corporation could often be earned through a domestic corporation instead, Congress believed that a major motivation of U.S. persons in earning such income through foreign corporate vehicles often was the tax benefit expected to be gained thereby. Congress believed that it was generally appropriate to impose current U.S. tax on such income earned through a controlled foreign corporation, since there is likely to be limited economic reason for the U.S. person's use of a foreign corporation. Congress believed that by eliminating the U.S. tax benefits of such transactions, U.S. and foreign investment choices would be placed on a more even footing, thus encouraging more efficient (rather than more tax-favored) uses of capital.[14]

More recently, the IRS has stated:

> Subpart F was enacted by Congress to limit the deferral of U.S. taxation of certain income earned outside the United States by CFCs, which are foreign corporations controlled by United States shareholders. Limited deferral was retained after the enactment of subpart F to protect the competitiveness of CFCs doing business overseas. This limited deferral allows a CFC engaged in an active business, and located in a foreign country for appropriate economic reasons, to compete in a similar tax environment with non-U.S. owned corporations located in the same country.[15]

¶68.2.2 Definition of "Controlled Foreign Corporation"

A foreign corporation is a CFC for a particular taxable year if more than 50 percent of its stock is held by U.S. shareholders at any time during the year.[16] A U.S. shareholder is a U.S. person (citizen, resident, or domestic corporation, partnership, trust, or estate) owning at least 10 percent of the corporation's voting stock. In applying the 50 percent test, proportionate shareholdings are measured by voting power or value, whichever gives the highest percentage for

---

[14] Staff of Joint Comm. on Tax'n, 99th Cong., 2d Sess., General Explanation of the Tax Reform Act of 1986 at 964–65 (Comm. Print 1987) [hereinafter 1986 Bluebook].

[15] Notice 98-11, 1998-6 IRB 18.

[16] IRC §957(a). See generally Kuzma, Continued Use and Utility of a Control Test in Determining Subpart F Taxation, 41 Tax Lawyer 879 (1988).

U.S. shareholders.[17] Assume a domestic corporation owns exactly one half of a foreign corporation's voting common stock and one share more than one half of its nonvoting preferred stock; the remainder of the stock is owned by a nonresident alien.[18] The foreign corporation is a CFC because more than 50 percent of its stock, measured by value, is held by a U.S. shareholder.

1. *U.S. person.* Only U.S. persons can be U.S. shareholders, and whether a foreign corporation is a CFC depends on the stock ownership of U.S. shareholders. Normally, the term "United States person" includes U.S. citizens, resident aliens, domestic corporations and partnerships, and all estates and trusts not classified as nonresident aliens for U.S. tax purposes.[19] Special rules are provided, however, for corporations organized in Puerto Rico, Guam, American Samoa, and the Northern Mariana Islands.[20]

2. *U.S. shareholder.* A "United States shareholder" is a U.S. person who owns stock of a foreign corporation carrying at least 10 percent of the total combined voting power of all classes of stock entitled to vote.[21] Actual, indirect,

---

[17] For years beginning before 1987, control was measured by voting power only, and a foreign corporation owned predominantly by U.S. persons therefore avoided CFC status if at least one half of the voting power rested with foreign shareholders. IRC §957(a) (before amendment in 1986). The Treasury and IRS, however, insisted that the foreign shareholders have voting control in substance as well as in form. Reg. §1.957-1(b); Koehring Co. v. US, 583 F2d 313 (7th Cir. 1978) (implicit agreement that foreign stockholder with 55 percent of voting stock would vote as directed by U.S. shareholder), and cases there cited. The alternative reference to value was added in 1986 to make the rules less susceptible to manipulation. 1986 Bluebook, supra note 14, at 988.

For purposes of the rules on insurance income, the ownership threshold is lowered to 25 percent if more than 75 percent of the corporation's premium income is subpart F income. IRC §957(b); Reg. §1.957-2.

[18] Reg. §1.957-1(c) Ex. 8.

[19] IRC §§957(c); 7701(a)(30), (31).

[20] In determining whether a Puerto Rican corporation is a CFC, a shareholder who is a bona fide resident of Puerto Rico is not a U.S. person, even if he is a citizen of the United States, provided that a dividend received by the shareholder during the taxable year would be treated as income from sources within Puerto Rico for purposes of §933(1). IRC §957(c)(1); Reg. §1.957-4(b). For §933(1), which exempts bona fide residents of Puerto Rico from U.S. tax on income from sources in Puerto Rico, see supra ¶67.3.

A bona fide resident of Guam, American Samoa, or the Northern Mariana Islands is not considered a U.S. person in determining whether a corporation organized under the laws of one of those U.S. possessions is a CFC if (1) at least 80 percent of the corporation's gross income for the taxable year and the preceding two years is from sources within one of these possessions or is effectively connected with a trade or business conducted in the possession and (2) the corporation derives at least 50 percent of its gross income for this three-year period from the active conduct of a trade or business in the possession. IRC §957(c)(2).

[21] IRC §951(b). See Reg. §1.951-1(g)(2) (voting power generally consists of "power to elect, appoint, or replace a person, or persons, who ... exercise the powers ordinarily exercised by a member of the board of directors of a domestic corporation").

and constructive ownership are taken into account in applying the 10 percent threshold.[22]

a. *Indirect ownership.* Indirect ownership consists of stock beneficially owned by a U.S. person through foreign corporations, partnerships, trusts, and estates.[23] Stock held by a foreign entity is indirectly owned proportionately by its shareholders, partners, or beneficiaries. If a shareholder, partner, or beneficiary is itself a foreign entity, the stock indirectly held by the entity is treated as held indirectly by its shareholders, partners, or beneficiaries. Stock ownership thus flows through a chain of foreign entities until it is attributed to an individual (U.S. or foreign) or a domestic corporation, partnership, trust, or estate.

Assume domestic corporation P owns 80 percent of the only class of stock of foreign corporation $F1$; $F1$ owns 80 percent of the only class of stock of foreign corporation $F2$, and $F2$ owns 90 percent of the only class of stock of foreign corporation $F3$.[24] Through the direct ownership of 80 percent of $F1$'s stock, P is indirect owner of 64 percent of $F2$'s stock (80 percent of 80 percent) and 57.6 percent of $F3$'s stock (80 percent of 80 percent of 90 percent). However, if P is a wholly owned subsidiary of domestic corporation U, U is not indirect owner of stock of $F1$, $F2$, or $F3$ because the indirect ownership rule never attributes stock from a domestic entity to its owners.[25]

b. *Constructive ownership.* Constructive ownership is determined under §318(a), which treats stock owned by an individual as owned by his spouse, children, grandchildren, and parents and contains a variety of rules for attributing stock to and from entities.[26] The §318(a) rules, however, are modified in this context, as follows:

1. The rules apply only when their effect is to treat a U.S. person as a U.S. shareholder or a foreign corporation as a CFC.[27]

2. Stock owned, actually, indirectly, or constructively, by a nonresident

---

[22] Although indirect and constructive ownership are lumped together in determining whether a U.S. person is a U.S. shareholder, indirect and constructive ownership must be distinguished for other purposes. Most importantly, the gross income inclusions required by subpart F are based on actual and indirect ownership only. See infra ¶68.2.13.

[23] IRC §958(a)(2); Reg. §1.958-1.

[24] S. Rep. No. 1881, supra note 13, at 958.

[25] U is constructive owner of all shares actually and indirectly held by P under the rules described below, but the subpart F inclusions, which are based on actual and indirect ownership, go into the return of P, not U.

[26] IRC §958(b); Reg. §1.958-2. For §318, see infra ¶93.1.7. See generally Alexander, Controlled Foreign Corporations and Constructive Ownership, 18 Tax L. Rev. 531 (1963).

[27] Constructive ownership is also relevant under a few other provisions of subpart F. For example, the definition of "related person" under §954(d)(3) is applied with the constructive ownership rules of §318(a), but only when they have the effect of treating a person as a related person. For §954(d)(3), see infra ¶68.2.5 text accompanying notes 103-06.

alien may not be attributed to a U.S. citizen or resident under the family attribution rule.[28]

3. If a corporation, partnership, trust, or estate owns stock carrying more than 50 percent of the combined voting power of all outstanding stock, the rules attributing stock owned by that entity to its shareholders, partners, or beneficiaries are applied as though it owned all voting stock.[29]

4. Stock owned by a corporation is attributed ratably to its shareholders (according to the value of their stock), except that a shareholder is not constructive owner of any of stock owned by the corporation if he owns less than 10 percent by value of the shareholding corporation's stock (rather than 50 percent as in other applications of §318(a)).[30]

5. In applying the rules of §318(a)(3) for attributing stock from shareholders, partners, and beneficiaries to their corporations, partnerships, trusts, and estates, stock owned by a foreign shareholder, partner, or beneficiary is never attributed to a domestic entity.

To illustrate the third of the foregoing rules, assume three U.S. citizens each own 20 percent of the single class of stock of foreign corporation *F1*, whose other shareholders are foreigners; *F1* owns 60 percent of the single class of stock of foreign corporation *F2*.[31] Because *F1* owns more than 50 percent of *F2*'s voting stock, it is treated as owning 100 percent, and each of the 20 percent shareholders of *F1* is thus constructive owner of 20 percent of *F2*'s stock. *F2* is a CFC because more than 50 percent of its stock is constructively owned by U.S. persons.[32]

¶68.2.3　Insurance Income

Rules on insurance income were included in the original enactment of subpart F, but they were significantly revised in 1986. The original rules were enacted because many U.S. life insurance companies had "attempted to avoid tax on [underwriting] gains by reinsuring their policies abroad [or] by placing the initial policy with a foreign insurance company either controlled by an American insurance company or controlled by other American businesses."[33] Under these

---

[28] IRC §958(b)(1); Reg. §1.958-2(b)(3).

[29] IRC §958(b)(2).

[30] IRC §§318(a)(2)(C), 958(b)(3).

[31] See S. Rep. No. 1881, supra note 13, at 959 Ex. 1.

[32] Each of the U.S. shareholders, however, is indirect owner of only 12 percent of *F2*'s stock (20 percent of 60 percent) and thus is taxed on only 12 percent of *F2*'s subpart F income and earnings invested in U.S. property and excess passive assets. Although the 50 percent threshold of the CFC definition is exceeded, the subpart F inclusions are only 36 percent of the taxable items.

[33] S. Rep. No. 1881, supra note 13, at 787. See Ocean Drilling & Exploration Co. v. US, 24 Cl. Ct. 714, 92-1 USTC ¶50,018 (1991), aff'd, 988 F2d 1135 (Fed. Cir. 1993)

rules, income from insurance was subpart F income only if the policy insured risks located in the United States. In 1986, the scope of the rules was expanded to reach income from insuring any risk outside the country in which the CFC is incorporated because "insurance income generally represents the type of inherently movable income at which subpart F is aimed, since such income can frequently be routed through a corporation formed in any convenient jurisdiction."[34]

1. *Generally.* Under the 1986 revision, subpart F income includes "insurance income," which generally includes all income from the issuing or reinsuring of an insurance or annuity contract that covers risks outside the country in which the CFC is organized.[35] Income from insuring risks within the CFC's country of incorporation is also insurance income if "as the result of any arrangement . . . another corporation receives a substantially equal amount of premiums or other consideration" for insuring risks outside the CFC's country of incorporation. For this purpose, the risk is located (1) at the place of the insured property or activity in the case of casualty or liability insurance and (2) in the residence country of individuals covered by life or health insurance.

An item is usually insurance income only if, in the hands of a domestic insurance company, it would be taxable under subchapter L (the tax rules for domestic insurance companies). The subchapter L rules, however, are modified in several respects for this purpose.[36]

2. *Related person insurance income.* Several special rules apply if a U.S. person is both a shareholder of a foreign corporation and the insured under an insurance contract issued by the corporation.[37] As the Staff of the Joint Committee on Taxation explained when these rules were enacted in 1986:

> The related person insurance income of many offshore "captive" insurance companies avoided current taxation under the subpart F rules of prior law because, for example, the company's U.S. ownership was relatively dispersed, that is, no more than 25 percent of its voting stock was held by 10-percent U.S. shareholders. Generally, a captive insurance company is considered to be a company organized by one or more persons primarily to provide insurance protection to its owners or persons related to its owners. Congress decided to limit the unintended tax advantages received by U.S. taxpayers that jointly own, with a number of other persons, offshore captive insurers, by adopting a special rule which reduces subpart F's U.S. owner-

---

(under pre-1986 §953, reaching only income from insurance of U.S. risks, outer continental shelf is not part of United States; §638, which treats continental shelf as part of United States for certain purposes, does not apply under §953).

[34] 1986 Bluebook, supra note 14, at 968 ("indeed, several countries have promoted themselves as jurisdictions for the formation of such corporations").

[35] IRC §953(a).

[36] IRC §953(b).

[37] IRC §953(c).

ship requirements for current taxation of a foreign corporation's income in the case of certain related person insurance income.[38]

The term "related person insurance income" refers to a foreign corporation's income from insurance that covers U.S. persons owning stock in the corporation and persons related to them.[39] The special rules applied to this income are:

a. The corporation's U.S. shareholders include all U.S. persons who hold any of its stock (voting or nonvoting) and, if the corporation is a mutual insurance company, all of its U.S. policyholders.

b. The foreign corporation is a CFC if U.S. shareholders, so defined, own more than 25 percent, by value or voting power, of the corporation's stock.

c. The U.S. shareholders' pro rata shares of related person insurance income is determined as though (a) this income was the corporation's only subpart F income and (b) the stock held by U.S. shareholders constituted all of the corporation's outstanding stock.

The effect of the last of these rules is to tax the U.S. shareholders on related person insurance income, even if portions of the income are beneficially owned by foreign shareholders. None of the rules applies in determining the taxability of income other than related person insurance income.

The rules for related person insurance income apply whether the U.S. person holds shares of the corporation directly or indirectly through one or more foreign entities. They apply whether the U.S. person is directly insured under the contract or the contract reinsures a contract covering the U.S. person issued by another insurer. Moreover, a U.S. person is treated as the insured under all contracts that directly or indirectly insure persons, U.S. and foreign, who are related to the U.S. person.[40]

The rules are qualified by several exceptions. For example, they do not apply if, throughout the taxable year, less then 20 percent of the foreign corporation's stock (both by value and voting power) is held by U.S. persons who are insured or are related to persons insured under policies issued by the corporation.[41] Also, the rules do not apply if related person insurance income accounts for less than 20 percent of the corporation's insurance income for the year (including for this purpose income from insuring risks within the corporation's country of incor-

---

[38] 1986 Bluebook, supra note 14, at 968. See also id. at 979-82.

[39] IRC §953(c)(2).

[40] For the term "related person," see §954(d)(3), discussed infra ¶68.2.5 text accompanying notes 103-06. Also, a director, employee, or partner of the U.S. person is treated as a related person if the policy insures against liability arising from the insured's service as director, employee, or partner. IRC §953(c)(6)(B).

[41] IRC §953(c)(3)(A).

poration).[42] Moreover, if the corporation has never been a CFC apart from these rules at any time after 1986, it can elect to pay the effectively connected income tax on the related person insurance income in lieu of having it taxed to the U.S. shareholders.[43]

3. *Election to be treated as domestic corporation.* A foreign corporation may elect to be treated as a domestic corporation if (1) the election causes it to be subject to the rules of subchapter L for insurance companies and (2) the corporation is a CFC under either the general rules or the special rules for related person insurance income.[44]

¶68.2.4 Foreign Personal Holding Company Income

A CFC's subpart F income consists of the sum of its insurance income and foreign base company (FBC) income. FBC income includes foreign personal holding company (FPHC) income.[45] According to the Senate Finance Committee, reporting on the 1962 bill by which subpart F was enacted:

> Your committee, while recognizing the need to maintain active American business operations abroad on an equal competitive footing with other operating businesses in the same countries, nevertheless sees no need to maintain the deferral of U.S. tax where the investments are portfolio types of investments, or where the company is merely passively receiving investment income. In such cases there is no competitive problem justifying postponement of the tax until the income is repatriated.[46]

FPHC income generally consists of the sum of the CFC's income in the form of dividends, interest, annuities,[47] rents, royalties,[48] net gains on dispositions of property producing any of the foregoing types of income and property producing no income before sale,[49] net gains from commodities transactions,[50] net gains from foreign currency transactions,[51] and income

---

[42] IRC §953(c)(3)(B).

[43] IRC §§953(c)(3)(C), (D), (E).

[44] IRC §953(d).

[45] IRC §954(a)(1). See generally Laity, Defining the Passive Income of Controlled Foreign Corporations, 21 NC J. Int'l L. & Commercial Regulation 293 (1996); Yoder, Final and Proposed Subpart F Regulations: Determination of FBCI, Definitions of FPHCI and the Earnings and Profits Limitation, 25 Tax Mgmt. Int'l J. 3 (1996).

[46] S. Rep. No. 1881, supra note 13, at 789.

[47] For dividends, interest, and annuities, see infra text accompanying notes 53–68.

[48] For rents and royalties, see infra text accompanying notes 69–74.

[49] For these net gains, see infra text accompanying notes 75–79.

[50] See infra text accompanying notes 80–83.

[51] See infra text accompanying notes 84–90.

from notional principal contracts.[52]

1. *Dividends, interest, and annuities.* FPHC income generally includes dividends, interest (including original issue discount), income "equivalent to interest," and annuities.[53] Any income that predominantly reflects the time value of money or is compensation for the use or forbearance of money is equivalent to interest, including commitment fees and similar amounts for loans actually made.[54] Payments received in lieu of dividends under a securities lending transaction are also FPHC income.[55]

Related person factoring income is also treated as interest.[56] There are two types of related person factoring income—income from a trade or service receivable acquired from a related person and interest or other income on a loan by the CFC to finance a related person's purchase of inventory or performance of services.[57] The term "trade or service receivable" refers to an account receivable arising from a related person's sale of inventory or other property held primarily for sale to customers in the ordinary course of business or from a related person's performance of a service.[58] Assume a CFC's domestic parent sells goods for $100, payable in 60 days, and sells the account receivable to the CFC for $97. When the CFC collects $100 from the account receivable debtor, its income of $3 is related person factoring income and thus is classified as interest and FPHC income. The result would be the same if the parent sold the goods for $97 under an interest

---

[52] See infra text accompanying note 91. See Reg. §1.954-1(e)(4)(D) (FPHC income is excluded from all other categories of FBC income, except that if item is both FPHC income and insurance income, FBC shipping income, or FBC oil-related income, it is insurance income, FBC shipping income, or FBC oil-related income, not FPHC income).

[53] IRC §§954(c)(1)(A), (E). See 1986 Bluebook, supra note 14, at 967 ("dividends [and] interest . . . are inherently manipulable"). For original issue discount, see supra ¶56.1.

Income equivalent to interest was added to FPHC income in 1986 "to prevent taxpayers from . . . shelter[ing] passive interest-type income from current U.S. tax by rearranging the form of offshore passive investments so that the income they generate is not traditional interest income." 1986 Bluebook, supra.

See also Reg. §1.954-2(b)(3) (for CFC taxable years beginning after March 3, 1997, interest excluded from gross income under §103 is FPHC income). See supra ¶15.1 for §103 and infra ¶111.4 for the alternative minimum tax.

[54] Reg. §§1.954-2(h)(1), (2). For other items treated as interest equivalents, see Reg. §1.954-2(h)(4) (various factoring income); Reg. §1.954-2(h)(5) (deferred payments for services performed by CFC).

[55] IRC §954(c)(1)(G) (effective for taxable years beginning after August 5, 1997).

[56] IRC §§864(d)(2)(C).

[57] IRC §§864(d)(1), (6). The §267(b) definition of related person applies with one modification: A person related under §267(b) to a U.S. shareholder of the CFC is also related to the CFC. IRC §864(d)(4). See infra ¶78.3 for §267(b).

[58] IRC §864(d)(3).

bearing note, the CFC purchased the note for $97, and the obligor subsequently paid the CFC $100, including $3 of interest.

"[E]xport financing interest" is excluded from FPHC income if it is "derived in the active conduct" of a trade or business.[59] Export financing interest is interest earned in a banking business from financing sales of goods where the sales are made for use or consumption outside the United States but the goods were produced within the United States by the CFC or a related person. Related person factoring income cannot qualify for exclusion as export financing interest.[60]

Dividend or interest income is also excluded from FPHC income if (1) the CFC receives it from a related person, (2) the recipient and payor are organized under the laws of the same foreign country, and (3) a "substantial part" of the payor's assets are used in a trade or business in that country.[61] This exception was included in the 1962 legislation because Congress "saw no reason for taxing the U.S. shareholders on dividends received by a controlled foreign corporation from a related party where the U.S. shareholder would not have been taxed if he had owned the stock of the related party directly."[62] Assume a domestic corporation is beneficial owner of two CFCs organized in foreign country X, one of which manufactures goods in country X and the other of which owns stock of or makes loans to the manufacturing CFC. If the two CFCs were merged into one foreign corporation owned directly by the domestic corporation, there would be no subpart F income because manufacturing income comes within none of the categories of subpart F income. Dividends and interest paid by the manufactur-

---

[59] IRC §954(c)(2)(B); Reg. §1.954-2(b)(2).

[60] IRC §864(d)(5)(A)(iii).

[61] IRC §954(c)(3)(A)(i); Reg. §1.954-2(b)(4) ("substantial" usually means more than 50 percent; tests provided for determining location of assets). For the term "related person," see infra ¶68.2.5 text accompanying notes 103–06.

Under temporary regulations promulgated in 1998, a CFC's distributive share of partnership income can qualify for the same country exclusion only if (1) the exclusion would have applied had the CFC received the item directly, (2) the income does not result from a payment by the CFC to the partnership, and (3) at least one of the following is true: The partnership is organized in the same country as the CFC and uses a substantial part of its assets in a trade or business in that country; the partnership is fiscally transparent under the tax laws of all relevant countries; or the income is taxed at an effective rate that is at least 90 percent of, and not more than 5 percentage points less than, the rate that would have applied if the CFC received it directly. Reg. §1.954-2T(a)(5) (applicable to payments after March 22, 1998, under arrangements made after that date).

Also, if a payment between a CFC and a hybrid branch of a related CFC has the effect of reducing foreign taxes that would otherwise have been imposed, the same country exclusion can apply to the payment only if the payment would be excluded were the hybrid branch a separate CFC organized under the laws of the country in which the payment is subject to tax. Reg. §1.954-2T(a)(6) (applicable to payments after March 22, 1998, under arrangements made after that date). This rule also applies to payments between hybrid branches of related CFCs. For the term "hybrid branch," see Reg. §1.954-9T(a)(6), discussed infra ¶68.2.10A.

[62] S. Rep. No. 1881, supra note 13, at 789.

ing CFC to the financing CFC are excluded from the latter's FPHC income because they essentially consist of manufacturing income beneficially owned by the domestic corporation.

The same country exclusion is denied, however, for interest that reduces the payor's subpart F income or creates or increases a deficit that may reduce the subpart F income of the payor or another CFC, either presently or in the future.[63] Assume the active CFC in the example purchases and sells goods rather than manufacturing them. If income from the purchases and sales is FBC sales income and if an interest payment by this CFC to the financing CFC is deductible against the FBC sales income, the interest is included in the recipient's FPHC income because the funds used to pay the interest are generated in an activity productive of subpart F income but would be excluded from the subpart F incomes of both corporations if the same country exclusion applied.[64]

The same country exclusion is also inapplicable to interest income from sources within the United States that would be subject to the 30 percent tax of §881(a) but for the exemption of portfolio interest.[65]

This exclusion does not apply to related person factoring income, but the related person factoring rules contain their own same country exclusion.[66] Under the latter rule, income from a trade or service receivable is not related person factoring income if the following requirements are met. The related person must also be a foreign corporation, must be incorporated in the same foreign country as the CFC, and must use a substantial part of its assets in a trade or business in that country. Also, the related person's income from the sales or services transaction (measured as though it had retained and collected the receivable) may not include any FBC income or income effectively connected with a U.S. business. When these requirements are satisfied, the income is not related person factoring income and is usually excluded from FPHC income under the regular same country exclusion.

Finally, a dividend from earnings accumulated before the CFC acquired the stock does not qualify for the same country exception.[67] More completely, the exception is inapplicable to the extent a dividend comes from earnings and profits accumulated while the stock on which the dividend is distributed was not owned by the CFC receiving the dividend, either directly or indirectly though a chain of corporations that all met the conditions of the same country exclusion. Assume earnings are accumulated by F3 (a country X corporation) while F3 is a wholly owned subsidiary of another country X corporation (F2), which is in turn owned

---

[63] IRC §954(c)(3)(B). For the effects of deficits on subpart F income, see infra ¶68.2.10 text accompanying notes 227–38.

[64] See 1986 Bluebook, supra note 14, at 967.

[65] IRC §881(c)(4)(A)(iii). For the application of the 30 percent tax to interest, see supra ¶66.2.2.

[66] IRC §§864(d)(5)(A)(iv), (7).

[67] IRC §954(c)(3)(C), enacted by Pub. L. No. 103-66, §13233(a), 107 Stat. 312 (1993) (applicable for taxable years beginning after September 30, 1993).

by CFC *F1* (also a country *X* corporation); *F2* is subsequently liquidated, and the earnings are thereafter distributed by *F3* to *F1*.[68] The chain ownership rule allows the same country exception to apply to the dividend, even though *F1*, the CFC receiving the dividend, owned no *F3* stock directly when the earnings were accumulated.

2. *Rents and royalties.* FPHC income generally includes rents and royalties.[69] Rents are included whether the property is real or personal.

Rents or royalties are excluded, however, if they are "derived in the active conduct" of a trade or business and are received from a person that is not a related person with respect to the CFC.[70] Rents are considered earned in an active business if the CFC does one of the following: (1) manufactures or otherwise adds substantial value to the leased property and is regularly engaged in the activity by which this value is added; (2) "regularly performs substantial management and operational functions while the property is leased"; (3) normally uses the property in an active trade or business and leases the property temporarily while it is not needed in that business; or (4) performs a marketing function that is substantial in relation to rental income and is carried on by a staff of employees in a foreign country.[71] For example, rents received by a CFC operating an auto rental business are likely within the second and fourth of these rules. Royalties are active business income if the CFC (1) developed or added substantial value to the licensed property in the regular course of its business or (2) made the license as a result of marketing functions performed by the CFC through a staff of employees in a foreign country.[72]

Rents or royalties received from a related person are usually excluded if the rents or royalties are paid for the use or right to use property within the foreign country in which the CFC is incorporated.[73] This exclusion is lost, however, if the rents or royalties reduce the payor's subpart F income or create or increase a deficit that may reduce the subpart F income of the payor or another CFC, either presently or in the future.[74]

Assume *M*, a CFC incorporated in country *X*, licenses a country *X* patent to *N*, a CFC with the same parent as *M*. If *N* sublicenses the patent to an unrelated

---

[68] H.R. Rep. No. 213, 103d Cong., 1st Sess. 643–44 (Conf. Rep. 1993).

[69] IRC §954(c)(1)(A).

[70] IRC §954(c)(2)(A); Reg. §1.954-2(b)(6). For the term "related person," see infra ¶68.2.5 text accompanying notes 103–06.

[71] Reg. §1.954-2(c). For purposes of the fourth rule, a marketing function is considered substantial if "active leasing expenses" are at least 25 percent of "adjusted leasing profit." Reg. §1.954-2(c)(2).

[72] Reg. §1.954-2(d).

[73] IRC §954(c)(3)(A)(ii); Reg. §1.954-2(b)(5). For the application of the same country exclusion to a CFC's distributive share of partnership income, see Reg. §1.954-2T(a)(5).

[74] IRC §954(c)(3)(B). For the effects of deficits on subpart F income, see infra ¶68.2.10 text accompanying notes 227–38.

manufacturer in country X, royalties received from N are included in M's FPHC income because N is allowed a deduction for the royalties in determining its FPHC income and an exclusion of the royalties from M's FPHC income would allow the related group to avoid subpart F on the receipt of royalties from the unrelated country X manufacturer. On the other hand, if N uses the patent in manufacturing goods in country X rather than by sublicensing the patent, the royalties are excluded from M's FPHC income because they are essentially part of the related group's nonsubpart F income from manufacturing operations.

3. *Gains on sales of investment property.* FPHC income includes any excess of gains over losses from sales and exchanges during the taxable year of the following types of property: (1) property that produces FPHC income in the form of dividends, interest, royalties, rents, or annuities; (2) an interest in a trust, partnership, or REMIC; and (3) property that generates no income.[75] The last of these categories includes, for example, "gain on the sale of diamonds held for investment"[76] and options, forwards, and futures.[77] It does not, however, include inventory or other property held for sale to customers in the ordinary course of business, depreciable property held for a purpose other than rental or license, real property used in a nonrental business of the CFC, goodwill and other intangibles that are used in the CFC's business and are sold in a sale of the entire business, and notional principal contracts.

The CFC's holding purpose shortly before sale normally governs in applying the foregoing rules.[78] However, if the CFC's holding purpose changes from one that would cause gain or loss on sale to be included in FPHC income to a purpose that would bring it within an exclusion, the gain or loss is included in FPHC income unless the latter purpose was continuously held during a majority of the holding period and avoiding FPHC status was not a principal purpose for the change in purpose. Assume a CFC holds property for rental for two years, switches to an active business use for one year, and then sells the property at a gain. Gain on the sale is FPHC income, even though gains on sales of active business assets are not included, because the property was held for rental during most of the CFC's holding period.

Gain or loss on a disposition of property that the CFC simultaneously used for more than one purpose must be allocated between the two uses.[79] This rule applies, for example, to gain or loss on a sale of an office building if the CFC used a portion of the building in its business and rented out the remainder.

---

[75] IRC §954(c)(1)(B) Reg. §1.954-2(e).
[76] 1986 Bluebook, supra note 14, at 974.
[77] Reg. §1.954-2(e)(3).
[78] Reg. §1.954-2(a)(3).
[79] Reg. §1.954-2(e)(1)(iv).

4. *Gains in commodities transactions.* FPHC income includes any excess of gains over losses from commodities transactions during the taxable year, including futures, forwards, and similar transactions in commodities.[80]

The statutes, however, recognize two exceptions from this rule for commodities transactions in the normal course of business. First, gains and losses from "bona fide hedging transactions" are excluded if they are "reasonably necessary to the conduct of any business by a producer, processor, merchant, or handler of a commodity in the manner in which such business is customarily and usually conducted by others."[81]

Second, "active business" gains and losses from sales of commodities are excluded if "substantially all" of the CFC's business is "as an active producer, processor, merchant, or handler of commodities."[82] According to the Staff of the Joint Committee on Taxation:

> Congress intended this exception to apply only to foreign corporations actively engaged in commodities businesses, not those primarily engaged in such financial transactions as the trading of futures. Regularly taking delivery of physical commodities will generally indicate the existence of such a business, but such activity will not of itself determine the issue. For example, the business of a company that trades primarily in precious metals may be essentially financial, particularly if the company takes delivery of the metals through an agent such as a bank. . . . Active business gains and losses from commodity sales include gains and losses from financial transactions which constitute bona fide hedging transactions integrally related to a principal business of trading in physical commodities.
>
> Other characteristics of companies actively engaged in commodities businesses include: engaging in substantial processing activities and incurring substantial expenses with respect to commodities prior to their sale . . . ; engaging in significant activities and incurring substantial expenses relating to the physical movement, handling, and storage of commodities . . . ; owning and operating physical facilities used in the activities just described; owning or chartering vessels or vehicles for the transportation of commodities; and producing the commodities sold.[83]

Foreign currency gains and losses subject to the rule described immediately below are also excluded from the commodities hodgepot.

5. *Net gains in foreign currency transactions.* FPHC income includes any excess of gains over losses for the taxable year from transactions in currencies

---

[80] IRC §954(c)(1)(C); Reg. §1.954-2(f). For the terms "commodity" and "commodities transaction," see Reg. §§1.954-2(f)(2)(i), (ii).

[81] IRC §954(c)(1)(C)(i). For qualifying hedging transactions, see Reg. §1.954-2(f)(2)(iv).

[82] IRC §954(c)(1)(C)(ii). See Reg. §1.954-2(f)(2)(iii)(C) ("substantially all" means at least 85 percent).

[83] 1986 Bluebook, supra note 14, at 975. See Reg. §§1.954-2(f)(2)(iii)(B), (E).

other than the CFC's functional currency.[84] This category of FPHC income was added in 1986 because "Congress believed that income from trading in foreign currencies represents the type of income that can easily be routed through a controlled foreign corporation in a tax haven jurisdiction."[85]

An exception is provided, however, for foreign currency transactions "directly related to the [CFC's] business needs."[86] The exception covers foreign currency gains and losses from a CFC's "business as an active foreign currency dealer" or from hedging its inventory.[87] Also, if the CFC elects to treat exchange gain or loss on a forward, futures, or option contract as capital gain or loss, the gain or loss is treated as gain or loss on a sale of property, subject to rules described above, rather than as foreign currency gain or loss.[88]

If foreign currency gain or loss arises from an activity or investment generating subpart F income in a category other than FPHC income, an election may be made to include the gain or loss in that category and to exclude it from FPHC income.[89] Another election rule allows all foreign currency gains or losses to be treated as FPHC income.[90]

6. *Notional principal contracts.* Net income from notional principal contracts is FPHC income.[91] However, income or deduction from a contract entered into as a hedge is excluded from the net amount unless income from the hedged item is FPHC income.

7. *Regular dealers.* If the CFC is a "regular dealer" in property producing dividend, interest, royalty, rental, or annuity income or property that does not produce any income, FPHC income does not include any item of income or deduction (including gains and losses) "from any transaction (including hedging transactions) entered into in the ordinary course of such dealer's trade or business as a dealer."[92] This exclusion does not encompass dividends, payments in

---

[84] IRC §954(c)(1)(D); Reg. §1.954-2(g). For foreign currency gains and losses from nonfunctional currencies, see infra ¶71.5.

[85] 1986 Bluebook, supra note 14, at 966.

[86] IRC §954(c)(1)(D).

[87] Reg. §1.954-2(g)(2)(ii); 1986 Bluebook, supra note 14, at 976 (foreign currency gains from hedging inventory or other assets of a related person, however, are not directly related to CFC's business needs).

[88] Reg. §1.954-2(g)(5). For the capital gains election, see §988(a)(1)(B), discussed infra ¶71.9.5.

[89] Reg. §1.954-2(g)(3) (effective for taxable years beginning after November 5, 1995).

[90] Reg. §1.954-2(g)(4).

[91] IRC §954(c)(1)(F) (effective for taxable years beginning after August 5, 1997). Regulations under prior law income from interest rate swaps and other similar notional principal contracts denominated in CFC's functional currency, but income from equity swaps was not included. Reg. §1.954-2(h)(3).

[92] IRC §954(c)(2)(C) (effective for taxable years beginning after August 5, 1997). A similar exception, found in §954(c)(1)(B) (before amendment in 1997), applies for earlier years, but, unlike the present rule, it does not apply to dealers in financial instruments tied to commodities.

lieu of dividends under securities lending transactions, interest (including interest equivalents), royalties, rents, or annuity income. For example, if a CFC is a securities dealer, neither sales of securities nor futures and options acquired to hedge its securities inventory generate FPHC income, although dividends and interest on the securities are FPHC income. As another example, "gain of a regular art dealer on the sale of a painting" is not FPHC income, even though a CFC holding a painting for investment or display in its corporate offices would have FPHC income on sale (property producing no income before sale).[93]

8. *Active banking, financing and similar businesses.* In 1997, Congress enacted a provision that would exclude from FPHC all income derived in the CFC's active conduct of a banking, financing, or similar business if that business was the CFC's primary activity.[94] However, the provision, which was to apply only to taxable years beginning during 1998, was canceled by the President in exercise of his line-item veto power. It is therefore law only if the line-item veto power is ultimately found to be invalid.

¶68.2.5 Foreign Base Company Sales Income

A CFC's FBC income includes its FBC sales income,[95] which consists of income from transactions in goods where a related person is either the buyer or seller.[96] A CFC's gross profit on a sale of goods is usually FBC sales income if the CFC acquired the goods by purchase and either bought the goods from or sold them to a related person. If a CFC acts as an agent for a related person in arranging a transaction in goods, its commission or fee is normally FBC sales income whether the related person is the buyer or the seller. FBC sales income is limited to income from transactions involving related persons because Congress was "primarily concerned [with] income of a selling subsidiary [that] has been separated from manufacturing activities of a related corporation merely to obtain a lower rate of tax for the sales income."[97] Income from a sale can be FBC

For the term "regular dealer," see Reg. §1.954-2(a)(4)(iv). For "dealer property," see Reg. §1.954-2T(a)(4)(v). For the term "bona fide hedging transaction," see Reg. §1.954-2(a)(4)(ii).

[93] 1986 Bluebook, supra note 14, at 974.

[94] IRC §954(h).

[95] IRC §954(a)(2).

[96] IRC §954(d)(1). FBC sales income also includes "any income (whether in the form of profits, commissions, fees, or otherwise) derived in connection with (A) the sale of any unprocessed timber . . . , or (B) the milling of any such timber outside the United States." IRC §954(d)(4), enacted by Pub. L. No. 103-66, §13239, 107 Stat. 312 (1993) (effective for sales and other dispositions after August 10, 1993). The term "unprocessed timber" includes a "log, cant, or similar form of timber" that is softwood and was cut in the United States. IRC §863(b).

[97] S. Rep. No. 1881, supra note 13, at 790.

sales income whether or not the sale is in the ordinary course of the CFC's business.[98]

Exceptions are provided for income on sales of goods produced in the country in which the CFC is incorporated or sold for use, consumption, or disposition in that country.[99] Income on sales of goods manufactured or produced by the CFC is also excluded from FBC sales income,[100] but this exclusion may be lost if the goods are sold through a branch that is physically separate from the manufacturing facility and the manufacturing and sales operations are in different countries.[101] Also, income on a sale of an agricultural commodity is excluded if the commodity is of a kind not grown in the United States.[102]

1. *Related person.* As explained above, a sales transaction generates FBC sales income only if a related person is involved as seller or buyer. The term "related person" includes any individual or entity that controls the CFC, any entity controlled by the CFC, and any entity that is controlled by the person or persons that control the CFC.[103] For this purpose, "control" includes the ownership of more than 50 percent, by either voting power or value, of a corporation's stock. A partnership, trust, or estate is controlled by any person owning more than 50 percent of the beneficial interests. Ownership is determined with the indirect and constructive ownership rules of §958.[104]

Until 1986, the term "related person" did not explicitly include a partnership, trust, or estate controlled by a CFC or by the same persons who control the CFC, thus raising doubt as to whether income of such a partnership could be FBC income. In *Brown Group, Inc. v. CIR*,[105] the Tax Court accepted the IRS position that such a partnership could have FBC income,[106] holding that where

---

[98] Reg. §1.954-3(a)(1)(i).

[99] See infra text accompanying notes 107-10.

[100] See infra text accompanying notes 111-18.

[101] See infra text accompanying notes 119-27.

[102] See infra text accompanying notes 128-29.

[103] IRC §954(d)(3).

[104] For §958, see supra ¶68.2.2 text accompanying notes 20-31.

[105] Brown Group, Inc. v. CIR, 104 TC 105 (1995), rev'd, 77 F3d 217 (3d Cir. 1996) (nonacq.). See Levine & Littman, Aggregate Arrogance or Entity Error? Brown Group v. Comr., 23 Tax Mgmt. Int'l J. 336 (July 8, 1994); McIntyre, Tax Court's *Brown Group* Decision Threatens Subpart F, 65 Tax Notes 371 (Oct. 17, 1994); Shakow, How Now *Brown* K? 63 Tax Notes 1761 (1994); Staffaroni, Partnerships: Aggregate vs. Entity and U.S. International Taxation, 49 Tax Lawyer 55, 61-67 (1995).

The IRS has confirmed its disagreement with the Court of Appeals decision in *Brown Group*. "To permit a CFC to avoid subpart F by earning income through a partnership under circumstances in which the income would be subpart F income if earned directly by the CFC would be contrary to the purposes of subpart F." Notice 96-39, 1996-32 IRB 8. It intends to issue regulations "to confirm its position that whether a CFC partner's distributive share of partnership income is subpart F income generally is determined at the CFC partner level." See Osterberg, Partnerships in the International Context: What Should the New Regulations Provide? 74 Tax Notes 345 (Jan. 20, 1997).

[106] See Rev. Rul. 89-72, 1989-1 CB 257.

a CFC is a partner of a partnership, its distributive shares of partnership items have the same character for subpart F purposes as they would to the partnership if it were a CFC. The taxpayer in *Brown*, a domestic corporation, was sole shareholder of a foreign corporation (CFC), which was the principal partner of a partnership that acted as the taxpayer's agent in purchasing goods in Brazil. If the partnership's commission income from these transactions had been realized by the CFC, the income would have been FBC sales income. The Tax Court held that whether partnership income is subpart F income should be determined at the partner level, not the partnership level, and that in the hands of the partner (the CFC), the commission income was subpart F income. In reversing, the Court of Appeals for the Third Circuit decided that such a broad embrace of the aggregate approach is inappropriate in this context. Under the pre-1986 law applicable to the case, a partnership owned by a CFC could not have foreign base company sales income, the court concluded, because such income must be realized in transactions with related persons and, under pre-1986 definition of "related person," a partnership was related to a corporation only if the partnership owned a controlling interest in the corporation. Under the 1986 revision of the "related person" definition, a partnership controlled by a corporation and that corporation are related persons, and the court took pains to point out that the result would likely be different on the same facts after 1986.

2. *Country of incorporation exclusions.* Income from a sale is excluded from FBC sales income if the goods are manufactured, produced, grown, or extracted within the country in which the CFC is organized.[107] This exclusion applies if, for example, a CFC incorporated in country X purchases grapefruit grown in country X and resells them to its parent corporation for distribution in the United States. Sales income is also excluded if the goods are sold for use, consumption, or disposition within the country of the CFC's incorporation.[108] This exclusion applies if, for example, a CFC organized in country X purchases hula hoops manufactured by its parent in the United States and resells them to retailers in country X. These exclusions are provided because "a lower rate of tax for [sales income] is likely to be obtained only through purchases and sales outside of the country in which [the CFC] is incorporated."[109]

For purposes of the second of the exclusions, goods sold to an unrelated person are generally deemed to be used, consumed, or disposed of at the destination specified for delivery in the sales transaction in which the CFC participates.[110] For example, if a CFC delivers goods to a common carrier in Baltimore in a sale made F.O.B. Amsterdam, the goods are usually considered used, consumed, or disposed of in the Netherlands. The relevant destination, however, is

---

[107] IRC §954(d)(1). For what constitutes manufacturing, see Reg. §1.954-3(a)(4), described infra text accompanying notes 111–18.

[108] IRC §954(d)(1).

[109] S. Rep. No. 1881, supra note 13, at 790.

[110] Reg. §1.954-3(a)(3)(ii). See S. Rep. No. 1881, supra note 13, at 950.

the ultimate destination, not the place of any temporary interruption in the shipment of the goods. Also, if the CFC knows or ought to have known from the surrounding circumstances that the unrelated buyer would not use, consume, or dispose of the goods in the country of destination, the country of incorporation exclusion does not apply unless the CFC can demonstrate that the buyer actually used, consumed, or disposed of them in the country of the CFC's incorporation. Moreover, the place of actual use, consumption, or disposition must be shown in any sale to a related person, but the destination rule described above can be applied to a transaction in which the related person resells the goods to an unrelated person.

3. *Goods produced or assembled by CFC.* Congress intended that FBC sales income include only "income from the purchase and sale of property, without any appreciable value being added to the product by the selling corporation," and that it not include sales income "where any significant amount of manufacturing, major assembling, or construction activity is carried on with respect to the product by the selling corporation."[111] The regulations adopt this interpretation, stating that a CFC is engaged in manufacturing if the goods it sells are "in effect not the property which it purchased."[112] This test is satisfied if "purchased personal property is substantially transformed prior to sale."[113] Examples of substantial transformation are producing paper from wood pulp, making screws and bolts from steel rods, and canning fish.

Manufacturing also occurs if components are combined into a product, but only if these operations "are substantial in nature and are generally considered to constitute the manufacture, production, or construction of property."[114] For example, in *Bausch & Lomb Inc. v. CIR*,[115] the Tax Court held that the assembly of sunglasses from components purchased from related persons was manufacturing; although assembly operations did not require a large investment in physical capital and were not substantial in relation to the time and investment re-

---

[111] S. Rep. No. 1881, supra note 13, at 790.

[112] Reg. §1.954-3(a)(4)(i). See Rev. Rul. 97-48, 1997-49 IRB 5, revoking Rev. Rul. 75-7, 1975-1 CB 244 (in determining whether CFC is engaged in manufacturing, activities of contract manufacturer producing goods for CFC are not attributed to CFC; taxpayers may rely on contrary rule of Rev. Rul. 75-7 for CFC taxable years beginning before December 8, 1997); Dolan, DuPuy & Jackman, Contract Manufacturing: The Next Round, 27 Tax Mgmt. Int'l J. 59 (1998); Dolan, Contract Manufacturing; Is it Dead or Alive, 26 Tax Mgmt. Int'l J. 195 (1997); Fuller, Fuller, Schrotenboer, Clark & Colgin, Rev. Rul. 97-48 and the Revocation of Rev. Rul. 75-7, 15 Tax Notes Int'l 1783 (Dec. 1, 1997), reprinted in 77 Tax Notes 1271 (Dec. 15, 1997); Yoder, New IRS Ruling Rocks the Contract Manufacturing Boat, 9 J. Int'l Tax'n 6 (1998).

[113] Reg. §1.954-3(a)(4)(ii). See S. Rep. No. 1881, supra note 13, at 949.

[114] Reg. §1.954-3(a)(4)(iii).

[115] Bausch & Lomb Inc. v. CIR, 71 TCM (CCH) 2031 (1996). See Dave Fischbein Mfg. Co. v. CIR, 59 TC 338 (1972) (acq.) (CFC's activities found to be manufacturing rather than minor assembling); Yoder, Bausch & Lomb: The "Manufacturing" Exception to Foreign Base Company Sales Income, 25 Tax Mgmt. Int'l J. 427 (1996).

quired to fabricate the assembled parts, they required a substantial investment in human capital (skill, training, and experience in assembly techniques), included a broad range of activities, and were considered in the industry to be manufacturing. Under a safe harbor rule, substantial manufacturing is deemed to occur if direct labor costs and factory burden are at least 20 percent of the cost of goods sold. "On the other hand, activity such as minor assembling, packaging, repackaging or labeling will not be sufficient to exclude the profits."[116]

If a CFC assembles goods in operations that are not manufacturing, an apportionment might be necessary. Income on a sale of goods is not FBC sales income if the goods (1) are neither purchased from nor sold to a related person, (2) were produced in the country in which the CFC is incorporated, or (3) are sold for use, consumption, or disposition in the country of incorporation. If assembled goods are sold to an unrelated person for use, consumption, or disposition outside the country of incorporation, only part of the income on the sale is FBC sales income if (1) CFC purchases some of the components from related persons and others from unrelated persons or (2) some of the components are produced in the country of incorporation and others are not. The FBC sales income from such a sale equals the income on the sale multiplied by the ratio of (1) the costs of components produced outside the country of incorporation that the CFC acquires from related persons to (2) the costs of all components.[117]

Assume a CFC assembles goods from components acquired at a cost of $60; $40 of these components were produced outside the country in which the CFC is incorporated, and $30 of this $40 represents costs of components purchased from related persons.[118] One half of the components' costs ($30 of $60) consists of items that are produced outside the country of incorporation and purchased from related persons. One half of the income on a sale is therefore FBC sales income if the buyer is unrelated and purchases for use, consumption, or disposition outside the country of incorporation. No FBC sales income results from a sale for use, consumption, or disposition within the country of incorporation, whether the purchaser is related or unrelated. All income on a sale to a related person is FBC sales income unless the purchase is made for use, consumption, or disposition within the CFC's country of incorporation.

4. *Branch rules.* The exclusions for income on sales of goods manufactured by the CFC or produced in the CFC's country of incorporation can be lost, at least in part, if the goods are sold through a branch of the CFC. The exclusions are denied when "the combined effect of the tax treatment accorded the branch, by the country of incorporation of the [CFC] and the country of operation of the branch, is to treat the branch substantially the same as if it were a subsidiary corporation organized in the country in which it carries on its trade or busi-

---

[116] S. Rep. No. 1881, supra note 13, at 790.
[117] Reg. §1.954-3(a)(5).
[118] Reg. §1.954-3(a)(5) Ex. 1.

ness."[119] The technique for effectuating this concept is to treat the branch as a separate corporation in some circumstances, which can have the effect of denying an exclusion if the hypothetical separate corporation is neither a manufacturer nor incorporated in the country in which the goods are produced. The concept is expressed in two rules—one for sales or purchasing branches and another for manufacturing branches.

    a. *Sales or purchasing branches.* A branch engaged in selling or purchasing goods is treated as a separate corporation in applying the definition of FBC sales income if (1) it is located outside the country in which the CFC is incorporated and (2) the effective rate at which the CFC is taxed on the branch's income as it is earned falls below a threshold rate.[120] The threshold rate is the lesser of (1) 90 percent of the rate at which the country of incorporation would tax the income or (2) a rate five percentage points below the country of incorporation rate. The country of incorporation rate is the rate at which the income would be taxed by that country if the income were from sources within the country and were attributable to a permanent establishment in the country and the branch were a corporation managed or controlled in the country. The threshold test is applied only to the portion of the corporation's income from each transaction that is attributable to the branch's activities and only to income that is FBC sales income if the branch is treated as a separate corporation.

    If the test is failed, the branch is treated as a separately incorporated subsidiary of the actual corporation, organized under the laws of the country in which the branch is located.[121] Its income is tested under the general definition of FBC sales income, as though it functioned as sales agent for the remainder of the corporation.[122] If the CFC has two or more selling or purchasing branches outside the actual country of incorporation, the foregoing rules are applied separately to each branch.

    Assume a CFC manufactures goods in foreign country X, the country under whose laws it is organized, and sells the goods through a branch in foreign country Y.[123] Country X taxes corporate income at 50 percent, but it exempts all income of country X corporations from business operations in other countries, including the income of the CFC's country Y branch. Country Y imposes a 10 percent tax on the branch's income. The branch is treated as a separate country Y corporation because (1) it is located outside the country in which the CFC is incorporated and (2) the 10 percent tax rate in country Y is less than 90 percent of and more than five percentage points below the 50 percent rate of country X.

---

[119] S. Rep. No. 1881, supra note 13, at 790. See Vetco, Inc. v. CIR, 95 TC 579 (1990) (wholly owned foreign subsidiary of CFC may not be treated as CFC's branch for purposes of branch rules); Magee, Farmer & Katcher, Reexamining Branch Rules in the Context of Check-the-Box, 77 Tax Notes 1511 (Dec. 29, 1997).

[120] Reg. §1.954-3(b)(1)(i).

[121] Reg. §1.954-3(b)(2)(i)(*a*).

[122] Reg. §1.954-3(b)(2)(i)(*b*).

[123] Reg. §1.954-3(b)(4) Ex. 1.

The income of this hypothetical corporation may be FBC sales income because the sales are made on behalf of a related person (the actual corporation, which is deemed to be the hypothetical corporation's parent) and the goods are produced in a country (X) other than the country of the hypothetical corporation's incorporation (Y). However, because sales for use, consumption, or disposition in the country of incorporation do not generate FBC sales income, the branch's FBC sales income is limited to the income allocable to the branch from sales made for use, consumption, or disposition in countries other than Y. The income from these sales must be apportioned between the manufacturing and sales functions because the portion allocable to manufacturing is not FBC sales income.

Assume a CFC organized in country X purchases goods produced in that country by a related person and sells them through a branch in country Y.[124] Under the general rules, the CFC's income is not FBC sales income because the income is from sales of goods produced in the country in which the CFC is organized. The branch rule does not alter this result if the CFC is taxed by country X on its worldwide income. However, if country X exempts country X corporations from tax on income from operations in other countries and if the CFC's income from sales through the country Y branch qualifies for this exemption, income from sales for use, consumption, and disposition in countries other than Y may be FBC sales income under the branch rule. Whether the branch rule applies depends on whether the income is taxed by country Y or some other country at an effective rate that is at least 90 percent of or not more than five percentage points below the country X rate.

b. *Manufacturing branches.* If a CFC has a branch outside the country of its incorporation that is engaged in manufacturing, production, construction, growing, or extraction activities, the threshold test described above is applied to the income of the remainder of the corporation, not the branch.[125] The manu-

---

[124] Reg. §1.954-3(b)(4) Ex. 3.

[125] Reg. §1.954-3(b)(1)(ii). In Ashland Oil Co. v. CIR, 95 TC 348 (1990), the Tax Court rejected an innovative construction of the branch rules urged by the IRS. The taxpayer's CFC made a contract with an unrelated Belgian corporation under which the latter manufactured chemical products for the CFC, using various intangibles owned by the CFC and raw materials obtained largely from suppliers suggested by the CFC. The price charged by the Belgian corporation for the manufactured goods equaled the sum of its materials costs and a fixed fee. The IRS contended that (1) the Belgian corporation was a "branch or similar establishment" of the CFC, (2) the branch rules required that it be treated as a wholly owned subsidiary of the CFC, and (3) the CFC's income was therefore FBC sales income because it arose on resale of goods purchased from a related person. If the CFC had itself done the manufacturing outside the country in which its sales office was located, the IRS noted, the branch rule would have characterized the sales income as FBC sales income, and a more favorable result should not be obtainable, it argued, merely by entering into a contract manufacturing arrangement.

The court disagreed. It held that the ordinary usage of the term "branch" does not include "an unrelated corporation operating under an arm's-length contractual arrangement with" a CFC and that "similar establishment" refers to "an establishment that bears the typical characteristics of an ordinary-usage branch, yet goes by another name for

facturing branch is tentatively treated as a separate corporation, and its income is segregated from that of the remainder of the corporation. A pool of income is assembled, consisting of the income of the remainder of the corporation that becomes FBC income once the manufacturing branch is treated as a separate corporation. The effective rate at which the CFC is currently taxed on this income is compared with the effective rate that would apply in the country of the manufacturing branch if the income were from sources within the latter country and were attributable to a permanent establishment in the country and the corporation were organized and managed there. The manufacturing branch is treated as a separate corporation unless the actual effective rate is at least 90 percent of or no more than five percentage points less than the hypothetical effective rate in the country of manufacture. If this threshold test is failed, the definition of FBC sales income is applied to the income of the remainder of the corporation as though its sales or purchasing activities were performed as agent for the hypothetical manufacturing corporation.[126]

Assume a CFC incorporated in foreign country X manufactures goods in foreign country Y and sells them through an office of the corporation in country X.[127] Country Y taxes corporate income at 30 percent, but the CFC is only subject to the country Y tax on its manufacturing profits. Country X has no income tax, and the CFC pays no income taxes to any country on the portion of its income that Y does not tax as manufacturing profits. The manufacturing branch is treated as a separate corporation because (1) it is not located in the country in which the CFC is organized and (2) the zero rate of tax on income not allocable to manufacturing (the income of the remainder of the corporation) is less than 90 percent of and more than five percentage points below the 30 percent rate at which the income would be taxed by country Y. The hypothetical corporation has no FBC sales income because it is a manufacturer. The income of the remainder of the corporation, however, can be FBC sales income because (1) it is earned in sales made on behalf of a related person (the hypothetical manufacturing corporation) and (2) the goods are not produced in the country of incorporation (produced in Y, incorporated in X). None of the income from sales for use, consumption, or disposition in country X is FBC sales income because income from sales in the country of incorporation is always excepted. The non-manufacturing portion of the income from sales for use, consumption, or disposition in countries other than X, however, is FBC sales income because (1) the

accounting, financial reporting, local law, or other purposes." 95 TC at 357. The court therefore found that the CFC's income, being from sales of goods neither purchased from nor sold to related persons, was not FBC sales income. The result, the court thought, was not "unjustifiably permissive to taxpayers, primarily because neither" the CFC nor the taxpayer (the U.S. shareholder) had any claim to the manufacturer's income under the arrangement. 95 TC at 361.

[126] Reg. §1.954-3(b)(2)(i)(c).

[127] Reg. §1.954-3(b)(4) Ex. 2.

goods are sold on behalf of a related person and (2) the goods are neither produced nor sold in the country of incorporation (*X*).

5. *Agricultural commodities not grown in United States.* Income from a transaction in an agricultural commodity is excluded from FBC sales income if the commodity is not grown in the United States in "commercially marketable quantities."[128] This exclusion applies to income from sales of bananas, black pepper, cocoa, coconuts, coffee, crude rubber, tea, and any other commodity the taxpayer can demonstrate, on the basis of all relevant facts and circumstances, to be within the statutory description.[129]

¶68.2.6 Foreign Base Company Services Income

A CFC's FBC income includes its FBC services income, which consists of income from services transactions involving related persons.[130] The services may be "technical, managerial, engineering, architectural, scientific, skilled, industrial, commercial, or like services."[131] FBC services income may consist of compensation for the CFC's performance of services or a commission or fee received for arranging for a service to be performed by someone else.[132]

1. *For or on behalf of related person.* Income from services is FBC services income only if the services are "performed for or on behalf of" a related person.[133] This limitation is provided because the purpose of the FBC services rule is "to deny tax deferral where a service subsidiary is separated from manufacturing or similar activities of a related corporation and organized in another country primarily to obtain a lower rate of tax for the service income."[134] The regulations identify four situations where services are considered performed for or on behalf of a related person:

a. *Compensation from related person.* A CFC's services are performed on behalf of a related person if the CFC receives compensation or any other "substantial financial benefit from" a related person for performing the services.[135] For example, if a CFC's parent corporation pays the CFC to perform installation or maintenance services with respect to goods sold by the parent, the payment is FBC services income of the CFC.[136]

b. *Related person's obligation.* Services are performed on behalf of a related person if a related person is or has been obligated to perform the services per-

---

[128] IRC §954(d)(1).

[129] See Reg. §1.954-3(a)(1)(ii) (list of commodities that cannot qualify).

[130] IRC §954(a)(3).

[131] IRC §954(e)(1).

[132] Reg. §1.954-4(a).

[133] IRC §954(e)(1)(A). For the term "related person," see supra ¶68.2.5 text accompanying notes 103-06.

[134] S. Rep. No. 1881, supra note 13, at 790.

[135] Reg. §1.954-4(b)(1)(i).

[136] Reg. §1.954-4(b)(3) Ex. 1.

formed by the CFC.[137] Assume a domestic corporation agrees to construct a highway in a foreign country and, after work begins, assigns the contract to its foreign subsidiary.[138] The subsidiary's work under the contract is a service performed on behalf of the parent corporation, even if the other party to the contract releases the parent from its obligations when the contract is assigned to the subsidiary.

A mere guarantee by a related person of the CFC's performance is not covered by this rule, however, if neither the guarantor nor any other related person pays for the services or "any significant services related to such services."[139] Assume a CFC undertakes to build a highway in a foreign country; at the insistence of the government agency for which the work is to be done, the CFC's parent corporation agrees that it will construct the highway or have it done by someone else if the CFC defaults on its contract.[140] The parent's agreement is a mere guarantee and is not substantial assistance unless the parent is required to perform its guarantee. Also, the parent is considered a mere guarantor if it contracts to build the highway and immediately assigns the contract to the CFC without being released from liability, provided that any plans and specifications prepared in making a bid for the contract are done by the CFC, not the parent.[141]

    c. *Condition of sale by related person.* Services with respect to property sold by a related person are performed on behalf of the related person if the CFC's performance of the services is "a condition or a material term of such sale."[142] Assume a domestic corporation sells equipment to foreign purchasers at one price without provision for installation and at a lower price when the purchasers simultaneously contract to have the equipment installed by the corporation's foreign subsidiary.[143] The subsidiary's installation services are performed on behalf of the parent. Assume a domestic corporation sells goods to foreign purchasers under a warranty that is good only so long as maintenance work is done by a factory-authorized service agency, and a foreign subsidiary of the seller is the only such agency.[144] Maintenance services for the parent's customers are performed on behalf of the parent. On the other hand, if there are several authorized service agencies, including both the subsidiary and unrelated persons, maintenance work done by the subsidiary is not on behalf of the parent.[145]

    d. *Substantial assistance from related person.* A CFC's services are performed on behalf of a related person if the related person provides "substantial

---

[137] Reg. §1.954-4(b)(1)(ii).

[138] Reg. §1.954-4(b)(3) Ex. 5.

[139] Reg. §1.954-4(b)(2)(i).

[140] Reg. §1.954-4(b)(3) Ex. 4.

[141] Reg. §1.954-4(b)(3) Exs. 6, 7.

[142] Reg. §1.954-4(b)(1)(iii).

[143] Reg. §1.954-4(b)(3) Ex. 8.

[144] Reg. §1.954-4(b)(3) Ex. 9.

[145] See Reg. §1.954-4(b)(3) Ex. 10.

assistance contributing to the performance of" the services.[146] Examples of substantial assistance are "direction, supervision, services, know-how, financial assistance (other than contributions to capital), and equipment, material, or supplies."[147] However, direction, supervision, services, or know-how is substantial assistance in only two situations: (1) where this assistance provides the CFC with "skills" that are "a principal element in producing" the CFC's income from the performance of a service and (2) where the CFC's cost for this assistance accounts for at least 50 percent of its total costs in performing the service.[148] Moreover, this assistance is never substantial unless it "directly" aids the CFC in performing the service.[149]

Assume a CFC undertakes to drill an oil well in a foreign country for an unrelated person.[150] The CFC owns the equipment needed for the drilling project, but it does not have a regular staff of employees. Technical and supervisory personnel regularly employed by the CFC's parent corporation are assigned to be temporary employees of the CFC for the duration of the project, and the CFC hires unskilled and semiskilled laborers on the open market. The drilling work is considered performed on behalf of the CFC's parent because the technical and supervisory employees borrowed from the parent provide skills that are a principal element in the production of the CFC's income from the project. In contrast, if the CFC has a permanent staff of technical and supervisory employees and utilizes personnel of the parent to do only clerical and accounting work, no substantial assistance is provided by the parent because the clerical and accounting services do not assist the CFC "directly" in the performance of the contract.[151]

Financing, equipment, material, or supplies provided by a related person are considered assistance to the CFC only if the CFC pays less than an arm's length price for the items.[152] When an arm's length price is not paid, the CFC receives assistance equal to the excess of the arm's length price over the amount paid. Whether the assistance is substantial is determined by comparing the amount of the assistance received in this form from all related persons to the CFC's profits from the performance of the service.

Assistance in the form of direction, supervision, services, know-how, financing, equipment, material, or supplies, even if not substantial under the foregoing rules, may be substantial in combination with other assistance if it "directly" assists the CFC in the performance of services.[153]

---

[146] Reg. §1.954-4(b)(1)(iv).

[147] Reg. §1.954-4(b)(2)(ii)(a).

[148] The 50 percent test is applied after any appropriate adjustments to intercompany prices under §482. Reg. §1.954-4(b)(2)(ii)(b). For §482, see infra ¶79.1.

[149] Reg. §1.954-4(b)(2)(ii)(e). See Reg. §1.954-4(b)(3) Ex. 3.

[150] Reg. §1.954-4(b)(3) Ex. 2.

[151] See Reg. §1.954-4(b)(3) Ex. 3.

[152] Reg. §1.954-4(b)(2)(ii)(c).

[153] Reg. §1.954-4(b)(2)(ii)(d).

2. *Country of incorporation exception.* Income that would otherwise be FBC services income is excluded if the services are performed in the foreign country under whose laws the CFC is organized.[154] Generally, services are performed where the employees doing the work are physically located.[155] When only part of the work is done in the country of incorporation, the income is allocated on the basis of "employee-time spent" within and outside the country, giving "relative weight ... to the values of the various functions performed" by the employees. Clerical work is "assigned little value, while services performed by technical, highly skilled, and managerial personnel [are] assigned greater values."

3. *Presale services of manufacturing CFCs.* Income that would otherwise be FBC services income is excluded if the services are "directly related" to the CFC's sale of goods it manufactures, produces, grows, or extracts and are performed before the sale occurs.[156] This exclusion also applies if the services are directly related to an "offer or effort" to sell such goods.

¶68.2.7 Foreign Base Company Shipping Income

FBC income includes FBC shipping income,[157] which encompasses a broad range of income from foreign shipping operations.[158] Under the 1962 legislation by which subpart F was enacted, shipping income was excluded from subpart F income "primarily in the interests of national defense [and] to encourage a U.S.-owned maritime fleet and U.S.-owned airlines operating abroad."[159] In 1976, a new category of FBC income was added—FBC shipping income—but FBC shipping income was excluded from subpart F income if it was reinvested in shipping operations. The exclusion was repealed in 1986. According to the Staff of the Joint Committee on Taxation:

> Congress did not believe that this reinvestment exclusion was appropriate as a matter of tax policy. Nowhere else in subpart F is such an exception granted. ... Because shipping income is seldom taxed by foreign countries, earning such income through a foreign corporation could effectively exempt it from all current tax, U.S. and foreign. The prior exclusion thus served to promote U.S. investment in foreign-flag shipping operations by providing U.S. tax benefits to such investment. Congress questioned whether it was fully in the interests of the United States to promote U.S. investment in the shipping activities of other nations.[160]

---

[154] IRC §954(e)(1)(B).

[155] Reg. §1.954-4(c).

[156] IRC §954(e)(2)(A); Reg. §1.954-4(d).

[157] IRC §954(a)(4).

[158] IRC §954(f).

[159] S. Rep. No. 1881, supra note 13, at 791.

[160] 1986 Bluebook, supra note 14, at 970.

FBC shipping income includes income of the CFC from the use of an aircraft or vessel in "foreign commerce" whether the CFC operates the aircraft or vessel, is lessor of the aircraft or vessel, performs a service in connection with its use, or receives a fee or commission for arranging a lease or services transaction for someone else. Gain on a sale or other disposition of an aircraft or vessel used in foreign commerce is also FBC shipping income.

The term "foreign commerce" includes the transportation of passengers or goods between a foreign port or airport and a port or airport in the United States, a possession of the United States, or a foreign country.[161] A trawler, factory ship, or oil drilling ship is not used in foreign commerce, so defined, but a cruise ship is if it visits one or more foreign ports. A vessel or aircraft is used in foreign commerce if it is chartered to a person for such use, whether the charter is a bareboat or time charter or takes some other form.[162]

Services generating FBC shipping income include terminal services, stevedoring, and the services of tugs, lighters, barges, scows, launches, and floating cranes.[163] Also, maintenance, repairs, training of pilots and crew, and acting as booking, operations, or managing agent are covered if they are performed for a related person or pertain to the CFC's own use of the vessel or aircraft.

Dividends and interest received by a CFC from a foreign corporation and gains on sales of the corporation's stock or debt instruments can also be FBC shipping income if the foreign corporation has FBC shipping income and the dividends, interest, or gains are attributable to that income.[164] The dividends, interest, and gains are so tainted, however, only if (1) the CFC and the issuer of the stock or debt are related persons or (2) on a receipt of dividends from the issuer, the CFC would be deemed to have paid portions of any foreign income taxes actually paid by the issuer for purposes of determining the indirect foreign income tax credits allowable to the CFC's U.S. shareholders.[165] Also, if a CFC is a partner of a partnership, the CFC's FBC shipping income includes its distributive share of any FBC shipping income of the partnership.[166]

Moreover, FBC shipping income includes income from an activity conducted (1) in space, (2) "on or under water" that is not within the jurisdiction of any country (as recognized by the United States), and (3) in Antarctica.[167] This rule, however, does not cover income from communications activities and activities relating to natural deposits within the jurisdiction of a country.

An item that would otherwise be FBC shipping income is excluded from all categories of FBC income if it is earned in commerce between two points within

---

[161] Reg. §1.954-6(b)(3).

[162] Reg. §1.954-6(b)(4).

[163] Reg. §§1.954-6(d)(2), (3).

[164] IRC §954(f)(1).

[165] Reg. §1.954-6(f). For the indirect credit rules of §§902 and 960, see infra ¶69.8.

[166] IRC §954(f)(2); Reg. §1.954-6(g).

[167] IRC §§863(d)(2), 954(f).

the same foreign country and the CFC is organized and the vessel or aircraft is registered in that country.[168] This rule applies whether the income is earned by the CFC's operation of the vessel or aircraft or consists of rents for the hiring or leasing of the vessel or aircraft for this purpose.

For years before 1987, FBC shipping income was excluded from FBC income if it was reinvested in foreign shipping operations.[169] Although the reinvestment exclusion has been repealed, U.S. shareholders of CFCs that utilized the exclusion continue to be taxed on their pro rata shares of amounts withdrawn from investments that qualified the corporation for the exclusion.[170] Such a withdrawal occurs if (1) the CFC's qualified investments in FBC shipping operations decline during the taxable year and (2) the pre-1987 exclusions allowed to the CFC exceed the amounts deemed withdrawn in prior taxable years.[171] The term "qualified investments in foreign base company shipping operations" refers to investments in aircraft and vessels used in foreign commerce and other assets used in performing services directly related to such aircraft or vessels.[172] A qualified investment can consist of stock of another CFC that is a related person, but if the related CFC owns assets other than qualified investments, the stock qualifies only to the extent allocable to the related CFC's qualified investments.[173] Also, in some circumstances, one CFC's qualified investment can be treated as a qualified investment of a related CFC even if the former is not a shareholder of the latter.[174] The amount of a qualified investment is the adjusted basis of the qualifying property, reduced by any liability to which it is subject.[175]

The withdrawal of previously excluded earnings equals the decrease in the CFC's qualified investments during the taxable year.[176] The starting point for computing the decrease for any year is the CFC's qualified investments at the end of its last taxable year beginning before 1987.[177] This base is reduced by the sum of (1) the qualified investments at the end of the current year[178] and (2) the amounts considered withdrawn under this rule during prior post-1987 years. It is further reduced by any excess of losses over gains on dispositions of qualified investments during the taxable year. The resulting figure usually is the current decrease in qualified investments. The decrease, however, may not exceed the

---

[168] IRC §954(b)(7).

[169] IRC §954(b)(2) (before repeal in 1986).

[170] IRC §951(a)(1)(A)(iii).

[171] IRC §955(a)(1). See Reg. §§1.955A-1 through -4.

[172] IRC §955(b)(1).

[173] For the term "related person," see supra ¶68.2.5 text accompanying notes 103–06.

[174] IRC §955(b)(2).

[175] IRC §955(b)(4).

[176] IRC §955(a)(1).

[177] IRC §955(a)(2).

[178] This figure can sometimes be determined at the end of the succeeding taxable year. IRC §955(b)(3).

available earnings and profits, including both current earnings and profits and earnings and profits accumulated in earlier years (but usually excluding earnings and profits accumulated in years before 1976).

A CFC's withdrawal of previously excluded earnings is the lesser of the decrease in qualified investments during the taxable year or the previously excluded earnings. The previously excluded earnings consist of the FBC shipping income for years beginning before 1987 that was excluded from FBC income under the rule for qualified investments in FBC shipping operations, reduced by the portions of the earnings deemed withdrawn during years preceding the taxable year.[179]

The withdrawal of previously excluded earnings is allocated among the CFC's shareholders as though it was distributed pro rata to the shareholders at the end of the taxable year (or if earlier, the last day during the year when the corporation was a CFC).[180] Each U.S. shareholder must usually include in gross income the amount so allocated to the shares the shareholder owns actually and indirectly through foreign corporations.[181] If the corporation is a CFC for less than all of the current year, however, this inclusion is reduced by eliminating the portions ratably attributable to the periods during the year when the corporation was not a CFC.[182]

¶68.2.8 Foreign Base Company Oil Related Income

FBC income includes a CFC's FBC oil related income, which consists of income from the activities of processing, transporting, or distributing oil or gas if the activities are located in foreign countries other than the country in which the oil or gas is extracted. A CFC can have FBC oil related income, however, only if it or a related entity is a producer of significant amounts of crude oil or gas from wells located outside the United States.

More specifically, income is FBC oil related income only if it is "foreign oil related income," defined as income from sources outside the United States and its possessions from (1) the processing of oil or gas into its primary products, (2) the transportation or distribution of oil or gas or its primary products, or (3) the performance of a "related service."[183] Foreign oil related income also includes gains on dispositions of assets used in a trade or business of processing, transporting, or distributing oil or gas or its primary products. If the CFC is a partner of a partnership, the CFC's foreign oil related income also includes its distributive share of the partnership's foreign oil related income and foreign oil and gas extraction income.[184]

---

[179] IRC §955(a)(1)(A).

[180] IRC §955(a)(3).

[181] For indirect ownership, see supra ¶68.2.2 text accompanying notes 23–25.

[182] IRC §951(a)(3).

[183] IRC §§907(c)(2), 954(g)(1).

[184] IRC §907(c)(3). For the term "foreign oil and gas extraction income," see infra ¶69.10.2 text accompanying notes 12–41.

Income from sources within a particular foreign country is not FBC oil related income, however, if it arises in connection with oil or gas extracted within that country by the CFC or any other person.[185] Also, income from a sale is not FBC oil related income if the sale is of oil or gas or a primary product thereof for use or consumption within the country that is the source of the CFC's income from the sale.[186] Moreover, income on a sale of an oil or gas product for use as fuel by a vessel or aircraft is excluded if the fuel is loaded on the vessel or aircraft in the country that is the income's source.[187] The latter two rules apply whether the sale is made by the CFC or by a related person for whom the CFC acts as commission agent.

A CFC is wholly excused from the FBC oil related income rules if it is not a "large oil producer,"[188] defined as a CFC belonging to a "related group" whose "average daily production of foreign crude oil and natural gas" is at least 1,000 barrels during either the taxable year or the immediately preceding year.[189] The term "related group" refers to the CFC and all related persons.[190] Average daily production is total production for the year, expressed in barrels of crude oil (each containing 42 U.S. gallons), divided by the number of days in the year.[191] Only crude oil and natural gas from wells outside the United States are counted in the average.

An item within the definition of FBC oil related income is excluded from the CFC's FBC sales and services income.[192] However, an item encompassed by the definitions of both FBC oil related income and FPHC income is treated as FPHC income, not FBC oil related income.[193]

¶68.2.9 Foreign Base Company Income

FBC income, which is the principal component of subpart F income, is an aggregate of a CFC's FPHC income and FBC sales, services, shipping, and oil related income.[194] FBC income is determined in the following steps:

---

[185] IRC §954(g)(1)(A).

[186] IRC §954(g)(1)(B).

[187] Id.

[188] IRC §954(g)(2)(A).

[189] IRC §954(g)(2)(B).

[190] IRC §954(g)(2)(C). For the term "related person," see supra ¶68.2.5 text accompanying notes 103-06.

[191] IRC §613A(c)(2).

[192] IRC §954(b)(8).

[193] IRC §954(g)(1), as amended by Pub. L. No. 103-66, §13235(a)(3), 107 Stat. 312 (1993). This rule applies only for taxable years beginning after 1992. For prior years, such an item is FBC oil related income. See Reg. §§1.954-8(a), (c); 1.964-4(d)(4).

[194] IRC §954(a).

1. *Gross FBC income.* The items of gross income constituting FPHC income and FBC sales, services, shipping, and oil related income are combined into an aggregate called gross FBC income.[195]

2. *Adjusted gross FBC income.* Gross FBC income is tested under two all-or-nothing rules—a de minimis rule and a full inclusion rule. Adjusted gross FBC income is the amount remaining after these rules have been applied.[196]

Under the de minimis rule, a CFC's adjusted gross FBC income is zero if the sum of gross FBC income and gross insurance income is less than both $1 million and 5 percent of all gross income.[197] For example, if a CFC's gross income for a particular year is $15 million, the de minimis threshold is $750,000 (lesser of $1 million or 5 percent of $15 million). If gross income is $25 million, the threshold is $1 million (lesser of $1 million or 5 percent of $25 million). If the CFC has related person factoring income, however, this income is included in FBC income even if the sum of gross FBC income and gross insurance income is below the de minimis threshold.[198] The de minimis rule is also inapplicable to interest income from sources within the United States that would be subject to the 30 percent tax imposed by §881(a) but for the exemption of portfolio interest.[199]

Under the full inclusion rule, all of a CFC's gross income is FBC income if the sum of gross FBC income and gross insurance income exceeds 70 percent of all gross income for the taxable year.[200] When this rule applies, the items of gross income it adds to FBC income constitute a separate category of FBC income called "full inclusion FBC income."[201]

The de minimis and full inclusion rules are usually applied separately to each CFC. Two or more CFCs are aggregated in applying the rules, however, if "a principal purpose for separately organizing, acquiring, or maintaining such

---

[195] Reg. §1.954-1(a)(2).

[196] Reg. §1.954-1(a)(3).

[197] IRC §954(b)(3)(A). The term "gross insurance income" refers to the items of gross income that are included in determining insurance income. IRC §954(b)(3)(C). See supra ¶68.2.3 for insurance income. See Reg. §1.954-1(b)(1)(i)(B) (if functional currency is not U.S. dollar, $1 million ceiling is translated into functional currency).

[198] IRC §864(d)(5)(A)(ii); Reg. §1.954-1(b)(1)(i)(C). For the term "related person factoring income," see IRC §864(d)(3).

[199] IRC §881(c)(5)(A)(i). For the application of the 30 percent tax to interest, see supra ¶66.2.2.

[200] IRC §954(b)(3)(B); Reg. §1.954-1(b)(1)(ii).

[201] Reg. §1.954-1(b)(2).

multiple corporations" is to obtain the benefits of the de minimis rule.[202] The aggregation rule is intended to frustrate attempts, for example, to make the de minimis rule applicable to more than $1 million of FBC income by splitting an activity generating this income among commonly owned CFCs.

3. *Net FBC income.* Adjusted gross FBC income, reduced by all deductions (including taxes) "properly allocable" to it, is net FBC income.[203] Deductions are generally allocated for this purpose by the deduction rules used in applying the foreign tax credit limitation rules of §904(d).[204]

However, interest on obligations owing to the CFC's U.S. shareholders is allocated first to FPHC income that is classified as passive income for purposes of the foreign tax credit limitation.[205] This rule also applies to interest on an obligation to another CFC that is related to a U.S. shareholder.

4. *Adjusted net FBC income.* Net FBC income may be adjusted by removing any item that is subject to an income tax imposed by a foreign country at an "effective rate" exceeding 90 percent of the highest rate under §11.[206] Presently, the highest §11 rate is 35 percent, and this exclusion applies whenever an item is taxed by foreign countries at an effective rate exceeding 31.5 percent. The high tax exclusion is allowed because the policy of subpart F—to deny the deferral privilege to income susceptible to tax haven manipulation—does not require that U.S. shareholders be immediately taxed when foreign countries tax an item at rates approximating or exceeding the U.S. corporate rate.[207]

The effective rate of foreign income taxes is the amount of the taxes, divided by the excess of the gross income over the deductions allocated to it (other than

---

[202] Reg. §1.954-1(b)(4)(i). In three specified circumstances, related CFCs are presumed to be infected with the forbidden purpose. Reg. §1.954-1(b)(4)(ii).

[203] IRC §954(b)(5).

[204] Reg. §1.954-1(c).

[205] IRC §954(b)(5).

[206] IRC §954(b)(4). This exclusion applies only if, in addition to establishing that foreign income taxes on the item exceed the 90 percent threshold, the U.S. shareholders elect to exclude the item from FBC income. Reg. §§1.954-1(d)(1), (5). The election is generally made item by item, but it must be made for all passive FPHC income or for none. Reg. §1.954-1(d)(4)(i). See 1986 Bluebook, supra note 14, at 983.

Until 1986, §954(b)(4) excluded income from foreign base company income if neither the choice of the CFC's place of organization nor the decision to effect the transaction through the CFC had as one of its "significant purposes a substantial reduction of income . . . taxes." See Dietz Corp. v. US, 939 F2d 1 (2d Cir. 1991) (interest on bank deposits excluded from foreign base company income under former §954(b)(4) where CFC was engaged in trade or business in foreign country and deposits were maintained "to keep cash reserves of U.S. dollars to meet its obligations payable in U.S. dollars [and] to hedge against currency exchange losses occasioned by extreme devaluations in H.K. dollars"); Bruckner, The Exception to Foreign Base Company Income Under Former Section 954(b)(4), 45 Tax Lawyer 621 (1992).

[207] 1986 Bluebook, supra note 14, at 983.

deductions for foreign income taxes).[208] The amount of foreign tax on an item is generally the indirect credit that a corporate U.S. shareholder would get if the item were fully included in its gross income under subpart F.[209] The gross income and deductions are determined with U.S. tax principles. Assume a CFC has FPHC income of $100, to which deductions of $10 are allocated, and the income is subject to foreign taxes of $30. The exclusion applies because the effective foreign tax rate is 33 percent ($30 divided by excess of $100 over $10).

The rule generally applies item by item, but some aggregation is allowed.[210] For items other than FPHC income, all items within the same category of FBC income (e.g., FBC sales income) are aggregated and treated as a single item if they are within the same limitation category under the foreign tax credit limitation rules of §904(d).[211] For FPHC income that is included in the passive basket for purposes of the credit limitation, aggregation rules are borrowed from those used in applying a high tax rule under §904(d).[212] For other FPHC income, dividends, interest, rents, royalties, and annuities are aggregated, and net gains on sales of property make up another aggregate.

The high tax exclusion does not apply to two types of income: interest from sources within the United States that would be subject to the 30 percent tax of §881(a) but for the exemption of portfolio interest, and FBC oil related income.[213]

¶68.2.10 Subpart F Income

A CFC's subpart F income normally consists of the sum of its adjusted net FBC income and insurance income.[214] Additions are made to subpart F income,

---

[208] Reg. §1.954-1(d)(2) (foreign taxes, gross income, and deductions are stated in U.S. dollars). See Rev. Proc. 98-7, 1998-1 CB—, §3.01(3) (IRS will not rule in advance on effective rate in particular case); Rev. Proc. 87-61, 1987-2 CB 765, superseded by Rev. Proc. 90-6, 1990-1 CB 430 ("determining the effective rate of tax imposed by a foreign jurisdiction is inherently factual and therefore not appropriate for an advance ruling").

[209] Reg. §1.954-1(d)(3). For the indirect credit for §951(a)(1) inclusions, see infra ¶68.2.13.

[210] See 1986 Bluebook, supra note 14, at 983.

[211] Reg. §1.954-1(c)(1)(iii).

[212] For these rules, see infra ¶69.6.2 text accompanying notes 34–38.

[213] IRC §§881(c)(4)(A)(ii); 954(b)(4). For the application of the 30 percent tax to interest, see supra ¶66.2.2.

[214] IRC §952(a). Under regulations proposed in 1998, if a CFC is a partner of a partnership, its distributive share of an item of partnership income is within a particular category of subpart F income to the extent the item would have been within that category if the CFC had realized it directly. Prop. Reg. §1.952-1(b)(1). For example, if a CFC owns 80 percent of the interests in a partnership that receives $100 of interest income (other than export financing interest) from an unrelated debtor, the CFC's $80 share of the interest income is FPHC income. Prop. Reg. §1.952-1(b)(2) Ex. According to the IRS,

The legislative history of [the partnership tax rules] indicates that a partnership distributive share should be characterized by using the approach that best serves the

however, if the CFC engages in proscribed activities or does business in a proscribed country.[215] On the other hand, income is excluded from subpart F income if the CFC pays an effectively connected income tax to the U.S. on the income.[216] Also, subpart F income may not exceed the CFC's current earnings and profits, and earnings and profits deficits incurred in earlier years and by related CFC's are sometimes applied in reduction of subpart F income.[217]

1. *Bad conduct inclusions.* Various additions are made to subpart F income if a CFC does business in a country on bad terms with the United States, pays illegal bribes or kickbacks, or participates in an international boycott.

Subpart F income includes the entirety of any income "derived from" a particular country if (1) the United States does not recognize its government (unless the country is eligible to purchase defense articles under the Arms Export Control Act), (2) the United States has severed diplomatic relations with the country, (3) the United States technically has diplomatic relations with the country but "does not conduct such relations," or (4) the country has been designated by the Secretary of State as a repeated supporter of acts of international terrorism.[218]

If the CFC pays an illegal bribe or kickback to an official, employee, or "agent in fact" of a government, the amount of this payment is added to subpart F income for the year in which it is made.[219] A bribe or kickback is considered illegal for this purpose if a payment by a U.S. person under the same circumstances would be unlawful under the Foreign Corrupt Practices Act.

Code or regulations section at issue. . . . To allow a CFC to avoid subpart F treatment for items of income by the simple expedient of receiving them as distributive shares of partnership income, rather than directly, is contrary to the intent of subpart F.

REG-104537-97, 1998-16 IRB 21, 22. One court reached a contrary result under pre-1987 law. Brown Group, Inc. v. CIR, 77 F3d 217 (3d Cir. 1996) (nonacq.). See Osterberg, Partnerships in the International Context: What Should the New Regulations Provide? 74 Tax Notes 345 (Jan. 20, 1997).

Also, in applying rules that depend on whether the payor and payee are related or on where an entity is created or organized, these "determination[s] shall be made by reference to such [CFC] and not by reference to the partnership." Prop. Reg. §1.954-1(g)(1). Assume X Corp. and Y Corp., two commonly controlled CFCs, own 80 percent and 20 percent, respectively, of the interests in partnership PRS, and PRS purchases goods from Y and resells them to unrelated persons. Prop. Reg. §1.954-1(g)(2) Ex. X's distributive share of PRS's income from these transactions may be FBC sales income because X is, for these purposes, treated as having purchased the goods from Y, a related person.

[215] Infra text accompanying notes 219–22.

[216] Infra text accompanying notes 223–24.

[217] Infra text accompanying notes 225–38.

[218] IRC §§901(j)(2), 952(a)(5). For the countries encompassed by this sanction, see infra ¶69.4.8.

[219] IRC §952(a)(4); Reg. §1.952-1(a)(4).

Another addition to subpart F income is made if the CFC participates in an international boycott.[220] This addition equals the corporation's income (exclusive of income yielding earnings and profits includable in subpart F income under other rules and income from U.S. sources that is taxed to the CFC as income effectively connected with a trade or business in the United States) multiplied by the international boycott factor.[221]

2. *Exclusion of U.S. income.* An item of income, although within one of the components of subpart F income, is excluded from aggregate subpart F income if it is (1) from sources within the United States, (2) effectively connected with a U.S. trade or business, and (3) not eligible for a reduced rate or exemption under an income tax treaty.[222] The purpose of subpart F is to deny deferral of U.S. taxation. When a CFC is itself subject to U.S. tax at the normal corporate rates, tax is not deferred, and the policies of subpart F are satisfied without the imputation of the income to the CFC's U.S. shareholders. An item is not excluded from subpart F income, however, merely because it is subject to the 30 percent tax on nonbusiness income imposed by §881(a).[223]

3. *Earnings and profits limitations.* Subpart F income may not exceed the CFC's earnings and profits for the taxable year.[224] The purpose of subpart F to deny deferral of U.S. taxation never requires that U.S. shareholders of a CFC be taxed on amounts exceeding the dividends they would have received if all income had been distributed currently, and earnings and profits are the measure of dividend income. Assume a CFC's subpart F income for 1991 is $100 before application of the earnings and profits limitation, but it has a $25 loss from other

---

[220] IRC §952(a)(3); Reg. §1.952-1(a)(3).

[221] For the international boycott factor, see infra ¶68.8.

[222] IRC §952(b). An item is not considered exempt from U.S. taxation merely because an income tax treaty exempts it from the branch taxes imposed by §884. Thus, if a CFC has U.S. source income that is effectively connected with a U.S. trade or business, the income is not tax-exempt, even if a repatriation of the item is exempted by treaty from the branch profits tax, so long as the effectively connected income tax applies to the item.

If the CFC is also a foreign sales corporation (FSC), interest, carrying charges, dividends, royalties, and other investment income are deemed to be from U.S. sources for this purpose. For FSCs, see supra ¶68.1.4.

[223] Reg. §1.952-1(b)(2). For the 30 percent tax, see supra ¶66.2.

[224] IRC §952(c)(1)(A); Reg. §1.952-1(e). See Reg. §1.952-1(c)(1) (earnings and profits computed as of end of year without diminution by distributions).

For purposes of this rule and the earnings and profits rules described below, earnings and profits are determined without three rules: the rules requiring that, for earnings and profits purposes, (1) FIFO inventory must be used if LIFO is used in determining taxable income, (2) gains on installment sales must be reported when made if the installment method is used in determining taxable income, and (3) income under a long-term contract must be determined with the percentage of completion method if the completed contract method is used in determining taxable income. IRC §§312(n)(4), (5), (6); 952(c)(3). For earnings and profits determinations generally, see Reg. §1.964-1.

operations that reduces current earnings and profits to $75.[225] Subpart F income for the year is $75.

The earnings and profits ceiling, however, is modified by three subsidiary rules. First, when subpart F income exceeds the ceiling, the excess is carried forward to subsequent years, and any excess of earnings and profits over subpart F income for a carryover year is recharacterized as subpart F income, up to the amount of the excess.[226] Assume a CFC has subpart F income of $100 and earnings and profits of $85 for year 1 and $85 of subpart F income and $100 of earnings and profits for year 2. Subpart F income for year 1 is reduced to $85 by the earnings and profits rule, but the amount of the reduction ($15) is carried to year 2, where the $15 excess of current earnings and profits ($100) over current subpart F income ($85) is recharacterized as additional subpart F income. As a consequence, subpart F income and earnings and profits over the two-year period are both $185 ($85 plus $100).

The other two modifications, described in more detail below, (1) allow a deficit in earnings and profits for an earlier year to be carried forward to reduce subpart F income of a later year and (2) permit a current deficit of one CFC to be applied in reduction of the subpart F income of another CFC if the two CFCs are parent and subsidiary and both are incorporated in the same country.

a. *Offsets for deficits of earlier years.* The offset for prior deficits is applied shareholder by shareholder. Generally, a U.S. shareholder's inclusion under §951(a)(1) for current subpart F income is reduced by the shareholder's pro rata share of an earnings and profits deficit for an earlier year if both the current inclusion and the prior deficit are "qualified."[227]

Some items included in subpart F income can never be offset by prior years' deficits, including income earned in countries with which the United States has bad relations and amounts included in subpart F income because of illegal bribes or kickbacks or participation in an international boycott.[228] Insurance or FPHC income can be offset by an earlier deficit only if, in both the current and the deficit years, the CFC is "predominantly engaged in the active conduct of an insurance business [or] a banking, financing, or similar business."[229] All other items included in subpart F income can be offset by any qualified deficit.

A deficit in earnings and profits of an earlier year qualifies as an offset against a current §951(a)(1) inclusion only if the deficit was incurred in a qualifying year and the corporation was a CFC for that year.[230] The qualifying years

---

[225] S. Rep. No. 1881, supra note 13, at 945 Ex. 1.

[226] IRC §952(c)(2); Reg. §1.952-1(f).

[227] IRC §952(c)(1)(B)(i).

[228] IRC §952(c)(1)(B)(iii).

[229] IRC §§952(c)(1)(B)(iii)(V), (iii)(VI), (v), (vi). For the term "banking, financing, or similar business," see Reg. §1.864-4(c)(5)(i); Stanford v. CIR, 108 TC 344 (1997) ("Administrative and management services" are not banking, even if performed for subsidiary corporation that is bank).

[230] IRC §952(c)(1)(B)(ii).

are all years after 1962 for a deficit from activities generating FBC sales and services income, after 1982 for FBC oil related income, and after 1987 for deficits arising in all other activities.

A qualified deficit, however, may be offset against the U.S. shareholder's current inclusion under §951(a)(1) only to the extent it arises from the same activity in which the deficit was incurred.[231] A deficit incurred in an activity of selling goods, for example, may only be used against the portion of the current inclusion consisting of foreign base company sales income.

Also, to ensure that a qualified deficit may be used only once, the amount carried to any year consists of the excess of the deficit over the portions of it used as offsets in years intervening between the deficit year and the current year.[232]

The offset against a U.S. shareholder's §951(a)(1) inclusion equals the shareholder's pro rata share of the qualified deficit carried to the current year.[233] A shareholder's pro rata share is the amount the shareholder would receive with respect to stock actually owned and owned indirectly through foreign entities if the corporation made a cash distribution equal to the amount allowed as an offset for the current year. Actual and indirect shareholdings are determined as of the end of the taxable year or the year of the deficit, whichever produces the smaller offset for the shareholder.

b. *Chain deficit rule.* A CFC may reduce its subpart F income by an earnings and profits deficit of another CFC if (1) the other CFC is a "qualified chain member," (2) the deficit was incurred in a taxable year ending with or within the current taxable year of the taxpayer CFC, and (3) the taxpayer CFC elects to apply this rule.[234] Even if these requirements are satisfied, the reduction is allowed only if the income and deficit arise from the same type of activity and the income is not disqualified.

A CFC is a qualified chain member if it is organized under the laws of the same foreign country as the taxpayer CFC and an ownership test is satisfied.[235] The ownership test requires that the taxpayer CFC own all the stock of the other CFC or that the other CFC own all the stock of the taxpayer CFC. In either case, directors' qualifying shares are ignored, and the shares can be held directly or indirectly through other corporations (but not through the common parent).[236] Assume *CFC1* is sole shareholder of *CFC2*, *CFC2* is sole shareholder of *CFC3*, and all three corporations are incorporated in foreign country *X*. Each of the corporations is a qualified chain member with respect to each of the other

---

[231] IRC §952(c)(1)(B)(ii)(I).

[232] IRC §952(c)(1)(B)(ii)(II).

[233] IRC §952(c)(1)(B)(iv).

[234] IRC §952(c)(1)(C)(i). For the chain deficit rule of pre-1986 law, see Unisys Corp. v. US, 30 Ct. Fed. Cl. 552, 94-1 USTC ¶50,069 (1994), aff'd without opinion, 39 F.3d 1197 (Fed. Cir. 1994).

[235] IRC §952(c)(1)(C)(ii).

[236] See Stanford v. CIR, 108 TC No. 17 (1997) (exclusion of indirect ownership through common parent applies whether common parent is foreign or domestic).

corporations. For example, because *CFC1* owns all of *CFC3*'s stock indirectly through *CFC2*, *CFC1* is a qualified chain member with respect to *CFC3* and vice versa. The chain deficit rule thus allows a deficit incurred by any of the corporations to be applied in reduction of the subpart F income of any of the other corporations. In contrast, if the stock of the three corporations was held by domestic corporation *P*, the chain deficit rule would not apply because none of the corporations has any direct or indirect shareholdings in the others except through the common parent.

A CFC's subpart F income may be offset by a deficit of a qualified chain member, however, only if two additional requirements are met. First, subpart F income of a particular type (e.g., FBC sales income) may be offset only by the portion of the qualified chain member's deficit that arose from an activity that, if profitable, would have generated income of the same type. Second, a qualified chain member's deficit may not be offset against FPHC income (unless the taxpayer CFC is an active insurance company or bank), insurance income (unless the taxpayer CFC is an active insurance company), income earned in a proscribed country, or amounts included in subpart F income because of bribes, kickbacks, or participation in international boycotts.

When the chain deficit rule applies, each CFC first reduces its subpart F income by its own deficits from prior years under the offset rule described above, and a deficit of a qualified chain member may only be applied against any subpart F income remaining after the CFC's own prior deficits have been fully utilized.[237] When a CFC's deficit is used to reduce current subpart F income of another CFC, the deficit may not be carried forward to offset the CFC's own subpart F income for a subsequent year.

¶68.2.10A   Hybrid Arrangements

Temporary regulations issued in 1998 deny tax benefits sought through arrangements using hybrid branches and partnerships.[238] "A hybrid branch is one

---

[237] IRC §952(c)(1)(C)(iii).

[238] See generally Cooper, Melcher & Stretch, Suddenly Saving Foreign Taxes Is Abusive? An Untenable Proposal, 79 Tax Notes 885 (May 18, 1998); Gannon, Calianese, Layden, Moreland & Seo, Subpart F, Hybrid Entities, and Other Little Things, 79 Tax Notes 473 (Apr. 27, 1998), reprinted in 16 Tax Notes Int'l 1467 (May 4, 1998); Ganz & Stange, Subpart F Inclusion Income Under Hybrid Branch Regs: How the Regs Work, 79 Tax Notes 487 (Apr. 27, 1998); New York State Bar Ass'n Tax Section, Notice 98-11: Tax Treatment of Hybrid Entities, 79 Tax Notes 877 (May 18, 1998), reprinted in 16 Tax Notes Int'l 1669 (May 25, 1998); Tax Executives Institute, Hybrid Arrangements Notice "Poor Tax Policy," 16 Tax Notes Int'l 1003 (Mar. 30, 1998); Tillinghast, An Old-Timer's Comment on Notice 98-11, 78 Tax Notes 1739 (Mar. 30, 1998); Yoder, Hybrid Branches: Temporary Regulations Create Something Out of Nothing for Subpart F Purposes, 27 Tax Mgmt. Int'l J. 219 (1998).

The regulations generally apply to payments made or accrued after January 15, 1998, under "arrangements" made after that day, but the effective date is delayed to March 23,

that is viewed under United States tax principles to be part of the CFC (i.e., fiscally transparent), but under the law of the CFC's country of incorporation as an entity separate from the CFC (i.e., non-fiscally transparent)."[239] A hybrid partnership is an entity that is considered a partnership for U.S. tax purposes but is not fiscally transparent under the tax laws of a foreign country in which the CFC is subject to tax.

The arrangements targeted by the regulations "involve the use of deductible payments to reduce the taxable income of a [CFC] under foreign law, thereby reducing the CFC's foreign tax and, also under foreign law, the corresponding creation in another entity of low-taxed, passive income of the type to which subpart F was intended to apply." The check-the-box regulations issued in 1996 "have facilitated" these arrangements because they allow many foreign entities to be treated, at the taxpayer's election, either as a corporation or as a branch (if it has one owner) or a partnership (if it has more than one owner).[240] For example, taxpayers can elect to treat entities organized under foreign equivalents of the U.S. limited liability company laws as branches or partnerships for U.S. tax purposes, even if they are taxed as separate corporate entities under foreign laws.

Assume D, a domestic corporation, is sole shareholder of F-1, a corporation organized under the laws of country A, and F-1 owns all of the stock of another country A corporation, F-2, that carries on an active manufacturing business in country A.[241] F-1 is also sole owner of a limited liability company (LLC) organized under the laws of country B, a tax haven. The LLC is treated as a separate corporation under the tax laws of countries A and B, but D elects to treat it as a branch for U.S. tax purposes. The LLC makes a loan to F-2. Interest on this loan is deductible by F-2 in determining its country A tax, but the LLC's interest income is not taxed, because country A does not impose a withholding tax on interest payments to foreign persons and country B exempts from tax all interest received by country B entities from foreign persons. Because the LLC is not a separate entity for U.S. tax purposes, the interest paid by F-2 is considered received by F-1. Although a CFC's interest income is normally included in its

---

1998, for cases involving hybrid branches of partnerships in which CFCs are partners. Reg. §1.954-9T(d).

An entity that elected to be treated as a partnership for U.S. tax purposes can avoid the hybrid branch rules by electing to be classified instead as an association, beginning with its first taxable year beginning after 1997. Reg. §1.954-9T(b). This election, which must be made by the end of that taxable year, is a waiver of the usual rule that a classification election may not be changed until it has been in effect for at least 60 months. Reg. §301.7701-3T(c)(1)(iv).

[239] Notice 98-11, 1998-6 IRB 18, II.

[240] For the check-the-box regulations, see infra ¶90.1.3. See also TD 8767, 1998-16 IRB 4 ("This administrative provision was not intended to change substantive law. Particularly in the international area, the ability to more easily achieve fiscal transparency can lead to inappropriate results").

[241] Notice 98-11, 1998-6 IRB 18, II Ex. 1.

subpart F income as foreign personal holding company income,[242] this interest income of *F-1* is not subpart F income, because (1) *F-1* and *F-2* are incorporated under the laws of the same foreign country (*A*) and (2) *F-2* uses a substantial part of its assets in the active conduct of a trade or business in that country.[243]

The Treasury finds these results to be "inconsistent with the policies and rules of subpart F" because "one of the purposes of subpart F is to prevent CFCs from converting active income that is not easily moveable and is earned in a jurisdiction in which a business is located for non-tax reasons, into passive, easily moveable income that is shifted to a lower tax jurisdiction primarily for tax avoidance."[244] The premise underlying the same country exception is that the interest, being paid by a corporation actively engaged in business in its country of incorporation to a commonly owned corporation organized in the same country, will, in the hands of the recipient, be subject to the same tax regime as the payor's active business income. However, because *F-1*'s LLC is considered a separate corporation under country *A*'s tax laws, country *A* does not tax *F-1* on this income. "One of the purposes of subpart F is to prevent CFCs (including those engaged in active businesses) from structuring transactions designed to manipulate the inconsistencies between foreign tax systems to inappropriately generate low- or non-taxed income on which United States tax might be permanently deferred."[245]

Similar results might follow if the LLC made the loan to *F-1*, rather than *F-2*. Because country *A* recognizes the LLC as a separate taxable entity, interest on the loan may be deductible in determining *F-1*'s country *A* tax, but the LLC will not be taxed by either country on its interest income. The result under foreign law is the same as an interest payment by a CFC in a nonhaven country to a related CFC in a tax haven, a transaction that generates interest income included in foreign personal holding company income and hence subpart F income. However, because *F-1* and its LLC are not separate entities under U.S. law, the loan and interest payments are ignored.

1. *Hybrid branches.* The regulations sometimes recharacterize income other than subpart F income as subpart F income if a CFC or a partnership of which the CFC is a partner makes a payment to a "hybrid branch," which is an "entity"[245.1] that has all of the following characteristics:

a. It has only one owner, whose ownership may be direct or "through branches."

---

[242] IRC §954(c)(1)(A).

[243] IRC §954(c)(3)(A)(i).

[244] TD 8767, 1998-16 IRB 4.

[245] Notice 98-11, 1998-6 IRB 18, I.

[245.1] An "entity" is a "person" that is treated "as other than an individual" by the United States or any other "jurisdiction." Reg. §1.954-9T(a)(6). See IRC §7701(a)(1) ("person" includes "an individual, a trust, estate, partnership, association, company or corporation").

b. Its owner is a CFC or a partnership at least one of whose partners is a CFC ("directly or indirectly through one or more branches or partnerships").

c. It is "fiscally transparent" for U.S. income tax purposes.

d. It is not fiscally transparent under the tax laws of a country in which the CFC, the "payor entity," an owner of a fiscally-transparent payor entity, or "any intermediary partnership" is organized or "has substantial assets."[245.2]

Moreover, the regulations apply only to a "hybrid branch payment," which is a payment that, under foreign tax laws to which the payor is subject, is considered made between separate entities but that is disregarded under "U.S. income tax principles" because it is considered made "between two parts of a single entity."

The regulations recharacterize income other than subpart F income as subpart F income if four requirements are met:

a. The hybrid branch payment must be between (1) the CFC and a hybrid branch of the CFC, (2) two hybrid branches of the CFC, (3) a partnership in which the CFC is a partner and a hybrid branch of the partnership, or (4) two hybrid branches of a such a partnership.[245.3] The term "partnership" apparently includes any entity that is classified as a partnership for purposes of U.S. law.[245.4]

b. The hybrid branch payment must reduce foreign income taxes. Specifically, foreign income taxes of the payor of the hybrid branch payment (or of an owner of the payor) must be "less than the foreign tax that would have been imposed on such income had the hybrid branch payment not been made."[245.5] This lesser tax may result from a loss, deficit, or "other tax attribute" that is created or increased by the hybrid branch payment and is carried back or forward to reduce foreign income taxes for another year.

c. The hybrid branch payment must be a type of FPHC income. Whether

---

[245.2] Reg. §1.954-9T(a)(6).

[245.3] Reg. §1.954-9T(a)(2). For purposes of the partnership rules, the CFC's partnership interest may be held directly or through one or more branches or other partnerships.

[245.4] In cases involving partnerships and their hybrid branches, the CFC is usually treated as making or receiving its "proportionate share" of a hybrid branch payment made or received by the partnership, and a hybrid branch of the partnership is usually considered a hybrid branch of the CFC. Reg. §1.954-9T(a)(2)(ii). Assume X Corp., a CFC organized under the laws of country A, is a 90 percent partner of partnership PRS, which borrows money from BR, a hybrid branch of PRS; country A's tax laws allow X to deduct 90 percent of the interest paid by PRS to BR, but they do not tax X on any portion of BR's interest income. The regulation's recharacterization rule is applied by treating X as paying to BR 90 percent of the interest actually paid by PRS. However, if the partnership is not fiscally transparent under foreign tax laws applicable to the CFC, the recharacterization rules are applied as if the partnership were a CFC.

[245.5] Reg. §1.954-9T(a)(3).

a hybrid branch payment is within a category of FPHC income is determined by treating the hybrid branch as a separate wholly-owned subsidiary of the CFC that is incorporated in the country where the branch is organized or has substantial assets.[245.6]

d. Under a "tax disparity rule," the effective rate of tax on the hybrid branch payment in "the year when earned" must be "less than 90 percent of, and at least 5 percentage points less than, [a] hypothetical effective rate of tax."[245.7] The hypothetical rate is a fraction whose numerator is (1) the income taxes that would have been paid or accrued by the payor of the hybrid branch payment in the absence of the payment, less (2) the income taxes actually paid or accrued by the payor; the denominator is the amount of the hybrid branch payment.[245.8]

If all four of these requirements are met, income of the CFC other than subpart F income is recharacterized as subpart F income, usually in an amount equal to the lesser of the hybrid branch payment or the excess of the CFC's earnings and profits for the year over its subpart F income (as determined before the recharacterization rule is applied).[245.9] If the hybrid branch payment exceeds the non-subpart F earnings and profits, the excess is not carried to any other year. For foreign tax credit purposes, the recharacterized amount is allocated among the separate categories of §904(b) in proportion to the amounts of non-subpart F income of the CFC in the various baskets.[245.10]

Assume X Corp., a CFC organized in country A, has taxable income from manufacturing for country A tax purposes of $70, after deducting $30 of interest paid to its hybrid branch in country B; the interest payment is not taxed by either country A or country B. All four of the requirements are likely met. The interest payment is made by a CFC to a hybrid branch of the CFC. Because the payment is deductible by the CFC and not taxable to the branch, it reduces foreign tax. If the branch were treated for U.S. tax purposes as a separate country B corporation, its interest receipt would be FPHC income. If X's country A tax for the year is $35, but would have been $50 without the deduction for the interest payment, the hypothetical effective rate is 50 percent (($50 − $35)/$30), and the tax

---

[245.6] Reg. §1.954-9T(a)(4). However, for all purposes other than this requirement, the hybrid branch is not treated as a separate entity. For example, a hybrid branch payment is not deductible by the CFC in determining its foreign base company income, and earnings and deficits of the hybrid branch are included in the CFC's earnings and profits in determining whether the CFC has an overall deficit for purposes of the deficit rules of §952(c). For the deductions allowable in determining foreign base company income, see infra ¶68.2.9. For §952(c), see infra ¶68.2.10.

[245.7] Reg. §1.954-9T(a)(5)(iv).

[245.8] If the payment creates or increases a loss or deficit for the year, the numerator is the tax that would have been imposed if the payor's taxable income for the year equaled the amount of the payment.

[245.9] Reg. §1.954-9T(a)(5).

[245.10] Reg. §1.954-9T(c).

disparity rule is met because the effective rate of tax on the branch payment (zero) is less than 90 percent of the hypothetical rate (50 percent) and is also at least 5 percentage points less than that rate. Since the four requirements are met, part of X's non-subpart F income (from manufacturing) is recharacterized as subpart F income. The amount so recharacterized is $30, which is the lesser of the amount of the hybrid branch payment ($30) or X's earnings and profits for the year (pretax income of $100, less country A tax of $35).[245.11]

However, the recharacterization rule does not apply if the non-subpart F income that would otherwise be recharacterized is subject to foreign taxes at an effective rate of at least 31.5 percent (90 percent of the maximum U.S. corporate rate under §11).[245.12] The effective tax rate is the foreign income taxes on this income, divided by the amount of the income, as determined under U.S. tax rules. In the example, X's non-subpart F income is taxed at an effective rate of 35 percent—the country A tax ($35), divided by the pretax amount of X's manufacturing income ($100). However, although the regulations are not clear on the matter, the recharacterized amount is probably the $30 of the manufacturing income that is offset by the interest deduction for country A purposes, which is not taxed by any country. If so, the effective rate is zero, and the exception does not apply.

2. *Hybrid partnerships.* The regulations take a different route to similar results for deductible payments by CFCs to hybrid partnerships in which they have interests. In determining FBC income, the CFC's deduction for such a payment may not be allocated against the CFC's distributive share of the partnership's income from the payment, to the extent the distributive share is subpart F income, if

a. The payee entity, although classified as a partnership for U.S. tax purposes, is not fiscally transparent under the tax laws of a country in which the CFC does business or has substantial assets,

b. The CFC's foreign tax liabilities are less than they would have been if the payment had not been made, and

c. The effective rate of tax on the partnership's income from the payment is less than 90 percent of, and at least 5 percentage points less than, the effective rate of tax on the additional income that the CFC would have had if the payment had not been made.[245.13]

The rule does not affect the CFC's deduction for the excess of the payment over its distributive share of the partnership's corresponding income.[245.14]

[245.11] Earnings and profits are determined without any deduction for the interest because the payor (X) and payee (the branch) are one person for U.S. tax purposes.

[245.12] Reg. §1.954-9T(a)(5)(v).

[245.13] Reg. §1.954-1T(c)(1)(B). This rule generally applies to amounts paid or accrued after March 22, 1998, under arrangements made after that date. Reg. §1.954-1T(c)(1)(i)(E).

[245.14] Reg. §1.954-1T(c)(1)(i)(C).

Assume X Corp., a CFC organized and doing business in country A, owns 70 percent of the interests in a country B entity (*PRS*), which is a partnership for U.S. tax purposes but is not fiscally transparent under the laws of country A.[245.15] X borrows $100 from *PRS* at 10 percent annual interest. X's income is taxed by country A at 30 percent, but *PRS*'s interest income is subject only to 5 percent imposed by country B. X's $7 distributive share of *PRS*'s $10 of annual interest income is FPHC income. Of the $10 of interest on the loan from *PRS*, $7 is not deductible against this subpart F income, because *PRS* is not fiscally transparent under country A law, the deduction for the interest payment reduces X's country A tax, and the tax on the partnership's interest income (5 percent of $10) is less than 90 percent of, and more than 5 percentage points less than, the tax rate that would have applied to the increase income X would have had if it had not made the payment (country A tax of 30 percent of $10). The normal deduction allocation rules apply only to the remaining $3. The effect of the rule is to give X additional subpart F income of $7, which is X's share of the income shifted by the loan arrangement out of X's income (taxed by country A at 30 percent) and into *PRS*'s income (taxed only at 5 percent).

The rule does not apply, however, to the extent the CFC has no non-subpart F income against which to allocate the deduction.[245.16]

¶68.2.11 Earnings Invested in U.S. Property

In addition to a ratable share of subpart F income, a U.S. shareholder must include in gross income its pro rata share of any increase in the CFC's investment of earnings in U.S. property.[246] "Generally, earnings brought back to the United States are taxed to the shareholders [because] this is substantially the equivalent of a dividend being paid to them."[247]

1. *U.S. property.* The term "U.S. property" includes, very generally, tangible property located in the United States, stock and debt obligations of related domestic corporations, and patents, copyrights, and other intangibles acquired or developed for use in the United States.[248] Although §956 only applies for years in which a foreign corporation is a CFC, a CFC's U.S. property for such a year may include property acquired previously when it was not a CFC.[249] Various exceptions are provided, many of which are intended to cover property held in the United States incident to "normal commercial transactions without intention to

---

[245.15] Reg. §1.954-1T(c)(1)(i)(D) Ex.

[245.16] Reg. §1.954-1T(c)(1)(i)(C).

[246] IRC §951(a)(1)(B). See Laity, Anatomy of Sections 951(a)(1)(B) and 956 of the Internal Revenue Code, 14 Va. Tax Rev. 71 (1994).

[247] S. Rep. No. 1881, supra note 13, at 794.

[248] IRC §956(c)(1).

[249] Reg. §1.956-2(a)(1).

permit the funds to remain in the United States indefinitely."[250] Portfolio investments in stock and debt of unrelated U.S. companies are also excluded.

Normally, an item of U.S. property is taken into account under §956 only if it is owned by the CFC.[251] Property held by a trustee or nominee for the CFC, however, is considered owned by the CFC.[252] Also, property held by a foreign corporation controlled by the CFC is treated as owned by the CFC if avoidance of §956 is "one of the principal purposes for creating, organizing, or funding (through capital contributions or debt) such other foreign corporation."[253] The latter rule is intended to prevent taxpayers from circumventing §956 by using a CFC with no earnings and profits to hold U.S. property that is effectively acquired with the earnings of a related CFC.

a. *Tangible property.* Tangible property is usually U.S. property if it is located in the United States.[254] Goods purchased in the United States "for export to, or use in," foreign countries are excluded, however, even if the CFC takes title before the goods leave this country.[255] Also, an aircraft, railroad rolling stock, vessel, motor vehicle, or container is excluded if it is used to transport people or goods in foreign commerce and its use is "predominantly" outside the United States.[256] Moreover, "movable property" other than vessels and aircraft is excluded when used on the Continental Shelf of the United States in "exploring for, developing, removing, or transporting resources from ocean waters or under waters."[257]

b. *Corporate stock and debt instruments.* Generally, stock of a domestic corporation is U.S. property,[258] and a debt instrument is U.S. property if the obligor is a U.S. person (a U.S. citizen or resident or a domestic corporation,

---

[250] S. Rep. No. 1881, supra note 13, at 794. A U.S. shareholder claiming the benefit of any exception must file a statement with its return identifying the property covered by the exception. Reg. §1.956-2(b)(2).

In addition to the exceptions described below, all property acquired before 1963 is excluded from U.S. property. See Reg. §1.956-2(d)(1)(i)(c) (exclusion of property acquired before 1963 also applies to property acquired after 1962 in exchange for pre-1963 property if no gain or loss was recognized on exchange and basis carried over).

[251] See Reg. §1.956-2(d)(1)(i) (U.S. property is acquired when CFC obtains basis for it); Rev. Rul. 90-112, 1990-2 CB 186 (CFC treated as owner of ratable share of U.S. property owned by domestic or foreign partnership of which it is partner, even if CFC owns only minority interest in partnership).

[252] Reg. §1.956-1T(b)(4)(i).

[253] Id. A CFC is deemed to control another foreign corporation for this purpose if the two corporations are related under §267(b). For §267(b), see infra ¶78.3.

[254] IRC §956(c)(1)(A).

[255] IRC §956(c)(2)(B).

[256] IRC §956(c)(2)(D); Reg. §1.956-2(b)(1)(vi) (predominantly used outside United States if at least 70 percent of miles traversed during taxable year are outside country or if located outside country at least 70 percent of time).

[257] IRC §956(c)(2)(G); Reg. §1.956-2(b)(1)(ix).

[258] IRC §956(c)(1)(B). See Rev. Rul. 82-171, 1982-2 CB 161 (obligation of Canadian or Mexican corporation is U.S. property where corporation's U.S. parent has elected to

partnership, trust, or estate).[259] For this purpose, a CFC is treated as owning any obligation of a U.S. person that the CFC guarantees or secures with a pledge of its property.[260] For example, if a CFC pledges assets to secure a loan obtained by its domestic parent corporation from a foreign bank, the CFC is considered owner of the parent's obligation to the bank.[261]

Several exceptions, described below, are provided, which cover stock and obligations of unrelated domestic corporations, bank deposits, obligations of the U.S. government, and some accounts receivable.

Stock and debt instruments issued by a domestic corporation are not U.S. property unless, immediately after the CFC's acquisition of the property, (1) the corporation is a U.S. shareholder of the CFC or (2) 25 percent or more of the corporation's voting stock is owned, actually, indirectly, or constructively, by persons who are U.S. shareholders of the CFC.[262] Since a CFC's U.S. shareholders are constructive owners of at least part of any stock owned by the CFC, the CFC's stock ownership affects the application of the 25 percent rule.

Also, deposits "with persons carrying on the banking business" are not U.S. property even if the bank is domestic.[263] Money and obligations of the U.S. government are excluded too.[264] A deposit of cash or securities by or with a securities or commodities dealer is excluded if it is made or received "on commercial terms in the ordinary course" of the dealer's business as collateral or

---

treat it as domestic corporation under §1504(d) in order to include it in parent's consolidated return).

[259] IRC §§956(c)(1)(C); 7701(a)(30). See Jacobs Engineering Group Inc. v. US, 97-1 USTC ¶50,340 (CD Cal. 1997) (series of short-term loans to domestic parent, none outstanding at year-end, treated as one continuous loan, which was U.S. property); Yoder & McGill, Treatment of CFC Loans to U.S. Affiliates: The Sword and Sickle of Subpart F, 26 Tax Mgmt. Int'l J. 454 (1997).

[260] IRC §956(d). See Reg. §1.956-2(c)(2) (pledge includes any arrangement by which CFC's assets secure obligation of U.S. person; pledge of two thirds or more of CFC's stock may be treated as pledge of CFC's assets), §1.956-2(c)(3) Ex. 3(illustrating rule on pledge of CFC stock); Rev. Proc. 98-7, 1998-1 CB—, §4.01(19) (IRS ordinarily will not rule on "whether a pledge of the stock of a controlled foreign corporation is an indirect pledge of the assets of that corporation").

[261] Reg. §1.956-2(c)(3) Ex. 1. See Reg. §1.956-2(c)(3) Ex. 2 (under guarantee branch of rule, same result if CFC agrees to purchase parent's note from bank at face in event of parent's default).

[262] IRC §956(c)(2)(F); Reg. §1.956-2(b)(1)(viii). For the indirect and constructive ownership rules, see supra ¶68.2.2. See Rev. Rul. 87-89, 1987-2 CB 195, declared obsolete in part, Rev. Rul. 95-56, 1995-2 CB 322 (where CFC makes deposit in unrelated bank and bank lends to U.S. shareholder, CFC is treated as loaning directly to shareholder unless loan would have been made on same terms without deposit; right of bank to offset deposit against shareholder's obligation is "presumptive evidence" that loan would not have been made without deposit).

[263] IRC §956(c)(2)(A). Under the pledge rule described above in notes 260-61 and the accompanying text, this exclusion is lost if the deposit is used to secure an obligation of a U.S. person. Reg. §1.956-2(b)(1)(iii).

[264] IRC §956(c)(2)(A).

margin for a securities loan, notional principal contract, option, or forward or futures contract.[265] Moreover, a U.S. person's obligation under a repurchase agreement or reverse repurchase is not U.S. property if the agreement is made by or with a securities or commodities dealer in the ordinary course of the dealer's business; this exclusion applies only to the extent the obligation's "principal amount . . . does not exceed the fair market value of readily marketable securities sold or purchased pursuant to [the] agreement or otherwise posted or received as collateral."[266]

Accounts receivable from U.S. debtors are usually excluded.[267] Since debt obligations of unrelated domestic corporations are excluded under a broader rule described above, the exclusion of accounts receivable is most often useful for accounts arising in sales to related persons. In this context, however, the exclusion is denied unless the amount outstanding during the taxable year never exceeds what unrelated parties would find "ordinary and necessary to carry on the trade or business of both the other party to the . . . transaction and the U.S. person."[268]

Also, a trade or service receivable from a U.S. obligor cannot qualify under any of the exclusions described above if the CFC acquired the receivable from a related U.S. person.[269] This rule most often applies when a CFC factors accounts receivable of its domestic parent corporation. The term "trade or service receivable" covers any indebtedness arising in a sale by a related person of property held for sale to customers in the ordinary course of business or from the performance of services by a related person.[270] A person is related to a CFC for this purpose if it is a U.S. shareholder of the CFC or if the CFC and the original account receivable creditor are related within the meaning of §267(b).[271]

Finally, a debt "arising out of the involuntary conversion of property" is not U.S. property if the converted property was not U.S. property.[272] This exception most often applies to insurance claims arising from damage to or theft of property located outside of the United States but insured by a domestic insurance company.

c. *Other intangibles.* A patent, copyright, invention, model, design, secret formula or process, or "other similar property right" is U.S. property if the CFC acquired or developed it for use in the United States.[273] An intangible "actually

---

[265] IRC §956(c)(2)(J) (effective for CFC taxable years beginning after 1997).

[266] IRC §956(c)(2)(K) (effective for CFC taxable years beginning after 1997).

[267] IRC §956(c)(2)(C) (exclusion for accounts "in connection with the sale or processing of property"); Reg. §1.956-2T(d)(2)(i)(B) (exclusion for accounts receivable for services rendered by CFC).

[268] IRC §956(c)(2)(C); Reg. §§1.956-2(b)(1)(v), 1.956-2T(d)(2)(i)(B).

[269] IRC §956(c)(3); Reg. §1.956-3T.

[270] IRC §§864(d)(3), 956(c)(3)(A).

[271] IRC §864(d)(4). For §267(b), see infra ¶78.3.

[272] Reg. §1.956-2T(d)(2)(i)(A).

[273] IRC §956(c)(1)(D).

used principally in the United States" is presumed acquired or developed for use in this country.[274]

d. *Insurance assets.* An insurance company's investments of unearned premiums and reserves are excluded from U.S. property if the premiums and reserves are not attributable to the insurance of U.S. risks and, in the case of investments of reserves, do not exceed the amounts "ordinary and necessary for the proper conduct of [the CFC's] insurance business."[275]

e. *Investments of U.S. earnings.* If a CFC has U.S. source income that is taxed as income effectively connected with a U.S. trade or business (or has had such income during any earlier year), its U.S. property is reduced by an amount equal to the earnings and profits accumulated from this income.[276] U.S. source earnings taxed as effectively connected income, in other words, can be invested in U.S. property without causing the earnings to be taxed a second time to U.S. shareholders.

f. *FSC earnings.* If a CFC is also a foreign sales corporation (FSC), property related to its export activities is excluded from U.S. property.[277] This exclusion, however, does not apply to a trade or service receivable acquired from a related person.[278]

2. *Investment in U.S. property.* As of the end of any taxable year, a CFC's earnings invested in U.S. property equals the aggregate amount of this property or, if less, the portion that would be a dividend if cash equal to this amount was distributed to shareholders on the last day of the year.[279]

The amount of each investment is the property's adjusted basis as determined for purposes of computing earnings and profits, less the amount of any liability to which the property is subject.[280] A liability is taken into account only if it is a "specific charge" on the property; liabilities incurred on the CFC's general credit are therefore ignored.[281] Liabilities created "for the purpose of artificially increasing or decreasing the . . . investment of earnings in United States property" are also disregarded.[282] Moreover, a recourse liability is ignored

---

[274] Reg. §1.956-2(a)(1)(iv).

[275] IRC §956(c)(2)(E). See Reg. §1.956-2(b)(1)(vii).

[276] IRC §956(c)(2)(H) (only earnings accumulated after 1962 qualify). See Reg. §1.956-2(b)(1)(x).

[277] IRC §956(c)(2)(I). For FSCs, see supra ¶68.1.4.

[278] IRC §956(c)(3), discussed supra text accompanying notes 269–71.

[279] IRC §956(a)(1). See Rev. Rul. 89-73, 1989-1 CB 258 (obligation of U.S. person is deemed held at end of taxable year where obligation is disposed of shortly before year-end and substantially identical obligation is reacquired early in next year; also, "factors in addition to the period of disinvestment may be indicative of a repatriation of earnings"); Mogenson & Rogers, IRS Curbs Parent's Ability to Roll Over Loans From a CFC, 72 J. Tax'n 44 (1990).

[280] IRC §956(a). For earnings and profits rules affecting adjusted basis, see §§316(k) and (n), discussed infra ¶92.1.3.

[281] Reg. §1.956-1(e)(1).

[282] Reg. §1.956-1(e)(3).

if the U.S. property securing it is a debt instrument issued by a related person.[283] An item of U.S. property is so valued as of the last day of each quarter of the year.

Earnings and profits are computed in the normal manner, with the following modifications:[284] Earnings included in the gross income of U.S. shareholders under the U.S. property rules for prior years are excluded unless the shareholders have received nontaxable distributions of the earnings. If U.S. property acquired in prior years has been treated as an investment of previously taxed subpart F income, these earnings are also excluded from earnings and profits until distributed. A further exclusion is provided for earnings currently taxed to a U.S. shareholder under the foreign personal holding company rules and undistributed earnings from prior years that were included in the U.S. shareholder's gross income under these rules. The purpose of these exclusions is to ensure that earnings taxed to the shareholder for earlier years or taxed currently under other rules are not included in the shareholder's gross income a second time. The exclusions apply only for purposes of the U.S. property rules.

3. *Increase in earnings invested in U.S. property.* The inclusion in a U.S. shareholder's gross income under the U.S. property rules is the lesser of the following two amounts:[285]

    a. (1) The shareholder's pro rata share of the average of the amounts of U.S. property held by the CFC, directly or indirectly, as of the close of the four quarters of the taxable year, less (2) the undistributed earnings and profits that were taxed to the shareholder under §956 for prior years or would have been so taxed but were traced to previously taxed subpart F income.[286]

    b. The shareholder's pro rata share of the CFC's "applicable earnings."[287]

Generally, the "applicable earnings" are the CFC's current and accumulated earnings and profits, less the sum of the following amounts:

    a. Distributions made during the taxable year.

    b. Earnings and profits treated by §959(c)(1) as amounts that either (1) were previously taxed to the U.S. shareholder under §956 or the excess passive assets rules of §956A or (2) would have been taxed under one of these provisions but were traced to previously taxed subpart F income.[288]

---

[283] Reg. §1.956-1T(e)(5)(i).

[284] Reg. §1.956-1(b)(3). See generally Reg. §1.964-1.

[285] As described here, these rules apply for taxable years beginning after September 30, 1993. Pub. L. No. 103-66, §13232, 107 Stat. 312 (1993). The rules for prior years are similar except that they are based on the bases of the U.S. property at the end of the year and E&P adjustments to adjusted basis are not required.

[286] IRC §956(a)(1). More technically, the reduction consists of the earnings and profits described in §959(c)(1)(A), discussed infra ¶68.2.14.

[287] IRC §956(a)(2).

[288] IRC §§956(b)(1), 956A(b). For §956A, see infra ¶68.2.12.

If the CFC has an earnings and profits deficit at the beginning of the taxable year, the deficit is ignored, and "applicable earnings" consists of current earnings and profits, less current distributions and the §959(c)(1) amounts.[289]

U.S. property acquired by the corporation before it became a CFC is generally excluded in applying the foregoing rules, but the amount so excluded cannot exceed the applicable earnings accumulated before the first day the corporation was a CFC.[290] Applicable earnings are reduced both by actual distributions and by the inclusion of amounts in gross income under §§956 and 956A. However, as noted by the legislative history:

> Under the . . . ordering rules for the attribution of actual distributions or income inclusions to years of earnings, earnings from more recent years are treated as distributed or included before earnings from earlier years. Thus, the pre-acquisition earnings, which operate as a limit to the exclusion of certain U.S. property acquired before the foreign corporation became a controlled foreign corporation, will not be treated as distributed or included until actual distributions or income inclusions from the controlled foreign corporation carry out all more recent earnings.[291]

If the corporation ceases to be a CFC during the taxable year, the shareholder's pro rata shares of the relevant items are based on the stock owned on the last day on which the corporation was a CFC, U.S. property is determined only for the quarters ending before that day, and only a ratable share of current earnings and profits is included in applicable earnings.[292]

4. *Exclusion of investments of subpart F income.* A U.S. shareholder's share of the increase in earnings invested in U.S. property is included in the shareholder's gross income, except to the extent the earnings consist of subpart F income that was previously taxed to the shareholder or a prior owner of the shares.[293] Subpart F income, in other words, may be invested in U.S. property without causing it to be taxed a second time to U.S. shareholders. Moreover, earnings invested in U.S. property are treated as consisting first of subpart F income of the current year and, to the extent not distributed or used to cover an increase in earnings invested in U.S. property or excess passive assets during any earlier year, subpart F income of prior years.[294] Earnings invested in U.S. property thus are taxed to U.S. shareholders only when the U.S. investment exceeds subpart F income.

Assume a CFC wholly owned by a domestic corporation (1) has U.S. property of $250 for 1997, but has never had excess passive assets, (2) has earnings and profits of $50 for 1997 and accumulated earnings and profits of $175 at the

---

[289] H.R. Rep. No. 213, 103d Cong., 1st Sess. 637 (Conf. Rep. 1993).

[290] IRC §956(b)(2).

[291] H.R. Rep. No. 213, supra note 289, at 643 n.76.

[292] IRC §§956(b)(3), 956A(e).

[293] IRC §959(a).

[294] Reg. §1.959-1(c). See S. Rep. No. 1881, supra note 13, at 787.

end of 1996, of which $100 were included in the shareholder's gross income under §956 for 1996 and prior years, (3) has subpart F income of $35 for 1997, and (4) distributes $50 to its shareholder during 1997.[295] The 1997 increase in earnings invested in U.S. property is shown in Example 68-1.

Example 68-1
Investment of Subpart F Income in U.S. Property

1. a. U.S. shareholder's ratable share of average U.S. property held by CFC during 1997, over $250

    b. Less undistributed earnings previously taxed as investment in U.S. property   100 $150

2. U.S. shareholder's ratable share of "applicable earnings" (current and accumulated E&P of $225, less current distributions of $50 and less undistributed earnings already taxed under §956 ($100)) $ 75

3. Earnings invested in U.S. property (lesser of line 1 or line 2) $ 75

4. Less exclusion under §959(a) (subpart F income not previously treated as investment of U.S. property or excess passive assets, consisting of current subpart F income) $ 35

5. Amount includable in gross income as earnings invested in U.S. property (line 3, less line 4) $ 40

¶68.2.12 Earnings Invested in Excess Passive Assets

Section 956A, enacted in 1993, repealed in 1996, and effective for CFC taxable years beginning after September 30, 1993, and before 1997, taxes U.S. shareholders on CFC earnings to the extent that the CFC's investments in passive assets exceed 25 percent of all assets.[296] Since subpart F was adopted in 1962, income from passive assets (foreign personal holding company income) has been

---

[295] Id. at 954–55.

[296] See Pub. L. No. 103-66, §13231, 107 Stat. 312 (1993) (§956A applies for taxable years of U.S. shareholders that include last days of CFC taxable years beginning after September 30, 1993); Pub. L. No. 104-188, §1501, 110 Stat. 1755 (1996) (repeal is effective for taxable years of foreign corporations beginning after 1996). See Adess, Angus & Villmow, The Erosion of Deferral: Subpart F After the 1993 Act, 47 Tax Lawyer 933 (1994); Burke, Excess Passive Asset Rules of RRA '93 Require Current Inclusion in Income, 79 J. Tax'n 314 (1993); Gottschalk, Tax Planning Options Under New Section 956A for U.S. Multinationals with Retained Earnings Abroad, 7 Tax Notes Int'l 1319 (Nov. 22, 1993); Stoffregen & Lipeles, The Impact of Section 956A and Related Legislative Changes on U.S. Multinationals, 8 Tax Notes Int'l 1325 (May 11, 1994), reprinted in 63 Tax Notes 751 (May 11, 1994).

taxed to U.S. shareholders as subpart F income.[297] More generally, the rules defining subpart F income are designed to restrict the opportunity to defer U.S. taxation through the use of CFCs to income from active business operations. Under §956, which has also been part of subpart F since 1962, earnings from active business operations are taxed to U.S. shareholders if the CFC invests them in U.S. property, on the theory that the acquisition of U.S. property is equivalent to a repatriation of the earnings to the United States and should therefore have the same consequences as a direct repatriation as a dividend.[298] Section 956A takes matters one step further by taxing U.S. shareholders on earnings accumulated from active business operations if an excessive amount of the CFC's assets are passive. The idea underlying §956A is that deferral of U.S. taxation is justified only so long as the tax-deferred earnings are invested in active business operations; small amounts of holdings of passive assets can be justified as a cushion against the ups and downs of business, but if passive holdings become excessive, accumulated earnings, to the extent of the excess, should be taxed to the U.S. shareholders. Congress chose a fixed percentage—25 percent—as the dividing line between reasonable and excessive holdings of passive assets. According to the House Ways and Means Committee:

> [D]eferral of U.S. tax on income of U.S. persons earned through foreign corporations may tend to favor foreign investment over U.S. investment, and can provide an incentive to engage in certain tax-haven activities. . . . [P]rior enactments that permit deferral of U.S. tax on most types of active business income derived through controlled foreign corporations have been justified as enhancing the competitiveness of U.S.-owned business operations abroad. . . . The committee believes, however, that deferral of U.S. tax on accumulated active business profits is not necessary to maintain the competitiveness of [CFC's] business activities . . . where such accumulated profits are held in the form of excessive accumulations of passive assets. . . . The committee believes that neither [the inclusion of passive income in subpart F income nor the PFIC rules] sufficiently restricts the benefits of deferral in the case of controlled foreign corporations that accumulate excessive quantities of earnings and profits, without reinvesting them in active business assets, and without subjecting them to U.S. income taxation (with proper allowance for foreign tax credits) in the hands of the U.S. shareholders.[299]

The inclusion in a U.S. shareholder's gross income under §956A is the lesser of two amounts. The first amount is the excess of the shareholder's pro rata share of the CFC's "excess passive assets" over the earnings and profits identified in §959(c)(1)(B) as having been previously included in the shareholder's gross income under §956A.[300] The second amount is the shareholder's pro rata share of

---

[297] See supra ¶68.2.4.
[298] See supra ¶68.2.11.
[299] H.R. Rep. No. 111, 103d Cong., 1st Sess. 691 (1993).
[300] IRC §956A(a)(1).

the CFC's "applicable earnings."[301] If the corporation ceases to be a CFC during a taxable year, the U.S. shareholder's pro rata share of the excess passive assets and applicable earnings is determined as of the last day during the taxable year on which the corporation is a CFC.[302]

1. *"Applicable earnings."* Generally, "applicable earnings" consist of current and accumulated earnings and profits from taxable years beginning after September 30, 1993, less the sum of the following amounts:

a. Distributions made during the taxable year.[303]

b. Accumulated earnings and profits identified under §959(c)(1)(B) as amounts that have been included in the shareholder's gross income for prior years under §956A or that would have been included but for the fact that the excess passive assets were treated as investments of previously taxed subpart F income.[304]

c. Accumulated earnings and profits identified under §959(c)(1)(A) as amounts that are or have been included in the shareholder's gross income for the current and prior years under §956 as earnings invested in U.S. property or that would have been so included but for the fact that the U.S. property was treated as an investment of previously taxed subpart F income.

If the CFC has an earnings and profits deficit at the beginning of the taxable year, the accumulated deficit is ignored, and "applicable earnings" consists of current earnings and profits, less current distributions and the §959(c)(1) amounts.[305]

2. *"Excess passive assets."* The term "excess passive assets" means the excess of the CFC's passive assets over 25 percent of its total assets.[306] The passive and total assets figures are averages of the amounts of passive and total assets at the end of the four quarters of the year.[307] Assets are valued at their adjusted bases, as determined for earnings and profits purposes, as of the last days of the four quarters.[308]

Generally, an asset is "passive" if it produces "passive income" or is held for the production of passive income.[309] The term "passive income" includes divi-

---

[301] IRC §956A(a)(2).

[302] IRC §956A(e)(1).

[303] IRC §956A(b). See IRC §956A(e)(3) (if corporation ceases to be CFC during taxable year, current earnings and profits are pro rated, and applicable earnings includes only amount so allocated to period while corporation is CFC).

[304] For §959(c), see infra ¶68.2.14.

[305] H.R. Rep. No. 213, 103d Cong., 1st Sess. 637 (Conf. Rep. 1993).

[306] IRC §956A(c)(1).

[307] However, if the corporation ceases to be a CFC during the year, figures are included only for the quarters ending while the corporation is a CFC. IRC §956A(e)(2).

[308] For earnings and profits rules affecting adjusted basis, see §§316(k) and (n), discussed infra ¶92.1.3.

[309] IRC §956A(c)(2)(A).

dends, interest, royalties, rents, net gains from sales and exchanges of property producing dividends, interest, royalties, or rents, net gains from commodities transactions, and net foreign currency gains.[310] However, U.S. property, as defined for purposes of §956, is considered not passive, regardless of the nature of the property.[311]

In measuring passive and total assets, the CFC is treated as owning intangible property it holds as lessee under leases with terms exceeding 12 months.[312] The CFC's adjusted basis for leased property is deemed to be the "unamortized portion . . . of the present value of the payments under the lease." Also, the adjusted basis of the CFC's total assets is increased by the sum of the corporation's research or experimental expenditures for the taxable year and the preceding two years.[313]

3. *Aggregation rule.* All members of a "CFC group" are treated as one CFC in applying the excess passive assets test, and if this hypothetical CFC has excess passive assets, the excess is allocated among the constituent CFCs in proportion to their applicable earnings.[314] A "CFC group" consists of one or more "chains" of CFCs "connected through stock ownership with a top tier corporation" that is a CFC.[315] The top tier corporation must directly own more than 50 percent, by vote or value, of the stock of at least one other member CFC, and more than 50 percent, by vote or value, of the stock of each member CFC (other than the top tier corporation) must be owned, directly or indirectly, by one or more other members of the group.

Under the CFC group rule, "intercompany stock and obligations generally are disregarded in the determination of excess passive assets."[316] For example, if *FS*, a foreign corporation wholly owned by domestic corporation *DP*, is sole shareholder of *FSS*, another foreign corporation, the *FS* and *FSS* are a CFC group, and their assets are treated as the assets of one corporation, except that stock and debt instruments of *FSS* held by *FS* are eliminated from the aggregate.

The CFC group rule can affect the character of assets as passive or nonpassive. Assume *FSS* makes credit sales of goods to unrelated customers in the ordinary course of an active business and sells its accounts receivable to *FS*. The aggregate of *FS* and *FSS* is both seller of the goods and the holder of the accounts

---

[310] Id. More completely, the definition of "passive income" in the PFIC rules is used for this purpose. For the PFIC definition of "passive income," see §1296(b), discussed ¶68.5.2 text accompanying notes 9–13.

[311] IRC §956A(c)(2)(B). For the term "United States property," see §956(c), discussed supra ¶68.2.11 text accompanying notes 248–78.

[312] IRC §956A(c)(3)(B), incorporating the rule of §1297(d), discussed infra ¶68.5.2 text accompanying notes 23–27.

[313] IRC §956A(c)(3)(C), incorporating the rule of §1297(e), discussed infra ¶68.5.2 text accompanying notes 28–32.

[314] IRC §956A(d)(1).

[315] IRC §956A(d)(2).

[316] H.R. Rep. No. 213, supra note 289, at 639.

receivable. The IRS has ruled that accounts receivable of a seller of goods are not passive assets, even if they bear interest.[317]

If the members of a CFC group have different functional currencies, the adjusted bases of the assets of all group members must be stated in a single currency, "ordinarily the U.S. dollar," as of each measurement date.[318] Translation procedures will be provided by the Treasury, but the legislative history indicates that the spot rate may be used. Alternatively, assets denominated in foreign currencies might be reported at their historical costs in U.S. dollars.

4. *Look-thru rule.* If a CFC is direct or indirect owner of at least 25 percent (by value) of the stock of another corporation, it is treated as owner of a proportionate part of any passive assets held by the other corporation.[319] This look-thru rule has no application within a CFC group. For example, *FS* is not treated as owner of *FSS*'s passive assets under the look-thru rule because *FS* and *FSS* are treated as one corporation under the CFC group rule. However, the look-thru rule applies whenever a member of a CFC group owns 25 percent or more of the stock of a corporation that is not a member of the group. For example, if the stock of another foreign corporation (*FS2*) is owned 35 percent by *FSS* and 65 percent by *DP* (the domestic parent), *FS2* is not a member of the CFC group because *FS* and *FSS* own less than 50 percent of the stock of *FS2*, but *FSS* (and hence the *FS-FSS* group) is treated as owning 25 percent of any passive assets of *FS2*.

¶68.2.13 Taxation of Subpart F Income and Earnings Invested in U.S. Property and Excess Passive Assets

Under §951(a)(1), a U.S. shareholder of a CFC must report as gross income his ratable share of the CFC's subpart F income and increase in earnings invested in U.S. property.

1. *Shareholders subject to inclusion rule.* Section 951(a)(1) applies for a particular taxable year of a foreign corporation only if the corporation is a CFC for an uninterrupted period during the year of at least 30 days. It applies to a particular shareholder only if, on the last day during the year when the corporation is a CFC, the shareholder is a U.S. shareholder and owns some of the CFC's stock, either directly or indirectly through foreign entities.

Indirect ownership must be distinguished from constructive ownership. Whether a U.S. citizen or resident or domestic entity is a U.S. shareholder is determined with a broad set of constructive ownership rules that, for example, treat an individual as owner of stock actually owned by family members and attribute stock between entities and their owners. Under the constructive own-

---

[317] Notice 88-22, 1988-1 CB 489.

[318] H.R. Rep. No. 213, supra note 289, at 640.

[319] IRC §956A(c)(3)(A), incorporating look-thru rule of §1296(c), discussed infra ¶68.5.2 text accompanying notes 33-37.

ership rules, a U.S. person may be constructive owner of stock actually owned by another U.S. person.[320] It would be inappropriate to tax two or more actual or constructive shareholders on the same items of corporate income. A U.S. shareholder is thus taxed under §951(a)(1) on the amounts allocable to shares actually owned and shares owned indirectly through foreign entities, but not shares only owned constructively. Under the indirect ownership rule, stock owned by a foreign entity is attributed ratably to the entity's shareholders, partners, or beneficiaries—successively through a chain of foreign entities, if necessary, until the stock reaches a U.S. person or a nonresident alien.[321]

Assume M and S, parent and child, own 5 and 9 percent, respectively, of the single class of stock of a CFC.[322] M and S are both U.S. shareholders because each is constructive owner of the other's stock, and the total of 14 percent exceeds the 10 percent threshold. M's inclusions under §951(a)(1), however, are based solely on her actual ownership of 5 percent because she is not actual or indirect owner of S's stock. Similarly, S's §951(a)(1) inclusions are based on his 9 percent alone.

2. *Inclusion of subpart F income.* A U.S. shareholder's §951(a)(1) inclusion includes a pro rata share of the CFC's subpart F income.[323] The application of this rule is simplest when one U.S. person holds all of a CFC's stock throughout the taxable year and the shareholder and CFC have the same taxable year. Assume domestic corporation P owns all stock of foreign corporation F, both corporations use the calendar year as their taxable years, and for 1997, F has $50 of subpart F income.[324] The $50 is included in P's taxable income for 1997.

In more complex cases, a U.S. shareholder's pro rata share is determined by assuming the CFC made a distribution ratably to its shareholders.[325] If the corporation was a CFC throughout the entire year, the hypothetical distribution is deemed made on the last day of the year and equals subpart F income for the year. If the corporation was a CFC for only part of the year, the hypothetical distribution takes place on the last day during the year on which the corporation was a CFC, and it equals the portion of the subpart F income for the year that

---

[320] IRC §958(b), discussed supra ¶68.2.2 text accompanying notes 26–32.

[321] IRC §958(a)(2), discussed supra ¶68.2.2 text accompanying notes 23–25.

[322] See S. Rep. No. 1881, supra note 13, at 944.

[323] IRC §951(a)(1)(A)(i). If the CFC was allowed to exclude foreign base company shipping income reinvested in foreign base company shipping operations, any withdrawal of this investment is included ratably in the U.S. shareholder's §951(a)(1) inclusions. IRC §951(a)(1)(A)(iii). The exclusion for reinvestments in foreign base company shipping operations was repealed in 1986. IRC §954(b)(2) (repealed in 1986). The inclusions for withdrawals of these reinvestments, however, continue until excluded amounts have been withdrawn. See supra ¶68.2.7.

Also, until 1975, subpart F income was reduced by amounts invested in less developed countries. Withdrawals of such investments are included in the §951(a)(1) inclusions. IRC §951(a)(1)(A)(ii).

[324] See S. Rep. No. 1881, supra note 13, at 942 Ex. 1.

[325] IRC §951(a)(2)(A).

is ratably attributable to the days during the year when the corporation was a CFC.[326] A U.S. shareholder's pro rata share of subpart F income consists of the portion of the hypothetical distribution that would have been distributed with respect to stock the shareholder owns actually and indirectly through foreign entities on the date of the hypothetical distribution.

Assume a domestic corporation owns all of a foreign corporation's stock on January 1, 1997 (the beginning of the foreign corporation's taxable year); 60 percent of the shares are sold to a nonresident alien on May 26, 1997.[327] If the foreign corporation's subpart F income for 1997 is $100, the domestic corporation must include $40 in gross income under §951(a)(1) for its taxable year including May 26. The foreign corporation ceases to be a CFC on May 26, which is the 146th day of the year. The hypothetical distribution thus occurs on May 26 and its amount is $40 ($146/365$ of $100). In contrast, if the domestic corporation owns 40 percent of the shares at the beginning of 1997 and purchases the remaining 60 percent from a nonresident alien on May 26, the hypothetical distribution occurs on December 31 and is $60 ($219/365$ of $100). As a third case, assume the domestic corporation owns 40 percent at the beginning of 1997, and the remainder is owned by another (but unrelated) domestic corporation, which sells its stock to the first domestic corporation on May 26. The foreign corporation is a CFC for all of 1997, and the hypothetical dividend occurs on December 31 and consists of all of the CFC's subpart F income of $100. The corporation owning the CFC's stock at the end of the year reports the entire amount even though 40 percent of the stock was held for 40 percent of the year by an unrelated corporation.

A U.S. shareholder's pro rata share of subpart F income may be reduced, however, if any portion of the shareholder's stock was acquired during the year and the corporation made a distribution during the year to the prior owner of the stock.[328] The reduction equals the distribution to the prior owner or, if less, the portion of the subpart F income allocable to the stock that is ratably attributable to the time within the year when the taxpayer did not own the stock. For purposes of this rule, gain on sale of the stock is treated as a distribution to the extent §1248 recharacterizes the gain as a dividend.[329]

Assume that at the beginning of 1998, A, a U.S. citizen, owns 20 percent of the stock of Z, a CFC that accounts by the calendar year; on July 1, 1998, A sells the stock to B, also a U.S. citizen; A recognizes gain on the sale, $12 of which is a dividend under §1248.[330] If Z's subpart F income for 1998 is $100, B's inclusion is $10, computed as shown in Example 68-2.

---

[326] See Reg. §1.951-1(f) (U.S. shareholder deemed to hold shares starting with day after day of acquisition and ending with day of disposition).

[327] Reg. §1.951-1(b)(2) Ex. 2.

[328] IRC §951(a)(2)(B).

[329] IRC §951(a)(2)(B) (last sentence) (applicable to dispositions after August 5, 1997). For §1248, see infra ¶68.2.16.

[330] S. Rep. No. 1881, supra note 13, at 943 Ex. 1.

Example 68-2
Adjustments for Dividends to Prior Shareholders

1. Total amount deemed distributed by Z ($12 divided by 20%)	$60
2. Subpart F income allocable to portion of year A held stock (one half of $100)	$50
3. Reduction of B's inclusion (20 percent of lesser of line 1 or 2)	$10
4. B's inclusion (20 percent of $100 of subpart F income less line 3)	$10

3. *Inclusion of earnings invested in U.S. property and excess passive assets.* In addition to the pro rata share of subpart F income, a U.S. shareholder's gross income under §951(a)(1) includes amounts determined under §§956 and 956A if the CFC has earnings invested in U.S. property or excess passive assets. The procedures for determining these amounts are described above.[331]

4. *Special rules for FSCs, foreign investment companies, foreign personal holding companies, and passive foreign investment companies.* If the CFC is also a foreign sales corporation (FSC), the corporation's foreign trade income, which is specially treated under the FSC rules, is excluded in determining the U.S. shareholder's §951(a)(1) inclusions.[332] Moreover, the §951(a)(1) inclusion is wholly abrogated if the CFC is a foreign investment company that has elected under §1247 to distribute at least 90 percent of its income currently and meets various other requirements.[333] On the other hand, if the CFC is also a foreign personal holding company (FPHC) or passive foreign investment company (PFIC), the §951(a)(1) inclusion is determined first and is excluded from any inclusion in the shareholder's gross income under the FPHC or PFIC rules.[334]

5. *Indirect credit.* If a U.S. shareholder is a domestic corporation and is the direct or indirect owner of at least 10 percent of a CFC's voting stock, it is entitled to credit against its U.S. tax for foreign income taxes paid by the CFC with respect to earnings of the CFC taxed to the U.S. shareholder under §951(a)(1). This credit, which is discussed elsewhere in this work,[335] gives the U.S. shareholder the same allowance for the CFC's foreign income taxes that it would have enjoyed in the absence of subpart F if the items taxed under §951(a)(1) had been distributed as dividends.

6. *Individual election to be taxed as corporation.* A U.S. shareholder who is an individual may elect to be taxed on the §951(a)(1) inclusion as though the

---

[331] Supra ¶¶68.2.11, 68.2.12. See Rev. Rul. 90-31, 1990-1 CB 147 (CFC's earnings and profits are not reduced when transferor shareholder's gain is taxed as dividend, in whole or in part, under §1248; instead, earnings and profits are reduced by actual distributions of amounts excluded from transferee's gross income under §959(e)).

[332] IRC §951(e). For FSCs, see supra ¶68.1.4.

[333] IRC §951(c); Reg. §1.951-2. For §1247, see infra ¶68.4.1.

[334] IRC §§951(d), (f). For FPHCs and PFICs, see infra ¶¶68.3 and 68.5.

[335] Infra ¶69.8.1.

shareholder were a corporation.[336] The purpose of the election is to make sure that an individual taxed under §951(a)(1) is not required to pay more tax than he "would have [if he had] invested in an American corporation doing business abroad."[337] If the individual is a U.S. shareholder of more than one CFC, the election applies to the §951(a)(1) inclusions from all of them.

An electing shareholder's tax on §951(a)(1) inclusions is determined under §§11 and 55 as though the includable amounts had been received by a domestic corporation. Generally, the §11 rate structure is applied as though the hypothetical corporate recipient had no other income. If the §951(a)(1) inclusions include less than all of the shareholder's ratable share of the CFCs' current earnings and profits, however, each rate bracket is reduced in size according to the ratio of (1) the §951(a)(1) inclusions to (2) the shareholder's ratable share of the earnings and profits for the taxable year of all CFCs contributing to the inclusions.[338]

An electing shareholder is also entitled to the indirect credit for foreign income taxes paid by the CFC.[339] The credit, like the U.S. tax against which it is allowed, is determined as though the §951(a)(1) inclusions had been received by a domestic corporation.

If a distribution is traced to CFC earnings of a year for which the election is made, the electing shareholder is taxed on the distribution even if, in the absence of the election, the distribution would be a nontaxable distribution of previously taxed earnings.[340] The shareholder must recognize gross income equal to the excess of the distribution over the tax previously paid on the distributed earnings. The distribution is thus treated essentially as though it was first received by the hypothetical domestic corporation that was taxed on the §951(a)(1) inclusion and then redistributed to the individual taxpayer.

Assume a U.S. citizen is sole shareholder of a CFC that has subpart F income for 1997 of $100. The CFC pays $20 of foreign taxes on this income and distributes the remaining $80 to the shareholder. If the shareholder elects to be taxed as a corporation and the U.S. corporate rate for the year is a flat 35 percent, the shareholder's tax on the subpart F income is $15 (precredit tax of $35 less $20 credit for the CFC's foreign income taxes). In addition, the shareholder's gross income includes dividend income of $65 ($80 distribution received less $15 tax on §951(a)(1) inclusion).

The election is made year by year.[341] Once made for a particular year, it may be revoked only with IRS consent.

---

[336] IRC §962(a). See Pollack, Individual Investors in CFCs May Benefit From Electing to Be Taxed as Corporations, 81 J. Tax'n 112 (1994).

[337] S. Rep. No. 1881, supra note 13, at 798.

[338] IRC §962(c).

[339] IRC §962(a)(2).

[340] IRC §962(d). For the tracing rules, see infra ¶68.2.14.

[341] IRC §962(b).

¶68.2.14   Exclusion of Distributions of Previously Taxed Earnings

A distribution received from a CFC is excluded from the shareholder's gross income if it is traced to earnings and profits that were taxed to the shareholder or a prior holder of the shares under §951(a)(1).[342] The exclusion applies whether the earnings are taxed to the shareholder for the current year or a prior year and whether the earnings are taxed as subpart F income or earnings invested in U.S. property or excess passive assets. Also, if gain on a sale of CFC stock is taxed as a dividend under §1248, the earnings and profits included in this constructive dividend are excluded from gross income when actually distributed to a subsequent owner of the stock.[343]

Assume a domestic corporation owns all of the stock of a CFC that has subpart F income and earnings and profits of $100 for 1997, which is the CFC's first year, and the CFC distributes $50 to the shareholder during 1997.[344] The distribution is nontaxable because it comes from subpart F income currently included in the shareholder's gross income. In contrast, if the distribution occurs in 1998, the subpart F income is included in the shareholder's gross income for 1997, but the 1998 distribution is still nontaxable.

To illustrate the exclusion for an amount taxed to a previous owner of the taxpayer's shares, assume X, a U.S. shareholder of a CFC, owns 20 of the 100 outstanding shares of the CFC's stock at the end of 1996; for 1996, the CFC has subpart F income of $100, and X reports its $20 share as gross income under §951(a)(1).[345] In January of 1997, X transfers nine of her shares to Y, and the CFC pays a dividend of $1 per share in June of 1997. Both the $11 received by X and the $9 received by Y are nontaxable distributions of the subpart F income taxed to X for 1996.

Also, income of a lower-tier CFC that is included in a U.S. shareholder's gross income under §951(a)(1) is excluded from the gross income of upper-tier CFCs for purposes of subpart F when the income is distributed through a chain of ownership.[346] Because of this exclusion, the distribution cannot be FPHC income of the upper-tier CFC even though dividends are usually FPHC income and hence FBC and subpart F income. Moreover, the amount of the distribution is transferred out of the distributing CFC's earnings and profits to the distributee CFC's earnings and profits, where it retains its character as previously taxed subpart F income or earnings invested in U.S. property.[347] When the income is distributed up the chain to the U.S. shareholder, the distribution is nontaxable.

Assume domestic corporation P is sole shareholder of foreign corporation $F1$, which owns all of the stock of foreign corporation $F2$; for 1997, $F2$'s only income is

---

[342] IRC §959(a). For information that must be supplied to document an exclusion based on an inclusion in a prior owner's gross income, see Reg. §1.959-1(d).

[343] IRC §959(e). For §1248, see infra ¶68.2.17.

[344] Reg. §1.959-1(b) Ex.

[345] S. Rep. No. 1881, supra note 13, at 960.

[346] IRC §959(b); Reg. §1.959-2.

[347] Reg. §1.959-2(b) Ex. (c).

subpart F income of $100, which it distributes to *F1*.[348] As indirect owner of *F2*'s stock, *P* is taxed under §951(a)(1) on *F2*'s subpart F income. The distribution of this income to *F1* is therefore excluded from *F1*'s gross income, thus blocking its inclusion in *P*'s gross income a second time as FPHC income of *F1*. Also, any investment by *F1* in U.S. property or excess passive assets is traced first to *F1*'s earnings and profits consisting of subpart F income, which include the distribution received from *F2*, and is excluded from *P*'s gross income to this extent. Moreover, *P* can receive a nontaxable distribution from *F1* of the subpart F income *F1* received from *F2*. The results would be the same if the distribution from *F2* to *F1* occurred in a later year, so long as it is traced to *F2*'s 1996 subpart F income.

A distribution excluded from the recipient's gross income reduces the distributing CFC's earnings and profits whether the recipient is a U.S. shareholder or another CFC, but it is not otherwise treated as a dividend.[349] Amounts included in a U.S. shareholder's gross income under §951(a)(1) thus are treated as a special class of earnings and profits from which nontaxable distributions may be made, but once these distributions have occurred, they are removed from the earnings and profits account.[350]

Under rules described above, amounts otherwise taxable to a U.S. shareholder as a result of CFC investments in U.S. property and excess passive assets are included in the shareholder's gross income under §951(a)(1) only to the extent they exceed the portions that can be traced to previously taxed subpart F income.[351] When such an amount is traced to subpart F income, a contemporaneous transfer is made from the second earnings and profits pool (subpart F income) to the first pool (earnings invested in U.S. property and excess passive assets).[352]

For purposes of the foregoing rules, distributions and investments in U.S. property and excess passive assets are traced to particular pools of earnings and profits as follows: Distributions are traced first to the pool consisting of earnings invested in U.S. property and excess passive assets, second to previously taxed subpart F income (to the extent not traced to U.S. property and excess passive assets for prior years), and third to other earnings and profits.[353] A distribution is excluded from gross income unless it is traced to the third category.[354] The sources of distributions are determined before it is decided whether investments in U.S. property and excess passive assets come from previously taxed subpart F income or are included in gross income.[355] The ordering is thus as follows:

---

[348] S. Rep. No. 1881, supra note 13, at 960–61.

[349] IRC §959(d).

[350] See S. Rep. No. 1881, supra note 13, at 961.

[351] Supra ¶68.2.11 text accompanying notes 293–95.

[352] IRC §959(c)(1)(B).

[353] IRC §959(c).

[354] IRC §959(c)(1) (distribution is allocated ratably between §956 amount and §956A amount).

[355] IRC §959(f)(2).

1. Determine the amounts includable under §§956 and 956A (applied without regard to §959).
2. Treat current distributions as made first from these amounts (first for the current year and then for prior years), then from the shareholder's pro rata share of subpart F income (first for the current year and then for prior years), and finally from other earnings and profits.
3. Exclude the current §§956 and 956A amounts from gross income to the extent any subpart F income remains after Step 2.

Assume a CFC is organized at the beginning of 1997 as a wholly owned subsidiary of a domestic corporation.[356] For 1997, the CFC has earnings and profits of $200, of which $100 is subpart F income. The CFC distributes $20 to its shareholder during the year, and it has U.S. property of $50 at the end of the year. Its earnings and profits at year-end are $180 ($200 less $20 distributed), classified as follows:

Invested in U.S. property ($50 less $20 distributed during year)	$ 30
Subpart F income ($100 less $50 deemed invested in U.S. property)	$ 50
Potentially taxable to shareholders ($200 less $80 in other pools and $20 distributed)	$100

The domestic parent is taxed under §951(a)(1) on the $100 of subpart F income. The $50 of earnings invested in U.S. property is not taxed because it is traced to the subpart F income, and the $20 distribution is nontaxable because it is traced to the earnings invested in U.S. property.

Assume the CFC has $300 of earnings and profits for 1998, of which $75 is subpart F income, and a distribution of $250 is made to the domestic parent during 1998. The investment in U.S. property remains at $50 throughout the year.[357] The earnings and profits pools at the end of 1998 are as follows:

Invested in U.S. property ($30 from 1997 and $20 from 1998 less $50 of 1998 distribution)	-0-

---

[356] See S. Rep. No. 1881, supra note 13, at 962.

[357] Nevertheless, absent an exclusion under §959, $20 is taxable under §956 for 1998, computed as the lesser of the following:

1. Shareholder's pro rata share of U.S. property	$ 50
Less earnings in §959(c)(1)(A) pool	30
	$ 20
2. Shareholder's pro rata share of applicable earnings (current and accumulated earnings and profits of $300 and $180, less current distribution of $250 and less $30 of earnings in §959(c)(1) pool)	$200

Subpart F income ($50 from 1997 plus $75 from 1998
less $20 current transfer to earnings invested in U.S.
property and less $105 of 1998 distribution)   -0-
Potentially taxable ($100 from 1997 plus $225 from
1998 less $95 of 1998 distribution) $230

The domestic parent's 1998 gross income includes $75 of subpart F income and $95 of dividends from the third pool.

¶68.2.15 Basis Adjustments

When an amount is included in the gross income of a U.S. shareholder under §951(a)(1), an equal addition is made to the shareholder's adjusted basis.[358] If the U.S. shareholder holds shares of the CFC directly, the addition is made to the basis of those shares. If the CFC's stock is held indirectly through other foreign entities, the addition is made to the basis of the property that causes the taxpayer to be indirect owner, which might be stock of another foreign corporation or an interest in a foreign partnership, trust, or estate. The basis addition is denied, however, if the U.S. shareholder fails to report the gross income as required by §951(a)(1) and this omission is not corrected on audit.

Assume a domestic corporation is sole shareholder of foreign corporation F1, which owns all of the stock of foreign corporation F2; for 1997, §951(a)(1) taxes the domestic parent on $50 of F1's income and $60 of F2's income.[359] Both §951(a)(1) inclusions are added to the parent's basis for its F1 stock.

When a U.S. shareholder receives a tax-free distribution of amounts previously included in gross income under §951(a)(1), the basis of the stock (or the partnership, trust, or estate interest) is reduced by the amount of the distribution.[360] If the nontaxable distribution exceeds the shareholder's basis, the excess is taxed as capital gain.[361]

As explained above, an individual may elect to be taxed as a corporation on §951(a)(1) inclusions.[362] When this election is made, the basis increase for a §951(a)(1) inclusion is limited to the tax paid, and basis is reduced in like amount when the inclusion is distributed.[363] Assume an individual shareholder of a CFC is required to include $100 in gross income under §951(a)(1) and, pursuant to an

---

This increase is traced to the CFC's subpart F income and does not increase the §951(a)(1) inclusion for 1998.

[358] IRC §961(a).

[359] S. Rep. No. 1881, supra note 13, at 966 Exs. 1, 2.

[360] IRC §961(b)(1).

[361] IRC §961(b)(2).

[362] IRC §962, discussed supra ¶68.2.13 text accompanying notes 336–41.

[363] IRC §§961(a), (b)(1).

election to be taxed as a corporation, pays tax of $35 on the inclusion. The individual's stock basis is increased by $35, not $100. If the $100 is distributed, basis is reduced by $35, and the remaining $65 of the distribution is included in gross income as a dividend.

If a U.S. shareholder is indirect owner of CFC stock that is actually owned by another CFC, the shareholding CFC's basis for the stock is increased under the rules described above to reflect the U.S. shareholder's inclusions under §951(a) with respect to its indirect ownership, and this basis is reduced by actual distributions with respect to the stock.[364] Assume domestic corporation DC owns all of the stock of foreign corporation F-1, which owns all of the stock of foreign corporation F-2. If F-2 has subpart F income that is included in DC's gross income under §951(a), F-1's basis for its F-2 stock (as well as DC's basis for its F-1 stock) is increased by the amount so included. If F-2 makes a distribution to F-1, both F-1's basis for the F-2 stock and DC's basis for F-1 stock are reduced by the amount distributed.

¶68.2.16   Gains on Dispositions of CFC Stock

Under §1248(a), gain on a U.S. person's disposition of CFC stock is treated as dividend income to the extent of the earnings and profits attributable to the stock that were accumulated while the taxpayer held the shares.[365] The Senate Finance Committee described the purposes of this rule, enacted in 1962, as follows:

> Under [pre-1963] law, through an ordinary taxable liquidation or sale or exchange, it is possible to bring earnings accumulated by a foreign corporation back to this country merely by paying a capital gains tax on such earnings included in the gain. [The 1962 legislation] has as one of its objectives in the foreign income area the imposition of the full U.S. tax when income earned abroad is repatriated. Full U.S. taxation will occur in the case of the ordinary taxable liquidations or sales or exchanges only if the earnings and profits are in effect taxed as dividends (to the extent of any gain) at the time the funds are brought back to the United States.[366]

Section 1248 was enacted principally to deny the preferential capital gains rate to gain on a sale of CFC stock to the extent the gain represents the selling shareholder's interest in undistributed earnings and profits of the CFC that have not previously been taxed to the shareholder under subpart F. Section 1248,

---

[364] IRC §961(c) (applicable for taxable years of U.S. shareholders beginning after 1997).

[365] IRC §1248(a). See generally Klein, Scope of Section 1248—Dispositions of Stock in a Controlled Foreign Corporation—As Expanded by the Tax Reform Act of 1976, 4 J. Corp. Tax'n 336 (1978); Yoder, Section 1248: Treatment of Gain from the Disposition of Stock in a Controlled Foreign Corporation, 25 Tax Mgmt. Int'l J. 483, 589 (1996).

[366] S. Rep. No. 1881, supra note 13, at 813.

however, has significant effects for taxable years for which no preferential rate is provided for capital gains. For example, while capital losses can be deducted against capital gains, they cannot be offset against a gain that §1248 treats as a dividend. On the other hand, and most importantly, if the selling shareholder is a domestic corporation, the characterization of gain as a dividend may qualify the shareholder for an indirect credit for foreign income taxes paid by the CFC.[367]

1. *Transactions covered.* Section 1248(a) applies to gain on a sale or exchange of CFC stock, including a redemption of such stock or the liquidation of a CFC if the redemption or liquidation is treated as an exchange under §302 or §331. However, §1248 applies to a disposition of stock of a foreign corporation only if, immediately before the sale, exchange, redemption, or liquidation or at some time during the preceding five years, (1) the taxpayer owned at least 10 percent of the corporation's voting stock, either directly or indirectly through other foreign entities, and (2) the corporation was then a CFC.[368] In the discussion below, the term "CFC stock" is used when these requirements are met or would be met if a disposition occurred at a particular time.

Normally, §1248(a) applies only if the property directly disposed of is CFC stock. However, if a domestic corporation is "formed or availed of principally for the holding, directly or indirectly," of CFC stock, a disposition of stock of the domestic corporation is deemed to include a disposition of the CFC stock that is indirectly held by the taxpayer through the domestic corporation.[369] Assume a U.S. citizen organizes domestic corporation D to hold stock of foreign corporation F. If the F stock is CFC stock, a sale of the D stock is treated as a sale of the F stock, and §1248(a) may apply.

A related rule applies when a domestic corporation owns CFC stock and a shareholder exchanges stock of the domestic corporation for stock of the CFC.[370] The stock received in the exchange is treated as though it had been issued to the domestic corporation and the domestic corporation had then transferred it to the shareholder in a distribution in redemption or liquidation. The domestic corporation usually recognizes gain or loss on the constructive distribution, either under the general rules for corporate distributions or under §1248(f), discussed below; §1248(a) usually applies to any gain.

Normally, §1248(a) only applies to gain that is recognized apart from §1248. Section 1248(f), however, overrides some nonrecognition rules by requiring that gain be recognized on certain distributions of CFC stock by domestic corporations. Specifically, although §337 generally provides nonrecognition for liquidating distributions by a subsidiary corporation to its parent, gain must be recognized under §1248(f) where the liquidating corporation is a domestic corporation

---

[367] For the indirect credit, see infra ¶69.8.1.
[368] IRC §1248(a)(2).
[369] IRC §1248(e).
[370] IRC §1248(i).

and the property distributed is CFC stock.[371] Section 1248(f) also requires that a domestic corporation recognize gain on a distribution of CFC stock to shareholders pursuant to a plan of reorganization, even though §361(c)(1) provides nonrecognition for reorganization distributions of other kinds of property.[372] When §1248(f) applies, gain is recognized and characterized as a dividend in an amount equal to the §1248(a) dividend the distributing corporation would have recognized if it had instead sold the CFC stock for a price equal to its fair market value.[373]

In both contexts, however, the distribution is excepted from §1248(f) if the distributee (1) is also a domestic corporation, (2) succeeds to the distributing corporation's holding period for the CFC stock, and (3) would be subject to §1248(a) on a sale of the stock immediately after the distribution.[374] The purpose of §1248(f) is to ensure that tax-free distributions not be an avenue for escaping the §1248(a) dividend, and the exception covers cases where this backstop is not needed because the distributee steps into the distributing corporation's shoes for purposes of §1248(a).

Neither §1248(a) nor §1248(f) applies if, apart from §1248, gain on a disposition of CFC stock is recognized and is characterized as a dividend, ordinary income, or short-term capital gain.[375] A corporation's distribution of CFC stock in a redemption of its own stock is also excepted from §1248 if §303 applies to the redemption.[376]

2. *Measuring §1248 dividend.* The §1248 dividend equals the gain recognized on the sale, exchange, redemption, or liquidation or, if less, the earnings and profits attributable to the stock sold or exchanged.[377] The restriction of the §1248 dividend to allocable earnings and profits, however, applies only if the taxpayer establishes the amount of earnings and profits.[378]

The earnings and profits allocable to the stock disposed of consist of a pro rata share of the earnings that were accumulated (1) after 1962, (2) while the taxpayer held the stock, and (3) while the corporation was a CFC.[379] Assume a domestic corporation purchases 35 shares of a foreign corporation's stock at the beginning of year 1, when the foreign corporation's other shareholders are a U.S. citizen (10 shares) and a nonresident alien (55 shares).[380] The domestic corpora-

---

[371] See infra ¶93.6.1 for §337.

[372] For §361(c)(1), see infra ¶94.4.3.

[373] IRC §1248(f)(1).

[374] IRC §1248(f)(2).

[375] IRC §1248(g)(2).

[376] IRC §1248(g)(1). For §303, which provides capital gains treatment to the shareholder where stock is redeemed to pay death taxes and estate administration expenses, see ¶93.3.

[377] IRC §1248(a).

[378] IRC §1248(h).

[379] IRC §1248(a).

[380] See S. Rep. No. 1881, supra note 13, at 1005 Ex. 3.

tion purchases 10 of the nonresident alien's shares at the beginning of year 2, purchases the 10 shares of the U.S. citizen at the beginning of year 3, and at the beginning of year 4, sells all of its stock at a gain of $400. The foreign corporation has earnings and profits of $100 for each of the years 1 through 3. The earnings and profits attributable to the domestic corporation's shareholdings include none of year 1's earnings because the foreign corporation does not become a CFC until the beginning of year 2 (when the aggregate ownership of the domestic corporation and the U.S. citizen goes from 45 percent to 55 percent). The §1248(a) dividend on the domestic corporation's stock sale is $100, consisting of 45 percent of the $100 of earnings and profits for year 2 and 55 percent of the $100 of earnings for year 3. The remaining $300 of the gain on the sale is capital gain.

A CFC's earnings and profits are computed by the rules applied in determining the earnings and profits of a domestic corporation,[381] but several exclusions are provided for earnings accumulated in particular circumstances. Most importantly, earnings accumulated from income included in the taxpayer's gross income under §951(a)(1) are excluded from earnings and profits for this purpose unless they were distributed before the stock disposition.[382]

Assume a domestic corporation purchases all of the stock of a foreign corporation (CFC) for $100 at the beginning of year 1 and sells the stock for $140 at the beginning of year 3. For year 1, all of the CFC's earnings and profits of $10 are subpart F income and are included in the domestic corporation's gross income under §951(a)(1). For year 2, the CFC has earnings and profits of $15, none of which is taxed to the shareholder under §951(a)(1), and it distributes $5 to the shareholder. The distribution is nontaxable to the shareholder because it is traced to the subpart F income taxed to it for year 1.[383] The shareholder's gain on the sale is $35 (amount realized is $140; adjusted basis is $105—cost of $100 plus subpart F income of $10 less nontaxable distribution of $5).[384] The earnings and profits allocable to the stock are $15 (earnings and profits of $25 for period stock held, less $5 distributed and less $5 remaining undistributed from amounts included in gross income under §951(a)(1)). The §1248 dividend is therefore $15 (lesser of gain of $35 or earnings allocable to stock of $15), and the remaining $20 of the gain is capital gain.

Other exclusions from earnings and profits include:

a. Earnings previously included in the taxpayer's gross income under the rules for foreign investment companies that distribute substantially all income currently.[385]

b. Earnings previously included in the taxpayer's gross income under the rules for passive foreign investment companies (PFICs) that are also

---

[381] IRC §1248(c)(1).

[382] IRC §1248(d)(1).

[383] See IRC §959, discussed supra ¶68.2.14.

[384] For the basis adjustments, see supra ¶68.2.15.

[385] IRC §1248(d)(5). For foreign investment companies, see infra ¶68.4.1.

qualified electing funds, exclusive of the portions of these earnings that have been distributed to the taxpayer in nontaxable distributions of previously taxed income.[386]

c. Earnings accumulated from income that was effectively connected with a U.S. trade or business of the CFC if the effectively connected income tax on the income was neither reduced nor eliminated by treaty.[387]

d. Earnings accumulated from the foreign trade income of a foreign sales corporation (FSC), except that this exclusion does not encompass the portion of the foreign trade income that does not qualify for a special tax exemption allowed to FSCs and is not subject to the effectively connected income tax in the FSC's hands.[388]

If the stock disposed of caused the taxpayer to be treated as indirect owner of stock of one or more other CFCs (lower-tier CFCs), the earnings and profits allocated to the stock disposed of may include earnings and profits of the lower-tier CFCs.[389] A lower-tier CFC is covered by this rule only if, at some time during the preceding five years, (1) the taxpayer owned at least 10 percent of the lower-tier CFC's voting stock and (2) the corporation was a CFC.[390] In applying the 10 percent threshold, both stock owned by the taxpayer directly and stock owned indirectly through foreign entities is counted.[391] When a lower-tier CFC is covered, the portion of its earnings and profits that is allocated to the stock disposed of by the taxpayer is determined as follows:

a. Earnings and profits accumulated during a particular period are included only if, during that period, (1) the taxpayer held the stock disposed of and through this stock was indirect owner of stock of the lower-tier CFC and (2) the lower-tier corporation was a CFC.[392]

b. Earnings for periods meeting these requirements are included only to the extent they are ratably attributable to stock of the lower-tier CFC that the taxpayer then owned indirectly through its ownership of the stock sold or exchanged.[393]

c. Stock owned indirectly in the past but not at the time of the §1248 transaction is not counted unless the taxpayer's indirect ownership existed at some time during the preceding five years.

d. The earnings attributed to stock indirectly owned during the preceding

---

[386] IRC §1248(d)(7). For PFICs, see infra ¶68.5.

[387] IRC §1248(d)(4).

[388] IRC §1248(d)(6). The exclusion is also denied for accumulations from foreign trade income earned by the performance of engineering or architectural services for foreign construction projects. For FSCs, see supra ¶68.1.4.

[389] IRC §1248(c)(2).

[390] IRC §1248(c)(2)(B).

[391] For indirect ownership, see supra ¶68.2.2 text accompanying notes 23-25.

[392] IRC §1248(c)(2)(D).

[393] IRC §1248(c)(2)(C).

five years but not at the time of the §1248 disposition may not exceed the excess of the stock's fair market value over its cost immediately before the taxpayer ceased being the indirect owner.

3. *Taxing §1248 dividend.* The §1248 dividend is included in gross income as a dividend. If the taxpayer is a domestic corporation, it is allowed credit under §902 for foreign income taxes paid by the CFC in the same manner as if the taxpayer had actually received a cash dividend equal to the §1248 dividend.[394] Assume a domestic corporation recognizes gain of $400 on a sale of CFC stock, and $100 of the gain is a dividend under §1248(a); the dividend is drawn from an earnings and profits pool of $400, consisting of pretax income of $500 on which the CFC paid foreign income taxes of $100.[395] The domestic corporation is entitled to an indirect credit under §902 of $25 (dividend of $100 multiplied by ratio of CFC's post-1986 foreign income taxes ($100) to its post-1986 undistributed earnings ($400)). It has dividend income of $125 (sum of §1248(a) dividend of $100 and $25 gross-up under §78) and a capital gain of $300 ($400 gain on sale less $100 characterized by §1248(a)).

A ceiling is imposed on the tax on the §1248 dividend if the taxpayer is an individual and the stock disposed of is a capital asset that the taxpayer held for more than one year. The purpose of the ceiling is to ensure that the shareholder is left after taxes with no less than he would have had if the CFC had been fully taxed on its income, with credit for foreign taxes on the income, and the shareholder paid only a capital gains tax on the earnings remaining after the corporate tax.[396] The ceiling has a meaningful effect only when capital gains are taxed at a preferential rate; when capital gains are taxed at the same rate as ordinary income (including dividends), a corporate tax plus an individual capital gains tax on what remains after the corporate tax cannot be less than an individual ordinary income tax on the entire amount.

The ceiling consists of the sum of two amounts. The first is a portion of the U.S. taxes the CFC would have paid if the CFC had been taxed as a domestic corporation for all years after 1962 when the corporation was a CFC and the taxpayer held the stock. This hypothetical tax is applied to all income of the corporation for these periods with the exception of amounts taxed to shareholders under §951(a)(1) and amounts distributed before the taxpayer's stock disposition. The hypothetical tax is reduced by a credit for all foreign income taxes paid by the CFC on the income included in the hypothetical tax base.[397] The first

---

[394] For §902, see infra ¶69.8.1.

[395] See S. Rep. No. 1881, supra note 13, at 1005 Ex. 3.

[396] IRC §1248(b). See S. Rep. No. 1881, supra note 13, at 813 (without the ceiling, "the individual might be treated much worse than if the corporation had been a domestic corporation subject to the U.S. corporate tax, against which foreign tax credits could be taken, and then the balance distributed and taxed to the individual at capital gains rates").

[397] See IRC §1248(h) (§1248(b) inapplicable unless taxpayer establishes amount of these foreign income taxes).

component of the ceiling is the portion of the hypothetical tax, after the foreign tax credit, that is ratably allocable to the stock disposed of.

The second component is the addition to the taxpayer's tax for the year that results from including in gross income as long-term capital gain an amount equal to the excess of the §1248(a) gain over the first component. The sum of the two components approximates the U.S. taxes that would have been collected in the absence of §1248 if the CFC had been fully taxed on all of its income.

¶68.2.17　CFC's Taxable Year

If more than 50 percent of a CFC's stock, by voting power or value, is owned by one U.S. shareholder, the CFC must adopt the same taxable year as the shareholder or a taxable year beginning one month earlier.[398] According to the IRS, this rule, enacted in 1989, is intended

> to eliminate the deferral of income and, therefore, the understatement in income, by United States shareholders of certain controlled foreign corporations and foreign personal holding companies . . . Deferral results when certain income earned by these corporations is subject to United States income tax in a taxable year of the United States shareholder subsequent to the taxable year during which it was earned. The elimination of deferral is accomplished by requiring a specified foreign corporation to conform its taxable year to the required year, which is generally the majority U.S. shareholder year . . .[399]

---

[398] IRC §§898(a), (b)(1), (2). This rule, which also applies to foreign personal holding companies (IRC §898(b)(1)), is applicable for taxable years beginning after July 10, 1989. Pub. L. No. 101-239, §7401(d), 103 Stat. 2106 (1989).

The usual definition of "U.S. shareholder" applies for this purpose, except that if the CFC has related person insurance income, any person treated as a U.S. shareholder under the related person insurance rules is similarly treated under the rules described here. IRC §898(b)(3)(A); Prop. Reg. §1.898-2(b)(3)(ii). See supra ¶68.2.2 text accompanying notes 21–32 for the term U.S. shareholder and ¶68.2.3 text accompanying notes 37–43 for related person insurance income.

When the rule requires a change in a CFC's taxable year (e.g., on a U.S. shareholder's acquisition of a majority interest), IRS consent to the change must be obtained unless the change is made for the year including July 10, 1989. H.R. Rep. No. 386, 101st Cong., 2d Sess. 588 (Conf. Rep. 1989). The proposed regulations would allow the change to be deferred until the first year for which some amount is includable in the U.S. shareholder's gross income under subpart F or the foreign personal holding company rules. Prop. Reg. §1.898-1(c). For procedures for making the required change, see Prop. Reg. §§1.898-4(a), (b); Rev. Proc. 90-26, 1990-1 CB 512. The added tax resulting from a change required by this rule can sometimes be spread over four years. Pub. L. No. 101-239, supra, §7401(d)(2)(C); Prop. Reg. §1.898-4(d).

[399] INTL-848-89, 1993-1 CB 831, 832.

Both actual and constructive ownership are counted in applying the 50 percent test,[400] and the test thus may be satisfied by more than one U.S. shareholder. The test is normally applied only on the first day of the CFC's taxable year, but the IRS has proposed regulations that would require the test to be reapplied on any subsequent day during the year when the CFC has a new majority shareholder.[401]

The application of the taxable year rule is simplest if the same taxable year is used by all U.S. shareholders meeting the 50 percent test and all other U.S. shareholders whose stock is constructively owned by U.S. shareholders meeting the test. In this case, the CFC must use either the common taxable year of these U.S. shareholders or a year beginning one month earlier.[402] If these U.S. shareholders do not have a common taxable year, the CFC's taxable year is determined under regulations yet to be issued.[403]

¶68.3 FOREIGN PERSONAL HOLDING COMPANIES

¶68.3.1 Introductory

A U.S. shareholder of a foreign personal holding company (FPHC) must annually include in gross income as a dividend his share of the corporation's undistributed FPHC income. In recommending the 1937 legislation by which the FPHC rules were enacted, the House Ways and Means Committee said:

[F]oreign personal holding companies have afforded one of the most flagrant loopholes for tax avoidance [because they pay no tax on their foreign earnings and under pre-1937 law, their shareholders were not taxed on the earnings until repatriated by dividend distributions]. The use of such corporations has greatly increased within the last few years. . . . On account of

---

[400] IRC §898(b)(2)(B). For constructive ownership, see supra ¶68.2.2 text accompanying notes 26–32.

[401] IRC §898(c)(1)(C)(ii); Prop. Reg. §1.898-3(a)(5). The proposed regulations also include an anti-abuse rule, allowing the IRS to apply the test on any other day if the U.S. shareholders "engage in a transaction (or transactions) that has as its principal purpose the avoidance of the principles" of these rules. Prop. Reg. §1.898-3(a)(5)(v).

[402] IRC §898(c)(1). For the election to use a taxable year beginning one month earlier than the taxable year of the U.S. shareholders, see Prop. Reg. §1.898-3(a)(2).

For complications arising when this rule requires a CFC to use a taxable year for U.S. tax purposes that differs from the year used in computing tax liability under foreign law, see Prop. Reg. §1.898-4(c); INTL-848-89, supra note 399, at 833 (since foreign income tax accrues on last day of foreign-tax taxable year, different U.S. year can result in mismatch between U.S. taxation of CFC income and credit for foreign income taxes on that income).

[403] Under the proposed regulations, the required year in this situation is the taxable year that "results in the least aggregate deferral of income to all United States shareholders." Prop. Reg. §1.898-3(a)(4).

lack of direct jurisdiction over such companies, substantial difficulties have been encountered [in fashioning legislation to plug the loophole.] Your committee is of the opinion that it is justifiable on all grounds, including constitutional grounds, to provide for a method of taxation which will reach the shareholders who own stock in such companies and over whom the United States has jurisdiction. A new method of taxation is therefore proposed ... which treats the income of the foreign corporate entity as the income of the shareholders within the jurisdiction of the United States and requires them to report as their income the undistributed net income of such foreign personal holding companies.[1]

Forty-seven years later, Congress reaffirmed that the FPHC rules "serve an important purpose in removing the tax incentive to shift assets offshore, often to tax havens."[2] The rules' importance, however, was diminished by the enactment in 1962 of subpart F, which taxes U.S. shareholders on certain classes of earnings of controlled foreign corporations (CFCs).[3] Subpart F and the FPHC rules often apply to the same corporations, and passive investment income is a target of both regimes. A further erosion of the importance of FPHC status resulted from the addition in 1984 of a rule that whenever subpart F and the FPHC rules would both include the same item in a U.S. shareholder's gross income, the item is included under subpart F, not the FPHC rules.[4]

¶68.3.2 Definition of "Foreign Personal Holding Company"

The FPHC regime applies only if a foreign corporation is an FPHC for a particular taxable year, and this is so only if the corporation meets two tests for the year—a gross income requirement and a stock ownership requirement.

1. *Gross income requirement.* The gross income test is met if at least 60 percent of the corporation's gross income for the year is FPHC income.[5] Once the corporation is an FPHC for any year, however, the 60 percent threshold is lowered to 50 percent for subsequent years, except that it returns to 60 percent if (1) the stock ownership requirement is not met at any time during a taxable year or (2) FPHC income is less than 50 percent of gross income for each of three consecutive years. The 50 percent rule is provided "to prevent companies from

---

[1] H.R. No. 1546, 75th Cong., 1st Sess., reprinted in 1939-1 CB (Pt. 2) 704, 713. The courts confirmed Congress's belief that the FPHC scheme is constitutional. See, e.g., Eder v. CIR, 138 F2d 27 (2d Cir. 1943).

[2] Staff of Joint Comm. on Tax'n, 98th Cong., 2d Sess., General Explanation of the Revenue Provisions of the Deficit Reduction Act of 1984 at 440 (Comm. Print 1984) [hereinafter 1984 Bluebook].

[3] For subpart F, see supra ¶68.2.

[4] IRC §951(d), discussed infra ¶68.3.3 text accompanying note 67.

[5] IRC §552(a)(1).

going in and out of the foreign personal holding company classification merely by small changes in the character of their income."[6]

a. *Gross income.* A foreign corporation's gross income is determined for this purpose as though it were a domestic corporation and a personal holding company.[7] Items from foreign sources are therefore included in applying the gross income test, even if they are not effectively connected with a U.S. trade or business.[8] The object of the FPHC rules is to tax U.S. shareholders as though they owned the corporate assets directly. Since a U.S. person is taxed on worldwide income, an FPHC's gross income must also include worldwide income.[9]

Moreover, if the corporation is a shareholder of another FPHC, its gross income includes portions of the income of the other FPHC.[10] This rule is provided "in order to prevent the use of a chain of corporations to avoid [the] statute."[11] The amount included in the corporation's gross income is determined as though the other FPHC distributed its undistributed FPHC income to shareholders on the last day of its taxable year.[12] If the taxable years of the two corporations are not congruent, the relevant year of the lower-tier FPHC is the year ending within the upper-tier corporation's taxable year. If more than two FPHCs are assembled in a chain, this rule is applied successively until the undistributed FPHC income of all other FPHCs is attributed to the upper-tier FPHC.[13]

b. *FPHC income.* Dividends, interest, and annuities usually are FPHC income.[14] If the corporation is a shareholder of another FPHC and its gross income includes a constructive dividend from the other FPHC under a rule described above,[15] the constructive dividend is FPHC income. Assume a foreign

---

[6] H.R. No. 1546, supra note 1, at 714.

[7] IRC §555(a). For personal holding companies, see infra ¶95.2.

[8] H.R. No. 1546, supra note 1, at 714; Reg. §1.555-1. If the corporation owns stock of a controlled foreign corporation (CFC), dividends from the CFC are excluded from gross income in determining the application of the FPHC rules to a U.S. shareholder who is also a U.S. shareholder of the CFC if the dividends are distributed from amounts taxed to the shareholder under subpart F. IRC §959(b). For distributions of amounts taxed under subpart F, see supra ¶68.2.14.

[9] H.R. No. 1546, supra note 1, at 714-15.

[10] IRC §§552(a)(1), 555(c)(2). See Reg. §1.555-2.

[11] H.R. No. 1546, supra note 1, at 715.

[12] IRC §555(b). If the lower-tier FPHC does not meet the stock ownership requirement on the last day of its taxable year, the constructive dividend is deemed distributed on the last day during the year when this requirement is met, and it equals the portion of the undistributed FPHC income that is ratably allocable to the portion of the year from the beginning through the last day on which the stock ownership test is met. For illustrations of the computation of the constructive dividend, see Reg. §1.555-2(b).

[13] Reg. §1.555-2(a).

[14] IRC §553(a)(1). See Rev. Rul. 72-527, 1972-2 CB 456 (municipal bond interest not FPHC income because it is not gross income).

[15] IRC §555(b), discussed supra text accompanying notes 10-13.

corporation has gross income of $50 for a particular year, consisting of $35 from manufacturing operations and $15 of interest; the corporation owns 90 percent of the shares of another foreign corporation that is an FPHC and has undistributed FPHC income of $100 for the year.[16] The manufacturing corporation is also an FPHC because its gross income, including the constructive dividend from the other FPHC, is $140 ($50 actually and constructive dividend of $90), and more than 60 percent of this gross income ($105 of $140 or 75 percent) is FPHC income.

An exclusion is provided, however, for some dividends and interest from related foreign corporations that are not FPHCs.[17] The exclusion applies only if the payor of the dividends or interest (1) is a corporation organized under the laws of the same foreign country as the recipient corporation, (2) uses a substantial part of its assets in a trade or business in that country, (3) is a related person with respect to the recipient,[18] and (4) is not itself an FPHC.[19] This exclusion is allowed because "there appears to be no shifting of income to a tax haven when a foreign personal holding company receives interest or dividends from a related corporation organized and operating in the same country."[20] When applicable, the exclusion is restricted to the portion of the dividends or interest that is not attributable to the payor's FPHC income.

FPHC income generally includes royalties, including mineral, oil and gas, copyright, and patent royalties.[21] An exclusion is allowed, however, for "active business computer software royalties."[22]

Rents are also FPHC income unless they account for 50 percent or more of gross income.[23] The 50 percent rule is provided "principally so as not to interfere with bona fide and legitimate operating companies whose business consist[s] of the ownership and operation of office buildings, apartment houses, etc."[24] Regardless of the 50 percent rule, however, rents are FPHC income if (1) a person owning 25 percent or more of the corporation's stock is the lessee, a sublessee of the corporation's lessee, or entitled to use the property through any other ar-

---

[16] H.R. No. 1546, supra note 1, at 716.

[17] IRC §552(c)(1).

[18] The term "related person" includes any corporation controlled by or controlling the recipient or controlled by the same persons as the recipient; control is defined as ownership of more than 50 percent of the stock, by either voting power or value. IRC §954(d)(3), discussed supra ¶68.2.5 text accompanying notes 103–06.

[19] IRC §§552(c)(2), 954(c)(3)(A)(i).

[20] 1984 Bluebook, supra note 2, at 441.

[21] IRC §553(a)(1); Reg. §1.553-1(b)(1).

[22] IRC §553(a)(1).

[23] IRC §553(a)(7). Rents include all "compensation, however designated, for the use of, or right to use, property." Id.

[24] H.R. No. 1546, supra note 1, at 708.

rangement and (2) the corporation has FPHC income other than rents exceeding 10 percent of gross income.[25]

Unless the corporation is a regular dealer in stocks or securities, FPHC income includes any excess of gains over losses on sales and exchanges of stocks and securities during the taxable year.[26] An excess of losses over gains on such sales diminishes neither gross income nor FPHC income.

An excess of gains over losses from futures transactions in commodities is also FPHC income.[27] Only gains and losses from transactions on or subject to the rules of a board of trade or commodity exchange are included. Also, gain on a futures transaction is excluded if the corporation is a "producer, processor, merchant, or handler of the commodity" and the gain arises "out of a bona fide hedging transaction . . . reasonably necessary to the conduct of its business in the manner in which such business is customarily and usually conducted by others."[28]

If the corporation is a beneficiary of a trust or estate, FPHC income includes any income of the trust or estate that is included in the corporation's gross income and any gain on a sale of the corporation's interest in the trust or estate.[29] This rule is intended to prevent the FPHC rules from being "circumvented by creating a trust which pays its income to the corporation."[30]

Finally, compensation for personal services performed by the corporation is FPHC income if (1) the services are performed under a contract that either designates the individual who is to perform the service or gives a person other than the corporation the right to designate that individual and (2) the compensation is for the services of an individual who owns 25 percent or more (by value) of the corporation's stock.[31] Amounts received on a sale or other disposition of such a contract are also FPHC income. These rules are principally intended to cover the situation "where an individual with unique talents, whose compensation for personal services was large, formed a corporation which contracted with him for his services at a relatively modest figure, and then contracted out his services with third persons at a much higher figure."[32]

---

[25] IRC §553(a)(6). The user's stock ownership is determined with constructive ownership and other rules found in §554, discussed below in the text accompanying notes 33–38.

[26] IRC §§553(a)(2), (b)(1). See US v. Ross, 368 F2d 455 (2d Cir. 1966) (corporation found to be investor or speculator rather than dealer).

[27] IRC §§553(a)(3), (b)(2).

[28] IRC §553(a)(3).

[29] IRC §553(a)(4).

[30] H.R. No. 1546, supra note 1, at 707.

[31] IRC §553(a)(5). An individual's stock ownership is determined with constructive ownership and other rules found in §554, discussed below in the text accompanying notes 33–38.

[32] H.R. No. 1546, supra note 1, at 707.

2. *Stock ownership requirement.* The stock ownership test is met if, at any time during the taxable year, five or fewer U.S. citizens or residents own more than 50 percent of the corporation's stock.[33] Stock ownership is measured by voting power or value, whichever gives U.S. citizens and residents the largest proportionate interest.

Also, stock ownership is determined with a battery of constructive ownership and other rules. Stock owned by an entity is treated as owned proportionately by its shareholders, partners, or beneficiaries, and in the case of a chain of entities, this rule is applied repeatedly until the stock is attributed to individuals.[34] An individual is constructive owner of stock owned by the individual's family (including spouse, ancestors, lineal descendants, brothers, and sisters), but stock constructively owned under the family rule may not be reattributed to another person by a second application of this rule.[35] An individual who is a member of a partnership is constructive owner of stock owned by other partners.[36] The holder of an option to acquire stock is treated as the owner of the stock, and stock constructively owned under this rule may be reattributed to other persons by another application of the constructive ownership rules.[37]

Securities convertible into stock are treated as stock, even if the conversion privilege is not exercisable until a future year, but only if the effect is to cause the stock ownership requirement to be met.[38] Moreover, securities convertible at an

[33] IRC §552(a)(2).

[34] IRC §554(a)(1).

[35] IRC §§554(a)(2), (5). Stock owned by a nonresident alien is not attributed under the family rule to a U.S. citizen or resident unless the citizen or resident is the shareholder's spouse or owns stock of the corporation apart from the family rule. IRC §554(c)(1); 1984 Bluebook, supra note 2, at 440–41. Assume a brother and sister own 40 percent and 60 percent of the stock of a foreign corporation. If the brother is a U.S. citizen and the sister is a nonresident alien, the stock ownership requirement is met because the brother, actually owning some stock on his own, is constructive owner of the sister's stock. On the other hand, if both shareholders are nonresident aliens but a third sibling is a U.S. citizen, none of the stock is attributed to the citizen sibling because she owns no stock apart from the family rule. This limitation does not apply to foreign trusts and estates, even though they are generally classified as nonresident aliens for other purposes. See Miller's Est. v. CIR, 43 TC 760 (1965) (nonacq.) (for year prior to 1984 enactment of foregoing rules, nonresident alien's stock not attributed to U.S. citizen or resident under family rule).

[36] This rule may not be used to attribute stock owned by a foreign partner to a partner who is a U.S. citizen or resident unless the latter owns stock of the corporation apart from the partner rule. IRC §554(c)(2); 1984 Bluebook, supra note 2, at 442.

[37] IRC §554(a)(3). An individual who has an option to acquire stock of a family member is constructive owner of the stock under the option rule, not the family rule, and the stock may therefore be reattributed to a family member of the optionee under the family rule. IRC §554(a)(6).

[38] IRC §554(b). Similarly, in determining whether a services performer or a user of the corporation's property owns at least 25 percent of the corporation's stock for purposes of §553(a)(5) or (6), convertible securities are treated as stock only if the result is to push the services performer or user over the 25 percent threshold. For §§553(a)(5) and (6), see supra text accompanying notes 25 and 31.

earlier date may be treated as stock, while securities convertible at later dates are not, if the result is to make the corporation an FPHC.

3. *Tax-exempt organizations and foreign banks.* Even if the gross income and stock ownership requirements are both met, a foreign corporation is not an FPHC if it is a tax-exempt organization or qualifies under an exemption for foreign banks. The exemption for tax-exempt organizations applies if the foreign corporation qualifies for exemption from tax under §501 or is an exempt farmers' cooperative, shipowners' protection and indemnity association, political organization, or home-owners association.[39] Under the bank exemption, a corporation "organized and doing business under the banking and credit laws of a foreign country" is not an FPHC unless it is "formed or availed of for the purpose of evading or avoiding United States income taxes which would otherwise be imposed upon its shareholders."[40] The bank exemption applies only if the lack of tax avoidance purpose is annually certified by the IRS and a copy of the certificate is included with the shareholder's return.[41]

¶68.3.3 Taxation of U.S. Shareholders

The U.S. shareholders of an FPHC must report as dividends their ratable shares of the corporation's undistributed FPHC income. According to the House Ways and Means Committee:

> It is believed that in the ordinary case the stock of a foreign personal holding company is owned by the American individual (including the members of his family) for whom the corporation was created as a foreign "incorporated pocketbook." However, the set-up is not always so simple and in some instances the tax avoidance plan may involve a division of the stock of the foreign company among controlled domestic corporations, partnerships, estates, and trusts. For that reason, and since all such controlled domestic interests are within the jurisdiction of the United States, [the rule taxing undistributed FPHC income] applies not only to citizens or residents of the United States who are shareholders in the foreign personal holding company but also to any domestic corporation, partnership, estate, or trust which may be a shareholder therein.[42]

1. *Undistributed FPHC income.* An FPHC's undistributed FPHC income consists of its taxable income, subject to various adjustments and reduced by a

---

[39] IRC §552(b)(1).

[40] IRC §552(b)(2). See Rev. Rul 82-209, 1982-2 CB 157 (corporation organized under banking laws of foreign country failed to qualify for exception where it made only one loan during taxable year).

[41] For the certification procedure, see Reg. §1.552-4(b). For the requirement that a copy of the certificate be attached to each U.S. shareholder's return, see Reg. §1.552-5.

[42] H.R. No. 1546, supra note 1, at 717.

deduction for dividends paid.[43] As noted above, the FPHC's gross income includes income from both domestic and foreign sources, and taxable income thus also consists of worldwide income. Moreover, gross income includes constructive dividends from other FPHCs of which the taxpayer FPHC is a shareholder.[44]

Undistributed FPHC income must be distinguished from FPHC income. All gross income, regardless of its character, is included in calculating undistributed FPHC income. Since all gross income is included, regardless of source or character, taxable income is generally determined with the deductions that would be allowed if the corporation were domestic. With the adjustments and deduction for dividends paid, undistributed FPHC income approximates the corporation's earnings and profits.

The adjustments made in converting taxable income to undistributed FPHC income are:

a. A deduction is allowed for income taxes imposed on the FPHC by the United States, foreign countries, and possessions of the United States.[45]

b. The deduction for charitable gifts is allowed up to 50 percent of taxable income (before the charitable deduction, the deduction for capital loss carrybacks, and the constructive dividends from lower tier FPHCs), and the usual rule restricting the charitable deduction for corporations to 10 percent of taxable income is disregarded.[46]

c. No dividends received deduction is allowed.[47]

d. The usual deductions for net operating losses are disallowed, but a net operating loss from the immediately preceding year may be carried forward as a reduction of current income.[48]

e. Depreciation and other expenses relating to the operation and maintenance of the FPHC's property are allowed only to the extent of rents received unless the property is held in the course of a business carried on for profit, the rent is the highest obtainable, and the property either was acquired and held with an expectation that profit would be realized or is necessary for the conduct of the business.[49]

---

[43] IRC §556(a). For the deduction for dividends paid, see §561, discussed infra ¶95.2.5. For an illustration of the computation of undistributed FPHC income, see Reg. §1.556-3.

[44] IRC §555(c)(1). For the computation of these constructive dividends, see §555(b), discussed supra ¶68.3.2 text accompanying note 12.

[45] IRC §556(b)(1). See Reg. §1.556-2(a)(1)(i) (U.S. taxes deducted when accrued even if corporation uses cash method of accounting). No deduction is allowed, however, for the U.S. accumulated earnings and personal holding company taxes. See infra ¶¶95.1 and 95.2 for the accumulated earnings and personal holding company taxes.

[46] IRC §556(b)(2).

[47] IRC §556(b)(3). For the dividends received deduction, see infra ¶90.2.3.

[48] IRC §556(b)(4).

[49] IRC §556(b)(5); Reg. §1.556-2(e).

f. No deduction is allowed for contributions to qualified pension, profit sharing, stock bonus, or annuity plans.[50]

2. *U.S. shareholder.* Only U.S. shareholders are taxed on their shares of undistributed FPHC income. For this purpose, the term "United States shareholder" refers to a shareholder of an FPHC who is a U.S. citizen or resident, a domestic corporation or partnership, or a trust or estate that is not a foreign trust or estate.[51] No minimum shareholding is required to be a U.S. shareholder. Moreover, if stock of an FPHC is held by a foreign partnership, trust, or estate or a foreign corporation that is not an FPHC, this stock is attributed proportionately to the entity's shareholders, partners, or beneficiaries in determining the shareholdings of U.S. shareholders.[52] The attribution rule is applied repeatedly until the FPHC stock is attributed to an individual (U.S. or foreign) or a domestic entity.

The definition of U.S. shareholder must be distinguished from the stock ownership test applied in determining whether the corporation is an FPHC.[53] Only ownership by U.S. citizens and residents is counted under the stock ownership test, but broad constructive ownership rules are used in determining this ownership.[54] In identifying the corporation's U.S. shareholders, the only constructive ownership rule is the rule attributing stock from foreign entities to their owners, but the U.S. shareholders may include domestic entities as well as U.S. citizens and residents. Assume a U.S. citizen is sole shareholder of a domestic corporation that owns all of the stock of a foreign corporation. If the foreign corporation meets the gross income test, it is an FPHC because its stock is constructively owned by the U.S. citizen. The FPHC's U.S. shareholder, however, is the domestic corporation.

A U.S. person holding a very small minority interest in an FPHC is taxed under the FPHC rules as a U.S. shareholder, but Congress thought it unlikely that an independent minority shareholder would be affected by the rules.

---

[50] IRC §556(b)(6).

[51] IRC §551(a). A trust is foreign if it is not subject to supervision by a U.S. court or if U.S. persons do not have authority for or control over substantial trust decisions, and an estate is foreign if it is subject to U.S. tax under the rules for nonresident aliens. See supra ¶¶65.3.3, 65.3.4. See Rev. Rul. 82-150, 1982-2 CB 110 (where U.S. citizen paid $70 for option to purchase FPHC stock for $30, individual treated as owner of stock and taxed as U.S. shareholder).

[52] IRC §551(f). This rule was added in 1984 because "the prior rules allowed taxpayers to take the position that they could circumvent the foreign personal holding company rules by interposing foreign entities between themselves and foreign personal holding companies." 1984 Bluebook, supra note 2, at 441. See also id. at 442–43 (Treasury should allow adjustments to ensure U.S. shareholder is not taxed second time when undistributed FPHC income is distributed through intermediate foreign entity to shareholder).

[53] See Reg. §1.551-2(a).

[54] See supra ¶68.3.2 text accompanying notes 33–38.

In the ordinary course of events, strangers do not hold stock in a family owned "incorporated pocketbook".... If any individual is a minority shareholder of a foreign personal holding company, it is more than likely that such individual is a member of, or is in some way connected with, the family owning and controlling the foreign company. If by chance an individual should be a minority shareholder in a foreign corporation under such circumstances that he would not be aware of the company's classification as a foreign personal holding company, he would not be subjected to any penalties for failing to comply with [the FPHC rules].[55]

3. *Constructive dividend.* A U.S. shareholder of an FPHC has dividend income equal to the amount the shareholder would have received if the corporation had distributed its undistributed FPHC income on the last day of the taxable year.[56] If the stock ownership test is met during a portion of the taxable year but not on the last day of the year, the constructive dividend equals the undistributed FPHC income ratably allocable to the portion of the year beginning with the first day of the year (whether or not the stock ownership test was met on that day) and ending with the last day on which the stock ownership test is met.[57] Also, the constructive dividend is deemed distributed in this case on the last day during the year when the stock ownership test is met.

According to the Ways and Means Committee:

The respective amount to be returned by each United States shareholder depends not only upon the number of shares of stock owned by him but also upon the relative rights of the several classes of shareholders, if the foreign company has more than one class of stock outstanding. Thus, if the foreign company has both common and preferred stock outstanding and the preferred stock, whether cumulative or noncumulative, ranks ahead of the common stock with respect to dividend distributions, the assumed distribution of the undistributed [FPHC] income will first be applied to the preferred shareholders according to their relative and respective interests.[58]

The allocation of the constructive dividend among shareholders is based on their shareholdings when the dividend is deemed distributed.[59] When shares change hands during the year, a successor U.S. shareholder therefore must report undistributed FPHC income that is allocable to the time when the predecessor

---

[55] H.R. No. 1546, supra note 1, at 718.

[56] IRC §551(b).

[57] See Gray v. CIR, 71 TC 719 (1979) (acq.). If the shareholder is a U.S. citizen or resident for only part of the year, a further allocation may be permitted to restrict the constructive dividend to the amount allocable to the period of citizenship or residence. Gutierrez v. CIR, 72-1 USTC ¶9121 (DC Cir. 1971) (not officially reported); Marsman v. CIR, 205 F2d 335 (4th Cir. 1953).

[58] H.R. No. 1546, supra note 1, at 718. See Reg. §1.551-2(c).

[59] IRC §551(b). If the FPHC made a distribution in liquidation during the year by which it retired some but not all of its shares, the allocation of the constructive dividend is made as though the liquidating distribution had not occurred.

held the shares. Conversely, undistributed FPHC income beneficially accruing to a U.S. shareholder escapes tax under these rules if the shareholder's stock is transferred to a nonresident alien before the year ends or the corporation ceases to be a FPHC.

Regardless of the day on which the constructive dividend is deemed distributed, however, it is included in the shareholder's gross income for his taxable year that includes the last day of the FPHC's taxable year.[60] Assume a foreign corporation whose taxable year is the calendar year ceases being an FPHC on September 30, 1997; U.S. shareholder *A* uses the calendar year, and U.S. shareholder *B* uses a fiscal year ending November 30.[61] Although the constructive dividend for 1997 consists of the undistributed FPHC income allocable to the period ending September 30 and is allocated on the basis of shareholdings on September 30, each shareholder's share of the dividend is included in gross income for the taxable year of the shareholder including December 31, 1997, which is calendar 1997 for *A* and the year ending November 30, 1998 for *B*.

If the constructive dividend is not reported on the U.S. shareholder's return, the statute of limitations on the assessment of the resulting deficiency is extended to six years after the return is filed.[62]

The FPHC's earnings and profits are reduced by the amount of the constructive dividend, including any portion allocable to foreign shareholders.[63] The reduction is made so that U.S. shareholders will not be taxed a second time when the undistributed FPHC income is distributed.[64] A distribution is deemed made from these previously taxed amounts, however, only after distributions have exhausted the corporation's earnings and profits remaining after the reduction for constructive dividends.[65] For example, if the corporation is an FPHC in some years but not in others, a tax-free distribution can be received only after earnings and profits from non-FPHC years are exhausted. Also, it is possible for the corporation to accumulate earnings and profits in years for which it is an FPHC because undistributed FPHC income and earnings and profits, although similar, are not identical. When a nontaxable distribution is received, stock basis is reduced by the amount distributed.[66]

4. *Elimination of subpart F income.* If an FPHC is also a controlled foreign corporation (CFC) and if a U.S. shareholder is also a U.S. shareholder for purposes of subpart F, the constructive dividend to the shareholder under the FPHC rules is reduced by eliminating any portion included in the shareholder's

---

[60] IRC §551(b).

[61] See Reg. §1.551-2(d).

[62] IRC §6501(e)(1)(B).

[63] IRC §551(d).

[64] H.R. No. 1546, supra note 1, at 719.

[65] See Reg. §1.551-5(b) Ex. 1.

[66] IRC §301(c)(2).

gross income under §951(a)(1) as subpart F income.[67] This rule significantly narrows the impact of the FPHC rules because FPHC income is also included in subpart F income and the definitions of FPHC income in the FPHC and subpart F rules are similar.

For an FPHC that is also a CFC, the principal effect of the FPHC rules may be to tax U.S. shareholders on the corporation's active business income. Subpart F income consists principally of items Congress believed susceptible to tax haven abuse, and it includes FPHC income but not most income from active business operations. U.S. shareholders of an FPHC, in contrast, are taxed on the corporation's undistributed FPHC income, which includes income of all types. The income that causes the corporation to be an FPHC—its FPHC income—thus may be taxed under subpart F, and the FPHC rules may be relegated to taxing the residue of the corporation's income.

An FPHC, however, is not necessarily a CFC. In broadest outline, the tests for FPHC and CFC status are the same—U.S. ownership of more than 50 percent of a foreign corporation's stock, by voting power or value. Under the CFC definition, however, a U.S. person's ownership is counted toward the 50 percent threshold only if the person owns at least 10 percent of the corporation's voting stock. The FPHC definition contains no such limitation. Assume a U.S. citizen owns 60 shares of a foreign corporation's stock, and a nonresident alien owns the remaining 40 shares; all shares are identical except the citizen's stock is nonvoting. The corporation is not a CFC because the citizen, owning no voting stock, is not a U.S. shareholder for subpart F purposes. If the gross income test is met, however, the corporation is an FPHC because the ownership of nonvoting shareholders is counted under the FPHC rules and the citizen owns more than 50 percent of the corporation's stock by value.

As another example, assume a foreign corporation has three shareholders—A, a U.S. citizen who owns 45 shares, B, an unrelated resident alien who owns six shares, and C, an unrelated nonresident alien who owns 49 shares; all shares are voting common stock. The corporation is not a CFC because A is the only U.S. shareholder under subpart F and her ownership is only 45 percent. It may be an FPHC, however, because no minimum shareholding is required to be counted under the FPHC definition and five or fewer U.S. citizens or residents (A and B) thus own more than 50 percent of the stock (51 of 100 shares).

¶68.3.4   Stock Basis

The adjusted basis of a U.S. shareholder's shares is normally increased by the amount of any constructive dividend included in the shareholder's gross income under the FPHC rules.[68] The shareholder is thus treated as though the

---

[67] IRC §951(d). For subpart F income, see supra ¶68.2.10.
[68] IRC §551(e).

constructive dividend had actually been distributed but was immediately returned to the corporation as a capital contribution. The basis increase ensures that the shareholder will not be taxed a second time when the undistributed FPHC income represented by the constructive dividend is actually distributed or is indirectly realized by a sale of the shareholder's stock.[69] The basis increase is lost, however, if the shareholder fails to include the dividend in gross income and this omission is not corrected on audit or by amended return before the statute of limitations runs on deficiency assessments for the year.[70]

On the death of a U.S. citizen or resident owning stock of an FPHC, the decedent's estate and heirs take a basis for the stock equal to the lesser of the decedent's basis or the stock's fair market value on the estate tax valuation date.[71] Generally, the basis of appreciated property is stepped up to fair market value at death.[72] According to the Ways and Means Committee:

> [The] more severe rule [for FPHC stock] is justified by the character of the corporations to whose stock and securities its application is limited. Such foreign personal holding companies are, with few exceptions, it is believed, formed or availed of by their owners to evade or avoid the payment of their just share of Federal income taxes by the accumulation of income abroad. Sound fiscal policy demands that all possible lawful means be invoked to protect the integrity of the revenues from the destructive effects of widespread resort to this type of tax-dodging device.[73]

¶68.3.5 Return Requirements and Taxable Years

If a U.S. shareholder owns at least 5 percent by value of the FPHC's stock on the date of the constructive dividend, a statement must be included with the shareholder's return for the year that itemizes "in complete detail" the corporation's gross income, deductions, credits, taxable income, FPHC income, and undistributed FPHC income.[74] "This requirement is necessary since a return may not be filed by the foreign company from which such information may otherwise be procured."[75] It applies only for years the shareholder is required to report a constructive dividend under the rules described above.[76]

---

[69] See IRC §551(d) (earnings and profits—the measure of future dividends—is reduced by constructive dividend), §301(c)(2) (nondividend distributions excluded from gross income to extent of shareholder's stock basis).

[70] The statute of limitations is six years in this context. IRC §6501(e)(1)(B), discussed supra ¶68.3.3 text accompanying note 62.

[71] IRC §1014(b)(5).

[72] IRC §1014(a), discussed supra ¶41.4.

[73] H.R. No. 1546, supra note 1, at 721.

[74] IRC §551(c).

[75] H.R. No. 1546, supra note 1, at 719.

[76] Reg. §1.551-4.

Also, each U.S. citizen or resident who owns 10 percent or more of the FPHC's stock or is an officer or director of the corporation must file a return providing information on both the corporation's shareholders and income.[77] The shareholder information includes the names and addresses of all shareholders, a description of the various classes of the FPHC's stock, and information on changes in shareholdings during the year. The income information is the same as the "complete detail" required of 5 percent shareholders.

If an FPHC has a majority shareholder, it usually must adopt the same taxable year as the shareholder. More specifically, this rule applies for a particular taxable year of the FPHC if, on the first day of the year, more than 50 percent of its stock, by voting power or value, is owned by one U.S. shareholder.[78] Both actual and constructive ownership are counted in applying the 50 percent test,[79] and the test thus may be satisfied by more than one U.S. shareholder.

The application of the taxable year rule is simplest if the same taxable year is used by all U.S. shareholders meeting the 50 percent test and all other U.S. shareholders whose stock is constructively owned by U.S. shareholders meeting the test. In this case, the FPHC must use the common taxable year of these U.S. shareholders or a taxable year beginning one month earlier.[80] If they do not have a common taxable year, the FPHC's taxable year is determined under regulations yet to be issued.

¶68.4   FOREIGN INVESTMENT COMPANIES

¶68.4.1   Introductory

Foreign investment companies, typically based in Canada, Bermuda, or Curacao, were popular accumulation devices for U.S. investors before 1962. Since their foreign source income was exempt from U.S. taxes and was either exempt or taxed at nominal rates in the country of origin, they offered U.S. investors an opportunity to hold the tax collector at bay until they were ready to

---

[77] IRC §6035. In determining whether a shareholder is subject to this requirement, stock owned actually and constructively is taken into account, and stock ownership is measured by value or voting power, whichever gives the U.S. shareholder the greater proportionate interest. IRC §6035(e). Normally, the requirement applies only if an individual is a 10 percent shareholder, officer, or director when the return is due.

[78] IRC §§898(b)(1), (2). For a more detailed description of this rule, see supra ¶68.2.17.

The 50 percent test is applied as of the beginning of the year that would be the FPHC's taxable year in the absence of this rule. The Treasury may require that the test instead be applied on one or more days during a "representative period." IRC §898(c)(1)(C)(ii).

[79] IRC §898(b)(2)(B). For constructive ownership, see supra ¶68.3.2 text accompanying notes 25-31.

[80] IRC §898(c)(1).

sell their stock, when their profits, reflecting the reinvested earnings, were taxable as long-term capital gain.[1]

Section 1246, added in 1962, curbs this practice by requiring gain on sales of a foreign investment company's stock to be reported as ordinary income to the extent of the shareholder's pro rata share of the company's accumulated earnings and profits. Moreover, payment of a toll charge measured by §1246's standards is ordinarily required by the IRS as a condition to a ruling permitting appreciated stock of a foreign investment company to be transferred in a tax-free exchange.[2] Under a grandfather clause, companies in existence when §1246 was enacted were permitted to avoid the application of §1246 to their shareholders by electing irrevocably to distribute substantially all their income to their shareholders, who are taxed on these current earnings in substantially the same manner as shareholders of domestic mutual funds.[3]

In 1986, Congress added rules on passive foreign investment companies (PFICs).[4] A foreign corporation is a PFIC if at least 75 percent of its income is passive or at least 50 percent of its assets produce passive income. Generally, a U.S. shareholder's gain on a sale of PFIC stock is all ordinary income, regardless of the earnings and profits attributable to the stock, and the shareholder is assessed an interest charge to compensate the government for the delay in the imposition of the tax. Since 1986, §1246 has been like the cop on the beat after marshall law has been declared and the army has filled the neighborhood with troops; he is still there, but his authority has been so overwhelmed that it is easily overlooked.

¶68.4.2 Definition of "Foreign Investment Company"

A foreign corporation is a "foreign investment company" whenever it simultaneously meets a U.S. ownership test and a registration or business test.[5] The U.S. ownership test is met if at least 50 percent of the corporation's stock, by voting power or value, is held by U.S. persons, including U.S. citizens and residents and domestic corporations, partnerships, trusts, and estates.[6] The registration or business test is met if one of the following is true: (1) the corporation is registered as a management company or unit investment trust under the Investment Company Act of 1940; (2) its primary business is investing or trading in securities or commodities, including futures and forward contracts and options

---

[1] See Rev. Rul. 60-192, 1960-1 CB 142.

[2] See Reg. §7.367(b)-6, discussed infra ¶68.7.3.

[3] For §§851–855, relating to mutual funds, see infra ¶95.7.1.

[4] See infra ¶68.5.

[5] IRC §1246(b).

[6] For this purpose, a U.S. person is deemed to own shares owned indirectly through foreign entities and shares subject to options held by the person. For indirect ownership, see §958(a), discussed supra ¶68.2.2 text accompanying notes 23–25.

in securities or commodities; or (3) it holds itself out as primarily engaged in such a business. Registration under the Investment Company Act is a prerequisite to public sales of investment company stock in the United States. A closely held corporation, however, can be a foreign investment company if it is engaged primarily in the business of investing or trading in securities or commodities, although a closely held corporation is more likely to be ensnared by the foreign personal holding company rules or subpart F—which tax shareholders currently on undistributed earnings rather than merely taxing gains on stock sales as ordinary income.[7]

¶68.4.3   Ordinary Income Rule

Section 1246 requires ordinary income treatment for at least part of the gain on any sale or exchange of stock of a foreign investment company, including a redemption or liquidation treated as an exchange.[8] The rule applies if the corporation was a foreign investment company at any time while the taxpayer held the stock.[9] It does not apply, however, if, apart from §1246, the gain is characterized as short-term capital gain, ordinary income, or a dividend.[10] For example, gain treated as a dividend under §1248, which applies to sales of stock of controlled foreign corporations, is not affected by §1246.[11]

When §1246 applies, the taxpayer recognizes ordinary income equal to the stock's share of the post-1962 earnings and profits accumulated while the taxpayer held the stock or, if less, the gain on the sale or exchange.[12] If the foreign investment company is also a controlled foreign corporation, earnings and profits included in the taxpayer's gross income under subpart F are excluded. Earnings and profits of years preceding the first year the corporation was a foreign investment company are also excluded if the corporation became a foreign investment company by being in the business of investing or trading in stock or securities, not by registering under the Investment Company Act of 1940. All of the gain is ordinary income, however, unless the taxpayer establishes the amount of the earnings and profits allocable to the stock under the foregoing rules.[13]

Although applied with reference to earnings and profits, the rule characterizes gain as ordinary income, not a dividend. For taxpayers not entitled to a

---

[7] For subpart F and foreign personal holding companies, see supra ¶¶68.2, 68.3.

[8] IRC §1246(a)(1).

[9] See IRC §1246(c) (rule also applies to stock of corporation that has never been foreign investment company while taxpayer held it if its basis derives from stock, whether held by taxpayer or another person, of corporation that was foreign investment company).

[10] IRC §§1246(a)(4), (f).

[11] For §1248, see supra ¶68.2.16.

[12] IRC §§1246(a)(1), (2). The holding period rules of §1223 apply in determining the time the taxpayer is deemed to have held the stock. IRC §1246(c). For §1223, see supra ¶53.1.

[13] IRC §1246(a)(3).

preferential rate for capital gains, its principal effect is to preclude capital losses from being deducted against the recharacterized gain.[14] The rule does not entitle a domestic corporation to indirect credit for foreign income taxes paid by the foreign investment company because indirect credit is allowed only when dividend income is recognized.[15]

On the death of an individual owning foreign investment company stock, §1014(a) provides the estate or heirs with a basis for the stock equal to its fair market value on the estate tax valuation date.[16] This basis, however, is reduced by the ordinary income the decedent would have recognized under §1246 if the stock had been sold immediately before death.[17] Also, the ordinary income under §1246 on a sale by the estate or heirs includes earnings and profits accumulated while the decedent held the stock. Moreover, if the corporation was a foreign investment company while the decedent held the stock, the §1246 taint applies to the stock in the hands of the estate and heirs, even if the corporation ceased being a foreign investment company before the decedent died and is not a foreign investment company at any time while the estate or heirs hold the stock. When the estate or heirs sell, however, they are allowed an income tax deduction equal to the estate tax on the amount removed from the stock's basis under the rule described above.[18]

¶68.4.4 Election to Distribute Income Currently

Foreign investment companies that were registered under the Investment Company Act at the end of 1962 were allowed to elect under §1247 to be subject to a tax regime resembling that for domestic mutual funds. U.S. persons holding shares of an electing company are usually exempted from the ordinary income rule of §1246. Although corporations organized after 1962 have never been eligible to make this election, most foreign investment companies are also PFICs, and a PFIC may elect to be a qualified electing fund, which is also treated like a domestic mutual fund.[19]

A foreign investment company that made the §1247 election must annually distribute to shareholders at least 90 percent of its taxable income.[20] Taxable income is computed for this purpose as though the corporation were a domestic corporation, but net capital gain is excluded, and no deduction is allowed for net operating losses or dividends received.[21] Also, the corporation must notify share-

---

[14] For the limitations on deductions for capital losses, see supra ¶50.2.5.
[15] For the indirect credit, see infra ¶69.8.
[16] For §1014(a), see supra ¶41.4.
[17] IRC §1246(e)(1).
[18] IRC §1246(e)(2).
[19] For qualified electing funds, see infra ¶68.5.4.
[20] IRC §1247(a)(1).
[21] IRC §1247(a)(2)(A).

holders within 45 days after the close of each taxable year of their pro rata shares of the corporation's net capital gain for the year (computed as though the corporation were domestic) and the portions of this gain being distributed currently.[22] A distribution of taxable income or net capital gain is deemed made currently if it occurs before the sixteenth day of the third month of the next taxable year (by March 15 for corporations accounting on calendar year).

A U.S. shareholder of an electing company must annually include in his return as long-term capital gain his share of the corporation's net capital gain, including both the distributed and undistributed portions of this gain as designated in the corporation's notice to the shareholder.[23] A U.S. shareholder is exempted from the ordinary income rule of §1246 unless, for one or more years while he held the shares sold or exchanged, he failed to report his share of the undistributed net capital gain.[24]

If more than one half of the value of an electing corporation's portfolio at the end of a taxable year is represented by stocks and debt instruments of foreign corporations, an additional election can be made for the year, which has the effect of passing through to shareholders credits for foreign income taxes paid by the corporation.[25] If this election is made, (1) the corporation's taxable income and net capital gain are computed without deductions for foreign income taxes, (2) the amounts of these taxes are treated as distributed to shareholders, and (3) each shareholder has additional gross income equal to his share of this deemed distribution, but is treated as having paid an equal amount in foreign income taxes, which usually can be credited against the shareholder's U.S. tax. The corporation must provide notice to shareholders of their shares of the foreign income taxes, and a shareholder's credit for these taxes may not exceed the amount designated in this notice.[26] Moreover, the credit is completely lost if the shareholder fails to report his share of the corporation's undistributed net capital gain.

¶68.5   PASSIVE FOREIGN INVESTMENT COMPANIES

¶68.5.1   Introductory

With the enactment in 1986 of the rules for passive foreign investment companies (PFICs), Congress chipped away further at the deferral privilege for

---

[22] IRC §1247(a)(1).

[23] IRC §1247(d). If a shareholder holds his stock for one year or less, any loss on the sale or exchange of the stock is treated as long-term capital loss up to the amount of any undistributed net capital gain included in the shareholder's return as long-term capital gain. IRC §1247(i).

[24] IRC §§1247(a), (c).

[25] IRC §1247(f).

[26] IRC §1247(g).

earnings accumulated in foreign corporations.[1] The PFIC rules generally apply to shareholders of a foreign corporation if at least 75 percent of the corporation's income is passive or at least 50 percent of its assets produce passive income. Although the rules apply only to shareholders who are U.S. persons (U.S. citizens and residents and domestic corporations, partnerships, trusts, and estates), no minimum ownership by U.S. shareholders is required. A U.S. person owning PFIC stock is subject to these rules even if the shareholder holds only one of a million outstanding shares and all other shareholders are unrelated foreigners. Moreover, if a corporation is a PFIC at any time while a U.S. person is shareholder, the shareholder may be subject to the PFIC rules after the corporation ceases to be a PFIC.

Three alternative regimes are provided for PFIC shareholders. One allows tax to be deferred until dividends are distributed or the stock is sold, but often imposes interest on the tax when it is finally imposed. The other two, which only apply when elected, either taxes undistributed PFIC income to the shareholders as it is earned by the corporation or taxes the PFIC shareholder annually on the appreciation or depreciation in the stock's value during the year.

Under the first of these regimes, an interest charge is imposed when a PFIC shareholder recognizes gain on a sale of stock or receives an extraordinary distribution. Interest is computed essentially as though the gain or distribution had been included in gross income ratably over the period the taxpayer held the stock but payment of the resulting tax had been delayed until the sale or distribution. The interest rate is the rate for underpayments of tax. Also, gain on a sale of PFIC stock is ordinary income under this regime, thus eliminating any possibility that the deferral might have the collateral effect of converting ordinary income into capital gains.

One alternative regime, which only applies for taxable years after 1997, is a mark-to-market rule that requires an electing PFIC shareholder to report annually as ordinary income any increase in the stock's value during the year and usually allows the shareholder a deduction for any decrease in the stock's value during the year.[2]

The other alternative regime applies to PFIC shareholders who elect to treat the corporation as a qualified electing fund (QEF), but only if the corporation provides the IRS with the information it needs to administer the QEF rules. QEF

---

[1] See generally Dunn, PFIC Rules: Tax Policy Gone Awry, 39 Tax Notes 625 (1988); Shay, The Post-TAMRA Treatment of U.S. Shareholders of PFICs, 70 J. Tax'n 296 (1989); Tuerff, Renfroe & Gordon, Unpleasant Surprises: Life in the Section 1291 Ditch, 5 Tax Notes Int'l 1105 (Nov. 23, 1992).

For 1997 statutory amendments, see O'Donnell, PFICs and the Taxpayer Relief Act of 1997: Genuine Relief or Traps for the Unwary? 26 Tax Mgmt. Int'l J. 515 (1997). See also Rollinson, O'Connor & Baik, The Year of the PFIC?—First the 1997 Act, and Now Comprehensive PFIC Guidance on Making QEF Election, 16 Tax Notes Int'l 371 (Feb. 2, 1998), reprinted in 78 Tax Notes 1163 (Mar. 2, 1998).

[2] IRC §1296, discussed infra ¶68.5.5.

shareholders are taxed on their shares of the PFIC's income as it is realized by the corporation, but they generally are not burdened by special taxes or interest charges when they sell their stock or receive distributions from the corporation.

Congress concluded that "eliminating the economic benefit of deferral [for PFIC shareholders] is necessary to eliminate the tax advantages that U.S. shareholders in foreign investment funds have heretofore had over U.S. persons investing in domestic investment funds."[3] A domestic investment fund is either a conduit entity, whose shareholders are taxed on its income whether distributed or not, or it is itself taxed on its earnings.[4] A foreign investment company pays no U.S. income tax on its foreign earnings, and in the absence of the PFIC rules, its shareholders are not taxed on undistributed income unless the shares are sufficiently concentrated in a small group of U.S. shareholders to make the corporation a controlled foreign corporation (CFC) or foreign personal holding company (FPHC).[5]

The QEF rules closely resemble those applied to domestic mutual funds and thus directly carry out the policy to equate investors in domestic and foreign funds. Why then did Congress make them an elective alternative to a regime allowing deferral with an interest charge? According to the Staff of the Joint Committee on Taxation:

> Although Congress believed current taxation was more appropriate than continuation of deferral of tax on income derived from passive assets, Congress recognized that current taxation of U.S. investors in passive foreign investment companies could create difficulties for certain investors in cases where the U.S. investors did not have the ability to obtain relevant information relating to their share of the funds' earnings and profits, did not have enough control to compel dividend distributions, or did not have sufficient liquidity to meet a current tax liability before actual income was realized from their investment.[6]

The congressional preference for the pass-through model is evident, however, in the structure of the deferral alternative. A shareholder in a domestic mutual fund or QEF pays no interest charge when the fund defers gain by letting unrealized appreciation accumulate in its assets. Moreover, if the shareholder sells or redeems stock before the fund realizes such gains, gain on the sale or redemption, which is an indirect realization of the shareholder's share of the corporation's unrealized gains, is taxed as capital gain. A shareholder of a PFIC that is not a QEF, in contrast, is subject to an interest charge computed as though the gain inherent in the shares accrued in equal daily increments. This mechanism ignores the possibility that part of the shareholder's gain might derive from

---

[3] H.R. Rep. No. 841, 99th Cong., 2d Sess. II-641 (Conf. Rep. 1986).

[4] See infra ¶95.7.1.

[5] For CFCs and FPHCs, see supra ¶¶68.2, 68.3.

[6] Staff of Joint Comm. on Tax'n, 99th Cong., 2d Sess., General Explanation of the Tax Reform Act of 1986 at 1023 (1987) [hereinafter 1986 Bluebook].

unrealized appreciation in the value of corporate assets, appreciation that would not have been taxed at any earlier time under the rules for domestic mutual funds and QEFs. Also, because all gain on a sale of a nonelecting PFIC shareholder's stock is ordinary income, the shareholder is denied the possibility that domestic mutual fund and QEF shareholders have of cashing in as capital gains their shares of the unrealized appreciation in corporate assets. These and other disadvantages burdening nonelecting shareholders suggest that the rules are designed to force the QEF election to be made whenever feasible.

Although the purpose of the PFIC rules is to equate investors in domestic and foreign mutual funds, the rules apply to shareholders of foreign corporations that do not look much like mutual funds. A foreign corporation can be a PFIC whether its shares are widely dispersed or closely held. Although the intention was to limit a deferral opportunity, the rules can apply to shareholders of foreign corporations that are also subject to the antideferral rules for FPHCs or CFCs.[7] The definition of PFIC, in sum, refers only to the income and assets of the corporation, not to the composition of its shareholder group or its status under other provisions of the Code.

¶68.5.2 Definition of "Passive Foreign Investment Company"

A foreign corporation is a PFIC if it meets a passive income test or a passive assets test.[8] The passive income test is met if at least 75 percent of the corporation's income consists of dividends, interest, and other passive items. The passive assets test is met if at least 50 percent of the corporation's assets produce passive income.

1. *Passive income test.* Under the passive income test, a foreign corporation is a PFIC for a taxable year if 75 percent or more of its gross income for the year is "passive income," defined to include dividends, interest, passive rents and royalties, net gains on sales of property producing passive income, and other income classified as foreign personal holding company income for purposes of subpart F.[9] Exclusions are provided for income earned in the active conduct of a banking business,[10] income "derived in the active conduct of a securities busi-

---

[7] Rev. Rul. 87-90, 1987-2 CB 216 (wholly owned foreign subsidiary of domestic corporation can be PFIC).

[8] IRC §1297(a).

[9] IRC §§954(c), 1297(b)(1). For the subpart F definition of FPHC income, see supra ¶68.2.4.

[10] IRC §1297(b)(2)(A); Notice 89-81, 1989-2 CB 399. For proposed regulations on the exception for banking income, see INTL-65-93, 1995-1 CB 978, promulgating Prop. Reg. §1.1296-4; Klien & Blum, Proposed IRS Guidance on Characterization of Foreign Banks' and Securities Dealers' Income as Passive, 24 Tax Mgmt. Int'l J. 324 (1995); Lederman & Hirsh, Prop. Regs. Implement PFIC Exceptions for Foreign Banks and Securities Dealers, 83 J. Tax'n 38 (1995); Van Brunt, The Proposed PFIC Rules for Foreign Banks and Foreign Securities Dealers, 11 Tax Notes Int'l 453 (Aug. 14, 1995).

ness,"[11] and insurance income of a corporation "actively [and] predominantly engaged" in an insurance business.[12] Also, interest, dividends, rents, or royalties received from a related person are passive only to the extent "allocable" to passive income of the payor.[13]

2. *Passive assets test.* Under the passive assets test, a foreign corporation is a PFIC if at least 50 percent of its assets during the taxable year produce passive income or are held for the production of passive income.[14] When this 50 percent threshold is reached or exceeded, the corporation is a PFIC even if it carries on an active business and utilizes a substantial portion of its assets (but no more than 50 percent) in this business.[15]

According to the IRS, an asset is passive "if it has generated [passive income for the corporation] (or is reasonably expected to generate [such income] in the reasonably foreseeable future)."[16] This "passive income" can be of a type that

---

[11] IRC §1297(b)(3) (applicable for taxable years beginning after September 30, 1993 and before 1998). The exclusion applies only if the foreign corporation is a CFC and is registered under the Securities Exchange Act of 1934 as a securities broker or dealer or a government securities broker or dealer. When these conditions are satisfied, the exclusion applies only for the purpose of applying the PFIC rules to the corporation's U.S. shareholders (U.S. persons owing at least 10 percent the corporation's voting stock). For the terms "controlled foreign corporation" and "U.S. shareholder," see §§951(b), 957(a), discussed supra ¶68.2.2. For proposed regulations on this exclusion, see INTL-65-93, 1995-1 CB 978, promulgating Prop. Reg. §1.1296-6.

The exclusion, combined with the exclusion for income from active banking businesses, can cover all income of an active business "that consists in part of banking activities and in part of securities activities." H.R. Rep. No. 213, 103d Cong., 1st Sess. 641 (Conf. Rep. 1993). According to the House Ways and Means Committee:

> there is considerable overlap between . . . bona fide banking activities . . . and the activities conducted by foreign securities dealers. For example, foreign securities dealers may regularly arrange and engage in foreign exchange transactions, enter into interest rate and currency swaps and other hedging transactions and underwrite issues of stock, debt obligations and other securities. Each of these activities is . . . a bona fide banking activity.

H.R. Rep. No. 111, 103d Cong., 1st Sess. 693 (1993).

[12] IRC §1297(b)(2)(B). An insurance company, however, has passive income if it "maintain[s] financial reserves in excess of the reasonable needs of [its] insurance business"; also, "a foreign corporation established to acquire insurance coverage on behalf of related persons (a captive insurance company) may [be] a PFIC [if] there is no shifting of risk to the foreign entity." 1986 Bluebook, supra note 6, at 1025. Moreover, the income of a foreign bank or insurance business is passive if it operates as an "incorporated investment vehicle . . . on behalf of shareholders or other related parties." Id. at 1026.

[13] IRC §1297(b)(2)(C). For the term "related person," see §954(d)(3), discussed supra ¶68.2.5 text accompanying notes 103–06.

[14] IRC §1297(a)(2).

[15] Rev. Rul. 87-90, 1987-2 CB 216 (foreign corporation more than 50 percent of whose assets produce passive income is PFIC even though it carries on manufacturing business).

[16] Notice 88-22, 1988-1 CB 489.

would be tax-exempt in the hands of a U.S. person. For example, a municipal bond is a passive asset. "Cash and other assets readily convertible into cash" are passive even when held as working capital in an active business.

Accounts receivable are not passive unless the transaction in which the receivable arises generates passive income. For example, an account receivable for the price of goods sold or services performed in the ordinary course of the corporation's business is not passive even if it bears interest.

Corporate stock generally is passive.[17] A securities dealer's inventory, however, is not passive, notwithstanding the receipt of interest and dividends on securities in inventory, if inventory securities are adequately distinguished in the corporation's records from investment securities and the quantity of inventory securities "does not exceed the reasonable needs of the dealer's trade or business."[18]

Assets that generate both passive and nonpassive income during the taxable year are considered "partly passive and partly nonpassive assets in proportion to the relative amounts of income generated by those assets in that year."[19]

The passive assets test is normally applied with reference to the fair market values of the corporation's assets.[20] However, if the corporation is not "publicly traded," its assets are valued at their adjusted bases for purposes of determining earnings and profits if the corporation is a CFC or if it elects to use adjusted basis in lieu of fair market value.[21] The election to use basis rather than value must be made by the corporation, and once made for any year, it applies in all subsequent years until revoked with IRS consent. Asset value or basis is determined as of the end of each quarter during the taxable year, and the ratio of passive assets to all assets for the year consists of the average of the quarterly values of the assets in the two categories.[22] Each asset is taken into the ratio at its gross value or basis, undiminished by liabilities.

---

[17] 1986 Bluebook, supra note 6, at 1024.

[18] Notice 89-81, 1989-2 CB 399, 401; Notice 88-22, 1988-1 CB 489.

[19] Notice 88-22, 1988-1 CB 489.

[20] IRC §1297(a)(2).

[21] IRC §1297(f) (effective for taxable years beginning after 1997). For earnings and profits rules affecting adjusted basis, see §§316(k) and (n), discussed infra ¶92.1.3.

A similar rule, found in §1296(a) applied for taxable years beginning after September 30, 1993 and before 1998. According to the House Ways and Means Committee:

[M]any foreign corporations that are subject to the PFIC rules hold assets (such as tangible or intangible business assets) the fair market value of which is difficult to determine. This difficulty is faced primarily by those PFICs that are also controlled foreign corporations, rather than those PFICs that are foreign-controlled investment funds (which tend to hold marketable assets). The committee is aware that the process of determining the fair market value of such foreign assets is a source of complexity and administrative burden for taxpayers, and is an enforcement problem for the Internal Revenue Service.

H.R. Rep. No. 111, 103d Cong., 1st Sess. 692 (1993).

[22] Notice 88-22, 1988-1 CB 489.

3. *Leased property.* The PFIC rules are usually applied treating a foreign corporation as owner of any "tangible personal property" that it possesses as lessee under "a lease with a term of at least 12 months."[23] Presumably, a lease for 12 months or more is covered throughout its term, including the final 12 months of the term.

At any point in time, the adjusted basis of leased property is deemed to be the "unamortized portion . . . of the present value of the payments under the lease."[24] Present value is determined using a discount rate equal to the applicable Federal rate (AFR) in effect for the month during which the term begins.[25] The AFR is separately determined for short-term, mid-term, and long-term obligations; the rate for a lease is the AFR that would apply to a debt instrument issued at the beginning of the lease term and maturing at the end of the term. Options to renew or extend the lease are ignored. The "unamortized portion" of the "present value" is presumably the present value of the remaining payments (including an appropriate portion of a payment already made for the rent period in progress at the valuation date), determined with the AFR identified at the beginning of the lease term.

Assume a foreign corporation leases an airplane under a 10-year lease for an annual rental of $100 (payable at the beginning of each lease year). If the AFR is 7 percent at the beginning of the lease term, the corporation's deemed adjusted basis for the airplane is initially $752 (present value, at 7 percent compounded annually, of 10 annual payments of $100 each, the first being immediately payable). At the beginning of, say, the fourth year of the lease term, the deemed adjusted basis is $577 (present value, at 7 percent compounded annually, of seven annual payments of $100 each).

A lessee is not treated as owner of leased property if the lessor is a related person.[26] The leased property rule is also inapplicable if "a principal purpose of leasing the property was to avoid" the PFIC rules or §956A.[27]

4. *Intangibles.* For purposes of the PFIC rules, the adjusted basis of a CFC's assets is increased by the sum of the corporation's research or experimental expenditures for the taxable year and the preceding two years.[28] The legislative history explains the purpose of this provision as follows:

> When a controlled foreign corporation incurs research and experimental expenditures, the practical effect may be to enhance the corporation's ability to generate active business income over an extended period; yet inasmuch as

---

[23] IRC §1298(d) (applicable for taxable years beginning after September 30, 1993).

[24] IRC §1298(d)(2)(A).

[25] For the AFR, see §1274(d), discussed supra ¶57.2.

[26] IRC §1298(d)(3). For the term "related person," see §954(d)(3), discussed supra ¶68.2.5 text accompanying notes 103–06.

[27] For §956A, which borrows the leased property rule of §1298(d), see supra ¶68.2.12.

[28] IRC §1298(e)(1) (effective for taxable years beginning after September 30, 1993).

such expenditures are commonly deductible under section 174, these types of expenditures may affect the corporation's adjusted basis in its assets differently than . . . purchase[s] of tangible or intangible assets.[29]

However, an expenditure is not taken into account under this rule if the CFC has been reimbursed for it (e.g., under a cost sharing arrangement).

Also, if a CFC is a licensee of intangible property that it uses in "the active conduct of a trade or business," the adjusted basis of its assets is usually increased by 300 percent of the payments made during the taxable year for the CFC's use of the property.[30] However, this rule does not apply if the payments are to a foreign person that is related to the CFC or if "a principal purpose of entering into such license was to avoid" the PFIC rules or §956A.[31] For example, if a domestic corporation licenses a patent to a wholly owned foreign subsidiary and the subsidiary sublicenses the patent to an unrelated foreign person, the subsidiary's royalty payments to the parent do not boost the subsidiary's adjusted basis under the 300 percent rule if "one principal purpose for licensing the property indirectly [through the subsidiary] was to increase the measurement of the controlled foreign corporation's active assets."[32] The antiavoidance limitation also applies if a CFC licenses an intangible to its domestic parent, which sublicenses it to another CFC owned by the parent and "one principal purpose for licensing the property indirectly was to increase the measurement of the second controlled foreign corporation's active assets."

5. *Income and assets of subsidiaries.* A look-through rule is provided so that "foreign corporations that own subsidiaries primarily engaged in active business operations [are not] treated as PFICs."[33] Specifically, if a foreign corporation owns 25 percent or more of the stock of another corporation (a subsidiary), the passive income and assets tests are applied by treating the foreign corporation's income and assets as including a ratable share of the subsidiary's income and assets.[34] For example, if a foreign corporation's only assets are stock and debt instruments of operating subsidiaries and its only income is dividends and interest from the subsidiaries, the corporation is not a PFIC because (1) its income is deemed to consist of the nonpassive income of the subsidiaries, not the dividends and interest actually received from the subsidiaries, and (2) its assets are deemed

---

[29] H.R. Rep. No. 213, 103d Cong., 1st Sess. 642 (Conf. Rep. 1993). "[T]axpayers have argued that the practical effect of marketing expenditures that are properly deductible under section 162 as ordinary and necessary business expenses may also be to enhance the corporation's ability to generate active business income over an extended period." Id. Congress provided no relief to such taxpayers, but directed the Treasury to study the issue.

[30] IRC §1298(e)(2)(A). The term "intangible property" includes patents, formulas, knowhow, copyrights, trademarks, trade names, franchises, licenses, contracts, and "any similar item." IRC §936(h)(3)(B).

[31] IRC §1298(e)(2)(B).

[32] H.R. Rep. No. 213, 103d Cong., 1st Sess. 642 (Conf. Rep. 1993).

[33] 1986 Bluebook, supra note 6, at 1026.

[34] IRC §1297(c).

to consist of the operating assets of the subsidiaries, not the stock and debt instruments it actually owns.[35]

The rule, however, can have the opposite effect. Assume an operating foreign corporation is sole shareholder of another foreign corporation, all of whose assets are portfolio investments. The operating corporation is treated as owner of the assets of the investment corporation, and these assets are included in applying the passive assets test at their full value or basis, undiminished by liabilities. If the deemed held assets account for at least 50 percent of all assets, the operating company is a PFIC, even if the stock of the investment company has a value or basis that is less than one half of the aggregate. Similarly, in applying the passive income test, the operating company's income includes the subsidiary's gross passive income, whereas the dividends it receives on its stock of the subsidiary are necessarily net of expenses and taxes.

The look-through rule applies if a foreign corporation is the direct or constructive owner of at least 25 percent of the stock of another corporation. Under constructive ownership rules described below, a corporation is deemed to own stock actually held by subsidiaries.[36] The rule thus can bring the income and assets of lower-tier subsidiaries into the testing hodgepots.[37]

6. *Exceptions for new corporations and corporations changing businesses.* A newly organized corporation is given a one-year reprieve if it meets the passive income or assets test because of temporary investments incident to the launching of its business.[38] The year of reprieve, called the "start-up year," is the first year the corporation has gross income. To qualify for the reprieve, three requirements be met: (1) The IRS must be satisfied that the corporation will not be a PFIC for either of the two taxable years immediately following the start-up year; (2) the corporation must not in fact be a PFIC for either of those years; and (3) the corporation must not be a successor to another corporation that was a PFIC.

Another exception is made for corporations that hold passive assets as temporary investments while changing businesses.[39] This exception applies for a particular year if the following requirements are met: (1) Neither the corporation nor any predecessor may have been a PFIC for any prior year; (2) "substantially all" of the corporation's passive income for the year must be from investments of the proceeds of the sale of one or more active businesses; (3) the IRS must be satisfied that the corporation will not be a PFIC for either of the succeeding two taxable years; and (4) the corporation must not in fact be a PFIC for either of those years.

---

[35] H.R. Rep. No. 841, 99th Cong., 2d Sess. II-644 (Conf. Rep. 1986).
[36] Infra ¶68.5.5.
[37] 1986 Bluebook, supra note 6, at 1026.
[38] IRC §1298(b)(2).
[39] IRC §1298(b)(3).

7. *Exception for U.S. shareholders of controlled foreign corporations.* A foreign corporation is not a PFIC with respect to a shareholder for any period after 1997 during which the shareholder is a U.S. shareholder and the corporation is a controlled foreign corporation (CFC).[40] Very generally, a U.S. shareholder is a U.S. person who owns, actually, indirectly, or constructively, at least 10 percent of the corporation's voting stock, and the corporation is a CFC if more than 50 percent of its stock, by value or by vote, is owned, actually, indirectly, or constructively, by U.S. shareholders.[41]

Accordingly, a shareholder that is subject to current inclusion under the subpart F rules with respect to stock of a PFIC that is also a CFC generally is not subject also to the PFIC provisions with respect to the same stock. The PFIC provisions continue to apply ... to shareholders that are not subject to subpart F (i.e., to shareholders that are U.S. persons and that own (directly, indirectly, or constructively) less than 10 percent of the corporation's stock by vote).[42]

Also, as generally happens when a PFIC ceases to be a PFIC,[43] if a shareholder owned PFIC stock before the shareholder became a U.S. shareholder or before the corporation became a CFC, "the stock held by such shareholder continues to be treated as PFIC stock unless the shareholder makes an election to pay tax and an interest charge with respect to the unrealized appreciation in the stock or the accumulated earnings of the corporation."[44]

8. *Foreign investment companies.* A PFIC may also be a foreign investment company under §1246.[45] A foreign corporation is a foreign investment company if at least 50 percent of its shares are held by U.S. persons and if it is registered under the Investment Company Act of 1940 or its primary business is investing in or trading securities or commodities. When a foreign corporation is both a foreign investment company and a PFIC, §1246—which requires that gain on a stock sale be reported as ordinary income to the extent of the stock's share of earnings and profits accumulated while the taxpayer held the stock—is usually trumped by the PFIC rules, which taint all gain as ordinary income and impose an interest charge in addition. However, if the corporation has elected under §1247 to distribute substantially all of its income as earned, it is exempted from PFIC status.[46]

---

[40] IRC §1297(e). If the shareholder ceases to be a U.S. shareholder or the corporation ceases to be a CFC, the shareholder is usually deemed, for purposes of the PFIC rules, to have purchased the stock on that day.

[41] IRC §§951(b), 957(a), discussed supra ¶68.2.2.

[42] Staff of Joint Comm. on Tax'n, 105th Cong., 1st Sess., General Explanation of Tax Legislation Enacted in 1997, at 310 (Comm. Print 1997).

[43] IRC §1298(b)(1).

[44] Id.

[45] For foreign investment companies, see supra ¶68.4.

[46] IRC §1297(d).

¶68.5.3   Treatment of Shareholders of PFICs That Are Not QEFs

Generally, a special tax computation and interest charge apply whenever a U.S. PFIC shareholder receives an "excess distribution" from the corporation or recognizes gain on a sale of all or a portion of the shareholder's stock.[47] Very generally, (1) the excess distribution or gain on sale is spread over the post-1986 years the shareholder held the stock, (2) the amounts allocated to years before the taxable year are taxed at the highest ordinary income rates in effect for those years, and (3) the IRS collects interest as though these amounts had actually been taxed in the prior years and the taxpayer simply failed to pay the tax until the year in which the excess distribution or sale occurs. These rules apply to an excess distribution or sale if, at any time during the shareholder's holding period for the stock, the corporation or any predecessor was a PFIC and no QEF election was in effect.[48]

1. *Excess distributions.* The term "excess distribution" is defined as the excess of (1) the distributions received from the corporation during the taxable year over (2) 125 percent of the average of the distributions received by the shareholder over the preceding three taxable years.[49] For example, if the taxpayer receives distributions during the current year of $150 and average distributions over the preceding three years were $100, the excess distribution is $25 ($150 less 125 percent of $100). If the taxpayer held the stock for less than all of the three preceding years, average distributions are computed over the period the stock was held prior to the taxable year. No distribution received during the year the stock is acquired can be an excess distribution, regardless of its size.

Several rules are provided for computing average distributions. If the taxpayer's holding period for the stock begins during the three-year averaging period, distributions received during the year the stock is acquired are annualized. If PFIC stock is acquired by a calendar year taxpayer on December 1 and a dividend of $1 is received during December, dividends for the year of acquisition are deemed to be $12. If another person's holding period is tacked on to the taxpayer's under §1223, distributions received by the prior owner are treated as though they had been received by the taxpayer.[50] Also, an excess distribution for a prior year is included in the average only to the extent it was allocated to the year of the distribution in computing the special tax and interest charge for the prior year.[51]

If more than one distribution is received during the year, the excess is prorated among the distributions, and the amount allocated to each distribution is treated as a separate excess distribution. Assume a PFIC shareholder receives

---

[47] IRC §1291(a). The tax computation is done on Form 8621.

[48] IRC §1298(b)(1). For the QEF election, see infra ¶68.5.4.

[49] IRC §1291(b).

[50] IRC §1291(b)(3)(D). For §1223, see supra ¶53.1.

[51] For the allocation of an excess distribution over the taxpayer's holding period, see infra text accompanying notes 69–75.

distributions of $100 and $55 during a particular taxable year of the PFIC. If distributions to the shareholder over the previous three years have averaged $100, the excess distribution is $30 ($155 of current distributions less 125 percent of $100), and the excess is deemed to consist of $19.4 of the $100 distribution ($100/$155 of $30) and $10.6 of the $50 distribution.[52] The allocation of the excess between the two distributions is necessary because, under rules described below, an excess distribution is prorated over the shareholder's holding period for the stock up to the date of the distribution.

If the taxpayer has been taxed on undistributed corporate income under the subpart F, FPHC, or QEF rules, some of the distributions received during the current year or during the averaging period might be excluded from gross income as distributions of previously taxed income.[53] The statute requires that "proper adjustment" be made for these excluded amounts, but does not specify what the adjustments might be.[54]

If the taxpayer is a domestic corporation and qualifies for the indirect credit under §902 on receiving a distribution from a PFIC, the addition to gross income under §78 is included as part of the distribution.[55] Assume a domestic corporation receives a dividend of $60 from a PFIC and, as a consequence, is deemed under §902 to have paid $40 of the PFIC's foreign income taxes. Under §78, the domestic corporation has additional gross income of $40. The distribution is deemed to be $100, the sum of the actual distribution of $60 and the deemed paid taxes of $40, whether the distribution is received during the averaging period or the current year.

If distributions are received in a foreign currency, the excess distribution is measured in that currency, and the amount so determined is then translated into dollars at the spot rate on the date of the distribution.[56]

The definition of excess distribution is applied separately with respect to each share of PFIC stock held by the taxpayer, except that a block of stock with a common holding period can be treated as a unit.

2. *Dispositions subject to tax and interest charge.* The special tax and interest charge are triggered by a disposition of PFIC stock as well as by the receipt of an excess distribution. They apply to gain on a stock disposition if the corporation has been a PFIC (but not a QEF) for any year after 1986 while the taxpayer held the stock, whether or not it is a PFIC at the time of sale.[57]

---

[52] See H.R. Rep. No. 841, 99th Cong., 2d Sess. II-642 (Conf. Rep. 1986).

[53] IRC §551(d) (discussed supra ¶68.3.3 text accompanying note 63), §959(a) (discussed supra ¶68.2.14), §1293(c) (discussed infra ¶68.5.4 text accompanying note 101).

[54] IRC §1291(b)(3)(F).

[55] IRC §1291(g)(1)(A). For §§902 and 78, see infra ¶69.8.1.

[56] IRC §§986(b)(2), 986(b)(1), 1291(b)(3)(E). For the currency translation rules generally, see supra ¶71.1.

[57] IRC §1298(b)(1).

A disposition is usually a triggering event only if gain is recognized.[58] The Treasury, however, may require that gain be recognized on dispositions of PFIC stock in transactions in which gain or loss is not ordinarily recognized.[59] For example, recognition of gain might be required on a gift of PFIC stock to a charity, nonresident alien individual, foreign corporation, or other person not likely to be subject to U.S. tax on a subsequent sale of the stock.[60]

In contrast, as described below, these rules usually do not trump a nonrecognition rule if the potential for imposing the special tax and interest charge can follow the stock into the transferee's hands or can attach to other property of the taxpayer.[61] Also, shareholders are deemed to make sales of PFIC stock in various circumstances where no sale occurs in fact.[62]

a. *Stock transferred or received in nonrecognition exchanges.* When gain is not recognized on a disposition of PFIC stock, the special tax and interest charge usually are merely delayed, not avoided. In most nonrecognition transactions (e.g., a gift or reorganization exchange), the transferor's basis for the stock becomes the basis of the stock in the transferee's hands or the basis of other stock in the transferor's hands, and the transferor's holding period usually tacks onto the holding period of the transferee or of the transferor for other stock. As a consequence, on a subsequent taxable disposition, gain inherent in the stock when transferred in the nonrecognition transaction can be recognized and subjected to the special tax and interest charge. The nonrecognition transaction, in other words, postpones rather than avoids the day of reckoning under the PFIC rules, just as under the income tax rules generally.

Several special rules are provided to ensure that the postponement does not become an avoidance. If PFIC stock is transferred in a transaction in which the transferee's basis derives from the transferor's, the stock is PFIC stock to the transferee, even if the corporation is never a PFIC while the transferee holds the stock, because the transferee's holding period dates back to include that of the transferor.[63] For example, if a gift is made of stock of a corporation that was a PFIC while the donor held the stock, the stock is PFIC stock in the donee's hands, even if the corporation ceased to be a PFIC before the gift. This rule is made applicable to PFIC stock received from a decedent by an additional rule

---

[58] IRC §1291(a)(2).

[59] IRC §1291(f). In cases where the Treasury so provides, the gain equals the excess of the stock's fair market value over its adjusted basis, and the recognized gain is added to adjusted basis if the taxpayer's basis for the stock transfers to another person or to other property of the taxpayer.

[60] See 1986 Bluebook, supra note 6, at 1028.

[61] Infra text accompanying notes 63–66.

[62] Infra text accompanying notes 67–68.

[63] IRC §§1246(c), 1291(e).

requiring that such stock take the decedent's basis rather than the usual fair market value basis under §1014(a).[64]

Moreover, if PFIC stock is exchanged for stock in another foreign corporation, the attributes of the stock exchanged attach to the stock received.[65] Assume that in a tax-free reorganization, stock of a foreign corporation is received in exchange for stock in another corporation that was a PFIC while the taxpayer held the stock. Because the stock given in the exchange is PFIC stock, the stock received is also PFIC stock, even if the issuer of this stock is never a PFIC. A grantor's interest in a grantor trust holding PFIC stock is also treated as PFIC stock.[66]

b. *Deemed sale rules.* PFIC stock used "as security for a loan" is treated as sold when the security interest is given.[67] Presumably, this means that the shareholder-borrower is treated as though a proportionate part of the pledged stock had been sold for a price equal to the loan proceeds. For example, if PFIC stock worth $100 is pledged to secure a $70 borrowing, a sale of 70 percent of the stock is deemed made for $70.

Another deemed sale rule applies to U.S. persons who are constructive owners of PFIC stock owned by foreign persons under attribution rules described below.[68] Constructively owned PFIC stock is deemed sold if the actual owner of the stock makes a disposition that cuts off the constructive ownership. Also, if a U.S. person's ownership of an interest in a foreign entity causes the person to be constructive owner of PFIC stock, a disposition of that interest is treated as including a sale of the constructively owned stock. Assume a domestic corporation owns all of the stock of a foreign operating company that owns PFIC stock. Because the domestic corporation is constructive owner of the PFIC stock, it is deemed to make a disposition of that stock if it disposes of its stock in the foreign operating company or if the operating company disposes of the PFIC stock. Moreover, a U.S. person with an option to acquire PFIC stock held by a foreign person is constructive owner of the stock, and a disposition of the option is treated as a disposition of the stock.

3. *Computation of special tax and interest charge.* An excess distribution or gain on a disposition of PFIC stock is prorated, day by day, over the period from the date the stock was acquired to the date of the sale or distribution, with two exceptions:[69] Amounts allocated to years before 1987 and amounts allocated to

---

[64] IRC §§1246(e)(1), 1291(e)(1). If the heir sells the stock, a deduction is allowed for the year of the sale equal to the estate tax attributable to the excess of the stock's estate tax value over the heir's basis for it. IRC §1246(e)(2). Stock received from a nonresident alien decedent is not subject to these rules. IRC §1291(e)(2).

[65] IRC §§1246(c), 1291(e).

[66] IRC §§1246(d), 1291(e).

[67] IRC §1298(b)(6).

[68] IRC §1298(b)(5). For the constructive ownership rules, see infra ¶68.5.5.

[69] IRC §1291(a)(1)(A). A taxpayer's holding period is determined under the holding period rules of §1223, except that (1) in applying the excess distribution rules, the holding

periods before the first year in which the corporation was a PFIC are reallocated to the year of the sale or distribution.[70] Because the special tax and interest charge do not apply to amounts allocated to the year of the distribution or disposition, the pre-1987 and pre-PFIC rules have the effect of allowing the benefits of deferral with respect to gain and excess distributions allocated to years before 1987 and before the corporation became a PFIC.

The amounts allocated to the year of the sale or distribution (including the amounts allocated to pre-1987 and pre-PFIC years) are included in gross income for the year as ordinary income, but the amounts allocated to other years are excluded from the regular tax calculation for this year and are instead subject to the special tax and interest charge.[71] The special tax on the amount allocated to each prior year is computed at the highest tax rate under §1 or §11, which is 39.6 percent for a noncorporate taxpayer or 35 percent for a corporation.[72] Interest on each increment of special tax accrues for the period beginning with the due date of the return for the year to which the taxable amount is allocated and ending with the return due date for the year of the sale or excess distribution. Extensions of filing due dates are ignored. The interest is computed at the rates for underpayments of tax in effect during the interest accrual period.[73] The special taxes for all prior years and the interest charges on them are added together, and the sum is an addition to the tax for the year of the sale or distribution.[74]

Several special rules are provided to coordinate the rules on excess distributions with the foreign tax credit rules.[75] The foreign income taxes with respect to the distribution (including taxes deemed paid under §902) are prorated between the excess distribution and the remainder of the distribution. For example, if dividends of $100 are received from a PFIC and $25 of these dividends are considered an excess distribution, 25 percent ($25/$100) of any foreign income taxes on the distribution are allocated to the excess distribution. The taxes allocated to the excess distribution are divided among the years of the taxpayer's holding period for the stock in the same proportions as the excess distribution. The taxes assigned to the year of the distribution are creditable for that year, subject to the normal limitations. The taxes assigned to each prior year in the taxpayer's holding period are applied in reduction of the special tax on the

---

period is deemed to end on the day of the distribution and (2) if the mark-to-market election of §1296 applied for any prior year, the holding begins with the first day of the first year following the last year for which this election applied. IRC §1291(a)(3)(A). See supra ¶53.3 for §1223.

[70] More specifically, this rule applies to the amounts allocated to periods before the first taxable year of the PFIC beginning after 1986.

[71] IRC §1291(a)(1)(B).

[72] IRC §1291(c)(2).

[73] IRC §1291(c)(3). For the underpayment rate, see §6621, discussed infra ¶114.1.

[74] IRC §1291(a)(1)(C). The interest, however, retains its separate character as interest. IRC §1291(c)(1). For individuals, this is little consolation because interest on tax deficiencies is nondeductible personal interest. IRC §163(h), discussed supra ¶31.5.

[75] IRC §1291(g).

portion of the excess distribution allocated to that year. The special taxes may not be offset by any other foreign income taxes.

4. *Exemptions for QEFs and former PFICs.* A shareholder is exempted from the special tax and interest rules if the shareholder elected to treat the corporation as a QEF for every year in the shareholder's holding period that the corporation was a PFIC.[76] Also, under rules described below, if a QEF election is made for a year after the first PFIC year in which the taxpayer is a shareholder, an election may be made to compute the special taxes and interest as though the stock had been sold at the beginning of the first QEF year.[77] If this election is made and the QEF election remains in effect continuously thereafter, subsequent distributions and sales are exempted from the special tax and interest charge.

A shareholder can also cut off the taint with respect to stock of a former PFIC by electing to treat the stock as having been sold on the last day of the last PFIC year.[78] This constructive sale causes the special tax and interest charge to apply as though the stock had been sold on that day for an amount equal to its fair market value.

¶68.5.4 Qualified Electing Funds

A PFIC shareholder who chooses to treat the corporation as a qualified electing fund (QEF) is taxed annually on a ratable share of corporate earnings, as follows: The QEF's income for each year is split between its "ordinary earnings" (earnings and profits reduced by net capital gain) and its "net capital gain" (excess of net long-term capital gain over net short-term capital loss, but not more than earnings and profits).[79] Each category of income is prorated among the days of the year, and the amount for each day is deemed distributed on that day.[80] An electing shareholder includes in gross income the amounts deemed distributed with respect to stock the shareholder actually owns and stock owned indirectly through foreign entities or options to purchase.[81] This inclusion appears on the shareholder's return for the taxable year of the shareholder that includes the last day of the QEF's taxable year. The shareholder's share of ordinary earnings is ordinary income, and the net capital gain is long-term capital gain.

---

[76] IRC §1291(d)(1). This rule generally does not apply if the taxpayer has elected to use the mark-to-market rule of §1296.

[77] Infra ¶68.5.4 text accompanying notes 105–07.

[78] IRC §1298(b)(1); Reg. §1.1297-3T. The election is made on the shareholder's return for the last PFIC year. Since that return often falls due before it is known that the year was in fact the last PFIC year, the election may be made by amending the return. Reg. §1.1297-3T(b)(1).

[79] IRC §§1293(a), (e).

[80] IRC §1293(b). If a QEF determines its income more frequently than annually, it may use these determinations in allocating its income among shareholders.

[81] IRC §1293(a). For the constructive ownership rules, see infra ¶68.5.5. The QEF inclusions are reported on Form 8621.

If a QEF shareholder is a domestic corporation and owns at least 10 percent of the QEF's stock, the shareholder is allowed credit for portions of the QEF's foreign income taxes.[82] This indirect credit is computed by treating the QEF inclusion in the shareholder's gross income as though it was required by subpart F, thus making applicable §960, the indirect credit rule of subpart F.[83]

Under rules described more fully below, various exclusions are allowed if a QEF is also a CFC,[84] a QEF shareholder may elect to defer the payment of tax on the QEF passthrough,[85] adjustments are made to prevent QEF shareholders from being taxed a second time on the undistributed amounts included in their gross incomes,[86] and QEF shareholders are exempted from the special tax and interest charge imposed on other PFIC shareholders when they sell their stock or receive large distributions.[87] The details of the QEF election are also described below.[88]

1. *Coordination with subpart F.* If a QEF is also a CFC and the taxpayer is a U.S. shareholder under the subpart F definition of that term, several exclusions are made in determining the QEF's ordinary earnings and net capital gain.[89] First, an item of income is excluded if the QEF is subject to a foreign income tax on the income at an effective rate exceeding 90 percent of the highest rate under §11 (31.5 percent).[90] Second, if the QEF is engaged in a trade or business in the United States, income effectively connected with the business is excluded if it is from U.S. sources and U.S. tax on the income is neither reduced nor eliminated by treaty. Income covered by these exclusions also is usually excluded from the amounts taxed to the shareholder under subpart F.[91]

An item of income not within either exclusion might be includable in the shareholder's gross income under both the QEF rules and subpart F. When this happens, the item is taxable to the shareholder under subpart F, not the QEF rules.[92] Also, if a QEF is also an FPHC, an amount includable in a shareholder's gross income under both the QEF and FPHC rules is included only under the FPHC rules.[93]

2. *Election to defer payment of tax on QEF passthrough.* Because "U.S. investors may not have sufficient ownership in the PFIC to compel distributions," they are sometimes allowed to defer payment of the tax on undistributed

---

[82] IRC §1293(f).
[83] For §960, see infra ¶¶69.8.1, 69.8.6.
[84] Infra text accompanying notes 89–93.
[85] Infra text accompanying notes 94–100.
[86] Infra text accompanying notes 101–02.
[87] Infra text accompanying notes 103–07.
[88] Infra text accompanying notes 108–15.
[89] For the subpart F definitions of CFC and U.S. shareholder, see supra ¶68.2.2.
[90] IRC §1293(g)(1).
[91] See supra ¶68.2.10.
[92] IRC §951(f).
[93] IRC §551(g). For the FPHC rules, see infra ¶68.3.

QEF earnings, but interest must be paid on the deferred tax.[94] The deferral, which is elective with the taxpayer,[95] applies to the "undistributed PFIC earnings tax liability," defined as the excess of (1) the taxpayer's tax for the year over (2) the tax that would have been imposed if the inclusion under the QEF rules had been restricted to the amounts distributed by the QEF to the taxpayer during the year.[96] The election is unavailable if the QEF is a FPHC or CFC and any amount is includable in the shareholder's gross income for the year under the FPHC rules or subpart F.

When the election is made, the time for payment of the deferred tax is extended until the deferred earnings are distributed, the taxpayer sells some of his stock, or the corporation ceases to be a QEF. Under the rule for distributions, the deferral period ends, at least in part, if a distribution made to the shareholder in a subsequent year is traced back to earnings of the QEF for the deferral year.[97] For this purpose, distributions are deemed made first from current earnings and then from accumulated earnings in order of time, starting from those most recently accumulated. Distributions thus reduce the deferral of current tax, rather than terminating the deferral of tax for earlier years, unless they exceed current earnings. Assume a QEF shareholder makes the deferral election for 1997. The election defers payment of the 1997 tax attributable to the amount by which the QEF inclusion for the year exceeds any distributions received by the shareholder during 1997. The deferral continues indefinitely if the QEF never makes distributions exceeding current earnings. However, if distributions received during, say, 1998 exceed the shareholder's share of 1998 earnings, the excess is a distribution of tax-deferred amounts from 1997 and the 1997 tax on these amounts becomes payable with the 1998 return.

Under the rule for dispositions, the deferral period is terminated by any disposition of QEF stock (including a gift, transfer at death, or other disposition in which gain or loss is not recognized), but only with respect to the deferred taxes attributable to the shares disposed of.[98]

Rather draconian rules apply to lending transactions. If a shareholder pledges QEF stock as security for a loan, the deferral period ends for tax on undistributed earnings equal to the loan proceeds.[99] Assume an individual pledges QEF stock worth $100 to secure a $40 loan. The individual is treated as though she had received distribution of $40 of tax-deferred earnings or, if less, all tax-deferred earnings attributable to the pledged stock. A similar result occurs if

---

[94] IRC §1294; H.R. Rep. No. 841, 99th Cong., 2d Sess. II-643 (Conf. Rep. 1986). For an illustration of the computation of the deferred tax, see Reg. §1.1294-1T(f).

[95] For election procedures, see Reg. §§1.1294-1T(c), (d), (h).

[96] IRC §1294(b).

[97] IRC §1294(c).

[98] See 1986 Bluebook, supra note 6, at 1029. The Treasury may exempt a transfer in a nonrecognition transaction from this rule if the transferee of the stock succeeds to the taxpayer's obligation to eventually pay the deferred tax. IRC §1293(c)(2).

[99] IRC §1294(f); Reg. §1.1294-1T(e)(2).

the QEF makes a loan to the shareholder or a related person or makes a pledge or guarantee to secure a loan by a third party to the shareholder or a related person. In this case, deferral terminates for tax on undistributed earnings equal to the amount of the loan made, secured, or guaranteed by the QEF.[100]

If the corporation ceases to be a QEF or ceases to be a PFIC, the deferral period ends as to all deferred taxes. Also, the IRS may terminate the deferral if it determines that collection of the deferred taxes is in jeopardy.

When the deferral terminates for any reason other than jeopardy, the deferred tax (or the portion of it affected by the termination) becomes payable on the due date of the shareholder's return for the taxable year during which the terminating event occurs. Extensions of the filing date are ignored. For example, if a calendar year taxpayer sells QEF stock during 1997, taxes deferred with respect to the stock are payable on April 15, 1998. When a jeopardy termination is made, the deferred tax is immediately due and payable. Since the deferral election causes no change in the tax for the deferral year, but only delays its payment, the termination of the deferral has no effect on the shareholder's income or tax for the year of the terminating event.

Because the deferral takes the form of an extension of the time for payment of the deferred tax, interest accrues on the tax at the usual rates for underpayments of tax. The interest, however, is not payable until the tax falls due. Because interest is compounded daily, the interest bill can be substantial when tax is deferred for a substantial period. Assume a shareholder's share of undistributed QEF earnings for 1997 is $100, and an election is made to defer the resulting tax of $39.6. The shareholder receives no distributions from the corporation and holds the stock for an additional 10 years, over which period the interest rate on underpayments of tax is 7 percent. When the stock is sold 2007, the shareholder owes $119.3—$39.6 of deferred tax and $79.7 of interest thereon—in addition to the tax on any gain on the sale.

3. *Distributions and basis adjustments.* Actual distributions from a QEF are tax free to the extent made from earnings and profits taxed under the QEF pass-through mechanism.[101] Also, stock basis is increased by amounts taxed to

---

[100] Reg. §1.1294-1T(e)(4).

[101] IRC §1293(c). Although a tax-free distribution is not a dividend to the shareholder, it reduces earnings and profits.

For taxable years beginning after September 30, 1993, §1293(c) does not apply to a U.S. shareholder of a PFIC that is also a CFC, but an equivalent rule in §959 applies to prevent double taxation. Generally, a U.S. person owning stock of a foreign corporation is a U.S. shareholder if the person owns at least 10 percent of the corporation's voting stock, and a foreign corporation is a CFC if more than 50 percent of its stock is owned by U.S. shareholders. IRC §§951(b), 957(a), discussed supra ¶68.2.2. Section 959 provides rules ensuring that U.S. shareholders of a CFC who have been taxed on subpart F income of the CFC are not taxed a second time when the income is distributed as dividends. See supra ¶68.2.14. For taxable years beginning after September 30, 1993, amounts included

the shareholder and is reduced by tax-free distributions.[102] If a taxpayer is constructive owner of QEF stock, these basis adjustments are made to the property that causes the taxpayer to be constructive owner, which may be stock in a foreign corporation, an interest in a foreign partnership, trust, or estate, or an option to purchase QEF stock from a foreign person.

The distribution and basis rules are not affected by the deferral election described above because the election only defers payment of the tax on QEF inclusions and does not delay the time when they are brought into the taxpayer's gross income.

4. *Taxation of gains and excess distributions of QEF shareholders.* Generally, the annual pass through of corporate income to QEF shareholders supersedes the special tax and interest charge described earlier.[103] Specifically, the special tax and interest charge do not apply to an excess distribution or gain on a stock sale if the taxpayer elected to treat the corporation as a QEF for all years after 1986 that are included in the taxpayer's holding period, with the exception of years when the corporation was not a PFIC.[104]

If a shareholder makes the QEF election for a year after the first year the shareholder holds the stock (or, if later, the first year the corporation is a PFIC), an additional election may be made that avoids the application of the special tax and interest rules on a subsequent distribution or sale.[105] When this election is made, gain or loss is computed as though the stock had been sold on the first day of the first QEF year for an amount equal to its fair market value. If gain results, the gain is subjected to the special tax and interest charge, and the basis of the stock is stepped up to fair market value.[106] The election can be made whether the constructive sale yields gain or loss.[107] Although loss is not recognized, the election has the desirable effect of purging depreciated stock of the PFIC taint, and it costs nothing because stock basis is unaffected when there is loss.

---

in a U.S. shareholder's gross income under §1293 are treated as subpart F income for purposes of §959.

[102] IRC §1293(d).

[103] For the special tax and interest charge, see supra ¶68.5.3.

[104] IRC §1291(d)(1).

[105] IRC §1291(d)(2)(A); Reg. §1.1291-10, promulgated by TD 8701, 61 Fed. Reg. 68149 (Dec. 27, 1996). Alternatively, if the PFIC is a controlled foreign corporation (CFC), the shareholder may elect to recognize dividend income as of the first day of the first QEF year equal to the shareholder's share of the corporation's post-1986 earnings and profits. IRC §1291(d)(2)(B); Reg. §1.1291-9, promulgated by TD 8701, supra. See Brewer & Forouhar, Final and Proposed Passive Foreign Investment Company Regulations, 26 Tax Mgmt. Int'l J. 160 (1997).

[106] IRC §1291(d)(2)(C). Also, the taxpayer's holding period for the stock begins anew with the date of the constructive sale.

[107] Reg. §1.1291-10T(b)(1).

5. *QEF election.* The QEF election is made by the shareholder-taxpayer.[108] Any U.S. person holding PFIC stock may elect, including a domestic partnership, S corporation, domestic nongrantor trust, or a U.S. person who holds PFIC stock in bearer form.[109] The election may also be made by a U.S. person who holds an interest in a foreign partnership owning PFIC stock, is grantor of a trust owning such stock, or is a beneficiary of a foreign trust or estate. Generally, a qualified shareholder must elect independently of any related person who may also own stock in the PFIC. When a group of corporations files a consolidated return, however, the group's parent must elect for the group, and an election by the parent applies to all stock of the PFIC held by all members of the group. If the taxpayer owns stock in more than one PFIC, the election is made corporation by corporation. For example, if members of a group of corporations filing a consolidated return own stock in several PFICs, a separate election must be made with respect to each PFIC.

The PFIC and each intermediary through which the taxpayer owns PFIC stock must supply the information needed by the IRS to administer the QEF rules.[110] The corporation must provide to an electing shareholder a "PFIC Annual Information Statement," in which it specifies (1) its taxable year, (2) the shareholder's ratable share of the corporation's ordinary earnings and net capital gain for the year and the amounts distributed to the shareholder during the year, and (3) that the shareholder may inspect and copy the PFIC's books to whatever extent necessary to establish that ordinary earnings and net capital gain have been computed in accordance with U.S. tax rules.[111] If the PFIC stock is held through an "intermediary" (a nominee or other shareholder of record in the

---

[108] IRC §1295(a); Reg. §1.1295-1. The IRS has proposed regulations providing a "special preferred QEF election" that may be made by a holder of "qualified preferred stock" if the shareholder does not own as much as 5 percent, by vote or value of any class of stock. REG-209040-88, 61 Fed. Reg. 68,149 (Dec. 27, 1996), proposing Reg. §§1.1293-2, 1.1295-2. Preferred stock is "qualified" if it is registered, was issued for cash, is limited and preferred as to dividends, has a fixed redemption price, requires all distributions to be denominated in U.S. dollars, and meets various other requirements. Electing preferred shareholders would

> accrue annually ordinary dividend income with respect to the preferred shares regardless of the holder's pro rata share of ordinary earnings or net capital gain of the PFIC for the year. Because shareholders would accrue income regardless of the earnings and net capital gain of the PFIC, shareholders that elect to be subject to the regime would not have to report and collect any U.S. tax accounting information regarding the PFIC in order to make the special section 1295 election.

REG-209040-88, supra. See Brewer & Forouhar, Final and Proposed Passive Foreign Investment Company Regulations, 26 Tax Mgmt. Int'l J. 160 (1997).

[109] Reg. §1.1295-1T(d).

[110] IRC §1295(a).

[111] Reg. §1.1295-1T(g)(1). In "rare and unusual circumstances," and only pursuant to a private letter ruling and closing agreement, "alternative documentation" may be substituted for the PFIC Annual Information Statement. Reg. §1.1295-1T(g)(2).

"chain of ownership" between the taxpayer and the PFIC), the intermediary must furnish an Annual Intermediary Statement "reporting the indirect owner's pro rata shares of the ordinary earnings and net capital gain of the QEF."[112] The PFIC Annual Information Statement and Annual Intermediary Statement must be attached to a form included with the electing shareholder's tax return.[113] The IRS may terminate the election if the PFIC or an intermediary does not satisfy these requirements.[114]

The election may be made for any taxable year, but once made, it applies to all subsequent years until revoked with IRS consent.[115] The election must usually be made by the due date of the return for the first year to which the election is to apply.[115.1] A late election is allowed, however, if the failure to elect timely results from a reasonable belief that the corporation is not a PFIC.[115.2]

¶68.5.5 Mark-to-Market Election

For taxable years beginning after 1997, a U.S. owner of "marketable" PFIC stock can elect a mark-to-market regime. According to the Staff of the Joint Committee on Taxation,

> the interest-charge method for income inclusion provided in the PFIC rules is a substantial source of complexity for shareholders of PFICs. . . . [S]ome taxpayers have argued that they would have preferred choosing the current-inclusion method afforded by the qualified fund election, but were unable to do so because they could not obtain the necessary information from the PFIC. Accordingly, Congress believed that a mark-to-market election would provide PFIC shareholders with a fair alternative method for including income with respect to the PFIC.[116]

For purposes of the mark-to-market regime, PFIC stock is marketable if it is traded on a national securities exchange registered with the U.S. Securities and Exchange Commission or a national market system recognized under the Securities and Exchange Act of 1934.[117] The Treasury may extend this definition to

---

[112] Reg. §1.1295-1T(g)(3).

[113] Reg. §1.1295-1T(f)(2).

[114] Reg. §1.1295-1T(i)(1).

[115] IRC §1295(b)(1). See Reg. §1.1295-1T(i)(2) (revocation allowed only "upon a finding of a substantial change in circumstances"; request for consent to revoke must be made within 12 months "after the discovery of the substantial change of circumstances"), §1.1295-1T(i)(3) (effect of termination).

[115.1] IRC §1295(b)(2); Reg. §1.1295-1T(e) (due date determined with any extensions). For the forms used in making the election, see Reg. §1.1295-1T(f)(1).

[115.2] See Reg. §1.1295-3T.

[116] Staff of Joint Comm. on Tax'n, 105th Cong., 1st Sess., General Explanation of Tax Legislation Enacted in 1997, at 309 (Comm. Print 1997).

[117] IRC §1296(c). All PFIC stock held by a regulated investment company with shares redeemable at net asset value is considered marketable.

include (1) stock traded on any other exchange or market that "has rules sufficient to ensure that the market price represents a legitimate and sound fair
market value"[118] and (2) stock in a foreign corporation that is comparable to a
regulated investment company (mutual fund) and has stock redeemable at net
asset value. Options on marketable stock may also be treated as marketable.

Under the mark-to-market regime, an electing shareholder must report as
gross income any amount by which the stock's fair market value at year-end
exceeds the taxpayer's basis for the stock.[119] Any amount by which the stock's
basis exceeds fair market value at year-end is allowed as a deduction to the extent
it does not exceed "the unreversed inclusions with respect to such stock,"[120]
which equal the sum of the gross income inclusions for all prior years, less the
amount of any deductions allowed under this rule for prior years.[121] The gross
income inclusions and deductions are ordinary income or loss, as is gain or loss
on a sale or exchange of the stock.[122] The gross income is from the same source
as would be a gain on a sale of the stock, and the deduction is also allocated to
gross income from that source.[123] Under §865(a), such a gain is nearly always
from U.S. sources.[124] The stock's adjusted basis is increased by the amount
included in gross income and decreased by the amount allowed as a deduction.[125]

The mark-to-market election may be made by a controlled foreign corporation (CFC) owning PFIC stock, in which case the gross income inclusions are
treated as foreign personal holding company (FPHC) income and any deduction
allowed under these rules is allocable to such income.[126]

For purposes of these rules, PFIC stock owned by a foreign partnership,
trust, or estate is considered owned proportionately by its partners or beneficia-

---

[118] Staff of Joint Comm. on Tax'n, 105th Cong., 1st Sess., General Explanation of
Tax Legislation Enacted in 1997, at 311 (Comm. Print 1997).

[119] IRC §1296(a)(1). If the PFIC stock is held by a regulated investment company
(RIC), the gross income inclusion is treated as a dividend for purposes of the RIC rules.
IRC §1296(h).

[120] IRC §1296(a)(2).

[121] IRC §1296(d).

[122] IRC §1296(c)(1). For a noncorporate taxpayer, an annual deduction or a loss on
a sale or exchange of the stock is allowed in determining adjusted gross income.

[123] IRC §1296(c)(2).

[124] See infra ¶70.6.4.

[125] IRC §1296(b)(1). If PFIC stock is inherited from a decedent who made the
mark-to-market election, the heir's stock's basis is the lesser of the decedent's basis or the
stock's fair market value on the estate tax valuation date. IRC §1296(i).

If the taxpayer becomes a U.S. citizen or resident during any taxable year beginning
after 1997, the taxpayer's adjusted basis for the stock as of the beginning of that year is,
for purposes of the mark-to-market rules, the greater of the stock's fair market value or
taxpayer's adjusted basis at that time. IRC §1296(l).

[126] IRC §1296(f). For FPHC income of a CFC, see supra ¶68.2.4. See Staff of Joint
Comm. on Tax'n, 105th Cong., 1st Sess., General Explanation of Tax Legislation Enacted
in 1997, at 313 (Comm. Print 1997) ("The source of such amounts, however, is determined
by reference to the actual residence of the CFC").

ries, and, in the case of tiered entities, stock constructively owned under this rule is considered actually owned for purposes of applying the rule successively.[127] A U.S. person constructively owning PFIC stock is deemed to sell or exchange the stock if the stock is disposed of by the actual owner or the U.S. person or any intermediate owner disposes of property that causes the U.S. person to be constructive owner. The basis adjustments for gross income inclusions and deductions are made both to the actual owner's basis for the stock and to the U.S. taxpayer's basis for the property that caused the taxpayer to be constructive owner.[128]

An election of the mark-to-market rules applies for the year of the election and all subsequent years until the stock ceases to be marketable or the IRS consents to a revocation of the election.[129]

¶68.5.6 Stock Attribution Rules

Attribution rules are provided for use whenever stock ownership is relevant under the PFIC and QEF rules. The rules attribute PFIC stock directly owned by foreign persons to U.S. persons who beneficially own the stock. They apply only when their effect is to treat a U.S. person as owner of PFIC stock.[130] Stock actually owned by a U.S. person is not attributed to anyone else, and stock actually owned by a foreign person, once attributed to a U.S. person, is not reattributed to any other person.

Under a corporation-to-shareholder attribution rule, a person owning at least 50 percent of a foreign corporation's stock is deemed to own a proportionate part of any stock owned by the corporation.[131] For example, if a domestic corporation owns 60 percent of the stock of a foreign operating company, it is constructive owner of 60 percent of any PFIC stock owned by the operating company. In contrast, if the domestic corporation owns only 40 percent of the operating company's stock and the remaining shares are held by unrelated persons, no stock held by the operating company is attributed to the domestic corporation because the 50 percent threshold is not crossed.

---

[127] IRC §1296(g).

[128] IRC §1296(b)(2).

[129] IRC §1296(k). If the taxpayer elects the mark-to-market regime after the year during which the stock is acquired, §1291 applies to distributions with respect to the stock and dispositions of the stock during the year of election and to the gross income under §1296(a) for that year unless a QEF election was in effect throughout the taxpayer's holding of the stock. IRC §1296(j)(1). A somewhat different set of rules applies in this situation if the taxpayer is a RIC. IRC §1296(j)(2). These "coordination rule[s]" are meant "to ensure that the taxpayer does not avoid the interest charge with respect to amounts attributable to periods before such election." Staff of Joint Comm. on Tax'n, 105th Cong., 1st Sess., General Explanation of Tax Legislation Enacted in 1997, at 313 (Comm. Print 1997).

[130] IRC §1298(a)(1)(A).

[131] IRC §1298(a)(2)(A).

If a PFIC owns stock in another PFIC, however, the stock is attributed ratably to all shareholders of the shareholding PFIC, including shareholders with less than 50 percent interests.[132] Assume *T*, a U.S. citizen, owns one percent of the stock of foreign corporation *X*, and *X* owns one percent of the stock of foreign corporation *Y*. If *X* and *Y* are both PFICs, *T* is constructive owner of one one-hundredth of one percent of *Y*.

Also, stock owned by a foreign partnership, trust, or estate is deemed owned proportionately by its partners or beneficiaries, regardless of the sizes of their interests.[133] Moreover, the holder of an option is constructive owner of stock covered by the option.[134]

The attribution rules are applied successively.[135] PFIC stock buried in a lower-tier foreign subsidiary of a domestic corporation, for example, is deemed owned by the corporation through repeated applications of the corporation-to-shareholder rule. Once PFIC stock is attributed to a U.S. person, however, the attribution process stops.

The constructive ownership rules have two principal applications. If a PFIC is not a QEF, a transaction that cuts off constructive ownership is usually treated as a sale of the constructively owned stock, thus triggering the special tax and interest charge that apply to gains on sales of PFIC stock.[136] A constructive owner, like a direct owner, can avoid the special tax and interest charge by electing to treat the PFIC as a QEF, thereby causing corporate earnings attributable to the constructively owned stock to be included annually in the taxpayer's gross income.[137]

¶68.6　TRANSFERS OF PROPERTY TO FOREIGN ENTITIES

¶68.6.1　Introductory

Because foreign entities are ordinarily not taxed on foreign earnings, transfers of property by U.S. persons to foreign entities would, if not checked, offer a variety of tax-avoidance opportunities. For example, if a U.S. citizen owning appreciated securities could transfer them tax free to a wholly owned foreign corporation, such a corporation could be used as a tool for turning over a securities portfolio without immediately incurring U.S. tax on gains inherent in the securities. After the securities were transferred to the foreign corporation, it

---

[132] IRC §1298(a)(2)(B).
[133] IRC §1298(a)(3).
[134] IRC §1298(a)(4).
[135] IRC §1298(a)(5).
[136] IRC §1298(b)(5), discussed supra ¶68.5.3 text accompanying note 68.
[137] Supra ¶68.5.4 text accompanying notes 108-115.2.

could sell them without incurring U.S. tax (and perhaps without any foreign taxes), and the U.S. transferor would not be taxed on the resulting gains until she elected to repatriate them to the United States by liquidating the corporation or otherwise cashing in her interest in the corporation. A similar result might be obtained by transferring the securities to an irrevocable trust for the transferor's family.

Congress enacted two sets of rules for stymieing such tactics. Section 367(a)(1) denies the benefit of a broad range of nonrecognition rules that would otherwise apply to transfers of property by U.S. persons to foreign corporations. When §367(a)(1) applies, gain inherent in the property is recognized under the regular income tax. In contrast, under the alternative provision, §1491, a 35 percent excise tax, separate from the regular income tax, is imposed on gain inherent in property transferred by a U.S. person to a foreign partnership, trust, or estate.[1]

The general rule of §367(a)(1) is that gain is recognized when a U.S. person transfers property to a foreign corporation in any of the following transactions: (1) a U.S. person's transfer of property to a foreign corporation in exchange for the corporation's stock where the transferor, alone or together with others making contemporaneous transfers, controls the corporation immediately after the exchange; (2) a U.S. person's exchange of stock or securities of a domestic corporation for stock or securities of a foreign corporation pursuant to a plan of reorganization; and (3) a domestic corporation's transfer of its assets to a foreign corporation in a reorganization exchange for stock or securities of the foreign corporation.[2] A companion rule usually requires that a domestic subsidiary recognize gain on distributing its assets to a foreign parent corporation.[3]

The recognition rule of §367(a)(1) is modified by a few exceptions.[4] Transfers of stock or securities to a foreign corporation are excepted in several situations where Congress or the Treasury found little potential for tax evasion.[5] Also, nonrecognition is allowed for transfers of some types of assets to be used by a transferee foreign corporation in the active conduct of a trade or business in a foreign country.[6] Generally, the active business rule allows nonrecognition for gains not likely to be realized quickly by the transferee. A loss recapture rule,

---

[1] See infra ¶68.6.8.

[2] See infra ¶68.6.2. See generally Dolan, U.S. Taxation of International Mergers, Acquisitions and Joint Ventures (Warren, Gorham & Lamont 1995); Davis, Outbound Transfers of Tangible Property Under Section 367(a), 23 Tax Mgmt. Int'l J. 55, 103 (1994); Kingson, The Theory and Practice of Section 367, 37th Annual NYU Inst. on Fed. Tax'n (1994); Wells, Section 367(a) Revisited, 12 Tax Notes Int'l 1963 (June 17, 1996), reprinted in 71 Tax Notes 1511 (June 10, 1996). See also Tuerff & Moreland, U.S. Multinationals and International Joint Ventures, 78 Tax Notes 725 (Feb. 9, 1998).

[3] Infra ¶68.6.6.

[4] For an additional exception for transfers to foreign sales corporations (FSCs), see Reg. §1.367(a)-4T(h). For FSCs, see supra ¶68.1.4.

[5] Infra ¶68.6.3.

[6] Infra ¶68.6.4.

however, requires that even such gains be recognized on the incorporation of a foreign branch that has sustained losses.

Transfers of copyrights, patents, and similar intangibles come in for especially hard treatment, even when the property will be used in an active business of the transferee in a foreign country.[7] Such transfers are treated as though the property had been licensed to the transferee for a royalty payable over the property's economic life. Moreover, the constructive royalties are adjusted periodically to be commensurate with the transferee's income from the property throughout its life and are classified as income from U.S. sources.

¶68.6.2   Recognition Rule of §367(a)(1)

Section 367(a)(1) denies the benefits of various corporate nonrecognition rules when a U.S. person (including a U.S. citizen or resident or domestic corporation, partnership, trust, or estate) transfers property to a foreign corporation. The nonrecognition provisions affected by this rule are the following:

1. Section 351 (no gain or loss recognized on a transfer of property to a corporation in exchange for stock of the corporation if the transferor, alone or together with others making contemporaneous transfers, owns at least 80 percent of the corporation's stock immediately after the transfer).[8]
2. Section 354 (no gain or loss recognized when stock or securities are exchanged for other stock or securities pursuant to a reorganization).
3. Section 356 (where §354 would apply but for the receipt of other property in addition to stock, recognized gain is limited to the value of the other property, and no loss is recognized).[9]
4. Section 361 (corporation recognizes no gain or loss on a transfer of its property pursuant to a plan of reorganization in exchange for stock or securities of another corporate party to the plan).[10]

When the transferor is a U.S. person and the transferee is a foreign corporation, §367(a)(1) denies the benefit of these nonrecognition rules by providing that the transferee is deemed not to be a corporation. The reach of this principle is further extended by a rule that a U.S. person's contribution to the capital of a foreign corporation is treated as made in exchange for stock equal in value to the contributed property if the U.S. person, alone or together with others making con-

---

[7] Infra ¶68.6.5.
[8] For §351, see infra ¶91.1.
[9] For §§354 and 356, see infra ¶94.4.5.
[10] For §361, see infra ¶94.4.3.

temporaneous contributions, owns (actually or constructively) at least 80 percent of the foreign corporation's stock immediately after the transfer.[11]

The effects of these rules are illustrated by the following examples:

1. *Organization exchanges and contributions to capital.* Assume *A*, a U.S. citizen, transfers property to a newly organized foreign corporation, *F*, in exchange for all of *F*'s stock. Absent §367(a)(1), §351(a) would excuse *A* from recognizing gain or loss on the transfer because only stock of *F* is received in exchange and *A* owns more than 80 percent of *F*'s stock immediately after the exchange. Section 351(a), however, only applies to a transfer to a "corporation," and because *A* is a United States person and *F* is a foreign corporation, §367(a)(1) denies corporate status to *F* for purposes of applying §351 to gains. *A* therefore recognizes gain as though the transferred property had been sold for a price equal to the value of the *F* stock.

Assume *A* decides sometime later to make an additional contribution to *F*'s capital. Since *A* already owns all of *F*'s stock, it would be meaningless for *F* to issue additional shares in exchange for this contribution, and *A* therefore receives nothing in exchange. Stock equal in value to the contribution, however, is deemed issued to *A* in exchange for the contribution.[12] Absent an exception, gain is recognized on this constructive exchange because, as explained in the preceding paragraph, §367(a)(1) denies the benefit of §351, the only nonrecognition rule that could apply to the exchange.

2. *Reorganization exchanges.* Assume *A*, a U.S. citizen owning stock of corporation *T*, transfers the stock to foreign corporation *R* in exchange for *R* stock. If *R* owns at least 80 percent of the *T* stock immediately after this exchange, the transaction is a reorganization under §368(a)(1)(B), and absent §367(a)(1), §354(a)(1) would provide nonrecognition for *A*'s gain on the exchange. Section 354(a)(1), however, only applies when stock or securities of one corporation are exchanged in a reorganization for stock or securities of "another corporation." Because *R* is a foreign corporation, §367(a)(1) requires that it be treated as a noncorporate entity in applying §354 to an exchange by a U.S. person, such as *A*. The nonrecognition rule is therefore inapplicable, and *A* must

---

[11] IRC §367(c)(2). See Rev. Rul. 91-5, 1991-1 CB 114, modified and amplified, Rev. Rul. 92-86, 1992-2 CB 19 (domestic corporation sells all outstanding stock of foreign corporation (*FY*) to another foreign corporation (*FX*), which is wholly owned subsidiary of domestic corporation's parent; under §§304(a)(1) and 302(d), selling price is treated as received in redemption of stock of *FX* and is taxed as dividend to extent of combined earnings and profits of *FX* and *FY*, and *FY* stock is deemed transferred to *FX* as capital contribution; held, §367(a) applies to deemed capital contribution); Dolan, International Aspects of Section 304 Transactions, 24 Tax Mgmt. Int'l J. 75, 123 (1995); Hoke & Dablain, Taxpayer Relief Act of 1997: Impact on Foreign Taxable Restructurings, 79 Tax Notes 1169 (June 1, 1998); Oosterhuis & Hobbet, Musings on Revenue Ruling 91-5 and Its Implications for Section 304 Transactions, 50 Tax Notes 1291 (Mar. 20, 1991).

[12] IRC §367(c)(2).

recognize her gain on the exchange unless the transaction is encompassed by an exception described below.[13]

Assume D, a domestic corporation, transfers all of its assets to F, a foreign corporation, in exchange for F stock, and the stock is immediately distributed to D's shareholders in liquidation. The transaction is a reorganization under §368(a)(1)(C), and absent §367(a)(1), §361(a) would exempt D from recognizing gain or loss on the exchange of its assets for F stock. However, because D is a U.S. person and F is a foreign corporation, F is considered a noncorporate entity in applying §361, and the nonrecognition rule is inapplicable. Absent an exception, D therefore recognizes gain as though it had sold its assets for cash equal to the value of the F stock received in the exchange.

Section 367(a)(1) applies to a U.S. person's transfer to a foreign corporation whether the transfer is direct or indirect.[14] Assume domestic corporation T is merged into a domestic subsidiary of foreign corporation F, and in exchange for their T stock, the T shareholders receive F stock rather than stock of F's domestic subsidiary. Although no transfer is actually made to a foreign corporation, U.S. shareholders of T are deemed to have transferred their T stock to F in exchange for F stock. So viewed, the transaction is covered by §367(a)(1) because the transferor is a U.S. person and the transferee is a foreign corporation. More generally, a reorganization transaction in which a U.S. person exchanges stock of a domestic corporation for stock of a foreign corporation is treated as an indirect transfer to the foreign corporation even if the foreign corporation actually receives nothing from the U.S. person.[15]

Also, if a U.S. person transfers a partnership interest to a foreign corporation, §367(a) is applied as though the transfer consisted of the partner's pro rata share of the partnership's assets.[16] Assume a partnership carrying on a business in a foreign country is incorporated by the partners' transfer of their interests to a newly organized foreign corporation in exchange for stock. Each partner is deemed to have made an indirect transfer of her ratable share of the partnership's assets, and §367(a) applies to each partner who is a U.S. person. In this case, the rule may be helpful to the partners because the partnership's assets are to be used by the transferee in the active conduct of a foreign business and the transaction thus may be excepted from §367(a)(1) by the active business rule described

---

[13] Infra ¶68.6.3.

[14] Reg. §1.367(a)-1T(c)(1). See Reg. §1.367(a)-1T(c)(5) (where domestic corporation has elected under §1504(d) to treat Canadian or Mexican subsidiary as domestic corporation in order to allow subsidiary to join in consolidated return, termination of election is treated as indirect transfer by domestic to foreign corporation).

[15] Reg. §1.367(a)-1T(c)(2).

[16] IRC §367(a)(4); Reg. §1.367(a)-1T(c)(3)(ii). See Reg. §1.367(a)-1T(c)(3)(ii)(C) (transfers of limited partnership interests that are regularly traded on established securities market are treated as transfers of stock or securities, rather than as transfers of ratable shares of partnership assets).

below, whose application would be unclear if the transaction were analyzed as a transfer of partnership interests rather than partnership assets.[17]

A partnership's transfer of assets to a foreign corporation is treated as an indirect transfer of the assets by the partners, thus causing §367(a)(1) to apply to any partner that is a U.S. person.[18] Assume the partnership in the example is incorporated by the partnership transferring its assets to a newly organized corporation and distributing the stock received in exchange to the partners. Section 367(a) applies to the U.S. partners of the partnership because each partner is deemed to have made an indirect transfer of a portion of the partnership's assets. This rule is most significant where the partnership is organized in a foreign country because, absent the indirect transfer rule, the transfer would be a transfer from one foreign entity to another and thus outside the ken of §367(a)(1).

Section 367(a)(1) only applies to gain. Moreover, when several items are transferred simultaneously, the provision is applied item by item, denying nonrecognition to gains but letting the nonrecognition rules apply to losses on other items.[19] The character and source of gain required to be recognized by §367(a)(1) is determined by the usual rules for taxable exchanges.[20] Basis is determined as though the nonrecognition rules applied, but appropriate adjustments are made for gain recognized under §367(a)(1).

¶68.6.3 Transfers of Stock and Securities

Although §367(a)(1) generally requires that a U.S. person recognize gain on a transfer to a foreign corporation of stock or securities of another corporation, its application in this context is subject to two qualifications.[21] First, §367(a) generally does not interfere with the normal application of the corporate nonrecognition rules to transfers of stock or securities of one foreign corporation to another foreign corporation, probably because the exchange of an investment in one foreign corporation for an investment in another foreign corporation does not have much potential for removing appreciation from U.S. tax jurisdiction. Since the basis of property transferred in a nonrecognition exchange carries over

---

[17] For the active business rule, see infra ¶68.6.4.

[18] Reg. §1.367(a)-1T(c)(3)(i) (rule applicable whether partnership is domestic or foreign). See Reg. §1.367(a)-1T(c)(4) (transfer by trust or estate is treated as transfer by entity, not by beneficiaries, except that transfer by grantor trust is indirect transfer by grantor).

[19] Reg. §§1.367(a)-1T(b)(1), (3).

[20] Reg. §1.367(a)-1T(b)(4)(i).

[21] Also, if a domestic corporation transfers its own stock or securities to a person performing services for a foreign corporation of which the domestic corporation is a shareholder, §367(a)(1) does not apply merely because, under §1.83-6(d)(1), the stock or securities are deemed transferred by the domestic corporation to the foreign corporation and then by the foreign corporation to the services performer. Reg. §1.367(a)-3(c)(8).

to the property received in the exchange, any gain that would have been recognized on a sale of the old investment may be taxed on a subsequent sale of the new investment.

Second, a U.S. person's transfer of stock or securities of a domestic corporation may also qualify as a nonrecognition transaction, but the rules are more complicated in this situation.[22] Generally, a nonrecognition rule can apply to such a transfer only if the foreign corporation is not U.S. controlled after the transaction. For example, if domestic corporation DC transfers all of the stock of a domestic subsidiary (DS) to a foreign subsidiary (FS) in exchange for FS stock, DC fully recognizes its gain on the exchange, even though the exchange is covered by the nonrecognition rule of §351, because FS is controlled by DC after the transfer.[23]

In contrast, assume FP, a foreign corporation with only foreign shareholders, acquires all of the stock of domestic corporation DT in exchange for voting stock of FP in a transaction qualifying as B reorganization. If the former DT shareholders own no more than 50 percent of the FP stock after the exchange, they are allowed nonrecognition on the exchange. However, even in this situation, U.S. persons owning 5 percent or more of the foreign transferee's stock after the transaction qualify for nonrecognition only if the transferee holds the transferred stock or securities for at least five years. The underlying rationale seems to be that 5 percent or greater shareholders of the domestic corporation should be allowed nonrecognition only if the transferred stock or securities become a long-term investment of the transferee foreign corporation; that a disposition of the

---

[22] The regulations on the subject presently consist of final regulations issued in 1996 and temporary regulations from 1995. TD 8702, 1997-1 CB 92; TD 8638, 1996-1 CB 43. See Davis, New Section 367(a) Regulations Restrict Outbound Transfers of Domestic Stock or Securities, 25 Tax Mgmt. Int'l J. 238 (1996); Stankee, Section 367(a) Final Regs. Toughen the "Active Trade or Business" Test, 8 J. Int'l Tax'n 258 (1997). For the proposed regulations, issued in 1991, see NY State Bar Ass'n Tax Section, Report on Proposed Sections 367(a) and (b) Regulations, 55 Tax Notes 105 (1992); Elliott, Outbound Stock Transfers: A Commentary on the Proposed Section 367(a) Regulations, 5 Tax Notes Int'l 31 (July 8, 1992).

[23] In determining that nonrecognition should be denied in this situation, the IRS expressed most concern about a somewhat different transaction. See Notice 94-46, 1994-1 CB 356. Assume DC's shareholders are nine U.S. citizens, one of whom owns 40 percent of DC's stock and the other eight of whom own 7.5 percent each; DC's shareholders transfer their stock to FS in exchange for FS stock. Before this transaction, FS is a controlled foreign corporation (CFC), and DC is taxed under subpart F on FS's subpart F income and other items. See supra ¶68.2. After the transaction, FS is not a CFC because less than 50 percent of its stock is owned by U.S. shareholders (U.S. persons owning at least 10 percent of the foreign corporation's voting stock). Because the transaction has the effect of removing FS from the ambit of subpart F, the IRS decided that it should not be possible to accomplish the transaction tax free. However, the rule requires recognition in cases, like the example in the text, where the transaction does not have the effect of decontrolling a CFC.

stock or securities by the transferee within five (or 10) years after the transfer should be imputed back to these shareholders because it demonstrates a lack of this long-term investment commitment. Shareholders with less than 5 percent interests in the domestic corporation, on the other hand, are not likely to play any major role in the management of the transferee and therefore should not be charged with subsequent actions of the transferee.

1. *Transfers of stock of foreign corporations.* Section 367(a)(1) does not apply to a U.S. person's transfer to a foreign corporation of stock or securities of another foreign corporation if the issuer of the stock or securities is a party to the exchange or is a party to a reorganization that includes the transfer.[24] For example, if a U.S. person owning stock of foreign corporation T transfers the stock to foreign corporation A in exchange for voting stock of A in a transaction qualifying as a B reorganization, §367(a)(1) does not apply to the exchange, and §354(a), which provides the shareholder with nonrecognition for a stock-for-stock exchange in a reorganization, therefore applies in its normal manner.

However, such an exchange might cause the U.S. person to recognize gain (or dividend income) under §367(b).[25] This is most likely to occur, for example, if T is a controlled foreign corporation (CFC) and the U.S. person is a U.S. shareholder (generally, a 10 percent or greater voting shareholder) of T, while A is not a CFC or the U.S. person is not a U.S. shareholder of A.

2. *Transfers of stock or securities of domestic corporations.* A U.S. person's transfer to a foreign corporation of stock or securities of a domestic corporation (the U.S. target) is exempted from §367(a)(1) only if all of the following requirements are met:[26]

    a. The stock of the transferee foreign corporation received by U.S. persons in the transaction accounts for not more than 50 percent, by vote and by value, of the transferee's outstanding stock after the transaction.[27]

    b. Immediately after the transaction, not more than 50 percent of the transferee's stock, by both vote and value, is owned by U.S. persons who are officers or directors of the U.S. target or "five-percent target shareholders." A five-percent target shareholder is a person owning at least 5 percent of the U.S. target's stock, by vote or by value, immediately before

---

[24] IRC §367(a)(2); Reg. §§1.367(a)-1T(b)(2)(i); 1.367(a)-3T(b)(1).

[25] See infra ¶68.7.5.

[26] Reg. §1.367(a)-3(c)(1). These rules apply to all transfers after January 29, 1997, but taxpayer may usually elect to apply them to transfers after April 17, 1994. Reg. §1.367(a)-3(c)(11).

For purposes of these requirements, stock or securities transferred by a partnership (domestic or foreign) are treated as transferred ratably by the partners. Reg. §1.367(a)-3(c)(4)(i).

[27] The "transferee foreign corporation" is the corporation whose stock is received in the exchange, which is not necessarily the corporation to which the U.S. transferors transfer their stock. Reg. §1.367(a)-3(c)(5)(vi).

the transaction.[28] In applying this test, all stock owned by these U.S. persons is taken into account, including stock that they owned before the transaction.

c. The transferee has been actively engaged in a trade or business outside the United States for at least 36 months before the transaction.[29]

d. At the time of the transfer, the fair market value of the transferee equals or exceeds that of the U.S. target.[30]

e. The taxpayer (U.S. transferor) either is not a five-percent transferee shareholder or enters into an agreement with the IRS to recognize gain on the transfer if the U.S. target's stock or securities are transferred again within five years. A "five-percent transferee shareholder" is a transferor who, immediately after the transaction, owns at least 5 percent of the stock of the transferee foreign corporation, either by vote or by value.[31]

The constructive ownership rules of §958 apply in determining stock ownership for purposes of all of these requirements.[32]

---

[28] Reg. §1.367(a)-3(c)(5)(iii). SEC filings may sometimes be relied upon to identify five-percent target shareholders.

[29] Reg. §1.367(a)-3(c)(3)(i). This requirement may be met by a trade or business with a history of at least 36 months that acquired during the 36-month period from a person other than the U.S. target or an affiliate. Reg. §1.367(a)-3(c)(3)(ii). Moreover, the requirement may be satisfied by a trade or business carried on or acquired by a "qualified" subsidiary or partnership. A subsidiary is qualified if the transferee owns at least 80 percent of its stock, both by value and voting power, and the U.S. target did not own as much as 50 percent of the stock, directly or indirectly, during the 36 months preceding the transfer. Reg. §1.367(a)-3(c)(5)(vii). A partnership is generally qualified if the transferee has "active and substantial management functions as a partner with regard to the partnership business" and has an interest of at least 25 percent in partnership profits and capital. Reg. §1.367(a)-3(c)(5)(viii).

The IRS will consider issuing a letter ruling allowing nonrecognition for a transaction failing to meet this requirement or the fair market value requirement described in the next note and accompanying text if (1) all of the other requirements are met and (2) the active trade or business and fair market value requirements are "substantially" satisfied. Reg. §1.367(a)-3(c)(9).

[30] Reg. §1.367(a)-3(c)(3)(iii). The transferee's fair market value is determined with regard to an asset acquired during the preceding 36 months if it produces passive income, was acquired for the purpose of satisfying this requirement, or is stock of a qualified subsidiary or an interest in a qualified partnership. This fair market value of the transferee's interest in a qualified subsidiary or partnership excludes any value attributable to assets of the subsidiary or partnership that would be excluded under the 36-month rule if held by the transferee. Moreover, an asset received within the 36-month period from the U.S. target or an affiliate is excluded whether held by the transferee or a qualified subsidiary or partnership.

[31] Reg. §1.367(a)-3(c)(5)(ii).

[32] Reg. §1.367(a)-3(c)(4)(iv). For §958, see supra ¶68.2.2. If this rule causes a transaction to fail any of the requirements for nonrecognition, the IRS will consider issuing a letter ruling allowing nonrecognition. Reg. §1.367(a)-3(c)(9).

In determining whether either of the 50 percent thresholds is exceeded (requirements *a* and *b*), all transferring shareholders of the U.S. target are presumed to be U.S. persons.[33] Thus, if the stock issued to all target shareholders in the transaction exceeds one half of the foreign corporation's outstanding stock after the transaction, requirement *a* is not met unless this presumption is rebutted with respect to at least some of the shareholders.[34] The presumption is rebutted as to a particular shareholder only if the U.S. target holds a statement from the shareholder representing that the shareholder is not a U.S. person.[35] Also, for purposes of the thresholds, an option is treated as exercised "if a principal purpose of the issuance or the acquisition of the option . . . was the avoidance of [§367(a)(1)]."[36] Moreover, for these purposes, the U.S. target's shareholdings in the transferee foreign corporation are deemed not outstanding.[37]

The gain recognition agreement required of five-percent transferee shareholders (requirement *e*) obligates them to recognize gain on the transfer in the event the transferee foreign corporation, during the term of the agreement, disposes of the transferred stock or securities of the U.S. target by any means other than a liquidation of the target.[38] The agreement's term begins on the date of the transfer and ends with the close of the fifth taxable year following the year in which the transfer occurs.[39] If the transferred stock or securities are disposed of during the agreement's term, the transferor must, within 90 days after the disposition, amend its return for the year of the transfer to report any gain realized

---

[33] Reg. §1.367(a)-3(c)(2).

[34] Reg. §1.367(a)-3(c)(10) Ex. 1.

[35] Reg. §1.367(a)-3(c)(7). The U.S. target must also include with its U.S. return for the year of the transaction a statement summarizing the shareholder statements that it holds.

For the content of the shareholder statement, which must be "signed under penalties of perjury," see Reg. §1.367(a)-3(5)(i).

[36] Reg. §1.367(a)-3(c)(4)(ii).

[37] Reg. §1.367(a)-3(c)(4)(iii).

[38] Reg. §1.367(a)-3T(g)(1).

A disposition by the U.S. target, out of the ordinary course of its business, of "all or a substantial portion of its assets," other than by distribution to the transferee foreign corporation, is treated as a disposition by the transferee of a proportionate part of its target stock. Reg. §1.367(a)-3T(g)(3)(iii). A disposition by the transferee foreign corporation of assets received in distributions from the U.S. target may also be treated as a disposition of target stock. Reg. §1.367(a)-3T(g)(3)(iv).

On the other hand, if the transferee foreign corporation disposes of target stock in a transaction in which no gain or loss would be recognized under U.S. tax principles, this disposition does not trigger gain recognition under the agreement if the taxpayer notifies the IRS of the disposition and makes a new gain recognition agreement covering future dispositions by the new owner of the stock or securities or by the original transferee foreign corporation of the consideration received in the nonrecognition transaction. Reg. §1.367(a)-3T(g)(7).

[39] Reg. §1.367(a)-3T(g)(3)(i).

but not recognized on the transfer. If the foreign corporation disposes of only a portion of the transferred stock or securities, only a proportionate part of the taxpayer's realized but not previously recognized gain is recognized.[40] Any increase in tax resulting from the amendment bears interest from the due date of the return for the year of the transfer to the date on which the tax is paid.[41] The agreement, which must include a waiver of the limitations period on assessments for the year of the transfer,[42] must be signed under penalties of perjury and must be attached to the return required to be filed reporting the transaction under §6038B.[43]

By the gain recognition agreement, the five-percent transferee shareholder must warrant that arrangements have been made to ensure that the shareholder will be informed of any disposition covered by the agreement.[44] The shareholder must also agree to include a statement with its U.S. return for each year during the term of the agreement,[45] which will either certify that the transferee foreign corporation has not yet disposed of the transferred stock or securities or, if such a disposition has occurred, provide information on the disposition.

In addition to the requirements outlined above, the U.S. target must file a report on the transaction with its return for the year of the transfer if the stock transferred by U.S. persons in the transaction is more than 10 percent of the U.S. target's stock, by either vote or value.[46] The report must, among other things, (1) describe the transaction, the stock issued by the transferee foreign corporation in exchange for stock or securities of the U.S. target, and the stock of the transferee held by the U.S. target (directly and indirectly) immediately after the transaction, (2) represent that requirements c (transferee actively engaged in business) and d (transferee's fair market value at least equal to U.S. target's), and (3) list the U.S. persons who are officers or directors of the U.S. target or five-percent target shareholders.

The regulations qualify all of the foregoing with an antiabuse rule. Even if all of the requirements are met, a U.S. person transferring stock of a domestic corporation to a foreign corporation is taxed on gain on the transfer if (1) the taxpayer would recognize gain under §367(a)(1) on a transfer to the foreign corporation of any property owned by the domestic corporation, (2) that property was transferred to the domestic corporation by a U.S. person in a nonrec-

---

[40] Reg. §1.367(a)-3(g)(3)(ii).

[41] Reg. §1.367(a)-3T(g)(3)(i). Appropriate basis adjustments are made to reflect the gain recognized, but not the tax or interest thereon. Reg. §1.367(a)-3T(g)(13).

[42] Reg. §1.367(a)-3T(g)(4). The waiver must extend the limitations period until the end of the eighth taxable year following the year of the transfer. Reg. §1.367(a)-3T(g)(4).

[43] Reg. §1.367(a)-3T(g)(2). For §6038B, see infra ¶68.6.7.

[44] Reg. §1.367(a)-3T(g)(6).

[45] Reg. §1.367(a)-3T(g)(5).

[46] Reg. §1.367(a)-3(c)(6)(i). The report must usually be included with a timely filed return for the year, but the report may be waived on a showing of reasonable cause for the target's failure to file timely. Reg. §1.367(a)-3(c)(6)(ii).

ognition transaction, and (3) avoiding §367(a) was "one of the principal purposes" for the transfer of the property to the domestic corporation.[47] Any transfer to the domestic corporation during the two years preceding the transfer of the corporation's stock or securities is presumed made principally for the purpose of avoiding §367(a). This presumption also arises "if it otherwise appears that the transfer of stock to the foreign corporation was planned or contemplated at the time of the transfer of the property to the domestic corporation."

¶68.6.4 Active Foreign Businesses

A U.S. person's transfer of property to a foreign corporation is usually exempted from §367(a)(1) if the property is to be used by the corporation in "the active conduct of a trade or business outside of the United States."[48] For example, when a domestic corporation incorporates a foreign branch, the active business exception often permits the transferor to enjoy nonrecognition under §351 even if the newly organized corporation is foreign. The exception also sometimes applies where a domestic subsidiary is reorganized into a foreign subsidiary.[49] In these contexts, the policy of the corporate nonrecognition rules to allow business adjustments to occur unimpeded by tax consequences is generally considered more weighty than the policy of §367(a)(1) to require that gain be recognized when property leaves U.S. tax jurisdiction.

The §367(a)(1) policy, however, is given preference by subsidiary rules requiring that gain must be recognized on transfers of certain types of property, principally assets that will quickly be converted into cash, even if the transferee uses the property in the active conduct of a foreign business.[50] Also, depreciation must be recaptured on a transfer of depreciable tangible property that the transferor used in the United States.[51] Moreover, a loss recapture rule requires recognition of gain on the incorporation of a foreign branch if the taxpayer has taken deductions for losses sustained by the branch.[52]

1. *Basic requirements.* For purposes of the active business rule, a "trade or business" is

---

[47] Reg. §1.367(a)-3T(h)(2).

[48] IRC §367(a)(3)(A). See Rev. Proc. 98-7, 1998-1 CB—, §4.01(1) (IRS ordinarily will not rule on whether property is transferred for use in active conduct of trade or business if "the determination requires extensive factual inquiry").

The active business exemption is denied if the taxpayer fails to comply with the reporting requirements of §6038B, discussed infra ¶68.6.7. Reg. §1.367(a)-2T(a). Also, the exemption may be lost if the transferee corporation retransfers the assets within six months after receiving them. Reg. §1.367(a)-2T(c). See Reg. §1.367(a)-4T(d).

For the application of the active business rule to transfers of working interests in oil and gas, see Reg. §1.367(a)-4T(e).

[49] Infra text accompanying notes 59-60.

[50] Infra text accompanying notes 60-68.

[51] Infra text accompanying notes 69-72.

[52] Infra text accompanying notes 73-89.

a specific unified group of activities that constitute (or could constitute) an independent economic enterprise carried on for profit. .... To constitute a trade or business, a group of activities must ordinarily include every operation which forms a part of, or a step in, a process by which an enterprise may earn income. .... The group of activities must ordinarily include the collection of income and the payment of expenses.[53]

The active business exception thus cannot apply if the transferee's activities will be merely an aspect of a trade or business it shares with a related person. However, the selling of goods may be a separate trade or business, even if the goods are produced by the transferee's parent or other affiliates and its operations are fully integrated with the parent's, provided that the transferee's activities "could be independently carried on for profit."[54] The holding of investments for the corporation's own account, however, cannot be a trade or business.

Even if the transferee has a separate trade or business, the active business rule does not apply unless the business is "actively conducted," which requires that "the officers and employees of the corporation carry out substantial managerial and operational activities."[55] Work done by officers and employees on loan from related entities is taken into account in applying this test if the work is supervised and paid for by the transferee corporation. Work done by independent contractors is not counted as corporate activity, however, and the use of independent contractors for more than "incidental activities" may preclude the corporation from being actively engaged in business.

The transferee's active business must be carried on outside the United States. Generally, an active business is considered carried on outside the United States if substantially all of the transferred assets are located outside the country immediately after the transfer and "the primary managerial and operational activities" are outside the United States.[56]

When applicable, the active business rule only exempts transfers of assets used or held for use in the trade or business. Property is considered used in a business if it is "held to meet the present needs of that trade or business and not its anticipated future needs."[57]

Transfers compelled by foreign law or foreign governmental action are sometimes presumed made for use in an active business of the transferee. The presumption applies if (1) the property was previously used by the transferor in the country in which the transferee is incorporated and (2) the transfer either is required as a condition of doing business in that country or is made in response to a "genuine threat of immediate expropriation."[58]

---

[53] Reg. §1.367(a)-2T(b)(2).
[54] Id.
[55] Reg. §1.367(a)-2T(b)(3).
[56] Reg. §1.367(a)-2T(b)(4).
[57] Reg. §1.367(a)-2T(b)(5).
[58] Reg. §1.367(a)-4T(f).

2. *Reorganizations.* Generally, the active business rule applies to incorporation exchanges under §351 but not to reorganization exchanges. Assume a domestic corporation owned by U.S. citizens carries on its business in foreign countries; it transfers its assets to a foreign corporation in exchange for voting stock of the latter and distributes the stock to its shareholders in complete liquidation. Even if the transaction qualifies as a reorganization, the domestic corporation recognizes gain under §367(a)(1) on the transfer of its assets to the foreign corporation. The active business rule is inapplicable because it generally does not restore nonrecognition under §361(a) or (b)—the nonrecognition rules for corporate transferors in reorganizations.[59]

However, §361 nonrecognition is allowed under the active business rule if at least 80 percent of the stock of the transferor domestic corporation is owned by five or fewer domestic corporations.[60] For example, if domestic corporation P is sole shareholder of domestic corporation S, whose business is located in a foreign country, the active business rule can apply to a reincorporation of S in a foreign country.

3. *Tainted assets.* Congress identified several types of property, principally "liquid or passive investment assets," that it decided should not escape U.S. tax jurisdiction without the recognition of gain.[61] Specifically, the active business rule is inapplicable to the following: (1) inventory and other property held for sale to customers in the ordinary course of business; (2) installment obligations and accounts receivable, unless the principal amount was included in determining gross income when the obligation or receivable was accepted; (3) foreign currency and obligations denominated in foreign currencies; and (4) copyrights, patents, and similar intangibles.[62] Goodwill and going concern value, in contrast, are not tainted if they were developed in the foreign business before the incorporation transaction.[63]

Gain must usually be recognized on the transfer of property of any type if the transferor held the property as lessor and the transferee foreign corporation is not the lessee immediately before the transfer.[64] The regulations, however, allow two exceptions from this rule. First, tangible property to be held by the transferee in the active conduct of a leasing business can qualify for nonrecog-

---

[59] IRC §367(a)(5).

[60] Id. For this purpose, all members of an affiliated group are treated as one corporation. The transferor corporation thus can have numerous shareholders so long as all of them are domestic corporations belonging to no more than five affiliated groups.

[61] Staff of Joint Comm. on Tax'n, 98th Cong., 2d Sess., General Explanation of the Revenue Provisions of the Deficit Reduction of 1984 at 427 (Comm. Print 1984) [hereinafter 1984 Bluebook] (tainted asset rule largely codifies prior administrative practice).

[62] IRC §367(a)(3)(B); Reg. §§1.367(a)-5T(b), (c). For more on obligations denominated in foreign currencies, see Reg. §1.367(a)-5T(d). For the treatment of transfers of intangibles not qualifying under the active business rule, see §367(d), described infra ¶68.6.5.

[63] 1984 Bluebook, supra note 61, at 435; Reg. §1.367(a)-5T(e).

[64] IRC §367(a)(3)(B)(v); Reg. §1.367(a)-5T(f).

nition if the property is leased for use outside the United States and "the transferee has need for substantial investment in assets of the type transferred."[65] To be in an active leasing business, the foreign corporation's employees must "perform substantial marketing, customer service, repair and maintenance, and other substantial operational activities with respect to the transferred property outside the United States." This exception cannot apply to property held for sale to customers in the ordinary course of business.

The second exception for leased property is a de minimis rule, applicable to tangible property that will be used primarily by the foreign corporation but will be leased to others "during occasional brief periods" when not needed in the corporation's business.[66] An example is an airplane leased during periods of excess capacity. Also, if foreign real property is used primarily by the foreign corporation in its active business, the de minimis rule allows up to 10 percent of the property to be leased to others.

Property not tainted by any of the foregoing rules is disqualified from nonrecognition under the active business rule if "it is reasonable to believe" the transferee will dispose of "any material portion" of the property "in the reasonably foreseeable future" in a transaction not in the ordinary course of business.[67]

Where assets transferred for active use in a foreign business include both tainted assets and other assets, the active business rule applies to the other assets, but gain must be recognized on the transfer of the tainted assets.[68]

4. *Depreciation recapture.* If otherwise untainted property was used by the transferor in the United States, depreciation recapture inherent in property must be recognized as ordinary income on the incorporation transfer.[69] Aircraft, rolling stock, motor vehicles, vessels, and containers are also subject to the recapture rule if used in transporting passengers or freight between the United States and foreign locations.[70] Assume an airplane, purchased several years ago for $5 million and subsequently fully depreciated, is transferred by its owner, a domestic corporation, to a foreign subsidiary; the airplane was and will be used in an active foreign business. If the airplane is worth $8 million at the time of the transfer, the domestic corporation recognizes gain on the transfer of $5 million (lesser of gain of $8 million or depreciation previously taken of $5).

If property other than transportation equipment is used partly within and partly without the United States, only a ratable portion of the recapture income is recognized.[71] Property used wholly without the United States is not subject to

---

[65] Reg. §1.367(a)-4T(c)(1).

[66] Reg. §1.367(a)-4T(c)(2).

[67] Reg. §1.367(a)-4T(d).

[68] 1984 Bluebook, supra note 61, at 432.

[69] Reg. §1.367(a)-4T(b). See 1984 Bluebook, supra note 61, at 434-35. For depreciation recapture, see supra ¶¶55.2, 55.3.

[70] Reg. §1.367(a)-4T(b)(2), referring to §48(a)(2)(B) (before amendment in 1990).

[71] Reg. §1.367(a)-4T(b)(3) (amount recognized equals total recapture multiplied by number of months of U.S. use and divided by number of months of total use).

recapture under this rule, probably because accelerated methods of depreciation are not available for such property.[72]

5. *Loss recapture.* Nonrecognition under the active business rule is denied, in whole or in part, if the transfer is of assets of a "foreign branch" of the U.S. transferor and the branch sustained net losses before the transfer.[73] The idea underlying this rule is as follows: Goodwill, going concern value, and perhaps other intangibles are usually created in the startup period of a new business, even if the business reports losses during this period. Losses incurred by a U.S. person in establishing a foreign branch are usually deductible in determining U.S. tax. If the branch is incorporated as a foreign corporation once the business becomes profitable, the taxpayer often gets the best of both worlds—immediate deduction of losses during the startup period and deferral of tax on profits earned thereafter. Congress decided these advantages should be curbed when the profits result in material part from intangibles created and other unrealized appreciation arising during the startup period. Its solution is to require the recognition of gain on the incorporation transfer up to the amount of the previously deducted losses, thereby effectively recapturing the loss deductions.

The gain recognized under this rule is the lesser of the gain on the incorporation transfer or the previously deducted branch losses. Goodwill and going concern value developed by the foreign branch are included in computing the gain on the transfer.[74] Assume a domestic corporation transfers the assets of a foreign branch (fair market value, $2,500; adjusted basis, $1,000) to a newly organized foreign corporation after having taken deductions for net branch losses of $350.[75] The recapture rule requires recognition of gain of $350—the lesser of the realized gain of $1,500 ($2,500 less $1,000) or the previously deducted losses of $350.

The gain has the same character as the branch losses.[76] For example, if the net branch loss includes a capital loss, an equal amount of the gain recognized on the incorporation transaction is capital gain.[77] Also, the gain is deemed to be from

---

[72] See IRC §168(g), discussed supra ¶23.3.5.

[73] IRC §367(a)(3)(C). See Reg. §1.367(a)-6T(g)(1) ("'foreign branch' means an integral business operation carried on by a U.S. person outside the United States"). See generally Spudis, Lemein & Waimon, Using Partnerships in International Tax Planning, 73 Taxes 834 (1995).

This rule was adopted in 1984. For prior law, see Rev. Rul. 78-201, 1978-1 CB 91, revoked, Rev. Rul. 82-146, 1982-2 CB 84 (adopting similar rule administratively); Mars, Inc. v. CIR, 88 TC 428 (1987) (acq.) (rejecting Rev. Rul. 78-201); Hershey Foods Corp. v. CIR, 76 TC 312 (1981) (same).

[74] Reg. §1.367(a)-6T(c)(3). See 1984 Bluebook, supra note 61, at 434.

[75] Reg. §1.367(a)-6T(f).

[76] IRC §367(a)(3)(C).

[77] 1984 Bluebook, supra note 61, at 434. Also, if the branch sustained a loss in foreign oil or gas extraction activities, a corresponding portion of the incorporation gain is treated as foreign oil and gas extraction (FOGE) income in determining the transferor's foreign tax credit limitation. Reg. §1.367(a)-6T(c)(1) (recapture gain is FOGE income in same

foreign sources, regardless of how it might be characterized under the source rules of general application.[78]

The previously deducted branch losses normally equal the sum of the losses of the branch for all years, including the year of the incorporation transfer (through the date of the transfer).[79] The characterization rule described in the preceding paragraph requires that the branch losses be segregated between ordinary and capital losses.[80] This is done by computing the ordinary income or loss for each taxable year (branch gross income for the year less the deductions allocated and apportioned to this income, exclusive of capital gains and losses) and capital gain net income or loss for the year (sum of capital gains and losses allocable to the branch). Normally, the total ordinary loss is the sum of the taxpayer's ordinary income and losses for the branch for all years up to and including the year of the transfer, and the total capital loss is the sum of the capital gain net income or loss figures for these years. The following adjustments, however, are made:

a. If the ordinary loss for any year is part of a net operating loss (NOL) sustained by the taxpayer for the year, the ordinary loss is reduced by any portion of the NOL that has not yielded tax benefit under the carryback and carryover rules for any year before the year in which the branch is incorporated.[81]

b. If an NOL from another year is carried to one or more years in which ordinary branch losses are sustained, any portion of the carryback or carryover that has not yielded tax benefit for any year before the year of the branch incorporation is applied in reduction of the ordinary branch losses, starting with the loss for the earliest year to which the NOL is carried.[82]

c. Reductions similar to those described in paragraphs a and b are made to branch capital losses to reflect net capital losses and carrybacks and carryovers of net capital losses.[83]

d. If a credit for foreign income taxes has been denied under the credit limitation rules and the carryover for the noncreditable taxes expired unused during the time the branch was in existence, ordinary and capital losses are reduced by the deduction equivalent of the expired carryover

---

proportion as previously deducted FOGE losses bore to all previously deducted losses). For the foreign tax credit rules on FOGE income, see infra ¶69.10.2.

[78] IRC §367(a)(3)(C).

[79] Losses from property abandoned as worthless before the incorporation are included. 1984 Bluebook, supra note 61, at 434.

[80] Reg. §1.367(a)-6T(d)(1).

[81] Reg. §1.367(a)-6T(d)(2).

[82] Id.

[83] Reg. §1.367(a)-6T(d)(3).

(the carryover divided by the U.S. tax rate), starting with the earliest year of branch operations to which the taxes were carried.[84]

e. A similar reduction is made for expired investment credit carryovers.[85]

f. Taxable income of the branch for any year (including the portion of the current year ending with the date of the transfer) is applied in reduction of branch losses for other years.[86]

g. If the incorporation of the branch also triggers recognition of gain under §904(f)(3), an overlapping rule found in the foreign tax credit rules, branch losses for all years are reduced by the gain recognized under §904(f)(3).[87]

h. A further reduction is made for any gain on the incorporation transfer that is recognized under §367(a)(1) apart from the branch rule.[88]

i. Finally, if more than one incorporation transfer is made of assets of the branch, previously deducted losses, as computed for any subsequent transfer, are reduced by gain recaptured under the branch rule on earlier transfers.[89]

¶68.6.5 Transfers of Intangibles

Special rules apply to a U.S. person's transfer of a patent, trade name, customer list, or other intangible to a foreign corporation in a transaction described in §351 (incorporation transfers) or §361 (transfers by corporations in reorganization).[90] The transferor is treated as having sold the property for a series

---

[84] Reg. §1.367(a)-6T(d)(4). For the foreign tax credit carryover rules, see §904(c), discussed infra ¶69.5.4.

[85] Reg. §1.367(a)-6T(d)(5). For investment credit carryovers, see supra ¶27.1.2.

[86] Reg. §1.367(a)-6T(e)(2).

[87] Reg. §1.367(a)-6T(e)(3). For the application of this rule when §904(f)(3) applies to more than one transfer of assets of the branch, see Reg. §1.367(a)-6T(e)(5).

Section 904(f)(3) applies if the taxpayer has experienced an "overall foreign loss" (excess for any taxable year of deductions allocated and apportioned to gross income from foreign sources over that gross income, less amounts recaptured under §904(f)(1) from foreign source taxable income of subsequent years). See infra ¶69.7. If the taxpayer's foreign source income has derived solely from the incorporated branch, the overall foreign loss generally equals the branch loss, and the branch recapture rule applies to nothing. The branch rule has a meaningful application only where the taxpayer has had other foreign income. In general, §904(f)(3) recaptures foreign losses that have been deducted against U.S. income, while the branch rule recaptures foreign losses that have been deducted against income from other foreign ventures or investments.

[88] Reg. §1.367(a)-6T(e)(4).

[89] Reg. §1.367(a)-6T(e)(6).

[90] IRC §367(d)(1). See Reg. §1.367(d)-1T(g)(6) (where U.S. person transfers intangible to domestic corporation and later transfers domestic corporation's stock to foreign corporation, latter transfer is treated as transfer of intangible by U.S. person to foreign corporation if transfer to domestic corporation was primarily to avoid rules described here).

of payments contingent on the property's productivity, use, or disposition.[91] The payments are commensurate with the transferee's income from the property and usually continue annually over the property's useful life.[92] A final lump sum payment is deemed received if, before the end of the useful life, the transferee disposes of the intangible or the transferor disposes of the stock received in exchange for the property.[93]

Before the adoption of this rule in 1984, the IRS generally allowed tax-free transfers of manufacturing intangibles under the active business rule described above. According to the Staff of the Joint Committee on Taxation:

> In light of this favorable ruling policy, a number of U.S. companies adopted a practice of developing patents or similar intangibles at their facilities in the United States, with a view towards using the intangibles in foreign operations. When these intangibles were ready for profitable exploitation, they were transferred to a manufacturing subsidiary incorporated in a low-tax foreign jurisdiction (or in a high-tax jurisdiction that offered a tax holiday for specified local manufacturing operations). By engaging in such practices, the transferor U.S. companies hoped to reduce their U.S. taxable income by deducting substantial research and experimentation expenses associated with the development of the transferred intangible and, by transferring the intangible to a foreign corporation at the point of profitability, to ensure deferral of U.S. tax on the profits generated by the intangible. By incorporating the transferee in a low-tax jurisdiction, the U.S. companies also avoided any significant foreign tax on such profits.[94]

1. *Property subject to rule.* The deemed royalty rules apply to a transfer of a patent, invention, formula, process, design, pattern, know-how, trademark, trade name, brand name, franchise, license, contract, method, program, system, procedure, campaign, survey, study, forecast, estimate, customer list, technical data, or "any similar item" that has substantial value apart from the services of particular individuals.[95] It does not apply to the goodwill or going concern value of a business conducted outside of the United States or to the right to use a corporate name in a foreign country.[96] It may apply to a copyright or a literary, musical, or artistic composition, but not if the transferor created the property by

---

[91] IRC §367(d)(2)(A). See generally Davis, Outbound Transfers of Intangible Property Under Section 367(d) After the New Section 482 Regulations, 23 Tax Mgmt. Int'l J. 471 (1994); Parnes, United States Tax Considerations in Organizing a Foreign Joint Venture, 20 J. Corp. Tax'n 3 (1993).

[92] Infra text accompanying notes 102-04.

[93] Infra text accompanying notes 104-08 (stock transfer) and 109-11 (transfer of intangible).

[94] 1984 Bluebook, supra note 61, at 427.

[95] IRC §936(h)(3)(B).

[96] Reg. §§1.367(a)-1T(d)(5)(iii), 1.367(d)-1T(b).

his personal efforts or has a basis for the property determined with reference to the creator's basis.[97]

2. *Term and character of deemed royalties.* The deemed royalties continue for the property's "useful life," defined as "the entire period during which the property has value," except that this period may not exceed 20 years.[98] If the property's value is dependent on secrecy or legal protections, its value ceases when the secret is disclosed or the legal protection expires or is otherwise lost.

The deemed royalties are ordinary income to the U.S. transferor from sources within the United States.[99] They reduce the foreign corporation's earnings and profits.[100] Also, they may be treated as a deduction allocable to the foreign corporation's subpart F income, which may have the effect of reducing the amounts included in the U.S. transferor's gross income under subpart F.[101]

3. *Amounts of deemed royalties.* The constructive periodic payments under the deemed royalty rules must be "commensurate with the [foreign corporation's] income attributable to the intangible" and do not necessarily equal the amounts that would have been paid if the transferor had made a contingent payment sale of the property to an unrelated person in an arm's length transaction.[102] According to the Staff of the Joint Committee on Taxation, commenting on the 1986 enactment of this rule:

> Transfers between related parties do not involve the same risks as transfers to unrelated parties. . . . Congress thus concluded that it is appropriate to assure that the division of income between related parties reasonably reflects the relative economic activities undertaken by each. . . .
>
> In making this change, Congress intended to make it clear that industry norms or other unrelated party transactions do not provide a safe-harbor payment for related party intangibles transfers. Where taxpayers transfer intangibles with a high profit potential, the compensation for the intangibles should be greater than industry averages or norms. In determining whether the taxpayer could reasonably expect that projected profits would be greater than the industry norm, Congress intended that there should be taken into account any established pattern of transferring relatively high profit intangibles to U.S. possessions or low tax foreign locations.
>
> Congress did not intend, however, that the inquiry as to the appropriate compensation for the intangible be limited to the question of whether it was appropriate considering only the facts in existence at the time of the transfer. Congress intended that consideration also be given to the actual profit experience realized as a consequence of the transfer. Thus, Congress intended

---

[97] Reg. §§1.367(a)-5T(b)(2), 1.367(d)-1T(b).

[98] Reg. §1.367(d)-1T(c)(3).

[99] IRC §367(d)(2)(C); Reg. §1.367(d)-1T(c)(1).

[100] IRC §367(d)(2)(B); Reg. §1.367(d)-1T(c)(2).

[101] Reg. §1.367(d)-1T(c)(2).

[102] IRC §367(d)(2)(A).

to require that the payments made for the intangible be adjusted over time to reflect changes in the income attributable to the intangible. [Although] annual adjustments [are not required] when there are only minor variations in revenues, . . . adjustments will be required when there are major variations in the annual amounts of revenue attributable to the intangible. . . .

[In ascertaining the payments commensurate with the income stream, it is relevant whether] the transferee bears real risks with respect to its ability to make a profit from the intangible or, instead, sells products produced with the intangible largely to related parties (which may involve little sales risk or activity) and has a market essentially dependent on, or assured by, such related parties' marketing efforts. However, the profit or income stream generated by or associated with the intangible is to be given primary weight.[103]

4. *Transferor's disposition of stock in transferee.* Two sets of rules are provided for cases where the U.S. transferor of an intangible subject to the deemed royalty rule disposes of the stock received in exchange for the intangible during the term of the deemed royalties. Whether the transfer is subject to one set or the other depends on whether the person receiving the stock is related to the U.S. transferor.[104]

a. *Disposition to unrelated person.* If the stock is sold or otherwise transferred to an unrelated person, the deemed royalties cease as of the date of the disposition, but the U.S. transferor is deemed to make a simultaneous sale of the intangible.[105] Gain (but not loss) is recognized on this deemed sale equal to the value of the intangible at that time, less the transferor's basis for the intangible when it was transferred to the foreign corporation. The gain must be recognized, even if the stock is transferred in a nonrecognition exchange, and it is considered income from sources within the United States. Any additional gain otherwise recognized on the disposition of the stock is characterized and sourced by rules of general application.

When this rule applies, the buyer or other transferee of the stock is deemed to have purchased the intangible for a price equal to its fair market value and contributed it to the corporation's capital.[106] The principal effect of this rule is to give the corporation a basis for the intangible equal to the fair market value figure used in computing the U.S. transferor's gain under the rule described in the preceding paragraph. The deemed capital contribution does not cause a new stream of deemed royalties to be attributed to the purchaser of the stock, even if

---

[103] Staff of Joint Comm. on Tax'n, 99th Cong., 2d Sess., General Explanation of the Tax Reform Act of 1986 at 1015-16 (Comm. Print 1987). The commensurate with income standard also applies under §482, and the IRS has provided greater elaboration on the standard in that context. See infra ¶79.8.4.

[104] For the term "related person," see Reg. §1.367(d)-1T(h) (borrowing relatedness definitions of §§267(b) and 707(b)(1), but lowering ownership thresholds in those provisions from 50 percent to 10 percent).

[105] Reg. §1.367(d)-1T(d)(1).

[106] Reg. §1.367(d)-1T(d)(2).

the purchaser is a U.S. person. Also, the corporation's earnings and profits are not affected by these gyrations, except in so far as future earnings and profits are reduced by amortization of the new basis for the intangible.

b. *Transfer to related person.* If the stock is transferred by the U.S. transferor to a related person who is also a U.S. person, the deemed royalties continue, but are thereafter considered received by the new owner of the stock.[107] The deemed royalties to the new shareholder, like those to the original U.S. transferor, are ordinary income from sources within the United States. If the stock is transferred to a related foreign corporation, the U.S. transferor continues to include the deemed royalties in gross income as though the stock had not been transferred.[108]

5. *Transferee's transfer of intangible.* The deemed royalties cease with a disposition of the intangible by the transferee foreign corporation during the term of the deemed royalties if the person receiving the intangible in this transaction is not related to the U.S. transferor.[109] The U.S. transferor, however, must recognize gain equal to any excess of the intangible's fair market value at that time over the U.S. transferor's basis for the intangible when it was transferred to the original transferee. The foreign corporation's earnings and profits are reduced as though it had distributed a dividend to the U.S. transferor equal to the gain taxed to the transferor.[110]

If the foreign corporation transfers the intangible to a related person, the deemed royalties continue as though the transfer had not occurred.[111] After the transfer, however, earnings and profits and other adjustments reflecting the deemed royalties are made in the accounts of the related transferee of the intangible.

6. *Payment of deemed royalties.* The deemed royalties can be paid by the transferee foreign corporation to the U.S. transferor without further tax consequence.[112] A tax-free payment can also be made of the gain imputed to the U.S. transferor when the transferee foreign corporation disposes of the intangible to an unrelated person. If a deemed royalty or gain is not paid within the year it is included in the U.S. transferor's gross income, a noninterest-bearing account receivable may be established in the U.S. transferor's books for the amounts imputed but not paid for the year, and payments received on the account receivable during the succeeding two taxable years are tax free if they are appropriately reflected in the account. If payment is not made within these two years, the account receivable is deemed contributed to the capital of the transferee foreign corporation, thus causing the amount of the account to be added to the U.S.

---

[107] Reg. §1.367(d)-1T(e)(1).
[108] Reg. §1.367(d)-1T(e)(3).
[109] Reg. §1.367(d)-1T(f)(1).
[110] Reg. §1.367(d)-1T(f)(2).
[111] Reg. §1.367(d)-1T(f)(3).
[112] Reg. §1.367(d)-1T(g)(1).

transferor's stock basis but ending the right to receive payment tax free before earnings and profits are exhausted.

7. *Election of cash sale treatment.* In some cases, a U.S. transferor of an intangible is allowed to elect to treat the transfer of the intangible as a cash sale, rather than as a sale for a series of payments contingent on the intangible's productivity, use, or disposition.[113] When this election is made, the transferor must recognize ordinary income for the year of the transfer equal to the excess of the intangible's fair market value over the transferor's adjusted basis for it. The income is from U.S. sources. The election, however, is available in only three cases:

    a. Where the property is an "operating intangible," defined as an intangible of a type not ordinarily licensed, such as a customer list, purchase or supply contract, survey, or study.[114]

    b. Where the transfer to the foreign corporation is compelled by either foreign law or a "genuine threat of immediate expropriation."[115]

    c. Where all of the following requirements are met: (1) The property is transferred within three months of the foreign corporation's incorporation and as part of the plan for its original capitalization; (2) the U.S. transferor holds at least 40 percent but not more than 60 percent of the transferee's stock, both by value and voting power, immediately after the transfer; (3) at least 40 percent of the foreign corporation's stock, both by value and voting power, is then owned by unrelated foreign persons; (4) at least 50 percent of the property transferred by the U.S. transferor is intangible; (5) the intangible covered by the election will be used by the transferee in the active conduct of a business in a foreign country; and (6) the intangible will not be used in the production of goods for use or consumption in the United States.[116]

8. *Coordination with loss recapture rules.* Section 904(f)(3) requires the recognition of gain on the incorporation of a foreign branch if the taxpayer has previously sustained an overall foreign loss.[117] Also, §367(a)(3)(C) requires that gain be recognized on the incorporation of a branch that has itself sustained losses.[118] If an intangible is among the property transferred in a transaction that triggers either or both of these recapture rules, the deemed royalties and gains under the intangibles rule are reduced to reflect the gain recognized under the branch rules.[119]

---

[113] Reg. §1.367(d)-1T(g)(2).
[114] Reg. §§1.367(a)-1T(d)(5)(ii), 1.367(d)-1T(g)(2)(i).
[115] Reg. §1.367(d)-1T(g)(2)(ii).
[116] Reg. §1.367(d)-1T(g)(2)(iii).
[117] See infra ¶69.7.
[118] See supra ¶68.6.4 text accompanying notes 73–89.
[119] Reg. §1.367(d)-1T(g)(3).

¶68.6.6 Liquidations of Domestic Corporations With Foreign Parent Corporations

Section 367(a)(1) does not apply to a liquidating distribution made by a domestic corporation to a foreign shareholder if the shareholder is a foreign corporation owning at least 80 percent of the liquidating corporation's stock, but regulations under §367(e)(2) provide results similar to those that would apply under the §367(a) regulations.

Section 332 provides that a parent corporation recognizes no gain or loss on the receipt of property in complete liquidation of a subsidiary if the parent owns at least 80 percent of the subsidiary's stock. Under §337, the subsidiary recognizes no gain or loss on distributing property in liquidation to a parent qualifying for nonrecognition under §332.[120] Since foreign corporations typically are not subject to U.S. tax on capital gains, §337 is the crucial provision where the liquidating corporation is domestic and the parent is foreign.

The §367(e)(2) regulations generally override §337 in this situation, requiring that a domestic corporation recognize gain on a liquidating distribution of its assets to a foreign parent corporation.[121] The gain is computed, asset-by-asset, as the excess of fair market value over the distributing corporation's adjusted basis for the property. Loss is also recognized, except that, in the aggregate, capital losses recognized on the liquidation cannot exceed capital gains and ordinary losses may not exceed ordinary gains; also, no loss is recognized on the distribution of property that the distributing corporation received in a nonrecognition transaction during the preceding five years.[122] The distributee's adjusted basis for the property is the distributing corporation's basis, increased or decreased by gain or loss recognized on the distribution.[123]

The regulations provide two exceptions from this recognition requirement.

1. *Exception for assets of U.S. business.* An exception is allowed for some distributions of assets used by the distributing corporation in a trade or business located in the United States. Specifically, no gain or loss is recognized on a §337 distribution of property used in a U.S. business of the distributing corporation if all of the following requirements are met:

   a. The foreign parent corporation must not be a controlled foreign corporation (CFC).[124]

   b. For at least 10 years after the liquidation, the parent must continue the

---

[120] For §§332 and 337, see infra ¶93.8.

[121] Reg. §1.367(e)-2T(b)(1)(i). For the application of these rules where the distributed property includes a partnership interest, see Reg. §1.367(e)-2T(b)(1)(iii).

[122] Reg. §1.367(e)-2T(b)(1)(ii).

[123] Reg. §1.367(e)-2T(b)(3)(i).

[124] Reg. §1.367(e)-2T(b)(2)(i)(A)(*1*). A CFC is a foreign corporation, more than one half of the stock of which (by vote or by value) is owned by U.S. persons, each of whom own at least 10 percent of the corporation's stock. IRC §957(a), discussed supra ¶68.2.2.

U.S. business and continue to use the property in that business.[125] If any of the property ceases to be used in the business during this 10-year period (e.g., because it is sold), the subsidiary's return for the year of the liquidation must be amended to report gain on the liquidating distribution of the property unless the triggering event is a disposition by the distributee and the distributee recognizes gain on disposition as effectively connected income.[126]

c. The liquidating subsidiary and the parent must attach to their U.S. tax returns for the year of the liquidation a statement representing that this exception applies, identifying the parties, describing the distributed property, and providing various other information.[127]

d. The subsidiary and parent must include with this statement a waiver of any treaty benefits that might apply to income from an activity in which the property is used or to gain on a disposition of the property by the distributee.[128]

e. The statement must also extend the statute of limitations on assessment of tax on gains realized in the liquidation until three years after the property ceases to be used in a U.S. business (or, if sooner, until 13 years after the liquidation).[129]

The exception does not apply to a distribution of an intangible.[130]

2. *Exception for distributions of U.S. real property interests.* The requirement that a U.S. subsidiary recognize gain on liquidating distributions to a foreign parent does not apply to distributions of U.S. real property interests.[131] The term "U.S. real property interests" generally includes interests in real property located in the United States and stock in domestic corporations, more than one half of whose assets are U.S. real property interests.[132]

---

[125] Reg. §1.367(e)-2T(b)(2)(i)(A)(2). Property is considered used in a U.S. trade or business if income from the activity in which the property is deployed is effectively connected with such a trade or business and any gain on the property's sale would also be effectively connected income. Inventory is considered used in the business if it is held for sale to customers of the business until it is sold.

[126] Reg. §1.367(e)-2T(b)(2)(i)(C).

[127] Reg. §§1.367(e)-2T(b)(2)(i)(A)(3), (B).

[128] Reg. §1.367(e)-2T(b)(2)(i)(B)(4).

[129] Reg. §1.367(e)-2T(b)(2)(i)(B)(5).

[130] Reg. §1.367(e)-2T(b)(2)(i)(A).

[131] Reg. §1.367(e)-2T(b)(2)(ii).

[132] IRC §897(c)(1), discussed supra ¶¶66.4.2–66.4.4. However, gain must be recognized on a liquidating distribution of one type of U.S. real property interest. If a domestic corporation's U.S. real property interests at one time comprise more than one half of its assets, but the U.S. real property interests subsequently fall below one half of the corporation's assets, stock of the corporation continues to be a U.S. real property interest for five years thereafter. If a liquidating subsidiary holds stock that is within this five-year period, it must recognize gain on distributing this stock in liquidation to a foreign parent.

¶68.6.7 Reporting Requirements

A U.S. person making a transfer to a foreign corporation described in §367(a) must file a notice of the transaction with the IRS.[133] The notice is required even if all or part of the gain on the transaction is within an exception to the recognition rule of §367(a)(1). Failure to file subjects the taxpayer to a penalty equal to 25 percent of the gain on the transfer unless reasonable cause for the delinquency is shown.[134] The regulations also deny the benefit of the active business exception to a noncomplying taxpayer and toll the statute of limitations on the assessment of any deficiency resulting from the transfer until a complying notice is filed.[135]

¶68.6.8 Transfers by U.S. Persons Not Subject to §367(a)(1)

1. *Transfers to trusts.* Section 684, enacted in 1997, requires a U.S. person to recognize gain (but not loss) on any transfer of property to a foreign trust or estate unless the transferor is treated as owner of the trust under the grantor trust rules.[136] If a domestic trust becomes a foreign trust (e.g., because authority to control all substantial decisions of the trust is transferred to a foreign person), the trust is deemed to transfer all of its assets to a foreign trust immediately before it becomes a foreign trust.

2. *Transfers to partnerships.* A U.S. person who transfers property to a foreign partnership in exchange for a partnership interest must report the exchange to the IRS if (1) the person's direct or indirect interest in partnership profits or capital exceeds 10 percent immediately after the transfer or (2) the value of the transferred property, combined with the value of any other property transferred to the partnership during the preceding 12 months, exceeds $100,000.[137] A transferor who fails to make this report is generally subject to a penalty of 10 percent of the fair market value of the transferred property.[138]

3. *Transfers before August 6, 1997.* Until its repeal in 1997, §1491 imposed a 35 percent excise tax on gain inherent in property transferred by a U.S. person to a foreign partnership, estate, or trust.[139] The taxable gain equals the fair market value of the transferred property, reduced by the transferor's adjusted basis for

---

[133] IRC §6038B(a). See Reg. §1.6038B-1T(b)(1) (notice given by filing Form 926 with return for year in which transfer occurs). For the persons required to file, see Reg. §1.6038B-1T(b)(2).

[134] IRC §6038B(b).

[135] Reg. §1.6038B-1T(f)(1).

[136] Section 684 applies to transfers after August 5, 1997.

[137] IRC §§6038B(a), (b)(1). For the application of this requirement to transfers during the period August 6 through December 31 of 1998, see Notice 98-17, 1998-1 CB __.

[138] IRC §6038B(c).

[139] The repeal applies to transfers after August 5, 1997. Pub. L. No. 105-34, §1131 (1997). See Lederman & Hirsh, New Reporting Rules for Departing U.S. Persons and

it and any gain recognized on the transfer apart from §1491.[140] The tax thus does not apply if gain is fully recognized under the regular income tax. The transactions reached by §1491 include "[t]ax-free exchanges, gifts, sales in which any portion of the gain realized is deferred, and private annuity transactions."[141] If a domestic trust becomes a foreign trust (e.g., by the substitution of foreign trustees for U.S. trustees), the trust is deemed, for purposes of §1491, to have transferred all of its assets to a foreign trust immediately before the change in status.[142]

The tax is also technically applicable to a U.S. person's transfer to a foreign corporation as a contribution to capital. A transfer "described in section 367," however, is exempt from the §1491 tax,[143] and capital contributions to foreign corporations are usually brought within §367(a)(1) by a rule that treats such contributions as made in exchange for stock.[144]

Moreover, the statute allows two avenues for escaping the excise tax when it would otherwise apply. The taxpayer may elect to have the transfer governed by "principles similar to the principles of section 367," which causes gain on the transfer to be recognized under the regular income tax unless an exception to §367(a)(1) applies.[145] Alternatively, the taxpayer may elect to treat the transac-

---

Property After IRS Guidance and TRA '97, 87 J. Tax'n 149 (1997); Tello, The Repeal of Chapter 5 and Other Outbound Amendments, 27 Tax Mgmt. Int'l J. 24 (1998).

For §1491, as it existed immediately before the repeal, see Notice 97-18, 1997-1 CB 389, VI (transfer to foreign partnership is not subject to §1491 if partnership has validly elected under §761(a) not to be treated as partnership); Yu & McClellan, Notice 97-18: Some Results Unforeseen, 26 Tax Mgmt. Int'l J. 325 (1997).

[140] IRC §1491. See generally Davis, Outbound Transfers of Intangible Property Under Section 367(d) After the New Section 482 Regulations, 23 Tax Mgmt. Int'l J. 471 (1994); Parnes, United States Tax Considerations in Organizing a Foreign Joint Venture, 20 J. Corp. Tax'n 3 (1993). See also Lubin, Recent Developments Underscore Hazards of Outbound Transfers, 8 J. Int'l Tax'n 264 (1997).

[141] Notice 97-18, 1997-1 CB 389.

[142] IRC §1491, as amended by Pub. L. No. 104-188, §1907(b) (1996) (amendment effective as of August 20, 1996). The definition of "foreign trust" was changed in 1996. A trust that has been classified as domestic may become a foreign trust solely as a result of this change. However, the IRS has provided transition relief to allow trusts time to rearrange their affairs to avoid this consequence. Notice 96-65, 1996-2 CB 232; Notice 97-18, 1997-1 CB 389, III.B.

[143] IRC §1492(2)(A). Also, the §1491 tax does not apply to a transfer to an organization exempt from tax under §§501-505 (e.g., a qualifying foreign charity) unless the organization is a qualified pension, profit sharing, or stock bonus trust. IRC §1492(1). For §501, see infra ¶100.1.1.

[144] IRC §367(c)(2), discussed supra ¶68.6.2 text accompanying note 11.

[145] IRC §1492(2)(B). This election may be made on a Form 926 filed with the transferor's income tax or information return for the year in which the transfer is made. Notice 97-18, 1997-1 CB 389, III.B. According to the statutes, the election can be as a matter of right before the transfer, and the IRS has discretion to allow it to be made after the transfer. IRC §1494(b).

tion as a fully taxable exchange under the regular income tax.[146] Under the latter election, gain is recognized as though the property had been sold for a price equal to its fair market value. Since the regular income tax rates are often less than the 35 percent rate of the §1491 excise tax, the taxpayer is usually advantaged by making one of these elections.

The excise tax imposed by §1491 is due and payable on the day of the transfer, and the IRS may collect it without assessment or notice.[147] The transferor must report the transfer on Form 926, which must be filed either on the day of the transfer or with the transferor's income tax or information return for the year including that day.[148] A transfer to a foreign trust also triggers a reporting obligation under §6048(a).[149] A penalty is imposed if the return or the §6048(a) report is not filed or the transfer is not reported accurately and if the failure to file is not excused by reasonable cause.[150] The penalty normally equals 35 percent of the value of the transferred assets immediately after the transfer. If the penalty is not paid within 90 days after the IRS mails a notice of the penalty to the transferor, an additional penalty of $10,000 accrues for each 30 days that this delinquency continues, except that the aggregate of the original and additional penalties can never exceed the fair market value of the transferred property at the time of the transfer.

The obligation to file Form 926 generally applies to all transfers described in §1491, including transfers of unappreciated property and transfers exempted from the excise tax by one of the rules described above.[151] However, the duty to file is waived for several types of transactions. For example, filing is not required if, apart from §1491, the transferor immediately recognizes gain on the transfer equal to any excess of fair market value over adjusted basis and the transferor

---

[146] IRC §§1057, 1492(3). The election may be made on a Form 926 filed with the transferor's income tax or information return for the year during which the transfer is made. Notice 97-18, 1997-1 CB 389, III.B.

[147] IRC §1494(a). The tax may be paid with the transferor's return for the year, but interest is charged from the day of the transfer until the time of payment. Notice 97-18, 1997-1 CB 389, III.D.

[148] Notice 97-18, 1997-1 CB 389, III.A. For the time for filing for the taxable year including August 20, 1996, see Notice 97-42, 1997-2 CB—.

[149] As described more fully below, a filing under §6048(a) satisfies the reporting obligation under §1494.

[150] IRC §§1494(c), 6677, as amended by Pub. L. No. 104-188, §1907(b) (1996) (effective as of August 20, 1996); Notice 97-18, 1997-1 CB 389, V. If the report understates the value of the transferred property, the penalty applies only to the amount of the understatement.

A failure to file is excused by reasonable cause if, for example, the transfer is a deemed capital contribution to a foreign subsidiary resulting from an allocation of income from the subsidiary to the transferor under §482 and the accuracy-related penalty is not triggered by the §482 allocation. Notice 97-18, supra, V.

[151] Reg. §1.1494-1(a).

does not have "a significant interest in the transferee" after the transfer.[152] The transferor has a significant interest if, very generally, the transferor holds an interest in the transferee, or vice versa, of at least 10 percent.[153] If the transferor holds a significant interest, the transfer must be reported, even if it is for full value or consists of money or property worth less than the transferor's adjusted basis.

Form 926 need not be filed if the transfer is reported by Form 5471 (for transactions between U.S. persons and controlled foreign corporations, reportable under §6038), Form 5472 (for transactions with related foreign persons of U.S. corporations at least 25 percent of whose stock is held by foreign persons), or Form 3520 (U.S. person's transfer to foreign trust).[154] Also, if the transfer is by a domestic corporation to a foreign corporation and is covered by the reporting rules for §367 transactions (§6038B), no additional filing is required under §1491.

Other transactions exempted from the filing requirement include the following:

1. Transfers by a transferor that is exempt from U.S. tax under §501(a) or §664(c) (relating to charitable remainder trusts).
2. A domestic corporation's transfer of its own stock to a foreign partnership, trust, or estate if the corporation recognizes no gain under §1032.
3. A domestic partnership's transfer of an interest in the partnership to a foreign partnership, trust, or estate if §721 applies to the transfer.[155]
4. Most distributions by corporations and partnerships to foreign shareholders and partners.[156]

¶68.7 PROPERTY TRANSFERS BY FOREIGN CORPORATIONS

¶68.7.1 Introductory

Section 367(b) authorizes regulations denying nonrecognition under §§332, 351, 354, 355, 356, and 361 where "necessary or appropriate to prevent the avoidance of Federal income taxes." This regulatory authority only applies to transactions, here called §367(b) transactions, that involve foreign corporations

---

[152] Notice 97-18, 1997-1 CB 389, II.A.1. The requirement that gain be "immediately" recognized excludes installment sales and private annuity transactions from this rule.

[153] Id. II.A.2, adopting and modifying related person definitions of §§267, 643(i)(2)(B), and 707(b).

[154] Notice 97-18, 1997-1 CB 389, II.B.

[155] Id. II.A.1.

[156] Id. VII.

but do not consist of transfers by U.S. persons to foreign corporations. Transfers by U.S. persons to foreign corporations are excluded because they are governed by §367(a).[1]

Two distinct goals underlie the regulations issued pursuant to this authority.[2] First, where a U.S.-owned foreign corporation transfers its assets to a domestic corporation in a nonrecognition transaction, the regulations immediately tax U.S. shareholders of the foreign corporation on their shares of the corporation's earnings if the transaction is the first and last opportunity for imposing the U.S. corporate tax on these earnings. Assume a foreign subsidiary of a domestic corporation completely liquidates by distributing its assets to the parent. A subsidiary to parent liquidation causes the earnings and profits of the subsidiary to be merged into those of the parent. Where the subsidiary is foreign and the parent is domestic, however, the earnings and profits of the two corporations are not usually comparable. Because the parent is taxed by the United States on its worldwide income, its earnings and profits are an after-tax amount. The subsidiary's foreign earnings, in contrast, may never have been taxed by the United States, and if they are simply absorbed by the parent, the potential for subjecting them to a U.S. corporate tax may be forever lost. The regulations therefore require that on a liquidation of a foreign subsidiary into a domestic parent, the parent must recognize dividend income equal to the subsidiary's accumulated earnings and profits. Because the policy is to impose the U.S. corporate tax once but no more than once, an exclusion is allowed for earnings of the subsidiary that have previously been taxed by the United States to either the parent (e.g., under subpart F) or to the subsidiary.

The second concern of the regulation writers, which is principally expressed in the rules for reorganization exchanges, is to prevent nonrecognition transactions from erasing the potential for taxing the earnings of foreign corporations to U.S. shareholders under §1248. Under §1248, a U.S. person selling stock of a foreign corporation must report gain as dividend income to the extent of the earnings and profits attributable to the stock if, at some time during the preceding five years, the corporation was a controlled foreign corporation (CFC) and the taxpayer owned at least 10 percent of the voting stock.[3] The §1248 dividend consists of the earnings and profits of the foreign corporation and its subsidiaries that are attributable to the stock sold, exclusive of earnings accumulated before the taxpayer acquired the stock or while the corporation was not a CFC.

Tax-free exchanges in reorganization could be a means of skirting §1248. For example, even if §1248 is potentially applicable to a sale of the stock received

---

[1] See supra ¶68.6.

[2] See Rev. Proc. 98-7, 1998-1 CB __, §4.01(2) (IRS ordinarily will not issue advance ruling under §367(b) unless "significant legal issue" is presented or transaction is liquidation or reorganization of foreign corporation). See generally Dolan, U.S. Taxation of International Mergers, Acquisitions, and Joint Ventures (Warren, Gorham & Lamont 1995).

[3] For §1248, see supra ¶68.2.16.

in the exchange, the reorganization exchange would arguably give the shareholder a fresh start in the absence of §367(b), thus avoiding the dividend tax under §1248 on earnings accumulated before the exchange. The regulations head off this possibility by allowing such an exchange to be tax free, but requiring that the earnings and profits attributable to the stock exchanged become a tax attribute of the stock received, awaiting eventual recognition on a §1248 disposition of the latter stock.

A more immediate remedy is provided where, in a reorganization, a U.S. shareholder exchanges stock within §1248's ambit for stock that is not (e.g., stock of a corporation that is not a CFC). In such a case, dividend income is recognized at the time of the exchange equal to the §1248 dividend that would have been recognized if no nonrecognition rule applied to the exchange.

For many §367(b) transactions, the regulations allow nonrecognition only if the taxpayer complies with various requirements. Occasionally, taxpayers are advantaged by avoiding nonrecognition and may intentionally disregard these requirements in order to obtain this advantage. The IRS, however, retains discretion to allow nonrecognition where the requirements are not met.[4] This discretion can be exercised to force nonrecognition on taxpayers. It can also be exercised to allow nonrecognition where the taxpayer's noncompliance is inadvertent.

The IRS has proposed regulations to replace the existing temporary regulations under §367(b). The proposed regulations yield results similar to those of the existing regulations, but they differ significantly in structure. They are therefore discussed separately.[5]

¶68.7.2 Definitions

The §367(b) regulations rest on a foundation consisting of a complex set of definitions described below.

1. *CFC.* The regulations borrow the subpart F definition of "controlled foreign corporation."[6] Very generally, a foreign corporation is a CFC if more than 50 percent of its stock (by voting power or value) is owned by U.S. persons, excluding those owning (actually and constructively) less than 10 percent of the corporation's voting stock. The term "United States person" includes U.S. citizens, resident aliens, and domestic corporations, partnerships, trusts, and estates.[7]

2. *U.S. shareholder.* A U.S. shareholder is a U.S. person to whom §1248 would apply on a sale of the shareholder's stock in the foreign corporation.[8]

---

[4] Reg. §7.367(b)-1(b).

[5] Infra ¶¶68.7.8–68.7.13.

[6] See supra ¶68.2.2.

[7] IRC §7701(a)(30).

[8] Reg. §7.367(b)-2(b). For §1248, see supra ¶68.2.16.

Under §1248, gain on a U.S. person's sale of stock of a foreign corporation is treated as a dividend, at least in part, if, at some time during the preceding five years, the corporation was a CFC and the shareholder actually or constructively owned at least 10 percent of the corporation's voting stock. The amount of the dividend is the lesser of the gain on the sale or the earnings and profits attributable to the stock. The term "CFC stock" is used in the ensuing discussion to refer to stock held by a U.S. shareholder, the sale of which would invoke §1248.

3. *Section 1248 amount.* The §1248 amount is the "net positive earnings and profits" that would be attributed to a U.S. shareholder's CFC stock if the stock were sold in a transaction subject to §1248.[9] It generally consists of the stock's ratable share of the earnings and profits accumulated while the shareholder held the stock and the corporation was a CFC. The §1248 amount plays a dual role under the §367(b) regulations. When a reorganization or other corporate adjustment cuts off the application of §1248 to a future sale of a U.S. shareholder's stock, the regulations require that the shareholder recognize gain on the transaction up to the §1248 amount. When a U.S. shareholder exchanges CFC stock for other CFC stock in a corporate nonrecognition exchange, the §1248 amount for the stock exchanged attaches to the stock received so that on a sale of the stock received, the §1248 dividend can include earnings accumulated before as well as after the exchange.

The §1248 amount includes the U.S. shareholder's share of corporate earnings that were previously taxed to the shareholder under subpart F or to the foreign corporation as income effectively connected with U.S. business, even though, on a sale of CFC stock, previously taxed earnings are excluded from the shareholder's §1248 dividend.[10] The §1248 amount, however, has the same character as the corporate earnings included in it.[11] The rules requiring that the §1248 amount be reported as gross income in various circumstances are thus qualified by the §1248 exclusions for previously taxed amounts.

In contrast, earnings accumulated before 1963, which are also excluded in determining a shareholder's §1248 dividend, are omitted from the §1248 amount rather than being included as a nontaxable element.

Subject to the same limitations, earnings and profits of lower-tier foreign corporations are included in the §1248 amount to the extent they are ratably attributable to stock in these corporations that the U.S. shareholder holds indirectly through actual shareholdings in the upper-tier foreign corporation. Assume domestic corporation *P* is sole shareholder of foreign corporation *F1*, and *F1* is sole shareholder of *F2*. *P* is indirect owner of the *F2* stock,[12] and the §1248 amount attributable to *P*'s *F1* stock thus includes earnings and profits of both *F1*

---

[9] Reg. §1.367(b)-2(d).

[10] Reg. §7.367(b)-2(I). For the exclusion of previously taxed earnings under §1248, see §1248(d), discussed supra ¶68.2.16 text accompanying notes 373–75.

[11] Reg. §7.367(b)-3(c).

[12] See supra ¶68.2.2 text accompanying notes 22–24.

and *F2*. Earnings and profits of a lower-tier corporation, however, are included only to the extent accumulated while the U.S. shareholder was indirect owner of the lower-tier shares and the lower-tier corporation was a CFC. In the example, the §1248 amount does not include *F2* earnings from any period before *P* acquired the *F1* stock or *F1* acquired the *F2* stock, whichever occurred last.

In some contexts, the §367(b) regulations require immediate taxation of the §1248 amount. For example, if a U.S. shareholder exchanges CFC stock for stock of a domestic corporation in a reorganization, the §1248 amount, or if less the gain on the exchange, is included in gross income as a dividend for the year of the exchange.[13] In such a case, the §1248 amount is either a positive number or zero. In other contexts, the §1248 amount is not taxed but is attached to the stock received in the exchange as an additional tax attribute. For example, if a U.S. shareholder exchanges CFC stock for other CFC stock in a reorganization, the exchange is tax free, but the §1248 amount for the old stock attaches to the new stock and is added to the §1248 dividend if the shareholder subsequently sells the new stock. As a preserved tax attribute, the §1248 amount may be positive or negative. In the example, if the target sustained losses while the shareholder held its stock, its share of the deficit is a negative §1248 amount and reduces any §1248 dividend on a subsequent sale of the new stock.

4. *All earnings and profits amount.* The all earnings and profits amount generally equals the §1248 amount, except that earnings accumulated before 1963 are included and earnings of lower-tier subsidiaries are omitted.[14] The principal role of the all earnings and profits amount is under a rule requiring that it be included in a U.S. shareholder's gross income when the foreign corporation liquidates if the U.S. shareholder is a domestic corporation and qualifies for nonrecognition under §332 by owning at least 80 percent of the foreign corporation's stock.[15] Pre-1963 earnings are included in the all earnings and profits amount because the §367(b) rules on subsidiary to parent liquidations predate the enactment of §1248 in 1962. The earnings of lower-tier subsidiaries are excluded because the liquidation of an upper-tier subsidiary does not significantly change the parent's relationship to a lower-tier subsidiary or its earnings.

In applying the rule taxing the all earnings and profits amount when a foreign subsidiary liquidates into a domestic parent, the all earnings and profits amount is either a positive number or zero. In various corporate adjustments, however, the all earnings and profits amount attributable to stock exchanged is attached as a tax attribute to stock received in the exchange. As a tax attribute, the all earnings and profits amount may be positive or negative. Assume a reorganization occurs in which domestic corporation *P* exchanges a 100 percent interest in foreign corporation *FT* for an 80 percent interest in foreign corporation *FA*. The exchange is tax free, but the all earnings and profits amount for *FT*

---

[13] See infra ¶68.7.4.

[14] Reg. §§1.367(b)-2(f), 7.367(b)-2(h)(1).

[15] See infra ¶68.7.3.

attaches to *P*'s *FA* stock and thus may be taxed to *P* when *FA* liquidates. If *FT* incurred a deficit while *P* held its stock, *P*'s share of the deficit comprises the all earnings and profits amount and thus reduces the amount taxable to *P* on a subsequent liquidation of *FA*.

5. *Additional earnings and profits amount.* The additional earnings and profits amount consists of the earnings and profits or deficit accumulated before 1963, to the extent attributable to particular stock of the foreign corporation.[16]

6. *Section 1248(c)(2) amount.* The §1248(c)(2) amount is a tax attribute of a foreign corporation's stock in another foreign corporation.[17] It consists of the earnings and profits of the latter corporation (and lower-tier subsidiaries) that are attributable to the stock held by the shareholding foreign corporation, computed under §1248 as though the shareholder was a domestic corporation making a sale of the stock. The role of the §1248(c)(2) amount is to preserve the potential for taxing lower-tier earnings and profits to U.S. shareholders of the shareholding foreign corporation after the latter makes an exchange of its stock in the lower-tier corporation. The §1248(c)(2) amount is often computed together with the additional earnings and profits amount, which in this context is the amount by which the §1248(c)(2) amount would increase if pre-1963 earnings and profits were taken into account.

¶68.7.3 Complete Liquidation of Foreign Subsidiary

Under §332(a), a corporation recognizes no gain or loss on receiving a distribution in complete liquidation of another corporation if the shareholder corporation (the parent) owns at least 80 percent of the stock of the liquidating corporation (the subsidiary).[18] The §367(b) regulations significantly modify §332 if the parent is domestic but not if it is foreign.

1. *Domestic parent.* When the parent in a §332 liquidation is a domestic corporation and the subsidiary is foreign, the parent must recognize its gain unless it includes the all earnings and profits amount in gross income for the year of the liquidation.[19] Under §381, the earnings and profits of the liquidating subsidiary are absorbed into the earnings and profits account of the parent.[20] The earnings and profits of a foreign subsidiary may never have been subject to U.S. taxation, while those of the domestic parent were taxed when earned and are largely protected against being subjected to corporate taxation a second time. The liquidation thus is the last opportunity for the corporate tax to be imposed on the

---

[16] Reg. §7.367(b)-2(g).

[17] Reg. §7.367(b)-2(e).

[18] For §332, see infra ¶93.8.

[19] Reg. §7.367(b)-5(b). For the all earnings and profits amount, see supra ¶68.7.2 text accompanying notes 14–15.

[20] For §381, see infra ¶95.5.2.

subsidiary's earnings, and taxing the parent on the all earnings and profits amount is the mechanism for seizing this opportunity.

Normally, the all earnings and profits amount is fully included in gross income even if it exceeds the parent's gain on the liquidation. An exclusion is allowed, however, for amounts previously taxed by the United States and other earnings of the subsidiary that would be excluded in computing the §1248 dividend if the parent had sold the subsidiary's stock. The inclusion is treated as a cash dividend received from the subsidiary immediately before the liquidation.[21] As a consequence, it is ordinary income, but it qualifies the parent under §902 for credit for foreign income taxes paid by the subsidiary on the earnings and profits taxed to the parent.[22]

Assume domestic corporation P receives property with a net value of $1,000 in a distribution in complete liquidation of FS, a wholly owned foreign subsidiary; P's basis for its FS stock is $250. FS's earnings and profits are $600, of which $70 has been taxed to P under subpart F and $30 has been taxed to FS as effectively connected income. On a cash distribution of the $500 of earnings not previously taxed by the United States, P would be deemed to pay $200 of foreign income taxes actually paid by FS. The consequences of the liquidation are as follows:

a. P's gain on the liquidation is $750 (amount realized of $1,000 less $250 basis).

b. The all earnings and profits amount is $600.

c. P can comply with the §367(b) regulations by reporting dividend income for the year of the liquidation of $500 (all earnings and profits amount of $600 less previously taxed amounts of $70 and $30).

d. If this $500 dividend is included in P's gross income, it is deemed under §902 to have paid FS's foreign income taxes of $200, and it has $200 of additional dividend income under §78.

e. By reporting the $500 dividend, P qualifies under §332 for nonrecognition of the remaining $250 of the liquidation gain.

f. As a consequence of §332's application, §334(b) requires that P take FS's adjusted bases for the distributed assets (without any increase for the dividend income recognized on the liquidation).

g. Under §381(c)(2), FS's earnings and profits of $600 are added to P's accumulated earnings and profits, but the aggregated earnings and profits are reduced by P's tax for the year, including the portion of this tax attributable to the inclusion of the all earnings and profits amount.

If a domestic parent of a liquidating foreign subsidiary fails to include the all earnings and profits amount in gross income, its gain on the liquidation is recognized. The gain is a dividend under §1248 to the extent it would have been so

---

[21] Reg. §7.367(b)-3(b).
[22] Reg. §7.367(b)-3(f). For §902, see infra ¶69.8.1.

characterized if the subsidiary's stock had been sold for a price equal to the net value of the property received in the liquidation. Moreover, the rules auxiliary to §332 apply as though nonrecognition had been allowed under §332.[23] The parent thus takes the subsidiary's adjusted bases for the distributed assets under §334(b) and inherits the subsidiary's earnings and profits under §381(c)(2).

In the example, if P fails to include the all earnings and profits amount in gross income, it recognizes gain of $750 ($1,000 received, less basis of $250), and §1248 characterizes $500 of the gain as dividend income. Its failure to follow the all earnings and profits rule thus has only adverse consequences unless it is in the unusual position of being advantaged by the recognition of additional gain. A parent corporation is more likely to intentionally disregard the all earnings and profits rule if the all earnings and profits amount, after the exclusion of previously taxed amounts, exceeds the gain on the liquidation. Assume the all earnings and profits amount in the example is $900, of which $100 was previously taxed by the United States. The all earnings and profits inclusion is $800, but the §1248 dividend is limited to P's gain of $750. However, if P disregards the all earnings and profits rule and recognizes its §1248 dividend, the IRS apparently may force the inclusion of the all earnings and profits amount by allowing nonrecognition under §332 subject to the all earnings and profits rule even though the rule completely swallows §332 in such a case.[24]

On the other hand, nonrecognition under §332, where advantageous, can be lost by an inadvertent failure to report the all earnings and profits amount or a miscalculation of the amount. The IRS, however, has discretion to allow nonrecognition under §332, with the inclusion of the all earnings and profits amount, if the taxpayer's failure to comply with the inclusion requirement resulted from a good faith error.[25]

2. *Foreign parent.* Section 332(a) applies without modification under §367(b) when a foreign parent receives a distribution in complete liquidation of a foreign subsidiary.[26] Also, under §337, a foreign corporation generally recognizes no gain or loss on a liquidating distribution to a foreign parent corporation.[27] However, the subsidiary must recognize gain on the distribution of property used in a U.S. trade or business unless the parent uses the property in a U.S. business immediately after the distribution.[28] Gain must also be recognized on a

---

[23] Reg. §7.367(b)-5(b).

[24] Reg. §7.367(b)-1(b)(2).

[25] Id. See Reg. §7.367(b)-13 Ex. 2(b)(iii).

[26] Reg. §7.367(b)-5(c). See Reg. §7.367(b)-13 Exs. 1, 2.

[27] Reg. §1.367(e)-2T(c)(1).

[28] Reg. §1.367(e)-2T(c)(2)(i). This rule generally applies to distributions after July 1986. Reg. §1.367(e)-2T(d).

Generally, the subsidiary avoids recognition on distributions of U.S. business assets only if, for 10 years after the distribution, the parent continues the U.S. business and uses the distributed property in that business; the parent must also submit a statement to the IRS to facilitate enforcement of the 10-year requirement. However, if the subsidiary and

distribution of property used in a U.S. trade or business within 10 years before the distribution, but not so used at the time of the distribution.[29] However, neither of these rules requires recognition of gain on a distribution of a U.S. real property interest.[30]

Under §381(c)(2), the foreign parent inherits the liquidating subsidiary's earnings and profits or deficit. If the parent is a subsidiary of a domestic corporation, the inherited earnings or deficit become part of the all earnings and profits amount attributable to the stock held by the domestic corporation. For purposes of §§367(b) and 1248, the inherited earnings or deficit has the same character to the parent as it did to the subsidiary.[31] For example, if portions of the liquidated subsidiary's earnings were taxed by the United States under subpart F or as income effectively connected with a U.S. business of the subsidiary, the exclusions for previously taxed earnings continue to apply when the all earnings and profits amount or some other amount calculated under the §367(b) regulations is included in the gross income of a U.S. shareholder.

¶68.7.4   Shareholder Exchanges in Reorganization

Under §354, no gain or loss is recognized on an exchange of stock or securities for other stock or securities pursuant to a reorganization. Section 356 provides for nonrecognition of loss and partial nonrecognition of gain if an exchanging shareholder or security holder receives boot in addition to stock or securities in a reorganization exchange.[32]

The §367(b) regulations make no alterations in these rules for reorganization exchanges of securities other than stock. For example, in a reorganization, bonds of a foreign corporation may be exchanged tax free for stock or bonds of a domestic corporation.

For reorganization exchanges of stock of foreign corporations, the §367(b) regulations modify §§354 and 356 for only two classes of cases: (1) where the exchanging shareholder is a U.S. shareholder of the foreign corporation and (2) where the exchanging shareholder is itself a foreign corporation and has at least one U.S. shareholder who is also a U.S. shareholder of the corporation whose stock is being exchanged. In other words, the modifying rules apply to an exchange by a U.S. person only if §1248 would have applied to a cash sale of the stock immediately before the reorganization and to an exchange by a foreign

---

parent are both controlled foreign corporations, it is sufficient that the parent use the property in any U.S. trade or business immediately after the distribution.

For basis and other collateral consequences of the recognition of gain under this rule, see Reg. §1.367(e)-2T(c)(3).

[29] Reg. §1.367(e)-2T(c)(2)(ii).
[30] For the term U.S. real property interest, see supra ¶¶66.4.2–66.4.4.
[31] Reg. §7.367(b)-3(e).
[32] For §§354 and 356, see infra ¶94.4.5.

corporation if the exchange could affect the application of §1248 to a U.S. shareholder of the exchanging corporation.

Assume a domestic corporation owns 80 percent of the single class of stock of foreign corporation *F1*, which owns 70 percent of the single class of stock of foreign corporation *F2*. The domestic corporation is a U.S. shareholder of both foreign corporations because its stock ownership (80 percent of *F1* and 80 percent of 70 percent of *F2*) makes both corporations CFCs (more than 50 percent U.S. ownership) and exceeds the 10 percent threshold of the definition of U.S. shareholder. The regulation modifications of §§354 and 356 thus apply if, in a reorganization, the domestic corporation exchanges its *F1* stock or *F1* exchanges its *F2* stock. On the other hand, if a U.S. citizen owns 5 percent of *F1*'s stock and is not related to any other shareholder, §§354 and 356 apply without modification to a reorganization exchange of her stock because she does not own enough stock to be a U.S. shareholder.

The modifying rules fall into two categories. If §1248 would apply to an immediate sale of stock received in a reorganization exchange, nonrecognition is allowed under §§354 and 356, but the §1248 amount and other tax attributes of the stock exchanged attach to the stock received in the exchange. This rule applies to an exchange by a U.S. shareholder if the issuer of the stock received in the exchange is a CFC and the taxpayer becomes a U.S. shareholder of it. In contrast, if the taxpayer receives stock of a corporation that is not a CFC or if that corporation is a CFC but the taxpayer is not a U.S. shareholder of the corporation, the reorganization exchange cuts off the possibility of a subsequent application of §1248. In this situation, the shareholder is taxed on the §1248 dividend that would have been recognized if the stock exchanged had been sold for cash, but any excess of the gain on the exchange over this amount qualifies for nonrecognition under §§354 and 356. Analogous rules apply when the exchanging shareholder is a foreign corporation.

1. *Exchanges of CFC stock for CFC stock.* Nonrecognition is allowed under §§354 and 356 for a reorganization exchange by a U.S. shareholder of stock in a foreign corporation if, immediately after the exchange, the issuer of the stock received in the exchange is a CFC and the taxpayer is a U.S. shareholder of that corporation.[33] Such an exchange, however, invokes a series of rules meant to preserve the §§367(b) and 1248 attributes of the stock exchanged. These rules also apply to a reorganization exchange made by a foreign corporation if CFC stock is received in the exchange and, immediately after the exchange, all U.S. shareholders of the exchanging foreign corporation are also U.S. shareholders of the issuer of the stock received.

a. *Tax attributes assigned to stock received.* When the exchanging shareholder is a U.S. person, the §1248 amount and the all earnings and profits

---

[33] Reg. §7.367(b)-7(b).

amount are computed with respect to the stock exchanged.[34] If the exchanging shareholder is a foreign corporation, the §1248(c)(2) amount and additional earnings and profits amount are computed. All of these amounts are computed as of the time immediately before the reorganization exchange.[35]

The amounts become tax attributes of the stock received in the exchange.[36] For an exchanging U.S. shareholder, the §1248 amount is added to the earnings and profits included in computing the §1248 dividend on a subsequent sale of the stock received. If the exchanging shareholder is a domestic corporation, the all earnings and profits amount for the stock exchanged, together with any all earnings and profits amount accumulated after the reorganization, will be taxed to the shareholder in the event the subsidiary subsequently liquidates when the exchanging shareholder owns at least 80 percent of its stock. If the exchanging shareholder is a foreign corporation, the §1248(c)(2) amount will be included in computing a U.S. shareholder's §1248 dividend on a subsequent stock sale; if the U.S. shareholder is a domestic corporation with an 80 percent or greater interest, the additional earnings and profits amount may be included in the all earnings and profits amount on a subsequent liquidation into the domestic parent under §332.

These various amounts may be reduced by distributions occurring after the reorganization.[37] Postreorganization distributions, however, are deemed made first from postreorganization earnings, and the attributed amounts are thus invaded by distributions only after postreorganization distributions have exhausted postreorganization earnings.

b. *Transfer of earnings and profits.* The corporation issuing the stock received in the reorganization usually inherits the earnings and profits or deficit of the corporation whose stock is exchanged.[38] If earnings and profits or deficits of lower-tier corporations are included in the §1248 or §1248(c)(2) amount with respect to the stock exchanged, the earnings and profits or deficits of the lower-tier corporations are also transferred to the issuer of the stock received. When the issuer of the stock received is the acquiring corporation in the reorganization this

---

[34] Reg. §7.367(b)-9(b)(1). The all earnings and profits amount can be disregarded if the exchanging shareholder is not a corporation.

[35] For illustrations, see Reg. §7.367(b)-13 Ex. 5(a)(i) (exchange by U.S. shareholder), Exs. 10–13 (exchange by foreign corporation having U.S. shareholders).

[36] Reg. §7.367(b)-12(e). See Reg. §7.367(b)-12(b) (if exchanging shareholder's stock is subsequently transferred in transaction allowing transferee to tack transferor's holding period on to his own (e.g., a transfer by gift), attributes stick to stock in transferee's hands).

[37] Reg. §7.367(b)-12(c). See Reg. §7.367(b)-13 Exs. 7, 8.

[38] Reg. §7.367(b)-9(c)(1). See Reg. §7.367(b)-11(b) (inherited deficit may only be applied against earnings and profits accumulated after exchange). For an illustration, see Reg. §7.367(b)-13 Ex. 9.

transfer of earnings and profits or deficits occurs under §381(c)(2).[39] If this stock is issued by a corporation other than the acquiring corporation or if there are lower-tier corporations not absorbed into the acquiring corporation, the transfer occurs under the §367(b) regulations, which apply §381 as though the issuer of the stock acquired all assets of all corporations whose earnings and profits are included in the §1248 or §1248(c)(2) amount. No earnings and profits transfer occurs under the §367(b) regulations, however, if one U.S. shareholder owns more than 50 percent of the stock of both the target corporation and the issuer of the stock received.[40]

Assume domestic corporation P is sole shareholder of foreign corporation FT1, which owns all stock of foreign corporation FT2; P transfers the FT1 stock to foreign corporation FA in exchange for voting stock of FA in a reorganization under §368(a)(1)(B). Because FT1 and FT2 remain in existence, §381 normally would not transfer any of their tax attributes to FA. The §367(b) regulations, however, require that FA absorb the entire earnings and profits or deficits of both FT1 and FT2 unless P owns more than 50 percent of the FA stock immediately after the reorganization.

Also, in cases where §381 is otherwise applicable, the §367(b) regulations sometimes send the target's earnings and profits to a corporation different from that identified as the acquiring corporation under §381. Assume FT1 transfers its assets to foreign corporation FAS in exchange for stock of foreign corporation FAP, which is FAS' sole shareholder, and FT1 distributes the FAP stock to P in complete liquidation. In this case, FAS, the acquirer of the assets of FT1, generally succeeds to FT1's tax attributes under §381, but the §367(b) regulations alter §381 by requiring that the earnings and profits of both FT1 and FT2 go to FAP, the issuer of the stock received by P in the reorganization.

If the issuer of the stock received owns less than all of the stock or assets of the target or a lower-tier corporation immediately after the reorganization, it assumes only a proportionate part of the earnings and profits or deficits.[41] Both direct and indirect ownership are taken into account, however, in applying this rule. In the last example, FAP inherits the earnings and profits of FT1 and FT2, even though it owns no stock of either corporation, because it indirectly owns all of the stock of both corporations.

When earnings and profits or deficits are transferred under the foregoing rules, the earnings and profits or deficits of the corporations from which the transfers come are correspondingly reduced.[42] In the last example, FT1 and FT2 have no earnings and profits or deficits immediately after the reorganization.

---

[39] For §381, see infra ¶95.5.2.
[40] Reg. §1.367(b)-9(c)(4).
[41] Reg. §7.367(b)-9(c)(2).
[42] Reg. §7.367(b)-9(d).

The earnings and profits transfer does not occur, however, if one U.S. shareholder participating in the stock for stock exchange owns more than 50 percent of the stock of both the corporation whose stock is exchanged and the corporation issuing the stock received in the exchange.[43] For purposes of the 50 percent threshold, both actual and constructive ownership is counted, and the threshold is crossed if a U.S. shareholder's interest in the two corporations exceeds 50 percent by value or voting power.[44] When this rule applies, §381 applies without modification under §367(b).

c. *Adjustments to stock basis.* When a lower-tier corporation loses earnings and profits or a deficit under the foregoing rules, the stock bases of the corporation's shareholders may be increased or decreased by the amount of the transferred earnings or deficit.[45] Normally, a decrease is mandatory, but an increase is allowed only if the U.S. shareholders agree to treat the transferred earnings as though they had been distributed as dividends. These constructive dividends, although deemed received by foreign corporations, are often taxed to the U.S. shareholders under subpart F.

d. *Tax attributes other than earnings and profits and stock basis.* Section 381 applies without modification under §367(b) to all corporate tax attributes other than earnings and profits.[46]

2. *Exchanges by U.S. shareholders of CFC stock for non-CFC stock.* A U.S. shareholder exchanging stock for stock in a reorganization must recognize gain on the exchange if the issuer of the stock received is (1) a domestic corporation, (2) a foreign corporation that is not a CFC, or (3) a CFC of which the shareholder is not a U.S. shareholder immediately after the exchange. Stock falling within any of these three categories is here called non-CFC stock. Gain is recognized on such an exchange because §1248, which was potentially applicable to the stock exchanged, cannot apply to a disposition of the stock received in the exchange.

Assume domestic corporation *S* owns 10 percent of the single class of stock of foreign corporation *FT*, whose remaining stock is also held by U.S. shareholders; *FT* is acquired in a reorganization in exchange for stock of corporation *A*. *S* recognizes gain on its exchange of *FT* stock for *A* stock if *A* is (1) a domestic corporation, (2) a foreign corporation but not a CFC, or (3) a CFC but *S* owns less than 10 percent of *A*'s voting stock.

Normally, the gain recognized in such an exchange is the lesser of the §1248 amount for the stock exchanged or the gain on the exchange.[47] The gain on the

---

[43] Reg. §1.367(b)-9(b)(4). This exception only applies to exchanges after March 2, 1989.

[44] For the constructive ownership rules, see §958, discussed supra ¶68.2.2 text accompanying notes 26–32.

[45] Reg. §§7.367(b)-9(e), (f).

[46] Reg. §7.367(b)-9(c)(1).

[47] For the §1248 amount, see supra ¶68.7.2 text accompanying notes 9–13. See Rev. Rul. 81-32, 1981-1 CB 131 (if U.S. shareholder is individual, special tax computation of

exchange is the excess of the fair market value of the stock exchanged over its adjusted basis. If the §1248 amount is less than the gain on the exchange, the rest of the gain qualifies for nonrecognition under §§354 and 356. The amount recognized is treated as a dividend distributed immediately before the exchange.[48] If the U.S. shareholder is a domestic corporation, it thus may qualify under §902 for credit for foreign income taxes paid by the corporation whose stock is exchanged, providing that the U.S. shareholder owns at least 10 percent of the voting stock of this corporation.[49]

The U.S. shareholder, however, must report the all earnings and profits amount as gross income if (1) it is a domestic corporation, (2) it receives stock of a domestic corporation in exchange for its CFC stock, and (3) the CFC's assets are transferred to a domestic corporation in the reorganization.[50] Assume FT transfers its assets to A, an unrelated domestic corporation, in exchange for A stock in a reorganization under §368(a)(1)(C), and FT then liquidates by distributing the A stock to its shareholders, including domestic corporation S. If S is a U.S. shareholder of FT immediately before the reorganization and recognizes gain on the exchange, the gain is ineligible for nonrecognition under §354 unless S reports its share of FT's all earnings and profits amount as gross income. If the all earnings and profits amount is included in S's gross income, it is added to S's basis for the A stock and A's basis for the FT assets.

If a domestic corporation subject to the foregoing rule fails to so report the all earnings and profits amount, the nonrecognition rules of §§354 and 356 are inapplicable to any gain on the exchange.[51] Section 1248 applies as it would to any taxable exchange, thus likely causing at least part of the gain to be ordinary dividend income. As a further penalty, the corporation's basis for the stock received equals its basis for the CFC stock exchanged, and the acquiring corporation takes the CFC's adjusted basis for its assets. Neither the shareholder corporation (S in the example) nor the acquiring corporation (A) is allowed any increase in basis for the gain recognized by the shareholder in the exchange.

When a U.S. shareholder includes the §1248 amount or all earnings and profits amount in gross income under the foregoing rules, the amounts are treated as though they had been taxed to the shareholder under subpart F.[52] As a consequence, subsequent distributions to the shareholder are tax free to the shareholder until the previously taxed amounts are exhausted.[53]

---

§1248(b) applies). See supra ¶68.2.16 text accompanying notes 396–97 for §1248(b). For an illustration of the rules described in the text, see Reg. §7.367(b)-13 Ex. 5(a)(ii).

[48] Reg. §7.367(b)-3(b).

[49] Reg. §7.367(b)-3(f). For §902, see infra ¶69.8.1.

[50] Reg. §7.367(b)-7(c)(2)(i). See Rev. Rul. 88-25, 1988-1 CB 116 (all earnings and profits amount taxed to U.S. shareholder when CFC reincorporated as domestic corporation under state domestication statute).

[51] Reg. §7.367(b)-7(c)(2)(ii).

[52] Reg. §7.367(b)-12(d).

[53] IRC §959, discussed supra ¶68.2.14. See Reg. §7.367(b)-13 Ex. 6.

3. *Exchanges by foreign corporations of CFC stock for non-CFC stock.*
When a foreign corporation exchanges CFC stock for non-CFC stock, the
§1248(c)(2) amount for the stock exchanged must be included in the exchanging
corporation's earnings and profits.[54] The effect of such an exchange is to eliminate the lower-tier foreign corporation's earnings and profits from the §1248
amounts of the exchanging corporation's U.S. shareholders. The inclusion in the
exchanging corporation's earnings and profits replaces the eliminated earnings,
thus keeping the U.S. shareholders' §1248 amounts constant. The inclusion may
be positive or negative. For example, the exchanging CFC's earnings and profits
are reduced by the CFC's share of any deficit incurred by the lower-tier corporation while the exchanging CFC held the stock.

The exchanging CFC's basis for the stock received in the exchange is usually
increased or decreased by the amount of the adjustment to its earnings and
profits, just as though this amount had been recognized as gain or loss on the
exchange.[55] A basis increase is allowed, however, only if the CFC's U.S. shareholders consent to treat the earnings and profits addition as though it had been
received by the CFC as a dividend. The consent often causes the U.S. shareholders to be taxed on their shares of the constructive dividend under the subpart F
rules taxing U.S. shareholders on a CFC's foreign personal holding company
income.[56]

The foregoing rules do not apply if the exchanging CFC receives stock of a
commonly owned domestic corporation but the lower-tier foreign corporation
does not transfer its assets to a domestic corporation (e.g., remains in existence).[57]
Specifically, §§354 and 356 apply without modification to a reorganization exchange by a foreign corporation if two requirements are met. First, the issuer of
the stock received in the exchange must be a domestic corporation that could be
included in a consolidated return with the exchanging CFC but for the exclusion
of foreign corporations from affiliated groups eligible to file consolidated returns.[58] Second, the assets of the foreign corporation whose stock is exchanged
cannot be absorbed by a domestic corporation in the reorganization.

Assume domestic corporation *P* is sole shareholder of foreign corporation
F1, which owns all stock of foreign corporation *F2*; *F1* transfers its *F2* stock to
D, a domestic subsidiary of *P*, in exchange for *D* stock in a reorganization under
§368(a)(1)(B).[59] Even though the *F2* stock transferred in the exchange is CFC
stock and the *D* stock received in the exchange is not, §§354 applies without
modification because *F1* and *D* would be members of the same affiliated group if
foreign corporations could belong to such groups. No modifying rules are re-

---

[54] Reg. §1.367(b)-7(c)(1)(ii).
[55] Reg. §7.367(b)-7(c)(1)(iv).
[56] See supra ¶68.2.4.
[57] Reg. §§1.367(b)-7(c)(ii), (iii) (applicable only to exchanges after March 3, 1989).
[58] For consolidated returns, see ¶90.4.
[59] Reg. §1.367(b)-7(c)(iii) Ex. 1.

quired for this case because §1248 can apply to D's subsequent sale of the $F2$ stock or the all earnings and profits amount can be taxed to D on $F2$'s liquidation. In contrast, $F2$'s earnings and profits would be added to $F1$'s earnings and profits if the reorganization consisted of $F2$'s transfer of its assets to D in exchange for D stock, followed by $F2$'s liquidating distribution of the D stock to $F1$. The modifying rule is needed in this case because D's absorption of $F2$'s assets would otherwise cut off the possibility of $F2$'s ever being taxed to any domestic member of the group on a future stock sale or liquidation.

¶68.7.5 Transfers of CFC Stock by Foreign Corporations Under §351

The rules described above for shareholder exchanges in reorganizations also apply to a foreign corporation's transfer of CFC stock to another corporation in an exchange to which §351 applies.[60] Under §351(a), no gain or loss is recognized on a transfer of property to a corporation in exchange for stock of the corporation if the transferor, alone or together with others making contemporaneous transfers, owns at least 80 percent of the corporation's stock immediately thereafter. If such a transfer is made in exchange for stock and other property or money, no loss is recognized, and gain is recognized only up to the amount of the money or other property.

Section 351 applies without modification under the §367(b) regulations to transfers by individuals and by entities other than foreign corporations. Moreover, with one limited exception,[61] regulation modifications for §351 transfers by foreign corporations apply only if the property transferred is stock of a foreign corporation that has at least one U.S. shareholder. The modifications for these cases are as follows:

First, the §1248(c)(2) and all earnings and profits amounts for the stock transferred attach to the stock received if, immediately after the exchange, the transferee corporation is a CFC and all U.S. shareholders of the transferor are also U.S. shareholders of the transferee.[62] Assume domestic corporation P is sole shareholder of foreign corporation $F1$, which owns all of the stock of foreign corporation $F3$; $F1$ transfers its $F3$ stock to newly organized $F2$ in exchange for all of the stock of $F2$. The §1248(c)(2) amount and all earnings and profits for $F1$'s stock in $F3$ are switched over to the $F2$ stock that $F1$ receives in the exchange because (1) the transferor ($F1$) is a foreign corporation, (2) the transferred property is stock in another foreign corporation ($F3$) that has a U.S. shareholder (P)

---

[60] See infra ¶91.1 for §351. See Reg. §7.367(b)-4(b) (if §351 transfer is also reorganization under §368(a)(1)(B), exchange is governed by reorganization rules, not §351).

[61] The exception is that if the §351 transfer is also described in §361 (asset transfers by target corporations in reorganizations) and if the transferor remains in existence after the transaction, the target's earnings and profits are not transferred to the acquiring corporation, as usually occurs in reorganizations. Reg. §7.367(b)-8(b).

[62] Reg. §7.367(b)-8(c)(1). For the shifting of these tax attributes from one block of stock to another, see Reg. §7.367(b)-9, discussed supra ¶68.7.4 text accompanying note 45.

immediately before the exchange, (3) the transferee (*F2*) is a CFC immediately after the exchange, and (4) *F1*'s only U.S. shareholder also becomes a U.S. shareholder of the transferee (*F2*).

Second, the §1248(c)(2) amount and the additional earnings and profits amount for the exchanged stock are added to the transferor corporation's earnings if the transferee corporation is a domestic corporation, a foreign corporation that is not a CFC, or a CFC whose U.S. shareholders do not include all of the transferor's U.S. shareholders.[63] Assume domestic corporation *P* is sole shareholder of foreign corporation *F1*, which owns all of the stock of foreign corporation *F3*; *F1* transfers its *F3* stock to newly organized *F2* in exchange for 5 percent of the stock of *F2*. If the remaining shareholders of *F2* are unrelated to *P*, the rule described in the preceding paragraph does not apply because *F1*'s U.S. shareholder (*P*) is indirect owner of only 5 percent of *F2* and therefore is not a U.S. shareholder of *F2*. *F1* thus must include the §1248(c)(2) and additional earnings and profits amounts for the *F3* stock in its earnings and profits.

¶68.7.6 Corporate Divisions Involving Foreign Corporations

Under §355, a shareholder recognizes no gain or loss on receiving a distribution of stock of another corporation if (1) the distributing corporation owns at least 80 percent of the stock of the other corporation (the controlled corporation) immediately before the distribution, (2) the distributed stock includes at least 80 percent of the outstanding stock of the controlled corporation, (3) both corporations are engaged in active businesses that have been carried on for at least five years, and (4) the distribution is not a device for distributing the distributing corporation's earnings.[64] A §355 distribution may be a spin-off (a ratable distribution of the stock of an existing or newly created subsidiary), a split-off (a distribution of the subsidiary's stock in exchange for portions of the parent's stock, which need not be ratable among all of the parent's shareholders), or a split-up (parent transfers all of its assets to subsidiaries and distributes the subsidiaries' stock in complete liquidation).

For purposes of §367, stock received in a §355 distribution is deemed received in exchange for stock of the distributing corporation, whether or not the distributee actually surrenders any stock in connection with the distribution.[65] The distributee is thus referred to as the "exchanging shareholder" in the §367(b) regulations and in the ensuing discussion.

If the corporation making a §355 distribution is domestic, §367(b) has no application unless the distribution consists of stock of a foreign corporation and the distributing corporation was a U.S. shareholder of the foreign corporation

---

[63] Reg. §1.367(b)-8(c)(2). For the consequences of this inclusion in earnings and profits, see Reg. §7.367(b)-7(c)(1)(iv), discussed supra ¶68.7.4 text accompanying note 55.

[64] For §355, see infra ¶94.1.

[65] IRC §367(c)(1).

immediately after the exchange. As described more fully below, when these conditions are present, the distributing corporation recognizes dividend income under §1248, and the §367(b) regulations require that the earnings and profits or deficits of the distributing and controlled corporations be allocated between them in proportion to net asset values.[66]

However, a domestic distributing corporation must usually recognize gain on a §355 distribution, whether the distributed stock is of a domestic or foreign corporation, if the distributee is a foreign person.[67]

When a foreign corporation makes a §355 distribution, the §367(b) regulations intervene only if the distributing corporation has at least one U.S. shareholder.[68] If the distribution does not reduce or eliminate the amounts potentially taxable to U.S. shareholders under §1248, the §367(b) regulations merely assure that the §1248 amount and related tax attributes are properly aligned among the shares held after the distribution. If the distribution reduces the potential §1248 dividends of U.S. shareholders, either the shareholders are immediately taxed or adjustments are made in earnings and profits accounts to restore the §1248 potential.

1. *Domestic distributing corporation—generally.* If the corporation making a §355 distribution is domestic and the controlled corporation is foreign, the distributing corporation often recognizes gain as a dividend under §1248(f). Section 361(c)(1) usually provides nonrecognition treatment for the distributing corporation on a distribution under §355. When the controlled corporation is foreign, however, §1248(f) overrides §361(c)(1) by requiring the distributing corporation to recognize a dividend equal to the §1248 dividend that would have been realized if the distributed stock had been sold for a price equal to its fair market value.[69] If the controlled corporation has been profitable, a §1248 dividend results from this hypothetical sale because the distributing corporation cannot satisfy §355's 80 percent control requirement without the controlled corporation being a CFC and the distributing corporation being a U.S. shareholder.

---

[66] Infra text accompanying notes 69–71.

[67] Infra text accompanying notes 72–83.

[68] See infra text accompanying notes 84–91.

[69] For §1248(f), see supra ¶68.2.16 text accompanying notes 372–74.

Section 1248(f) applies to a variety of corporate distributions of CFC stock in addition to §355 distributions. A distribution is excepted from §1248(f) if the distributee's holding period for the distributed stock includes the distributing corporation's holding period and the distributee is a U.S. shareholder immediately after the exchange. IRC §1248(f)(2). This exception cannot apply to a §355 distribution. The distributee's basis for stock distributed under §355 derives from the distributee's basis for stock of the distributing corporation, not the distributing corporation's basis for the distributed stock. IRC §§358(a)(1), (c). The distributee's holding period thus includes his holding period for his stock of the distributing corporation, not the latter's holding period for the distributed stock. IRC §1223(1).

The §367(b) regulations supplement §1248(f) by requiring that the earnings and profits or deficits of the distributing and controlled corporations be reallocated between them. If the distribution includes all outstanding stock of the controlled corporation and neither corporation controls any other corporation immediately after the distribution, the reallocation is simple in concept: The earnings and profits or deficits of the two corporations are added together, and the aggregate is split between them in proportion to the net values of their assets immediately after the distribution.[70]

The allocation is more complex if one or both of the corporations controls other corporations after the distribution. Moreover, adjustments are often made to the stock basis of the shareholders of lower-tier corporations whose earnings and profits or deficits are reduced in the reallocation. The distributing or controlled corporation is deemed to control a lower-tier corporation for this purpose if it owns 80 percent or more of the stock of the lower-tier corporation, directly or indirectly through intermediate subsidiaries.

a. *Earnings and profits of lower-tier corporations.* Separate determinations are made of the accumulated earnings and profits or deficit of the distributing corporation, the controlled corporation, and each corporation controlled by either of them. The earnings and deficits of all of these corporations are added together. The aggregate is split between the distributing corporation and the corporations it controls immediately after the distribution (the distributing group) and the controlled corporation and the corporations it then controls (the controlled group) in proportion to the net values of the assets of the two groups. The assets of each group exclude group members' shareholdings in other corporations in the group, but include all other assets of all group members. For the group whose aggregate earnings or profits or deficit increases in the reallocation, the increase is made to the earnings or deficit of the distributing or controlled corporation only. If one group's earnings and profits decrease in the reallocation, the decrease is prorated among group members in proportion to their separate earnings and profits before the reallocation. If one group's aggregate deficit is decreased by the reallocation, each member with a deficit reduces it by an amount equal to the total reduction multiplied by the ratio of the member's deficit to the sum of the deficits of all deficit members of the group.

b. *Basis adjustments.* The rules for basis adjustments apply only if the distributing or controlled corporation controls at least one other corporation immediately after the distribution.[71] If the earnings and profits of a lower-tier controlled corporation are reduced, its direct shareholder's stock basis is increased if each U.S. shareholder agrees to treat the transferred earnings and profits as though they had been distributed up the chain as a dividend to the

---

[70] Reg. §7.367(b)-10(d). See Reg. §7.367(b)-3(e) (earnings and profits or deficit received in reallocation has same character to recipient as to corporation from which transferred).

[71] Reg. §§7.367(b)-10(e), (f).

distributing or controlled corporation immediately after the §355 distribution. This constructive distribution may be taxed to the U.S. shareholders under subpart F or the foreign personal holding company rules. Any amounts so taxed to them are added to their stock bases, thus adding a final step to the chain of basis adjustments. If a lower-tier controlled corporation's deficit is reduced in the reallocation or earnings and deficits, its shareholder or shareholders must reduce the basis of their stock. The basis increase or decrease equals the earnings and profits or deficit transferred from that corporation and other corporations in still lower tiers.

Assume foreign corporation *C1*, a controlled corporation whose stock is distributed in a §355 distribution, is sole shareholder of foreign corporation *C2*, which in turn owns the stock of foreign corporation *C3*; *C1*'s U.S. shareholders after the distribution consent to treat earnings and profits transferred from *C2* and *C3* as though they had been distributed as dividends to *C1*. Any earnings and profits or deficit of *C3* that is transferred to the distributing group is added to or subtracted from *C2*'s basis for its *C3* stock. *C1*'s basis for the *C2* stock is adjusted for the earnings and profits or deficits transferred from both *C2* and *C3*.

2. *Domestic distributing corporation; foreign distributee.* Generally, a corporation recognizes no gain or loss on making a §355 distribution of stock or securities (hereinafter "stock").[72] However, a domestic distributing corporation must generally recognize gain (but not loss) on making a §355 distribution to a foreign person (any person other than a U.S. citizen or resident or domestic corporation).[73] The gain is the excess of the fair market value of the stock distributed to the foreign distributee over the distributing corporation's adjusted basis for the stock.[74] If the distributee is a partnership, trust, or estate, this rule is applied as though the distribution were made ratably to the partners or beneficiaries.[75] Moreover, if the distributee is a domestic corporation that was formed or availed of by one or more foreign persons to hold stock of the dis-

---

[72] IRC §§355(c), 361(c).

[73] IRC §367(e)(1); Reg. §1.367(e)-1T(b)(1). These rules generally apply to distributions after September 13, 1996. Reg. §1.367(e)-1T(f). An earlier, similar version of the regulations applies to distributions after January 15, 1993 and before September 13, 1996. Reg. §1.367(e)-1(f) (before elimination in 1996).

Such a distribution is also described in §367(a)(1), but the rule described here trumps any exception from gain recognition under §367(a)(1). Reg. §1.367(e)-1T(b)(3).

[74] Reg. §1.367(e)-1T(b)(2). For this purpose, the stock's adjusted basis is a ratable portion of the distributing corporation's basis for all of its stock of a particular class.

If the distribution is of stock of a foreign corporation, all or part of the gain may be a dividend under §1248. Reg. §1.367(e)-1T(d)(2). For §1248, see supra ¶68.2.16.

[75] Reg. §1.367(e)-1T(b)(5)(i). This rule is applied successively until the stock is attributed to an individual or corporation. See Reg. §1.367(e)-1T(e) Ex. 8.

A partner's proportionate share of stock distributed to a partnership is the same as the partner's proportionate share of any gain that would have been recognized if the partnership had sold its stock in the distributing corporation immediately before the distribution. Stock distributed to a trust or estate is deemed distributed to the persons who are constructive owners of the stock under §§318(a)(2)(A) and (B).

tributee corporation "for a principal purpose of avoiding" tax under this rule, the stock is deemed distributed to the foreign persons, not the domestic corporation.[76] The distributing corporation's recognition of gain does not affect the taxation of the distributee, who is treated as receiving a §355 distribution.[77]

However, distributions of stock of domestic corporations are excepted from this rule in three situations. First, the rule does not apply if, immediately after the distribution, the distributing and controlled corporations are both U.S. real property holding corporations.[78] A U.S. real property holding corporation is a domestic corporation, more than one half of whose assets are U.S. real property interests (generally, interests in real property located in the United States and stock in other U.S. real property holding corporations).[79] This exception is apparently allowed on the theory that since foreign persons are subject to U.S. tax on gains on sales of stock of U.S. real property holding corporations, the distribution does not, in this situation, remove the distributed stock from U.S. tax jurisdiction.

Second, distributions by publicly held corporations of stock of domestic subsidiaries are usually excepted from the rule. Specifically, the rule does not apply to a distribution of stock of a domestic controlled corporation if at least 80 percent (by value) of the controlled corporation's stock is distributed to holders of classes of stock of the distributing corporation that are regularly traded on an established securities market in the United States.[80] However, this exemption applies to the distribution to a particular foreign distributee only if the distributee does not, in so far as the distributing corporation knows or has reason to know, own more than 5 percent of the class of the distributing corporation's stock with respect to which the distribution is made, either actually or constructively.[81]

Third, a distributing corporation can, at least temporarily, avoid recognizing gain on a §355 distribution of stock of a domestic corporation to a maximum of

---

The distributing corporation may determine the identity, status, and proportionate interests of the partners or beneficiaries by any means. If it receives a written statement from a partner or beneficiary certifying under penalties of perjury that the partner or beneficiary is a U.S. person, it is not liable for tax on the distribution allocable to the partner or beneficiary, regardless of the truth or falsity of the statement, unless the corporation knows or has reason to know that the statement is false. Reg. §1.367(e)-1T(b)(5)(ii).

[76] Reg. §1.367(e)-1T(b)(6). See Reg. §1.367(e)-1T(e) Ex. 9.

[77] Reg. §1.367(e)-1T(b)(3).

[78] Reg. §1.367(e)-1T(c)(1). See Reg. §1.367(e)-1T(e) Ex. 2.

[79] IRC §897(c), discussed supra ¶66.4.3.

[80] Reg. §1.367(e)-1T(c)(2)(i). See Reg. §1.367(e)-1T(e) Ex. 3.

If the distributing and controlled corporations are both U.S. real property holding corporations, the distribution is excepted under the rule described in the preceding paragraph of the text, not this rule. Reg. §1.367(e)-1T(c)(2)(v).

[81] Reg. §§1.367(e)-1T(c)(2)(ii), (b)(1)(i). Constructive ownership rules and other details in the application of the 5 percent threshold are borrowed from §897(c)(3), discussed supra ¶66.4.3 text accompanying notes 41–42.

10 qualified foreign distributees by filing with the IRS an agreement to recognize the gain on the distribution to each distributee covered by the agreement in the event the distributee, before the end of the tenth year following the taxable year of the distribution, disposes of either the distributed stock or the distributee's stock in the distributing corporation.[82] This exception usually applies only if, immediately after the distribution and on each "testing date," the distributing corporation's net worth (fair market value of assets, less liabilities) exceeds the gain that the distributing corporation realized but did not recognize.[83] Each of the distributees covered by the agreement must be a resident of a country with which the United States has an income tax treaty.

3. *Foreign distributing corporation.* When the distributing corporation in a §355 distribution is foreign, a U.S. shareholder participating in the distribution is taxed on it unless the issuer of the stock received is a foreign corporation and the distributee is a U.S. shareholder of that corporation immediately after the distribution. If these conditions are met, nonrecognition is allowed under §355, but the regulations attach various attributes to the stock in order to preserve the potential for future taxation of past earnings. Attribute preservation rules also apply when both the distributing corporation and the distributee are foreign corporations. In addition, whether the distribution is subject to immediate taxation or attribute preservation, the earnings and profits or deficits of the distributing and controlled corporations and lower-tier corporations are reallocated under the rules described above for distributions by domestic corporations, and lower-tier reallocations are reflected by the same adjustments to stock basis.

a. *Reallocation of §1248 and §367(b) attributes.* In all cases, the first step under the rules for §355 distributions by foreign corporations is to reallocate various §367(b) attributes of the stock held before the distribution among the stock held after the distribution, as follows: The §1248 amount and the all earnings and profits amount are computed for each U.S. shareholder's stock in the distributing corporation immediately before the distribution, including the stock of U.S. shareholders not participating in the §355 distribution.[84] Similarly, the §1248(c)(2) and additional earnings and profits amounts are determined with respect to the stock of each lower-tier corporation having one or more U.S. shareholders. The amounts for the stock held before the distribution are pro rated among the stock held after the distribution according to the values the various blocks held.[85]

b. *U.S. shareholder's receipt of non-CFC stock.* A U.S. shareholder of the distributing foreign corporation that receives non-CFC stock in the distribution

---

[82] Reg. §1.367(e)-1T(c)(3). See Reg. §1.367(e)-1(e) Exs. 4–7.

[83] Reg. §1.367(e)-1T(c)(3)(ii)(B). The testing dates are the last day of each taxable year of the distributing corporation during which the gain recognition agreement is in effect and each day on which the distributing corporation distributes property to its shareholders under §301(a).

[84] Reg. §7.367(b)-10(g).

[85] Reg. §7.367(b)-10(h).

must recognize gain under §1248.[86] The term "non-CFC stock" is used here to refer to stock of (1) a domestic corporation, (2) a foreign corporation that is not a CFC, or (3) a CFC as to which the exchanging shareholder is not a U.S. shareholder. When this rule applies, the exchanging shareholder must usually recognize gross income equal to the lesser of (1) the §1248 amount for the non-CFC stock or (2) the gain the shareholder would have recognized on a sale of the shareholder's stock in the distributing corporation immediately before the distribution for a price equal to its fair market value.

However, the exchanging shareholder's gross income inclusion equals the all earnings and profits amount allocated to the non-CFC stock if the shareholder is a domestic corporation and the distribution is also a reorganization under §368(a)(1)(D) in which a domestic corporation succeeds to the assets of a foreign corporation.[87] If the all earnings and profits amount is not so reported in this case, gain must be recognized on the exchange as though §355 did not exist, but basis is determined under the reorganization rules as though no gain had been recognized.

Any amount included in a U.S. shareholder's gross income under these rules is treated as a cash dividend received immediately before the §355 distribution from the corporation making that distribution.[88] The shareholder thus may qualify under §902 for credit for foreign income taxes paid by the distributing corporation if the shareholder is a domestic corporation and owned at least 10 percent of the distributing corporation's voting stock immediately before the distribution.[89] In any event, a shareholder taxed under these rules is exempted from tax on subsequent distributions with respect to the non-CFC stock until these distributions have fully exhausted the amount taxed.[90]

 c. *Foreign corporation's receipt of non-CFC stock.* If a foreign corporation receives non-CFC stock in a §355 distribution by another foreign corporation, the exchanging shareholder's earnings and profits are adjusted.[91] The stock received is "non-CFC stock" if the issuer of the stock is (1) a domestic corporation, (2) a foreign corporation that is not a CFC, or (3) a CFC whose U.S. shareholders do not include all of those who were U.S. shareholders of the distributing corporation before the distribution. When this rule applies, the exchanging shareholder's earnings and profits are increased (or its deficit reduced) by the §1248(c)(2) amount allocated to the non-CFC stock.

---

[86] Reg. §7.367(b)-10(i). See Rev. Rul. 83-23, 1983-1 CB 82 (where U.S. shareholder received 60 of foreign controlled corporation's 100 shares and unrelated foreign persons received 40, stock treated as non-CFC stock because U.S. shareholder immediately transferred 20 shares to foreign shareholders pursuant to agreement made before distribution).

[87] Reg. §7.367(b)-10(j). For §368(a)(1)(D), see infra ¶94.3.4.

[88] Reg. §7.367(b)-3(b).

[89] Reg. §7.367(b)-3(f). For §902, see infra ¶69.8.1.

[90] Reg. §7.367(b)-12(d), incorporating the rules of §959, discussed supra ¶68.2.14.

[91] Reg. §7.367(b)-10(i).

¶68.7.7 Reporting and Recordkeeping Requirements

A person who realizes gain in a §367(b) transaction must give the IRS notice of the transaction if the person is obligated to file U.S. income tax returns.[92] The notice must be filed no later than the due date (with extensions) of the taxpayer's return for the year in which the transaction occurs. The notice must describe the transaction and include other information relevant to the rules applied to the transaction, such as the earnings and profits attributable to stock received by the taxpayer in the transaction.[93] Failure to give notice is treated as a noncompliance with the §367(b) regulations unless reasonable cause is shown.[94] Noncompliance usually results in recognition of the taxpayer's gain on the transaction.

If a corporation's earnings and profits are adjusted under the §367(b) regulations, it must "keep records adequate to establish the adjustment."[95] The same exhortation is given to a U.S. person when the regulations attribute any amount to stock owned by the person.[96]

¶68.7.8 Proposed §367(b) Regulations—Generally

The IRS has proposed regulations to replace the existing temporary regulations under §367(b).[97] The proposed regulations are generally less complex than the temporary regulations. The remaining complexity, however, is not inconsiderable.

Under §367(b) and the regulations thereunder, foreign corporations are sometimes deemed not to be corporations for purposes of various corporate nonrecognition rules. When this happens, the nonrecognition rule becomes inapplicable, and the 367(b) regulations require either that gain on the exchange covered by the nonrecognition rule be recognized, in whole or in part, or that one or more parties to the transaction report deemed dividends. The nonrecognition rules affected by §367(b) are

1. Section 332, providing that a parent corporation recognizes no gain or loss on the liquidation of a subsidiary if it owns at least 80 percent of the subsidiary's stock.[98]
2. Section 351, excusing a transferor from recognizing gain or loss on a transfer to a controlled corporation in exchange for stock.[99]

---

[92] Reg. §7.367(b)-1(c)(1).

[93] Reg. §7.367(b)-1(c)(2).

[94] Reg. §7.367(b)-1(c)(3).

[95] Reg. §7.367(b)-1(d)(1).

[96] Reg. §7.367(b)-1(d)(2).

[97] INTL-178-86, 1991-2 CB 1070. See NY State Bar Ass'n Tax Section, Report on Proposed Sections 367(a) and (b) Regulations, 55 Tax Notes 105 (Jan. 30, 1992).

[98] For §332, see infra ¶93.6.

[99] For §351, see infra ¶91.2.

3. Section 354, providing that gain or loss shall not be recognized on an exchange of stock or securities for other stock or securities pursuant to a plan of reorganization.[100]

4. Section 355, allowing nonrecognition on the distribution and receipt of stock or securities in various corporate divisions.[101]

5. Section 356, requiring partial recognition of gain (and denying recognition of loss) if boot is received in an exchange otherwise encompassed by §354 or §355.

Section 367(b) may affect the application of these provisions whenever the "status of a foreign corporation as a corporation is relevant for determining the extent to which income shall be recognized or for determining the effect of the transaction on earnings and profits, basis of stock or securities, or basis of assets."[102] Section 367(b) does not apply, however, to a transfer by a U.S. person to a foreign corporation if, under §367(a)(1), the foreign corporation is deemed not to be a corporation.[103]

Generally, under the proposed regulations, a foreign corporation is considered to be a corporation for purposes of a nonrecognition rule subject to §367(b) unless the exchange is covered by a rule of the regulations that denies corporate status or alters the nonrecognition rule.[104] Very generally, the proposed regulations override or alter nonrecognition rules in two types of situations:

1. When the assets of a foreign corporation are transferred to a domestic corporation in a transaction otherwise within a corporate nonrecognition rule, U.S. shareholders of the foreign corporation are usually required to report deemed dividends equal to their shares of the foreign corporation's earnings and profits.[105]

2. When a U.S. shareholder of a controlled foreign corporation exchanges its stock in the corporation for stock in another foreign corporation, the U.S. shareholder is deemed to receive a dividend unless the potential for taxing the U.S. shareholder on the first foreign corporation's accumulated earnings is essentially unchanged by the transaction.[106]

A person realizing income or gain on a §367(b) exchange must file a notice on the transaction with the IRS whether or not the income or gain is recognized.[107] The notice must be attached to the person's return for the year during which the income or gain is realized. If the person is not required to file a return,

---

[100] For §354, see infra ¶94.4.5.
[101] For §355, see infra ¶94.1.
[102] Prop. Reg. §1.367(b)-1(a).
[103] For §367(a)(1), see supra ¶68.6.
[104] Prop. Reg. §1.367(b)-1(b).
[105] See infra ¶68.7.9.
[106] See infra ¶68.7.10.
[107] Prop. Reg. §1.367(b)-1(c).

the notice must be filed with the IRS office and by the time that would be required if a return were due.

¶68.7.9 Proposed Regulations—Repatriations of Foreign Assets

When the assets of a foreign corporation are acquired by a domestic corporation in a reorganization or a §332 (subsidiary to parent) liquidation, the shareholders of the foreign corporation usually have deemed dividend income equal to their ratable shares of the foreign corporation's earnings and profits.[108] Some shareholders are excused from the deemed dividend rule but may be required to recognize gain on the reorganization exchange.

According to the preamble to the proposed regulations:

> The United States generally does not tax a foreign corporation on its foreign source earnings and profits. If the foreign corporation is owned in whole or in part ... by a United States person, ... the United States does not [usually] tax the United States person on the foreign corporation's earnings and profit until those earnings and profits are repatriated (for example, through the payment of dividends) or the United States person disposes of an interest in the foreign corporation. One of the principles of the proposed regulations under 367(b) is that the repatriation of a United States person's share of earnings and profits of a foreign corporation through what would otherwise be a nonrecognition transaction ... should generally cause recognition of income by the foreign corporation's shareholders. A domestic acquirer of the foreign corporation's assets should not succeed to the basis or other tax attributes of the foreign corporation except to the extent that the United States tax jurisdiction has taken account of the United States person's share of the earnings and profits that gave rise to those tax attributes.[109]

Assume domestic corporation D owns the stock of foreign corporation F, which has accumulated substantial earnings and profits by actively carrying on business operations in foreign countries; F sells its assets and distributes the selling proceeds to D. If F has steered clear of subpart F, its earnings and profits were not subjected to U.S. taxation at any time before the liquidation. Normally, §§332 and 337 would excuse D and F from recognizing gain or loss on the liquidation, and under §381, F's earnings and profits account would be added to D's earnings and profits. Without more, F's earnings would escape U.S. corporate taxation permanently because D's earnings and profits consist of amounts already subjected to the corporate tax. For example, if D distributes a dividend to another corporation that owns D stock, the dividend qualifies for the dividends received deduction under §243. F's liquidation is thus the last chance to apply a U.S. corporate tax to F's earnings, and §367(b) seizes the opportunity by requiring D to report a deemed dividend on the liquidation.

---

[108] Prop. Reg. §1.367(b)-3(a).
[109] INTL-178-86, supra note 97, at 1072.

1. *Shareholders subject to dividend rule.* Two categories of shareholders are subject to this rule: U.S. shareholders and certain foreign corporations.[110] A U.S. shareholder is a U.S. person (citizen or resident of the United States or domestic corporation or partnership) that owns at least 10 percent of the foreign corporation's stock, actually or constructively.[111] A foreign corporation owning stock of the foreign corporation acquired or liquidating in the transaction is subject to the dividend rule if a U.S. person might sometime be affected by the foreign corporation's dividend income, and this is so in two situations.

First, a foreign shareholder corporation is subject to the deemed dividend rule if a U.S. person is a §1248 shareholder of the shareholder corporation. A §1248 shareholder is a U.S. person who owns (actually or constructively) at least 10 percent of the voting stock of a foreign corporation at a time (during the preceding five years) when the corporation is a controlled foreign corporation (CFC).[112] A foreign corporation is a CFC if more than 50 percent of its stock, by vote or value, is owned (actually or constructively) by U.S. persons, each of whom owns (actually or constructively) at least 10 percent of the voting stock.[113] A deemed dividend imputed to a foreign corporation under these rules might be taxed to a §1248 shareholder immediately under subpart F or in the future when the §1248 shareholder sells his stock.[114]

Second, a foreign shareholder corporation is subject to the dividend rule if a domestic corporation owns stock in the foreign corporation that meets the stock ownership requirement of §902. Section 902 allows a domestic corporation receiving dividends from a foreign corporation to take credit for foreign income taxes paid by the foreign corporation if the domestic corporation owns at least 10 percent of the foreign corporation's voting stock. Also, credit may pass through from a second-tier or third-tier foreign corporation if the domestic corporation's indirect interest in the lower-tire foreign corporation's voting stock is at least 5 percent and the stock ownership at each link in the chain of ownership includes at least 10 percent of the voting stock.[115]

2. *Measuring deemed dividend.* Each exchanging shareholder subject to the dividend rule must report a deemed dividend equal to the all earnings and profits amount attributable to the shareholder's stock.[116] The all earnings and profits amount is the stock's ratable share of the foreign corporation's net positive earnings and profits.[117] Earnings and profits are determined by "principles substantially similar to those applicable to domestic corporations." However, earn-

---

[110] Prop. Reg. §1.367(b)-3(b).

[111] IRC §951(b), discussed supra ¶68.2.2 text accompanying notes 20-31.

[112] Prop. Reg. §1.367(b)-2(b). For constructive ownership, see §958(b), discussed supra ¶68.2.2 text accompanying notes 26-32.

[113] IRC §957, discussed supra ¶68.2.2.

[114] See supra ¶68.2 for subpart F and ¶68.2.16 for §1248.

[115] See infra ¶69.8.2.

[116] Prop. Reg. §1.367(b)-3(b)(2)(i)(A).

[117] Prop. Reg. §1.367(b)-2(d).

ings and profits are included only for the period the corporation was a CFC and the taxpayer held the stock. Also, the all earnings and profits amount excludes earnings previously taxed to a U.S. shareholder under subpart F, earnings taxed to the foreign corporation as income effectively connected with a trade or business carried on in the United States, and a few other amounts. On the other hand, earnings and profits accumulated before 1963 (when subpart F and §1248 went into effect) are included. The all earnings and profits amount may exceed the gain that would be realized on a sale of the stock for its fair market value. However, it does not include earnings and profits of lower-tier corporations.

Assume foreign corporation F liquidates by distributing all of its assets to its sole shareholder, domestic corporation D.[118] D must report a dividend equal to F's all earnings and profits amount. Otherwise, the normal rules for subsidiary to parent liquidations apply: Under §337, F recognizes no gain or loss on distributing its assets, §332 excuses D from recognizing gain or loss on exchanging its F stock for F's assets, and D succeeds to F's basis for its assets, earnings and profits, and various other tax attributes.[119]

The results are slightly more complicated if the liquidating foreign corporation has minority shareholders. Assume D owns 80 percent of F's stock, and the remaining 20 percent is owned by an unrelated U.S. citizen.[120] Sections 337 and 332, which require only 80 percent ownership by the parent, still apply to the liquidating distribution to D, but the distribution to the individual shareholder is subject to §336, which requires the recognition of gain or loss by the liquidating corporation, and §331, which requires the shareholder to recognize gain or loss with respect to her stock.[121] Assume F's earnings and profits were $20 immediately before the liquidation, and D's all earnings and profits amount was then $16 (80 percent of $20); F's liquidating distribution to the minority shareholder consists of assets worth $20 with a basis of $5. Under §336(a), F recognizes gain on this distribution of $15 (excess of fair market value over basis).[122] If no foreign tax is imposed on the gain, it adds $15 to F's earnings and profits. D's all earnings and profits amount thus becomes $28 (sum of $16 immediately before liquidation and 80 percent of $15), and the dividend to D on the liquidation is thus $28.

The application of the dividend rule is essentially the same for a reorganization in which a domestic corporation acquires the assets of a foreign corporation. Assume domestic corporation D is sole shareholder of both foreign corporation FS and domestic corporation DS; in a D reorganization, DS acquires all of the assets of FS, issuing additional DS stock to D in exchange for D's FS stock.[123] D must report a dividend equal to the all earnings and profits amount with

---

[118] Prop. Reg. §1.367(b)-3(b)(2)(B) Ex. 1.

[119] See infra ¶93.6.

[120] Prop. Reg. §1.367(b)-3(b)(2)(B) Ex. 2.

[121] See supra ¶93.5.

[122] In addition, the minority shareholder recognizes gain or loss under §331(a) equal to the difference between $20 and the adjusted basis of her F stock.

[123] Prop. Reg. §1.367(b)-3(b)(2)(B) Ex. 3. For D reorganizations, see infra ¶94.3.4.

respect to its *FS* stock. Otherwise, the normal reorganization rules apply. Under §354(a), *D* recognizes no gain or loss on the exchange of its *FS* stock for *DS* stock, §361(a) excuses *FS* from recognizing gain or loss on the transfer of its assets to *DS*, and *DS* inherits *FS*'s basis, earnings and profits, and other tax attributes.[124]

If the deemed dividend is recognized by a foreign corporation that is not a U.S. taxpayer, it nevertheless has tax consequences, immediate or potential. Assume domestic corporation *D* owns the stock of foreign corporation *F1*, which owns the stock of foreign corporation *F2*; in a D reorganization, *F2* transfers its assets to *DS*, a domestic subsidiary of *D*, in exchange for *DS* stock, and *F2* distributes the *DS* stock to *F1* and goes out of existence.[125] Because the reorganization includes a transfer of the assets of a foreign corporation (*F2*) to a domestic corporation (*DS*), *F1*, as the shareholder *F2*, must report as a dividend the all earnings and profits amount with respect to its *F2* stock. Because *F1* is a foreign corporation, it is not subject to U.S. tax on the deemed dividend. The dividend, however, is foreign personal holding company income and therefore subpart F income. *D*, as U.S. shareholder of *F1*, must include the subpart F income in its gross income under §951. Moreover, although a dividend from one CFC to another may be excluded from gross income if both of them are organized in the same foreign country, the proposed regulations deny this exclusion to a deemed dividend of the all earnings and profits amount.[126]

3. *Exchange gain or loss.* An exchanging shareholder subject to the deemed dividend rule must recognize exchange gain or loss to the extent its share of the foreign corporation's capital has appreciated or depreciated "by reason of changes in the relative exchange rates of the foreign acquired corporation's functional currency and the exchanging shareholder's functional currency during the exchanging shareholder's holding period."[127] Assume domestic corporation *D*, whose functional currency is the U.S. dollar, paid $200 for its stock in a U.K. subsidiary (*F*) when the subsidiary was organized, and the subsidiary exchanged the $200 for 100£; several years later, when the all earnings and profits amount is 20£ and 1£ is worth $2.20, *F* liquidates by distributing its assets, consisting of 120£, to *D*.[128] *D*'s deemed dividend is $44 (20£ times 2.2). In addition, *D* has exchange gain of $20, computed as the excess of the dollar value of the repayment of the capital it contributed to *F* (100£ times 2.2) over the dollar value of the capital when contributed ($200). In other words, because the dollar value of the 100£ of capital increased from $200 to $220 while *F* held the capital, *D* has exchange gain of $20 on the liquidation. *D*'s basis for the 120£ received in the liquidation is $264 (120£ times 2.2).

---

[124] See infra ¶94.4.

[125] Prop. Reg. §1.367(b)-3(b)(2)(i)(B) Ex. 4.

[126] Prop. Reg. §1.367(b)-3(b)(2)(i)(A).

[127] Prop. Reg. §1.367(b)-3(b)(2)(ii)(A). For more on currency translation and exchange gain and loss for shareholders of CFCs, see infra ¶71.4.

[128] Prop. Reg. §1.367(b)-3(b)(2)(ii)(B) Ex. 1.

Exchange loss recognized under this rule may not exceed the deemed dividend.[129] Assume the pound is worth $1.60 when F is liquidated.[130] The deemed dividend is $32 (20£ times 1.6). The exchange loss is $40 ($200 invested less capital return of $160), but only $32 (an amount equal to the deemed dividend) may be recognized. The basis of the 120£ received in the liquidation is apparently $192 (120£ times 1.6). If so, the $8 of exchange loss disallowed by the dividend ceiling disappears permanently.

The exchange gain or loss apparently has the same source characterization as the deemed dividend.

4. *Taxable exchange election.* In lieu of recognizing the deemed dividend and exchange gain or loss under the foregoing rules, the exchanging shareholder may elect to recognize gain (but not loss) on the exchange.[131] The gain so recognized is usually characterized as a dividend, at least in part, by §1248, but the §1248 dividend, unlike the all earnings and profits amount, does not include earnings and profits accumulated before 1963 and may not exceed the gain on the exchange.[132]

Assume foreign corporation F distributes its assets in complete liquidation to its sole shareholder, domestic corporation D.[133] The distributed assets consist of land (value $60, basis $30) and tangible depreciable property (value $40, basis $80), and D's basis for the F stock is $80. The all earnings and profits amount is $30 (including $11 accumulated before 1963), but the earnings and profits picked up by §1248 are only $19. If D makes the election, it recognizes gain of $20 ($100 value of property received less $80 stock basis), of which $19 (§1248 earnings and profits) is a dividend.

When the election is made, any excess of the all earnings and profits amount over the gain recognized by the exchanging shareholder (the "excess earnings and profits amount") is applied in reduction of tax attributes that follow the distributed assets.[134] If the foreign corporation carried on a trade or business in the United States and has net operating loss (NOL) or capital loss carryovers from the trade or business, the excess earnings and profits amount is applied first against the NOL carryovers and then against the capital loss carryovers. In the usual case where the corporation has such carryovers, the excess is applied against the basis of the distributed assets, starting with tangible property subject to depreciation or depletion and continuing with other tangible assets apart from inventory, then intangible assets subject to amortization, and finally all other assets (except "dollar-denominated money"). Within the last of these categories that is reached in a particular case, the taxpayer may choose the assets to absorb the basis reduction.

---

[129] Prop. Reg. §1.367(b)-3(b)(2)(ii)(A).

[130] Prop. Reg. §1.367(b)-3(b)(2)(ii)(B) Ex. 2.

[131] Prop. Reg. §1.367(b)-3(b)(2)(iii)(A).

[132] See supra ¶68.2.16.

[133] Prop. Reg. §1.367(b)-3(b)(2)(iii)(B) Ex.

[134] Prop. Reg. §1.367(b)-3(b)(2)(iii)(A).

Assume *F* had no U.S. trade or business. The all earnings and profits amount ($30) exceeds *D*'s recognized gain ($20) by $10. The adjusted basis of *F*'s depreciable property ($80 immediately before the distribution) is thus reduced by $10. *D*'s bases for the distributed assets are $70 ($80 less $10) for the depreciable property and $30 (*F*'s basis, without change) for the land.

5. *Shareholders not subject to dividend rule.* In a reorganization in which assets of a foreign corporation are transferred to a domestic corporation, an exchanging shareholder not subject to the dividend rule must recognize all gain on the exchange, but loss remains subject to the nonrecognition rules of §§354 and 356.[135] This rule applies, for example, to a U.S. person owning less than 10 percent of the foreign corporation's voting stock, actually and constructively. The gain is capital if the stock exchanged was a capital asset.

6. *Gain recognition by foreign corporation liquidating into foreign parent.* Under §337, a corporation generally recognizes no gain or loss on a liquidating distribution to a parent corporation if §332 applies to the parent. Section 337 generally applies on the liquidation of a foreign subsidiary.[136] However, if the parent is also a foreign corporation, the subsidiary must recognize gain on the distribution of property used in a U.S. trade or business unless the parent uses the property in a U.S. business immediately after the distribution.[137] Gain must also be recognized on a distribution of property that the liquidating corporation used in a U.S. trade or business within 10 years before the distribution, but does not so use at the time of the distribution.[138] However, neither of these rules requires recognition of gain on a distribution of a U.S. real property interest.[139]

¶68.7.10 Proposed Regulations—Stock or Assets of Foreign Corporation Acquired by Another Foreign Corporation

When a foreign acquiring corporation acquires stock or assets of a foreign acquired corporation in a reorganization or §351 exchange, various categories of

---

[135] Prop. Reg. §1.367(b)-3(c).

[136] Reg. §1.367(e)-2T(c)(1).

[137] Reg. §1.367(e)-2T(c)(2)(i). This rule generally applies to distributions after July 1986. Reg. §1.367(e)-2T(d).

Generally, the subsidiary avoids recognition on distributions of U.S. business assets only if, for 10 years after the distribution, the parent continues the U.S. business and uses the distributed property in that business; the parent must also submit a statement to the IRS to facilitate enforcement of the 10-year requirement. However, if the subsidiary and parent are both controlled foreign corporations, it is sufficient that the parent use the property in any U.S. trade or business immediately after the distribution.

For basis and other collateral consequences of the recognition of gain under this rule, see Reg. §1.367(e)-2T(c)(3).

[138] Reg. §1.367(e)-2T(c)(2)(ii).

[139] For the term U.S. real property interest, see supra ¶¶66.4.2–66.4.4.

shareholders of the acquired corporation are deemed to receive dividends.[140] A deemed dividend is imputed where the reorganization or exchange either cuts off the potential for §1248 applying to a subsequent stock sale or diminishes this potential by shifting beneficial interests in earnings and profits. Under §1248, gain on a sale of stock of a foreign corporation is treated as a dividend, in whole or in part, if the seller is a U.S. person who, during the preceding five years, held at least 10 percent of the foreign corporation's stock while the corporation was a controlled foreign corporation (CFC).[141] The dividend usually equals the earnings and profits allocable to the stock sold, exclusive of earnings accumulated while the seller did not hold the stock or the corporation was not a CFC, earnings accumulated before 1963, earnings previously taxed by the United States (e.g., under subpart F), and a few other categories of earnings.

Assume domestic corporation D has held all stock of foreign corporation FS since its organization, and FS has accumulated substantial earnings and profits from active business operations in foreign countries; in a B reorganization, D exchanges its FS stock for a minority interest in foreign corporation FA, whose other shareholders are unrelated foreign persons. Normally, under §354, no gain or loss is recognized on a stock for stock exchange pursuant to a plan of reorganization. However, if D had made a cash sale of its FS stock, gain on the sale would have been a dividend under §1248 to the extent of FS's earnings and profits, but §1248 will not apply to D's disposition of the FA stock received in the reorganization because less than 50 percent of FA's stock is owned by U.S. persons and FA is therefore not a CFC. If D recognized no income or gain on the reorganization, the reorganization would therefore have the effect of avoiding the application of §1248 and thereby permanently exempting D from a U.S. dividend tax on the earnings accumulated by FS while D held the FS stock. Section 367(b) frustrates the avoidance by requiring D to report at the time of the reorganization the same §1248 dividend that D would have had if it had instead sold the FS stock for cash.

The exchanging shareholders subject to the deemed dividend rule are described immediately below, and the measurement of the dividend is described thereafter.

1. *Exchanges cutting off potential application of §1248.* A U.S. person is subject to the deemed dividend rule if the person is a "section 1248 shareholder"

---

[140] Prop. Reg. §1.367(b)-4(a). The proposed regulations omit A reorganizations from the list of transactions subject to this rule, but a foreign corporation cannot be the acquired or acquiring corporation in an A reorganization because such a reorganization must be "effected pursuant to the corporation laws" of the United States, one of the states, or the District of Columbia. Reg. §1.368-2(b)(1).

[141] See supra ¶68.2.16. A foreign corporation is a CFC if more than 50 percent of its stock, by vote or value, is owned (actually or constructively) by U.S. persons, each of whom owns (actually or constructively) at least 10 percent of the voting stock. IRC §957, discussed supra ¶68.2.2.

and meets various other requirements.[142] A §1248 shareholder is a U.S. person (U.S. citizen or resident or domestic corporation or partnership) that owns (actually or constructively) at least 10 percent of the voting stock of a foreign corporation at a time (during the preceding five years) when the corporation was a CFC.[143] A §1248 shareholder, in other words, is a shareholder who would have had dividend income under §1248 if the stock had been sold for cash rather than exchanged in the reorganization or §351 transaction. A foreign corporation that exchanges stock in a covered transaction may be subject to the deemed dividend rule if, immediately before the exchange, at least one U.S. person is a §1248 shareholder of both the exchanging corporation and the foreign acquired corporation.[144]

A §1248 shareholder or a foreign corporation with a §1248 shareholder must report a deemed dividend under the rule if one of the following is true:

a. The issuer of the stock received in the exchange is not a CFC immediately after the exchange.

b. The issuer is a CFC but the §1248 shareholder is not a §1248 shareholder of the issuer immediately after the exchange.

c. The foreign acquiring corporation (or in a B reorganization, the foreign acquired corporation) is not a CFC immediately after the exchange.

d. The §1248 shareholder is not a §1248 shareholder of the foreign acquiring corporation (or in a B reorganization, the foreign acquired corporation) immediately after the exchange.[145]

In other words, the deemed dividend is recognized unless, immediately after the exchange, the §1248 shareholder continues to be a §1248 shareholder of the foreign corporation holding the acquired corporation's assets and, if different, the foreign corporation whose stock is received in the exchange. Stated yet another way, the deemed dividend is imputed whenever (1) stock potentially subject to §1248 is exchanged for stock not subject to §1248 or (2) the potential application of §1248 is eliminated by an exchange of stock of a lower-tier corporation. However, the deemed dividend need not be reported if the stock received in the exchange is stock of a domestic corporation.

Assume domestic corporation D exchanges the stock of its foreign subsidiary FS for stock of foreign corporation FA in a C reorganization in which FA acquires all assets of FS and FS liquidates; D receives 30 percent of FA's voting stock in the exchange, and the remainder of FA's stock is owned by unrelated foreign persons.[146] Immediately before the exchange, FS is a CFC, and D is a

---

[142] Prop. Reg. §1.367(b)-4(b)(1).

[143] Prop. Reg. §1.367(b)-2(b). For constructive ownership, see §958(b), discussed supra ¶68.2.2 text accompanying notes 26–32.

[144] Prop. Reg. §1.367(b)-4(b)(1).

[145] Prop. Reg. §1.367(b)-4(b)(1)(ii).

[146] Prop. Reg. §1.367(b)-4(e) Ex. 1.

§1248 shareholder of *FS*. Immediately after the exchange, *D* is not a §1248 shareholder of *FA* because *FA* is not a CFC. *D* must therefore recognize a deemed dividend on the reorganization exchange equal to the dividend income it would have had if it had sold the *FS* stock for cash.

In contrast, if the *FA* stock received by *D* in the reorganization exchange is, say, 60 percent of *FA*'s outstanding stock immediately after the exchange, *D* has no deemed dividend because *FA* is a CFC and *D* is a §1248 shareholder.[147] Assume *D* receives voting stock of foreign corporation *FP*, which is *FA*'s sole shareholder, rather than stock of *FA*, and this stock constitutes 60 percent of *FP*'s stock outstanding immediately after the exchange.[148] No deemed dividend is recognized in this case either because both *FP* (the issuer of the stock received) and *FA* (the acquiring corporation) are CFCs immediately after the exchange and *D* is a §1248 shareholder of both of them.

To illustrate the application of the dividend rule where the exchanging shareholder is a foreign corporation, assume domestic corporation *D* is sole shareholder of foreign corporation *FS*, which owns all of the stock of foreign corporation *FSS*; *FS* transfers the *FSS* stock to another foreign corporation, *FA*, in exchange for 30 percent of *FA*'s stock in a B reorganization.[149] If the remainder of *FA*'s stock is held by unrelated foreign persons, *FS* must recognize the §1248 amount as dividend income because (1) *D* was a §1248 shareholder of the acquired corporation (*FSS*) and (2) immediately after the exchange, *D* is not a §1248 shareholder of either the acquired corporation (*FSS*) or the acquiring corporation (*FA*) because neither of them is a CFC. As discussed more fully below, the deemed dividend is not immediately subject to U.S. tax because its principal purpose is to transfer *D*'s share of *FSS*'s §1248 earnings and profits to *FS* so that *D* can be taxed on them when *FS* makes distributions to *D* or *D* disposes of the *FS* stock.[150]

A B reorganization can be subject to §§367(a)(1) as well as 367(b) where the acquired and acquiring corporations are both foreign. Assume domestic corporation *D* exchanges all of the outstanding stock of foreign corporation *FS* for 30 percent of the voting stock of foreign corporation *FA*; the remainder of *FA*'s stock is owned by unrelated foreign persons.[151] The exchange is a B reorganization because *FA* acquires stock of another corporation (*FS*) solely in exchange for its own voting stock and owns at least 80 percent of *FS* immediately thereafter.[152] Section 367(a)(1) applies because *D*, a U.S. person, transfers property (*FS* stock) to a foreign corporation (*FA*) in a transaction described in §354 (stock for stock exchange in reorganization). If gain is recognized on the exchange under

---

[147] Prop. Reg. §1.367(b)-4(e) Ex. 3.

[148] Prop. Reg. §1.367(b)-4(e) Ex. 4.

[149] Prop. Reg. §1.367(b)-4(e) Ex. 2.

[150] See infra text accompanying note 162.

[151] Prop. Reg. §1.367(b)-4(e) Ex. 5.

[152] See infra ¶94.3.2.

§367(a)(1), §367(b) does not apply. However, the §367(a)(1) regulations allow *D* to avoid immediate recognition of its gain on the exchange by filing a gain recognition agreement requiring that *D* amend its return for the year of the reorganization to treat the reorganization as fully taxable if *FA* sells the *FS* stock within five years.[153] If the gain recognition agreement is filed, §367(b) applies to the reorganization exchange because the reorganization consists of a foreign corporation's acquisition of stock of another foreign corporation. Under the §367(b) regulations, *D* has a deemed dividend on the reorganization exchange because it was a §1248 shareholder of *FS* before the exchange but is not a §1248 shareholder of either *FS* or *FA* after the exchange (neither is a CFC). The deemed dividend reduces the gain on the exchange; the remainder of the gain on the exchange is not recognized unless *FA* sells the *FS* stock during the life of the gain recognition agreement.

2. *Excessive shifts of earnings and profits.* An exchanging shareholder in a foreign to foreign reorganization or §351 exchange must recognize the deemed dividend, even if the exchange does not cut off the future application of §1248, if all of the following are true.

   a. The foreign acquired and acquiring corporations are not members of the same affiliated group immediately before the exchange.

   b. Immediately after the exchange, a domestic corporation has sufficient ownership of the foreign acquiring corporation (directly or indirectly) to qualify for credit under §902 for foreign income taxes imposed on the acquiring corporation.

   c. The exchanging shareholder receives preferred stock in exchange for common stock or receives stock that in the opinion of the IRS, will allow the exchanging shareholder to "participate ... disproportionately" in earnings generated by particular assets of the acquired or acquiring corporation.[154]

For purposes of requirement *a*, an "affiliated group" is a group of corporations (foreign, domestic, or both) joined to a common parent in parent-subsidiary or brother-sister relationships, with more than 50 percent stock ownership (by vote and value) at each link in the chain. For purposes of requirement *c*, stock is not considered preferred if it participates fully in dividends, redemptions, and corporate growth.

Assume domestic corporation *D* is sole shareholder of foreign corporation *FS*, whose assets are acquired by unrelated foreign corporation *FA* in a C reorganization in exchange for voting preferred stock of *FA*, which *FS* distributes to *D* in complete liquidation.[155] Assume the voting preferred stock received by *D* carries 10 percent of the total voting power of all *FA* stock, thus qualifying *D* for

---

[153] Reg. §1.367(a)-3T, discussed supra ¶68.6.3.
[154] Prop. Reg. §1.367(b)-4(b)(2).
[155] Prop. Reg. §1.367(b)-4(e) Ex. 7.

indirect credit under §902 when it receives dividends from *FA*, and *FA*'s other shareholders are U.S. persons (unrelated to *D*), thus causing *FA* to be a CFC. Even though *D* is a §1248 shareholder of *FA* immediately after the reorganization exchange, *D* has deemed dividend income because (1) *FS* and *FA* were not members of the same affiliated group before the exchange, (2) *D*'s ownership of *FA* qualifies it for §902 credit, and (3) *D* receives preferred stock in the exchange.[156] The results would be the same if *D* received voting common stock of *FA* but *FA* and its shareholders agreed that dividends on *D*'s stock would depend solely on *FS*'s earnings and profits and any distribution in redemption or liquidation or *D*'s stock of *FA* would equal the value of the *FS* stock.[157]

3. *Recapitalizations.* An exchanging shareholder must recognize the deemed dividend in a recapitalization if

a. In the recapitalization, the shareholder receives preferred stock or a disproportionately participating interest described in requirement *c* of the rules described immediately above.

b. Within 24 months before or after the recapitalization, a reorganization occurs that meets requirements *a* and *b* of those rules.[158]

4. *Amount of deemed dividend; §1248 amount.* The deemed dividend under these rules equals the §1248 amount for the stock exchanged.[159] The §1248 amount equals the net earnings and profits that would be included in gross income as a dividend under §1248 on an arm's length sale of the exchanged stock.[160] Generally, this amount is the lesser of (1) the gain recognized on the sale or (2) the post-1962 earnings and profits that are ratably allocable to the stock and were accumulated while the taxpayer held the stock and the foreign corporation was a CFC.[161] The latter amount excludes earnings previously taxed to a U.S. shareholder under subpart F, earnings taxed to the foreign corporation as income effectively connected with a trade or business carried on in the United States, and a few other amounts. Earnings and profits of lower-tier corporations are attributed through the chain of ownership. If the corporation has an earnings and profits deficit, the §1248 amount is zero.

Although §1248 only applies to sales by U.S. persons, the §1248 amount for stock held by a foreign corporation is determined as though the corporation was a U.S. person. Assume domestic corporation *D* purchases the stock of foreign corporation *F1* from foreign persons at the beginning of year 2; *F1* then owns 60 percent of the stock of *F2* (the remainder then being held by foreign persons), but

---

[156] See Prop. Reg. §1.367(b)-4(e) Ex. 8 (no deemed dividend if *D* owns all *FA* stock before reorganization because *FS* and *FA* both belong to *D* affiliated group before reorganization).

[157] Prop. Reg. §1.367(b)-4(e) Ex. 9.

[158] Prop. Reg. §1.367(b)-4(b)(3).

[159] Prop. Reg. §1.367(b)-4(b).

[160] Prop. Reg. §1.367(b)-2(c).

[161] See supra ¶68.2.16.

F1 purchases the remainder of the *F2* stock at the beginning of year 3; at the beginning of year 4, *F1* exchanges the *F2* stock in a B reorganization for 15 percent of the stock of *FA*, whose other shareholders are unrelated foreign persons. *F1* has deemed dividend income equal to the §1248 amount for the *F2* stock because, (1) immediately before the reorganization, a U.S. person (*D*) is a §1248 shareholder of *F1* and *F2* and (2) as a result of the reorganization, *D* ceases to be a §1248 shareholder of *F2* (which ceases to be a CFC). *F1* is treated as a U.S. person for this purpose, except in determining when *F2* was a CFC and when the stock was held indirectly by a U.S. person. The §1248 amount includes (1) none of the earnings and profits accumulated by *F2* before *F2* became a CFC on *D*'s acquisition of the *F1* stock at the beginning of year 2, (2) only 60 percent of *F2*'s earnings and profits for year 2 because 40 percent of *F2*'s stock was held by foreign persons during this year, and (3) 100 percent of the earnings and profits accumulated in year 3, when *D* indirectly owned all of *F2*'s stock.

When a foreign corporation recognizes a deemed dividend under these rules, the dividend is excluded from subpart F income by treating it as a dividend from a corporation incorporated in and actively doing business in the country of organization of the corporation recognizing the deemed dividend, thereby qualifying it for exclusion under §954(c)(3)(A)(i).[162] The effect of the deemed dividend is therefore to add to the earnings and profits of the exchanging shareholder (*F1* in the example), thus potentially adding to the dividend income of the §1248 shareholder (*D*) when distributions are made or stock is sold.

5. *Subsequent applications of §§1248 and 367(b)*. Special rules are provided for applying §§1248 and 367(b) to transactions occurring after a reorganization acquisition of one foreign corporation by another where the exchanging shareholder was within one of the groups of shareholders subject to the deemed dividend rule (a §1248 shareholder or a foreign corporation with a §1248 shareholder), but the reorganization fit within one of the exceptions to the rule (e.g., the §1248 shareholder continued to be such after the exchange).[163] Any earnings and profits inherited by the acquiring corporation under §381 are deemed to have been accumulated by the acquiring corporation at the same times as they were actually accumulated by the acquired corporation, even if the acquiring corporation did not come into existence until later. Also, the exchanging shareholder is deemed to have held the stock received in the exchange for the periods the exchanged stock was held. These rules are intended to preserve the potential for taxing the §1248 shareholder on the earnings and profits of the acquired corporation on some subsequent occasion (e.g., a sale of the stock received in the reorganization).

---

[162] Prop. Reg. §1.367(b)-4(c). For §954(c)(3)(A)(i), see supra ¶68.2.4 text accompanying notes 61-68.

[163] Prop. Reg. §1.367(b)-4(d).

¶68.7.11 Proposed Regulations—Corporate Divisions

Under §355, when a corporation makes a distribution to one or more of its shareholders consisting of stock of a corporation controlled by the distributing corporation, neither the distributing corporation nor the shareholders recognize gain or loss on the distribution if various qualification criteria are satisfied.[164] The proposed regulations under §367(b) modify this nonrecognition regime in various particulars where the distributing or controlled corporation is foreign.

1. *Domestic corporation's distribution of foreign controlled corporation.* The rules for §355 distributions by a domestic corporation of stock of a controlled corporation that is foreign depend on whether the distributee is a corporation or an individual. If the distributee shareholder is a corporation, the controlled corporation is deemed not to be a corporation.[165] Since §355 applies only to a distribution of stock or securities of a "corporation" controlled by the distributing corporation, this rule makes §355 wholly inapplicable, and both the distributing corporation and the distributee shareholder recognize gain or loss on the distribution. If the distributee shareholder is an individual, the controlled corporation is considered a corporation for all purposes except §355(c), the provision that normally allows nonrecognition to the distributing corporation.[166] As a consequence, the distributee qualifies for nonrecognition under §355(a), but the distributing corporation recognizes gain (but not loss) on the distribution as though it sold the distributed stock and securities for a cash price equal to fair market value.

The distributee is always either a corporation or an individual because stock owned by a partnership, trust, or estate is considered owned proportionately by its partners or beneficiaries.[167] However, the distributing corporation must treat the distributee as an individual (and thus not recognize loss) unless it "has reason to know that the distributee shareholder is a corporation."[168]

2. *Distributions by CFCs.* If a §355 distribution is made by a controlled foreign corporation (CFC), the results depend on the effect of the distribution on the "predistribution amounts" with respect to the distributing corporation and the controlled corporation. The predistribution amounts are determined as though the distributee sold all of its stock in the distributing corporation immediately before the §355 distribution.[169] The dividend recognized by the distributee under §1248 on this hypothetical sale is divided into two parts—the portion consisting of earnings and profits of the controlled corporation and the corporations it controls and the portion consisting of earnings and profits of the

---

[164] See infra ¶94.1.

[165] Prop. Reg. §1.367(b)-5(b)(1).

[166] Prop. Reg. §1.367(b)-5(b)(2).

[167] Prop. Reg. §1.367(b)-2(*l*).

[168] Prop. Reg. §1.367(b)-5(b).

[169] Prop. Reg. §1.367(b)-5(e).

distributing corporation and all corporations it controls (other than the controlled corporation and the corporations it controls). The former is the predistribution amount with respect to the controlled corporation, and the latter is the predistribution amount for the distributing corporation.

Assume domestic corporation D owns 60 percent of the stock of foreign corporation $F1$, which is sole shareholder of foreign corporation $F2$; $F1$ has earnings and profits of $30, and $F2$'s earnings and profits are $20; all of these earnings and profits were earned when D held its 60 percent interest in $F1$ and $F1$ owned $F2$, and none of them are excluded under §1248.[170] Assume $F1$ distributes the $F2$ stock in a §355 distribution. If D had sold its $F1$ stock immediately before the distribution and the basis of this stock was then at least $30 less than its value, D would have had a dividend under §1248 of $30 (sum of 60 percent of $F1$'s earnings and profits of $30 and 60 percent of $F2$'s earnings and profits of $20). The predistribution amounts are thus $18 (60 percent of $30) for $F1$ and $12 (60 percent of $20) for $F2$.

If the §355 distribution is pro rata, the distributee must reduce the basis of its stock in the distributing or controlled corporation by any amount by which the §1248 amount on a hypothetical sale of the stock immediately after the distribution is less than the predistribution amount for the stock immediately before the distribution.[171] Assume the distribution by $F1$ in the example is pro rata, and D, as 60 percent shareholder of $F1$, receives 60 percent of the $F2$ stock. If D sold its $F1$ stock and its post-distribution basis for this stock is at least $18 less than the stock's value, the §1248 dividend on this sale would be $18, which equals the predistribution amount for this stock. If D sold the $F2$ stock received in the distribution and its basis for this stock is at least $12 less than the stock's value, the §1248 dividend on this sale would be $12, which also equals the predistribution amount for the stock. Since the §1248 dividends on hypothetical postdistribution sales of the two blocks of stock equal the predistribution amounts, no adjustment is needed. In contrast, assume D's predistribution basis for the $F1$ stock is allocated between the $F1$ stock and $F2$ stock in a way that leaves only $10 of gain on the hypothetical sale of the $F2$ stock. Because the §1248 dividend may not exceed the gain on the sale, the distribution reduces the §1248 amount for the $F2$ stock by $2; this reduction is eliminated under the regulations by taking away $2 of D's basis for the $F2$ stock.

If the §355 distribution is not pro rata, any decrease in the §1248 amount for the stock of the distributing or controlled corporation must usually be recognized as a dividend out of the earnings and profits of the corporation for which the decrease occurs.[172] Assume $F1$ distributes the stock of $F2$ to D in exchange for all of D's stock in $F1$. On a sale of the $F2$ stock immediately after the distribution, the §1248 dividend would be $12 (60 percent of $F2$'s earnings and profits of

---

[170] See Prop. Reg. §1.367(b)-5(h) Ex. 1.

[171] Prop. Reg. §1.367(b)-5(c).

[172] Prop. Reg. §1.367(b)-5(d)(2).

$20),[173] which equals the predistribution amount for this stock. However, *D's* §1248 amount for the *F1* stock is zero after the distribution because *D* no longer owns *F1* stock. The predistribution amount for this stock ($18) is therefore a deemed dividend to *D* at the time of the distribution.[174]

For purposes of the rule on non-pro rata distributions, all shareholders of the distributing corporation are deemed to be distributees.[175] Assume *F1* distributes the *F2* stock to the owner of the other 40 percent of its stock, foreign corporation *F*, in exchange for all of *F's F1* stock, and *D* receives nothing in the distribution.[176] *D's* §1248 amount with respect to the *F2* stock, which was $12 (60 percent of *F2's* earnings and profits of $20) before the distribution, is zero immediately thereafter because the distribution eliminates *D's* indirect ownership of 60 percent of *F2*. *D* thus has deemed dividend income of $12 for the year of the distribution, even though *D* receives nothing in the distribution. Because the deemed dividend is from the earnings and profits of *F2*, it is treated as distributed from *F2* to *F1* and from *F1* to *D*.

A special election is provided for a shareholder, such as *D* in the last example, who does not participate in the distribution, either by exchanging stock of the distributing corporation or receiving stock of the controlled corporation, but is nevertheless visited with a deemed dividend under the rule described in the preceding paragraph.[177] If the shareholder makes the election, the deemed dividend need not be recognized, but both the distributing corporation and the controlled corporation are deemed not to be corporations "for the purpose of recognition of income (but not loss) by all persons affected by the taxable status of the transaction." If the election is made in the example, *D* has no deemed dividend income, but §355(c), which would normally protect *F1* from recognizing gain on the distribution, is rendered inapplicable, and *F1* thus recognizes gain under §311(b) as though it had sold the *F2* stock for an amount equal to its fair market value. The resulting gain becomes earnings and profits of *F1* and part of the §1248 amount of its sole shareholder *D*. *D* thus avoids immediate taxation on a deemed dividend, but subjects itself to the possibility of increased taxation on a later transaction (e.g., a sale of the *F1* stock) where the §1248 amount is relevant. Since the gain recognized by *F1* on the distribution is not limited to *D's* §1248 amount with respect to *F2*, the future tax could be greater than the tax avoided by the election.

---

[173] Even though *D* now owns all of the *F2* stock, the §1248 amount is only 60 percent of the earnings and profits because *D* owned (indirectly) only 60 percent of the *F2* stock when the earnings and profits were accumulated.

[174] The regulations say the deemed dividend is treated as having been distributed from *F2* to *F1* and then to *D* (Prop. Reg. §1.367(b)-5(h) Ex. 1), but this is a slip; the deemed dividend is from the earnings and profits of the corporation with respect to which the §1248 amount decreases—*F1* in this case.

[175] Prop. Reg. §1.367(b)-5(d)(3)(i).

[176] Prop. Reg. §1.367(b)-5(h) Ex. 2.

[177] Prop. Reg. §1.367(b)-5(d)(3)(ii).

The election can be made by any shareholder who would otherwise have a deemed dividend without directly participating in the distribution. If there are two such shareholders and only one elects, the results can be bizarre. Assume *D*'s 60 percent interest in *F1* was instead held equally by two unrelated domestic corporations, *D1* and *D2*. If *D1* elects, *D1* avoids the deemed dividend, but the distribution is fully taxable to *F1*; if *D2* does not elect, it is taxable on the deemed dividend, but its §1248 amount is apparently increased by its share of the gain recognized by *F1* because of *D1*'s election. Moreover, the election causes the distribution to be taxable to the actual distributee, even though the distributee does not participate in the election.

If the distributing corporation transfers property to the controlled corporation as part of the same transaction as the distribution of the controlled corporation's stock (a divisive D reorganization), the distributing corporation's earnings and profits are allocated between the distributing corporation and the controlled corporation in proportion to the relative adjusted bases (net of liabilities) of the property transferred and retained by the distributing corporation.[178] Assume domestic corporation *D* owns 60 percent of the stock of foreign corporation *F*, which has earnings and profits of $50; *F* transfers to newly organized *FS* (in exchange for *FS* stock) a portion of *F*'s assets having a net adjusted basis equal to 40 percent of the net basis of all of *F*'s pretransfer assets; *F* then distributes the *FS* stock to *D* in exchange for all of *D*'s *F* stock. The transaction is a D reorganization.[179] Because *FS* gets assets with a net basis equal to 40 percent of *F*'s total net basis, *F*'s earnings and profits ($50) are allocated 40 percent ($20) to *FS* and 60 percent ($30) to *F*. *D*'s predistribution amounts are thus $18 (60 percent of $30) for its *F* stock and $12 (60 percent of $20) for the *FS* stock. Although the §1248 amount for the *FS* stock remains unchanged, *D* owns no *F* stock after the distribution, and the predistribution amount for this stock ($18) must be reported as a deemed dividend.

¶68.7.12   Proposed Regulations—Reincorporations of Foreign Corporations

An F reorganization (mere change in identity, form, or place of organization) of a foreign corporation is deemed to consist of the following steps:

1. A transfer of the foreign corporation's assets to the acquiring corporation in exchange for stock of the acquiring corporation and the assumption of the foreign corporation's liabilities.
2. A distribution of the acquiring corporation's stock to the foreign corporation's shareholders.

---

[178] Prop. Reg. §1.367(b)-5(f). This rule applies in lieu of the allocation rules normally used in divisive D reorganizations, which are found in §312(h) and Reg. §1.312-10(b).
[179] See infra ¶94.3.4.

3. An exchange by the foreign corporation's shareholders of their stock in the corporation for the stock in the acquiring corporation received in the reorganization.[180]

If securities other than stock are surrendered or received in the reorganization, they are deemed issued, distributed, and received together with the stock.

Once an F reorganization has been so restructured, the rules described earlier are applied. If a foreign corporation is reincorporated as a domestic corporation, the rules for repatriation of foreign assets are applied to steps 1 and 3.[181] For example, if a foreign subsidiary of a domestic corporation is reincorporated as a domestic subsidiary, the domestic parent has a deemed dividend equal to the all earnings and profits amount of the foreign subsidiary. If the corporation emerging from the reincorporation is also a foreign corporation, the rules for transfers from foreign corporation to foreign corporation apply.[182] For example, if a foreign subsidiary of a domestic corporation is reincorporated in a different foreign jurisdiction, no deemed dividend results because the §1248 amount for the old subsidiary becomes the §1248 amount for the new subsidiary.

Also, if a foreign corporation is reincorporated as a domestic corporation or if the old corporation has earnings and profits effectively connected with the conduct of a trade or business in the United States, the corporation's taxable year ends with the reorganization, and the acquiring corporation's taxable year ends with the day the transferor's taxable year would have ended if the reorganization had not occurred. Assume a foreign corporation with a taxable year ending June 30 is reincorporated as a domestic corporation on April 20, 1997. The foreign corporation has a taxable year beginning on July 1, 1996 and ending April 20, 1997, and the domestic corporation has a taxable year beginning April 21, 1997 and ending June 30, 1997.

If a domestic corporation and a foreign corporation are "stapled entities"—that is, if at least 50 percent of the stock in both corporations is coupled so that the stock of one can be sold only as a unit together with stock of the other—the foreign corporation is deemed to be a domestic corporation.[183] When an entity previously treated as a foreign corporation is stapled to a domestic corporation, the resulting conversion of the foreign corporation into a deemed domestic corporation is considered an F reorganization subject to the rules described above.[184] Also, when a foreign insurance company elects under §953(d) to be treated as a domestic corporation, the election is treated as an F reorganization for this purpose.[185] An election under §1504(d), allowing the parents of certain Canadian and Mexican subsidiaries to treat the subsidiaries as

---

[180] Prop. Reg. §1.367(b)-2(f).

[181] See supra ¶68.7.9.

[182] See supra ¶68.7.10.

[183] IRC §269B, discussed supra ¶65.3.

[184] Prop. Reg. §1.367(b)-2(g).

[185] Prop. Reg. §1.367(b)-2(h).

domestic corporations, has the same effect unless the election is effective from the inception of the subsidiaries' existence.[186]

¶68.7.13 Proposed Regulations—Deemed Dividends

In many circumstances described above, the §367(b) regulations require exchanging shareholders to report deemed dividends. Such a deemed dividend is treated as a dividend for all federal income tax purposes.[187] Assume foreign corporation F completely liquidates by distributing its assets to its sole shareholder, domestic corporation D.[188] D must report a deemed dividend equal to the all earnings and profits amount.[189] Under §902(a), a domestic corporation receiving a dividend from a foreign corporation, of which it is a 10 percent or greater voting shareholder, is deemed to have paid portions of the foreign income taxes actually paid by the foreign corporation.[190] The deemed dividend required by §367(b) is a dividend for purposes of §902, and for the year of the liquidation, D may therefore be eligible for credit for some or all of F's foreign income tax payments.

The deemed dividend is considered paid out of the earnings and profits with respect to which it was determined, usually the all earnings and profits amount or the §1248 amount.[191] For example, a deemed dividend is never excluded from gross income as a distribution of amounts previously taxed to the shareholder under subpart F because these previously taxed amounts are not included in either the all earnings and profits amount or the §1248 amount.[192]

If the deemed dividend is treated as coming from earnings and profits of a lower-tier subsidiary, it is deemed distributed through the chain of ownership.[193] Assume domestic corporation D owns the stock of foreign corporation F1, which owns the stock of foreign corporation F2; in a B reorganization, D exchanges its F1 stock for a minority interest in a foreign corporation that is not a CFC.[194] D is deemed to receive a dividend equal to the §1248 amount with respect to its F1 stock, and this amount includes earnings and profits of both F1 and F2. The portion of the deemed dividend consisting of F2 earnings and profits is treated as distributed by F2 to F1 and by F1 to F2. As a consequence, foreign income taxes imposed on F2 are deemed paid by F1 under §902(b), and D, by reason of the

---

[186] Prop. Reg. §1.367(b)-2(j).

[187] Prop. Reg. §1.367(b)-2(e)(2).

[188] Prop. Reg. §1.367(b)-2(e)(4) Ex. 1.

[189] Prop. Reg. §1.367(b)-3, discussed supra ¶68.7.9.

[190] See infra ¶69.8.

[191] Prop. Reg. §1.367(b)-2(e)(2).

[192] For the exclusion of previously taxed amounts, see §959, discussed supra ¶68.2.14.

[193] Prop. Reg. §1.367(b)-2(e)(2).

[194] Prop. Reg. §1.367(b)-2(e)(4) Ex. 2.

deemed dividend from *F1*, is deemed to have paid taxes actually paid by *F1* and taxes of *F2* deemed paid by *F1*.

The dividend is deemed distributed immediately before the exchange triggering the dividend and is added to the shareholder's basis for the stock exchanged.[195] For example, if boot is received in a reorganization exchange, the deemed dividend is added to the shareholder's stock basis before the gain recognized on account of the boot under §356 is computed. Assume domestic corporation *D* realizes gain of $100 on a reorganization exchange of stock of foreign corporation *F* for stock of another corporation and $70 in cash; the §367(b) regulations require *D* to report a deemed dividend of $40.[196] The added basis resulting from the deemed dividend reduces the realized gain to $60 ($100 less $40), and the gain recognized under §356(a) is thus $60 (lesser of boot received ($70) or gain realized). Also, under §358(a)(1), the deemed dividend is included in the basis of the stock or securities the shareholder receives in the exchange. For example, if *D* had a basis of $200 for its *F* stock, the basis of the stock received in the exchange is $230—the basis of the stock exchanged ($200 before adjustment plus $40 deemed dividend), plus the gain recognized ($60), less the boot received ($70). Under §362, the deemed dividend is also included in the transferee's basis for the stock surrendered by the shareholder in the exchange.

¶68.8 PARTICIPATION IN INTERNATIONAL BOYCOTTS

In 1976, to discourage U.S. businesses from honoring the Arab boycott of Israel, Congress enacted §999, which penalizes a wide range of acts entailing participation in or cooperation with international boycotts and requires operations in a boycotting country or with its government, companies, or nationals to be reported to the Treasury.[1]

---

[195] Prop. Reg. §1.367(b)-2(e)(3).

[196] Prop. Reg. §1.367(b)-2(e)(4) Ex. 3.

[1] See Reg. §7.999-1; International Boycott Guidelines, 1978-1 CB 521 (detailed analysis in question-and-answer form), supplemented by Notice, 44 Fed. Reg. 66,272 (1979); U.S. Dep't of Treasury, The Operation and Effect of the International Boycott Provisions of the Internal Revenue Code—Fourth Annual Report (April 1985) (relating to 1982; annual reports not issued for subsequent years). See generally Flynn & McKenzie, International Boycotts, 1977 S. Cal. Tax Inst. 139; Rubenfeld, Legal and Tax Implications of Participation in International Boycotts, 32 Tax L. Rev. 613 (1977); Kaplan, Income Taxes and the Arab Boycott, 32 Tax Lawyer 313 (1979). See Hines, Taxed Avoidance: American Participation in Unsanctioned International Boycotts (NBER 1997) ("U.S. anti-boycott legislation significantly reduces the willingness of American firms to participate in the boycott of Israel, reducing boycott participation rates by as much as 15–30 percent"); Data Release, International Boycott Reports, 1995, 17 Stat. Income Bull. 118 (Winter 1997–1998) (for 1995, 1,336 international boycott reports were filed, 207 filers reported receiving requests to participate in international boycott, 49 reported agreeing to participate, and 20 reported tax effect from boycott participation).

The reports must be filed by U.S. taxpayers doing business in or with boycotting countries and by domestic members of controlled groups whose foreign members are engaged in such business.[2] The Treasury maintains an official list of boycotting countries,[3] but operations involving other countries must also be reported if the company or its affiliates know or have reason to know that participation in or cooperation with an international boycott is required as a condition of doing business within the country or with its government, companies, or nationals. In addition, requests for actual participation in or cooperation with a boycott must be reported.[4] Section 999, however, does not apply to boycotts approved by our government.[5]

A person participates in or cooperates with an international boycott if, as a condition of doing business within a country or with its government, companies, or nationals, the person agrees to refrain from doing business with (1) the boycotted country, (2) U.S. persons engaged in business in the boycotted country, or (3) companies owned or managed by persons of a particular nationality, race, or religion.[6] Boycott participation also includes an agreement to refrain from employing persons of a particular nationality, race, or religion and an agreement, made as a condition of a sale of goods, to refrain from shipping or insuring the goods on a carrier that does not participate in the boycott.

If a person participates in or cooperates with a boycott in any way, all operations of the person and its affiliates in the same taxable year in all boycotting countries are usually treated as violations of §999.[7] A "clearly separate and identifiable operation," however, can be purged of the taint by "clearly" demonstrating that no participation or cooperation with the boycott occurred in this operation during the year. Also, a ban on trade between boycotting and boycotted countries may be honored without violating §999 if this consists of no more than complying with prohibitions on importing into a boycotting country

[2] IRC §999(a)(1). The affected group is defined by §993(a)(3) (modifying §1563 for DISC purposes). See also §999(e) (where any person controls a corporation, corporation or controlling person is presumed to be boycott participant if other is).

[3] IRC §999(a)(3); Notice 95-41, 1995-2 CB 328 (list as of June 14, 1995 includes Bahrain, Iraq, Jordan, Kuwait, Lebanon, Libya, Oman, Qatar, Saudi Arabia, Syria, United Arab Emirates, and Republic of Yemen).

[4] IRC §999(a)(2).

[5] IRC §999(b)(4)(A). But see Holden & Brown, A Paradox: Why Does the Federal Tax Law Penalize United States Taxpayers Who Observe the Boycott of South Africa By United States Allies? 42 Tax Lawyer 211 (1989).

[6] IRC §999(b)(3). See IRC §999(d) (IRS must rule on whether particular operations entail participation in international boycott); Rev. Proc. 98-1, 1998-1 CB __, §3.04 (procedures for obtaining determination letter on issue).

[7] IRC §§999(b)(1), (2).

goods produced in a boycotted country or exporting goods from a boycotting country to a boycotted country.[8]

If a taxpayer or any member of its controlled group participates in or cooperates with an international boycott, the taxpayer's foreign tax credit is reduced.[9] Also, the subpart F income of a controlled foreign corporation (CFC) is increased if it is a member of a controlled group that includes a boycott participant.[10] Moreover, the benefits allowed to foreign sales corporations (FSCs) and their shareholders are reduced if the foreign sales corporation or a member of its controlled group participates in or cooperates with a boycott.[11] The size of these penalties is usually computed by reference to an "international boycott factor," which is a fraction whose numerator reflects the taxpayer's operations in boycotting countries and whose denominator reflects its total foreign operations.[12] The penalty, however, is restricted to the taxes and income attributable to specific tainted operations if these amounts can be clearly shown.

---

[8] IRC §§999(b)(4)(B), (C). The rule permitting compliance with a prohibition on importation is not explicitly limited to importation into a boycotting country, but that is its evident meaning.

[9] IRC §908. For the foreign tax credit, see infra ¶69.1.

[10] IRC §952(a)(3). For CFCs and subpart F income, see supra ¶68.2.

[11] IRC §927(e)(2).

[12] IRC §999(c).

Foreign Tax Credit

¶69.1 INTRODUCTORY

Section 901(a) allows a credit for foreign income taxes paid or deemed paid by qualifying taxpayers who elect to take the credit in lieu of deducting the taxes under §164(a).[1] The policy of the credit is to alleviate the double taxation that results when income earned in a foreign country is taxed by both the United States and the country of source. Since the United States taxes its citizens, residents, and domestic corporations on their worldwide income, this double taxation typically occurs whenever a U.S. person is taxed by another country.

Assume a domestic corporation does business in country X through a branch that has profits of $100 for a particular year; country X taxes foreign corporations on domestic profits at 25 percent, while the United States taxes U.S. corporations at 35 percent on worldwide income. In the absence of relief from double taxation, the corporation's tax burden on country X income would be 60 percent (25 plus 35). A country X corporation doing business in the United States would face the same burden. Because both countries tax local companies much more lightly on local source income (25 percent or 35 percent), it would rarely be profitable for a U.S. corporation to do business in country X or for a country X corporation to do business in the United States.

Relief from double taxation can be given by either the source country or the taxpayer's home country. Unilaterally and through treaties, source countries often relinquish tax jurisdiction over selected items of domestic source income of foreigners or adopt low tax rates for these items. For example, the United States exempts foreigners from tax on portfolio interest income from U.S. sources, and treaties commonly limit to 5 percent or 15 percent the tax on dividends paid by a corporation of the taxing country to residents of the other country.[2] Business income, however, is typically taxed at the point of source at the normal rates for such income prevailing in the source country.[3] For business income and other income taxed at source, the job of alleviating double taxation is left to the taxpayer's home country.

The foreign tax credit is the home-country relief provided by the United States. Other countries use a similar credit system, exempt their residents from tax on foreign source income, or use a mixture of the credit and exemption methods. The principal difference between these two methods is that when the

---

[1] For the election between the credit and deduction for foreign income taxes, see infra ¶69.14. See Nutter, Corporate Foreign Tax Credit, 1993: An Industry and Geographic Focus, 17 Stat. Income Bull. 97 (Fall 1997) (for 1993, foreign tax credit was claimed by 6,322 domestic corporations, which reported foreign tax liabilities of $23.7 billion on $97.7 billion of foreign source taxable income (comprising 41.4 percent of worldwide income) and claimed credits, after limitation, of $22.9 billion); Data Release, Corporate Foreign Tax Credit, 1992: An Industry and Geographic Focus, 15 Stat. Income Bull. 111 (Winter 1996).

[2] See supra ¶66.2.2 (interest), ¶66.2.3 (dividends).

[3] See supra ¶66.3.1.

source country's rate is lower than that of the home country, the credit system allows the home country to impose tax equal to the difference, whereas under the exemption system, the only tax is that of the source country, whether it is at a rate that is lower, higher, or the same as the home country's rate.

Consistently with the role of the credit as home-country relief, the foreign tax credit under U.S. law is generally allowed only to citizens and residents of the United States and domestic corporations.[4] In the example used earlier, the pre-credit taxes on a domestic corporation's $100 of country X profits are $35 to the United States and $25 to country X. The country X tax, however, is creditable against the U.S. tax, and the corporation's final liabilities thus are $25 to country X and $10 ($35 less $25) to the United States. The sum of these amounts ($35) equals the tax the corporation would have paid to the United States if it had earned the $100 in this country.

A deduction for the country X tax would reduce double taxation, but it would not eliminate it. With a deduction, the corporation's U.S. tax would be $26.25 (35 percent of the excess of $100 over $25), and the sum of the U.S. and country X taxes would be $51.25, an amount substantially larger than the tax that the corporation would have paid if it had earned the $100 in the United States.

Under §904(a), the credit for foreign income taxes is limited to an amount equal to the precredit U.S. tax on the taxpayer's foreign source income.[5] Assume the country Y tax rate is 46 percent, and a domestic corporation pays $46 of country Y tax on $100 of income earned in country Y. If the tax were fully creditable, the after-credit U.S. tax on the $100 of country Y profits would be negative $11 ($35 of precredit U.S. tax less $46 of credit). The credit would thus eliminate U.S. tax on the country Y income and also reduce U.S. tax on other income by $11. The latter effect is not necessary to alleviate double taxation. If the corporation has no other foreign income, §904(a) bars this effect by restricting the credit to $35, the U.S. tax on foreign source income.

In the simple examples used so far, the taxpayer's total tax on foreign source income is the greater of the precredit U.S. tax on the income or the foreign tax. In the last example, the total equals the foreign tax ($46 of country Y tax plus zero U.S. tax). In the earlier example, where the foreign rate is less than the U.S. rate, the total tax equals the precredit U.S. tax of $35 ($25 of country X tax plus $10 of U.S. tax after the credit).

The policy of §904(a) is less clear in more complex situations. Assume the corporation in the example earns $100 in country Y (taxed at 46 percent) and $100 in country Z, whose income tax rate is 24 percent. If the income from countries Y and Z and the taxes paid to those countries are aggregated in applying §904(a), the taxes are fully creditable because the sum of the foreign income taxes ($46 plus $24, or $70) equals the precredit U.S. tax on foreign

---

[4] For a limited credit for nonresident aliens and foreign corporations, see §906, discussed infra ¶69.9.

[5] See infra ¶69.5.

income (35 percent of $200, or $70). Arguably, double taxation would be fully eliminated by a lesser credit; double taxation of the country Y income would be eliminated by a $35 credit (reducing U.S. tax on this income to zero), and a $24 credit would eliminate double taxation of the country Z income. In other words, the credit should perhaps be $59 rather than $70, leaving a U.S. tax liability of $11 after the credit.

Congress has responded to this dilemma with a solution of notable complexity. The general rule of §904(a) is that all foreign income and taxes are lumped together in computing the credit limitation, thus allowing the sort of rate averaging illustrated by the example in the preceding paragraph. This rule, however, is supplemented, and in many applications entirely superseded, by rules requiring that the limitation be computed separately for various categories of foreign source income and the taxes on this income.[6] Very generally, the rules isolate into separate baskets various types of income that are frequently subject to foreign taxes at very high or very low rates and thereby limit the ability of taxpayers to manipulate the credit limitation by averaging rates in the way illustrated by the example in the preceding paragraph. However, because most income from active business operations falls into one basket, taxpayers continue to enjoy the benefits of rate averaging if they do business in both high and low tax countries. Under the overall limitation of §904(a), a taxpayer with foreign source income taxed abroad at rates exceeding U.S. rates has a strong incentive to obtain other foreign source income that bears less foreign tax. Congress generally has no objection to a taxpayer responding to this incentive by doing business in both high and low tax countries. The separate basket system, however, is meant to frustrate schemes for increasing the limitation by mixing together different kinds of income that typically face very different foreign tax regimes, even within a single country.

The credit system is further complicated by §902, which generally allows domestic corporations credit for foreign income taxes paid by their foreign subsidiaries.[7] To illustrate the reason for §902, assume a domestic corporation owns all of the stock of a foreign corporation that earns $100 in country X and pays $25 of country X tax; the foreign corporation distributes its after-tax income of $75 to its parent as a dividend. In the absence of §902, the parent would pay U.S. tax on the dividend of $26.25 (35 percent of $75), and would be left with $48.75 after taxes. If the country X business had been carried on through a branch, in contrast, the total tax on the $100 of country X income would have been $35 (country X tax of $25 plus U.S. tax of $35 less $25), and the domestic corporation would have had $65 after taxes. Without §902, in other words, double taxation would go largely unremedied where the foreign tax is paid by a foreign subsidiary and the U.S. tax is paid by a domestic parent.

---

[6] See infra ¶69.6.
[7] For §902, see infra ¶69.8.

Section 902 solves this problem as follows: The parent in the example is taxed as though the subsidiary had distributed its pretax income of $100 ($75 actual dividend plus $25 of foreign tax). The pretax U.S. tax is thus $35 (35 percent of $100). The subsidiary's taxes, however, are treated as having been paid by the parent, and the credit for the taxes reduces the parent's U.S. tax on the income to $10, leaving the parent with $65 after taxes (dividend of $75 less $10 of U.S. tax). In this simple example, §902 equates the branch and subsidiary situations. In more complex cases, the equivalence of the branch and subsidiary cases is only approximate, reflecting the fundamental differences between the tax treatments of branch earnings, which are subject to U.S. taxes as earned, and the earnings of foreign subsidiaries, which are generally taxed by the United States only when distributed as dividends.

¶69.2   TAXES AGAINST WHICH CREDIT ALLOWED

The foreign tax credit is generally allowed against the taxes imposed by §1 (for individuals, estates, and trusts) and §11 (for corporations).[1] A nonresident alien or foreign corporation may not take the credit against the withholding taxes imposed by §§871(a) and 881, and a foreign corporation is denied the credit against the branch profits tax.[2] No taxpayer is allowed the credit against (1) several penalty taxes on distributions from annuities, endowment contracts, and employee plans,[3] (2) the accumulated earnings and personal holding company taxes,[4] (3) the taxes on built-in gains and passive investment income of S corporations that were formerly C corporations,[5] and (4) a few other taxes.[6] The credit

---

[1] IRC §§26(b), 901(a).

[2] IRC §§26(b)(2)(K), (M). See supra ¶66.2 for the withholding taxes and ¶66.5 for the branch profits tax. In very limited circumstances, a nonresident alien or foreign corporation may take the foreign tax credit against the effectively connected income tax. IRC §906, discussed infra ¶69.9.

[3] IRC §26(b)(2)(C). These taxes are four penalties, each at the rate of 10 percent, on:

1. Distributions from an employee plan in excess of the distributee's plan entitlements if the distributee is an owner-employee with a 5 percent or greater interest in the employer. IRC §72(m)(5)(B).
2. Premature annuity payments. IRC §72(q), discussed supra ¶12.4.2.
3. Amounts received prematurely under a modified endowment contract. IRC §72(v), discussed supra ¶12.4.5.
4. Premature distributions from qualified retirement plans. IRC §72(t), discussed supra ¶61.12.2.

For purposes of the latter three taxes, a distribution or payment is premature if it is made before the annuitant, policy owner, or employee reaches age 59½, dies, or becomes disabled.

[4] IRC §§26(b)(2)(E), (F). For the accumulated earnings and personal holding company taxes, see infra ¶¶95.1, 95.2.

[5] IRC §§26(b)(2)(H), (I). For these taxes, see infra ¶¶95.6.6, 95.6.9.

is allowed in determining the alternative minimum tax under §55, but with several modifications described later in this chapter.[7]

¶69.3 TAXPAYERS QUALIFYING FOR CREDIT

The credit for foreign income taxes is generally allowed to U.S. persons, but only when they elect the credit in lieu of the deduction otherwise allowable for the taxes.[1] Only rarely is credit allowed to a foreign person.

More specifically, for citizens and domestic corporations, the credit is allowed for income taxes imposed by foreign countries and possessions of the United States, including Puerto Rico.[2] A "bona fide" resident of Puerto Rico is also allowed credit for both foreign and possessions income taxes, even if he is not a U.S. citizen.[3]

For aliens residing in the United States, the credit is limited to income taxes of foreign countries.[4] The credit is even more sharply restricted if a resident alien is a citizen of a country that does not allow a comparable dispensation to U.S. citizens residing in that country.[5] Specifically, a resident alien is allowed credit for taxes imposed by the taxpayer's country of citizenship only if that country allows U.S. citizens residing there either a credit for U.S. taxes or an exemption from tax on U.S. source income. Moreover, a resident alien is allowed credit for taxes imposed by a third country only if the taxpayer's country of citizenship allows U.S. citizens residing there a credit for taxes imposed by the third country or an exemption from tax on income from sources within the third country.

Foreign corporations and nonresident aliens are allowed the credit in the limited circumstances permitted by §906.[6] This credit applies only where income effectively connected with a U.S. business is also taxed by a foreign country other than the taxpayer's home country. The credit for foreign persons is generally intended only to alleviate the double taxation that arises when the United States and another country both claim to be the source of particular income.

---

[6] The other taxes are the environmental tax imposed by §59A, the tax imposed by §1351(d)(1) on recoveries of previously deducted foreign expropriation losses, the tax imposed by §7518(g)(6) on withdrawals from merchant marine capital construction funds, the tax on certain transfers of residual interests in REMICs under §860E(e), and the recapture tax under §143(m) on sales of residences financed with tax-exempt bonds issued by a state or local government. IRC §26(b)(2).

[7] Infra ¶69.12.

[1] For the election, see infra ¶69.14.

[2] IRC §§901(b)(1), 7701(d).

[3] IRC §§901(b)(2), (3).

[4] IRC §901(b)(3).

[5] IRC §901(c); Reg. §1.901-1(b).

[6] See infra ¶69.9.

[7] IRC §901(b).

A person qualifying for credit is allowed credit only for foreign income taxes "paid or accrued during the taxable year."[7] A tax is considered paid or accrued only by "the person on whom foreign law imposes legal liability for such tax, even if another person (*e.g.*, a withholding agent) remits such tax"[8] and even if the tax is assumed by another party to the transaction by which the taxpayer earns or receives the income subject to the tax.[9] Assume *D*, a domestic corporation, loans $1,000 to *F*, a resident of country *X*, under an agreement requiring *F* to pay interest at 6 percent, net of any withholding tax that may be imposed by country *X*.[10] If country *X* imposes a 10 percent withholding tax on interest paid by country *X* residents to nonresidents and treats the tax as part of the interest income, the withholding tax on each $60 annual payment of net interest is $6.7 (10 percent of the sum of $60 and $6.7), and *D* has gross income of $66.7 and is treated as paying a foreign income tax of $6.7.

If a tax is imposed on the combined income of two or more persons who are jointly and severally liable for the tax, each of these persons is considered the taxpayer with respect to the tax "attributable [to] its portion of the base of the tax."[11] For example, if a domestic corporation's subsidiaries in country *X* file a consolidated country *X* return, each subsidiary is the taxpayer with respect to the country *X* tax on its portion of the consolidated income. The same rule applies to a husband and wife filing a joint foreign income tax return.

A partner or a beneficiary of an estate or trust is allowed credit for a proportionate share of the foreign income taxes imposed on the partnership, estate, or trust if credit would have been allowed had the tax been imposed on the partner or beneficiary rather than the entity.[12] In expressing this rule, §901 and the regulations thereunder refer only to partners and beneficiaries who are individuals. Section 702(a), however, allows every partner to "take into account separately his distributive share of the partnership's . . . taxes, described in section 901." The regulations under §702(a) allow "a partner" to "elect to treat his total amount of such taxes, including his distributive share of such taxes of the partnership, as a deduction under section 164 or as a credit under section 901."[13]

---

[8] Reg. §§1.901-2(f)(1), (g)(1). See Peaslee, Economic Substance Test Abused: Notice 98-5 and the Foreign Law Taxpayer Rule, 79 Tax Notes 79 (Apr. 6, 1998), reprinted in 16 Tax Notes Int'l 1153 (Apr. 13, 1998).

A significant exception to this principle is §902, which sometimes treats a domestic corporation as having paid foreign income taxes actually paid by a foreign corporation from which it receives dividends. See infra ¶69.8.

A foreign tax withheld from wages is considered imposed on the wage earner if the tax finances retirement, old-age, death, survivor, unemployment, illness, or disability benefits. Reg. §1.901-2(f)(1).

[9] Reg. §1.901-2(f)(2)(i).

[10] Reg. §1.901-2(f)(2)(ii) Ex. 1.

[11] Reg. §1.901-2(f)(3).

[12] IRC §901(b)(5); Reg. §1.901-1(a)(1).

[13] Reg. §1.702-1(a)(8).

The lack of any evident reason for distinguishing between individual and other partners in this context argues for reading §702 to allow the credit to pass through to all partners rather than implying negatively from §901's reference to partners and beneficiaries that only individuals qualify.

¶69.4 "FOREIGN INCOME TAX" DEFINED

¶69.4.1 Introductory

The foreign tax credit is only allowed for "income, war profits, and excess profits taxes" of foreign countries and U.S. possessions.[1] The quoted words can effectively be reduced to "income taxes" because excess profits taxes are a type of tax on income and a war profits tax is an excess profits or other income tax imposed in time of war. To be a creditable income tax, a foreign impost must be a tax, and its "predominant character" must be "that of an income tax in the U.S. sense."[2] The principal characteristics of a tax are that it is a compulsory levy that goes into government coffers and is not payment for a specific benefit received by the taxpayer, such as a right to extract oil and gas from government-owned deposits.[3]

Consistently with the purpose of the credit to alleviate double taxation, the predominant character test restricts the credit to foreign taxes that duplicate the U.S. tax against which the credit is taken. Since the latter is an income tax, the credit is restricted to foreign income taxes. Foreign property and consumption taxes are not creditable, for example, because they do not duplicate the U.S. income tax any more than property and sales taxes imposed by state and local governments within the United States, which are deductible but not creditable.[4] Similarly, credit is not allowed for a foreign tax that is denominated an income tax but bears little resemblance to and hence does not duplicate the U.S. income tax. On the other hand, an income tax imposed by "any political subdivision of any foreign state" is creditable,[4.1] even though income taxes imposed by the U.S. states and their political subdivisions are deductible, but not creditable, for federal income tax purposes.

---

[1] IRC §901(b).

[2] Reg. §1.901-2(a)(1). This test derives from comments made by the Supreme Court in Biddle v. CIR, 302 US 573 (1938). Although the meaning of the term "income tax" was not at issue in *Biddle*, the Court's comments have been the touchstone of the definitional inquiry ever since. See Gleason Works v. CIR, 58 TC 464 (1972).

See Smith & Valente, Italian Tax Reform: Eligibility of New Taxes for U.S. Foreign Tax Credit, 15 Tax Notes Int'l 1793 (Dec. 1, 1997).

[3] See infra ¶69.4.2.

[4] IRC §164(a), discussed supra ¶32.1.

[4.1] Reg. §1.901-2(g)(2).

The credit is not limited, however, to foreign taxes imposed under laws that are substantially identical to the U.S. Internal Revenue Code (the Code). The U.S. income tax law is not an embodiment of a theoretically coherent conception of income taxation, common to the thinking of all enlightened lawmakers throughout the world; it is rather a product of complex political, administrative, and economic factors, many of which are unique to the United States. A close correspondence between U.S. and foreign law thus cannot be expected and is not necessary to achieve the policy of alleviating double taxation.

What is required is that the predominant character of the U.S. and foreign taxes be enough alike that, in most cases, it can realistically be said that the same thing is being taxed by the two countries. That depreciation allowances are more or less accelerated in country X than in the United States, for example, does not prevent country X tax from being creditable. If, over the long run, both countries tax the same profits, a denial of credit for the country X tax on account of the differing depreciation policies would frustrate rather than serve the policy to alleviate double taxation.

Moreover, the need for a close correspondence between U.S. and foreign law is lessened by the fact that the definition of "foreign income tax" is not the Code's only mechanism for restricting the credit to its role of alleviating double taxation. Section 904, discussed below,[5] limits a taxpayer's credits for foreign income taxes to the precredit U.S. tax on income from foreign sources. If a foreign tax is an income tax in the U.S. sense in its predominant character but in its application to a particular taxpayer hits items that are not taxed under U.S. law, the §904 limitation may deny credit.

The predominant character requirement is met if two subsidiary tests are satisfied. First, the foreign tax must be "likely to reach net gain [in] the normal circumstances in which it applies."[6] Second, the tax cannot be a so-called soak-up tax; that is, "liability for the tax [cannot be] dependent . . . on the availability of a credit for the tax against income tax liability to another country."[7] The net gain test is further subdivided into three requirements: (1) The foreign tax law must generally adhere to a realization concept similar to the realization doctrine of the U.S. income tax; (2) tax computations must usually begin from actual gross receipts, rather than from fictional amounts; and (3) costs incurred in earning these gross receipts must be allowed as deductions.[8] Generally, "a tax either is or is not an income tax, in its entirety, for all persons subject to the tax."[9]

---

[5] Infra ¶69.5.

[6] Reg. §1.901-2(a)(3)(i), discussed infra ¶69.4.3.

[7] Reg. §1.901-2(a)(3)(ii), discussed infra ¶69.4.4.

[8] Reg. §1.901-2(b)(1).

[9] Reg. §1.901-2(b)(2)(i). See Texasgulf Inc. v. CIR, 107 TC 51, 71 (1996) ("This phrase does not mean that, to be creditable, a tax must be an income tax for each taxpayer subject to it; it means that a tax is creditable by either all, or none, of the taxpayers subject to it, regardless of variations in how the tax applies to each taxpayer subject to it.").

A tax that fails the net gain requirement is nevertheless creditable as a tax in lieu of an income tax if the taxing country also has a general income tax that satisfies the net gain requirement and the tax in question substitutes for the general income tax for certain groups of taxpayers or types of income or for income from particular activities.[10] For example, a gross income tax on nonbusiness income of foreigners does not meet the net gain requirement, but such a tax often qualifies as an in lieu tax because income subject to the tax typically is exempted from the taxing country's general income tax. Credit thus is usually allowed when U.S. taxpayers are subject to foreign levies analogous to the withholding tax imposed by the United States under §§871(a) and 881.

Although the foreign tax credit is usually determined on an accrual basis,[11] credit is allowed only for amounts that are ultimately "paid." This requirement has several implications. A tax is considered not paid if it is actually paid but the payment is virtually certain to be refunded either directly or through a related subsidy to the taxpayer, a person related to the taxpayer, or a person involved in a transaction in which the taxpayer participates.[12] Also, if a nonincome tax is allowed as a credit against an income tax, the amount paid as an income tax consists of the net amount after the credit.[13] Moreover, because a tax must be compulsory, a payment is considered not paid as an income tax to the extent it exceeds the taxpayer's liability under the foreign law.[14]

These several requirements are applied "independently for each separate foreign levy."[15] Generally, a separate foreign levy is an impost on a tax base that is separate from the base on which other levies are imposed.

Finally, if all of the foregoing hurdles are overcome, credit is still denied if the tax is imposed by one of several countries that is identified with terrorism or is on bad terms with the United States for other reasons.[16]

¶69.4.2 What Is a "Tax"?

A "tax" is "a compulsory payment pursuant to the authority of a foreign country to levy taxes."[17] Whether a payment is compulsory and is exacted pursuant to the payee's taxing powers are questions of U.S. tax law. A foreign country's "assertion" that a levy is pursuant to its authority to levy taxes is not determinative of the issue. Penalties, fines, interest, and customs duties are not taxes; however, they might be denominated by the governments imposing them.

---

[10] Infra ¶69.4.5.
[11] See infra ¶69.13.1.
[12] Infra ¶69.4.6 text accompanying notes 105–13.
[13] Infra ¶69.4.6 text accompanying notes 126–29.
[14] Infra ¶69.4.6 text accompanying notes 130–45.
[15] Reg. §1.901-2(a)(1), discussed infra ¶69.4.7.
[16] Infra ¶69.4.8.
[17] Reg. §1.901-2(a)(2)(i).

The most difficult issues in determining whether an impost is a tax arise when the taxpayer receives benefits from the foreign government that are not available to all taxpayers. Generally, a payment for a "specific economic benefit" is not a tax.[18] A person receiving a specific economic benefit, however, may be a "dual capacity taxpayer," a person who both receives a specific economic benefit from a foreign government and pays a tax to the country providing the benefit.[19] Such a tax is not creditable unless the taxpayer shows it is not a payment for specific economic benefits.

1. *Specific economic benefits.* If a specific economic benefit is received in exchange for a payment to a foreign government, the payment is not a tax because it is not levied pursuant to the government's taxing power.[20] A specific economic benefit is "an economic benefit that is not made available on substantially the same terms to substantially all persons" subject to the foreign country's general income tax or, if there is no such tax, to "the population of the country in general."[21] For example, a "concession to extract government-owned petroleum is a specific economic benefit" because the government is necessarily selective in granting such concessions. In contrast, the right to travel on a government-owned airline or to ship freight on the airline is not a specific economic benefit if the airline's services are available to all on a nondiscriminatory basis. Also, "the right or privilege merely to engage in business generally . . . or in a particular form" is not a specific economic benefit.

A specific economic benefit can be received in the form of money, property, services, or "a reduction or discharge of a contractual obligation."[22] For example, if a bank lends money to foreign country X, interest on the loan is a specific economic benefit because a person does not become entitled to such a payment merely by being a country X taxpayer.[23] A specific economic benefit can consist of a right to use a patent or other property owned by the foreign government or a right to extract resources the government owns. A right to extract, acquire, or use resources or property is a specific economic benefit, even if the taxing government does not own the property or resources, if the government "exhibits substantial indicia of ownership" by, for example, "both regulating the quantity of property that may be extracted and establishing the minimum price at which it may be disposed of."[24]

A specific economic benefit can be received either directly or indirectly. The payor of a levy imposed by a foreign government is considered the indirect recipient of a benefit received by any entity that the payor owns or controls,

---

[18] Infra text accompanying notes 20–27.
[19] Infra text accompanying notes 27–36.
[20] Reg. §1.901-2(a)(2)(i).
[21] Reg. §1.901-2(a)(2)(ii)(B).
[22] Reg. §1.901-2(a)(2)(ii)(B).
[23] Reg. §1.901-2A(c)(2)(ii) Ex. 1.
[24] Reg. §§1.901-2(a)(2)(ii)(B), (D).

directly or indirectly.[25] A benefit received by a person who owns or controls the payor is also deemed received indirectly by the payor. Further, a payor is the indirect recipient of a benefit received by a person with whom the payor deals if the "terms and conditions" of the transaction pass on to the payor any part of "the value of the specific economic benefit."[26]

In contrast, "a foreign levy imposed on individuals to finance retirement, old age, death, survivor, unemployment, illness, or disability benefits" is not considered a payment for a specific economic benefit unless the amount of the levy is "computed on a basis reflecting the respective ages, life expectancies or similar characteristics of [the] individuals" required to pay it.[27] Foreign taxes analogous to the U.S. social security (FICA) taxes are thus considered taxes, not payments for social security benefits. The same rule applies to a levy imposed for any "substantially similar purpose."

2. *Dual capacity taxpayers.* A "dual capacity taxpayer" is a person that is subject to a foreign levy but also receives a specific economic benefit from the government imposing the levy or an agency or political subdivision thereof.[28] A payment by a dual capacity taxpayer can qualify as a tax if it is pursuant to a single foreign levy that applies to both dual capacity and other taxpayers and no distinction is made, either explicitly or in practice, in applying the levy to these two groups.[29] In this case, none of the levy is considered payment for the specific economic benefit. Assume a U.S. company engaged in extracting oil and gas from deposits owned by the country X government is subject to a general income tax of country X that applies to all persons doing business in the country, including many who do not exploit natural resources owned by the government. Any amount paid by the company pursuant to this levy is a tax, not payment for the right to extract minerals owned by the government, if, in applying the levy, no distinction is made between those who do and do not exploit governmentally owned deposits.

If the levy applies differently to dual capacity and other taxpayers, it is deemed to consist of two separate levies, one for dual capacity taxpayers and another for all others.[30] In this case and in cases where a levy applies only to dual capacity taxpayers, credit may be allowed to such a taxpayer for "the distinct element of the levy that is a tax."[31] The burden, however, is on the taxpayer to

---

[25] Reg. §1.901-2(a)(2)(ii)(E)(*1*).

[26] Reg. §1.901-2(a)(2)(ii)(E)(2).

[27] Reg. §1.901-2(a)(2)(ii)(C).

[28] Reg. §1.901-2(a)(2)(ii)(A).

[29] Reg. §1.901-2A(b)(1).

[30] Reg. §1.901-2A(a), discussed infra ¶69.4.7 text accompanying notes 158-65.

[31] Reg. §1.901-2A(b)(1). See Phillips Petroleum Co. v. CIR, 104 TC 256, 296, 297 (1995) (under earlier version of regulations, "special charge" imposed by Norway only on petroleum producers was not for specific economic benefit; "Norway imposed the special charge pursuant to . . . its sovereign taxing power, not pursuant to its proprietary rights, as an owner of petroleum resources"; unlike typical royalty, special charge was computed

show this distinct element, and no credit is allowed if the burden is not discharged.[32] The amount not proven to be a tax is considered a payment for the specific economic benefit and takes its character from the nature of the benefit.[33] The nontax payment may, for example, be a royalty for the right to extract minerals owned by the government, part of the purchase price of goods received from the government, or a reduction of interest on a loan to the government.

Assume country X imposes a tax on the net income of corporations engaged in the banking business through country X branches; all banks doing business in the country loan money to the government but also have substantial income from business with private persons.[34] Because interest received on loans to the government is a specific economic benefit, taxpayers have the burden of establishing that the levy is a tax rather than compensation for the specific economic benefit (a partial rebate of the interest). This burden can be discharged by showing that the tax applies equally to interest on government loans and income from other aspects of the banking business.

If a dual capacity taxpayer fails to show that the entirety of a levy is a tax rather than payment for a specific benefit, a portion of it may nevertheless be shown to be a tax.[35] A safe harbor rule is provided for establishing this amount.[36]

¶69.4.3   "Net Gain" Requirement

A tax is an income tax only if it is calculated to reach net gain, and this requirement is met only if the tax satisfies three tests—the realization, gross receipts, and net income requirements.[37]

1. *Realization requirement.* The realization requirement is met unless income or gain is recognized under the foreign tax law earlier than is permitted by any of four rules described below.[38] The first of these rules usually requires that the foreign law follow U.S. conceptions of realization, but the second, third, and fourth rules relax this stricture in several situations. Further, strict adherence to

---

as percentage of profit, after subtraction of expenses, and "was not inextricably interwoven with the grant to exploit Norwegian petroleum resources"); Nordberg, Fischl & Greenhouse, Tax Court Provides Guidance on Creditability of Foreign Taxes, 67 Tax Notes 679 (May 1, 1995).

[32] Reg. §1.901-2A(c)(2)(i). See Rev. Proc. 98-7, 1998-1 CB —, §4.01(16) (IRS ordinarily will not rule on whether credit claimant has established "the amount (if any) paid by a dual capacity taxpayer under a qualifying levy that is not paid in exchange for a specific economic benefit").

[33] But see Reg. §1.901-2A(b)(2) (if levy is labeled a tax by treaty between United States and taxing country, it is considered a tax, not payment for specific economic benefit, unless taxpayer claims credit under statute rather than treaty).

[34] Reg. §1.901-2A(c)(2)(ii) Ex. 1.

[35] Reg. §1.901-2A(c)(1).

[36] Reg. §1.901-2A(e).

[37] Reg. §1.901-2(b)(1).

[38] Reg. §1.901-2(b)(2)(i).

the four rules is not required because a foreign tax need only meet the realization requirement in its "predominant character."

    a. *General rule.* Generally, the realization requirement is satisfied only if income or gain is recognized under the foreign tax law no sooner than the event that triggers realization of the item under U.S. law.[39] For example, an increase in the value of property is usually realized under U.S. law only when the property is sold or exchanged, and a foreign tax law thus satisfies the realization requirement with respect to such income or gain if it is taxed in the year of sale or exchange or some subsequent year. Assume the profits of a branch within foreign country X are taxed by country X when they are distributed or deemed distributed to the taxpayer's home office outside the country.[40] If the profits include only realized income in the U.S. sense, the tax meets the realization requirement because the event triggering the tax (distribution or deemed distribution of the profits) comes after the U.S. realization event.[41]

    b. *Recapture.* A foreign tax law may require recognition before the U.S. realization event if the income or gain is a "recapture . . . of a tax deduction, tax credit or other tax allowance previously accorded to the taxpayer."[42] Under U.S. law, for example, an investment credit is sometimes recaptured if the property that qualified the taxpayer for the credit ceases to be used for a qualifying purpose, even if the change in use does not involve a sale or exchange.[43] Similar departures from the realization doctrine are also tolerated in foreign tax laws.

    c. *Unrealized items.* The realization requirement is not violated by the imposition of a foreign tax before realization in the U.S. sense if (1) the income, gain, or loss under foreign law consists of the change in the value of property over a period of time or (2) recognition of the income or gain is triggered under foreign law by "the physical transfer, processing, or export of readily marketable property."[44] A foreign tax on unrealized appreciation in stocks and bonds (e.g., under a mark-to-market regime) is an example of the first branch of the rule.[45] The second is illustrated by a foreign tax law that treats goods as sold or exchanged at fair market value when exported from the taxing country, even if the taxpayer continues to own the goods after export.

---

[39] Reg. §1.901-2(b)(2)(i)(A).

[40] For the U.S. analogue of such a branch profits tax, see supra ¶66.5.

[41] Reg. §1.901-2(b)(2)(iv) Ex. 3.

[42] Reg. §1.901-2(b)(2)(i)(B).

[43] IRC §47(a)(1), discussed supra ¶27.2.5.

[44] Reg. §1.901-2(b)(2)(i)(C).

[45] Compare IRC §1256 (mark-to-market rule under U.S. law for commodities futures, foreign currency contracts, and some options), discussed supra ¶45.2.

The second branch of the rule applies only to readily marketable property, a requirement that is satisfied if (1) the goods are inventory or other property held primarily for sale to customers and (2) they either can be "sold on the open market without further processing" or are exported from the taxing country.[46] For example, partially processed minerals are considered readily marketable for purposes of a tax imposed when they are exported, even if they are never sold in this form. In contrast, an intermediate good of a type that is rarely sold is not readily marketable for purposes of a foreign tax imposed at a time other than the point of export.

A further requirement qualifies both branches of the rule: The foreign law must either have a mechanism that ensures the item will not reappear in the tax base at any subsequent time, or it must provide a credit to prevent the item from being taxed twice.[47] Assume a mining company is subject to country X tax both when minerals are extracted from a country X mine and when the extracted minerals are sold. The former tax fails to meet the realization requirement unless an exclusion, deduction, or credit is allowed at the time of sale to relieve double taxation.

As another illustration of this qualification, assume a foreign country X has both a stock appreciation tax on annual increases in the value of stock and a general income tax that includes in its base capital gains measured from original cost.[48] A taxpayer buys stock in June 1996 for 100 units of the local currency (100u). The taxpayer holds the stock at the end of 1996 (when its value is 120u) and at the end of 1997 (when its value is 155u). She sells in May 1998 for 160u. Assume the country X taxes are computed as follows: Under the stock appreciation tax, 20u is taxed for 1996 (120u value at end of 1996 less cost of 100u), and 35u is taxed for 1997 (155u value at end of 1997 less 120u value at end of 1996). On sale, the gain under the country's general income tax is 60u (amount realized of 160u less original cost of 100u). Since the investment produces only 60u of gain, the amounts taxed under the stock appreciation tax are taxed a second time under the general income tax, and the stock appreciation tax does not satisfy the realization requirement.

In contrast, the stock appreciation tax satisfies the realization requirement if, under the general income tax, gain or loss on a sale of stock acquired before the year of sale is computed as the excess of the amount realized over the stock's value at the end of the prior year. If this is done, gain on sale is 5u (selling price of 160u over the 155u value of the stock

---

[46] Reg. §1.901-2(b)(2)(iii).

[47] Reg. §1.901-2(b)(2)(i)(C). This double tax prohibition is not breached, however, by a second tax imposed when the income is distributed or deemed distributed.

[48] Reg. §1.901-2(b)(2)(iv) Ex. 1.

at the end of 1997), and the general income tax does not tax amounts already subject to the stock appreciation tax.[49]

d. *Deemed distributions.* A creditable foreign income tax may be imposed on a corporate shareholder or beneficiary of a trust or estate even though the income of the entity being taxed has not been distributed to the shareholder or beneficiary.[50] This rule applies, however, only if the income has been realized by the entity under one of the foregoing rules. For example, the realization requirement is not breached by a foreign country taxing a shareholder on a deemed distribution if the corporate profits included in the deemed distribution have been realized by the corporation. Also, the rule is inapplicable if the foreign law lacks a mechanism for precluding a second tax on the shareholder or beneficiary when the income is actually distributed.[51]

e. *Predominant character test.* A foreign tax satisfies the realization requirement if, "judged on the basis of its predominant character," it is a tax on income covered by the four rules described above.[52] A tax that includes items not encompassed by any of the four rules thus meets the realization requirement if the inclusion of these items does not affect the predominant character of the tax. For example, a foreign tax on the imputed rental value of a personal residence is not an income tax because this income is never realized under U.S. law,[53] but a foreign tax on a base that includes imputed income can be an income tax if, in its predominant character, it is a tax on income covered by the four realization rules described above.

A tax either meets or fails to meet the realization requirement for all taxpayers.[54] If the predominant character of a tax satisfies the requirement, it is met for all taxpayers, even those who are only taxed on items that meet none of the realization tests. For example, if imputed income is included in a foreign tax base, but the tax is nevertheless found to be predominantly on realized income, a taxpayer who is taxed only on imputed income may qualify for credit. Conversely, if a foreign tax does not satisfy the realization requirement in its predominant character, the tax is not considered an income tax in any application, including those cases where the taxpayer's income consists entirely of items that are realized in the U.S. sense.

2. *Gross receipts requirement.* Generally, the starting point for the calculation of income subject to a creditable foreign income tax must be actual gross

---

[49] Reg. §1.901-2(b)(2)(iv) Ex. 2.

[50] Reg. §1.901-2(b)(2)(ii).

[51] For a scheme satisfying this requirement, see Reg. §1.901-2(b)(2)(iv) Ex. 4.

[52] Reg. §1.901-2(b)(2)(i).

[53] See supra ¶5.3.3.

[54] Reg. §1.901-2(b)(2)(i).

receipts.[55] For example, a foreign tax on income from the extraction of petroleum fails this test if the law imposing the tax specifies that all petroleum is deemed sold for 105 percent of its fair market value.[56]

Amounts other than actual gross receipts can be substituted in two situations. First, a substitution may be made where "it is reasonable to believe that gross receipts may not otherwise be clearly reflected."[57] "[T]ransactions between related parties" are an example.[58] The substituted amount, however, must be "computed under a method that is likely to produce an amount that is not greater than fair market value."[59] Assume a corporation sells goods to a subsidiary, which resells them to an unrelated person at a higher price. The gross receipts requirement is not violated by a foreign tax law that disregards the corporation's actual gross receipts on the sale to the subsidiary and substitutes the price at which the goods would have been sold between unrelated persons dealing at arm's length.[60]

Assume country X imposes a "headquarters company tax" on corporations that have headquarters in country X but carry on operations through affiliates in other countries. Because of the difficulties that would arise in case-by-case determinations of arm's length charges for management services provided by a headquarters organization to affiliates, country X law provides that a headquarter's gross receipts are deemed equal to 110 percent of its expenses.[61] A substitution for actual gross receipts is allowed in this situation because it is reasonable to expect that actual gross receipts do not clearly reflect income. The gross receipts test is thus met if the substituted amount, 110 percent of expenses, is not likely to be greater than the fair market value of the services that headquarters typically perform for their affiliates. If this is so, the requirement is met for all taxpayers, including those for whom the notional gross receipts demonstrably exceed the fair market value of their services.

A substitution for actual gross receipts is also allowed where the realization rules allow income to be recognized under the foreign tax law in the absence of gross receipts. For example, the realization requirement can be met by a periodic foreign tax on unrealized appreciation or a foreign tax imposed when minerals are lifted from the ground or goods are exported. Substitutes for actual gross receipts are obviously needed for such taxes. In this situation also, however, the

---

[55] Reg. §1.901-2(b)(3)(i).

[56] Reg. §1.901-2(b)(3)(ii) Ex. 3.

[57] Reg. §1.901-2(b)(3)(i)(B)(*1*).

[58] Id. See Phillips Petroleum Co. v. CIR, 104 TC 256 (1995) (finding this requirement met with respect to Norwegian taxes on petroleum producers under which "norm price" was substituted for actual gross receipts).

[59] Reg. §1.901-2(b)(3)(i)(B).

[60] For an analogous substitution under U.S. law, see §482, discussed infra ¶79.1.

[61] Reg. §1.901-2(b)(3)(ii) Exs. 1, 2.

substituted amount must be computed in a way likely to keep it from exceeding the goods' fair market value.[62]

A foreign tax need meets the gross receipts requirement only in its "predominant character."[63] The inclusion of amounts other than actual gross receipts in situations where the regulations do not allow a substitution does not automatically disqualify a foreign tax. If the predominant character of the levy is a tax computed from actual gross receipts or acceptable substitutes, the presence of a few ciphers is not fatal. The regulations give no examples of deviations that would destroy a predominantly acceptable character.

3. *Net income requirement.* To satisfy the net income requirement, a foreign tax law must provide for the "recovery of the significant costs and expenses (including significant capital expenditures) attributable, under reasonable principles, to [the] gross receipts" included in the tax base.[64] The regulations do not identify the "significant costs and expenses" attributable to particular gross receipts, except to say that a tax can satisfy the net income requirement without allowing a deduction for other income taxes.[65] For example, if a foreign country and one of its political subdivisions each impose an income tax on the same income, both taxes can satisfy the net income requirement even if neither tax is allowable as a deduction in determining the other.[66] However, a tax that does not satisfy the realization, gross receipts, and net income requirements (e.g., a real property or value added tax) is a significant cost that must reduce the base of a creditable income tax. In lieu of direct deductions of costs and expenses, the foreign law can allow reductions of the tax base "under a method that is likely to produce an amount that approximates, or is greater than, recovery of such significant costs and expenses."[67]

---

[62] Reg. §1.901-2(b)(3)(i)(B).

[63] Reg. §1.901-2(b)(3)(i).

[64] Reg. §1.901-2(b)(4)(i).

[65] Reg. §1.901-2(b)(4)(i). See Texasgulf, Inc. v. US, 17 Cl. Ct. 275, 89-1 USTC ¶9385 (1989) (Ontario Mining Tax not creditable because no deductions allowed for interest, depletion, royalties, and other significant expenses).

[66] Reg. §1.901-2(b)(4)(iv) Ex. 5.

[67] Reg. §1.901-2(b)(4)(i)(B). The regulations further state: "A foreign tax law that does not permit recovery of one or more significant costs of expenses, but that provides allowances that effectively compensate for nonrecovery of such significant costs or expenses, is considered to permit recovery of such costs or expenses." Reg. §1.901-2(b)(4)(i). In Texasgulf Inc. v. CIR, 107 TC 51 (1996), the court held that a "processing allowance" under the Ontario Mining Tax effectively compensated for disallowed deductions for interest, royalties, and other items because multiyear data for the taxpayer and most other companies subject to tax showed that the allowance exceeded the disallowed deductions in the aggregate and in most years. "Use of aggregate data is appropriate because a tax is or is not creditable for all taxpayers subject to it." Id. at 72. The court rejected the IRS' objection that use of such data would require the IRS to reevaluate the creditability of the tax annually, but it did not specify how creditability would be affected by periodic fluctuations in the data. The court also held that the issue under the quoted sentence from the

It is not necessary that the deductions or other reductions be allowed at the same time as the costs are deductible under U.S. law. For example, a depreciation system allowing cost recovery more slowly than U.S. law is usually not disqualifying; neither is a foreign rule requiring capitalization of costs that are immediately written off under U.S. law. The requirement is not met, however, if the timing of the "recovery is such that under the circumstances there is effectively a denial of such recovery."[68]

Similarly, foreign rules for allocating and apportioning costs between gross receipts of various classes need only be reasonable.[69] The rules for allocating costs between gross receipts included in and excluded from the foreign tax base are not required to be the same as the detailed rules provided for this purpose in the U.S. regulations.[70]

A tax that fails the net income requirement may be creditable as a tax in lieu of an income tax under §903, discussed below,[71] if the taxing country also has an income tax that meets the requirement and the items taxed on a basis other than net income are exempted from the general income tax.

4. *Loss deductions.* The net gain test usually does not require that losses from one period be deductible against profits of other periods.[72] The net operating loss deduction, in other words, is a feature of U.S. law that is not a necessary ingredient of a qualifying foreign tax law. A foreign tax law, however, must usually allow losses incurred in any aspect of a trade or business in the taxing country to be offset against profits earned in other aspects of the business.[73] This is often accomplished by pooling all costs against all gross receipts of the business. In lieu of such a pooling, losses incurred in one activity in a particular taxable period can be allowed against profits of other activities of the trade or business in other periods, as long as any delay in the allowance of the offset is not so great as to effectively deny a right of offset.

If a loss in one activity of the business is never allowed against income from other activities of the business, the loss must be carried to other periods as a deduction against profits from the loss activity, and the period of carryover and carryback must not be so restricted "that under the circumstances there is effectively a denial of the ability to offset such loss against profit."[74] Assume

---

regulations was whether the allowance effectively compensated in fact for the nondeductible costs, not whether it was intended to compensate for them.

[68] Reg. §1.901-2(b)(4)(i).

[69] Id.

[70] See Reg. §1.861-8, discussed infra ¶70.10.1.

[71] Infra ¶69.4.5.

[72] Reg. §1.901-2(b)(4)(iii).

[73] Reg. §1.901-2(b)(4)(ii).

[74] Id. See Phillips Petroleum Co. v. CIR, 104 TC 256 (1995) (net income requirement not violated by Norwegian rule that losses from activities other than petroleum extraction (onshore activities) could not offset more than 50 percent of petroleum-extraction income; onshore losses could be carried forward for 10 years).

country X law provides that losses incurred in oil and gas exploration in the area covered by one contract with the country X petroleum authority may not be deducted against income earned in another contract area. The tax satisfies the net income requirement only if (1) losses incurred in a particular contract area during any year may be deducted against profits earned in this contract area during other years and (2) the carryover and carryback periods are long enough to provide a realistic prospect of gaining tax benefit from the deduction.

Generally, profits and losses of related persons need not be pooled under a qualifying foreign tax law.[75] If separate activities of a unified business are required to be organized as separate entities, however, the tests described in the two preceding paragraphs must be met. Assume country X law requires that oil companies form a separate subsidiary for each exploration contract and does not allow a pooling of profits and losses of subsidiaries owned by a common parent company. Under the rule described in the preceding paragraph, each subsidiary must be allowed to carry losses of one period to other periods over a sufficiently long time to allow a realistic chance for offsetting losses against profits.

Losses from one trade or business in the taxing country need not be allowed against income from another business, and business profits and losses need not be pooled with investment income and loss.[76] For example, if a taxpayer both extracts oil and gas and has an oil and gas refinery in the taxing country, the net income test does not require that losses from the extraction business be allowed against refining profits or vice versa.

5. *Predominant character test.* A foreign tax need only satisfy the net income requirement in its "predominant character."[77] A denial of allowances for some significant costs therefore does not necessarily disqualify the tax.

However, a tax on gross receipts or gross income fails the requirement unless two restrictive conditions are met.[78] First, the tax must be "almost certain to reach some net gain in the normal circumstances in which it applies because costs and expenses will never be so high as to offset gross receipts or gross income." Second, "the rate of the tax [must be] such that after the tax is paid persons subject to the tax are almost certain to have net gain." If imposed on businesses, such a tax fails the test unless "businesses subject to the tax are almost certain never to incur a loss (after payment of the tax)."

The regulations suggest that it is a "rare situation" where these conditions are met.[79] Assume country X imposes a bank tax equal to one percent of the gross interest incomes of banking branches in the country. Because a banking business incurs substantial costs in earning interest, such a business is almost certain never to incur a loss on interest income, and the tax, which is computed without

---

[75] Reg. §1.901-2(b)(4)(ii).

[76] Id.

[77] Reg. §1.901-2(b)(4)(i).

[78] Id.

[79] Id.

deductions for these costs, thus fails the net income requirement.[80] In contrast, if country X taxes net interest income of banking branches within the country and also imposes a one percent tax on gross interest received by banks without local branches from loans to country X residents, the net income tax on banking branches meets the net income requirement, but the tax on gross interest income does not.[81] On the other hand, a gross wage tax of 40 percent meets the requirement because an employee is very unlikely to sustain a loss.[82]

   6. *Source rules.* The source rules used to identify items subject to the foreign tax need not match their U.S. counterparts. Assume foreign country X imposes a tax on net income from services rendered to country X residents, regardless of where the services are performed. Under U.S. law, services income has its source where the services are performed.[83] The country X tax, however, may qualify as a creditable income tax even though, in a particular case, it might tax a U.S. person on items that are from U.S. sources under U.S. law.[84]

¶69.4.4   Soak-Up Taxes

   A foreign tax does not qualify for credit "to the extent that liability for the . . . tax is . . . dependent . . . on the availability of a credit for the tax against income tax liability to another country."[85] The forbidden dependency exists "if and to the extent that the foreign tax would not be imposed on the taxpayer but for the availability of such a credit." A tax that fails this test is known as a soak-up tax.

   The dependency on credit in another country need not be stated in the foreign tax law. If, in fact, some portion of the tax is imposed only on persons who qualify for credit in another country, that portion of the tax is disallowed. Assume foreign country X imposes a tax on nonresidents receiving royalties from country X sources.[86] The rate of tax is generally 15 percent, but it is 20 percent for residents of the United States and four other specified countries. Each of the four specified countries, like the United States, allows its residents credit for foreign taxes on foreign source income. Because the 20 percent rate only applies to residents of countries that have foreign tax credits, one fourth of the tax on a U.S. resident—the excess of the 20 percent tax over the 15 percent tax—is considered imposed only because it is creditable elsewhere, and this portion of the

---

[80] Reg. §1.901-2(b)(4)(iv) Ex. 1.
[81] Reg. §1.901-2(b)(4)(iv) Ex. 2.
[82] Reg. §1.901-2(b)(4)(iv) Ex. 3.
[83] IRC §861(a)(3), discussed infra ¶70.4.
[84] Reg. §1.901-2(b)(4)(iv) Ex. 4.
[85] Reg. §1.901-2(c)(1).
[86] Reg. §1.901-2(c)(2) Ex. 1.

tax is noncreditable. It is apparently not relevant whether the higher rate applies to residents of all countries with credit systems.

However, a discrimination against foreigners from countries with credit systems does not disqualify a tax if the tax (or the portion of it in question) is imposed on a significant group of persons who get no credit for it in any other country. Assume country X provides a tax holiday to locally organized corporations owned by foreign shareholders, under which these corporations are exempted from the country's general income tax for their first 10 years of business operations.[87] The holiday is only allowed to corporations certified eligible by an administrative agency, and the agency never issues the certificate to corporations owned predominantly by corporations organized in the United States and other countries whose tax laws contain indirect credit rules like §902.[88] The forbidden dependency on the credit is not present. Because the country's corporate income tax is regularly imposed on many corporations that are owned by residents of country X or are foreign-owned but have been in business in the country for more than 10 years, the tax applies to a substantial group of taxpayers having no opportunity to credit it against another country's tax, and it is therefore creditable.[89]

Moreover, a dependency on credit is disqualifying only if it results from a feature of the foreign tax law or its administration, not from the fact that only residents of credit countries carry on taxable activities. Assume country X imposes a tax on the realized net income of every nonresident engaged in business in the country, but all persons so engaged are residents of the United States. The tax is not dependent on the allowance of credit because the tax applies equally to all persons who carry on the activity subject to the tax and the right to engage in this activity is not restricted to residents of the United States.[90]

¶69.4.5 Taxes in Lieu of Income Taxes

Under §903, a foreign tax not meeting the net gain requirements is nevertheless treated as an income tax if it is imposed "in lieu of a tax on income . . . generally imposed" by a foreign country or U.S. possession. According to the regulations, a foreign levy qualifies as an in lieu tax if it is a tax, a substitution

---

[87] Reg. §1.901-2(c)(2) Ex. 3.

[88] Section 902(a) provides that when a U.S. corporation receives a dividend from a foreign corporation in which it owns at least 10 percent of the voting stock, the U.S. corporation is treated as having paid a ratable share of the foreign income taxes paid by the foreign corporation. See infra ¶69.8.

[89] The result is the same if the foreign country initially allows the holiday to corporations owned by residents of countries that have §902-type credits, but effectively cancels out the holiday's effect by imposing tax when earnings are distributed to the corporations' shareholders. Reg. §1.901-2(c)(2) Ex. 4.

[90] Reg. §1.901-2(c)(2) Ex. 2.

requirement is met, and the tax is not a soak-up tax.[91] In lieu taxes are often imposed on particular groups of taxpayers because of administrative difficulties in determining their net incomes. A foreign country's reasons for a particular tax, however, are not relevant to whether it qualifies as an in lieu tax. The base on which an in lieu tax is imposed need not approximate net income; it may consist of gross income, gross receipts, or the number of units produced or exported.

1. *Substitution requirement.* A tax meets the substitution requirement if it "in fact operates as a tax imposed in substitution for, and not in addition to, an income tax or a series of income taxes otherwise generally imposed."[92] The tax need not be a complete substitute for a particular taxpayer's regular income tax. A tax on a portion of a taxpayer's income (e.g., passive investment income) can be an in lieu tax even if the taxpayer is subject to the regular income tax on other income (e.g., active business income).

The most common type of in lieu tax is a foreign tax analogous to the withholding taxes imposed by the United States on nonbusiness income of nonresident aliens and foreign corporations under §§871(a) and 881.[93] Assume country X has a general income tax that satisfies the net gain requirement, but nonbusiness income of foreigners from country X sources is exempted from this tax and is instead subject to a 20 percent gross income tax.[94] The 20 percent tax is an in lieu tax because it substitutes for the general income tax for a particular class of taxpayers. The tax may be collected by requiring country X payors to withhold tax and remit it to the country X tax authorities.[95]

Another common type of in lieu tax is a gross income tax on particular types of business activities. Assume country X has an income tax that generally applies to all persons doing business within the country, but banks are exempt from this tax and are instead subject to a one percent tax on gross interest income from bank branches within the country.[96] The bank tax is an in lieu tax because, for a particular type of business, it substitutes for a general income tax. The same conclusion is reached if banks with branches in country X are subject to the general income taxes but a bank having no branch in the country is subject to a tax of one percent of gross interest income from loans to country X residents.[97]

Like a regular income tax, an in lieu tax need not be based on source rules identical to those of U.S. law. Assume country X imposes a tax on foreigners' gross incomes from the performance of services for country X residents, regard-

---

[91] Reg. §1.903-1(a). For whether a levy is a tax, see supra ¶69.4.2. See Moore, The Foreign Tax Credit for Foreign Taxes Paid in Lieu of Income Taxes: An Evaluation of the Rationale and a Reform Proposal, 7 Am. J. Tax Pol'y 207 (1988).

[92] Reg. §1.903-1(b)(1).

[93] See supra ¶66.2 for §§871(a) and 881.

[94] Reg. §1.903-1(b)(3) Ex. 1.

[95] Reg. §1.903-1(b)(3) Ex. 2.

[96] Reg. §1.901-2(b)(4)(iv) Ex. 1. See Reg. §1.903-1(b)(3) Ex. 4 (same for special taxes on income from construction activities).

[97] Reg. §1.901-2(b)(4)(iv) Ex. 2.

less of where the services are performed, and it enforces the tax by requiring the payors to withhold tax from the payments.[98] The tax can qualify as an in lieu tax even if it applies when the services are performed outside country X and U.S. law would characterize the income as not from country X sources.

A tax does not meet the substitution requirement, however, unless a taxpayer subject to it is exempted, in whole or as to discrete portions of the taxpayer's income, from the general income tax. Assume an individual is subject in country X to both an income tax and an excise tax, the latter being allowed as a credit against the income tax.[99] For a particular year, the individual's precredit income tax is 100u, the excise tax is 30u, and the final income tax is 70u (100u less 30u credit for the excise tax). The taxpayer is treated as paying 70u of income tax and 30u of excise tax.[100] The credit of the excise tax against the income tax does not make the former an in lieu tax, because neither the taxpayer nor any portion of her income is exempt from the income tax.

2. *Soak-up taxes.* An in lieu tax, like a regular income tax, may not be a soak-up tax.[101] That is, liability for the tax may not be dependent on the availability of credit for the tax in another country. However, liability for a tax meeting the substitution requirement is deemed dependent on another country's credit only to the extent of the lesser of (1) the portion of the substitute tax that would not be imposed in the absence of the credit or (2) the amount by which the tax actually imposed exceeds the tax that would have been imposed under the general income tax if the taxpayer had been subject to that tax instead of the substitute tax.

Assume country X has a general income tax, but it makes an agreement with a U.S. company doing business in the country that fixes the company's annual country X tax liability at the greater of 5u for each unit produced in the country or the maximum credit for country X tax allowable in determining the company's U.S. tax.[102] For a particular year, the company produces 16 units in country X, and the limitation on its foreign tax credit for U.S. tax purposes is 125u. Under the agreement, the country X tax for the year thus is 125u (greater of 125u or 5u times 16). If the company were subject to the general country X income tax, its tax for the year would be 150u. The tax actually paid satisfies the substitution requirement because the company is exempted from the general country X income tax, and none of the tax is a soak-up tax because the substitute tax is less than the tax the company would have paid under the general income tax. On the other hand, if the company's general income tax would be 90u, the tax actually

---

[98] Reg. §1.903-1(b)(3) Ex. 3.

[99] Reg. §1.903-1(b)(3) Ex. 5.

[100] Reg. §1.901-2(e)(4)(i), discussed infra ¶69.4.6 text accompanying notes 126-29.

[101] Reg. §1.903-1(b)(2). For the soak-up test applied to regular income taxes, see supra ¶69.4.4.

[102] Reg. §1.903-1(b)(3) Ex. 6.

paid qualifies only to the extent of 90u (greater of non-soak-up portion of substitute tax (5u times 16 units produced) or hypothetical regular tax of 90u).[103]

¶69.4.6 Creditable Amount

If a tax is found to be an income tax or a tax in lieu of an income tax, credit is usually allowed under §901 for the amount that is "paid" by the taxpayer.[104] A tax actually paid is considered not paid if (1) it is reasonably certain to be refunded, (2) it is indirectly refunded through a subsidy given by the taxing country, (3) it is offset in the computation of a nonqualifying tax, or (4) the taxpayer could reduce or eliminate the tax by exhausting its remedies under foreign law. These limitations are discussed below.

1. *Refunds and credits.* "An amount is not tax paid to a foreign country to the extent that it is reasonably certain that the amount will be refunded, credited, rebated, abated, or forgiven."[105] Credit is allowed, in contrast, for "a reasonable approximation of final tax liability to the foreign country."[106]

Assume country X imposes a withholding tax on gross interest income of nonresidents.[107] The statutory rate is 25 percent, but it is reduced to 10 percent for U.S. residents by a treaty between the United States and country X. Tax is withheld at the statutory rate, and the benefit of the treaty can be had only by filing a claim for refund. T, a citizen of the United States, has 100u of interest income from sources within the taxing country. The payor withholds 25u, remits it as tax, and pays 75u to T. If T files a timely claim for refund, the tax paid is 10u because 15u of the tax withheld is reasonably certain to be refunded. If T fails to file a timely claim for refund, the refundable 15u is noncreditable under the rules for noncompulsory payments discussed below.[108]

Refunds are taken into account under this rule if they will be received in money or other property. Assume country X law provides that every taxpayer is entitled to receive a bond issued by country X with a face amount equal to 10 percent of the tax paid.[109] T pays tax under the law of 380u and thereby becomes

---

[103] Reg. §1.903-1(b)(3) Ex. 7.

[104] Reg. §1.901-2(e)(1). The credit, however, is usually allowed when the tax accrues, not when it is paid. IRC §905(a), discussed infra ¶69.13.2.

[105] Reg. §1.901-2(e)(2)(i).

[106] Id. As such an approximation is refined, adjustments in the credit must be made under §905, discussed infra ¶¶69.13.3, 69.13.4.

[107] Reg. §1.901-2(e)(2)(ii) Ex 1.

[108] Infra text accompanying notes 130–45.

[109] Reg. §1.901-2(e)(2)(ii) Ex. 4. Revenue Ruling 90-107, 1990-2 CB 178, applied this test to a Brazilian law that allowed a corporation to designate a portion of its income tax for investment in an investment fund. An investment certificate was issued to evidence the designation. The holder of an investment certificate was a shareholder of the fund, and the certificate could be exchanged for direct ownership of fund assets or sold on a Brazilian stock exchange. The IRS held that the corporation's Brazilian tax was the excess of the

entitled to a 38u bond. Because a refund equal to the fair market value of the bond is reasonably certain, the tax paid is the excess of 380u over that fair market value.[110]

The filing of a claim for refund does not establish that a refund is reasonably certain. Assume T incurs a cost related to its country X business, but the allowability of the cost as a deduction in computing country X tax is uncertain.[111] T files a return in which the cost is not claimed as a deduction and pays tax of 100u with this return. A claim for a refund of 90u, based on the uncertain deduction, is promptly filed. The tax paid is 100u, unreduced by the refund claimed, because T's entitlement to a refund is uncertain.[112]

The tax considered paid is net of credits as well as assured refunds. Assume T's tax in a foreign country is initially computed as 100u, but this amount is reduced by an investment credit of 15u and a credit for charitable gifts of 5u.[113] The tax paid is 80u.

2. *Subsidies.* Under §901(i), a foreign income tax is deemed not to be a tax if the amount paid as tax is used to provide a subsidy to the taxpayer, either directly or indirectly through a related person or a person with whom the taxpayer deals.[114] Any "benefit conferred, directly or indirectly, by a foreign coun-

---

amount paid to the Brazilian tax collector over the fair market value of the investment certificate because it was reasonably certain that the latter amount would be refunded to the taxpayer.

[110] A distinction is made between this example and the example described in the preceding paragraph of the text that is not as clear-cut as the regulation writers may have assumed. In both examples, the tax payment creates a claim against the taxing government that will be paid in the future. In the first example, payment is reduced by the amount of the claim; in the second, it is reduced by the claim's fair market value (present value). The difference between the two examples is that the claim in the first example is expected to be paid relatively soon, whereas payment is delayed in the second example until the bond matures. The time value of money can reasonably be ignored when a refund will be paid promptly, but the line between promptly and delayed is not easily drawn. Perhaps, a cue can be taken from the time value of money rules, which generally impute no interest to obligations payable within a year of issue. See supra ¶56.5.3.

When received, the bond in the second example should have a basis equal to the fair market value figure used in determining the credit, and the bond should thereafter be treated as an investment unrelated to foreign taxes. The excess of the bond's face amount over its fair market value when received should be treated as original issue discount (OID), not as a further reduction of foreign income tax, because it is an amount earned by the forbearance of money and thus is in the nature of interest. For OID, see supra ¶56.1.

[111] Reg. §1.901-2(e)(2)(ii) Ex. 3.

[112] If the claim is allowed in any part, the credit is adjusted under §905(c), discussed infra ¶69.13.3.

[113] Reg. §1.901-2(e)(2)(ii) Ex. 2.

[114] See Reg. §1.901-2(e)(3)(i). The subsidy rule was originally provided by regulations, but Congress added §901(i) in 1986 to confirm and perhaps broaden it. See Reg. §1.901-2(e)(3)(v) (regulations under §901(i) apply to foreign taxes paid or accrued in taxable years beginning after 1986); Norwest Corp. v. CIR, 69 F3d 1404 (8th Cir. 1995),

try" is considered a subsidy, and "substance and not form shall govern in determining whether a subsidy exists."[115] The subsidy may take the form of a rebate, refund, credit, deduction, payment, or discharge of an obligation, or it may be provided by "any other method."[116] A tax payment is considered used to provide a subsidy if the "subsidy is determined (directly or indirectly) by reference to the amount of such tax, or the base used to compute the amount of such tax."[117] Section 901(i) applies if the subsidy is provided to the taxpayer, a related person, a "party to the transaction," or a "party to a related transaction."[118] Relatedness is determined under §482, which generally encompasses persons that own or control the taxpayer or are owned or controlled by the taxpayer or by the same persons that own or control the taxpayer.[119]

Assume foreign country X imposes a 30 percent withholding tax on interest received by nonresidents on obligations of country X residents, and this tax qualifies under §903 as a tax in lieu of an income tax.[120] To encourage borrowing from foreigners, country X provides a subsidy to its residents equal to 20 percent of the interest on their obligations to foreign lenders. A U.S. bank is entitled to interest of 100u of country X currency on a loan to a resident of country X. The borrower withholds 30u for remittance to the X tax authorities, pays 70u to the bank, and receives 20u from the X government. The bank is deemed to pay country X tax of 10u, the excess of the nominal tax of 30u over the subsidy of 20u. The subsidy is subtracted from the nominal tax because (1) it is provided to a party to the transaction giving rise to the income subject to the foreign tax, (2) the amount of the subsidy is determined with reference to the base on which the bank is taxed (both the tax and the subsidy are a percentage of the interest on the obligation of the country X resident), and (3) the subsidy is thus considered made from the tax payment. Also, the bank's gross interest income is 80u, the sum of

---

cert. denied, 116 S. Ct. 1704 (1996) (sustaining and applying prior regulations); Continental Ill. Corp. v. CIR, 998 F2d 513 (7th Cir. 1993), cert. denied, 510 US 1041 (1994) (same); Riggs Nat'l Corp. v. CIR, 107 TC 301 (1997) (same); Bankers Trust NY Corp. v. US, 36 Fed. Cl. 30, 96-2 USTC ¶50,384 (1996) (same); Vallez, Note, Foreign Tax Credit Disallowed for Subsidized Foreign Tax: *Bankers Trust New York Corporation v. United States*, 50 Tax Lawyer 443 (1997); Rev. Rul. 84-143, 1984-2 CB 127 (effect of Mexican Exchange Control Decree for taxes paid or accrued in taxable years beginning before 1987).

[115] Reg. §1.901-2(e)(3)(ii).

[116] Reg. §1.901-2(e)(3)(i)(A).

[117] IRC §901(i)(2); Reg. §1.901-2(e)(3)(i)(B).

[118] Reg. §1.901-2(e)(3)(i)(A).

[119] See infra ¶79.2.

[120] Reg. §1.901-2(e)(3)(iv) Ex. 1. See Reg. §1.901-2(e)(3)(iv) Ex. 4 (U.S. company produces oil and gas in country X under production-sharing agreement with country X government and its petroleum authority; petroleum authority is subject to country X income tax but is allowed credit for one half of country X taxes paid by U.S. company; held, one half of company's country X income taxes are noncreditable under §901(i)).

the 70u actually received and the 10u of withholding tax deemed paid on its behalf.[121]

Section 901(i) can also apply where the subsidy is received by a party to a transaction that is related to the transaction out of which the foreign tax liability arises. Assume a U.S. bank lends money to the development bank of country X, which relends the money to several country X companies.[122] Country X imposes a 30 percent withholding tax on interest paid by residents to foreign lenders. Under country X law, however, the development bank remits to the X tax authorities only one third of the tax it withholds, and the other two thirds is paid over to the borrowing companies. Two thirds of the taxes withheld from interest payable to the U.S. bank is not creditable because this amount is used to provide subsidies to parties to transactions that are related to the lending transaction in which the bank earns the income subject to the country X tax.

The last example leads down a slippery slope. Assume a U.S. lender lends to the country X development bank at 10 percent, and the development bank relends to country X companies at 8 percent. The development bank withholds and remits to the country X treasury a 30 percent tax on each interest payment to the U.S. lender, but the X government covers the development bank's losses. If the losses are covered by crediting to the development bank two thirds of each withholding tax payment it makes, the economic effect is identical to that in the preceding example, and the subsidy rule denies credit for two thirds of the nominal tax. But, suppose the losses are met by annual appropriations that relate to the bank's overall operations and are not matched with particular transactions.[123] Suppose the bank's capital comes from many sources so that the U.S. lender's funds cannot be traced to particular borrowers from the bank. Suppose, more generally, that the pattern of the development bank borrowing abroad at high rates and relending to local borrowers at lower rates can be seen in the general outlines of the bank's operations but not in particular transactions. Whether a taxpayer benefits from a subsidy provided through a related transaction, in other words, is often a difficult factual issue for which neither the statute, the legislative history, nor the regulations provides much guidance.

Use of an official exchange rate of a foreign government is not considered a subsidy subject to §901(i), even if the rate is more beneficial to the taxpayer than an available free exchange rate, providing that all of the following requirements are met:

---

[121] Rev. Rul. 78-258, 1978-1 CB 239, modified by Rev. Rul. 89-119, 1989-2 CB 132.

[122] See Reg. §1.901-2(e)(3)(iv) Ex. 2; Staff of Joint Comm. on Tax'n, 99th Cong., 2d Sess., General Explanation of the Tax Reform Act of 1986, at 914 (Comm. Print 1987).

[123] See Reg. §1.901-2(e)(3)(iv) Ex. 5 (U.S. company produces oil and gas in country X under production-sharing agreement with country X government and its petroleum authority; petroleum authority receives subsidies from country X in amounts not related to country X taxes paid by U.S. company; held, §901(i) not applicable to company's country X income taxes).

a. The benefit flowing from the official rate may not be "targeted to or tied to transactions that give rise to a claim for a foreign tax credit."

b. The official rate must apply "to a broad range of international transactions, in all cases based on the total payment to be made without regard to whether the payment is a return of principal, gross income, or net income, and without regard to whether it is subject to tax."

c. "Any reduction in the overall cost of the transaction [must be] merely coincidental to the broad structure and operation of the official exchange rate."[124]

Assume country X has a dual exchange rate system, consisting of a controlled official rate, which is used in a broad range of export and international lending transactions, and a free-market exchange rate used in all other transactions.[125] A U.S. bank lends dollars to a country X borrower under a lending agreement requiring that interest and principal payments also be in dollars. Country X imposes a 30 percent withholding tax on interest payments by resident borrowers to nonresident lenders. For a particular period, the country X borrower owes the U.S. bank interest of US $100. It pays the bank US $70, which it obtains at the official exchange rate, and remits as country X tax an amount of country X currency worth US $30 at the official rate. Any benefit to the U.S. bank or its borrower from the use of the official rate is not a subsidy subject to §901(i) because the official rate is not directed specifically to transactions yielding foreign tax credits, the rate applies to both principal and interest, and the resulting benefits are incidental to the official rate's normal operation. Also, the U.S. bank may value the country X tax payment at $30 even though the units of foreign currency used to pay the tax are worth less at the free exchange rate.

3. *Cross-credited levies.* If liability for one foreign tax is reduced by credit for a second tax, the first tax equals the amount payable after the credit, and the second tax is the amount paid, unaffected by the credit.[126] Assume a foreign country imposes an income tax, but provides a credit against income tax liability for a separate excise tax. T, whose tentative income tax liability for a particular year is 100u, is allowed a credit against this liability for 30u of excise tax paid for the year. T's tax liabilities are 70u of income tax and 30u of excise tax.[127] In contrast, the IRS ruled that where a Mexican income tax was allowed as a credit against a Mexican assets tax, the creditability of the income tax was not affected by the cross-crediting arrangement because the income tax was the credited tax, not tax against which credit was allowed.[128]

This rule can contradict the foreign country's purpose in allowing one tax to be credited against another. Under U.S. law, for example, an income tax credit

---

[124] Reg. §1.901-2(e)(3)(iii).
[125] Reg. §1.901-2(e)(3)(iv) Ex. 3.
[126] Reg. §1.901-2(e)(4)(i).
[127] Reg. §1.903-1(b)(3) Ex. 5.
[128] Rev. Rul. 91-45, 1991-2 CB 336.

is used as a means of refunding gasoline taxes to farmers and users of other off-road vehicles who, Congress decided, should be effectively exempt from the gasoline tax.[129] If a foreign country used an identical scheme, the rule described in the preceding paragraph would treat the taxpayer as having a gasoline tax liability, notwithstanding the refund of this tax through the income tax credit, and the income tax would be reduced by the credit, even though the credit is merely a payment device meant to accomplish a purpose extraneous to the income tax system. The rule can probably be justified on the ground that a rule turning on the policies underlying cross-crediting devices in foreign tax laws would not be administratively feasible for taxpayers or the IRS and that a simple rule of thumb is therefore needed for these devices.

4. *Noncompulsory amounts.* A payment is not a tax unless it is compulsory, and it is not compulsory "to the extent that [it] exceeds the amount of liability under foreign law for tax."[130] To keep its foreign tax payments within its liability, a taxpayer must take all reasonable steps to "reduce, over time, the taxpayer's reasonably expected" foreign tax liability.

The Treasury probably included this rule because it recognized that some taxpayers would otherwise have a strong incentive to follow the path of least resistance in dealing with foreign tax authorities. Assume T's foreign income tax liabilities, however calculated, are less than the credit limitation of §904. Country X undertakes an audit of T's return. In the absence of the compulsory payment rule, T would likely pay any additional tax claimed in the audit without argument. If T's country X tax is increased, the credit against U.S. tax would increase in like amount, and T's worldwide tax liability and after-tax profits would remain unchanged. In contrast, expenses incurred in the audit are deductible but not creditable, and they therefore reduce after-tax profits. After-tax profits would thus be maximized by incurring no expense in minimizing country X taxes, and simply paying whatever the country X authorities demand.

Under the compulsory payment rule, a taxpayer subject to a foreign self-assessment system must determine its liabilities under "a reasonable interpretation and application of the substantive and procedural provisions of foreign law (including applicable tax treaties)."[131] Assume DP, a domestic corporation, buys

---

[129] IRC §34.

[130] Reg. §1.901-2(e)(5)(i). The IRS argued in several cases that U.S. lenders to Brazilian borrowers were not entitled to credit for Brazilian withholding taxes because only the borrowers were liable for payment of the taxes. Norwest Corp. v. CIR, 69 F3d 1404 (8th Cir. 1995), cert. denied, 116 S. Ct. 1704 (1996); Continental Ill. Corp. v. CIR, 998 F2d 513 (7th Cir. 1993), cert. denied, 114 S. Ct. 685 (1994); Nissho Iwai Am. Corp. v. CIR, 89 TC 765 (1987). The courts consistently rejected the argument. See Norwest Corp. v. CIR, supra ("under United States tax law . . . the person obligated to pay the tax is not necessarily the same person to whom legal liability attaches"). But see Riggs Nat'l Corp. v. CIR, 107 TC 301 (1997) (under Brazilian law, remittances by Brazilian Central Bank were exempt from withholding taxes, and taxes bank withheld from interest paid to taxpayer were therefore noncreditable noncompulsory amounts).

[131] Reg. §1.901-2(e)(5)(i).

goods for $1,000 and resells them for $600 to its foreign subsidiary, *FS*, which resells the goods to unrelated persons for $1,200.[132] *FS*, which is subject to tax in its home country (country *X*) at the rate of 3 percent of its net income, pays foreign income tax of $18 (3 percent of the excess of $1,200 over $600). Assume country *X* law requires that transactions between related persons be reported as though they were made at arm's length prices, and the arm's length price for *DP*'s sale to *FS* would be $1,050, as *FS*'s officers know when the foreign tax return is filed. *FS*'s reporting of the transaction at a price of $600 is not a reasonable application of the foreign tax law, and a portion of the foreign tax payment fails to qualify as a tax. This portion is $13.5—the excess of the amount paid ($18) over *FS*'s maximum liability under a reasonable application of foreign law (3 percent of the excess of $1,200 over $1,050, or $4.5).

Tax paid under a particular interpretation or application of foreign law is creditable, even if this interpretation or application is ultimately determined to be wrong, unless the taxpayer either knew or had reason to know that the interpretation or application is not reasonable. An interpretation or application ceases to be reasonable once the taxpayer has "actual notice or constructive notice . . . that the interpretation or application is likely to be erroneous."[133] For example, an adverse court decision can give notice that an interpretation likely is erroneous.

This notice need not come before the foreign tax return is filed; notice received at any time while the foreign tax liability is subject to adjustment must be acted upon. Assume *DP*, a domestic corporation, has regular transactions with *FS*, its country *X* subsidiary.[134] For a particular year, the combined income of *DP* and *FS* from these transactions is $1,000, and it is divided among them on their U.S. and country *X* returns in the proportions $300 to *DP* and $700 to *FS*. A treaty between the United States and country *X* requires that transactions between related persons must be reported using arm's length prices. When *FS* initially determines its country *X* tax liability, it has "no actual or constructive notice" that its treatment of the transactions on its return is "likely to be erroneous" under the treaty rule. Later, the IRS audits *DP*'s return for the year, and $200 of the income reported by *FS* is reallocated to *DP* under §482 of U.S. law and the treaty. The IRS's action is actual notice to *DP* and constructive notice to *FS* that the application of foreign and treaty law in the filing of *FS*'s return is likely to be erroneous. If *FS* does not seek a refund of the foreign tax paid on the $200 of reallocated income, this tax no longer qualifies as a creditable tax.

A taxpayer must "exhaust . . . all effective and practical remedies" for minimizing its foreign income taxes, including any available "foreign audit adjustment" and "competent authority procedures available under applicable tax trea-

---

[132] Reg. §1.901-2(e)(5)(ii) Ex. 1.

[133] Reg. §1.901-2(e)(5)(i).

[134] Reg. §1.901-2(e)(5)(ii) Ex. 2.

ties."[135] Assume a U.S. citizen qualifies for a treaty reduction of a foreign withholding tax, but the foreign country allows the benefit of the reduction to be obtained only by claim for refund of the excess of the statutory withholding rate over the reduced treaty rate.[136] Credit for the refundable amount is denied even if the taxpayer fails to file a claim for refund.

A remedy is considered effective and practical "if the cost thereof . . . is reasonable in light of the amount at issue and the likelihood of success."[137] Assume in the example in the second preceding paragraph that FS files a claim for refund of its home country tax on the reallocated $200 and invokes the competent authority provision of the treaty.[138] Neither of these remedies produces any refund for FS. FS decides that a judicial remedy is not a reasonable alternative in light of the amount at issue and the likelihood of success, and it does nothing further to eliminate the tax on the $200. FS has done all that is required in exhausting its remedies.[139] Similarly, if the statute of limitations has run on FS's right to a refund under foreign and treaty law when the IRS reallocation occurs, FS need not press any claim because it has no effective remedy.[140] Moreover, the risk that "offsetting or additional tax liability" might be asserted against the taxpayer is a cost that may be considered in deciding whether to pursue a remedy.

---

[135] Reg. §1.901-2(e)(5)(i). See International Bus. Mach. v. US, 38 Fed. Cl. 661, 97-2 USTC ¶50,602 (1997) (taxpayer found to have exhausted all practical remedies, even though its claim for refund of foreign tax was still pending in court). Under most income tax treaties, a resident of either country who is subjected to double taxation of a sort meant to be eliminated by the treaties can request that designated tax officials of the two countries (called competent authorities) confer on the taxpayer's situation. See supra ¶65.6.

[136] Reg. §1.901-2(e)(5)(ii) Ex. 6.

[137] Reg. §1.901-2(e)(5)(i).

[138] Reg. §1.901-2(e)(5)(ii) Ex. 3.

[139] The example passes over several difficult issues. How vigorously must FS pursue its claim for refund and request for competent authority consideration? Who decides, the IRS or FS, whether the cost of a judicial remedy is unreasonable in the circumstances? Generally, the question should be asked: "What would a reasonable person do if the person's own money were on the line and there was no possibility of credit against U.S. tax?" If FS's actions and decisions fall within the range of what a reasonable person would do, it should be regarded as having exhausted its remedies, even if some other equally reasonable taxpayer might have pursued the case more vigorously.

[140] Reg. §1.901-2(e)(5)(ii) Ex. 4. Suppose the foreign statute of limitations is open when the IRS begins its audit of DP, but runs before the audit is concluded. Does the constructive notice provided by the IRS reallocation come before or after the statute runs? The overall tone of the compulsory payment rules is one of reasonableness rather than technicality. Given this, FS should be required to file a protective claim for refund if the IRS provides DP with even a preliminary calculation of a §482 adjustment soon enough to allow the preparation and filing of FS's claim before the running of the statute. If a notice of deficiency or final action on judicial proceedings commenced by DP was needed to put FS to its foreign remedies, the statute would frequently run in all foreign countries before the notice came.

The same standard of reasonableness applies to settlements. "A settlement . . . of two or more issues [is] evaluated on an overall basis, not on an issue-by-issue basis."[141]

A taxpayer is not required to avail itself of every tax minimization opportunity. Where foreign law offers timing options, the taxpayer need not exercise these options in any particular way.[142] Credit is not denied, for example, merely because the taxpayer did not defer foreign taxes as long as legally permitted. Assume a foreign tax law allows machinery purchase costs to be expensed immediately or to be depreciated over two, four, six, or 10 years. A taxpayer can elect a 10-year recovery period without jeopardizing the credit.[143] Also, "a taxpayer is not required to alter its form of doing business . . . or the form of any business transaction in order to reduce its liability under foreign law for tax."[144]

"In interpreting foreign tax law, a taxpayer may generally rely on advice obtained in good faith from competent foreign tax advisors to whom the taxpayer has disclosed the relevant facts."[145]

¶69.4.7   Definition of "Separate Foreign Levy"

The tests for determining whether a foreign levy is an income tax or a tax in lieu of an income tax are independently applied to each "separate" exaction under the laws of the taxing country.[146] Whether foreign laws impose a single levy or several separate levies can determine whether the tax on a particular taxpayer is creditable. Assume a foreign tax, as applied to the taxpayer, reaches only realized net income, but in other applications, it also taxes items falling outside the boundaries set by the realization requirement of the regulations. If there is but one tax and its predominant character fails to satisfy the realization requirement, the tax is not creditable because a tax that fails the regulation tests is noncreditable for all taxpayers, including those not affected by the offending features of the foreign tax law. In contrast, if the foreign rules taxing unrealized items can be characterized as a tax separate from the tax paid by the taxpayer, the taxpayer may qualify for credit.

1. *Generally.* Separate levies exist if the base on which the levy is imposed on one class of taxpayers differs "in kind, and not merely in degree," from the base for another class.[147] A separate base may consist of "a particular type of

---

[141] Reg. §1.901-2(e)(5)(i).

[142] Id.

[143] Reg. §1.901-2(e)(5)(ii) Ex. 5. Neither is the credit affected if the taxpayer's selection of recovery period turns out to be unfortunate because, for example, income in later years is insufficient to absorb the depreciation deductions.

[144] Reg. §1.901-2(e)(5)(i).

[145] Id.

[146] Reg. §1.901-2(a).

[147] Reg. §1.901-2(d)(1).

income or . . . an amount unrelated to income, *e.g.*, wages paid." Whether there is one foreign levy or several separate levies is an issue of U.S. law. Whether the levy or levies are imposed by one or several foreign statutes is not determinative.

For example, under U.S. law, the tax on foreign persons doing business in the United States is separate from the tax on citizens, residents, and domestic corporations because the base of the former tax (taxable income effectively connected with U.S. business) differs in kind from the base of the latter (worldwide income).[148] If a foreign tax system mirrors U.S. law in this respect, the creditability of the effectively connected income tax is considered separately from the creditability of the tax on residents. Moreover, if a foreign country has a levy analogous to the effectively connected income tax and also has a withholding tax similar to the one the United States imposes on foreign persons' nonbusiness income, the two are separate taxes.[149]

If a foreign tax liability is "the sum of two or more separately computed amounts," each "computed by reference to a separate base," each element of the sum is a separate levy.[150] Assume a foreign country imposes an annual tax on corporations equal to 15 percent of realized net income plus 3 percent of net wealth. Because the tax is the sum of two amounts computed on different bases, it consists of two levies that are evaluated separately.[151] The portion based on net income probably qualifies as a creditable income tax, whereas the portion based on wealth does not.

------

[148] Also, in the U.S. system, the general corporate income tax, the personal holding company tax, the withholding tax on nonbusiness income of foreign persons, the tax imposed by §1491 on transfers to foreign entities, and the FICA tax on employers are separate taxes because the bases on which they are imposed differ in kind from each other. Reg. §1.901-2(d)(1).

[149] Reg. §1.901-2(d)(3) Ex. 2.

[150] Reg. §1.901-2(d)(1).

[151] Reg. §1.901-2(d)(3) Ex. 1. Assume a foreign country has a schedular tax imposed at the rates and on the bases indicated below:

Base is net income from:	Rate
Mining	45%
Manufacturing	50%
Technical services	50%
Other services	45%
Investments	15%
All other activities	50%

The deductions against gross income of each type are limited to expenses incurred in earning that income. A loss in one category is not allowed as a deduction in any other category. Because of the loss limitation, the bases are separate, and the levy on each category of income is evaluated separately. Reg. §1.901-2(d)(3) Ex. 3. The differing rates are not relevant, and the conclusion would be the same if a single rate applied to all categories. It is also not relevant whether the taxes on the various categories are imposed by one statute or several.

In contrast, separate computations preliminary to an aggregation into a single tax base do not mark separate levies.[152] Assume a foreign tax law provides that gross receipts and allowable costs must initially be computed separately for various types of income, but a loss in any category is deductible against net income of another category subject to the same rate. The loss rule has the effect of aggregating all amounts taxed at the same rate, and each rate category is thus one tax notwithstanding the initial schedular computation.[153] This is so even if the offset of loss against income is deferred to a year after the year in which the loss is incurred.

Levies imposed by one taxing authority are always separate from the levies of other taxing authorities in the same country.[154] A levy of a national government, for example, is separate from a levy of a provincial government or other political subdivision of the national government.

A single tax need not be imposed at a single rate on all taxpayers.[155] Different rate schedules for taxpayers of different family or filing statuses (e.g., married filing jointly, unmarried, married filing separately) do not indicate separate levies. A tax imposed at graduated rates is one tax even though taxpayers are taxed at differing marginal rates. Also, various categories of income can be taxed at different rates, as long as losses can cross category lines.[156]

If a foreign tax law is modified by agreement between the taxing country and one or more taxpayers, the tax on persons governed by the agreement is separate from the tax on all others.[157]

2. *Dual capacity taxpayers.* If the application of a foreign levy is different for dual capacity taxpayers than for other taxpayers, separate levies are considered imposed on these two groups unless the only difference is a lower rate for

---

[152] Reg. §1.901-2(d)(1).

[153] In the example in the second preceding note, if losses are deductible against income of other categories taxed at the same rate, the levy on manufacturing, technical services, and residual net income (taxed at 50 percent) is one tax, the levy on mining and other services income (45 percent) is one tax, and the levy on investment income (15 percent) stands alone. Reg. §1.901-2(d)(3) Ex. 4.

Assume losses of any type are first offset against income subject to the same rate, but if a net loss occurs in any rate category, it is offset against income of other categories according to a prescribed priority. Special treatment is reserved for the investment category; a net loss in all other categories combined is offset against investment income, but a loss in the investment category is never allowed against income of other types. The levies on all types of income are a single tax. Reg. §1.901-2(d)(3) Ex. 5. The rules for ordering loss deductions relate to rates, and a single tax need not be imposed at a constant rate on all income. The special rule for the investment category operates as a limitation on deductions for investment losses, and, as long as other types of losses are allowable against investment income, this limitation does not have the effect of walling this income off into a separate base. Compare IRC §469, discussed supra ¶28.1.

[154] Reg. §1.901-2(d)(1).

[155] Id.

[156] Reg. §1.901-2(d)(3) Ex. 5, discussed supra note 153.

[157] Reg. §1.901-2(d)(2).

dual capacity taxpayers.[158] A dual capacity taxpayer is a person subject to a foreign levy who also receives a specific economic benefit from the government imposing the levy or from a political subdivision or agency of that government.[159] An example is a company that extracts oil and gas from deposits owned by a foreign government and is also subject to an income tax imposed by the government. A levy applied differently to dual capacity and other taxpayers is usually treated as two levies because the difference is considered related to the specific economic benefit received by dual capacity taxpayers and is therefore a distinction in kind, not merely in degree, in the application of the levy to taxpayers in various capacities.

Assume country X has a general income tax under which income is determined with deductions for substantially all business expenses, except that taxpayers engaged in extracting designated minerals, all deposits of which are owned by the government, are permitted no allowance for exploration expenses.[160] Because the rule on exploration expenses applies only to dual capacity taxpayers, the country X tax is treated as two levies, one for dual capacity taxpayers and another for all other taxpayers. For the latter group, the levy is probably a qualifying income tax. The levy on dual capacity taxpayers, however, does not qualify because the denial of any allowance for exploration expenses violates the net income requirement. In contrast, assume the country X government owns only some of the deposits exploited by taxpayers subject to the rule on exploration expenses.[161] In this case, the impost is considered to be a single levy. The nondeductibility of exploration expenses could jeopardize the credit for all taxpayers, but if the predominant character of the country X tax satisfies the net income and all other requirements, the tax is creditable for all taxpayers, including dual capacity taxpayers.

Even if the law imposing a levy makes no distinction between dual capacity and other taxpayers, it is presumed that it is applied differently in practice to the two groups unless the absence of a difference is demonstrated.[162] Assume country X has a general income tax that draws no explicit distinction between dual capacity and other taxpayers, but it is graduated, bars interest paid to related persons from being deducted against income from some activities but not others, and provides net operating loss carrybacks and carryovers for losses incurred in some activities but not others.[163] The tax is treated as a single levy only if it is shown that in practice, the higher rates under the graduated rate table and the limitations on interest and net operating loss deductions apply to both dual capacity and other taxpayers.

---

[158] Reg. §1.901-2A(a)(1).

[159] For the terms "dual capacity taxpayer" and "specific economic benefit," see supra ¶69.4.2.

[160] See Reg. §1.901-2A(a)(2) Ex. 1.

[161] Reg. §1.901-2A(a)(2) Ex. 2.

[162] Reg. §1.901-2A(a)(1).

[163] Reg. §1.901-2A(a)(2) Exs. 3, 4.

If the only difference in the application of a levy to dual capacity and other taxpayers is that the former are given a lower rate, the levy is treated as a single impost, and none of it is considered payment for the specific economic benefit received by dual capacity taxpayers.[164] Assume country X imposes a tax on interest income from country X sources received by foreign corporations not engaged in business in the country; the rate is generally 30 percent, but it is 15 percent for a specified category of corporations, all of which are dual capacity taxpayers.[165] Since the only distinction between dual capacity and other taxpayers is that the former are taxed at a lower rate, the impost is a single levy.

¶69.4A NONCREDITABLE FOREIGN INCOME TAXES

¶69.4A.1 Taxes Paid to Misbehaving Countries

Section 901(j) denies credit for income taxes paid to various foreign countries with which the United States has bad relations.[1] A country's taxes fall under this ban if (1) the United States does not recognize its government,[2] (2) the United States has severed diplomatic relations with the country or does not carry on such relations,[3] or (3) the Secretary of State has designated the country as a repeated provider of "support for acts of international terrorism."[4] As of September 1995, the rule applied

---

[164] Reg. §1.901-2A(a)(1).

[165] Reg. §1.901-2A(a)(2) Ex. 7.

[1] IRC §901(j)(1)(A). Credit for these taxes is denied whether the taxpayer pays them directly or is deemed to have paid them under the indirect credit rules of §902 or §960. See ¶69.8 for the indirect credit.

[2] IRC §901(j)(2)(A)(i). Taxes imposed by such a country are excepted from the disallowance rule, however, if its government is "eligible to purchase defense articles or services under the Arms Export Control Act." The exception is probably intended to allow credit for taxes paid to the Republic of China (Taiwan).

[3] IRC §§901(j)(2)(A)(ii), (iii).

[4] IRC §901(j)(2)(A)(iv). This designation must be made under the Export Administration Act of 1979.

The disallowance rule applies to taxes paid or accrued to such a country after 1986 or, if later, taxes paid or accrued more than six months after the country first comes within one of the proscribed categories. IRC §901(j)(2)(B)(i). The rule ceases to apply when the Secretary of State certifies to the Treasury that the country is no longer within any of the categories. IRC §901(j)(2)(B)(ii). See Rev. Rul. 92-62, 1992-2 CB 193 (when foreign country ceases to be within described categories during taxpayer's taxable year, §901(j) denies credit only for taxes paid to country on income allocated to period ending with cessation date).

The rule also applied to taxes paid to South Africa beginning in 1988 and continuing

to taxes imposed by seven countries.[5]

Deductions are allowed for some taxes made noncreditable by this rule. Normally, §275(a)(4)(A) forbids a taxpayer from deducting any foreign income taxes for a year if credit is claimed for any such taxes for the year. This bar is lifted for taxes that are noncreditable under the misbehaving country rule.[6] Deductions are allowed, however, only for taxes paid directly by the taxpayer. Sections 902 and 960 sometimes treat a domestic corporation as having paid foreign income taxes actually paid by its foreign subsidiaries, but they apply only for credit purposes. The relaxation of the deduction rule thus does not provide any deduction for deemed paid taxes.[7]

¶69.4A.2   Withholding Taxes on Short-Term Holders of Stock

A shareholder is denied credit for a foreign withholding tax on a dividend if the taxpayer held the stock for fewer than 16 days during the 30-day period beginning 15 days before the stock "becomes ex-dividend with respect to such dividend."[8] This rule applies if, for example, a taxpayer purchases stock the day before the ex-dividend date and sells the stock five days later. It was enacted in 1997 because some U.S. persons have "engaged in tax-motivated transactions designed to transfer foreign tax credits from persons that are unable to benefit from such credits (such a tax-exempt entity or a taxpayer whose use of foreign tax credits is prevented by the limitation) to persons that can use such credits."[9]

---

until it abandoned the apartheid system (July 10, 1991), even though that country never fell within any of the categories described in the text. IRC §901(j)(2)(C) (before repeal in 1993).

[5] The countries are Cuba, Iran, Iraq, Libya, North Korea, Sudan, and Syria. Rev. Rul. 95-63, 1995-2 CB 85. Other countries that have been subject to this ban at various times in the past are Afghanistan, Albania, Angola, Cambodia, South Africa, Vietnam, and People's Democratic Republic of Yemen.

[6] IRC §901(j)(3).

[7] See infra ¶69.8.1 text accompanying notes 11–13.

[8] IRC §901(k)(1)(A) (effective for dividends received after September 4, 1997). See Staff of Joint Comm. on Tax'n, 105th Cong., 1st Sess., General Explanation of Tax Legislation Enacted in 1997, at 248 (Comm. Print 1997) [hereinafter 1997 Bluebook] ("No inference is intended as to the treatment under [prior] law of tax-motivated transactions intended to transfer foreign tax credit benefits").

A "withholding tax" is a tax "determined on a gross basis" that is not "in the nature of a prepayment of a tax imposed on a net basis." IRC §901(k)(1)(B). Somewhat redundantly, the statute exempts a securities dealer from the limitation if the dealer is taxed on the dividend on a net basis and the taxing country allows any tax withheld from the dividend to be credited against the net income tax. IRC §901(k)(4).

For the computation of the holding period, see §246(c)(3).

[9] 1997 Bluebook, supra note 8, at 246.

The rule also applies "to the extent that the [taxpayer] is under an obligation (whether pursuant to a short sale or otherwise) to make related payments with respect to positions in substantially similar or related property."[10] If the taxpayer is a domestic corporation owning at least 10 percent of the voting stock of the foreign distributing corporation, no indirect credit is allowed under §902 or §960 with respect to a dividend if a withholding tax on the dividend would not be creditable.[11]

The minimum holding period is extended to 46 days out of the 90-day period beginning 45 days before the ex-dividend date if (1) the stock has "preference in dividends" and (2) the dividends "are attributable to a period or periods aggregating in excess of 366 days."[12] For example, if preferred stock is purchased 10 days before the ex-dividend date for an annual dividend on the stock, credit for a withholding tax on the dividend is allowed only if the taxpayer holds the stock for at least 35 days after the ex-dividend date.

The taxpayer's holding period does not include any time when the taxpayer has an option or contract to sell the stock, has an unclosed short sale of substantially identical stock, is the grantor of an option to buy substantially identical stock, or "has diminished his risk or loss" by a position or positions in "substantially similar or related property."[13] For example, if a taxpayer buys foreign common stock and immediately "enters into an equity swap under which the taxpayer is entitled to receive payments equal to the losses on the stock," the 16-day or 46-day clock does not run as long as the taxpayer retains the swap position.[14]

A tax made noncreditable by these rules is generally allowed as a deduction, even if the taxpayer claims the foreign tax credit for the year.[15]

¶69.4A.3 Antiabuse Rules

Foreign income taxes are generally creditable only to the extent of the precredit U.S. tax on taxable income from foreign sources.[16] Moreover, §904(d) groups foreign source income and the taxes thereon into nine

---

[10] This language is intended to frustrate "the use of derivatives to allow a person that cannot benefit from the foreign tax credits with respect to a dividend to retain the economic benefit of the dividend while another person receives the foreign tax credit benefits." 1997 Bluebook, supra note 8, at 246.

[11] IRC §901(k)(2). The gross-up rule of §78 does not apply when indirect credit is lost under this rule. IRC §901(k)(7).

[12] IRC §901(k)(3).

[13] IRC §§246(c)(4), 901(k)(5), (6).

[14] 1997 Bluebook, supra note 8, at 247.

[15] IRC §901(k)(7).

[16] See infra ¶69.5.

categories (baskets) and restricts the credit for foreign income taxes on income in any basket to the precredit U.S. tax on foreign source taxable income within that basket. Excess foreign tax on an item taxed abroad at rates exceeding the U.S. rate may thus be "cross-credited" against U.S. tax on foreign source income taxed abroad at lesser rates only to the limited extent allowed by §904(d). However, the government has recently expressed concern about a perceived cross-crediting abuse that is not addressed by §904(d).

> Multinational corporations that are subject to relatively low rates of tax on their foreign-source income may be in an excess limitation position. Generally, [except as blocked by the separate limitation rules of §904(d),] such taxpayers may properly use credits for foreign taxes imposed on high-taxed foreign income to offset residual U.S. tax on their low-taxed foreign income. Treasury and the service are concerned, however, that such taxpayers may enter into foreign tax credit-generating schemes designed to abuse the cross-crediting regime and effectively transform the U.S. worldwide system of taxation into a system exempting foreign-source income from residual U.S. tax. . . . No statutory purpose is served by permitting credits for taxes generated in abusive transactions designed to reduce residual U.S. tax on low-taxed foreign-source income. The foreign tax benefits derived from such transactions represent subsidies from the U.S. Treasury to taxpayers that operate and earn income in low-tax or zero-tax jurisdictions.[17]

The IRS has identified two types of transactions, described below, that are abusive of the foreign tax credit rules, and it has promised to issue regulations denying credit in these transactions. Under the regulations, a transaction of either type will be considered abusive if "the reasonably expected economic profit [from the transaction] is insubstantial compared to the value of the foreign tax credits expected to be obtained as a result of the arrangement."[18] The regulations will apply to foreign taxes paid or accrued after December 22, 1997, but "other principles of existing law" may limit credits for foreign taxes incurred earlier.[19]

---

[17] Notice 98-5, 1998-3 IRB 49, I ("The effect is economically equivalent to the tax sparing benefits for U.S. taxpayers that Congress and the Treasury have consistently opposed in the tax treaty context because such benefits are inconsistent with U.S. tax principles and sound tax policy").

[18] Notice 98-5, 1998-3 IRB 49, III. See Dolan, DuPuy & Bower, Notice 98-5: Shoot Now, Aim Later, 27 Tax Mgmt. Int'l J. 174 (1998); Peaslee, Economic Substance Test Abused: Notice 98-5 and the Foreign Law Taxpayer Rule, 79 Tax Notes 79 (Apr. 6, 1998), reprinted in 16 Tax Notes Int'l 1153 (Apr. 13, 1998).

[19] Notice 98-5, 1998-3 IRB 49, IV. See id. V (IRS has established "early coordination procedures" for application of "existing law" to transactions of types identified in Notice).

1. *Purchases of income streams subject to foreign withholding taxes.* If a taxpayer purchases "an asset that generates an income stream subject to foreign gross basis taxes such as withholding taxes," the regulations will treat the transaction as abusive if "the expected economic profit from the arrangement is insubstantial compared to the foreign tax credits generated."[20]

Assume D, a domestic corporation, purchases a foreign patent for $75 shortly before its expiration, when the only anticipated return from the patent is a royalty of $100, which is payable one day after the purchase and which country X will subject to a 30 percent withholding tax.[21] If the expectations hold true, D will incur a pretax loss of $5 ($100 royalty, less $30 of foreign withholding tax and $75 cost basis). However, if, apart from this transaction, D's foreign tax limitation in the relevant basket is at least $30 larger than D's foreign tax liabilities in that basket, the transaction would, in the absence of an antiabuse rule, yield an after-tax profit of $25 ($100 royalty, less $30 withholding tax, plus $30 reduction of U.S. tax, less $75 cost basis). Since the expected pretax profit (zero) is insubstantial in relation to the expected foreign tax credit ($30), the transaction is considered abusive, and the regulations will deny the credit. D might obtain similar results by purchasing a bond of a foreign issuer shortly before an interest payment date and selling the bond a few days after the payment is received.[22]

Other varieties of this type of transaction are "acquisitions in combination with total return swaps."[23] Assume D does the following:

a. Purchases for $1,000 a bond of a foreign issuer providing for annual interest payments of $100, which are subject to country X withholding tax at 4.9 percent,

b. Borrows $1,000 at the LIBOR, and

c. Enters into a three-year swap with F, a foreign corporation, under which (1) D will annually pay $96 to F and receive from F an amount equal to $1,000 times the LIBOR and, (2) at the end of the swap period, D will pay to F or F will pay to D the amount by which the bond's value then exceeds or falls short of $1,000.[24]

If all payments are made when due, D will have an annual pretax loss of $.9 ($100 interest received, less withholding tax of $4.9, and less $96 paid to F); D's annual obligation on its LIBOR borrowing is canceled out by its LIBOR receipt from F. However, if credit is fully allowed for the withholding tax, D has an after-tax profit from the transaction of $4 (U.S. tax reduction of $4.9, less pretax loss of $.9). Since the anticipated economic profit

---

[20] Notice 98-5, 1998-3 IRB 49, II.
[21] Notice 98-5, 1998-3 IRB 49, II Ex. 1.
[22] Notice 98-5, 1998-3 IRB 49, II Ex. 2.
[23] Notice 98-5, 1998-3 IRB 49, II.
[24] Notice 98-5, 1998-3 IRB 49, II Ex. 3.

(negative $.9) is not substantial in relation to the expected foreign tax credit ($4.9), the regulations will deny the credit.

More generally, the regulations will provide that "a purchase of a foreign security coupled with an asset swap that is designed to hedge substantially all of the taxpayer's risk of loss with respect to the security for the duration of the arrangement generally will constitute an abusive foreign tax credit arrangement."[25] However, a hedge of interest rate and currency risks under a debt instrument will not be considered abusive if "other risks (e.g., creditor risk)" are not reduced "for a significant portion of the taxpayer's holding period."

"Transactions described in this class may [also] include acquisitions of income streams through securities loans and similar arrangements."[26]

2. *Cross-border tax arbitrage transactions.* Foreign tax credit abuse can also arise from "cross-border tax arbitrage transactions that permit effective duplication of tax benefits . . . when the U.S. grants benefits and, in addition, a foreign country grants benefits."[27] In this context, the U.S. benefit is the foreign tax credit, and the foreign country benefits can be provided by, for example, "a full or partial imputation or exemption system, or a preferential rate for certain income."

Assume the following:

a. D organizes a subsidiary, S, under the laws of country X and pays $1,000 for all of S's common stock,

b. S receives $9,000 from F, an unrelated country X person, in a transaction that is treated as a loan for U.S. tax purposes but as an equity investment under country X's tax laws,

c. The instrument that S issues to F obligates S to pay F $675 annually,

d. S purchases for $10,000 bonds or preferred stock of unrelated country X corporations on which S will receive annual interest or dividends of $1,000, and

e. Country X, which taxes corporate and individual income at 30 percent, has an imputation system that allows shareholders credit for corporate taxes attributable to dividends received.[28]

S's annual income tax obligation to country X is $300 (30 percent of $1,000 of interest or dividends received). Country X allows S no deduction for the annual payment to F, because it considers the payment to be a dividend, but no country X tax is imposed on F with respect to the dividend, because the imputation credit fully offsets the dividend tax. For U.S. tax purposes, S's earnings and profits are $25 (receipts of $1,000, less interest of $675 paid to F and less country X tax of $300). The earnings and profits are subpart F income (foreign personal holding

---

[25] Notice 98-5, 1998-3 IRB 49, III.

[26] Notice 98-5, 1998-3 IRB 49, II.

[27] Notice 98-5, 1998-3 IRB 49, II.

[28] Notice 98-5, 1998-3 IRB 49, II Ex. 4.

company income) and are therefore included in D's gross income.[29] Absent the antiabuse rule, the inclusion of this gross income would entitle D to a credit for all of F's foreign income taxes ($300).[30] However, under the antiabuse rule, the credit will be denied because the arrangement "exploit[s] the inconsistency between U.S. and country X tax law in order to generate foreign tax credits in a transaction with respect to which the reasonably expected profit [$25] is insubstantial in relation to the expected U.S. foreign tax credits [$300]."[31]

3. *Promised regulations.* The IRS has promised to issue regulations denying the foreign tax credit otherwise flowing from a transaction if "the reasonably expected economic profit [from the transaction] is insubstantial compared to the value of the foreign tax credits expected to be obtained as a result of the arrangement."[32] "The regulations will emphasize an objective approach to calculating expected economic profit and credits, and will require that the determination of expected economic profit reflect the likelihood of realizing both potential gain and potential loss (including loss in excess of the taxpayer's investment)." Notional principal contracts, forwards, and other "executory financial contracts" will be ignored in determining expected economic profit if they "do not represent a real economic investment or potential for profit" or "are not properly treated as part of the arrangement." Future payments will be discounted to present value.

Foreign tax consequences will usually be included in the computation of reasonably expected economic profits, but "foreign tax savings" resulting from the transaction may be ignored. U.S. taxes are always ignored at this point in the analysis.

The regulations will apply separately to each "discrete" arrangement, purportedly separate transactions will be aggregated, and purportedly integrated transactions will be disaggregated as necessary to achieve the regulations' purposes.

---

[29] See IRC §§951(a)(1), 954(c), discussed supra ¶68.2.

[30] Under §960, a domestic corporation including earnings and profits of a foreign corporation in gross income under §951(a)(1) is treated as having paid foreign income taxes equal to the foreign corporation's foreign income taxes ($300), multiplied by the amount of the gross income inclusion ($25) and divided by the foreign corporation's earnings and profits ($25). See infra ¶69.8.7.

[31] In another example, S's receipts are dividends from country Y corporations, subject to country Y withholding taxes, but because country X treats F as a shareholder, whereas F is a creditor under U.S. tax law and because S is treated as fiscally transparent under the tax laws of both country X and the United States, F takes a foreign tax credit under country X law for most of S's country Y tax, and D takes credit for the entire tax under U.S. law. Notice 98-5, 1998-3 IRB 49, II Ex. 5.

[32] Notice 98-5, 1998-3 IRB 49, III.

¶69.5 CREDIT LIMITATION—IN GENERAL

¶69.5.1 Introductory

Under §904(a), the credit for foreign income taxes may not exceed the U.S. tax (before the credit) on income from foreign sources.[1] This limitation is an important aspect of determining the policy of the credit to eliminate double taxation for U.S. persons. A U.S. person is subject to double taxation when income from foreign sources is taxed both by the United States (which taxes U.S. persons on worldwide income) and by the foreign country in which the income is earned. Double taxation is eliminated by allowing foreign income taxes to be credited against U.S. tax on foreign source income only. Section 904 thus bars the credit from being taken against U.S. tax on U.S. income.

The effect of §904(a) is that a taxpayer's worldwide tax liability on foreign source income equals the precredit U.S. tax on the income or the foreign tax, whichever is higher. If the precredit U.S. tax is higher than the foreign tax, the latter is fully creditable; however, it does not fully offset U.S. tax on the income, with the result that the sum of the foreign and U.S. taxes, after the credit, equals the precredit U.S. tax. If the foreign tax is the higher of the two, the credit reduces U.S. tax on foreign source income to zero, but the excess of the foreign tax over the precredit U.S. tax produces no immediate U.S. tax benefit. The foreign tax thus is the final tax liability on the income.

1. *Source rules.* The §904 limitation is determined using the source rules of U.S. law.[2] When foreign countries tax U.S. persons on income that the United States treats as U.S. source income, the limitation can frustrate the fundamental purpose of the credit to alleviate double taxation. Assume a domestic corporation performs architectural services in the United States for a construction project in foreign country *X*. Under U.S. law, services income has its source where the services are performed—the United States in this case.[3] Assume that under the tax laws of country *X*, the domicile of the recipient of a service is the source of the services performer's income. The corporation is thus taxed by country *X* on income that the U.S. source rules treat as domestic income. Unless the corpo-

---

[1] See IRC §904(i) (authorizing regulations requiring corporations to compute credit limitation on consolidated basis if they are affiliated corporations or would be under broader definition of "affiliation"); TD 8627, 1995-2 CB 86 (issuing such regulations as Reg. §1.904(i)-1); Fischl & Panitch, IRS Issues Final Section 904(i) Deconsolidated Regulations, 25 Tax Mgmt. Int'l J. 104 (1996).

See also Grubert, Randolph & Rousslang, Country and Multi-National Company Responses to the Tax Reform Act of 1986, 49 Nat'l Tax J. 341 (1996) (1986 reduction of U.S. corporate tax rate caused §904 limitation to be substantially less than foreign income tax liabilities for many U.S. multinationals, which created incentives for companies to reduce foreign taxes; probably as result, average foreign tax rates declined from 1983 to 1992).

[2] See infra ¶69.5.2.

[3] IRC §861(a)(3), discussed infra ¶70.4.

ration has other income from foreign sources, its §904 limitation is zero, and the foreign tax is not creditable.

As a consequence, double taxation may go unabated. The U.S. approach, however, is not necessarily wrong. When a country undertakes to mitigate double taxation for its residents, it gives up primary taxing jurisdiction over income its residents earn in other countries. This undertaking need not extend to whatever income other countries might choose to tax. A country's source rules are a means of classifying income between income the country claims primary jurisdiction to tax and income as to which it yields primary jurisdiction to other countries. When countries disagree on source characterizations, the country of the taxpayer's residence, even though generally committed to a policy of eliminating double taxation of its residents, is not necessarily the country that should concede the disputed point. For example, bilateral income tax treaties may be used as a vehicle for resolving source disputes.

2. *Overall limitation.* Section 904(a) states the limitation on an overall basis, restricting the credit for any taxable year to the U.S. tax, before credit, multiplied by the following fraction:

$$\frac{\text{Taxable income from sources without the United States}}{\text{Entire taxable income}}$$

By rearranging the terms of this formula, the limitation may be stated as taxable income from sources without the United States, multiplied by

$$\frac{\text{Precredit U.S. tax}}{\text{Entire taxable income}}$$

The fraction is the effective rate of precredit tax. Thus, for a corporation taxed under §11 at a flat 35 percent, the maximum credit is 35 percent of taxable income from sources without the United States.

Assume a domestic corporation has taxable income for a particular year of $1,000, $100 of which is from foreign sources; the corporation's U.S. tax, before credit, is $350. The overall limitation is:

$$(\$350)\ (\$100/\$1,000) = \$35$$

The credit is the lesser of the taxpayer's foreign income taxes or the §904 limitation. If foreign income taxes for the year are $40, the credit is $35. If foreign taxes are $30, the credit is $30.

3. *Modifications for capital gains and losses.* The limitation is modified in several ways for taxpayers who have capital gains and losses.[4] These modifications were introduced in 1976 so that the limitation would better reflect the restrictions on capital loss deductions and the preferential treatment of net capital gain.

4. *Separate limitations.* Further complications are added by §904(d), which requires that the limitation be computed separately with respect to nine categories of income—eight specially defined categories and a residual category consisting of all income not within any of the special categories.[5] Section 904(d), enacted in its present form in 1986, is intended to limit the averaging of foreign tax rates that otherwise occurs under the overall limitation. Under an overall limitation, foreign income taxes are fully creditable if the average foreign tax rate does not exceed the U.S. rate.[6]

Assume a domestic corporation has two items of foreign source income, $100 of business income subject to a foreign tax of $50 and $100 of interest income on which foreign tax of $10 is paid. If the taxpayer is taxed in the United States at 35 percent and the §904 limitation is computed on an overall basis, the foreign taxes of $60 are fully creditable because they are less than the precredit U.S. tax on foreign source income of $70 (35 percent of $200). In other words, full credit is allowed because the average foreign tax rate of 30 percent (sum of $50 and $10 divided by the sum of $100 and $100) is less than the U.S. rate of 35 percent.

The policy to eliminate double taxation requires no more than that the foreign tax on an item of foreign source income be creditable against U.S. tax on that income. In the example, double taxation would be fully ameliorated if credit were allowed for $35 of the $50 tax on the highly taxed item and all of the $10 tax on the lightly taxed item. Just as credit against U.S. tax on U.S. income is not needed to eliminate double taxation, double taxation can be avoided without allowing foreign tax on one foreign item to be credited against U.S. tax on another foreign item.

A per-income-item limitation, however, probably is neither feasible nor desirable. Because of the "integrated nature of U.S. multinational operations abroad," income items and their associated taxes are often not as distinct from one another as the example implies, and a certain amount of cross crediting is

---

[4] See infra ¶69.5.3.

[5] See infra ¶69.6.

[6] See Staff of Joint Comm. on Tax'n, 99th Cong., 2d Sess, General Explanation of the Tax Reform Act of 1986, at 862 (Comm. Print 1987) [hereinafter 1986 Bluebook] ("The overall limitation allows taxpayers to credit high foreign taxes paid on one stream of income against the residual U.S. tax otherwise due on other, lightly taxed foreign income").

needed to reflect business realities.[7] Congress believed, however, that rate averaging "distort[s] the purpose of the foreign tax credit limitation" when it provides "an incentive at the margin to place new investments abroad rather than in the United States."[8] Under an overall limitation, this incentive arises whenever a taxpayer has income taxed abroad at rates higher than the U.S. rate because the high-rate foreign taxes can be credited against U.S. tax on any more lightly taxed items the taxpayer can generate.[9] In the example, the 50 percent tax on the taxpayer's business income encourages the taxpayer to seek out or retain the investment producing income taxed at 10 percent. "[I]nvestments that can quickly and easily be made in foreign countries rather than at home" are especially affected by any such incentive; "portfolio investments in stock in publicly traded companies" are an example.[10]

Congress decided that the proper balance between necessary rate averaging and perverse investment incentives can be obtained by grouping income into categories and limiting credit for foreign taxes on income in each category to the precredit U.S. tax on that income. Each of the eight separate limitation categories set up by §904(d) consists of an income type that "frequently bear[s] little foreign tax or abnormally high foreign tax, or [is] relatively manipulable as to source."[11] The residual category consists primarily of business income that is taxed under the general income tax rates of the source countries.

5. *Overall foreign losses.* Section 904(f) restricts the limitation in another way to meet problems perceived to arise when U.S. persons have foreign losses.[12] The provision has two aspects, one designed to preserve the walls between the various categories of foreign income under §904(d) and the other to preserve the wall between foreign and U.S. income. The policy of §904(f) is as follows: If, for a particular taxable year, a taxpayer has a loss of one type and income of another type, the loss is deductible against the income, with the consequence that U.S. tax is reduced in the income category. If the taxpayer later has income in the loss category, Congress decided, the income should be reassigned to the income

---

[7] 1986 Bluebook, supra note 6, at 862. See id. at 867 ("it is frequently appropriate to allow cross-crediting of taxes paid by one unit of a worldwide business against income earned by another unit of that business")

[8] Id. at 862.

[9] Another consequence of an overall limitation is that as long as aggregate foreign income taxes do not exceed the limitation, the U.S. credit relieves pressure to minimize foreign taxes. Such a taxpayer may have little incentive to be tough with foreign tax administrators because a reduction of a foreign tax is matched by an equal increase in U.S. tax. (Less foreign tax means less credit, which means more U.S. tax after the credit.) But see Reg. §1.901-2(e)(5) (no credit unless taxpayer exhausts reasonable and practical remedies for minimizing foreign tax), supra ¶69.4.6 text accompanying notes 130–45. Similarly, foreign governments have little incentive to alter tax rules that impact harshly on U.S. businesses but do not affect others. See 1986 Bluebook, supra note 6, at 862.

[10] 1986 Bluebook, supra note 6, at 862.

[11] Id. at 863.

[12] See infra ¶69.7.

category to make up the loss deduction so that the integrity of the categorization is preserved over the long run.

Assume a domestic corporation has a category 1 loss of $100 in year 1 and category 1 income of $100 in year 2; in category 2, it has income of $200 in both years. In year 1, the category 1 loss is deducted against category 2 income, and net income of $100 in category 2 is reported. In year 2, $100 of category 1 income is reallocated to category 2, and $300 of category 2 income is reported. Over the two years, the taxpayer has no category 1 income, and $400 of category 2 income, which faithfully reflects reality (offsetting loss and income in category 1 and $200 of category 2 income in each year). Categories 1 and 2 could be two of the nine limitation categories of §904(d), or they could be overall foreign and U.S. income. Under §904(f), the details of the rules differ some in these two contexts, but the basic approach is the same.

6. *Carrybacks and carryovers of noncreditable taxes.* Under §904(c), foreign income taxes in excess of the §904 limitation are carried back two years and forward five years. Credit is allowed in a year to which the taxes are carried to the extent foreign income taxes for the carryback or carryover year are less than the limitation for that year.[13]

¶69.5.2 Source Rules

The numerator of the §904 fraction is taxable income from sources without the United States—that is, gross income from foreign sources less the deductions allocated and apportioned to that income.[14] If the taxpayer has income in more than one of the §904(d) categories, a separate fraction is constructed for each category, and the numerator of each fraction is foreign source taxable income within that category.[15] The source of gross income is usually determined for this purpose by the source rules that apply throughout the Code, and the allocation and apportionment rules of general application are used to identify the deductions that enter into the computation of the numerator.[16]

One source rule, however, is provided for exclusive use in applying the credit limitation. This rule, §904(g), was enacted in 1984 to block credit claimants from artificially increasing the limitation by routing U.S. source income through foreign corporations in order to attach a foreign source label to the income.[17] Assume a domestic corporation borrows from a foreign subsidiary that is actively engaged in business only in foreign countries; the parent pays interest on the loan, but the

---

[13] See infra ¶69.5.4.

[14] IRC §§862(b), 904(a).

[15] For §904(d), see infra ¶69.6.

[16] See infra ¶70.1. See generally Finlayson, U.S. Source Income Earned by Foreign Branches and Affiliates, 47 Tax Lawyer 349, 372-84 (1994).

[17] For the relationship of §904(g) to the separate limitation rules of §904(d), see Reg. §§1.904-5(m), (n).

subsidiary returns the amount so paid to the parent as a dividend. The subsidiary's interest income is from U.S. sources, but it might not be taxed by the United States or any foreign country.[18] When the subsidiary distributes this income to the parent as a dividend, the parent's dividend income is from foreign sources under the usual source rules for dividends,[19] and, in the absence of §904(g), it would increase the parent's credit limitation. If this occurred without any increase in foreign tax liabilities, the inflated limitation would permit credit to be taken for foreign taxes imposed on other income at rates exceeding U.S. rates.

Congress found this result inconsistent with "a fundamental premise of the credit—that it should offset only U.S. tax on foreign income, and not U.S. tax on U.S. source income."[20] Domestic income beneficially owned by U.S. persons, Congress concluded, should retain its U.S. source characterization for credit purposes, even if it is earned indirectly through a foreign corporation. Section 904(g) accomplishes this in the example by reassigning the parent's dividend income, at least in part, to domestic sources and thereby deflating the limiting fraction.[21]

1. *Taxpayers and income subject to resourcing.* Section 904(g) applies to various types of income recognized by shareholders and creditors of a foreign corporation if U.S. persons own at least 50 percent of the corporation's stock, by voting power or value.[22] For purposes of the 50 percent test, stock owned by a foreign entity is attributed ratably to its shareholders.[23] For example, if domestic corporation P owns 50 percent of the stock of foreign corporation $F1$, which owns all of the stock of foreign corporation $F2$, 50 percent of $F1$'s $F2$ stock is attributed to P, and both $F1$ and $F2$ thus meet the 50 percent test. Also, a U.S.

---

[18] The subsidiary, for example, might be a resident of a country that has a treaty with the United States by which each country agrees not to tax interest income of residents of the other. Even in the absence of a treaty, the internal tax laws of the subsidiary's country of residence might not tax residents on portfolio interest income from foreign sources.

[19] Under §862(a)(2), a dividend from a foreign corporation is from foreign sources if the corporation has no income effectively connected with business carried on in the United States. See infra ¶70.3.

[20] Staff of Joint Comm. on Tax'n, 98th Cong., 2d Sess., General Explanation of the Revenue Provisions of the Tax Reform Act of 1984, at 347 (Comm. Print 1984) [hereinafter 1984 Bluebook].

[21] This deflation occurs even if the taxpayer has an overall loss for the year in which the §904(g) item is recognized because §904(g) is applied before the overall foreign loss rule of §904(f). IRC §904(g)(8). In a year in which a taxpayer has an overall foreign loss, the resourcing of gross income items from foreign to domestic thus has the effect of increasing the overall foreign loss. Under §904(f), an overall foreign loss is applied in subsequent years in reduction of foreign source taxable income. By increasing the overall foreign loss, §904(g) thus has the effect of causing more future income to be resourced from foreign to domestic. See infra ¶69.7 for §904(f).

[22] IRC §§904(g)(1), (6). The term "U.S. persons" includes U.S. citizens and residents, domestic corporations, and estates and trusts that are taxed as residents. IRC §§904(g)(6), 7701(a)(30).

[23] IRC §§904(g)(6), 958(a)(2).

person is treated as owner of any stock it has an option to acquire.[24] If *P* in the example owns no *F1* stock but has an option to acquire 50 percent of the stock, it is treated as a 50 percent shareholder of both *F1* and *F2*.

When the 50 percent test is satisfied, §904(g) applies to the following types of income:[25]

a. Dividends and interest from the foreign corporation.
b. Income of the corporation taxed to U.S. shareholders under subpart F if the corporation is a controlled foreign corporation (CFC).[26]
c. Amounts taxed to U.S. persons under the foreign personal holding company (FPHC) rules if the corporation is an FPHC.[27]
d. Amounts taxed to U.S. owners under the rules for passive foreign investment companies (PFICs) if the corporation is a PFIC and an election has been made to pass the PFIC's income through to its shareholders.[28]

Section 904(g) also applies to two types of items from domestic corporations—interest from so-called 80-20 companies and dividends from a corporation qualifying for the possessions credit of §936.[29] An 80-20 company is a domestic corporation at least 80 percent of whose gross income is from foreign sources and is earned in the active conduct of business in foreign countries.[30] Interest received from an 80-20 company is usually from foreign sources, but it is subject to resourcing under §904(g) under the same circumstances as interest received from foreign corporations, with one difference. Interest from a foreign corporation is subject to §904(g) only if the corporation is at least 50 percent U.S. owned. This limitation does not apply to interest from an 80-20 corporation.

2. *Dividends.* When §904(g) applies, a dividend that would otherwise be from foreign sources is recharacterized as U.S. source income to the extent it is paid from domestic source earnings and profits of the distributing corporation.[31] In applying this rule, a dividend is first traced to the earnings and profits of a particular year or years.[32] A dividend from any year's earnings and profits is

---

[24] IRC §§318(a)(4), 904(g)(6).

[25] IRC §904(g)(1)(A).

[26] For CFCs, see supra ¶68.2.

[27] For FPHCs, see supra ¶68.3.

[28] For PFICs, see supra ¶68.5.

[29] IRC §904(g)(9). For the §936 credit, see supra ¶67.2.

[30] IRC §§861(a)(1)(A), (c), discussed infra ¶70.2 text accompanying notes 7-15.

[31] IRC §904(g)(4). The term "dividend" includes gain on a sale of stock of a foreign corporation if (1) the corporation is or has been a CFC and §1248 characterizes the gain as a dividend or (2) the corporation is a foreign investment company and §1246 makes the gain ordinary income. IRC §904(g)(7). See supra ¶68.2.16 for §1248 and ¶68.4 for §1246.

[32] The statute does not provide an ordering rule for determining what year's earnings and profits are the source of a dividend. Generally, earnings and profits are lumped into two pools—earnings and profits of the current year, which are the first source of a dividend, and accumulated earnings and profits, which is dipped into when current earnings and profits are exhausted. IRC §316(a). In this context, however, prior years' earn-

recharacterized as U.S. source income in an amount equal to the dividend multiplied by the following fraction:

$$\frac{\text{Earnings and profits from U.S. sources for the year}}{\text{Earnings and profits for the year}}$$

For example, if one third of a foreign corporation's earnings and profits for a particular year[33] are from U.S. sources, one third of a dividend from these earnings is U.S. source income if §904(g) applies.

The dividend rule is subject to a de minimis limitation: None of a foreign source dividend is reassigned to U.S. sources if U.S. source income accounts for less than 10 percent of the earnings and profits from which the dividend is paid.[34] Earnings and profits, however, are determined for purposes of the de minimis rule without deductions for interest subject to the resourcing rules described immediately below.

3. *Interest.* When §904(g) applies, interest that would otherwise be from foreign sources is U.S. source income to the extent it is attributable to U.S. source income of the payor and is paid or accrued to a U.S. shareholder of the payor or a person related to a U.S. shareholder.[35] The rules for allocating and apportioning the payor's deduction for the interest also determine the portion of the recipient's interest income that is traced to the payor's U.S. source income.[36] Interest income subject to §904(g) thus is from U.S. sources to the extent the payor's deduction for the interest is taken against U.S. source income. Under the deduction rules, interest expense is usually allocated among income of various classes in proportion to the values of the assets used in activities and investments that produce the income.[37] If the payor is a CFC, however, interest paid to U.S. shareholders is

---

ings and profits are not pooled into a single accumulated earnings account. Perhaps an ordering rule can be drawn from the pre-1987 version of §902, under which dividends are first traced to current earnings and then to prior years' earnings, beginning with the immediately preceding year. See infra ¶69.8.3 text accompanying notes 60-74.

[33] The term "earnings and profits . . . from sources within the United States" is not defined. It should consist of the foreign corporation's taxable income from U.S. sources for the year, increased and decreased by the adjustments normally made in converting taxable income into earnings and profits, but taking into account only adjustments associated with U.S. source taxable income. For example, the subtraction for income taxes, which is the most common and often the largest of the adjustments, should be limited in this context to taxes on U.S. source income. See Reg. §1.904-5(m)(4). See infra ¶92.1.3 for more on earnings and profits.

[34] IRC §904(g)(5).

[35] IRC §904(g)(3).

[36] H.R. Rep. No. 861, 98th Cong., 2d Sess. 919 (Conf. Rep. 1984).

[37] IRC §863(e); Reg. §1.861-8(e)(2), discussed infra ¶70.10.2.

allocated first to income of the CFC that is passive income under the separate limitation rules of §904(d).[38]

Assume a foreign corporation pays interest of $30 to its U.S. parent.[39] For the year of the payment, the corporation's income (before the allocation of interest expense) consists of $10 of interest income on a $100 deposit with a U.S. bank, $15 of interest on a $100 obligation of a domestic subsidiary of the parent, and a net loss of $25 from foreign manufacturing operations in which assets of $300 are used. Because the CFC's interest income is passive, it is the first source for the interest payment to the parent; $25 (the sum of $10 and $15) of the $30 paid as interest to the parent is traced to this income. Because the income is from U.S. sources, $25 of the parent's interest income is also from U.S. sources. The remaining $5 of the parent's interest income is allocated to the CFC's manufacturing income. It is foreign source income if the manufacturing income is from foreign sources. If the manufacturing income is partially from U.S. sources, the interest allocable to this income is further subdivided, this time in proportion to the values of the assets of the U.S. and foreign operations, and the portion placed on the U.S. side is domestic source income to the parent.

The interest rule is subject to two limitations. First, it does not apply unless the recipient of the interest either is a U.S. shareholder of the payor or is related to such a shareholder.[40] A U.S. shareholder is a U.S. person who owns at least 10 percent of the foreign corporation's voting stock.[41] Second, if the payor has earnings and profits for the year in which interest is paid or accrued, the rule does not apply unless at least 10 percent of the earnings and profits consists of U.S. income.[42]

---

[38] IRC §954(b)(5); Reg. §§1.904-5(c)(2), (m)(2); 1986 Bluebook, supra note 6, at 894. See infra ¶69.6.2 for passive income under §904(d).

[39] H.R. Rep. No. 861, supra note 36, at 922-23.

[40] IRC §904(g)(3)(B). Relatedness is determined under §267(b). See infra ¶78.3 for §267(b).

The Treasury has the power to extend the provision by regulations to cover interest received by persons who are neither U.S. shareholders nor related to such shareholders. IRC §904(g)(11)(B). No such regulations have yet been promulgated. "Such regulations might be necessary in the case of U.S.-owned foreign corporations not all of whose U.S. owners are 10-percent U.S. shareholders." 1984 Bluebook, supra note 20, at 349. Since the term "U.S. shareholder" applies only to shareholders of foreign corporations, regulatory clarification is also needed in the application of the rules to interest from domestic corporations classified as 80-20 corporations. See supra notes 29–30 and accompanying text.

[41] IRC §§904(g)(3)(B), 951(b), discussed supra ¶68.2.2.

[42] IRC §904(g)(5). Earnings and profits are determined for this purpose without deduction for interest that is resourced under §904(g), apart from the earnings and profits limitation.

Assume a foreign corporation has an earnings and profits deficit for the year of $25, determined with a deduction for $100 of interest paid to a U.S. shareholder. For purposes of this limitation, earnings and profits are $75 (the $25 deficit, restated by eliminating the

4. *Gross income inclusions under subpart F, foreign personal holding company rules, and passive foreign investment company election.* When §904(g) applies to income of a foreign corporation taxable to a U.S. person under subpart F, the FPHC rules, or a PFIC election, the income has the same source to the U.S. taxpayer as it has in the hands of the foreign corporation.[43] Assume a foreign subsidiary of a domestic corporation has $100 of insurance income that is subpart F income and therefore taxable to the parent.[44] If $90 of the $100 is earned by the insurance of U.S. risks, this $90 is domestic source income to the subsidiary, and §904(g) requires that this source characterization adhere to the income in the parent's return.

The rules for subpart F, FPHC, and PFIC inclusions contain no analogue to the de minimis limitations for dividends and interest.[45] Assume that for a particular year, a CFC has earnings and profits of $100 and accrues interest of $20 on an obligation owing to a domestic corporation owning 90 percent of its stock; the CFC's only U.S. source income for the year is a dividend of $6, to which is allocated $1 of the interest payment and no other deductions.[46] Because less than 10 percent of the CFC's earnings and profits are from domestic sources,[47] none of the parent's interest income is resourced. However, the parent's subpart F inclusion (90 percent of subpart F income) includes domestic source income of the CFC of $4.5 (90 percent of the net dividend income of $5). This portion of the inclusion is resourced under §904(g) even though the U.S. portion of earnings and profits is less than 10 percent.

5. *Coordination with treaties.* If §904(g)'s characterization of an item conflicts with the source characterization given the item by a treaty, §904(g) overrides the treaty unless the taxpayer elects to give precedence to the treaty.[48] If the election is made, a separate credit limitation is computed for this item alone, and the indirect credit rules of §§902 and 960 are also applied separately to the item.

When §904(g) applies to a U.S. shareholder's gross income inclusion under subpart F, the election can be made whether or not the treaty provides a source characterization for the inclusion if a taxable dividend distribution of the corporate income comprising the inclusion would be from foreign sources under the treaty. When the election applies to a subpart F inclusion, the inclusion is from

---

deduction for the $100 of interest), and the earnings and profits limitation applies if less than 10 percent of this $75 is from U.S. sources.

[43] IRC §904(g)(2); Reg. §§1.904-5(m)(5), (6). See supra ¶68.2.1 for subpart F, ¶68.3.1 for FPHCs, and ¶68.5.1 for PFICs.

[44] H.R. Rep. No. 861, supra note 36, at 921. For insurance income under subpart F, see supra ¶68.2.3.

[45] 1984 Bluebook, supra note 20, at 349.

[46] H.R. Rep. No. 861, supra note 36, at 921-22.

[47] Earnings and profits are specially restated as $120 (the sum of $100 under the usual definition of "earnings and profits" and the $20 paid as interest to the parent). IRC §904(g)(5) (last sentence), discussed supra text accompanying note 42. The U.S. source portion of these earnings and profits is 5 percent ($6/$120).

[48] IRC §904(g)(10).

foreign sources, but the limitation and indirect credit rules are applied separately to the inclusion.

6. *Antiavoidance regulations.* The Treasury is instructed to take special care to assure that §904(g) is not avoided by the use of multiple entities.[49] Assume a domestic corporation is sole shareholder of foreign corporation *F1*, which receives U.S. source dividends that would normally be taxable to the parent under subpart F.[50] The rule described in the preceding paragraph would characterize the subpart F inclusion as domestic source income. *F1*, however, pays interest to another foreign subsidiary of the parent (*F2*) in an amount sufficient to reduce its earnings and profits to zero. Because a subpart F inclusion cannot exceed current earnings and profits, the parent has no subpart F inclusion on account of *F1*. The interest received by *F2* is included in the parent's gross income under subpart F. Strictly applied, §904(g) would not reach this inclusion because *F2*'s interest income, having been received from a foreign corporation, is not from U.S. sources. The legislative history directs that the regulations apply §904(g) to resource the inclusion by carrying the U.S. source character of *F1*'s dividends through to *F2*'s interest income and then to the parent's subpart F inclusion from *F2*. No such regulations have yet been promulgated.

¶69.5.3 Capital Gains and Losses

Section 904(b) requires several adjustments to the credit limitation to reflect the special treatment of capital gains and losses. Some of them are adjustments for a preferential rate for long-term capital gains and thus have no application for years when no rate preference is allowed (1987 through 1990 for individuals and after 1986 for corporations).[51] Other adjustments reflect the limitations on capital loss deductions, and they apply in all years.

1. *Gains and losses subject to the rules.* The §904(b) rules apply to all capital gains and losses. Normally, a gain or loss is capital if it is recognized on a sale or exchange of a capital asset.[52] Depreciable property and land used in a trade or business are not capital assets.[53] Under §1231(a), however, gains and losses on dispositions of such property are treated as capital if net gain is recognized on all such dispositions for the year or as ordinary income and loss if net loss is recognized on these transactions.[54] Gains and losses treated as capital under §1231 are considered capital for purposes of §904(b).[55] In applying §904(b),

---

[49] IRC §904(g)(11)(A).

[50] H.R. Rep. No. 861, supra note 36, at 920-21.

[51] For the capital gains rate preference, see supra ¶50.3.1.

[52] IRC §§1222(1)-(4).

[53] IRC §1221(2).

[54] See supra ¶54.1.

[55] IRC §904(b)(3)(C).

§1231 gains and losses are first netted without regard to source.[56] If the netting produces gain, the §1231 gains and losses are treated as capital in determining the credit limitation, even if there is net loss on foreign transactions. Conversely, if the overall net amount is a loss, the gains and losses are ordinary gains and losses, and no adjustments are made for them under §904(b).

On the other hand, gain or loss on a sale or exchange of a capital asset is excluded in applying §904(b) if any provision of the Code requires that it be treated as ordinary income or loss.[57] For example, gain on a sale of stock of a foreign corporation is excluded to the extent §1248 treats it as a dividend.[58]

2. *Foreign gains offset by U.S. losses.* If a taxpayer has net gain for the year from all foreign capital transactions, but net loss from all domestic capital transactions, the net foreign gain is reduced in the numerator of the §904 fraction by the net domestic loss.[59] Assume a taxpayer has two capital transactions during a year; one yields foreign source gain of $100, and a domestic loss of $80 is recognized on the other. Ordinarily, a loss enters into the computation of taxable income from foreign sources (the numerator of the §904 fraction) only if the deduction for the loss is allocated to foreign income. In the example, however, because the taxpayer has net foreign gain and net domestic loss from capital transactions, the domestic capital loss is deducted from the foreign gain in the numerator, and capital gains transactions thus add only $20 to foreign source taxable income.

The concept underlying this rule is as follows: Because capital losses are usually deductible only against capital gains,[60] a net domestic loss from capital transactions is only deductible to the extent of net foreign gain from such transactions. The net domestic loss thus effectively eliminates U.S. tax on an equal amount of net foreign gain. When foreign gain is taxed abroad but is effectively sheltered from U.S. tax by the deduction for domestic loss, the foreign tax is the only tax on the gain, and no credit for that tax is needed to abrogate double taxation. Foreign gain offset by domestic loss is removed from the numerator of the §904 fraction in order to restrict credit in this situation.

Mechanically, the rule works as follows: Taxable income from foreign sources (the numerator of the fraction) includes gains from sales and exchanges of capital assets only to the extent of "foreign source capital gain net income."[61]

---

[56] Reg. §1.904(b)-1(b)(8).

[57] Reg. §1.904(b)-1(b)(1).

[58] For §1248, see supra ¶68.2.16.

[59] IRC §§904(b)(2)(A), (B)(i). For purposes of these rules, the source of income rules determine whether a gain is domestic or foreign, and the rules for allocating and apportioning deductions are used in sourcing losses. Reg. §1.904(b)-1(b)(7). For the source and deduction allocation rules, see infra ¶70.1.

[60] Corporations are never allowed an immediate deduction for an excess of capital losses over capital gains. IRC §1211(a). Other taxpayers can deduct up to $3,000 of such an excess. IRC §1211(b). See supra ¶¶50.2.5, 50.3.2.

[61] IRC §§904(b)(2)(A), (B)(i).

The latter term is defined as the lesser of "capital gain net income from sources without the United States or . . . capital gain net income."[62] Capital gain net income is an excess of capital gains—short-term and long-term—over capital losses.[63] Capital gain net income from sources without the United States is an excess of capital gains from foreign sources over capital losses allocated to foreign income.

When capital gain net income from all sources is larger than foreign source capital gain net income, this rule has no effect because it says no more than that capital gains and losses enter into foreign source taxable income only if they are from foreign sources. When foreign source capital gain net income is larger than capital gain net income from all sources—that is, when domestic capital gains transactions produce a net loss—the rule effectively removes from foreign source taxable income an amount of gain from foreign transactions equal to the net domestic capital loss.

In the example, foreign source capital gain net income is $20—the lesser of capital gain net income from sources without the United States ($100) or capital gain net income ($20, consisting of the foreign gain of $100 reduced by the domestic loss of $80). Only $20 of the foreign gain is included in the numerator of the §904 fraction.

3. *Adjustments for rate preference.* For noncorporate taxpayers, the numerator and denominator of the §904 fraction are adjusted for the preferential rate for net capital gain. The adjustment converts the preference into an equivalent exclusion from gross income and removes the excluded amounts from the fraction.

More specifically, capital gains are included in the numerator of the limiting fraction to the extent of foreign source capital gain net income (determined under the rules described above), less "the rate differential portion of foreign source net capital gain," and in the denominator, capital gain net income is reduced by "the rate differential portion of net capital gain."[64] Net capital gain is an excess of net long-term capital gain over net short-term capital loss.[65] Foreign source net capital gain is computed in the same way, except that it includes only gains from sources outside the United States and losses allocable to foreign source income and may not exceed net capital gain from all sources.[66] A "rate differential" exists only for taxpayers other than corporations, since the rates for corporations make no distinction between capital gains and ordinary income. For noncorporate taxpayers for the taxable years 1994 through 1996, the rate differential is 29.29 percent, which is (1) the excess of the highest tax rate under §1 (39.60 percent) over the maximum tax rate for net capital gain under §1(h) (28 percent), divided

---

[62] IRC §904(b)(3)(A).
[63] IRC §1222(9).
[64] IRC §904(b)(2)(B)(i).
[65] IRC §1222(11).
[66] IRC §904(b)(3)(B).

by (2) the highest §1 rate.[67] For these years, the rate differential portion is 29.29 percent of the foreign source net capital gain or the net capital gain, as the case may be. The computation is not affected by whether any of the taxpayer's income is actually taxed at the 39.60 percent rate. For 1997 and subsequent years, these mechanics are complicated by the introduction of multiple capital gains rates, and the Treasury is invited to draft regulations solving this dilemma.[68]

Assume an unmarried couple has taxable income for 1995 of $356,500, including $100,000 of net capital gain, and $50,000 of the taxable income and $10,000 of the net capital gain are from foreign sources.[69] The numerator of the §904 fraction (foreign source taxable income) would normally be $50,000, but it is reduced by the rate differential portion (29.29 percent) of foreign source net capital gain, which is the lesser of net capital gain from foreign sources ($10,000) or net capital gain from all sources ($100,000). The numerator is therefore

$$\$50,000 - (0.2929)(\$10,000) = \$47,071$$

The denominator, which would otherwise be $356,500, is reduced by 29.29 percent of net capital gain of $100,000 ($29,292) and is therefore $327,207. The credit limitation is:

$$(\$109,710)(\$47,071/\$327,207) = \$15,783$$

4. *Foreign net capital loss offsetting domestic net capital gain.* A noncorporate taxpayer must make a further adjustment if the taxpayer has net capital gain from domestic sources and net capital loss from foreign sources.[70] The adjustment is to reduce foreign net capital loss by "the rate differential portion of the excess of net capital gain from sources within the United States over net capital gain."[71] The idea underlying this adjustment is that because the foreign capital loss is deductible only against the U.S. net capital gain, which is taxed at the preferential rate, the loss should be reduced to reflect the lesser rate applicable to the offset gain.

Assume the net capital gain of the taxpayer in the preceding example consists of $110,000 of net gain from U.S. sources and a loss of $10,000 from foreign sources, and the foreign source taxable income consists of $60,000 of ordinary

---

[67] IRC §904(b)(3)(E).

[68] IRC §904(b)(2)(C).

[69] For the sake of simplicity, it is assumed that all of the taxpayer's income and foreign income taxes are within the general limitation category for purposes of §904(d). If the taxpayer has income or foreign taxes within one of the eight separate baskets of §904(d), the procedures described here must be applied separately within each basket, including the general limitation basket. For §904(d), see infra ¶69.6.

[70] Net capital loss is an excess of all capital losses (short-term and long-term) over all capital gains. IRC §1222(10).

[71] IRC §904(b)(2)(B)(iii).

income and the \$10,000 net capital loss.[72] The net capital loss from foreign sources is reduced by the rate differential portion (29.29 percent). The numerator is thus:

$$\$60,000 - (\$10,000 - (0.2929)(\$10,000)) = \$52,929$$

The denominator is reduced as in the original example by the rate differential portion (29.29 percent) of net capital gain (\$100,000), and it is thus:

$$\$356,500 - (0.2929)(\$100,000) = \$327,207$$

The credit limitation is:

$$(\$109,710)(\$52,929/\$327,207) = \$17,747$$

¶69.5.4 Carryovers and Carrybacks

If a taxpayer's foreign income taxes for any year exceed the §904 limitation for the year, the excess is carried back to the second year preceding the taxable year and then forward through the fifth year following the taxable year until the carryback or carryover is used.[73] An amount carried to a particular year is creditable for that year to the extent of the excess limitation for the year (the excess limitation year). The excess limitation is the credit limitation for the excess limitation year, less the foreign income taxes actually and deemed to have been paid for that year.[74] Assume a corporation has foreign income taxes of \$830 for 1997, a year for which its credit limitation is \$100. Credit of \$100 is allowed for 1997, and \$730 is carried back to 1995. If the limitation for 1995 is \$175 and foreign income taxes for 1995 are \$75, an additional \$100 of 1997 taxes is creditable for 1995.

If the amount carried to a particular year is larger than the excess limitation for that year, the unused amount is carried to the next succeeding year in the carryback and carryover period. In the example, only \$100 of the \$730 carried to 1995 produces tax benefit in that year, and the remaining \$630 is therefore carried to 1996. Assume the limitation for 1996 is \$150, and foreign income taxes for that year are \$60. An additional \$90 of the foreign income taxes for 1997 is creditable for 1996, and the carryover to 1998 is \$540 (the excess of \$630 carried to 1996 over the \$90 absorbed in that year).

---

[72] It is assumed that all of the taxpayer's income and foreign income taxes are within the general limitation category for purposes of §904(d). See supra note 68.

[73] IRC §904(c). A taxpayer claiming a carryback or carryover must include a Form 1116 or Form 1118 with its return for each year in which any portion of the carryback or carryover is applied. Reg. §1.904-2(f).

[74] Reg. §1.904-2(c)(2)(ii).

A carried amount expires unused to the extent it cannot be used by the fifth year succeeding the excess credit year. In the example, the last year to which the 1997 taxes can be carried is 2002. A taxable year of less than 12 months counts as a full year of the carryback and carryover period.[75]

If foreign income taxes originating in two different years are carried to one carryback or carryover year, the amount carried from the earliest year of origin is used first. This rule is illustrated in Example 69-1.

Example 69-1
Carryovers From More Than One Year

	1998	1999	2000	2001	2002	2003
1. Limitation	$100	$100	$300	$400	$200	$600
2. Current foreign taxes	$170	$150	$100	$200	$140	$400
3. Credit for current taxes (lesser of line 1 or 2)	$100	$100	$100	$200	$140	$400
4. Excess credit	$ 70	$ 50				
5. Excess limitation			$200	$200	$ 60	$200
6. Carryovers from						
a. 1997	$540	$540	$540	$340	$140	
b. 1998		$ 70	$ 70	$ 70	$ 70	$ 70
c. 1999			50	50	50	50
d. Total	$540	$610	$660	$460	$260	$120
7. Usable carryover (lesser of line 5 or 6d)			$200	$200	$ 60	$120
8. Total credit (sum of lines 3 and 7)	$100	$100	$300	$400	$200	$520

The carryback and carryover rules are part of the credit mechanism, and there is no analogue in the deduction rules. This has two consequences. First, there can be no carryback or carryover of excess taxes from a year in which the deduction for foreign income taxes is used. For example, if the taxpayer in Example 69-1 chooses the deduction for 1998, none of the 1998 taxes can be carried to any other year.[76]

Second, when excess taxes are carried to a year for which foreign income taxes are deducted, they produce no tax benefit, but they are nevertheless absorbed by any excess limitation in the deduction year. The amount carried to the next carryback or carryover year is the excess of (1) the amount carried to the deduction year, over (2) the excess limitation for that year.[77] Assume the taxpayer in the example deducts foreign income taxes for 2000.[78] The excess of the limitation over current taxes for the year ($300 less $100, or $200) is neither

---

[75] Reg. §1.904-2(e).
[76] See Reg. §1.904-2(g) Ex. 2.
[77] Reg. §1.904-2(d).
[78] See Reg. §1.904-2(g) Ex. 3.

creditable nor deductible, but the carryover from 2000 to 2001 is reduced by that excess, as shown in Example 69-1.

When husband and wife file jointly, the carryover rules are applied on the basis of joint computations in both the excess credit year and all carryback and carryover years.[79] Special complications arise when spouses file jointly in the excess credit year and separately in a carryback or carryover year or vice versa. These complications are the subject of detailed regulations.[80]

¶69.5.5 Increased Limitation for Taxpayers Receiving Distributions of Previously Taxed Amounts

Under §959(a), income of a controlled foreign corporation (CFC) that has been taxed to a U.S. shareholder under subpart F is excluded from the shareholder's gross income when distributed as a dividend.[81] A U.S. shareholder receiving such a distribution might qualify for credit for two types of taxes: foreign income taxes imposed directly on the shareholder's receipt of the distribution (e.g., a withholding tax), and if the taxpayer is a domestic corporation, taxes of an upper-tier CFC that are deemed paid by the U.S. shareholder under §902.[82] Assume domestic corporation P is sole shareholder of foreign corporation F1, and F1 is sole shareholder of foreign corporation F2, which has had subpart F income that was taxed directly to P. This income is distributed as a dividend by F2 to F1, which is taxed by a foreign country on the dividend, and F1 redistributes the income as a dividend to P, which incurs a withholding tax liability on the dividend. On the receipt of the latter dividend, P may qualify for credit for both the withholding tax and all or part of the income tax imposed on F1's receipt of the dividend from F2.

If the distribution is received after the year of the subpart F inclusion, §904 would often deny the credit for these taxes because a distribution from previously taxed income is not gross income, and the §904 limitation equals the precredit U.S. tax on foreign taxable income (gross income from foreign sources less deductions allocated and apportioned to this income). Section 960(b) provides the needed relief by increasing the §904 limitation sufficiently to make room in many cases for the taxes actually and deemed paid with respect to distributions from previously taxed amounts. The increase is available whether the taxpayer is a corporation or an individual.

Section 960(b) applies only if the taxpayer receives an excludable distribution of amounts included in the taxpayer's gross income under subpart F for a

---

[79] Reg. §§1.904-3(b), (c).

[80] Reg. §1.904-3.

[81] See supra ¶68.2.14.

[82] Generally, on a distribution of previously taxed earnings, the indirect credit is allowed only for taxes not credited to the taxpayer under §960 for the year of the subpart F inclusion. IRC §§960(a)(2), (3), discussed infra ¶69.8.6.

prior year and pays or is deemed to pay foreign income taxes on the distribution.[83] Moreover, the taxpayer must have elected the foreign tax credit, in lieu of the deduction for foreign income taxes, for both the year for which the subpart F inclusion was recognized and the year in which the taxpayer receives the excludable distribution.[84]

If §960(b) applies, the §904 limitation for the year of the distribution is increased by the lesser of (1) the foreign income taxes paid or accrued and deemed paid on the distribution or (2) the balance in an "excess limitation account."[85] Every U.S. shareholder of a CFC has an excess limitation account, which is a multiyear pool.[86] For each year that any amount is included in the U.S. shareholder's gross income under subpart F, an addition is made to the shareholder's excess limitation account equal to (1) the amount by which the §904 limitation is increased for the year as a result of the subpart F inclusion, less (2) the foreign income taxes for the year that are creditable solely as a result of the inclusion.[87] Assume a subpart F inclusion is $100, the U.S. shareholder's pre-credit U.S. tax is at a flat 35 percent, and indirect credit of $20 is allowed under §960 on account of the inclusion. The excess limitation account is increased by $15 — 35 percent of $100, less $20. As of the close of each year during which an excludable distribution is received, the account is reduced by the amount of credit allowed for the year as a result of §960(b). If the subpart F income in the example is subsequently distributed to the shareholder and the shareholder incurs a withholding tax of $14 on the distribution, which is allowed as credit, the account is reduced by $14.

The excess limitation account applies only to distributions of amounts that were included in the U.S. shareholder's gross income under subpart F for taxable years beginning after September 30, 1993.[88] For excludable distributions of subpart F inclusions for earlier years, the limitation increase under §960(b) is computed year by year. For the year the distribution is received, the credit limitation

---

[83] IRC §960(b)(1).

[84] This requirement is waived if the taxpayer had no foreign income taxes for the year of the subpart F inclusion.

If the taxpayer elects the foreign tax credit for the year of the subpart F inclusion, but chooses the deduction for foreign income taxes for the year it receives an excludable distribution traced to that inclusion, no deduction is allowed for foreign income taxes on the distribution. IRC §960(b)(4).

[85] IRC §960(b)(1).

[86] See H.R. Rep. No. 111, 103d Cong., 1st Sess. 693-94 (1993) (pooling mechanism adopted in 1993 to be more consistent with pooling rules under §902 adopted in 1986).

[87] IRC §960(b)(2)(B). Additions to the account are made only for taxable years beginning after September 30, 1993.

If foreign income taxes for either of the subsequent two years are carried back to the taxable year, the account addition for the taxable year is reduced by any portion of the carryback that is creditable solely as a result of the subpart F inclusions for the taxable year. For the carryback, see §904(c), discussed supra ¶69.5.4.

[88] IRC §960(b)(2)(B).

is usually increased by (1) the amount by which the subpart F inclusion increased the limitation for the year of the inclusion, less (2) the foreign income taxes creditable for the year of the inclusion solely by reason of the inclusion.[89] The limitation increase, however, may not exceed the foreign income taxes actually and deemed paid on receipt of the distribution.

Assume domestic corporation *P*, which is sole shareholder of foreign corporation *F*, was required to report $100 of *F*'s subpart F income as gross income for 1990. This inclusion increased *P*'s §904 limitation by $34 (34 percent of $100), but *P*'s indirect credit under §960 for the inclusion was only $10. If *P* receives a distribution of $100 from *F* during 1997 and this distribution is traced to the amount taxed to *P* in 1990, *P*'s §904 limitation for 1997 is increased by the lesser of (1) the actual and deemed paid taxes for 1997 with respect to the distribution or (2) $24 ($34 of precredit U.S. tax for 1990 on the subpart F inclusion less $10 of taxes deemed paid in 1990).

Whether the excludable distribution is traced to a post-1993 or pre-1994 subpart F inclusion, if the limitation increase under §960(b) exceeds the precredit U.S. tax for the year the distribution is received, the excess is refunded to the taxpayer as though it were an overpayment of tax.[90]

¶69.5.6 Exemption for Individuals With Small Foreign Income Tax Liabilities

An individual taxpayer may elect to be wholly exempted from the limitation rules of §904 if (1) the individual's gross income from sources without the United States consists exclusively of "qualified passive income" and (2) the individual's creditable foreign income taxes for the year do not exceed $300 ($600 for a joint return).[91] The term "qualified passive income" includes dividends, interest, royalties, rents, net gains from property producing dividends, interest, royalties, and rents, net gains from commodities transactions, net foreign currency gains, and other income classified as passive for purposes of the separate basket rules.[92] However, passive income is not qualified unless the taxpayer receives a "payee statement" showing the amount of the foreign source income and the foreign tax. The exemption is allowed only to natural persons, not to trusts and estates, even though they are normally governed by tax rules for individuals.

---

[89] IRC §960(b)(3) (referring to §960(b)(2) (before amendment in 1993)).

[90] IRC §960(b)(5).

[91] IRC §904(j) (applicable for taxable years after 1997). See Staff of Joint Comm. on Tax'n, 105th Cong., 1st Sess., General Explanation of Tax Legislation Enacted in 1997, at __ (Comm. Print 1997) ("The Congress intended that an individual electing this exemption will not be required to file Form 1116 in order to obtain the benefit of the foreign tax credit").

[92] See infra ¶69.6.2. The separate basket limitation is applied for this purpose without the exclusion of export financing interest, high-taxed income, and other items falling into baskets other than the passive basket.

No carryover under §904(c) is permitted for foreign income taxes paid or accrued for a taxable year for which an individual validly elects this exemption, and no foreign taxes carried from other years are deemed paid for an election year.

¶69.6   CREDIT LIMITATION—SEPARATE BASKET RULES

¶69.6.1   Introductory

Under §904(d), the credit limitation must be determined separately for foreign taxes on each of eight specified types of income and a residual category (the general limitation basket) consisting of all income not within any of the eight separate baskets.[1] The separate baskets consist of:

1. Passive income.[2]
2. Interest subject to foreign withholding taxes at rates of 5 percent or more.[3]
3. Financial services income of banks, insurance companies, and other financing businesses.[4]
4. Shipping income.[5]
5. Three categories of income relating to domestic international sales corporations and foreign sales corporations.[6]
6. Dividends received by a domestic corporation from a foreign corporation that is not controlled by U.S. shareholders.[7]

The credit for foreign taxes on income within each basket equals the taxpayer's precredit U.S. tax multiplied by the following fraction:

---

[1] See generally Fischl, An Analysis of the Final Section 904(d) Regulations, 42 Tax Notes 859 (Feb. 13, 1989); Parnes, United States Tax Considerations in Organizing a Foreign Joint Venture, 20 J. Corp. Tax'n 3 (1993); Tarris, Foreign Tax Credit Limitation After Tax Reform: The Separate Limitation Categories and the Application of the Look-Through Rule, 42 Tax Lawyer 275 (1989). See also Desai & Hines, "Basket" Cases: International Joint Ventures After the Tax Reform Act of 1986 (NBER 1996) (suggesting that separate limitation rules caused sharp decline in U.S. participation in international joint ventures, particularly ventures operating in low-tax countries); Nutter, Corporate Foreign Tax Credit, 1993: An Industry and Geographic Focus, 17 Stat. Income Bull. 97, 122 (Fall 1997) (for 1993, about 64 percent of domestic corporations claiming foreign tax credit reported income subject to general limitation, amounting to about 61 percent of all foreign source taxable income).

[2] Infra ¶69.6.2.
[3] Infra ¶69.6.3.
[4] Infra ¶69.6.4.
[5] Infra ¶69.6.5.
[6] Infra ¶69.6.6.
[7] Infra ¶69.6.7.

Foreign source taxable income within the basket
Entire taxable income

Both U.S. and foreign source income must be allocated among the baskets, even though the U.S. source income is aggregated with all other income in the denominator, because credit for foreign taxes on income that is from domestic sources under U.S. rules is restricted to the §904(d) limitation for the basket that includes the income.[8] A taxpayer's foreign income taxes, including both those actually paid and those deemed paid under §§902 and 960, must also be allocated among the baskets.[9]

The separate limitation rules are applied with several look-through rules, under which income of a CFC retains its character in the returns of the CFC's U.S. shareholders.[10] When a U.S. shareholder is taxed directly on a CFC's subpart F income, the amounts included in the shareholder's return have the same character as they have to the CFC. For example, if a CFC's subpart F income is passive income, the portion that is taxed to a particular U.S. shareholder is included in the shareholder's passive basket. Also, when a CFC pays interest, rents, royalties, or dividends to a U.S. shareholder, the shareholder's income has the same character as the income of the CFC from which the payment is made. For example, if a CFC pays interest to its domestic parent and the payment is from shipping income of the CFC, the parent's interest income is included in its shipping basket rather than the passive basket, which is the usual place for interest income.

¶69.6.2 Passive Income

A separate limitation is determined for foreign income taxes on passive income.[11] The term "passive income" generally has the same meaning as the term "FPHC income" has under subpart F.[12] It includes:

---

[8] Reg. §1.904-6(a)(1)(i).

[9] Infra ¶69.6.10.

[10] Infra ¶69.6.8.

[11] IRC §904(d)(1)(A). See Nutter, Corporate Foreign Tax Credit, 1993: An Industry and Geographic Focus, 17 Stat. Income Bull. 97, 122 (Fall 1997) (for 1993, about one third of domestic corporations claiming foreign tax credit reported passive income, amounting to less than 2 percent of all foreign source taxable income).

[12] IRC §904(d)(2)(A)(i), adopting the definition of "FPHC income" in §954(c), discussed supra ¶68.2.4. Only a CFC can have FPHC income under subpart F, whereas §904(d) applies to all taxpayers. Section 954(c) and the regulations thereunder thus are applied substituting "taxpayer" for "controlled foreign corporation." See Reg. §1.904-4(b)(2)(i).

1. Dividends and interest.[13]
2. Rents and royalties unless derived in the active conduct of a trade or business and received from an unrelated person.[14]
3. The excess of gains over losses from sales and exchanges of stocks, bonds, and property (other than inventory and dealer property) that produces rents, royalties, or no income.[15]
4. The excess of gains over losses from commodities transactions.[16]

---

[13] Interest includes "any income equivalent to interest, including income from commitment fees (or other similar amounts) for loans actually made." IRC §954(c)(1)(E).

Related person factoring income is also treated as interest. IRC §864(d), discussed supra ¶68.2.4. Related person factoring income comes in two varieties: income from a trade or service receivable acquired from a related person, and interest or other income on a loan by the CFC to finance a related person's purchase of inventory or performance of services. A "trade or service receivable" is an account receivable arising from a related person's sale of inventory or other property held primarily for sale to customers in the ordinary course of business or from a related person's performance of a service. The §267(b) definition of "related person" is used. See infra ¶78.3 for §267(b).

Assume a corporation sells goods for $100, payable in 60 days, and sells the account receivable to a subsidiary corporation for $97. When the subsidiary collects $100 from the account receivable debtor, its income of $3 is related person factoring income and thus is interest included in the passive basket. The result would be the same if the parent sold the goods for $97 under an interest-bearing note, the subsidiary purchased the note for $97, and the obligor subsequently paid the subsidiary $100, including $3 of interest.

[14] IRC §904(d)(2)(A)(i), Reg. §1.904-4(b)(2), adopting the rules of §954(c)(2)(A) and §1.954-2(d)(1), discussed supra ¶68.2.4 text accompanying notes 66-71.

Some adaptations are needed in this context. For example, §954(c)(2)(A) and the regulations thereunder only apply to rents and royalties received by CFCs, whereas §904(d) applies to all rent and royalty recipients. Also, the Treasury is urged to develop regulations "substitut[ing] for the facts and circumstances test . . . more objective rules for distinguishing between active and passive rents and royalties." Staff of Joint Comm. on Tax'n, 99th Cong., 2d Sess., General Explanation of the Tax Reform Act of 1986, at 877 (Comm. Print 1986) [hereinafter 1986 Bluebook].

In this context, unlike under subpart F, the active business requirement can be satisfied by an affiliated corporation rather than the entity receiving the rents or royalties. Reg. §1.904-4(b)(2)(ii). Assume domestic corporation P licenses trademarks, tradenames, and related intangibles to its foreign subsidiary S, and S sublicenses them to franchisees in a foreign country. If P is actively engaged in a franchising business, S's royalty income from its franchisees is nonpassive whether or not S meets the active business requirement on its own. Reg. §1.904-4(b)(2)(iv) Ex.

[15] To the extent characterized as a dividend under §1248, gain on a sale of stock of a foreign corporation is included in the passive basket as a dividend, not as gain on a sale of stock. 1986 Bluebook, supra note 14, at 874 n.11. A §1248 dividend thus is excluded in determining whether gains on sales of property exceed losses. For §1248, see supra ¶68.2.16.

[16] Three types of gains and losses are excluded from this aggregate: Gain or loss on a hedging transaction is excluded if it is incident to the taxpayer's business as producer, processor, merchant, or handler of the commodity. Also, gain or loss on a sale of a commodity is excluded if "substantially all of [the seller's] business is as an active producer, processor, merchant, or handler of commodities" and the sale is made in the active conduct of the business. Finally, a foreign currency gain or loss is excluded if it arises from

5. The excess of foreign currency gains over foreign currency losses from transactions in currencies other than the taxpayer's functional currency, exclusive of transactions "directly related to . . . business needs."[17]

6. Amounts included in a shareholder's gross income under the rules for FPHCs and PFICs.[18]

Congress provided a separate basket for passive income because this income "tends to bear little or no foreign tax" and is often "manipulable as to source."[19] Without a separate basket for passive income, the overall limitation would thus provide an "incentive at the margin to place new investments abroad rather than at home, if the taxpayer has excess foreign tax credits that can be used to shelter additional foreign income from U.S. tax."

The definition of "passive income" is narrowed by several exceptions described below, most of which are crafted to further the policy of isolating income that can easily be shifted to foreign sources without incurring substantial foreign tax or otherwise significantly affecting the taxpayer's economic situation.

1. *Income in other baskets.* Income included within any of the other separate baskets is not passive income.[20] The basket for high withholding tax interest, for example, consists entirely of income that would otherwise be passive.[21]

Also, income that would normally be passive is shifted to the basket for financial services income if (1) the recipient is a corporation principally engaged in the active conduct of a banking, insurance, or other financing business and (2) the income is earned in that business.[22] If the recipient carries on a banking, financing, or insurance business, but not as its predominant activity, the passive income basket has its usual content, and it can include income earned in the active conduct of that business.

The shipping basket absorbs some income that would otherwise be passive.[23] An example is "rental payments for the use of a vessel."[24]

Further, the look-through rules for dividends, interest, rents, and royalties received from a CFC reclassify these items with reference to the character of the

---

a transaction in a currency other than the taxpayer's functional currency; however, such a gain or loss is usually included in the aggregate of foreign currency gains and losses described below in paragraph 5. IRC §954(c)(1)(C).

[17] IRC §§904(d)(2)(A)(i), 954(c)(1)(D).

[18] IRC §904(d)(2)(A)(ii). See supra ¶68.3 for FPHCs and ¶68.5 for PFICs.

[19] 1986 Bluebook, supra note 14, at 863.

[20] IRC §904(d)(2)(A)(iii)(I).

[21] See infra ¶69.6.3.

[22] See infra ¶69.6.4.

[23] See infra ¶69.6.5 for the shipping basket. "This priority rule parallels the . . . subpart F priority rule for income that is otherwise both subpart F foreign personal holding company income and foreign base company shipping income," and it thereby "simplifies the application of the separate limitation rules." 1986 Bluebook, supra note 14, at 877.

[24] 1986 Bluebook, supra note 14, at 876.

CFC's income.[25] A recharacterized item stays in the passive basket only if it is deemed paid from the CFC's passive income.

2. *High-tax kickout.* "[H]igh-taxed income" cannot be passive.[26] Income is high taxed if it is subject to foreign income taxes at an effective rate that exceeds the highest U.S. tax rate for corporations (if the taxpayer is a corporation) or individuals (if the taxpayer is not a corporation).[27] This high-tax kickout is provided to preclude "substantial averaging within the passive basket."[28]

The effective foreign rate is the sum of the foreign taxes on the income divided by the income. The numerator of the ratio includes taxes imposed on the taxpayer with respect to the income by any foreign country or possession of the United States, and it also includes taxes deemed paid under §§902 and 960.[29] The income figure—the denominator—is net of expenses, and it is "measured under the United States' tax rules, not foreign countries' tax rules."[30] When taxes are deemed paid under §902 or §960, the denominator includes the fictional dividend imputed by §78.

Assume a domestic corporation receives rents of $100 from foreign sources that are subjected to a foreign withholding tax of $30; for U.S. tax purposes, deductions of $40 are allocated to the rental income.[31] The effective rate of the foreign tax is 50 percent, computed as the foreign tax on the income ($30) divided by the excess of the rents over the deductions allocated to them ($100 less $40). If the highest U.S. corporate tax rate for the year is 35 percent, the rents are excluded from the passive basket, even though the nominal foreign rate of 30 percent is lower than the U.S. rate.

When an item of passive income is earned by a foreign entity but is taxable to a U.S. person who claims the foreign tax credit, the kickout rule is applied by the credit claimant, not the foreign entity. Assume a foreign subsidiary of a domestic corporation has $100 of passive income that bears $34 of foreign taxes; the income is included in the parent's return as subpart F income.[32] Subject to the §904 limitation, §960 allows the parent credit for the taxes paid by the subsidiary. Assume $5 of the parent's expenses are allocated to the $100 subpart F inclusion. The effective foreign rate is 35.8 percent—the ratio of the taxes actually and

---

[25] See infra ¶69.6.8.

[26] IRC §904(d)(2)(A)(iii)(III). The legislative history refers to this exception as a high-tax kick-out; it is intended as an antiabuse rule. H.R. Rep. No. 841, 99th Cong., 2d Sess. II-565 (Conf. Rep. 1986).

[27] IRC §904(d)(2)(F).

[28] 1986 Bluebook, supra note 14, at 880.

[29] IRC §904(d)(2)(F). See infra ¶69.8 for §§902 and 960.

[30] H.R. Rep. No. 841, supra note 26, at II-567; 1986 Bluebook, supra note 14, at 880.

[31] H.R. Rep. No. 841, supra note 26, at II-568.

[32] 1986 Bluebook, supra note 14, at 881-82.

deemed paid by the parent ($34) to the net income reported by the parent ($100 less $5). The ratio of tax to income at the subsidiary level is irrelevant.[33]

The high-tax rule is generally applied income item by income item. For any year, however, items may be aggregated as follows:[34]

    a. Generally, a U.S. person may group passive income received directly into three aggregates: (1) income subject to foreign withholding taxes of 15 percent or higher; (2) income subject to withholding taxes but at rates less than 15 percent; and (3) income not subject to withholding taxes.[35]

    b. Passive income received directly but through a qualified business unit (QBU) in a foreign country is excluded from the foregoing aggregates, but it may be grouped into four other aggregates: (1) income from sources within the QBU's country of operation and (2) income from sources in other countries, subgrouped into three aggregates according to withholding tax rates, as described in paragraph a.[36]

    c. If passive income of a CFC is included in the taxpayer's gross income

---

[33] Assume the parent has a second foreign subsidiary, which receives a royalty payment from the first subsidiary, and subpart F also includes the second subsidiary's royalty income in the parent's gross income. The look-through rules probably characterize the gross income inclusion from the second subsidiary by tracing income characterizations from the first subsidiary to the second subsidiary to the parent. However, the first subsidiary's foreign income taxes are irrelevant to the application of the kickout rule to the inclusion on account of the second subsidiary because this inclusion does not bring into the parent's return any portion of the first subsidiary's taxes. 1986 Bluebook, supra note 14, at 882.

[34] 1986 Bluebook, supra note 14, at 881 (regulations should "balance the administrative convenience that might be gained from grouping particular items of income against the increased sheltering opportunities that might be created by such grouping").

[35] Reg. §1.904-4(c)(3). For each group, the numerator of the testing fraction includes all foreign income taxes on income within the group, whether the income is from foreign or U.S. sources under the U.S. source rules, but only foreign source income is included in the denominator. Reg. §1.904-4(c)(1).

Assume P Corp. has $100 of passive royalty income that is from U.S. sources under U.S. law, but the income is categorized by foreign country X as from X sources and is subject to a 15 percent withholding tax imposed by X; for the same year, P has $100 of passive dividend income that is from sources within foreign country Y and is subject to Y's 15 percent withholding tax. See Reg. §1.904-4(c)(8) Ex. 10. Since the royalties and dividend are both subject to foreign withholding taxes at 15 percent or more, they are grouped together. The numerator of the fraction for this group is $30 (sum of two $15 taxes). Assume $15 of deductions are allocable to the dividends. The denominator is $85—$100 of dividend income, less $15 of deductions allocated to it. The ratio is 35.3 percent ($30/$85). Because it is exceeds 35 percent, the income and the taxes on it are kicked out of the passive basket by the high-tax rule. The inclusion of the country X tax on the U.S. source royalties increases the ratio from 17.6 percent ($15/$85) to 35.3 percent.

[36] Reg. §1.904-4(c)(4). Whether the income is from sources within or without the country of operation is determined under "the laws of the foreign country of the payor of the income." Reg. §1.904-4(c)(4)(iii). A QBU is a "separate and clearly identified unit of a trade or business" for which the taxpayer maintains separate books and records. IRC §989(a), discussed infra ¶71.3.

under subpart F, passive income of each QBU of the CFC is grouped as described in paragraph b.[37]

d. If the taxpayer is taxed on passive income of a CFC that is not attributable to any QBU of the CFC, this income is separately grouped into four categories as described in paragraph b.

e. If rent or royalty expense is allocable to an item of rent or royalty income, the income is excluded from all of the foregoing aggregates.[38]

Assume domestic corporation P is sole shareholder of foreign corporation S, which constitutes a single QBU; for a particular year, S's passive income consists of gross royalty income of $130 from sources within the country in which the QBU operates; the costs allocable to this income consists of expenses of $30 (none of which is royalty expense) and foreign income taxes of $30.[39] Under subpart F, P's inclusion on account of this income is $70 ($130 of gross income less $60 of expenses and taxes), but P is treated as having paid S's taxes of $30 on the income and must include this amount in gross income under §78. Assume $50 of P's own expenses are allocable to the subpart F inclusion. The effective rate of foreign taxes is 60 percent (deemed paid tax of $30 divided by $50, computed as the sum of $70 of subpart F inclusion and $30 of §78 dividend reduced by $50 of P's expenses). Because the effective rate exceeds the U.S. rate of 35 percent, both the subpart F inclusion and the §78 dividend are kicked out of the passive basket and are therefore general limitation income.

Assume S also has $65 of passive interest income from sources outside the QBU's country of operation, and it incurs $15 of expenses and $10 of foreign income taxes with respect to the interest income.[40] P's subpart F inclusion for the interest is $40 ($65 less S's expenses of $15 and taxes of $10), P is deemed to pay the $10 of foreign income taxes actually paid by S, and it also has a $10 con-

---

The income subject to this rule includes dividends from a CFC that are treated as passive income under the look-through rule of §904(d)(3). Reg. §1.904-4(c)(5)(iv).

[37] Reg. §1.904-4(c)(4). The grouping rules are applied after the taxpayer's gross income inclusion has been characterized under the look-through rules described below in ¶69.6.8. Generally, whether passive subpart F income is highly taxed is determined when it is included in the shareholder's gross income, not when it is distributed. Reg. §1.904-4(c)(6). But see Reg. §1.904-4(c)(7) (special rules for where foreign tax on CFC's passive income is refunded or otherwise reduced on income's distribution).

The rules for CFCs are also applied to a partner's inclusions for passive income of a partnership if the inclusions are characterized under the look-through rules. Reg. §1.904-4(c)(5)(ii). If the look-through rules do not apply, the partner's share of the partnership's passive income is treated as one passive item that cannot be aggregated with any others. For the look-through rules for partnerships, see infra ¶69.6.8 text accompanying notes 133–35.

[38] Reg. §1.904-4(c)(5)(i). A foreign currency gain or loss with respect to the taxpayer's receipt of an otherwise tax-free distribution of a CFC's previously taxed income is also evaluated as a separate item. Reg. §1.904-4(c)(5)(iii).

[39] Reg. §1.904-4(c)(9) Ex. 1.

[40] See Reg. §1.904-4(c)(8) Ex. 2.

structive dividend under §78. Because a CFC's passive income from sources within the QBU's country of operation cannot be aggregated with passive income from other sources, the interest income must be separately evaluated. If $20 of *P*'s expenses are allocable to the interest income, the effective rate of foreign tax on the interest is 33 percent ($10 of foreign tax divided by $30, computed as the sum of the subpart F inclusion of $40 and the §78 dividend of $10 reduced by $20 of *P*'s expenses). Because 33 percent is less than the U.S. corporate rate of 35 percent, the interest stays in the passive basket.

3. *Export financing interest.* Interest is not passive income if it is "export financing interest," defined as interest on an obligation financing a sale of property that meets all of the following requirements: (1) The sale must be made "for use or consumption outside the United States"; (2) the property must be produced by the person receiving the interest; (3) the property must have been produced in the United States; and (4) no more than 50 percent of the fair market value of the property may be attributable to components imported into the United States.[41] For example, when a domestic corporation makes an export sale on credit, interest on the buyer's obligation can be export financing interest if the obligation is held by the seller but not if the sale is financed by a loan from an unrelated lender.

Export financing interest can also arise from a financing that satisfies all of the foregoing requirements except that the interest is received by a person related to the producer of the property, rather than the producer itself.[42] "Thus, for example, interest received by a U.S. finance company on loans made to foreign purchasers of inventory manufactured in the United States by and purchased from the finance company's manufacturing affiliate generally will qualify for the export financing exception."[43] Producer and lender are related if either controls the other or if both are controlled by the same person.[44] "Control" means ownership of more than 50 percent of a corporation's stock (by value or voting power, whichever gives the higher percentage) or more than 50 percent of the beneficial interests in a partnership, trust, or estate.[45]

Export financing interest covered by this exception usually falls into the general limitation basket. The exception arose out of a fear that the separate

---

[41] IRC §§904(d)(2)(A)(iii)(II), (G). For this purpose, the term "sale" includes an exchange or "other disposition" on which gain is recognized. 1986 Bluebook, supra note 14, at 875.

Also, "the United States" consists of the 50 states, the District of Columbia, and Puerto Rico. Reg. §1.904-4(h)(1)(i). The "fair market value" of imported property is its value as determined for tariff purposes when imported. IRC §904(d)(2)(G).

[42] However, related person factoring income cannot be export financing interest. IRC §864(d)(5)(A)(i). For the term "related person factoring income," see supra note 13. For the interrelationship between the definition of "export financing interest" and the related person factoring income rules, see Reg. §1.904-4(h)(3).

[43] 1986 Bluebook, supra note 14, at 876.

[44] IRC §§904(d)(2)(H), 954(d)(3); Reg. §1.904-4(h)(1)(iii).

[45] IRC §954(d)(3).

limitation rules might otherwise "have the effect of reducing the availability of export financing in some cases, which could, in turn, have a negative impact on the volume of exports."[46]

4. *Foreign oil and gas extraction income.* For years beginning before 1993, foreign oil and gas extraction income is excluded from passive income because §907 provides a separate limitation for foreign taxes on this income.[47]

¶69.6.3   High Withholding Tax Interest

A separate limitation is provided for foreign taxes on "high withholding tax interest," defined as interest subject to a withholding tax imposed by a foreign country or U.S. possession at a rate of 5 percent or more.[48] The term "withholding tax" includes any tax "determined on a gross basis,"[49] except that it does not include withholding merely as prepayment toward a final tax that will be computed on a net basis when a return is filed.[50] It encompasses foreign taxes similar to the U.S. taxes imposed by §§871(a) and 881 on foreign persons' nonbusiness incomes from U.S. sources.[51]

As its title implies, this basket is meant to isolate income likely to be taxed abroad at rates exceeding U.S. rates. Whether a 5 percent tax on gross income exceeds the U.S. tax on the income depends on the amount of deductions associated with the income. Assume a U.S. bank, whose cost of funds is 9 percent, lends to a foreign borrower at 10 percent. If interest on the loan is taxed by the borrower's home country at 5 percent of gross income, the foreign tax is 0.5 percent of principal (5 percent of 10 percent). Because the bank's net income from the loan is one percent of principal, the 5 percent gross income tax is equivalent to a 50 percent tax on net income (0.5 percent is 50 percent of one percent), and it thus exceeds the U.S. tax of 35 percent of net income. However, interest subject to a foreign withholding tax of 5 percent or more is placed in the high withholding basket whether or not the effective rate exceeds the U.S. rate.

The rule for high withholding tax income derives in part from Congress's observation that several "foreign countries, particularly developing countries,

---

[46] H.R. No. 841, supra note 26, at II-565.

[47] IRC §904(d)(2)(A)(iii)(IV). For §907, see infra ¶69.10. For the repeal of the exclusion of foreign oil and gas extraction income from passive income, see Pub. L. No. 103-66, §13235(a)(2), 107 Stat. 312 (1993).

[48] IRC §904(d)(2)(B). See Nutter, Corporate Foreign Tax Credit, 1993: An Industry and Geographic Focus, 17 Stat. Income Bull. 97, 122 (Fall 1997) (for 1993, about 6 percent of domestic corporations claiming foreign tax credit reported high withholding tax interest, amounting to less than one percent of all foreign source taxable income).

[49] IRC §904(d)(2)(B)(i)(I). The rule also applies to taxes on interest that are "substantially similar" to gross withholding taxes "in the sense that their imposition results in heavier taxation by the levying country of foreign lenders than residents." 1986 Bluebook, supra note 14, at 887.

[50] Reg. §1.904-4(d).

[51] IRC §§871(a)(1), 881(a), 1441(a), 1442(a), discussed supra ¶66.2.

impose gross withholding taxes on interest earned by nonresident lenders that significantly exceed the general income taxes that would be imposed on the associated net interest income were it taxed on a net basis."[52] For U.S. lenders with less heavily taxed income from other transactions, high gross income taxes on interest were often fully creditable under the pre-1987 overall limitation. As a consequence, "the U.S. Treasury, in effect, bore the burden of those high levels of foreign tax on foreign loans."

Congress also perceived that under pre-1987 law, these high gross income taxes sometimes created a perverse incentive for U.S. lenders to lend abroad rather than at home. Lenders were often able to pass the burden of the taxes back to borrowers, sometimes by provisions guaranteeing the lender a stated after-tax interest return. As long as the lender's overall limitation absorbed the foreign tax, a lender who could pass on the tax would likely take the view that the higher the foreign tax the better because the credit for the foreign tax reduced U.S. tax without any economic cost to the lender.[53] In this scenario, the foreign tax on the lender is passed on once to the foreign borrower and a second time to the U.S. Treasury, thus leaving the lender with after-tax interest on the foreign loan at a higher rate than the pretax rate on a U.S. loan.[54]

The effect of the separate basket is to bar a lender from averaging the tax on high withholding tax interest together with the tax on other income. It is a rough mechanism. Because there is no constant relation between lenders' gross and net incomes, the 5-percent-of-gross test is not certain to reach all highly taxed income or only such income. Congress, however, decided that a more precise test would introduce unwarranted complexities. The Treasury is empowered to broaden this basket to include interest that bears a foreign tax of less than 5 percent "where necessary to prevent avoidance of the purposes" of the high withholding basket.[55]

The rule for high withholding tax interest usually trumps the rules for passive income (a low-tax basket) and financial services income (an overall limitation for banks). Export financing interest, however, is excluded from this basket and usually falls into the overall basket.[56] For a corporation primarily engaged in an active banking, financing, or insurance business, the financial services

---

[52] 1986 Bluebook, supra note 14, at 864.

[53] Id. at 864-65. The Bluebook refers to a case where the Mexican government's repeal of a withholding tax on interest on foreign loans was rescinded at the urging of U.S. lenders. Id. at 865.

[54] In a competitive market, this scenario would not occur unless the demand for borrowings drew into the market lenders who could not credit the foreign tax. If all lenders could credit the tax, the lender's windfall would be competed away by an erosion of the net interest rate charged to borrowers. Even in this case, however, a transfer from the U.S. to the foreign treasury occurs in an amount equal to the excess of the foreign tax on the income over the U.S. tax.

[55] IRC §904(d)(2)(B)(iii).

[56] IRC §904(d)(2)(B)(ii). For "export financing interest," see supra ¶69.6.2 text accompanying notes 41-46.

basket includes export financing interest that is subject to a 5 percent or greater withholding tax.[57]

¶69.6.4   Financial Services Income

A separate basket is composed of "financial services income" if the taxpayer is "predominantly engaged in the active conduct of a banking, insurance, financing, or similar business."[58] This basket includes most income connected with the business and most passive income. It is intended to be similar to the overall limitation of pre-1987 law, allowing "credit [for] foreign taxes on one type of financial income against U.S. tax liability on another type of financial income."[59] "This reflects the judgment of Congress that a bona fide financial services company, . . . while it should not be able to average its financial services . . . income with any other, unrelated types of income, generally should be able to obtain the benefits of foreign tax rate averaging with respect to its active business income to the same extent that, for example, a manufacturing or service enterprise can."[60] Passive income is included in this basket regardless of its connection with business activities because of "the practical difficulty of distinguishing passive income of a bank . . . —most or all of the income of which arises from financial activity—from its active income."[61]

1. *Active financing income.* The financial services basket consists of income that the regulations call "active financing income,"[62] including:

   a. Income from the active conduct of a banking, financing, or similar business.

   b. An insurance company's income from the investment of unearned premiums or "reserves ordinary and necessary for the proper conduct of its insurance business."

   c. Income that is "insurance income" for purposes of subpart F.[63]

   d. All income that would otherwise be passive income.

---

[57] See infra ¶69.6.4.

[58] IRC §904(d)(2)(C)(i). See Nutter, Corporate Foreign Tax Credit, 1993: An Industry and Geographic Focus, 17 Stat. Income Bull. 97, 122 (Fall 1997) (for 1993, about 5 percent of domestic corporations claiming foreign tax credit reported financial services income, amounting to about one third of all foreign source taxable income).

[59] 1986 Bluebook, supra note 14, at 864. See also H.R. Rep. No. 841, supra note 26, at II-571.

[60] 1986 Bluebook, supra note 14, at 883.

[61] Id. at 884.

[62] Reg. §1.904-4(e)(2).

[63] For the subpart F definition of "insurance income," see supra ¶68.2.3. Although subpart F insurance income normally does not include income from the insurance of risks located in the country in which the corporation is organized, this limitation does not apply in this context. IRC §904(d)(2)(C)(ii)(III).

e. Interest that is both export financing interest and high withholding tax interest.[64]

Income from the active conduct of a banking or financing business may include:

> service fee income from investment and correspondent banking, income earned by broker-dealers in the ordinary course of business (such as commissions), earnings from interest rate and currency swap businesses, income from services provided to unrelated parties with respect to the management of funds, income from fiduciary services provided to unrelated parties, bank-to-bank participation income, charge and credit card services income from financing purchases from third parties, gains on the disposition of tangible personal property that was used in the active conduct of a financial services business and that generated only financial services income prior to its disposition, hedging gains with respect to other financial services income, and income from travelers' check services.[65]

Income "integrally related to active financing income" is also active financing income.[66] For example, active financing income can include income from property acquired on foreclosure of a loan made in an active financing business; even income from the operation of a nonfinancial business whose assets are acquired on foreclosure can qualify.[67] Income from trading in precious metals or commodities is also included if the trading is integrally related to futures income of an active financing business.

Income from a "nonfinancial activity," however, is never included.[68] For example, income from data processing or travel services is not financial services income, even if the taxpayer is predominantly engaged in financial businesses. Income on sales of goods also cannot be financial services income.

A few types of income cannot be financial services income even if integrally connected with a financial services business, including (1) high withholding tax interest unless it is also export financing interest,[69] (2) export financing interest unless it is also high withholding tax interest, and (3) noncontrolled §902 dividends.[70]

2. *Financial services entities.* A person has income in the financial services basket only if it is predominantly and actively engaged in a banking, insurance, financing, or similar business (an "active financing business"). A person has an

---

[64] Section 904(d)(2)(B)(ii) normally precludes export financing interest from being high withholding tax interest, but this limitation is ignored for this purpose. IRC §904(d)(2)(C)(i)(III).

[65] 1986 Bluebook, supra note 14, at 883. For a complete list, see Reg. §1.904-4(e)(2).

[66] Reg. §1.904-4(e)(4).

[67] Reg. §1.904-4(e)(4)(i)(B) Exs. 1-2. Generally, collateral or other assets received on foreclosing or otherwise settling a loan are presumed to be incident to the financing business for five years, but they are thereafter presumed held as investments. Reg. §1.904-4(e)(4)(i)(A).

[68] 1986 Bluebook, supra note 14, at 885; Reg. §1.904-4(e)(4)(ii).

[69] IRC §904(d)(2)(C)(iii)(I).

[70] IRC §904(d)(2)(C)(iii)(II). For noncontrolled §902 dividends, see infra ¶69.6.7.

active financing business if at least 80 percent of its gross income for the taxable year is active financing income.[71] For this purpose, gross income includes items of a type that are gross income under §61 but fall within a statutory exclusion. If an entity is a member of an affiliated group that meets the 80 percent test, the entity is usually treated as a financial services entity even if it does not meet the test on its own.[72] Special rules are provided for applying the test in conjunction with the look-through rules.[73]

¶69.6.5   Shipping Income

Another separate basket is composed of "shipping income," which includes income from (1) the use of a vessel or aircraft in foreign commerce, (2) the leasing or hiring of a vessel or aircraft for such use, or (3) the performance of services in connection with such a use.[74] Income from activities in space or international waters (other than transportation, communications, and mining activities) is also shipping income.[75]

Shipping income is segregated into a separate basket because it "frequently is not taxed by any foreign country or is subject to very limited foreign tax."[76] Inclusion of this income in an overall limitation would allow excess credits on other income to reabsorb U.S. tax on the shipping income, thus effectively exempting the shipping income from U.S. tax as well. The limitation, however, applies on an overall basis to all shipping income, regardless of the rates at which foreign countries tax it. "This reflects the judgment of Congress that a . . . shipping company, while it should not be able to average its . . . shipping income with any other, unrelated types of income, generally should be able to obtain the benefits of foreign tax rate averaging with respect to its active business income to the same extent that, for example, a manufacturing or service enterprise can."[77]

However, if the taxpayer is a financial service entity, financial services income is excluded from the shipping income basket and falls instead into the

---

[71] Reg. §1.904-4(e)(3). See 1986 Bluebook, supra note 14, at 884-85 (person is actively engaged in such a business if "a high percentage of [its] income is attributable to financial services activities").

[72] Reg. §1.904-4(e)(3)(ii).

[73] Reg. §§1.904-4(e)(3)(i), (iii).

[74] IRC §§904(d)(2)(D), 954(f); Reg. §1.904-4(f). Shipping income generally includes all income treated as foreign base company shipping income for purposes of subpart F. See supra ¶68.2.7.

See also Nutter, Corporate Foreign Tax Credit, 1993: An Industry and Geographic Focus, 17 Stat. Income Bull. 97, 122 (Fall 1997) (for 1993, 61 domestic corporations claiming foreign tax credit reported shipping income, amounting to somewhat more than one percent of foreign source taxable income reported by all corporate credit claimants).

[75] IRC §§863(d)(2), 904(d)(2)(D), 954(f).

[76] 1986 Bluebook, supra note 14, at 864.

[77] Id. at 883.

financial services basket.[78] For example, if a bank owns a ship that it charters to shipping companies, charter rents are financial service income, not shipping income. Also, a noncontrolled §902 dividend may not be shipping income.[79]

¶69.6.6   Income Relating to FSCs and DISCs

Three separate baskets are provided for (1) dividends from domestic international sales corporations (DISCs) and former DISCs to the extent they are treated as foreign source income,[80] (2) taxable income attributable to foreign trade income of a foreign sales corporation (FSC),[81] and (3) distributions received from a FSC from earnings and profits attributable to foreign trade income.[82]

¶69.6.7   Dividends From Noncontrolled Foreign Corporations

A separate basket is established for dividends from a foreign corporation if the dividends entitle the taxpayer to the indirect credit under §902 but the foreign corporation is not a CFC.[83] More specifically, a dividend is subject to this rule if (1) the taxpayer is a domestic corporation and owns at least 10 percent of the voting stock of the foreign corporation paying the dividend and (2) the dividend is a distribution of earnings and profits for a period when the payor was not a CFC.[84] Very generally, a foreign corporation is a CFC whenever more than 50 percent of its stock (by voting power or value) is owned by U.S. persons, counting only the holdings of U.S. persons who each own 10 percent or greater voting interests.[85] The statutory term for a foreign corporation whose dividends are

---

[78] IRC §904(d)(2)(D). For the term "financial services entity," see supra ¶69.6.4 text accompanying notes 71-73.

[79] See infra ¶69.6.7 for noncontrolled §902 dividends.

[80] IRC §904(d)(1)(F). See supra ¶68.1.3 for DISCs.

[81] IRC §904(d)(1)(G). For FSCs, see supra ¶68.1.4.

[82] IRC §904(d)(1)(H).

[83] See infra ¶69.8 for §902. See Nutter, Corporate Foreign Tax Credit, 1993: An Industry and Geographic Focus, 17 Stat. Income Bull. 97, 122 (Fall 1997) (for 1993, about 11 percent of domestic corporations claiming foreign tax credit reported dividends from noncontrolled 902 corporations, amounting to less than one percent of all foreign source taxable income).

[84] IRC §§904(d)(1)(E), (2)(E)(i). Whether the foreign corporation is a CFC when the dividend is distributed is not relevant. 1986 Bluebook, supra note 14, at 887. See Reg. §1.904-4(g)(1) (if partnership holds stock of foreign corporation, tests are applied at partner level); Handler, Avoiding 10/50 Status Through CFC Classification: CFC Attribution Rules and Usufructs, 75 Taxes 419 (1997).

If the foreign corporation is a passive foreign investment company and elects to have its income included in the gross incomes of its shareholders under §1293, the gross income inclusion for a domestic corporation owning at least 10 percent of the foreign corporation's voting stock is subject to this rule. IRC §904(d)(2)(E)(iii).

[85] See supra ¶68.2.2.

covered by this rule is "noncontrolled §902 corporation," but in common parlance, such a corporation is known as a 10/50 company.[86] For taxable years beginning after 2002, the 10/50 rule will apply only to the extent the dividends come from earnings and profits accumulated in taxable years beginning before 2003.[87]

If dividends are received from two or more 10/50 companies, dividends from each corporation comprise a separate basket for taxable years beginning before 2003, but the dividends are aggregated into a single 10/50 basket for subsequent years.[88] A recipient of a noncontrolled §902 dividend is deemed to have paid some portion of the foreign income taxes actually paid by the distributing corporation, but it must also recognize additional gross income under §78 equal to the deemed paid taxes. The effect of this basket thus is that a domestic corporation receiving dividends from a 10/50 company is allowed credit for the taxes deemed paid on receipt of the dividends, together with foreign income taxes actually paid on the dividends, in an amount that may not exceed the precredit U.S. tax on the sum of the dividends and the §78 gross income.

Assume domestic corporation T owns 40 percent of the single class of stock of foreign corporation F, which is otherwise foreign-owned. For taxable years beginning before 2003, dividends received by T on this stock comprise a separate basket because T owns at least 10 percent of F's voting stock and F, being predominantly foreign-owned, is not a CFC. Assume that during a particular year, (1) T receives dividends from F of $80, from which a foreign income tax of $4 is withheld, and (2) as a consequence of the dividends, T is deemed to have paid $40 of F's foreign income taxes. The separate limitation for the dividends is $42, computed as the U.S. corporate rate of 35 percent applied to the sum of the $80 of dividends and the related $40 gross income inclusion required by §78. The foreign income taxes associated with the dividends are $44 (sum of $4 actually paid and $40 deemed paid under §902). Only $42 is immediately creditable. The remaining $2 is allowable only under the carryback and carryover rule of §904(c).[89] However, the carryback and carryover are also confined to the separate

---

[86] IRC §904(d)(2)(E)(i). The legislative history uses the term "10- to 50-percent U.S.-owned foreign corporations." H.R. Rep. No. 841, supra note 26, at II-584. The term "10-50 corporation" is sometimes used.

[87] This limitation was enacted in 1997 because Congress concluded that the 10/50 rule "imposes a substantial record-keeping burden on companies and has the additional negative effect of discouraging minority-position joint ventures abroad." Staff of Joint Comm. on Tax'n, 105th Cong., 1st Sess., General Explanation of Tax Legislation Enacted in 1997, at 302 (Comm. Print 1997) ("The Congress believed that the joint venture can be an efficient way for American business to exploit its know-how and technology in foreign markets").

[88] Reg. §1.904-4(g)(2)(i). See IRC §904(d)(2)(E)(iv) (for taxable years beginning after 2002, all 10/50 companies other than passive foreign investment companies are treated as one corporation for this purpose).

[89] See supra ¶69.5.4.

basket for dividends from F, and they thus are allowable only against U.S. tax on F dividends received in the carryback and carryover years.[90]

A separate basket may also be required under this rule if a CFC receives dividends from another foreign corporation that is not a CFC.[91] If the CFC owns at least 10 percent of the voting stock of the payor of the dividends, the CFC is deemed under the lower-tier rules of §902(b) to have paid a portion of the foreign income taxes of the payor.[92] When a U.S. shareholder of the CFC recognizes income of the CFC under subpart F or on the receipt of dividends, the U.S. shareholder is deemed under §960 or §902 to have paid some portion of the foreign income taxes actually and deemed paid by the CFC, including a portion of the deemed paid taxes from the noncontrolled §902 corporation. If the look-through rules trace any part of the U.S. shareholder's subpart F inclusion or dividend to the CFC's dividend from the noncontrolled §902 corporation, that portion is placed in a separate noncontrolled §902 basket.[93] Also, if the U.S. shareholder receives interest, rents, or royalties from the CFC, the look-through rules might trace portions of this income to the CFC's noncontrolled §902 dividend; if so, these portions are placed in the noncontrolled §902 basket. Even though no indirect credit is allowed on the receipt of interest, rents, or royalties, the inclusion of such income in this basket limits the credit for taxes actually paid on these items. If no taxes are paid on the interest, rents, or royalties, their inclusion in this basket increases the limitation on credit for taxes actually and deemed paid on dividends and subpart F inclusions that fall into the same basket.

The separate basket for noncontrolled §902 dividends takes priority over other baskets that can contain dividends, including the passive income, financial services, and shipping income baskets. "If, for example, a 30 percent U.S.-owned foreign banking company pays a dividend to its [30 percent] U.S. owner, also a banking company, then the dividend is subject to the separate limitation for dividends from noncontrolled section 902 corporations, not to the separate limitation for financial services income."[94]

¶69.6.8 Look-Through Rules for Income From CFCs, Partnerships, and 10/50 Companies

A U.S. shareholder of a CFC is subject to look-through rules under which dividends, interest, rents, and royalties received from the CFC are allocated between the various baskets by tracing them back to the CFC's income in those categories. Also, amounts included in the shareholder's gross income under subpart F have the same character for purposes of the separate basket rules as

---

[90] H.R. Rep. No. 841, supra note 26, at II-584.

[91] Reg. §1.904-4(g)(2).

[92] See infra ¶69.8.5.

[93] 1986 Bluebook, supra note 14, at 888. For the look-through rules, see infra ¶69.6.8.

[94] 1986 Bluebook, supra note 14, at 887.

they have in the CFC's hands. The regulations provide similar rules for partnership income,[95] and, under a 1997 amendment, a look-through rule will also apply after 2002 to dividends received by a domestic corporation from a non-CFC foreign corporation in which the recipient holds a voting interest of at least 10 percent.[96]

The look-through rules are intended "to make the foreign tax credit limitation treatment of income earned through foreign branches and income earned through foreign subsidiaries more alike by, in effect, treating income earned by a foreign subsidiary as if it were earned directly by its U.S. parent."[97] Whether foreign business is done through a branch or a CFC, "it is frequently appropriate to allow cross-crediting of taxes paid by one unit of a worldwide business against income earned by another unit of that business."[98]

The CFC look-through rules apply to U.S. shareholders. A U.S. shareholder is a citizen or resident of the United States, domestic corporation, or nonforeign estate or trust owning (directly or constructively) stock of a foreign corporation carrying at least 10 percent of the voting power of all of the corporation's stock.[99] Also, if a U.S. shareholder is a corporation, all other members of the same controlled group are treated as U.S. shareholders for this purpose.[100]

Moreover, the look-through rules only apply if the foreign corporation is a CFC. A foreign corporation is a CFC if more than 50 percent of its stock, by voting power or value, is held by U.S. shareholders.[101] The look-through rules are restricted to CFCs because "[w]hen the U.S. interest in a foreign entity falls below a majority interest, [the] entity frequently no longer substantially resembles a branch operation of U.S. persons."[102] Also, this restriction avoids "the difficulty that some shareholders in minority U.S.-owned corporations might have encountered in obtaining the additional income and tax information necessary to apply the look-through rules to payments of such corporations."[103]

1. *Subpart F income.* One of the three look-through rules applies in conjunction with the rule requiring U.S. shareholders to report as gross income their ratable shares of the CFC's subpart F income.[104] In applying §904(d), subpart F income has the same character in a U.S. shareholder's return as it has to the

---

[95] See infra text accompanying notes 133–35.

[96] See infra text accompanying notes 138–40.

[97] H.R. Rep. No. 841, supra note 26, at II-573.

[98] 1986 Bluebook, supra note 14, at 867.

[99] IRC §§904(d)(4)(B), 951(b). See supra ¶68.2.2.

[100] Reg. §1.904-5(a)(3). The consolidated return definition of "controlled group" is used, except that the 80 percent threshold in that definition is reduced to 50 percent. For consolidated returns, see infra ¶90.4.

[101] IRC §904(d)(4)(A), 957. See supra ¶68.2.2.

[102] 1986 Bluebook, supra note 14, at 866.

[103] Id. at 866–67.

[104] IRC §951(a)(1)(A)(i), discussed supra ¶68.2.1.

CFC.[105] Subpart F income can fall within several of the separate limitation categories. Assume domestic corporation P is sole shareholder of foreign corporation S; S's income for a particular year consists of $85 of FBC shipping income (a component of subpart F income), $15 of FPHC income (another component of subpart F income), and nonsubpart F income of $100.[106] If no foreign income taxes are imposed on S's income, S has $100 of subpart F income (sum of $85 and $15), all of which is included in P's gross income. In applying §904(d) to P, the $85 of FBC shipping income is included in the shipping basket, and the $15 of FPHC income falls into the passive basket. Within each of these baskets, the income is combined with any other income of the same character earned by P directly or through other CFCs.

When a domestic corporation is taxed under subpart F as a CFC shareholder, §960 usually treats some portion of the foreign income taxes paid by the CFC as though it was paid by the U.S. shareholder. When this happens, the shareholder has additional income under §78 equal to the deemed paid taxes. The look-through rule applies to the §78 income as well as to the subpart F inclusion that triggered it.[107]

Assume S in the example pays foreign income taxes of $15 on its shipping income and $5 on its FPHC income. Subpart F income is $80 ($100 of gross income less $20 in taxes). This $80 is included in P's gross income and is allocated between the shipping and passive baskets—to the former, $70 ($85 of gross income less $15 in taxes) and to the latter, $10 ($15 of gross income less $5 in taxes). P is deemed to have paid the $20 of foreign income taxes on the income, and the same amount is included in P's gross income under §78. Of this $20, $15 is included in the shipping basket, and $5 is in the passive basket.

2. *Interest, rents, and royalties.* The look-through principle also applies to interest, rents, and royalties received by a U.S. shareholder from a CFC. If the CFC has income within a separate limitation category, an allocable portion of a U.S. shareholder's interest, rent, or royalty receipts from the CFC is placed in the same basket.[108] For example, interest on a debt owed by a CFC to a U.S. share-

---

[105] IRC §904(d)(3)(B). Also, if a CFC had shipping income that was excluded from subpart F income under a rule that formerly permitted such an exclusion when the income was reinvested in shipping operations, the look-through rule applies to the income U.S. shareholders must recognize when the CFC reduces its investment in shipping operations. IRC §904(d)(3)(B). See supra ¶68.2.7 for the withdrawal of previously excluded shipping income.

Moreover, if a CFC is also a passive foreign investment company (PFIC) and elects to have its income taxed directly to shareholders under §1293, the look-through rule is used to characterize the gross income inclusion for any U.S. shareholder. IRC §904(d)(3)(I). For §1293, see supra ¶68.5.4.

[106] Reg. §1.904-5(c)(1)(ii) Ex. 1.

[107] IRC §904(d)(3)(G).

[108] IRC §§904(d)(3)(A), (C). The regulations also apply these rules to interest, rents, and royalties received by one domestic corporation from another domestic corporation if (1) the income is from foreign sources and (2) one of the corporations controls the other

holder is passive income to the extent it is allocable to passive income of the CFC. To the extent not traced to CFC income in a separate limitation category, the interest, rents, and royalties are general limitation income.

Congress enacted the look-through rule for interest, rents, and royalties because "such payments often serve as alternatives to dividends as a means of removing earnings from a controlled foreign corporation."[109] Also, Congress wanted to make sure these alternatives are not discouraged. Because interest, rents, and royalties are usually deductible under foreign tax laws, while dividends usually are not, the repatriation of foreign earnings as interest, rents, and royalties typically "reserve[s] for the United States more of the pre-credit U.S. tax on [the] earnings than the payment of dividends." Apart from the look-through rule, interest, rents, and royalties are usually in the passive basket, which is frequently one of the most restrictive baskets because of the lack of substantial foreign taxes. By shifting some of the income into other baskets, the look-through rule often has the effect of increasing the limitation for baskets containing substantial foreign taxes.

a. *Allocations.* A key aspect of the application of this rule is the allocation of a CFC's interest, rent, and royalty payments among income of the CFC in the various separate baskets. Generally, the recipient's income is allocated in the same way as the CFC's deduction for the payment.[110] For example, a royalty paid to a U.S. shareholder is placed in the recipient's general limitation basket to the same extent that the payor CFC's deduction for the royalty is allocated and apportioned to its general limitation income.

A special rule is provided for allocating interest payments. If the CFC has income that is both passive income for purposes of §904(d) and FPHC income under subpart F, interest paid or accrued to a U.S. shareholder is deemed to come first from this income.[111] The regulations, which refer to these payments as related person interest, correlate this rule with the general rules on allocating deductions as follows:[112]

1. The CFC's gross income in each of the §904(d) baskets is determined.

---

or they are controlled by the same U.S. persons, "control" being defined as ownership of at least 50 percent of a corporation's stock by voting power or value. Reg. §1.904-5(g).

[109] 1986 Bluebook, supra note 14, at 866.

[110] Id. at 890. For the allocation and apportionment of deductions, which is always done under U.S. rules, see Reg. §1.861-8, discussed infra ¶70.10.

[111] IRC §§904(d)(2)(A), 954(b)(5). According to the Staff of the Joint Committee on Taxation, this rule was enacted

under the theory that it would generally be as easy for the ultimate passive income recipient to have received the passive income directly as to have channeled it through a related corporation. In addition, this treatment of passive income prevents avoidance of tax through the use of back to back loans.

1986 Bluebook, supra note 14, at 892.

[112] Reg. §1.904-5(c)(2).

2. The general rules for allocating deductions are applied to divide the CFC's expenses among the baskets, except that three categories of expenses—those not definitely related to any gross income, those definitely related to all gross income, and related person interest—are excluded from this step.
3. Related person interest is allocated to the passive basket up to the net amount remaining in the basket after step 2.
4. If related person interest exceeds the amount allocated under step 3, it is allocated among the nonpassive baskets by the general rules for allocating deductions.
5. Expenses not definitely related to any gross income and expenses definitely related to all gross income are allocated last.

Apart from the rule for related person interest, interest expense is usually definitely related to all gross income and is apportioned among all classes of gross income in proportion to the values of the CFC's assets.[113] Unrelated person interest thus is typically allocated in step 5, and the passive income allocated to related person interest in step 3 thus is usually net of only expenses other than interest.

Assume S is a wholly owned foreign subsidiary of domestic corporation P. For a particular year, S's income consists of $200 of FPHC income and $100 of FBC sales income, which falls into the general limitation basket; S pays interest for the year of $150 on a $1,500 loan from P and interest of $100 to an unrelated person on a $1,000 loan. Because the passive basket ($200) is larger than the related person interest ($150), this interest is allocated solely to the passive basket. The unrelated person interest is apportioned according to asset value, except that passive assets are reduced by the amount of the related person debt. Assume S has $2,000 of passive assets and $2,000 of general limitation assets. The passive assets are deemed to be $500 ($2,000 actually held less $1,500 of related person debt), and total assets are $2,500 ($4,000 less $1,500). The allocation of the unrelated person interest is thus as follows:

Passive basket: ($100)($500/$2,500) = $20
General limitation: ($100)($2,000/$2,500) = $80

As a consequence, the $150 of interest received by P is passive income, and P must report subpart F income of $40, consisting of passive income of $30 ($200 less $150 of related person interest and $20 of unrelated person interest) and FBC sales income of $20 ($100 less $80 of unrelated person interest).

Although the related person interest rule applies only to interest payments, the general rules for allocating deductions often provide similar treatment for

---

[113] See infra ¶70.10.2.

rents and royalties.[114] Assume a domestic corporation licenses a patent to its foreign subsidiary, and the subsidiary relicenses the patent to an unrelated foreign user. The CFC's deductions for royalties paid to the parent are allocated to the royalties received under the sublicense because the royalty obligation "is incurred . . . in connection with property from which [the CFC's royalty income] is derived."[115] The parent's royalty income is thus deemed paid from the CFC's royalty income, and it is therefore passive unless the CFC earned its royalties in the active conduct of a licensing business. In contrast, if the CFC instead uses the patent in its manufacturing business, its deduction for the royalty is allocated to manufacturing income, and the look-through rule places the parent's royalty income in the general limitation basket.

b. *High withholding tax interest received from financial services entity.* A special rule applies to interest received from a CFC predominantly engaged in an active banking, insurance, financing, or similar business.[116] If the interest is financial services income under the look-through rule, but it would be high withholding tax interest in the absence of the rule, it is placed in the high withholding basket, not the financial services basket. The amount subject to this rule, however, may not exceed the portion of the CFC's financial services income that consists of interest and interest equivalents. The principal application of the rule is to U.S. shareholder-creditors of foreign banks and insurance companies who are subjected to foreign withholding taxes on interest received from their banking and insurance subsidiaries. The rule's effect is to preclude these withholding taxes from being averaged together with the taxes on other financial services income.

3. *Dividends.* Generally, a taxable dividend from a CFC falls within a separate basket in the same proportion as the distributed earnings and profits consist of income of the type contained in that basket.[117] For example, if 65 percent of a CFC's earnings and profits are financial services income, 65 percent of a dividend is financial services income to a U.S. shareholder. The dividends subject to this rule include dividends actually received, undistributed earnings of a CFC that are taxed to a U.S. shareholder under subpart F because the CFC has invested them in U.S. property, and gains on sales of CFC stock that are treated as dividends under §1248.[118]

In determining the indirect credit under §902, distributions from a foreign corporation are deemed made first from a pool consisting of all earnings and profits for years after 1986, reduced by distributions made from this pool in prior

---

[114] See 1986 Bluebook, supra note 14, at 894.

[115] Reg. §1.861-8(b)(2).

[116] IRC §904(d)(3)(H); Reg. §1.904-5(f)(1). For an illustration of the rule, see Reg. §1.904-5(f)(4) Ex. For whether a CFC is predominantly and actively engaged in such a business, see supra ¶69.6.4.

[117] IRC §904(d)(3)(G).

[118] IRC §904(d)(3)(G); Reg. §1.904-5(c)(4)(iii) Ex. 2. For investments of earnings in U.S. property, see §956, discussed supra ¶68.2.11. For §1248, see supra ¶68.2.16.

years.[119] The same tracing rule applies for purposes of the look-through rule.[120] A CFC's post-1986 earnings and profits thus must be divided among the separate and general limitation baskets, and a dividend from post-1986 earnings and profits is allocated ratably among them. If a CFC begins a taxable year with a post-1986 deficit, but has earnings and profits for the year, the allocation for current dividends is based on current earnings and profits.[121]

Assume a CFC's post-1986 earnings and profits are $1,000, consisting of $700 from manufacturing operations (general limitation income) and $300 of dividends from a noncontrolled §902 corporation that have not previously been taxed to U.S. shareholders under subpart F.[122] If a U.S. shareholder receives a $200 dividend from the CFC's post-1986 earnings and profits, the dividend is split between the noncontrolled §902 and general limitation baskets in the proportions $60 to the former ($200 times $300/$1,000) and $140 to the latter ($200 times $700/$1,000).

In the allocation of a CFC's post-1986 earnings and profits among the various baskets, the composition of the baskets is modified if the CFC's earnings and profits include income that was subject to foreign tax at an effective rate higher than 31.5 percent (90 percent of the maximum U.S. corporate rate of 35 percent).[123] If this income would otherwise be in the passive, financial services, or shipping basket, it is transferred over to the general limitation basket.[124] Put another way, the income is general limitation income unless it is high withholding tax interest or dividends from a noncontrolled §902 corporation.

Under §959(a), a distribution from a CFC is excluded from gross income to the extent it is a distribution of amounts previously taxed to the shareholder under subpart F.[125] A distribution that is nontaxable under this rule falls within none of the baskets because the baskets include only gross income. Also, amounts taxed to shareholders under subpart F are removed from post-1986 earnings and profits in applying the look-through rules to taxable dividends.

Assume a CFC's earnings and profits for its first year of existence are $100, consisting of (1) $20 of FPHC income, (1) $20 of dividends from a 50 percent

---

[119] See infra ¶69.8.3.

[120] 1986 Bluebook, supra note 14, at 895.

[121] Id. at 895-96.

[122] Id. at 895. See supra ¶69.6.7 for noncontrolled §902 dividends. Dividends received by a CFC are usually FPHC income and thus taxed immediately to U.S. shareholders under subpart F. Dividends may be excluded from FPHC income, however, if the payor and recipient are incorporated in the same foreign country or if the CFC is taxed on the dividends at a rate exceeding 90 percent of the maximum U.S. rate. IRC §954(c)(3)(A), discussed supra ¶68.2.4 text accompanying notes 58-65. Also, because subpart F income cannot exceed earnings and profits, dividends received in a year for which the CFC has a net loss are not immediately taxed to U.S. shareholders. See supra ¶68.2.10.

[123] Reg. §1.904-5(d)(2).

[124] IRC §904(d)(3)(E).

[125] See supra ¶68.2.14.

owned noncontrolled §902 corporation that are excluded from FPHC income because payor and payee are incorporated in the same country, and (3) $60 of manufacturing income.[126] The FPHC income is included in the U.S. shareholders' gross incomes as subpart F income (passive basket because FPHC income is passive). Post-1986 earnings and profits are $80 ($100 less the portion thereof taxed as subpart F income), and they consist of $20 of noncontrolled §902 dividends and $80 of general limitation income. Assume $40 is distributed to U.S. shareholders during the year. Of this amount, $20 is excluded from gross income as a distribution of previously taxed subpart F income. Of the remaining $20, $5 ($20 times $20/$80) goes into the shareholders' noncontrolled §902 basket and $15 ($20 times $60/$80) is general limitation income.

4. *De minimis rule.* The two principal components of subpart F income, FBC income (including FPHC income) and gross insurance income, are deemed to be zero if the sum of these items for the year is less than both $1 million and 5 percent of the CFC's gross income for the year.[127] When this de minimis rule applies, the CFC's FBC income and gross insurance income are treated as general limitation income for purposes of the look-through rules.[128] This is done to "avoid the recordkeeping burden of applying the look-through rules to limited amounts of separate limitation income earned by controlled foreign corporations."[129]

Assume a CFC has $100 of gross income for a year, consisting of $96 of manufacturing income that is not subpart F income, $1 of FBC sales income (an ingredient of subpart F income), and $3 of FPHC income (another element of subpart F income).[130] Subpart F income, determined without the de minimis rule, is less than both $1 million and 5 percent of gross income. The de minimis rule therefore reduces it to zero, and the CFC's FBC sales and FPHC income is general limitation income, like the manufacturing income. As a consequence, any interest, rents, or royalties the CFC pays or accrues to its U.S. shareholders during the year are general limitation income to the shareholders, and any dividends from the year's earnings and profits are also general limitation income, regardless of when paid.

The de minimis rule is inapplicable, however, if the look-through rules, applied without the de minimis rule, label an item financial services income.[131]

5. *Successive look-throughs.* If one CFC receives dividends, interest, rents, or royalties from a related CFC, the look-through rules are applied once to characterize the receipt and again when the item is included in the gross income

---

[126] 1986 Bluebook, supra note 14, at 896. For the same country exclusion for dividends, see IRC §954(c)(3)(A), discussed supra note 120.

[127] IRC §954(b)(3)(A), discussed supra ¶68.2.9.

[128] IRC §904(d)(3)(E).

[129] H.R. Rep. No. 841, supra note 26, at II-575.

[130] 1986 Bluebook, supra note 14, at 878.

[131] IRC §904(d)(3)(E).

of a U.S. shareholder or another related CFC.[132] Two CFCs are related for this purpose if (1) either owns at least 50 percent of the other's stock, by voting power or value, or (2) the same U.S. shareholders own at least 50 percent, by vote or value, of the stock of both CFCs.

Assume a domestic corporation has two foreign subsidiaries, *F1* and *F2*; *F1* pays interest to *F2*.[133] The interest comes first from *F1*'s passive income,[134] and to that extent, it is passive income to *F2*. This characterization can then pass through to the parent by a second application of the look-through rules. For example, if *F2*'s interest income is subpart F income, the portion of it traced to *F1*'s passive income is passive in the parent's return.

6. *Partnerships.* Generally, for purposes of §904(d), a partner's distributive share of partnership income has the same character in the partner's return as the income has to the partnership.[135] Also, if a partner receives a payment from the partnership in a capacity other than as partner, the partner's income is placed in the same basket as the partnership's deduction for the payment if the payment is interest, rent, or royalties and the partner owns at least 10 percent of the interests in the partnership.[136] For example, if a 10 percent partner makes a loan to the partnership, interest received or accrued on the loan is placed in the partner's general limitation basket to the extent the partnership's deduction for it is allocated to general limitation income of the partnership.

The look-through rule usually does not apply to a partner whose interest in partnership profits is less than 10 percent by value if the partner is either a limited partner or a corporate general partner.[137] In this case, the partner's distributive share of all partnership income and deductions is usually placed in the passive basket. If the partnership has high withholding tax interest, however, such a partner's distributive share of it must be included in the partner's high withholding basket.

7. *Noncontrolled section 902 corporations.* A look-through rule also applies to dividends received from noncontrolled section 902 corporations, popularly known as 10/50 companies, during taxable years beginning after 2002.[138] Dividends are subject to this rule if (1) the taxpayer is a domestic corporation and owns at least 10 percent of the voting stock of the foreign corporation paying the

---

[132] Reg. §1.904-5(i)(1).

[133] See Reg. §1.904-5(*l*) Ex. 1.

[134] See Reg. §1.904-5(c)(2), discussed supra text accompanying notes 109-11.

[135] Reg. §1.904-5(h)(1).

[136] For these payments, see §707, discussed infra ¶86.5. The same rule applies to a partnership's payments to other members of a controlled group that includes a 10 percent or greater partner.

[137] Reg. §1.904-5(h)(2). For the valuation of partnership interests, see Reg. §1.904-5(h)(4). See Reg. §1.904-5(i)(2) (in case of tiered partnerships, look-through applies if nonpartnership partner owns at least 10 percent of first-tier partnership, regardless of size of indirect ownership of lower-tier partnerships).

[138] IRC §904(d)(4).

dividends and (2) the dividends are distributed from earnings and profits of taxable years beginning after 2002, excluding earnings and profits for any period when the payor was a CFC.[139] Very generally, a foreign corporation is a CFC whenever more than 50 percent of its stock (by voting power or value) is owned by U.S. persons, counting only the holdings of U.S. persons who each own 10 percent or greater voting interests.[140] Under the look-through rule, post-2002 dividends from a 10/50 company are in a separate basket in proportion to the following ratio:

$$\frac{\text{Earnings and profits of } {}^{10}\!/\!{}_{50} \text{ company in that basket}}{\text{Total earnings and profits}}$$

The dividends are traced to earnings and profits for particular years, and the ratio for the dividends traced to a particular year is composed solely of earnings and profits of the 10/50 company for that year.

¶69.6.9   U.S. Losses

If a taxpayer has taxable income from foreign sources but an overall loss from U.S. sources, the U.S. loss is apportioned among the several §904(d) baskets.[141] Assume a corporation has worldwide taxable income of $100, consisting of $100 of U.S. loss and $200 of foreign source taxable income, and the foreign income is composed of $150 of general limitation income and $50 of passive income.[142] The loss is prorated among the two categories of foreign income, leaving general limitation income of $75 ($150, less $150/$200 of $100) and passive income of $25 ($50, less $50/$200 of $100).

¶69.6.10   Allocation of Taxes

The separate limitation for each of the nine income baskets under §904(d) is the ceiling on the credit for foreign taxes on that income. For example, foreign taxes on shipping income are creditable up to the amount of the separate limitation for the shipping basket. A taxpayer's foreign income taxes thus must be allocated among the nine baskets.

If a foreign income tax is imposed on a base consisting of income within only one basket, the tax is assigned to that basket.[143] For example, credit for a foreign

---

[139] IRC §§904(d)(1)(E), (2)(E)(i). Whether the foreign corporation is a CFC when the dividend is distributed is not relevant. 1986 Bluebook, supra note 14, at 887.

[140] See supra ¶68.2.2.

[141] IRC §904(f)(5)(D). For rules on foreign losses, see infra ¶69.7.

[142] 1986 Bluebook, supra note 14, at 913.

[143] Reg. §1.904-6(a)(1)(i).

withholding tax on a dividend classified as passive income is subject to the separate limitation for the passive basket.

If the base on which a foreign tax is imposed includes income within two or more baskets, the tax for each year is allocated among the baskets.[144] The tax allocable to a particular basket is the tax multiplied by the following fraction:

$$\frac{\text{Net income within the basket subject to the foreign tax}}{\text{Entire net income subject to the foreign tax}}$$

In calculating the net income subject to the tax, gross income is determined under the laws of the country or U.S. possession imposing the tax. If the taxpayer is a CFC, any deduction allowed by the foreign tax law for interest payable to U.S. shareholders is allocated to the passive basket up to the amount of gross income (determined under foreign law) that is included within that basket.[145] Other deductions are first allocated according to any rules of the foreign law that identify particular deductions with particular income. The remaining deductions are apportioned among the baskets under rules provided by the foreign law or, if there are no such rules, under the U.S. deduction rules.

Assume domestic corporation P is sole shareholder of foreign corporation S.[146] For a particular year, S's gross income consists of $200 of manufacturing income and $50 of passive income, and its only expense is $100 paid to another of P's foreign subsidiaries for shipping S's goods. Although the shipping payment withstands scrutiny under §482, country X, where S is incorporated and does its business, allows a deduction for only $50 of it. S's country X tax is $40, computed as 20 percent of taxable income of $200 (gross income of $200 and $50, less deduction of $50). Of the country X taxable income, $50 is allocated to the passive basket (gross passive income of $50 less no deductions), and the general limitation basket contains $150 ($200 of gross income less $50 of deductions). The country X tax of $40 is therefore allocated $10 to the passive basket ($40 times $50/$200) and $30 to the general limitation basket ($40 times $150/$200). Although foreign tax rules are used to associate taxes with particular income, foreign tax characterizations of the income do not govern. Assume domestic corporation T receives a $50 royalty during year 1 from foreign corporation F; T is a 50 percent shareholder of F, but F is not a CFC.[147] During year 2, the IRS determines that an arm's length royalty would be $100 rather than $50, and it increases T's year 1 gross income by $50 under §482. F pays this additional $50 to T during year 2, and the payment is treated for U.S. tax purposes as a nontaxable collection of an account receivable. The country in which F is incorporated, however, treats the payment as a dividend and requires that F withhold

---

[144] Reg. §1.904-6(a)(1)(ii).

[145] For an illustration of this rule, see Reg. §1.904-6(c) Ex. 6.

[146] Reg. §1.904-6(c) Ex. 4.

[147] Reg. §1.904-6(c) Ex. 5.

$10 of tax. The tax is treated as tax on the royalty reported for year 1, and it is therefore assigned to the basket containing the royalty. If the royalty was passive income, the tax is assigned to the passive basket.

Taxes allocated to the passive basket must be further allocated among items of passive income in order to apply the rule excluding income from the passive basket if it is subject to foreign taxes at a rate exceeding the highest U.S. rate.[148] If the high-tax kickout rule excludes one or more items of income from the passive basket, the taxes on the income follow the income into the general limitation basket.

When a domestic corporation receives a dividend from a foreign corporation in which it has a 10 percent or greater voting interest or is taxed under subpart F on earnings and profits of the foreign corporation, the domestic corporation is deemed under §902 or §960 to have paid a portion of the foreign income taxes actually paid by the foreign corporation.[149] Deemed paid taxes must also be allocated among the domestic corporation's separate limitation baskets. This is easiest if the foreign corporation is a noncontrolled §902 corporation rather than a CFC.[150] All noncontrolled §902 dividends from one foreign corporation comprise a separate basket, and taxes deemed paid on receipt of the dividends are assigned to that basket, together with any foreign taxes imposed directly on the dividends.

When a domestic corporation is taxed on earnings and profits of a CFC (either under subpart F or on receipt of dividends), the earnings are allocated among the several baskets by looking through to the sources of the CFC's income, and the taxes on each category of earnings is allocated to the same basket.[151] In this context, the regulations leave a host of questions unanswered. The most pervasive problem is that while §904(d) is applied by identifying particular taxes with particular income, the deemed paid taxes are determined under §§902 and 960 by pooling together all post-1986 earnings and profits and all post-1986 foreign income taxes. The regulations fail to describe how the transformation is made from pooling under the indirect credit rules to particularity under §904(d). Proposed regulations under §§902 and 960 answer some of these questions.[152]

¶69.6.11 Misbehaving Countries

Another separate limitation is required for income earned in some countries. Section 901(j) denies credit for income taxes paid to several countries whose

---

[148] Reg. §1.904-6(a)(1)(iii). For the high-tax kickout, see supra ¶69.6.2 text accompanying notes 26–40.

[149] See infra ¶69.8.1.

[150] See supra ¶69.6.7 for noncontrolled §902 dividends.

[151] For the look-through rules, see supra ¶69.6.8.

[152] See infra ¶69.8.4.

governments are on bad terms with the U.S. government.[153] Section 901(j)(1)(B) backs up this denial by providing that the limitation rules of §904 are applied separately to income from sources in a country whose income taxes are noncreditable under §901(j). In determining the limitations on credit for taxes paid to other countries, such income is therefore excluded from all of the nine baskets under §904(d). As a consequence of the denial and separate limitation rules, U.S. tax on income from a misbehaving country cannot be offset by taxes paid to that or any other foreign country.

¶69.7 CREDIT LIMITATION—FOREIGN LOSSES

Section 904(f) contains an elaborate set of rules for allocating and recapturing foreign losses. The principle underlying the rules is that when a foreign loss of any character is deducted against income of another character, an equal amount of subsequent income of the first character should be reclassified as income of the second character. If income of type A is offset by loss of type B, future income of type B must be recharacterized as type A income so that over the long run the separation between the two income types is maintained.

The principle is applied by separately computing foreign source taxable income and loss within each of the nine baskets under §904(d).[1] A loss in any basket is first deducted ratably against foreign income in the other baskets. If the taxpayer has a loss in all baskets combined (an overall foreign loss), it is deducted against income from U.S. sources. In subsequent years, income of the same character as the loss is reclassified as income of the character offset by the loss.

For example, if a foreign source loss in the general limitation basket for one year is deducted against foreign source passive income for that year, general limitation income for subsequent years is shifted to the passive basket. If a foreign general limitation loss is deducted against U.S. source income, subsequent foreign general limitation income is recharacterized as U.S. source income. In both cases, the effect is that the earlier general limitation loss is ultimately deducted against later general limitation income. The deduction against foreign passive income in the first case or U.S. income in the second is only temporary because it is restored by the later recapture.

1. *Foreign loss in one basket deducted against foreign income in other baskets.* As a first step in the application of the loss recapture rules, gross income from foreign sources and the deductions allocated and apportioned to that income are split among the eight separate baskets and the general limitation bas-

---

[153] For §901(j), see supra ¶69.4.8.
[1] For §904(d), see supra ¶69.6. See Reg. §1.904(f)-12 (providing for recapture after 1986 of overall foreign loss incurred before 1987 and treatment of post-1986 overall foreign losses included in net operating losses carried to pre-1987 years).

ket.[2] If a loss appears in any basket, it is apportioned ratably among income in the other baskets.[3]

Assume corporation T's taxable income from foreign sources for year 1 consists of $20 in the passive basket, $5 in the separate basket for distributions from FSCs, and a loss of $10 in the general limitation basket.[4] The loss is prorated among the income in the other baskets. After the proration, passive income is $12 ($20 less $^{20}/_{25}$ of $10) and FSC distributions are $3 ($5 less $^{5}/_{25}$ of $10). None of the loss is allocated against U.S. income.

When a loss in one basket has been allocated as a deduction in another basket, it is recaptured out of the first income subsequently recognized in the loss basket.[5] In the example, T's first general limitation income from foreign sources is recaptured by reallocating it to the two baskets to which the loss was allocated. Assume T's foreign source taxable income for year 2 consists of $25 of passive income, $5 of FSC distributions, and $50 of general limitation income.[6] Of the latter amount, $8 is reallocated to the passive basket to reflect the deduction of $8 of the prior year's general limitation loss against passive income, and $2 is reclassified as FSC distributions. After the reallocations, foreign source taxable income for year 2 consists of $33 of passive income ($25 and $8), $7 of FSC distributions ($5 and $2), and $40 of general limitation income ($50 less $10).

If income for the year immediately following the loss year is insufficient to cover the recapture, the available income is prorated among the previously offset categories, and the shortfall carries over to the next year.[7] Assume T's foreign general limitation taxable income for year 2 is only $5 before reallocation. This $5 is recharacterized as $4 of passive income and $1 of FSC distributions (raising these two categories to $29 and $6), and an additional $5 of general limitation income remains to be reclassified in subsequent years. For example, if T's foreign general limitation taxable income is $15 for year 3, $4 is shifted to the passive basket, $1 becomes FSC distribution, and only $10 remains in the general limitation basket.

If losses are sustained in two or more of the nine baskets, each loss is prorated among the foreign source categories that have income. Assume corporation U's foreign source taxable income for year 1 consists of $20 of passive income, $5 of FSC distributions, $5 of loss in the shipping basket, and $20 of general limitation loss. Of the $5 shipping loss, $4 ($^{20}/_{25}$ of $5) is deducted against

---

[2] Staff of Joint Comm. on Tax'n, 99th Cong., 2d Sess., General Explanation of the Tax Reform Act of 1986 at 911 (Comm. Print 1987) [hereinafter 1986 Bluebook]. A net operating loss (NOL) deduction (a deduction for a NOL carryback or carryover) is not allocated and apportioned among the nine baskets because, under rules described below, the NOL is split among the baskets when it is sustained.

[3] IRC §904(f)(5)(B).

[4] 1986 Bluebook, supra note 2, at 909–10.

[5] IRC §904(f)(5)(C).

[6] 1986 Bluebook, supra note 2, at 910.

[7] IRC §904(f)(5)(B); 1986 Bluebook, supra note 2, at 910.

passive income, and $1 ($^5/_{25}$ of $5) is deducted against FSC distributions. The $20 general limitation loss is similarly allocated, $16 against passive income and $4 against FSC distributions. Assume U's only foreign source item for year 2 is general limitation taxable income of $30. Of this $30, $16 becomes passive income, $4 becomes FSC distributions, and $10 keeps its character as general limitation income. Recapture of the shipping loss awaits the realization of shipping income in subsequent years.

The recapture rule may either increase or decrease a taxpayer's credits over the long run.[8] If a loss is allocated to a basket containing highly taxed income, the loss deduction might reduce the limitation for that basket below the foreign taxes paid on income in the basket, and the recapture, which has the effect of adding to that limitation in subsequent years, may be the vehicle by which carryovers become creditable. In contrast, if a loss is allocated to a basket containing lightly taxed income, the loss deduction might merely absorb excess limitation in that basket, and the recapture might increase that excess in subsequent years, at the expense of other categories where foreign taxes exceed the limitation.

a. *Allocation and recapture of NOL carryovers.* The allocation and recapture rules apply to net operating loss (NOL) carryovers as well as current losses.[9] When the NOL is sustained, it is allocated between U.S. and foreign sources, and the foreign source portion is allocated again among the §904(d) baskets. An NOL is traceable to foreign sources to the extent that the deductions allocated and apportioned to gross income from foreign sources exceed that gross income. If any portion of an NOL is from foreign sources, it is allocated among the §904(d) baskets, probably as follows:

1. Reduce the gross income within each basket by the deductions allocated and apportioned to that income.
2. If taxable income remains in any basket, prorate it among the baskets with losses.
3. If the sum of the separate basket losses remaining after step 2 exceeds the worldwide NOL (that is, if taxable income from U.S. sources is positive), the loss in each basket is reduced by its ratable share of taxable income from sources within the United States.

The loss remaining in each basket after step 3 is its portion of the NOL. As the NOL carries forward, the separate basket NOLs retain their character. In each carryover year, the NOL is deductible in an amount equal to the lesser of (1) the carryover (after the elimination of any portions of it deducted with tax benefit in

---

[8] 1986 Bluebook, supra note 2, at 909.

[9] Id. at 911. An NOL is an excess of all deductions over all gross income. IRC §172(c). It can be carried back to the three years preceding the loss year and, to the extent not used in a carryback year, it can be carried forward for 15 years after the loss year. IRC §§172(b)(1)(A), (B). A taxpayer can elect to forego the carryback. IRC §172(b)(3). A peculiarity in the rules for overall foreign losses makes this election attractive for most taxpayers with such losses. For NOLs generally, see supra ¶25.11.

earlier years) or (2) taxable income for the carryover year before the carryover is taken into account.[10] If the NOL is fully deductible in one carryover year, the portion of the NOL allocated to each basket is treated as a deduction allocable to that basket for the year. If some but less than all of the NOL is deductible for a particular carryover year, a ratable portion of each basket's share of the NOL is treated as a deduction within the basket. A separate basket NOL carryover might produce loss for the carryover year in the basket to which it is allocated. If this occurs, the separate basket loss is deducted against income of other baskets under the rules described earlier, but the recapture rule requires that income for later years in the loss basket be shifted over to the basket against which the loss was deducted.

Assume a corporation incurs an NOL for year 1, $200 of which is composed of foreign source general limitation income and deductions allocated and apportioned to that income.[11] The NOL is carried forward to year 2, when the corporation has taxable income from foreign sources, consisting of $180 of general limitation income and $30 of passive income. If the NOL is fully deductible for year 2, the foreign portion of it ($200) is deducted first against general limitation income and second, ratably, against income of other separate baskets (passive income in this case). The corporation's foreign source taxable income for year 2 is $10 ($180 and $30, less $200), and all of it is passive.[12]

---

[10] IRC §172(b)(2).

[11] 1986 Bluebook, supra note 2, at 911.

[12] The situation is more complicated if the taxpayer has foreign source gross income within more than one category in the loss year. Assume the $200 foreign NOL for year 1 consists of $100 of passive income, $75 of shipping loss, and $225 of overall limitation loss. The passive income is prorated among the two losses, leaving a shipping NOL of $50 ($75 less $75/$300 of $100) and overall limitation NOL of $150 ($225 less $225/$300 of $100). Regardless of the use subsequently made of the carryovers for the NOL, the allocation of shipping and overall limitation loss against passive income for year 1 triggers the recapture rule; for some later year or years, $25 of shipping income and $75 of overall limitation income will be shifted to the passive basket.

Assume the corporation's foreign source taxable income for year 2 (before taking the NOL carryover into account) consists of $180 of overall limitation income and $30 of passive income. The deduction for the carryover does not step aside for the recapture rule. The carryover should therefore be allocated before the recapture rule is applied. The $150 overall limitation carryover thus reduces overall limitation income from $180 to $30, and the $50 shipping carryover is prorated between the remaining $30 of overall limitation income and the $30 of passive income, reducing each of these baskets by $25 ($30/$60 of $50). This leaves $10 of foreign source taxable income for year 2, consisting of $5 of overall limitation income and $5 of passive income. The $5 of overall limitation income, however, is recharacterized as passive income in partial recapture of the overall-to-passive deduction taken in year 1, and foreign source taxable income thus is all passive.

The following remains to be recaptured in years after year 2: from year 1 allocations, (1) $25 to be reallocated from shipping income to passive income and (2) $70 ($75 less $5) to be reallocated from overall limitation income to passive income; from year 2 allocations, (1) $25 to be reallocated from shipping income to overall limitation income and (2) $25 to be reallocated from shipping income to passive income.

Once an NOL carryover has been allocated to income of a different type, it is subject to recapture under the same rules that apply to current losses.[13] Assume the corporation in the example has foreign source taxable income in year 3 consisting of $220 of general limitation income. Because $20 of the general limitation NOL was deducted in year 2 against passive income, $20 of general limitation income for year 3 is recaptured by shifting it to the passive basket.

b. *Application with U.S. loss rule.* The legislative history suggests two rules for coordinating the rules for separate limitation losses with a rule described earlier under which a U.S. loss is allocated ratably among foreign income in the separate baskets.[14]

If a taxpayer has foreign loss in one or more of the §904(d) baskets and also has a U.S. loss, the foreign loss or losses are fist allocated among the foreign income in the other baskets, and the U.S. loss is then prorated among the income remaining in the baskets.[15] Assume corporation V has worldwide taxable income for year 1 of $850, consisting of (1) $100 of U.S. loss, (2) a foreign general limitation loss of $50, (3) $600 of foreign shipping income, and (4) $400 of foreign passive income. The general limitation loss is first allocated to the baskets with foreign income, leaving shipping income of $570 ($600 less $600/1,000 of $50) and passive income of $380 ($400 less $400/1,000 of $50). The U.S. loss is then allocated among the income remaining in these baskets, reducing the shipping income to $510 ($570 less $570/950 of $100) and the passive income to $340 ($380 less $380/950 of $100).

U.S. losses, however, are allocated before the recapture of losses within the separate baskets.[16] Assume V has entire taxable income for year 2 of $20, consisting of a U.S. loss of $780, general limitation income of $200, and shipping income of $600. The U.S. loss is first prorated among the foreign income baskets, reducing general limitation income to $5 ($200 less $200/800 of $780) and shipping income to $15 ($600 less $600/800 of $780). The remaining $5 of general limitation income is then reallocated in partial recapture of the $50 of general limitation loss for the preceding year. Of the $5 to be reallocated, $3 is shipping income, and $2 is passive income, reflecting the allocation of the prior year's loss deduction—$30 against shipping income and $20 against passive income. In sum, the taxpayer's taxable income for year 2 consists of shipping income of $18 and passive income of $2, and the recapture remaining for subsequent years is $45 ($27 from overall to shipping and $18 from overall to passive).

c. *No reallocation of taxes.* The recapture rule recharacterizes only income, not the foreign taxes on the income.[17] For example, if V pays $100 of foreign income taxes on $220 of general limitation income for year 3, those taxes remain

---

[13] 1986 Bluebook, supra note 2, at 911.

[14] For the U.S. loss rule, see supra ¶69.6.9.

[15] 1986 Bluebook, supra note 2, at 913.

[16] Id. at 913-14.

[17] IRC §904(f)(5)(C).

subject to the general limitation even though $45 of year 3's general limitation income is shifted to the shipping and passive baskets.

d. *Rules applied on consolidated basis.* The loss allocation and recapture rules are applied on a consolidated basis to an affiliated group filing a consolidated return.[18] For example, if a member of an affiliated group has a loss within one basket but the group does not, the rules do not apply, even if the member sustaining the loss leaves the consolidated group before it recoups the loss.

e. *No credit years.* If a taxpayer claims the foreign tax credit for some years but not others, the loss allocation and recapture rules are applied for all years to determine their effects in the years for which credit is claimed.[19] Assume a corporation's foreign source income for a particular year consists of passive income of $20 and general limitation loss of $15; the corporation pays no foreign income taxes for the year. The general limitation loss is nevertheless treated as a deduction against the passive income, with the consequence that general limitation income of subsequent years will be shifted to the passive basket, and the credit limitation for foreign taxes on general limitation income will thereby be reduced.

2. *Overall foreign losses.* If foreign taxable income in the §904(d) baskets is insufficient to fully absorb foreign losses in other baskets, the unabsorbed amount (an overall foreign loss) is a deduction against U.S. income.[20] Assume a corporation has $200 of U.S. income, $20 of foreign passive income, and $25 of foreign general limitation loss. The deduction for the loss is allocated $20 against the foreign passive income and $5 against U.S. income. The corporation has a $5 overall foreign loss for the year.

An "overall foreign loss" is an excess of deductions allocated and apportioned to gross income from foreign sources over that gross income.[21] A few deductions, however, are excluded. One of these exclusions—the NOL deduction (a deduction for an NOL carryback or carryover)—is required by accounting considerations. Because the deductions that create an NOL are included in determining whether there is an overall foreign loss for the loss year, the exclusion of the carryback or carryover is needed to avoid double counting. The deductions for foreign expropriation, casualty, and theft losses are also excluded. These exclusions are not required by the logic of the system, and to the extent of the excluded deductions, they have the effect of allowing foreign losses to be deducted against U.S. income without possibility of future recapture.

An overall foreign loss is recaptured by recharacterizing subsequent foreign source income as U.S. income.[22] Generally, recapture of overall foreign losses has

---

[18] 1986 Bluebook, supra note 2, at 911.
[19] Id.
[20] IRC §904(f)(5)(A); 1986 Bluebook, supra note 2, at 910.
[21] IRC §904(f)(2).
[22] IRC §904(f)(1).

priority over recapture within the separate baskets.[23] Assume that for year 1, corporation *W* has $200 of U.S. income, $20 of passive income, and $25 of general limitation loss. The deduction for the loss is allocated $20 against the foreign passive income and $5 against U.S. income. Assume *W*'s foreign source taxable income for years 2 and 3 consists of general limitation income of $15 and $40. The year 2 amount is all recharacterized, $5 as U.S. income to recapture year 1's overall foreign loss and $10 as foreign passive income to recapture a portion of the year 1 deduction of $20 of foreign general limitation loss against passive income. In year 3, recapture of the $20 is completed by shifting $10 of foreign general limitation taxable income to the passive basket.

Recapture of an overall foreign loss, however, is subject to an additional limitation: The overall foreign loss recapture rule applies to no more than 50 percent of foreign source taxable income unless the taxpayer elects a higher percentage.[24] Assume that for year 2, *W* has only $8 of foreign source income (all in the general limitation basket). If *W* does not choose to raise the 50 percent ceiling, recapture of the overall foreign loss is limited to $4. The $8 of general limitation income is thus recharacterized as $4 of U.S. income and $4 of foreign passive income. There remains to be recaptured in future years $1 of overall foreign loss ($5 less $4) and $16 of the loss deduction against passive income ($20 less $4).

The 50 percent limitation is subject to two modifications described below:[25]

a. *Dispositions of foreign business assets.* The recapture rule is applied without the ceiling to gain recognized on a disposition of property used in a foreign business.[26] Moreover, if property used in a foreign business is disposed of in a nonrecognition transaction while an overall foreign loss awaits recapture, gain is recognized up to the amount of the unrecaptured loss. Assume a domestic corporation incurs an overall foreign loss in a foreign branch operation, but the branch's assets are transferred to a newly organized foreign corporation just as the branch operations begin to be profitable. The incorporation, by shifting foreign profits out of the domestic corporation's return, could delay the recapture of the foreign loss. The possibility of such a delay is reduced, however, by the rules described here, which require that (1) gain must be recognized on the incorporation even though recognition might otherwise be avoided under §351 and (2) the overall loss is recaptured out of all of this gain, notwithstanding the 50 percent ceiling.[27]

---

[23] 1986 Bluebook, supra note 2, at 910.

[24] IRC §904(f)(1)(B).

[25] Also, the limitation is inapplicable to an accumulation distribution of foreign source income from a foreign trust. IRC §904(f)(4); Reg. §1.904(f)-4.

[26] IRC §904(f)(3)(A).

[27] For §351, see infra ¶91.1. For the application of §351 to transfers by U.S. persons to foreign corporations, see supra ¶68.6.1.

A transfer of property is subject to these rules if the property "has been used predominantly without the United States in a trade or business."[28] The predominant use test is applied taking into account only use during the three years preceding the disposition or if less, the period the taxpayer has held the property for business use.

These rules apply to the unrecaptured portions of the overall losses for all years prior to the disposition. The unrecaptured portion of an overall foreign loss is the amount of the loss, reduced by the portions recaptured in prior years and by the portion recaptured in the current year from foreign source income other than gains on dispositions of foreign business property. Up to the amount of the unrecaptured loss, gain on a disposition of a foreign business asset is initially considered foreign source income, regardless of how it might be classified by the source rules of general application, and it is then reclassified as U.S. income by the recapture rule.

The rules apply to all dispositions of foreign business property, including gifts and distributions to shareholders.[29] Exceptions are made for (1) a disposition of property that "is not a material factor in the realization of income by the taxpayer" and (2) a transfer to a domestic corporation in a reorganization or a liquidation of a subsidiary corporation into its parent.[30]

b. *Recapture limited to same basket.* Although the ceiling is normally 50 percent of all foreign source taxable income, the legislative history indicates that an overall foreign loss is recaptured (up to the ceiling) only from foreign source income from the same basket or baskets as the overall foreign loss.[31] Assume corporation X has an overall foreign loss for year 1 of $125—all traceable to the general limitation basket—and this loss is deducted against X's U.S. source taxable income of $300. For year 2, X has foreign source taxable income consisting of $50 of general limitation income and $150 of passive income. The ceiling is $100 (50 percent of the sum of $50 and $150). Only $50 is recaptured in year 2, however. Because the overall foreign loss arose in the general limitation basket, it is only recaptured from general limitation income, a source that contains only $50 in year 2.[32] The remaining $75 of the overall foreign loss is recaptured in subsequent years, subject to the same limitations.

---

[28] IRC §904(f)(3)(A).

[29] IRC §904(f)(3)(B)(i).

[30] IRC §904(f)(3)(C).

[31] 1986 Bluebook, supra note 2, at 912.

[32] The statute contains not a hint of this limitation, and another solution is more consistent with the statutory language. Up to the amount allowed by the 50 percent limitation, overall foreign loss could be recaptured first from foreign income of like kind and thereafter from income from other baskets, and the latter use could be subsequently recaptured by reallocating income from the loss category. In the example, $100 of overall foreign loss could be recaptured in year 2, first from the $50 of overall limitation income and then from $50 of the $150 of passive income; from the first overall limitation income of subsequent years, $50 could be shifted to the passive basket.

¶69.8 INDIRECT CREDIT

¶69.8.1 Introductory

Under §902, a domestic corporation is treated as having paid foreign income taxes actually paid by a foreign corporation from which it receives dividends if the domestic corporation owns at least 10 percent of the foreign corporation's voting stock.[1] The amount deemed paid is determined by prorating the foreign corporation's foreign income taxes among its earnings and profits and attributing to the domestic corporation the amount allocated to the earnings it receives as a dividend. For example, if a domestic corporation receives a dividend comprising one third of a foreign corporation's earnings and profits, the domestic corporation is deemed to have paid one third of the foreign income taxes paid by the foreign corporation. The amount deemed paid under §902 is creditable under §901, generally subject to the same limitations that apply to taxes actually paid by the domestic corporation. For example, deemed and actually paid taxes are often aggregated in applying the credit limitation of §904(a).[2]

The function of §902 is to mitigate double taxation where U.S. and foreign income taxes do not converge in the same entity.[3] Generally, a taxpayer cannot take credit for taxes paid by another person, even if the two are related as, for example, parent and subsidiary corporations. If this rule were strictly applied to domestic corporations doing business abroad through foreign subsidiaries, the credit rules would fall seriously short of the goal of eliminating double taxation.

---

[1] For the regulations under §902, see TD 8708, 1997-1 CB 137; Moetell, IRS Issues Final Regulations Under Section 902, 26 Tax Mgmt. Int'l J. 111 (1997). For the proposed regulations, see INTL-933-86, 1995-1 CB 959; Carr & Moetell, IRS Issues Proposed Regulations Under Section 902, 24 Tax Mgmt. Int'l J. 219 (1995); Hoke, Proposed Section 902 Regulations Raise Major Issues, 11 Tax Notes Int'l 49 (July 3, 1995). The prior regulations, interpreting the pre-1987 §902, are retained; the prior §1.902-1 is now §1.902-3, and §1.902-2 became §1.902-4. The regulations are effective for distributions made during taxable years beginning after 1986. Reg. §1.902-1(g).

See also Bouma, The U.K. Advance Corporation Tax and the Deemed Paid Foreign Tax Credit Under Section 902, 23 Tax Mgmt. Int'l J. 549 (1994); Dolan & Walsh, Use of Holding Companies in International Tax Planning, 73 Taxes 873 (1995); Pugh, The Interaction of the U.S. Deemed Paid Foreign Tax Credit and the German Integration System, 7 Tax Notes Int'l 1429 (Dec. 6, 1993).

[2] See supra ¶69.5 for the §904 limitation. For the interrelationships between §§902 and 904, see infra ¶69.8.4.

Also, deemed paid taxes (1) can be subject to reduction under §901(e), which applies to foreign taxes on mineral income, (2) are sometimes made noncreditable by §901(f), which applies to foreign taxes on income from purchases and sales of oil and gas, and (3) can be subject to the special limitation of §907(a) for foreign taxes on oil and gas extraction income. See Reg. §§1.902-1(c)(4), (5), (6). See infra ¶69.10 for §907.

[3] See US v. Goodyear Tire & Rubber Co., 493 US 132, 135 (1989) ("The credit protects domestic corporations that operate through foreign subsidiaries from double taxation of the same income: taxation first by the foreign jurisdiction, when the income is earned by the subsidiary, and second by the United States, when the income is received as a dividend by the parent").

Typically, foreign taxes on income earned in this way are primarily imposed on the subsidiary, an entity that is exempt from U.S. taxation on foreign income, while U.S. taxes on the income are imposed on the parent, usually when the income is distributed as dividends. Only by treating foreign taxes on the subsidiary as paid by the parent can double taxation of the income be avoided.

Under §78, a domestic corporation qualifying for the indirect credit under §902 must report additional dividend income equal to the amount of the deemed paid taxes. The purpose of this fictional gross income item, commonly known as a gross-up, is to roughly equate the tax treatment of income earned through foreign subsidiaries with the treatment of income of foreign branches.[4] U.S. taxable income is a pretax amount.[5] Dividends are necessarily paid from after-tax earnings, net of all taxes paid by the distributing corporation. Equivalence between the branch and subsidiary situations can only be achieved by augmenting a parent's dividend income to be a pretax amount.[6] Section 78 accomplishes this.

Assume a foreign branch of a domestic corporation has net income (before taxes) of $100, and foreign income taxes of $40 are imposed on the income. U.S. taxable income includes the entire $100, not just the $60 remaining after taxes. Assume the income is instead earned by a foreign subsidiary that distributes all earnings currently to its domestic parent. The subsidiary's earnings and profits, and hence the parent's dividends, are $60 because earnings and profits are an after-tax amount. By reason of the distribution, §902 treats the parent as having paid the subsidiary's foreign income taxes of $40, and §78 requires that this amount also be reported as gross income. As a consequence, foreign operations add $100 to the parent's taxable income and $40 to its potential credit, just as in the branch case.

Indirect credit is allowed under §902 only when dividends are distributed by a foreign corporation to a domestic corporation.[7] However, U.S. shareholders of CFCs are sometimes taxed under subpart F on undistributed earnings of the CFCs.[8] When a domestic corporation is a CFC shareholder, the subpart F rules create the same potential for double taxation as that addressed by §902—foreign taxation of the foreign corporation and U.S. taxation of the domestic parent on the same income. Congress therefore provided in §960 that a subpart F inclusion

---

[4] See US v. Goodyear Tire & Rubber Co., 493 US 132, 135, 140 (1989) (legislative history of indirect credit "clearly reflects an intent to equalize treatment between domestic corporations that operate through foreign subsidiaries and those that operate through unincorporated foreign branches").

[5] See IRC §275(a)(4) (credit claimant allowed no deduction for foreign income taxes), discussed supra ¶69.1.

[6] "The 'gross-up' prevents the U.S. corporate taxpayer from effectively obtaining a deduction as well as a credit for foreign taxes, since the amount of the actual distribution or subpart F inclusion reflects only after-foreign tax profits." Staff of Joint Comm. on Tax'n, 99th Cong., 2d Sess., General Explanation of the Tax Reform Act of 1986 at 858 n.6 (Comm. Print 1987) [hereinafter 1986 Bluebook].

[7] IRC §902(a).

[8] See supra ¶68.2.

is treated as a dividend for purposes of the credit rules and thus brings §§902 and 78 into play.[9]

Sections 902, 960, and 78 apply only for purposes of the foreign tax credit. Foreign income taxes deemed paid by a domestic corporation under these provisions can never be taken as deductions, even for years for which the taxpayer chooses the deduction rather than the credit for foreign income taxes it actually pays.[10] Generally, the denial of the deduction is a matter of little consequence. If §§902 and 78 applied to a taxpayer who deducts foreign income taxes, the amount of the deemed taxes would first be added to gross income under §78 and then deducted under §164(a), and the net result would be the same as under present law.

However, denial of the deduction may have a harsh effect in one context. Under §901(j), credit is denied for income taxes imposed by several countries having bad relations with the United States.[11] Nevertheless, §§902(a) and 78 seemingly apply if the taxpayer claims credit for other taxes.[12] In consequence, when a taxpayer is deemed under §902 to have paid taxes imposed by a misbehaving country, an amount equal to the deemed paid taxes is included in gross income under §78, but no credit or deduction is allowed for the deemed paid taxes. If the taxes had been paid directly, in contrast, credit would have been denied, but a deduction would have been allowed.[13] The Treasury could avoid this inequity by construing §§902 and 960 to be inapplicable to foreign income taxes paid to misbehaving countries, thus treating them in the same way as foreign taxes not qualifying as income taxes.

¶69.8.2 Qualification Criteria

To qualify for indirect credit under §902 or §960, a taxpayer must be a domestic corporation, and it must meet an ownership requirement and a dividend test.

The ownership requirement is that the domestic corporation must own at least 10 percent of the voting stock of a foreign corporation.[14] The requirement must be satisfied by stock owned directly by the credit claimant; no constructive

---

[9] Section 551 taxes U.S. shareholders of foreign personal holding companies (FPHCs) on their ratable shares of undistributed FPHC income. The FPHC rules have no analogue to §960, and the IRS ruled that a constructive dividend under §551 is not a dividend for purposes of §902. Rev. Rul. 74-59, 1974-1 CB 183. The regulations reverse this position, defining "dividend" to include deemed dividends under, among other provisions, §551. Reg. §1.902-1(a)(11). See TD 8708, supra note 1, at 15–16.

[10] Reg. §1.902-1(c)(3).

[11] See supra ¶69.4.8.

[12] See IRC §901(j)(1)(B).

[13] IRC §901(j)(3).

[14] IRC §902(a). See Willens, What Restrictions on Voting Rights Will Affect Voting Stock Status? 75 J. Tax'n 208 (1991).

ownership rules apply.[15] Assume domestic corporation P owns nonvoting preferred stock of foreign corporation F whose voting stock is owned by a subsidiary of P. Although P is beneficial owner of F's voting stock, it does not satisfy §902's ownership test because it owns none of the voting stock itself.

Under §902, the dividend requirement is that the ownership test must be met when a dividend is received from the foreign corporation.[16] The analogous requirement under §960 is that the ownership test must be met at the end of the CFC's taxable year for which the subpart F inclusion is recognized (or if the foreign corporation ceases to be a CFC during the year, on the last day during the year on which it is a CFC).

The usual tax definition of "dividend"—a distribution from current or accumulated earnings and profits—generally applies under §902.[17] A dividend is considered received "when the cash or other property is unqualifiedly made subject to the demands of the distributee."[18] Amounts characterized as dividends by other Code provisions, even though not distributed, are also treated as dividends for purposes of §902.[19] For example, dividend treatment might result under §367(b) from any one of several types of transactions involving stock of a foreign corporation,[20] under §551 if the foreign corporation is a foreign personal holding company,[21] or under §1248 on a U.S. shareholder's sale of stock of a

---

[15] First Chicago NBD Corp. v. CIR, 135 F3d 457 (7th Cir. 1998) (stock owned by commonly controlled corporations may not be aggregated to reach 10 percent threshold, even if they file consolidated return); Rev. Rul. 85-3, 1985-1 CB 222 (same); Rev. Rul. 74-459, 1974-2 CB 207 (no indirect credit where dividend was received on nonvoting stock in foreign corporation in which shareholder had no direct voting interest, even though shareholder's wholly owned foreign subsidiary owned 50 percent of distributing corporation's voting stock); Rev. Rul. 74-459, 1974-2 CB 207 (no indirect credit where dividend was received on nonvoting stock in foreign corporation in which shareholder had no direct voting interest, even though shareholder's wholly owned foreign subsidiary owned 50 percent of distributing corporation's voting stock).

In Revenue Ruling 71-141, 1971-1 CB 211, the IRS allowed the indirect credit to two domestic corporations, each of which was a 50 percent partner of a domestic general partnership that owned 40 percent of the voting stock of a foreign corporation and received dividends from the corporation. The IRS intends to propose additional regulations on whether the indirect credit should also be allowed to domestic corporations that are partners in domestic limited partnerships or foreign partnerships owning stock of a foreign corporation or are members of limited liability companies or trusts owing such stock. TD 8708, supra note 1, at 14.

[16] A DISC or former DISC is treated as a foreign corporation for this purpose to the extent dividends received from it are treated as foreign source income under §§861(a)(2)(D) and 862(a)(2), which are discussed infra ¶70.3. Reg. §1.902-1(a)(2).

[17] Reg. §1.902-1(a)(11). See IRC §316(a), discussed infra ¶92.1.2.

[18] Reg. §1.902-1(a)(12).

[19] Reg. §1.902-1(a)(11). Deemed dividends are treated as received at the times indicated by the statutes under which they arise. Reg. §1.902-1(a)(12).

[20] See supra ¶68.7.

[21] See supra ¶68.3.

CFC.[22] However, the term "dividend" does not encompass inclusions under §§951(a) (subpart F) and 1293 (passive foreign investment companies electing to be treated as pass-through entities) because §§960 and 1293(f) contain indirect credit rules for these inclusions.

In Revenue Ruling 92-86, the IRS held that §902 credit may be allowed with respect to amounts treated as dividends under §304.[23] The ruling involves a sale by domestic corporation DX to foreign corporation FX of all of the stock of foreign corporation FY; DX and FX are wholly owned subsidiaries of domestic corporation P. Under §304(a)(1), the selling price, assumed to be $40, is treated as a distribution in redemption of stock of FX (the acquiring corporation) because FX and FY (the corporation whose stock is acquired) are controlled by the same person (P). Under §302(d), the distribution is equivalent to a dividend because the distributee (DX) actually owned all FY stock before the transaction and, through P, constructively owns the stock after the transaction. Under §304(b)(2), the distribution ($40) is deemed to come first from the earnings and profits of the acquiring corporation (FX), assumed to be $30, and then from the earnings and profits of the corporation whose stock was sold (FY), which are also $30. The $40 is thus a dividend in its entirety. The ruling holds that the deemed dividend brings with it §902 credit.

Section 902(a) limits the indirect credit to corporate dividend recipients owning at least 10 percent of the voting stock of the distributing corporation. Normally, only direct ownership is counted toward the 10 percent minimum, and DX (the deemed dividend recipient) never owned stock of FX and disposes of its FY stock in the transaction. However, the legislative history of 1984 amendments to §302 indicates that §902 credit should be allowed in at least some §304 cases, and the ruling therefore holds that constructive ownership is counted under §902(a) for this limited purpose. Since DX constructively owned all stock of FX and FY at the time of the deemed dividend, §902 credit is allowable. Where, as here, constructive ownership is a crucial factor in the characterization of a receipt as a dividend, fairness perhaps demands that constructive ownership be considered also in determining eligibility for indirect credit with respect to the dividend, even though constructive ownership cannot otherwise qualify a dividend recipient for indirect credit.

Although only voting stock counts toward satisfying the ownership test, a domestic corporation whose voting stock satisfies the test is also entitled to the

---

[22] See supra ¶68.2.16.

[23] Rev. Rul. 92-86, 1992-2 CB 199. For §304, see infra ¶93.3. The positions taken in the 1992 ruling were initially stated in Rev. Rul. 91-5, 1991-1 CB 114. See Birnkrant & Croker, IRS Clarifies Redemptions Through Related Corporations in Cross-Border Transactions, 78 J. Tax'n 38 (1993); Dolan, International Aspects of Section 304 Transactions, 24 Tax Mgmt. Int'l J. 75 (1995); Oosterhuis & Hobbet, Musings on Revenue Ruling 91-5 and Its Implications for Section 304 Transactions, 50 Tax Notes 1291 (Mar. 18, 1991); Staffaroni, The International Boundaries of Section 304, 46 Tax Lawyer 125 (1992).

indirect credit with respect to dividends and subpart F inclusions on nonvoting stock.[24]

The indirect credit is not allowed to an S corporation, even if it satisfies all of the requirements outlined above.[25] An S corporation is treated as a partnership for purposes of the foreign tax credit rules,[26] and it thus cannot be a "domestic corporation," as required by §902(a). Shareholders of an S corporation are allowed credit for foreign income taxes paid by the corporation, but the shareholders cannot qualify for the indirect credit because corporations cannot be shareholders of S corporations.[27]

¶69.8.3　　Computation of Amount Deemed Paid

The foreign income taxes deemed paid under §902 equal the foreign corporation's foreign income taxes multiplied by the following fraction:

$$\frac{\text{Amount of dividend}}{\text{Foreign corporation's earnings and profits}}$$

The computation under §960 is the same except that the subpart F inclusion is substituted for the amount of the dividend. The effect of this formula is to prorate the foreign income taxes among the earnings and profits, treating the domestic corporate shareholder as having paid the taxes prorated to the portion of the earnings and profits that is taxed to it. If a domestic corporation qualifies for indirect credit with respect to two or more foreign corporations, §§902 and 960 are applied separately to each foreign corporation.[28]

The foregoing scheme requires that a dividend or subpart F inclusion be traced to particular earnings of the foreign corporation and that the foreign taxes on these earnings be identified. The statutes provide two schemes for doing this, one for earnings accumulated after 1986 and the other for pre-1987 earnings. The post-1986 scheme pools together all earnings and profits of a foreign corporation accumulated after 1986 and also pools the foreign taxes on these earnings. Under the rules for distributions from pre-1987 earnings, dividends are traced to the earnings of particular years, and the deemed paid taxes are a ratable share of the foreign corporation's foreign income taxes for the year in which the distributed earnings were realized. Generally, dividends are traced first to post-1986 earnings and, when they are exhausted, to earnings accumulated in years before 1987,

---

[24] See Rev. Rul. 79-74, 1979-1 CB 242 (domestic corporation owning 10 percent of voting stock and 5 percent of nonvotingstock of foreign corporation gets §902 credit when dividends are distributed on nonvoting stock only).

[25] Reg. §1.902-1(a)(1). For S corporations, see infra ¶95.6.

[26] IRC §1373(a)(1).

[27] IRC §1361(b)(1)(B).

[28] Reg. §1.902-1(c)(1)(i). See Reg. §1.902-1(f) Ex. 2.

starting with the taxable year beginning in 1986 and proceeding backwards in time.[29]

Congress adopted the pooling method in 1986 because it found the year-by-year method excessively susceptible to manipulation.[30] The rules for distributions from pre-1987 earnings encouraged taxpayers to distribute dividends traced to heavily taxed profits and to avoid distributions traced to profits taxed more lightly. Assume domestic corporation P has a foreign subsidiary, F, that has a steady flow of income, as measured by U.S. rules, but is subject to tax in a foreign country that allows income to be shifted from year to year. In years prior to 1987, F bunched its income in alternate years for foreign tax purposes and distributed dividends to P in the high-income years. This device (called the rhythm method) caused deemed paid taxes to flow through at a higher rate than the long-run effective rate of foreign tax.[31]

Assume F's annual pretax income under U.S. rules was 100u (100 units of country X's currency), but under the foreign tax rules, it was 200u every second year and zero in the other years. If the foreign tax rate was 30 percent, and 40u was distributed in each of the high-income years, (1) the foreign income taxes for each dividend year were 60u (30 percent of 200u), (2) earnings and profits for the year were 40u (100u pretax income by U.S. standards less 60u tax), and (3) the deemed paid taxes under the pre-1986 rules were:

$$(60u)(40u/40u) = 60u$$

Although the foreign tax rate was 30 percent, the deemed paid taxes were at an effective rate of 60 percent (60u is 60 percent of the sum of the 40u dividend and the 60u gross-up under §78). Also, although the dividends were less than 30 percent of after-tax earnings (over each two-year period, earnings of 200u less 60u in taxes, as against dividends of 40u), all of F's taxes were deemed paid by the parent.

Under the method adopted in 1986, the pooling of foreign income taxes and earnings and profits causes the indirect credit to reflect more closely the long-run effective rate of foreign tax. Assume F continues the same income and distribution pattern after 1986; the second year governed by the pooling rules, 1988, is a high-income/dividend year. If 1u equals $1 at all relevant times, post-1986 foreign income taxes are $60 (the sum of the taxes for 1987 and 1988), post-1986

---

[29] Reg. §1.902-1(b)(2). See Reg. §1.902-1(b)(5) Ex. 1.

If the foreign corporation has more than one shareholder, post-1986 undistributed earnings are considered distributed ratably to the shareholders, and the earnings and profits of each pre-1987 year are similarly prorated among the shareholders. Reg. §1.902-1(b)(2).

[30] 1986 Bluebook, supra note 6, at 868-70. Also, the pre-1987 rules did not work well when a foreign corporation sustained losses in some years, a problem that is discussed below in ¶69.8.6.

[31] 1986 Bluebook, supra note 6, at 869.

undistributed earnings are 140u (the pretax income for these two years of 200u less the foreign income taxes of 60u), and the deemed paid taxes are:

$$(\$60)(40u/140u) = \$17.14$$

The effective rate of the deemed paid taxes equals the foreign tax rate of 30 percent ($17.14 is 30 percent of the sum of the 40u dividend and the 17.14u gross-up).

The pre-1987 rules continue to apply to post-1986 distributions of pre-1987 earnings. The rules have a somewhat greater contemporary significance than might be apparent. Under §1248, gain on a sale of stock of a foreign corporation is treated as a dividend to the extent of the earnings and profits attributable to the stock if, when the earnings were accumulated, the taxpayer held at least 10 percent of the corporation's voting stock and the corporation was a CFC.[32] Also, under §367(b), when a foreign corporation liquidates into a domestic parent corporation, the parent must usually recognize dividend income equal to its ratable share of the subsidiary's earnings and profits.[33] Moreover, if a CFC invests foreign earnings in U.S. property or excess passive assets, U.S. shareholders are taxed on their ratable shares of these earnings.[34] Earnings and profits from periods in the distant past thus can become taxable to U.S. shareholders even if dividend distributions never exceed current earnings.

1. *Foreign corporation's foreign income taxes.* The rules for both pre-1987 and post-1986 earnings require an annual determination of a foreign corporation's foreign income taxes. Under the post-1986 rules, foreign income taxes must be ascertained for the years included in the pool of post-1986 foreign income taxes. Under the pre-1987 rules, when a dividend is traced to the accumulated profits of a particular year, the foreign income taxes of the foreign corporation for that year are included in the formula for determining the taxes deemed paid on account of the dividend.

The U.S. definition of "foreign income tax" is used for this purpose.[35] The foreign income taxes of a foreign corporation for a particular year are the taxes

---

[32] See supra ¶68.2.16.

[33] See supra ¶68.7.

[34] See supra ¶¶68.2.11, 68.2.12.

[35] IRC §902(c)(4); Reg. §1.902-1(a)(7). See supra ¶69.4 for this definition. Also, if the foreign corporation is shareholder of another foreign corporation, taxes deemed paid by the foreign corporation on account of dividends from lower-tier corporations are included in the foreign corporation's foreign income taxes. See infra ¶69.8.5.

If the foreign subsidiary is a resident of a country with which the United States has an income tax treaty, the treaty may identify the taxes of that country qualifying as "foreign income taxes" and may affect the computation of the taxes paid by the subsidiary. See Xerox Corp. v. US, 41 F3d 647 (Fed. Cir. 1994) (nonacq.) (treatment under U.S.-U.K. treaty of United Kingdom's Advance Corporation Tax); Bouma, The U.K. Advance Corporation Tax and the Deemed Paid Foreign Tax Credit Under Section 902, 23 Tax Mgmt. Int'l J. 549 (1994).

imposed by foreign tax authorities for the year on income as measured under foreign law.[36]

However, for years after 1986, portions of the foreign income taxes on high withholding tax interest are excluded from a foreign corporation's tax pool if the corporation is a noncontrolled §902 corporation.[37] High withholding tax interest is interest income that is subject to a withholding tax imposed by a foreign country or U.S. possession at a rate exceeding 5 percent.[38] A noncontrolled §902 corporation is a foreign corporation with respect to which the taxpayer (domestic corporation) qualifies for indirect credit under §902 but whose U.S. shareholders, in the aggregate, own not more than 50 percent of its stock, by value or voting power.[39] When these conditions are present, there is excluded from the foreign corporation's foreign tax pool the excess of (1) the foreign withholding tax, over (2) the amount the tax would have been if the rate were 5 percent.[40]

Assume F, a foreign banking corporation that is owned 40 percent by a domestic corporation and 60 percent by unrelated foreign persons, receives interest income of $1,000 that is subject to a 10 percent withholding tax imposed by foreign country X.[41] The limitation described in the preceding paragraph applies because U.S. ownership of F does not exceed 50 percent, the tax is a withholding tax, the rate exceeds 5 percent, and the income subject to the tax is interest. Thus, only $50 of the $100 tax (5 percent of the gross interest income subject to the tax) is included in F's foreign tax pool. The remaining $50 is not altogether ignored in assembling the formula because F's earnings and profits are reduced by the entire tax, including the portion made noncreditable by this rule.[42] Assume (1) F's only other income is $1,000, which is not taxed by any country, (2) its expenses are $1,700, and (3) its earnings and profits of $200 ($2,000 less expenses of $1,700 and foreign income taxes of $100) are distributed as dividends to the shareholders. The domestic corporation, which owns 40 percent of the stock, receives $80 and is deemed under §902 to pay $20 of F's foreign income taxes, computed as follows:

---

[36] See Rev. Rul. 74-310, 1974-2 CB 205 (foreign corporation used completed contract method in determining accumulated profits for U.S. tax purposes, but used percentage of completion method in reporting income to foreign tax authorities; held, foreign income taxes on the foreign base are creditable under §902); Rev. Rul. 70-303, 1970-1 CB 161 (foreign income taxes accrued for year are fully included in §902 calculation even though payment of one half of taxes was deferred for four years by agreement between taxpayer and taxing country).

[37] IRC §904(d)(2)(E)(ii).

[38] See supra ¶69.6.3.

[39] See supra ¶69.6.7.

[40] The excess is measured in the foreign corporation's functional currency, and the amount not disallowed is translated into U.S. dollars at the spot rate on the date of the foreign corporation's payment of the tax. Reg. §1.902-1(a)(8)(iii). See Reg. §1.902-1(f) Ex. 2.

[41] 1986 Bluebook, supra note 6, at 886–87.

[42] Reg. §1.902-1(a)(9)(iii).

$$(\$50)(\$80/\$200) = \$20$$

If U.S. shareholders own more than 50 percent of a foreign corporation's stock, the foregoing limitation does not apply, but a look-through rule in the credit limitation rules of §904 subjects high withholding tax interest to a separate limitation that has a similar effect.[43]

2. *Distributions from post-1986 earnings.* When a qualifying domestic corporation receives a dividend from a foreign corporation's post-1986 earnings, the domestic corporation is deemed to have paid foreign income taxes equal to the foreign corporation's "post-1986 foreign income taxes" multiplied by the following fraction:[44]

$$\frac{\text{Amount of the dividend}}{\text{Foreign corporation's post-1986 undistributed earnings}}$$

Under §960, the same rule applies when subpart F requires an inclusion in a qualifying domestic corporation's gross income for a year after 1986, except that the amount of the inclusion is substituted for the dividend in the numerator of the fraction.[45] Under both provisions, post-1986 foreign income taxes are stated in U.S. dollars,[46] while the dividend or subpart F inclusion and post-1986 undistributed earnings are stated in the foreign corporation's functional currency.[47]

Assume domestic corporation P receives a dividend from foreign corporation F of 15u (15 units of F's functional currency); F's post-1986 foreign income

---

[43] For the look-through rules, see supra ¶69.6.8.

[44] IRC §902(a). If the taxpayer satisfies the qualification criteria for more than one foreign corporation, §902 is applied separately with respect to each foreign corporation. See Reg. §1.902-3(b)(1)(ii).

[45] Subpart F inclusions are of three kinds—subpart F income, earnings invested in U.S. property, and earnings taxed to U.S. shareholders as a result of excess passive assets of the CFC. See supra ¶68.2.1. Subpart F income—primarily income from transactions considered susceptible to tax haven abuse—consists only of current earnings and profits. IRC §952(c)(1). Earnings invested in U.S. property and excess passive assets can be either current or accumulated earnings and profits. See IRC §§956(a), 956A(a), discussed supra ¶¶68.2.11, 68.2.12.

Generally, the pooling principles of §902 apply with respect to all kinds of subpart F inclusions because it was thought necessary to restrict the temptation "to avoid the effect of pooling by creating subpart F inclusions." 1986 Bluebook, supra note 6, at 907. However, Congress anticipated that "technical difficulties" might arise in applying the pooling rules to subpart F income, and it therefore provided regulatory authority to modify pooling for these inclusions. Also, earnings invested in U.S. property come from pre-1987 earnings once the post-1986 pool is exhausted, and in this case, the year-by-year regime for such earnings applies rather than pooling.

[46] Foreign income taxes paid in foreign currencies are translated into U.S. dollars at the exchange rate prevailing at the time of payment. IRC §986(a).

[47] For the term "functional currency," see infra ¶71.2.

taxes are $40, and its post-1986 undistributed earnings are 60u. If *P* owns at least 10 percent of *F*'s voting stock, it is deemed to pay foreign income taxes of:

$$(\$40)(15u/60u) = \$10$$

The result would be the same if *P* received no dividend but included 15u of *F*'s post-1986 earnings in its gross income under subpart F.

A foreign corporation's "post-1986 undistributed earnings" (the denominator of the fraction) is the sum of its earnings and profits for the period beginning with the foreign corporation's first taxable year beginning after 1986 and ending with the year of the dividend or subpart F inclusion.[48] This sum is reduced by the amounts of earnings distributed as dividends for prior post-1986 years and earnings included in shareholder gross income under subpart F, §1248, or any other provision for any such prior year.[49] However, dividend distributions or subpart F inclusions for the current year do not affect post-1986 undistributed earnings.[50] Earnings and profits are determined from the foreign tax base, adjusted to reflect U.S. accounting and tax rules.[51] Assume a foreign corporation organized in 1995 has earnings and profits of 60u for 1995 and zero for 1996; it makes distributions to shareholders of 40u in 1995 and 20u in 1996. Post-1986 undistributed earnings for 1995 are 60u (earnings and profits in taxable years beginning after 1986, unreduced by current distributions) and for 1996 are 20u (the sum of earnings and profits for 1995 and 1996, less distributions in 1995).

Generally, all of a foreign corporation's earnings and profits comprise a single pool. "Special allocations of earnings and taxes to particular shareholders, whether required or permitted by foreign law or a shareholder agreement, shall be disregarded."[52] For example, if the corporation is subject to a foreign income tax that applies only to corporate income ratably attributable to shareholders not

---

[48] IRC §902(c)(1); Reg. §1.902-1(a)(9)(i).

[49] Reg. §1.902-1(a)(8)(i). Under §1248, a U.S. shareholder's gain on a sale or exchange of stock of a controlled foreign corporation (CFC) is treated as a dividend from the CFC to the extent of the earnings and profits ratably allocated to the stock, exclusive of earnings accumulated before the shareholder acquired the stock or the corporation became a CFC. See supra ¶68.2.16. Other provisions under which earnings and profits might be included in shareholder gross income without a dividend distribution include §§304, 367(b), 551, and 1293.

[50] 1986 Bluebook, supra note 6, at 906.

[51] The earnings and profits of a foreign corporation are "determined according to rules substantially similar to those applicable to domestic corporations." IRC §§902(c)(1), 964(a). This idea is worked out in considerable detail in the regulations. Reg. §1.964-1. Also, the foreign currency provisions contain earnings and profits rules that must be applied in this context. IRC §§902(c)(1), 986. See infra ¶71.4 for the foreign currency rules.

Post-1986 undistributed earnings are reduced by all taxes imposed on the foreign corporation, whether or not creditable. Reg. §1.902-1(a)(9)(iii).

[52] Reg. §1.902-1(a)(9)(iv).

resident in the taxing country, all earnings and profits, including nontaxable earnings allocable to resident shareholders, are included in post-1986 undistributed earnings.[53]

A foreign corporation's "post-1986 foreign income taxes" usually consist of the sum of its foreign income taxes for the year of the dividend or subpart F inclusion and all prior years after 1986, reduced by the portions of the taxes allocable to dividends paid and subpart F inclusions in these prior years.[54] "If, however, there is an agreement to pay dividends only out of earnings in the separate categories for passive or high withholding tax interest income, then only

---

[53] The Tax Court and the IRS have disagreed over the treatment of this situation under pre-1987 law. Vulcan Materials Co. v. CIR, 96 TC 410 (1991), aff'd per curiam, 959 F2d 973 (11th Cir. 1992) (nonacq.); Rev. Rul. 87-14, 1987-1 CB 181, discussed infra text accompanying note 70. The IRS follows the approach described in the text, including all earnings and profits in the numerator of the §902 fraction, but the Tax Court has excluded the nontaxable earnings from accumulated profits under pre-1987 law. The proposed "regulations are intended to make clear that the decision in Vulcan is not applicable to distributions out of post-1986 undistributed earnings." INTL-933-86, supra note 1, at 960.

[54] IRC §902(c)(2). The statute says the reduction for prior years' distributions equals the "foreign taxes . . . deemed paid with respect to dividends distributed by the foreign corporation in prior taxable years." Since foreign taxes are deemed paid only by shareholders that are domestic corporations owning at least 10 percent of the foreign corporation's voting stock, the quoted language literally does not cover foreign taxes allocable to dividends to individuals and foreign persons and to domestic corporations with smaller than 10 percent interests. Post-1986 undistributed earnings, however, are reduced by all distributions in prior years, including distributions to shareholders not eligible for indirect credit. The statutory mechanism thus can work properly only if post-1986 foreign income taxes are also reduced for all prior years' dividends, including those to ineligible shareholders. The regulations so provide. Reg. §1.902-1(a)(8)(i). See TD 8708, supra note 1, at 14-15.

Assume (1) foreign corporation F has two shareholders, a domestic corporation (D) holding 25 percent of the stock and a U.S. citizen owning 75 percent, (2) F's earnings and profits and foreign income taxes are 60u and $40 for 1995 and zero for 1996, and (3) the corporation distributes dividends of 40u in 1995 and 20u in 1996. D receives a dividend of 10u in 1995 (25 percent of 40u). The dividend equals one sixth of F's post-1986 undistributed earnings, and D thus is deemed to have paid foreign income taxes of $6.67 (one sixth of the post-1986 foreign income taxes of $40). For 1996, the post-1986 undistributed earnings are 20u (the sum of 1995 and 1996 earnings, reduced by 1995 dividends to both shareholders), and post-1986 foreign income taxes should be $13.3 (the $40 tax for 1995 less the two thirds thereof allocable to the 1995 distribution of two thirds of 1995 earnings). On the 1996 distribution, D receives 5u (25 percent of post-1986 undistributed earnings of 20u), and it should be deemed to have paid foreign income taxes of $3.3 (one fourth of $13.3). If this is so, D, which receives distribution of one fourth of the 60u earned in 1995, is deemed to have paid one fourth of the taxes on those earnings (the sum of $6.7 for 1995 and $3.3 for 1996 is one fourth of F's foreign income taxes of $40).

However, post-1986 foreign income taxes are not reduced by a dividend that is distributed out of current earnings and profits when the foreign corporation has a deficit in post-1986 undistributed earnings. Reg. §1.902-1(a)(8)(i). Such a dividend carries no indirect credit and thus should not affect post-1986 foreign income taxes. TD 8708, supra note 1, at 15.

taxes imposed on passive or high withholding tax interest earnings shall be treated as related to the dividend."[55]

A special rule applies if no domestic corporation owns a 10 percent or greater voting stock interest in the foreign corporation until some time after 1986. In this case, earnings and profits and foreign income taxes for years before the year during which a domestic corporation first meets the 10 percent test are excluded from post-1986 undistributed earnings and post-1986 foreign income taxes.[56] Earlier years, including years after 1986, are treated as pre-1987 years.[57] Assume domestic corporation P, in 1995, acquires all shares of foreign corporation F from a nonresident alien individual.[58] If no domestic corporation has owned as much as 10 percent of F's voting stock at any time since 1986, dividends received by P are first traced to earnings of F accumulated after 1994. Distributions from this pool carry with them §902 credit under the post-1986 rules, but only for taxes for 1995 and subsequent years. Once this pool is exhausted, distributions are traced to accumulated profits for years before 1995, proceeding in reverse order of time starting with 1994, and distributions from these profits carry with them §902 credit under the pre-1987 rules.

Under the foregoing rules, earnings and profits, foreign income taxes, and the various adjustments are determined taxable year by taxable year and then aggregated. A foreign corporation's taxable year for this purpose is apparently the accounting period used in determining its foreign tax liabilities.[59]

3. *Distributions from pre-1987 earnings.* If a foreign corporation distributes a dividend that exceeds post-1986 undistributed earnings, the distribution is deemed made from earnings and profits accumulated before 1987. Such a dividend is traced to the foreign corporation's accumulated profits for a particular year or years, starting with the taxable year beginning in 1986 and proceeding backward in time.[60] The amount traced to a particular year's accumulated profits

---

[55] Reg. §1.902-1(a)(9)(iv).

[56] IRC §902(c)(3); Reg. §1.902-1(a)(13)(i). This rule also applies to a lower-tier foreign corporation if no domestic corporation satisfies the ownership requirements for the indirect credit with respect to the foreign corporation until a year subsequent to 1986. For the indirect credit for foreign income taxes paid by lower-tier foreign corporations, see infra ¶69.8.5.

[57] Reg. §1.902-1(a)(10)(i).

[58] See Reg. §1.902-1(a)(13)(ii) Ex.

[59] The statute says only that when foreign income taxes "are determined on the basis of an accounting period of less than 1 year," that accounting period is a taxable year. IRC §902(c)(5). It makes no sense to track short years unless, as a general rule, the U.S. taxable year is the same as the foreign taxable year. Generally, a CFC must adopt as its U.S. taxable year the taxable year of its majority shareholder. IRC §§898, discussed supra ¶68.2.17. It is not clear how that requirement applies in this context.

[60] IRC §902(c)(1) (before amendment in 1986). See Rev. Rul. 69-447, 1969-2 CB 153 (pre-1987 dividend is from current earnings and profits to extent of earnings and profits for entire year, not just earnings and profits allocated to portion of year preceding dividend).

carries with it deemed paid taxes equal to the foreign income taxes of the foreign corporation for that year, multiplied by the following fraction:[61]

$$\frac{\text{Dividend from that year's accumulated profits}}{\text{Foreign corporation's earnings and profits for the year}}$$

The deemed paid taxes are translated from the foreign corporation's functional currency into U.S. dollars at the spot exchange rate prevailing at the time of the distribution.[62]

Assume foreign corporation F paid foreign income taxes of $40 for 1985, has $60 of earnings and profits for the year, and distributes a dividend of $30 from these earnings and profits to a domestic corporation that qualifies for the indirect credit.[63] The domestic corporation is deemed to pay foreign income taxes of:

$$(\$40)(\$30/\$60) = \$20$$

Earnings and profits are determined under U.S. law, applied as though the foreign corporation were domestic.[64] Various adjustments must be made, however, to account for foreign accounting rules and currency translations. These

---

In Brunswick Corp. v. CIR, 100 TC 6 (1993), the taxpayer, before 1987, made a taxable exchange of the stock of a foreign subsidiary. Under §1248, its gain on the exchange was dividend income in an amount equal to all of the subsidiary's earnings and profits immediately before the exchange. The court held that in applying §902(a), the §1248 dividend had to be traced to accumulated profits of particular years. Tracing could not be skipped on the theory that because the deemed dividend included all of the subsidiary's earnings and profits, all foreign income taxes of the subsidiary not previously credited under §902 should be creditable at time of the exchange.

If a pre-1987 dividend was paid during the first 60 days of the year, the dividend was deemed paid from accumulated profits of prior years, not those of the year of distribution, unless the IRS was "shown otherwise." See Snap-On Tools, Inc. v. US, 26 Cl. Ct. 1045, 92-2 USTC ¶50,425 (1992) (IRS cannot disregard 60-day rule unless it is "shown" that distribution during first 60 days of taxable year came from accumulated profits of current year).

In all cases not covered by the foregoing rules, the district director for the district in which the taxpayer's return was filed has "power" to trace dividends to accumulated profits of particular years. Reg. §1.902-3(g)(4).

[61] IRC §902(a) (before amendment in 1986). The statute states the denominator as "the amount of such accumulated profits in excess of such income . . . taxes (other than those deemed paid)," but the regulations confirm that these words refer to the corporation's earnings and profits. Reg. §1.902-3(e).

[62] Reg. §1.902-1(a)(10)(iii).

[63] See Reg. §1.902-3(k) Ex. 1.

[64] Reg. §1.902-1(a)(10)(ii); US v. Goodyear Tire & Rubber Co., 493 US 132, 133 (1989) ("tax provisions should generally be read to incorporate domestic tax concepts absent a clear congressional expression that foreign concepts control"). See generally Henrey, *Goodyear* Affirms Supremacy of U.S. Tax Accounting Rules, 72 J. Tax'n 164 (1990).

adjustments may, but need not, be made according to rules provided in regulations promulgated under subpart F.[65]

The use of U.S. rules in computing earnings and profits sometimes causes dividends to be traced to years in which a foreign corporation has no income for foreign tax purposes and thus pays no foreign income taxes. In *Goodyear Tire & Rubber Co. v. United States*, for example, the taxpayer's foreign subsidiary initially paid substantial income taxes to the United Kingdom for 1970 and 1971, but it later obtained a refund of these taxes because of a net operating loss carryback from 1973.[66] The 1973 deductions that created the carryback were peculiar to U.K. law, and there was no net operating loss under U.S. rules. The foreign carryback had the effect of increasing earnings and profits for 1970 and 1971 because it reduced the subtraction for foreign taxes without otherwise affecting gross income or deductions. The dividends paid in 1970 and 1971 thus continued to be traced to accumulated profits for those years. The §902 credit that had originally passed through with the dividends disappeared because the foreign income taxes paid for those years were refunded.[67] The Court rejected the taxpayer's argument that the foreign corporation's accumulated profits should be determined under U.K. law and that the carryback's elimination of 1970 and 1971 earnings should cause the dividends for those years to be traced to earlier years when foreign income taxes were paid. In the Court's view, 1970 and 1971 were years for which the subsidiary had earnings but paid no foreign income taxes, and these earnings should not be excluded as a source of dividends merely because no foreign country chose to tax them.

The multiplicand of the §902 formula (the foreign corporation's foreign income taxes) includes all foreign income taxes imposed for the year to which the dividend is traced, with one exception:[68] If the foreign corporation has income subject to U.S. taxation, an exclusion is made for the foreign income taxes "on or with respect to" an amount of accumulated profits equal to the U.S. tax. Assume foreign corporation F's accumulated profits for a particular year are $100, including $10 of income from sources within the United States that is subject to a U.S. tax of $3.5. F pays $40 of foreign income taxes, which are imposed at a uniform rate of 40 percent on its $100 of pretax profits. The foreign income taxes taken into account in applying §902 are $38.6, consisting of the foreign income taxes imposed on the $96.5 of accumulated profits remaining after subtraction of the U.S. tax (40 percent of $96.5 is $38.6). The remaining $1.4 of foreign taxes reduces F's earnings and profits, but it is excluded from F's foreign income taxes.

According to the proposed regulations, "[s]pecial allocations of accumulated profits and taxes to particular shareholders with respect to distributions of

---

[65] Reg. §1.902-3(g)(1). See Reg. §1.902-3(g)(3) for the procedures for electing to use the subpart F rules.

[66] US v. Goodyear Tire & Rubber Co., 493 US 132, 133 (1989).

[67] The credit for any year is recomputed if foreign income taxes initially credited for the year are refunded. IRC §905(c).

[68] Reg. §1.902-3(f).

pre-1987 accumulated profits in taxable years beginning after December 31, 1986, whether required or permitted by foreign law or a shareholder agreement, shall be disregarded."[69] One application of this statement is a foreign corporate income tax that applies only to the earnings allocable to some shareholders. In cases involving pre-1987 distributions by foreign corporations subject to such taxes, the IRS held that all earnings and profits of the foreign corporation, including the nontaxable earnings, are pooled together in the denominator of the §902 fraction, but the Tax Court held that only income subject to the tax is included in the fraction.[70]

Assume foreign corporation F, which is incorporated under the laws of and does business only in foreign country X, is subject to a country X income tax that only applies to earnings allocable to shareholders who are not country X residents. F has two equal shareholders, a country X resident and a Delaware corporation. F's income is $100, and the country X tax rate is 45 percent. F's tax liability is $22.5 (45 percent of the 50 percent of the income that is allocable to the nonresident shareholder). Earnings and profits are $77.5 (income of $100 less taxes of $22.5). If a dividend of $10 is received by the corporate shareholder, the deemed paid taxes, according to the IRS, are:

$$(\$22.5)(\$10/\$77.5) = \$2.9$$

The deemed paid taxes are at an effective rate of 22.5 percent ($2.9 is 22.5 percent of the sum of the $10 dividend and the §78 gross-up of $2.9), not the nominal foreign rate of 45 percent, because the tax, nominally imposed on only one half of the income, is prorated among all earnings and profits.

In contrast, the Tax Court applied §902 in such a situation by restricting the corporation's earnings and profits to those that were subject to the foreign income tax, thereby excluding the nontaxable earnings allocated to shareholders resident in the taxing country. Under this approach, the relevant earnings and profits in the example are $27.5 (one half of $100, less tax of $22.5), and the deemed paid taxes on the U.S. shareholder's receipt of a $10 dividend is:

$$(\$22.5)(\$10/\$27.5) = \$8.18$$

"The intent of the . . . regulations is to reverse the Tax Court's decision . . . for distributions in taxable years beginning after December 31, 1986, out of pre-1987 accumulated profits."[71]

Pre-1987 earnings and profits are reduced by amounts distributed therefrom or included in shareholder gross income without distribution under subpart F,

---

[69] Reg. §1.902-1(a)(10)(ii).

[70] Vulcan Materials Co. v. CIR, 96 TC 410 (1991), aff'd per curiam, 959 F2d 973 (11th Cir. 1992); Rev. Rul. 87-14, 1987-1 CB 181.

[71] INTL-933-86, supra note 1, at 960.

§1248, or some other provision.[72] Assume *OP*, a domestic corporation, sells all of the stock of foreign corporation *F* to domestic corporation *NP*. For purposes of determining indirect credits subsequently allowed to *NP*, pre-1987 earnings and profits are reduced by the portion of *OP*'s gain on the sale of the stock that is characterized as a dividend under §1248.[73] Similarly, foreign income taxes for a pre-1987 year are reduced by amounts deemed paid by shareholders by reason of prior distributions and gross income inclusions.[74]

4. *Coordinating the rules for pre- and post-1986 earnings.* Dividends paid after 1986 are considered distributed out of post-1986 undistributed earnings to the extent thereof.[75] Once this pool is exhausted, post-1986 dividends usually come from the accumulated profits of earlier years, starting with the accumulated profits of the taxable year beginning in 1986 and proceeding backwards from there. The pre-1987 version of §902(a) applies to the latter dividends.[76]

However, a post-1986 distribution in excess of post-1986 undistributed earnings is not traced to pre-1987 accumulated profits if it comes from post-1986 earnings and profits. This happens only if post-1986 earnings and profits exceed post-1986 undistributed earnings. A common example is where a foreign corporation with a post-1986 accumulated deficit distributes a dividend from current earnings and profits.

Assume a foreign corporation has an earnings and profits deficit of 75u for the years 1987 through 1995, has 60u of earnings and profits for 1996, and distributes 50u to its shareholder, a domestic corporation, during 1996. The distribution is a dividend because it is fully covered by current earnings and profits. Post-1986 undistributed earnings for the year are a negative 15u (accumulated deficit of 75u, less current earnings of 60u), but because the dividend comes from current earnings and profits, it is not traced to a pre-1987 year.[77] As a result, the dividend carries with it no deemed paid taxes. However, the dividend reduces undistributed earnings for the next year (1997), which, before 1997 results are taken into account, is a deficit of 65u (minus 15u for 1996, less the 1996 distribution of 50u). Assume post-1986 foreign income taxes are zero at the beginning of 1996 and $40 for 1996. Post-1986 foreign income taxes for 1997 are the sum of $40 and any taxes for 1997. The results are somewhat arbitrary in that if post-1986 undistributed earnings for 1996, taking into account the accumu-

---

[72] Reg. §1.902-1(a)(10)(ii).

[73] For §1248, see supra ¶68.2.16.

[74] Reg. §1.902-1(a)(10)(iii). This reduction is determined as though all shareholders, including individuals and foreign persons, were eligible for the indirect credit.

[75] IRC §902(c)(6)(B).

[76] IRC §902(c)(6)(A). If no domestic corporation owns 10 percent or more of the foreign corporation's voting stock until some time after 1986, years before a domestic corporation first becomes a 10 percent shareholder are treated as pre-1987 years. IRC §902(c)(3), discussed supra text accompanying notes 56-58.

[77] Reg. §1.902-1(b)(4); Notice 87-54, 1987-2 CB 363. See S. Rep. No. 313, 99th Cong., 2d Sess. 321 (1986); Reg. §1.902-1(b)(5) Ex. 2.

lated deficit and current earnings, were positive by as much as a penny, the dividend would, to that extent, be from post-1986 undistributed earnings, and the $40 of post-1986 foreign income taxes for 1995 would be deemed paid by the shareholder.

A similar but more obscure example arises from a requirement in the pre-1987 rules that a foreign corporation's earnings and profits be separately computed for purposes of §§902 and 960, respectively.[78]

5. *Reallocations under §482.* Section 482 allows the IRS to reallocate income and deductions among commonly controlled entities whenever necessary "to prevent evasion of taxes or clearly to reflect the income of any of such organizations."[79] When a foreign corporation's income is changed by a reallocation made under §482, at least one, and possibly two, changes ensue in the §902 arithmetic.

First, the reallocation alters the foreign corporation's earnings and profits, the denominator of the §902 fraction. Assume foreign corporation F initially reports earnings and profits of 60u and distributes a dividend of 10u, and indirect credit is claimed for one sixth (10u/60u) of F's foreign income taxes. If additional deductions of 30u are allocated to F under §482, the indirect credit is recomputed using a redetermined earnings and profits figure as the denominator of the fraction.[80] For example, if the deductions reduce earnings and profits from 60u to 30u, the dividend recipient is deemed to pay one third (10u/30u) of F's foreign income taxes rather than one sixth.

Second, foreign income taxes can also change as a result of a §482 allocation. A foreign levy qualifies as a foreign income tax only if it is compulsory, and a levy is not compulsory unless the taxpayer exhausts all practical remedies for minimizing it.[81] One of the principal functions of the compulsory payment rule is to require taxpayers to seek a redetermination of foreign taxes when the IRS reallocates income away from a foreign corporation under §482.[82]

Assume F originally paid foreign income taxes of 40u on pretax income of 100u, the foreign income taxes are translated as $40, and F's parent, a domestic corporation, claimed §902 credit on receiving a dividend of 10u, as follows:

$$(\$40)(10u/60u) = \$6.7$$

If 30u of F's income is reallocated to the parent, but the reallocation does not

---

[78] See Notice 88-70, 1988-2 CB 369, Ex. 4.

[79] See infra ¶79.1.

[80] Rev. Rul. 74-158, 1974-1 CB 182.

[81] Reg. §1.901-2(e)(5), discussed supra ¶69.4.6 text accompanying notes 130–45.

[82] The first expression of the compulsory payment rule was in this context. Rev. Rul. 76-508, 1976-2 CB 225, superseded by Rev. Rul. 92-75, 1992-2 CB 197. The regulations presently stating the rule illustrate it with examples involving §482 allocations. Reg. §1.901-2(e)(5)(ii) Exs. 1, 2.

change the foreign tax liability, the deemed paid taxes are recalculated as follows:

$$(\$40)(10u/30u) = \$13.3$$

This is the result, however, only if the foreign tax remains unchanged after the exhaustion of all practical remedies under foreign law to reduce the tax. Assume the foreign tax law contains a rule similar to §482, and it is determined that a reduction in F's income is also appropriate under foreign law, diminishing the foreign tax liability to $20. The indirect credit becomes:

$$(\$20)(10u/30u) = \$6.7$$

Because $20 of the original foreign tax of $40 is refundable to F, it is removed from the multiplicand of the formula whether or not the refund is actually obtained.[83]

6. *Distributions of property.* When a qualifying domestic corporation receives a distribution from a foreign corporation of property other than money, the dividend (the numerator of the §902 fraction) is the lesser of the fair market value of the property or the distributing corporation's earnings and profits.[84] The dividend reduces earnings and profits by the greater of the property's fair market value or its basis to the distributing corporation.[85] Any excess of fair market value over basis is recognized by the distributing corporation as gain on the distribution, and this gain, less any tax on it, adds to earnings and profits. When distributed property is worth more than its adjusted basis and the corporation has adequate earnings and profits, fair market value is the measure of both the dividend and the reduction of earnings and profits, and the §902 computations

---

[83] Normally, when a foreign income tax is redetermined, the redetermination is reflected by prospective adjustments to the tax and earnings pools for the year of the redetermination and future years, rather than by amending the indirect credit on returns already filed. See infra ¶69.13.4. However, when income is reallocated under §482, any resulting change in foreign income taxes is reflected by amending the indirect credit (as illustrated in the example), not by prospective adjustments in the pools. This is done because the foreign tax paid on the reallocated income is considered a voluntary payment, an amount that never qualified as a tax. If the foreign corporation obtains a refund of this amount, the refund should be treated as a recovery of a debt to the corporation, not as a redetermination of its taxes.

[84] IRC §§301(b), (c)(1), 316; Central Aguirre Sugar Co. v. CIR, 24 TC 630 (1955), acq.; Rev. Rul. 71-65, 1971-1 CB 212. See infra ¶92.3.

[85] Under §312(a)(3), earnings and profits are reduced by the distributing corporation's adjusted basis for the distributed property, but §312(b) requires that fair market value be the measure of the reduction if fair market value exceeds adjusted basis. Section 312(b) is a companion to §311(b), which requires that the distributing corporation recognize gain equal to any excess of fair market value over basis.

are the same as they would be on a distribution of cash equal to the property's fair market value.[86]

The results are a bit less obvious when depreciated property is distributed. Assume a foreign corporation, whose post-1986 undistributed earnings are 60u and post-1986 foreign income taxes are $40, distributes to its shareholder (a domestic corporation) property that is worth 15u and has an adjusted basis of 60u. The distribution is a dividend of 15u, which carries with it indirect credit of:

$$(\$40)(15u/60u) = \$10$$

Post-1986 undistributed earnings, however, are reduced by 60u (the adjusted basis of the distributed property), and the undistributed earnings pool falls to zero. Although $30 remains in post-1986 foreign income taxes, no indirect credits are allowable until the corporation has additional earnings and profits. The result is not unwarranted because there can be no dividends without additional earnings and profits and the purpose to avoid double taxation requires no credit until the shareholder has U.S. gross income.

¶69.8.4 Relationship With §904

Foreign income taxes deemed paid under §§902 and 960 are creditable subject to the limitations of §904.[87] The dividend and taxes must be allocated among the separate limitation categories (baskets) under §904(d), a matter of some complexity that is discussed below.

1. *Source.* The credit limitation is generally the product of the taxpayer's taxable income from foreign sources and the effective rate of U.S. tax before credit.[88] A dividend or subpart F inclusion triggering §902 or §960 is usually foreign source income, includable in the domestic corporation's foreign source taxable income. More specifically, a §902 dividend is usually treated as income from sources within the country or U.S. possession under whose laws the distributing corporation is organized, and the deemed paid taxes are treated as having been paid to that country.[89] The identification of a particular country as the source of the dividend and the deemed recipient of the taxes is significant principally in applying §901(j), which denies credit for taxes imposed by some countries on bad terms with the United States and excludes income from sources within these countries in computing the §904 limitations.[90] The gross income

---

[86] See Rev. Rul. 71-65, 1971-1 CB 212 (for years before 1987, dividends distributable out of any year's accumulated profits are limited to that year's earnings and profits, before reduction for any distributions).

[87] For §904, see supra ¶69.5.

[88] See supra ¶69.5.1.

[89] Reg. §§1.902-3(h)(1), (2).

[90] See supra ¶¶69.4.8, 69.6.11.

inclusion under §78 for the amount of the deemed taxes has the same source as the dividend or subpart F inclusion.[91]

However, under §904(g), a dividend from a foreign corporation or a subpart F inclusion is U.S. source income to the extent it comes from U.S. source income of the foreign corporation if at least 50 percent of the foreign corporation's stock, by vote or by value, is owned by U.S. persons.[92] Assume foreign corporation F's earnings and profits for its first year of existence consists of 150u of general limitation income, none of which is taxed to its shareholder (domestic corporation P) under subpart F but 50u of which is from U.S. sources.[93] If F pays a dividend during the year of 75u, one third of the dividend (25u) is U.S. source income to P. Because one third of the dividend is from U.S. sources, one third of the §78 dividend ($10) is also assigned to U.S. sources.

2. *Distributions and subpart F inclusions from post-1986 undistributed earnings.* The post-1986 pooling rules, which lump together foreign income taxes and undistributed earnings for all years after 1986, contrast with the separate limitation rules of §904(d), which parse a taxpayer's taxable income and foreign income taxes for each year into nine separate categories (baskets).[94] The technical means for coordinating these two sets of rules is far from obvious from the statutes. The regulations answer some but not all of the questions.

a. *Noncontrolled §902 corporations.* The coordination is quite simple when a domestic corporation is entitled to the indirect credit on receiving a dividend from a noncontrolled §902 corporation—a foreign corporation that is not a CFC. A separate basket (sometimes called the 10-50 basket) is set up for dividends from each noncontrolled §902 corporation, containing no income other than these dividends and the gross income imputed by §78 because of the dividends.[95] The taxes deemed paid on account of these dividends are placed in this basket, together with any taxes actually paid by the shareholder on the dividends (e.g., a foreign withholding tax on the dividends). The separate limitation on credit for these taxes is the taxpayer's precredit U.S. tax, multiplied by:

$$\frac{\text{Sum of dividends and §78 gross-up, less allocable deductions}}{\text{Entire taxable income}}$$

Although the separate basket contains only items for the taxable year, the amount of the deemed paid taxes is determined by pooling all post-1986 items in the usual way.

A post-1986 dividend from earnings and profits accumulated by a foreign corporation when it was not a CFC, whether after 1986 or before 1987, is placed

---

[91] Reg. §1.902-1(c)(2)(i).

[92] See supra ¶69.5.2.

[93] Reg. §1.902-1(c)(2)(iii) Ex.

[94] For §904(d), see supra ¶69.6.

[95] IRC §904(d)(1)(E), (2)(E), discussed supra ¶69.6.7.

in the 10-50 basket, even if the corporation is a CFC when the dividend is distributed.[96] For example, if foreign corporation F, organized in 1980, had no U.S. shareholders before domestic corporation P purchases 60 percent of its stock in 1996, dividends received by P from earnings accumulated in years before 1996 are 10-50 dividends.[97]

A dividend distributed by a CFC from earnings accumulated while the corporation was a CFC is also assigned to a 10-50 basket if (1) when the dividend is received, the CFC has a U.S. shareholder that owns at least 90 percent of the CFC's voting stock, directly or indirectly, and (2) this shareholder was not a U.S. shareholder when the CFC accumulated the distributed earnings.[98] This rule applies to dividends from a lower-tier CFC to a higher-tier CFC as well as to dividends from a first-tier CFC to the U.S. shareholder. Assume OP, a domestic corporation that has owned all shares of foreign corporation F since F was organized, sells the stock during 1996 to domestic corporation NP.[99] Since NP owns at least 90 percent of F's stock, dividends it receives from earnings accumulated by F before 1996, when NP is first a U.S. shareholder, are in the 10-50 basket. This rule is administered by requiring a 90 percent shareholder to "begin a new set of post-1986 undistributed earnings and post-1986 foreign income taxes pools on the first day of the first taxable year in which it owns more than 90% of the voting stock."[100]

In contrast, if OP had owned and sold to NP only 85 percent of F's stock, the remaining shares being owned by unrelated foreign persons, dividends received by NP from post-1986, pre-1996 earnings would not be 10-50 dividends, but would instead be governed by the look-through rules described below, because NP owns less than 90 percent of F's stock. Similarly, if F was originally owned 90 percent by OP and 10 percent by NP and NP buys out OP's interest in 1996, the look-through rules apply to all dividends received by NP because NP's 10 percent interest made it a U.S. shareholder throughout F's lifetime.

---

[96] Reg. §1.902-1(d)(3)(i).

[97] Prop. Reg. §1.902-1(d)(3)(v) Ex. 1. Because F first has a U.S. shareholder in 1996, the indirect credits for dividends from pre-1996 earnings are determined under the pre-1987 §902. IRC §902(c)(3), discussed supra ¶69.8.3 text accompanying notes 56-58.

[98] Prop. Reg. §1.902-1(d)(3)(ii). The 90 percent test is applied taking into account all stock owned directly, indirectly, and constructively within the meaning of §958. For §958, see supra ¶68.2.2.

If the recipient of the dividend acquired its stock from a fellow member of its affiliated group, the rule described in the text applies only if it also applied to the corporation from which the stock was acquired. Prop. Reg. §1.902-1(d)(3)(iii).

Paragraph §§1.902-1(d)(3)(ii)-(iv) of the proposed regulations were not included in the final regulations, because the IRS intends to adopt the rules as regulations under §904(d).

[99] Prop. Reg. §1.902-1(d)(3)(v) Ex. 2.

[100] INTL-933-86, supra note 1, at 962.

For purposes of the foregoing two rules, a dividend is traced first to earnings accumulated after the foreign corporation became a CFC or the 90 percent owner became a U.S. shareholder, and it is deemed to come from pre-CFC earnings for purposes of the first rule or from preacquisition earnings under the second rule only after post-CFC or postacquisition earnings have been exhausted.[101] Earnings for the year the corporation became a CFC or the 90 percent owner became a U.S. shareholder are treated as post-CFC or postacquisition earnings.

b. *CFCs.* The application of §904(d) is more complex for dividends and subpart F inclusions from foreign corporations that were CFCs when the distributed earnings were accumulated. Such cases are governed by a look-through procedure, under which indirect credits are separately computed for each of the §904(d) baskets.[102]

For each taxable year beginning after 1986, a CFC's pretax net income (determined under U.S. rules) and foreign income taxes are allocated among the §904(d) baskets as though the corporation were itself claiming the foreign tax credit. Foreign income taxes are placed in a particular basket to the extent they were imposed on income within that basket.[103] The foreign income taxes within a particular basket are aggregated with the foreign income taxes so allocated for other post-1986 years. This aggregate, reduced by the portions of it allocable to dividends and subpart F inclusions for previous years,[104] comprises the post-1986 foreign income taxes within this basket. Post-1986 undistributed earnings allocable to the basket consist of the foreign corporation's aggregate pretax income in the basket for all post-1986 years, reduced by (1) the foreign income taxes allocable to the income for all post-1986 years[105] and (2) dividends paid and subpart F inclusions for prior years to the extent allocable to this basket.[106]

Dividends from a CFC (including constructive dividends under §§304, 367(b), 551, and 1248) are allocated among the §904(d) baskets in proportion to the CFC's earnings and profits in the various separate limitation categories.[107] The §902 formula is applied separately for each basket, and the taxes deemed paid within a particular basket consists of the CFC's post-1986 foreign income

---

[101] Prop. Reg. §1.902-1(d)(3)(iv).

[102] Reg. §1.902-1(d)(1).

[103] Reg. §1.904-6(b)(3); Reg. §1.902-1(c)(2)(ii). See supra ¶69.6.8.

[104] The foreign income taxes allocable to dividends and subpart F inclusions for prior years are the taxes deemed paid by shareholders on account of these dividends and inclusions, determined as though all shareholders (including individuals and foreign persons) were eligible for the deemed paid credit.

[105] This subtraction should equal the post-1986 foreign income taxes before reduction for amounts allocable to dividends paid and subpart F inclusions for prior years.

[106] For this purpose, a dividend or subpart F inclusion should be allocated to a particular basket if it was so allocated under §904(d) for the year in which it was distributed or reported under subpart F.

[107] Reg. §1.902-1(d)(2)(i). See supra ¶69.6.8.

taxes within the basket multiplied by

$$\frac{\text{Portion of dividend coming from earnings within basket}}{\text{Post-1986 undistributed earnings within basket}}$$

Income taxed to a U.S. shareholder under subpart F has the same character for purposes of §904(d) as the income has in the hands of the CFC.[108] The taxes within a particular basket deemed paid on account of a subpart F inclusion are computed by the same approach as is used for dividends, except that the portion of the inclusion consisting of CFC income within the basket is the numerator of the fraction.[109]

The gross income inclusion under §78 is within a particular basket to the extent the deemed paid taxes come from that basket.[110]

Assume domestic corporation P is sole shareholder of F, a foreign corporation whose net income (before taxes) is 200u for 1995 and 300u for 1996, the first two years of its existence.[111] The income falls into the financial services and general limitation baskets in the amounts shown in line 1 of Example 69-2. F distributes no dividends in 1995, but distributes 90u to P during 1996. P is not required to include any amount under subpart F for either year. The exchange rate is 1u for $1 at all relevant times. The computation of the deemed paid taxes within each basket is shown in Example 69-2.

Example 69-2
Allocation of Post-1986 Undistributed Earnings and Foreign Income Taxes Among §904(d) Baskets

1. Allocation of income and taxes among baskets

Basket		1995	1996
Financial services:	Pretax income	150u	200u
	Foreign income taxes	$ 45	$ 60
General Limitation:	Pretax income	50u	100u
	Foreign income taxes	$ 15	$ 30
Total:	Pretax income	200u	300u
	Foreign income taxes	$ 60	$ 90

2. Post-1986 undistributed earnings (UE) and foreign income taxes (FIT) for 1996

	Pretax earnings		
	FIT	UE	
a. Financial services			
1995	150u	$ 45	105u
1996	200u	60u	140u

---

[108] IRC §904(d)(3)(B).
[109] Reg. §1.902-1(d)(2)(ii).
[110] Reg. §1.902-1(c)(2)(i).
[111] See Reg. §1.902-1(f) Ex. 5.

Example 69-2
Allocation of Post-1986 Undistributed Earnings and
Foreign Income Taxes Among §904(d) Baskets *(continued)*

b. General Limitation

1995	50u	$15	35u
1996	100u	30	70u
Total	150u	$45	105u

3. Allocation of 1996 dividend
   a. Financial services   (90u)(245u/350u) =   63u
   b. General limitation   (90u)(105u/350u) =   27u

   c. Total   90u
4. Computation of deemed paid taxes
   a. Financial services   ($105)(63u/245u) = $ 27
   b. General limitation   ($45)(27u/105u) = $ 11.60

Still more complexity arises if the CFC has losses within some of the §904(d) baskets but has positive post-1986 undistributed earnings overall.[112] If a foreign source deficit occurs in the post-1986 undistributed earnings account within any basket, the deficit is prorated among baskets with positive post-1986 undistributed earnings.[113] If the deficit exceeds the earnings pools within all foreign source baskets, the excess is applied against the CFC's post-1986 U.S. source earnings. However, the deficit allocation is made for a particular year only if there is a dividend distribution or subpart F inclusion for the year (i.e., only if the post-1986 earnings pools are used in computing deemed paid taxes for the year). Even in this case, the allocation is only made for the purpose of doing the indirect credit calculations for that year. As of the beginning of the next year, the deficit is removed from the baskets to which it was allocated and is brought back into the basket in which it arose.

Assume foreign corporation *F*, which is organized in 1995 as a wholly owned subsidiary of domestic corporation *P*, has current earnings and profits and deficits for 1995, 1996, and 1997, which fall into three baskets as follows:[114]

Year	*Shipping income*	*General limitation*	*Noncontrolled §902 dividends*
1995	100u	(300u)	-0-
1996	100u	100u	50u
1997	120u	300u	55u

Assume *P* is not taxed under subpart F during any of these years, and *F* distributes dividends of 25u in 1996 and 100u in 1997. Since there are no dividends or

---

[112] Notice 88-71, 1988-2 CB 374.

[113] For a comparable allocation in the return of the U.S. taxpayer, see supra ¶69.7.

[114] See Notice 88-71, 1988-2 CB 374, Ex. 3.

subpart F inclusions for 1995, the deficit allocation rule does not apply for that year. It applies, however, when the dividend of 25u is distributed in 1996, as shown in Example 69-3. The collating adjustments for 1997 are shown in Example 69-4.

Example 69-3
Allocation of Deficits

	Shipping income	General limitation	Noncontrolled §902 dividends	Overall
1. Post-1986 undistributed earnings				
1995	100u	(300u)	–0–	(200u)
1996	100u	100u	50u	250u
Total before deficit allocation	200u	(200u)	50u	50u
Deficit allocation	(160u)		(40u)	
After allocation	40u	–0–	10u	50u
2. 1996 dividend	20u		5u	25u
3. Post-1986 foreign income taxes	$ 100	$ 50	$ 25	$ 175
4. Deemed paid taxes	$ 50		$ 12.50	$ 62.50

Example 69-4
Adjustments for Year Following Deficit Allocation

	Shipping income	General limitation	Noncontrolled §902 dividends	Overall
1. Post-1986 undistributed earnings				
After deficit allocation	40u	–0–	10u	50u
Reverse allocation	160u	(200u)	40u	
	200u	(200u)	50u	50u
Less 1996 dividend	20u		5u	25u
	180u	(200u)	45u	25u
Plus 1997 earnings	120u	300u	55u	475u
1997 total	300u	100u	100u	500u
2. 1997 dividend	60u	20u	20u	100u
3. Post-1986 foreign income taxes				
For 1996	$ 100	$ 50	$ 25	$ 175
Deemed paid in 1996	(50)	(12.50)	(62.50)	
For 1997	60	150	27.50	237.50
1997 total	$ 110	$ 200	$ 40	$ 350
4. Deemed paid in 1997	$ 22	$ 40	$ 8	$ 70

3. *Post-1986 dividends from profits accumulated before 1987.* The pre-1987 indirect credit rules could be coordinated with §904(d) by either of two approaches. Under one of these approaches, when a post-1986 dividend is traced to the earnings and profits for a particular pre-1987 year, these earnings and profits would be allocated among the separate limitation baskets under the present §904(d), and the dividend would be prorated among the baskets. Foreign income taxes for the year would also be allocated among the baskets under the tax allocation rules of the §904(d) regulations.[115] Within each basket, the deemed paid taxes would equal the foreign corporation's foreign income taxes for the year within the basket, multiplied by:

$$\frac{\text{Dividend allocated to basket}}{\text{Earnings and profits within basket}}$$

The principal problem with this approach is that it requires the allocation of pre-1987 taxes and earnings under rules not enacted until 1986, and the records necessary to apply the rules may not have been kept for these years.

This problem is avoided under a second approach, which is suggested by rules for allocating pre-1987 losses and deficits.[116] Under this approach, taxes and earnings for each pre-1987 year are allocated among baskets in accordance with §904(d) as it existed during that year. Immediately before the 1986 amendments, §904(d) provided separate limitations for (1) most interest income, (2) dividends from a DISC or former DISC, (3) foreign trade income of a FSC, and (4) distributions received from a FSC or former FSC. Under this approach, each separate basket under pre-1987 law is assigned to the most closely analogous basket under post-1986 law. For example, the pre-1987 interest basket goes into the passive basket under post-1986 law, and the pre-1987 DISC and FSC baskets are subsumed into the DISC and FSC baskets under post-1986 law. If the taxpayer can demonstrate that particular items of pre-1987 income and deduction would be in particular baskets under post-1986 law, had it applied for the year, the items are also assigned to these baskets. All other income and deductions are placed in the general limitation basket. Foreign income taxes for the year are allocated among the baskets in the same way.

4. *Pre-1987 deficits carried to post-1986 years.* If a foreign corporation had an accumulated deficit as of the end of its last pre-1987 year, the deficit is carried over to the first post-1986 year as a negative balance in the corporation's post-

---

[115] See supra ¶69.6.10.

[116] See Reg. §1.904(f)-12(a); Notice 88-71, 1988-2 CB 374. See infra text accompanying notes 117–18 for the deficit allocation rules.

1986 undistributed earnings.[117] The deficit must also be allocated among the separate limitation categories under §904(d) as follows:

Identify the items of income and loss for all pre-1987 years that are allocable to each separate basket under §904(d) as it existed during the years in which the items were recognized. The items in each separate basket under pre-1987 law are placed in the most closely analogous basket under post-1986 law. The taxpayer is also allowed to show that additional items of pre-1987 income and deduction would have been in particular baskets under post-1986 law if it had been applicable for the years in which the items were recognized.[118] The general limitation basket contains all pre-1987 items that are not in a separate limitation basket under pre-1987 law and are not shown to be of a type that would be in separate limitation basket under post-1986 law.

Once the income and deductions for all pre-1987 years have been assigned to baskets under post-1986 law, the items in each basket are added together, and the sum becomes the opening balance in the basket for the first post-1986 year. Typically, the balances are deficits. An overall deficit, however, can consist of net loss in some baskets that is partially but not fully offset by net income in other baskets. Under the deficit carryover rule, some post-1986 baskets can thus have positive opening balances.

¶69.8.5 Rules for Lower-Tier Corporations

A domestic corporation that meets the 10 percent ownership requirement of §902(a) is sometimes deemed to have paid foreign income taxes actually paid by lower-tier foreign corporations in which its ownership is indirect. For example, if domestic corporation P owns stock of foreign corporation F1, which owns stock of foreign corporation F2, P might qualify for credit for foreign income taxes paid by F2 as well as by F1. The policy of the rule for lower-tier taxes is the same as that for taxes of first-tier foreign corporations—to alleviate double taxation where income is taxed abroad to one entity and in the U.S. to another. The rule is therefore subject to similar limitations: Credit for lower-tier taxes is allowed only if the domestic corporation has a substantial interest in the lower-tier corporation and only when the domestic corporation is taxed on the lower-tier corporation's earnings. For taxable years beginning before August 6, 1997,

---

[117] Notice 88-71, 1988-2 CB 374.

[118] The rule is expressed in a way that may give the taxpayer an election. Assume a dividend received by a CFC during a pre-1987 year would, under post-1986 law, be in the basket for noncontrolled §902 dividends. The taxpayer, however, prefers to include the dividend in the computation of the deficit carryover to the general limitation basket and therefore offers no evidence as to the nature of the income. Is the dividend in the noncontrolled §902 or general limitation basket? The IRS notice says an item is in a separate limitation basket if the taxpayer "can demonstrate" it would fall into that basket under post-1986 law, suggesting that the item is so classified if the taxpayer can demonstrate the crucial facts, even if it chooses not to make this demonstration.

the lower-tier rules allow a domestic corporation to be treated as having paid taxes actually paid by a second- or third-tier foreign corporation, and credit is never allowed for foreign income taxes paid by a fourth- or lower-tier foreign corporation. For subsequent taxable years, indirect credit can pass through as many as six tiers of foreign corporations.

If a domestic corporation's foreign subsidiaries join in filing a consolidated return under foreign law, the consolidated tax liability is apportioned among the corporations jointly liable for the tax, ratably according to the contribution of each to consolidated taxable income.[119]

1. *Post-1997 years.* For taxable years beginning after August 5, 1997, a foreign corporation receiving a dividend from another foreign corporation is deemed to have paid portions of the foreign income taxes of the payor corporation if both corporations are part of a "qualified group" and the recipient owns at least 10 percent of the payor's voting stock.[120] A "qualified group" consists of (1) a foreign corporation (first-tier corporation) that pays dividends to a domestic corporation (the taxpayer) that owns at least 10 percent of the first-tier corporation's voting stock and (2) other foreign corporations meeting the following requirements:

   a. At least 10 percent of each such corporation's voting stock must be owned by another member of the qualified group;
   b. The taxpayer must indirectly own at least 5 percent of the corporation's voting stock through a chain of ownership that includes both the first-tier corporation and the foreign corporation described in a.;
   c. The corporation cannot be more than six tiers removed from the taxpayer; and
   d. If the corporation is more than three tiers removed from the taxpayer, it must be a CFC and the taxpayer must be a U.S. shareholder of the CFC.[121]

Very generally, a foreign corporation is a CFC if more than 50 percent of its stock, either by voting power or by value is owned by U.S. shareholders, who are U.S. persons who each own, directly, indirectly, or constructively, at least 10 percent of the foreign corporation's stock.[122] Moreover, for a foreign corporation below the third tier, indirect credit is only allowed for foreign income taxes for periods when the corporation was a CFC.

Assume a domestic corporation (*D*) owns voting stock of a foreign corporation (*F-1*), which owns voting stock of foreign corporation *F-2*, which owns voting stock of foreign corporation *F-3*, which owns voting stock of foreign corporation *F-4*, which owns voting stock of foreign corporation *F-5*, which owns

---

[119] Rev. Rul. 77-209, 1977-1 CB 238.
[120] IRC §902(b)(1).
[121] IRC §902(b)(2).
[122] IRC §§951(b), 957(a), discussed supra ¶68.2.2.

voting stock of foreign corporation F-6, which owns voting stock of foreign corporation F-7; the corporations simultaneously distribute dividends. If the voting stock interest at each level is 10 percent, D is only deemed to have paid foreign income taxes of F-1 because its indirect voting interest in F-2 is only one percent (10 percent of 10 percent) and its interest in lower-tier corporations is even less. If the interest at each level is 50 percent, D's indirect credit includes foreign income taxes of F-1 through F-4; its interest in F-5 is only 3.125 percent. If the interest at each level is 70 percent, the indirect credit reaches foreign income taxes imposed on F-1 through F-6; although D's indirect interest in F-7 is 8.24 percent, the indirect credit never reaches lower than six tiers.

When dividends pass through a qualified group, each corporation receiving dividends from another member of the group is deemed to pay foreign income taxes imposed on the distributing corporation in an amount determined under §902(a), as though that corporation were a domestic corporation. The taxes deemed paid by the dividend recipient are aggregated with the taxes actually imposed upon it in determining the taxes deemed paid by the next higher corporation in the chain.[123]

Many aspects of these rules are developed further by the regulations, which were promulgated under pre-1997 law and are described below.

2. *Taxes paid by second-tier foreign corporations; pre-1997 law.* On receipt of a dividend, a domestic corporation is deemed to pay a portion of the taxes actually paid or deemed to have been paid by the foreign corporation distributing the dividend.[124] Assume domestic corporation P receives dividends from foreign corporation F1, in which P has a 10 percent or greater voting interest. The foreign income taxes deemed paid by P include taxes that F1 actually paid or is deemed to have paid. F1 is deemed to have paid taxes actually paid by another foreign corporation if the requirements described below are met.

a. *Qualification criteria.* A foreign corporation distributing a dividend to a domestic corporation (the first-tier foreign corporation) is deemed to have paid taxes actually paid by another foreign corporation (the second-tier corporation) if the following tests are met: (1) The domestic corporation must own at least 10 percent of the first-tier corporation's voting stock; (2) the first-tier corporation must own at least 10 percent of the voting stock of the second-tier corporation; (3) the domestic corporation's indirect interest in the second-tier corporation's voting stock must be at least 5 percent; (4) the first-tier corporation must have received a dividend from the second-tier corporation; and (5) the domestic corporation must receive a dividend from the first-tier corporation.[125]

The first two of these requirements, the direct stock ownership tests, must be met when the dividends are received. That is, the first-tier corporation's voting interest in the second-tier corporation must be 10 percent or more when it

---

[123] IRC §902(c)(4)(B).
[124] IRC §902(c)(4)(B).
[125] IRC §§902(b)(1),(3)(A).

receives a dividend from the second-tier corporation, and the domestic corporation's shareholdings in the first-tier corporation must meet the 10 percent test when it receives a dividend from the first-tier corporation.[126] If the test is not met at either level at the time of a dividend, the dividend carries with it no deemed paid taxes.[127] Assume dividends are distributed by F2 to F1 on February 16, 1995, and by F1 to P on January 27, 1996.[128] Taxes actually paid by F2 can flow through to F1 and then to P only if the requisite 10 percent is held by F1 in F2 on February 16, 1995, and P in F1 on January 27, 1996.

The third requirement, the 5 percent indirect ownership test, is applied by multiplying together the percentages of the voting stock held by the domestic corporation in the first-tier corporation and by the first-tier corporation in the second-tier corporation. The requirement is met if the product is five or more.[129] The relevant percentages are the same as those used in applying the direct ownership tests: (1) the domestic corporation's ownership of the first-tier corporation's voting stock when the domestic corporation receives the dividend and (2) the first-tier corporation's voting interest in the second-tier corporation when the first-tier corporation receives dividends.[130]

Assume P owns 10 percent of the voting stock of F1, and F1 has an 80 percent voting interest in F2. If F1 receives a dividend from F2, it is deemed to have paid some portion of the foreign income taxes actually paid by F2 because (1) the domestic corporation owns at least 10 percent of the stock of F1, (2) F1 owns at least 10 percent of the voting stock of F2, and (3) the domestic corporation's indirect interest in F2 is at least 5 percent (10 percent of 80 percent is 8 percent).

Because the availability of the indirect credit for taxes paid by a second-tier corporation depends on the stockholdings of particular shareholders at particular times, the computation of the pass-through from second-tier to first-tier corporation is specific to a particular shareholder of the first-tier corporation. Assume F1 owns 40 percent of the voting stock of F2, and F1's shareholders are two domestic corporations, P1 (holding 90 percent of F1's voting stock) and P2 (holding 10 percent). P1 qualifies for indirect credit for F2's taxes, but P2 does not because P2's indirect interest in F2 is less than 5 percent (10 percent of 40 percent is 4 percent). However, both P1 and P2 are allowed §902 credit for taxes actually paid by F1. F1's foreign income taxes thus must be computed twice—once including taxes of F2 deemed paid by F1 (for determining P1's indirect credit) and once without deemed paid taxes (for determining P2's indirect credit). Assume F1 receives a dividend of 24u from F2, which carries with it deemed paid taxes of $16. F1's post-1986 undistributed earnings and post-1986

---

[126] Reg. §1.902-1(b)(1).

[127] Reg. §§1.902-3(a)(2), (3).

[128] See Reg. §1.902-3(c)(1) Ex.

[129] IRC §902(b)(3)(A).

[130] Reg. §1.902-3(c)(1).

foreign income taxes, before taking the dividend from $F2$ into account, are 120u and $80. The dividend increases $F1$'s post-1986 undistributed earnings to 144u (sum of 120u and 24u). Post-1986 foreign income taxes for purposes of determining $P1$'s indirect credit are $96 (sum of $80 and $16), but are only $80 for purposes of determining $P2$'s indirect credit. Assume $F1$ distributes 100u to its shareholders (90u to $P1$ and 10u to $P2$). The shareholders are deemed to have paid $F1$'s foreign income taxes in the following amounts:

$$P1: (\$96)(90u/144u) = \$60$$
$$P2: (\$80)(10u/144u) = \$5.6$$

b. *Computation of deemed paid taxes.* When the direct and indirect ownership requirements are met, the amount of foreign income taxes deemed paid by the first-tier foreign corporation is determined under §902(a) as though the corporation were a domestic corporation.[131] It is thus deemed to pay taxes actually paid by the second-tier corporation only if the latter pays a dividend to the former. In the example, $F1$ is deemed to pay some portion of $F2$'s foreign income taxes when $F1$ receives a dividend from $F2$. If the dividend is from $F2$'s post-1986 undistributed earnings, the deemed paid taxes equal $F2$'s post-1986 foreign income taxes, multiplied by:

$$\frac{F2\text{'s dividend to } F1}{F2\text{'s post-1986 undistributed earnings}}$$

If the dividend is from accumulated profits for a pre-1987 year of $F2$, the amount deemed paid by $F1$ is $F2$'s foreign income taxes for the year multiplied by:

$$\frac{F2\text{'s dividend to } F1}{F2\text{'s earnings and profits for the year}}$$

If a first-tier corporation owns qualifying voting interests in two or more second-tier corporations, §902(a) is applied separately to each second-tier corporation.[132]

Whether distributed from pre-1987 or post-1986 earnings of the second-tier corporation, a dividend distributed after 1986 is added to the first-tier corporation's post-1986 undistributed earnings,[133] and the taxes deemed paid on account

---

[131] IRC §902(b)(1).

[132] Reg. §1.902-1(c)(1)(i).

[133] Reg. §1.902-1(a)(9)(ii). Section 78 does not apply at this level. Reg. §1.902-1(c)(2)(ii). Earnings and profits of $F1$ are thus increased by the amount of the dividend (less any taxes imposed on the dividend income), not the sum of the dividend and the deemed paid taxes. This is appropriate because the addition is being made to earnings and profits, an after-tax account. The desired equivalence to the branch situation is fully accomplished by applying §78 to P alone because P's taxable income is the first pretax

of the dividend are added to its post-1986 foreign income taxes, even if the second-tier corporation paid these taxes before 1987.[134] These additions are made for the year the dividend is received. Some portion of the deemed paid taxes pass through to the domestic corporation if it receives a dividend from the first-tier corporation's post-1986 undistributed earnings during the year the additions are made or some subsequent year.

Assume $F1$ receives a dividend of 24u from $F2$ in 1996, and the dividend carries deemed paid taxes of \$16; for 1996, $F1$'s post-1986 undistributed earnings and post-1986 foreign income taxes are 120u and \$80 before taking the dividend from $F2$ into account. The dividend increases $F1$'s post-1986 undistributed earnings to 144u (sum of 120u and 24u), and its post-1986 foreign income taxes to \$96 (sum of \$80 and \$16). Assume $F1$ distributes a dividend of 12u during 1996 to its sole shareholder, domestic corporation P. P is deemed to pay foreign income taxes actually and deemed paid by $F1$ of:

$$(\$96)(12u/144u) = \$8$$

A dividend from a second-tier corporation, and the taxes deemed paid as a result, are included in the first-tier corporation's undistributed earnings and foreign income tax pools for the year of the dividend's receipt. Section 902(a) must therefore be applied for a particular taxable year first to the second-tier corporation's dividends to the first-tier corporation and then to the first-tier corporation's dividends to the domestic corporation, even if the former dividends occur later in the year than the latter.[135]

3. *Taxes paid by third-tier foreign corporations; pre-1997 law.* A similar procedure allows foreign income taxes imposed on a third-tier foreign corporation to be passed through to a domestic corporation. The rules described in the preceding paragraphs are applied first to dividends paid by the third-tier corporation to the second-tier corporation. Foreign income taxes deemed paid by the second-tier corporation are lumped with taxes actually paid by that corporation in reapplying the rules to dividends from the second-tier corporation to the first-tier corporation.[136] Assume $F2$ is the sole shareholder of foreign corporation $F3$ (a third-tier corporation); $F3$ distributes dividends to $F2$, which distributes dividends to $F1$, which distributes dividends to P. Taxes actually paid by $F3$ may be deemed paid by $F2$ and thereby included in the pool of taxes that can flow through to $F1$ and ultimately to P.

---

figure that enters into the computation. See Reg. §1.902-1(a)(9)(iii) (earnings and profits of upper-tier foreign corporation are not reduced by foreign income taxes of lower-tier corporation deemed paid by upper-tier corporation on latter's receipt of dividends).

[134] Reg. §1.902-1(a)(8)(ii); 1986 Bluebook, supra note 6, at 906–07.

Foreign income taxes deemed paid by the first-tier corporation on a post-1986 distribution of pre-1987 earnings of the second-tier corporation are translated into U.S. dollars at the spot rate on the distribution date. Reg. §1.902-1(a)(8)(ii).

[135] Reg. § 1.902-1(c)(1).

[136] IRC §902(c)(4)(B).

A second-tier foreign corporation is deemed to have paid taxes actually paid by a third-tier foreign corporation if three requirements are met.[137] First, 10 percent or greater voting interests must be held by the domestic corporation in the first-tier foreign corporation, by the first-tier corporation in the second-tier foreign corporation, and by the second-tier corporation in the third-tier foreign corporation. Second, the domestic corporation's indirect interests in the second-tier corporation and the third-tier corporation must each be at least 5 percent. Third, dividends must be distributed by the third-tier corporation to the second-tier corporation, by the latter to the first-tier corporation, and by the first-tier corporation to the domestic corporation.

Each dividend recipient must own at least 10 percent of the voting stock of the distributing corporation when the dividend is received. If a dividend is received when the recipient does not hold the required 10 percent, no deemed paid taxes pass through with the dividend.[138] Assume dividends are distributed by (1) $F3$ to $F2$ on March 3, 1994, (2) $F2$ to $F1$ on February 16, 1995, and (3) $F1$ to P on January 20, 1996.[139] Taxes actually paid by $F3$ flow through to $F2$, then to $F1$, and finally to P if the requisite 10 percent is held by $F2$ in $F3$ on March 3, 1994, by $F1$ in $F2$ on February 16, 1995, and P in $F1$ on January 20, 1996.

The same percentages are used in applying the 5 percent requirement. In the example, the percentages representing the voting interests of $F2$ in $F3$ on March 3, 1994, of $F1$ in $F2$ on February 16, 1995, and of P in $F1$ on January 20, 1996, are multiplied together, and the 5 percent requirement is met if the product is at least five. Assume the voting interests on these dates are: $F2$ owns 75 percent of $F3$, $F1$ owns 80 percent of $F2$, and P owns 10 percent of $F1$. The ownership requirements are met because, (1) when the dividends are distributed, at least 10 percent voting interests are held by P in $F1$, by $F1$ in $F2$, and by $F2$ in $F3$, and (2) the product of the voting percentages is at least 5 percent (10 percent of 80 percent of 75 percent is 6 percent).

When these requirements are met and the dividend distributed by the third-tier corporation is from its post-1986 earnings and profits, the taxes deemed paid by the second-tier corporation equal the third-tier corporation's post-1986 foreign income taxes (including only taxes actually paid), multiplied by:[140]

$$\frac{\text{Dividend received by second-tier corporation}}{\text{Third-tier corporation's post-1986 undistributed earnings}}$$

If the third-tier corporation's dividend is from pre-1987 earnings and profits, the dividend is traced to the earnings and profits of a particular year, and the deemed paid taxes are the corporation's foreign income taxes for that year, multiplied by:

---

[137] IRC §§902(b)(2),(3)(B).
[138] Reg. §§1.902-3(a)(2), (3), (4).
[139] See Reg. §1.902-3(d)(1) Ex.
[140] IRC §§902(b)(2), (c)(4)(B).

Dividend received by second-tier corporation

Third-tier corporation's earnings and profits for that year

If the dividend is received after 1986, it is included in the second-tier corporation's post-1986 undistributed earnings, whether it comes from pre-1987 or post-1986 earnings of the third-tier corporation, and the deemed paid taxes are included in post-1986 foreign income taxes.

Assume in the example that before taking account of the effects of the dividends, the dividends paid, post-1986 undistributed earnings (UE), and post-1986 foreign income taxes (FIT) are as follows:

Corporation	Dividend Paid	UE	FIT
F3	20u	30u	$20
F2	30u	120u	80
F1	40u	60u	40

F2, as 75 percent shareholder of F3, receives a dividend of 15u (75 percent of 20u), and it is deemed to have paid foreign income taxes actually paid by F3 of:

$$(\$20)(15u/30u) = \$10$$

F2's dividend income and deemed paid taxes are added to its post-1986 undistributed earnings and foreign income taxes, making these amounts 135u (sum of 120u and 15u) and $90 (sum of $80 and $10).[141] F1, as 80 percent shareholder of F2, receives a dividend of 24u (80 percent of 30u), and it is deemed to pay taxes of:

$$(\$90)(24u/135u) = \$16$$

F1's dividend income and deemed paid taxes increase its post-1986 undistributed earnings to 84u (sum of 60u and 24u) and its foreign income taxes to $56 (sum of $40 and $16). P, as 10 percent shareholder of F1, receives a dividend of 4u (10 percent of 40u). Its deemed paid taxes are:

$$(\$56)(4u/84u) = \$2.667$$

Since a dividend from a lower-tier corporation, and the taxes deemed paid as a result, are included in the shareholder corporation's undistributed earnings and foreign income tax pools for the year of the dividend's receipt, §902(a) must be applied for a particular taxable year first to the third-tier corporation's divi-

---

[141] Section 78 does not apply at this level. It is assumed that no taxes are imposed on the dividend income of F2 or F1.

dends to the second-tier corporation, then to the second-tier corporation's dividends to the first-tier corporation, and finally to the first-tier corporation's dividends to the domestic corporation, regardless of the order of these dividends within the year.[142]

4. *Coordination with §904 limitations.* A dividend from a lower-tier CFC to an upper-tier CFC is deemed to come ratably from the distributing corporation's earnings in the various §904(d) baskets.[143] The §902 formula is applied separately for each basket, and the taxes deemed paid within a particular basket consist of the lower-tier corporation's post-1986 foreign income taxes within the basket multiplied by

$$\frac{\text{Portion of dividend coming from earnings within basket}}{\text{Post-1986 undistributed earnings within basket}}$$

¶69.8.6　Deficits

The treatment of deficits is troublesome under the pre-1987 rules, and the elimination of these difficulties was one of the stated goals of the 1986 revisions.[144] The rules described below for dealing with these difficulties generally apply to deficits incurred by first-, second-, and third-tier foreign corporations.

1. *Post-1986 losses.* Under the post-1986 rules, a foreign corporation's loss for any year is pooled with earnings for other years, reducing post-1986 undistributed earnings. A loss for a post-1986 year thus increases the likelihood of dividends being traced back to years before 1987. Also, because the loss reduces the denominator of the §902 fraction (post-1986 undistributed earnings), it increases the proportion of post-1986 foreign income taxes that flows through with each dollar of dividend from any remaining post-1986 undistributed earnings.

When losses of prior years cause post-1986 undistributed earnings to be less than current earnings and profits, the numerator of the fraction (the dividend or subpart F inclusion) is limited so that the fraction cannot exceed one.[145] Assume foreign corporation F has an earnings and profits deficit of 75u for the years 1987 through 1995, has 125u of earnings and profits for 1996, and distributes 100u in 1996. The distribution is a dividend because it is fully covered by current earnings and profits. Post-1986 undistributed earnings, however, are 50u (the excess of 1996 earnings and profits of 125u over the 1987–1995 deficit of 75u), and the dividend from post-1986 undistributed earnings is thus limited to 50u. If F's post-1986 foreign income taxes are $120, the deemed paid taxes are:

---

[142] Reg. §1.902-1(c)(1).

[143] Reg. §1.902-1(d)(2)(i).

[144] 1986 Bluebook, supra note 6, at 869.

[145] Notice 87-54, 1987-2 CB 363. See H.H. Robertson Co. v. CIR, 59 TC 53 (1972), aff'd without opinion, 500 F2d 1399 (3d Cir. 1974).

$$(\$120)(50u/50u) = \$120$$

To the extent a dividend from current earnings and profits exceeds post-1986 undistributed earnings, it carries no deemed paid taxes, but it creates a deficit in the post-1986 earnings pool.[146] At the end of 1996, F's post-1986 undistributed earnings are a negative 50u (predividend balance of 50u less dividend of 100u). The same result would occur if the corporation distributed no dividend but had subpart F income for the year of 100u.[147]

If post-1986 undistributed earnings remain in deficit after current earnings and profits are added in, the indirect credit from post-1986 foreign income taxes is zero, even if current earnings bear foreign taxes and are included in U.S. shareholders' gross incomes as dividends or subpart F inclusions.[148] Assume that at the end of 1995, foreign corporation G has a deficit of 200u in post-1986 undistributed earnings and post-1986 foreign income taxes of zero; in 1996, the corporation has current earnings and profits of 100u, pays foreign income taxes of $50, and distributes 100u to its shareholder. The distribution is a dividend because it is covered by current earnings and profits, but deemed paid taxes are zero. The denominator of the §902 fraction is zero because post-1986 undistributed earnings are still in deficit at the end of 1996 (200u deficit at the end of 1995 less 100u of current earnings and profits). In order to prevent the fraction from exceeding one, the numerator—the dividend from post-1986 undistributed earnings—must also be zero. Since the dividend is from earnings and profits of a post-1986 year, the pre-1987 rules are inapplicable, and the dividend carries no deemed paid taxes from any period.

In the last example, however, the taxes paid for 1996 remain in the post-1986 foreign income taxes pool, and the shareholder may get indirect credit for them with a later dividend. Assume that for 1997, G has 250u of earnings and profits, pays foreign income taxes of $100, and makes a distribution to its shareholder of 50u. The distribution is a dividend from current earnings and profits. Post-1986 undistributed earnings for 1997 are 50u (200u deficit at the end of 1995, plus 1996 earnings and profits of 100u, less 1996 distribution of 100u, and plus 1997 earnings and profits of 250u). Post-1986 foreign income taxes are $150 (the sum of $50 of taxes paid for 1996 and $100 for 1997). The deemed paid taxes accompanying the 1997 dividend are:

$$(\$150)(50u/50u) = \$150$$

The dividend from 1997 current earnings and profits thus carries with it all foreign income taxes paid in 1996 and 1997.

---

[146] Notice 87-54, 1987-2 CB 363.
[147] Notice 88-70, 1988-2 CB 369, Ex. 3.
[148] Notice 87-54, 1987-2 CB 363.

2. *Post-1986 losses carried to pre-1987 years.* If a foreign corporation has a deficit in its post-1986 undistributed earnings account at the end of any taxable year in which the corporation distributes a dividend to shareholders, the deficit is carried back against earnings and profits for years before 1987, beginning with the most recent of these years, unless the corporation also has an overall deficit for all years preceding 1987.[149] This rule applies to any distribution that is a dividend, except a dividend from current earnings and profits (which carries no deemed paid taxes if post-1986 undistributed earnings are in deficit). The same rule applies if such a post-1986 deficit exists for a year for which an inclusion in the shareholder's gross income is required under subpart F or a year for which the shareholder is taxed on a constructive dividend under §367(b) or §1248.[150]

If there are adequate earnings in pre-1987 years to absorb the deficit, the deficit is eliminated from the post-1986 earnings pool, which thus begins the succeeding year with a zero balance.[151] If pre-1987 earnings do not fully absorb the deficit, the unabsorbed amount continues as a negative balance in post-1986 undistributed earnings. Post-1986 foreign income taxes are not affected by the deficit or its carryback to pre-1987 years. For example, if foreign income taxes are paid for the year of the dividend or subpart F inclusion, they remain part of the post-1986 foreign income taxes.

Assume foreign corporation F has a deficit of 100u for 1987 and earnings and profits of 150u for 1986. Because of differences between U.S. and foreign law, F paid foreign income taxes of $10 for 1987; F distributed dividends of 50u during 1987 to its shareholders, domestic corporation D (which owns 10 percent of F's sole class of stock) and unrelated foreign corporation FP (which owns 90 percent of F's stock).[152] The 1987 deficit, which comprises post-1986 undistributed earnings, is carried back against earnings and profits for 1986, reducing them from 150u to 50u. The dividend comes from the remaining 50u of 1986 earnings and profits.[153] If F's foreign income taxes for 1986 are 120u,[154] the deemed paid taxes flowing through with the 1987 dividend to D (5u) are:

---

[149] Reg. §§1.902-2(a)(1),(b)(2); Notice 87-54, 1987-2 CB 363. If the stock ownership requirements for obtaining indirect credit for the foreign corporation's foreign income taxes are first satisfied by a domestic corporation during a year subsequent to 1987, all years prior to this year are treated as pre-1987 years for this purpose. See IRC §902(c)(3), discussed supra ¶69.8.3 text accompanying notes 56–58.

[150] Notice 88-70, 1988-2 CB 369.

[151] Reg. §1.902-2(a)(1).

[152] Reg. §1.902-2(a)(2) Ex. 1; Notice 87-54, 1987-2 CB 363.

[153] If the 1987 deficit were 150u, rather than 100u, it would completely offset 1986 earnings and profits, thereby forever barring the 1986 foreign income taxes from being deemed paid by the domestic corporation, in any part, and the 1987 distribution would be from 1985 earnings and profits. Reg. §1.902-2(a)(2) Ex. 2.

[154] The foreign tax figure used in this computation is the tax liability for the year after reduction by any refund obtainable by carrying back the 1987 loss. IRC §905(c).

$$(120u)(5u/50u) = 12u$$

At the beginning of 1988, post-1986 undistributed earnings are zero because the 100u deficit for 1987 was fully absorbed against 1986 earnings. If 1988 earnings and profits are, for example, 100u, post-1986 undistributed earnings are 100u for 1988.[155] Assume this is so, and F (1) pays foreign income taxes of $50 for 1988, (2) has no earnings and profits and pays no foreign income taxes for 1989, and (3) distributes 50u in 1989 to its shareholders. For 1989, post-1986 foreign income taxes are $60 ($10 from 1987 and $50 from 1988). The 1987 taxes are included in the tax pool even though the 1987 deficit was eliminated from the earnings pool by the carryback to 1986. Post-1986 undistributed earnings are 100u (from 1988), and the taxes deemed paid by D on account of its share of the 1989 dividend (5u) are:

$$(\$60)(5u/100u) = \$3$$

However, a deficit in post-1986 undistributed earnings is carried back to a pre-1987 year only if, for the year of the deficit, dividends are distributed or a U.S. shareholder is taxed under subpart F, §367(b), or §1248.[156] Assume foreign corporation G has an earnings and profits deficit of 50u for 1987, distributes no dividends in that year, and has earnings and profits of 150u for 1988, when it makes its first post-1986 distribution—dividends of 120u to its shareholders, domestic corporation D, and unrelated foreign corporation Z.[157] Because no dividend is paid in 1987, the 1987 deficit is not carried back. Post-1986 undistributed earnings for 1988 are thus 100u (sum of the 1987 deficit of 50u and the 1988 earnings and profits of 150u), and the 1988 dividends of 120u come 100u from that source and 20u from the earliest pre-1987 with earnings and profits remaining undistributed.

3. *Pre-1987 losses carried to pre-1987 years.* Under the pre-1987 rules, there is no overall pooling of losses with earnings. The IRS has ruled, however, that an earnings and profits deficit for a pre-1987 year is carried back against the earnings and profits of prior years, starting with the year immediately preceding the loss year.[158] Assume foreign corporation F has a deficit in earnings and profits for 1986 of 150u, but it has earnings and profits of 100u for each of the years 1985 and 1984. The deficit is carried back, offsetting all of the 1985 earnings and 50u of the 1984 earnings. If F makes a distribution that is traced back to pre-1987

---

[155] See Notice 87-54, 1987-2 CB 363.
[156] Notice 88-70, 1988-2 CB 369; Notice 87-54, 1987-2 CB 363.
[157] Reg. §1.902-2(a)(2) Ex. 3.
[158] Rev. Rul. 74-550, 1974-2 CB 209.

earnings, the distribution comes first from the remaining 50u of 1984 earnings and profits.[159]

When a loss is carried back to a particular year, it reduces both accumulated profits (pretax profits) and earnings and profits.[160] Assume F paid foreign income taxes of 30u on 1984 profits. It distributes a dividend of 50u to its shareholder, a domestic corporation, and the dividend is traced back to 1984 profits. The carryback of 50u of the 1986 loss to 1984 reduces 1984 earnings and profits to 50u,[161] and the taxes deemed paid by the shareholder are:

$$(30u)(50u/50u) = 30u$$

If a loss for a pre-1987 year exceeds accumulated earnings and profits for all prior years, the excess is carried forward against earnings and profits of subsequent years, beginning with the year immediately following the loss year.[162] The carryover, however, has no effect on the application of §902 to a distribution from a subsequent year's current earnings and profits.

The foregoing rules are applied without regard to the loss carryback and carryover rules of foreign tax laws.[163] The rules work well only in the unusual case where foreign tax laws parallel the scheme outlined above. Assume a post-1986 distribution of 50u made by foreign corporation G to its sole shareholder, a domestic corporation, is traced to pre-1987 earnings, and G's earnings and profits and foreign income taxes, before taking loss carrybacks and carryovers into account, are as follows:

Year	Earnings and profits or (deficit) under U.S. tax rules	Foreign income taxes
1986	(150u)	-0-
1985	100u	40u
1984	100u	30u

First, assume that under the foreign tax law, the 1986 deficit is carried back to 1985 and then to 1984, but that the foreign law is otherwise identical to U.S. law. Under the foreign law, the deficit is applied against 1985's pretax income of 140u (the sum of earnings and profits of 100u and taxes of 40u), thereby reducing 1985 income to zero and allowing G a refund of all 1985 taxes. Only 10u of the 1986 loss remains to be carried back to 1984. The carryback reduces 1984 income by one thirteenth (from 130u to 120u), and the 1984 tax is therefore reduced by one thirteenth to 27.7u. For U.S. tax purposes, earnings and profits for 1985 and

---

[159] See Rev. Rul. 87-72, 1987-2 CB 170.

[160] Champion Int'l Corp. v. CIR, 81 TC 424 (1983); Rev. Rul. 87-72, 1987-2 CB 170.

[161] If the loss is also carried back to 1984 for foreign tax purposes, foreign income taxes for 1984 are reduced by any portion of the initial 1984 tax liability that is refunded to F as a result of the carryback. IRC §905(c).

[162] Rev. Rul. 87-72, 1987-2 CB 170.

[163] Id. Cf. Champion Int'l Corp. v. CIR, 81 TC 424 (1983). However, foreign income taxes are reduced by any refunds resulting from carrybacks.

1984 increase by the amounts of foreign tax refunded to *G*—from 100u to 140u for 1985 and from 100u to 102.3u for 1984. The 150u of loss for 1986 is carried to 1985, offsetting all 140u of the earnings and profits for that year, and then to 1984, where it offsets 10u of the 102.3u of earnings and profits. On receiving the 1987 dividend of 50u, *G*'s shareholder is deemed to pay foreign income taxes of:

$$(27.7u) (50u/92.3u) = 15u$$

The results are quite logical because the foreign carryback regime exactly parallels the U.S. application of the deficit.

However, assume the foreign carryback rules are the same as the U.S. carryback rules, under which a net operating loss is carried first to the third preceding taxable year. If *G*'s profits for 1983 and 1984 are adequate to absorb the 1986 loss, the 1985 foreign tax liability remains unchanged, but 1985 earnings and profits are fully offset by the 1986 loss. As a result, the 1987 dividend is traced to 1984 and possibly to 1983, years for which *G*'s foreign tax liabilities may have been eliminated by the net operating loss carryback under foreign law, and no dividend can ever be traced to 1985, a year for which *G* paid foreign income taxes. The U.S. shareholder is permanently denied credit for the *G*'s 1985 taxes, and the goal of eliminating double taxation is frustrated.

4. *Pre-1987 deficit carried to post-1986 years.* If a foreign corporation has a deficit in its earnings and profits account as of the beginning of the first taxable year beginning after 1986, the deficit is carried over as the opening balance in the post-1986 undistributed earnings account.[164] Assume a foreign corporation has an accumulated earnings and profits deficit of 100u as of the end of 1986, has earnings and profits of 200u and 100u for 1987 and 1988, and makes no distributions during 1987. Post-1986 undistributed earnings for 1988 are 200u (the sum of the pre-1987 accumulated deficit of 100u and the earnings and profits of 200u and 100u for 1987 and 1988).

Foreign income taxes paid before 1987 never carry over into the post-1986 pool.[165] When there is an overall deficit at the end of 1986, no post-1986 dividend can be traced back to a pre-1987 year, and pre-1987 taxes can never become creditable.

For years before 1987, the rules for computing earnings and profits for purposes of §902 differed in some respects from those used under §960. The principal difference was that the §902 earnings and profits account was kept in the foreign corporation's functional currency, whereas the accounting under

---

[164] Reg. §1.902-2(b)(1); Notice 87-54, 1987-2 CB 363. See Reg. §1.902-2(b)(3) Exs. 1, 2.

If the stock ownership requirements for obtaining indirect credit for the foreign corporation's foreign income taxes are first satisfied by a domestic corporation during a year subsequent to 1987, all years prior to this year are treated as pre-1987 years for this purpose. IRC §902(c)(3), discussed supra ¶69.8.3 text accompanying notes 56–58.

[165] Reg. §§1.902-2(b)(1), (2).

§960 was in dollars. The deficit carryover rule described in the preceding paragraph applies to the deficit, if any, in the §902 account, not to a deficit in the §960 account. The foreign corporation thus has a single post-1986 undistributed earnings account that is used for purposes of both §§902 and 960, regardless of any differences in the pre-1987 accounts.[166]

¶69.8.7 Special Problems Under §960

Section 960, which allows the indirect credit when a domestic corporation is taxed on earnings of a CFC under subpart F, is the counterpart of §902, which allows the indirect credit when a domestic corporation receives dividends from a foreign corporation. Generally, §§902 and 960 apply alike. For example, a domestic corporation does not qualify for the indirect credit under either §902 or §960 unless it owns at least 10 percent of the voting stock of the foreign corporation. When a domestic corporation qualifies for the indirect credit under §960, the deemed paid taxes are computed as though the subpart F inclusion were a dividend that qualified the corporation for the indirect credit under §902. However, §960 has some unique features, which are described below.

1. *Requirement of subpart F inclusion and ownership requirement.* Whereas the basic jurisdictional prerequisite of §902 is a domestic corporation's receipt of a dividend from a foreign corporation, §960 applies when a domestic corporation is taxed under §951(a)(1) on earnings and profits of a foreign corporation.[167] Section 951(a)(1) requires that a U.S. shareholder of a CFC include in gross income its pro rata share of the CFC's subpart F income and earnings invested in U.S. property or excess passive assets. Very generally, (1) a CFC is a foreign corporation more than 50 percent of whose stock is held by U.S. shareholders, (2) a U.S. shareholder is a domestic corporation or U.S. citizen or resident owning (actually or constructively) at least 10 percent of the foreign corporation's voting stock, and (3) subpart F income consists of income Congress found to be susceptible to tax haven abuse or, for other reasons, wanted to tax directly to U.S. shareholders, whether distributed or not.

The basic ownership requirement for a claimant of the indirect credit is that the domestic corporation own at least 10 percent of the voting stock of the

---

[166] Notice 88-70, 1988-2 CB 369. However, a foreign corporation that existed before 1987 has two accounts for pre-1987 earnings and profits, one for accumulations as computed for purposes of §902 and the other for accumulations computed under the pre-1987 §960 rules. For example, it is possible that an actual distribution by the foreign corporation of a given dollar amount would be dividend (causing §902 to apply), while an investment of that amount in U.S. property (treated as a constructive distribution under subpart F) would not be a dividend for lack of earnings and profits. See Notice 88-70, supra, Ex. 2. After 1986, however, both earnings and profits accounts are kept in the corporation's functional currency; the pre-1987 §960 account (originally in dollars) is translated into the functional currency at the spot rate prevailing on the first day of the foreign corporation's first post-1986 year.

[167] For subpart F, see supra ¶68.2.

foreign corporation. Under §960, this requirement must be satisfied at the end of the foreign corporation's taxable year or, if the corporation ceases to be a CFC during the year, on the last day during the year when it is a CFC.[168] Assume *F*, a foreign corporation whose taxable year is the calendar year, is initially wholly owned by domestic corporation *P*, but its stock is sold on July 15, 1996, to an unrelated foreign corporation that retains the stock for the remainder of the year. For the taxable year 1996, the ownership test is applied on July 15, 1996 (just before *P*'s sale of its *F* stock) because that is the last day during *F*'s taxable year 1996 when it is a CFC. This rule parallels §951(a)(1), under which the amount taxable to a U.S. shareholder is also based on the shareholder's stockholdings as of the last day in the year on which the foreign corporation is a CFC.

2. *Computation of §960 credit.* Under §960(a)(1), a domestic corporation taxed on earnings of a CFC under §951(a)(1) is deemed to have paid foreign income taxes of the CFC in an amount equal to the CFC's post-1986 foreign income taxes multiplied by:

$$\frac{\text{Amount of §951(a)(1) inclusion}}{\text{CFC's post-1986 undistributed earnings}}$$

Post-1986 foreign income taxes and undistributed earnings (the tax and earnings pools) are computed in the same way as they are for purposes of §902.[169]

Assume *P*, a domestic corporation that is sole shareholder of foreign corporation *F*, is required to report as gross income for 1996 a 50u increase in *F*'s earnings invested in U.S. property. *F*'s post-1986 foreign income taxes are $20, and its post-1986 undistributed earnings are 80u.[170] *P* is deemed to have paid foreign income taxes of *F* of:

$$(\$20)(50u/80u) = \$12.5$$

When a domestic corporation is taxed on a CFC's earnings invested in U.S. property, the earnings are traced back to years before 1987 to the extent post-1986 undistributed earnings are not sufficient. The taxes deemed paid on account of earnings from a particular pre-1987 year are the foreign income taxes imposed on the CFC for that year multiplied by:

$$\frac{\text{Portion of §951(a)(1) inclusion traced to year's earnings}}{\text{Earnings and profits for the year}}$$

---

[168] Reg. §1.960-1(d)(1).

[169] Supra ¶69.8.3. See Reg. §1.960-1(i)(2) (if domestic corporation is entitled to credit under both §902 and §960 for same corporation for same year, §960 is applied first, and post-1986 foreign income taxes and undistributed earnings are reduced by §960 amounts before §902 is applied).

[170] See Reg. §1.960-1(c)(4) Ex. 1.

3. *Correlation with separate limitation rules of §904(d)*. When a subpart F inclusion causes §960 to apply, the tax and earnings pools must be coordinated with the separate limitation rules of §904(d).[171] Under §904(d), the shareholder's inclusion is allocated among nine baskets by a look-through rule that gives each item the same character in the shareholder's return as it has to the CFC.[172] Assume domestic corporation P owns all of the stock of foreign corporation F, which has subpart F income for 1996 that would be included in the passive basket if F were eligible for the foreign tax credit. P's inclusion under §951(a)(1) is also placed in its passive income basket.

The tax and earnings pools are determined "in accordance with" the separate basket rules.[173] Presumably, this means that the CFC's post-1986 foreign income taxes and post-1986 undistributed earnings are allocated among the baskets by applying §904(d) for each post-1986 year as though the CFC were a credit claimant. The foreign income taxes deemed paid on account of a subpart F inclusion within a particular basket is therefore the CFC's post-1986 foreign income taxes allocable to income within that basket, multiplied by the following fraction:

$$\frac{\text{Subpart F inclusion within the basket}}{\text{Post-1986 undistributed earnings within the basket}}$$

Assume P is required to report as gross income $100 of subpart F income of F that is in the passive income basket. Post-1986 undistributed earnings consists of F's gross income within the passive basket for all years after 1986, reduced by the sum of (1) F's deductions allocable to this income, (2) foreign income taxes imposed on F with respect to this income, and (3) amounts from this pool that, during prior years, were distributed to shareholders as dividends or taxed under subpart F. Post-1986 foreign income taxes are item 2 in the foregoing, less amounts attributable to earnings taxed to shareholders in prior years. The statute provides no method for determining whether a dividend distribution is made from a particular basket (item 3 above), but the characterization of the dividend or inclusion in applying §904(d) to the recipient should govern. For example, if a 90u dividend received by P from F is allocated 60u to P's passive income basket and 30u to its general limitation basket, the dividend should be deemed to come from F's post-1986 undistributed earnings in these two baskets in the same amounts.

A similar problem of coordinating §960 with the separate limitation rules arises when a domestic corporation is taxed on a CFC's earnings invested in U.S.

---

[171] For §904(d), see supra ¶69.6.

[172] IRC §904(d)(3)(B).

[173] IRC §960(a)(1).

property or excess passive assets.[174] The statutes provide no guidance on how this is to be done. Since earnings invested in U.S. property or excess passive assets are not attributable to any particular segment of the CFC's earnings, the increase should be allocated among the CFC's §904(d) baskets in the same way as the U.S. shareholder's gross income inclusion is split among the baskets in the shareholder's return.

4. *Lower-tier rules.* Section 960, like §902, allows foreign income taxes to be passed through to a domestic corporation from a first-, second-, or third-tier foreign corporation.[175] The basic ownership requirements for lower-tier corporations are the same under both provisions: The domestic corporation must own at least 10 percent of the voting stock of the first-tier corporation, the first-tier corporation must own at least 10 percent of the voting stock of the second-tier corporation, and the second-tier corporation must own at least 10 percent of the voting stock of the third-tier corporation. Also, a second- or third-tier foreign corporation's taxes pass through to the domestic corporation only if the latter's indirect interest in the foreign corporation is at least 5 percent.

There is, however, a fundamental difference between §§902 and 960 in their application to lower-tier corporations. Under §902, foreign income taxes pass through from a lower-tier corporation only if dividends are distributed through the tiers, ultimately reaching the domestic corporation. Congress structured §902 in this way because these successive dividends are the mechanism by which income of a lower-tier corporation enters into the tax return of the domestic corporation and the dividends are therefore what cause the double taxation meant to be alleviated by §902. In contrast, when a lower-tier CFC has subpart F income or earnings invested in U.S. property or excess passive assets, a U.S. shareholder of the CFC is taxed directly on the CFC's earnings, without these earnings passing through intervening foreign corporations in the chain of ownership. Under §960, a lower-tier foreign corporation's foreign income taxes also go directly from a lower-tier corporation to the domestic corporation.

Consistent with this approach, the stock ownership requirements are applied at all levels as of the same date: the last day of the taxable year of the foreign corporation whose income is being taxed to the domestic corporation (or if the foreign corporation ceases to be a CFC during the year, the last day on which it is a CFC).[176] Assume that during 1996, domestic corporation *P* is the sole shareholder of foreign corporation *F1*, *F1* owns the stock of *F2*, and *F2* owns the stock of *F3*. If *F3* has subpart F income for the year, the income is taxable directly to *P* under §951(a)(1) because *P* indirectly owns all of *F3*'s stock. *P* qualifies for the indirect credit under §960 because, on the last day of *F3*'s taxable year, the ownership requirements are satisfied by *P*'s ownership of *F1*, *F1*'s ownership of

---

[174] For CFC earnings invested in U.S. property, see supra ¶68.2.11; for earnings attributable to excess passive assets, see supra ¶68.2.12.

[175] For the lower-tier rules under §902, see supra ¶69.8.5.

[176] Reg. §1.960-1(d)(1).

F2, and *F2*'s ownership of *F3*. If *F3* also has subpart F income for 1997, but *P* sells its *F1* stock to an unrelated nonresident alien individual on July 15, 1997, §960 is also available to *P* for some portion of *F3*'s 1997 taxes because *F1*, *F2*, and *F3* cease to be CFCs when the sale occurs and the stock ownership requirements are therefore satisfied on the last day on which *F3* is a CFC (the last day of *P*'s ownership of the *F1* stock). In contrast, if *P* sold the *F1* stock to another domestic corporation on July 15, 1997, it would get no §960 credit for 1997 because *F3* would continue to be a CFC after the sale and the required stock ownership link between *P* and *F3* would not exist on the last day of the year.

5. *Constructive ownership.* The ownership rules of §960 resemble the definition of "U.S. shareholder," which determines which U.S. persons are taxable under §951(a)(1): A 10 percent voting interest is the basic requirement for both purposes. The two, however, are not identical because indirect and constructive ownership rules apply under the U.S. shareholder definition but not under §960's ownership test.[177] Assume domestic corporation *P* owns all of the stock of foreign corporation *F1*; *P* and *F1* each own 5 percent of the voting stock of *F2*, which is also a CFC. *P* is a U.S. shareholder of *F2* because it is indirect owner of the stock held by *F1* and thus passes the 10 percent threshold of the U.S. shareholder definition. *P* is therefore taxed on 10 percent of *F2*'s subpart F income and earnings invested in U.S. property or excess passive assets. However, no such attribution rules apply under §960. Because neither *P* nor *F1* owns at least 10 percent of the voting stock of *F2*, *P* is not deemed to pay any of *F2*'s foreign income taxes on income taxed to *P* under subpart F.

6. *Credits on distributions of previously taxed earnings.* Several rules come into play when a CFC distributes earnings that have been taxed to a U.S. shareholder under subpart F. Some of the rules are intended to ensure that any indirect credit allowed at the time of the subpart F inclusion is not duplicated by a second credit when the earnings are distributed. Others are meant to remove blocks that might otherwise deny credit for taxes not previously credited by the U.S. shareholder.

a. *Indirect credit generally denied.* Because a U.S. shareholder is allowed indirect credit under §960 when it is taxed on CFC earnings under subpart F, the indirect credit is usually denied when the earnings are subsequently distributed.[178] When a CFC makes a distribution, the distribution is deemed to come first from earnings previously taxed under subpart F and, to this extent, it is excluded from the recipient's gross income.[179] A dividend excluded from gross income under the foregoing rule is generally ignored in determining indirect credit.

---

[177] For the indirect and constructive ownership rules, see §958, discussed supra ¶68.2.2.

[178] IRC §960(a)(2).

[179] IRC §959, discussed supra ¶68.2.14.

Assume foreign corporation F distributes 175u to its sole shareholder, domestic corporation P. P has been taxed under subpart F on 150u of F's earnings and has not previously received distribution of any of these earnings. Of the 175u, 150u is excluded from gross income as a distribution of previously taxed income and is ignored in computing P's indirect credit. The numerator of the §902 fraction includes only the 25u of the distribution that remains after the 150u has been excluded.

b. *Subsequently imposed taxes.* If previously taxed income is subject to foreign income taxes that were not deemed paid when the income was taxed to the U.S. shareholder, additional indirect credit is allowed when the earnings are distributed to the U.S. shareholder.[180] Such not previously credited taxes most commonly exist where the U.S. shareholder was taxed under subpart F on earnings of a lower-tier CFC and the earnings bore additional taxes as they passed through a chain of foreign corporations.

Assume domestic corporation P owns all of the stock of foreign corporation $F1$, which is sole shareholder of foreign corporation $F2$. For 1995, P is taxed on 150u of $F2$'s subpart F income and is deemed to pay $37.5 of $F2$'s foreign income taxes under §960. During 1996, $F2$ distributes a dividend of 150u to $F1$, which is subject to a foreign tax of $15 (50u) on this income; $F1$ has no other income and pays no other foreign income taxes for any post-1986 year. $F1$'s post-1986 undistributed earnings are 100u (150u of dividend income less 50u in tax), and its post-1986 foreign income taxes are $15. If $F1$ distributes 100u as a dividend to P during 1996, P is deemed to have paid taxes actually paid by $F1$ of:

$$(\$15)(100u/100u) = \$15$$

Given more complex facts, the foregoing rule requires modifications of the normal pooling of foreign income taxes and undistributed earnings, but neither the statutes nor the regulations give much guidance on the subject. Normally, post-1986 foreign income taxes of a first-tier CFC are determined by lumping taxes deemed paid by the CFC together with taxes actually paid by the CFC. With respect to taxes on previously taxed income, this aggregation is probably inconsistent with the directive in §960 that a distribution of previously taxed income does not carry indirect credit unless the income has been subjected to additional taxes that have not yet been credited by the U.S. shareholder.

The regulations under §904(d) contain an example indicating that when previously taxed earnings are distributed, tax and earnings pools must be established including only the previously taxed income and the foreign income taxes imposed after the subpart F inclusion.[181] If the previously taxed income falls within more than one of the §904(d) baskets, a set of such pools is established within each basket. It would seem appropriate that the previously-taxed-income

---

[180] IRC §960(a)(3).
[181] Reg. §1.904-6(c) Ex. 8.

pools within a particular basket contain all previously taxed income for years after 1986 and all subsequently imposed taxes on this income; however, the example in the regulations is not clear on this point.

¶69.9   CREDIT ALLOWED TO FOREIGN PERSONS

Under §906, a nonresident alien individual or foreign corporation is entitled to credit for foreign income taxes only if engaged in business in the United States and then in only two relatively rare situations. First, if the taxpayer's income effectively connected with the U.S. business includes income from foreign sources, foreign taxes are creditable against the U.S. tax on this income. The effectively connected income tax on foreign source income is primarily intended to prevent the United States from being used as a tax haven, and this policy, Congress decided, does not require that U.S. tax be collected to the extent the income is burdened by foreign taxes.

Second, a foreign tax on U.S. source income is potentially creditable if (1) the country imposing the tax is not the taxpayer's country of residence (in the case of an individual) or the country in which the taxpayer is incorporated or domiciled (in the case of a corporation) or (2) the foreign tax is imposed by the taxpayer's country of residence, incorporation, or domicile, but it would have been imposed even in the absence of this tie. Moreover, a noncreditable foreign tax on U.S. source income is not deductible either.

A primary function of the credit for foreign persons is to provide relief when taxpayers are subjected to conflicting source claims. For example, when U.S. source effectively connected income is taxed by a country other than the taxpayer's country of residence, incorporation, or domicile, the taxpayer is often subject to triple taxation—by the taxpayer's home country and by two other countries (including the United States) that each claim to be the source of the income. In such a case, the credit effectively subordinates the U.S. tax claim to that of the other source country.

1. *Trade or business in United States.* No credit is allowed to a nonresident alien or foreign corporation unless the taxpayer is engaged in a trade or business in the United States during the taxable year.[1] The credit is only allowed against the effectively connected income tax, and this tax usually applies only for years in which the taxpayer carries on a trade or business in this country.[2] Thus, the requirement of a U.S. trade or business normally demands only that the taxpayer must be subject to the tax against which credit is claimed.

The requirement, however, creates ambiguity in some situations. For example, a foreign owner of U.S. real property can treat the property as a trade or business even if the taxpayer's activities relating to the property are too minimal

---

[1] IRC §906(a).

[2] IRC §864(c)(1)(B), discussed supra ¶66.3.1.

to be a business under the usual definition of that term.[3] Does the §906 credit apply if the taxpayer is not engaged in a business but is treated as so engaged?

Also, income and gain is sometimes taxed as effectively connected income even if the taxpayer is not engaged in a U.S. trade or business during the taxable year. If reported on the installment or cash method, gain on a sale of property or income from services is treated as effectively connected income, whether or not the taxpayer has a U.S. business during the year, provided that the income or gain would have been so characterized had it been recognized when the property was sold or the services performed.[4] If property used in a U.S. business is switched to another use (e.g., use in a foreign business), gain on a sale or exchange of the property at any time during the succeeding 10 years is effectively connected income if it would have been so treated had the disposition occurred immediately before the U.S. business use ceased.[5] Moreover, a foreign person's gain on a disposition of a U.S. real property interest is taxed as effectively connected income, whether or not the taxpayer is actually engaged in business in this country.[6] Is a foreign person entitled to credit if the person does not actually carry on business in the United States during the taxable year but has income treated as effectively connected income?

Credit should be allowed in these cases. The requirement that the taxpayer be engaged in a U.S. business should be construed to deny §906 credit only for years in which the taxpayer is not subject to the effectively connected income tax. The policies underlying §906 would be defeated rather than served by denying credit to a taxpayer not actually engaged in a U.S. trade or business if the taxpayer is treated as so being engaged or is treated as having income effectively connected with such a business. For example, the policy to provide relief to foreign taxpayers subjected to conflicting source claims is particularly relevant where the United States taxes as effectively connected income a gain on a sale of property that was formerly used in a U.S. business but is used in a foreign business immediately before the sale.

2. *Foreign tax must be imposed on effectively connected income.* The §906 credit is restricted to taxes of foreign countries and U.S. possessions that are imposed "with respect to income effectively connected with the conduct of a trade or business within the United States."[7] No rules are given for determining whether a particular tax is "with respect to" effectively connected income. A handy analogy, however, is provided by the rules for identifying the foreign taxes on income within the nine baskets established by the separate limitation rules of §904(d).[8] These rules should also be used in this context.

---

[3] IRC §§871(d), 882(d), discussed supra ¶66.3.6.
[4] IRC §864(c)(6), discussed supra ¶66.3.5.
[5] IRC §864(c)(7), discussed supra ¶66.3.5.
[6] IRC §897(a), discussed supra ¶66.4.
[7] IRC §906(a).
[8] Reg. §1.904-6, discussed supra ¶69.6.10.

3. *Credit only allowed against effectively connected income tax.* The §906 credit is only allowed against the tax under §1 or 11 on income effectively connected with the conduct of a U.S. trade or business. Sections 871(a) and 881 impose tax at 30 percent (or lower treaty rate) on selected items of U.S. source income not effectively connected with U.S. business.[9] The foreign tax credit is never allowed against the §§871(a) and 881 taxes.[10] Section 884 taxes branch profits and interest payments of foreign corporations engaged in business in the United States.[11] The §884 branch taxes are also noncreditable because they are substitutes for the taxes that would be imposed on shareholders and lenders under §§871(a) and 881 if the branch were separately organized as a domestic corporation.[12]

4. *Foreign taxes on U.S. source income.* Credits and deductions for foreign taxes on income from sources within the United States is further restricted. For a nonresident alien, such a tax is neither creditable nor deductible if (1) the taxpayer is a citizen or resident of the foreign country or U.S. possession imposing the tax and (2) the tax would not have been imposed in the absence of this citizenship or residence.[13] Assume individual A is a resident of country X, which taxes its residents on worldwide income. If A has U.S. source income that is effectively connected with a U.S. business, the country X tax on the income is neither creditable nor deductible in determining U.S. effectively connected income tax unless country X categorizes the income as country X income that it would tax even if the taxpayer were not a citizen or resident. Similarly, a foreign corporation can neither credit nor deduct a foreign tax on U.S. source income if (1) it was organized under the laws of the taxing country or possession or is considered domiciled in that country or possession under its laws and (2) the tax would not have been imposed in the absence of this link.

Credit for foreign taxes on U.S. source income is also affected by §904(a), described more fully immediately below, under which the §906 credit cannot exceed the U.S. tax on effectively connected taxable income from foreign sources. If a foreign person's effectively connected income is all from U.S. sources, the §904 limitation is zero. Even when allowed under the rules described in the preceding paragraph, foreign taxes on U.S. source income thus are creditable only to the extent that the precredit U.S. tax on effectively connected income from sources outside the United States exceeds the foreign taxes on that income.

5. *Section 904 limitation.* Section 904(a) restricts the credit for foreign income taxes to the portion of the U.S. tax (before the credit) that is ratably attributable to taxable income from sources outside the United States. In applying §904 to a taxpayer eligible for credit under §906, taxable income consists only

---

[9] See supra ¶66.2.
[10] IRC §906(b)(3).
[11] See supra ¶66.5.
[12] IRC §906(b)(7).
[13] IRC §906(b)(1).

of income effectively connected with the taxpayer's U.S. businesses.[14] The maximum credit for a foreign person is thus the precredit tax under §1 or §11 on taxable income effectively connected with trades or businesses in the United States multiplied by:

$$\frac{\text{Effectively connected taxable income from foreign sources}}{\text{Entire effectively connected taxable income}}$$

Assume a foreign corporation has $100 of taxable income effectively connected with U.S. businesses, of which $28.6 is from sources without the United States. If the corporation's effectively connected income tax is $35 before the credit, the maximum §906 credit is:

$$(\$35)\ (\$28.6/\$100) = \$10$$

Although the numerator of the limiting fraction includes only foreign source income, foreign taxes on U.S. as well as foreign source income are creditable, up to the amount of the limitation, unless the taxes are disqualified under rules other than §904.

   6. *Indirect credit.* Section 906(a) allows credit for both taxes paid or incurred directly by a foreign person and, if the taxpayer is a corporation, taxes that it would have been deemed to have paid under the indirect credit rules of §902 if it were a domestic corporation. Under §902(a), if a domestic corporation receives dividends from a foreign corporation in which it holds at least 10 percent of the voting stock, the domestic corporation is treated as having paid foreign income taxes actually imposed on the foreign corporation.[15]

   When §902 is applied in conjunction with §906, both the shareholder corporation (the credit claimant) and the distributing corporation are foreign.[16] Like the credit for taxes paid directly, the indirect credit is allowed to a foreign corporation only if the corporation is engaged in business in the United States, and it is restricted to foreign taxes on effectively connected income. A foreign corporation is thus entitled to indirect credit only in the rare case where it receives dividends from another foreign corporation that are effectively connected with the conduct of the taxpayer corporation's trade or business in the United States. Moreover, even in this rare case, if the distributing corporation has income effectively connected with U.S. business, this income and foreign taxes on it are excluded in computing the §902 credit.[17]

---

[14] IRC §906(b)(2).
[15] See supra ¶69.8.
[16] IRC §906(b)(4).
[17] IRC §906(b)(6).

7. *FSCs.* If the taxpayer is an FSC, §906 credit is not allowed for foreign taxes on its foreign trade income.[18]

¶69.10   TAXES ON FOREIGN OIL AND GAS INCOME

¶69.10.1   Introductory

Section 907 imposes two additional restrictions on credits for foreign taxes on income from the extraction, refining, transportation, or distribution of oil and gas and their primary products. First, under §907(a), credits for foreign taxes on income from the extraction of oil or gas may not exceed the precredit U.S. tax on this income.[1] This rule functions much like the separate limitation rules of §904(d).[2] To the extent creditable after the application of §907(a), however, foreign taxes on extraction income are also subject to §904. Section 907(a) is thus a limitation rule layered on top of other limitation rules.

Second, under §907(b), discriminatory foreign taxes on income from refining, transporting, or distributing oil and gas or their primary products are partially recharacterized as business expenses rather than as foreign income taxes.[3] A foreign tax is discriminatory for this purpose if, either by the terms of the foreign tax law or the way in which it is administered, oil-related income is taxed at effective rates higher than those applied to other types of income. The recharacterized portion of such a tax generally equals the excess of the tax over the amount that would have been imposed on a like amount of nonoil income.

Also, under §901(f), foreign taxes on income from purchases and sales of oil or gas extracted in the taxing country do not qualify as income taxes for purposes of §901, and therefore are deductible but not creditable, if (1) the taxpayer has no economic interest in the oil or gas deposits and (2) the purchase or sale is at a price differing from fair market value. A taxpayer has an economic interest if it "has acquired, by investment, any interest in the oil in place, and secures, by any form of legal relationship, income derived from the extraction of the oil, to which he must look for a return of his capital."[4]

¶69.10.2   Taxes on Extraction Income

Section 907(a) imposes a ceiling on the credit for foreign "oil and gas extraction taxes" (FOGEI taxes). In general, this ceiling equals the precredit U.S.

---

[18] IRC §906(b)(5). For FSCs and the term "foreign trade income," see supra ¶68.1.4.

[1] See infra ¶69.10.2.

[2] For §904(d), see supra ¶69.6.

[3] See infra ¶69.10.3.

[4] Palmer v. Bender, 287 US 551, 557 (1933), applied in this context by Gulf Oil Co. v. CIR, 914 F2d 396 (3d Cir. 1990) (under this test, taxpayer found to have economic interest in Iranian oil and gas, even though Iranian government held title to deposits).

tax on the taxpayer's "foreign oil and gas extraction income" (FOGEI), including income from the extraction of oil and gas and the sale of related business assets. The purpose of the limitation is to prevent high foreign taxes on FOGEI from offsetting U.S. tax on less heavily taxed income from trading, refining, and shipping oil and gas and from activities unrelated to oil and gas.[5] Taxes subject to the §907(a) limitation are additionally limited by §904.[6]

The §907(a) limitation operates on an overall basis; the credit for all FOGEI taxes is limited to the precredit U.S. tax on all FOGEI.[7] Assume a domestic corporation has extraction activities in country X that generate taxable income of $300, but it sustains a loss of $100 from extraction activities in country Y. A tax of $138 is imposed by country X on the $300 of extraction income from that country. FOGEI is $200 ($300 less $100). If the U.S. tax rate is 35 percent, the precredit U.S. tax on the FOGEI is $70, and §907(a) denies current credit for $68 ($138 less $70) of the country X tax. Under a carryover rule described below, the disallowed taxes are carried to the two preceding and five succeeding taxable years, and they are allowed in the earliest of those years in which the §907(a) limitation exceeds current foreign taxes on FOGEI.[8]

1. *Computation and application of §907(a) limitation.* For a corporation, the §907(a) ceiling is the corporation's FOGEI for the taxable year multiplied by the highest tax rate for corporations under §11. For years in which the highest corporate rate is 35 percent, the cap is 35 percent of FOGEI. Assume a domestic corporation has $200 of FOGEI for a particular year and pays taxes to foreign countries X and Y of $115 on the income.[9] Credit for these taxes is restricted to $70 (35 percent of $200). For an individual, the ceiling is FOGEI multiplied by the effective U.S. tax rate, which is the ratio of the individual's precredit U.S. tax for the year to entire taxable income.[10]

The §907(a) ceiling is a limitation on the taxes eligible for credit under §901. Up to the amount of the ceiling, FOGEI taxes are creditable, subject to the §904 limitation. If the foreign tax credit is elected for a taxable year in which FOGEI taxes exceed the ceiling, the excess is neither creditable nor deductible for the year, but it is potentially creditable in other years under a carryover rule de-

---

[5] Staff of Joint Comm. on Tax'n, 97th Cong., 2d Sess., General Explanation of the Revenue Provisions of the Tax Equity and Fiscal Responsibility Act of 1982 at 71 (Comm. Print 1982) [hereinafter 1982 Bluebook].

[6] See Reg. §1.907(a)-1(f). For §904, see supra ¶69.5.

[7] For taxable years beginning before 1983, the limitation was applied on a per country basis. This approach was rejected in 1982 because, when a taxpayer had extraction losses in one country and extraction income in another, the per country rule had the effect of allowing the extraction losses to offset nonextraction income rather than extraction income, which was "contrary to the general goal of segregating oil and gas extraction income and taxes." 1982 Bluebook, supra note 5, at 71.

[8] See infra text accompanying note 63.

[9] See Reg. §1.907(a)-1(d) Ex. 1.

[10] Reg. §1.907(a)-1(c)(3).

scribed below.[11] If a taxpayer chooses to deduct rather than credit foreign income taxes for the taxable year a FOGEI tax is imposed, §907(a) has no application to the tax.

2. *FOGEI.* FOGEI consists of foreign source taxable income from (1) "the extraction . . . of minerals from oil or gas wells" located outside the United States and its possessions and (2) sales and exchanges of assets used in the business of extracting these minerals.[12] The term "minerals" encompasses "hydrocarbon minerals extracted from oil and gas wells," including crude oil, natural gas, and "incidental impurities from these wells, such as sulphur, nitrogen, or helium."[13] Minerals from shale oil and tar sands are excluded.

The taxpayer need not be the person who extracts the minerals, but it must usually have "an economic interest in the minerals in place."[14] Whether income is from extraction or the sale of assets used in an extraction business depends on the substance of the transaction, not its form.[15] For example, if a foreign government gives a discount on purchases of oil and gas as payment for extraction assets taken when the government nationalized the taxpayer's facilities in the country, the discount is treated as gain on a sale of extraction assets.

FOGEI is distinguished from foreign oil related income (FORI), which includes income from oil and gas activities subsequent to the extraction phase.[16] FOGEI does not include income "attributable to marketing, distributing, processing or transporting minerals or primary products."[17] Income from purchases and sales of oil and gas also are not FOGEI.

When a taxpayer extracts oil or gas but does not sell it at the wellhead, oil and gas income is allocated between FOGEI and FORI. FOGEI is determined as though the oil or gas were sold for an amount equal to "the fair market value of the minerals in the immediate vicinity of the well."[18] An "independent market" in the vicinity of the well provides the best evidence of this fair market value; however, the market value at a port can be used as the starting point if the taxpayer's relationship with the foreign government and other relevant circumstances are taken into account in adjusting the port price to be a fair estimate of the field price.[19]

Generally, if oil or gas is sold at a price that differs from fair market value, FOGEI is determined as though the sale were made at fair market value.[20] For

---

[11] Reg. §1.907(a)-1(e)(1). For the carryover rule, see infra text accompanying note 63.

[12] IRC §907(c)(1).

[13] Reg. §1.907(c)-1(f)(1).

[14] Reg. §§1.907(c)-1(b)(1), (7). For the meaning of the term "economic interest," see Reg. §1.611-1(b)(1), discussed supra ¶24.1.2.

[15] Reg. §1.907(c)-1(b)(3).

[16] For FORI, see infra ¶69.10.3 text accompanying notes 65–75.

[17] Reg. §1.907(c)-1(b)(5).

[18] Reg. §1.907(c)-1(b)(2).

[19] Reg. §1.907(c)-1(b)(6).

[20] IRC §907(d).

example, if oil or gas is sold to a foreign government at a posted price, this price is ignored unless it equals fair market value.[21]

In addition to income on sales of oil and gas extracted by the taxpayer and royalties from an exploiter of oil or gas deposits in which the taxpayer has an economic income, FOGEI can include interest on bank deposits and other temporary investments held as working capital for an extraction business and foreign exchange gain or loss.[22] A recovery under a business interruption insurance policy is FOGEI if the covered loss arose in extraction activities.[23] FOGEI can also include income from the performance of services directly related to oil and gas extraction and from the lease or license of related property.[24]

a. *Gains and losses on assets sales.* Gain or loss on a sale of property other than oil and gas is included in FOGEI if the taxpayer used the property primarily in a trade or business of extracting oil and gas.[25] Property is used in a trade or business if it is described in §1231(b) (applied without regard to holding period or the normal requirement that §1231 property be depreciable). Stock in a corporation cannot be an asset of an extraction business, although gain on a sale of stock is sometimes brought into FOGEI by a rule for dividends described below.[26] If gain or loss on an installment sale is included in FOGEI, interest on the installment obligation is also included.[27] Gain recognized on an insurance recovery for a casualty loss or on an expropriation is FOGEI if the property destroyed in the casualty was primarily used in an extraction business.[28]

b. *Dividends and subpart F inclusions.* If the taxpayer is a domestic corporation, FOGEI includes a dividend from a foreign corporation that qualifies the taxpayer for indirect credit under §902, but only to the extent the dividend is "attributable" to FOGEI of the distributing corporation.[29] If §1248 characterizes gain on a sale of stock as a dividend, it is considered a dividend for this purpose as well.[30] Also, if the taxpayer is taxed under subpart F on income of a CFC and

---

[21] Reg. §1.907(d)-1.

[22] Reg. §§1.907(c)-1(f)(3), (4), (5). Interest income cannot be FOGEI, however, if it is passive income for purposes of the credit limitation rules of §904(d). IRC §907(c)(1), as amended by Pub. L. No. 103-66, §13235(a), 107 Stat. 312 (1993) (effective for taxable years beginning after 1992). For the §904(d) meaning of "passive income," see supra ¶69.6.2.

[23] Reg. §1.907(c)-1(f)(6).

[24] Reg. §§1.907(c)-1(b)(4), (g).

[25] Reg. §1.907(c)-1(e)(1). See Reg. §1.907(c)-1(e)(2) (if property is used primarily in extraction activities, entire gain or loss is FOGEI even if some use is in other activities; if primary use is not in extraction, none of gain or loss is FOGEI even if some use is in extraction).

[26] Reg. §1.907(c)-1(e)(3).

[27] Reg. §1.907(c)-1(e)(7).

[28] Reg. §1.907(c)-1(f)(6).

[29] IRC §907(c)(3)(A). See Reg. §1.907(c)-2(c)(2) (if taxpayer qualifies for §902 credit, dividend may be FOGEI even if foreign corporation paid no foreign income taxes). For §902, see supra ¶69.9.

[30] Reg. §1.907(c)-2(b)(1). For §1248, see ¶68.2.16.

if this qualifies the taxpayer for the indirect credit under §960, the subpart F inclusion is FOGEI to the extent it is attributable to FOGEI of the CFC.[31] When indirect credit is allowed under §902 or §960, a constructive dividend must be recognized under §78 equal to the taxes imputed to the taxpayer under the indirect credit rules.[32] A constructive dividend under §78 is FOGEI to the extent the taxes imputed to the taxpayer under §902 or §960 are FOGEI taxes.[33]

The portion of a dividend that is "attributable" to the distributing corporation's FOGEI, and is therefore included in the taxpayer's FOGEI if the rule described above applies, equals the amount of the dividend multiplied by a fraction.[34] Usually, the fraction is the distributing corporation's post-1986 undistributed FOGEI earnings, divided by the corporation's post-1986 undistributed earnings. Post-1986 undistributed FOGEI earnings equal the corporation's post-1986 FOGEI, reduced by the sum of (1) post-1986 FOGEI taxes and (2) dividends distributed in prior years from post-1986 undistributed FOGEI earnings. Assume foreign corporation *F* has post-1986 undistributed earnings of 100u, 60u of which are of FOGEI. If the dividend rule described above applies to a dividend received from *F*, the recipient's FOGEI includes 60 percent (60u/100u) of the dividend and 60 percent of the related constructive dividend under §78.

FOGEI does not include a dividend to the extent that the dividend is passive income for purposes of the credit limitation rules of §904(d).[35] Generally, if a dividend from a foreign corporation qualifies the recipient for indirect credit under §902, the dividend is passive income only if the corporation is a CFC and only to the extent the dividend is assigned to the passive basket under a look-through procedure.[36]

The portion of a subpart F inclusion that is attributable to FOGEI is the amount of the inclusion multiplied by the portion of the CFC's current earnings and profits that consists of FOGEI, and divided by the corporation's entire earnings and profits for the year.[37] This procedure can have the odd effect of characterizing part of an inclusion as FOGEI even though the inclusion consists

---

[31] IRC §907(c)(3)(B). See Reg. §1.907(c)-2(c)(3) (inclusion may be FOGEI even if CFC paid no foreign income taxes). For subpart F, see supra ¶68.2.

[32] The amount of this constructive dividend is not affected by §907(a). Reg. §1.907(a)-1(e)(3). Assume a domestic corporation receives a $60 dividend from a foreign corporation and, as a consequence, is deemed to have paid $40 of foreign income taxes actually paid by the foreign corporation. The taxpayer has a §78 dividend of $40 even if immediate credit for some of the $40 of deemed paid taxes is denied by §907(a).

[33] Reg. §1.907(c)-2(d)(5).

[34] Reg. §1.907(c)-2(d)(1).

[35] IRC §907(c)(1), as amended by Pub. L. No. 103-66, §13235(a), 107 Stat. 312 (1993) (effective for taxable years beginning after 1992).

[36] For the look-through rule, see supra ¶69.6.8. If the distributing corporation is not a CFC, the dividend is assigned to a separate basket and cannot be passive income. IRC §904(d)(1)(E), discussed supra ¶69.6.7.

[37] Reg. §1.907(c)-2(d)(4).

of particular items that are unrelated to extraction activities. Assume a CFC's current earnings consist of FOGEI and dividends and interest that are not FOGEI but are taxed to the CFC's U.S. shareholders under subpart F. Even though the subpart F inclusion consists exclusively of non-FOGEI items, a portion of the inclusion is considered FOGEI because some of the CFC's earnings and profits are FOGEI.

c. *Partnership items.* If the taxpayer is a partner in a partnership, domestic or foreign, the taxpayer's distributive share of the partnership's FOGEI is FOGEI of the taxpayer.[38]

d. *Deductions.* FOGEI consists of taxable income, not gross income. From the items of gross income described above are subtracted the deductions allocated and apportioned to this income under the general rules for allocating and apportioning deductions.[39]

e. *Source.* FOGEI only includes foreign source income.[40] Income is from foreign sources for this purpose if its source is outside the United States and its possessions (including Puerto Rico). Source is determined for this purpose without regard to §904(f), which sometimes recharacterizes foreign source income as domestic source income as a means of recapturing overall foreign losses sustained in prior years.[41]

3. *FOGEI taxes.* The term "oil and gas extraction taxes" (FOGEI taxes) includes all foreign taxes "with respect to" FOGEI.[42] Generally, the foreign law imposing a tax determines the amount of the tax that is imposed on FOGEI.[43] The first step in determining the effect of foreign law is to identify the base on which the tax is levied. A tax base consists of income and deductions that are mixed together and subject to tax as a unit under a single rate schedule. Generally, if an excess of deductions over gross income of one class is allowable against income of another class, the two classes of income and related deductions constitute one tax base. If a tax base includes only FOGEI, all taxes on this base are FOGEI taxes. If the base includes both FOGEI and other income, the taxes on the base are apportioned according to the relative net amounts of FOGEI and other income, determined as far as possible by the accounting rules of the foreign tax law. Foreign law, however, usually does not require that a tax base be divided between FOGEI and other income, and the division thus is often made by a mixture of foreign and U.S. tax principles. If a foreign income tax is collected by

---

[38] IRC §907(c)(3)(C); Reg. §1.907(c)-2(f).

[39] Reg. §1.907(c)-1(f)(2). For the allocation and apportionment of deductions, see infra ¶70.10.

[40] For the source of income, see infra ¶70.1.

[41] Reg. §1.907(a)-1(c)(3)(iii). For §904(f), see supra ¶69.7.

[42] IRC §907(c)(5).

[43] Reg. §1.907(c)-3(a). See Reg. §1.907(a)-1(c)(4)(ii) (foreign tax for particular year may be FOGEI tax even if, under U.S. rules, taxpayer has net operating loss in taxing country).

withholding, it is apportioned according to the amounts of FOGEI and non-FOGEI in each payment subject to withholding.[44]

Assume that a domestic corporation extracts crude oil in country Y, transports the oil to a port in that country by a pipeline owned by the corporation, and exports the oil from the port.[45] Country Y imposes tax at 50 percent on all mineral income, computed as though crude oil was sold at a posted price of $12 per barrel at the time of export. The tax is assumed to qualify as a foreign income tax for purposes of §901.[46] In addition, country Y collects a royalty of 12 percent of the posted price ($1.44 per barrel) and allows as deductions 20 cents per barrel for lifting costs and 80 cents per barrel for transportation costs. The country Y tax for each barrel exported is shown in line 1 of Example 69-5. Because the tax base includes both FOGEI and income from transporting and exporting the oil, the tax must be apportioned. If the fair market value of the oil in the vicinity of the wells (the starting figure for computing FOGEI) is $9, while the fair market value at the point of export is $10 ($2 less than the posted price used in computing country Y tax), the apportionment is as shown in line 2 of Example 69-5.

Example 69-5
Computation of FOGEI Taxes

1. Foreign tax per barrel:		
Sales		$12.00
Less:		
Royalties	$ 1.44	
Lifting costs	.20	
Transporting costs	.80	$ 2.44
Tax base		$ 9.56
Country Y tax (at 50 percent)		$ 4.78
2. Portion qualifying as FOGEI taxes:		
Modified gross income ($9 fair market value at wellhead plus $2 excess of posted price over fair market value)	$11.00	
Less:		
Royalties	$ 1.44	
Lifting costs	.20	1.64
FOGEI tax base		$ 9.36
Country Y tax on this base (FOGEI tax)		$ 4.68

A domestic corporation's FOGEI taxes can include both taxes imposed directly on the taxpayer and taxes paid by foreign corporations that the taxpayer

---

[44] Reg. §1.907(c)-3(a)(7).

[45] Reg. §1.907(c)-3(e) Ex. 3.

[46] But see supra ¶69.4.3 text accompanying notes 55–63 (qualifying tax must usually be computed from actual gross receipts).

is deemed to pay under the indirect credit rules of §§902 and 960.[47] Deemed paid taxes are FOGEI taxes in an amount equal to the deemed paid amount multiplied by:[48]

$$\frac{\text{Foreign corporation's post-1986 FOGEI taxes}}{\text{Corporation's post-1986 foreign income taxes}}$$

For example, if foreign corporation *F* has \$120 of post-1986 foreign income taxes, \$80 of which are FOGEI taxes, two thirds of the deemed paid taxes recognized on account of a dividend or subpart F inclusion from *F* are FOGEI taxes.[49]

If, for U.S. tax purposes, the taxpayer has a loss for the year from oil and gas extraction activities, a foreign tax is nevertheless a FOGEI tax if it is imposed on items taken into account (either currently or in some other year) in determining FOGEI. Moreover, if the taxpayer incurred an extraction loss for a prior year and the loss is carried over to the current year under a recapture rule described below, the recapture rule (which recharacterizes FOGEI as non-FOGEI income) is ignored in determining whether a foreign tax is a FOGEI tax.[50]

Section 907(a) only applies to amounts qualifying as "foreign income taxes," as that term is defined by the regulations under §901, or as foreign taxes in lieu of income taxes, qualifying under §903.[51] An amount that fails to qualify as a foreign income tax or a tax in lieu thereof is not creditable under any circumstance, but it might be deductible under §164.[52]

4. *Recapture of foreign oil and gas extraction losses.* If a taxpayer sustains a "foreign oil extraction loss" (FOEL), FOGEI of subsequent years is recharacterized as income that is not FOGEI until the FOEL is fully recaptured.[53] A FOEL is an overall loss for the taxable year from foreign oil and gas extraction activities. Since the §907(a) limitation consists of the precredit tax on FOGEI, the effect of this recapture rule is to reduce the limitation until the FOEL is recaptured.

The theory underlying the rule is that because the FOEL, when incurred, usually offsets income other than FOGEI, credit for FOGEI taxes should be

---

[47] However, taxes deemed paid under §902 are not FOGEI taxes to any extent if the taxpayer's dividend income is passive income and therefore excluded from FOGEI. See supra text accompanying note 36. For the indirect credit rules, see supra ¶69.8.

[48] Reg. §1.907(c)-3(b). See supra text accompanying notes 29–36 for the related computation of the portion of the dividend or subpart F inclusion that is characterized as FOGEI.

[49] See Reg. §1.907(c)-3(e) Ex. 1.

[50] For the recapture rule, see infra text accompanying notes 53–62.

[51] See supra ¶69.4.

[52] For §164, see supra ¶32.1.1.

[53] IRC §907(c)(4)(A). See Reg. §1.907(c)-1(c)(1) (FOEL carries forward indefinitely until recaptured from FOGEI). For the converse situation, where a non-FOGEI loss from foreign sources is deducted against FOGEI, see Reg. §1.907(c)-2(d)(7).

denied until foreign extraction activities generate sufficient income to restore the loss. Until then, there is no net U.S. tax on FOGEI because the tax on FOGEI of later years merely offsets the tax saved by deducting the FOEL against other income. The fundamental policy of §907(a) to allow credit for FOGEI taxes only against U.S. tax on FOGEI thus requires that credit for these taxes be deferred until the FOEL is recaptured. The recapture rule applies, however, whether or not "the taxpayer obtained . . . tax benefit from the loss."[54]

A FOEL is the amount by which gross income taken into account in determining FOGEI for any year is exceeded by the deductions allocated and apportioned to the gross income.[55] In other words, a FOEL is negative FOGEI. If a consolidated return is filed for the loss year, the FOEL is determined on a consolidated basis.[56] A FOEL may exist for a taxable year whether or not the taxpayer elects the foreign tax credit for the year; however, only losses in taxable years beginning after 1982 may be FOELs.

Net operating losses carried from other years are ignored in computing a FOEL because the deductions making up these losses are taken into account in determining whether there is FOGEI or a FOEL for the years the net operating losses are sustained.[57] Also, the deduction for an uninsured casualty or foreign expropriation loss is not allocated or apportioned to FOGEI for this purpose, even if the loss relates directly to foreign oil and gas extraction activities. The effect of the latter rule is effectively to exempt a FOEL from recapture to the extent it is attributable to a casualty or foreign expropriation loss.

A FOEL is recaptured by carrying it to the year immediately following the loss year and recharacterizing FOGEI for the carryover year as non-FOGEI up to the amount of the FOEL. If the FOEL exceeds that year's FOGEI (before recapture), the excess is carried to the second succeeding year, where it is subject to the same procedure. If full recapture is not accomplished in the second year, the procedure is repeated in subsequent years until the FOEL is fully recaptured. If a second FOEL is incurred before the first is recaptured, it is added to the unrecaptured portion of the first FOEL, and the aggregate is carried forward from year to year until it is recaptured.

The recharacterization of FOGEI under the recapture rule does not change the character of foreign taxes on that income.[58] Taxes on recharacterized FOGEI thus are not currently creditable unless FOGEI, before recharacterization, ex-

---

[54] 1982 Bluebook, supra note 5, at 73.

[55] IRC §907(c)(4)(B).

[56] Reg. §1.907(c)-1(c)(4); 1982 Bluebook, supra note 5, at 73 ("[i]f no overall foreign extraction loss has been sustained in the case of an affiliated group of corporations filing a consolidated return, then no such loss is subject to recapture . . . even if a member of the group had an extraction loss and the member is subsequently sold or otherwise leaves the group").

[57] Reg. §1.907(c)-1(c)(3)(ii).

[58] Reg. §§1.907(a)-1(c)(4)(i), 1.907(c)-1(c)(5). See 1982 Bluebook, supra note 5, at 74 (FOGEI "taxes always retain their character as extraction taxes").

ceeds the FOEL carried to the year and the §907(a) ceiling, after recharacterization, is sufficient to cover them. When current credit is lost under the recapture rule, however, the uncredited taxes are carried to other years under the carryover rule described below.[59]

Under §904(f)(1), an overall foreign loss for any year is recaptured by recharacterizing future foreign source income as domestic.[60] Since an "overall foreign loss" is defined as the amount by which gross income from foreign sources (including oil and gas extraction income) is exceeded by the deductions allocated and apportioned to this income, it is possible for an FOEL, or some part of it, to be included in an overall foreign loss. When this happens, the amount included in both categories is recaptured under §904(f), but only from subsequent FOGEI. The residue of the FOEL is recaptured under the FOEL rule.[61]

Assume that for 1996, a domestic corporation has a FOEL of $100, $75 of foreign source taxable income from activities other than the extraction of oil and gas, and $200 of taxable income from domestic sources.[62] For 1996, the FOEL effectively offsets $75 of non-FOGEI foreign source income and $25 of domestic income. The corporation has an overall foreign loss of $25 for 1996, all of which is included in the FOEL. In 1997 and subsequent years, $25 of the $100 FOEL will be recaptured under §904(f) by recharacterizing $25 of FOGEI as domestic source income. This $25 will be neither FOGEI in computing the §907(a) limitation nor taxable income from foreign sources in computing the §904 limitation. The remaining $75 of the FOEL will be recaptured under the FOEL rule by recharacterizing $75 of FOGEI as non-FOGEI (but still foreign source) income.

5. *Carryover rule.* If the taxpayer's FOGEI taxes exceed the §907(a) limitation for any year (an unused credit year), the excess is carried to the second preceding taxable year, then to the first preceding year, and then to each of the five years following the taxable year.[63] Subject to the §904 limitations, the carryback or carryover is creditable for a year to which it is carried to the extent the §907(a) limitation for that year exceeds the FOGEI taxes for the year.

If carryovers or carrybacks from two or more years are carried to the same year, the amount carried from the earliest year is used first. The amount of a carryover or carryback that can be used in a particular year is thus the excess of the current §907(a) limitation over the sum of (1) current FOGEI taxes and (2) carryovers and carrybacks from taxable years before the unused credit year.

A carryback or carryover allowed under the foregoing rules must also run the gauntlet of §904, which has its own carryback and carryover rules in §904(c). Under §904(c), a carryback or carryover is allowed in a particular year to the extent the §904 limitation for the year exceeds the sum of (1) current foreign

---

[59] For the carryover rule, see infra text accompanying note 63.

[60] See supra ¶69.7 for §904(f).

[61] 1982 Bluebook, supra note 5, at 74.

[62] See id. For additional examples, see Reg. §1.907(c)-1(c)(6).

[63] IRC §907(f)(1); Reg. §1.907(f)-1.

income taxes and (2) amounts carried to the current year from years before the unused credit year. If both FOGEI taxes and other foreign taxes are carried from the same unused credit year, the FOGEI taxes are allowed first, subject to §904(c)'s carryover and carryback ceiling, and the other taxes are allowable only to the extent some portion of this ceiling remains unused by FOGEI taxes.

Carryovers and carrybacks may only be used as credits. They are unavailable for any carryover or carryback year for which the taxpayer elects the deduction for foreign income taxes in lieu of the foreign tax credit.

¶69.10.3   Discriminatory Taxes on Foreign Oil Related Income

Under §907(b), a foreign tax on "foreign oil related income" (FORI) does not qualify as a foreign income tax to the extent that under the law imposing the tax, the income is taxed more heavily than other income. FORI is more heavily taxed if the tax on this income "will generally be materially greater, over a reasonable period of time, than the amount generally imposed on income" not connected with foreign oil operations. This rule applies whether the excess tax on FORI results from the way the foreign tax law is "structured" or from the way it "in fact operates." However, a foreign tax is structured or operates to discriminate against FORI "only if, under the facts and circumstances, there has been a shifting of tax by the foreign country from a tax on FOGEI to a tax on FORI."[64] The FORI rule is thus a backstop for the separate limitation for FOGEI under §907(a).

FORI is foreign source taxable income from postextraction activities relating to oil and gas.[65] Income from processing crude oil and gas into their primary products is FORI whether the oil or gas was extracted by the taxpayer or some other person, related or unrelated. "The term 'processing' means the destructive distillation, or a process similar in effect to destructive distillation, of crude oil and the processing of natural gas into their primary products including processes used to remove pollutants from crude oil or natural gas."[66]

Income from transporting oil and gas and their primary products is FORI whether the transportation is by "vessel, pipeline, truck, railroad, or aircraft."[67] Income from "time or voyage charter hires" can be FORI, but income from "a bareboat charter hire" cannot.

Income from distributing or selling oil or gas or their primary products is FORI whether the sales are made to processors, wholesalers, retailers, or retail customers.[68] For example, income from the operation of gasoline stations in

---

[64] Reg. §1.907(b)-1.

[65] IRC §907(c)(2).

[66] Reg. §1.907(c)-1(d)(4). For an itemization of the primary products of oil and gas, see Reg. §§1.907(c)-1(d)(5), (6).

[67] Reg. §1.907(c)-1(d)(2).

[68] Reg. §1.907(c)-1(d)(3). See Phillips Petroleum Co. v. CIR, 97 TC 30 (1991) (taxpayer extracted natural gas from wells in Alaska, processed it into liquid natural gas

foreign countries is FORI. Interest received in credit sales of oil or gas or their primary products is also FORI.[69]

Gain or loss recognized on a disposition of assets used in such a refining, transportation, distribution, or sales business is FORI.[70] FORI can also include income from "the performance of any other related service."[71]

Only foreign source income can be FORI. An item is from foreign sources for this purpose if its source is outside the United States and its possessions.

Dividends and interest income are FORI in various circumstances. FORI includes a dividend received by a domestic corporation from a foreign corporation if the dividend qualifies the domestic corporation for indirect credit under §902, but only to the extent the dividend is "attributable" to FORI of the distributing corporation.[72] Moreover, if the taxpayer would qualify for the indirect credit on receiving a dividend from a foreign corporation, interest received from the foreign corporation is also FORI to the extent it is attributable to the foreign corporation's FORI and is not passive income for purposes of the credit limitation rules of §904(d).[73] The exclusion of passive dividends and interest income generally means that dividends and interest can be FORI only if the foreign corporation is a CFC. Also, if a domestic corporation is taxed under subpart F as a U.S. shareholder of a CFC and, as a consequence, the domestic corporation qualifies for the indirect credit under §960, the subpart F inclusion is FORI to the extent it is attributable to the CFC's FORI.[74]

(LNG) in Alaska, and sold it in Japan; held, income on sales is partly from U.S. sources and partly from foreign sources, and foreign source portion is FORI).

[69] However, interest income cannot be FORI if it is passive income for purposes of the credit limitation rules of §904(d). IRC §907(c)(2), as amended by Pub. L. No. 103-66, §13235(a), 107 Stat. 312 (1993) (applicable for taxable years beginning after 1992). For the passive basket under §904(d), see supra ¶69.6.2.

[70] IRC §907(c)(2)(D).

[71] IRC §907(c)(2)(E); Reg. §1.907(c)-1(g).

[72] IRC §§907(c)(3)(A). Whether a dividend is attributable to the distributing corporation's FORI is determined by the same rules used in deciding whether a dividend is attributable to the corporation's FOGEI. See supra ¶69.10.2 text accompanying note 34.

A dividend cannot be FORI if it is passive income for purposes of the credit limitation rules of §904(d). IRC §907(c)(2) (applicable for taxable years beginning after 1992). This limitation, however, rarely applies to dividends described in the text because, if the taxpayer qualifies for credit under §902, the dividend is either in a separate (10-50) basket or is subject to a look-through rule that seldom assigns the dividend to the passive basket. For §904(d), see supra ¶69.6.

[73] IRC §§907(c)(2),(3)(A); Reg. §1.907(c)-2(c)(1). Interest is attributable to the payor's FORI if its deduction for the interest is matched with FORI under the general rules for allocating and apportioning deductions. Reg. §1.907(c)-2(d)(2). For the allocation and apportionment of deductions, see ¶70.10. The exclusion of passive interest from FORI applies for taxable years beginning after 1992.

[74] IRC §907(c)(3)(B). The extent to which the inclusion is attributable to the CFC's FORI is determined by the same rules used to trace a subpart F inclusion to FOGEI. See supra ¶69.10.2 text accompanying note 34.

If the taxpayer is a partner in a partnership, domestic or foreign, the tax-payer's distributive share of the partnership's FORI is FORI of the taxpayer.[75]

¶69.11   CREDIT REDUCTION FOR PARTICIPANTS IN INTERNATIONAL BOYCOTTS

If a taxpayer "participates in or cooperates with an international boycott," the foreign tax credit is reduced for each taxable year in which the taxpayer so participates or cooperates.[1] This reduction is also made if the taxpayer is a member of a consolidated group of corporations and another member of the group participates in or cooperates with an international boycott during the taxable year.[2] Moreover, if a foreign corporation participates in or cooperates with an international boycott, the reduction is made in the indirect credits under §§902 and 960 that would otherwise be available to the domestic corporation on receiving dividends from the foreign corporation or being taxed on its income under subpart F.[3]

In each of these cases, otherwise creditable taxes are reduced by a fraction referred to as the international boycott factor, which generally represents the proportion of the taxpayer's business that is done in the countries imposing the boycott. If the taxpayer or another member of its consolidated group participates in or cooperates with an international boycott, all otherwise creditable foreign income taxes are reduced by this fraction. If the taxpayer is subject to these rules only because it is a shareholder in a foreign corporation that participates in or cooperates with a boycott, the foreign income taxes of the foreign corporation deemed paid by the taxpayer under §§902 and 960 are reduced, but the credit for other taxes is not affected.

When taxes imposed directly on the taxpayer are reduced under the international boycott rule, a deduction is allowed for the disallowed amount.[4] When the indirect credit is reduced, §78, which normally requires that a constructive dividend be reported equal to the taxes of the foreign corporation deemed paid by the taxpayer, does not apply to the amount lost in the reduction.

---

[75] IRC §907(c)(3)(C).

[1] IRC §908(a). For the meaning of "international boycott" and "participates in or cooperates with," see supra ¶68.8.

[2] The term "consolidated group" is defined as a group of corporations that is eligible to file a consolidated return or that would be eligible if the usual 80 percent ownership requirement for groups filing consolidated returns were reduced to 50 percent. IRC §993(a)(3).

[3] For §§902 and 960, see supra ¶69.8.

[4] IRC §908(b).

¶69.12 CREDIT AGAINST ALTERNATIVE MINIMUM TAX

The foreign tax credit is allowed in determining the alternative minimum tax (AMT) under §55, but with several modifications.[1] The limitations on the credit under §904 are specially tailored to the AMT rules unless the taxpayer elects not to apply these modifications. Also, the credit, so limited, usually may not exceed 90 percent of the AMT. If a taxpayer's foreign income taxes exceed these ceilings, the excess is carried to other years under §904(c), but the amounts and application of the carrybacks and carryovers are specially computed for AMT purposes.

1. *Alterations of §904.* The general rule of §904(a) is that the foreign tax credit cannot exceed an amount equal to the precredit tax multiplied by a fraction whose numerator is foreign source taxable income and whose denominator is entire taxable income.[2] Assume a corporation has taxable income of $100, including $10 from sources without the United States, and the corporation's tax liability, computed before the credit, is $35. The credit limitation is:

$$(\$35)(\$10/\$100) = \$3.5$$

Under §904(d), if the taxpayer has income within any one of eight separate baskets, a separate limitation is computed for foreign taxes on that income.[3] When the general and separate limitations are computed for purposes of the AMT foreign tax credit, three changes are made.

The numerator of the fraction is alternative minimum taxable income (AMTI) from sources without the United States, and the denominator is entire AMTI.[4] AMTI is taxable income with various adjustments meant to eliminate many tax preferences. Generally, the sources of AMTI are determined by the rules used in sourcing taxable income.[5]

The separate limitation rules of §904(d) generally apply for AMT purposes in the same way as they apply for regular tax purposes. For each basket, the numerator of the limiting fraction is foreign source AMTI within the basket. One change, however, is made in assembling the passive basket. For regular tax purposes, income is excluded from the passive basket if it is subject to foreign

---

[1] For the alternative minimum tax, see infra ¶111.4.

[2] See supra ¶69.5.1.

[3] See supra ¶69.6.

[4] IRC §59(a)(1)(B).

[5] For taxable years beginning in 1987, 1988, and 1989, a source rule unique to the AMT rules applies to an addition to AMTI of corporations that is made when book income exceeds AMTI (computed without this addition). The addition is not computed from gross income and thus has no source under the regular source rules, which only apply to items of gross income. The addition is allocated to sources within and without the United States in the same proportions as AMTI, without this addition, is split between these two sources. IRC §59(a)(1)(C) (before amendment in 1990). For example, if 10 percent of AMTI without the addition is from foreign sources, 10 percent of the addition is also from foreign sources.

taxes at an effective rate exceeding the highest tax rate under §1 or §11.[6] For AMT purposes, this high-tax kickout applies if the effective foreign tax rate exceeds the AMT rate of 20 percent (for corporations) or 28 percent (for other taxpayers).[7]

The §904 fractions are applied against the tentative minimum tax, not against the precredit regular tax.[8] The tentative minimum tax is 20 percent of AMTI for corporations and 26 or 28 percent for other taxpayers. Assume a corporation has AMTI of $150, of which $15 is from foreign sources and falls within the general limitation basket. The tentative minimum tax is $30 (20 percent of $150), and the §904 limitation on the AMT foreign tax credit is:

$$(\$30)(\$15/\$150) = \$3$$

Instead of recomputing its credit limitation based on the sources of AMT taxable income, a taxpayer can elect to use as its AMT foreign tax credit limitation the precredit AMT, multiplied by regular taxable income from sources outside the United States (but not more than AMT taxable income) and divided by entire AMT taxable income.[9]

2. *Ninety percent ceiling.* The AMT foreign tax credit is usually the lesser of the taxpayer's foreign income taxes for the year (including taxes deemed paid under §§902 and 960) or the §904 limitation (as modified for AMT purposes). The credit, however, is subject to a further limitation that is unique to the AMT: It cannot exceed 90 percent of precredit tentative minimum tax.[10] This limitation

---

[6] IRC §§904(d)(2)(A)(iii)(III), (F), discussed supra ¶69.6.2 text accompanying notes 26–40.

[7] IRC §59(a)(1)(C).

[8] IRC §59(a)(1)(A).

[9] IRC §59(a)(4). The election, which applies only for taxable years beginning after 1997, must be made for the first taxable year beginning after 1997 for which the taxpayer claims an AMT foreign tax credit. Once made, the election applies for all subsequent years unless it is revoked with IRS consent.

If regular-tax foreign source taxable income exceeds AMT taxable income and the taxpayer has income in more than one of the separate limitation categories of §904(d), the AMT taxable income ceiling is applied by proportionately reducing regular-tax foreign source taxable income in each category (basket). Staff of Joint Comm. on Tax'n, 105th Cong., 1st Sess., General Explanation of Tax Legislation Enacted in 1997, at 299–300 (Comm. Print 1997).

The election was provided because of the difficulties taxpayers encountered in reallocating deductions between U.S. and foreign sources for AMT purposes, a task that had little ultimate effect because the items of tax preference are predominantly from U.S. sources. Staff of Joint Comm., supra, at 299.

[10] IRC §59(a)(2)(A). See Lindsey v. CIR, 98 TC 672 (1992), aff'd without opinion, 73 AFTR2d ¶94-1089 (DC Cir. 1994) (90 percent limitation prevails over any conflicting treaty predating its enactment).

The ceiling does not apply, however, if (1) the taxpayer is a domestic corporation, (2) the taxpayer is not a member of an affiliated group, (3) more than 50 percent of its stock, by both vote and value, is held by U.S. persons, (4) all of the taxpayer's activities are

applies on an overall basis, not basket by basket. It derives from the underlying philosophy of the AMT that everyone with substantial economic income should pay some tax. It is, however, a significant departure from the goal of eliminating double taxation. It also makes the AMT applicable to some taxpayers utilizing no tax preferences. Assume all of a U.S. citizen's income is earned in a foreign country that taxes the income at 50 percent. Even though the income has been taxed abroad at rates exceeding the maximum U.S. rate, the individual's U.S. tax liability may not be fully eliminated because of the 90 percent limitation.[11]

Normally, the limitation applies only if more than 90 percent of AMTI is from foreign sources. If an AMT net operating loss deduction is carried to the year, however, the limitation is further reduced so that the AMT, after the credit, cannot be less than 10 percent of what the tentative minimum tax would be in the absence of the foreign tax credit and net operating loss deduction.

Assume a corporation's AMTI (determined without the net operating loss deduction) is $100. Without the net operating loss deduction or the foreign tax credit, the corporation's AMT is $20 (20 percent of $100). The AMT cannot be reduced below $2 by the foreign tax credit, the net operating loss deduction, or the two of them together.

3. *Credit carrybacks and carryovers.* To the extent credit for foreign income taxes is denied by §904, as modified for AMT purposes, or the 90 percent limitation, they are carried to other years under the carryback and carryover rules of §904(c).[12] The carrybacks and carryovers, however, are computed using the AMT rules for all years beginning after 1986.[13]

¶69.13 ACCRUAL OF FOREIGN INCOME TAXES; ADJUSTMENTS OF FOREIGN TAX LIABILITIES

¶69.13.1 Introductory

Section 905 modifies normal accounting rules in two significant respects. First, it allows the foreign tax credit to be determined on an accrual basis, regardless of the taxpayer's general method of accounting.[1] Second, it modifies

---

located in one foreign country, (5) that country has an income tax treaty with the United States that provides for exchanges of tax information, (6) the taxpayer makes annual distributions of all of its earnings, excepting only earnings retained for "normal maintenance or capital replacements or improvements of an existing business," and (7) all U.S. persons holding stock of the taxpayer use the amounts received in the annual distributions in their own businesses in the United States. IRC §59(a)(2)(C) (applicable for taxable years beginning after March 31, 1990).

[11] See Lindsey v. CIR, 98 TC 672 (1992), aff'd without opinion, 73 AFTR2d ¶94-1089 (DC Cir. 1994).

[12] IRC §59(a)(2)(B).

[13] IRC §59(a)(1)(A).

[1] See infra ¶69.13.2.

the annual accounting concept by requiring that an adjustment in a foreign tax occurring after the year in which the tax is credited must be reflected by amending the return for the year in which the credit was taken, rather than by reporting it for the year in which the adjustment is determined. The regulations apply the latter rule quite rigorously for foreign taxes imposed directly on the taxpayer,[2] but they often allow changes in foreign tax liabilities of foreign corporations to be reflected prospectively in the indirect credits of U.S. shareholders of the corporations.[3] The rules on foreign tax redeterminations are complemented by various other rules, including a requirement that the IRS be notified of a redetermination,[4] a waiver of interest on a U.S. tax deficiency resulting from a foreign tax refund that itself bears no interest,[5] and rules extending the statutes of limitations for deficiencies and refunds relating to changes in foreign tax liabilities.[6]

If a taxpayer accounts for foreign income taxes on an accrual basis, the taxes, including adjustments to the tax liabilities, are usually translated into dollars at the "average exchange rate for the taxable year to which such taxes relate."[7] However, this rule does not apply to a foreign income tax liability denominated in an inflationary currency or to a tax denominated in any currency that is paid before the taxable year begins or more than two years after the year ends.

If a foreign income tax is covered by one of these exceptions or if the taxpayer accounts for foreign income taxes on a cash basis, the tax or taxes are translated into dollars as of the date of payment or, if the tax is collected by withholding, as of the date of withholding.[8] This rule also applies to all foreign income taxes for taxable years beginning before 1998, whether the taxpayer accounts for foreign income taxes on a cash or accrual basis. When applicable, it applies to estimated tax payments as well as to payments of taxes for which returns have been filed.

¶69.13.2   Accrual of Foreign Income Taxes

Section 905(a) allows foreign income taxes to accrue for credit purposes, even if the taxpayer generally uses the cash method of accounting. Once a taxpayer exercises this election, it must be adhered to for all subsequent years. The election, however, only applies for years in which foreign taxes are credited

---

[2] See infra ¶69.13.3.

[3] See infra ¶69.13.4.

[4] See infra ¶69.13.5.

[5] See infra ¶69.13.6.

[6] See infra ¶69.13.7.

[7] IRC §986(a)(1). This rule applies for taxable years beginning after 1997.

[8] IRC §986(a)(2)(A); Reg. §1.905-3T(b)(2). The Treasury may, by regulations, allow the translation to be made by an average exchange rate, rather than the rate on the date of payment.

under §901. For years in which the deduction for foreign income taxes is taken instead of the credit, the taxpayer's general accounting method is used in determining the deduction, except that taxes claimed as credits when accrued cannot be taken as deductions in a subsequent year when paid.

A foreign income tax generally accrues during the year for which it is imposed. For example, a country X tax on 1996 income usually accrues in 1996, even if no return or payment is due to the country X tax authorities until 1997.

However, if an accrued tax is not paid within two years after the close of the taxable year for which it accrues, it is creditable only when paid.[9] The effects of this rule, which applies for taxable years beginning after 1997, were illustrated by the Staff of the Joint Committee on Taxation as follows:

> [A]ssume that in year 1 a taxpayer accrues 1,000 units of foreign tax that relate to year 1 and that the currency involved is not inflationary. Further assume that as of the end of year 1 the tax is unpaid. . . . If the 1,000 units of tax are paid by the taxpayer in either year 2 or year 3, no redetermination of foreign tax is required. If any portion of the tax so accrued remains unpaid as of the end of year 3, however, the taxpayer is required to redetermine its foreign tax accrued in year 1 to eliminate the accrued but unpaid tax, thereby reducing its foreign tax credit for such year. If the taxpayer pays the disallowed taxes in year 4, the taxpayer again redetermines its foreign taxes (and foreign tax credit) for year 1. . . .[10]

This rule applies in conjunction with a currency translation rule described above, under which accrued foreign income taxes are generally translated by the average exchange rate for the year of accrual but taxes not paid within two years after that year ends must be translated at the exchange rate prevailing on the date of payment.[11]

Also, foreign tax probably does not accrue if the taxpayer takes no action to comply with the foreign tax law. In *United States v. Cruz*, a criminal tax evasion case, the taxpayer's defense was that as a citizen of the Dominican Republic, he owed income taxes to that country that were creditable against U.S. tax.[12] No Dominican Republic return had been filed, however, and no Dominican Republic tax had been paid. The defense was rejected because the foreign tax was found not to have accrued. Generally, an item accrues when liability is fixed and the amount can be determined with reasonable accuracy. If a taxpayer fails to com-

---

[9] IRC §905(c)(2). If the taxpayer claimed indirect credit under §902 or §960 for a tax accrued by a foreign corporation and that corporation failed to pay the accrued tax within this two-year period, credit is permanently denied for the accrued tax, and the foreign corporation's ultimate payment of the tax is reflected in its foreign income tax and undistributed earnings pools for the year of payment and subsequent years.

[10] Staff of Joint Comm. on Tax'n, 105th Cong., 1st Sess., General Explanation of Tax Legislation Enacted in 1997, at 298 (Comm. Print 1997).

[11] IRC §§986(a)(1),(2).

[12] US v. Cruz, 698 F2d 1148 (11th Cir.), cert. denied, 464 US 960 (1983).

ply with foreign tax laws, the court decided, a foreign tax does not accrue under this standard until it is levied or paid.

¶69.13.3 Changes in Foreign Taxes Imposed Directly on Taxpayer

Under §904(c), if the amount of a foreign income tax is either increased or decreased after the year for which credit is claimed for the tax, the adjustment is reflected by an amendment of the original credit and does not affect the credit for the year in which the foreign tax adjustment occurs. Assume credit is claimed in 1996 for a foreign income tax accruing in 1996, but the tax, when paid in 1997, is higher than the accrued amount. If the 1996 return is filed before the tax is paid, it may be amended to restate the credit using the higher amount paid in 1997 in place of the amount accrued in 1996. Assume a portion of the 1997 payment is refunded to the taxpayer in 1999. The 1996 return must again be amended, this time to reduce the credit to reflect the refund in 1999.

The regulations identify three types of changes in foreign tax liabilities that trigger a redetermination of U.S. tax: (1) a refund of a foreign income tax previously paid by the taxpayer; (2) a foreign tax payment of an amount (stated in the currency in which the tax was paid) that is more or less than the amount previously reported; and (3) a foreign tax payment whose dollar value is more or less than the dollar value of the amount accrued because of a change in currency exchange rates.[13]

1. *Actual refunds and additional assessments.* An adjustment of a foreign tax liability (other than an adjustment for exchange rate fluctuation) occurs when an addition to the tax is paid, when a portion of the tax is refunded, or (if the taxpayer's general method of accounting is the accrual method) when the fact of liability for additional tax or an entitlement to a refund is fixed and the amount can be determined with reasonable accuracy.[14]

Assume domestic corporation T's 1996 tax return to country X is audited in 1998, and country X tax authorities assert in 1998 that T underpaid its 1996 tax by $100. T contests this assertion, but, during 1998, pays an additional $5 of country X tax for 1996 in partial satisfaction of the asserted deficiency. The dispute is settled in 2001 by an agreement that the 1996 deficiency is $20, and T pays the remaining $15 of the agreed deficiency in 2001. T's foreign tax credits for 1996 are revised twice. The first revision occurs in 1998, when the 1996 country X taxes are increased by the $5 payment. The unpaid $95 of the amount claimed in 1998 by the country X authorities is ignored because it is disputed and T's liability for it thus is not fixed. A second redetermination is made in 2001 by adding $15 more to 1996 country X taxes because, in that year, liability for this amount becomes fixed and is paid.

---

[13] Reg. §1.905-3T(c).
[14] Rev. Rul. 84-125, 1984-2 CB 125.

When an earlier year's tax is refunded to any extent, a redetermination is made under §905(c) regardless of the reason for the refund. Assume a taxpayer pays taxes to a foreign country on foreign income earned in 1996, but a loss sustained in the foreign business in 1998 is carried back under foreign law to 1996 and causes the 1996 tax to be refunded. Credit for 1996 is recomputed by excluding the 1996 country X tax that is refunded in 1998 on account of the loss carryback. That the refund results from a subsequent event, not from a correction in the original calculation of the 1996 tax, is not relevant.[15]

When a foreign tax is refunded, the credit redetermination takes into account any additional foreign income tax that may become due on account of the refund.[16] A refund of one tax might result in an increase of another tax because, for example, the refunded tax was deducted in determining the other tax and the refund is therefore added to gross income for purposes of the other tax. In the U.S. credit redetermination, the refund is deemed to be the excess of the actual refund over the resulting additional tax, and the additional tax is not creditable or deductible in any other way. For example, if $100 of a foreign income tax is refunded to the taxpayer, but the refund causes an addition of $10 to some other foreign income tax, the credit is redetermined on the basis of a $90 refund, and the additional tax of $10 is not otherwise deductible or creditable.

In adjusting the credit to account for a foreign tax redetermination, the additional tax or refund must be related to the separate baskets under §904(d).[17] A refund is allocated to the basket to which the original payment of the refunded amount was allocated.[18] An additional tax is allocated among the baskets by the rules generally used for allocating foreign taxes.[19]

Although an adjustment in a foreign tax is reflected by changing the foreign taxes reported on the return for the year the tax was paid or accrued, the adjustment can affect U.S. tax liability for other years through the carryover mechanism of §904(c).[20] Assume a domestic corporation makes an additional payment in 1998 of 1996 country X tax; the corporation's 1996 U.S. return, as filed, reported foreign income taxes in excess of the §904 limitation, and the excess was carried to 1994 and 1995, fully utilizing the excess limitations for those years.[21] The 1998 payment adds to the excess foreign taxes for 1996 and thus increases the carryover, which now goes to 1997.

2. *Currency translation rules.* When foreign income taxes are translated as of the dates of payment, the redetermination process raised additional issues.

---

[15] Goodyear Tire & Rubber Co. v. US, 14 Cl. Ct. 23, 87-2 USTC ¶9656 (1987), aff'd, 493 US 132 (1989).

[16] IRC §905(c); Reg. §1.905-3T(e).

[17] For §904(d), see supra ¶69.6.

[18] Reg. §1.905-3T(b)(4).

[19] See supra ¶69.6.10.

[20] See supra ¶69.5.4 for §904(c).

[21] See Rev. Rul. 84-125, 1984-2 CB 125.

3. *Redetermination when dollar amount of payment differs from dollar amount of accrual.* If credit is claimed for an accrued foreign income tax that has not been paid by the last day of the U.S. taxable year, the tax is translated into dollars as of the last day of the year.[22] The accrued amount, however, is only tentative because the tax, when paid, must be retranslated at the exchange rate for the date of payment.[23] Assume that as of the end of its taxable year 1996, a corporation owes foreign income tax of 100u (100 units of foreign currency), but none of the tax has been paid. If the exchange rate on the last day of 1996 is 5u for $1, the tax is initially reported as $20 (100u divided by 5). When the tax is paid, however, the credit must be redetermined using the exchange rate as of the date of payment. If the exchange rate is then 4u for $1, the credit is restated using $25 rather than $20 as the amount of the tax.

The regulations allow one exception: The adjustment can be taken into account for the year of payment rather than the year for which the tax accrued if the dollar amount of the difference between the accrual and payment exceeds neither $10,000 nor 2 percent of the foreign tax initially accrued to the taxing country.[24] When this exception applies, the credit for the year of accrual is not altered, but "an appropriate adjustment" is made to U.S. tax liability for the year of payment. The regulations do not describe this "appropriate adjustment," but it presumably is an exchange rate gain or loss equal to the difference between the dollar amounts of the accrual and payment.

Assume a country X tax liability of 1,000u is accrued when the exchange rate is 5u for $1, but it is paid when the rate is 5.1u to the dollar. The accrued amount is $200. The revised figure on payment would be $196 (1,000u divided by 5.1), but the exception applies because the revision of $4 does not exceed either $10,000 or 2 percent of $200. The $200 tax accrual thus is not altered, but the taxpayer has exchange gain of $4 for the year in which the payment is made. When the exception applies, the exchange rate fluctuation is presumably accounted for in the same way as it would have been if the accrued liability had been owed to a trade creditor rather than to a government as tax.[25]

Exchange gain or loss might also be recognized when a foreign income tax is paid in a foreign currency that is not the taxpayer's functional currency.[26] Assume an individual whose functional currency is the dollar pays $100 for 500u and later uses the 500u to pay a foreign income tax in that amount. If the 500u are worth $125 on the date of payment, the individual is considered to have paid $125 of foreign income taxes, but has an exchange gain of $25.

---

[22] Reg. §1.905-3T(b)(1).

[23] Reg. §1.905-3T(c)(3).

[24] Reg. §1.905-3T(d)(1).

[25] See infra ¶71.8.

[26] Reg. §1.905-3T(b)(5) (penultimate sentence). For the term "functional currency," see infra ¶71.2.

4. *Translation of foreign tax refunds.* A refund of a foreign income tax is translated into dollars as of the date the refunded amount was paid.[27] If the refunded tax was paid on more than one date, the refund is deemed to consist of the portions paid most recently. Assume T pays 100u of foreign income taxes in 1996 when the exchange rate is 5u to $1, and this tax is refunded in 1998 when the exchange rate is 4u to $1. The exchange rate as of the date of payment in 1996 determines both the amount of the payment and the refund. The 1996 payment and 1998 refund therefore are both $20 (100u divided by five). The exchange rate as of the date of the refund is irrelevant to the credit redetermination.

If a refund is received by a unit of the taxpayer's business for which the dollar is the functional currency, the foreign currency received in payment of the refund takes an adjusted basis in dollars equal to the dollar amount of the refund, determined under the rules described in the preceding paragraph.[28] If the dollar is T's functional currency, the 100u received in the refund has a basis of $20 even though its value when received is $25 (100u divided by four). If T exchanges the 100u for $25, an exchange gain of $5 results.

If a unit whose functional currency is not the dollar receives a foreign tax refund in a foreign currency other than its functional currency, the adjusted basis of the currency received is an amount, stated in the functional currency, determined by translating the dollar amount of the refund at the exchange rate prevailing when the tax was paid.[29] When a refund is received in a nondollar functional currency, the currency's basis equals its face amount.[30]

¶69.13.4 Changes in Foreign Taxes Deemed Paid by Taxpayer

Under the indirect credit rules of §§902 and 960, a domestic corporation that owns at least 10 percent of a foreign corporation's voting stock is treated as though it had paid taxes actually paid by the foreign corporation if it receives dividends from the foreign corporation or is taxed on its earnings under subpart F.[31] If §905(c) were read literally, amounts deemed paid under §902 or §960 would have to be changed to reflect any subsequent redetermination of the foreign corporation's tax liabilities. The Treasury apparently concluded that these changes would raise excessive administrative problems and has therefore provided that a redetermination of a foreign corporation's income taxes is generally reflected prospectively, rather than by amending indirect credits claimed on returns already filed. This general rule, however, is subject to several exceptions, including:

1. A retroactive adjustment is made to the indirect credit if the foreign

---

[27] Reg. §1.905-3T(b)(3).
[28] Reg. §1.905-3T(b)(5)(i).
[29] Reg. §1.905-3T(b)(5)(ii).
[30] Reg. §1.905-3T(b)(5)(iii).
[31] See supra ¶69.8 for §§902 and 960.

corporation receives a tax refund that would otherwise cause a deficit in its post-1986 foreign income taxes.[32]

2. The post-1986 foreign income taxes of an upper-tier corporation is sometimes retroactively adjusted to reflect a tax refund received by a lower-tier corporation.[33]

3. If a foreign corporation is subject to a tax imposed by a foreign country with a hyperinflationary currency, a redetermination of the tax is reflected by retroactive adjustments to indirect credits.[34]

4. The IRS may require a retroactive adjustment if a foreign tax payment falls more than 2 percent short of the amount accrued for the tax.[35]

5. The indirect credit allowed when a domestic corporation is taxed under subpart F on undistributed earnings of a foreign corporation is retroactively adjusted if a portion of the tax is refunded on a distribution of the earnings.[36]

1. *Generally.* A foreign tax redetermination is usually reflected by an adjustment in the foreign tax and earnings and profits pools, which is made at the time of the redetermination and therefore affects deemed paid taxes only for the year in which the redetermination occurs and subsequent years.[37] Where a re-

---

[32] Infra text accompanying notes 45–46.

[33] Infra text accompanying notes 47–49.

[34] Infra text accompanying note 50.

[35] Infra text accompanying notes 51–52.

[36] Infra text accompanying note 53.

[37] Reg. §1.905-3T(d)(2). As originally issued, the regulations distinguished between three situations. First, a redetermination of the foreign corporation's foreign income taxes was reflected in the original computation of the domestic corporation's indirect credit for the redetermined taxes if the redetermination occurred (1) more than 90 days before the due date (with extensions) of the return on which the indirect credit was claimed and (2) before the return was filed. Second, if the redetermination occurred after the domestic corporation's return was filed, no amendment was made to the original computation, but the redetermination was reflected in the indirect credits for the year of the redetermination and subsequent years. Third, if the redetermination occurred before the return was filed but 90 or fewer days before the return's due date (as extended), the domestic corporation could chose to reflect the redetermination in either the original computation of the indirect credits or the indirect credit computations for the year of the redetermination and subsequent years. These rules, however, were "suspended" retroactively to the effective date of the 1986 statutory amendments. Notice 90-26, 1990-1 CB 336.

Assume domestic corporation P, which uses a fiscal year ending June 30, is sole shareholder of foreign corporation S, which accounts by the calendar year. For 1996, S is liable for a foreign income tax of 20u. The exchange rate is 4u for $1 when the tax accrues at the end of 1996, but it is 2u for $1 when the tax is paid. P's U.S. return for the year ending June 30, 1997, is filed on its due date, September 15, 1997. The suspended rules applied as follows: If S pays its 1996 tax before June 16, 1997 (that is, more than 90 days before September 15, 1997), the indirect credit on the return filed September 15, 1997, is determined using the exchange rate on the date of payment, when the 20u is worth $10. In this case, the redetermination of the foreign tax resulting from the fluctuation in exchange rates between the dates of accrual and payment is reflected in the original

determination of the foreign corporation's taxes is not reflected in the original computation of indirect credit for the taxes, the domestic corporation must give notice of the redetermination. Notice is given by attaching a statement describing the redetermination to the domestic corporation's return for its taxable year including the last day of the taxable year of the foreign corporation during which the redetermination occurs.[38] Assume S's 1996 foreign taxes are paid on October 16, 1997 (after the September 15 filing of P's return for the year ending June 30, 1997). The exchange rate for the date of payment may not be used in determining P's indirect credits for that year, but P must attach a statement to its return for the year ending June 30, 1998, notifying the IRS of the redetermination of S's 1996 tax.

Also, appropriate adjustments must be made in the foreign corporation's accounts. The indirect credit allowed for a dividend or subpart F inclusion is computed as the foreign corporation's post-1986 foreign income taxes (the tax pool) multiplied by a fraction whose numerator is the dividend or subpart F inclusion and whose denominator is the foreign corporation's post-1986 undistributed earnings (the earnings pool). When a redetermination of the foreign corporation's taxes is not reflected in the domestic corporation's indirect credit for the year the taxes are imposed on the foreign corporation, it is reflected in the latter's tax and earnings pools for the year in which the redetermination is made.

Assume the redetermination of S's 1996 taxes is not reflected in the computation of P's indirect credit for the year ending June 30, 1997, because the redetermination results from S's payment of its 1996 taxes after September 15, 1997. The additional $5 of foreign income taxes resulting from the exchange rate redetermination is reflected by adjusting S's tax and earnings pools in determining P's indirect credits for the year ending June 30, 1998, and subsequent years. Neither of the pools is changed in determining the indirect credits for the year ending June 30, 1997, or any earlier year.

The adjustments are as follows: If the redetermination consists of a refund to the foreign corporation of an earlier payment of a foreign income tax, the refund is subtracted from the tax pool and added to the earnings pool.[39] This treatment reverses the effect of the original payment of the tax (increase in foreign income taxes, decrease in undistributed earnings). The adjustments are allocated among the various baskets under §904(d) in the same proportions as the

---

computation of the indirect credit. In contrast, if S's 1996 tax is paid after P's return is filed on September 15, 1997, the indirect credit in that return is based on the exchange rate as of the date of accrual (the last day of S's taxable year), when 20u is worth $5. In this case, when the tax is paid, it is redetermined as $10 rather than $5, but the additional $5 is reflected only in indirect credits for dividends and subpart F inclusions reported by P for years subsequent to the year ending June 30, 1997. On the other hand, if S's 1996 tax is paid during the period June 16, 1997, through September 15, 1997 (the date 90 days before the return's due date through the due date), P can determine the indirect credit on the return using either the exchange rate as of the end of 1996 or as of the date of payment.

[38] Reg. §1.905-3T(d)(2)(iii).

[39] Reg. §1.905-3T(d)(3)(ii).

original payment of the tax.[40] If the refund is received in a currency other than the taxpayer's functional currency, the refund is translated into the functional currency using the exchange rate in effect when the tax was paid.[41]

Assume S, a foreign corporation wholly owned by domestic corporation P, pays foreign income taxes for year 1 of 200u, of which 100u is allocated to manufacturing income within the general limitation basket under §904(d) and 100u is allocated to shipping income.[42] The payment is made (before the filing of P's return for year 1) when 1u is worth $1. The payment is thus reflected in the tax and earnings pools for year 1 as $200 of post-1986 foreign income taxes (allocated $100 to the general limitation basket and $100 to the shipping basket) and as a 200u reduction of post-1986 undistributed earnings (100u allocated to each of the two baskets). After the filing of P's year 1 return, S receives a 75u refund of year 1 taxes, consisting of 25u of tax on general limitation income and 50u on shipping income. The refund does not affect the tax and earnings pools for year 1 or any other year before the year of the refund. For the year in which the refund is received, post-1986 foreign income taxes are reduced by $75 (the 75u refund translated into dollars at the exchange rate prevailing when the refunded tax was paid), and post-1986 undistributed earnings are increased by 75u. The reduction in the tax pool is allocated $25 to general limitation income and $50 to shipping income, and the increase in the earnings pool is allocated 25u to the former basket and 50u to the latter.

If the redetermination is an addition to the tax (an "assessment"), post-1986 foreign income taxes are increased by the additional tax and post-1986 undistributed earnings are reduced in the same amount.[43] The tax is allocated among the separate baskets for purposes of §904(d) by the same rules as are applied to an initial assessment.[44]

If a foreign tax redetermination results solely from exchange rate fluctuation between the dates of accrual and payment, the redetermination is reflected in the tax pool (which is kept in dollars), but not usually the earnings pool (which is kept in the foreign corporation's functional currency). Assume a domestic corporation bases its indirect credit for a particular year on its foreign subsidiary's accrual of 100u of foreign income taxes. Because the taxes are not paid by the time the domestic corporation's return is filed, the credit is based on the exchange rate of 4u to $1 at the end of the subsidiary's taxable year, and $25 (100u divided by 4) is included in post-1986 foreign income taxes. If the taxes are paid when the exchange rate is 5u for $1, the foreign corporation is deemed to have received a refund on the date of payment of $5 ($25 accrual less $20 payment). In contrast,

---

[40] Reg. §1.905-3T(b)(4). For the §904(d) baskets, see supra ¶69.6.

[41] Reg. §1.905-3T(d)(3)(ii). For more on currency translation, see supra ¶69.13.3 text accompanying notes 22–30.

[42] Reg. §1.905-3T(d)(3)(v) Ex. 2.

[43] Reg. §1.905-3T(d)(3)(ii).

[44] For these rules, see Reg. §1.904-6, discussed supra ¶69.6.10.

if the exchange rate is 3u to $1 on the date of payment, an additional assessment of $8.3 ($33.3 payment less $25 accrual) is deemed made on the date of payment. If the tax is paid in the foreign corporation's functional currency, however, no adjustment is made to the earnings pool because it is kept in the corporation's functional currency and, in the functional currency, the amounts accrued and paid are identical.

2. *Amendment required to avoid deficit in tax pool.* A domestic corporation is required to amend its indirect credit to reflect a refund of the tax deemed paid if the refund causes a deficit in the foreign corporation's tax pool.[45] Moreover, where the tax pool is divided into more than one basket under §904(d), an amendment is required if the refund creates a deficit in the tax pool for any of the separate baskets. In either case, the amendment is required even if the return claiming the indirect credit has been filed.

Assume that in year 1, foreign corporation S has income of 200u (all within the general limitation basket), pays foreign taxes of 100u (when 1u equals $1), and distributes 50u (one half of its earnings and profits) as a dividend to P, a domestic corporation that owns all of S's stock.[46] For year 1, P is entitled to an indirect credit of:

$$(\$100) \ (50u/100u) = \$50$$

S's post-1986 foreign income taxes are reduced to $50 ($100 paid less $50 deemed distributed). For year 2, S has 90u of general limitation income (subject to foreign taxes of 45u) and 200u of shipping income (subject to foreign taxes of 100u). The value of 1u remains $1. Also, during year 2, all of S's year 1 income taxes of 100u are refunded. If reflected in the pools for year 2, the refund would create a deficit in the general limitation tax pool of $5 ($50 at end of year 1, plus $45 paid in year 2, less $100 refunded in year 2). P's indirect credit for year 1 therefore must be amended. Since all of S's foreign income taxes for year 1 are refunded, the amended indirect credit is zero. S's tax pool begins year 2 with a zero balance, but the year 2 taxes add $45 to the general limitation pool and $100 to the shipping pool.

3. *Redeterminations of foreign income taxes of lower-tier foreign corporations.* The foregoing rules usually apply alike to upper-tier and lower-tier foreign corporations. A refund or additional assessment of a lower-tier foreign corporation is usually reflected by adjustments to the tax and earnings pools of that corporation alone.

A special rule is provided, however, to prevent the tax pool of a lower-tier foreign corporation from being pushed into deficit by a tax refund. The special rule applies only if the foreign corporation distributed a dividend in the year the refunded tax was imposed or in some subsequent year before the refund is

---

[45] Reg. §1.905-3T(d)(4)(iv).
[46] Reg. §1.905-3T(d)(4)(v) Ex.

received. Under the special rule, at least a portion of the tax pool adjustment for a refund received by a lower-tier foreign corporation is made to the tax pool of its shareholder (an upper-tier foreign corporation) if, (1) before the year of the refund, the lower-tier corporation distributed a dividend causing a portion of its foreign income taxes and undistributed earnings to shift into the tax and earnings pools of the distributee and (2) making the adjustment for the refund solely to the lower-tier foreign corporation's tax pool would create a deficit in that pool.[47] In this situation, the tax pool of the upper-tier foreign corporation that received the dividend is reduced by the excess of (1) the foreign income taxes it is deemed to have paid on account of its receipt of the dividend, over (2) the taxes it would have been deemed to have paid if the foreign tax refund had been received by the lower-tier corporation before the dividend was distributed. The lower-tier foreign corporation reduces its tax pool by the remainder of the refund. The reductions for both corporations are expressed as dollar amounts determined using the exchange rate as of the date the refunded tax was paid. The increase in post-1986 undistributed earnings reflecting the refund is made solely in the earnings pool of the lower-tier corporation receiving the refund.

Assume domestic corporation P is sole shareholder of foreign corporation $S1$, which owns all shares of foreign corporation $S2$.[48] For year 1, $S2$ has post-1986 foreign income taxes of $100 and post-1986 undistributed earnings of 100u. When the taxes are paid, 1u is worth $1. For years 2 and 3, $S2$ has no earnings or losses and pays no taxes. $S2$ distributes 50u to $S1$ during year 2. In year 3, it receives a refund of 75u of the 100u tax paid for year 1. For years 1, 2, and 3, $S1$ has no earnings or losses other than dividends from $S2$, and it pays no taxes.

By reason of the dividend distribution in year 2, $S1$ is deemed under §902 to have paid taxes actually paid by $S2$ of:[49]

$$(\$100)\ (50u/100u) = \$50$$

The distribution reduces $S2$'s post-1986 foreign income taxes from $100 to $50, and gives $S1$ a tax pool of $50. In year 3, when $S2$ receives the tax refund of 75u ($75 as translated at the rate of exchange prevailing when the refunded tax was paid in year 1), the special rule described above applies because $S2$'s tax pool would otherwise be thrust into deficit ($50 less $75). $S1$'s tax pool is thus reduced to reflect the refund received by $S2$. The reduction is the excess of (1) the $50 of deemed paid tax determined in year 2 when the dividend was distributed, over (2) the taxes that would have been deemed to have been paid if the refund had been received before the dividend. The computations are shown in Example 69-6.

---

[47] Reg. §1.905-3T(d)(3)(iv).

[48] See Reg. §1.905-3T(d)(3)(v) Ex. 3.

[49] For the application of §902 to dividends distributed by lower-tier foreign corporations to upper-tier foreign corporations, see supra ¶69.8.5.

Example 69-6
Adjustment of Upper-Tier Tax Pool for Lower-Tier Refund

1. Adjusted tax pool of *S2* for year 2 (before dividend)
   a. As originally stated $ 100
   b. Less refunded amount $ 75

   c. Amount remaining after refund $ 25
2. Adjusted earnings pool of *S2* for year 2 (before dividend)
   a. As originally stated 100u
   b. Plus refunded tax 75u

   c. Amount after refund 175u
3. Taxes deemed paid by *S1* for year 2 (after refund)
   a. Adjusted tax pool (line 1c) $ 25
   b. Multiplied by ratio of dividend to adjusted
      earnings pool (line 2c) (50u/175u)
   c. Deemed paid taxes $ 7.14
   d. Reduction of *S1*'s tax pool ($50 originally
      deemed paid less $7.14 deemed paid after
      adjustment) $ 42.86
4. Adjusted tax pool of *S2* at end of year 2
   a. Predividend pool (line 1c) $ 25
   b. Less amount deemed paid by *S1* 7.14

   c. Adjusted year-end balance $ 17.86
5. Adjusted earnings pool of *S2* at end of year 2
   a. Predividend pool (line 2c) 175u
   b. Less dividend 50u

   c. Adjusted year-end balance 125u

4. *Taxes paid in hyperinflationary currencies.* If the foreign corporation is subject to an income tax imposed by a foreign country with a hyperinflationary currency, the indirect credit must be amended to reflect a redetermination of the tax even if the redetermination occurs after the return claiming the credits has been filed.[50] The amendment is determined by substituting the redetermined tax for the tax as originally reported. A principal objective of this rule is probably to deny credit for the dollar amount of a foreign tax accrual to the extent it is effectively eliminated by inflation occurring between the accrual and payment dates.

A foreign country's currency is considered hyperinflationary if cumulative inflation in the currency was 100 percent or more during the 36-month period ending with the taxable year for which the original tax was reported. Inflation rates are taken from International Financial Statistics, a publication of the International Monetary Fund.

---

[50] Reg. §1.905-3T(d)(4)(i).

5. *Adjustment for excess accrual.* The IRS reserves the right to require an amendment of the indirect credit where the foreign corporation accrues foreign tax liability in an amount at least 2 percent larger than the tax subsequently paid.[51] For this purpose, the tax accrual and payment are stated in the foreign currency in which the tax is imposed, and the 2 percent rule therefore cannot be triggered by exchange rate fluctuation.

Assume foreign corporation *F* accrues a foreign income tax of 120u for year 1.[52] The tax is not paid before *F*'s domestic parent files its return for the year, and the accrued amount (translated into dollars at the exchange rate at the end of *F*'s taxable year) is therefore used in computing the parent's indirect credit. When paid, however, the tax amounts to only 100u. Because the payment is more than 2 percent less than the accrual, the IRS may require an amendment of the parent's indirect credit for year 1, even though the general rule would require only a prospective adjustment in *F*'s tax and earnings pools.

6. *Reduction of foreign corporate tax on distribution of earnings.* A domestic corporation must amend its indirect credit if (1) the corporation became entitled to the credit because it was taxed under subpart F on undistributed earnings of a foreign corporation and (2) a subsequent distribution of these earnings causes the foreign corporation's foreign tax on the earnings to be reduced.[53]

Assume foreign country *X* imposes a corporate income tax at the rate of 45 percent on undistributed earnings and 30 percent on distributed earnings. If earnings are accumulated but the accumulation is later distributed, the 45 percent tax initially applies, but one third of the tax is refunded when the distribution occurs. For year 1, domestic corporation *P* is taxed under subpart F on $100 of income of foreign corporation *S*, which is subject to country *X*'s tax and has no other income for the year. Under §960, as initially applied for year 1, *P* is deemed to have paid the $82 of country *X* tax actually paid by *S* ($82 is 45 percent of the sum of $100 and $82). During year 2, *S* distributes a $70 dividend to *P*, which causes *S* to receive a refund of $19 of the $82 of country *X* tax paid for year 1. *P*'s indirect credit for year 1 must be amended. The amended indirect credit is $63, the unrefunded portion of tax paid by *S* on the $100.

¶69.13.5 Notification Requirement

When a redetermination of a foreign income tax requires a change in the foreign tax credit claimed on a previously filed return, the taxpayer must give notice of the redetermination.[54] The notice must "provide the Service with in-

---

[51] Reg. §1.905-3T(d)(4)(ii).

[52] See Reg. §1.905-3T(d)(4)(iii) Ex.

[53] Reg. §1.905-3T(f).

[54] Reg. §1.905-4T(b). Notice is given by filing an amended return (Form 1120X for corporations and 1040X for individuals) together with the foreign tax credit form (Form 1118 for corporations and Form 1116 for other taxpayers). Reg. §1.905-4T(b)(1). The

formation sufficient to redetermine the tax," and the information must be "in a form that will enable the Service to verify and compare the original computations with respect to a claimed foreign tax credit, the revised computations resulting from the foreign tax redeterminations, and the net changes resulting therefrom."[55] For example, when a foreign tax redetermination results in a refund of foreign tax, the required information includes "the amount of foreign taxes paid in foreign currency; the date or dates the foreign taxes were paid; the rate of exchange on each date the foreign taxes were paid; [and] the amount of the foreign taxes refunded in foreign currency."[56]

If the foreign tax redetermination results in a reduction of the foreign income taxes paid or deemed paid by the taxpayer, the notice of the redetermination must be given within 180 days after the redetermination occurs.[57] A failure to meet this deadline is subject to a penalty of 5 percent of the deficiency for each month (or portion thereof) the notice is late, up to a maximum of 25 percent of the deficiency.[58] A tardy filer is excused from the penalty only if the failure to file timely "is due to reasonable cause and not due to willful neglect."

In contrast, if the foreign tax redetermination causes a decrease in U.S. tax liability, notice of the redetermination need only be given before the expiration of the statute of limitations on claims for refund.[59] The notice of redetermination constitutes a claim for refund.[60]

Upon receiving such a filing, the IRS redetermines the taxpayer's tax for the year.[61] Any tax due as a result of the redetermination must be paid on notice and demand. No notice of deficiency is sent, and the deficiency procedures (including Tax Court review) are unavailable. If the IRS determines the taxpayer has overpaid, the overpayment is refunded or credited.

¶69.13.6   Interest on Overpayments and Deficiencies

If a foreign tax redetermination causes a decrease in U.S. tax liability, the overpayment bears interest, computed under the usual rules for interest on overpayments.[62] Interest on U.S. tax deficiencies resulting from foreign tax refunds, however, are subject to a special limitation. Such a deficiency bears no interest for the period from the due date of the return claiming the credit to the date of the

---

instructions for Form 1118 give further guidance. The filing must be with the Internal Revenue Service Center where the original return was filed.

[55] Reg. §1.905-4T(b)(3)(i).

[56] Reg. §1.905-4T(b)(3)(ii)(A). For detail on the information required in other situations, see Reg. §1.905-4T(b)(3).

[57] Reg. §1.905-4T(b)(2).

[58] IRC §6689.

[59] For the applicable statute of limitations, see infra ¶69.13.7.

[60] Reg. §1.905-4T(b)(2).

[61] Reg. §1.905-4T(b)(1).

[62] For interest on overpayments and deficiencies, see infra ¶114.1.

foreign tax refund unless the foreign tax authority pays interest on the refund.[63] If the foreign tax refund bears interest, the interest on the U.S. deficiency for this period may not exceed the interest on the refund received from the foreign tax authority. Once the foreign tax refund is received, interest accrues on the deficiency in the usual way. The limitation applies whether the foreign tax refund is received by the taxpayer or by a foreign corporation whose foreign income taxes are included in the taxpayer's indirect credit under §902 or §960. In contrast, if a U.S. deficiency arises from exchange rate fluctuation between the dates of accrual and payment, interest accrues under the general rules.

¶69.13.7   Statutes of Limitation

Because the usual statutes of limitations would often bar adjustments reflecting foreign tax redeterminations, Congress enacted rules extending the statutes of limitations to facilitate the adjustments.

1. *Limitations period for assessments.* The statute of limitations on assessments is lifted to allow a deficiency in U.S. tax resulting from a refund or other decrease in a foreign tax to be assessed at any time.[64] If made after the normal three-year limitations period has expired, however, the assessment cannot exceed the deficiency attributable to the change in foreign income taxes. Even computational errors in the determination of the credit cannot be touched if they are unrelated to the amount of the foreign income taxes.[65]

2. *Limitations period for refund claims.* If an increase in a foreign tax liability causes a reduction of U.S. tax, the taxpayer is allowed 10 years from the due date of the U.S. return to make claim for refund of the resulting overpayment.[66] If the claim is made after the expiration of the limitations period that would otherwise apply, the refund is limited to the reduction in U.S. tax resulting from the redetermination of the foreign tax.[67] Moreover, the IRS can raise any defense to the refund claim, whether or not related to the amount of foreign income taxes, because even when the statute of limitations has run on the assessment of deficiencies, a refund is allowable only to the extent the taxpayer's taxes have been overpaid.[68]

According to the IRS, the 10-year period runs from the due date of the return in which the foreign tax is reported, even if the addition to that tax is

---

[63] IRC §905(c); Reg. §1.905-4T(c).

[64] IRC §6501(c)(5). The regulations say that when the IRS receives notice of a foreign tax adjustment, it "will redetermine" U.S. tax. Reg. §1.905-4T(b)(1). The Tax Court, however, has held that there is no statute of limitations on assessments in this situation. Pacific Metals Corp. v. CIR, 1 TC 1028 (1943).

[65] Rev. Rul. 72-525, 1972-2 CB 443. See also Texas Co. v. CIR, 12 TC 925 (1949) (acq.).

[66] IRC §6511(d)(3)(A).

[67] IRC §6511(d)(3)(B).

[68] Rev. Rul. 83-80, 1983-1 CB 130. See also infra ¶115.7.

carried under §904(c) to another year.[69] Although this position finds support in legislative history, it has been rejected by the court of claims, which holds that when the newly paid tax becomes part of a carryover, the 10-year period is measured from the year for which the refund of U.S. tax is sought, which is the year to which the carryover is carried and used with tax benefit.[70]

Assume a corporation pays an additional amount in 1998 as a deficiency in 1991 country X income taxes. The additional tax is reported by an amendment to the corporation's 1991 U.S. return, but, because previously reported 1991 foreign income taxes exceed the §904 limitation, the additional tax becomes a carryover and is allowed as a credit in 1993. The statute of limitations on the corporation's claim for refund of 1993 tax resulting from this carryover is (1) 10 years from the due date of the 1991 return under the IRS view and (2) 10 years from the due date of the 1993 return under the court of claims view.

The regulations say that the 10-year limitations period only applies to adjustments in the foreign tax credit, and that the initial election to claim the credit rather than the deduction for foreign income taxes must be made within the normal limitations period.[71] This restriction, however, has been held invalid as contrary to the plain meaning of the statute.[72]

¶69.14 ELECTION OF CREDIT

The foreign tax credit is elective. The election is made by filing a return claiming the credit. The cost of the election is that the taxpayer loses the deduction otherwise allowed under §164(a) for foreign income taxes.[1]

The choice between the credit and the deduction applies to all foreign income taxes for the taxable year. If the credit is taken for any taxes for a taxable year, the deduction for foreign income taxes is denied for all such taxes.[2] The election is made year by year, however, and a taxpayer can freely elect the credit one year and the deduction the next. The election for any year can be made or revoked at any time before the expiration of the statute of limitations on refunds.[3] An election on a joint return applies to the foreign income taxes of both spouses.[4]

The deduction is only occasionally preferable to the credit. Because the credit reduces tax dollar for dollar whereas the deduction only reduces the amount subject to tax, the deduction would never be advantageous in the absence

---

[69] Rev. Rul. 84-125, 1984-2 CB 125. For §904(c), see supra ¶69.5.4.
[70] Ampex Corp. v. US, 620 F2d 853 (Ct. Cl. 1980).
[71] Reg. §1.901-1(d).
[72] E.g., Hart v. US, 585 F2d 1025 (Ct. Cl. 1978).
[1] IRC §275(a)(4). For §164, see supra ¶32.1.
[2] IRC §275(a)(4)(A); Reg. §1.901-1(c).
[3] Reg. §1.901-1(d). For the applicable statute of limitations, see supra ¶69.13.7.
[4] Reg. §1.901-1(e).

of the credit limitation of §904. That limitation, however, sometimes suppresses the credit sufficiently to make the taxpayer's tax less with the deduction.

Assume domestic corporation T has taxable income of $150 (before taking foreign income taxes into account), consisting of $150 of income from sources within the United States, $100 of income from a business in country X (which is subject to a tax of $30), and a $100 loss from a business in country Y. Because taxable income from sources outside the United States is zero (country X income of $100 less country Y loss of $100), the §904 limitation is zero, and no credit can be taken for the $30 paid in tax to country X. A deduction for the tax, however, is allowable. If T is taxed by the United States at a flat 35 percent, the deduction reduces T's tax by $10.5 (35 percent of $30).

Even in this situation, however, the choice of the deduction has a cost. Under §904(c), if the credit is elected, foreign income taxes made noncreditable by §904(a) are carried to the second year preceding the taxable year and then forward to the succeeding six years (skipping the taxable year) until used.[5] If the deduction is taken in lieu of the credit, the carryback and carryover opportunity is lost. Since a carryback or carryover is a credit rather than a deduction, the deduction is usually disadvantageous unless the carrybacks and carryovers are unlikely to produce tax benefit.

For example, if T earns an after-tax rate of return of 8 percent, a credit in the last (fifth) year of the carryover period has a present value (as of the year for which the foreign tax is imposed) equal to 68 percent of the amount of the tax, whereas the immediate deduction reduces tax by only 35 percent. Since future income is unpredictable, the value of a carryover is often speculative. However, if T estimates that it has, for example, a 70 percent chance of utilizing the carryover, the value of the carryover (70 percent of 56.74 percent, or 39.71 percent) still exceeds that of the deduction.

¶69.15   FILING AND SUBSTANTIATION REQUIREMENTS

The election of the foreign tax credit is made by including with the taxpayer's return a Form 1118 (for corporations) or 1116 (for other taxpayers).[1] Also, the IRS has the power to require that a return claiming a foreign tax credit be accompanied by a bond.[2]

1. *Receipt or return requirement.* According to the regulations, a credit claimant must, "upon request," provide to the IRS either a receipt for payment

---

[5] For §904(c), see supra ¶69.5.4.

[1] Reg. §1.905-2(a)(1). The same reporting and substantiation requirements apply when a domestic corporation claims the indirect credit under §960 for income taxes of a controlled foreign corporation whose earnings are taxed to the domestic corporation under subpart F. Reg. §1.960-1(e).

[2] See infra text accompanying note 12 for the bond requirement.

of the tax if it has been paid or a copy of the return reporting the tax liability if it has not been paid.[3] This receipt or return must be "the original, a duplicate original, or a duly certified or authenticated copy." Moreover, if the receipt or return is in a foreign language, a certified translation must be furnished.

Under the regulations, the receipt or return requirement is waived if the taxpayer shows it is impossible to supply a receipt or return complying with the foregoing rules.[4] The amount of the tax, however, must be shown by secondary evidence acceptable to the IRS. For example, as a substitute for a receipt for payment, the taxpayer might provide "a photostatic copy of the check, draft, or other medium of payment showing the amount and date thereof, with certification identifying it with the tax claimed to have been paid, together with evidence establishing that the tax was paid for taxpayer's account as his own tax on his own income."[5] If the foreign tax was withheld by a person remitting income to the taxpayer and the taxpayer is unable to obtain a receipt for amounts withheld, some other form of substitute must be supplied; the acceptability of a particular substitute is determined with "due regard to the taxpayer's books of account and to the rates of taxation prevailing in the particular foreign country during the period involved."[6]

Under the regulations, if the taxpayer finds it impossible to supply a copy of a foreign return to document an accrued but unpaid tax, a certified statement of the amount accrued must be attached to the taxpayer's U.S. return, together with copies of excerpts from the taxpayer's books showing the accrual of foreign income and tax and copies of other available documents showing the computa-

---

[3] Reg. §1.905-2(a)(2). The regulations formerly required the taxpayer to attach the receipt to the Form 1118 or 1116. The IRS, however, acquiesced in an early decision holding that failure to furnish a receipt with the return does not bar a taxpayer from later establishing its right to the credit claimed. U.S. Fidelity & Guaranty Co. v. CIR, 5 BTA 23 (1926) (acq.). Moreover, the IRS suspended the receipt or return requirement as of January 1, 1988, pending completion of a study undertaken when it was discovered that "many taxpayers cannot timely obtain and prepare the necessary information in a form suitable for submission with the tax return." See REG-2082288-90, 1997-11 IRB 14 (proposing to amend Reg. §1.905-2(a)(2) to eliminate requirement that receipt or foreign return be attached to U.S. return). Notice 88-65, 1988-1 CB 552. The rule described in the text is effective for returns due after 1987.

[4] Reg. §1.905-2(b).

[5] Reg. §1.905-2(b)(1). See Continental Ill. Corp. v. CIR, 998 F2d 513 (7th Cir. 1993), cert. denied, 510 US 1041 (1994) (taxpayer made "net" loans to foreign borrowers, who were required to pay stipulated interest, free of foreign taxes, and also bear any foreign taxes; held, letters from borrowers were insufficient to prove amount of foreign taxes paid on taxpayer's behalf by borrowers).

If the taxpayer uses the accrual method, evidence must also be furnished that the tax accrued during the taxable year.

[6] Reg. §1.905-2(b)(3). See REG-2082288-90, 1997-1 CB 722 (proposing to amend Reg. §1.905-2(b)(3) to require that, on IRS request, "taxpayer must prove that any taxes withheld at the source were paid to the foreign country").

tion of the tax.[7] Also, the IRS may require that a taxpayer claiming credit for an accrued but unpaid tax furnish a bond or an undertaking to adjust the credit claimed when the foreign tax is finally determined.

A taxpayer filing a return with a substitute for a receipt or return must furnish the normally required receipt or return if one later becomes available.[8]

2. *Bond requirement.* The IRS may require that a bond be filed "as a condition precedent to the allowance of a credit."[9] The bond, filed on Form 1117, must be in whatever amount the IRS determines necessary to protect its right to any tax resulting from a redetermination of the credit.

3. *Reporting requirement.* Section 6038(a) requires a U.S. person having control of a foreign corporation to file an annual information return providing various information regarding the foreign corporation. Control is defined as ownership of at least 50 percent, by vote or value, of the foreign corporation's stock, taking into account both actual and constructive ownership under §318(a). One of the penalties for failure to file this return is a reduction of the foreign tax credit.[10] Generally, the foreign corporation's foreign income taxes are reduced by 10 percent in determining the noncomplying U.S. shareholder's indirect credits under §§902 and 960, and the shareholder's credits for other foreign income taxes are also reduced by 10 percent. However, the total reduction may not exceed the foreign corporation's income for the year or, if greater, $10,000.

---

[7] Reg. §1.905-2(b)(2).
[8] Reg. §1.905-2(b).
[9] IRC §905(c); Reg. §1.905-2(c).
[10] IRC §6038(c).

CHAPTER
70

Sources of Income

¶70.1   INTRODUCTORY

Many statutory provisions governing the taxation of foreign income and foreign persons distinguish between income from sources within the United

States and income from sources without the United States. For example, the withholding tax imposed by §§871(a)(1) and 881(a) applies to various items of nonbusiness income of nonresident aliens and foreign corporations, but only if the income is from U.S. sources.[1] A nonresident alien or foreign corporation engaged in business in the United States is taxed under §1 or §11 on income effectively connected with this business, and the rules identifying the items considered effectively connected with U.S. business distinguish between income from sources within and without the United States.[2] A U.S. citizen or resident or domestic corporation is entitled to credit against U.S. tax for foreign income taxes, but the credit for any year may not exceed the precredit U.S. tax on taxable income from foreign sources.[3] Also, §911 exempts from tax certain foreign source income earned by citizens who are bona fide residents of a foreign country for an entire taxable year.[4]

Sections 861 and 862 classify various types of income by source.[5] Interest income is usually from U.S. sources if the debtor is a domestic corporation or "noncorporate resident" or is from foreign sources if the debtor is a nonresident or foreign corporation.[6] Dividends from domestic corporations are from domestic sources, while dividends from foreign corporations are usually from foreign sources.[7] Income from the performance of personal services usually has its source where the services are performed.[8] Rents and royalties are from sources within the country in which the lessee or licensee uses the property that is the subject of the lease or license.[9] Gain on a disposition of real property is from domestic sources if the property is located in the United States or from foreign sources if it is located outside the United States.[10]

Income on sales of goods manufactured by the taxpayer is bifurcated between the manufacturing and selling aspects of the taxpayer's business.[11] The portion of the income allocated to the manufacture of the goods has its source at the place of the taxpayer's manufacturing activities, whereas the portion allocated to the sale is from sources in the country in which the goods are sold. Income on sales of goods acquired by purchase and held for sale to customers in

---

[1] See supra ¶66.2.1.

[2] See supra ¶66.3.

[3] See supra ¶69.5.1.

[4] See supra ¶65.5.

[5] See generally Finlayson, U.S. Source Income Earned By Foreign Branches and Affiliates, 47 Tax Lawyer 349 (1994).

[6] IRC §§861(a)(1), 862(a)(1), discussed infra ¶70.2.

[7] IRC §§861(a)(2), 862(a)(2), discussed infra ¶70.3.

[8] IRC §§861(a)(3), 862(a)(3), discussed infra ¶70.4.

[9] IRC §§861(a)(4), 862(a)(4), discussed infra ¶70.5.

[10] IRC §§861(a)(5), 862(a)(5), discussed infra ¶70.6.2.

[11] IRC §§863(a), (b), discussed infra ¶70.6.3.

the ordinary course of business is entirely allocated to the place of sale.[12] A sale is usually deemed to occur where title passes from seller to buyer.

Gains on sales of personal property not held for sale in the ordinary course of business are assigned to the taxpayer's country of residence.[13] For example, gains recognized by a U.S. resident on sales of stocks and securities held for investment are from domestic sources regardless of where the sale occurs or where the issuer of the securities is organized or does business. If a U.S. resident speculates in stocks listed on the Hong Kong stock exchange, gains from these trades are from U.S. sources.

The source rules generally apply to items of gross income. Taxpayers are often required to determine the sources of their taxable incomes. For example, the ceiling on the credit for foreign income taxes is the precredit U.S. tax on taxable income from sources without the United States. Taxable income from a particular source consists of the gross income from that source, reduced by the deductions allocated and apportioned to that gross income.[14] Generally, deductions for business and investment expenses are allocated to the items of gross income produced in the activities and investments in which the expenses are incurred, but many complexities are encountered in the application of this principle.[15]

The source rules generally recognize only two sources of income—domestic and foreign, but the operational rules sometimes demand a more refined allocation. For example, §933(1) refers to income "from sources within Puerto Rico."[16] Section 901(j) demands that income from sources within various countries on bad terms with the United States must be excluded from foreign source taxable income in computing the ceiling on credits for income taxes paid to other foreign countries.[17] Income from sources within a particular country or possession is ordinarily determined by substituting the name of the country or possession for the "United States" in the source rules.[18] In a few situations, the statutory source rules are supplanted by treaty.

The source rules allocate items of gross income and deduction to domestic or foreign sources but do not determine whether particular items are includable in gross income or deductible. In effect, the rules take hold only after these threshold determinations have been made by more general statutory provisions. Moreover, having allocated an item to domestic or foreign sources, the rules do not attach any substantive consequences to the allocation. This function is discharged by numerous operational provisions.

---

[12] IRC §§861(a)(6), 862(a)(6), discussed infra ¶70.6.3.
[13] IRC §865, discussed infra ¶70.6.4.
[14] IRC §§861(b), 862(b).
[15] See infra ¶70.10.
[16] See supra ¶67.3.
[17] See supra ¶69.6.11.
[18] Reg. §1.863-6.

¶70.2　INTEREST

Interest income is from U.S. sources if it is paid or accrues on an obligation of a domestic corporation, a noncorporate resident of the United States, the federal government, or an agency or instrumentality of the federal government.[1] Interest on obligations of foreign corporations, nonresidents (including U.S. citizens residing abroad), and foreign governments is usually from foreign sources.[2] It is not relevant where the interest is paid, the evidence of the indebtedness is situated, or the transaction giving rise to the debt occurred.[3] In the case of guaranteed debt, the residence of the primary obligor is controlling, even if the guarantor pays the interest, unless the guarantor becomes the primary debtor.[4] The term "interest" includes not only interest on bonds, notes, and other interest-bearing obligations but also such less common items as original issue discount and unstated interest under §483.[5]

---

[1] IRC §861(a)(1); Reg. §1.861-2(a)(1). For the residence of citizens and aliens, see supra ¶65.2. For partnerships, see Reg. §1.861-2(a)(2) (partnership, domestic or foreign, is resident in the United States if engaged in U.S. business at any time during taxable year). For the residence of estates and trusts, see supra ¶65.3.

Interest is also from domestic sources if it is gross income and is received on an obligation of one of the states, a political subdivision of a state, the District of Columbia, or an agency or instrumentality of any of the foregoing. IRC §861(a)(1); Reg. §1.861-2(a)(1). Interest on state and local obligations, however, is usually excluded from gross income. IRC §103(a), discussed supra ¶15.1.

[2] IRC §862(a)(1).

[3] See Iglesias v. US, 848 F2d 362 (2d Cir. 1988) (prejudgment interest included in judgment against domestic corporation is from U.S. sources); A.C. Monk & Co. v. CIR, 10 TC 77 (1948) (interest paid to Chinese national by Chinese branch of U.S. corporation was from U.S. sources, even though it was paid by checks drawn on Chinese bank and accrued on debt arising from dealings in China); McKinnon's Est. v. CIR, 6 BTA 412 (1927)(acq.) (location of negotiable coupon bonds irrelevant in determining source of interest); Rev. Rul. 71-516, 1971-2 CB 264 (place of payment and nationality of paying agent not determinative of source).

[4] Reg. §1.861-2(a)(5). See Tonopah & Tidewater R.R. v. CIR, 39 BTA 1043 (1939), rev'd on other grounds, 112 F2d 970 (9th Cir. 1940) (foreign parent's payment as guarantor of domestic subsidiary's defaulted interest payment is U.S. source income); Rev. Rul. 78-118, 1978-1 CB 219 (party bearing risk of loss is true obligor in financing transaction).

[5] IRC §861(a)(1); Reg. §1.861-2(a)(4). See supra ¶31.1.2 for general discussion of the meaning of "interest," ¶56.1 for original issue discount, and ¶57.1 for unstated interest under §483. See also Bank of America v. US, 680 F2d 142 (Ct. Cl. 1982) (acceptance and confirmation commissions of domestic bank on export letters of credit were in the nature of interest, not compensation for services, because bank substituted its credit for credit of foreign issuing bank, thereby effectively making loan to issuing bank).

Under regulations issued in 1997, if a person who transferred a debt instrument in a securities lending or "sale-repurchase transaction" receives payments as substitutes for interest on the instrument, the source of these substitute payments is determined as though the payments were interest on that instrument. Reg. §1.861-2(a)(7); see Reg. §1.861-2(e) (this provision applies to payments made after November 13, 1997); Swartz, Securities

The debtor-residence rule is subject to a few exceptions, including a rule that interest from a domestic corporation is foreign source income if at least 80 percent of the debtor's gross income is from the active conduct of foreign businesses and a rule attaching a foreign source label to interest on deposits with foreign branches of U.S. banks.[6]

1. *80-20 rule.* Interest on an obligation of a resident alien or domestic corporation is not U.S. source income if, during a testing period, at least 80 percent of the debtor's gross income was "active foreign business income."[7] A debtor's active foreign business income includes any gross income from sources outside the United States that is derived in the "active conduct of a trade or business" in a foreign country or U.S. possession.[8] The testing period is usually the three taxable years of the debtor preceding the year in which the interest is paid.[9] If the debtor existed for less than three years before the taxable year of the payment, the testing period is the term of its existence before the current year. If the payment is made during the debtor's first taxable year, that year is the testing period.

If the debtor is a domestic corporation with one or more subsidiaries, income received by the corporation from the subsidiaries is active foreign business income to the extent attributable to the subsidiaries' active foreign business income.[10] A dividend from a subsidiary is active foreign business income in the same proportion as the subsidiary's gross income is active business income.[11] For example, if 60 percent of a subsidiary's gross income is active foreign business income, 60 percent of the dividends is foreign active business income of the parent, regardless of the source of the dividend. Also, interest, rents, and royalties received from a subsidiary is considered active foreign business income to the extent the subsidiary's deduction for the item is allocated to the subsidiary's active foreign business income.[12] A corporation is a subsidiary for this purpose if

---

Lending Transactions, in Taxation of Financial Instruments (Avi-Yonah, Newman & Ring, eds. Clark Boardman Callaghan 1996).

[6] In addition, special rules are provided for interest on various obligations subject to special treatment under an interest equalization tax imposed in the 1960s and repealed in 1974. IRC §§861(a)(1)(C), (D); Reg. §1.861-2(b)(6). By 1989, all of the obligations covered by these rules had matured.

[7] IRC §§861(a)(1)(A), (c)(1)(A); Reg. §1.861-2(b)(2).

[8] IRC §861(c)(1)(B).

[9] IRC §861(c)(1)(C).

[10] IRC §861(c)(1)(B).

[11] H.R. Rep. No. 841, 99th Cong., 2d Sess. II-602-03 (Conf. Rep. 1986). Neither the statute nor the legislative history states what year's or years' gross income is taken into account for this purpose. An example in the Bluebook indicates that a dividend from current earnings and profits is allocated according to gross income for the current year. Staff of Joint Comm. on Tax'n, 99th Cong., 2d Sess., General Explanation of the Tax Reform Act of 1986 at 939-40 (Comm. Print 1987) [hereinafter 1986 Bluebook].

[12] 1986 Bluebook, supra note 11, at 939. For the allocation of deductions, see infra ¶70.10. For an analogous look-through regime, see §904(d)(3), discussed supra ¶69.6.8.

the payor corporation owns at least 50 percent of its stock, both by value and voting power.[13] This pass-through treatment, however, does not apply to interest received from the subsidiary.

Normally, when at least 80 percent of the debtor's income is active foreign business income, all interest on the debtor's obligations is from foreign sources. However, if the interest recipient is related to the debtor, the interest is split between U.S. and foreign sources in the same proportions as the debtor's gross income for the testing period is divided between these sources.[14] The debtor and interest recipient are related if (1) either of them is an entity and the other owns at least 10 percent of its stock or beneficial interests, by voting power or value, or (2) both of them are entities and the same persons own at least 10 percent of their stock or beneficial interests.[15]

2. *Interest paid by foreign banking branches.* Interest on deposits with a domestic corporation or partnership are foreign source income if the deposits are "with" a foreign branch of the corporation or partnership and the branch is engaged in "the commercial banking business."[16] For purposes of this rule, it is not relevant whether the corporation or partnership also carries on a banking business in the United States, whether the recipient of the interest is a U.S. or foreign person, or whether the deposits are denominated in a foreign currency or U.S. dollars.[17]

3. *Interest from foreign corporations.* For periods after 1986, interest on an obligation of a foreign corporation is generally not from domestic sources.[18] However, interest paid by a U.S. trade or business of a foreign corporation is treated as paid by a domestic corporation and is therefore from sources within the United States.[19] Also, if the interest deducted in determining income effectively connected with a U.S. trade or business exceeds the interest paid by the trade or business, the excess is treated as paid by a domestic corporation to the foreign corporation itself, creating notional interest income from U.S. sources.

For periods before 1987, a proportionate part of a foreign corporation's interest payments was U.S. source income to the recipients if the corporation was engaged in a trade or business in the United States during the year in which the interest was paid or accrued and at least 50 percent of the corporation's gross

---

[13] IRC §§861(c)(1)(B), 1504(a)(2); H.R. Rep. No. 841, supra note 11, at II-602. Stock owned indirectly by the parent is counted, but the statute does not say how indirect ownership is determined.

[14] IRC §861(c)(2)(A).

[15] IRC §§861(c)(2)(B), 954(d)(3).

[16] IRC §861(a)(1)(B)(i). This rule also applies to amounts paid or credited on accounts of foreign branches of savings institutions chartered under federal or state law. IRC §§861(a)(1)(B)(ii), 871(i)(3)(B). Branches in U.S. possessions are treated as foreign branches. Reg. §1.861-2(b)(5).

[17] Reg. §1.861-2(b)(5).

[18] IRC §§861(a)(1), 862(a)(1).

[19] IRC §884(f)(1)(A), discussed supra ¶66.5.3.

income from all sources during the preceding three years was effectively connected with this trade or business.[20] In making the three-year computation, the debtor's gross income included that of predecessors whose tax history it inherited by mergers and similar acquisitions.[21]

4. *Treaties*. Tax treaties generally follow the residence principle of the statute. For example, the OECD model treaty provides that "[i]nterest shall be deemed to arise in a Contracting State when the payer is that State itself, a political subdivision, a local authority or a resident of that State."[22] However, under most treaties, interest received from a resident of either country is treated as income from sources within the other country if the payor has a permanent establishment in the other country and the debt was incurred in connection with, and the interest is borne by, the permanent establishment.

¶70.3 DIVIDENDS

Dividends received from a domestic corporation are U.S. source income unless the corporation has elected the §936 credit or is a DISC or former DISC.[1] Dividends from foreign corporations are usually foreign source income, but they are assigned to domestic sources in a few cases where a substantial portion of the foreign corporation's earnings derive from the United States.[2]

The source rules use the term "dividend" as it is defined by §316 (a corporate distribution out of earnings and profits).[3] They do not apply to nondividend

---

[20] IRC §§861(a)(1)(C), (D) (before amendment in 1986); Reg. §1.861-2(c)(1). In applying the 50 percent test, the corporation's effectively connected gross income was compared with its gross income from sources throughout the world, even though foreign source income not effectively connected with U.S. business is normally excluded from a foreign corporation's gross income under §882(b). Reg. §1.861-2(c)(4)(iii). See IRC §861(d) (before amendment in 1986) (special rule for corporations with no gross income during three-year period).

[21] Rev. Rul. 76-300, 1976-2 CB 217.

[22] See, e.g., Organisation for Economic Co-operation and Development, Model Tax Convention on Income and Capital art. 11(5) (1992). The model defines "interest" as "income from debt-claims of every kind," exclusive of "[p]enalty charges for late payment." Id. art 11(3).

[1] IRC §§861(a)(2)(A), (D). For the §936 credit, which is allowed to some corporations doing business in Puerto Rico and U.S. possessions, see supra ¶67.2. For DISC dividends, see infra text accompanying note 15.

[2] See infra text accompanying notes 6–14.

[3] Reg. §1.861-3(a)(1). Also, in determining source, gain on a sale of stock is treated as a dividend to the extent it is ordinary income under §306. IRC §306(f). See infra ¶92.1.2 for §316 and ¶95.3 for §306.

If a person who transferred stock in a securities lending or "sale-repurchase transaction" receives payments as substitutes for dividends on the instrument, the source of these substitute payments is determined as though the payments were dividends on the transferred stock. Reg. §1.861-3(a)(6); see Reg. §1.861-3(d) (this provision applies to distributions, such as payments to redeem stock in a disproportionate redemption and distributions in excess of earnings and profits. The rules for gains on sales of personal property provide source characterizations for many nondividend distributions that are included in gross income, such as gains on nondividend redemption and liquidation distributions.[4] To the extent treated as a recovery of the taxpayer's stock basis, a nondividend distribution is excluded from gross income, and the source rules, which only cover gross income, have no application.

Income tax treaties typically do not have source rules for dividends but allow dividends to be taxed on the basis of source whenever the company paying the dividends is a resident of the taxing country.[5]

1. *Dividends from foreign corporations.* A dividend from a foreign corporation is U.S. source income, in whole or in part, if (1) at least 25 percent of the corporation's gross income for the preceding three years was effectively connected with a trade or business in the United States, (2) the dividend is distributed from earnings and profits that the corporation inherited from a domestic corporation, or (3) the taxpayer qualifies for a dividends received deduction and source is being determined for purposes of the foreign tax credit.[6]

a. *Twenty-five percent rule.* Generally, dividends from a foreign corporation are entirely from foreign sources unless, for the three years preceding the taxable year during which the dividend is declared, at least 25 percent of the corporation's gross income was effectively connected with the conduct of a trade or business in the United States.[7] If the corporation existed for less than all of the three years preceding the declaration year, the testing period is the period of the corporation's existence before the declaration year. If the dividend is declared in

---

payments made after November 13, 1997); Swartz, Securities Lending Transactions, in Taxation of Financial Instruments (Avi-Yonah, Newman & Ring, eds. Clark Boardman Callaghan 1996).

[4] See infra ¶¶70.6.3, 70.6.4; Hay v. US, 145 F2d 1001 (4th Cir. 1944), cert. denied, 324 US 863 (1945) (liquidating distribution has source in country of incorporation).

[5] See, e.g., Organisation for Economic Co-operation and Development, Model Tax Convention on Income and Capital art. 10(2) (1992). Treaties usually define "dividend" as "income from shares... or other rights, not being debt-claims, participating in profits, as well as income from other corporate rights which is subjected to the same taxation treatment as income from shares by the laws of the State of which the company making the distribution is a resident." Id. art. 10(3).

[6] Even if dividends from a foreign corporation are from U.S. sources, they are exempted from the withholding tax imposed by §§871(a)(1) and 881(a) if the distributed earnings and profits are from a taxable year for which the corporation is subject to the branch profits tax. IRC §884(e)(3). For the branch profits tax, see §884(a), discussed supra ¶66.5.1.

[7] IRC §861(a)(2)(B). For this purpose, a foreign corporation's gross income from all sources includes noneffectively connected income from foreign sources, even though such income is usually excluded from a foreign corporation's gross income under §882(b). Reg. §1.861-3(b)(3)(iii). Items covered by other statutory exclusions from gross income are also included in gross income from all sources, but not effectively connected gross income.

the corporation's first year, that year is the testing period.[8] The corporation's effectively connected income for the testing period includes all gross income treated as effectively connected income, excepting gains on dispositions of U.S. real property interests and a few other items.[9] When the 25 percent threshold is reached or exceeded, dividends from the foreign corporation are U.S. source income in an amount equal to the dividends multiplied by:

$$\frac{\text{Effectively connected gross income for testing period}}{\text{All gross income for testing period}}$$

b. *Inherited earnings and profits.* If a foreign corporation succeeded to the earnings and profits of a domestic corporation by merger or liquidation, dividends distributed by the foreign corporation from these earnings are U.S. source income.[10]

c. *Dividends received deduction allowed.* When a dividends received deduction is allowed for a dividend from a foreign corporation, the source determination is coordinated with the deduction mechanism for purposes of the foreign tax credit.[11] Under §245(a), a corporation is allowed a dividends received deduction for dividends received from a foreign corporation if (1) the taxpayer corporation owns at least 10 percent of the foreign corporation's stock, both by value and voting power, (2) the foreign corporation is neither a foreign personal holding company nor a passive foreign investment company, and (3) some portion of the corporation's post-1986 undistributed earnings consists of effectively connected income or dividends from a domestic subsidiary corporation.[12] When these re-

---

[8] IRC §861(d); Reg. §1.861-3(b)(1). This rule also applies if the corporation existed before the declaration year but had no gross income during the three years preceding the start of the declaration year.

[9] IRC §§861(a)(2)(B), 884(d). For the treatment of U.S. real property gains as effectively connected income, see supra ¶66.3.6. The other types of gross income excluded from effectively connected income for this purpose are (1) certain income of foreign sales corporations (FSCs) under §921(d), (2) distributions received by a foreign person from a FSC's foreign trade income under §926(b), (3) related person insurance income of a controlled foreign corporation under §953(c)(3)(C), and (4) interest on obligations of the U.S. government held by a bank organized and doing business in a U.S. possession under §882(e). IRC §§861(a)(2)(B), 884(d). See supra ¶68.1.4 for FSCs and ¶68.2.3 for related person insurance income.

[10] IRC §§243(e), 861(a)(2)(C); Reg. §1.861-3(a)(4).

[11] IRC §861(a)(2)(B).

[12] A domestic corporation is considered a subsidiary of the distributing foreign corporation if the latter owns at least 80 percent of the domestic corporation's stock, by both value and voting power, either directly or through one or more other corporations. IRC §245(a)(5)(B). See supra ¶68.3 for foreign personal holding companies, ¶68.5 for passive foreign investment companies, and ¶69.8.3 text accompanying notes 48–53 for the term "post-1986 undistributed earnings."

Section 245(a) does not apply if the foreign distributing corporation is a wholly owned subsidiary of the shareholder corporation and all of the foreign corporation's gross

quirements are met, the dividends received deduction equals a stipulated percentage of the portion of the dividend that is ratably attributable to the distributing corporation's post-1986 U.S. undistributed earnings, including both effectively connected income and dividends from domestic subsidiaries. The stipulated percentage is 80 if the taxpayer owns at least 20 percent of the distributing corporation's stock and is otherwise 70 percent.[13]

For purposes of the foreign tax credit, the U.S. source portion of a dividend qualifying for the §245(a) deduction equals the portion of the dividend received from the distributing corporation's post-1986 U.S. undistributed earnings.[14] If the 80 percent deduction is allowed, the U.S. source portion is $100/80$ of the deduction; if the 70 percent deduction rate applies, an amount equal to $100/70$ of the deduction is domestic source income.

Assume domestic corporation P receives a $100 dividend from foreign corporation F, of which P is a 30 percent shareholder (by both vote and value). F has post-1986 undistributed earnings of $1,000, of which $200 consist of income effectively connected with U.S. businesses of F. F owns no stock of domestic corporations. Because $200 of F's post-1986 undistributed earnings of $1,000 derive from effectively connected income, $20 of the $100 dividend comes from post-1986 undistributed U.S. earnings. Because D owns more than 20 percent of F's stock, the deduction rate is 80 percent, and the dividends received deduction is $16 (80 percent of the $20 received from post-1986 undistributed U.S. earnings). The U.S. source portion of the dividend is $20 ($100/80$ times the $16 dividends received deduction).

2. *DISC dividends.* Dividends from a domestic international sales corporation (DISC) or a former DISC are from foreign sources to the extent attributable to qualified export receipts.[15] A DISC must be a domestic corporation, and dividends from earnings and profits not attributable to qualified export receipts are U.S. source income, like dividends from domestic corporations generally.

¶70.4   SERVICES

Compensation for labor and personal services performed in the United States is from U.S. sources, except for income from certain services by nonresident aliens temporarily present in the United States for not more than 90 days during the taxable year and from services of nonresident alien crew members on

---

income is effectively connected with U.S. business. In this case, a 100 percent dividends received deduction is allowed under §245(b), and the dividends are entirely from U.S. sources. Reg. §1.861-3(a)(3)(ii)(b).

[13] IRC §§243(a)(1), (c).

[14] IRC §§245(a)(3), 861(a)(2)(B).

[15] IRC §861(a)(2)(D); Reg. §1.861-3(a)(5).

foreign vessels.[1] Compensation for services performed outside the United States is foreign source income.[2] The residence of the recipient of the service, the place of contracting, and the time and place of payment are irrelevant.[3] Special rules are provided for income from transportation and international communications activities.[4]

The place-of-performance principle embraces fringe benefits as well as regular wages and salaries.[5] It applies not only to individuals but also to corporations and other enterprises, and it reaches advertising income,[6] sales commissions,[7] and amounts received under a covenant not to compete.[8] However, the distinction

---

[1] IRC §861(a)(3). For the exceptions, see infra text accompanying notes 16–21. See Reg. §1.861-4(c) (wages of "alien seaman earned on a coastwise vessel" are from U.S. sources).

The "United States" excludes Puerto Rico and the U.S. possessions, but it includes continental shelf areas for the purpose of sourcing income relating to oil and gas and other natural deposits, including salaries and wages of individuals. IRC §§638, 7701(a)(9); Reg. §1.861-4(a)(5).

See also Glicklich, Levine, Goldberg & Brody, Electronic Services: Suggesting a Man-Machine Distinction, 87 J. Tax'n 69 (1997); Gordon, Services, Licensing, and Technical Sales Contracts Under U.S. Income Tax Treaties, 14 Tax Notes Int'l 1033 (Sept. 29, 1997); Lowell, Tilton, Sheldrick & Donahue, Tax Issues in the Provision of Outbound Services, 8 J. Int'l Tax'n 296 (1997).

[2] IRC §862(a)(3).

[3] Reg. §1.861-4(a)(1).

[4] See infra text accompanying notes 22–32, 33–39.

[5] Rev. Rul. 84-144, 1984-2 CB 129 (where service covered by pension plan of U.S. employer was partly within and partly without United States, pension benefits are from foreign sources to extent attributable to employer contributions on account of foreign service; benefits attributable to contributions for U.S. services and trust earnings are from U.S. sources). See Clayton v. US, 33 Fed. Cl. 628, 95-2 USTC ¶50,391 (1995), aff'd without published opinion, 96-1 USTC ¶50,314 (Fed. Cir. 1996) (distribution from U.S. employee stock ownership trust (ESOP) is from U.S. sources, even if participant's work for employer was entirely outside United States, to extent of trust earnings and appreciation credited to participant's account and included in distribution); Dammers v. CIR, 76 TC 835 (1981) (reimbursement of moving expenses incurred by employee on returning to United States from foreign employment was compensation for services performed outside United States); Rev. Rul. 73-252, 1973-1 CB 337 (unemployment compensation assigned to place where qualifying services were performed).

[6] See CIR v. Piedras Negras Broadcasting Co., 127 F2d 260 (5th Cir. 1942) (advertising revenue received by Mexican radio station beaming programs to United States ascribed to foreign sources in absence of evidence warranting allocation).

[7] Rev. Rul. 60-55, 1960-1 CB 270 (sales commissions for soliciting orders abroad are compensation for labor performed outside the United States), and cases there cited.

[8] Korfund Co. v. CIR, 1 TC 1180 (1943) (payments under covenant not to compete in United States are U.S. source income); Rev. Rul. 74-108, 1974-1 CB 248 (allocation between domestic and foreign sources, where recipient must refrain from both domestic and foreign competition). See Rev. Rul. 83-177, 1983-2 CB 112 (amount received in settlement of suit for employer's breach of services contract is foreign source income where services were to be performed outside United States).

between services income and income subject to other source rules is not always easily drawn.[9]

    1. *Services performed partly in United States.* If services are performed both within and without the United States, the compensation for the services is allocated between U.S. and foreign sources.[10] This is more easily accomplished for services performed by an individual, whose whereabouts can be ascertained with relative accuracy, than for services performed by a corporation, whose compensation reflects work by a staff of persons with a wide range of skills, especially if they travel extensively in the course of the taxable year.[11]

    If a "specific amount" is paid for the services performed in the United States, this amount is domestic source income.[12] For example, if an employee is paid an hourly wage, wages for hours worked in the United States are from U.S. sources. In other cases, an apportionment by time may be appropriate.[13] Assume

---

[9] See Bank of America v. US, 680 F2d 142 (Ct. Cl. 1982) (acceptance and confirmation commissions of domestic bank on export letters of credit were in the nature of interest, not compensation for services, because bank substituted its credit for credit of foreign issuing bank); CIR v. Hawaiian Philippine Co., 100 F2d 988 (9th Cir.), cert. denied, 307 US 635 (1939) (payments by sugar planters to manufacturer were for services, not for manufacturing or selling goods).

For the distinction between services income and royalties, see Boulez v. CIR, 83 TC 584 (1984) (amounts received by orchestral conductor for recordings were personal services income even though calculated as percentage of sales receipts and called royalties in recording contract; not royalties because conductor had no ownership interest in recordings and thus had nothing to license); Ingram v. Bowers, 47 F2d 925 (SDNY 1931), aff'd, 57 F2d 65 (2d Cir. 1932) (same result for estate of Enrico Caruso); Karrer v. US, 152 F. Supp. 66 (Ct. Cl. 1957); infra ¶70.5.

For the distinction between services income and income on sales of property produced by the taxpayer, see Cook v. US, 599 F2d 400 (Ct. Cl. 1979) (sculptor's income on sale of sculpture was from sources in country where taxpayer worked; court applied services rule rather than rule for property sales).

[10] Reg. §1.861-4(b)(1)(i).

[11] See British Timken, Ltd. v. CIR, 12 TC 880 (1949) (acq.) (payments to foreign corporation were compensation for services of sales agents outside United States, with source at place of performance rather than at situs of sales); Yardley & Co. v. CIR, ¶42,482 P-H Memo TC (1942) (payments were compensation for managerial services, not royalties; allocation between U.S. and foreign sources based on facts); Rev. Rul. 60-55, 1960-1 CB 270 (commissions received by foreign corporation from U.S. corporation were foreign source income to extent paid for services).

[12] Reg. §1.861-4(b)(1)(i).

[13] Rev. Rul. 77-167, 1977-1 CB 239 (pilot's compensation allocated on basis of flight time). See Stemkowski v. CIR, 690F2d 40 (2d Cir. 1982) (income of professional hockey player allocated according to number of days on which services were performed within and without United States, including preseason training camp and postseason playoff games); Hanna v. CIR, 763 F2d 171 (4th Cir. 1985) (*Stemkowski* followed on substantially identical facts); Favell v. US, 16 Cl. Ct. 700, 89-1 USTC ¶9287 (1989) (same); Rev. Rul. 87-38, 1987-1 CB 176 (following *Stemkowski* and *Hanna*); Linseman v. CIR, 82 TC 514 (1984) (signing bonus to hockey player allocated in proportion to games played by team within and without United States during first season covered by contract).

an employee receives a salary of $12,240 for a period of 104 consecutive days, of which 59 days are spent in the United States; the employee is on call at all times and receives the same salary regardless of how many hours are worked.[14] The compensation may be allocated on a daily basis, assigning to U.S. sources $6,944 ($12,240 times $59/104$).

However, an apportionment on a time basis is not allowed if it does not reflect economic reality.[15] Assume an engineering firm works on a construction project in a foreign country. Some of the services are performed at the firm's office in the United States, and some are performed at the construction site. Some of the work is done by highly skilled professional employees, but employees with varying degrees of lesser skills are also active in the project. The firm's fee for the service cannot be apportioned between U.S. and foreign sources according to the number of hours worked by all employees within and without the United States because the amount of fee income generated by each hour varies from employee to employee. An allocation according to hours worked, weighted by employee skill level, is acceptable.

2. *Nonresident aliens temporarily present in United States.* Compensation for services performed by a nonresident alien individual in the United States is foreign source income if all of the following conditions are satisfied:[16] (1) The services are performed while the individual is temporarily present in the United States; (2) the individual is not present in the United States during the taxable year for more than 90 days;[17] (3) the compensation for the services does not exceed $3,000;[18] and (4) the services are performed as an employee or independent contractor of a foreign employer. A nonresident alien or a foreign corporation or partnership is a foreign employer unless it is engaged in a trade or business in the United States.[19] A U.S. citizen or resident or a domestic corporation or partnership is a foreign employer only if the services are performed for an office of the employer in a foreign country or U.S. possession.

The 90-day rule is intended as a de minimis rule, allowing foreigners to come to the United States for brief periods in the course of their employment without becoming subject to U.S. tax. However, its application has steadily been diminished by inflation because the $3,000 ceiling has not been raised since 1954. For

---

[14] Reg. §1.861-4(b)(1)(ii) Ex. 1.

[15] Reg. §1.861-4(b)(1)(i). See Le Beau Tours v. US, 547 F2d 9 (2d Cir. 1976), cert. denied, 431 US 904 (1977) (allocation of services of travel agency). For the use of time as the exclusive basis of apportionment under earlier regulations, see Tipton & Kalmbach, Inc. v. US, 480 F2d 1118 (10th Cir. 1973).

[16] IRC §861(a)(3).

[17] See Reg. §1.861-4(a)(2) (calendar day counted against 90-day ceiling if individual is physically present in United States for any portion of day).

[18] See Reg. §1.861-4(a)(4) (employer's reimbursement of travel expenses is not counted against $3,000 ceiling if recipient is required to and does account to employer for expenses; pensions and retirement pay also not counted).

[19] See Reg. §1.861-4(a)(3) (for this purpose alone, employer is not considered engaged in U.S. trade or business because of individual's work in United States).

example, the rule applies to an employee who is present in the United States for 90 days during a particular year only if the employee's annual pay is $12,000 or less, and an employee earning $100,000 annually is covered by the rule only if the employee spends no more than seven working days in the United States during the year. Most income tax treaties contain an analogous but more generous rule, allowing up to 183 days of presence in the United States and containing no dollar ceiling.[20]

A more specialized rule provides that compensation for a nonresident alien individual's services in the United States is foreign source income if the services are "in connection with the individual's temporary presence in the United States as a regular member of the crew of a foreign vessel engaged in transportation between the United States and a foreign country" or U.S. possession.[21]

3. *Transportation services.* One half of the income from the furnishing of transportation is U.S. source income if the trip or voyage begins or ends in the United States.[22] If the trip or voyage both begins and ends in the United States, all income is from U.S. sources, even if some portion of the trip or voyage is in or over international waters or the territory of a foreign country. An airline's income from flights between the U.S. mainland and Hawaii, for example, is entirely from U.S. sources.

In enacting these rules in 1986, Congress focused primarily on the role of the source rules in applying the foreign tax credit:

> Congress generally did not believe that U.S. persons should be allowed to generate foreign source income (or loss) unless the income (or loss) is generated within a foreign country's tax jurisdiction and subject to foreign tax. Congress believed that the United States has the right to assert primary tax jurisdiction over income earned by its residents that is not within any other country's tax jurisdiction.[23]

The rules, however, apply to all taxpayers, including nonresident aliens and foreign corporations. According to the staff of the Joint Committee on Taxation,

---

[20] See, e.g., Organisation for Economic Co-operation and Development, Model Tax Convention on Income and Capital art. 15(2) (1992) (salaries and wages of resident of treaty country are exempt from U.S. tax if employer is not U.S. resident, compensation is not borne by U.S. permanent establishment of employer, and employee is not present in United States for more than 183 days during any 12-month period beginning or ending during taxable year). For an unsuccessful effort to exploit a similar French treaty provision by becoming an employee of a specially formed French corporation wholly owned by the purported employee, see Johansson v. US, 336 F2d 809 (5th Cir. 1964), discussed supra ¶66.2A.3.

[21] IRC §861(a)(3) (last sentence) (applicable for services performed in taxable years beginning after 1997). The rule does not apply for purposes of §79 (group life insurance), §105 (employer-provided medical benefits), and the rules on qualified pension, profit sharing, stock bonus, and annuity plans.

[22] IRC §863(c)(2)(A).

[23] Staff of Joint Comm. on Tax'n, 99th Cong., 2d Sess., General Explanation of the Tax Reform Act of 1986 at 926–27 (Comm. Print 1987) [hereinafter 1986 Bluebook].

"prior law's understatement of U.S. source income tended to subject foreign persons to too little U.S. tax."[24]

The rules generally apply to all "transportation income," defined as income earned through the use of a vessel or aircraft or the performance of personal services in connection with the use of the vessel or aircraft.[25] All income of a shipping company or an airline is thus transportation income. Income from the use of a container in connection with a vessel or aircraft is also transportation income. Moreover, rents received on the "hiring or leasing" of a vessel, aircraft, or container used in connection with a vessel or aircraft are transportation income.[26] Income from trucking and other land transportation, however, is not transportation income.

Whether transportation begins or ends in the United States is determined by looking to the points of origin and destination of each passenger or item of cargo.[27] Assume an airline flight begins in Frankfurt, stops in London, and flies from there to New York. For passengers or cargo flying from Frankfurt to New York or London to New York, the airline's income is from transportation ending in the United States. For passengers or cargo flying from Frankfurt to London, in contrast, none of the income is from transportation beginning or ending in the United States.

A round trip is analyzed as two trips, an outbound and an inbound trip.[28] Assume a cruise begins and ends in the United States but calls at several foreign ports. The cruise is treated as two trips, one beginning in the United States and ending in a foreign country and the other beginning in a foreign country and ending in the United States. One half of the income from the cruise is therefore from U.S. sources.

The 50-50 source rule does not apply to salaries and wages of seamen and airline employees earned in voyages and trips that begin in the United States and end in a foreign country or vice versa.[29] Under the general rule for services, this income has its source where the employee's work is done. However, for seamen who are U.S. citizens or residents and for airline employees, regardless of citizenship or residence, salaries and wages for a trip or voyage beginning and ending

---

[24] Id. at 927.

[25] IRC §863(c)(3).

[26] Income from a lease of a vessel may be either transportation income or ocean activity income subject to rules described in ¶70.8. According to the staff of the Joint Committee on Taxation, income from a lease of a vessel is transportation income if the vessel "is used to transport cargo or persons for hire between ports-of-call," but it is ocean activity income if the vessel is "not used to transport cargo or persons for hire." 1986 Bluebook, supra note 23, at 929, 934. For example, a lease is an ocean activity if a vessel is chartered for personal use by the lessee or for use in fishing or ocean exploration.

[27] 1986 Bluebook, supra note 23, at 929.

[28] Id.

[29] IRC §863(c)(2)(B); H.R. Rep. No. 841, 99th Cong., 2d Sess. II-599 (Conf. Rep. 1986).

in the United States is all U.S. source income,[30] and one half is from U.S. sources if the trip or voyage begins in the United States and ends in a foreign country or U.S. possession or vice versa.[31] Salaries and wages of nonresident alien seamen is wholly from foreign sources.[32]

4. *International communications income.* International communications income of a U.S. person is split in half; 50 percent is from U.S. sources and 50 percent is foreign source income.[33] Congress concluded in enacting this rule in 1986 that while the income has "some potential to be taxed in a foreign country," the portion earned outside the jurisdiction of all countries should be U.S. source income because treating it as foreign source income caused an inflation of the limitation under §904 on the foreign tax credit.[34] International communications income of a foreign person is usually entirely from foreign sources, but if the taxpayer has an office or other fixed place of business in the United States, international communications income attributable to the office is from U.S. sources.[35]

International communications income consists of income from "the transmission of communications or data" between the United States and a foreign country or U.S. possession.[36] The quoted words include "signals, images, sounds, or data transmitted in whole or in part by buried or underwater cable or by satellite."[37]

A communication between two points in the United States yields only U.S. source income, not international communications income, even if it is routed through a satellite and even if the satellite is located over international waters or a foreign country.[38] Moreover, a communication between the United States and a ship at sea or airborne aircraft is deemed to be between two points in the United States unless the ship or aircraft is then within the jurisdiction of a foreign country or U.S. possession.[39]

---

[30] IRC §863(c)(1).

[31] IRC §§863(c)(2).

[32] IRC §861(a)(3).

[33] IRC §863(e)(1)(A). See IRC §7701(a)(30) (U.S. persons include U.S. citizens and residents and domestic corporations, partnerships, trusts, and estates).

[34] 1986 Bluebook, supra note 23, at 933-34. For §904, see supra ¶69.5.1.

[35] IRC §863(e)(1)(B). The Treasury has authority to assign other international communications income of foreign persons to U.S. sources. See 1986 Bluebook, supra note 23, at 935 (suggesting this power might be exercised where the income is earned by a controlled foreign corporation).

[36] IRC §863(e)(2).

[37] 1986 Bluebook, supra note 23, at 935.

[38] Id.

[39] Id.

¶70.5 RENTS AND ROYALTIES

Rents from lessees of tangible property have their source where the property is located.[1] Royalties from licensees of intangible property, such as patents, copyrights, secret processes, and franchises, are assigned to the place where the intangibles are used. For example, royalties for the exhibition of movies have their source in the place of exhibition, not where the films were produced. Lump sum payments for the worldwide use of intangibles are apportioned between domestic and foreign sources on the basis of the relative values of the use rights.[2]

In 1980, the IRS ruled that where a foreign person (A) licenses a U.S. patent to another foreign person (X) and X licenses the patent to a U.S. person for use in the United States, royalties paid by X to A, as well as royalties from the U.S. user to X, are from sources in the United States.[3] At both levels, the IRS decided, the royalties were "for the use of [the patent] in the United States."[4] Thus, both royalties are subject to U.S. withholding tax. On the facts of the ruling, the royalty from the U.S. user to X was exempted from this tax by treaty, but no treaty exempted the royalty from X to A. However, in *SDI Netherlands BV v. CIR*,[5] the Tax Court rejected this approach in a case involving the same basic fact pattern. The court concluded that "the two licenses were separate and distinct from each other with the result that the royalties paid to $[X]$ by [the U.S. user] did not retain their U.S. source character as part of the royalties paid by $[X]$ to $[A]$." The IRS' recourse in such a case is to disregard the intermediate recipient (X) if it is a mere conduit between the U.S. user and the owner of the intellectual property, and, on the facts, X was found not to be a mere conduit.

Where an intangible is created by the taxpayer's personal efforts, difficulties often arise in deciding whether the taxpayer's income constitutes royalties or compensation for services.[6] Also, it is necessary to distinguish royalties from sales

---

[1] IRC §§861(a)(4), 862(a)(4).

[2] See Wodehouse v. CIR, 178 F2d 987 (4th Cir. 1949), and cases there cited. See generally Lokken, The Sources of Income From International Uses and Dispositions of Intellectual Property, 36 Tax L. Rev. 233, 277-86 (1981); Colden, Alien Artists, Intangible Property, and United States Taxation, 52 S. Cal. L. Rev. 429 (1979).

[3] Rev. Rul. 80-362, 1980-2 CB 208.

[4] IRC §861(a)(4).

[5] SDI Netherlands BV v. CIR, 107 TC 161 (1996). See Cunningham, Sourcing Royalties Paid by Foreign Intermediaries, 76 Tax Notes 959 (Aug. 18, 1997); King, Note, Royalty Payments from U.S. Source to Foreign Corporation Did Not Retain Character: *SDI Netherlands v. Commissioner*, 50 Tax Lawyer 863 (1997); McIntyre, The Royalty Source Rule, Treaty Shopping, Cascading Effects, and the U.S. Tax Court's Indefensible Decision in *SDI Netherlands*, 15 Tax Notes Int'l 2031 (Dec. 22, 1997), reprinted in 78 Tax Notes 115 (Jan. 5, 1998); Ruchelman & Adrion, *SDI Netherlands* Begets Confusion by IRS, Tax Court, and Commentators, 76 Tax Notes 841 (Nov. 17, 1997); Short & Fried, Tax Court Rejects Cascading Royalty Theory: *SDI Netherlands BV v. Comr.*, 26 Tax Mgmt. Int'l J. 18 (1997).

[6] Commercial Solvents Corp. v. CIR, 42 TC 455 (1964) (acq.) (payments for right to use secret process in Japan; held, royalties rather than sale price); Rev. Rul. 74-555,

proceeds because the source rules for gains on sales of personal property apply to an outright sale of a patent, copyright, or other intangible.[7] If an intangible is produced in one country and sold in another, gain on a sale is presumably allocated between the two sources under §863(b)(2), although there are no cases or rulings in point.[8] Moreover, income on sales of goods takes its source under the rules for property sales, even if intellectual property is used in the production or sale of the goods.[9]

Special rules are provided for railroad rolling stock that the taxpayer owns and leases to a domestic common carrier by railroad or to a corporation controlled by such a railroad. If the lessee's use of the rolling stock is expected to be in the United States, all gross income from the property, including gain on its sale, is from U.S. sources.[10] Also, the foreign tax credit may not be taken for foreign taxes on this income, but the taxes are probably deductible even if the taxpayer claims the foreign tax credit for the year.[11] A lessee's use is expected to be in the United States if the only anticipated use outside this country is temporary use in Canada or Mexico for not more than 90 days annually. These rules do not apply to rolling stock leased between two members of the same controlled group of corporations if the group includes a domestic common carrier by rail-

---

1974-2 CB 202, modified by Rev. Rul. 76-283, 1976-2 CB 222 (where author made contract with publisher giving publisher exclusive right to publish all books, stories, and articles written by author during contract's term, amounts received by author were royalties, not compensation for services, because contract gave publisher no control over what and when author wrote); Rev. Rul. 84-78, 1984-1 CB 173 (same where fight promoter granted foreign corporation right to broadcast fight in one foreign country). See also Rev. Rul. 75-254, 1975-1 CB 243 (on sale of trademarked product for flat price, no imputed royalty). See generally Gordon, Services, Licensing, and Technical Sales Contracts Under U.S. Income Tax Treaties, 14 Tax Notes Int'l 1033 (Sept. 29, 1997); Lokken, supra note 2, at 269–77. For more on the distinction between royalties and services income, see supra ¶70.4 note 9.

[7] See CIR v. Wodehouse, 337 US 369 (1949); Bloch v. US, 200 F2d 63 (2d Cir. 1952), cert. denied, 345 US 935 (1953); Rohmer v. CIR, 153 F2d 61 (2d Cir.), cert. denied, 328 US 862 (1946); Rev. Rul. 84-78, 1984-1 CB 173 (transfer of exclusive right to use copyright in particular country in particular medium (e.g., broadcasting) is sale if exclusive right continues for remaining life of copyright but not if it expires before copyright). But see AMP, Inc. v. US, 492 F. Supp. 27 (MD Pa. 1979), aff'd by unpublished order (3d Cir. 1980) (subsidiaries' payments to parent corporation for patent rights treated as royalties for source purposes even though characterized as sale proceeds for capital gains purposes). See generally Lokken, supra note 2, at 247–69.

[8] See IRC §864(a) ("produced" includes "created"). For §863(b)(2), see supra ¶70.6.3. See generally Lokken, supra note 2, at 292–94.

[9] See Rev. Rul. 68-443, 1968-2 CB 304 (royalties for use of trademark on products to be used in foreign country are foreign source income, even though products sold in United States). See generally Lokken, supra note 2, at 294–98.

[10] IRC §861(e)(1).

[11] IRC §861(e)(3). For the foreign tax credit, see supra ¶69.1.

road or a switching or terminal company;[12] instead, income from such property is governed by the usual rules for rents and gains on sales of personal property.

¶70.6 GAINS ON SALES OF PROPERTY

¶70.6.1 Introductory

Gains on sales and exchanges of real property have their source at the property's location.[1] Income and gains on dispositions of personal property are governed by a complex pastiche of rules, including the following:

1. Income on a sale of inventory acquired by purchase has its source at the place of sale, and a sale is deemed to occur where title to the property is transferred from the taxpayer to the buyer.[2]
2. Income on sales of goods manufactured or produced by the taxpayer is divided between the places of manufacture and sale.[3]
3. On a disposition of depreciable property, gain, up to the amount of depreciation deductions taken on the property, has the same source as the income against which those deductions were taken.[4]
4. Gain on a sale or exchange of a patent, copyright, or similar property has its source where the buyer uses the property if the price consists of payments contingent on the property's productivity, use, or disposition.[5]
5. Most income and gain on dispositions of personal property not covered by the foregoing rules, including most capital gains, are from sources in the country of the taxpayer's residence.[6]

¶70.6.2 Real Property

Gain on a disposition of a U.S. real property interest is U.S. source income, whereas gain on a sale or exchange of real property located outside the United States is foreign source income.[7] The term "U.S. real property interest" includes real property located in the United States, certain personal property associated

---

[12] IRC §861(e)(2).
[1] See infra ¶70.6.2.
[2] See infra ¶70.6.3 text accompanying notes 9–12, 36–39.
[3] See infra ¶70.6.3 text accompanying notes 13–35.
[4] See infra ¶70.6.4 text accompanying notes 58–66.
[5] See infra ¶70.6.4 text accompanying notes 67–74.
[6] See infra ¶70.6.4 text accompanying notes 51–57.
[7] IRC §§861(a)(5), 862(a)(5).

with the realty, and stock of a domestic corporation if at least 50 percent of the corporation's assets are U.S. real property interests.[8]

These rules conform to the conventional view that real property has an unusual affinity to the country of location. A more sophisticated analysis suggests, however, that gains from sales of real property can arise in part from activities in another country. For example, if condominiums in the Caribbean are promoted and sold to commuters by high-pressure tactics in a booth in Grand Central Station, it is questionable whether all the income should be assigned to the country where the property is located.

¶70.6.3　Personal Property Held for Sale to Customers

The source of income on a sale of inventory or other personal property held for sale to customers in the ordinary course of business depends on whether the taxpayer acquired the goods by purchase or produced them itself.

1. *Goods acquired by purchase.* Generally, income on a sale of inventory property acquired by purchase has its source in the country in which the sale occurs.[9] However, income on a sale of inventory property purchased in a U.S. possession and sold in the United States is apportioned between U.S. and possessions sources.[10] Income on a sale of "unprocessed timber" is from U.S. sources, regardless of the place of sale, if the timber is "softwood and was cut from an area in the United States."[11] Also, income on a foreign person's sale of inventory property is from U.S. sources, regardless of the place of sale, if the income is attributable to an office or other fixed place of business of the taxpayer in the United States.[12]

---

[8] IRC §897(c), discussed supra ¶¶66.4.2, 66.4.3.

[9] IRC §861(a)(6). See generally Krass, A Guide to the Source of Income Rules for the Sale and Purchase of Inventory Property, 45 Tax Lawyer 857 (1992); Roussiang, The Sales Source Rules for U.S. Exports: How Much Do They Cost? 62 Tax Notes 1047 (1994) (attempt to quantify effects of rules on tax revenues, exports, and U.S. and global welfare).

[10] IRC §863(b)(3); Reg. §1.863-3A(c)(4) (method of allocation). The IRS has proposed a restatement of the regulations under §863(b)(3). REG-251985-96, 1997-48 IRB 18, proposing Reg. §1.863-3(f)(3). For the history of §863(b)(3), see H.R. Rep. No. 1860, 75th Cong., 3d Sess. (1938), reprinted in 1939-1 (Part 2) CB 728, 760. Although there has been an abundance of litigation concerning the place where the property was sold, there are no reported decisions about the place of "purchase." The issue can be resolved by applying the same principles; the place where the property is sold by the seller can be treated as the place of its purchase by the buyer.

Section 863(b)(3) is a one-way street: Income from property purchased in the United States and sold in a possession is not allocated but is instead assigned in full to possession sources.

[11] IRC §865(b), as amended by Pub. L. No. 103-66, §13239, 107 Stat. 312 (1993) (applicable to sales and other dispositions after August 10, 1993). The term "unprocessed timber" is defined as a "log, cant, or similar form of timber."

[12] IRC §865(e)(2), discussed infra ¶70.6.4 text accompanying notes 67–74.

2. *Goods manufactured or produced by seller.* Gross income on a U.S. sale of goods produced by the taxpayer outside the United States, or a sale outside the United States of goods produced in this country, is from sources partly within and partly without the United States.[13] The term "produced" includes manufactured, produced, created, fabricated, extracted, processed, cured, or aged.[14] Only production activities "conducted directly by the taxpayer" are considered for this purpose.[15]

The regulations describe two methods that may be used for allocating or apportioning income from these transactions (§863 sales)—a 50/50 method and an independent factory price (IFP) method.[16] The regulations also permit the allocation to be made by a method devised by the taxpayer if the taxpayer obtains advance permission from the IRS. The 50[5]0 method applies to any §863 sale unless the taxpayer properly elects the IFP or books and records for those sales.[17]

Each of the methods utilized for §863 sales must be applied separately to U.S. sales of goods produced outside the United States and foreign sales of goods produced in the United States.[18]

a. *50/50 method.* Under the 50/50 method, one half of the income from §863 sales is allocated to production activities, and one half is allocated to the sales function.[19] For example, if *P* Corp. produces goods in the United States at

---

[13] IRC §863(b)(2). The regulations under §863(b)(2) were restated in 1996. TD 8687, 1996-2 CB 47; Mogenson, Rollinson & Jennings, Final Section 863(b) Regulations Solidify 50/50 Method as General Rule for Inventory Sales—but No Relief for Natural Resource Exporters, 26 Tax Mgmt. Int'l J. 121 (1997). See Reg. §1.863-3(h) (restated regulations apply for taxable years beginning after December 29, 1996, but taxpayers may elect to apply them for years beginning after July 11, 1996). For the proposed regulations, see INTL-0003-95, 60 Fed. Reg. 63,478 (1995); Nadel & Gates, 863(b) Prop. Regs. May Increase Some Taxpayers' Foreign-Source Income, 7 J. Int'l Tax'n 265 (1996).

The regulations, unlike their predecessor, apply to U.S. sales of goods produced in international waters or in space and sales in international waters or in space of goods produced in the United States. See TD 8687, supra, at 6. Also, "the general rules" of the regulations may be used "where a product is produced in one country but is destined for use either on the high seas or in space." Id.

[14] IRC §864(a); Reg. §1.863-3(c)(1)(i).

[15] Reg. §1.863-3(c)(1)(i). For the possibility of attributing a partnership's production or sales activities to the partners, see Reg. §1.863-3(g); TD 8687, supra note 13, at 6-7.

[16] A taxpayer with §863 sales "must fully explain the methodology used, the circumstances justifying use of that methodology, the extent that sales are aggregated, and the amount of income so allocated." Reg. §1.863-3(e)(2).

[17] Reg. §1.863-3(e)(1). If the taxpayer is eligible to use the IFP method for a sale, this method may be elected by using it to report income from the sale "on a timely filed original return."

[18] Reg. §1.863-3(a)(2).

[19] Reg. §1.863-3(b)(1)(i). Under the prior regulations, income on §863 sales was apportioned under a sales-property method if the taxpayer did not have an independent factory price for the goods. Under this method, gross income on the sale of personal property produced in the United States and sold outside the United States, or vice versa, is divided into two equal parts. Reg. §1.863-3T(b)(2) Ex. 2(ii) (before amendment in 1996).

a cost of $40 and sells them in a foreign country for $100, the gross income on the sales of $60 ($100, less $40) is allocated $30 to the United States as the place of production and $30 to the foreign country as the place of sale.[20] The 50/50

One of the halves is assigned to the place of sale. This half is apportioned according to sales, but the apportionment is based solely on sales of goods produced in the United States and sold elsewhere and goods produced elsewhere and sold in the United States. Reg. §1.863-3(b)(2) Ex. 2(iii) (before amendment in 1996). Thus, the sales half is entirely foreign source income if the taxpayer produces goods in the United States and sells them in foreign countries but does not produce goods abroad for sale in the United States. Phillips Petroleum Co. v. CIR, 101 TC 78 (1993), aff'd, 96-1 USTC ¶50,006 (10th Cir. 1995). Conversely, the sales half is entirely U.S. source income if the taxpayer produces goods in a foreign country and sells them in the United States but does not produce goods in the United States for sale in foreign countries. The sales half is apportioned only if the taxpayer produces goods both in the United States and foreign countries, exports U.S. produced goods, and imports foreign produced goods.

The other half of the gross income is apportioned according to the value of the taxpayer's property within and without the United States. Only property used to produce and sell goods in these transactions is included in the apportionment. Reg. §1.863-3(b)(2) Ex. 2(iv) (before amendment in 1996). See Phillips Petroleum Co. v. CIR, supra, at 108 (only property owned by taxpayer is included in apportionment, not leased property used by taxpayer in its production activities; because regulations speak of "property within the United States and within the foreign country," inventory located in international waters is omitted from apportionment). However, if the same property is also used to produce or sell other goods, the property's full value is apparently included. Assume a corporation manufactures goods in the United States, and it sells 90 percent of the goods in this country and exports the remaining 10 percent for sale by its branch in a foreign country. Although the apportionment applies to gross income from only 10 percent of the taxpayer's sales, 100 percent of the manufacturing assets are apparently included in the apportionment.

For purposes of the property apportionment, property is normally valued at "book value," which probably is its adjusted basis for U.S. tax purposes. The taxpayer, however, may use the property's "actual value" if "affirmative evidence" of this value is given. See Phillips Petroleum Co. v. CIR, supra, at 114–15 ("actual value" is "fair market value"; value determined for purposes of state ad valorem tax is not controlling; reference in regulations to appraisals for "purposes of taxation" includes "only valuation or appraisals for purposes of *Federal* tax law"). Usually, the property figure for a taxable year may be the average of the values at the beginning and end of the year, but a monthly or daily average must be used if "material changes" during the taxable year cause the yearly average not to be a fair representation of average value throughout the year.

Deductions allocated and apportioned to the gross income from §863 sales are prorated between the U.S. and foreign segments of the gross income. Reg. §1.863-3T(b)(2) Ex. 2(ii) (before amendment in 1996). This proration primarily applies to selling expenses, but it may also apply to any production expenses that are not included in the cost of goods sold.

[20] Reg. §1.863-3(b)(1)(ii) Ex. Unless the taxpayer undertakes substantial activities in selling the goods, the 50/50 rule usually allocates more than can reasonably be justified to the place of sale. As a result, it is often much more favorable for companies exporting goods from the United States than for importers. See Hufbauer & DeRosa, Costs and Benefits of the Export Source Rule, 75 Tax Notes 1401 (June 9 1997); Rousslang, Comments on Hufbauer & DeRosa, "Costs and Benefits of the Export Source Rule," 76 Tax

method is the default method that applies unless the taxpayer elects the independent factory price or books and records method.

b. *Independent factory price (IFP) method.* If an independent factory price (IFP) is "fairly established," the taxpayer may elect to apportion gross income from §863 sales by the IFP method, which operates as though the taxpayer's factory sold the goods to its sales branch for the IFP.[21] Gross receipts from the sale equal to the IFP are apportioned to production activities, and that amount, less the taxpayer's cost of goods sold (including only costs incurred at the place of production), is gross income from production activities, which has its source at the place of production.[22] The remainder of the sales price, less any additional cost of goods sold incurred in sales activities, is gross income from sources at the place of sale. Assume a domestic corporation produces goods in the United States at a cost of $80 and sells them to a retail outlet in a foreign country for $110; the corporation sells identical goods for $100 in transactions establishing an IFP in that amount.[23] Under the IFP method, U.S. source income on the sale to the retail outlet (income from production activities) is $20 (sales revenues of $100 less $80 cost of goods sold), and foreign source income (income from sales activities) is $10.

An IFP is "fairly established . . . only if the taxpayer regularly sells part of its output to wholly independent distributors or other selling concerns in such a way as to reasonably reflect the income earned from production activity."[24] Sales

---

Notes 541 (July 28, 1997); Hufbauer & DeRosa, The Costs and Benefits of the Export Source Rule: A Rejoinder, 14 Tax Notes Int'l 933 (Sept. 22, 1997).

[21] Reg. §1.863-3(b)(2). If a taxpayer does not have an IFP, but is able to establish a factory price by some other means, it can possibly use this methodology under the books and records method. TD 8687, supra note 13, at 7. For example, if the taxpayer sells to a related distributor at a price that passes muster under §482, this price might be used as a factory price under the books and records method.

[22] Reg. §§1.863-3(b)(2)(ii), (iii).

[23] Reg. §1.863-3(b)(2)(iv) Ex. 1.

[24] Reg. §1.863-3(b)(2)(i). Under the prior regulations, a taxpayer had an IFP if it "regularly sells part of [its] output to wholly independent distributors or other selling concerns in such a way as to establish fairly an independent factory or production price . . . unaffected by considerations of tax liability." Reg. §1.863-3(b)(2) Ex. 1 (before amendment in 1996). The IRS parsed this language in detail:

1. The words "regularly sells" mean that an IFP is not established by sales that are "sporadic and occasional" or "represent an insubstantial part of the total output of the relevant product." Notice 89-10, 1989-1 CB 631, ¶2.

2. The requirement that IFP sales be to "distributors" is satisfied by sales to buyers that use the taxpayer's goods as materials or components in products they manufacture for resale, but not by sales to buyers who customarily retain the goods for their own use. Id. at ¶3. However, the IRS' inclusion of a purchaser producing "a product into which [the purchased goods are] integrated or transformed" was rejected by the Tax Court, which defined "distributors" to include only "an entity that does not change the product it acquires, [but] merely acts as a middleman in

activities in connection with these sales may not be "significant in relation to all of the activities with respect to that product." A particular IFP may only be used for sales that are "reasonably contemporaneous" with the sales establishing the IFP and sales in "geographic markets" that are not "substantially different" from the markets in which the IFP sales were made.[25]

The IFP method is elective, but once elected for any §863 sales, it must be used for all sales of goods "that are substantially similar in physical character- istics and function, and are sold at a similar level of distribution," including the

---

the sale of the property to the retailer or . . . ultimate consumer." Phillips Petro- leum Co. v. CIR, 101 TC 78, 102 (1993).

3. The requirement that a distributor be "wholly independent" is not satisfied if the taxpayer and the distributor are related in a way that allows the IRS to test transactions between them under §482. Notice 89-10, supra, ¶4.

4. Sales to wholly independent distributors "establish [an IFP] fairly" only if they "reasonably reflect the income earned from manufacturing or production," to the exclusion of other functions. Id. ¶5. This requirement is not met if, in the sales to distributors, "income-generating activity of the taxpayer other than manufactur- ing or production activity . . . is significant in relation to manufacturing or pro- duction," as where expenses of marketing or selling are significant in relation to gross receipts in the sales. Id. ¶5A. Moreover, the requirement is not met if expenses of nonmanufacturing activities are substantial in absolute amount (re- gardless of their relationship to the selling price) and the goods bear a trademark of the taxpayer that has "significant value." Transportation costs, duties, excise taxes, and insurance costs are not indicative of significant nonmanufacturing activity, but these costs must be subtracted out in determining the IFP.

5. When all other requirements are met, an IFP may usually be established by sales in the country in which the taxpayer's manufacturing operation or sales branch is located, but sales in a third country do not establish an IFP if the markets in the distributor and branch countries are "materially different" with respect to the product. Id. ¶5B. Whether the two markets are materially different is usually determined by comparing the prices at which the goods are sold to unrelated persons at the same level of distribution.

6. The distributor and branch sales must be "reasonably contemporaneous," a re- quirement that in the absence of "significant price instability," is met if the distributor sales occur during the same taxable year as the branch sales or in the preceding year. Id. ¶5C.

7. An IFP may be established only by sales of products that are "substantially similar in physical characteristics [and] function" to the goods sold through the sales branch. Id. ¶6.

8. If the goods sold in distributor and branch sales are offered for resale "to unre- lated parties at the same level of distribution," the prices in these resales must be "substantially similar."

A taxpayer may also establish an IFP by evidence other than sales to independent dis- tributors. Id. ¶1. This evidence might consist of "market prices, analysis of economic functions, or transactions of other taxpayers," including sales by other members of the same affiliated group. The IRS, however, may not require a taxpayer to use an IFP unless it is established by sales to independent distributors.

[25] Reg. §1.863-3(b)(2)(ii).

sales establishing the IFP.[26] All income from the IFP sales thus has its source where the goods are produced. Moreover, the election binds the taxpayer for all taxable years subsequent to the year for which the election is made,[27] and the IFP method must be used for sales of all goods for which IFPs are established during the election year or any subsequent year. Assume *X* Corp. manufactures three dissimilar products; initially, it establishes an IFP for one of the products and elects the IFP method for sales of that product, using the 50/50 method for the other two products.[28] *X* must continue using the IFP method for the one product for as long as it has an IFP for the product. Also, if *X* later establishes an IFP for one of the other products, income on sales of that product must thereafter be apportioned by the IFP method.

c. *Books and records method.* The taxpayer may apportion income from §863 sales by the method it uses in keeping its books and records if the taxpayer "has received in advance the permission of the District Director having audit responsibility over its tax return."[29] This permission is given only if the taxpayer has demonstrated that, "in good faith and unaffected by considerations of tax liability, [it] will regularly employ in its books of account a detailed allocation of

---

[26] Reg. §1.863-3(b)(2)(ii). Under the prior regulations, the independent factory price method was required to be used if the taxpayer had an IFP for the goods sold through a sales branch. Phillips Petroleum Co. v. CIR, 97 TC 30 (1991), aff'd without opinion, 96-1 USTC ¶50,006 (10th Cir. 1995); Rev. Rul. 88-73, 1988-2 CB 173. However, the regulations stated that the IFP method applied only for sales made by a "selling or distributing branch or department of the [taxpayer's] business [that] is located in a different country from that in which the factory is located or the production carried on." Reg. §1.863-3(b)(2) Ex. 1(before amendment in 1996). The Tax Court held that this language blocked the IRS from requiring the IFP method if the taxpayer's selling or distributing branch or department was located in the country in which the taxpayer produced the goods. Intel Corp. v. CIR, 100 TC 616 (1993), aff'd, 76 F3d 976 (9th Cir. 1996). See Ingwalson, Sourcing Income From Cross-Border Sales, 47 Tax Lawyer 549 (1994); McIntyre, Overruling *Intel* to Pay for GATS, 9 Tax Notes Int'l 979 (Sept. 26, 1994).

[27] However, the taxpayer can abandon the IFP method with IRS consent, which "will not be withheld unless the change would result in a substantial distortion of the source of the taxpayer's income." Reg. §1.863-3(e)(1).

[28] Reg. §1.863-3(2)(iv) Ex. 2.

[29] Reg. §1.863-3(b)(3). Once this permission is obtained, the books and records method must be used for all taxable years until the District Director consents to a change, but permission to change "will not be withheld unless the change would result in a substantial distortion of the source of the taxpayer's income." Reg. §1.863-3(e)(1).

Under the prior regulations, the books and records method could be used if the IRS was satisfied that (1) the taxpayer "regularly employs" this method, (2) that taxpayer's adoption of the method was "in good faith and unaffected by considerations of tax liability," and (3) the method "reflects" U.S. source income "more clearly" than either of the methods described above. Reg. §1.863-3(b)(2) Ex. 3 (before amendment in 1996). See INTL-0003-95, 60 Fed. Reg. 63,478, 63,483 (1995) ("The books and records method is rarely, if ever, used"). For variations on this procedure in the case of income partly from sources within a U.S. possession, see Reg. §1.863-3A(c); Rev. Rul. 71-387, 1971-2 CB 264 (allocation formula illustrated).

receipts and expenditures which clearly reflects the amount of the taxpayer's income from production and sales activities." Permission may be granted subject to conditions, and it may be revoked if these conditions are not satisfied.

d. *Sources of gross and taxable income from production and sales activities.* Under each of the foregoing methods, gross income on a sale is divided between production activities and sales activities. The production share is from sources in the country or countries in which production activities occur, and the place of the sale is the source of the sales share.[30]

The production share is wholly from U.S. sources or foreign sources if the taxpayer's "production assets" are located solely in the United States or solely outside the United States.[31] If the production assets are located both within and without the United States, the production share is split between U.S. and foreign sources in proportion to the average adjusted basis of the production assets.[32] The

---

[30] Reg. §1.863-3(c)(2). The place of sale is determined under §1.861-7(c), discussed infra text accompanying notes 36–39, and is usually the place where title passes from seller to buyer.

The place of sale is "presumed to be the United States" if the goods are wholly produced, and are sold for use, consumption, or disposition, in the United States. Reg. §1.863-3(c)(2). Moreover, for this purpose, goods are considered produced wholly in the United States, even if "packaging, repackaging, labeling, or other minor assembly operations" occur outside the country. The presumption probably cannot be rebutted simply by demonstrating that, under the contract of sale, title passes to the buyer in a foreign country, but, if so, it is not clear what evidence might rebut the presumption. This rule was included in anticipation of possible abuses involving sales of goods produced or sold in international waters or in space. TD 8687, supra note 13, at 6. However, the presumption is not expressly so limited and apparently applies if, for example, goods are produced in New York, exported to Canada, where they are packaged and labeled, and sold to a buyer in Michigan by a contract passing title in Canada.

[31] Reg. §1.863-3(c)(1)(i)(A). The term "production assets" means "tangible and intangible assets owned by the taxpayer that are directly used by the taxpayer to produce inventory" sold in §863 sales. Reg. §1.863-3(c)(1)(i)(B). Production assets do not include accounts receivables, marketing intangibles and other intellectual property "not related to production of inventory," property used in transporting goods, "warehouses, the inventory itself, raw materials, or work-in-process." Cash and other liquid assets, even if serving as working capital for production activity, are not production assets. Intangible production assets are deemed located at the same place as the tangible assets used in the same production activity. Reg. §1.863-3(c)(1)(i)(C); see Reg. §1.863-3(c)(1)(iii) Ex. 2.

[32] Reg. §1.863-3(c)(1)(ii)(A). The average adjusted basis of the assets is determined by averaging basis as of the first and last days of the taxable year "unless by reason of material changes during the taxable year such average does not fairly represent the average for such year." Reg. §1.863-3(c)(1)(ii)(B). If the assets are used to produce both goods sold in §863 sales and other goods (e.g., goods sold in the country where they are produced), only a portion of the adjusted basis of these assets is included, and this portion must be determined by some method that "reasonably reflects the portion of the assets that produces inventory sold in Section 863 Sales." See Reg. §1.863-3(c)(1)(iii) Ex. 1 (apportioning production assets in proportion to same-country and export sales revenues).

If the taxpayer enters into or structures a transaction "with a principal purpose of reducing its U.S. tax liability by manipulating" the basis formula, the IRS "may make appropriate adjustments so that the source of the taxpayer's income from production

latter rule applies if, for example, the taxpayer produces goods in two stages, one located in the United States and the other in a foreign country.[33] Only production assets owned directly by the taxpayer are taken into account for this purpose, and no part of the production share of the income may be assigned to the place of manufacturing done by another person under contract with the taxpayer, whether the contract manufacturer is related to the taxpayer or unrelated.[34]

Deductions are allocated and apportioned between the U.S. and foreign portions of the gross income under the usual rules for allocating and apportioning deductions.[35] The allocation and apportionment rules must be applied separately to income governed by each of the three methods. If the 50/50 method is used for any sales, deductions allocated and apportioned to gross income from these sales are divided proportionately between the U.S. and foreign portions of that income.

3. *Place of sale.* As discussed above, income on a sale of inventory property has its source, in whole or in part, at the place of sale. The regulations prescribe the following principles for determining whether a sale occurs within or without the United States:

> [A] sale of personal property is consummated at the time when, and the place where, the rights, title, and interest of the seller in the property are transferred to the buyer. Where bare legal title is retained by the seller, the sale shall be deemed to have occurred at the time and place of passage to the buyer of beneficial ownership and the risk of loss. However, in any case in which the sales transaction is arranged in a particular manner for the primary purpose of tax avoidance, the foregoing rules will not be applied. In such cases, all factors of the transaction, such as negotiations, the execution of the agreement, the location of the property, and the place of payment, will be considered, and the sale will be treated as having been consummated at the place where the substance of the sale occurred.[36]

---

activity more clearly reflects the source of that income." Reg. §1.863-3(c)(1)(iii). An example of such a transaction is a sale of the taxpayer's U.S. production assets, followed by a leasing of the assets back from the purchaser, in order to reduce the portion of production income apportioned to U.S. sources. Reg. §1.863-3(c)(1)(iv) Ex. 3 (appropriate adjustment is to apply formula as though taxpayer continues to own assets sold and leased back).

[33] Reg. §1.863-3(c)(1)(iii) Ex. 1.

[34] TD 8687, supra note 13, at 7. For the possibility of attributing a partnership's production assets to the partners, see Reg. §1.863-3(g); TD 8687, supra, at 6-7.

[35] Reg. §1.863-3(d). For allocations and apportionments of deductions, see §§1.861-8 to 1.861-14T, discussed infra ¶70.10.

[36] Reg. §1.861-7(c). For title passage rules under the laws of the states of the United States, see UCC §§2-401(1) through 2-401(2), 2-501.

The title passage rule is notorious for being susceptible to manipulation. A major objective of §865, as first drafted by the Ways and Means Committee, was to do away with it. H.R. Rep. No. 841, 99th Cong., 2d Sess. II-595 (Conf. Rep. 1986). See infra ¶70.6.4 for §865. However, the Senate Finance and Conference Committees worried about effects on trade and wondered whether incentives to manipulate source might be reduced by the

Under conventional commercial contracts for sales made FOB point of shipment or CIF, title to the goods passes when they are delivered by the seller to the carrier at the port of embarkation. In a series of cases involving a tax preference for foreign source income of Western Hemisphere Trade Corporations (WHTCs), it was held that the title passage principle applies even if title to goods was retained by a U.S. sales corporation until they arrive at their destination in a foreign country in order to generate foreign source income qualifying for the preference.[37] In *CIR v. Pfaudler Inter-American Corp.*, for example, the Court of Appeals for the Second Circuit refused to apply the "vague and uncertain" tax-avoidance qualification in the regulations:

> The Commissioner's reliance on the . . . Regulation is misplaced, inasmuch as [it] applies solely in cases "in which the sales transaction is arranged in a particular manner for the primary purpose of tax avoidance." It is not tax avoidance in this sense to take advantage of a provision of law [the WHTC rules] especially enacted to favor those who do business in a certain area of the world and who otherwise meet the statutory conditions as Pfaudler does. It is clear that Pfaudler's sales were no mere shams; retention of title carried with it the risk of loss or damage to the goods prior to ultimate delivery as well as the benefits linked to reservation of control over the goods while in transit.[38]

It is true, as the court stated, that the retention of title until the goods arrived at their destination in a foreign country meant that the seller retained the risk of loss through destruction of the goods or default by the purchaser. However, these risks approach the vanishing point in a commercial world characterized by solvent insurance companies and irrevocable letters of credit. This suggests that certainty in this area has been achieved by ascribing more importance to the formal documents than to the facts of life. Moreover, the rationale of *Pfaudler*—that in postponing passage of title to qualify for the WHTC benefits, the taxpayer merely responded to a legislative invitation—can be extended to many other tax allowances. Thus, although some room is left for the tax-avoidance qualification of the regulations, it seems reserved for egregious ar-

---

lower tax rates provided by the 1986 Act. H.R. Rep. No. 841, supra, at II-596. The title passage rule was thus left in place for inventory sales by US residents, and the Treasury was instructed to study the effects of the rule. Pub. L. No. 99-514, §1211(d), 100 Stat. 2085 (1986).

[37] For WHTCs, which lost their preference at the end of 1979, see supra ¶68.1.2.

[38] CIR v. Pfaudler Inter-American Corp., 330 F2d 471, 474-75 (2d Cir. 1964). See Rev. Rul. 64-198, 1964-2 CB 189 (agreeing to follow *Pfaudler*). See also Hunt v. CIR, 90 TC 1289 (1988) (income from purchase and sale of oil had its source at ports where buyers took delivery); Miami Purchasing Serv. Corp. v. CIR, 76 TC 818 (1981) (determination of where title passed); East Coast Oil Co. v. CIR, 31 BTA 558 (1934) (acq.), aff'd, 85 F2d 322 (5th Cir.), cert. denied, 299 US 608 (1936) (buyer's right to inspect goods does not delay passage of title).

rangements. Few reported decisions have assigned income to domestic sources when title passed outside the United States, or vice versa.[39]

¶70.6.4 Other Personal Property

Under §865(a), income or gain on a U.S. resident's sale or exchange of personal property other than inventory is from U.S. sources, and income or gain on a disposition by a nonresident is from sources outside the United States.[40] The source, in other words, is at the taxpayer's place of residence. Neither the place of sale nor the place of the taxpayer's activities with respect to the holding or sale of the property is relevant. These principles generally apply to both tangible and intangible property.

Before §865 was enacted in 1986, the place of sale rule, and the attendant title passage rule, applied alike to sales of inventory and noninventory personal property.[41] Although recognizing the ease with which these rules can be manipulated, Congress feared that their "repeal for sales of inventory would create difficulties for U.S. businesses competing in international commerce."[42]

> In other cases where manipulation of the place-of-sale rule was relatively easy (for example, sales of portfolio stock investments), Congress . . . believe[d] that the United States should assert taxing jurisdiction by reference to more meaningful criteria than under prior law. Congress realized that in cases where manipulation of source occurs, there is little likelihood that foreign countries tax this income. Congress believed in these circum-

---

[39] See US v. Balanovski, 236 F2d 298 (2d Cir. 1956), cert. denied, 352 US 968, reh's denied, 352 US 1019 (1957) (title passage test applied); Philipp Bros. Inter-Continent Corp. v. US, 66-1 USTC ¶9421 (SDNY 1966) (not officially reported) (same result whether title passage or substance-of-sale test applied); Ardbern Co. v. CIR, 41 BTA 910 (1940), modified on other grounds, 120 F2d 424 (9th Cir. 1941) (title to securities passed in United States, even though certificates were taken to Canada by messenger for formal transfer there). For a remarkable but unsuccessful effort to manipulate the allocation of income by passing title to minerals while they were in midair, falling from a dockside conveyor belt into a ship's hold, see U.S. Gypsum Co. v. US, 304 F. Supp. 627, 639 (ND Ill. 1969) (schematic diagram), modified on other grounds, 452 F2d 445 (7th Cir. 1971). See generally Chao, "Substance of the Sale" Test: From the *Balanovski* Case up to Date, 48 Taxes 68 (1970).

[40] IRC §§865(a),(i)(2). Section 865 generally applies in taxable years beginning after 1986. Pub. L. No. 99-514, §1211(c),100 Stat. 2085 (1986). For the exclusion of income on sales of inventory and other property held for sale to customers in the ordinary course of business, see §§865(b),(i)(1). See generally Brennan, Revising the Source of Income Rule for the Purchase and Sale of Personal Property: The Tax Reform Act of 1986, 41 Tax Lawyer 169 (1987).

[41] For the place of sale and title passage rules, see supra ¶70.6.3.

[42] Staff of Joint Comm. on Tax'n, 99th Cong., 2d Sess., General Explanation of the Tax Reform Act of 1986 at 918 (Comm. Print 1987) [hereinafter 1986 Bluebook].

stances that the residence of the seller should govern the source of the income since countries rarely tax personal property gains on a source basis.[43]

In large part, the residence rule is designed to carry out the broader policy that "income not taxed, or not likely to be taxed, by a foreign country generally should not be treated as foreign source income for purposes of the foreign tax credit limitations."[44] In applying the residence rule to foreign persons, Congress recognized that the income and gain covered by the rule has never been taxed by the United States, even when it has borne a U.S. source label.

The residence rule is qualified by several exceptions, including rules that (1) assign gains of U.S. citizens residing abroad to U.S. sources if the gains are not subject to substantial foreign taxes,[45] (2) source gains on sales of depreciable property by looking to the treatment of depreciation deductions taken by the taxpayer,[46] (3) subject gains on sales of intangibles to the source rule for royalties when the gains are recognized on receipt of contingent payments,[47] (4) sometimes allow domestic corporations to report gains on sales of foreign subsidiaries as foreign source income,[48] (5) assign some income attributable to an office outside the taxpayer's country of residence to the location of the office,[49] and (6) occasionally allow treaty rules to prevail over §865.[50]

1. *Residence.* Domestic corporations are U.S. residents for purposes of §865, as are estates and trusts not taxed as nonresident aliens, but all other corporations, estates, and trusts are nonresidents.[51]

Generally, individuals are residents of the country in which they maintain their tax homes. A person has a tax home in a particular country if expenses incurred in traveling away from the country on business would be deductible under §162(a)(2).[52] A U.S. citizen is a resident of the United States for purposes of §865 unless he has a tax home in a foreign country.[53] The same test is applied to an alien who is a U.S. resident under the general residence test of §7701(b).[54]

---

[43] Id.

[44] Id. at 919.

[45] See infra text accompanying note 57.

[46] See infra text accompanying notes 58–66.

[47] See infra text accompanying notes 67–74.

[48] See infra text accompanying notes 75–77.

[49] See infra text accompanying notes 83–88.

[50] See infra text accompanying notes 89–92.

[51] IRC §865(g)(1). For whether a corporation, trust, or estate is domestic or foreign, see supra ¶65.3.

[52] IRC §911(d)(3). For the deduction for traveling expenses, see supra ¶21.1. According to the regulations, "an individual's tax home is considered to be located at his regular or principal (if more than one regular) place of business or, if the individual has no regular or principal place of business because of the nature of the business, then at his regular place of abode in a real and substantial sense." Reg. §1.911-2(b).

[53] IRC §865(g)(1)(A)(i)(I).

[54] For §7701(b), see supra ¶65.2.

It is thus possible for an alien to be a U.S. resident for all other purposes but a nonresident for purposes of §865. An alien who is not a U.S. resident under §7701(b) is a resident for purposes of §865 only if he has a tax home in the United States.[55]

A partnership is neither a resident nor a nonresident for purposes of §865. Partnership income and gain subject to §865 has no source characterization in the partnership's return, and each partner separately applies §865 to the partner's distributive share of these items.[56] For example, when the residence rule applies to a partnership item, the distributive share of the item allocated to each partner residing in the United States is from U.S. sources.

2. *U.S. citizens and alien residents with foreign tax homes.* A special rule applies to an individual with a tax home in a foreign country who is either a U.S. citizen or an alien classified as a U.S. resident under §7701(b). For such a person, a §865 gain is from U.S. sources unless a foreign income tax of 10 percent or more of the gain is "actually paid."[57] For example, if a U.S. citizen lives and works in a foreign country, gains on sales of securities are U.S. source income, even if the securities are issued by companies resident in the taxpayer's country of residence and the gains are realized in transactions taking place in that country, unless the residence country (or some other foreign country) taxes the gains at a rate of at least 10 percent.

3. *Depreciable property.* The place of residence rule does not apply to gain on a property disposition if depreciation deductions have been allowed with respect to the property for U.S. tax purposes. Under a recapture rule, the gain, up to the amount of the depreciation, has the same source characterization as the depreciation deductions.[58] For example, if 60 percent of the depreciation allowed for particular property was deducted from gross income from U.S. sources, 60 percent of the gain (or, if less, gain equal to 60 percent of the depreciation) is also U.S. source income. If the gain exceeds the depreciation deductions, the excess has its source at the place of sale.[59]

Under the recapture rule, the gain is divided between (1) an amount equal to the aggregate of the depreciation deductions allowed in determining U.S. tax (or if less the entire gain) and (2) any excess of the gain over the depreciation deductions. The recapture rule applies to the former amount, and the latter is subject to the place of sale rule. The depreciation with respect to the property consists of all depreciation deductions reflected in the property's adjusted basis, including (1) depreciation taken on other property whose adjusted basis was

---

[55] IRC §§865(g)(1)(A)(i)(II), (B).

[56] IRC §865(i)(5).

[57] IRC §865(g)(2). This rule does not apply to some gains of bona fide residents of Puerto Rico on sales of stock of corporations deriving most of their incomes from active businesses in Puerto Rico. IRC §865(g)(3), discussed infra text accompanying notes 81–82.

[58] IRC §865(c).

[59] IRC §865(c)(2). See supra ¶70.6.3 for the place of sale rule.

transferred to the property in some prior nonrecognition transaction and (2) depreciation on the property taken by a prior owner whose basis carried over to the taxpayer.[60] Assume gain is recognized on a sale of property (Asset Two) that the taxpayer acquired some years earlier in an exchange of like-kind property.[61] Because the basis of the exchanged property (Asset One) was the foundation for the basis of the Asset Two,[62] the depreciation taken into account on the sale of Asset Two is the sum of the depreciation deductions allowed to the taxpayer with respect to Assets One and Two. Similarly, on a sale of property transferred to the taxpayer in a §351 exchange, both the transferor's and the taxpayer's depreciation are taken into account because the transferor's basis carried over to the taxpayer under §362(a).[63]

The first segment of the gain (the recapture amount) is split between U.S. and foreign sources in the same proportions as the depreciation deductions were allocated.[64] This is done by constructing a fraction. The numerator of the fraction is the sum of the depreciation on the property that was allowed in determining taxable income from sources within the United States.[65] The denominator is the sum of all depreciation allowed with respect to the property in determining taxable income from both domestic and foreign sources. The fraction is multiplied by the recapture amount. The product is gain from U.S. sources, and the remainder of the recapture amount is from foreign sources.[66]

Assume equipment used in the taxpayer's business is sold in a foreign country at a gain of $50. If $40 of depreciation was allowed on the equipment for U.S.

---

[60] IRC §865(c)(4)(B). See IRC §865(c)(4)(C) ("depreciation" includes amortization and "any other deduction [that] treats an otherwise capital expenditure as a deductible expense").

[61] For like-kind exchanges, see supra ¶44.2.

[62] IRC §1031(d).

[63] For §§351 and 362(a), see infra ¶91.1.

[64] IRC §865(c)(1).

[65] IRC §865(c)(3)(A). This rule is applied strictly to depreciation on aircraft, railroad rolling stock, and trucks used in international commerce and a few other items described in §48(a)(2)(B). For other property, depreciation for a particular year is deemed to have been allocated to U.S. source income alone if the property was used predominantly in the United States during the year, and depreciation on property used predominantly outside the country during a year is deemed allocable to foreign source income only. IRC §865(c)(3)(B).

[66] IRC §865(c)(1). The statutory procedure is flawed in its application to foreign persons. Some foreign source income is taxed by the United States as effectively connected income, and depreciation allocable to foreign source income thus can reduce effectively connected taxable income. IRC §864(c)(4), discussed supra ¶66.3.4. However, gain on a disposition of property used in a U.S. business is effectively connected income only if it is from U.S. sources. IRC §§864(c)(3), (4). If a foreign person is allowed depreciation that is allocated to effectively connected income from foreign sources, a like amount of gain on sale is foreign source income under the §865(c) recapture rule, but this amount is not effectively connected income. In this case, the depreciation reduces the U.S. tax base, but the recapture does not increase it.

tax purposes, the recapture rule determines the source of $40 of the gain. This $40 is from U.S. sources if the equipment has been used exclusively in the United States and all depreciation has been deducted against income from U.S. sources. In contrast, if the depreciation deductions have been allocated 75 percent to U.S. source income and 25 percent to foreign income, $30 is income from sources within the United States and $10 is foreign source income. The $10 excess of the gain over the sum of the depreciation deductions is from sources in the country in which the sale occurs.

4. *Intangibles.* The residence rule applies to gain on a sale or exchange of an intangible only if the gain is recognized on a payment that is "not contingent on the productivity, use, or disposition of the intangible."[67] Gain with respect to a contingent payment is treated as a royalty for source purposes and thus has its source at the place of the buyer's use of the intangible.[68] However, if the taxpayer has been allowed depreciation or amortization deductions with respect to the intangible, the rules for depreciable property apply to an amount of gain equal to these deductions, and the rules for intangibles apply only to gain in excess of the deductions.[69] The term "intangible" includes "any patent, copyright, secret process or formula, . . . trademark, trade brand, franchise, or other like property."[70]

If an intangible is sold for a price that is partly fixed and partly contingent on the property's productivity, use, or disposition, gain is bifurcated. Gain attributable to the fixed payments is sourced under the residence rule, while the royalty rule applies to the contingent payments.[71] Assume a nonresident alien not engaged in business in the United States sells a U.S. patent to a domestic corporation for $100 plus an annual payment equal to 2 percent of the corporation's revenues from goods produced under the patent. Gain on the $100 payment is from foreign sources and thus is exempt from U.S. tax. The annual payments, in contrast, are from U.S. sources under the place of use rule for royalties, and they therefore are subject to the withholding tax imposed by §871(a).[72]

The place of residence rule is wholly inapplicable to gain on a sale or exchange of goodwill. Gain on receipt of a contingent payment for goodwill is treated as a royalty, as on dispositions of other intangibles, and gain on receipt of a noncontingent payment is "from sources in the country in which such goodwill was generated."[73]

---

[67] IRC §865(d)(1)(A).

[68] IRC §865(d)(1)(B). See supra ¶70.5 for the source of royalties.

[69] IRC §865(d)(4).

[70] IRC §865(d)(2).

[71] See 1986 Bluebook, supra note 42, at 923.

[72] For §871(a), see supra ¶66.2.1.

[73] IRC §865(d)(3). See International Multifoods Corp. v. CIR, 108 TC No. 3 (1997) (taxpayer-franchisor sold its operations in Asia and Pacific, including franchise agreements, rights to system used by franchisee, and goodwill, for fixed price; held, §865(d)(3) inapplicable because taxpayer failed to "establish that it transferred any goodwill separate and apart from the goodwill inherent in the franchisor's interest and trademarks").

When gain on a sale of an intangible (including goodwill) is U.S. source income under §865 and foreign source income under a treaty, the taxpayer may elect to follow the treaty rule rather than §865, but the credit limitation rules of §904 are applied separately to gain covered by the election and to foreign taxes on the gain.[74]

5. *Domestic corporation's disposition of stock of foreign affiliate.* Gain on a domestic corporation's sale of stock of a foreign corporation is from foreign sources if (1) the two corporations would be members of the same affiliated group, but for the exclusion of foreign corporations from affiliated groups,[75] (2) the foreign corporation is actively engaged in a trade or business in a particular foreign country, (3) for the three-year period ending with the taxable year of the foreign corporation preceding the year in which the stock disposition occurs, at least 50 percent of its gross income derived from the foreign trade or business, and (4) title to the stock passes to the purchaser within the foreign country in which the business is located.[76] If any of these requirements is not met, the gain is from U.S. sources under the residence rule. Whether or not the requirements are met, the gain subject to these rules does not include any amount characterized by §1248 as a dividend because the source rules for dividends apply to this amount.[77]

Assume domestic corporation P is sole shareholder of foreign corporation F, which carries on manufacturing operations in foreign country X. Gain on a sale of the F stock is foreign source income if (1) more than 50 percent of F's gross income for the preceding three years was from the country X business and (2) the stock is delivered to the buyer in country X.

6. *Stock of corporations organized or doing business in U.S. possessions.* Two special rules are provided for gains on dispositions of stock of corporations deriving most of their income from active businesses in U.S. possessions. First, a shareholder's gain on the liquidation of a corporation organized in a possession is from sources outside the United States if, for the three taxable years preceding the taxable year of its liquidation, more than 50 percent of the corporation's gross income was from the active conduct of a trade or business in the possession.[78] The credit limitation rules of §904 are applied separately to the gain, thus precluding the gain's foreign source label from increasing the maximum credit for foreign taxes on other income.[79] Also, if the shareholder is a U.S.-owned foreign corpo-

---

[74] IRC §865(h), discussed infra text accompanying notes 90–92.

[75] IRC §§865(f)(1), (i)(4). An affiliated group is a chain of corporations or a series of chains of corporations, where all corporations are connected to a common parent by 80 percent or greater stock ownership. IRC §1504(a).

[76] IRC §§865(f), (i)(4). The taxpayer can elect to treat the foreign affiliate and its wholly owned subsidiaries as one corporation in applying these requirements.

[77] 1986 Bluebook, supra note 42, at 922.

[78] IRC §§865(h)(1), (2)(B).

[79] See supra ¶69.5 for §904.

ration, the gain is segregated in applying the indirect credit rules of §§902 and 960.[80]

The second rule applies to gain on a sale of stock by an "individual who is bona fide resident of Puerto Rico" if the corporation is actively engaged in a trade or business in Puerto Rico and more than 50 percent of its gross income for the preceding three years derived from this business.[81] This gain is exempted from the normal rule assigning gains of nonresident U.S. citizens to U.S. sources unless the gain bears a foreign tax of at least 10 percent.[82] The gain thus has its source at the taxpayer's place of residence, usually Puerto Rico. Unlike the rule described in the preceding paragraph, this rule is not limited to stock of corporations organized in a possession, and gains subject to it are not specially limited under §904.

7. *U.S. resident with foreign office.* Income or gain of a U.S. resident on a disposition of personal property is from foreign sources if (1) the taxpayer has an office or other fixed place of business in a foreign country, (2) the income or gain is "attributable" to the foreign office,[83] (3) a foreign income tax of at least 10 percent of the income is "actually paid,"[84] and (4) the property is not inventory, depreciable property, an intangible, or stock of a foreign affiliate.[85] Because of the many restrictions, the rule has a limited application. It gives a foreign source characterization to gain on a sale of a portfolio investment, for example, if the property sold was a temporary investment of working capital of a business carried on through a foreign office and the gain is subject to a substantial tax in the country in which the foreign office is located.

8. *Foreign person with U.S. office.* Generally, income or gain of a nonresident on a disposition of personal property is from U.S. sources if (1) the taxpayer has an office or other fixed place of business in the United States and (2) the income or gain is attributable to the office.[86] This rule can apply to income or gain on a sale of personal property of any character, including inventory and depreciable property.

---

[80] See supra ¶69.8 for the indirect credit rules.

[81] IRC §865(g)(3).

[82] For the 10 percent rule, see §865(g)(2), discussed supra note 57.

[83] See infra note 86 for whether income is attributable to a particular place of office.

[84] See H.R. Rep. No. 841, supra note 36, at II-596 (requirement met "only if the income is taxed abroad at an effective rate of at least 10 percent"); 1986 Bluebook, supra note 42, at 921 ("the 10-percent tax rule is designed to reflect Congress' general intent that the source of income for U.S. residents be the United States unless the income is subject to meaningful foreign tax"; foreign tax must qualify as foreign income tax under foreign tax credit rules).

[85] IRC §865(e)(1). The exclusion of intangibles does not apply to an intangible other than goodwill that is sold for a fixed price.

[86] IRC §865(e)(2)(A). The rules of §864(c)(5) are used in determining whether a taxpayer has an office or other fixed place of business in a particular country and whether income on a sale is attributable to that place of business. IRC §865(e)(3). For §864(c)(5), see supra ¶66.3.4.

An exception is provided for income on a sale of inventory property if (1) the sale is outside the United States under the title passage rule, (2) the property is sold for use, disposition, or consumption outside the United States, and (3) a fixed place of business of the taxpayer in a foreign country participates materially in the sale.[87] Income covered by the exception is from foreign sources under the place of sale rule. Assume a foreign corporation buys goods in the United States for export to a foreign country, and offices of the corporation in the United States and the foreign country of destination both participate materially in the sale. If title passes to purchasers in the country of destination, income on the sales is from foreign sources and is exempt from U.S. tax. If title passes in the United States, in contrast, the income is from U.S. sources under the U.S. office rule, and it is taxed as income effectively connected with the corporation's U.S. business.[88]

9. *Treaty election.* At least in its application to U.S. persons, Congress intended that §865 override inconsistent treaty rules.[89] However, an election is allowed to follow a treaty source rule rather than §865 for gain on a sale of an intangible or stock in a foreign corporation.[90] The election may be made only if the gain is U.S. source income under §865 and foreign source income under a treaty to which the United States is a party. When the election is made, the credit limitation rules of §904 are applied separately to the gain and any foreign taxes on it.[91] As a consequence, even if foreign taxes on the gain are less than the precredit U.S. tax on it, the gain's foreign source label does not increase the maximum credit for foreign taxes on other income. The indirect credit rules of §§902 and 960 and the foreign tax rules for foreign oil related income are also applied separately to the gain.[92]

10. *Losses.* A deductible loss on a sale of property does not have a source characterization. It is instead allocated as a deduction against U.S. or foreign source income or apportioned between these two groupings of income. Under the regulations, losses on sales of capital assets and depreciable property used in business are allocated to income of the same source as the income produced by the property before its sale.[93] For example, loss on a sale of stock from which the taxpayer received U.S. source dividends is allocated as a deduction from income from U.S. sources. Loss on a sale of equipment used in a foreign factory is deductible against foreign source income.

The regulations often lead to asymmetrical treatments of gains and losses. For example, if a U.S. resident sells stock on which she received foreign source dividends, §865(a) typically makes gain on the sale U.S. source income, but the

---

[87] IRC §865(e)(2)(B).

[88] For the effectively connected income tax, see supra ¶66.3.1.

[89] 1986 Bluebook, supra note 42, at 919–20.

[90] IRC §865(h).

[91] See supra ¶69.5 for §904.

[92] See supra ¶69.8 for §§902 and 960 and ¶69.10 for the credit rules on foreign oil related income.

[93] Reg. §1.861-8(e)(7)(i), discussed infra ¶70.10.

regulations treat loss as a deduction from foreign source income. Section 865 directs the Treasury to promulgate such regulations "relating to the treatment of losses from sales of personal property . . . as may be necessary or appropriate to carry out the purpose" of §865.[94] Most logically, the Treasury should respond with regulations providing that a loss on a sale of personal property is allocated to income of the same source as gain from the sale, had the sale produced a gain.[95]

¶70.7 NATURAL RESOURCES

The regulations long provided that income from the ownership or operation of farms, mines, oil and gas wells, other natural deposits, and timber was from U.S. sources if the underlying property was located in the United States, even if the products were sold abroad.[1] Conversely, if the property was located outside the United States, the income was from foreign sources, even if the products were sold within the United States.[2] These rules applied even if the minerals, crops, or other products were processed to a limited extent in the country of origin.[3] However, the Tax Court held the regulations invalid in *Phillips Petroleum Co. v. CIR*, which involved sales of liquefied natural gas (LNG) produced in Alaska to Japanese buyers under contracts passing title to the buyers in Japan.[4] Under the regulations, all income from the sales was from U.S. sources because the gas was extracted from wells located in the United States. The court found the regulations to be contrary to "the clear and unambiguous language" of §863(b)(2), which provides that income on a sale of inventory property is from sources partly within and partly without the United States if the goods are "produced" within

---

[94] IRC §865(j).

[95] See 1986 Bluebook, supra note 42, at 923 ("it is anticipated that regulations will provide that losses from sales of personal property generally will be allocated consistently with the source of income that gains would generate but that variations of this principle may be necessary").

The IRS has proposed regulations providing that loss on a sale of stock (other than portfolio stock) usually has the same source as would gain on the sale; that is, the loss is usually allocated to income from sources in the taxpayer's country of residence, just as gain on the sale of the stock would be from sources in that country. Prop. Reg. §1.865-2. See Wilson & Womack, Proposed Section 865 Regs Offer Potentially Favorable Treatment on Losses on the Disposition of Foreign Stock, 13 Tax Notes Int'l 521 (Aug. 12, 1996).

[1] Reg. §1.863-1(b) (before amendment in 1996).

[2] Rev. Rul. 67-194, 1967-1 CB 183. See Rev. Rul. 71-198, 1971-1 CB 210 (foreign source income realized on sale of fish caught in international waters and sold without further treatment or processing to canneries in United States).

[3] Rev. Rul. 67-194, 1967-1 CB 183 (minerals treated or processed at foreign mine). Compare the "ordinary treatment" concept formerly applied in computing percentage depletion, discussed in ¶24.3.4.

[4] Phillips Petroleum Co. v. CIR, 97 TC 30 (1991), aff'd without published opinion, 70 F3d 1282 (10th Cir. 1995).

and sold without the country or vice versa, and §864(a), which defines the "produced" to include "extracted."[5]

In response to the *Phillips Petroleum* decision, the Treasury restated the regulations.[6] Under the restated regulations, gross receipts on a foreign sale of products derived from the taxpayer's ownership or operation of a U.S. farm, mine, oil or gas well, other natural deposit, or timber are allocated between U.S. and foreign sources "based on the fair market value of the product at the export terminal."[7] Conversely, gross receipts on a U.S. sale of products derived from the ownership or operation of a foreign farm, deposit, or timber are allocated with reference to the value at the foreign export terminal. The title passage rule determines whether a sale is made in the United States or a foreign country.[8] The "export terminal" is the "final point . . . from which goods are shipped from a foreign country to the United States" or from the United States to a foreign country.[9] For this purpose, the United States includes certain continental shelf areas.[10]

Under the export terminal rule, gross receipts equal to fair market value at the terminal are from sources in the country in which the farm, deposit, or uncut timber is located.[11] The sources of the remaining gross receipts on the sale are as follows:

1. "If the taxpayer engages in additional production activities subsequent to shipment from the export terminal" and these activities occur outside the country of sale, the sources of the remainder are determined under the rules for goods produced in one country and sold in another (§863(b)(2) and the regulations thereunder).[12]

---

[5] Id. at 32–35.

[6] TD 8687, 1996-52 IRB 4. The regulations are effective for taxable years beginning after December 29, 1996, but taxpayers may elect to apply them for years beginning after July 11, 1995 but before December 30, 1996. Reg. §1.863-1(e). For the proposed regulations, see INTL-0003-95, 60 Fed. Reg. 63,478 (1995).

[7] Reg. §1.863-1(b)(1).

[8] For the title passage rule, see Reg. §1.186-7(c), discussed supra ¶70.6.3.

[9] Reg. §1.863-1(b)(3)(iii). If there is no shipment point in any country (because, for example, the product is produced on the high seas), the export terminal is the place of production.

[10] IRC §638(1) (United States includes "the seabed and subsoil of those submarine areas which are adjacent to the territorial waters of the United States and over which the United States has exclusive rights, in accordance with international law, with respect to the exploration and exploitation of natural resources").

[11] Fair market value must be determined from "all of the facts and circumstances," including the arm's length standard of §482 if the goods are sold to a related person. Reg. §1.863-1(b)(4). The taxpayer must attach a statement to its return explaining how it determined fair market value. Reg. §1.863-1(b)(6).

[12] Reg. §1.863-1(b)(1)(i). For the allocation between the places of the production activities and sale, see Reg. §1.863-3, discussed supra ¶70.6.3. In applying §1.863-3, only

2. In all other cases, the remainder is from sources in the country of sale (generally, the country in which title passes to the buyer).[13]

For purposes of the first of these rules, "production activities" include the creation, fabrication, manufacture, extraction, processing, curing, or aging of inventory property.[14] The term "additional production activities" means "substantial production activities performed directly by the taxpayer in addition to activities from the ownership or operation of any farm, mine, oil or gas well, other natural deposit, or timber."[15] Preparation of the products for export, including any activity "designed to facilitate the transportation of the natural resource to or from the export terminal," is not additional production activity. For example, liquefaction of natural gas is not additional production because it merely "prepares the natural gas for transportation from the export terminal."[16]

The regulations illustrate the foregoing rules as follows:

1. A U.S. company mines gold in country X, makes jewelry from the gold in the United States, and sells the jewelry in country Y.[17] An amount equal to the fair market value of the gold when exported from country X is from sources in country X. The remainder of the gross receipts on the sale of the jewelry is from U.S. and country Y sources, in amounts determined under §863(b)(2).

2. A domestic corporation extracts crude oil from wells in country X, transports it through a pipeline to an export terminal in country Y, and ships the oil to the United States, where it is refined and the refined products are sold.[18] An amount equal to the fair market value of the oil at the export terminal in country Y is from country X sources, and the remainder of the gross receipts are from U.S. sources.

3. A U.S. company mines copper in foreign country X, mills the copper ore into a concentrate, dries the concentrate, and exports it from a terminal

---

production assets used in the additional production activity subsequent to the export terminal are taken into account.

[13] Reg. §1.863-1(b)(1)(i).

[14] Reg. §1.861-1(b)(3)(i).

[15] Reg. §1.863-1(b)(3)(ii). The "principles of §1.954-3(a)(4)" determine whether production activities are substantial. Under these principles, production activities are substantial only if they "substantially transform" the materials used or "are substantial in nature and are generally considered to [be manufacturing]." See supra ¶68.2.4.

The taxpayer must attach a statement to its return describing any additional production activities. Reg. §1.863-1(b)(6).

[16] Reg. §1.863-1(b)(7) Ex. 2. See TD 8687, 1996-52 IRB 4 ("Even though liquefaction may be an expensive, complex process, liquefied natural gas retains its character as a natural resource, so that liquefaction should be treated no differently than other processes that prepare natural resources for export").

[17] Reg. §1.863-1(b)(7) Ex. 3.

[18] Reg. §1.863-1(b)(7) Ex. 4.

in country X in sales occurring in the United States.[19] Because the milling and drying are not additional production activities, gross receipts from the export sales are from country X sources to the extent of the value of the concentrate at the point of export, and the remainder is from U.S. sources.

Additional rules apply if the taxpayer subjects the products to additional production activities before they are shipped from the export terminal.[20] In this case, the gross receipts allocable to the ownership or operation of the farm, deposit, or uncut timber equal the fair market value of the product immediately before the additional production activities. The remaining gross receipts are allocated between the production and sale activities under §863(b)(2). Assume a U.S. company mines copper in foreign country X, mills the ore into concentrate at the mine, transports the copper to a smelter that the company operates in country X, and exports the smelted copper to the United States.[21] The smelting, but not the milling, is an additional production activity. The taxpayer's gross receipts from mining thus equal the fair market value of the copper concentrate as it enters the smelter, and the remainder of the gross receipts on export sales is allocated between U.S. and foreign sources under §863(b)(2).

Gross income from ownership or operation of the farm, deposit, or timber stand is the fair market value of the product at the export terminal (or, in the case of production activities in the country of the farm, deposit, or timber, the fair market value immediately before those activities), less the taxpayer's cost for the product, determined under normal cost accounting methods.[22] The gross income from sources in the country or countries in which the sale and any additional production activities occur is the excess of the revenues on the sales over the fair market value of the product at the export terminal or commencement of the additional production activities. Taxable income from each source is determined by allocating and apportioning deductions in the usual ways.[23]

¶70.8 SPACE, OCEAN, AND ANTARCTIC ACTIVITIES

Income from a space or ocean activity is assigned to U.S. sources if the taxpayer is a U.S. person (a U.S. citizen or resident or a domestic corporation, partnership, trust, or estate).[1] For all other taxpayers, such income is from

---

[19] Reg. §1.863-1(b)(7) Ex. 1.

[20] Reg. §1.863-1(b)(2).

[21] Reg. §1.863-1(b)(7) Ex. 5.

[22] Reg. §1.863-1(b)(5).

[23] Reg. §1.863-1(c). For the allocation and apportionment of deductions, see infra ¶70.10.

[1] IRC §§863(d)(1), 7701(a)(30). See generally Kelly, Taxing Space and Ocean Activities, 37 Tax Notes 735 (Nov. 16, 1987); Pratt, Three Knots or Twelve? At What

foreign sources. Before this rule was enacted in 1986, income from these activities was usually from sources outside the United States. According to the staff of the Joint Committee on Taxation:

> Congress concluded that asserting primary tax jurisdiction only over income generated within the United States and its territorial waters was inappropriate .... Congress [therefore] enacted source rules the policy of which is to assert primary tax jurisdiction over income earned by U.S. residents that is not within any foreign country's taxing jurisdiction .... [W]hen a U.S. taxpayer conducted activities in space or international waters, Congress noted that foreign countries had no apparent right to tax the income and generally did not tax the income. Thus, the foreign tax credit limitation was inflated by income that was not within any foreign country's tax jurisdiction such that a taxpayer with excess foreign tax credits from other operations could eliminate all tax (U.S. and foreign) on this income rather than eliminating double tax. Similarly, a taxpayer's foreign tax credit limitation might have been inappropriately reduced if the operations had been conducted at a loss.[2]

The term "space or ocean activity" refers to activities conducted "in space," in Antarctica, or on or under water that is not recognized by the United States as being within the jurisdiction of any country.[3] It includes:

> the performance and provision of services in space or on or beneath the ocean, the leasing of equipment for use on or beneath the ocean (for purposes other than providing transportation) or in space (for example, spacecraft and satellites), the licensing of technology or other intangibles for use in space or on or beneath the ocean, and the manufacturing of property in space or on or beneath the ocean.[4]

By regulations, the Treasury may also include "underwriting income from the insurance of risks on activities conducted in space or on or beneath the ocean."[5]

The rules for space and ocean activities do not apply to transportation or international communications activities or to activities relating to mines, oil and gas wells, and other natural deposits in certain continental shelf areas.[6] Other rules enacted in 1986 provide for income from transportation and international communications activities.[7] The rules for international communications income

---

Distance from Shore Do U.S. Waters Become the International High Seas for Federal Income Tax Purposes? 26 Tax Mgmt. Int'l J. 332 (1997).

[2] Staff of Joint Comm. on Tax'n, 99th Cong., 2d Sess., General Explanation of the Tax Reform Act of 1986 at 933 (Comm. Print 1987) [hereinafter 1986 Bluebook].

[3] IRC §863(d)(2)(A).

[4] 1986 Bluebook, supra note 2, at 934.

[5] Id. at 935.

[6] IRC §§863(d)(2)(B)(i)-(iii). See 1986 Bluebook, supra note 2, at 934 ("ocean activities" do not include "the operation or lease of a vessel if such vessel is used to transport cargo or persons for hire between ports-of-call").

[7] See supra ¶70.4 text accompanying notes 22-32, 33-39.

apply "even if the communication is routed through a satellite located in space."[8]
The exclusion for continental shelf activities applies if (1) the activities occur in an area that is adjacent to the territorial waters of the United States, a U.S. possession, or a foreign country, (2) the United States or a foreign country "has exclusive rights, in accordance with international law, with respect to the exploration and exploitation of natural resources" in the area, and (3) in the case of an area claimed by a foreign country, the United States recognizes the country's rights to the area and the country exercises taxing jurisdiction with respect to the exploration and exploitation of natural resources within the area.[9] Income from the exploitation of natural deposits in a continental shelf area to which the United States has exclusive rights is from U.S. sources, whether the taxpayer is a U.S. or foreign person, and income from an area in which a foreign country or U.S. possession has exclusive rights is from foreign or possessions sources.[10] When a natural deposit is not within the jurisdiction of any country, the space and ocean rule applies to income from the exploitation of the deposit, including income from "the leasing of drilling rigs, the extraction of minerals, and the performance and provision of services related thereto."[11]

¶70.9   OTHER ITEMS OF GROSS INCOME

Many types of gross income are not covered by any of the statutory source rules. The omitted items include alimony, prizes, fellowships, debt cancellation income, recovery of deducted items, annuity payments, compensation for injuries or sickness, damages for breach of contract, windfalls, and gains on surrender of life insurance policies. These items are generally "separately allocated to sources within or without the United States."[1] The IRS has announced that "in the absence of an overriding Code provision, the main factor in determining the source of income . . . is whether the location of the property to which the payment related or the situs of the activities that resulted in its being made was in the United States or abroad."[2] Few cases or rulings put any flesh on this skeleton.[3] Alimony has been held to be from sources within the country of the payor's

---

[8] 1986 Bluebook, supra note 2, at 935.

[9] IRC §§638, 863(d)(2)(B)(iii).

[10] See supra ¶70.7.

[11] 1986 Bluebook, supra note 2, at 935.

[1] Reg. §1.863-1(a).

[2] Rev. Rul. 73-252, 1973-1 CB 337.

[3] See Helvering v. Suffolk Co., 104 F2d 505 (4th Cir. 1939) (refund to foreign corporation of U.S. tax paid by predecessor domestic corporation is U.S. source income); Int'l Multifoods Corp. v. CIR, 108 TC No. 3 (1997) (IRS conceded that domestic corporation's income under covenant not to compete in foreign countries was from foreign sources); Corporaciòn de Ventas de Salitre y Yoda de Chile v. CIR, 44 BTA 393 (1941), rev'd on other grounds, 130 F2d 141 (2d Cir. 1942) (foreign corporation's purchase of its

residence by analogy to the statutory source rule for interest.[4] The regulations provide source rules for two categories of income: scholarships, grants, prizes, and awards and income from notional principal contracts.

1. *Scholarships, grants, prizes, and awards.* Under the regulations, the source of a scholarship, fellowship grant, other type of grant, prize, or award generally depends on the residence or status of the grantor.[5] Such an item is usually from U.S. sources if the grantor is a U.S. person (a U.S. citizen or resident, a domestic corporation or partnership, or a nonforeign trust), the United States, one of the states, or the District of Columbia; it is from foreign sources if the grantor is anyone else.[6] For example, amounts received from foreign governments and international organizations are from foreign sources.

A special rule classifies some payments to foreign persons for foreign activities as foreign source income, even if the grantor is a U.S. person or government. Under this rule, a scholarship, fellowship grant, targeted grant, or achievement award received by a foreign person is from foreign sources if it is awarded "with respect to activities . . . conducted . . . or to be conducted . . . outside the United States."[7] The terms "targeted grant" and "achievement award" refer to

---

debentures at discount in United States generates U.S. source debt discharge income); IT 3119, 1937-2 CB 227 (same); Rev. Rul. 70-293, 1970-1 CB 282 (IT 3119 declared obsolete); Rev. Rul. 70-304, 1970-1 CB 163 (insurance proceeds for loss of goods in transit have source at original situs of goods unless they acquired permanent situs elsewhere before loss).

[4] Manning v. CIR, 614 F2d 815 (1st Cir. 1980); Howkins v. CIR, 49 TC 689 (1968).

[5] TD 8615, 1995-2 CB 83. For purposes of these rules, the terms "scholarship," "fellowship grant," "prize," and "award" are defined as they are for purposes of §§117 and 74. Reg. §§1.863-1(d)(3)(i), (ii), (iii). See supra ¶11.2.2 for §117 and ¶11.1 for prizes and awards. The term "grant" refers to a grant to an individual "to achieve a specific objective, produce a report or other similar product, or improve or enhance a literary, artistic, musical, scientific, teaching, or other similar capacity, skill or talent of the grantee." Reg. §1.863-1(d)(3)(iv), incorporating the definition of §4945(g)(3).

With respect to scholarships and fellowship grants, the regulations generally apply to payments made after 1986. Reg.§1.863-1(d)(4)(i). The regulations apply to grants, prizes, and awards paid after September 25, 1995, except that the taxpayer may elect to apply them to payments made after 1986. Reg. §1.863-1(d)(4)(ii).

Before the regulations were issued, the IRS ruled that a scholarship, fellowship, or prize for solving a puzzle had its source at the residence of the payor because the payor's residence, not the place where the recipient does the subsidized study or solves the puzzle, is "the principal economic nexus with the payments." Rev. Rul. 89-67, 1989-1 CB 233. See Blum, Raising the U.S. Tax Threshold for Foreign Students and Teachers Visiting the United States, 34 Va. J. Int'l Law 145, 162-78 (1993); Turro, U.S. Colleges and Foundations Seek Solution to Scholarship Sourcing Misstep, 50 Tax Notes 10 (Jan. 7, 1991) (discussing complaints of U.S. foundations awarding scholarships and fellowships for study in foreign countries about Rev. Rul. 89-67). For the proposed regulations, see INTL-41-92, 1993-2 CB 634.

[6] Reg. §§1.863-1(d)(2)(i), (ii).

[7] Reg. §1.863-1(d)(2)(iii). Although the regulations generally apply to payments made after 1986, this rule need not be applied to payments made during the period May 15, 1989, through June 15, 1993 (the period beginning with the issuance of Rev. Rul.

grants and awards from an educational or charitable organization or government that are "for an activity [or past activity] undertaken in the public interest and not primarily for the private financial benefit of a specific person or persons or organization."[8]

2. *Income from notional principal contracts.* Income under a notional principal contract usually has its source at the taxpayer's residence.[9] A "notional principal contract" is "a financial instrument that provides for the payment of amounts by one party to another at specified intervals calculated by reference to a specified index upon a notional principal amount in exchange for specified consideration or a promise to pay similar amounts."[10] An example is an interest rate swap contract under which a taxpayer agrees to make semiannual payments to another person of $50 each (interest on $1,000 at a fixed rate of 10 percent per annum) and the other person agrees to make simultaneous payments to the taxpayer equal to interest on $1,000 at a rate two percentage points higher than the six-month London Interbank Overnight Rate (LIBOR). The taxpayer might make such a contract if, for example, it had borrowed $1,000 under a note obligating it to pay interest at a floating rate tied to the LIBOR but wanted to substitute a fixed rate obligation.

Generally, income under a notional principal contract is from sources in the country of the taxpayer's residence.[11] For this purpose, domestic corporations and partnerships are U.S. residents, foreign corporations and partnerships are residents of the countries under whose laws they are organized, trusts and estates are U.S. residents unless they are classified as nonresident aliens for U.S. tax purposes, and individuals are generally considered residents of the countries in which they maintain their principal places of business.[12]

89-67, 1989-1 CB 233, and ending with the issuance of proposed regulations). Reg. §1.863-1(d)(4)(i).

[8] Reg. §§1.863-1(d)(3)(v), (vi).

[9] Reg. §1.863-7(b)(1). See May, Taxing Foreign Counterparties and Cross-Border Derivative Transactions, 1 Derivatives 148 (1996); Rosenbloom, Source-Based Taxation of Derivative Financial Instruments: Some Unanswered Questions, 50 U. Miami L. Rev 597 (1996).

[10] Reg. §1.863-7(a)(1).

[11] If a notional principal contract requires the other party to pay a "fee" to the taxpayer for late payment, the fee is not notional principal contract income. Reg. §1.863-7(d)(2).Presumably, the source of the fee is determined under the rules for interest income. See supra ¶70.2.

[12] Reg. §1.863-7(b)(1) (borrowing definition of §988(a)(3)(B)(i)). For the classification of entities as domestic or foreign, see supra ¶65.3.

More fully, individuals are generally considered residents of the country in which they maintain their "tax homes." An individual has a tax home at a particular place if expenses incurred in traveling away from that place on business are deductible business expenses under §162(a)(2). IRC §911(d)(3). This usually means that the tax home is at the individual's principal place of business. See Reg. §301.7701(b)-2(c)(1). However, an individual with an "abode" in the United States is a U.S. resident for this purpose, regardless of the location of the tax home, and an individual with no principal place of business is a

There is one exception to the place of residence rule: Income under a notional principal contract has its source at the principal place of business of a "qualified business unit" (QBU), not the place of the taxpayer's residence, if all of the following requirements are met: (1) The taxpayer must be a U.S. resident under the rules described in the preceding paragraph; (2) the QBU's principal place of business must be outside the United States; (3) the QBU must be engaged in business in the country in which its principal place of business is located; and (4) the contract must be "properly reflected" on the QBU's books.[13] Generally, any trade or business of the taxpayer is a QBU if a separate set of books is maintained for it.[14] Whether a notional principal contract is properly reflected on a QBU's books depends on "the degree of [the QBU's] participation in the negotiation and acquisition" of the contract, whether the QBU was interjected into the negotiation and acquisition of the contract in order to affect the source of the income, and any other facts and circumstances that might be relevant.

¶70.10 ALLOCATION AND APPORTIONMENT OF DEDUCTIONS

¶70.10.1 Introductory

Section 904(a) limits the foreign tax credit to the precredit U.S. tax on taxable income from sources outside the United States.[1] Foreign source taxable income consists of gross income from non-U.S. sources, reduced by the deductions allocated and apportioned to that gross income.[2] Also, a nonresident alien or foreign corporation engaged in business in the United States is taxed on taxable income effectively connected with the U.S. business.[3] Effectively connected taxable income is the excess of gross income effectively connected with U.S. trades or businesses over the deductions allocated and apportioned to the gross income.[4] Various other provisions of the Code also require the computation of taxable income from one source or another.[5]

Until 1977, the requirement that expenses, losses, and other deductions be properly apportioned or allocated among gross income from various sources was implemented by rather sketchy regulations. Deductions were matched with items of gross income to the extent possible, and unassigned deductions were allocated

---

U.S. resident if he is a U.S. citizen or resident alien but is otherwise considered a resident of a foreign country. For the term "resident alien," see supra ¶65.2.

[13] Reg. §1.863-7(b)(2).

[14] See infra ¶71.2.

[1] See supra ¶69.5.

[2] IRC §862(b).

[3] IRC §§871(b), 882(a), discussed supra ¶66.3.

[4] IRC §§871(b)(1), (2); 873(a); 882(a), (c).

[5] For a list of these provisions, see Reg. §1.861-8(f).

to domestic (or foreign) sources in the ratio that domestic (or foreign) gross income bore to total gross income. If a domestic corporation with both domestic and foreign income wished to increase its foreign source taxable income to increase the foreign tax credit limitation, it could often do so by allocating a large part of its expenses to gross income from domestic sources. As a justification for this practice, domestic corporations commonly asserted that overhead, research and development expenses, interest on indebtedness, and some other expenses were incurred primarily or solely to serve domestic operations and that foreign income was a marginal by-product of these expenses rather than a deliberately sought objective. In the absence of a definitive regulation to the contrary, the argument often succeeded.

Extensive regulations on the allocation and apportionment of deductions were promulgated in 1977, principally to ensure that foreign operations of domestic corporations are charged with a proper share of deductions.[6] However, foreign corporations usually use the same rules in allocating expenses to gross income effectively connected with U.S. business.

The regulations are based on "the factual relationship of deductions to gross income."[7] Generally, their application is a two step process. Deductions are first allocated to income from the activities and investments in which the deductible costs were incurred.[8] If the income class to which a deduction is allocated consists solely of income within or outside the relevant taxable income category (usually, foreign source taxable income or taxable income effectively connected with U.S. business), which is called the "statutory grouping," the allocation is the final step in the process. In other cases, the deduction is apportioned between the portion of the income class that is included in the statutory grouping and the portion falling outside the category (the residual grouping).[9] The apportionment must be done on a basis that reasonably reflects the factual relationships between deductions and income.[10]

Special rules are provided for several types of deductions, including expenses incurred by shareholders,[11] income taxes,[12] losses on dispositions of capital and quasi-capital assets,[13] net operating losses,[14] deductions not related to income

---

[6] See generally Fuller & Granwell, The Allocation and Apportionment of Deductions, 31 Tax Lawyer 125 (1977).

[7] Reg. §1.861-8(a)(2).

[8] See infra text accompanying notes 19–24.

[9] See infra text accompanying notes 25–27.

[10] See infra text accompanying note 28.

[11] See infra text accompanying notes 29–30.

[12] See infra text accompanying notes 31–34.

[13] See infra text accompanying notes 35–50.

[14] See infra text accompanying note 51.

producing activities and investments,[15] the personal and dependency exemptions,[16] interest expense,[17] and research costs.[18]

1. *Allocations to gross income classes.* When none of these special rules applies, a deduction is allocated to the class of income to which it is "definitely related."[19] Income is grouped into classes on the basis of the factual relationships between gross income and deductions, not on the basis of predetermined categories. A deduction is definitely related to a class of gross income if "it is incurred as a result of, or incident to, an activity or in connection with property from which such class of gross income is derived."[20] A deduction may be definitely related to all of the taxpayer's gross income.[21]

Assume a taxpayer manufactures goods in a foreign country and sells them through a sales branch in the United States. Gross income on sales of the goods is split between U.S. and foreign sources.[22] Expenses of the sales branch are definitely related to the U.S. portion of gross income because they are incurred in the activity in which this gross income is earned. Expenses of manufacturing activities are definitely related to the foreign source income from the goods' manufacture in a foreign country. Expenses of general management, in contrast, are definitely related to manufacturing and selling, and they are therefore allocated to a class that includes both the U.S. and foreign portions of the gross income.

If an activity or an item of property is expected to generate income of a particular class, expenses of the activity or property are allocated to that class whether or not the activity or property yields gross income for the taxable year and if there is gross income, whether the deductions definitely related to it are greater or less than the gross income.[23] For example, a shareholder's expenses are allocated to the class of gross income consisting of dividends on the stock, even if no dividends are received during the taxable year or the expenses exceed the dividends. In some cases, it may be easiest to identify the gross income that is not definitely related to particular deductions and allocate the deductions to the class consisting of all other gross income.[24]

2. *Statutory and residual groupings.* Gross income is also divided between "statutory groupings" and "residual groupings." A statutory grouping consists of gross income that when reduced by deductions, becomes relevant under par-

---

[15] See infra text accompanying note 52.
[16] See infra text accompanying notes 53–55.
[17] Infra ¶¶70.10.2, 70.10.3, 70.10.4.
[18] Infra ¶70.10.5.
[19] Reg. §1.861-8(b)(1).
[20] Reg. §1.861-8(b)(2).
[21] Reg. §1.861-8(b)(5).
[22] IRC §863(b)(2), discussed supra ¶70.6.3 text accompanying notes 13–35.
[23] Reg. §1.861-8(d)(1).
[24] Reg. §1.861-8(b)(2).

ticular operative provisions.[25] The residual grouping consists of all gross income not included in the statutory grouping. For example, for a taxpayer claiming the foreign tax credit, gross income from foreign sources is a statutory grouping because taxable income from foreign sources is the foundation of the §904 limitation. If the taxpayer has gross income in two or more of the separate limitation categories of §904(d) (the §904(d) baskets), each basket is a statutory grouping, and in determining taxable income within the basket, the residual grouping consists of all gross income outside the basket, including foreign source income in other baskets.[26] For a nonresident alien or foreign corporation carrying on a trade or business in the United States, the statutory grouping is gross income effectively connected with the U.S. business because that gross income, reduced by deductions, is the base on which the effectively connected income tax is imposed.

If a deduction is definitely related to a class of gross income that is wholly within the statutory grouping, it is allowed in full in determining the statutory taxable income amount. Conversely, if the class is wholly within the residual grouping, none of it is allowed. Assume domestic corporation D manufactures goods in the United States and sells them through a branch in a foreign country. Gross income on the sales is split between U.S. source manufacturing income and foreign source selling income. Expenses of the sales branch are definitely related to the foreign source gross income, and they are therefore deducted in determining taxable income from foreign sources. Expenses of manufacturing operations are definitely related to the U.S. gross income from manufacturing, which is included in the residual grouping, and these expenses thus are excluded from the computation of foreign source taxable income.[27]

3. *Apportionments.* If a deduction is definitely related to a class of gross income that includes gross income of both a statutory grouping and the residual grouping, an apportionment is required. Assume D incurs general management expenses in connection with the manufacture and sale of its goods, some of which are sold domestically and some are exported in transactions generating foreign source income. If these expenses relate to both manufacturing and selling, they are definitely related to a class of gross income that includes both U.S. and foreign source income, and because the income falls partly in the statutory grouping and partly in the residual grouping, the expenses must be apportioned.

An apportionment must be done in a way that "reflects to a reasonably close extent the factual relationship between the deduction and the grouping of gross

---

[25] Reg. §1.861-8(a)(4).

[26] Reg. §1.861-8T(c)(1). For §904(d), see supra ¶69.6.

[27] This is strictly true only if D has an independent factory price for the goods. If it does not and if it determines the U.S.-source portion of the gross income by a sales-property apportionment method, deductions are allocated to all gross income from these sales and are apportioned between the U.S. and foreign portions ratably according to the amounts of the gross income assigned to U.S. and foreign sources. Reg. §1.863-3(d), discussed supra ¶70.6.3 text accompanying note 35.

income."[28] Depending on the facts of the particular case, an acceptable apportionment may consist of a proration according to the number of units sold, gross receipts, cost of goods sold, gross income, assets used, space utilized, or time spent. Record-keeping burdens are taken into account in determining whether a particular apportionment is sufficiently precise.

4. *Shareholder expenses.* Expenses incurred by a shareholder in looking after an investment in stock are allocated to the class of gross income consisting of dividends received or to be received from the corporation. This rule applies to expenses incurred by a corporation in overseeing its investments in other corporations.[29] However, activities "undertaken for the corporation's own benefit as an investor in the related corporation" must be distinguished from services performed by the shareholder corporation for the related corporation. Costs incurred in performing services for a related corporation are allocated to the gross income from the services, and if no charge is made for the services, income is imputed to the services performer under §482.[30]

Generally, the distinction between an overseeing activity and a service for a related corporation is that the former duplicates activities of the related corporation, while the latter does not. Assume a subsidiary corporation develops a business plan, accompanied with financial analyses and projections made by its own staff, and submits the plan to its parent corporation for review. If the parent's review merely repeats steps taken by the subsidiary, the costs of the review are overseeing expenses.

5. *Income taxes.* A deduction for state, local, or foreign income taxes is allocated to the income on which the tax is imposed.[31] If the tax base includes income in two or more groupings, the tax is apportioned ratably. Because the U.S. states do not use the same source concepts as the federal government, the tax base for a state income tax can include income from foreign sources under the federal rules, and a state income tax thus may be subject to apportionment.[32] A state income tax is presumed to be imposed on foreign source income, at least in part, if state taxable income exceeds U.S. source taxable income, as computed for

---

[28] Reg. §1.861-8T(c)(1).

[29] Reg. §1.861-8(e)(4).

[30] For §482, see infra ¶79.1.

[31] Reg. §1.861-8(e)(6). See Chevron Corp. v. CIR, 104 TC 719 (1995) (finding Reg. §1.861-8(e)(6) valid and applying it to California Corporate Franchise Tax, which is imposed on a worldwide "unitary" basis); Rev. Rul. 87-64, 1987-2 CB 166 (state corporate franchise tax measured by income is allocated and apportioned in same way as state income tax; application of rules to foreign corporation explained); Rev. Rul. 87-65, 1987-2 CB 173 (same for domestic corporation); Bodner, Bryan & Kennedy, Tax Court Refines State Tax Apportionment and Allocation Issues for FTC Purposes, 83 J. Tax'n 280 (1995).

[32] Reg. §1.861-8(e)(6)(ii)(A) (deduction for state income taxes is allocated and apportioned "by reference to the taxable income that the law of the taxing jurisdiction attributes to the taxpayer ('state taxable income')").

federal income tax purposes.[33] Two elective safe harbor rules are provided for allocating and apportioning state income taxes.[34]

6. *Losses.* Generally, loss on a sale or exchange of a capital asset or property described in §1231(b) is allocated to the class of gross income that includes or included the income ordinarily produced by the property while the taxpayer held it.[35] For example, loss on a sale of stock is allocated to foreign source income under this rule if dividends on the stock were from foreign sources (generally, if the corporation is foreign). Gains on sales of such property usually have their source where the taxpayer resides.[36] For example, gain on a U.S. resident's sale of stock is U.S. source income, even if foreign source dividends were received on the stock.

The lack of symmetry in the gain and loss rules led Congress to suggest that the Treasury reconsider the loss rule.[37] Before the Treasury revised the regulations, the Tax Court seized upon the congressional suggestion to hold that loss on a domestic corporation's sale of stock of a foreign subsidiary should be allocated to income from sources in the United States, the country of the taxpayer's residence.[38] The regulations, adopted before 1986, were held inapplicable to noninventory property because they were promulgated under §861(b), which refers to deductions "from the items of gross income specified in subsection (a)," and, since 1986, the sources of income on sales of noninventory personal property have been determined under §865(a), not §861(a). Section 865(j)(1), which authorizes the Treasury to promulgate regulations "relating to the treatment of losses from sales of personal property . . . as may be necessary or appropriate to the purpose of this section," was construed as a directive to issue regulations allocating losses to the taxpayer's country of residence. The court pointed to a statement by the Staff of the Joint Committee on Taxation: "It is anticipated that regulations will provide that losses from sales of personal property generally will be allocated consistently with the source of income that gains would generate but

---

[33] Reg. §1.861-8(e)(6)(ii)(C).

[34] Reg. §1.861-8(e)(6)(ii)(D)(*1*). The safe harbor rules apply for taxable years ending after March 11, 1991. Reg. §1.861-8(e)(6)(iii).

[35] Reg. §1.861-8(e)(7)(i). See Black & Decker Corp. v. CIR, 986 F2d 60 (4th Cir. 1993) (loss on worthlessness of stock of foreign subsidiary was allocable solely to income from foreign sources because dividends from subsidiary would have been from foreign sources; not relevant that subsidiary actually paid no dividends); Trinova Corp. v. CIR, 73 TCM (CCH) 2118, 2124 (1997) (foreign exchange losses apportioned by general rules, not rules for losses on sales and exchanges of property, because "foreign currency, while qualifying as property, would not ordinarily produce a type of income itself, independent of the assets that were denominated in that currency").

[36] IRC §865(a), discussed supra ¶70.6.4.

[37] IRC §865(j)(1).

[38] Int'l Multifoods Corp. v. CIR, 108 TC No. 26 (1997). See Erdahl, The Domestic Source Rule for Foreign Affiliates Stock Losses—How Far Will it Extend? 87 J. Tax'n 236 (1997); Wood & Chestnut, International Multifoods Corp. v. Comr.—The Tax Court Does the Best It Can, 26 Tax Mgmt. Int'l J. 531 (1997).

that variations of this principle may be necessary."[39] According to the court: "When Congress directs that regulations be promulgated to carry out a statutory purpose, the fact that regulations are not forthcoming cannot be a basis for thwarting the legislative objective."

In 1996, the year before the Tax Court's decision, the Treasury proposed regulations taking more nuanced steps toward implementing the congressional suggestion.[40] Under the proposed regulations, the existing rules continue to apply to losses on dispositions of "portfolio stock," stock of mutual funds and S corporations, and personal property other than stock.[41] A taxpayer's shareholdings in a corporation are "portfolio stock" if the taxpayer owns less than 10 percent of all of the corporation's stock, both by value and by vote. For example, if a U.S. citizen recognizes loss on a sale of a portfolio holding of stock in a foreign corporation, all of whose dividends are foreign source income, loss on a sale of the stock is allocated to income from foreign sources, even though gain on a sale of the stock would have been from U.S. sources.

The proposed regulations generally allocate loss on a sale or exchange of other stock to the class of gross income that would have embraced gain on the disposition if it had resulted in gain.[42] This allocation applies both in allocating deductions by source and in dividing them among the separate baskets established for purposes of the foreign tax credit limitation. Since gains on sales and exchanges of stock are generally assigned to sources in the taxpayer's country of residence, this rule usually matches loss on a stock disposition with U.S. source

---

[39] Staff of Joint Comm. on Tax'n, 99th Cong., 2d Sess., General Explanation of the Tax Reform Act of 1986, at 923 (Comm. Print 1986).

[40] INTL-4-95, 1996-36 IRB 8. See generally Anson & McMahon, Generally Favorable 865(j) Prop. Regs. Should Be Extended, 7 J. Int'l Tax'n 499 (1996); Mogenson, Wood & Leiman, Section 865 Proposed Regulations Finally Bring Certainty to the Sourcing of Losses on Stock Sales, 25 Tax Mgmt. Int'l J. 741 (1996); Wilson & Womack, Proposed Section 865 Regs Offer Potentially Favorable Treatment on Losses on the Disposition of Foreign Stock, 13 Tax Notes Int'l 521 (Aug. 12, 1996), 72 Tax Notes 1421 (Sept. 9, 1996).

[41] Prop. Reg. §1.865-1. See INTL-4-95, supra note 40, at 8 ("The treatment of portfolio stock . . . will be reviewed in the context of a broader project dealing with similar portfolio investments").

[42] Prop. Reg. §1.865-2(a)(1). The classification of the hypothetical gain is determined without regard to §1248, which sometimes treats gain on a sale of stock as a dividend. See supra ¶68.2.16.

Prop. Reg. §1.865-2 will generally be effective 60 days after final regulations are published, but taxpayers will be allowed to elect to apply them to all post-1986 years that are not closed by the statute of limitations when final regulations are issued. Prop. Reg. §1.85-2(e).

The proposed regulations contain two rules of application that qualify all of Prop. Reg. §1.865-2. First, if loss is recognized by a partnership on a sale or exchange of stock, each partner's distributive share of the loss is allocated under the foregoing rules as though the sale or exchange had been made by the partner. Prop. Reg. §1.865-2(c)(1). If the partnership has an office or other fixed place of business, it is, for this purpose, treated as an office of the partner. Second, for purposes of the regulation, loss on the worthlessness of stock is treated as loss on a sale or exchange. Prop. Reg. §1.865-2(c)(2).

income if the taxpayer is a U.S. resident or with foreign source income if the taxpayer is a nonresident alien individual or foreign corporation.

The foregoing rule is qualified by two special rules: First, if a foreign person recognizes loss on a sale or exchange of stock that is a U.S. real property interest, the loss is allocated as a deduction against income from U.S. sources.[43] This parallels the rule assigning gain on a sale of U.S. real property interest to U.S. sources.[44] Under the second rule, which applies if the taxpayer is a U.S. resident, the loss is attributable to an office or other fixed place of business outside the United States, and the stock is not inventory, the loss is matched with foreign source income if gain on the sale or exchange would have been taxed by a foreign country and the highest marginal rate of the foreign tax is at least 10 percent.[45] This rule is the mirror image of §865(e)(1), under which noninventory gains allocable to a foreign office are assigned to foreign sources if the gain is subject to a foreign income tax at a rate of at least 10 percent. If U.S. resident's noninventory stock gain is attributable to a foreign office but is not taxed by a foreign country, it is usually allocated to U.S. source income under the rule described in the preceding paragraph.

The foregoing rules are subject to two exceptions: First, to the extent of dividends distributed on the stock during the preceding 24 months, the loss is allocated to the class of gross income containing the dividends if the dividends received during these 24 months, in the aggregate, are at least 10 percent of the loss.[46] Assume domestic corporation *P* receives a dividend of $100 during year 1 from its wholly owned foreign subsidiary *FS*; the dividend is subject to a foreign withholding tax of $5, and by reason of its receipt of the dividend, *P* is deemed to have paid $45 of *FS*'s foreign income taxes; during year 2, *P* sells its *FS* stock at a loss of $110.[47] Because the dividend was received within 24 months before the sale and exceeds 10 percent of the loss, the loss must, to the extent of the dividend, be allocated to income of the same class as the dividend. For example, if the dividend was from foreign sources and was within the passive basket for purposes of the foreign tax credit limitation, $100 of the loss is allocated to foreign-source passive income for year 2.

---

[43] Prop. Reg. §1.865-2(a)(3). For stock as U.S. real property interests, see supra ¶66.4.3.

[44] IRC §865(a).

[45] Prop. Reg. §1.865-2(a)(2).

[46] Prop. Reg. §1.865-2(b)(1),(d)(2),(d)(5). For this purpose, earnings and profits of a controlled foreign corporation (CFC) are treated as having been distributed as dividends to the extent they have been included in shareholder gross income under the rules for U.S. investments of CFC earnings and excess passive assets. Prop. Reg. §1.865-2(d)(2). Also, dividends received by a CFC or passive foreign investment company (PFIC) are treated as having been distributed to shareholders to the extent they have been included in shareholder gross income and, in the shareholders' hands, included in a limitation basket other than the passive basket or the general limitation basket.

[47] Prop. Reg. §1.865-2(b)(4) Ex.

Second, loss recognized by a domestic corporation on a sale or exchange of stock of a foreign affiliate (or former foreign affiliate) is allocated to foreign sources if, during the five-year period ending with the close of the taxable year, (1) the taxpayer or another member of its consolidated group recognized gain on a disposition of stock of this or any other foreign affiliate and (2) this gain was assigned to foreign sources by §865(f).[48] A foreign affiliate is a foreign corporation within the same affiliated group as the taxpayer.[49] This rule applies only to the extent the loss is not covered by the dividend recapture rule described in the preceding paragraph. For example, if, during the five-year period ending with year 2, P recognized §865(f) gain on a sale of stock of another foreign subsidiary, the last $10 of the loss on the sale of FS stock is allocated to foreign source income under this rule.

The proposed regulations contain two antiabuse rules. First, the allocation of a loss on a sale or exchange of stock is determined as though the sale or exchange occurred before a reorganization, liquidation, tax-free transfer to a corporation, partnership, or trust, distribution from a partnership or trust, or transfer to or from a qualified business unit if a principal purpose of the reorganization, liquidation, transfer, or distribution was to alter the allocation of the loss.[50] Second, if loss on a sale or exchange of stock is "primarily attributable" to one or more financial instruments held by the corporation, the loss is allocated as though it were recognized on a sale or exchange of the financial instruments if affecting the allocation of the loss is a principal purpose for holding the instruments through the corporation. Factors relevant to the issue of primary purpose include whether the corporation carries on business activities and whether the taxpayer or a related person holds positions that offset the loss on the stock sale. Manipulation of the loss allocation may be a principal purpose, even if it is not the sole purpose and even if it "is outweighed by other purposes (taken together or separately)."

7. *Net operating losses.* A deduction for a net operating loss carried to the taxable year is allocated in the same way as the deductions that created the net operating loss in the loss year.[51] Assume a domestic corporation sustains a net operating loss of $100, consisting of foreign source taxable income of $50 and domestic source loss of $150. Because the net operating loss is entirely attributable to deductions allocated and apportioned in the loss year to domestic income,

---

[48] Prop. Reg. §1.865-2(b)(2)(i). This rule applies only if the gain was recognized after September 6, 1996. Prop. Reg. §1.865-2(b)(2)(ii).

[49] The consolidated return definition of affiliated group (chain of corporations connected to a common parent by 80 percent stock ownership at each link in the chain) is used for this purpose, except that foreign corporations are not excluded. IRC §§864(i)(4), 1504. A former foreign affiliate is a foreign corporation that was an affiliate during the five years preceding the sale or exchange. Prop. Reg. §1.865-2(b)(2)(i).

[50] Prop. Reg. §1.865-2(b)(3).

[51] Reg. §1.861-8(e)(8).

the deduction for the carryback or carryover of the loss is allocated exclusively to income from U.S. sources.

8. *Deductions not definitely related to any gross income.* Deductions unrelated to the taxpayer's business and investment activities are apportioned ratably among all gross income.[52] This rule applies to deductions for real estate taxes on a personal residence, medical expenses, charitable gifts, and alimony.

9. *Personal and dependency exemptions.* The deduction allocation and apportionment rules do not apply to the personal and dependency exemptions.[53] For purposes of the foreign tax credit limitation under §904, these exemptions are ignored in determining both foreign source taxable income and entire taxable income.[54] In computing effectively connected taxable income of a nonresident alien, the personal exemption and any dependency exemptions available to the taxpayer are allowed in full.[55]

¶70.10.2 Interest Expense—U.S. Persons

Because "money is fungible," the regulations usually attribute interest expense to all of the taxpayer's activities and property, "regardless of any specific purpose for incurring an obligation."[56] "The fungibility approach recognizes that all activities and property require funds and that management has a great deal of flexibility as to the source and use of funds." Because a borrowing for one purpose generally frees other funds for other purposes, the borrowing costs relate to both the purpose that triggered the decision to borrow and to other purposes.

Because interest expense is related to all of the taxpayer's activities and assets, the interest deduction is usually apportioned among all gross income in proportion to the values of the assets used by the taxpayer in generating the income.[57] For example, if one third of a domestic corporation's assets are used in activities and investments that produce foreign source income, one third of its interest expense is deductible in determining taxable income from foreign sources. Generally, the asset apportionment can be based on either the adjusted basis or the fair market value of the taxpayer's assets.

A few exceptions are made. Interest on nonrecourse debt financing rental property is usually allocated exclusively to income from the property.[58] For

---

[52] Reg. §§1.861-8(c)(3),(e)(9).

[53] Reg. §1.861-8(e)(11).

[54] IRC §904(b)(1).

[55] IRC §873(b)(3). However, unless the taxpayer is a resident of Canada or Mexico, no more than one exemption is allowed.

[56] Reg. §1.861-9T(a). See generally Andrus, Allocating Interest Expense for the Foreign Tax Credit, 41 Tax Notes 1105 (Dec. 5, 1988); New York State Bar Ass'n Tax Section, Comments on Proposed Regulations Allocating Interest and Expenses for Foreign Tax Credit, 38 Tax Notes 837 (Feb. 22, 1988).

[57] See infra text accompanying notes 76–88.

[58] See infra text accompanying notes 89–93.

foreign corporations doing business in the United States, the asset apportionment scheme is modified in a way that usually allows the interest expense of the U.S. business to be determined without valuing foreign assets.[59] Generally, for a U.S. citizen or resident, business interest expense is apportioned with reference to business assets only, the apportionment of investment interest expense depends on investment assets only, and the deduction for home mortgage interest is prorated among all gross income.[60] Nonresident aliens, who are allowed deductions only in determining taxable income effectively connected with a U.S. trade or business, may deduct interest expense only if the underlying liability is carried on the books of a U.S. business and is secured by assets of the business.[61]

An affiliated group of corporations must allocate and apportion the interest expense of all of its members as though the group were one corporation.[62] Since an affiliated group can include only domestic corporations,[63] this rule applies only for purposes of the foreign tax credit limitation.[64]

1. *Deductions subject to interest rules.* The interest rules apply to interest expense for the year it is deductible.[65] They never apply to interest expense that is nondeductible because, for example, it is matched with tax-exempt interest income under §265 or is personal interest made nondeductible by §163(h).[66] Neither do they apply to interest required to be capitalized as part of the basis of property constructed or produced by the taxpayer.[67] If interest is capitalized into the basis of depreciable property, for example, it is ultimately deducted as depreciation, not as interest. When the deduction for interest is suspended by §163(d), §465, or §469, the apportionment rules apply when the interest ultimately becomes deductible.[68]

Various "interest equivalents" are treated as interest expense for this purpose. More specifically, any deductible expense or loss is treated as interest if it

---

[59] See infra ¶70.10.3.

[60] See infra text accompanying notes 100–06.

[61] See infra ¶70.10.4.

[62] IRC §864(e)(1); Reg. §§1.861-11T, -14T. The term "affiliated group" has the same meaning as under the consolidated return regulations, except that corporations electing under §936 (possessions corporations) are included. Reg. §1.861-14T(d).

[63] IRC §§864(e)(5)(A), 1504.

[64] Reg. §§1.861-11T(b)(1), 1.861-14T(b)(1). See Reg. §§1.861-11T(b)(2), 1.861-14T(b)(2) (rule does not apply in computing subpart F income of controlled foreign corporations or in determining effectively connected taxable income of foreign corporations).

[65] Reg. §1.861-9T(c).

[66] Reg. §1.861-9T(c)(1). See supra ¶31.3 for §265 and ¶31.5 for §163(h).

[67] Reg. §1.861-9T(c)(2). For the capitalization of interest see infra ¶105.10.

[68] Reg. §§1.861-9T(c)(3), (4). For §163(d), which allows investment interest expense to be deducted only to the extent of investment income but permits disallowed amounts to be carried forward indefinitely, see supra ¶31.6. For §465, which limits loss deductions from property financed with nonrecourse debt, see supra ¶25.10. For §469, which disallows deductions for passive activity losses but carries the disallowed amounts forward indefinitely, see supra ¶28.1.

(1) is "incurred in a transaction or series of integrated or related transactions in which the taxpayer secures the use of funds for a period of time" and (2) is "substantially incurred in consideration of the time value of money."[69] Assume a domestic corporation, whose functional currency is the U.S. dollar,[70] borrows 100 British pounds, converts the pounds into dollars, and enters into a currency swap under which it will receive (in exchange for dollars) pounds equal to the interest and principal payments under the loan.[71] The borrowing and currency swap are a series of related transactions by which the corporation effectively borrows U.S. dollars. Any currency loss on the swap is thus incurred in consideration of the time value of money and is allocated and apportioned as interest expense.

If the taxpayer borrows in a nonfunctional currency at an interest rate below the applicable federal rate (AFR),[72] a swap, forward, future, option, or other financial arrangement is presumed to be part of an integrated series of transactions with the borrowing if it "substantially diminishes currency risk with respect to the borrowing or interest expense thereon."[73] More broadly, if a "derivative financial product . . . potentially alter[s] a taxpayer's effective cost of borrowing with respect to an actual liability," loss from the product is treated as additional interest expense, and net income from the product is treated as an offset against interest expense.[74] The latter rule can apply to interest rate swaps, options, forwards, caps, and collars. Also, if loss is incurred on a sale of an account receivable, the loss is usually treated as interest expense unless the receivable bears interest at a rate equal to or exceeding 120 percent of the AFR for short-term obligations in effect when the receivable came into being.[75]

2. *Asset method.* Generally, interest expense is apportioned according to "the average total value of [the] assets" producing income within the statutory

---

[69] Reg. §1.861-9T(b)(1)(i).

[70] The term "functional currency" generally refers to the currency in which the taxpayer carries on business and maintains its books. See infra ¶71.2.

[71] Reg. §1.861-9T(b)(1)(ii) Ex. 2.

[72] For the AFR, which generally equals the interest rate on obligations of the U.S. government with similar maturities, see supra ¶57.2.

[73] Reg. §1.861-9T(b)(2)(i). This rule applies whether the swap, forward, future, option, or other financial arrangement is entered into by the borrowing taxpayer or by a related person.

[74] Reg. §1.861-9T(b)(6)(i). These rules do not apply to "financial services entities," but rules for derivatives transactions of these entities have not yet been provided.

These regulations predate the regulations on notional principal contracts and hedging and have yet to be coordinated with the latter regulations. For notional principal contracts and hedging, see supra ¶¶45.7, 45.8.

[75] Reg. §1.861-9T(b)(3)(iii). The loss is not treated as interest to the extent that the selling price of the receivable is less than the receivable's present value, determined with a discount rate equal to the AFR. Any amount not treated as interest is allocated to "the gross income generated by the receivable."

and residual groupings, respectively.[76] Assume a domestic corporation has interest expense of $150 for a taxable year, and the average total value of its assets for the year is $3,600, including $600 for assets used in activities producing gross income from foreign sources.[77] The interest expense deductible in determining foreign source taxable income (the statutory grouping for purposes of the foreign tax credit limitation) is:

$$(\$150)(\$600/\$3,600) = \$25$$

The remaining $125 is assigned to the residual grouping. The same principle governs if there is more than one statutory grouping, as where the taxpayer has income within two or more of the limitation baskets prescribed by §904(d). Its application to a more complex case is illustrated by Example 70-1, where it is assumed that a domestic corporation with interest expense of $1,500 for a particular year has assets producing domestic source income and foreign source income falling within the general limitation, passive, and shipping baskets under §904(d).

Example 70-1
Allocation of Interest Expense by Asset Method
for Taxpayer With Several Statutory Groupings

Income class	Average asset value	Computation	Interest expense
Domestic	$ 9,000	($1,500)($9,000 ÷ $20,000)	$ 675
Foreign general limitation	6,000	($1,500)($6,000 ÷ $20,000)	450
Foreign passive	4,000	($1,500)($4,000 ÷ $20,000)	300
Foreign shipping	1,000	($1,500)($1,000 ÷ $20,000)	75
Total	$20,000		$1,500

Assets are placed in a statutory grouping if "they generate, have generated, or may reasonably be expected to generate" income within that grouping, and assets not matched with a statutory grouping are placed in the residual grouping.[78] The physical location of the assets is not relevant. For example, inventory

---

[76] Reg. §1.861-9T(g)(1)(i).

[77] Reg. §1.861-9T(g)(1)(v) Ex. 1.

[78] Reg. §1.861-9T(g)(3). If the taxpayer uses fair market values in apportioning interest expense, stock in related corporations is categorized by treating the taxpayer as owner of a ratable portion of each asset held by the related corporation. Reg. §1.861-

is classified according to the sources and character of the income on sales out of the inventory during the taxable year.[79] Generally, assets are divided among three categories: (1) assets producing income exclusively within one statutory grouping or the residual grouping; (2) assets producing income within two or more groupings; and (3) "assets that produce no directly identifiable income yield or that contribute equally to the generation of all income of the taxpayer (such as assets used in general and administrative functions)." An asset in the second category is prorated according to the gross income in the various groupings generated by the asset during the taxable year. For example, if one third of the income produced by an asset during the taxable year is in the statutory grouping and two thirds of the asset's income is in the residual grouping, the asset is split between the two groupings in the same proportions. An asset in the third category (no identifiable income) is disregarded.

The value figure for each asset may be its "tax book value" or its fair market value.[80] Tax book value generally is the asset's adjusted basis, but if the taxpayer owns 10 percent or more of the stock of a corporation not included in the taxpayer's affiliated group, the stock's tax book value is its adjusted basis increased or decreased by the taxpayer's share of the corporation's earnings and profits or deficit.[81]

Fair market values are determined as follows: If the taxpayer is a corporation whose stock is publicly traded, the aggregate value of its assets is the sum of the value of all outstanding stock and the corporation's liabilities.[82] In other cases, aggregate asset value is determined by capitalizing the taxpayer's earnings. Tangible assets are valued by "generally accepted valuation techniques."[83] The aggregate value of the taxpayer's intangible assets is the value of all assets, reduced by the sum of the values of the tangible assets.[84] The aggregate intangible value is apportioned among particular intangibles in proportion to net income.[85]

9T(h)(5). See Trinova Corp. v. CIR, 73 TCM (CCH) 2118 (1997) (asset value apportioned between statutory and residual grouping if asset produces gross income in both groupings).

[79] Reg. §1.861-12T(b).

[80] Reg. §1.861-9T(g)(1)(ii). Once a taxpayer elects to use fair market value for this purpose, the taxpayer and all related persons must use fair market value until the IRS "expressly authorize[s]" a change. Reg. §1.861-8T(c)(2).

[81] IRC §864(e)(4); Reg. §1.861-12T(c).

[82] Reg. §1.861-9T(h)(1)(i). Liabilities to related persons are excluded, but a ratable share of the liabilities of related persons to unrelated persons is included.

[83] Reg. §1.861-9T(h)(1)(ii).

[84] Reg. §1.861-9T(h)(1)(iii). Generally, the fair market value of stock in a related person is the taxpayer's pro rata share of the value of the related person's assets, determined under the rules described in the text. Reg. §1.861-9T(h)(5).

[85] Reg. §1.861-9T(h)(2). Net income is determined before interest expense and income taxes and does not include dividends or interest from related persons or other passive income.

If a taxpayer elects to use fair market value but fails to establish the fair market value of all of its assets, the IRS may either "determine the appropriate asset value" or require that tax book value be used.[86]

Normally, the asset figures for a taxable year are averages of asset values at the beginning and end of the year.[87] Assume a taxpayer's assets are valued at $2,000 at the end of year 1 and $2,200 at the end of year 2, of which amounts $400 and $600 represent assets within the statutory grouping. For year 2, average asset value in the statutory grouping is $500 ($400 plus $600 divided by two), and the overall average is $2,100 ($2,000 plus $2,200 divided by two).

If substantial distortion results from averaging year-end figures, the averages must be computed by a method "that more clearly reflects the average value of assets weighted to reflect the time such assets are held by the taxpayer during the taxable year."[88] Such a distortion often results if the taxpayer acquires or disposes of a large amount of assets during the year. Assume a domestic corporation owns foreign assets of $500 at the beginning of a taxable year and maintains roughly this level of foreign investment throughout the year, but it sells all foreign assets in a transaction closed during the last week of the year. The level of foreign investment throughout the year is seriously understated by an average of the values as of the beginning and end of the year (the sum of $500 and zero divided by two). A more realistic average might be determined by, for example, averaging asset values at the beginning and end of each month and averaging the 12 monthly averages.

3. *Direct allocations.* In three situations described below, interest expense is allocated exclusively to income from the property financed with the underlying indebtedness. Also, amortizations of bond premium are allocated exclusively to interest on the bond.

a. *Nonrecourse debt.* Interest is allocated exclusively to income from the property secured by the debt (or, in the absence of such income, to income that the property "could reasonably be expected to generate") if all of the following requirements are met:[89]

(1) The debt must have been incurred to purchase, construct, or improve

---

[86] Reg. §1.861-9T(g)(1)(iii).

[87] Reg. §1.861-9T(g)(2)(i). If interest is allocated to an asset under one of the direct allocation rules described below (infra text accompanying notes 89–99), the asset's value, to the extent of the directly allocated liability, is removed from the averaged sums. Reg. §1.861-9T(g)(2)(iii). For special rules for domestic corporations that have qualified business units using functional currencies other than the U.S. dollar, see Reg. §1.861-9T(g)(2)(ii). For the term "functional currency," see infra ¶71.2.

[88] Reg. §1.861-9T(g)(2)(i).

[89] Reg. §§1.861-10T(b)(1),(2); Notice 89-91, 1989-2 CB 408. If all of the requirements are satisfied when the indebtedness is incurred, they are deemed satisfied as well by a subsequent owner of the property who assumes the indebtedness unless details of the transaction relevant to the requirements have been changed. Reg. §1.861-10T(b)(11).

real property or depreciable personal property (including amortizable intangibles) with a useful life exceeding one year.[90]

(2) The debt proceeds must actually have been used for this purpose.

(3) The debt must be secured exclusively by the acquired, constructed, or improved property, and the taxpayer must have no personal liability on it.

(4) The expected cash flow from the property must be sufficient to cover debt service.

(5) The loan agreement must contain restrictions adequate to protect the creditor's security interest and expectation to be paid from the property's cash flow.

For purposes of requirements (4) and (5), "cash flow"—generally defined as the excess of cash receipts over all cash disbursements other than debt service—does not include revenues from sales of goods or services (except services "ancillary and subsidiary to the use of property").[91] The rule for nonrecourse financing thus is largely restricted to rental property, to the exclusion of property used by the taxpayer in a manufacturing, retailing, or services business. Also, the rule is inapplicable if the debt is (1) lacking in economic significance, (2) not truly nonrecourse because of cross collateralization, letters of credit, or other arrangements giving the debtor more than a mere security interest in the property, (3) incurred in a purchase of inventory, corporate stock, debt obligations, or a partnership interest, or (4) qualified residence interest.[92] Moreover, the rule cannot apply to indebtedness between related persons or to indebtedness to an unrelated person that was incurred to purchase property from a related person or property that is leased to a related person.[93]

　　b. *Integrated financial transactions.* If a taxpayer borrows as part of an "integrated financial transaction," interest on the borrowing is allocated exclusively to income from the transaction.[94] An integrated financial transaction consists of "an identified term investment" and a borrowing to finance the investment. An identified term investment might consist, for example, of a purchase of a portfolio of stocks approximating the composition of a stock index coupled

---

[90] If an indebtedness meets this requirement, a refinancing of the indebtedness (e.g., a substitution of permanent financing for construction financing) may also satisfy the requirement. Reg. §§1.861-10T(b)(9),(10).

[91] Reg. §§1.861-10T(b)(3)(i),(iii). If the property is constructed by the taxpayer, construction activities are not "services" for this purpose unless the property is constructed for resale or is actually sold within one year after it is placed in service. Reg. §1.861-10T(b)(3)(ii).

[92] Reg. §§1.861-10T(b)(4)-(8). For qualified residence interest, see supra ¶31.5 text accompanying notes 14-32.

[93] Reg. §1.861-10T(d)(1).

[94] Reg. §1.861-10T(c)(1).

with a forward contract to sell a specified quantity of the stocks in the index at a designated future date for a specified price.[95]

An integrated financial transaction must meet all of the following requirements:

(1) The indebtedness must be incurred to make an identified term investment.

(2) The debt must be so identified at the time of the borrowing.

(3) The term investment must be acquired within 10 business days after the borrowing.

(4) The reasonably expected return on the term investment must be sufficient to cover debt service.

(5) The income produced by the term investment must be interest or an interest equivalent.

(6) The maturity dates of the debt and term investment may not be separated by more than 10 days.

(7) The investment may not relate to the normal operation of the taxpayer's trade or business.[96]

For example, if a credit card company borrows to finance its purchase of credit card receivables of merchants, the last of these requirements excludes the borrowing from the application of this rule even if all other requirements are met.

c. *U.S. shareholders of controlled foreign corporations.* If a U.S. shareholder lends money to controlled foreign corporations (CFCs) that it controls, it may be required to allocate portions of its interest expense exclusively to interest received from the CFCs.[97] This rule is seemingly intended to limit the ability of a U.S. parent corporation to boost its foreign tax credit limitation by borrowing funds from unrelated persons and reloaning the funds to its CFCs, rather than having the CFCs borrow directly. Interest received from the CFCs would usually be entirely from foreign sources, but in the absence of this rule, the parent's interest payments would be allocated among all of its assets, including those producing U.S. source income. Consistently with this purpose, the rule requires the parent to allocate interest expense exclusively to interest received from CFCs only if (and to the extent that) the CFCs' debt to the parent, as a percentage of the value of the CFCs' stock, is greater than the average of such percentages for the preceding five years.

---

[95] Reg. §1.861-10T(c)(4) Ex. 1. A taxpayer might borrow to finance such an investment in order to exploit a difference between the interest rate on the borrowing and the interest rate implicit in the difference between the current and forward prices for the stocks.

[96] Reg. §1.861-10T(c)(2).

[97] Reg. §1.861-10(e). For the terms "U.S. shareholder" and "controlled foreign corporation," see supra ¶68.2.2.

d. *Bond premium.* When a debt instrument is issued at a premium, the premium is amortized over the instrument's life, and the amount recognized for any taxable year is gross income for the issuer and a deduction for the holder.[98] To the extent of the premium for any year, the issuer's deduction for interest on the instrument is allocated to premium income, and the holder's deduction for premium is allocated to interest income on the instrument.[99]

4. *U.S. citizens, resident aliens, and nonforeign trusts and estates.* Interest expense of a U.S. citizen, resident alien, or domestic trust or estate (U.S. individual) is separated into as many as four categories.[100]

a. Interest incurred in a trade or business is apportioned by the asset method, but only business assets are included in the apportionment.[101]

b. Investment interest is apportioned with reference solely to the taxpayer's investment assets.[102]

c. Interest incurred in a passive activity is apportioned on the basis of the assets of the individual's passive activities.[103]

d. Qualified residence interest is prorated among all gross income, including business, investment, and passive activity income but not amounts excluded by §911.[104]

For example, if a U.S. individual's only foreign source income is from investment assets, no interest on business borrowings is deductible in determining foreign source taxable income, but this income is reduced by portions of both investment interest (determined by the ratio of foreign investment assets to all investment) and qualified residence interest (determined by the ratio of foreign source gross income to all gross income).[105]

---

[98] See supra ¶59.7.

[99] Reg. §1.861-9T(b)(5).

[100] Reg. §1.861-9T(d)(1) (applicable for taxable years beginning after 1986).

[101] Reg. §1.861-9T(d)(1)(i).

[102] Reg. §1.861-9T(d)(1)(ii). For the term "investment interest," see §163(d)(3), discussed supra ¶31.6 text accompanying notes 9–13.

[103] Reg. §1.861-9T(d)(1)(iii). For passive activities, see supra ¶28.1.

[104] Reg. §1.861-9T(d)(1)(iv). Qualified residence interest includes most interest on mortgages on the taxpayer's primary or secondary residence. See supra ¶31.5 text accompanying notes 15–32. For §911, which allows a U.S. citizen residing abroad to exclude from gross income up to $70,000 of earned income from foreign sources, see supra ¶65.5.

Interest for any period that the residence is rented out is subject to the rule for business or passive activity interest, not the rule for qualified residence interest. Reg. §1.861-9T(d)(1)(iv).

[105] Reg. §1.861-9T(d)(1)(v) Ex.

If a U.S. individual has less than $5,000 of gross income from foreign sources, the complexities of the foregoing rules can be avoided by allocating all interest expense to U.S. source income.[106]

5. *Partnerships.* If a partnership has interest expense allocable exclusively to the income from particular property under one of the direct allocation rules described above,[107] each partner's distributive share of the expense is allocable to the partner's share of partnership income from the property.[108] The allocation of other interest expense of a partnership depends on the status of the partner, as follows:

a. If the partner is a corporation and has an interest in the partnership of 10 percent or more,[109] the partner's distributive share of the expense is allocated under the asset method "by reference to the partner's assets, including the partner's pro rata share of partnership assets."[110]

b. If a noncorporate partner is a general partner or is a limited partner with a partnership interest of 10 percent or more and is also a U.S. person,[111] the partner's distributive share of the interest expense is classified as active business interest, passive activity interest, or investment interest, and the interest is allocated by the rule described above for interest of that type,[112] treating the partner's assets of any type as including a ratable share of the partnership assets of that type.[113] For example, if the interest is incurred in an activity that is a passive activity for the partner, it is allocated in proportion to the partner's passive activity assets, including a ratable share of the assets of the partnership activity.

c. If the partner is a corporation or a noncorporate limited partner and has less than a 10 percent interest in the partnership, the partner's distribu-

---

[106] Reg. §1.861-9T(d)(1). Amounts excluded from gross income by §911 count against the $5,000 ceiling.

[107] See supra text accompanying notes 89–99.

[108] Reg. §1.861-9T(e)(1).

[109] The percentage interests in the partnership are the ratios by which partnership income for the taxable year is shared. Reg. §1.861-9T(e)(1). Both direct and indirect interests are taken into account.

[110] Reg. §1.861-9T(e)(2). If the corporation applies the asset method by book values, the book values of partnership assets are used. Otherwise, the apportionment is based on the fair market values of partnership assets.

For the application of this rule to a foreign corporation holding a partnership interest, see Reg. §1.861-9T(e)(7)(i).

[111] If the partner is a nonresident alien, the partner's distributive share of interest expense is allocated between effectively connected income and other income by reference to the relative values of the partnership's assets generating income of these kinds. Reg. §1.861-9T(e)(7)(ii). No interest expense incurred directly by a nonresident alien partner may be allocated to the partner's share of effectively connected income of the partnership.

[112] See supra text accompanying notes 100–05.

[113] Reg. §1.861-9T(e)(3).

tive share of partnership interest expense is allocated to the partner's distributive share of partnership income.[114] In applying the asset method to other interest expense of the partner, the partner's interest in the partnership is included among the partner's assets, but no portion of the partnership's assets is included.[115]

6. *Controlled foreign corporations.* Generally, interest expense of a controlled foreign corporation (CFC) may be apportioned by either the asset method or a modified gross income method.[116] Under the modified gross income method, a CFC's interest expense is apportioned ratably according to gross income if the CFC does not own stock of a lower-tier CFC.[117] For a multi-tier CFC structure, the interest expense of the lowest-tier CFC is apportioned by gross income, and the interest expense of each higher-tier CFC is apportioned by a modified gross income amount, consisting of (1) the corporation's gross income (exclusive of dividends from CFCs that are not subject to the look-through rule of §904(d)(3)) and (2) its ratable share of the gross income of all lower-tier CFCs (exclusive of subpart F income and net of interest expense).[118]

Generally, the modified gross income method may be elected by either the CFC or its controlling U.S. shareholders.[119] The election, even if made by the CFC, binds all U.S. shareholders. However, if the CFC is controlled by one U.S. shareholder and its affiliates, the method may not be elected unless the affiliated group applies the asset method by reference to tax book value, rather than fair market value.[120] Also, the election must either be made or not made by or for all CFCs in which a particular U.S. person is a U.S. shareholder, and if a CFC is required to make the election under this rule, the election applies to all of its U.S. shareholders.[121]

¶70.10.3 Interest Expense—Foreign Corporations Engaged in Business in the United States

If a foreign corporation carries on a trade or business in the United States, the interest deduction allowed in computing taxable income effectively connected with the business is generally computed by a three-step process based on the value of the corporation's U.S. assets, its worldwide debt to assets ratio, and the

---

[114] Reg. §1.861-9T(e)(4)(i).
[115] Reg. §1.861-9T(e)(4)(ii).
[116] Reg. §1.861-9T(f)(3)(i).
[117] Reg. §1.861-9T(j)(1).
[118] Reg. §1.861-9T(j)(2).
[119] Reg. §1.861-9T(f)(3)(ii).
[120] Reg. §1.861-9T(f)(3)(i).
[121] Reg. §1.861-9T(f)(3)(iii).

liabilities recorded on the books of the U.S. business.[122] If the corporation has U.S. assets denominated in more than one currency (e.g., is a bank whose U.S. branch makes loans in one or more foreign currencies as well as in U.S. dollars), this three-step procedure may be applied separately with respect to assets and liabilities in each of these currencies.[123] Also, interest on a few liabilities, including most nonrecourse debt, is allocated to the income from the property finances by the indebtedness, and this interest, debt, and property is ignored in applying the three-step procedure to other interest.[124] However, the interest expense deducted in determining effectively connected income, however determined, may not exceed the total of the interest expense paid or accrued by the taxpayer during the taxable year.[125]

If the corporation is a resident of a country with which the United States has an income tax treaty, deductions are typically allowed under the treaty for expenses "incurred for the purposes of" a permanent establishment of the corporation in the United States.[126] The rules described here are the "exclusive" means of determining the interest expense of a U.S. permanent establishment.[127]

1. *General rule.* Generally, the interest deduction allowed in determining effectively connected income is determined by a procedure, described more fully below, that consists of the following steps:

    a. The corporation's U.S. assets (generally, the assets of the U.S. business) are identified and valued.

    b. U.S.-connected liabilities are computed as the product of the U.S. assets

---

[122] Reg. §1.882-5(a)(1)(i). The present regulations on interest allocations for foreign corporations, promulgated by TD 8658, 1996-1 CB 161, apply for taxable years beginning after June 6, 1996. Reg. §1.882-5(f)(1). See generally Epstein, Final and Proposed Interest Expense Allocation Regulations for Foreign Corporations, 25 Tax Mgmt. Int'l J. 339 (1996); Katcher & Vogel, Interest Expense Allocation for Foreign Corporations: A Continuing Source of Discontent? 71 Tax Notes 811 (May 6, 1996), reprinted in 12 Tax Notes Int'l 1551 (May 13, 1996); McCahill, Favre, Lamantia & Bajaj, Final Interest Expense Regs. Give Taxpayers a "Fresh Start," 7 J. Int'l Tax'n 244 (1996).

[123] Reg. §1.882-5(e), discussed infra text accompanying notes 157-62.

[124] Reg. §1.882-5(a)(1)(ii), discussed infra text accompanying notes 163-66.

[125] Reg. §§1.882-5(a)(3). See Reg. §1.882-5(a)(8) Ex. 2.

For this purpose, interest denominated in a currency other than the U.S. dollar is translated into dollars at the weighted average exchange rate for that currency for the year. Reg. §§1.882-5(a)(3). The weighted average rate is "the simple average of the daily exchange rates," exclusive of weekends and other nonbusiness days. Reg. §1.989(b)-1.

[126] See, e.g., U.S. Treasury Dep't, Model Income Tax Treaty art. 7(3) (1981); Organisation for Economic Co-operation and Development, Model Tax Convention on Income and Capital art. 7(3) (1992).

[127] Reg. §1.882-5(a)(2). See TD 8658, supra note 122, at 14 ("[T]he methodology provided in these regulations is [believed to be] fully consistent with all of the United States's treaty obligations, including the Business Profits article of our tax treaties . . . [because] our treaties do not compel the use of any particular method"). For the application of prior regulations under treaties, see Rev. Rul. 89-115, 1989-2 CB 130 (treaty with United Kingdom); Rev. Rul. 85-7 1985-1 CB 188 (Japan).

and a fraction whose numerator is the corporation's worldwide liabilities and whose denominator is worldwide assets.

c. The liabilities shown on the books of the U.S. business are identified and compared with the U.S.-connected liabilities. If these two amounts are equal, the U.S. branch's interest expense is the interest on the U.S. booked liabilities. If the U.S. booked liabilities are greater than the U.S.-connected liabilities, a ratable portion of the interest on the U.S. booked liabilities is disallowed. If the U.S. booked liabilities are less than the U.S.-connected liabilities, the U.S. interest expense is the sum of the interest on the U.S. booked liabilities and interest on the excess U.S.-connected liabilities at the average interest rate on the corporation's U.S. dollar liabilities not booked in the United States.[128]

First step. The first of the three steps is to determine the aggregate value of the corporation's U.S. assets,[129] which consist of the following:[130]

a. Cash balances needed in the present conduct of a U.S. trade or business.

b. Inventory that is taken into account in determining the cost of goods sold by a U.S. business.

c. Depreciable property if depreciation on the property is allocable to effectively connected income.

d. An account receivable if income on the sale, services, or leasing transaction generating the receivable is effectively connected income and if the receivable does not bear interest and matures within six months.

e. An installment obligation if both gain on the installment sale and interest on the obligation are effectively connected income.[131] .

f. An interest in a partnership engaged in business in the United States.[132]

g. Any other asset if income from its use and gain on its disposition would be effectively connected income.[133]

---

[128] Reg. §1.882-5(a)(1)(i). See TD 8658, supra note 122, at 16 (government "believe[s] that the calculation of a taxpayer's interest deduction should reflect, to the greatest extent possible, the taxpayer's economic interest expense").

[129] Reg. §1.882-5(b)(1)(i).

[130] Reg. §1.884-1(d).

[131] Reg. §1.884-1(d)(2)(iii).

[132] Detailed rules are provided for determining the portion of a partnership interest to be treated as a U.S. asset where the partnership has businesses or property in addition to its U.S. business. Reg. §1.884-1(d)(3). The rules allow this determination to be based, at the taxpayer's election, on the relative adjusted bases of the partnership's assets or on the relative amounts of effectively connected and other income for the partnership taxable year ending with or within the taxpayer's taxable year.

[133] Several more specialized types of property are also U.S. assets:

1. U.S. real property held by a foreign bank's wholly owned domestic subsidiary if the property was acquired by the bank by foreclosure or is occupied by the bank.

If the income or gain generated by an asset includes both effectively connected income and other income, only a proportionate part of it is treated as a U.S. asset.

An asset is not a U.S. asset if one of the corporation's principal purposes for acquiring the property or using it in a U.S. business is to increase U.S. assets "artificially."[134] Factors indicative of the corporation's purposes include "the length of time during which the asset was used in a U.S. trade or business, whether the asset was acquired from a related person, and whether the aggregate value of the U.S. assets of the foreign corporation increased temporarily on the determination date." Also, no U.S. asset can arise from transactions between the corporation's various offices or branches.[135]

Generally, each U.S. asset is valued at its adjusted basis for determining gain on a disposition of the property,[136] but the corporation can elect to use the property's fair market value.[137] Each U.S. asset is valued "at the most frequent, regular intervals for which data are reasonably available," but at least semian-

---

2. Assets producing income that is treated as effectively connected income under the rules for foreign sales corporations (FSCs).
3. Assets of a captive insurance company producing income that the corporation has elected to treat as effectively connected income under §953(c)(3)(C).
4. Obligations issued by the United States and held by a foreign corporation carrying on a banking business in a U.S. possession, interest on which is effectively connected income under §882(e).

Reg. §1.882-5(b)(1)(ii). With respect to the first category, see TD 8658, supra note 122, at 15 ("banks frequently hold property acquired by foreclosure in special purpose subsidiaries in order to limit their exposure to environmental or other liabilities" but "must service the debt they incurred to acquire the real property").

If the corporation is a beneficiary of a trust, this beneficial interest is not a U.S. asset, even if the trust is engaged in business in the United States. Reg. §1.884-1(d)(4)(i). However, if, under the grantor trust rules, the corporation is treated as the owner of a trust, an asset of the trust so treated as owned by the corporation may be a U.S. asset. Reg. §1.884-1(d)(4)(ii).

[134] Reg. §1.882-5(b)(1)(v) ("A purpose may be a principal purpose even though it is outweighed by other purposes (taken together or separately)").

[135] Reg. §1.882-5(b)(1)(iv).

[136] Reg. §1.882-5(b)(2)(i). See Prop. Reg. §1.882-5(b)(2)(iv) (adjusted basis of security or contract marked to market under §475 or §1256 is fair market value on last day of year; financial instrument with fair market value of less than zero is liability not asset); Prop. Reg. §1.882-5(c)(5) Exs. 6, 7 (securities dealer subject to §475).

[137] Reg. §1.882-5(b)(2)(ii)(A). For the determination of fair market values, see Reg. §1.861-9T(h), discussed supra ¶70.10.2 notes 82–86 and accompanying text.

The fair market value of a partnership interest is deemed to be the sum of the fair market value of the interest and the partner's share of partnership liabilities. Reg. §1.882-5(b)(2)(ii)(B). For this purpose, a partner's percentage share of each partnership liability is the same as the partner's percentage share of the interest and other expense attributable to the liability for the taxable year. Reg. §1.882-5(c)(2)(vi).The value of a partnership interest cannot be less than zero.

If a taxpayer elects to use fair market value but fails to establish the fair market value of all of its assets, the IRS may either "determine the appropriate asset value" or require that tax book value be used. Reg. §1.861-9T(g)(1)(iii).

nually (at least monthly if the taxpayer is a "large bank").[138] The aggregate value is the average of these valuations during the taxable year.[139]

   Step two. Next, the taxpayer must determine its "U.S.-connected liabilities," which equal the aggregate U.S. assets for the year, multiplied by either the "actual ratio" or, if the taxpayer so elects, the "fixed ratio."[140] The fixed ratio is generally 50 percent (93 percent if the U.S. business is a bank).[141]

   The actual ratio is the sum of the taxpayer's worldwide liabilities, divided by the aggregate value of its worldwide assets.[142] Liabilities and assets must be valued at least annually (at least semiannually if the taxpayer is a large bank). Asset values are determined by the procedures described in *Step one* for valuing U.S. assets.[143] The classification of items as liabilities or assets must be "consistent from year to year and in accordance with U.S. tax principles."[144] For example, if the foreign corporation has issued "perpetual subordinated debt," which is classified as equity under U.S. tax rules, the corporation cannot treat it as a liability in determining the actual ratio.[145] The determination of the amounts of the liabilities and the valuation of the assets must also be consistent from year to year and must be "substantially in accordance with U.S. tax principles."[146]

---

   [138] Reg. §1.882-5(b)(3). See TD 8658, supra note 122, at 14 ("the rule is applied separately with respect to each U.S. asset").

   [139] Id. If the taxpayer is a bank, the aggregate value of loans qualifying as U.S. assets is reduced by a reserve for bad debts if additions to the reserve are deductible under §585. Reg. §1.882-5(b)(2)(iii).

   [140] Reg. §1.882-5(c)(1). See TD 8658, supra note 122, at 15 (because government believes that "a taxpayer's interest deduction should be based on the taxpayer's actual ratio of liabilities to assets whenever possible, the final regulations adopt rules that are intended to encourage taxpayers to use their actual ratio[s]").

   [141] Reg. §1.882-5(c)(4).

   [142] Reg. §1.882-5(c)(2)(i).

   [143] Reg. §1.882-5(c)(2)(iv).

   [144] Reg. §1.882-5(c)(2)(ii).

   [145] Reg. §1.882-5(c)(5) Ex. 1.

   [146] Reg. §§1.882-5(c)(2)(iii),(iv). The phrase "substantially in accordance" means that any differences between the taxpayer's determination and the amounts resulting from a strict application of U.S. tax rules must not "materially affect" the aggregate value of worldwide liabilities or worldwide assets or the taxpayer's actual ratio. Compare Reg. §1.882-5(c)(5) Ex. 2 (large bank, which cannot have reserve for loan losses under U.S. tax rules, maintains such reserve under tax laws of home country; held, loan values may not be reduced by reserve if doing so would materially affect value of worldwide assets) with Reg. §1.882-5(c)(5) Ex. 3 (valuing worldwide assets at book value, determined with depreciation adjustments under tax laws of home country, is acceptable if deviation between U.S. and foreign depreciation rules does not materially affect aggregate asset value).

   See Prop. Reg. §1.882-5(c)(2)(v) (transaction that hedges asset or liability or pool of assets or liabilities is taken into account in determining value, amount, and currency denomination of hedged item or items).

The actual ratio may be determined in either U.S. dollars or the functional currency of the taxpayer's home office.[147] The IRS may adjust the actual ratio to prevent the taxpayer "from intentionally and artificially increasing its actual ratio."[148] For example, liabilities arising from loans between related persons may be disregarded if "one of the principal purposes for entering into the loans was to increase artificially the actual ratio."[149]

Step three. Next, the U.S.-connected liabilities computed in *Step two* are compared with the "U.S. booked liabilities," which usually consist of liabilities that are reflected on the books of the corporation's U.S. trade or business and satisfy at least one of the following requirements:

a. "The liability is secured predominantly by a U.S. asset."
b. The liability is entered, "reasonably contemporaneously" with the incurring of the liability, on a set of books relating to activities producing effectively connected income.
c. The corporation maintains a set of books relating to activities producing effectively connected income, and the IRS "determines that there is a direct connection or relationship between the liability and that activity."[150]

A liability is not a U.S. booked liability if "one of the principal purposes for

---

[147] Reg. §1.882-5(c)(2)(ix). The IRS may require the ratio to be computed in dollars if the functional currency of the home office is a hyperinflationary currency "that materially distorts the actual ratio." A currency is "hyperinflationary" if cumulative inflation was at least 100 percent during the 36 calendar months immediately preceding the taxable year. Reg. §1.985-1(b)(2)(ii)(D), discussed infra ¶71.3.3 text accompanying note 76.

[148] Reg. §1.882-5(c)(3) ("A purpose may be a principal purpose even though it is outweighed by other purposes (taken together or separately)").

[149] See Reg. §1.882-5(c)(5) Ex. 5 (unrelated foreign corporation deposits $100 with bank's home office, and bank's U.S. branch loans $80 to corporation's U.S. subsidiary; held, if one of purposes of bank's participation in these transactions is to increase bank's actual ratio, $80 loan is offset against $100 deposit, foreign corporation is treated as directly loaning $80 to its subsidiary, and transactions produce net liability of $20 and no U.S. asset for bank).

[150] Reg. §1.882-5(d)(2)(ii)(A). If the U.S. trade or business is a bank, a liability (e.g., a deposit with the bank) is a U.S. booked liability only if, (1) before the close of business on the day on which the liability is incurred, it is entered on books kept by the taxpayer for activities producing effectively connected income and (2) the liability is "direct[ly]" connected or related to the activities. Reg. §1.882-5(d)(2)(iii)(A). The first of these requirements is waived if the failure to enter the liability on the appropriate books by the close of business on that day is "inadvertent." Reg. §1.882-5(d)(2)(iii)(B).

If the corporation is a partner of a partnership, U.S. booked liabilities include its share of partnership liabilities that are properly reflected on the books of a U.S. trade or business of the partnership under at least one of the rules described in the text or the preceding paragraph of this note. Reg. §1.882-5(d)(2)(vii).

No U.S. booked liability can arise from transactions between the taxpayer's various offices or branches. Reg. §1.882-5(d)(2)(viii).

incurring or holding the liability is to increase artificially the interest expense on" these liabilities.[151] Whether such a purpose underlies a liability depends on such factors as whether the interest on the liability is "excessive" in comparison with the interest on other liabilities denominated in the same currency and "whether the currency denomination of the liabilities of the U.S. branch substantially matches the currency denomination of the U.S. branch's assets."

U.S. booked liabilities must be determined throughout the taxable year "at the most frequent, regular intervals for which data are reasonably available," but at least semiannually (at least monthly for a large bank).[152] The amounts so determined are averaged.

If U.S. booked liabilities equal U.S.-connected liabilities, as computed in *Step two*, the interest deduction is the interest paid or accrued on the U.S. booked liabilities.[153] If average U.S. booked liabilities for the year exceed the U.S.-connected liabilities, the interest expense deductible in determining effectively connected income is the interest on the U.S. booked liabilities, multiplied by a fraction whose numerator is U.S.-connected liabilities and whose denominator is U.S. booked liabilities.

If average U.S. booked liabilities are less than U.S.-connected liabilities, the interest deduction is the sum of the interest paid or accrued on the U.S. booked liabilities and interest on the excess of U.S.-connected liabilities over U.S. booked liabilities.[154] The latter amount is the product of this excess and the weighted average interest rate on the U.S.-dollar denominated liabilities reflected on the books of the taxpayer's foreign offices and branches.

Example. Assume foreign corporation *FC* has three assets, rental real property located in the United States (value $2,500), rental property located in another country (value $5,500), and all of the stock of a domestic corporation engaged in a real estate business (value $2,000); its liabilities consist of a U.S. booked liability of $800 (bearing interest of $56 for the taxable year), and a $3,200 liability booked in the taxpayer's home country (interest of $256).[155] *FC*'s only U.S. asset is the U.S. rental property, valued at $2,500 (*Step one*). Although the stock of the domestic corporation has connections with the United States, it does not produce effectively connected income or fall within any of the other categories of U.S. assets described above. Assume that in *Step two*, *FC* uses the actual ratio, which is the average of *FC*'s worldwide liabilities (sum of $800 and

---

[151] Reg. §1.882-5(d)(2)(v) ("A purpose may be a principal purpose even though it is outweighed by other purposes . . . ").

[152] Reg. §1.882-5(d)(3). See Prop. Reg. §1.882-5(d)(2)(vi) (if liability is hedged, hedge is taken into account in determining currency denomination, amount of, and interest rate on liability); Prop. Reg. §1.882-5(d)(6) Ex. 4.

[153] Reg. §1.882-5(d)(4). Income, expense, gain, or loss from a hedging transaction is also reduced to the amount resulting from multiplying the item by the same fraction.

[154] Reg. §1.882-5(d)(5).

[155] Reg. §1.882-5(d)(6) Ex. 1.

$3,200), divided by the average amount of worldwide assets (sum of $2,500, $5,500, and $2,000). The ratio is 40 percent ($4,000/$10,000). The U.S.-connected liabilities are therefore $1,000—the product of the U.S. asset ($2,500) and the actual ratio (40 percent). Since the U.S.-connected liabilities ($1,000) exceed the U.S. booked liabilities ($800), the interest deductible in determining effectively connected income is $72—the sum of the interest on the U.S. booked liability ($56) and the product of the excess ($200) and the ratio of the interest on foreign-booked U.S. dollar liabilities ($256) to the amount of those liabilities ($3,200). In contrast, if *FC* uses the fixed ratio in *Step two*, the U.S. connected liabilities are $1,250 (50 percent of the value of the U.S. asset), and the interest deduction is $92—the sum of the interest on the U.S. booked liability ($560) and interest on the excess of the U.S.-connected liabilities ($1,250) over the U.S. booked liability ($800) at the average rate on the dollar liabilities booked abroad (8 percent).[156]

2. *Alternative separate currency pools method.* If a foreign corporation's U.S. assets are denominated in more that one currency, it can elect to determine its deductible interest expense by a separate currency pools method.[157] Under this method, which is probably most often useful for banks, the three steps are applied separately for each currency, as follows:

a. The U.S. assets in each currency are identified and valued by procedures described above.[158]

b. The U.S.-connected liabilities in each currency pool are computed as the value of the U.S. assets in that currency, multiplied by the actual ratio (the ratio of worldwide liabilities to worldwide assets) or, at the taxpayer's election, by the fixed ratio (usually, 50 percent, but 93 percent for banks).[159]

c. The interest deduction for a particular currency pool consists of interest on the U.S.-connected liabilities in that currency at the weighted average interest rate of the corporation's worldwide liabilities in that currency

---

[156] Reg. §1.882-5(d)(6) Ex. 2.

[157] Reg. §1.882-5(e)(1). See TD 8658, supra note 122, at 16 (this method "allows taxpayers to treat their U.S. assets in each currency as funded by the worldwide liabilities of the taxpayer in that same currency").

The separate currency pools method may not be used if more than 10 percent of the corporation's U.S. assets (by value) are denominated in a hyperinflationary currency. Reg. §1.882-5(e)(4). A currency is "hyperinflationary" if cumulative inflation was at least 100 percent during the 36 calendar months immediately preceding the taxable year. Reg. §1.985-1(b)(2)(ii)(D), discussed infra ¶71.3.3 text accompanying note 76.

[158] Reg. §1.882-5(b), discussed supra text accompanying notes 130-39. If the U.S. assets in any currency represent less than 3 percent of all U.S. assets, they may be translated into dollars. Also, any hedge of the U.S. asset is "taken into account [in] determining the currency denomination and the value of the U.S. asset."

[159] Reg. §1.882-5(e)(1)(ii). For the "actual ratio," see Reg. §1.882-5(c)(2), discussed supra text accompanying notes 142-49. For the "fixed ratio," see Reg. §1.882-5(c)(4), discussed supra text accompanying note 141.

(that is, the corporation's worldwide interest expense for the year in that currency divided by its average worldwide liabilities in the currency).[160]

Assume a foreign corporation carries on a banking business through a branch in the United States.[161] For a particular year, its U.S. assets consist of loans denominated in U.S. dollars (average value of $20,000) and loans denominated in the currency of foreign country X (average value of 5,000u). Its actual ratio for the year is 95 percent. Its U.S.-connected liabilities are therefore $19,000 (95 percent of $20,000) and 4,750u (95 percent of 5,000u). Assume the weighted average interest rates on worldwide liabilities is 6 percent on dollar denominated liabilities and 12 percent on liabilities denominated in the u. The interest expense allowed in determining effectively connected income is therefore $1,140 (6 percent of $19,000) and 570u (12 percent of 4,750u). The latter amount is translated into dollars by the procedures generally used for translating interest expense incurred in a foreign currency.[162]

3. *Direct allocations.* In two situations, interest "may" be allocated solely to income from investments financed by the indebtedness.[163]

First, interest on nonrecourse indebtedness may be allocated solely to income from the property securing the indebtedness if all of the following requirements are met:

a. The debt was incurred to finance the purchase, construction, or improvement of the property, and the loan proceeds were actually applied for this purpose.

b. The property is depreciable tangible property, real property, or an amortizable intangible, and has a useful life exceeding one year.

c. The creditor can look only to the property for payment of the debt and interest thereon.

d. The cash flow from the property is "reasonably expected" to be sufficient to cover debt service.

e. Restrictions in the loan agreement ensure that none of the foregoing requirements can be defeated by a transfer of the property.[164]

Second, interest on debt incurred as part of an "integrated financial transaction" may be allocated solely to income from the investment funded by the

---

[160] Reg. §§1.882-5(e)(1)(iii), (2). "The interest expense and liabilities are to be stated in that currency."

[161] Reg. §1.882-5(e)(5) Ex. 1.

[162] See infra ¶71.7.2.

[163] Reg. §1.882-5(a)(1)(ii)(A). For the application of these rules when the interest expense is incurred by a partnership of which the corporation is a partner, see Reg. §§1.882-5(a)(1)(ii)(B), 1.882-5(a)(8) Ex. 1.

[164] Reg. §1.882-10T(b), described more fully above in the text accompanying notes 89–92.

borrowing.[165] An integrated financial transaction consists of "an identified term investment" and a borrowing to finance the investment. An example of an identified term investment is a purchase of a portfolio of stocks approximating the composition of a stock index coupled with a forward contract to sell a specified quantity of the stocks in the index at a designated future date for a specified price.

If the taxpayer utilizes either of these direct allocation rules, two changes are made in the procedures described above in allocating the remainder of the taxpayer's interest expense: The basis or value of the financed property is reduced by the principal amount of the indebtedness subject to the direct allocation rule, and the liabilities subject to the rule are omitted from the corporation's liabilities.[166]

4. *Rules applicable under all methods.* Interest expense denominated in a currency other than the U.S. dollar is translated into dollars at the spot exchange rate for the date on which the expense is paid or incurred.[167] Other nondollar amounts relevant to the application of these rules are translated by the procedures used by the taxpayer for financial accounting purposes if those procedures are applied consistently from year to year.

The interest expense allocable to effectively connected income is determined before the application of rules that might require the capitalization, deferral, or nondeductibility of interest expense.[168] For example, interest allocated to effectively connected income under the rules described above may be required to be capitalized under §265[169] or deferred under the matching rule of §267(a)(3),[170] or it may be nondeductible under the earnings stripping rules of §163(j)[171] or under §265(a)(2), denying deductions for interest on debt incurred or carried to purchase or continue tax-exempt bonds.[172]

5. *Elections.* A foreign corporation must make all elections under the interest allocation rules by its original return for its first taxable year or, if the corporation carried on business in the United States before June 6, 1996, for the first taxable year beginning after June 5, 1996.[173] The election is made by the corporation calculating its interest deduction for that year in accordance with the elections made. If the taxpayer fails to make a timely election, the election may be made by the IRS on the taxpayer's behalf.[174] An election may be changed after

---

[165] Reg. §1.882-10T(c), discussed more fully above in the text accompanying notes 94-96.

[166] Reg. §1.882-5(a)(1)(ii)(A).

[167] Reg. §1.882-5(a)(4), adopting the rules of Reg. §1.988-2, discussed infra ¶71.8.

[168] Reg. §1.882-5(a)(5).

[169] See infra ¶105.10.

[170] See infra ¶78.2.3.

[171] See supra ¶31.12.

[172] See supra ¶31.3. See also Reg. §§1.882-5(a)(8) Ex. 3 (bonds exempt under §103), 1.882-5(a)(8) Ex. 4 (obligations bearing interest exempted by treaty).

[173] Reg. §§1.882-5(a)(7)(i), 1.882-5(f)(1).

[174] Reg. §1.882-5(a)(7)(ii).

it has been in effect for at least five years; before then, a change can be made only with IRS consent, which is given "only in rare and unusual circumstances."[175]

¶70.10.4 Interest Expense—Nonresident Aliens and Foreign Trusts and Estates

A nonresident alien (including a trust or estate taxed as a nonresident alien) is allowed deductions only in determining taxable income effectively connected with a U.S. trade or business.[176] Interest expense is deductible only if the underlying liability appears on the books and records of the U.S. business and is secured by assets that generate effectively connected income.[177] The security test is not met by liabilities secured by both assets of the U.S. trade or business and other assets. Moreover, if the liabilities meeting the booking and security tests exceed 80 percent of the "gross assets" of the U.S. trade or business, interest on the excess is nondeductible.

¶70.10.5 Costs of Research and Experimentation

A complex set of rules is provided for allocating and apportioning research and experimental expenditures deductible under §174 (R&D costs).[178] Costs incurred solely to meet legal requirements pertaining to the improvement or marketing of particular products or processes are allocated solely to the jurisdiction imposing the requirements if the costs are not expected to generate more than a de minimis amount of gross income elsewhere.[179] The remainder of the taxpayer's R&D costs is allocated and apportioned, at the taxpayer's election, by a sales method or a gross income method. Under the sales method, one half of the R&D costs is allocated to the country that is the situs of the activities in which the costs were incurred, and one half of the costs is prorated according to sales.[180] In the

---

[175] Reg. §1.882-5(a)(7)(i).

[176] IRC §873(a).

[177] Reg. §1.861-9T(d)(2)(i) (effective for taxable years beginning after 1987).

[178] Reg. §§1.861-8(e)(3), 1.861-17. For the regulations on R&D costs, see TD 8646, 1996-1 CB 144, promulgating Reg. §1.861-17. For the proposed regulations, see INTL-23-95, 1995-1 CB 987; Renfroe & Gordon, The Proposed Regulations for Allocation and Apportionment of Research and Experimental Expenditures—"And the Beat Goes On . . . ," 24 Tax Mgmt. Int'l J. 528 (1995). For §174, which allows research and experimentation costs to be deducted as incurred, see supra ¶26.3. See generally Brown, Neutral International Tax Rules Allocating Costs: Successful Formula for U.S. Research and Development, 1 Fla. Tax Rev. 333 (1993). See St. Jude Medical, Inc. v. CIR, 34 F3d 1394 (8th Cir. 1994), rev'g 97 TC 457 (1991) (nonacq.) (prior regulations on allocating and apportioning research and development costs, as incorporated by regulations on applying combined taxable income method for DISCs, are valid).

[179] See infra text accompanying notes 188-90.

[180] See infra text accompanying notes 191-213.

latter apportionment, sales revenues and R&D costs are grouped into broad product categories, and the costs in each category are apportioned according to sales revenues within the category. Under the gross income method, one fourth of the costs is allocated exclusively to the place at which the R&D activities are located, and the remainder is apportioned according to gross income.[181] However, under the gross income method, the amounts assigned to the statutory grouping or groupings and to residual gross income must each be at least 50 percent of the amount assigned to this income under the sales method.

The treatment of research and development costs has long been a source of controversy. The regulations, which derive from regulations adopted in 1977, require portions of a domestic corporation's R&D costs to be allocated to foreign source income whenever sales are made or gross income is obtained in foreign countries, even if all of these costs are incurred in the United States. Some foreign countries allow deductions for research costs only when the research work is done locally. Thus, when research activities are located in the United States, the regulations sometimes reduce foreign source taxable income for costs that do not reduce the amounts taxed by foreign countries. This incongruence between U.S. and foreign rules may cause the foreign tax credit limitation to be less than the taxes imposed by foreign countries, even when U.S. and foreign rates are similar. As a result, some have argued, U.S. companies are encouraged to shift portions of their research activities to foreign countries in order to bring foreign tax liabilities more in line with the foreign tax credit limitation.[182]

Congress imposed a moratorium on the application of the 1977 regulations during the years 1981 through 1985, allowing all R&D costs incurred in the United States to be allocated to U.S. source income.[183] In 1986, 1988, 1989, 1991, and 1993, Congress enacted temporary rules that allowed the regulations to go into effect but altered them in several particulars (e.g., by increasing the automatic allocation to the country in which the costs are incurred).[184] The temporary

---

[181] See infra text accompanying notes 214-17.

[182] See H.R. Rep. No. 247, 101st Cong., 1st Sess. 57 (1989).

[183] More precisely, the moratorium extended from the first taxable year beginning after August 13, 1981, and ended with the last taxable year beginning before August 1, 1986. See Brown, supra note 178, at 335-39. See also Intel Corp. v. CIR, 76 F3d 976 (9th Cir. 1995) (1981 moratorium did not apply in determining DISC's combined taxable income (CTI) because geographic source of income is not at issue in CTI calculation; regulations thus were fully applicable in determining CTI); St. Jude Medical, Inc. v. CIR, 34 F3d 1394 (8th Cir. 1994) (same).

[184] Under the 1977 regulations, the allocation to the place of the R&D activities was 30 percent and was allowed only if R&D costs were allocated by sales. The temporary rules adopted in 1986 increased this allocation to 50 percent and allowed it whether the costs were allocated by the sales method or the gross income method. The 1988 extension increased the allocation to 64 percent, and this allocation was continued in 1989, when the temporary rules were embodied in a Code provision, §864(f). Section 864(f) was renewed for successive one-year periods in 1990 and 1991. The 1991 extension expired with the end of the first six months of the first taxable year beginning after August 1, 1991. However,

rules have expired, but the IRS has amended the regulations to adopt most, but not all, of the temporary statutory rules.[185] The regulations are described below.

An affiliated group of corporations must generally apply these regulations, like other aspects of the regulations on allocating and apportioning deductions, as though all members of the group were one corporation.[186] If the taxpayer is a member of a partnership, the regulations apply to the taxpayer's distributive share of R&D costs of the partnership.[187]

1. *Research pursuant to government mandate; research in space and international waters.* If research and development is undertaken "solely" to satisfy "legal requirements imposed by a political entity with respect to improvement or marketing of specific products or processes" and the work "cannot reasonably be expected" to generate more than a de minimis amount of income outside the jurisdiction imposing the requirements, the costs of the work are allocated exclusively to income from sources within that country.[188] For example, if a drug company conducts tests to meet requirements of the U.S. Food and Drug Administration, the costs of the tests can be allocated to U.S. source income alone unless the tests are reasonably expected to generate more than de minimis gross income from foreign sources.[189]

Under the temporary statutory rules, a residence rule applied to costs of research and experimental activities conducted in space, "on or under water" that is outside the jurisdiction of any country (as recognized by the United States), or in Antarctica.[190] These costs were allocated to U.S. sources for U.S. persons (citizens, resident aliens, and domestic corporations and trusts) and were

---

the IRS provided a "transition method" that allowed taxpayers to continue using the allocation and apportionment mechanism of §864(f) for the succeeding 18 months. Rev. Proc. 92-56, 1992-2 CB 409. See Brown, supra note 178, at 339-40. In 1993, Congress reenacted §864(f), reducing to 50 percent the automatic allocation to the place of the R&D activities and making the provision applicable only for the taxable year immediately following the last year to which the Revenue Procedure 92-56 applied or would have applied if the taxpayer had elected to utilize the procedure—the taxable year beginning after July 1993 but before August 1994. IRC §864(f)(6), as enacted by Pub. L. No. 103-66, §13234, 107 Stat. 312 (1993).

[185] The present regulations generally apply for taxable years after 1995, but taxpayers may elect to apply them for all taxable years beginning after July 1995 (the first year following the last year to which §864(f) applied). Reg. §1.861-17(g).

[186] Reg. §1.861-17(a)(3).

[187] Reg. §1.861-17(f)(1).

[188] Reg. §1.861-17(a)(4). The temporary statutory rules were the same. IRC §864(f)(1)(A).

For this purpose, the taxpayer's distributive share of the R&D costs of a partnership is deemed incurred for the purpose that motivated the partnership's R&D activities. Reg. §1.861-17(f)(2).

[189] Reg. §1.861-17(h) Ex. 5. See Reg. §1.861-17(h) Ex. 3 (research "made solely to meet pollution standards mandated by [U.S.] law").

[190] IRC §864(f)(3).

allocated to foreign sources if the taxpayer is not a U.S. person. Neither the 1977 regulations nor the proposed regulations has an analogue.

2. *Sales method.* Under the sales method, which applies unless the taxpayer properly elects to use the gross income method, one half of the taxpayer's R&D costs (exclusive of those allocated under the rules described above) is allocated to the country in which the R&D activities are located and one half is apportioned ratably by sales.[191]

a. *Exclusive allocation to place of research.* One half of the R&D costs apportioned by the sales method is deductible against income from sources within the country that is the location of activities accounting for more than 50 percent of the deduction for R&D costs.[192] If the activities are so dispersed that the activities at no one "geographic source" account for more than 50 percent of the costs, no exclusive apportionment is made to the situs country, and the entire deduction is apportioned by sales.

The regulations justify this exclusive allocation to the place of the research as follows:

> [R]esearch and development is often most valuable in the country where it is performed, for two reasons. First, research and development often benefits a broad product category, consisting of many individual products, all of which may be sold in the nearest market but only some of which may be sold in foreign markets. Second, research and development often is utilized in the nearest market before it is used in other markets, and, in such cases, has a lower value per unit of sales when used in foreign markets.[193]

More than 50 percent of the R&D deduction can be allocated under this rule to the situs of the R&D activities if the taxpayer can establish that an allocation

---

[191] See Perkin-Elmer Corp. v. CIR, 103 TC 464 (1994) (upholding validity of substantially identical prior regulations on sales method).

[192] Reg. §1.861-17(b)(1)(i). For this purpose, the taxpayer's distributive share of the R&D costs of a partnership is deemed incurred at the place of the partnership's R&D activities. Reg. §1.861-17(f)(2).

The portion of the R&D costs subject to this rule has varied over time. Under the 1977 regulations, this portion was normally 30 percent, but the taxpayer could use a higher percentage if "the research and development is reasonably expected to have very limited or long delayed application outside the geographic source where it was performed." Reg. §1.861-8(e)(3)(ii)(A) (1977). This portion was 50 percent of the R&D costs under the temporary statutory rules enacted in 1986. It was 64 percent under the temporary rules adopted in 1988, 1990, and 1991 and under the administrative rules promulgated in 1992. Rev. Proc. 92-56, 1992-2 CB 409. The 1993 restoration of §864(f) reduced this allocation to 50 percent of the costs.

Also, under the statutory rules and the 1992 administrative action, the exclusive allocation to the place of the R&D activities was allowed whether the taxpayer used the sales method or the gross income method, whereas, under the 1977 regulations, it is part of the sales method only. The 1995 regulations allow an exclusive apportionment under the gross income method of 25 percent of the R&D costs. Reg. §1.861-17(b)(1)(ii), discussed infra text accompanying note 214.

[193] Reg. §1.861-17(b)(2)(i).

"significantly greater" than 50 percent is justified "because the research and experimentation is reasonably expected to have very limited or long delayed application outside the geographic source where it was performed."[194] Very limited foreign application can be established only by comparing the "commercial production of individual products in domestic and foreign markets made by" (1) the taxpayer, (2) uncontrolled persons under intangible property licensed or sold by the taxpayer to those persons, and (3) controlled corporations "that can reasonably be expected to benefit directly or indirectly from any of the taxpayer's research expense connected with the product category."[195] In establishing a long delayed application, the taxpayer must "compare the commercial introduction of its own particular products and processes" in domestic and foreign markets, including sales by the taxpayer and the controlled and uncontrolled persons described in the preceding sentence.[196] Delays in application are evaluated by discounting expected future cash flows at 10 percent annually unless the taxpayer shows a different discount rate to be more appropriate.

b. *Apportioned by sales.* The remainder of the R&D deduction is allocated among product categories, and the amount assigned to each category is split between the statutory and residual groupings in proportion to the taxpayer's sales of goods and services within the product category.[197] According to the regulations, "research and experimentation is an inherently speculative activity, . . . findings may contribute unexpected benefits, and . . . the gross income derived from successful research and development must bear the cost of unsuccessful research and development."[198] Deductions for R&D costs are therefore "definitely related to all income reasonably connected with the relevant broad product category" and should be allocated to a class consisting of all gross income related to that category, which may include income realized by the taxpayer on sales of goods, royalties from licensees of intangibles produced by the taxpayer's research, and dividends.

The product categories are taken from the Standard Industrial Classification Manual, a publication of the Office of Management and Budget.[199] Examples of

---

[194] Id.

[195] Reg. §1.861-17(b)(2)(ii).

[196] Reg. §1.861-17(b)(2)(iii).

[197] Reg. §1.861-17(c)(1).

[198] Reg. §1.861-17(a)(1).

[199] Reg. §1.861-17(a)(2)(ii). The regulations generally require research and development expenses to be allocated to three-digit SIC product codes. Two-digit codes were utilized under prior versions of the regulations. "Use of three digit SIC code product categories . . . enable[s] taxpayers to allocate research and experimental expenditures to narrower classes of gross income than the classes of gross income permitted by the [prior] regulations." INTL-23-95, supra note 178, at 987. See TD 8646, supra note 178, at 11 (rejecting suggestion that five-digit codes should be permitted; "such a rule would too narrowly restrict the necessarily broad scope of the deduction"; research is "inherently speculative," and income from successful projects must bear costs of unsuccessful projects).

product categories are engines and turbines, construction, mining, and materials handling machinery and equipment, electric lighting and wiring equipment, and drugs.[200] The categories may be combined if the taxpayer carries on research or development in more than one product category, but subdivisions of categories are not allowed.[201] If research or development work is not "clearly identified" with any product category, it is deemed related to all of the taxpayer's product categories.

Under the sales formula, the deduction for R&D costs within a particular product category (reduced by the amounts allocated under the rules described above) is apportioned to a statutory grouping in an amount equal to the costs, multiplied by a fraction whose numerator consists of revenues from sales within the product category that generated gross income in the statutory grouping and whose denominator consists of all sales revenues within the product category.[202] Assume a domestic corporation's deduction for research costs for a particular year is $100, $50 of which is allocated exclusively to U.S. source income because the United States is the situs of the research; within the product category in which the research is done, the corporation has sales revenues for the year of $1,000, including $600 yielding gross income from U.S. sources and $400 producing foreign source income. The portion of the R&D deduction taken in determining foreign source taxable income is $20 ($50 times $400/$1,000). The amount assigned to U.S. source income is $80 ($50 under the exclusive allocation rule and $50 times $600/$1,000 under the sales apportionment rule). The R&D costs matched with a particular product category can exceed the gross income of that category within the statutory grouping, in which case the excess is deducted against other gross income in the statutory grouping.[203]

The apportionment fraction usually includes all revenues from sales by the taxpayer of goods and services within the relevant product category. Rents received under equipment leases are treated as sales revenues for this purpose.[204]

The fraction also includes sales within the product category made by any "controlled" corporation that "can reasonably be expected to benefit, directly or

---

[200] Reg. §§1.861-17(h) Exs. 1, 4, 5, 6.

[201] Reg. §1.861-17(a)(2)(i). The taxpayer can thus utilize two-digit categories, or one-digit categories, by combining all three-digit categories within each one- or two-digit category. For restrictions on combining other categories with the two-digit categories "Wholesale trade" and "Retail trade," see Reg. §§1.861-17(a)(2)(iv),(v).

A change in product categories can be made only if the taxpayer demonstrates that the change is justified by "changes in the relevant facts." Reg. §1.861-17(a)(2)(iii). A change from two digit categories to three digit categories, or vice versa, is subject to this rule. See TD 8646, supra note 178, at 11 (regulations are intended to be "a simple and workable format for balancing the need for consistency with the desire for flexibility").

[202] Reg. §1.861-17(c)(1).

[203] Reg. §1.861-17(c)(1)(i).

[204] Reg. §1.861-17(c)(1)(ii).

indirectly . . . ," from the taxpayer's R&D work within the category.[205] A controlled corporation is reasonably expected to benefit from R&D "if the taxpayer can be expected to license, sell, or transfer intangible property to that corporation or transfer secret processes to that corporation, either directly or indirectly . . . ."[206] "Past experience" is taken as a guide in determining reasonable expectations. A corporation is related for this purpose if the relationship between the corporation and the taxpayer is described in §267(b) or if the corporation is a member of the same controlled group of corporations as the taxpayer.[207] If less than all of the controlled corporation's stock is owned by the taxpayer and other members of its controlled group, only a proportionate part of the controlled corporation's sales are included in the taxpayer's apportionment fraction.[208] Sales among members of the group are excluded to the extent necessary to avoid double counting.[209]

Sales by an uncontrolled person are also included in a taxpayer's apportionment formula if (1) the taxpayer licensed or sold a patent, know-how, or other intangible to that person or (2) another member of the taxpayer's controlled group sold or licensed intangible property to the uncontrolled person and the licensee or purchaser "can reasonably be expected to benefit directly or indirectly" from that other member's research and development.[210] The latter rule applies if the other member "can reasonably be expected to license, sell, or transfer intangible property to that uncontrolled party or transfer secret processes to that uncontrolled party, directly or indirectly." "Past experience" is looked to in determining reasonable expectations. The uncontrolled person's sales are included only to the extent they derive from goods or services produced

---

[205] Reg. §1.861-17(b)(3). Although sales of controlled corporations are taken into account in the apportionment, research and experimental costs of these corporations are not. See Perkin-Elmer Corp. v. CIR, 103 TC 464 (1994) (noting taxpayer's complaint that by failing to take costs of related foreign corporations into account, regulations overstate amount properly allocable to foreign income, but nevertheless upholding regulations on this point).

[206] See Reg. §1.861-17(c)(3)(iv) (if taxpayer and controlled corporation have entered into cost sharing arrangement with respect to R&D costs, controlled corporation is not expected to benefit from taxpayer's share of costs), §1.861-17(h) Ex. 3 (cost sharing agreement between domestic parent and foreign subsidiary covering research performed in the United States).

[207] Reg. §1.861-17(c)(3)(i). For §267(b), see infra ¶78.3. The term "controlled group of corporations" means, very generally, corporations joined together by parent-subsidiary or brothers-sister relationships with stock ownership of more than 50 percent at each link. IRC §§927(d), 993(a)(3), 1563(a).

[208] Reg. §1.861-17(c)(3)(ii). See Reg. §1.861-17(h) Ex. 3 (taxpayer's apportionment formula included 60 percent of sales of 60 percent owned foreign subsidiary).

[209] Reg. §1.861-17(c)(3)(iii).

[210] Reg. §1.861-17(c)(2). A person is generally "uncontrolled" unless it is a controlled corporation within the meaning of that term as described in note 207 and accompanying text. Reg. §1.861-17(c)(2)(i).

or sold using the licensed or transferred intangible.[211] If these sales are unknown, as where a licensee uses the intangible to manufacture an item that is a component in a larger product, a "reasonable estimate" of these sales is acceptable.[212]

Finally, if the taxpayer is a member of a partnership, its share of the partnership's sales is treated as sales made by the taxpayer.[213] The taxpayer's proportionate share of the partnership's sales in each product category is the same as its proportionate share of the partnership's gross income in that category.

3. *Gross income method.* Under the gross income method, the R&D deduction, to the extent not covered by the rule of exclusive allocation for research done to meet legal requirements in one country, is allocated and apportioned as follows: If more than 50 percent of the deductible costs were incurred in activities located in one "geographic source," 25 percent of the deduction is assigned exclusively to that source.[214] The remainder is apportioned ratably according to gross income in the statutory and residuary groupings.[215]

R&D costs and gross income in all product categories are lumped together in this apportionment. However, the amount apportioned to the statutory grouping and to the residual grouping must each be at least 50 percent of what would be apportioned to this income under the sales method.[216] If the apportionment by gross income fails this test, the allocation to the statutory or residual grouping, as the case may be, is 50 percent of the amount apportioned to it by the sales method, and the remainder of the deduction goes to the other grouping.[217] If there is more than one statutory grouping, these groupings in the aggregate must be apportioned at least 50 percent of what would be assigned to them by the sales method, and if the apportionment to them would not otherwise satisfy the 50 percent requirement, the minimum allocation to the statutory groupings is apportioned among these groupings in proportion to gross income.

4. *Election.* In the absence of an election, the taxpayer must use the sales method.[218] An election to use the sales method must be made for the first taxable year to which these rules apply to the taxpayer, and once made, the election is

---

[211] Reg. §1.861-17(h) Ex. 6.

[212] Reg. §1.861-17(c)(2)(ii) (licenses; reasonable estimate should be "based on the principles of section 482"), §1.861-17(c)(2)(ii) (sales of intangibles; buyer's sales must be estimated annually, utilizing, "[i]f necessary, appropriate economic analyses"). See Reg. §1.861-17(h) Ex. 6 (licensee's sales estimated to be ten times royalties received from licensee).

[213] Reg. §1.861-17(f)(3).

[214] Reg. §1.861-17(b)(1)(ii).

[215] Reg. §1.861-17(d)(1)(i).

[216] Reg. §1.861-17(d)(2). The temporary rules of §864(f) required only that the amount apportioned to foreign source income be at least 30 percent of the amount that would have been apportioned to this income under the sales method. IRC §864(f)(1)(C).

[217] Reg. §1.861-17(d)(3).

[218] Reg. §1.861-17(d)(1)(i).

binding for the election year and the subsequent four years.[219] Within this five-year period, the election may be revoked only with IRS consent.[220] At any time after five years, the taxpayer may change the election, but the new election is binding for a new five-year period.

The gross income method must be made for all R&D costs or for none.[221] The sales method cannot be used for portions of the deduction (e.g., costs relating to particular product categories), and the gross income method for other portions.

5. *Examples.* Assume domestic corporation X, a manufacturer and distributor of small gasoline engines for lawn mowers, has R&D costs for a particular year of $60,000, all of which are incurred in the United States and deducted under §174.[222] The costs all fall within one product category—Engines and Turbines (SIC Industry Group 351).[223] X's wholly owned subsidiary, foreign corporation Y, manufactures and sells such engines in foreign countries using technology created by X's R&D and licensed to Y. For the taxable year, X's sales of the engines is $500,000, and Y's sales are $300,000. X's gross income for the year consists of $140,000 from engine sales (U.S. sources), $10,000 of royalties from Y (foreign sources), and $10,000 of interest income (U.S. sources). Because X allocates and apportions deductions solely for purposes of the foreign tax credit, the statutory grouping is gross income from foreign sources, and U.S. income is residual gross income.

Under the sales method, one half of the R&D costs ($30,000) is allocated exclusively to the United States as the situs of the activities in which the activities were incurred, and the remainder is apportioned by sales as follows:

Statutory grouping: ($30,000)($300,000/$800,000) = $11,250
Residual gross income: ($30,000)($500,000/$800,000) = $18,750

In total, the deduction of $60,000 is apportioned $11,250 to the statutory group-

---

[219] Reg. §1.861-17(e)(1). For taxpayers that previously allocated and apportioned R&D costs, a new election may be made for the first taxable year beginning after 1995 or, if the taxpayer chooses, the first taxable year beginning after August 1, 1994. Reg. §1.861-17(g).

Under the 1977 regulations and §864(f), the election was made annually, and from year to year, the taxpayer was free to switch from the sales method to the gross income method and vice versa. IRC §864(f)(1)(C); Reg. §1.861-8(e)(3)(iii) (1977).

[220] Reg. §1.861-17(e)(2).

[221] Reg. §1.861-17(d)(1)(ii).

[222] Reg. §1.861-17(h) Ex. 1.

[223] The costs need not be incurred with respect to the same product, so long as the research object is in the same product category. For example, if X also manufactured and sold steam turbines and part of the R&D costs pertained to turbines, all of the costs would be allocated and apportioned together because engines for lawn mowers and steam turbines are in the same product category. Reg. §1.861-17(h) Ex. 2. In apportioning the costs, turbine sales or gross income from turbines would be aggregated with engine sales or gross income, even if turbine sales are made only in the United States.

ing (foreign source income) and $48,750 (sum of $30,000 and $18,750) to U.S. income (residual gross income).

Under the gross income method, one fourth of the R&D costs ($15,000) is allocated to the United States as the place of the R&D activities, and the remaining $40,000 is tentatively allocated by gross income (including only the sales and royalty income allocable to the product category), as follows:

Statutory grouping: ($45,000)($10,000/$150,000) = $3,000
Residual gross income: ($45,000)($140,000/$150,000) = $42,000

However, the result is that the statutory grouping receives less than one half of what would be apportioned to it under the sales method ($11,250). Thus, if the taxpayer elects the gross income method, the apportionment to the statutory grouping is $5,625 (one half of $11,250).

CHAPTER
71

Foreign Currencies

¶71.1 INTRODUCTORY

All U.S. tax liabilities must be determined and paid in U.S. dollars. When taxpayers invest and do business in transactions denominated in foreign currencies, foreign currency amounts must be translated into dollars. Also, account must be taken of the gains and losses resulting when the relative values of the dollar and another currency change while a U.S. taxpayer owns or has a position denominated in the other currency. Sections 985 through 989, enacted in 1986 and amply supplemented with regulations, provide for rules for making these translations, measuring foreign currency gains and losses, and establishing when the translations must be made and the gains and losses determined.[1] The rules are most important to U.S. citizens and residents and domestic corporations, who are commonly taxed on income from foreign investments and businesses. Foreign persons, who are taxed by the United States only on U.S. income, are immune from this complication, except in the relatively unusual case of a U.S. investment or business transaction denominated in a foreign currency.

---

[1] See generally Dilworth, Andrus, Harter & O'Donnell, U.S. Tax Treatment of Financial Transactions Involving Foreign Currency (Tax Analysts 1990); Ring, Foreign Currency Transactions, in Taxation of Financial Instruments (Avi-Yonah, Newman & Ring, eds. Clark Boardman Callaghan 1996); Stodghill, Taxing the Yen for Foreign Currency: The Statutory Regime, 7 Va. Tax Rev. 57 (1987); Stodghill, The Foreign Currency Regulations, 40 Tax Notes 1063 (1988). See also Solway & Bothamley, Treasury Centers, Hybrid Instruments, and Foreign Currency Strategies, 11 Tax Notes Int'l 1679 (Dec. 4, 1995).

Under the foreign currency rules, transactions are generally accounted for in the taxpayer's functional currency.[2] The functional currency of a U.S. citizen or resident or a domestic corporation is usually the U.S. dollar.[3] A foreign currency is the functional currency for a unit of the taxpayer's operations if the unit is a "qualified business unit" (QBU) and its "economic environment" is in the foreign currency. Very generally, a QBU is a trade or business for which separate books are kept.

If a QBU's functional currency is not the U.S. dollar, profits and losses are usually determined annually in the functional currency and translated into dollars at an average exchange rate for the year.[4] Gains and losses in the QBU's assets resulting from exchange rate fluctuations generally are not recognized until earnings of the QBU are remitted. If the QBU operates in a hyperinflationary economy, however, the taxpayer may elect to tie accounting for the QBU much closer to the dollar.

Foreign currency gain or loss from transactions involving currencies other than the functional currency are computed transaction by transaction.[5] Moreover, what might be viewed as one transaction is often broken down into a series of events, each of which has independent significance under the foreign currency rules. Assume a business sells goods on credit for a price denominated in a nonfunctional currency, accrues interest on the account receivable pending payment, collects the price and accrued interest, and exchanges the nonfunctional currency for functional currency. The revenues on the sale are translated by the spot rate at the time of the sale, and interest income is translated at the average rate during the accrual period. Exchange gain or loss is realized on collection of both the price and accrued interest, measured by the difference between the spot rate at the time of collection and the rates used for the accruals of the price and interest. Unless the amount collected is immediately exchanged for the functional currency, another exchange gain or loss is realized on the currency exchange.

Numerous rules are also provided for various situations where a U.S. shareholder is taxed on earnings of a foreign corporation.[6]

---

[2] The term "taxpayer" is used here (and in the statutes) to include many foreign entities that pay no U.S. taxes, but have shareholders, partners, or beneficiaries that are taxed by the U.S. on the entities' income. See H.R. Rep. No. 841, 99th Cong., 2d Sess. II-671 (Conf. Rep. 1986); infra ¶71.4. Compare IRC §7701(a)(14) ("the term 'taxpayer' means any person subject to any internal revenue tax").

[3] Infra ¶71.2.

[4] Infra ¶71.3.

[5] Infra ¶71.5.

[6] Infra ¶71.4.

¶71.2 FUNCTIONAL CURRENCY

Generally, all income tax determinations are initially made in the taxpayer's "functional currency" or currencies.[1] The U.S. dollar is the functional currency for all transactions unless a taxpayer has a qualified business unit for which a foreign functional currency is permitted.[2]

1. *Qualified business unit.* A "qualified business unit" (QBU) is a "separate and clearly identified unit of a trade or business of a taxpayer which maintains separate books and records."[3] Every corporation, domestic or foreign, is a QBU.[4] For example, a holding company is a QBU whether or not its activities are sufficient to be a trade or business.[5] In addition, a particular activity of the corporation is a QBU if it is a trade or business and "a separate set of books and records" is maintained for the activity.[6] Assume a domestic corporation's activities are primarily in the United States, but it has a sales office in London.[7] If the activities of the London office are a trade or business and if separate books are kept for the office, the corporation has at least two QBUs, the London office and the remainder of the corporation.

A "trade or business" is a "unified group of activities that constitutes (or could constitute) an independent economic enterprise carried on for profit."[8] A trade or business "must ordinarily include every operation which forms a part of, or a step in, a process by which an enterprise may earn income or profit, . . . includ[ing] the collection of income and the payment of expenses." A "vertical,

---

[1] IRC §985(a). See Rev. Proc. 98-7, 1998-1 CB —, at §4.01(19) (IRS ordinarily will not rule in advance on whether particular currency is taxpayer's functional currency). See generally ABA Section of Tax'n Comm. on Foreign Activities of U.S. Taxpayers, Comments on Regulations Dealing With Foreign Currency Transactions, 44 Tax Lawyer 71, 116-35 (1990). See also Magee, Farmer & Katcher, Reexamining Branch Rules in the Context of Check-the-Box, 77 Tax Notes 1511 (Dec. 29, 1997).

For issues raised by the conversion of European Union countries' currencies to a single European currency (EURO), see Announcement 98-18, 1998-10 IRB 44 (soliciting comments on these issues); Cope & Dunahoo, Will European Monetary Convergence Be a Taxable Event? Some Thoughts on the Conversion to the Euro, 26 Tax Mgmt. Int'l J. 526 (1997); Fisher & Picciano, The Euro Is Coming: U.S. Companies May Be Caught Short by Complex Tax Issues, 9 J. Int'l Tax'n 12 (1998); Johnsen, U.S. Tax Issues Raised by Conversion to the Euro, 16 Tax Notes Int'l 847 (Mar. 16, 1998), reprinted in 79 Tax Notes 369 (Apr. 20, 1998); National Foreign Trade Council, Implications of European Economic and Monetary Union, 79 Tax Notes 361 (Apr. 20, 1998), reprinted in 16 Tax Notes Int'l 1383 (Apr. 27, 1998).

[2] IRC §985(b)(1)(A).

[3] IRC §989(a). See H.R. Rep. No. 841, 99th Cong., 2d Sess. II-660 (Conf. Rep. 1986). See also Rev. Proc. 98-7, 1998-1 CB —, §4.01(20) (IRS ordinarily will not rule in advance on whether particular operations are QBUs).

[4] Reg. §1.989(a)-1(b)(2)(i).

[5] Reg. §1.989(a)-1(e) Ex. 5.

[6] Reg. §1.989(a)-1(b)(2)(ii).

[7] Reg. §1.989(a)-1(e) Ex. 1.

[8] Reg. §1.989(a)-1(c).

functional, or geographic division of the same trade or business" is itself a trade or business if it is "capable of producing income independently."[9] For example, if domestic corporation D manufactures goods in the United States and sells them through a branch in a foreign country, the branch may be a trade or business separate from the manufacturing operations because it could be carried on as an independent economic enterprise.[10] Also, activities at a particular location may be a trade or business separate from identical activities at another location. For example, if D maintains sales offices in Paris and Frankfurt in addition to London, the three offices may be three separate trades or businesses.[11]

However, "merely ancillary" activities are not a trade or business.[12] For example, if D has an employee in Tokyo to deliver documents to Japanese customers relating to sales arranged by D from the United States, the employee's activities are not a trade or business because they are merely ancillary.[13] In contrast, if D creates a Japanese subsidiary to carry on the courier activities, the subsidiary is a QBU because a corporation is a QBU whether or not it has a trade or business.[14]

An individual is not a QBU, but an individual may have a QBU consisting of a trade or business for which separate records are kept.[15] Assume individual A, a U.S. citizen, carries on business in Spain as distributor of goods produced by various U.S. manufacturers.[16] A's activities in Spain are a trade or business and therefore are a QBU if separate records are kept for the activities. However, an individual's activities as an employee are not a trade or business for this purpose.[17] An employee of A's business, for example, has no QBU.

Investment and other activities, the expenses of which are deductible under §212 but not §162(a), are not a trade or business as that term is used in other contexts, but they are so treated under these rules.[18] Assume A hires a Japanese investment manager to manage her sizable portfolio of stocks and bonds of Japanese corporations.[19] The manager's activities on A's behalf are a QBU if the manager maintains a set of books in yen for A's investments because investment expenses are deductible under §212. Also, if A's investments are organized into

---

[9] Staff of Joint Comm. on Tax'n, 99th Cong., 2d Sess., General Explanation of the Tax Reform Act of 1986 at 1093 (Comm. Print 1987) [hereinafter 1986 Bluebook]; Reg. §1.989(a)-1(c).

[10] Reg. §1.989(a)-1(e) Ex. 1.

[11] See Reg. §1.989(a)-1(e) Ex. 2.

[12] Reg. §1.989(a)-1(c).

[13] See Reg. §1.989(a)-1(e) Ex. 3.

[14] Reg. §1.989(a)-1(e) Ex. 4.

[15] Reg. §1.988(a)-1(b)(2).

[16] Reg. §1.989(a)-1(e) Ex. 8.

[17] Reg. §1.989(a)-1(c).

[18] Reg. §1.989(a)-1(c). For §§162(a) and 212, see supra ¶20.1.

[19] See Reg. §1.989(a)-1(e) Ex. 6.

a separate holding company, the holding company is a QBU because a corporation is always a QBU.[20]

A partner is deemed engaged in any business carried on by the partnership,[21] and a QBU of the partnership is therefore a QBU of the partner.[22] Assume a domestic corporation is a partner in a partnership that is principally engaged in business activities in country X and uses the country $X u$ as its functional currency. The country X business is a QBU of both the partnership and the partner.

A QBU's separate books and records must include "books of original entry and ledger accounts, both general and subsidiary, or similar records."[23] For a taxpayer using the accrual method, the books of original entry must include "a journal to record sales (accounts receivable) and a journal to record expenses incurred (accounts payable)."

2. *Nondollar functional currencies.* A QBU's functional currency is the U.S. dollar unless a foreign currency is established as the functional currency.[24] A foreign currency is a QBU's functional currency if (1) it is "the currency of the economic environment in which a significant part of such unit's activities are conducted," (2) the QBU's "books and records" are kept in that currency, and (3) the QBU's activities are not "primarily conducted in dollars."[25] A QBU's activities are primarily conducted in dollars if "the currency of the economic environment in which the QBU conducts its activities is primarily the dollar."[26] The purpose of these requirements is to test whether "the foreign operation represents a sufficient commitment to the economic environment of the host country."[27]

The currency of the economic environment of a QBU's activities is determined from the facts and circumstances.[28] Consideration is given to the currencies in which the QBU (1) accrues revenues and incurs expenses, (2) receives revenues and pays expenses, (3) borrows and lends, and (4) makes pricing and other financial decisions. The location of the QBU's principal place of business is also relevant. The duration of the QBU's activities and the volume of its "independent activities" are taken into account because "the functional currency approach presupposes a long-term commitment to a specific economic environ-

---

[20] Reg. §1.989(a)-1(e) Ex. 7.

[21] For foreign partners, this proposition is made explicit by §875(1). For U.S. partners, it is, at a minimum, implicit in the overall scheme for taxing partnership income.

[22] Reg. §1.989(a)-1(b)(2)(i).

[23] Reg. §1.989(a)-1(d)(1).

[24] Reg. §1.985-1(b).

[25] IRC §§985(b)(1)(B), (2).

[26] Reg. §1.985-1(b)(2).

[27] 1986 Bluebook, supra note 9, at 1092.

[28] Reg. §1.985-1(c)(2); 1986 Bluebook, supra note 9, at 1093. Generally, the same factors are considered under U.S.financial accounting rules.

ment."[29] Whether a foreign activity is of sufficient duration to be a QBU depends, in part, on whether the host country taxes it. For example, an activity lasting only 12 months may be a QBU if it is taxed by the host country.[30] The rate of inflation in a particular currency is not considered. If the taxpayer has more than one trade or business, the economic environment standard must be applied consistently to all of them.

Sometimes, more than one currency satisfies the standard because, for example, the QBU does substantial business in two or more foreign currencies.[31] When this occurs, the taxpayer may choose any one of the qualifying currencies as the functional currency.[32]

The functional currency concept is borrowed from financial accounting principles.[33] In order to facilitate consistency in financial and tax accounting, the regulations allow the currency of a QBU's economic environment to be determined under U.S. financial accounting rules if the facts and circumstances taken into account are "substantially similar" to those described in the regulations.[34]

The currency in which a QBU's books are kept is presumed to be its functional currency.[35] The taxpayer may rebut this presumption by showing a substantial nontax reason for keeping the books in a currency other than the one asserted to be the QBU's functional currency. The IRS may disregard the presumption at will. Assume a domestic bank has a branch in a foreign country that requires the branch's books to be kept in that country's currency; the branch's principal activity, however, is making loans in dollars from funds it borrows in dollars.[36] Because the branch's activities are primarily conducted in dollars and the books are kept in a foreign currency for a substantial nontax reason (to comply with local law), the presumption is rebutted, and the dollar is the QBU's functional currency.

If a foreign corporation has two or more QBUs with different functional currencies, the economic environment standard may be applied a second time to the corporation's activities as an aggregate to determine the corporation's overall functional currency.[37] When this is done, each QBU of the corporation determines taxable income or loss and earnings and profits (or deficit) in its functional currency, and the figures for the several QBUs are translated into the corporation's overall functional currency at the weighted average exchange rate for the

---

[29] 1986 Bluebook, supra note 9, at 1092 (offshore construction project is of insufficient duration to be QBU).

[30] Id. at 1093.

[31] Id. at 1094.

[32] Reg. §1.985-1(c)(4).

[33] Financial Accounting Standards Board, Statement of Financial Accounting Standards No. 52 (1976).

[34] Reg. §1.985-1(c)(5).

[35] Reg. §1.985-1(c)(3).

[36] Reg. §1.985-1(f) Ex. 3.

[37] Reg. §1.985-1(d).

taxable year.[38] Since a foreign corporation is subject to U.S. tax only on U.S. source income and taxable income effectively connected with U.S. business, the overall figures are usually relevant only to the U.S. taxation of shareholders who are U.S. persons. For example, if the corporation is a controlled foreign corporation, the overall figures are needed to apply subpart F and §1248 to its U.S. shareholders.[39]

3. *Changes of functional currency.* A functional currency is a method of accounting, and the adoption or election of a new functional currency thus is a change of accounting method, which normally can be done only with IRS consent.[40] Permission to change is usually given only if "significant changes" have occurred "in the facts and circumstances of the QBU's economic environment."[41] Even if consent is given, various adjustments must be made to reflect the change.[42]

4. *Dollar election in lieu of hyperinflationary currency.* If a QBU operates in a hyperinflationary economy, the U.S. dollar may be used as its functional currency even if the QBU's books are kept in the local currency. This election, however, is essentially a method of translation and is discussed in the next section.[43]

¶71.3 QUALIFIED BUSINESS UNITS ACCOUNTING IN FOREIGN CURRENCIES

¶71.3.1 Introductory

If a taxpayer has one or more qualified business units (QBUs) with functional currencies different from the taxpayer's overall functional currency, taxable income or loss is computed separately for each such unit.[1] The computation

---

[38] The weighted average exchange rate is "the simple average of the daily exchange rates" during the year, exclusive of weekends and other nonbusiness days. Prop. Reg. §1.987-1(b)(1); Reg. §1.989(b)-1.

[39] See supra ¶68.2 for subpart F and §1248.

[40] IRC §985(b)(4); Reg. §1.985-4(a). See infra ¶105.12 for changes of accounting methods.

[41] Reg. §1.985-4(b).

[42] Reg. §1.985-5.

[43] Infra ¶71.3.3.

[1] IRC §987(1); Prop. Reg. §1.987-1(a). See Staff of Joint Comm. on Tax'n, 99th Cong., 2d Sess., General Explanation of the Tax Reform Act of 1986 at 1089–90 (Comm. Print 1987) [hereinafter 1986 Bluebook].

Except as noted below for particular provisions, the regulations under §987 will be effective for taxable years beginning more than 30 days after final regulations are promulgated. Prop. Reg. §1.987-1(c). For post-1986 years preceding the regulations' effective date, the profit and loss method must be applied in a way that is "reasonable" and "consistent with the principles" of the proposed regulations.

is done in the unit's functional currency, usually using a profit and loss method.[2] A QBU is called a "QBU branch" if its functional currency differs from the taxpayer's overall functional currency and it uses the profit and loss method.[3] However, if a QBU's functional currency is hyperinflationary, a U.S. dollar approximate separate transactions method (DASTM) may be elected and may sometimes be required.[4]

Under the profit and loss method, taxable income or loss is computed annually in the QBU's functional currency. This taxable income is generally translated into the taxpayer's overall functional currency (typically, U.S. dollars) at an average exchange rate for the year. However, if the taxpayer elects the credit for foreign income taxes, these taxes, and an amount of taxable income equal to the taxes, are translated at the exchange rate prevailing when the taxes were paid. Gains and losses from exchange rate fluctuation between the QBU's functional currency and the taxpayer's overall functional currency are not recognized as they accrue, but exchange gain or loss is instead recognized each time the QBU remits earnings to the head office or to another QBU that has a different functional currency—when assets of the QBU are removed from the foreign currency environment in which the QBU operates.

¶71.3.2 Profit and Loss Method

Under the profit and loss method, a QBU branch's taxable income or loss for the year, initially computed in the branch's functional currency, is translated into the taxpayer's overall functional currency, and the translated amount is combined in the taxpayer's return with all other gross income and deductions.[5] For example, the taxable income or loss of a domestic corporation using the U.S. dollar as its functional currency is an aggregate of (1) the sum of the separate taxable incomes and losses of its QBU branches, so computed and translated into dollars, and (2) gross income and deductions as to which the functional currency is the dollar.

The profit and loss method is also used in determining earnings and profits of a foreign corporation whose shareholders include U.S. persons, even if the corporation is not itself subject to U.S. tax.[6] Assume a domestic corporation has a subsidiary in country X that carries on business in countries X and Y; the subsidiary's overall functional currency is country X's, but the business in country Y is a QBU branch whose functional currency is the country Y currency. The

---

[2] For the dollar approximate separate transactions method, see infra ¶71.3.3.

[3] Prop. Reg. §1.987-1(a)(2).

[4] Infra ¶71.3.3. See INTL-965-86, 1991-2 CB 1032, 1034 (as an alternative to DASTM, IRS is "studying recharacterizing a portion of the QBU's interest expense (but not its interest income) as principal under the authority of section 989(b)").

[5] IRC §§987(1), (2); Prop. Reg. §1.987-1(b)(1).

[6] Prop. Reg. §1.987-1(b)(1).

subsidiary's earnings and profits for any year, which are stated in country X currency (the overall functional currency), are the sum of (1) the country Y branch's profit or loss for the year, determined in country Y currency but translated into country X currency at the average exchange rate for the year, and (2) country X profit or loss for the year.

1. *Generally.* Under the profit and loss method, taxable income or loss and earnings and profits are computed in three steps:

    a. A profit and loss statement is prepared from the branch's books and records in its functional currency.

    b. This statement is adjusted to conform to U.S. tax principles.

    c. The profit or loss shown on the adjusted statement is translated into dollars at the "average exchange rate for the taxable year," which is "the simple average of the daily exchange rates" during the year, exclusive of weekends and other nonbusiness days.[7]

However, actual dividends and deemed dividends under §1248 are translated at the spot rate for the date the amount is included in the taxpayer's gross income, not the average rate for the year.[8] Assume the assets of a domestic corporation's branch in country X include all of the stock of a country X corporation.[9] Dividends received by the branch from the X corporation are translated at the spot rate for the dates of distribution, and if the stock is sold at a gain, any portion of it that is characterized as a dividend under §1248 is translated at the spot rate for the date of sale. Also, if undistributed earnings of a foreign corporation are included in a U.S. shareholder's gross income under subpart F or the rules for qualified electing funds, these inclusions are excluded from the profit and loss statement, even if the stock is an asset of a QBU branch of the shareholder, because they are subject to separate translation rules described elsewhere.[10]

---

    [7] Prop. Reg. §1.987-1(b)(1); Reg. §1.989(b)-1. Exchange rates must be determined from a "qualified source," which is any source shown "to reflect actual transactions conducted in a free market and involving representative amounts." Reg. §1.964-1(d)(5). A publication of the International Monetary Fund called International Financial Statistics is used unless the taxpayer demonstrates that another source satisfies the free-market, representative-amounts test. See Travelers Ins. Co. v. US, 35 Fed. Cl. 138, 96-1 USTC ¶50,231 (1996) (under prior law, profit and loss method, applied with year-end exchange rates, clearly reflected taxpayer's income).

    [8] IRC §§989(b)(1), (2); Prop. Reg. §1.987-1(b)(1)(iv). Section 1248 characterizes a U.S. shareholder's gain on a sale of stock of a controlled foreign corporation as a dividend to the extent of the shareholder's ratable share of any earnings of the corporation not previously subjected to U.S. tax. See supra ¶68.2.16.

    [9] Prop. Reg. §1.987-1(b)(6) Ex. 6.

    [10] Prop. Reg. §1.987-1(b)(2), discussed infra ¶71.4 text accompanying notes 7-12.

A loss determined under the profit and loss method may be recognized even if it exceeds the taxpayer's investment in the branch.[11] Assume a domestic corporation organizes a branch in foreign country X and funds the branch with $100, which is then worth 100 units of the branch's functional currency (the country X u); for the first year of branch operations, the branch sustains a loss of 100u, which is translated as $150 under the rules described above.[12] The loss is fully recognized, even though the dollar amount of the loss ($150) exceeds the dollar amount of the taxpayer's investment in the branch ($100). However, this excess is foreign currency gain, and under rules described below, it will subsequently be recognized as such, thereby effectively recapturing the excess loss deduction, either when the branch makes a remittance to the taxpayer or when the branch terminates.

2. *Foreign income taxes.* If the taxpayer elects the foreign tax credit and accounts for foreign income taxes on an accrual basis, these taxes are usually translated into dollars at the average exchange rate for the year to which the taxes relate (the accrual year).[13] If the taxpayer accounts for foreign income taxes on a cash basis, the translation is at the exchange rate prevailing at the time of payment, even if the tax is prepaid under an estimated tax or withholding regime. This time-of-payment rule also applies to all taxpayers, regardless of accounting method, for taxable years beginning before 1998.

A subsequent increase in a QBU's income tax liability (e.g., a deficiency assessment) is translated at the average exchange rate for the accrual year or the exchange rate prevailing when the deficiency is paid, usually depending on whether the original liability was translated on a cash or accrual basis.[14] However, if a tax payment is refunded or credited against a later year's tax, the refund or credit is translated at the exchange rate used for the original payment.[15] Assume a QBU whose functional currency is the country X u pays a country X income tax of 100u in year 1 when 1u is worth 60 cents. The payment is translated as $60 (100u times $.6), and if 10u of the tax is refunded in year 2, the refund is translated as (10u times $.60), regardless of the exchange rate at the time of the refund.[16]

Without further modification, the time-of-payment rule would have the odd effect of translating a foreign income tax paid by a branch at the spot rate on the

---

[11] Prop. Reg. §1.987-1(b)(4). The legislative history indicates that the Treasury could, contrary to this proposed regulation, restrict the dollar amount of a branch's loss to "the taxpayer's dollar basis in the branch (that is, the original dollar investment plus subsequent capital contributions and advances, unremitted earnings, and indebtedness for which the taxpayer is liable)." H.R. Rep. No. 841, 99th Cong., 2d Sess. II-675 (Conf. Rep. 1986).

[12] Prop. Reg. §1.987-1(b)(6) Ex. 1.

[13] IRC §986(a); H.R. Rep. No. 841, supra note 11, at II-676. The translation rules are described more fully in ¶69.13.

[14] IRC §986(a)(1)(B)(i).

[15] IRC §986(a)(1)(B)(ii).

[16] See H.R. Rep. No. 841, supra note 11, at II-676.

date of payment, while the revenues of the branch used to pay the tax was translated at the average rate for the year. To eliminate this discrepancy, a taxpayer using the time-of-payment rule is required to translate taxable income of a QBU branch equal to the branch's foreign income taxes at the rates used to translate the taxes.[17] This amount is referred to as the "tax equivalent amount." If the taxpayer chooses to deduct foreign income taxes, rather than claiming the credit, this rule does not apply because foreign income taxes are not separately translated.

Assume a domestic corporation (U.S. dollar functional currency) has a QBU branch whose functional currency is the country X u; for a pre-1998 year, the branch has 100u of taxable income and pays country X taxes of 20u; the average exchange rate for the year is 1u = \$1, but the taxes are paid when the rate is 1u = \$1.2.[18] The 20u of taxes are translated as \$24 (20u times 1.2). If the taxpayer claims the foreign tax credit, taxable income equal to the excess of total income over the foreign income taxes (100u less 20u) is translated at the average rate of 1u = \$1, and the remaining income (20u) is translated at the rate used for translating the taxes. The branch's taxable income is therefore \$104 (sum of 80u times \$1 and 20u times \$1.2).

If a foreign income tax is redetermined after the taxable year, the redetermination is also reflected in the translation of taxable income. Assume the country X tax for the year in the example is redetermined during the next year, requiring the taxpayer to pay an additional 5u of country X tax when the exchange rate is 1u = \$1.4.[19] The additional tax is translated as \$7 (5u times \$1.4), and the total taxes for the year are thus \$31 (sum of \$24 and \$7). Taxable income equal to the taxes of 25u is translated at the same rates as the taxes (\$31), while the remaining taxable income is translated at the average rate (75u times \$1). Taxable income is therefore \$106 (\$31 plus \$75).

If a branch's foreign income taxes exceed total branch income, as computed under U.S. rules, taxable income equal to the taxes is nevertheless translated at the rates used for the taxes. Assume that for the following year, the branch in the example has taxable income of 10u under U.S. rules, but because of differences between U.S. and country X accounting rules, country X determines taxable income to be much greater than 10u and imposes taxes of 30u on branch income.[20] Assume the spot rate for the date these taxes are paid is 1u = \$1.2. The taxes are translated as \$36 (30 times \$1.2), and branch taxable income of 30u is also translated as \$36. The excess of this deemed taxable income over actual taxable income (30u − 10u) is treated as a loss and is translated at the average rate for the year. If the average rate is 1u = \$1, the deemed loss is \$20 (20u times

---

[17] Prop. Reg. §1.987-1(b)(3).
[18] Prop. Reg. §1.987-1(b)(6) Ex. 2.
[19] Prop. Reg. §1.987-1(b)(6) Ex. 4.
[20] Prop. Reg. §1.987-1(b)(6) Ex. 3.

$10). In total, branch taxable income is $16 ($36 of taxable income less loss of $20).

3. *Earnings remittances.* Foreign currency gain or loss, called §987 gain or loss, is recognized whenever property of a QBU branch is transferred to another unit of the taxpayer and when the branch terminates.[21] Assume a domestic corporation organizes a foreign branch whose functional currency is the country *X u*. The branch is capitalized with 10,000u, which the taxpayer purchased for $5,000, and the branch's taxable income for its first year is 1,000u, which is translated as $600 dollars at the average exchange rate for the year (1u = $.6). At the end of this year, the branch sells its only asset, 11,000u in cash, for $7,700 and transfers the $7,700 to the corporation's head office. The corporation invested $5,000 in this venture and recognized $600 as taxable income, but it comes away from the venture with $7,700. The amount by which the remittance from the branch ($7,700) exceeds sum of the investment and taxable income ($5,000 plus $600) is §987 gain. Because it results from changes in the exchange rate between the dollar and the *u* while the venture was underway, it is a form of currency gain and is therefore ordinary income. However, while other forms of exchange gain or loss are from sources within the country of the taxpayer's residence, the source of §987 gain or loss depends on the locations of the branch's assets or income.

The proposed regulations utilize two pools—an equity pool and a basis pool—as tools for determining §987 gain or loss.[22] The equity pool essentially represents the taxpayer's investment in the branch, including accumulated income, stated in the branch's functional currency; the basis pool represents this investment in the taxpayer's overall functional currency. Section 987 gain or loss is the difference between a branch remittance, translated into the overall functional currency at the spot rate for the date of the remittance, and the portion of the basis pool that is allocated to the remittance.

a. *"Remittance."* Section 987 gain or loss is recognized only when a QBU branch makes a "remittance" or terminates.[23] Any transfer from a branch to another unit of the taxpayer is a remittance if the aggregate of these transfers during the taxable year does not exceed the equity pool, determined at year-end but without regard to transfers made by the branch during the year.[24] If the transfers made by the branch during the year exceed the equity pool, the pool

---

[21] Prop. Reg. §1.987-2(a)(1). See H.R. Rep. No. 841, supra note 11, at II-675, which anticipates these rules but differs in many details.

Except as noted below, the rules on §987 gain or loss will become effective only for taxable years beginning more than 30 days after the promulgation of final regulations. Prop. Reg. §1.987-2(h). For post-1986 years preceding the first year to be governed by the regulations, §987 gain or loss must be calculated and characterized in ways that are "consistent" with "the principles" of the proposed regulations.

[22] Prop. Reg. §1.987-2(a)(1).

[23] Id.

[24] Prop. Reg. §1.987-2(b)(4).

must be allocated among the transfers by "a reasonable method" that is applied consistently for all of the taxpayer's QBU branches, and each transfer is a remittance to the extent of the equity pool allocated to it.

b. *Equity and basis pools.* The opening balance in the equity pool is the sum of the adjusted bases of the branch's property, less branch liabilities, on the first date the branch uses the profit and loss method (e.g., the date it commences business).[25] This balance is stated in the branch's functional currency. Each year, the equity pool is

(1) Increased or decreased by taxable income or loss for the year as determined in the branch's functional currency under the profit and loss method, except that taxable income equal to foreign income taxes on branch income that are claimed as credits (the "tax equivalent amount") is excluded from the pool.[26]

(2) Increased by any amounts transferred by the taxpayer to the branch during the year and decreased by transfers from the branch to another branch or the taxpayer's head office.

(3) Increased by distributions received from foreign corporations whose stock is among the branch's assets, but only if the distributions are tax-free dividends from amounts previously included in gross income under subpart F or the rules for qualified electing funds (previously taxed amounts).

Borrowings, and principal repayments of borrowings, normally have no effect on the pool, even if the loan is an obligation of the branch and is repaid from assets of the branch, because the borrowing and repayments (as distinguished from the use of the borrowed funds) neither creates nor reduces basis.[27] However, a repayment of a branch liability with funds not previously treated as a branch asset should be treated as though the money was transferred to the branch immediately before the payment, and a use of branch funds to repay a liability not previously treated as a branch liability should have the opposite consequence.

The basis pool is determined in the same way as the equity pool, except that

(1) The opening balance is translated into the taxpayer's overall functional currency (e.g., the dollar) at the spot rate for the date on which the profit and loss method is first used for the branch.[28]

---

[25] Prop. Reg. §1.987-2(c)(1). Special rules are provided for applying this rule for branches that operated before 1987.

[26] Prop. Reg. §1.987-1(b)(3)(iii) (tax equivalent amount excluded from pools).

[27] Prop. Reg. §1.987-2(c)(3) Ex. 3; INTL-965-86, supra note 4, at 1033.

[28] Special rules are provided for branches in operation before 1987.

The "spot rate" is a rate shown "to reflect a fair market rate of exchange available to the public for currency under a spot contract in a free market and involving represen-

(2) Branch profit or loss is translated into the overall functional currency under rules described above.[29]

(3) The pool is adjusted for remittances under rules described below.

(4) Transfers to the branch from other units of the taxpayer are translated at the spot rate on the date of transfer, as are transfers made by the branch that are not remittances because they exceed the equity pool.[30]

(5) Previously taxed amounts are translated at the spot rate as of the date of receipt.

If one or more contributions to or distributions by a QBU branch do "not have a significant business purpose," the IRS may "make appropriate adjustments to clearly reflect the income of the taxpayer."[31] Typically, such adjustments would consist of adding or removing property to or from the pools so that they reflect the true composition of the branch's assets.

c. *"Transfer."* A transfer to a QBU branch adds to the equity and basis pools, and a transfer by a branch is usually a remittance, which triggers §987 gain or loss and reduces the pools. The term "transfer" refers to "the net amount of property that, on any day, either is distributed from a QBU branch to the taxpayer (or to any other QBU branch of the taxpayer) or is contributed by the taxpayer (or by any other QBU branch of the taxpayer) to the QBU branch."[32]

A transfer denominated as a loan is treated the same as an outright transfer. For example, if a taxpayer's country X branch purports to "loan" 1,000u to the taxpayer's country Y branch, the loan is a distribution by the country X branch (and therefore a remittance to the extent of the equity pool) and a contribution to the country Y branch, and a payment of interest or principal on the loan is a distribution by the country Y branch and a contribution to the country X branch.[33]

If the transfer consists of property other than money, the amount of the transfer is the property's adjusted basis, stated in the functional currency of the transferor unit.[34] For example, if a domestic corporation's functional currency is

---

tative amounts." Prop. Reg. §1.987-2(b)(3), adopting definition of Reg. §1.988-1(d)(1), discussed infra ¶71.5 text accompanying notes 17–20.

[29] See supra text accompanying notes 7–12.

[30] This translation may be made with a "spot rate convention," under which a particular rate is used for all transactions during a period not longer than one quarter of the year (e.g., the average rate for the month). Prop. Reg. §1.987-2(b)(3), adopting rule of Reg. §1.988-1(d)(3), discussed infra ¶71.8 text accompanying notes 17–20.

[31] Prop. Reg. §1.987-2(a)(2). This rule is effective for all taxable years beginning after 1986. Prop. Reg. §1.987-2(h).

[32] Prop. Reg. §1.987-2(b)(2)(i).

[33] See Prop. Reg. §1.987-2(c)(3) Ex. 4.

[34] The transferee's basis is increased or decreased by any exchange gain recognized under §988 as a result of the transfer. Prop. Reg. §1.987-2(b)(2)(iii). Assume the country X branch distributes a bond denominated in dollars, which are nonfunctional currency to the branch but functional currency to the remainder of the corporation. The branch recognizes exchange gain under §988 on the distribution, and the bond's new basis is the

the dollar and its country X branch uses the u as its functional currency, the amount of a contribution to the branch of property other than money is the corporation's basis for the property in dollars, and the amount of a distribution by the branch is the property's adjusted basis in u. If the transferor and transferee units use different functional currencies, the transferee's basis is translated into the functional currency of the transferee unit at the spot rate for the date of transfer.[35] For example, if the domestic corporation transfers a machine with a basis of $100 to the country X branch when the spot rate is 1u = $1.25, the branch's basis for the property is 80u ($100/$1.25).

A transfer of a liability from another unit of the taxpayer to a QBU branch is treated as a distribution by the branch equal to the liability, and a transfer of a liability from a QBU branch to another unit of the taxpayer is treated as a contribution to the branch.[36] If the liability is denominated in the transferor unit's functional currency, it is translated into the transferee's functional currency at the spot rate for the date of transfer. For example, if the domestic corporation in the example transfers a $100 liability to the branch when 1u = $1.33, the liability is recorded in the branch's books as a nonfunctional currency liability with a functional currency basis of 75u ($100/$1.33). If the liability is denominated in a currency other than the transferor unit's functional currency, the transferor recognizes exchange gain under §988. Assume the branch in the example owes $100 under a note for which it has a functional currency basis of 80u. If the liability is transferred off the branch's books when 1u = $1, the branch has exchange loss of 20u (80u less $100/u).

All transfers to and by a QBU branch on any day are netted.[37] Assume the domestic corporation in the example transfers 1,000u to the county X branch, and the branch transfers 480u to the corporation's country Y branch. If the two transfers occur on the same day, the country X branch is treated as receiving a net transfer 520u (1,000u less 480u), and it therefore makes no remittance. If they occur on successive days, they are analyzed as a 1,000u transfer to the country X branch and a 480u transfer by the country X branch to the country Y branch, and the latter is a remittance on which the country X branch recognizes §987 gain or loss.

To illustrate the application of the foregoing rules to property other than money, assume the country X branch transfers to the corporation's head office a

---

sum of the branch's basis and the exchange gain, both stated in u, translated into dollars at the spot rate for the date of the distribution.

[35] This translation may be made with a spot rate convention of a kind described above in note 30.

[36] Prop. Reg. §1.987-2(b)(2)(iv).

[37] Prop. Reg. §1.987-2(b)(2)(i). See INTL-965-86, supra note 4, at 1033 (netting rule is "proposed to simplify compliance with section 987," but because it "deviate[s] from the rule for distributions from corporations, . . . the total amount of foreign source income of a business will vary slightly depending on whether the business is conducted in branch or corporate form").

machine worth 100u that has a basis of 25u, and the head office simultaneously transfers 100u to the branch.[38] The branch's transfer is counted at 25u, the amount of the machine's adjusted basis, whereas the head office's transfer is counted at 100u. The two transfers are therefore netted as a 75u transfer to the country X branch. If the spot rate is 1u = $1.2 on the date of the transfers, the adjusted basis of the machine immediately thereafter is $30 (25u times $1.2).

d. *Section 987 gain or loss on remittances.* On a remittance by a QBU branch, §987 gain or loss is recognized to the extent of the difference between the amount of the remittance and the portion of the basis pool allocated to the remittance.[39] The gain or loss is essentially treated as income or loss of the remainder of the corporation and is thus not reported on the branch's profit or loss statement.

The amount of the remittance usually is the basis of the remitted property in the branch's functional currency, translated into the taxpayer's overall functional currency at the spot rate on the date of the remittance.[40] The portion of the basis pool allocated to a remittance is the amount of the pool (reduced by prior remittances), multiplied by

$$\frac{\text{Amount of remittance, stated in branch's functional currency}}{\text{Equity pool (reduced by prior remittances)}}$$

Assume a domestic corporation (U.S. dollar functional currency) organizes a branch in country X that uses the country X u as its functional currency.[41] During the first year of branch operations (year 1), (1) the taxpayer transfers 1,000u to the branch when 1u = $1 and transfers $1,000 to the branch when 1u = $2, (2) the branch has profits of 1,000u, which is translated at the average rate for the year of 1u = $2, and (3) the branch transfers 1,000u to the taxpayer when 1u = $2. Before taking item 3 into account, the branch's equity and basis pools at year-end are

	Equity	Basis
Opening balances	-0-	-0-
Increased by		

---

[38] Prop. Reg. §1.987-2(c)(3) Ex. 1.

[39] Prop. Reg. §§1.987-2(d)(1), (2).

[40] Prop. Reg. §§1.987-2(b)(2)(i), (4). This amount is adjusted if the remittance consists of (1) functional currency of the unit of the taxpayer to which the remittance is made (e.g.,the functional currency of a QBU branch receiving the remittance or the taxpayer's overall functional currency if the remittance is not to another QBU branch) or (2) a financial instrument denominated in the functional currency of the recipient unit. In such a case, exchange gain or loss is recognized by the branch on the remittance under §988, and the amount of the remittance is the sum of the branch's basis for the currency or instrument and the §988 gain or loss. Reg. §1.988-1(a)(10), discussed infra ¶71.11.

[41] Prop. Reg. §1.987-2(c)(3) Ex. 4.

	Equity	Basis
Profits	1,000u	$2,000
Transfers to branch		
1,000u	1,000u	1,000
$1,000	500u	1,000
		$4,000
	2,500u	

Item 3, the branch's 1,000u transfer to the taxpayer, is a remittance because it does not exceed the year-end balance in the equity pool, determined without regard to remittances. The portion of the basis pool allocated to the remittance is

$$\text{(remittance in } u)/\text{(equity pool)} \times \text{(basis pool)} =$$
$$1{,}000u/2{,}500u \times \$4{,}000 = \$1{,}600$$

Section 987 gain or loss is $400—the excess of (1) the dollar value of the remittance, translated at the spot rate for the date of the transfer (1,000u times $2), over (2) the portion of the basis pool that is allocated to the distribution ($1,600). The remitted 1,000u is no longer functional currency because the taxpayer's overall functional currency is the dollar. The 1,000u are thus treated as property other than money and have a basis of $2,000 (1,000u times $2).

The equity pool is reduced by the amount of the remittance in the branch's functional currency, and the basis pool is reduced by the portion of the pool that is allocated to the remittance. After taking the remittance into account, the year-end pools are

	Equity	Basis
Balance exclusive of remittance	2,500u	$4,000
Less remittance	1,000u	1,600
	1,500u	$2,400

Assume the country X branch has a loss for year 2 of 1,000u, which is translated at the average exchange rate for the year of 1u = $2. During year 2, but on different days, (1) the taxpayer transfers 2,000u to the branch when 1u = $3, and (2) the branch "loans" 4,000u to another QBU branch of the taxpayer, also when 1u = $3. The loan characterization is ignored, and the 4,000u is treated as a remittance to the extent of the equity pool. Apart from this transfer, the year-end balances in the pools are

	Equity	Basis
Year-end balance from year 1	1,500u	$2,400
Increased by transfer to branch	2,000u	6,000

	Equity	Basis
Decreased by year 2 loss	(1,000u)	(2,000)
	2,500u	$ 6,400

The 4,000u loan is a remittance to the extent of 2,500u, the balance in the equity pool. The basis pool allocable to the remittance is

$$(2,500u)/(2,500u) \times \$6,400$$

The remittance results in §987 gain of $1,100—the excess of (1) the amount of the remittance translated into the overall functional currency at the spot rate on the date of distribution (2,500u times $3) over (2) the allocable basis pool ($6,400). The QBU branch receiving the 4,000u from the country X branch takes a basis for the 4,000u of $12,000 (4,000u times $3), translated into the recipient branch's functional currency at the spot rate for the date of the purported loan. Taking the transfer of the 4,000u into account, the country X branch's pools at year-end are

	Equity	Basis
Balance exclusive of remittance	2,500u	$6,400
Reduced by		
Remittance	2,500u	6,400
Nonremittance portion of transfer	1,500u	4,500
	(1,500u)	($4,500)

If a QBU branch has a positive balance in its equity pool while its basis pool is negative, a transfer by the branch results in §987 gain exceeding the amount of the transfer. Assume that during a subsequent year, on a day when the spot rate is 1u = $1, the country X branch in the example transfers 40u to the head office; apart from this transfer, the year-end balances are 120u in the equity pool and negative $60 in the basis pool.[42] The entire amount of the transfer (40u) is a remittance because it is less than the equity pool (120u). The basis pool allocable to the remittance is

$$40u/120u \times (\$60) = (\$20)$$

The remittance results in §987 gain of $60—the excess of the remittance, translated into dollars at the spot rate for the date of distribution (40u times $1), less the basis pool allocated to the remittance (minus $20). A remittance worth $40 thus triggers recognition of $60 of gain. This occurs because (1) an excess of the

---

[42] Prop. Reg. §1.987-2(c)(3) Ex. 5.

dollar value of the equity pool over the basis pool is foreign currency gain and (2) when the equity pool is positive and the basis pool negative, this difference necessarily exceeds the equity pool. In the example, one third of this difference is taxed because one third of the equity pool is distributed.

If a partnership's functional currency differs from a partner's, the partnership is a QBU branch of the partner, and a partnership distribution to the partner is thus a remittance on which the partner has §987 gain or loss, even if the distribution is otherwise tax-free.[43] Assume a citizen and resident of the United States (U.S. dollar functional currency) is a partner of a partnership whose operations are in country X (country X u functional currency), and the partnership distributes 100u to the partner. Under §731(a), the partner recognizes neither gain nor loss on the distribution.[44]

However, the partner has §987 gain or loss equal to the difference between the dollar value of the 100u at the time of distribution and the portion of the partner's basis for her interest that is allocated to the distribution under the rules described above.

When a QBU branch makes a transfer in the functional currency of the recipient or a transfer consisting of a financial instrument denominated in the recipient's functional currency, exchange gain or loss is recognized on the transmittal as well as the receipt of the remittance.[45] Assume a domestic corporation (U.S. dollar functional currency) has a country X branch (country X u functional currency), and the branch remits U.S. dollars to the corporation's head office. The branch has exchange gain or loss under §988 (included in its profit or loss for the year of the remittance) equal to the difference between its adjusted basis in u for the dollars and the value of the dollars in u at the spot rate for the date of the remittance.[46] The amount of the transfer in u is the sum of the branch's basis and the exchange gain or loss; in dollars, it equals the number of dollars transferred. Because units of functional currency cannot have a basis different from their face amount (e.g., for a taxpayer or QBU whose functional currency is the dollar, $1 cannot have a basis of more or less than $1), any difference between basis and face must be recognized when the currency switches from nonfunctional to functional currency. In the example, gain or loss in the branch's dollar holdings must be reckoned up when the dollars are remitted to the head office because the remittance changes the dollars from nonfunctional to functional currency.

---

[43] See INTL-965-86, supra note 4, at 1033–34 (IRS "is particularly interested in suggestions on how section 987 can best be coordinated with the partnership provisions").

[44] For §731(a), see infra ¶87.1.1. Under §731(a), a partner recognizes gain on a distribution only to the extent the amount of money distributed exceeds the partner's basis for her partnership interest. The distributed 100u should be considered property other than money because the u is not the partner's functional currency. The distribution is thus tax-free under §731(a), regardless of the partner's basis.

[45] H.R. Rep. No. 841, supra note 11, at II-675.

[46] For §988, see infra ¶71.5.

e. Section 987 gain or loss on branch termination. Section 987 gain or loss is recognized on the termination of a QBU branch.[47] "Generally, a QBU branch terminates when its activities cease," whether as a result of the transfer of its assets to another unit of the taxpayer or a sale or other disposition of substantially all of the assets or for any other reason.[48] Also, a deemed sale of a corporation's assets under §338 results in the termination of all of the corporation's QBU branches. Moreover, a foreign corporation's QBU branches terminate if, during a period of 12 months or less, a U.S. person sells or exchanges 10 percent or more (by vote or value) of the corporation's stock in transactions to which §1248 applies or is treated as disposing of the stock (e.g., on a sale or exchange of stock of the corporation's parent).[49]

However, asset transfers in nonrecognition transactions usually do not terminate QBU branches. Specifically, no termination results from a distribution of branch assets from subsidiary corporation to parent corporation in a liquidation subject to §332 unless (1) the distributing subsidiary is a domestic corporation and the parent is foreign, or vice versa, or (2) both corporations are foreign and the parent's functional currency is the same as that of the QBU branch.[50]

Similarly, a transfer of branch assets pursuant to a plan of corporate reorganization is generally not a termination because, under §381, the transferee succeeds to the transferor's tax attributes.[51] However, a reorganization terminates branches in three situations. First, if the reorganization includes a transfer of property from a U.S. person to a foreign corporation and is therefore subject to §367(a), the reorganization terminates all QBU branches of the transferor corporation. Second, if §367(a) does not apply but a foreign corporation is a party to the reorganization, the reorganization terminates (1) any QBU branch of the transferor whose functional currency is the same as the transferee's or (2) all of the transferor's QBU branches if a U.S. shareholder of the transferor is required to report a deemed dividend under §367(b).

A QBU branch terminates on the transfer of its assets to a controlled corporation in an exchange to which §351 applies if the transferor is a U.S. person and the transferee is a foreign corporation.[52] The IRS has reserved for

---

[47] Prop. Reg. §1.987-3(g) (effective for all taxable years beginning after 1986).

[48] Prop. Reg. §1.987-3(a). Except as noted, the provisions of §1.987-3 will be effective only for taxable years beginning more than 30 days after the regulations are finalized. Prop. Reg. §1.987-3(i). For earlier post-1986 years, "a taxpayer must determine what constitutes a termination using the principles of §1.987-3(a)."

[49] Prop. Reg. §1.987-3(d). See INTL-965-86, supra note 4, at 1034 ("consideration was given to requiring only the selling (or redeeming) shareholder in a section 1248 transaction to realize his pro-rata share of the unrealized section 987 gain or loss of a QBU branch of a CFC, rather than treating a section 1248 transaction as a termination event, which affects all shareholders[, but t]he pro-rata approach was rejected in the interest of simplicity").

[50] Prop. Reg. §1.987-3(b)(1). For §332 liquidations, see infra ¶93.6.

[51] Prop. Reg. §1.987-3(b)(2). For §381, see infra ¶95.5.2.

[52] Prop. Reg. §1.987-3(c). For §351, see infra ¶91.1.

future consideration the issue of whether other §351 transfers should trigger branch terminations.

For the year of a termination, §987 gain or loss is recognized under the usual rules for remittances that are made by the branch during the termination year but before the termination. Section 987 gain or loss is also recognized on the termination of the branch, computed as follows:[53]

(1) The branch's profit or loss is computed for the portion of the taxable year ending with the date of termination.[54]

(2) The equity and basis pools are adjusted for this profit or loss and for transfers to and by the branch during the year but before the termination.[55]

(3) If the equity pool exceeds zero after these adjustments, the §987 gain or loss on termination is the difference between (1) the equity pool, translated into the taxpayer's overall functional currency at the spot rate for the date of termination, and (2) the basis pool.

(4) If the equity pool is zero or less, (1) the taxpayer is deemed to make a transfer to the branch immediately before the termination sufficient to bring the pool to zero, (2) this transfer increases the basis pool by the amount of the deemed transfer, translated into the overall functional currency at the spot rate on the date of transfer, and (3) a negative balance in the basis pool after this increase is §987 gain, and a positive balance is §987 loss.

Assume a domestic corporation (U.S. dollar functional currency) has a country X branch (country X u functional currency) that terminates during year 10.[56] As of the beginning of year 10, the branch's equity and basis pools were 20u and $20, and the branch has profits of 12u for the portion of the taxable year ending with the termination. The average exchange rate for year 10 is 2u = $1, and the spot rate for the date of termination is 4u = $1. If there are no transfers to or by the branch during the year, the equity pool at the time of termination is 32u (20u at the beginning of the year plus current profit of 12u), and the basis pool is $26 ($20 plus 12u times $.5). Translated into dollars at the spot rate on the date of termination, the equity pool is $8 (32u times $.25). The difference

---

[53] Prop. Reg. §1.987-3(h) (effective for all taxable years beginning after 1986).

[54] If the branch holds units of the taxpayer's overall functional currency (which is nonfunctional currency to the branch) or holds or owes debt or contract rights denominated in the overall functional currency, the branch recognizes exchange gain or loss on these items under §988 as though the branch sold them at fair market value immediately before the termination. Reg. §1.988-1(a)(10), discussed infra ¶71.11.

[55] The basis adjustment for branch profit or loss for the year is determined with the average exchange rate for the portion of the taxable year ending with the termination. See Prop. Reg. §1.987-1(b)(5).

[56] Prop. Reg. §1.987-3(j) Ex. 1.

between the translated equity pool of $8 and the basis pool of $26 is §987 loss ($18).

In contrast, assume the branch's equity and basis pools were negative 16u and negative $5 at the beginning of year 10.[57] After adjustment for the year 10 profit, the pools are negative 4u (negative 16u plus 12u) and positive $1 (negative $5 plus 12u times $.50). Because the adjusted equity pool is less than zero, the taxpayer is deemed to have made a transfer to the branch equal to the deficit (4u), bringing the pool to zero. The corresponding increase to the basis pool, translated at the spot rate for the date of termination, is $1 (4u times $.25), bringing the basis pool to $2. This $2 is §987 loss.

4. *Character and source of §987 gain or loss.* Section 987 gain or loss is ordinary income or loss,[58] and according to the proposed regulations, its source and character are generally determined by "the same method the taxpayer uses to allocate and apportion its interest expense under [§]861."[59] Interest expense is usually apportioned ratably according to the values of the taxpayer's assets yielding income from various sources, but a "modified gross income method," under which interest expense is prorated according to the taxpayer's gross income from various sources, is also permitted.[60]

If the taxpayer uses the asset method, §987 gain or loss is also apportioned by the asset method, taking into account only assets of the QBU branch and ignoring various exceptions normally made to the fungibility principle that underlies the method.[61] Assume a country X branch of a domestic corporation has assets worth 2,000u, including 400u of assets generating income from sources within the United States, 400u generating foreign source income included in the general limitation basket for purposes of the separate limitation rules of §904(d),

---

[57] Prop. Reg. §1.987-3(j) Ex. 2.

[58] IRC §987(3)(B); Prop. Reg. §1.987-2(e). This rule is effective for all taxable years beginning after 1986. Prop. Reg. §1.987-2(h).

[59] Prop. Reg. §1.987-2(f)(1). The statute states that the source of income or loss is determined "by reference to the source of the income giving rise to post-1986 accumulated earnings." IRC §987(3)(B). The preamble to the proposed regulations states:

However, section 987 gain or loss is attributable not only to post-1986 earnings but also [to] contributions by the taxpayer to the branch and unremitted earnings from pre-1987 years. Therefore reliance upon post-1986 accumulated earnings would be inadequate. The "interest expense" method was chosen to avoid substantial complications in trying to determine the portion of the section 987 gain or loss attributable to transfers to the branch and pre-1987 earnings and how to allocate and apportion these amounts for purposes of sections 904(d) and 954. Using an interest expense method promotes the goal of regulation simplification by eliminating the need to maintain separate section 904(d) or subpart F "baskets" (and associated basis amounts) which are not otherwise needed or maintained for each branch.

INTL-965-86, supra note 4, at 1033.

[60] Reg. §1.861-9T.

[61] Prop. Reg. §1.987-2(f)(1)(i). For the ignored exceptions, see Reg. §1.861-10T.

and 1,200u generating foreign source income included in the passive basket.[62] Of any §987 gain or loss recognized during the year, 20 percent (400u/2,000u) is from domestic sources, 20 percent (400u/2,000u) is foreign source income (or deduction allocated to foreign source income) in the general basket, and 60 percent (1,200u/2,000u) is in the passive basket.

If the modified gross income method is used, it is applied to §987 gain or loss taking into account only gross income of the branch.[63] Assume the country X branch's gross income for the year is 500u, including 80u from domestic sources and 140u from foreign sources in the general limitation basket and 280u in the passive basket.[64] Under the modified gross income method, any §987 gain or loss for the year is assigned 16 percent (80u/500u) to domestic sources, 28 percent (140u/500u) to the general basket, and 56 percent (280u/500u) to the passive basket.

The IRS reserves the right to diverge from these source and character rules whenever necessary to avoid "significant distortion."[65] For example, if transfers to or from a branch cause the mix of its assets to differ "significantly" from the "historical composition," the IRS might block use of the asset method.

5. *Interaction with subpart F and qualified electing fund rules.* Several special rules apply if the assets of a QBU branch include stock of a controlled foreign corporation (CFC) or of a passive foreign investment corporation (PFIC) that is a qualified electing fund.[66] First, amounts included in gross income under subpart F (§951(a)) or the rules for qualified electing funds (§1293(a)(1)) are excluded from the profit and loss statement of a branch, even if the stock is an asset of the branch, because these items are subject to separate translation rules described elsewhere.[67] Second, these inclusions do not affect the equity and basis pools,[68] but the pools are increased by distributions received from the CFC or qualified electing fund if the distribution is treated as a nontaxable distribution of amounts previously included in the taxpayer's gross income under §951(a) or §1293(a)(1).[69] The increase in the equity pool is in the branch's functional currency, and the basis pool is increased by the same amount, translated into the taxpayer's overall functional currency at the spot rate for the date of distribution. The principal purpose of these rules is "to allow the rules of section 986(c), relating to foreign currency gain or loss on previously taxed earnings and profits,

---

[62] Prop. Reg. §1.987-2(f)(3) Ex. 1.

[63] Prop. Reg. §1.987-2(f)(1)(ii).

[64] See Prop. Reg. §1.987-2(f)(3) Ex. 2.

[65] Prop. Reg. §1.987-2(f)(2).

[66] See supra ¶68.2 for CFCs and ¶68.5.4 for qualified electing funds.

[67] Prop. Reg. §1.987-1(b)(2). For these separate translation rules, see infra ¶71.4 text accompanying notes 7-13.

[68] Prop. Reg. §1.987-2(b)(2)(ii).

[69] Prop. Reg. §§1.987-2(c)(1)(ii)(C), (2)(ii)(C).

to apply at the 'taxpayer' rather than the 'branch' level. Any other rule could convert section 986 gain or loss income into section 987 gain or loss."[70]

Assume the assets of a QBU branch in country X include all of the stock of a country X corporation (CFC); the country X u is the functional currency of the branch and the CFC.[71] If the CFC has subpart F income of 100u for year 1, this amount is included in the taxpayer's gross income under §951(a). Even though the CFC's stock is a branch asset, the gross income is neither included in the branch's profit or loss statement for year 1 nor reflected in the equity or basis pool. Assume the CFC distributes 75u to the branch during year 2, and the distribution is treated as a tax-free distribution from the subpart F income of year 1. At the time of distribution, the equity pool is increased by 75u, and the basis pool is increased by the dollar value of 75u according to the spot rate for the date of distribution.

¶71.3.3 Dollar Election for QBUs Operating in Hyperinflationary Currency

If the currency that would otherwise be a QBU's functional currency is hyperinflationary, the dollar must be used as the functional currency under a "U.S. dollar approximate separate transactions" method (DASTM), which supplants profit and loss method in this situation.[72] Under DASTM, costs are translated into dollars as they are incurred, other elements of the income and loss computation are determined and translated monthly or more frequently, and exchange gain and loss is recognized more or less as it accrues.

In providing for this method, Congress recognized that for "taxpayers operating in hyperinflationary economies, ... local-currency based accounting might not accurately reflect the income or loss ... because the local currency depreciation charge will become insignificant in relation to operating income."[73] More generally, tax computations based on historical cost, including the cost of goods sold and gains on sales of assets as well as depreciation, are distorted by

---

[70] INTL-965-86, supra note 4, at 1033.

[71] Prop. Reg. §1.987-2(c)(3) Ex. 2.

[72] Reg. §1.985-1(b)(2)(ii)(A) (applicable for taxable years beginning after August 24, 1994). See generally Cope & Katcher, Final DASTM Regulations Provide Significant Advantages to Businesses Operating in Hyperinflationary Countries, 9 Tax Notes Int'l 753 (Sept. 5, 1994); Hassman, Tuerff, Haecker & Gordon, A Practical Guide to Applying DASTM to the Current and Prior Taxable Years, 10 Tax Notes Int'l 662 (Feb. 20, 1995). For taxable years beginning before August 25, 1994, DASTM is elective for QBUs operating in hyperinflationary environments. Reg. §§1.985-1(b)(2)(i); 1.985-2. Taxpayers now required to use DASTM for operations previously reported under the profit and loss method may elect to use DASTM for all earlier years that are not barred by the statute of limitations. Reg. §1.985-3(a)(2)(ii).

For procedures for changing from the profit and loss method to DASTM, see Reg. §1.9854-7, promulgated by TD 8765, 1998-16 IRB 11.

[73] H.R. Rep. No. 841, supra note 11, at II-661.

inflation, as is interest income and expense, and the distortions are severe when inflation rates are high. DASTM largely insulates income computations from the effects of inflation in the hyperinflationary currency.

Although Congress expected that DASTM would be optional, the regulations make it mandatory because "the use of a hyperinflationary functional currency and the profit and loss method of accounting . . . does not clearly reflect income."[74] Although DASTM is advantageous to taxpayers in avoiding inflationary erosion of deductions based on historical cost, other deductions, especially interest expense, can be substantially overstated if DASTM is not used. An elective DASTM would typically be utilized only when the distortions under the profit and loss method run predominantly in the government's favor. The Treasury concluded that DASTM must be mandatory to protect the fisc from the mirror image of the distortions that Congress saw as unfairly disadvantaging taxpayers.

Assume *DC*, a domestic corporation, has a branch in country *Z*, whose functional currency would ordinarily be the country *Z u*. Country *Z* has experienced substantial inflation, and inflationary expectations are reflected in extraordinarily high interest rates. To finance operations of the country *Z* branch, *DC* borrows 1,000u from a country *Z* lender at 45 percent interest, which is the prevailing rate for bank loans to businesses in country *Z*. If *DC* is allowed to use the profit and loss method in accounting for the branch, *DC* is allowed a deduction for the annual interest of 450u, translated (like all other elements of profit and loss) at the average exchange rate for the year. However, much of the interest is effectively compensation to the lender for the erosion of principal through inflation. For example, if cumulative inflation in the *u* is 40 percent during the year, the value of the principal amount falls by 40 percent during the year, and the interest cost in constant *u*'s is only 50u (450u nominal interest, less 400u decline in value of principal). If the branch's assets do not include substantial amounts of long-lived property, *DC* likely would not elect DASTM because the election would cause the inflationary erosion of principal to be recognized at an earlier time, thereby offsetting the large interest deductions.

1. *QBUs required to use DASTM.* A QBU must usually adopt DASTM if its functional currency would otherwise be a "hyperinflationary currency,"[75] defined as a currency in which cumulative inflation was at least 100 percent over the 36 calendar months immediately preceding the taxable year.[76] Cumulative inflation is determined with compounding. For example, if inflation in a particular currency over the relevant three years is 29 percent, 25 percent, and 30 percent, the cumulative rate is 109.6 percent (129 percent times 125 percent times 130 percent, less 100 percent), not 84 percent (sum of 29, 25, and 30). The inflation rate is based on the consumer price index for the country issuing the

---

[74] TD 8556, 1994-35 IRB 6, 7.
[75] Reg. §1.985-1(b)(2)(ii)(A).
[76] Reg. §1.985-1(b)(2)(ii)(D). See H.R. Rep. No. 841, supra note 11, at II-662.

currency, as given in International Financial Statistics (a publication of the International Monetary Fund).

Although a functional currency can usually be changed only with IRS consent,[77] a change to DASTM required by the regulations is deemed made with IRS consent.[78] If a QBU is required to use DASTM for any year, DASTM becomes a method of accounting that, under the present regulations, cannot be changed without IRS consent, even if the foreign currency ceases to be hyperinflationary. However, the IRS has proposed regulations that would require a return to the profit and loss method, using the foreign currency of the QBU's economic environment as the functional currency, once that currency has not been hyperinflationary for three successive years.[79]

The regulations recognize one exception from the rule requiring use of DASTM: A foreign corporation need not use DASTM, either for the entire corporation or for a branch operating in a hyperinflationary environment, unless the corporation is a controlled foreign corporation (generally, a foreign corporation more than 50 percent owned by U.S. persons who each own at least 10 percent of the voting stock).[80] However, if a domestic corporation owns enough stock in the foreign corporation to qualify under §902 for indirect credit for foreign income taxes imposed on the foreign corporation, DASTM may be elected for purposes of determining §902 credits.

If a controlled foreign corporation's functional currency is a foreign currency that is not hyperinflationary but the corporation has a branch operating in a hyperinflationary environment, DASTM is applied substituting the corporation's functional currency for the U.S. dollar.[81] Assume a U.S. corporation has a German subsidiary, whose functional currency is the German mark, and the subsidiary has a branch operating in country X, whose hyperinflationary currency would otherwise be the branch's functional currency. The branch must use DASTM, but the method is applied by translating all items from the hyperinflationary currency to marks, rather than to dollars.

2. *Application of DASTM—generally.* When required, DASTM must be used in determining taxable income or loss and earnings and profits for all federal income tax purposes.[82] Under DASTM, annual income or loss and earnings and profits or deficit are computed by the following steps:

    a. Prepare an income or loss statement from the QBU's books in the hyperinflationary currency.

---

[77] Reg. §1.985-4, discussed supra ¶71.2 text accompanying notes 40–42.

[78] Reg. §1.985-1(b)(2)(ii)(C). Various adjustments are required to account for the change. Reg. §1.985-5.

[79] Prop. Reg. §1.985-1(b)(2)(ii)(E).

[80] Reg. §1.985-1(b)(2)(ii)(B)(2). For the definition of controlled foreign corporation, see §957, discussed supra ¶68.2.2.

[81] Reg. §1.985-1(b)(2)(ii)(B)(1).

[82] Reg. §1.985-3(a)(1).

b. Adjust the statement to conform to U.S. financial accounting and tax principles.

c. Translate the adjusted statement into U.S. dollars.

d. Add or subtract DASTM gain or loss.[83]

3. *Translation into dollars.* The translation into U.S. dollars (step 3) is usually done by breaking each item on the income or loss statement into monthly amounts and translating the amount for each month at the exchange rate for the month.[84] For example, sales revenues are determined separately for each month during the year and are translated into dollars at the exchange rate for the month. Taxpayers can adopt translation periods shorter than one month, but shorter periods must be equal in length, and, once elected, a shorter period can be changed only with IRS consent.[85]

Special translation rules are provided for several items. In determining the cost of goods sold, purchases for each month or shorter translation period are translated at the exchange rate for that period, and inventory costs are translated at the rate for the period when the costs were incurred.[86] For example, if the QBU uses the LIFO method, the cost of each LIFO layer is translated at the rate for the period when the layer was added to inventory; under FIFO, closing inventory is translated at the rate for the last month of the year unless closing inventory is larger than the purchases made during that month.[87] Also, depreciation on each item of depreciable property is translated at the rate for the period when the property's cost was incurred.[88] Prepaid income and expenses are translated at the rate for the period during which the prepayment was received or made.[89] These special rules are the primary mechanisms for preventing historical cost figures from being inflated away.

---

[83] Reg. §1.985-3(b). The present regulations on DASTM generally apply for taxable years beginning after August 24, 1994, but taxpayers can elect to use them for earlier years. Reg. §1.985-3(a)(2).

[84] Reg. §§1.985-3(c)(1), (6), (7). See Reg. §1.985-3(c)(10) Ex. 2.

However, if the QBU ever used the profit and loss method, items on its balance sheet as of the beginning of the first DASTM year are translated at the spot rate on the last day of the preceding year, and the dollar amounts resulting from this translation are used for as long as these items remain on the balance sheet. Reg. §1.985-3(c)(1).

[85] Reg. §1.985-3(c)(7)(ii).

[86] Reg. §§1.985-3(c)(2), (3). However, if inventory is valued at market, the translation is at the exchange rate as of the last day of the taxable year. Reg. §1.985-3(c)(3)(iii)(A). For example, the lower-of-cost-or-market rule is applied by comparing cost as determined under the rule described in the text with value on the last day of the year, determined in the hyperinflationary currency and translated into dollars at the rate for the last day of the year.

[87] See Reg. §1.985-3(c)(3)(iii)(B) (in ascertaining period when inventory cost was incurred, taxpayer may use "reasonable approximations and averages, including rates of turnover, provided that the method is used consistently from year to year").

[88] Reg. §1.985-3(c)(4).

[89] Reg. §1.985-3(c)(5).

The exchange rate for each translation period may be determined by "any reasonable method" that is used consistently and "conforms to the taxpayer's method of financial accounting."[90] For example, the rate for a period might be the average of the spot rates on the first and last days of the period or the spot rate on the last day.

If the QBU engages in a transaction in dollars, the dollar amount is used directly, rather than being translated into the foreign currency and retranslated back to dollars.[91] Moreover, transactions in which the taxpayer's entitlements or obligations are determined in (or with reference to) the U.S. dollar must be reported transaction-by-transaction. In contrast, transactions in foreign currencies other than the hyperinflationary currency may be reported by "any reasonable method" that is "consistent with" the taxpayer's financial accounting methods.[92]

4. *DASTM gain or loss.* For any year, currency gain or loss (called DASTM gain or loss) is recognized as ordinary income or loss.[93] DASTM gain or loss is the sum of:

  a. The QBU's net worth at the end of the year, and
  b. Dividends paid, remittances to the home office, credited income taxes, and other items for the year that reduce net worth without affecting income,

less the sum of:

  c. Net worth at the end of the preceding year,
  d. The QBU's income, loss, earnings and profits, or deficit for the current year, and
  e. Capital contributions for the year and other items that increase net worth without affecting income.[94]

Dividends, remittances, and capital contributions are translated at the spot rate for the date of the distribution or transfer.[95] Net worth as of the end of the current and preceding years are determined by preparing balance sheets from the QBU's books in the hyperinflationary currency, adjusting the balance sheets to conform to U.S. financial and tax accounting principles, and translating each figure on the adjusted balance sheets into dollars.[96] Costs and liabilities are generally translated at the exchange rate for the month or shorter translation

---

[90] Reg. §1.985-3(c)(6). A method for determining the exchange rate may be changed only with IRS consent.

[91] Reg. §1.985-3(c)(8). See Reg. §1.985-3(c)(10) Ex. 1.

[92] Reg. §1.985-3(c)(9).

[93] Reg. §1.985-3(d)(8).

[94] Reg. §1.985-3(d)(1). For an illustration of the computation of DASTM gain or loss, see Reg. §1.985-3(d)(9) Ex.

[95] Reg. §§1.985-3(d)(3), (4).

[96] Reg. §1.985-3(d)(2).

period in which they were incurred.[97] Specifically, (1) inventory costs are translated at the rate for the translation period in which incurred (as in the determination of taxable income), (2) bad debt reserves are translated at the rate for the last period in the taxable year, (3) prepaid income and expenses are translated at the rate for the period the prepayment was received or made, (4) cash, bank deposits, debt obligations, and derivatives contracts denominated in the hyperinflationary currency are translated at the rate for the last period of the year, (5) costs of plant and equipment, goodwill, patents, and other intangible property, as well as cost recovery allowances on these assets, are translated at the rate for the periods in which the costs were incurred, and (6) tax liabilities are translated at the rate for the last day of the taxable year in which they accrued. Assets and liabilities denominated in dollars are dropped from the balance sheet.[98] Transactions in currencies other than the dollar and the hyperinflationary currency can be accounted for by "any reasonable method" that is consistent with the taxpayer's financial accounting.[99]

The mechanics of the computation of DASTM gain or loss can perhaps be best understood by applying them to a case in which the exchange rate remains constant at all relevant times, where the gain or loss is appropriately zero. Assume a QBU's net worth at the end of the preceding year was 800u, and it has pretax earnings of 100u for the current year, remits 30u to the head office during the year, incurs a foreign income tax liability for the year of 40u (claimed as a credit), receives no capital contributions during the year, and has year-end net worth of 830u (800u at end of preceding year, plus current earnings of 100u, less remittances of 30u and foreign income taxes of 40u). If the exchange rate is $1 for 1u throughout the year, exchange gain or loss is:

$$\$830 + \$70 - (\$800 + \$100 + 0) = 0$$

In contrast, if the exchange rate fluctuates during the year, the amount produced by the formula (DASTM gain or loss) is more or less than zero.

Under §904(d), the limitation on the credit for foreign income taxes must be determined separately for various categories of taxable income from foreign sources.[100] If a QBU has income from more than one of these categories, DASTM gain or loss must be allocated among them.[101] If the adjusted basis of the QBU's assets does not exceed $10 million at year-end, the taxpayer may allocate DASTM gain or loss ratably among all categories of gross income. If the taxpayer is not eligible to or does not make this election, DASTM gain or loss is

---

[97] Reg. §1.985-3(d)(5). However, costs incurred before the QBU adopted DASTM are generally translated as of the day preceding the beginning of the first DASTM year.

[98] Reg. §§1.985-3(c)(8), (d)(6).

[99] Reg. §1.985-3(d)(7).

[100] For §904(d), see supra ¶69.6.

[101] Reg. §1.985-3(e).

allocated by a nine-step procedure, essentially in proportion to the amounts of monetary assets and liabilities affected by inflation that are deployed in generating gross income of each category.

¶71.4 TRANSLATIONS FOR U.S. SHAREHOLDERS OF FOREIGN CORPORATIONS

For several purposes, it is necessary to translate receipts and payments of foreign corporations into U.S. dollars to determine the tax liabilities of U.S. taxpayers owning shares of the corporation.

1. *Earnings and profits.* A foreign corporation's earnings and profits are initially determined in its functional currency.[1] Transactions denominated in the functional currency are recorded in that currency under the corporation's method of accounting. Transactions denominated in other currencies are translated into the functional currency transaction by transaction under §988.[2] Once recorded in the functional currency, a transaction enters into earnings and profits as indicated by U.S. tax rules. When a foreign corporation makes a distribution to a U.S. person, the portion that is a dividend is initially determined in the corporation's functional currency, and the distribution and the dividend portion are translated into U.S. dollars by the spot rate on the date the dividend is included in income.[3]

Because earnings and profits are first translated when distributed, exchange gain or loss does not arise merely because of fluctuations in exchange rates between the time the earnings and profits are realized and the time they are distributed.[4] However, the distributed earnings and profits may include exchange gain or loss of the corporation. For example, if the corporation engages in transactions in currencies other than its functional currency or has a QBU with a functional currency other than the overall functional currency of the corporation, exchange gain or loss from these transactions or QBUs is reflected in earnings and profits, like any other item of income or deduction of the corporation.

Also, if the corporation makes the distribution in its functional currency, it recognizes no exchange gain or loss on the distribution because a functional currency is money and gain or loss is never realized on a disposition of money. In contrast, if a foreign corporation's functional currency is not the U.S. dollar, but it distributes dollars to its shareholders, exchange gain is recognized because a nonfunctional currency is property other than money and a corporation rec-

---

[1] IRC §986(b)(1).

[2] See infra ¶71.5.

[3] IRC §§986(b)(2), 989(b)(1). For the "spot rate," see infra ¶71.5 text accompanying notes 18–20.

[4] H.R. Rep. No. 841, 99th Cong., 2d Sess. II-672 (Conf. Rep. 1986).

ognizes gain (but not usually loss) when it distributes property other than money to shareholders.[5]

Assume a foreign corporation, whose functional currency is the British pound, distributes £100 to its sole shareholder, a U.S. citizen, when the corporation has earnings and profits of £80. The distribution consists of an £80 dividend, and a £20 recovery of capital.[6] If the pound is worth $1.50 at the time of the distribution, the dividend is $120 (£80 times $1.50), and the capital recovery is $30 (£20 times $1.50). No exchange gain or loss is recognized by corporation or shareholder.

In contrast, assume the distribution consists of $150, which the corporation had earlier purchased for £105. On the distribution, the corporation has exchange loss of £5—the value in pounds of the dollars when distributed ($150 divided by the date-of-distribution exchange rate of $1.50 or £100) less the cost in pounds of the distributed dollars (£105). The exchange loss reduces earnings and profits to £75 (£80 less £5). The distribution (£100) thus consists of a dividend of £75, and capital recovery of £25. In dollars, the shareholder has a dividend of $112.5 (£75 times $1.50) and a capital recovery of $37.5 (£25 times $1.50).

2. *Subpart F, foreign personal holding company, and passive foreign investment company determinations.* U.S. shareholders of a controlled foreign corporation (CFC) must include in gross income their ratable shares of the corporation's subpart F income and earnings invested in U.S. property.[7] U.S. persons holding stock of a foreign personal holding company (FPHC) must report their ratable shares of the corporation's undistributed personal holding company income.[8] Also, U.S. persons holding stock in a passive foreign investment company are currently taxed on their shares of the corporation's earnings if the corporation elects to be a qualified electing fund (QEF).[9] When a CFC, FPHC, or QEF shareholder is taxed on undistributed corporate earnings, the taxable amounts are determined in the corporation's functional currency and translated into U.S. dollars by the "average exchange rate for the taxable year of the foreign corporation"; if these amounts are limited by the corporation's earnings and profits, the relevant earnings and profits figures are translated in the same way.[10]

When a U.S. shareholder is taxed on undistributed corporate earnings under the subpart F or QEF rules, subsequent distributions are tax free to the share-

---

[5] IRC §§311(a), (b), discussed infra ¶92.3.2.

[6] Under §301(c), discussed infra ¶92.1.1, the recovery of capital is excluded from gross income to the extent of the shareholder's basis for the stock, and any excess is included in gross income as a capital gain.

[7] IRC §951(a)(1), discussed supra ¶68.2.1.

[8] IRC §551(a), discussed supra ¶68.3.

[9] IRC §1293(a), discussed supra ¶68.5.4.

[10] IRC §§986(b)(2), 989(b)(3).

holder up to the amount of the previously taxed earnings.[11] The tax-free amount is determined in the foreign corporation's functional currency and is translated into dollars at the spot exchange rate on the date of distribution. If the exchange rate had fluctuated, the dollar amount of the prior inclusion differs from the dollar value of the tax-free distribution. This difference is "ordinary income or loss from the same source as the associated income inclusion."[12]

Assume a U.S. shareholder of a CFC is taxed in year 1 on 100u of the corporation's subpart F income and receives a distribution of 100u in year 2 that is treated as a tax-free distribution of the amount taxed in year 1. If the year 1 exchange rate is 60 cents, the shareholder has $60 of gross income for year 1. If the exchange rate is 50 cents when the distribution is made in year 2, the shareholder has ordinary loss for year 2 of $10 ($60 of gross income less dollar value of distribution (100u times $.50)). The deduction for this loss is allocated to income from the same source as the subpart F income taxed to the shareholder in year 1, unlike other exchange gain or loss, which is from sources in the taxpayer's country of residence.[13]

3. *Section 1248 dividends.* When a U.S. shareholder sells stock of a CFC, any gain recognized by the shareholder is treated as a dividend under §1248 up to the amount of earnings and profits attributable to the stock for the period the taxpayer held it.[14] Earnings and profits are translated into dollars for purposes of §1248 at the spot rate on the date of the §1248 transaction.[15]

Assume U.S. citizen *A*, who has been sole shareholder of foreign corporation *X* since its incorporation, sells 10 percent of the stock (basis of $15) for 100u when the corporation's accumulated earnings and profits are 600u and 1u is worth 50 cents. Gain on the sale is $35 (amount realized of 100u times $.50 less basis of $15). Of this gain, $30 is a dividend under §1248 (ten percent of 600u times $.50), and the remaining $5 is capital gain.

4. *Foreign income taxes.* Under §902, a domestic corporation receiving a dividend from a foreign subsidiary is allowed credit for foreign income taxes paid by the subsidiary.[16] Section 960 allows a similar credit when a domestic corporation is taxed under subpart F on earnings of a CFC. For purposes of §§902 and 960, foreign income taxes imposed on a foreign corporation are translated into dollars at the average exchange rate for the year for which the tax accrued if the taxpayer accounts for foreign income taxes on an accrual basis or at the spot rate prevailing when the taxes were paid if these taxes are accounted for on a cash

---

[11] See IRC §959(a) (subpart F rule, discussed supra ¶68.2.13); §1293(c) (QEF rule, discussed supra ¶68.5.4).

[12] IRC §986(c)(1).

[13] See supra ¶71.14.

[14] For §1248, see supra ¶68.2.15.

[15] IRC §§986(b)(2), 989(b)(2). For the spot rate, see supra ¶71.5 text accompanying notes 18–20.

[16] See infra ¶69.8.

basis.[17] When the date-of-payment rule applies, a refund or credit of a foreign income tax is translated "using the exchange rate as of the time of original payment," but a deficiency or other adjustment in a foreign tax liability is translated by "the exchange rate as of the time when such adjustment is paid."[18] These rules generally agree with those applied to taxes paid directly by a U.S. person.[19]

¶71.5   TRANSACTIONS IN NONFUNCTIONAL CURRENCIES—INTRODUCTORY

Foreign currency gain or loss is usually accounted for transaction-by-transaction when a taxpayer (or one of its QBUs) engages in a transaction in a nonfunctional currency.[1] The term "nonfunctional currency" includes any currency (including the European Currency Unit) that is not the functional currency of the taxpayer or QBU.[2] Assume a domestic corporation, whose overall functional currency is the dollar, has a QBU whose functional currency is the Belgian franc. For the QBU, all currencies other than the Belgian franc (including the U.S. dollar) are nonfunctional currencies, whereas in transactions not connected with any QBU of the taxpayer, all currencies other than the dollar (including the Belgian franc) are nonfunctional currencies.

The regulations elaborate in detail on the transaction-by-transaction approach for transactions in nonfunctional currencies, including:

     1. A nonfunctional currency is generally treated as property other than

---

[17] IRC §§986(a)(1), (2). The taxes are translated as of the date of payment, even if the taxpayer uses the accrual method, (1) for taxable years beginning before 1998, (2) if the taxes accrue in an inflationary currency, or (3) if the taxes are paid before the taxable year begins or more than two years after the year ends. See Rev. Rul. 91-21, 1991-1 CB 112 (for purposes of §902, foreign income taxes on accumulated profits of taxable years beginning before 1987 are translated as of date dividends are paid). See also Horner & Barge, Simplifying the Foreign Tax Translation Rules, 51 Tax Notes 1569 (June 24, 1991).

[18] IRC §986(a)(1)(B); H.R. Rep. No. 841, supra note 4, at II-677-76.

[19] See supra ¶69.13.

[1] See generally ABA Section of Taxation Committee on Foreign Activities of U.S. Taxpayers, Comments on Regulations Dealing With Foreign Currency Transactions, 44 Tax Lawyer 71, 74-116 (1990); Cathcart, New Final Regulations on Foreign Currency Transactions, 4 Tax Notes Int'l 985 (1992); Ponda, Economic Inconsistencies in the Taxation of Currency Swaps, 57 Tax Notes 1795 (1992). See also Solway & Bothamley, Treasury Centers, Hybrid Instruments, and Foreign Currency Strategies, 70 Tax Notes 883 (Feb. 12, 1996).

The transaction-by-transaction approach of §988 is summarized by the regulations as follows: "Exchange gain or loss from a section 988 transaction shall be separately computed for each section 988 transaction, and such amount shall not be integrated with gain or loss recognized on another transaction (whether or not such transaction is economically related to the section 988 transaction)." Reg. §1.988-1(e).

[2] Reg. §1.988-1(c).

money, and exchange gain or loss is recognized each time the currency is exchanged for a different currency or spent.[3]

2. A bank deposit in a nonfunctional currency is usually analyzed as currency itself.[4]

3. When a debt instrument is denominated in a nonfunctional currency, interest income or expense is translated at the exchange rate in effect when the interest is paid or accrues, and exchange gain or loss is usually recognized when either interest or principal is paid or received.[5]

4. Revenues or costs other than interest are translated at the exchange rate for the date the item is recognized under the taxpayer's method of accounting, and if it is not then received or paid, exchange gain or loss is recognized when the income is received or the cost paid.[6]

5. Income or loss under a forward, futures, or swap contract in a nonfunctional currency, or an option in such a currency, is usually characterized as exchange gain or loss.[7]

6. However, if a currency contract hedges a debt instrument issued or held by the taxpayer, the contract and instrument may be integrated into a synthetic debt instrument on which exchange gain or loss is not usually recognized.[8]

7. If a currency contract or bank deposit in a nonfunctional currency is used to hedge the taxpayer's obligation or entitlement under a contract to purchase or sell goods in the ordinary course of business, the hedge is subsumed into the purchase contract.[9]

8. A hedge against currency risk for the period between the trade and settlement dates in a securities transaction is integrated with the securities transaction.[10]

9. Exchange gain or loss is sometimes recognized when a nonfunctional currency or an instrument denominated in a nonfunctional currency is transferred to or from a QBU, even though the transfer is nothing more than a switch from the taxpayer's left to right pocket or vice versa.[11]

10. Regulations have been proposed allowing an election to recognize exchange gain or loss on a mark to market method.[12]

11. Individuals are usually exempted from recognizing exchange gain or

---

[3] Infra ¶71.6.1.
[4] Infra ¶71.6.2.
[5] Infra ¶71.7.
[6] Infra ¶71.8.
[7] Infra ¶71.9.
[8] Infra ¶71.10.2.
[9] Infra ¶71.10.3.
[10] Infra ¶71.10.4.
[11] Infra ¶71.11.
[12] Infra ¶71.12.

loss with respect to nonfunctional currency used for personal (as distinguished from business and investment) transactions.[13]

12. Exchange gain is usually income from sources within the taxpayer's country of residence, and the deduction for exchange loss is normally allocated to income from sources within the residence country.[14]

Exchange gain or loss is usually ordinary income.[15] Generally, it is not treated as interest income or expense.[16] If interest on a debt instrument is excluded from gross income under §103(a), however, exchange loss is treated as an offset against interest and thus is recognized only to the extent it exceeds interest on the instrument.[17]

The tax consequences of a transaction in a nonfunctional currency are usually determined by the spot rate as of a specified date. Generally, an exchange rate qualifies as a spot rate if it "reflect[s] a fair market rate of exchange available to the public for currency under a spot contract in a free market and involving representative amounts."[18] Exchange rates found in International Financial Statistics (published by the International Monetary Fund) usually qualify as spot rates, but rates published in newspapers, financial journals, and electronic financial news services may also be used.

A governmentally prescribed rate is disregarded in favor of the free market rate unless the prescribed rate more clearly reflects the taxpayer's income in a particular transaction.[19] Assume the government of country X establishes an exchange rate of 1u for $1, but the rate on a secondary market is 1u for 60 cents. A domestic corporation purchases 100u for $60 on the secondary market and transfers the 100u to its QBU in country X, which uses X's currency as its functional currency, and the QBU exchanges the 100u for $100 at the official rate. The transfer to the QBU triggers recognition of exchange gain or loss

---

[13] Infra ¶71.13.

[14] Infra ¶71.14.

[15] IRC §988(a)(1)(A). See Reg. §1.988-3(a) (ordinary income rule applies to exchange gain or loss recognized under §1256). However, an election can be made to treat gain or loss on some forward contracts as capital gain or loss. IRC §988(a)(1)(B), discussed infra ¶71.9.5.

[16] Reg. §1.988-3(c)(1). See Phillip Morris Inc. v. CIR, 71 F3d 1040 (2d Cir. 1996), cert. denied, 517 US 1220 (1996) (under pre-1986 law, currency gains realized on repayment of foreign-currency-denominated loans were not debt discharge income, even though taxpayer converted loan proceeds into dollars and purchased foreign currency with dollars shortly before repayment); Cunningham, The *Philip Morris* Case and Section 988, 68 Tax Notes 983 (Aug. 21, 1995).

[17] Reg. §1.988-3(c)(2) (applicable to instruments acquired after June 23, 1987). This rule generally applies only to taxpayers and QBUs with foreign functional currencies because §103(a) exempts interest on obligations of states and local governments of the United States, whose debt is nearly always denominated in U.S. dollars.

[18] Reg. §1.988-1(d)(1). See H.R. Rep. No. 841, 99th Cong., 2d Sess. II-663 (Conf. Rep. 1986).

[19] Reg. §1.988-1(d)(4)(i).

because the 100u are nonfunctional currency to the corporation's home office but functional currency to the QBU.[20] Because the purpose of the transactions is to exploit the difference between the official and free market exchange rates, the corporation's income on the transfer to the QBU is most clearly reflected by the official rate. The corporation thus has foreign currency gain on the transfer of $40 (dollar value of 100u at official rate of 1u to $1 less $60 basis for the 100u).

¶71.6 HOLDINGS AND DISPOSITIONS OF NONFUNCTIONAL CURRENCIES AND DEPOSITS DENOMINATED IN SUCH CURRENCIES

¶71.6.1 Nonfunctional Currencies

A nonfunctional currency is essentially treated as property other than money, except that gain or loss on its disposition is exchange gain or loss.[1] For example, if a taxpayer whose functional currency is the dollar buys 100u for $55, holds it for a time as a speculation, and exchanges it for $60, exchange gain is $5 ($60 amount realized less $55 adjusted basis).

When a nonfunctional currency is used to pay the purchase price of property, the currency is deemed exchanged for functional currency immediately before the payment, and the payment is deemed made in the functional currency.[2] Assume DC, a domestic corporation whose functional currency is the dollar, purchases 100u when the exchange rate is 60 cents and when the exchange rate is 70 cents, uses the 100u to purchase goods to be held as inventory. DC is deemed to exchange the 100u for $70 immediately before the inventory purchase and to purchase the inventory for $70, not 100u. The constructive exchange yields foreign currency gain of $10 ($70 amount realized less $60 basis).

The constructive exchange of nonfunctional for functional currency is inserted to ensure that any difference between the purchase price and the value of the purchased property is not recognized on the purchase as foreign currency gain or loss. Assume the purchase of goods in the example is pursuant to a contract made by DC several months earlier, and the inventory's value rises to 120u by the time the purchase is closed. If the payment was analyzed as an exchange of 100u for the goods, the gain would be $24, computed as the dollar value of the goods when received (120u times $.70 or $84) less the taxpayer's $60 basis of the 100u. This $24, however, includes appreciation in the value of the goods, and the exchange gain must consist exclusively of appreciation in the 100u.

---

[20] Reg. §1.988-1(a)(10), discussed infra ¶71.11.

[1] IRC §988(c)(1)(C)(i); Reg. §1.988-2(a)(1)(i). See Reg. §1.988-2(a)(1)(ii) (exchange of one nonfunctional currency for another nonfunctional currency is not like kind exchange qualifying for nonrecognition under §1031). See supra ¶44.2.1 for §1031.

[2] Reg. §1.988-2(a)(2)(ii)(B).

When a nonfunctional currency is received in a sale of property or services, its basis equals its value in the taxpayer's functional currency when it is received. Assume *DC* sells goods on credit for 100u when 1u = $.60, collects the account receivable when 1u = $.50, and later exchanges the 100u so received for $55. As explained below,[3] the selling price of the goods is $60 (100u times $.60), and exchange loss of $10 is recognized on collection of the receivable ($60 basis for the receivable less $50 value of 100u collected). In addition, *DC* has $5 of foreign currency gain on exchanging the 100u for dollars ($55 received less $50 basis for 100u).

¶71.6.2 Bank Deposits

A bank deposit denominated in a nonfunctional currency is treated as the currency itself, not as a debt instrument.[4] This rule applies to time and demand deposits, certificates of deposit, and any similar instrument issued by a financial institution. A 100u balance in a bank account thus is considered the same as a 100u bill. As a consequence, foreign currency gain or loss is not recognized when a nonfunctional currency is deposited in or withdrawn from a bank account denominated in that currency, when funds are switched to another account in the same currency, or on the maturity of a certificate of deposit in a nonfunctional currency.[5]

When a nonfunctional currency is deposited in or withdrawn from an account, its basis follows along.[6] Assume a taxpayer whose functional currency is the dollar purchases 100u for $60, deposits the 100u in a bank account a few days later, withdraws the 100u a month later, and exchanges the withdrawn funds for $55 a few days after the withdrawal. The taxpayer has exchange loss of $5 ($55 amount realized less $60 basis for the 100u). The exchange rates on the dates of deposit and withdrawal are not relevant because gain or loss is not recognized on the deposit or withdrawal and the $60 paid for the 100u becomes the basis of the funds in the account and the withdrawn funds.

Interest on a demand deposit in a nonfunctional currency is translated into the taxpayer's functional currency at the spot rate prevailing when it is accrued or received (actually or constructively), depending on the taxpayer's accounting method.[7] Interest on time deposits and certificates of deposit is translated under the rules for interest on debt instruments, described below.[8] The portion of the

---

[3] Infra ¶71.8.

[4] IRC §988(c)(1)(C)(ii).

[5] Reg. §1.988-2(a)(1)(iii).

[6] Id.

[7] Reg. §1.988-2(b)(1) (translation may be by any reasonable spot rate convention, such as translating as of last day of month, quarter, half year, or year, if all nonfunctional-currency accounts in same bank are treated alike).

[8] Reg. §1.988-2(b)(2), discussed infra ¶71.7.3.

account consisting of accumulated interest has a basis equal to the functional currency amount reported as interest income.

When a nonfunctional currency account contains funds with varying bases, "any reasonable method" may be used to identify the basis of amounts withdrawn, except that the same method must be used year after year for all accounts in a particular currency.[9] First-in first-out, last-in first-out, and pro rata are acceptable methods.

Assume a domestic corporation opens a bank account with a deposit of 2,000u on January 1 of year 1, allows interest to accumulate in the account throughout year 1, and withdraws 500u from the account on January 1 of year 2, as follows:

Date	Deposit	*Dollar basis* Interest	Exchange rate	Item total
1/01/1	2,000u	$.50	$1,000	$1,000
3/31/1	50u	.50	25	1,025
6/30/1	51u	.48	25	1,050
9/30/1	53u	.50	26	1,076
12/31/1	54u	.60	32	1,108

Under the pro rata method, the basis of the 500u withdrawn on January 1 of year 2 is:

$$(500u/2,208u)(\$1,108) = \$251$$

Under the first-in first-out method, the withdrawn 500u has a basis of $250 because it comes exclusively from the 2,000u deposited when the exchange rate was 1u = $0.50. Under the last-in, first-out, the basis is $254, the sum of the bases of the 208u of interest accumulations and 292u of the original deposit.

¶71.7 DEBT INSTRUMENTS

¶71.7.1 Introductory

Two groups of issues arise when a taxpayer issues or holds a debt instrument denominated in a nonfunctional currency (borrows or lends a nonfunctional currency): translating interest income or expense into the taxpayer's functional currency as it is recognized, and computing exchange gain or loss when interest or principal is paid.[1] The same issues are generally presented by a debt instrument

---

[9] Reg. §1.988-2(a)(2)(iii)(B).

[1] See generally Lopata, Current Issues in Foreign Currency Transactions, 51 Tax Notes 895 (1991).

that is payable in the taxpayer's functional currency if the amount of one or more payment is determined with reference to the current value of a nonfunctional currency (e.g. a zero coupon bond calling for a single payment in 10 years of a number of dollars then equal in value to 10,000 Swiss francs).

¶71.7.2　Interest Income and Expense

Interest income or expense on a nonfunctional currency instrument is initially determined in the nonfunctional currency and then translated into the taxpayer's functional currency.[2] The translation procedures depend on whether the interest is accounted for on a cash or accrual basis.

1. *Cash method reporting.* If interest income or expense is reported on a cash basis, it is translated at the spot rate on the date of receipt or payment.[3] No exchange gain or loss is realized when the interest is received or paid. However, under the rules for holdings of nonfunctional currencies, the payor can have exchange gain or loss on the disposition of the currency used to make the payment, and the recipient can subsequently have exchange gain or loss on disposing of the currency.

Assume a U.S. citizen using the cash method of accounting lends 1,000u under a three-year note requiring annual interest payments at 10 percent.[4] Interest income is translated into dollars at the spot rate on the date of receipt, and no exchange gain or loss is recognized on the receipt of interest. Assume 100u of interest is received when 1u is worth 60 cents. The taxpayer has $60 of interest income, has no foreign currency gain or loss on receiving the interest, and takes a $60 basis for the 100u. If the 100u is subsequently exchanged for $59, the taxpayer has exchange loss of $1.

Assume the borrower also accounts on the cash method and uses the U.S. dollar as its functional currency.[5] The borrower's interest expense, like the lender's interest income, is $60—the 100u payment translated at the exchange rate of 60 cents at the time of payment. But assume the 100u used in this payment was acquired a few weeks earlier for $62. Although there is no exchange gain or loss with respect to the interest obligation, the disposition of the 100u results in exchange loss of $2 (dollar value of 100u when disposed of ($60) less cost of $62).

2. *Accrual reporting.* Where interest income or expense is reported on an accrual basis, each accrual is translated at the average rate during the accrual period, except that if the period spans two taxable years, the translation is at the average rate for the portion of the period that is within the taxable year.[6] The

---

[2] Reg. §1.988-2(b)(2)(ii)(A).

[3] Reg. §1.988-2(b)(2)(ii)(B). For the "spot rate," see Reg. §1.988-1(d), discussed supra ¶71.5 text accompanying notes 18–20.

[4] See Reg. §1.988-2(b)(9) Ex. 1.

[5] See Reg. §1.988-2(b)(9) Ex. 6.

[6] Reg. §1.988-2(b)(2)(ii)(C).

average rate is normally "a simple average of the spot exchange rates for each business day of such period," but a "spot accrual convention" may also be used.[7] Under the convention, the average rate for an accrual period is usually the spot rate on the last day of the period or of the portion of the period that is within the taxable year, but if the interest is paid or received within five days of the end of the period or portion of the period, the spot rate on the date of payment or receipt may be used. Once the taxpayer elects the convention, it applies to all interest income and expense for all years until it is revoked with IRS consent.

Exchange gain or loss is realized on the payment or receipt of interest if the exchange rate at which the interest was translated differs from the spot rate on the date of payment or receipt. More completely, the issuer (obligor) realizes exchange gain or loss when the interest is paid or the interest obligation is extinguished or transferred,[8] and the holder has exchange gain or loss when the interest is received or, if earlier, when the debt instrument is disposed of.[9] The issuer's gain or loss on payment is the amount accrued in the functional currency, less the amount paid, translated into the functional currency at the spot rate on the date of payment. For an extinguishment or transfer, the computation is the same except that the number of nonfunctional currency units extinguished or transferred is substituted for the amount paid. The holder's exchange gain or loss is the amount received, translated into the functional currency at the spot rate for the date of receipt or disposition, reduced by the amount accrued in the functional currency.

Assume *DC*, a domestic corporation not engaged in business in any foreign country, borrows 1,000u on January 1 of year 1 under a note requiring semiannual payments of interest at 10 percent and a single principal payment 18 months after the date of the loan; *DC*'s taxable year ends on November 30. Exchange rates during the note's term are shown in Example 71-1A.

Example 71-1A
Assumed Exchange Rates

Date or period	Spot Rate	Average Rate
Calendar Year 1		
January 1	1u = $1	
January 1 thru June 30		1u = $1.10
June 30	1u = $1.20	
July 1 thru December 31		1u = $1.30
July 1 thru November 30		1u = $1.25
November 30	1u = $1.35	

---

[7] Reg. §1.988-2(b)(2)(iii).
[8] Reg. §1.988-2(b)(4).
[9] Reg. §1.988-2(b)(3).

Example 71-1A
Assumed Exchange Rates

Date or period	Spot Rate	Average Rate
December 1 thru 31		1u = $1.30
December 31	1u = $1.40	
Calendar Year 2		
January 1 thru June 30		1u = $1.20
June 30	1u = $1.30	

Alternative calculations are given in Example 71-1B of *DC*'s interest expense assuming the "average rate" used in translating the interest is (1) the true average of the exchange rates for the days during the accrual period or (2) the spot rate on the last day of the period within the taxable year.

Example 71-1B
Translation of Interest Accruals

	True average		Spot rate convention	
	Rate	Interest	Rate	Interest
Fiscal Year 1				
January 1 thru June 30 (interest of 50u)	$1.10	$ 55	$1.20	$ 60
June 30 thru November 30 (interest of 50u × ⁵/₆)	$1.25	52	$1.35	56
Total		$107		$116
Fiscal Year 2				
December (interest of 50u × ¹/₆)	$1.30	$ 11	$1.40	$ 12
January 1 thru June 30	$1.20	60	$1.30	65
Total		$ 71		$ 77

If *DC* uses the true average method, exchange loss is recognized on the payments of interest as shown in Example 71-1C.

Example 71-1C
Exchange Loss Under True Average Method

		Payment		
	Accrual	Rate	Gain or (loss)	Amount
Fiscal Year 1				
January 1 thru June 30	$55	$1.20	$60	($5)
June 30 thru November 30	$52	$1.35	$58	($4)
Fiscal Year 2				

Example 71-1C
Exchange Loss Under True Average Method

	Accrual	Payment Rate	Gain or (loss)	Amount
December 1 thru 31	$11	$1.40	$12	($ 1)
January 1 thru June 30	$60	$1.30	$65	($ 5)
Total				($15)

In contrast, if *DC* uses the spot accrual convention and interest is paid on the last day of each accrual period, the exchange gain is as shown in Example 71-1D.

Example 71-1D
Exchange Loss Under Spot Accrual Convention

	Accrual	Payment Rate	Gain or (loss)	Amount
Fiscal Year 1				
January 1 thru June 30	$60	$1.20	$60	0
June 30 thru November 30	$56	$1.35	$56	0
Fiscal Year 2				
December 1 thru 31	$12	$1.30	$11	$1
January 1 thru June 30	$65	$1.30	$65	0
Total				$1

The spot accrual convention thus eliminates exchange gain or loss whenever an interest accrual period falls wholly within a taxable year, but exchange gain or loss may still be realized when interest is received during the taxable year for an interest accrual period that began during the preceding year.[10]

3. *Bond premium.* If a debt instrument was purchased or issued at a premium, interest income or expense is offset by amortization of bond premium.[11] When a premium instrument is denominated in a nonfunctional currency, the premium amortization for each interest period is computed in the nonfunctional currency and reduces the interest for the period, also stated in the nonfunctional currency.[12] The net amount is translated into the functional currency under the rules described above.

Also, exchange gain or loss is recognized during each interest period with respect to the premium amortized to the period. For an instrument's holder,

---

[10] See TD 8400, 1992-1 CB 101, 103 ("elective spot rate convention eliminates the complexity of determining an average exchange rate and simplifies the computation of exchange gain or loss with respect to accrued interest").

[11] See supra ¶59.7.

[12] Reg. §1.988-2(b)(10)(i).

bond premium is paid when the instrument is acquired and is recouped in installments as part of the interest payments. The issuer receives the premium when the instrument is issued and repays a portion of it with each interest payment. The holder has exchange gain if the nonfunctional currency appreciates in relation to the functional currency between the times of payment and recoupment and has exchange loss if the nonfunctional currency depreciates. The issuer's situation is the exact opposite.

Assume a U.S. citizen using the cash method of accounting pays 10,799u for a four-year 10 percent note in the principal amount 10,000u.[13] For the first year, gross interest is 1,000u, premium amortization is 136u, and net interest is 864u (1,000u less 136u). Assume the exchange rate is 60 cents when the note is purchased and 50 cents when the first year's interest is paid. The holder's interest income for the first year is $432 (864u times $.50). She also has exchange loss for the year of $13.6, computed as the excess of (1) the dollar value of the taxpayer's cost for the premium amortized to the first year (136u times $.60 or $81.6) over (2) the dollar value of the holder's recoupment of this amount as part of the first year's interest (136u times $.50 or $68).

¶71.7.3 Market Discount

If a debt instrument is purchased for a price less than the instruments adjusted issue price (face amount if the instrument was issued at par), the excess of the adjusted issue price over the taxpayer's cost is market discount.[14] Market discount is allocated over the period beginning with the date the instrument is purchased and ending with the maturity date, and the portion allocated to the period the taxpayer holds the instrument is usually recognized as ordinary income when the instrument is paid, sold, or exchanged.[15] If an instrument is denominated in a nonfunctional currency, accrued market discount is computed in the nonfunctional currency and translated into the taxpayer's functional currency at the spot rate for the date of the payment, sale, or exchange.[16] There is no exchange gain or loss with respect to the discount.

Assume a 10,000u bond was issued years ago at par but is purchased by DC, whose functional currency is the dollar, two years before maturity for 9,653u.[17] If DC holds the bond to maturity and receives 10,000u in payment of the bond, market discount of 347u is recognized on receipt of the payment. If 1u = $.60 at maturity, the discount is reported as ordinary income of $208.2 (347u times $.60). Since the income is reported at the spot rate on the date of payment, no exchange gain or loss is realized on receipt of the payment.

---

[13] See Reg. §1.988-2(b)(10)(ii).

[14] IRC §1278(a)(2), discussed supra ¶59.3.2.

[15] IRC §1276(a)(1).

[16] Reg. §1.988-2(b)(11)(i).

[17] Reg. §1.988-2(b)(11)(ii) Ex.

In lieu of deferring market discount until the instrument is disposed of, a taxpayer can elect to accrue the discount over the instrument's remaining term.[18] When this election is made, the discount is translated under the rules for interest accruals, and exchange gain or loss is recognized on disposition under the rules for payments of accrued interest.[19]

¶71.7.4 Holders' Gains and Losses on Principal

1. *Generally.* The holder of a debt instrument has exchange gain or loss with respect to the principal when the instrument is paid or disposed of.[20] It is computed as (1) the principal amount in nonfunctional currency units, translated into the functional currency at the spot rate on the date payment is received or the instrument is disposed of, reduced by (2) the nonfunctional currency principal amount translated at the spot rate for the date the taxpayer acquired the instrument.

The principal amount is usually the holder's cost for the instrument, expressed in the nonfunctional currency in which the instrument is denominated.[21] For example, if *DC* purchases a 1,000u bond for 950u, the principal amount is 950u, regardless of whether the difference between the purchase price and the face amount is original issue discount (OID), market discount, or some combination thereof. Any OID will be recognized as interest under the rules described above, and other rules, also described above, provide for market discount. Assume 1u = $.60 when *DC* purchases the bond, and 1u = $.55 when *DC* subsequently sells the bond. At the time of sale, *DC* has exchange loss as follows:

Principal amount at spot rate for date of sale ($950 times $.55)	$523
Less principal amount at spot rate for date of purchase ($950 times $.60)	570
Exchange loss	$ 47

Assume the bond is sold for 1,000u. If the bond is without OID, *DC* recognizes market discount in addition to the exchange gain with respect to principal. The market discount is 50u (1,000u less 950u), and it is translated as $28 (50u times $.55).

---

[18] IRC §1278(b), discussed supra ¶59.3.4.

[19] Reg. §1.988-2(b)(11)(i).

[20] Reg. §1.988-2(b)(5).

[21] Id. If the holder received the instrument in a transfer in which the transferor realized but did not recognize exchange gain or loss, the holder's principal amount is the transferor's cost. Also, if the holder elects to amortize bond premium, the principal amount is reduced by premium amortized to periods during which the holder held the instrument.

2. *Ceiling rule.* A holder's exchange gain or loss on the payment or disposition of a debt instrument, including gain or loss with respect to both principal and interest, may not exceed the taxpayer's total gain or loss on the payment or disposition.[22] This ceiling applies whenever the taxpayer has gain in the nonfunctional currency and exchange loss or has loss in the nonfunctional currency and exchange gain.

Assume *DC* lends 1,000u when 1u is worth 60 cents, and the borrower's note is subsequently sold (immediately after an interest payment) for 980u, when the exchange rate is 65 cents.[23] By the normal calculation, exchange gain is $50—the principal translated at the spot rate for the date of the sale (1,000u times $.65 or $650), less the principal translated at the spot rate for the date the loan was made (1,000u times $.60 or $600). However, the entire gain on the sale is only $37—the amount realized on the sale (980u times $.65 or $637) less the note's adjusted basis (1,000u times $.60 or $600). The exchange gain is thus restricted to $37, and *DC* has no gain or loss on the sale of any other character. Even though a loss of 20u is sustained on the sale, no loss deduction is allowed because the loss is effectively applied in reduction of the exchange gain. The dollar value of the loss (20u times $.65 or $13) is the amount by which the exchange gain is reduced by the ceiling rule (from $50 to $37).

When the entire gain or loss exceeds the ceiling, it is usually bifurcated between exchange and other gain or loss. Assume the exchange rate at the time of the note's sale in the example is 55 cents.[24] The overall loss on the sale is $61—amount realized of $539 (980u times $.55), less basis of $600 (1,000u times $.60). Exchange loss (the decline in the dollar value of the 1,000u principal amount while the taxpayer held the note) is $50 (1,000u times $.55 less 1,000u times $.60). The overall loss of $61 thus consists of $50 of exchange loss, which is ordinary loss, and $11 of loss on the note's sale, which is capital loss if the note is a capital asset.

¶71.7.5   Issuers' Gains and Losses on Principal

The obligor under a debt instrument has exchange gain or loss with respect to principal when the instrument is paid or the liability is extinguished or transferred.[25] The gain or loss is (1) the principal amount, determined in the nonfunctional currency and translated into the obligor's functional currency at the spot

---

[22] IRC §§988(b)(1), (2); Reg. §1.988-2(b)(8).

[23] See Reg. §1.988-2(b)(9) Ex. 4.

[24] See Reg. §1.988-2(b)(9) Ex. 5.

[25] Reg. §1.988-2(b)(6). See Phillips, The "Amount Realized" on an Assumption of a Foreign Currency-Denominated Liability, 60 Tax Notes 217 (1993) (on sale of property subject to liability denominated in nonfunctional currency, seller's amount realized apparently includes amount of liability, translated into functional currency at exchange rate on date of sale, and seller has exchange gain or loss equal to difference between functional currency amounts of liability on date liability was incurred and date of sale); Tyson, U.S.

rate on the date of issue, less (2) the principal amount translated at the spot rate for the date the obligation is paid, extinguished, or transferred. The nonfunctional currency principal is usually the amount received by the issuer when the instrument was issued.[26] Assume *DC*, a domestic corporation using the dollar as its functional currency, borrows 100u when 1u = $.60 and repays the loan when 1u = $.58. The corporation has exchange gain on payment of the loan principal of $2—the excess of the dollar value of the borrowing (100u times $.60) less the dollar cost of the payment (100u times $.58).

The exchange gain or loss recognized when an obligation is paid, extinguished, or transferred, including gain or loss with respect to both principal and interest, may not exceed the issuer's total gain or loss on the transaction.[27] Assume *DC* issues a 1,000u bond at par when 1u = $.60 and subsequently repurchases the bond in a market transaction for 960u when 1u = $.62. Without regard to the ceiling, the corporation has exchange loss of $20—the principal amount translated at the spot rate as of the issue date (1,000u times $.60) less the principal amount translated at the spot rate for the date of repurchase (1,000u times $.62). Overall, however, the corporation has gain of $5—the excess of the dollar value of the issue price ($600) over the dollar cost of the repurchase (960u times $.62 or $595). The exchange loss thus is not recognized, and the overall gain is cancellation of indebtedness income.[28]

¶71.7.6 Original Issue Discount (OID) and Other Interest Equivalents

For purposes of these rules, the term "interest" includes OID, unstated interest under §483, and acquisition discount on obligations maturing within one year.[29] For a holder, OID is the amount reported as gross income, after adjustment for any acquisition premium paid for the instrument.[30]

The application of the rules to a discount obligation is illustrated by Example 71-2, in which a taxpayer whose functional currency is the U.S. dollar pays 8,227u at original issue for a two-year zero coupon note in the principal amount 10,000u and, two years later, collects 10,000u on the note's maturity.[31] OID

Taxation of Income From the Retirement of Nonfunctional Debt, 7 Tax Notes Int'l 647 (1993).

[26] If the obligor assumed the obligation from an obligor that realized but did not recognize exchange gain or loss on the transaction, the issuer's principal amount is the amount received by the prior obligor on original issue. Also, if the instrument was issued at a premium, the principal amount is reduced by premium amortized to periods ending with or before the date of the payment, transfer, or discharge.

[27] IRC §§988(b)(1), (2); Reg. §1.988-2(b)(8).

[28] See supra ¶6.4.

[29] Reg. §1.988-2(b)(2)(ii)(A). See supra ¶56.1 for OID, ¶57.5 for §483, and ¶59.4.2 for acquisition discount on short-term instruments.

[30] For acquisition premium, see supra ¶56.4.8.

[31] See Reg. §1.988-2(b)(9) Ex. 7.

accrues in four six-month increments. The dollar amounts of each accrual (column 3) is the product of the accrual in the nonfunctional currency (column 1) and the average exchange rate for the accrual period (column 2). No exchange gain or loss is recognized until the note is paid, but gain or loss is then recognized with respect to all OID accruals and the principal amount. The exchange gain or loss for each of these amounts (column 5) is the accrual in the nonfunctional currency (column 1) multiplied by the difference between the exchange rates at the times of accrual and payment (column 4 less column 2). The calculations are the same for the issuer, except that the holder's exchange gain is exchange loss for the issuer.

Example 71-2
Translation of OID and Exchange Gain
or Loss on Payment of OID Instrument

Exchange Period	(1) Nonfunctional Accrual	(2) Accrual Exchange Rate	(3) Functional Accrual	(4) Payment	(5) Exchange Gain or Rate (Loss)
1	411u	$.60	$247	$.62	$ 8
2	432u	.64	276	.62	(9)
3	454u	.62	281	.62	0
4	476u	.63	300	.62	(5)
Principal	8,227u	.58		.62	329
Total					$323

¶71.7.7 Dual and Multiple Currency Instruments

Special rules have been proposed for dual currency debt instruments.[32] A "dual currency debt instrument" is an instrument under which (1) qualified stated interest is denominated in one currency, (2) the stated redemption price at maturity is denominated in another currency, and (3) the payments in each currency are fixed when the instrument is issued.[33] Under the proposed regulations, such an instrument is bifurcated into a zero coupon bond in the currency

---

[32] See Hariton, New Foreign Currency Debt Regulations—An Analysis and a Recommendation, 56 Tax Notes 1201 (1992).

[33] Prop. Reg. §1.988-1(a)(4)(i). See Prop. Reg. §1.988-1(a)(4)(iii) (rules on dual currency contracts will apply only to transactions entered into after adoption of final regulations).
Qualified stated interest is interest payable unconditionally at least annually throughout the instrument's term at a fixed rate or a variable rate meeting various requirements. IRC §1273(a)(2), discussed supra ¶56.3.4. The stated redemption price at maturity consists of all payments other than qualified stated interest.

of the stated redemption price and an installment instrument in the currency of the qualified periodic interest.[34] The yield of each of these instruments is an interest rate agreed upon by the issuer and the holder, "based on the original yields of other debt instruments with similar maturities and security issued within the previous six months" and denominated in the same currency. The present value of the payment or payments, determined with these yields, must equal the instrument's issue price.

Assume an instrument issued for $999 requires semiannual interest payments of $40 each for 10 years and a single principal payment of 1,000u 10 years from the issue date; 1u = $1 on the issue date.[35] Assume the current market rate of interest for an instrument with a similar maturity and security is 7 percent if denominated in U.S. dollars and 8.6 percent if denominated in us. The issue price of the installment instrument is $569 (present value, at 7 percent compounded semiannually, of semiannual payments of $40 each for 10 years), and the issue price of the hypothetical zero coupon bond is 431u (present value, at 8.6 percent compounded semiannually, of 1,000u in 10 years). If the holder's functional currency is the dollar, §988 does not apply to the installment instrument because it is denominated in the functional currency. For the first six-month accrual period, the interest on the installment instrument is $20 (one half of 7 percent of issue price of $569). Section 988 applies to the zero coupon bond. For the first six-month accrual period, interest (OID) on this instrument is 19u (one half of 8.6 percent of issue price of 431u). If the average exchange rate for the first period is 1u = $1.10, interest is $41 ($20 plus 19u times $1.10).

An explanation of the theory underlying this treatment requires a brief digression into the world of forward exchange rates. Differences between the interest rates prevailing in two countries are necessarily reflected in forward exchange rates. In the example, the 10-year forward rate must be 1u = $0.858 when the instrument is issued. At the market interest rate in country X (8.6 percent), the right to 1,000u has a present value of 431u. At the exchange rate prevailing at the issue date, 431u is worth $431. The future value of $431 in 10 years at the interest rate prevailing in the United States (7 percent) is $858. If the 10-year forward rate differed from 1u = $0.858, arbitragers would either buy 10-year zero coupon bonds or 10-year forward contracts until the forward rate became 1u = $0.858.

The IRS concluded that given the connections between relative interest rates in two currencies and expectations as to future movements in exchange rates between the currencies, the yield on a payment or stream of payments denominated in a particular currency should be an interest rate reflecting the market in that currency. The instrument in the example could be treated more simply by honoring the instrument's nomenclature classifying the semiannual payments of $40 each as interest and the 1,000u payment as principal, requiring the holder to

---

[34] Prop. Reg. §1.988-1(a)(4)(ii).
[35] See Prop. Reg. §1.988-1(a)(6) Ex. 12.

report the $40 payments as interest and recognize exchange gain or loss on the 1,000u principal. However, this approach causes interest to accrue at an interest rate (8 percent) that is not the market rate in either the United States or country X but is instead a melding of the two countries' rates. The proposed regulations instead require interest to accrue at the U.S. rate on payments as to which the holder bears the currency risk of holding dollars and at the country X rate with respect to the payment as to which the currency risk is that of a holder of country X currency.

If payments under a debt instrument are in three or more currencies and the payments in each currency are fixed at issue, the instrument is split into several hypothetical instruments—one for each currency—"in a manner consistent with the principles" of the proposed regulation on dual currency obligations.[36]

¶71.7.8 Nonrecognition Transfers to Issuer

If a debt instrument is transferred by the holder to the issuer in a transaction covered by a nonrecognition rule, exchange gain or loss is nevertheless recognized by both parties, except that the loss limitations of §267 (sales and exchanges between related persons), §1091 (wash sales), and §1092 (straddles), if applicable, bar recognition of exchange loss.[37] Assume a U.S. citizen exercises the conversion privilege under a 1,000u bond that is convertible into stock of the issuer; 1u was worth $.50 when the taxpayer purchased the bond for 1,000u and is worth $.60 at the time of conversion.[38] Although gain or loss normally is not recognized on the conversion of a convertible bond, exchange gain or loss is recognized. If the holder paid 1,000u for the bond and no accrued interest is unpaid at the time of the conversion, the holder has exchange gain of $100—the principal amount translated at the spot rate on the date of conversion (1,000u times $.60) less the principal translated at the spot rate for the date the bond was acquired (1,000u times $.50).

For the obligor, exchange gain or loss in a transaction covered by a nonrecognition rule is computed before debt discharge income.[39] Assume a domestic corporation borrows 100u from its foreign parent when 1u is worth 65 cents, and the parent subsequently cancels the debt as a contribution to capital when the exchange rate is 60 cents.[40] The corporation has exchange gain on the cancellation of $5 ($65 value of 100u when borrowed less $60 value when the debt is canceled). Under §108(e)(6), when a shareholder contributes an obligation of the corporation to the corporation's capital, the corporation is deemed to have paid

---

[36] Prop. Reg. §1.988-1(a)(5) (applicable only to transactions entered into after adoption of final regulations).

[37] Reg. §1.988-2(b)(13)(i).

[38] See Reg. §1.988-2(b)(13)(iv) Ex. 1.

[39] Reg. §1.988-2(b)(13)(ii).

[40] See Reg. §1.988-2(b)(13)(iv) Ex. 2.

an amount equal to the shareholder's basis for the obligation.[41] The shareholder's basis (100u) and the amount of the obligation (100u) are translated at the exchange rate for the date of the capital contribution (60 cents). Under §108(e)(6), the corporation is thus deemed to pay $60 in retirement of a $60 debt, and no debt discharge income is recognized.

¶71.7.9 Instruments in Hyperinflationary Currencies

1. *High interest loans to foreign affiliates.* When a U.S. person makes a loan to a related foreign corporation at a high interest rate, the foreign tax credit limitation is adjusted by accruing exchange loss annually while the loan is outstanding.[42] The apparent purpose of the adjustments is to prevent the limitation from being artificially inflated by the high interest typically charged on loans in hyperinflationary currencies. The adjustments are made if (1) the borrower is a foreign corporation, (2) the lender is a U.S. person holding at least 10 percent of the corporation's voting stock or is related to a 10 percent or greater U.S. shareholder,[43] (3) the loan is denominated in a foreign currency, and (4) the interest rate is "at least 10 percentage points higher than the Federal mid-term rate" in effect when the loan is made.[44] Such a loan is "marked to market on an annual basis," but only for the purpose of determining the lender's foreign tax credit limitation.[45] This means that the lender computes exchange gain or loss annually as though (1) the loan was made on the first day of the year or such later day in the year on which it was actually made and (2) the loan was repaid in full on the last day of the year or such earlier day as it was actually repaid.

Assume *DC*, a domestic corporation, lends 1,000u to a foreign subsidiary operating in a country that has experienced high rates of inflation; the Federal mid-term rate is 8 percent when the loan is made, but the loan bears interest at 40 percent in order to compensate the lender for the erosion of principal expected to result from inflation. If the loan is outstanding throughout a taxable year during which the exchange rate for 1u declines from 60 cents to 40 cents, exchange loss on the loan for the year is $200 ($600 value of 1,000u at the beginning of the year less $400 value at year-end).

Exchange gain or loss computed by the mark to market procedure is not recognized as gross income or allowed as a deduction, but it is taken into account in two ways in determining the §904 limitation on the lender's credit for foreign

---

[41] See supra ¶7.5.

[42] IRC §988(a)(3)(C)(i).

[43] A lender is related to a 10 percent or greater U.S. shareholder if the lender controls the shareholder, the shareholder controls the lender, or both of them are controlled by a third person. IRC §§954(d)(3), 988(a)(3)(C). Control is defined as ownership of more than 50 percent, by vote or value, of the stock or other equity interests in the controlled person.

[44] IRC §988(a)(3)(C); Reg. §1.988-4(e). For the Federal mid-term rate, see supra ¶57.2.

[45] IRC §988(a)(3)(C)(i).

income taxes.[46] Section 904 limits the credit to an amount equal to the precredit U.S. tax multiplied by:

$$\frac{\text{Taxable income from foreign sources}}{\text{Entire taxable income}}$$

Exchange gain or loss under the mark to market rule is included in both entire taxable income and the taxable income figure used in computing the precredit U.S. tax.[47] It is treated as U.S. source income or loss and thus does not directly affect foreign source taxable income. However, interest on the loan, which would normally be foreign source income,[48] is recharacterized as U.S. source income up to the amount of exchange loss under the mark to market rule.[49]

Assume the interest income in the example is translated as $220 (400u times average exchange rate of 1u = $0.55), and *DC* has foreign source taxable income of $5,000 (including the $220 of interest), and entire taxable income of $20,000. If its income is taxed at 34 percent, its foreign tax credit limitation, before adjustment under the mark to market rule, is:

$$(\$6,800)(\$5,000/\$20,000) = \$1,700$$

The following adjustments are made: Of the $220 of foreign source interest income on the loan, $200—an amount equal to the exchange loss under the mark to market rule—is recharacterized as U.S. source income, thus reducing the numerator of the limiting fraction to $4,800. The denominator is reduced to $19,800 ($20,000 less $200 of exchange loss). The precredit U.S. tax is deemed to be $6,723 (34 percent of $19,800), and the limitation is:

$$(\$6,732)(\$4,800/\$19,800) = \$1,632$$

The $68 reduction in the limitation (from $1,700 to $1,632) equals the exchange loss multiplied by the U.S. tax rate (34 percent of $200 is $68). As a consequence, interest on the loan increases the §904 limitation by only 34 percent of the excess of the interest income ($220) over the accrued exchange loss ($200). The extraordinary interest charged to compensate for foreign inflation thus does not inflate the foreign tax credit limitation. However, because the adjustments are made solely for purposes of the foreign tax credit limitation, the extraordinary interest is included in gross income as received or accrued, depending on the taxpayer's method of accounting, and the offsetting exchange loss is not recognized until the loan is paid.

---

[46] See supra ¶69.5 for §904.

[47] IRC §988(a)(3)(C)(i).

[48] IRC §§861(a)(1), 862(a)(1), discussed supra ¶70.2.

[49] IRC §988(a)(3)(C)(ii).

2. *Other instruments.* Regulations have been proposed that would require exchange gain or loss to be recognized annually on any debt instrument (including a demand deposit) denominated in a nonfunctional currency that is hyperinflationary unless the taxpayer is subject to the rule described immediately above with respect to the instrument.[50] A country's currency is hyperinflationary if cumulative inflation in the currency was 100 percent or more during the 36 months ending with the preceding taxable year.[51]

When this rule applies, exchange gain or loss is recognized for each year equal to the difference between

a. The instrument's principal amount or basis as of the first day of the year or the first day during the year on which the taxpayer was obligor or holder of the instrument, determined in the functional currency and translated at the spot rate for this first day, and

b. The same principal amount or basis as of the last day of the year or the last day during the year on which the taxpayer was obligor or holder, translated at the spot rate for that day.[52]

The exchange gain or loss is offset against the interest income or expense under the instrument, except that if the gain or loss exceeds the interest income or expense, the character and source of the excess is determined by the usual rules for exchange gain and loss.[53] The principal amount or basis of the instrument is increased by exchange gain and decreased by exchange loss recognized under the rule.[54]

Assume *DC*, a domestic corporation whose taxable year is the calendar year, lends 1,000u to an unrelated country *X* corporation on January 1 of year 1 under a note requiring semiannual payments of interest at 40 percent per annum and a single principal payment 18 months after the date of the loan; the exchange rate declines from 1u = $1 to 1u = $0.70 during year 1, and the *u* is hyperinflationary. *DC* recognizes exchange loss for the year of $300—the principal amount in the nonfunctional currency, translated as of the first day of the year (1,000u times $1), less the same amount, translated as of the last day of the year (1,000u times $0.70). Assume interest for the first six-month accrual period is $180 (200u times average exchange rate of 1u = $0.90) and for the second six-month period is $140 (200u times $0.70). If the obligor is not engaged in business in the United

---

[50] Prop. Reg. §1.988-2(b)(15). See Prop. Reg. §1.988-2(b)(15)(v) (provision will be applicable only for transactions entered into after adoption of final regulations).

The provision is inapplicable to a qualified business unit using the U.S. dollar approximate separate transactions method (DASTM) because that method provides much the same results. Prop. Reg. §1.988-2(b)(15)(iv).

[51] Reg. §1.985-2(b)(2). Inflation is measured by the consumer price index listed in International Financial Statistics, a publication of the International Monetary Fund.

[52] Prop. Reg. §1.988-2(b)(15)(i).

[53] Prop. Reg. §1.988-2(b)(15)(ii).

[54] Prop. Reg. §1.988-2(b)(15)(iii).

States, the interest income for the year ($180 + $140 = $320) is from foreign sources.[55] The exchange loss is treated as a deduction allocable to this interest. The loan thus adds $20 ($320 less $300) to *DC*'s taxable income from foreign sources.

¶71.8 NONINTEREST INCOME AND DEDUCTIONS DENOMINATED IN NONFUNCTIONAL CURRENCIES

If an item of gross income, deduction, or credit (other than interest) is denominated in a nonfunctional currency, the item is translated into the taxpayer's functional currency at the spot rate prevailing when the revenue or cost is first recognized.[1] Assume U.S. citizen *A*, who accounts by the cash method, has gross income of 100u. The gross income is translated at the spot rate for the date on which the 100u is received. Assume *A* hires a foreign lawyer to perform a service for her business, and the lawyer bills 100u for the service. The deduction for the fee is the dollar value of 100u when the lawyer is paid.

For an accrual method taxpayer, revenues are translated at the spot rate for the date on which accrued, and exchange gain or loss is recognized on receipt of payment if exchange rates change between the dates of accrual and payment.[2] Assume *DC*, whose functional currency is the dollar, sells goods on credit for 100u during year 1 when 1u = $.55, and the price is collected during year 2 when 1u = $.53.[3] *DC* has sales revenues for year 1 of $55 (100u times $.55). For year 2, it has exchange loss of $2—100u times $.53, the spot rate at the time of payment, less the accrued $55. *DC*'s basis for the 100u is $53, and it will have exchange gain or loss if it subsequently converts the 100u into more or less than $53.[4]

The need to compute exchange gain or loss twice—on receipt of payment and on disposition of the currency received as payment—can be avoided by the taxpayer placing a standing order with its bank to convert all exchange receipts into dollars on receipt. If this is done, the payment is translated at the rate at which the deposited funds are actually exchanged.[5] For example, if *DC* places such an order and the bank exchanges the 100u for $54, exchange loss on the receivable and currency is $1 (amount realized of $54 less accrual of $55).

---

[55] IRC §862(a)(1).

[1] For the term "spot rate," see infra ¶71.5 text accompanying notes 18–20. The rules described here do not apply to foreign income taxes for which credit is claimed under §901. See supra ¶69.13.

[2] Reg. §1.988-2(c)(2).

[3] See Reg. §1.988-2(c)(4) Ex. 1.

[4] See supra ¶71.6.1.

[5] Reg. §1.988-2(c)(4) Ex. 3.

Similar principles apply when a cost accrues in a nonfunctional currency.[6] Assume *DC* purchases inventory on credit for 100u. The purchase is accrued at the dollar value of 100u when *DC*'s obligation becomes fixed (typically, by delivery of the goods). If 1u is then worth 52 cents, the purchase is booked at $52. Any change in the value of the 100u between the times of accrual and payment is exchange gain or loss. For example, if the exchange rate is 56 cents when the goods are paid for, *DC* has exchange loss of $4 ($52 accrual less $56 dollar value of payment).

If the deduction for a cost incurred in a nonfunctional currency is deferred, the cost is translated at the spot rate in effect when the cost is incurred, not when the deduction is allowed. Assume *DC* purchases depreciable property for 100u when 1u is worth 60 cents. The property's original basis is $60, and depreciation is computed from that basis.

A "spot rate convention" may be used in accounting for accounts receivable and payable denominated in nonfunctional currencies if the accounts arise in the ordinary course of the taxpayer's business.[7] Under such a convention, the same exchange rate is used for all transactions within a particular period, which may not be longer than one quarter. The rate may be the average of the spot rates on all business days during the period, the average of the rates on the first and last days of the period, or the rate on the last day of the period or the last day of the preceding period.[8] The convention and the taxpayer's application of it, however, must be "consistent with the taxpayer's financial accounting." Also, a spot rate convention is a method of accounting that can be changed only with IRS consent.[9]

Assume *DC* adopts a spot rate convention using the spot rate on the last day of each calendar month for all receivables and payables transactions during the month. If goods are sold in January and the price is collected in March, revenue on the sale is booked at the January 31 rate, and the payment is booked at the March 31 rate. The difference between the two is exchange gain or loss on the payment.

¶71.9 FORWARD CONTRACTS

¶71.9.1 Introductory

Generally, all gain or loss on a "forward contract, futures contract, option, or similar financial instrument" (hereinafter "forward contract") is exchange gain or loss if the instrument is denominated in a currency other than the

---

[6] Reg. §1.988-2(c)(3).
[7] Reg. §1.988-1(d)(3).
[8] See Reg. §1.988-2(c)(4) Ex. 2.
[9] For changes of accounting method, see infra ¶105.12.

taxpayer's functional currency.[1] A forward contract is "denominated" in a nonfunctional currency only if the "underlying property" is a nonfunctional currency or a debt instrument denominated in a nonfunctional currency.[2] For example, a forward contract to purchase wheat or a stock warrant is not denominated in a foreign currency, even if the contract or warrant price is payable in a nonfunctional currency, because the underlying property is wheat or stock, not a currency. On the other hand, an option to enter into a forward contract to purchase a nonfunctional currency or an option to purchase a bond denominated in a nonfunctional currency is a forward contract because the underlying property is the nonfunctional currency or an instrument denominated in the currency.

Under rules described below, if a forward contract is used to hedge currency risk on another asset, claim, or liability, it may be integrated with the other item, in which case exchange gain or loss is not separately computed on the forward contract.[3]

¶71.9.2   Computation and Recognition of Exchange Gain or Loss

1. *Realization of exchange gain or loss.* Normally, exchange gain or loss on a forward contract is the excess of the amount realized with respect to the contract over any amounts paid under the contract, including an amount paid to close out the taxpayer's position.[4] Assume S and B, who both use the U.S. dollar as their functional currency, make a contract under which S agrees to sell and B agrees to buy 100u for $60 in 90 days. The making of the contract has no immediate tax consequence. Assume B subsequently pays $2 to S to cancel the contract.[5] If neither party has any other costs in connection with the contract, S has exchange gain of $2, and B has exchange loss of $2. Alternatively, if S sells her position under the contract for $2, the gain on the sale is exchange gain.

If the taxpayer makes a payment to acquire a forward contract, the payment must be taken into account in computing exchange gain or loss. Assume DC, a domestic corporation, paid $1 for an option to purchase 100u for $60 in 90 days; on the expiration date, when 100u = $63, DC is paid $3 to close out the option.[6] DC has gain of $2 (amount realized of $3, less adjusted basis of $2). Also, on the lapse of a foreign currency option, the amount paid for the option is exchange gain and loss. For example, if DC holds the option until it expires unexercised, exchange loss of $1 is realized on the lapse of the option.

2. *Offsetting positions.* Generally, exchange gain or loss is not recognized on a forward contract merely because the taxpayer enters into one or more other

---

[1] IRC §§988(b)(3), (c)(1)(B)(iii).

[2] Reg. §1.988-1(a)(2)(iii)(A).

[3] Infra ¶71.10.

[4] Reg. §1.988-2(d)(4)(i).

[5] See Reg. §1.988-2(d)(2)(iv) Ex. 1.

[6] See Reg. §1.988-2(d)(4)(iii) Ex. 3.

transactions that offset the taxpayer's position under the contract.[7] However, if the contract is traded on an exchange, exchange gain or loss is recognized on the acquisition of an offsetting contract if the exchange's "general practice" is to terminate offsetting contracts. Also, even in the absence of such an exchange practice, exchange gain is recognized to the extent the taxpayer "derives, by pledge or otherwise, an economic benefit ... from any gain inherent in such offsetting positions." Assume *DC*, a domestic corporation, enters into a currency swap contract to exchange a series of payments in Japanese yen for a series of payments in U.S. dollars; sometime later, when its position under the contract has a substantial value, *DC* enters into an offsetting contract to lock in its profit.[8] The making of the offsetting contract does not cause *DC* to recognize its gain, but a pledge of the contracts to secure a loan would trigger recognition of the gain, apparently up to the amount borrowed. The taxpayer's basis for the contract is increased by any gain recognized under this rule.

3. *Making or taking delivery.* If a taxpayer takes or makes delivery under a forward contract, exchange gain or loss is recognized as though the contract had been sold on the delivery date.[9] Assume *A* enters into a forward contract on March 1 to purchase 100u for $60 on August 1; on August 1, when 1u is worth only 58 cents, *A* pays $60 for 100u under the contract.[10] *A* is deemed to have sold her position under the contract just before taking delivery of the 100u. Because the spot rate for 100u was then $2 less than the contract price, *A* would have had to pay $2 to cancel her obligation under the contract. She therefore has $2 of exchange loss and takes a basis of $58 for the 100u purchased under the contract.

However, a "spot contract"—a contract to buy or sell a nonfunctional currency within two business days after the contract is made—is not subject to the forward rules unless the contract is sold before delivery is made under the contract.[11] For example, if *DC* makes a contract on day 1 to purchase 100u for $60 on day 3, no exchange gain or loss is recognized when *DC* pays $60 for 100u on day 3, and the 100u takes a $60 basis, regardless of the spot rate on day 3. However, if *DC* sells the contract for $2 rather than taking delivery on day 3, the contract is treated as a forward contract, and the $2 is exchange gain.

4. *Extension of delivery date.* If the date for making or taking delivery on a forward contract is extended, exchange gain or loss is recognized on the original delivery date as though delivery had then been taken or made.[12] For example, in a "historical rate rollover," the maturity date of a forward contract is extended and the forward rate is restated as the rate prevailing on the date of the rollover,

---

[7] Reg. §1.988-2(d)(2)(ii).

[8] Reg. §1.988-2(d)(2)(iv) Ex. 2.

[9] IRC §988(c)(5); Reg. §1.988-2(d)(4)(ii) (applicable only if delivery is made or received after June 11, 1987). See Reg. §1.988-2(d)(2)(iii) (if contract expires before or after delivery date, delivery is deemed made or received on expiration date).

[10] See Reg. §1.988-2(d)(4)(iii) Ex. 1.

[11] Reg. §§1.988-1(b), 1.988-2(d)(1)(ii).

[12] Reg. §1.988-2(d)(2)(v).

adjusted for the gain or loss accrued as of the rollover date plus interest until the new delivery date.[13] Exchange gain or loss is recognized when a historical rate rollover is agreed upon. The interest factor (the excess of the future value of the gain or loss over its present value at the time of the rollover) is included in the exchange gain or loss if the rollover extends the delivery date by not more than 183 days, but is treated as interest income or expense if the extension exceeds 183 days.

The recognition of exchange gain or loss on a forward contract is subject to all recognition rules of the Code for gains and losses on sales and exchanges of property.[14] For example, if a forward contract is part of a straddle, recognition of exchange loss may be blocked by §1092.[15]

¶71.9.3 Notional Principal Contracts

A "notional principal contract" is subject to §988 if the payments made or received under the contract are "determined with reference to a nonfunctional currency."[16] A notional principal contract is a financial instrument "that provides for the payment of amounts by one party to another at specified intervals calculated by reference to a specified index upon a notional principal amount in exchange for specified consideration or a promise to pay similar amounts."[17] Common examples of notional principal contracts are swaps, caps, floors, and collars (none of which has anything to do with clothing or building construction).

Assume (1) A agrees to make five annual payments to B equal to the interest on a hypothetical 100u note bearing interest at 9 percent and (2) B agrees to pay A annually for five years an amount equal to interest on 100u at a floating rate that is 2 percentage points in excess of London Interbank Offered Rate (LIBOR). A might make such an agreement (an interest rate swap) because, for example, it borrowed 100u from a third party under a variable rate instrument, and it wishes to substitute a fixed interest obligation for the variable obligation. A's ultimate obligation in such a case is to pay 9 percent interest to B because the variable interest received from B and the variable interest payable to the third party are a wash.

The IRS has issued regulations under §446 governing the computation and timing of income and deduction from notional principal contracts.[18] The regulations generally treat payments under such a contract as income or expense when received or paid, except that a payment received or made when the contract is made is usually spread over the contract's life. The regulations generally apply

---

[13] Reg. §1.988-5(b)(2)(iii)(C).

[14] Reg. §1.988-2(d)(3).

[15] For §1092, see supra ¶45.3.

[16] Reg. §1.988-1(a)(2)(iii)(B)(1).

[17] Reg. §1.988-1(a)(2)(iii)(B)(2).

[18] Reg. §1.446-3, discussed supra ¶45.7.

to notional principal contracts subject to §988. In the example, a net amount received under the interest rate swap on any payment date is income, and a net amount paid under the swap is expense. Usually, the only significance of a notional principal contract being subject to §988 is that the income or deduction determined under the notional principal contract regulations is exchange gain or loss.[19]

The §988 regulations provide substantial detail on the treatment of one type of notional principal contract—currency swaps.[20] A currency swap contract requires the parties to exchange "periodic interim payments" in different currencies on or before maturity and to exchange the "swap principal amount" at maturity.[21] The swap principal amount may also be exchanged when the contract is made. The interim payments in each currency are "computed by reference to an interest index applied to the swap principal amount."

Generally, exchange gain or loss under a currency swap is determined by treating payments under the swap as though made under a hypothetical borrowing denominated in the currency of the payments and treating receipts as received under a hypothetical loan in the currency in which received.[22] The swap principal amount is the issue price of the hypothetical borrowing and loan, and the stated redemption price at maturity is the sum of all payments made or received, excepting an exchange of the swap principal at the outset and periodic interim payments that are qualified stated interest (interest payable at least annually at a fixed or qualifying variable rate). Exchange gain or loss on periodic interim payments made and received during any year is (1) the sum of interest income on the hypothetical loan and exchange gain or loss with respect to interest income, less (2) the sum of interest expense on the hypothetical borrowing and exchange gain or loss with respect to interest expense. Exchange gain or loss with respect to the swap principal amount is realized when principal payments are swapped at maturity, equal to the value of the swap principal amount received, less the value of the swap principal amount paid.[23] No exchange gain or loss is realized on a swap of principal amounts at the outset.

Assume DC, a domestic corporation using the accrual method of accounting, enters into a swap agreement with J in the notional principal amounts of $150 and 100 British pounds (£), which are equal in value when the contract is made.[24] Under the contract, (1) DC must pay $15 (10 percent of the dollar principal) to J on the last days of years 1 and 2, (2) simultaneously with each of these payments, J must pay £12 (12 percent of the pound principal) to DC, and (3) on the last day of year 2, DC must pay J $150, and J must pay DC £100. DC

---

[19] Reg. §1.988-2(e)(1).
[20] Reg. §1.988-2(e).
[21] Reg. §1.988-2(e)(2)(ii).
[22] Reg. §1.988-2(e)(2)(iii).
[23] Reg. §1.988-2(e)(2)(iv).
[24] Reg. §1.988-2(e)(5) Ex. 1.

might make such a contract to eliminate currency risk under a 100£ borrowing from a third party under a 12 percent note. Exchange gain or loss on the swap is computed as though (1) *DC* borrowed $150 at 10 percent interest and loaned £100 at 12 percent interest. Assume the average exchange rates are £1 = $1.45 for year 1 and £ = $1.35 for year 2. *DC* is treated as having received interest of $17.40 (£12 times $1.45) for year 1 and $16.20 (£12 times $1.35) for year 2. Assume spot rates are $1 = $1.40 at the end of year 1 and $1 = $1.30 at the end of year 2. On the receipt of the £12 payments, *DC* has exchange loss for year 1 of $.60 (£12 times exchange rate at time of receipt ($16.80), less $17.40 accrued) and exchange loss for year 2 of $.60 (£12 times $1.30 ($15.60), less accrual of $16.20). The exchange gain or loss with respect to the periodic interim payments is the sum of the foregoing amounts, less the dollar payments of $15 each.

	Year 1	Year 2
Hypothetical interest	$17.40	$16.20
Hypothetical exchange gain or loss	(.60)	(.60)
Total of hypothetical receipts	$16.80	$15.60
Less amounts paid	15.00	15.00
Exchange gain	$ 1.80	$ .60

DC also has exchange loss with respect to the swap principal, as follows:

Amount received (£100 times spot rate at maturity ($1.30))	$130
Less amount paid	150
	($ 20)

The aggregate results of the contract are:

	Year 1	Year 2
Exchange gain or (loss)	$1.80	($19.40)

If the present value of the swap payments to be made and received are not equal when the contract is made (that is, if the contract is "off-market"), the taxpayer typically makes or receives a payment (a "swap premium" or "swap discount") to equalize the values. A swap premium or discount is recognized as expense or income "in a manner which places the taxpayer in the same position it would have been in had the taxpayer entered into a currency swap contract under which" the present values of the future amounts to be paid and received are equal.[25] The premium or discount may arise because the "swap exchange rate"—"the single exchange rate set forth in the contract at which the swap principal amounts are determined"—differs from the spot rate when the contract

---

[25] Reg. §1.988-2(e)(3).

is made. When this is so, the premium or discount is recognized as expense or income at the time of the swap of principal amounts. Alternatively, a premium or discount may arise because the interest indices used in computing the periodic interim payments do not reflect "current values." When this is so, the swap premium or discount is amortized as an adjustment to interest income or expense by "the principles of economic accrual."

Gain or loss on a disposition of a currency swap contract is exchange gain or loss.[26]

¶71.9.4 Contracts Subject to §1256

A foreign currency contract that is traded on the interbank market is subject to both the §988 rules for forward contracts and the mark to market rules of §1256.[27] Under the latter rules, gain or loss is recognized as though contracts held at year-end had been sold on the last day of the taxable year at fair market value. Assume *DC*, a domestic corporation whose taxable year is the calendar year, makes a forward contract on October 1 of year 1 to purchase 100u on March 1 of year 2 for $60.[28] If the mark to market rule applies and *A*'s position under the contract is worth $3 on the last business day of year 1, *A* has $3 of exchange gain for year 1, and the contract takes a basis of $3. Although gain or loss recognized under the mark to market rules is normally 40 percent short-term capital gain or loss and 60 percent long-term gain or loss,[29] *A*'s exchange gain is ordinary because §988 trumps §1256 in this respect.[30] Assume the value of the dollar falls early during year 2, and *A* pays $2 during February of year 2 to cancel her obligation under the contract. *A* has exchange loss on the cancellation of $5 (sum of $3 basis and $2 paid).

Section 988 does not apply to a regulated futures contract or nonequity option subject to §1256 unless the taxpayer elects to have the rules apply.[31] The election must usually be made no later than the first day during the taxable year on which the contract is held. Once made for any taxable year, the election applies for all subsequent years until it is revoked with IRS consent. For contracts held by a partnership or S corporation, the election is made the partners or shareholders, not the entity.

Section 988 is also inapplicable to instruments subject to §1256, including foreign currency contracts traded on the interbank market, that are held by a "qualified fund," defined as a partnership that (1) has at least 20 partners, (2) has no partner owning more than 20 percent of the interests in capital or profits, (3)

---

[26] Reg. §1.988-2(e)(4).
[27] For §1256, see supra ¶45.2.
[28] See Reg. §1.988-2(d)(2)(iv) Ex. 3.
[29] IRC §1256(a)(3).
[30] See Reg. §1.988-2(d)(4)(iii) Ex. 2.
[31] IRC §988(c)(1)(D); Reg. §1.988-1(a)(7).

is principally engaged in buying and selling options, futures, and forwards in commodities, (4) elects to be subject to this rule, and (5) meets a few other requirements.[32]

¶71.9.5 Capital Gains Election

Exchange gain or loss is usually ordinary income.[33] However, an election can be made to treat gain or loss on a forward contract as capital gain or loss if (1) the contract is a capital asset and is not a part of a straddle, (2) the election is made by "clearly identifying" the contract in the taxpayer's records on the day the contract is acquired, and (3) the taxpayer attaches a statement to the return for the year identifying the contracts for which the election is made and declaring that the statutory requirements have been met.[34]

¶71.10 HEDGING

¶71.10.1 Introductory

The regulations provide several rules for integrating transactions and instruments denominated in nonfunctional currencies with hedges acquired to eliminate foreign currency risk.[1] For example, if a taxpayer borrows or lends in a nonfunctional currency, it might enter into one or more forward contracts to buy or sell the units of currency required to be paid or to be received under the borrowing or loan. In this case, the borrowing or loan may be integrated with the forward contracts (the hedge) into a "synthetic debt instrument," consisting of a series of payments to be made or received under the hedge.[2] Also, if a taxpayer makes a contract to buy or sell goods or services and the price is in a nonfunctional currency, the taxpayer may acquire units of the currency or make a contract to buy or sell currency, so that the price, expressed in the functional

---

[32] IRC §988(c)(1)(E); Reg. §1.988-1(a)(8).

[33] IRC §988(a)(1)(A); Reg. §1.988-3(a). See generally Cathcart, Effect of *Arkansas Best* on Foreign Currency Transactions, 39 Tax Notes 397 (1988).

[34] IRC §988(a)(1)(B); Reg. §1.988-3(b). For the term "straddle," see §1092(c), discussed supra ¶45.3.1.

[1] The IRS will consider requests for letter rulings on the income tax consequences of hedging systems not covered by the rules of the regulations on hedges. Such a ruling may cover a system for hedging "net nonfunctional currency exposure or anticipated nonfunctional currency exposure." Reg. §1.988-5(e). However, the IRS will not rule on "hedges of a taxpayer's investment in a foreign subsidiary"—so-called *Hoover* hedges. See Hoover Co. v. CIR, 72 TC 206 (1979).

See generally Homan, The Section 988(d) Hedging Rules: Room to Expand Integration Treatment, 46 Tax Lawyer 887 (1993).

[2] See infra ¶71.10.2.

currency, is locked in when the contract is made. In this case also, the contract and the hedge may be integrated to reflect the economic substance of the transactions.[3]

¶71.10.2 Fully Hedged Debt Instruments in Nonfunctional Currencies

A "qualified hedging transaction," consisting of a debt instrument in a nonfunctional currency and a hedge that eliminates foreign currency risk and that the taxpayer identifies as such, is collapsed into a single "synthetic debt instrument."[4] The taxpayer can be either the issuer or holder of the actual debt instrument and plays the same role under the synthetic instrument. The synthetic debt instrument is denominated in the currency in which payments are made or received under the hedge (usually, the taxpayer's functional currency). Assume *DC*, a domestic corporation whose functional currency is the dollar, borrows British pounds and hedges currency risk by entering into contracts to purchase for dollars the pounds it will need to pay interest and principal. If properly identified, the borrowing and the currency contracts are integrated and treated as a borrowing in dollars under a note payable in dollars. Similarly, if the corporation buys a bond denominated in pounds and simultaneously makes contracts to sell the pounds to be received under the bond, the bond and contracts may be integrated as a bond denominated in dollars, the payments under which consist of the amounts to be received under the forward contracts.

If the synthetic debt instrument is denominated in the taxpayer's functional currency, the taxpayer has no exchange gain or loss under either the actual debt instrument or the hedge.[5] If the synthetic instrument is in a nonfunctional currency, exchange gain or loss is recognized when interest or principal is paid or received, just as though the synthetic instrument was an actual nonfunctional currency instrument.[6] For example, if a taxpayer whose functional currency is the dollar acquires a debt instrument denominated in Israeli shekels and hedges the instrument in Swiss francs, the synthetic instrument is in francs, and exchange gain or loss is recognized as if the taxpayer actually held an instrument denominated in francs.

---

[3] See infra ¶70.10.3.

[4] Reg. §1.988-5(a)(9). The IRS is considering whether to permit the rules for hedged debt instruments to be applied treating a consolidated group of corporations as one corporation. TD 8400, 1992-1 CB 101, 104-05. See generally Lopata, Current Issues in Foreign Currency Transactions, 51 Tax Notes 895 (1991); Weinrib, Driscoll & Connors, Final and Proposed Regulations Expand Available Foreign Currency Hedging Opportunities, 77 J.Tax'n 110 (1992).

[5] Reg. §1.988-5(a)(1).

[6] However, the qualified hedging transaction rules do not apply, and the debt instrument and hedge are analyzed separately, if the Federal short-term rate is at least 20 percentage points lower than the rate most nearly resembling that rate in the currency in which the synthetic instrument is denominated. Reg. §1.988-5(a)(2). For the Federal short-term rate, see supra ¶57.2.

If a debt instrument and hedge are properly identified as a qualified hedging transaction, they are exempted from the straddle and mark to market rules of §§263(g), 1092, and 1256.[7] However, the synthetic instrument may be part of a straddle to which §263(g) or §1092 applies.

1. *Qualified hedging transaction.* The foregoing rules apply only to a "qualified hedging transaction" consisting of a "qualifying debt instrument" and a "hedge" that are an "integrated economic transaction."[8] A debt instrument qualifies unless it is an account receivable or payable.[9] Dual currency and multicurrency debt instruments are qualified. A contingent debt instrument also qualifies if, when it is combined with the hedge, a yield to maturity can be determined in a currency other than the one in which the debt instrument is denominated.[10] If the debt instrument is not fully hedged, but an identical proportion of each payment under the instrument is hedged, the hedged portion of the instrument may qualify.[11] The taxpayer may be either the issuer or holder of a qualifying debt instrument.

A hedge may consist of a spot contract, futures contract, forward contract, option, notional principal contract, currency swap contract, or a "similar financial instrument"; it may also consist of a "series or combination" of any of the foregoing.[12] When the contract or contracts are combined with the qualifying debt instrument, it must be possible to calculate "a yield to maturity in the currency (under principles of section 1272) in which the synthetic debt instrument is denominated."

The complexity and variety of the instruments and contracts that can be integrated under these rules is illustrated by the following example: Assume *DC* receives $1,000 on issuing a five-year note calling for annual interest payments of $80 each and a payment at maturity equal to the excess of $2,000 over the value at that time of 150,000 Japanese yen (but not less than zero); simultaneously, *DC* (1) enters into a forward contract to sell 150,000 yen for $1,000 on the note's

---

[7] Reg. §1.988-5(a)(9)(i)(A). But see Reg. §1.988-5(a)(7) (IRS can disqualify qualified hedging transaction if qualifying debt instrument is part of straddle before being identified as part of qualified hedging transaction). For the straddle and mark to market rules, see supra ¶45.1.

[8] Reg. §1.988-5(a)(1).

[9] Reg. §1.988-5(a)(3).

[10] See TD 8400, 1992-1 CB 101, 104.

[11] Reg. §1.988-5(a)(3)(i). See Reg. §1.988-5(a)(9)(iv) Ex. 8 (taxpayer borrows £200 under three-year note bearing interest at 10 percent payable annually and simultaneously enters into currency swap agreement under which it immediately exchanges £100 for $100 and agrees to pay $8 for 10 pounds on first two interest payment dates and $108 for 110 pounds at maturity; because swap covers 50 percent of each payment under debt instrument, one half of note is qualifying debt instrument, and this one half and swap contract may be integrated as synthetic debt instrument in dollars; other half of note is subject to usual rules for debt instruments in nonfunctional currency).

[12] Reg. §1.988-5(a)(4)(i). For a definition of "currency swap contract," see Reg. §1.988-2(e)(2)(ii), discussed supra ¶71.9.3.

maturity date and (2) acquires an option to purchase 150,000 yen for $2,000, which expires on the same date and requires *DC* to pay an annual premium of $5.[13] If the note, contract, and option are properly identified, they are integrated as a synthetic debt instrument in dollars with an issue price and stated redemption price at maturity of $1,000 and annual interest of $85 (sum of interest of $80 on the note and the $5 annual premium on the option)—a plain vanilla $1,000, 8.5 percent, five-year note. The forward contract and option guarantee that *DC* will be required to pay $1,000 (in addition to interest) at maturity. For example, if $1 = 100 yen at maturity, the principal payment on the bond will be only $500 ($2,000, less 150,000 yen divided by 100), but *DC* will have to make a payment to close out the forward contract of $500 ($1,500 value of 150,000 yen, less $1,000 forward price for 150,000 yen). In contrast, if $1 = 200 yen at maturity, the principal payment under the note will be $1,250 ($2,000, less 150,000 yen divided by 200), but the forward contract will have a value of $250 (excess of contract price of $1,000 over $750 value of 150,000 yen). If $1 = 50 yen at maturity, 150,000 yen will be worth $3,000, the principal payment under the note will be zero, and *DC* will exercise the option to acquire 150,000 yen for $2,000 and transfer the 150,000 yen under the forward contract, receiving $1,000 in exchange and thereby reducing its net cost to $1,000 ($2,000 paid less $1,000 received). The note, contract, and option may be integrated because, although contingencies abound in the individual components, *DC*'s net obligations under the package are fixed and a yield to maturity can therefore be computed.

A qualifying debt instrument and a hedge are an "integrated economic transaction" if all of following requirements are met:[14]

a. Before the close of business on the day the hedge is acquired, the instrument and hedge must be identified as a qualifying hedging transaction under the rules described below.[15] At the time of the identification, the taxpayer need not have acquired or issued the qualified debt instrument or all of the contracts comprising the hedge.

b. When the transaction is so identified, all payments under the debt instrument to be made or received in a nonfunctional currency must be "fully hedged" so that the taxpayer's costs or returns under the debt instrument will not be affected by exchange rate changes after the iden-

---

[13] Reg. §1.988-5(a)(9)(iv) Ex. 6. See Reg. §1.988-5(a)(9)(iv) Ex. 7 (five-year note issued for £504, requiring semiannual interest payments in pounds at 3.7 percent and principal payment at maturity equal to £504 plus product of £504 and percentage increase, if any, in Financial Times 100 Stock Exchange index during note's term; hedged with swap contract under which issuer exchanges issue price for $1,000 and agrees to pay interest on $1,000 semiannually at 8.15 percent and $1,000 at note's maturity in exchange for payments in pounds equal to those required by note).

[14] Reg. §1.988-5(a)(5). See Reg. §1.988-5(a)(7) (IRS can disqualify qualified hedging transaction if qualifying debt instrument is part of straddle before being identified as part of qualified hedging transaction).

[15] Reg. §1.988-5(a)(8)(i).

tification date.[16] If only a portion of the debt instrument is treated as a qualifying debt instrument, only that portion of each payment need be fully hedged.

c. When the transaction is so identified, it must be possible to determine a yield on the synthetic instrument resulting from combining the qualifying debt instrument and hedge. If the debt instrument calls for one or more contingent payments, the contingency must be offset by the hedge so that the synthetic instrument is not a contingent payment instrument.

d. The hedge must be entered into on the identification date.

e. The parties to the hedge must be unrelated.[17]

f. If the transaction is booked by a qualified business unit (QBU) of the taxpayer located outside the United States, the qualifying debt instrument and hedge must be properly reflected on the QBU's books throughout the transaction's life.

g. The qualifying debt instrument and hedge must be entered into by the same individual or entity. A debt instrument issued or held by one corporation may not be integrated with a hedge held by another corporation, even if the two corporations are members of the same affiliated group.

h. If the taxpayer is a nonresident alien or foreign corporation engaged in business in the United States and the qualifying debt instrument or hedge is entered into through the U.S. business, all items of income and expense under the instrument and hedge must, apart from the hedge rules, be effectively connected with the U.S. business.

A taxpayer identifies a qualifying debt instrument and hedge as a qualified hedging transaction by establishing a separate record on the date the hedge is entered into that contains the following information:

a. The date or dates on which the debt instrument and hedge are entered into.

b. The date on which the identification is made.

c. Descriptions of the debt instrument and hedge.

d. A summary of the cash flows under the synthetic debt instrument resulting from the integration of the qualified hedging transaction.[18]

---

[16] Reg. §1.988-5(a)(5)(i). The debt instrument, however, need not be fully hedged during all of the time the taxpayer owes or holds the instrument. For rules that apply when the hedge is acquired after the debt instrument is issued or purchased (legging in) or when the taxpayer disposes of the debt instrument or hedge before the maturity date of the hedging transaction (legging out), see Reg. §1.988-5(a)(6). For examples, see Reg. §1.988-5(a)(9)(iv) Ex. 3 (legging in), Reg. §1.988-5(a)(9)(iv) Ex. 4 (legging out).

[17] Relatedness is determined under §§267(b) and 707(b)(1), discussed infra ¶¶78.3, 87.2.4. See Ring, Risk-Shifting Within a Multinational Corporation: The Incoherence of the U.S. Tax Regime, 38 BC L. Rev. 667 (1997).

[18] Reg. §1.988-5(a)(8)(i). If the hedge is acquired after the debt instrument is entered into, the record must also state the amount, source, and character of any exchange gain or loss that is deferred under the legging in rule of §1.988-5(a)(6)(i).

If the taxpayer fails to satisfy some or all of the identification requirements, the IRS may nevertheless treat a qualifying debt instrument and hedge as a qualified hedging transaction if it concludes that the instrument and hedge "are, in substance, a qualified hedging transaction."[19] Moreover, although a qualifying debt instrument and hedge entered into by different entities cannot be integrated at the taxpayer's instance, the IRS can identify an instrument and hedge held by different entities as a qualified hedging transaction. For example, if a bond denominated in a nonfunctional currency is issued by one member of an affiliated group and another member of the group enters into a currency swap contract that hedges foreign currency risk under the bond, the affiliated group cannot treat the bond and contract as a qualified hedging transaction, but the IRS can do so.

2. *Treatment of qualified hedging transaction.* The synthetic debt instrument resulting from integrating the qualifying debt instrument and hedge is considered denominated in the currency to be paid under the hedge.[20] For example, if *DC* borrows British pounds and hedges the borrowing with a forward contract under which it will sell the pounds to be received under the instrument for dollars, the synthetic debt instrument is denominated in dollars.

The issue price of the synthetic instrument is the adjusted issue price of the qualifying debt instrument, translated into the currency of the taxpayer's payments under hedge at the spot rate on the date the qualified hedging transaction is identified.[21] If the qualifying debt instrument is a borrowing, the stated redemption price at maturity is determined by the payments to be made by the taxpayer under the hedge; if the qualifying debt instrument is a lending, the stated redemption price is determined by the payments to be received under the hedge.[22]

The term of the synthetic debt instrument begins with the date the qualifying debt instrument and hedge identified as a qualified hedging transaction, and it ends with the maturity date of the qualifying debt instrument or, if earlier, with the disposition or termination of that instrument or the hedge.[23] The accrual period under the synthetic instrument is six months in length unless another interval is "clearly indicated" by the payment interval under the hedge.[24]

If a trust enters into a qualified hedging transaction, the identification requirements may be satisfied by the trustee on behalf of the beneficiary or beneficiaries. Reg. §1.988-5(a)(8)(ii).

[19] Reg. §1.988-5(a)(8)(iii).

[20] Reg. §1.988-5(a)(9)(ii)(A).

[21] Reg. §1.988-5(a)(9)(ii)(C).

[22] Reg. §1.988-5(a)(9)(ii)(D).

[23] Reg. §1.988-5(a)(9)(ii)(B).

[24] The payment interval under the hedge need not be the same as the payment interval under the qualifying debt instrument, in which case the former determines the accrual period under the synthetic debt instrument. See Reg. §1.988-5(a)(9)(iv) Ex. 9 (taxpayer borrows £100 for three years at 10 percent payable annually and hedges with currency swap under which taxpayer makes monthly payments at LIBOR, less 65 basis points, and receives annual payments equal to those under note).

Assume *DC*, a domestic corporation whose functional currency is the dollar, borrows 100u on the last day of year 0 under a three-year note requiring annual payments of interest at 10 percent and a single principal payment on the last day of year 3.[25] Simultaneously, *DC* enters into a currency swap contract under which it immediately exchanges the borrowed 100u for $60 and agrees to the following future swaps:

On last day of year	DC pays	DC receives
1	$ 7	10u
2	$ 7	10u
3	$67	110u

If *DC* identifies the borrowing and swap as a qualified hedging transaction, the borrowing and swap are integrated as a synthetic dollar borrowing of $60. The borrowing of 100u and the payments of 10u, 10u, and 110u in years 1 through 3 are ignored, and effect is given only to the $60 into which *DC* immediately converts the 100u and the $7, $7, and $67 *DC* pays for the nonfunctional currency used to satisfy its obligations under the note. Because interest is payable annually in a fixed amount ($7) and because the stated redemption and issue prices are both $60, there is no original issue discount (OID), and *DC* simply reports interest expense of $7 for each of the years 1, 2, and 3. This interest is apportioned among U.S. and foreign source income by the usual rules for apportioning interest expense.[26]

Quite commonly, the synthetic debt instrument invokes more complicated applications of the OID rules. Assume *DC* makes a forward contract on December 24 of year 0 (when 1u = $1) to sell 100u on December 31 of year 0 for $100.04; as planned, on December 31, *DC* (1) uses the 100u to purchase a 100u, 3-year, 6 percent note and (2) enters into a series of forward contracts to purchase 6u for $6.12 on December 31 of year 1, 6u for $6.23 on December 31 of year 2, and 106u for $112.16 on December 31 of year 3.[27] If the identification requirements are met, all forward contracts are integrated with the note, with the following results: The note and contracts become a synthetic debt instrument in dollars, purchased for $100.04 (the amount paid under the first forward contract) and under which *DC* will receive payments of $6.12, $6.23, and $112.16 on the last days of years 1, 2, and 3 (the amounts to be received under the December 31 of year 0 forward contracts). The synthetic instrument is an installment obligation with periodic payments of interest of $6.12 annually and a stated redemption price of $106.15 (sum of $6.12, $6.23, and $112.16, less three stated interest payments of $6.12 each). The excess of the stated redemption price of $106.15 over the issue price of $100.04 is OID ($6.11). The synthetic instrument's yield

---

[25] See Reg. §1.988-5(a)(9)(iv) Ex. 1.

[26] Reg. §1.988-5(a)(9)(iii). See supra ¶70.10.2 for the apportionment of interest.

[27] Reg. §1.988-5(a)(9)(iv) Ex. 2.

is 8 percent. Interest for year 1 is $8 (8 percent of $100.04), of which $1.88 ($8 less stated interest of $6.12) is OID. For year 2, interest is $8.15 (8 percent of sum of $100.04 and $1.88), of which $2.03 ($8.15 less $6.12) is OID. For the third year, interest is $8.32 (8 percent of sum of $100.04, $1.88, and $2.03), of which $2.19 ($8.32 less $6.12) is OID.

3. *Source.* For a holder, the interest income under the synthetic instrument, including OID, has the same source as interest under the actual debt instrument, and its character for purposes of the separate limitations of §904(d) also derives from the actual instrument.[28] For example, if the 100u note held by *DC* is issued by a foreign corporation, the $6 of interest income in years 1, 2, and 3 is foreign source income. Similarly, if interest under the note is passive income for purposes of §904(d), the synthetic interest goes into the passive basket.

4. *Foreign persons engaged in U.S. business.* If the taxpayer is a nonresident alien or foreign corporation engaged in a trade or business in the United States, a qualifying debt instrument and hedge cannot be a qualified hedging transaction unless all items of income and expense relating to the instrument and hedge are effectively connected with the U.S. business.[29] When this test is met, the interest income under the synthetic debt instrument is effectively connected income, and interest expense is lumped with other interest paid by the taxpayer in determining the interest deduction allowable in determining the effectively connected taxable income.[30] When the test is not met, the instrument and hedge are analyzed separately in determining the foreign person's tax liability.[31] However, if a foreign corporation has U.S. shareholders, the qualified hedging transaction rules are applied in the usual way in determining the corporation's earnings and profits.

5. *Legging in.* If the taxpayer acquires a hedge after the debt instrument is entered into and properly identifies the hedge and instrument as a qualified hedging transaction (that is, if the taxpayer legs in), exchange gain or loss is recognized with respect to the qualifying debt instrument for the period preceding the acquisition of the hedge.[32] This gain or loss is measured, and its source and character are determined, as though the debt instrument had been paid or disposed of immediately before the hedge was acquired. However, recognition of the gain or loss is deferred until the debt instrument is actually paid or disposed of.

Assume *DC* borrows 100 British pounds under a three-year, 10 percent note on January 1 of year 1 and immediately sells them for $150; on December 31 of year 1, when 1£ = $1.60 and the pound interest rate is still 10 percent, *DC* enters into a currency swap under which it agrees to exchange £10 on December 31 of

---

[28] Reg. §1.988-5(a)(9)(iii). For the source of interest income, see supra ¶70.2. For §904(d), see supra ¶69.6.

[29] Reg. §1.988-5(a)(5)(vi).

[30] Reg. §1.988-5(a)(9)(i)(B).

[31] Reg. §1.988-5(a)(9)(i)(C).

[32] Reg. §1.988-5(a)(6)(i).

year 2 for $12.80 and £110 on December 31 of year 3 for $172.80.[33] If *DC* identifies the currency swap as a qualified hedging transaction, *DC* realizes exchange loss with respect to the borrowing for the term January 1 through December 31 of year 1 as follows:

Value of obligation when incurred on January 1 (£100 times $1.50)	$150
Less value of obligation when taxpayer legs in on December 31 (£100 times $1.60)	160
Exchange loss	($ 10)

This loss is deferred, to be recognized only when the qualified hedging transaction is closed out. Beginning with the acquisition of the hedge on December 31, the note and swap contract are treated as a synthetic debt instrument in dollars, whose issue price is $160 (sum of principal amount of the note when issued ($150) and the $10 of deferred exchange loss), whose accrual period is the calendar year, and whose stated redemption price at maturity is $160 (the price to be paid for £100 under the swap contract at maturity). Since the issue price and stated redemption price of the synthetic instrument are equal, there is no OID, and the stated interest (the $12.80 to be paid on December 31 of year 2 and year 3 for £10) is the only interest.

6. *Legging out.* Exchange gain or loss is recognized if a qualifying debt instrument and hedge are identified as a qualified hedging transaction but the taxpayer disposes of or closes out the instrument or hedge while continuing to hold the other (legs out).[34] The legging out rules also apply if a "material term" of the instrument or hedge is changed by, for example, exercising an option to change the interest rate, index, or maturity date on the debt instrument or changing the interest rate, exchange rate, or maturity date of the hedge. However, a simultaneous termination or disposition of the debt instrument and hedge is treated as a disposition of the synthetic debt instrument, not a legging out.[35]

Gain or loss is recognized under the usual rules on the leg that is disposed of or terminated. Also, the taxpayer is usually treated as selling or terminating the retained leg for a price equal to its fair market value on the date of the legging

---

[33] Reg. §1.988-5(a)(9)(iv) Ex. 3.

[34] Reg. §1.988-5(a)(6)(ii).

[35] See Reg. §1.988-5(a)(9)(iv) Ex. 10 (domestic corporation *K* loans £100 for three years at 10 percent interest, payable annually, and hedges with currency swap under which *K* will exchange pounds to be received under loan for dollars; *K* identifies loan and swap as qualified hedging transaction, but subsequently transfers loan and swap to domestic corporation *B*, which is wholly owned by *K*; transfer not legging out, but is instead treated as transfer of synthetic debt instrument).

out, and any gain or loss on this deemed sale or termination is recognized at that time.[36]

Assume DC exchanges $100 for 200u and immediately uses the 200u to purchase a three-year, 200u bond bearing interest payable annually at 5 percent; simultaneously, DC enters into a swap contract under which DC will sell 10u for $5.14 on the first interest payment date, 10u for $5.29 for 10u on the second interest payment date, and 210u for $114.26 on the instrument's maturity date.[37] The swap agreement implies that the interest rate in dollars is 8 percent because the dollar payments under the swap have a present value of $100 at 8 percent. If DC properly identifies the hedge, the bond and swap are integrated as a synthetic debt instrument in dollars whose issue price is $100 and whose yield is 8 percent. For the first year, interest is $8, consisting of stated interest of $5.14 (the amount receivable under the swap for the first year) and OID of $2.86 ($8 less $5.14).

Assume DC closes out the swap immediately after receiving the first interest payment but retains the bond; the interest rate in dollars is then 10 percent, while the u interest rate remains unchanged at 5 percent and 1u = $.5143. In order to close out the swap, DC must pay $3.62—the excess of (1) the present value at the u interest rate of the amounts payable under the swap (200u times $.5143 or $102.86) over (2) the present value at the dollar interest rate of the amounts receivable under the swap ($99.24). This payment is exchange loss. DC is deemed to sell the bond at its fair market value, but no gain or loss is realized on the deemed sale because the bond's value is 200u (present value of remaining interest and principal discounted at 5 percent), which translates at the date of the deemed sale as $102.86 (200u times $.5143) and the bond's basis is also $102.86 (original basis of $100 plus OID of $2.86).

A taxpayer who has legged out may not integrate the retained leg with another debt instrument or hedge, and exchange gain or loss may therefore be recognized with respect to the retained leg. Gain or loss with respect to the retained leg, including exchange gain or loss, is measured as though the retained leg was entered into at fair market value on the date of the legging out. In the example, the retained bond has a basis immediately after the legging out equal to its fair market value of $102.86, and $102.86 is also the principal amount for purposes of measuring exchange gain or loss with respect to the bond's principal.

The foregoing rules are modified if (1) the deemed disposition or termination of the retained leg would result in gain and (2) during the period beginning 30 days before the leg out date and ending 30 days after that date, the taxpayer enters into another transaction that hedges at least one half of the currency flows under the retained leg.[38] In this case, the deemed sale is deemed not to occur, and

---

[36] Reg. §§1.988-5(a)(6)(ii)(B), (C).

[37] Reg. §1.988-5(a)(9)(iv) Ex. 5.

[38] Reg. §1.988-5(a)(6)(ii)(E).

the basis and principal amount of the retained leg are the taxpayer's original cost for the instrument or contract.

¶71.10.3   Hedged Contracts to Purchase or Sell Goods or Services

A "hedged executory contract," consisting of an "executory contract" and a "hedge," is treated as an integrated transaction if they are identified in the taxpayer's records as a hedged executory contract and various other requirements are met.[39] Assume a domestic corporation makes a contract to purchase a machine several months in the future for a price denominated in a foreign currency, and to protect against exchange rate fluctuation while the contract is executory, the corporation simultaneously makes a forward contract to purchase the foreign currency needed to pay for the machine. Until the delivery date, the contract for the machine is executory and the forward contract is a hedge. The two contracts are therefore integrated, and the corporation is treated as agreeing to purchase the machine for the dollar amount to be paid under the forward contract. Since the forward contract eliminates foreign currency risk, no exchange gain or loss is recognized. As in the case of any executory contract, appreciation or depreciation between the contract date and the closing date is not recognized when the purchase transaction is closed.

1. *Executory contract.* To be an "executory contract," an agreement must satisfy three tests.[40] First, it must be a contract to (1) purchase property for use in the ordinary course of the taxpayer's business, (2) sell property used or held for sale in the ordinary course of business, (3) purchase a service, (4) perform a service, or (5) purchase or sell stock. An agreement to purchase or sell property can qualify whether the property is tangible or intangible. However, the ordinary course of business requirement excludes purchases and sales of investments other than stocks. Section 988 transactions, including agreements to purchase or sell nonfunctional currencies, are also excluded. Second, the purchase or selling price must be payable in a nonfunctional currency. Third, the agreement must be made before the accrual date, which is the date on which the obligation to make or entitlement to receive the nonfunctional currency payment accrues under the taxpayer's method of accounting.[41] On the accrual date, the agreement ceases to be an executory contract and becomes an account payable or receivable, but the hedge can continue until the account is paid or collected.[42]

2. *Hedge.* A hedge can consist of a deposit of nonfunctional currency in a bank, a futures or forward contract, an option, or a combination of these de-

---

[39] Reg. §1.988-5(b)(1).
[40] Reg. §1.988-5(b)(2)(ii).
[41] Reg. §1.988-5(b)(2)(iv).
[42] Reg. §1.988-5(b)(2)(ii)(A).

vices.[43] An option may be a hedge only if it expires on or before the accrual date of the executory contract. If an option treated as a hedge expires unexercised, the option premium is integrated with the executory contract.

When a bank deposit is used as a hedge, the deposit may either be in a separate account or in a "hedging account." A hedging account is an account with a bank or other financial institution that contains only deposits of nonfunctional currency deposits used to hedge executory contracts.[44] Any reasonable convention may be used for determining the basis of the units of nonfunctional currency in the account that comprise a particular hedge, but the same convention must be used for all such accounts, and the hedge must consist of units in the account on the accrual date.

Whatever device is used, it must reduce (but not necessarily eliminate) the risk that exchange rate fluctuation may cause loss by increasing or decreasing the value in the taxpayer's functional currency of a payment or receipt under the executory contract.[45] Assume DC, a domestic corporation whose functional currency is the U.S. dollar, enters into a contract to purchase a machine for 100u, payable in 18 months when delivery of the machine is due.[46] DC can hedge against currency risk under the contract by immediately purchasing 100u and depositing it in a separate bank account. Alternatively, DC can enter into a forward or futures contract to purchase 100u on the date payment is due under the machine contract. Either device eliminates currency risk by freezing the dollar cost of the machine at the exchange rate in effect when the purchase contract is made.

When a hedge consists of an interest bearing account in a nonfunctional currency, interest accruing up to the accrual date under the executory contract may be included in the hedge, but this interest is included in gross income under the usual rules for interest on bank accounts.[47] Assume DC purchases 86u for $51.6 when the machine contract is made and deposits the funds in a bank account bearing interest at the annual rate of 10 percent. Over the 18 months until payment for the machine is due, 14u of interest accumulates in the account, increasing the balance to 100u, and DC uses the 100u to pay for the machine. DC can treat all funds in the account as a hedge. If so, the machine contract and the

---

[43] Reg. §1.988-5(b)(2)(iii)(A). A "historical rate rollover" may also be a hedge. Reg. §1.988-5(b)(2)(iii)(C). A historical rate rollover is an extension of a forward contract where the forward rate for the new maturity date is adjusted for the value of the contract immediately before the extension and an interest factor on that value from the date of the extension until the new maturity date. A historical rate rollover may be a hedge only if the rollover occurs before the accrual date under the executory contract. Also, if the extension is for more than 183 days, the interest factor is broken out and treated as interest income or expense.

[44] Reg. §1.988-5(b)(2)(iii)(D).

[45] Reg. §1.988-5(b)(2)(iii)(A).

[46] Reg. §1.988-5(b)(4)(vi) Ex. 1.

[47] Reg. §1.988-5(b)(2)(iii)(E). For the translation of interest income on bank accounts, see supra ¶71.6.2.

bank deposit are integrated, and the machine's cost is the sum of $51.60 (the dollar cost of the initial deposit of 86u) and the dollar amounts recognized as interest income from the account.

Switching horses in midstream is generally allowed so long as currency risk is hedged continuously, at least in part, from the date the first hedge is identified until the accrual date under the executory contract.[48] For example, when the machine contract is made, *DC* could enter into a forward contract to purchase 100u for $60 in six months, and when the forward contract matures, the 100u could be deposited in a bank account until payment for the machine comes due.[49] The forward contract and deposit both qualify as hedges because they protect against currency loss continuously from the date the forward contract is made until payment for the machine is due.

3. *Hedged executory contract.* An executory contract and hedge qualify as a hedged executory contract if the following additional requirements are met.

a. The executory contract and hedge must be identified as a hedged executory contract.[50] Normally, the taxpayer does this by establishing a record before the end of the day the hedge is entered into that contains a "clear description" of the contract and hedge and states they are being identified as a hedged executory contract.[51] However, if all other requirements are met, the IRS may treat a contract and hedge as a hedged executory contract when the taxpayer fails to identify them or identifies them defectively.

b. The parties to the hedge must not be related.[52] A contract to buy from or sell between members of the same affiliated group can be an executory contract, but an executory contract cannot be hedged with a bank deposit or contract with another member of the affiliated group.

c. If the executory contract or hedge is properly recorded on the books of a QBU of the taxpayer with a principal place of business outside the United States, the other leg must also be properly reflected on the QBU's books.[53]

d. The same individual or entity must hold both the executory contract and the hedge.[54] An executory contract made by one member of an affiliated group of corporations and a hedge held by another member thus cannot

---

[48] Reg. §1.988-5(b)(2)(iii)(B) (hedges are continuous even if successor hedge is not entered into until business day following day on which old hedge is terminated).

[49] See Reg. §1.988-5(b)(4)(vi) Ex. 4.

[50] Reg. §1.988-5(b)(2)(i)(A).

[51] Reg. §1.988-5(b)(3).

[52] Reg. §1.988-5(b)(2)(i)(D). Relatedness is determined under §§267(b) and 707(b)(1), discussed infra ¶¶78.3, 87.2.4. See Ring, Risk-Shifting Within a Multinational Corporation: The Incoherence of the U.S. Tax Regime, 38 BC L. Rev. 667 (1997).

[53] Reg. §1.988-5(b)(2)(i)(E). For QBUs, see supra ¶71.2 text accompanying notes 3-23.

[54] Reg. §1.988-5(b)(2)(i)(F).

usually be a hedged executory contract. However, the IRS may integrate an executory contract held by one person with a hedge held by another person, although the circumstances where this is appropriate are not spelled out.[55]

e. If the taxpayer is a nonresident alien or foreign corporation engaged in a trade or business in the United States, all items of income and expense under the executory contract and hedge must be effectively connected with the U.S. trade or business, apart from the hedging rules.[56]

4. *Integration rules.* Generally, when an executory contract and a hedge are integrated as a hedged executory contract, payments made or received under the hedge are treated as made or received under the executory contract, and no exchange gain or loss is realized under the hedge.[57] Moreover, if payment is not made or received on the accrual date, exchange gain or loss is not recognized on the account payable or receivable existing between the accrual and payment dates to the extent it is hedged. The mark to market and straddle rules of §§263(g), 1092, and 1256 do not apply to a contract that is part of a hedged executory contract, but they may apply to the hedged executory contract as a whole if it is part of a straddle.[58]

Assume *DC* makes a contract on January 1 of year 1 to purchase a machine for 100u on June 1 of year 2, but the price is not payable until September 1 of year 2; on February 1 of year 1, *DC* enters into a forward contract to purchase 100u for $60 on September 1 of year 2.[59] If the purchase and forward contracts are integrated, *DC*'s cost for the machine is $60, its cost under the forward contract, and no exchange gain or loss is recognized with respect to the forward contract or the account payable existing between June 1 and September 1 of year 2. Although the mark to market rule of §1256 generally applies to a forward contract traded in the interbank market, *DC*'s forward contract is exempted from §1256 because it is part of a hedged executory contract.

If a hedge only partially covers exchange risk under an executory contract, payments under the hedge are treated as payments under the hedged portion of the executory contract.[60] Assume *DC* purchases 50u for $30, holds it in a separate bank account until the price of the machine becomes payable, and then pays for the machine with the deposit balance and another 50u purchased on the spot market for $35. *DC*'s cost for the machine is $65, the sum of the amounts paid in dollars for the two 50u purchases.

When an executory contract is not fully hedged and payment is not made until after the accrual date, exchange gain or loss is recognized on the unhedged

---

[55] Reg. §1.988-5(b)(3)(ii).

[56] Reg. §1.988-5(b)(2)(i)(G).

[57] Reg. §1.988-5(b)(4)(i).

[58] Reg. §1.988-5(b)(4)(v). For §§263(g), 1092, and 1256, see supra ¶45.1.

[59] Reg. §1.988-5(b)(4)(vi) Ex. 2.

[60] Reg. §1.988-5(b)(4)(ii).

portion of the account payable or receivable. Assume *DC* purchases 50u for $30 when the contract is made, holds the 50u in a bank account until the machine is paid for, and pays for the machine 30 days after it is delivered; the exchange rate is 66 cents on the accrual date and 70 cents on the payment date.[61] The machine's cost is $63—the sum of the cost of the deposited 50u ($30) and the remaining 50u of the price translated at the spot rate on the accrual date (50u times $.66). *DC* has exchange loss of $2 on the account payable, computed as the excess of the dollar cost of payment of the unhedged portion of the payable (50u times $.70) less the dollar amount of the accrual (50u times $.66).

If the taxpayer retains the hedge after the executory contract is disposed of or otherwise terminated, the hedge is treated as sold for its fair market value on the date the executory contract is disposed of or terminated, and any gain or loss on the deemed sale is treated as an adjustment to the amount received or paid on the disposition or termination of the executory contract.[62] Exchange gain or loss on the actual disposition or termination of the hedge is determined with reference to the spot rate on the date of the deemed sale.

If the taxpayer terminates the hedge before the executory contract or the account payable or receivable resulting from the performance of the contract is satisfied, disposed of, or otherwise terminated, gain or loss on the disposition of the hedge is not recognized but is instead treated as an adjustment to the price under the executory contract.[63] If the termination of the hedge occurs between the accrual and payment dates, exchange gain or loss will be realized on payment or collection of account payable or receivable, measured from the spot rate on the date the hedge is disposed of or terminated.[64]

Assume *DC* agrees on January 1 of year 1 to purchase a machine for 100u on June 1 of year 2, with the price being payable on September 1 of year 2; on February 1 of year 1, *DC* enters into a forward contract to purchase 100u for $60 on September 1 of year 2, but this contract is sold for $5 on August 1 of year 2.[65] The $5 is not recognized as gain but instead is applied in reduction of *DC*'s cost for the machine. Assume *DC*, on September 1 of year 2, purchases 100u for $64 and uses the 100u to pay the price for the machine. The cost of the machine is $59 ($64 value of 100u on payment date, less $5 deferred gain on disposition of the forward contract). Also, *DC* has exchange gain or loss with respect to the 100u account payable during the period it is unhedged—August 1 to September 1. If the spot rates are 1u = $.66 on August 1 and 1u = $.64 on September 1, there is exchange gain of $2 (obligation of 100u times $.66, less payment of 100u times $.64).

---

[61] See Reg. §1.988-5(b)(4)(vi) Ex. 5.

[62] Reg. §1.988-5(b)(4)(iii)(A).

[63] Reg. §1.988-5(b)(4)(iii)(A). See Reg. §1.988-5(b)(4)(iii)(B) (this rule applies if executory contract is hedged by a series of contracts but replacement hedge is acquired later than day following disposition or termination of prior hedge).

[64] Reg. §1.988-5(b)(4)(iv).

[65] Reg. §1.988-5(b)(4)(vi) Ex. 3.

If the executory contract is between related persons and the taxpayer disposes of or terminates the executory contract or the hedge before the accrual date, the IRS may redetermine the timing, source, or character of gain, loss, or expense from the hedge or executory contract if it determines that a "significant purpose" for the disposition or termination was to manipulate the timing, source, or character of the gain, loss, or expense.[66]

¶71.10.4 Purchases and Sales of Publicly Traded Securities

When a taxpayer using the cash method of accounting sells or purchases stock or securities traded on an established securities market for a price denominated in a foreign currency, the amount realized for the property sold or the basis of the property purchased is determined by the spot rate for the settlement date.[67] Assume a U.S. citizen sells shares of stock for 100u on December 30 of year 1 for settlement on January 5 of year 2. The amount realized is determined by the exchange rate on January 5, even though gain or loss on the sale is recognized for year 1.[68] For example, if the exchange rate is then 60 cents, the amount realized in the sale is $60, and the taxpayer's basis for the 100u received is also $60. For taxpayers using the accrual method, the amount realized or basis of the property sold or bought is usually determined by the spot rate on the date of the sale or purchase (the trade date), but such a taxpayer may elect to use the rule described above for cash method taxpayers.[69]

A purchase or sale of stock or securities is integrated with a hedge protecting against currency risk during the period between the trade and settlement dates if the purchase or sale is on an established securities market.[70] For a purchase, the integration rule gives the stock or securities a cost basis equal to the functional currency amounts paid under the hedge. For a sale, the amount received in the functional currency under the hedge is the amount realized for the stock or securities.

Assume a U.S. citizen sells stock for 100u on a foreign stock exchange where transactions are settled five business days after the trade date. On the trade date, the taxpayer enters into a forward contract to sell 100u for $60 on the settlement date. Because the forward contract hedges currency risk between the trade and settlement dates, the taxpayer's amount realized for the stock is the $60 received under the forward contract, not the 100u actually received in the sale. Assume a U.S. citizen purchases stock on the same foreign exchange for 100u. Simultaneously with the purchase, the taxpayer buys 100u for $62 in the spot market and

---

[66] Reg. §1.988-5(b)(4)(iii)(C).

[67] Reg. §1.988-2(a)(2)(iv).

[68] IRC §453(k).

[69] Reg. §1.988-2(a)(2)(v). Once made, the election must be applied consistently for the year of the election and all subsequent years, until it is revoked with IRS consent.

[70] Reg. §1.988-5(c).

deposits it in a separate account, which the taxpayer uses to pay for the stock when the transaction is settled. Because the bank deposit hedges against currency loss pending settlement of the purchase, the stock's cost is the $62 paid for the 100u deposited in the account, not the dollar value of the 100u when used to settle the transaction.

The integration rule applies if (1) the stock or securities are traded on an established securities market, (2) the hedge consists of a deposit of nonfunctional currency in a separate account or a forward or futures contract, (3) the hedge covers at least part of the purchase or selling price for any of the period between trade and settlement dates, (4) the taxpayer identifies the purchase or sale and the hedge as an integrated transaction under the rules for hedged executory contracts, and (6) various other requirements for hedged executory contracts are satisfied.[71]

¶71.10.5   Hedged Payments

The Treasury has proposed regulations that would provide rules for "hedged qualified payments" parallel to those for hedged executory contracts.[72] The term "qualified payment" includes (1) a declared but unpaid dividend that is denominated in a nonfunctional currency of the recipient and (2) unaccrued rent or royalties denominated in a nonfunctional currency of the taxpayer (who may be the payor or recipient), provided that the rent or royalties are fixed when the hedge is entered into. When a qualified payment is hedged in a way meeting these requirements, the payment and hedge are integrated by treating "amounts paid or received under the hedge as paid or received under the qualified payment."[73]

¶71.11   TRANSFERS TO AND FROM QBUS

Gain or loss is normally not recognized when a nonfunctional currency or an item denominated in a nonfunctional currency is transferred by a qualified business unit (QBU) to another aspect of the taxpayer's operations or vice versa (an "intrataxpayer transaction").[1] However, exchange gain or loss is recognized on such a transaction if the transferred currency or the currency in which the transferred property is denominated is the functional currency of the transferee unit.[2] Assume domestic corporation *DC* has a branch in foreign country *X* that

---

[71] For hedged executory contracts, see supra ¶71.10.3.
[72] Prop. Reg. §1.988-5(d).
[73] INTL-15-91, 1992-1 CB 1202, 1203.
[1] Reg. §1.988-1(a)(10)(i). For the term "qualified business unit," see supra ¶71.2 text accompanying notes 3–23.
[2] Reg. §1.988-1(a)(10)(ii).

is a QBU; the dollar is *DC*'s functional currency, but the QBU's functional currency is the country *X u*.[3] If the branch transfers $25 to *DC*'s head office, exchange gain or loss is recognized on the transfer because the $25 is a nonfunctional currency to the QBU but is functional currency to the head office. Exchange gain or loss is also recognized if the country *X* branch transfers a bond denominated in dollars to the head office. Conversely, exchange gain or loss is recognized if the corporation transfers *us* or an instrument or contract denominated in *u*'s to the country *X* branch.

Even if a particular currency is nonfunctional to both the transferor and the transferee, exchange gain or loss is recognized on an intrataxpayer transfer of the currency or property denominated in the currency if the transfer might otherwise change the source of exchange gain or loss.[4] Assume *DC* transfers a bond denominated in British pounds to the country *X* branch. Although the pound is a nonfunctional currency to both the head office and the branch, exchange gain or loss is recognized on the exchange because exchange gain or loss of the branch has a different source than such gain or loss recognized by the head office. Generally, exchange gain or loss of a domestic corporation is from sources within the United States, but exchange gain or loss of a QBU has its source in the country where the QBU's principal place of business is located.[5] If no gain or loss were recognized on *DC*'s transfer of the bond to the country *X* branch, exchange gain or loss inherent in the bond at the time of the transfer, which would have been from U.S. sources if recognized by *DC*, would be from country *X* sources when subsequently recognized by the branch. The regulations prevent this switch in source by requiring *DC* to recognize exchange gain or loss on the transfer to the branch; as a result, exchange gain or loss inherent in the bond at the time of transfer is recognized by *DC* as income from U.S. sources or deduction allocable to U.S. income, and the exchange gain or loss from country *X* sources will be restricted to gain or loss accruing after the transfer to the branch.

The IRS may defer recognition of gain or loss on an intrataxpayer transfer that does not have a "significant business purpose."[6] This qualification is intended "to prevent taxpayers from engaging in intra-taxpayer transfers . . . for the purpose of recognizing gains or losses on such transactions."[7]

¶71.12 MARK TO MARKET ELECTION

Regulations have been proposed that would allow taxpayers to elect a mark to market system for exchange gains and losses on §988 transactions, including

---

[3] Reg. §1.988-1(a)(10)(iii) Ex.
[4] Reg. §1.988-2(a)(10)(ii).
[5] IRC §§988(a)(3)(A), (B).
[6] Reg. §1.988-2(a)(10)(ii).
[7] TD 8400, 1992-1 CB 101, 102.

holdings of nonfunctional currencies, holdings of instruments and contracts denominated in nonfunctional currencies, and liabilities denominated in such currencies.[1] Under this method, exchange gain or loss is recognized periodically (not less often than quarterly) on holdings of nonfunctional currencies and assets and liabilities denominated in such currencies. The gains and losses are computed as though the currencies, assets, and liabilities were sold, paid, or otherwise closed out at fair market value at the end of each period. The method may be used for U.S. tax purposes only if it is "consistent" with the taxpayer's methods of financial accounting and those methods conform to U.S. generally accepted accounting principles. The method may not be elected by a dealer or trader in nonfunctional currencies or nonfunctional currency denominated instruments.

If properly elected, the mark to market method applies to all section 988 transactions, except those governed by hedging rules.[2] Once elected, the method applies in all years until revoked with IRS consent.

¶71.13   NONFUNCTIONAL CURRENCY HELD FOR PERSONAL USE

Section 988 generally does not apply to foreign currency transactions of an individual that are made for personal rather than business or investment reasons.[1] More specifically, an individual's transaction in a nonfunctional currency is a "personal transaction" not subject to §988 if costs of the transaction are not deductible as business expenses or expenses of a transaction entered into for profit or are deductible as business travel expenses.[2] These transactions are instead governed by the "principles of [pre-1986] law."[3] Under those principles, exchange gains and losses are realized when nonfunctional currency acquired in exchange for functional currency is subsequently spent or exchanged back to the functional currency.[4]

The principles of pre-1986 law are modified by a de minimis exclusion.[5] No gain is recognized "by reason of changes in exchange rates" while an individual

---

[1] Prop. Reg. §1.988-5(f) (effective for taxable years ending after final regulations are promulgated).

[2] For the hedging rules, see supra ¶71.10.

[1] IRC §988(e)(1); Reg. §1.988-1(a)(9).

[2] IRC §988(e)(3). A transaction is "personal" if expenses in connection with the transaction are deductible as costs incurred in connection with the determination, collection, or refund of any tax."

[3] TD 8400, 1992-1 CB 101, 102.

[4] Rev. Rul. 74-7, 1974-1 CB 198.

[5] In formulating regulations issued in 1992, the Treasury rejected a suggestion that it exempt de minimis amounts of exchange gains and losses of individuals from business and investment transactions: "The Service does not have authority to adopt such a rule in light of section 988(e)." TD 8400, 1992-1 CB 101, 102.

holds a nonfunctional currency ultimately disposed of in a personal transaction if "the gain which would otherwise be recognized on the transaction exceeds $200."[6] Assume *A*, a U.S. citizen, exchanges $600 for 1,000u for use on a foreign vacation, spends 900u on the vacation, and exchanges 100u for $70 on returning. *A* realizes exchange gain or loss on each expenditure from the 900u and on exchanging the last 100u. For example, on the conversion, she has exchange gain of $10 ($70 amount realized less $60 basis). However, if, as is likely, the gain does not exceed $200 on any expenditure or the conversion, none of the gain is recognized. In contrast, assume *A* exchanges $6,000 for 10,000u and, several weeks later when the exchange rate is $.70 = 1u, buys a painting for 9,000u. The exchange gain on the purchase is $900 (amount realized of $6,300 ($.70 times 9,000), less adjusted basis of $5,400 ($.60 times 9,000)). The gain is recognized because it exceeds $200.

The application of these rules to mortgages on personal residences was often disadvantageous to taxpayers.[7] Assume a U.S. citizen purchased a personal residence in country *X* for 95,000u, paying 10,000u in cash and borrowing the remaining 85,000u under a mortgage denominated in the foreign country's currency. At the time of the purchase, 1u was worth $1. Sometime later, when .95u = $1, the taxpayer sells the residence for 142,500u, of which 85,000u is used to repay the mortgage. The borrowing and repayment under a mortgage loan are considered separately from the purchase and sale of the property securing the mortgage.[8] The taxpayer's gain on the sale of the residence is:

Amount realized (142,500 divided by exchange rate of .95 at time of sale)	$150,000
Less adjusted basis (95,000u divided by exchange rate of 1.00 at time of purchase)	95,000
Gain	$ 55,000

In addition, the taxpayer has loss on the repayment of the mortgage as follows:

Dollar value of amount paid in satisfaction of mortgage (85,000u divided by exchange rate of .95 at time of repayment)	$89,474
Less dollar value of amount borrowed (85,000u divided by exchange rate of 1.00 at time of borrowing)	85,000
Loss	($ 4,474)

---

[6] IRC §988(e)(2) (effective for taxable years beginning after 1997). The provision refers only to gains because, under §165(c), losses in personal transactions are nondeductible. Staff of Joint Comm. on Tax'n, 105th Cong., 1st Sess., General Explanation of Tax Legislation Enacted in 1997, at 301 (Comm. Print 1997).

[7] See Rev. Rul. 90-79, 1990-2 CB 187.

[8] Helburn v. CIR, 214 F2d 815 (1st Cir. 1954); Church's English Shoes, Ltd. v. CIR, 24 TC 56 (1955), aff'd per curiam, 229 F2d 957 (2d Cir. 1956); Rev. Rul. 78-281, 1978-2 CB 204.

The loss is not deductible under §165 because it is not incurred in a trade or business or a transaction entered into for profit.

This approach can also be disadvantageous where the dollar appreciates against the nonfunctional currency in which the mortgage loan is denominated. Assume the sale in the example occurs when 1u = $1.05. The taxpayer's gain on the sale of the residence is $40,714 (amount realized of $135,714 (142,500 divided by exchange rate of 1.05 at time of sale), less adjusted basis of $95,000). In addition, the taxpayer has gain on repayment of the mortgage of $4,048—the dollar value of the amount borrowed ($85,000) less the dollar value of the amount repaid (85,000u divided by exchange rate of 1.05 at time of repayment, which is $80,952).[9] If the property is the taxpayer's principal residence, the gain on the sale is not recognized.[10] The gain on repayment of the mortgage, in contrast, is taxable because it is not realized on the sale of the taxpayer's personal residence.

¶71.14   SOURCES OF EXCHANGE GAINS AND LOSSES

Exchange gain is normally income from sources in the country of the taxpayer's residence, and the deduction for exchange loss is usually allocated to gross income from sources in the taxpayer's residence country.[1] Exchange gain or loss of a QBU, however, has its source in the country in which the QBU's principal place of business is located.[2] Also, if the taxpayer is a nonresident alien or foreign corporation and is engaged in a trade or business in the United States, exchange gain or loss is treated as fixed or determinable annual or periodic income from U.S. sources for the sole purpose of determining whether it is effectively connected with the U.S. business.[3]

1. *Residence.* For this purpose, domestic corporations and partnerships are residents of the United States, and all other corporations and partnerships are residents of foreign countries.[4] However, if a partnership is "formed or availed of to avoid tax by altering the source of exchange gain or loss," its residence is ignored, and each partner's distributive share of partnership exchange gain or

---

[9] But see H.R. Rep. No. 841, 99th Cong., 2d Sess. II-669 (Conf. Rep. 1986) (under pre-1986 law, "a U.S. individual residing outside of the United States [does not recognize exchange gain or loss] upon repayment of a foreign currency denominated mortgage on the individual's principal residence").

[10] IRC §121, discussed supra ¶44A.1.

[1] IRC §988(a)(3)(A); Reg. §1.988-4(a).

[2] IRC §988(a)(3)(B)(ii); Reg. §1.988-4(b)(1).

[3] Reg. §1.988-4(c).

[4] IRC §§988(a)(3)(B)(i)(II), (III). A corporation or partnership is domestic if it is organized under the laws of the United States, the District of Columbia, or one of the States. IRC §7701(a)(4).

loss has its source in the partner's residence country.[5] Estates and trusts are residents of the United States unless they are classified as nonresident aliens for U.S. tax purposes.[6]

Individuals are residents of the countries in which they have their tax homes.[7] Generally, a place is an individual's tax home if expenses incurred in traveling elsewhere on business are deductible under §162(a)(2) as expenses of traveling away from home.[8] An individual's tax home is in the United States, however, if his "abode" is located in this country, even if the abode is not the taxpayer's tax home for purposes of §162(a)(2). Also, an individual who does not have a principal place of business outside the United States is a U.S. resident if he is a citizen or an alien treated as a resident under §7701(b).[9]

2. *QBU items.* If an instrument, obligation, or other item giving rise to exchange gain or loss is "properly reflected" on the books of a QBU of the taxpayer, the gain or loss has its source at the QBU's "principal place of business."[10] The regulations offer little guidance on when an item is properly reflected on a QBU's books, except to warn that "inconsistent booking practices" of the taxpayer and its QBUs raises a presumption that an item is not properly reflected.[11]

Assume a domestic corporation has a branch in France that is a QBU and uses the French franc as its functional currency; the branch has an exchange loss arising out of a credit sale of goods for a price denominated in British pounds. The deduction for the loss is allocated to income from sources in France, the locus of the branch's principal place of business.

3. *Hedging low-interest nonfunctional currency borrowings.* Exchange gain or loss is usually not treated as interest income or expense.[12] In some cases, however, exchange loss on a forward contract acquired to hedge a borrowing in a nonfunctional currency is treated as interest expense for purposes of allocating the deduction for the loss between U.S. and foreign source income.[13] For a taxpayer or QBU whose functional currency is the dollar, this rule applies if (1) the interest rate on the nonfunctional currency borrowing is less than the applicable Federal rate (AFR), which, very generally, is the prevailing interest rate on

---

[5] Reg. §1.988-4(d)(1).

[6] IRC §§988(a)(3)(B)(i)(II); 7701(a)(30). For trusts and estates taxed as nonresident aliens, see supra ¶¶65.3, 65.4.

[7] IRC §988(a)(3)(B)(i)(I).

[8] IRC §911(d)(3); Reg. §1.988-4(d)(1).

[9] For §7701(b), see supra ¶65.2.

[10] IRC §§988(a)(3)(A), (B)(ii); Reg. §§1.988-4(b)(1), (d)(2). For QBUs, see supra ¶71.2 text accompanying notes 3–23.

[11] Reg. §1.988-4(b)(2)(ii).

[12] Reg. §1.988-3(c)(1).

[13] Reg. §1.861-9T(b)(2)(i). A swap, future, option, or similar arrangement is treated the same as a forward contract for this purpose. For the allocation and apportionment of interest expense, see supra ¶¶70.10.2, 70.10.3, 10.10.4.

U.S. government debt of equivalent maturity, (2) the forward contract "substantially diminishes" currency risk or interest expense with respect to the borrowing, and (3) the taxpayer fails to show the borrowing and the forward contract are unrelated. The borrowing and contract are unrelated if, for example, the contract was made to hedge a nonfunctional currency risk that arises in the ordinary course of its business rather than from the borrowing. The rule is the same for a taxpayer or QBU using a foreign functional currency, except that the interest rate on the borrowing is tested against the interest rate on debt of the government issuing the functional currency, rather than the AFR. Whether the taxpayer's functional currency is the dollar or a foreign currency, however, the rule does not apply if the borrowing and forward contract are integrated under a rule described above.[14]

Generally, an arm's length loan can be obtained in a foreign nonfunctional currency at an interest rate below the AFR only if inflation in the foreign currency is expected to be significantly less than inflation in the U.S. dollar. Currencies with higher inflation generally depreciate in relation to currencies with less inflation. For a person whose functional currency is the dollar, the apparently low interest rate on a borrowing in a low-inflation nonfunctional currency is usually an illusion because the number of dollars required to pay interest and principal under the loan steadily increases as the value of the nonfunctional currency increases. Foreign currency costs, in other words, are part of the anticipated costs of the loan repayments—that is, additional interest costs. The rule described in the preceding paragraph reflects this by treating currency costs incurred under a forward contract as interest expense.

---

[14] Infra ¶71.10.2.

CHAPTER
79

Reallocation of Income and Deductions Among Related Taxpayers

¶79.1   SECTION 482 REALLOCATIONS—INTRODUCTORY

Section 482 authorizes the IRS to allocate gross income, deductions, credits, and other allowances among two or more organizations, trades, or businesses under common ownership or control whenever it determines that this action is "necessary in order to prevent evasion of taxes or clearly to reflect the income of any of such organizations, trades, or businesses."[1] The sparse legislative history

---

[1] See generally Notice 88-123, 1988-2 CB 458 (IRS study of intercompany pricing under §482, with emphasis on income from intellectual property); Comptroller General, Report to House Committee on Ways and Means, IRS Could Better Protect U.S. Tax Interests in Determining the Income of Multinational Corporations (1981) (study of IRS methods of determining arm's length prices, with recommendations); Organisation for Economic Cooperation and Development, Transfer Pricing Guidelines for Multinational Enterprises and Tax Administrations (1995); Allegra, Section 482: Mapping the Contours of the Abuse of Discretion Standard of Judicial Review, 13 Va. Tax Rev. 423 (1994); Avi-Yonah, The Rise and Fall of Arm's Length: A Study in the Evolution of U.S. International Taxation, 12 Va. Tax Rev. 89 (1995); Fuller, Section 482 Revisited, 31 Tax L. Rev. 475, 476–78 (1976); Higinbotham, Asper, Stoffregen & Wexler, Effective Application of the Section 482 Transfer Pricing Regulations, 42 Tax L. Rev. 293 (1987); Horner, International Cooperation and Understanding: What's New about the OECD's Transfer Pricing Guidelines, 50 U. Miami L. Rev. 577 (1996), reprinted in 13 Tax Notes Int'l 1065(Sept. 23, 1996). See also Hannes, Taxpayers (and the Courts) Can Make Beneficial Retroactive Pricing Changes Under Section 482, 26 Tax Mgmt. Int'l J. 394 (1997).

of this broad charter, whose origin dates back to 1921 and 1928, refers to "the shifting of profits, the making of fictitious sales, and other methods frequently adopted for the purpose of 'milking'"—terms suggesting deliberate evasions of tax.[2] The legislative history also states that reallocations are authorized "in order to clearly reflect [each organization's] true tax liability."

Some early cases viewed §482 as directed against manipulative "milking" of a profitable organization in order to shift income to affiliated organizations subject to lower rates or having offsetting losses. Later decisions, however, make it clear that the IRS can compel each of the commonly controlled taxpayers to

---

The regulations under §482 were extensively revised in 1994. TD 8552, 1994-2 CB 93. See Birnkrant & Croker, Transfer Pricing Final Regs. Increase Flexibility, but Not Certainty, in Choice of Method, 81 J. Tax'n 268 (1994); Dolan & Bower, Final Transfer Pricing Regulations, 23 Tax Mgmt. Int'l J. 423 (1994); Hirsh, Lederman & Hughes, Final Transfer Pricing Regulations Restate Arm's Length Principle, 72 Taxes 587 (1994); Nolan, U.S. Final Transfer Pricing Regulations, 50 U. Miami L. Rev. 537 (1996).

For special procedures for resolving transfer pricing disputes, see Wrappe, Working with the New IRS Procedures: A Silver Lining in the Transfer Pricing Cloud, 26 Tax Mgmt. Int'l J. 27 (1997).

For §482's constitutionality, see Asiatic Petroleum Co. v. CIR, 79 F2d 234 (2d Cir.), cert. denied, 296 US 645 (1935) (§482 does not improperly tax one person on another's income); Foster v. CIR, 80 TC 34 (1983), aff'd & rev'd on other issues, 756 F2d 1430 (9th Cir. 1985), cert. denied, 474 US 1055 (1986) (§482 not improper delegation of legislative power to administrative agency).

For economic analyses of transfer pricing issues, see Berry, Bradford & Hines, Arm's-Length Pricing: Some Economic Perspectives, 54 Tax Notes 731 (Feb. 10, 1992); Langbein, A Modified Fractional Apportionment Proposal for Tax Transfer Pricing, 54 Tax Notes 719 (Feb. 10, 1992); Wills, Risk Measurement: Applying Financial Theory to Transfer Pricing, 52 Tax Notes 1311 (Sept. 9, 1991).

For the situation in other countries, see Ernst & Young Transfer Pricing 1997 Global Survey, 15 Tax Notes Int'l 761 (Sept. 8, 1997), reprinted in 76 Tax Notes 1609 (Sept. 22, 1997).

The IRS has proposed extensive regulations on the application of §482 to income from "global dealing operations," defined as "the execution of customer transactions, including marketing, sales, pricing and risk management activities, in a particular financial product or line of financial products, in multiple tax jurisdictions." Prop. Reg. §1.482-8, issued by REG-208299-90, 1998-16 IRB 26. See also Organisation for Economic Cooperation and Development, The Taxation of Global Trading of Financial Instruments: A Discussion Draft, 16 Tax Notes Int'l 1275 (Apr. 20, 1998); Neigbour, The Taxation of Global Trading of Financial Instruments, 16 Tax Notes Int'l 1269 (Apr. 20, 1998); Plambeck, Transfer Pricing Analysis of Global Trading Operations and Procedural Alternatives, 74 Taxes 1129 (1996).

See also Keller, At a Loss: A Half Century of Confusion in the Tax Treatment of Transfers of Depreciated Property Between Related Taxpayers, 44 Tax Lawyer 445 (1991); Lowell, Relationship of Section 482 to International Corporate Tax Planning, 23 J. Corp. Tax'n 36 (1996).

[2] S. Rep. No. 960, 70th Cong., 1st Sess. (1928), reprinted in 1939-1 (Part 2) CB 409, 426. See S. Rep. No. 275, 67th Cong., 1st Sess. (1921), reprinted in 1939-1 (Part 2) CB 181, 195; Foster v. CIR, 80 TC 34 (1983), aff'd & rev'd on other issues, 756 F2d 1430 (9th Cir. 1985), cert. denied, 474 US 1055 (1986) (tracing legislative history of §482 back to regulations promulgated under War Revenue Act of 1917).

report the taxable income that would have resulted from dealing at arm's length with the other members of the group, even if this disturbs legally enforceable arrangements that were established for business reasons and without any tax-avoidance motive. The Tax Court stated in 1972:

> [O]ur review of the statute and its legislative and judicial history indicates that section 482 is designed to remedy only one abuse: the shifting of income from one commonly controlled entity to another.... Tax-avoidance motives or the lack of a business purpose in forming several corporations are relevant in a section 482 case only to the extent that they prove that there has been an actual shifting of income from one corporation to another. Section 482 is not designed to punish the mere existence of commonly controlled entities nor the unexercised power to shift income among them. ... Similarly, if there has been an actual shifting of income, purity of purpose and the presence of sound business reasons for forming multiple corporations are no defense under section 482. In short, section 482 does not deal with motivation and purpose . . . but with economic reality.[3]

In short, the objective of §482 is to place "a controlled taxpayer on a tax parity with an uncontrolled taxpayer by determining the true taxable income of the controlled taxpayer."[4] The IRS' corrective authority is not limited to fraudulent and sham transactions but also embraces distortions attributable to inadvertence.[5]

True taxable income is determined by judging transactions between commonly controlled taxpayers against the standard of comparable transactions between unrelated persons dealing at arm's length.[6] The unstated premise of this standard is that the imposition of arm's length results necessarily leads to a "true" statement of income. As Stanley Surrey stated in 1978: "Presumably, most transactions are governed by the general framework of the market place and hence it is appropriate to seek to put intra-group transactions under that general framework."[7] However, as the staff of the Joint Committee on Taxation has reported:

> Many observers have questioned the effectiveness of the "arm's length" approach of the regulations under section 482. A recurrent problem is the absence of comparable arm's length transactions between unrelated parties, and the inconsistent results of attempting to impose an arm's length concept in the absence of comparables.
>
> A fundamental problem is the fact that the relationship between related parties is different from that of unrelated parties. Observers have noted that

---

[3] Your Host, Inc. v. CIR, 58 TC 10, 23-24 (1972), aff'd, 489 F2d 957 (2d Cir. 1973).

[4] Reg. §1.482-1(b)(1), quoted with approval in CIR v. First Sec. Bank of Utah, 405 US 394, 400 (1972).

[5] Reg. §1.482-1(f)(1).

[6] Reg. §1.482-1(b)(1).

[7] See Surrey, Reflections on the Allocation of Income and Expenses Among National Tax Jurisdictions, 10 Law & Pol'y Int'l Bus. 409, 414 (1978).

multinational companies operate as an economic unit, and not "as if" they were unrelated to their foreign subsidiaries. In addition, a parent corporation that transfers potentially valuable property to its subsidiary is not faced with the same risks as if it were dealing with an unrelated party. Its equity interest assures it of the ability ultimately to obtain the benefit of future anticipated or unanticipated profits, without regard to the price it sets. The relationship similarly would enable the parent to adjust its arrangement each year, if it wished to do so, to take account of major variations in the revenue produced by a transferred item.[8]

In recent years, a substantial literature has arisen advocating various alternatives to the arm's length standard.[9] However, the arm's length standard is firmly entrenched in U.S. law, in income tax treaties between the U.S. and many

---

[8] Staff of Joint Comm. on Tax'n, 99th Cong., 2d Sess., General Explanation of the Tax Reform Act of 1986 at 1014 (Comm. Print 1987) [hereinafter 1986 Bluebook]. For additional discussion of criticisms of the arm's length standard, see Notice 88-123, 1988-2 CB 458, 483–85.

[9] See Avi-Yonah, The Structure of International Taxation: A Proposal for Simplification, 74 Texas L. Rev. 1301 (1996); Avi-Yonah, Slicing the Shadow: A Proposal for Updating U.S. International Taxation, 58 Tax Notes 1511 (Mar. 15, 1993); Coffill & Wilson, Federal Formulary Apportionment as an Alternative to Arm's Length Pricing: From the Frying Pan to the Fire? 59 Tax Notes 1103 (May 24 1993); Hellerstein, Federal Income Taxation of Multinationals: Replacement of Separate Accounting with Formulary Apportionment, 60 Tax Notes 1131 (Aug. 23, 1993); Kauder, The Unspecific Federal Tax Policy of Arm's Length: A Comment on the Continuing Vitality of Formulary Apportionment at the Federal Level, 60 Tax Notes 1147 (Aug. 23, 1993); Kauder, Intercompany Pricing and Section 482: A Proposal to Shift From Uncontrolled Comparables to Formulary Apportionment Now, 58 Tax Notes 485 (Jan. 25, 1993); Langbein, A Modified Fractional Apportionment Proposal for Tax Transfer Pricing, 54 Tax Notes 719 (Feb. 10, 1992); Libin, Formulary Apportionment for "Global Trading" in the Manufacturing Industry: Can It Work? 11 Tax Notes Int'l 1375 (Nov. 20, 1995); McDaniel, Formulary Taxation in the North American Free Trade Zone, 49 Tax L. Rev. 691 (1994); McLure, U.S. Federal Use of Formula Apportionment to Tax Income from Intangibles, 75 Tax Notes 109 (Apr. 7, 1997); McIntyre, Contrasting Methodologies: A Systematic Presentation of the Differences Between and Arm's-Length/Source-Rule System and a Combined-Reporting/Formulary-Apportionment System, 1994 Proc. 87th Ann. Conf. on Tax'n 13 (1995); McIntyre & McIntyre, Using NAFTA To Introduce Formulary Apportionment, 6 Tax Notes Int'l 851 (Apr. 5, 1993); Miller, None Are So Blind as Those Who Will Not See, 66 Tax Notes 1023 (Feb. 13, 1995); Schadewald, Global Apportionment: How Would It Affect the Largest U.S. Corporations? 13 Tax Notes Int'l 131 (July 8, 1996); Sullivan, Economic Efficiency and Alternative International Tax Regimes for Related Party Transactions, 1994 Proc. 87th Ann. Conf. on Tax'n 13 (1995); Turro, An Interview with Senator Byron L. Dorgan on Formulary Apportionment, 9 Tax Notes Int'l 1886 (Dec. 19, 1994); Weiner, Using the Experience in the U.S. States to Evaluate Issues in Implementing Formula Apportionment at the International Level, 13 Tax Notes Int'l 2113 (Dec. 23, 1996); Wetzler, Should the U.S. Adopt Formula Apportionment? 48 Nat'l Tax J. 357 (1995); Wickham & Kerester, New Directions Needed for Solution of the International Transfer-Pricing Tax Puzzle, 56 Tax Notes 339 (July 20, 1992). See also McLure, U.S. Federal Use of Formula Apportionment to Tax Income from Intangibles, 14 Tax Notes Int'l 859 (Mar. 10, 1997).

foreign countries, and in the internal laws of numerous foreign countries.[10] Moreover, the advocated substitutions for the arm's length standard tend to be reminiscent of the old saw that for every complex problem, there is at least one solution that is simple, elegant, and just plain wrong.[11]

The IRS has employed §482 most extensively to question transfer prices and expense allocations between domestic corporations and foreign affiliates that are not subject to U.S. income taxes on foreign income, although allocations between foreign corporations and their domestic affiliates have assumed increasing importance in recent years.[12] For example, if a U.S. corporation could sell goods to foreign subsidiaries at cost, the profits from reselling the products abroad often would not be taxed by the United States until repatriated (e.g., by dividend payments). This advantage could be magnified if the cost of conducting the foreign operations could be deducted by the parent from its domestic income. When these intercompany arrangements are subjected to the arm's length standard enunciated by the regulations under §482, however, the prices at which the parent's products are transferred to the subsidiary must be revised to reflect a reasonable profit, and deductions attributable to the cost of conducting the foreign operations must be allocated to the subsidiary in an appropriate fashion.

Although §482 has particularly dramatic results when applied to transfer prices and other arrangements between domestic and foreign affiliates, it is by no means confined to these relationships. Thus, §482 can be invoked to prevent the shifting of income from an individual to a corporation that is subject to a lower marginal tax rate or from a profitable corporation to an affiliated enterprise with unused deductions or loss carryovers. Indeed, the IRS can apply §482 even if

---

[10] Notice 88-123, 1988-2 CB 458, at 475 ("overwhelming evidence" that arm's length standard is "international norm for making transfer pricing adjustments"; United States should continue to follow it "in the interest of avoiding extreme positions by other jurisdictions and minimizing the incidence of disputes over primary taxing jurisdiction in international transactions"); Committee on Fiscal Affairs, Task Force Recommendations on U.S. Transfer-Pricing Regulations (OECD 1993), executive summary reprinted in 6 Tax Notes Int'l 93 (Jan. 11, 1993); Organisation for Economic Cooperation and Development, Transfer Pricing and Multinational Enterprises (OECD 1979).

[11] See Wilkins & Gideon, Memorandum to Congress: You Wouldn't Like Worldwide Formula Apportionment, 65 Tax Notes 1259 (Dec. 5, 1994).

[12] See Grubert, Another Look at the Low Taxable Income of Foreign-Controlled Companies in the United States, 15 Tax Notes Int'l 1873 (Dec. 8, 1997); Hobbs, Foreign-Controlled Domestic Corporations, 1994, 17 Stat. Income Bull. 71 (Summer 1997). For IRS jurisdiction over a foreign corporation to obtain information relevant to §482 allocations and the consequent proper tax liability of its domestic subsidiary, see §6038A, discussed infra ¶112.4.4; US v. Toyota Motor Corp., 561 F. Supp. 354 (CD Cal. 1983) (extensive discussion of jurisdictional question in proceeding to enforce summons issued to foreign parent), in further proceedings, 569 F. Supp. 1158 (CD Cal. 1983) (enforcing summons directing foreign parent to provide prices charged dealers in its home country). See also Vetco v. US, 691 F2d 1281 (9th Cir.), cert. denied, 454 US 1098 (1981) (summons for books and records of Swiss controlled foreign corporation enforced notwithstanding potential violations of Swiss Penal Code).

related taxpayers are subject to the same marginal tax rate, because the reallocation can have such ancillary effects as increasing the earnings and profits of one of the corporations in order to characterize its distributions to shareholders as taxable dividends rather than tax-free returns of capital.[13]

A reallocation can also set off a chain reaction affecting members of the group that are not parties to the recast transaction. For example, under a 1969 ruling, if A, an individual, owns corporations X and Y and causes X to make a bargain sale to Y, the allocation of additional consideration to X under §482 may be treated as a constructive distribution of the same amount by X to A and as a contribution by A to Y's capital.[14]

In 1986, Congress made the first significant change to the language of §482 in decades, requiring that royalties or other consideration for a license or transfer of intellectual property "shall be commensurate with the income attributable to the intangible." The legislative history of this change indicates that the underlying congressional concern went beyond licenses and transfers of intellectual property and also extended to intercompany sales of goods and services produced or marketed with intellectual property.[15] All of the pricing methods detailed in the regulations under §482 then in effect required that controlled transactions be evaluated with reference to comparable transactions between unrelated persons. These methods rarely worked for controlled transactions involving intellectual property, whether the transactions were licenses or transfers of intangibles or sales of goods or services produced or marketed with intellectual property. Because intellectual property is, by definition, unique, goods and services produced or marketed with intellectual property are not comparable to fungible goods, and one item of intellectual property is not easily compared with any other intellectual property.

Congress recommended in 1986 that the IRS comprehensively reexamine the regulations under §482. The IRS responded with a "White Paper" issued in 1988 that proposed several alternative approaches for implementing the commensurate with income standard, including a "basic arm's length return method" (BALRM) and BALRM with profit split.[16]

> The BALRM generally assigned an average rate of return to the assets and functions devoted to the routine activities associated with the controlled transaction. When high profit intangibles were involved, any residual profit

---

[13] See O'Connor, Side Effects of Section 482 Can Be More Serious Than Original Allocation, 31 J. Tax'n 194 (1969).

[14] Rev. Rul. 69-630, 1969-2 CB 112. See Bell v. CIR, 45 TCM (CCH) 97 (1982) (income reallocated under §482 between corporations was constructive dividend to shareholders of corporation whose income was increased followed by contribution to capital of corporation whose income was reduced); infra ¶92.2.

[15] H.R. Rep. No. 841, 99th Cong., 2d Sess. II-637 (Conf. Rep. 1986); H.R. Rep. 426, 99th Cong., 1st Sess 424 (1985).

[16] Notice 88-123, 1988-2 CB 458.

would be divided on the basis of the estimated relative values of the intangibles that each party contributed to the activity.[17]

The White Paper was followed by proposed regulations issued in 1992,[18] which elicited extensive commentary, mostly critical of the proposals.[19] Temporary regulations followed the next year;[20] they also sparked lively debate, somewhat less critical than the commentary on the proposed regulations.[21] Final regulations were issued in 1994.[22]

The present regulations generally apply for taxable years beginning after October 6, 1994.[23] Taxpayers may elect to apply the regulations for any prior year that is not barred by the statute of limitations, but the regulations also apply to

---

[17] TD 8552, 1994-2 CB 93, 94.

[18] INTL-0371-88, 1992-1 CB 1164.

[19] OECD Committee on Fiscal Affairs, Task Force Recommendations on U.S. Transfer-Pricing Regulations (1993), executive summary reprinted in 6 Tax Notes Int'l 93 (Jan. 11, 1993); Carlson, DeMasi, Dicker, Godshaw, Haeussler, Jennings & Neumann, The Proposed New Transfer Pricing Rules: New Wine in an Old Bottle? 54 Tax Notes 691 (Feb. 10, 1992); Fuller & Aud, The Proposed Section 482 Regulations, 4 Tax Notes Int'l 599 (Mar. 23. 1992); Hannes, An Examination of the New U.S. Transfer Pricing Proposals, 4 Tax Notes Int'l 281 (Feb. 10, 1992); McLennan, Complying With the Proposed Section 482 Regulations: How To Create and Apply a Comparable Profit Interval, 4 Tax Notes Int'l 1201 (1992); Purnell, The Net Present Value Approach to Intangible Transfer Pricing Under Section 482: An Economic Model Takes the BALRM Floor, 45 Tax Lawyer 647 (1992).

[20] TD 8470, 1993-1 CB 90.

[21] Carlson, Dicker, Giosa, Godshaw, Haeussler, Harrington, Sullivan & Venuti, Deja Vu All Over Again: The New Section 482 Regulations, 58 Tax Notes 607 (Feb. 1, 1993); Fuller & Aud, The New Temporary and Proposed Section 482 Regulations: A Wolf in Sheep's Clothing? 6 Tax Notes Int'l 525 (Mar. 1, 1993); Glicklich & Goldstein, New Transfer Pricing Regs. Adhere More Closely to an Arm's-Length Standard, 78 J. Tax'n 306 (1993); Granfield, An Economic Analysis of the Documentation and Financial Implications of the New Section 482 Regulations, 7 Tax Notes Int'l 97 (July 12, 1993); Hannes, An Evaluation of IRS's 1993 Transfer Pricing and Related Penalty Proposals: Round Three, 6 Tax Notes Int'l 397 (Feb. 15, 1993); Higinbotham, Guerard & Jankowski, An Economic Perspective on the Best Method Rule: Intercompany Transfer Pricing Under the New Section 482 Regulations, 6 Tax Notes Int'l 731 (Mar. 22, 1993); Horst, The Comparable Profits Method, 59 Tax Notes 1253 (May 31, 1993), reprinted in 6 Tax Notes Int'l 1443 (1993); Morrison, Commensurate With Income Takes a Back Seat to Contemporaneous Documentation in New Transfer Pricing Regulations, 6 Tax Notes Int'l 857 (Apr. 15, 1993); Nolan, Magee, Zakupowsky, Farmer & Katcher, Initial Perspectives on the New Transfer Pricing and Penalty Regulations, 6 Tax Notes Int'l 271 (Feb. 1, 1993); O'Grady, An Overview of the New Temporary Transfer Pricing Regulations, 6 Tax Notes Int'l 211 (Jan. 25, 1993); Simpson, Stone, Williams & Gallagher, From "CPI or Die" to the Best Method Rule: An Economic Analysis of the Arm's Length Standard Under the New IRS Regulations for Intercompany Pricing, 58 Tax Notes 1089 (Feb. 22, 1993).

[22] TD 8552, 1994-2 CB 93.

[23] Reg. §1.482-1(j)(1).

all subsequent taxable years of an electing taxpayer.[24] The temporary regulations generally apply for taxable years beginning during the period April 22, 1993 through October 5 1994.[25] Earlier taxable years are governed by the 1968 regulations.

Although the 1993 temporary regulations were the Treasury's first definitive construction of the commensurate-with-income requirement, that requirement applies for all taxable years beginning after 1986. For taxable years beginning after 1986 but before April 22, 1993, the requirement "must be applied using any reasonable method not inconsistent with the statute."[26] Methods prescribed by the regulations and methods derived from "their general principles" are reasonable methods.

The discussion below of §482 is concerned with six main issues:

1. The conditions bringing §482 into play—two or more organizations, common ownership or control, and an IRS determination that corrective action is necessary.[27]
2. The standards determining each organization's proper tax liability.[28]
3. The effects of a reallocation under §482.[29]
4. The relationship of §482 to the assignment of income doctrine, §446(b) (accounting method must clearly reflect the computation of taxable income), and other doctrines.[30]
5. The application of the accuracy-related penalty to taxpayers subject to §482 adjustments.[31]
6. An advance pricing agreement (APA) procedure allowing taxpayers to clear transfer prices in advance with the IRS.[32]

¶79.2 PREREQUISITES TO §482 REALLOCATIONS

There are three statutory prerequisites to a reallocation under §482: (1) two or more organizations, trades, or businesses, (2) common ownership or control,

---

[24] Reg. §1.482-1(j)(2).

[25] Reg. §1.482-1T(h) (superseded in 1994).

[26] Reg. §1.482-1(j)(3).

[27] Infra ¶79.2.

[28] Infra ¶¶79.3–79.10.

[29] Infra ¶79.11.

[30] Infra ¶79.12.

[31] Infra ¶79.15.

[32] Infra ¶79.14. Various other alternative dispute mechanisms have also been tried. For example, some income tax treaties provide for arbitration of transfer pricing disputes. See Campos, Treaty Provision for the Arbitration of Transfer Pricing Disputes, 24 Intertax 370 (1996).

and (3) an IRS determination that a reallocation is necessary to prevent tax evasion or to reflect income clearly.

1. *Two or more organizations.* Section 482's threshold condition is the existence of "two or more organizations, trades, or businesses (whether or not incorporated, whether or not organized in the United States, and whether or not affiliated)."[1] The regulations give this language the broadest possible meaning. The term "organization" is defined to include any sole proprietorship, partnership, trust, estate, association, corporation, or other kind of organization, regardless of where it is organized, operated, or carries on business, whether it is taxable or tax-exempt, whether or not it is a member of an affiliated group, and, if so, whether or not the affiliated group files a consolidated return.[2] "Trade or business" includes any trade or business, regardless of the nature of the activity or where it is carried on and regardless of who owns it.[3] Transactions between two sole proprietorships owned by the same individual do not ordinarily affect the owner's tax liability; however, if the enterprises have different accounting methods, a reallocation under §482 could shift income from one year to another. The same is true of two partnerships owned by the same partners in the same proportions.

In several cases, shareholders have been held to be "organizations, trades, or businesses" separate from corporations controlled by them or members of their family, so that income realized by the corporation could be reallocated to them under §482.[4] By itself, this should not be surprising. A sole proprietorship can conduct a business whose transactions with the owner's wholly owned corporation cry out for adjustment under §482. According to the regulations, employment for compensation, whether as employee or independent contractor and whether for a related or unrelated employer, is considered a trade or business separate from that of the employer.[5]

---

[1] For the breadth of §482's reach, see Asiatic Petroleum Co. v. CIR, 79 F2d 234 (2d Cir.), cert. denied, 296 US 645 (1935) (holding company conducting business solely through subsidiary); Cooper v. CIR, 64 TC 576, 581 (1975) (leasing business assets to controlled corporation).

[2] Reg. §1.482-1(i)(1).

[3] Reg. §1.482-1(i)(2).

[4] E.g., Dolese v. CIR, 811 F2d 543 (10th Cir. 1987) (partnership distributions reallocated among partners, one of whom was sole shareholder and employee of second partner); Rubin v. CIR, 460 F2d 1216 (2d Cir. 1972) (management services furnished to controlled corporation, which contracted services to third party for higher amount); Borge v. CIR, 405 F2d 673 (2d Cir. 1968), cert. denied, 395 US 933 (1969) (entertainment services performed for controlled corporation, which subcontracted services to third parties, producing profits offset by losses from other activities); Ach v. CIR, 358 F2d 342 (6th Cir. 1966), cert. denied, 385 US 899 (1966) (where successful proprietorship was transferred to loss corporation controlled by owner's son, portion of business profits allocated to transferor, who continued to manage enterprise).

[5] Reg. §1.482-1(i)(2). The case law generally supports this proposition. E.g., Trent v. CIR, 291 F2d 669 (2d Cir. 1961).

The tantalizing, unanswered question in this area is whether a shareholder-employee's failure to take a reasonable salary for services to a controlled corporation can trigger a corrective adjustment. Since a shareholder-employee's trade or business of being a corporate executive is considered separate from the corporation's trade or business, it is difficult to find anything in §482 to bar an allocation of adequate compensation for the services rendered in order to replicate the result, in the words of the regulations, "of a taxpayer dealing at arm's length with an uncontrolled taxpayer."[6] Presented by a taxpayer's lawyer with "a parade of horribles wherein the Commissioner would utilize §482 to reallocate income so as to increase the salaries of all employees of controlled corporations whom he believes to have been intentionally underpaid," the Court of Appeals for the Second Circuit observed that "the prospect is not so shocking to us as counsel."[7] However, the court found it unnecessary to explore all of the "horribles" because the situation before the court—the taxpayer was essentially employed as an executive of an unrelated corporation but inserted his own corporation between himself and the employer—was not that of a typical employee of a closely held corporation.

The "horribles" came closer to reality in *Foglesong v. CIR*, where the taxpayer incorporated his business of working as an independent sales representative for two unrelated corporations.[8] The Tax Court held the taxpayer's employment by his corporation was a trade or business separate from the corporation's, and it applied §482 to reallocate nearly all of the corporation's taxable income to the taxpayer. The Court of Appeals for the Seventh Circuit reversed, stating:

> As section 482 is written, we do not believe that the statute can be stretched as far as the Tax Court contends. Rather, we believe that . . . an individual who does not work exclusively for his personal service corporation may have the income earned by it allocated to him under section 482. The section should not apply, however, to one who does work exclusively for his corporation. This interpretation of section 482 satisfies both the terms of the statute—one who does not work exclusively for his corporation may rightly be said to be engaging in a separate business—and the policy that legitimate personal service corporations should be recognized.[9]

The Tax Court, however, is sticking to its guns, holding in the later case of *Haag v. CIR* that under §482, a physician employed by his wholly owned professional corporation could be allocated portions of the income realized by the corporation as partner of a medical partnership:

> The requirement that there be two or more trades, businesses, or organizations for a section 482 allocation is to be construed broadly . . . .

---

[6] Reg. §1.482-1(b)(1).

[7] Rubin v. CIR, 460 F2d 1216, 1218 (2d Cir. 1972).

[8] Foglesong v. CIR, 691 F2d 848 (7th Cir. 1982).

[9] Id. at 851. See Rev. Rul. 88-38, 1988-1 CB 246 (IRS does not follow *Foglesong* on this issue).

Petitioner and the P.C. satisfy the dual business requirement. Petitioner is in the business of providing medical services as an employee of the P.C., and the P.C., as a partner in [the medical partnership], is in the business of providing medical services through [the taxpayer.][10]

However, the cases in which the IRS has prevailed have involved situations where the corporation was a relatively passive intermediary between the individual taxpayer and the person ultimately receiving the taxpayer's services. None of the cases has involved an IRS attempt to utilize §482 to increase the salary of a shareholder-employee of a corporation actively engaged in a business consisting of more than providing the shareholder-employee's services to third persons. In *Foglesong*, the case that is factually closest to this model, the IRS was rebuffed.

2. *Common ownership or control.* The second jurisdictional prerequisite for a reallocation under §482—that the organizations, trades, or businesses be "owned or controlled directly or indirectly by the same interests"—is also construed broadly. The regulations state that "any kind of control, direct or indirect, whether legally enforceable, and however, exercisable or exercised" and that the "reality" of control is "decisive, not its form or the mode of its exercise."[11] An arbitrary shifting of income or deduction raises a presumption of control.[12] Section 482 is frequently applied to enterprises owned by different members of the same family or in different proportions by the same persons.[13] Also, if two

---

[10] Haag v. CIR, 88 TC 604, 615 (1987), aff'd without published opinion, 855 F2d 855 (8th Cir. 1988).

[11] Reg. §1.482-1(i)(4). See generally Gazur, The Forgotten Link: "Control" in Section 482, 15 Nw. J. Int'l L. & Bus. 1 (1994).

[12] The IRS has applied this idea to "lease stripping transactions." Notice 95-53, 1995-44 IRB 21. Of the several stripping transactions described in the Notice, one works as follows: A partnership owning leased tangible property sells the right to all future rents for a price payable in cash or by notes. The partnership immediately recognizes the amount realized in the sale as income, and it allocates this income to partners who are not subject to substantial U.S. income taxes (e.g.,corporations with large net operating loss carryovers). Soon after the sale of the rents, the interests of these partners are redeemed or sold, and subsequent deductions from the property (e.g., depreciation) are allocated to partners whose incomes are subject to substantial U.S. taxes. According to the IRS, the participants in such a transaction (the nontaxable and taxable partners) are commonly controlled, notwithstanding the lack of formal ownership connections, "because, among other factors, they act in concert with the common goal of arbitrarily shifting income or deductions between the[m]." Since §482 applies, the IRS "intends to exercise its authority under §482 to reallocate gross income, deductions, credits or allowances between the parties as appropriate." The IRS has subsequently proposed regulations under §7701(l) on these "obligation-shifting transactions." REG-209817-96, 1997-7 IRB 41, proposing Reg. §1.7701(l)-2.

[13] See, e.g., Ach v. CIR, 358 F2d 342 (6th Cir. 1966), cert. denied, 385 US 899 (1966) (mother and son); Fuller, Section 482 Revisited, 31 Tax L. Rev. 475, 481–85 (1976). But see Brittingham v. CIR, 66 TC 373, 396-400 (1976), aff'd per curiam, 598 F2d 1375 (5th Cir. 1979) (ownership divided among independent members of family; no common control in absence of "common design for the shifting of income"; extensive analysis).

unrelated corporations own a third corporation equally, reallocations between the controlled corporation and its owners are permissible.[14]

3. *IRS determination of necessity.* The final threshold condition to the application of §482 is an IRS determination that a reallocation is "necessary" to prevent evasion of taxes or clearly to reflect the income of any member of the group. For practical purposes, "necessary" probably means "helpful" or "appropriate," since it is hard to imagine a judicial rejection of an IRS determination on the ground that resorting to §482 was not necessary because the distortion could be corrected under §446(b) or the assignment of income doctrine. On the other hand, the fact that the IRS determines that a reallocation is necessary does not mean that the determination is correct, although the courts have repeatedly stated that IRS determinations in this area will be upheld unless shown to be arbitrary or capricious.[15] Because of this heavy burden of proof, the taxpayer is entitled to a notice that the IRS intends to rely on §482 unless its intent is sufficiently obvious to protect the taxpayer against prejudicial surprise.[16]

Although taxpayers may not apply §482 "at will" or "compel" the IRS to apply the provision, a controlled taxpayer may, "if necessary to reflect an arm's length result," report "the results of its controlled transactions based upon prices different from those actually charged."[17] A taxpayer's failure to report its true taxable income from controlled transactions" may subject the taxpayer to an accuracy-related penalty of 20 percent of the resulting understatement of tax.[18] However, deviations from the prices charged must be reported on timely returns, at least if the deviations decrease taxable income; "no untimely or amended returns will be permitted to decrease taxable income based on" adjustments to controlled transactions.[19]

A taxpayer's ability to report arm's length results differing from the terms of its actual transactions with controlled taxpayers is limited by §1059A.[20] Under

---

[14] B. Forman Co. v. CIR, 453 F2d 1144 (2d Cir.), cert. denied, 407 US 934, reh'g denied, 409 US 899 (1972) (extensive analysis).

[15] See, e.g., Liberty Loan Corp. v. US, 498 F2d 225 (8th Cir.), cert. denied, 419 US 1089 (1973) (extensive analysis); Keller v. CIR, 77 TC 1014 (1981), aff'd, 723 F2d 58 (10th Cir. 1983) (same).

[16] CIR v. Transport Mfg. & Equip. Co., 478 F2d 731 (8th Cir. 1973). See Abatti v. CIR, 644 F2d 1385 (9th Cir. 1981) (IRS could reallocate related farming income without express mention of §482 in statutory notices of deficiency and pleadings; no surprise). But see Morton-Norwich Prods., Inc. v. US, 602 F2d 270 (Ct. Cl. 1979), cert. denied, 445 US 927 (1980) (interest on deficiency attributable to §482 allocation runs from due date of return, not from date IRS gave notice of intent to rely on §482).

[17] Reg. §1.482-1(a)(3). See TD 8552, 1994-2 CB 93, 98–99 ("section 482 is concerned only with whether the taxpayer reports its true taxable income, and whether or not this result is consistent with the taxpayer's books, or is corrected in the books, is generally irrelevant").

[18] IRC §6662(e), discussed infra ¶79.14.

[19] Reg. §1.482-1(a)(3).

[20] TD 8470, 1993-1 CB 90, 92.

§1059A, if property is imported into the United States in a transaction between related persons and a cost is included both in the property's customs value and its inventory cost or basis, the amount of the cost included in inventory or basis may not exceed the amount used in determining customs value.[21]

The IRS' power to take transactions at face value, even where transfer prices are not at arm's length, is illustrated by a 1990 ruling involving a domestic corporation that licensed copyrights on various sound recordings to a foreign corporation at royalties less than would have been agreed to at arm's length.[22] The foreign corporation sublicensed the copyrights to an unrelated sublicensee for arm's length royalties and performed no significant role in the license transactions other than as a conduit between the domestic corporation and the unrelated sublicensee. Initially, a resident alien individual owned the stock of both the domestic corporation and the foreign corporation, but the individual subsequently transferred the stock of the foreign corporation to a foreign trust that the IRS disregarded as a sham. The ruling notes that the IRS could utilize its power under §482 by reallocating to the domestic corporation the entire spread between the royalties received by the foreign corporation and the royalties it paid to the domestic corporation. However, the ruling holds that if the foreign corporation distributes this spread as dividends to the disregarded trust, §482 is not applied, and the spread is included in the individual's gross income as dividends on the stock nominally owned by the trust but owned in substance by the individual. In contrast, if the spread is retained by the foreign corporation it might either be taxed to the individual under the foreign personal holding company rules or reallocated to the domestic corporation under §482.[23]

4. *Nonrecognition transactions.* The courts have recognized that in appropriate circumstances, income and deductions may be reallocated under §482 even if the intercompany transaction was covered by a nonrecognition rule.[24] In *National Securities Corp. v. CIR*, where one corporation transferred property to another in an exchange qualifying for nonrecognition under §351 and the transferee promptly sold the property at a loss, the loss was allocated back to the transferee to the extent of the excess of the property's basis over its fair market value in the transferor's hands.[25] No business purpose for the transfer was shown,

---

[21] For §1059A, see infra ¶79.7.1.

[22] Rev. Rul. 90-106, 1990-2 CB 162.

[23] For the foreign personal holding company rules, see supra ¶68.3.

[24] See generally Barrett & Rafferty, Section 482 and Nonrecognition Transfers, 45 Tax Notes 1239 (Dec. 4, 1989); Berger, Gilman & Stapleton, Section 482 and the Nonrecognition Provisions: An Analysis of the Boundary Lines, 26 Tax Lawyer 523 (1973); Miller, The Application of IRC Section 482 to Transfers Under Section 351: The *National Securities* Risk, 1976 Ariz. St. LJ 227; Townsend, Reconciling Section 482 and the Nonrecognition Provisions, 50 Tax Lawyer 701 (1997).

[25] National Securities Corp. v. CIR, 137 F2d 600 (3d Cir. 1943), cert. denied, 320 US 794 (1943). For §351, which provides that no gain or loss is recognized on a transfer of property to a corporation in exchange for stock of the corporation if the transferor controls the corporation immediately after the exchange, see infra ¶91.2.

and the transfer was apparently made because the transferee had capital gains against which the loss could be deducted, while the transferor did not.[26] The regulations allow the IRS to make §482 allocations "with respect to transactions that otherwise qualify for nonrecognition of gain or loss" whenever "necessary to prevent the avoidance of taxes or to clearly reflect income," and they illustrate this principle with an example based on *National Securities*.[27] In a few cases involving §351 transfers of land with growing crops, expenses incurred by the transferor before the transfer have been reallocated under §482 to the transferee in order to match the deductions for the expenses with the transferee's income on selling the harvested crops.[28]

In several cases involving §351 transfers of patents and other intangibles by corporations that had developed the intangibles to their subsidiaries, the IRS contended that portions of the subsidiary's income from its use of the intangible may be allocated back to the parent under §482. In each of the cases, the parent was a domestic corporation that took full advantage of the deductions for expenses incurred in developing the intangibles, but the subsidiary was a possessions corporation that was effectively exempted from U.S. tax by §936.[29] The Tax Court found that a mismatch justifying the application of §482 resulted from the

---

[26] See General Elec. Co. v. US, 3 Ct. Cl. 289, 83-2 USTC ¶9532 (Ct. Cl. 1983) (parent corporation's loss on sale of property received on liquidation of subsidiary reallocated to subsidiary because sale was planned before liquidation; subsidiary derived no tax benefit from loss deduction because it was exempt possessions corporation); Foster v. CIR, 80 TC 34 (1983), aff'd and rev'd on other issues, 756 F2d 1430 (9th Cir. 1985), cert. denied, 474 US 1055 (1986) (gain recognized by corporations on sales of building lots reallocated to partnership that had earlier conveyed undeveloped land to corporation in §351 transaction; partnership played predominant role in developing land after its transfer to corporation). But see Ruddick Corp. v. US, 643 F2d 747, 751 (Ct. Cl. 1981) (when subsidiary distributes property to parent, §482 overrides nonrecognition rule of §311(a) only if distribution is tainted by "a significant element of tax avoidance or evasion"); Bank of America v. US, 79-1 USTC ¶9170 (ND Cal. 1978) (not officially reported) (no reallocation following tax-free distribution from subsidiary to parent).

See also Northwestern Nat. Bank v. US, 556 F2d 889 (8th Cir. 1977), where a subsidiary corporation transferred property as dividend to its parent and the parent immediately gave property to charity. The court used §482 to reallocate the charitable deduction to the subsidiary, saying:

> The dividend was simply the vehicle by which assets were moved to the parent corporation, which was in a better position to enjoy the deduction that would accrue from the previously planned contribution. Since such a strategy would be unavailable to an uncontrolled taxpayer, the Commissioner did not abuse his discretion in reallocating the deduction back to the subsidiary, the true donor under the standard of an uncontrolled taxpayer.

Id. at 892.

[27] Reg. §1.482-1(f)(1)(iii).

[28] Rooney v. US, 305 F2d 681 (9th Cir. 1962); Central Cuba Sugar Co. v. CIR, 198 F2d 214 (2d Cir. 1952), cert. denied, 344 US 874 (1952).

[29] For §936, see supra ¶67.2.

taxable parent's deduction of costs that ultimately produced income for the exempt subsidiary, and the court allocated income of the subsidiary to the parent equal to the royalty the parent would have received in an arm's length sale or license of the property.[30] The only appellate court to address the issue disagreed, finding neither evasion of tax nor a distortion of the transferor's income.[31] Even before these cases were decided, however, Congress intervened, indicating that the commensurate with income standard added to §482 in 1986 is applicable whenever an intangible is transferred to a commonly controlled entity, even if the transfer is a §351 transaction or a capital contribution.[32]

5. *Consolidated returns.* Section 482 applies whether or not commonly controlled taxpayers join in a consolidated return.[33] If a controlled taxpayer files a separate return, "its true separate taxable income" is determined under §482. If a consolidated return is filed, "the true consolidated taxable income of the affiliated group and the true separate taxable income of the controlled taxpayer [are] determined consistently with the principles of a consolidated return."

¶79.3 APPLICABLE STANDARDS—GENERALLY

¶79.3.1 Introductory

Section 482 authorizes the IRS to reallocate tax items in order "to prevent evasion of taxes or clearly to reflect the income" of the affected organizations, trades, or businesses, but it does not articulate the standards to which the taxpayers must conform to avoid IRS intervention. This gap is filled by the regulations, which state that §482 "places a controlled taxpayer on a tax parity with an uncontrolled taxpayer by determining the true taxable income of the controlled taxpayer."[1] If the results reported by a controlled taxpayer diverge from its true taxable income, the IRS may, under §482, reallocate income, deductions, credits, basis, or any "other item or element affecting taxable income" among the members of the "controlled group."[2] The reallocation "may take the form of an increase or decrease in any relevant amount."

A controlled taxpayer's "true taxable income" is determined "in every case" as though the taxpayer had dealt "at arm's length with an uncontrolled taxpayer."[3] To satisfy the arm's length standard, the results of a controlled trans-

---

[30] G.D. Searle & Co. v. CIR, 88 TC 252 (1987).

[31] Eli Lilly Co. v. CIR, 856 F2d 855 (7th Cir. 1988).

[32] See infra ¶79.8.4.

[33] Reg. §1.482-1(f)(1)(iv).

[1] Reg. §1.482-1(a)(1).

[2] Reg. §1.482-1(a)(2).

[3] Reg. §1.482-1(b)(1). See TD 8552, 1994-2 CB 93, 99 (ideally, "controlled and uncontrolled taxpayers should be placed on the same (rather than a merely similar) footing").

action must be "consistent with [those that] would have been realized [had] uncontrolled taxpayers . . . engaged in the same transaction under the same circumstances." In the common case where no identical transaction is available for comparison, the reported results of a controlled transaction are judged "by reference to the results of comparable transactions under comparable circumstances."

The IRS may make an adjustment under §482 in any case where the taxable income of a controlled taxpayer (generally, an entity controlled by the same interests as the entity with which it deals in the transaction) differs from what "it would have been had the taxpayer, in the conduct of its affairs, been dealing at arm's length with an uncontrolled taxpayer."[4] The adjustment may be made whether the divergence from "true taxable income" occurs "by inadvertence or design." Section 482 adjustments are not restricted to cases of "improper accounting," "fraudulent, colorable, or sham" transactions, or "device[s] designed to reduce or avoid tax by shifting or distorting income, deductions, credits, or allowances."[5]

A §482 allocation may be made "even if the income ultimately anticipated from a series of transactions has not been or is never realized."[6] For example, if a sale of goods between controlled taxpayers is at a price less than an arm's length price, the seller's income may be adjusted using the arm's length price, even if the buyer's resales of the goods to unrelated persons occurs in later years. An allocation increasing the income of one party to a controlled transaction may be made, even if the result is to create or increase a loss to the other party from the transaction. For example, if money is loaned to a controlled borrower at a below-market interest rate, additional interest income may be allocated to the lender, even if the borrower's use of the borrowed funds is unprofitable. Also, if a corporation sustains losses in its manufacturing operations, arm's length prices are nevertheless required for the corporation's sales to a distributing subsidiary, even if these prices produce profits for the subsidiary and even if the sum of the subsidiary's profits and the parent's losses allocable to the goods sold to the subsidiary is a net loss.[7]

An examination under §482 focuses on the results of transactions between controlled taxpayers, not the methods and procedures employed by the taxpayer in setting the prices paid or received in these transactions.[8] Assume a U.S. manufacturer of household appliances sells a portion of its output to a foreign subsidiary that acts as the manufacturer's distributor in Europe. The distributor's gross margin is 18 percent, and "after adjusting for minor differences in the level of inventory," the gross margin of an uncontrolled European distributor for a

---

[4] Reg. §1.482-1(f)(1).
[5] Reg. §1.482-1(f)(1)(i).
[6] Reg. §1.482-1(f)(1)(ii)(A).
[7] Reg. §1.482-1(f)(1)(ii)(B) Ex.
[8] Reg. §1.482-1(f)(2)(v).

competitor's products is also 18 percent. The correspondence in gross margins justifies the prices paid by the subsidiary to the U.S. parent. It is not relevant whether the "budgeting, production, and performance evaluation processes" of the controlled and uncontrolled distributors are similar.

The regulations provide "specific methods" for applying the arm's length standard to various types of transactions,[9] including the following:

1. For sales of tangible property, a comparable uncontrolled price (CUP) method, a resale price method, and a cost plus method.[10]

2. For transfers of intangible property, a comparable uncontrolled transaction (CUT) method.[11]

3. A comparable profits method that may be used for either sales of tangible property or intangibles transfers if one of the participants in the controlled transactions uses valuable non-routine intangibles.[12]

4. A profit split method, which may be used for transfers of tangible or intangible property where all of the participants in the controlled transactions use valuable nonroutine intangibles.[13]

In each case, the "method or methods most appropriate to the calculation of arm's length results . . . must be selected,"[14] subject to an overriding "best method" rule, which requires use of the method that provides the most reliable measure of arm's length results under the circumstances.[15] Two or more methods may be applied to a single transaction or group of related transactions. For example, if services are provided in connection with a sale of goods, the methods for services and sales of goods may both be applied.

¶79.3.2 Defined Terms

The regulations use several terms of art, which are defined as follows:

---

[9] Reg. §1.482-1(b)(2)(i). The IRS has proposed regulations for applying §482 to "global dealing operations" consisting of the execution of customer transactions in financial products. See Breindel, Considine, Mace, Sorrells & Wolosoff, U.S. Treasury Issues Proposed Global Dealing Regulations, 16 Tax Notes Int'l 837 (Mar. 16, 1998); Reich, Nijenhuis & Zarapkar, Proposed Regs on Global Dealing Operations, 78 Tax Notes 1689 (Mar. 30, 1998); Rosenbloom & Katz, U.S. Proposed Global Trading Regs: Preliminary Questions Regarding Application, 16 Tax Notes Int'l 943 (Mar. 23, 1998). See also OECD Analysis of Global Trading of Financial Instruments Spurs Comments From Financial Industry, 3 Derivatives 70 (1997).

[10] Reg. §1.482-3, discussed infra ¶79.7.

[11] Reg. §1.482-4, discussed infra ¶79.8.

[12] Reg. §1.482-5, discussed infra ¶79.9.

[13] Reg. §1.482-6, discussed infra ¶79.10.

[14] Reg. §1.482-1(b)(2)(ii). See TD 8552, supra note 3, at 99 (this standard applies whether §482 is being used by IRS or by taxpayer in its initial determination of true taxable income).

[15] Reg. §1.482-1(c), discussed infra ¶79.3.3. See Levey & Shapiro, OECD Transfer Pricing Avoids "Overpapering the Best Method," 6 J. Int'l Tax'n 52 (1995).

1. A *"controlled taxpayer"* is "any one of two or more taxpayers owned or controlled directly or indirectly by the same interests," including the controlling taxpayer as well as the controlled taxpayer.[16] In other words, two or more persons are "controlled taxpayers" if transactions between them are subject to adjustment under §482. An *"uncontrolled taxpayer"* is "any one of two or more taxpayers [that is] not owned or controlled directly or indirectly by the same interests."

2. *"Taxpayer"* includes any person, organization, or trade or business, whether or not subject to taxation in the United States.[17]

3. *"Organization"* includes any sole proprietorship, partnership, trust, estate, association, corporation, or other kind of organization, regardless of where it is organized, operated, or carries on business; whether it is taxable or tax-exempt; whether or not it is a member of an affiliated group; and, if so, whether or not the affiliated group files a consolidated return.[18]

4. *"Trade or business"* includes any trade or business, regardless of the nature of the activity or where it is carried on and regardless of who owns it.[19] An employee's or independent contractor's performance of services for an employer is a trade or business separate from that of the employer.

5. *"Controlled"* includes "any kind of control, direct or indirect, whether legally enforceable or not, and however exercisable or exercised."[20] The "reality" of control is "decisive, not its form or the mode of its exercise." An arbitrary shifting of income or deduction raises a presumption of control.

6. Two or more taxpayers owned or controlled by the same interests, directly or indirectly, are referred to as a *"group,"* a *"controlled group,"* or a *"group of controlled taxpayers."*[21]

7. A *"controlled transaction"* or *"controlled transfer"* is a transaction or transfer between two or more members of a controlled group.[22] An *"uncontrolled transaction"* is a transaction between two or more taxpayers that are not members of the same group.

8. *"Transaction"* includes any sale, assignment, lease, license, loan, advance, contribution, other "transfer of any interest in or a right to use any property (whether tangible or intangible, real or personal) or

---

[16] Reg. §1.482-1(i)(5).
[17] Reg. §1.482-1(i)(3).
[18] Reg. §1.482-1(i)(1).
[19] Reg. §1.482-1(i)(2).
[20] Reg. §1.482-1(i)(4).
[21] Reg. §1.482-1(i)(6).
[22] Reg. §1.482-1(i)(8).

money," and any performance of services, regardless of how the transaction is effected and whether or not it is formally documented.[23]

9. *"Uncontrolled comparable"* is an uncontrolled transaction or transfer that is compared with a controlled transaction in applying §482.[24]

10. *"True taxable income"* is the taxable income a controlled taxpayer would have had if it had dealt at arm's length with all other members of the controlled group.[25]

¶79.3.3 Best Method Rule

Each transaction reviewed under §482 must be judged "under the method that, under the facts and circumstances, provides the most reliable measure of an arm's length result."[26] There is no hierarchy of methods,[27] and the choice of a particular method is not conditioned on a showing that any other method is inapplicable. If a particular method can be applied in two or more ways that yield inconsistent results, the best method is the application that "provides the most reliable determination of an arm's length result."

Two factors are primary in determining whether a particular method is the best method under the circumstances: the "degree of comparability" between the controlled transaction and the "uncontrolled comparables" and "the quality of the data and assumptions used in the analysis."[28]

Generally, given "data and assumptions of equal quality," a method applied with uncontrolled comparables having "the highest degree of comparability to the controlled transaction is more reliable than the methods that employ uncontrolled comparables with a lesser degree of comparability."[29] Comparability is important because, "[a]s the degree of comparability increases, the number and extent of potential differences that could render the analysis inaccurate is reduced."[30] "Adjustments can and should be made for any differences if the reliability of the analysis is improved by making the adjustment."[31] However, "the number, magnitude, and reliability of those adjustments . . . affect[s] the reliability of the results of the analysis."[32]

---

[23] Reg. §1.482-1(i)(7).

[24] Reg. §1.482-1(i)(10).

[25] Reg. §1.482-1(i)(9).

[26] Reg. §1.482-1(c)(1).

[27] However, if data on "closely comparable uncontrolled transactions" is available, the CUP method "generally" yields the most reliable results because an analysis under this method "can be expected to achieve a higher degree of comparability and be susceptible to fewer differences than analyses under other methods." Reg. §1.482-1(c)(2)(i).

[28] Reg. §1.482-1(c)(2).

[29] TD 8552, supra note 3, at 99.

[30] Reg. §1.482-1(c)(2)(i).

[31] TD 8552, supra note 3, at 99.

[32] Reg. §1.482-1(c)(2)(i).

An analysis is "relatively more reliable as the completeness and accuracy of the data increases" because the completeness and accuracy of data "affects the ability to identify and quantify those factors that . . . affect the result."[33] Generally, the lack of identified material differences between two transactions makes the transactions "highly comparable" only if, given the comprehensiveness of the data on both transactions, "it is unlikely that any such differences exist," and adjustments for all identified differences make the transactions highly comparable only if the data "is sufficiently complete and accurate that the difference has a definite and reasonably ascertainable effect."[34]

"All methods rely on assumptions,"[35] but the reliability of an analysis "depends on the soundness" of underlying assumptions.[36] For example, it is reasonable to assume that differences in payment terms affect prices and that this effect may reasonably be accounted for as being solely a function of the time value of money. In contrast, it is usually less sound to assume that the relative values of intangibles can be determined for purposes of the profit split method by capitalizing the costs of developing the intangibles, and this assumption thus weakens the reliability of an analysis.

Deficiencies in data or assumptions may be more damaging under some methods than under others because "the reliability of some methods is heavily dependent on the similarity of property or services involved in the controlled and uncontrolled transactions."[37] For example, although "a difference in risks borne might be expected to affect all methods to some extent,"[38] an analysis under the resale price method is crucially affected by "the extent to which controlled and uncontrolled taxpayers undertake the same or similar functions, employ similar resources, and bear similar risks."[39] Similarly, "an inability to reliably allocate research and development expenses would have a serious effect on the reliability of a residual profit split . . . but would have little effect on an analysis under the CUT method."[40] Also, "differences in management efficiency may have a greater effect on a comparable profits method analysis than on a comparable uncontrolled price method analysis, while differences in product characteristics . . . ordinarily [has] a greater effect on a comparable uncontrolled price method analysis than on a comparable profits method analysis."[41]

---

[33] Reg. §1.482-1(c)(2)(ii)(A). See Levey, Lubick & Bossart, Defining "Quality" Data in a Transfer Pricing Analysis, 7 J. Int'l Tax'n 4 (1996).

[34] TD 8552, supra note 3, at 100.

[35] Id.

[36] Reg. §1.482-1(c)(2)(ii)(B).

[37] Reg. §1.482-1(c)(2)(ii)(C).

[38] TD 8552, supra note 3, at 100.

[39] Reg. §1.482-1(c)(2)(ii)(C).

[40] TD 8552, supra note 3, at 100.

[41] Reg. §1.482-1(c)(2)(ii)(C).

It may also be useful to consider the extent to which the results produced by the method are consistent with the results from other methods.[42] If none of several possible analyses is clearly better than the others,[43] a method yielding results consistent with other methods may be preferred over a method producing results inconsistent with those of all other plausible alternatives.[44] However, if comparability and quality of data indicate that a particular method is best, this method must be chosen over all other methods, even if consistent results emerge from two or more of the latter methods.

¶79.3.4 Comparability

Whether a controlled transaction is at arm's length is usually determined by comparing the results of the transaction with "the results realized by uncontrolled taxpayers engaged in comparable transactions under comparable circumstances."[45] The comparability of transactions depends on the functions performed by the parties to the transactions, the risks undertaken in the transactions, the contractual terms, the economic conditions, the nature of the goods or services that are the subject of the transactions, and all other "factors that could affect prices or profits in arm's length dealings." These factors "are relevant under all the methods,"[46] but the importance of particular factors in particular cases may depend on the pricing method being used.

An uncontrolled transaction may be comparable even if it is not "identical" to the controlled transaction, but it "must be sufficiently similar that it provides a reliable measure of an arm's length result."[47] Adjustments must be made for any differences between the uncontrolled and controlled transactions that would "materially affect" the arm's length result under the method being used if the effects of the differences on prices or profits "can be ascertained with sufficient accuracy to improve the reliability of the results." Although adjustments are not required for "differences that would have only a *de minimis* or minor effect on price or profit, . . . such adjustments will tend to increase the reliability of the result."[48]

---

[42] Reg. §1.482-1(c)(2).

[43] See TD 8552, supra note 3, at 100 ("this situation will arise when, after considering the comparability and the quality of the data and assumptions under two different methods (or under two different applications of the same method), it is not possible to determine which of the competing analyses provides a more reliable measure of an arm's length result").

[44] Reg. §1.482-1(c)(2)(iii).

[45] Reg. §1.482-1(d)(1).

[46] TD 8552, supra note 3, at 100.

[47] Reg. §1.482-1(d)(2). See TD 8552, supra note 3, at 100 ("so-called 'inexact' comparables [may be used] under all methods").

[48] TD 8552, supra note 3, at 100.

The adjustments must be "based on commercial practices, economic principles, or statistical analyses."[49] The reliability of the analysis is affected by the number, magnitude, and reliability of the adjustments. If adjustments cannot be made, the reliability of the analysis is reduced, although neither the pricing method nor the comparables used in applying it need necessarily be abandoned.[50] However, "unadjusted industry average returns themselves cannot establish arm's length results."[51]

The regulations identify several factors affecting comparability, each of which "must be considered in determining the degree of comparability between transactions or taxpayers and the extent to which comparability adjustments may be necessary."[52]

1. *Functional analysis.* A "functional analysis" is made in order to compare "the functions performed, and associated resources employed," by the parties to the controlled and uncontrolled transactions.[53] This analysis must identify and compare "the economically significant activities undertaken, or to be undertaken, by" the parties to the transactions and must take into consideration the resources "employed, or to be employed, in conjunction with the activities, including . . . the type of assets used, such as plant and equipment, or the use of valuable intangibles." Relevant functions include

research and development; product design and engineering; manufacturing, production and process engineering; product fabrication, extraction, and assembly; purchasing and materials management; marketing and distribution functions including inventory management, warranty administration, and advertising and marketing activities; transportation and warehousing; and managerial, legal, accounting and finance, credit and collection, training, and personnel management services.

2. *Contractual terms.* Comparability also depends on "the significant contractual terms that could affect the results of the [controlled and uncontrolled] transactions."[54] Contractual terms for controlled transactions are "respected" if they are agreed to in writing before the transactions take place and are "consistent with the economic substance of the underlying transactions."[55]

---

[49] Reg. §1.482-1(d)(2).

[50] "The number and magnitude of adjustments affects reliability because as the number or magnitude of adjustments increases, the potential for error also increases." TD 8552, supra note 3, at 100.

[51] See National Semiconductor Corp. v. CIR, 67 TCM (CCH) (1994) (under prior regulations, industry pricing guidelines not considered in determining arm's length prices).

[52] Reg. §1.482-1(d)(3).

[53] Reg. §1.482-1(d)(3)(i). See DeSouza, Functional Analysis, 8 J. Int'l Tax'n 223 (1997).

[54] Reg. §1.482-1(d)(3)(ii)(A).

[55] Reg. §1.482-1(d)(3)(ii)(B)(*1*). The parties' "conduct" and "respective legal rights" are given "greatest weight" in determining whether contractual terms are consistent with the transaction's economic substance.

"For two transactions to be comparable, the contractual terms that would affect the prices charged should be comparable."[56] The relevant contractual terms include

the form of consideration charged or paid; sales or purchase volume; the scope and terms of warranties provided; rights to updates, revisions or modifications; the duration of relevant license, contracts or other agreements, and termination or renegotiation rights; collateral transactions or ongoing business relationships between the buyer and the seller, including arrangements for the provision of ancillary or subsidiary services; and extension of credit and payment terms.

The regulations contain an example illustrating the effect of sales or purchase volume.[57] Assume domestic corporation P ships goods to overseas customers by boats owned and operated by its foreign subsidiary F. P provides 90 percent of F's business, with the remaining 10 percent coming from unrelated shippers. F's transactions with unrelated shippers may be comparable to its transactions with P; however, these prices must be adjusted for the differences in volume and the regularity of services if these differences "have a material effect on the price."[58] Also, if the time for payment differs between the controlled and uncontrolled transactions, an adjustment should be made for this difference if it has "a material effect on price," even if no interest is imputed under §482 or any other statutory provision.[59]

If there is no written agreement or if contractual terms are not consistent with economic substance, the IRS may "impute terms" consistent with economic substance.[60] Assume domestic corporation DS acts as exclusive distributor in the United States of goods produced by its parent, foreign corporation FP.[61] During the first years of DS's existence, when FP's trade name is not known in the United States, DS incurs expenses in building a market for the goods that are not reimbursed by FP and are substantially greater than those that would be incurred by comparable independent distributor. FP's trade name eventually becomes well

---

[56] TD 8470, 1993-1 CB 90, 94.

[57] Reg. §1.482-1(d)(3)(ii)(C) Ex. 1.

[58] The example is reminiscent of the facts of US Steel Corp. v. CIR, 617 F2d 942 (2d Cir. 1980), where the court rejected the IRS' argument that controlled transactions with a foreign shipping subsidiary were not comparable to the subsidiary's transactions with unrelated shippers because the controlled transactions represented a large majority of the subsidiary's business. According to the court, the IRS' argument, based on differing "expectations about duration and risk" in the controlled and uncontrolled transactions, "may ... recognize economic reality," but the argument, if adopted would "engraft a crippling degree of economic sophistication onto a broadly drawn statute, which ... would allow the taxpayer no safe harbor from the Commissioner's virtually unrestricted discretion to reallocate." Id. at 951. See Reg. §1.482-1(d)(3)(ii)(C) Ex. 2 (determining adjustments for quantity differences).

[59] Reg. §1.482-1(d)(3)(ii)(A).

[60] Reg. §1.482-1(d)(3)(ii)(B)(2).

[61] Reg. §1.482-1(d)(3)(ii)(C) Ex. 3.

known in the United States and commands a premium price for the goods. Even if *FP* and *DS* have no agreement relating to *DS'* use of *FP*'s trade name, *DS'* expenditures in developing the name in the United States "indicate a course of conduct that is consistent with an agreement [entitling *DS* to] a long-term right to use the tradename . . . in the United States." Thus, the IRS "may impute an agreement between [*DS* and *FP*] under which [*DS*] will retain an appropriate portion of the price premium attributable to the . . . tradename."

Similarly, if consistent with the taxpayer's conduct, an "established industry convention or usage of trade" may be followed in assigning a risk or resolving an issue.[62] In the absence of agreement to the contrary, payment is considered due in a sale of goods when and where the buyer takes delivery of the goods.

3. *Risk analysis.* Comparability also depends on the sharing of the business and financial risks "that could affect the prices that would be charged or paid, or the profit that would be earned, in the [controlled and uncontrolled] transactions."[63] The relevant risks include

> market risks, including fluctuations in cost, demand, pricing, and inventory levels; risks associated with the success or failure of research and development activities; financial risks, including fluctuations in foreign currency rates of exchange and interest rates; credit and collection risks; product liability risks; and general business risks related to the ownership of property, plant, and equipment.

The risks borne by each of the parties to a controlled transaction are generally determined by the contract between the parties, but the contract's terms are given effect only if they are congruent with the transaction's economic substance.[64] Also, the contract is supplemented by any terms imputed from the transaction's economic substance, industry convention, or usage of trade. The focus on economic substance is required because "allocation of risk is potentially subject to manipulation by controlled taxpayers, who may purport to allocate risk inconsistently with the substance of their transactions."[65]

A contractual allocation of risk among controlled taxpayers is disregarded as lacking in economic substance if it is made "after the outcome of such risk is known or reasonably knowable."[66] Other factors considered in evaluating consistency with economic substance include the following:

a. Whether the parties' "conduct over time is consistent with the purported allocation of risk between the controlled taxpayers."

b. Whether the party nominally bearing a risk "has the financial capacity to

---

[62] Reg. §1.482-1(d)(3)(ii)(B)(2).
[63] Reg. §1.482-1(d)(3)(iii)(A).
[64] Reg. §1.482-1(d)(3)(iii)(B).
[65] TD 8470, supra note 56, at 94.
[66] Reg. §1.482-1(d)(3)(iii)(B).

fund losses that might be expected to occur as the result of the assumption of the risk."

c. Since, in arm's length dealings, "parties ordinarily bear a greater share of those risks over which they have relatively more control," whether "each controlled taxpayer exercises managerial or operational control over the business activities that directly influence the amount of income or loss [it] realize[s]."

Assume domestic corporation P enters into a contract with its foreign subsidiary (F) under which F agrees to purchase 20,000 units of goods from P annually for five years for $10 each. The goods are a new product in F's market, and F finances marketing activities to introduce the goods into its market. During the first three years of the contract period, F sells only 10,000 units at $11 each, but demand rises substantially during the fourth year, enabling F to sell its entire inventory for $25 per unit during that year. If F has "adequate financial capacity" to finance inventory accumulations and any resulting losses, F bears the market risk of these losses because the allocation of this risk is documented before the outcomes of the risk were known or reasonably capable of being known.[67] In contrast, F does not bear this risk if its capital, "including loans," is only $100,000 and the inventory accumulation is financed by the parent extending credit for the price of the unsold inventory.[68]

Similarly, if a domestic corporation purchases goods manufactured by its foreign subsidiary under a long-term contract and this contract requires the subsidiary to bear the risk of currency fluctuations, this allocation of risk is given effect only if the subsidiary has "adequate financial capacity" to bear any resulting losses and the parties' conduct is consistent with the contract.[69] The requisite financial capacity might, for example, consist of currency contracts held by the subsidiary to hedge currency risks under the arrangement with its parent. The parties conduct is inconsistent with the contract if, for example, the contract price is adjusted in the event of a large shift in exchange rates.

4. *Economic conditions.* The comparability of controlled and uncontrolled transactions also depends on the extent of the similarities in "the significant economic conditions that could affect" prices or profits.[70] Among the relevant economic factors to be considered are

a. "The similarity of geographic markets."
b. The "relative size[s]" of the markets.
c. The "extent of the overall economic development in each market."
d. "The level of the market (*e.g.*, wholesale, retail, etc.)."
e. The parties' market shares for the particular goods, property, or services.

---

[67] Reg. §1.482-1(d)(3)(iii)(C) Ex. 1.
[68] Reg. §1.482-1(d)(3)(iii)(C) Ex. 2.
[69] Reg. §1.482-1(d)(3)(iii)(C) Ex. 3.
[70] Reg. §1.482-1(d)(3)(iv).

f. "The location-specific costs of the factors of production and distribution."
g. "The extent of competition in each market."
h. "The economic condition of the particular industry, including whether the market is in contraction or expansion."
i. "The alternatives realistically available to the buyer and seller."

5. *Property or services.* The comparability of controlled and uncontrolled transactions also depends on the extent of the similarities in the goods, other property, or services involved in the transactions.[71] The comparison may also be affected by "any intangibles that are embedded in" the property or services. For example, if the controlled transaction involves goods sold under an internationally recognized trademark, but the goods involved in the uncontrolled transaction bear no trademark, appropriate adjustments must be made for the economic value of the trademark.

6. *Market share strategies.* If the parties to controlled transactions undertake "a market share strategy" in order "to enter new markets or to increase a product's share of an existing market," the strategy may result in "market development expenses" or resale prices that "temporarily" differ from those for comparable products in the same market.[72] The strategy may affect the transfer price, "depend[ing] on which party to the controlled transaction bears the costs of the pricing strategy." "In such circumstances the amount charged in the controlled transaction, or the expenses borne by a controlled taxpayer, may for a short time differ from what normally would be observed at arm's length."[73]

Prices set in such a strategy are honored under §482 if it is "shown" that uncontrolled taxpayers would act similarly in comparable circumstances, taking into account all of the factors of analysis (particularly, the risk analysis) described above.[74] The taxpayer need not "locate a comparable uncontrolled transaction that would satisfy the standards of the CUP method."[75] It could, for example, sustain the transfer price with "evidence of an uncontrolled taxpayer in a different industry engaging in such a strategy, given evidence that the circumstances otherwise were comparable."

However, the market strategy rule applies only if the taxpayer maintains documents establishing the following:

a. There is a "reasonable likelihood" of future profits flowing from the strategy "reflect[ing] an appropriate return in relation to the costs incurred to implement it."
b. These costs are "borne" by the party that will realize any future profits resulting from the strategy.

---

[71] Reg. §1.482-1(d)(3)(v).
[72] Reg. §1.482-1(d)(4)(i).
[73] TD 8552, supra note 3, at 101.
[74] Reg. §1.482-1(d)(4)(i).
[75] TD 8552, supra note 3, at 101.

c. The strategy is not "pursued" for an unreasonably long time, "taking into consideration the industry and product."

d. The strategy, "the related costs and expected returns," and any agreement for the sharing of these costs "were established before the strategy was implemented."[76]

7. *Different geographic markets.* Uncontrolled comparable transactions should "ordinarily" be in the same "geographic market" as the controlled transactions because "economic conditions" may differ significantly from market to market.[77] The term "geographic market" refers to "a geographic area in which the economic conditions for the relevant product or service are substantially the same." Two or more countries can comprise a single geographic market, "depending on the economic conditions."

Uncontrolled transactions in a different market "may be considered" if "information from the same market is not available" and "adjustments are made to account for differences between the two markets."[78] If the data needed to make appropriate adjustments is not available, uncontrolled comparables from the most similar market should be used; however, the differences between the markets affect the reliability of the method for purposes of the best method rule.

Among the adjustments that may be required where the controlled and uncontrolled transactions come from different geographic markets is an adjustment "to account for significant differences in costs."[79] Lower costs in a controlled taxpayer's geographic market "ordinarily" justify higher profits "only if the cost differences would increase the profits of comparable uncontrolled [taxpayers] operating at arm's length, given the competitive positions of buyers and sellers in that market." "[S]ome or all of the location savings might inure to the benefit of the other party to the controlled transaction."[80] Assume a U.S. clothing designer with a well known reputation and trademark in the market for high-priced clothing, purchases clothing manufactured by its foreign subsidiary in country Y, where clothing production costs are significantly less than in the United States.[81] If the subsidiary's manufacturing does not require "significant specialized knowledge" and could be performed by many firms in locations comparable to country Y, the lesser production costs in country Y do not "justify additional profits."

8. *Unacceptable comparables.* An uncontrolled transaction is not "ordinarily" a reliable measure of arm's length results if it is "not made in the ordinary course of business."[82] For example, if a competitor of the taxpayer becomes

---

[76] Reg. §1.482-1(d)(4)(i).

[77] Reg. §1.482-1(d)(4)(ii)(A).

[78] Reg. §1.482-1(d)(4)(ii)(A).

[79] Reg. §1.482-1(d)(4)(ii)(C).

[80] TD 8552, supra note 3, at 102.

[81] Reg. §1.482-1(d)(4)(ii)(D) Ex.

[82] Reg. §1.482-1(d)(4)(iii)(A)(*1*).

bankrupt and its inventory is sold to independent distributors in liquidation of the bankruptcy estate, these sales are not comparable to the taxpayer's sales of comparable goods to its foreign subsidiary, acting as distributor for the parent's products in various foreign countries.[83] However, the uncontrolled transactions need not be numerous. "Transfers of some property may be few in volume, but nonetheless be in the ordinary course of business and provide a useful basis for determining and arm's length result."[84]

Also, an uncontrolled transaction is not "ordinarily" a reliable measure if a "principal" purpose of the transaction "was to establish an arm's length result" to be used as a comparable for a controlled transaction.[85] Assume a U.S. manufacturer, which generally distributes its goods only through subsidiaries, increases its production by 5 percent and sells the additional goods to an unrelated distributor operating in foreign country X.[86] If one of the manufacturer's purposes for the production increase is to establish comparable uncontrolled prices for the transactions with subsidiaries, the sales to the unrelated distributor may not be used in applying §482, even if the taxpayer was also motivated by a desire to make productive use of excess manufacturing capacity.

¶79.3.5 Arm's Length Ranges

If the application of a transfer pricing method produces more than one reliable result, no §482 adjustment is made unless the results reported by the taxpayer fall outside the range of reliable results, which is called the "arm's length range."[87] The regulations' recognition of arm's length ranges is an innovation; prior regulations implied that §482 methodologies always produced a single arm's length result. The authors of the new regulations believed that "requiring a single precise result was inconsistent with the fact that the various methods were not always precise measures of an arm's length result, and ignored the economic fact that there often will be more than one arm's length price."[88] "Given equal degrees of high comparability, it is impossible to conclude which of the uncontrolled comparables provides a more reliable measure of an arm's length result."[89]

An arm's length range is normally established by applying one pricing method (the best method) using "two or more uncontrolled transactions of simi-

---

[83] Reg. §1.482-1(d)(4)(iii)(B) Ex. 1.
[84] TD 8552, supra note 3, at 102.
[85] Reg. §1.482-1(d)(4)(v)(A)(2).
[86] Reg. §1.482-1(d)(4)(iii)(B) Ex. 2.
[87] Reg. §1.482-1(e)(1).
[88] TD 8470, supra note 56, at 94.
[89] Id. at 102.

lar comparability and reliability."[90] Uncontrolled comparables with "a significantly lower level of comparability and reliability" than other available comparables may not be used.[91] A valid range cannot be derived "from a mix of exact and inexact comparables" because such a mix "would accord the same weight to results with potentially widely varying degrees of reliability."[92]

More specifically, the range usually consists of all uncontrolled comparables meeting the following conditions:

1. The information on the controlled transaction and the comparables is complete enough so "that it is likely that all material differences have been identified,"
2. Each material difference "has a definite and reasonably ascertainable effect on price or profit," and
3. Adjustments are made to compensate for all material differences.[93]

Assume the IRS locates four uncontrolled comparables that, after identifying and adjusting for all material differences, establish transfer prices of $44, $45, $45, and $45.50.[94] If the effect of each material difference on the price is definite and reasonably ascertainable, the arm's length range is $44 to $45.50, and no §482 adjustment is made if the taxpayer used a price falling within that range.

If no uncontrolled comparables meet all of these conditions, the arm's length range is derived from the uncontrolled comparables at the highest "level of comparability and reliability."[95] The included comparables should be "of approximately equal comparability," but there may be "material differences for which adjustments have not been made."[96] Assume the IRS, in applying the comparable profits method to a U.S. manufacturer, identifies 50 uncontrolled manufacturing companies within the same industry.[97] If only 20 of these companies have "similar capital investments and technical know-how," the other 30 are discarded. Assume that, of the remaining 20, data on five "is very limited, and although some material differences can be identified and adjusted for, the level of comparability of these five uncontrolled comparables is significantly lower than that of the other 15." The arm's length range is derived from the other 15.

---

[90] Reg. §1.482-1(e)(2)(i). More than one pricing method may be used to the extent allowed by the best method rule.

[91] Reg. §1.482-1(e)(2)(ii). See Reg. §1.482-1(e)(5) Ex. 1 (of 10 available uncontrolled comparables, three eliminated because comparability is "significantly lower" than for other seven, and three more eliminated because only remaining four can "reliably" be adjusted for material differences).

[92] TD 8552, supra note 3, at 102.

[93] Reg. §1.482-1(e)(2)(iii)(A).

[94] Reg. §1.482-1(e)(5) Ex. 2.

[95] Reg. §1.482-1(e)(2)(iii)(B).

[96] TD 8552, supra note 3, at 102.

[97] Reg. §1.482-1(e)(5) Ex. 4.

Where one or more of the three conditions is not met, the reliability of the range must be enhanced to the extent possible with the use of "a valid statistical method."[98] A statistical refinement is necessary because the comparables are "of differing degrees of comparability and reliability" and, in the absence of statistical refinement, "the analysis would be distorted" by giving them "equal weight."[99] Ideally, the statistical method should produce a 75 percent probability of a particular result falling within the range. The interquartile range—consisting of all uncontrolled comparables of similar comparability and reliability, excluding the one fourth of them producing the lowest results and the one fourth producing the highest results—is "ordinarily" an acceptable statistical method.[100] Generally, "it is reasonable to assume that the results diverging significantly from the norm are not comparable to the controlled taxpayer."[101] However, some other method may be used if it "provides a more reliable measure."[102]

If the number of uncontrolled comparables is not evenly divisible by 4, the number of comparables in the excluded low and high quartiles is rounded up to the next whole number. For example, if there are 15 comparables, the excluded low end consists of the lowest four, and the high end of the highest four.[103] If the number of uncontrolled comparables is evenly divisible by 4, the lower end of the range is the average of the highest result among the lower 25 percent and the next highest result, and the upper end of the range is the average of the lowest result among the higher 25 percent and the next lowest result. Assume the IRS locates four uncontrolled comparables—prices of $42, $44, $45, and $47.50, but the interquartile range is used because available data is not sufficient to ensure that all material product and functional differences have been identified and their effects quantified.[104] The interquartile range is $43 to $46.25. Since the lowest price ($42) comprises exactly 25 percent of the results, the lower end of the range is the average of the lowest two prices (one half of the sum of $42 and $44). Similarly, because the highest price also is 25 percent of the results, the upper end of the range is the average of the two highest prices (one half of the sum of $45 and $47.50).

If the taxpayer has reported results falling outside the arm's length range, the IRS may make a §482 adjustment falling "at any point" within the range.[105] However, if the interquartile range is used, the adjustment is "ordinarily" to the fiftieth percentile in that range, and in other cases, the adjustment is usually to the "arithmetic mean" of the range.

---

[98] Reg. §1.482-1(e)(2)(iii)(B).
[99] TD 8552, supra note 3, at 102.
[100] Reg. §§1.482-1(e)(2)(iii)(B), (C).
[101] TD 8552, supra note 3, at 103.
[102] Reg. §§1.482-1(e)(2)(iii)(B), (C).
[103] Reg. §1.482-4(c)(4) Ex. 3.
[104] Reg. §1.482-1(e)(5) Ex. 3.
[105] Reg. §1.482-1(e)(3).

The IRS need not construct an arm's length range.[106] It may, for example, apply the CUP method using one uncontrolled comparable, in which case the taxpayer can defeat the allocation only by establishing an arm's length range that encompasses the results reported on the taxpayer's return.

¶79.3.6 Aggregation of Transactions

Most of the transfer pricing methods are normally applied transaction-by-transaction.[107] However, for taxpayers having numerous transactions, a transaction-by-transaction approach may be impractical, and the IRS therefore allows each pricing method to be applied to "the overall results for product lines or other groupings." Also, sampling and "other valid statistical techniques" may be used in testing the results of all of an entity's "related party transactions."

Moreover, the combined effect of two or more separate transactions may be considered in applying §482 if the transactions "are so interrelated that consideration of multiple transactions is the most reliable means of determining" arm's length results.[108] The aggregated transactions need not occur in the same year. The regulations illustrate this approach with several examples, including the following:

1. Assume corporation *P* licenses its subsidiary (*S1*) to use a proprietary manufacturing process, and *S1* uses the process to produce goods it sells to another subsidiary (*S2*), which *S2* resells to unrelated buyers.[109] In determining whether the royalty paid by *S1* to *P* is at arm's length, the IRS may consider whether the prices paid by *S2* to *S1* are at arm's length, and it may also consider the aggregate profits of *S1* and *S2* from these transactions.

2. Assume *P*, a U.S. computer manufacturer, has three subsidiaries in country *Z*—*S1*, which is exclusive country *Z* distributor of *P*'s products; *S2*, which provides marketing services relating to country *Z* sales of *P*'s products and uses "significant marketing intangibles" owned by *P*; and *S3*, which administers the country *Z* warranty for *P*'s computers.[110] In testing the prices paid by *S1* for *P* computers, the royalties paid by *S2* for its use of *P*'s marketing intangibles, and the service fees earned by *S2* and *S3*, the IRS "may consider the combined effects of these separate transactions because they are so interrelated that they are most reasonably analyzed on an aggregate basis."[111]

---

[106] Id.

[107] Reg. §1.482-1(f)(2)(iv).

[108] Reg. §1.482-1(f)(2)(i)(A).

[109] Reg. §1.482-1(f)(2)(i)(B) Ex. 1.

[110] Reg. §1.482-1(f)(2)(i)(B) Ex. 2.

[111] The interrelationships of the activities of the three subsidiaries may also affect the choice of comparable transactions. Reg. §1.482-1(f)(2)(i)(B) Ex. 3.

However, the combined effect of transactions is usually relevant only if the transactions "involve related products or services."[112] Assume a corporation licenses a subsidiary to use a proprietary manufacturing process to produce one product and also sells another, unrelated product to the subsidiary.[113] The combined effects of "these separate and unrelated transactions" is not relevant to the testing of either the royalty paid by the subsidiary or the prices charged by the parent for the other product.

¶79.3.7 Multiple Year Data

Controlled transactions are normally compared with comparable uncontrolled transactions occurring during the same taxable year.[114] However, where "appropriate," information about the uncontrolled comparables or the controlled taxpayer for one or more years before or after the taxable year may be considered. If data on uncontrolled comparables from other years is used, data from the controlled taxpayer for the same years "ordinarily must be considered." However, if data from the same years is not available, data from different years, appropriately adjusted, may be used.

Circumstances that may make multiple year data appropriate include the unavailability of complete and reliable data for the taxable year, "business cycles in the controlled taxpayer's industry," and "life cycles of the product or intangible being examined."[115] Assume goods are sold between affiliated corporations during a particular year for $60 per unit, and applying the resale price method, an arm's length range is established for the year of $52 to $59.[116] Normally, a §482 adjustment is appropriate in such a case. However, resort may be had to data for other years if "cyclical factors . . . affect the results of the uncontrolled comparables (and that of the controlled transaction) that cannot be adequately accounted for by specific adjustments to the data" for the taxable year. For example, the arm's length range might be reconstituted as the averages of the prices charged by each of the uncontrolled comparable companies during the taxable year and the preceding two years. If this is done, the controlled transfer prices are also averaged over the same three years, and no §482 adjustment is made if this average falls within the range of average uncontrolled comparables.

The appropriateness of multiple year data also depends on the pricing method being applied and "the issue being addressed."[117] Such data is ordinarily

---

[112] Reg. §1.482-1(f)(2)(i)(A). For the term "related products or services," see Reg. §1.6038A-3(c)(7)(vii), discussed infra ¶112.4.4 note 58.

[113] Reg. §1.482-1(f)(2)(i)(B) Ex. 4.

[114] Reg. §1.482-1(f)(2)(iii)(A).

[115] Reg. §1.482-1(f)(2)(iii)(B).

[116] Reg. §1.482-1(f)(2)(iii)(E) Ex. 1.

[117] Reg. §1.482-1(f)(2)(iii)(B).

necessary in applying the rules on business and financial risks,[118] market share strategies,[119] periodic adjustments to royalty rates,[120] and the comparable profits method.[121] Data for other years is not considered in applying the CUP method, except in resolving issues relating to risk or market share strategies.

Assume a domestic corporation acts as U.S. distributor for goods manufactured in country X by its parent, a country X corporation.[122] The subsidiary's purchases from the parent are at prices denominated in the currency of country X, and these prices are tested using comparable transactions of uncontrolled companies whose purchases and sales are denominated in U.S. dollars. If the country X currency substantially appreciated or depreciated against the dollar during the taxable year, multiple year data may be one way of improving the comparison between the taxpayer, which bears a currency risk by making purchases denominated in a foreign currency and selling the same goods in dollar transactions, and the uncontrolled transactions, which are entirely in dollars.

Also, data from several years may be examined to determine whether the results of controlled transactions were affected by "economic conditions" that also had an impact on the uncontrolled comparables.[123] For example, if a taxpayer repeatedly reports losses on controlled transactions, this circumstance arouses suspicion that transfer prices are not at arm's length, but the IRS may examine multiple year data to determine whether the losses were caused, in whole or part, by economic conditions that similarly affected uncontrolled comparables. Assume a domestic corporation, which acts as U.S. distributor of goods manufactured by its parent in country X, reports losses for all of the years 1 through 5. For each of these years, the corporation presents data showing a comparable distributor sustaining a comparable loss.[124] If a different comparable distributor is used for each of the years, the IRS might check whether the comparable distributors had losses for all of the years. If each of the comparable distributors had profits for many of the years and was profitable overall for the five-year period, the IRS will likely conclude that the comparable distributor data does not support the taxpayer's transfer prices.

Similarly, results in controlled transactions that appear to be within an arm's length range may be rejected if multiple year data show that average results in the controlled transactions is out of line with the average results of each of the uncontrolled comparables.[125] Assume a foreign corporation, which serves as the country Y distributor of products manufactured in the United States by its parent (a domestic corporation), has a gross profit margin of 13 percent for each of the

---

[118] Reg. §1.482-1(d)(3)(iii), discussed supra ¶79.3.4 text accompanying notes 63—69.
[119] Reg. §1.482-1(d)(4)(i), discussed supra ¶79.3.4 text accompanying note 76.
[120] Reg. §1.482-4(f)(2), discussed infra ¶79.8.4.
[121] Reg. §1.482-5, discussed infra ¶79.9.
[122] Reg. §1.482-1(f)(2)(iii)(E) Ex. 2.
[123] Reg. §1.482-1(f)(2)(iii)(C).
[124] Reg. §1.482-1(f)(2)(iii)(E) Ex. 3.
[125] Reg. §1.482-1(f)(2)(iii)(D).

years 1 through 3. Gross profit margins for four uncontrolled comparables are established for these years, showing an arm's length range of gross margins of 4 percent to 13 percent for year 1, 3 percent to 13 percent for year 2, and a 2 percent to 13 percent for year 3.[126] For each year, examined in isolation, the foreign corporation's results are within the arm's length range. However, a §482 adjustment is made if none of the four comparable distributors is near the high point in the range for more than one of the three years—if, for example, none of the comparable distributors has an average gross profit margin for the three years exceeding 8.67 percent.

¶79.3.8 Contractual Arrangements and Patterns of Dealing Between Controlled Taxpayers

In applying §482, the IRS takes each transaction as the taxpayers have structured it "unless its structure lacks economic substance."[127] However, alternative structures are considered "in determining whether the terms of the controlled transaction would be acceptable to an uncontrolled taxpayer faced with the same alternatives and operating under comparable circumstances." If an uncontrolled taxpayer would have adopted a different structure, but the taxpayer's structure does not lack economic substance, the transaction is not restructured, but the consideration in the transaction may be adjusted "to account for material differences between the alternative and the controlled transaction." For example, if a corporation licenses a subsidiary to use a proprietary manufacturing process, the transactions will not be restructured as though the manufacturing was done by the parent, rather than the subsidiary, but the fact that the parent could have done the manufacturing may be relevant to the arm's length amount of the royalty.[128] The IRS explains:

> This analysis is central to the arm's length standard and the traditional notion of comparability. For example, under the comparable uncontrolled price method, the objective is to identify an alternative price at which the taxpayer could have conducted the controlled transaction. This section merely broadens this traditional analysis by permitting examination of other alternatives when the controlled taxpayer has the option of internally obtaining the goods or services that it obtained in the controlled transaction. In such a case, an otherwise acceptable comparable transaction may not provide a reliable measure of an arm's length result if the controlled taxpayer could have obtained the object of the controlled transaction more cheaply by obtaining it from internal sources. This approach duplicates the analysis that an uncontrolled taxpayer would employ in considering whether to obtain a product from an unrelated party or to produce the product itself,

---

[126] Reg. §1.482-1(f)(2)(iii)(E) Ex. 4.

[127] Reg. §1.482-1(f)(2)(ii)(A).

[128] Reg. §1.482-1(f)(2)(ii)(B) Ex.

and the amount that it would be willing to pay an unrelated supplier of that product.[129]

In several cases decided before the regulations were issued, involving U.S. companies that purchased most or all of the output of affiliates (typically, foreign subsidiaries), usually consisting of goods manufactured under patents and other intangibles supplied by the U.S. companies, the IRS contended that the affiliate should be treated as a contract manufacturer for the corporation and that the arm's length price for the affiliate's services as contract manufacturer should be computed as cost plus a markup on cost. The courts were not receptive to this theory. For example, the Tax Court rejected the theory in *Sundstrand Corp. v. CIR*, saying:

> SunPac [the taxpayer's foreign subsidiary] did not act as a subcontractor in form or substance. As petitioner's licensee, it owned the right to use the intangible property transferred to it under the SunPac License Agreement; it had the right to sell SunPac parts throughout the world to unrelated parties; it purchased its own materials (albeit through petitioner) and bore the inventory, production, and market risks with respect to its products; it scheduled its own production runs and was responsible for its own quality control; and it performed a variety of machining operations and processes. Because [the IRS'] determination, using the cost-plus method, was premised on SunPac acting as a subcontractor of petitioner, we conclude that this determination was arbitrary, capricious, and unreasonable.[130]

Under the regulations, the *Sundstrand* situation would apparently be analyzed as follows: Since the license to the foreign subsidiary and the subsidiary's activities were not lacking in economic substance, the transactions are analyzed as the taxpayers structured them, not by recharacterizing the subsidiary as a contract manufacturer. However, if functions performed and risks assumed by the subsidiary are similar to those of a contract manufacturer, the royalty rate under the license will be tested by comparing the subsidiary's profits, as reported, with those it would have had if it had acted as contract manufacturer.

¶79.3.9 Legal Restrictions

In 1972, the Supreme Court held in *CIR v. First Security Bank* that §482 does not allow the IRS to attribute income to a taxpayer that could not legally

---

[129] TD 8470, supra note 56, at 95.

[130] Sundstrand Corp. v. CIR, 96 TC 226, 357-58 (1991). See Bausch & Lomb, Inc. v. CIR, 933 F2d 1084 (2d Cir. 1991) (also rejecting contract manufacturer theory, except where related person's commitment to purchase output amounts to guarantee that insulates producer from market risk).

receive it.[131] The taxpayers in the case were federally chartered banks that offered credit life insurance to their borrowers. The insurance was issued by an independent insurer that paid no sales commissions, but 85 percent of the premiums on insurance issued to the banks' customers was paid over as reinsurance premiums to an insurance company owned by the banks' holding company. The Court held that §482 did not empower the IRS to allocate portions of the insurance affiliate's reinsurance income to the banks as sales commission income because federal banking statutes precluded the banks from receiving insurance sales commissions.

The IRS ruled in 1982 that the *First Security Bank* principle does not apply when the receipt of income is blocked by foreign law, rather than a law of the United States or one of the states.[132] However, the Tax Court and Court of Appeals for the Sixth Circuit decided in *Procter & Gamble Co. v. CIR* that the Supreme Court would recognize no such limitation on its holding.[133] The taxpayer in *Procter & Gamble* licensed various intangibles to its Swiss subsidiary, which was required to pay royalties to the taxpayer based on usage of the intangibles by all of its subsidiaries. The Swiss corporation sublicensed the intangibles to a wholly owned Spanish corporation, but the latter paid no royalties. The IRS allocated income from the Spanish corporation to the Swiss corporation to reflect the Spanish corporation's use of the intangibles. The Tax Court rejected the allocation because Spanish law forbad Spanish corporations from paying royalties to foreign shareholders. The situation, in the court's opinion, was indistinguishable from *First Security*, which the court read to hold that "section 482 simply does not apply where restrictions imposed by law, and not the actions of the controlling interest, serve to distort income among the controlled group."[134] The court found it irrelevant that the restriction on royalty payments was imposed by foreign law. "[T]he Supreme Court focused on whether the facts supported a finding that the controlling interest utilized its power to shift income."[135] The court also rejected the IRS' argument that *First Security*, which involved an attempt to allocate to the taxpayer a type of income (insurance commissions) that the taxpayer could not legally receive from any person, did not apply in *Procter & Gamble* because the Spanish subsidiary was only prevented

---

[131] CIR v. First Sec. Bank, 405 US 394 (1972). See Salyersville Nat'l Bank v. US, 613 F2d 650 (6th Cir. 1980) (*FirstSecurity* barred IRS from allocating insurance premium income from bank president to bank where president was licensed insurance agent but bank was not; although bank could have obtained insurance license, it had legitimate business reasons for not obtaining license). See generally Pratt, *First Security Bank of Utah* Revisited-Ramifications in the 1990s, 57 Tax Notes 247 (Oct. 12, 1992).

[132] Rev. Rul. 82-45, 1982-1 CB 89.

[133] Procter & Gamble Co. v. CIR, 95 TC 323 (1990), aff'd, 961 F2d 1255 (6th Cir. 1992). See Texaco, Inc. v. CIR, 98 F3d 825 (5th Cir. 1996) (same; where Saudi government fixed price at which crude oil purchase in Saudi Arabia could be resold, IRS could not reallocate income using different resale price).

[134] 95 TC at 336.

[135] Id. at 339.

from paying royalties to foreign shareholders and could have paid royalties to any other licensor.

The regulations, promulgated since the decision in *Procter & Gamble*, are intended to sharply limit the decision in that case. They state that "a foreign legal restriction" is taken into account in applying §482 only "to the extent that [it] affects the results of transactions at arm's length."[136] This requirement can be met by "show[ing] that the restriction affected an uncontrolled taxpayer under comparable circumstances for a comparable period of time." Assume domestic corporation P licenses a patent to a subsidiary organized in foreign country X, whose laws forbid country X corporations from paying royalties exceeding 5 percent of sales.[137] Even if the arm's length royalty for the license would normally be 10 percent of sales, a 5 percent royalty from the subsidiary to P is not adjusted under §482 if P provides evidence of a comparable uncontrolled transaction in which an uncontrolled licensor accepted a 5 percent royalty from a country X licensee.

In the absence of uncontrolled comparables, foreign legal restrictions affect §482 determinations only if all of the following requirements are met:

1. The restrictions are "publicly promulgated" and are "generally applicable to all similarly situated persons (both controlled and uncontrolled),"
2. They are "not imposed as part of a commercial transaction between the taxpayer and the foreign sovereign,"
3. The taxpayer or another member of its controlled group has "exhausted all remedies prescribed by foreign law or practice for obtaining a waiver of such restrictions," except remedies with "a negligible prospect of success,"
4. The restrictions "expressly prevented the payment or receipt, in any form, of part or all of [an] arm's length amount,"
5. The controlled taxpayers subject to the restrictions did not violate the restriction "in any material respect" or "engage in any arrangement" having "the effect of circumventing the restriction," and
6. A "deferred income method of accounting" is elected by the taxpayer whose U.S. tax liability is affected by the legal restriction.[138]

If these requirements are met, the foreign restriction is taken into account whether it is temporary or permanent.

The fourth of these requirements may often be the most difficult to meet. For example, a restriction on the deductibility of a payment under foreign tax law does not satisfy it if no law forbids the making of a nondeductible payment. Moreover, the requirement is that the parties must be barred from paying the arm's length amount "in any form." Assume domestic corporation P licenses a

---

[136] Reg. §1.482-1(h)(2)(i).
[137] Reg. §1.482-1(h)(2)(v) Ex. 4.
[138] Reg. §§1.482-1(h)(2)(ii),(iii).

patent to a subsidiary organized in foreign country X, whose laws forbid country X corporations from paying royalties to recipients outside the country but do not prevent country X corporations from paying dividends to foreign shareholders.[139] The fourth requirement is not met because the arm's length royalty for the license could be paid to P in the form of dividends.

The fifth requirement—that the parties not "engage in any arrangement" having "the effect of circumventing the restriction"—may also limit the usefulness of the rules. For example, if P's country X subsidiary is barred from paying an arm's length royalty to P in any form, even as a dividend, but the subsidiary arranges for an unrelated intermediary to pay this amount to P on the subsidiary's behalf, the foreign legal restriction is ignored in applying §482.[140]

Under the deferred income method of accounting, the arm's length amount whose payment or receipt is blocked by the foreign legal restriction is "treated as deferrable" until payment or receipt is no longer prevented.[141] An electing taxpayer must also defer deductions and credits "properly chargeable against" income deferred under the method, "including the cost or other basis of inventory and other assets sold or exchanged."[142] Otherwise, deferrable gross income equal to any such deductions already claimed "in open taxable years" may not be deferred. Although the regulations are not explicit on the point, the latter rule apparently requires a foreign legal restriction to be ignored in determining an arm's length royalty on a license to the extent of research and development expenditures attributable to the licensed intangible that were deducted by the taxpayer for years not yet barred by the statute of limitations.

An election of the deferred income method is effective only if it is made by the taxpayer whose U.S. tax liability may be affected by the election and this taxpayer establishes that the five requirements outlined above are met.[143]

¶79.4 LOANS OR ADVANCES

A §482 allocation may be made if a member of a controlled group makes a loan or advance to, or otherwise becomes a creditor of, another member of the group but does not charge interest at an arm's length rate.[1] For example, interest

---

[139] Reg. §1.482-1(h)(2)(v) Ex. 3.

[140] Reg. §1.482-1(h)(2)(v) Ex. 2.

[141] Reg. §1.482-1(h)(2)(iv).

[142] Reg. §1.482-1(h)(2)(iv).

[143] Reg. §1.482-1(h)(2)(iii). The election must be made by a statement attached to a timely filed return or amended return that is filed before the IRS first contacts any member of the controlled group about an audit of a return for the year affected by the legal restriction.

[1] Reg. §1.482-2(a)(1)(i). See Aristar, Inc. v. US, 553 F2d 644 (Ct. Cl. 1977) (distortion arose from taxpayer's charging of interest only on loans to profitable subsidiaries); Liberty Loan Corp. v. US, 498 F2d 225 (8th Cir. 1973), cert. denied, 419 US 1089 (1974)

at an arm's length rate may be imputed on accounts receivable arising from sales of goods, leases, and services between controlled taxpayers unless the receivables are promptly paid.[2] Although concerned primarily with inadequate interest charges, the regulation also authorizes a reduction of excessive charges.

1. *Period for which interest must accrue.* Generally, to avoid an adjustment under §482, an intercompany debt must bear interest at an arm's length rate beginning with the day after the indebtedness arises and continuing until the day the debt is satisfied "by payment, offset, cancellation, or otherwise."[3]

However, an "interest-free period" is allowed for "intercompany trade receivables," defined as indebtedness that arises in the ordinary course of business from sales, leases, or services between related persons and is not evidenced by a written instrument requiring the payment of interest.[4] Usually, an intercompany trade receivable need not bear interest until the beginning of the third calendar month following the month in which the receivable arises,[5] but the interest-free period is longer in three situations:

a. The period is extended until the beginning of the fourth month if the receivable arises in the ordinary course of a business actively conducted by the debtor outside the United States.[6]

b. The period may be extended even further if the creditor or unrelated companies in the same industry allow more time for payment without interest "as a regular trade practice" in dealing with unrelated persons in transactions "similar to" the intercompany transaction.[7]

c. Where the intercompany transaction is a sale of goods that the buyer resells to unrelated persons in a foreign country, a longer interest-free period (not exceeding 183 days) may be determined with reference to the average period the related buyer must wait to collect from its customers in that country.[8] The related buyer does not have to be actively engaged in business in a foreign country to be eligible to utilize this rule.

In determining the period that an intercompany indebtedness is outstanding, a payment or other credit is generally applied first against the indebtedness that

---

(same); Rev. Rul. 82-135, 1982-2 CB 104 (§482 applied to prepayments for merchandise purchased from parent). But see Pitchford's, Inc. v. CIR, 34 TCM (CCH) 384 (1975) (IRS concession that allocation is not required in absence of reasonable expectation of payment).

[2] Reg. §1.482-2(a)(1)(ii)(A).

[3] Reg. §1.482-2(a)(1)(iii)(A) (applicable for indebtedness arising after June 30, 1988).

[4] Reg. §1.482-2(a)(1)(iii)(A).

[5] Reg. §1.482-2(a)(1)(iii)(B). An intercompany trade receivable "arises" at the time of economic performance in the underlying transaction. Reg. §1.482-2(a)(iii)(A). For the term "economic performance," see §461(h), discussed infra ¶105.6.4.

[6] Reg. §1.482-2(a)(1)(iii)(C).

[7] Reg. §1.482-2(a)(1)(iii)(D).

[8] Reg. §1.482-2(a)(1)(iii)(E).

has been outstanding longest.[9] Assume corporation X incurs intercompany trade receivables to related corporation Y of $100 in May and $200 in June, and its only payments after the beginning of May are $60 on July 15 and $240 on August 31. The first payment is applied to the May receivables, and the second to the remainder of those receivables and the June receivables. If the receivables are subject to the general rule, interest accrues for one month on $40 of the May receivables because that amount remains unpaid at the beginning of the third calendar month after the receivables arise (August) but is paid at the end of that month. The June receivables bear no interest because they are fully paid before the beginning of the third succeeding month (September).

However, controlled taxpayers can, by agreement or understanding, deviate from this first-in-first-out rule if it is shown that one of these taxpayers "or others in its industry, as a regular trade practice," use similar procedures in similar transactions with unrelated persons.[10]

2. *Interest rate.* Generally, an indebtedness between controlled taxpayers is at arm's length only if it bears interest at the rate that would be charged, "at the time the indebtedness arose, in independent transactions with or between unrelated parties under similar circumstances."[11] "All relevant factors" are considered in determining this rate, "including the principal amount and duration of the loan, the security involved, the credit standing of the borrower, and the interest rate prevailing at the situs of the lender or creditor for comparable loans between unrelated parties." If the lender is in the business of making loans to unrelated persons, the principal factor is the rate charged on loans "of a similar type" made to unrelated persons in the course of this business "at and about the time of" the intercompany loan or advance.[12]

This general rule is modified by two special rules. First, a safe harbor rule applies to an intercompany loan or advance denominated in U.S. dollars if the creditor is not regularly engaged in the business of making loans to unrelated persons.[13] When the safe harbor applies, arm's length interest is determined as follows:

a. Stated interest is considered to be at arm's length if it is at a rate not less than the "applicable Federal rate" (AFR) and not greater than 130 percent of the AFR. The AFR is redetermined monthly, based on the

---

[9] Reg. §1.482-2(a)(1)(iv)(A).

[10] Reg. §1.482-2(a)(1)(iv)(B).

[11] Reg. §1.482-2(a)(2)(i).

[12] Reg. §1.482-2(a)(2)(iii)(D).

[13] Reg. §1.482-2(a)(2)(iii). The rules described in the text apply to term loans made after May 8, 1986 and to demand loans, whenever made, for periods after that date. Reg. §1.482-2(a)(2)(iii)(A). For term loans made before May 9, 1986, the safe harbor encompasses rates between 11 and 13 percent simple interest, but if the actual rate is outside these limits (or if no interest is charged), an allocation is made at the rate of 12 percent unless the taxpayer established a different arm's length rate. Reg. §1.482-2(a)(2)(iii) (before amendment in 1988).

average interest rate on obligations of the federal government with similar maturity dates.[14]

b. If the loan or advance is interest-free or bears interest at a rate less than the AFR, the arm's length rate is usually the AFR.

c. If the stated interest rate exceeds 130 percent of the AFR, the arm's length rate is usually 130 percent of the AFR.

d. However, when the stated interest rate falls outside the 100–130 percent range, the taxpayer is allowed an opportunity to justify the stated rate under the general arm's length standard. It is unlikely that many borrowers can show an ability to borrow more cheaply than the federal government (whose borrowing experience establishes the AFR), but establishing an arm's length rate exceeding 130 percent may be a less daunting task.

Second, where a taxpayer borrows money from an unrelated person and reloans it to a related organization, trade, or business, the arm's length rate on the intercompany loan usually equals the rate on the loan from the unrelated person if the latter loan was obtained "at the situs of the borrower" on the intercompany loan.[15] Assume a domestic corporation borrows money from a bank in country X and reloans the funds to a subsidiary whose principal business is in country X. The loan from parent to subsidiary probably must generally bear interest at the same rate as the parent's loan from the bank. However, the interest rate on the intercompany loan may be marked up to cover costs other than interest incurred in borrowing from the unrelated person and reloaning the funds in the intercompany loan. Also, an entirely different rate may be used if it is shown to be "more appropriate" under the general arm's length standard. That the borrower in the intercompany loan is a less worthy credit risk than its lender should justify a different rate, but the right to use a different rate can be established only if divergences in credit worthiness are quantified.

3. *Bona fide indebtedness.* The interest rules apply only to "bona fide indebtedness."[16] They do not apply, for example, to a purported loan by shareholder to corporation that is in substance a contribution to capital or to a purported loan from corporation to shareholder that is properly characterized as a dividend. Explicit interest on such a loan is usually characterized as a series of

---

[14] IRC §1274(d), discussed supra ¶57.2. The AFR in effect when the loan or advance is made generally governs throughout loan's term, but the safe harbor rate for a demand loan fluctuates monthly. Reg. §1.482-2(a)(2)(iii)(C). Also, if the indebtedness arises in a sale or exchange between controlled taxpayers, the lower limit is the lowest of the AFRs in effect for the calendar month during which a binding contract for the sale or exchange is made and the two preceding months.

[15] Reg. §1.482-2(a)(2)(ii).

[16] Reg. §1.482-2(a)(1)(ii)(B). See Altama Delta Corp. v. CIR, 104 TC 424 (1995) (where parent corporation sold goods to subsidiary for price exceeding arm's length price, excess is essentially loan from parent to subsidiary on which interest may be imputed under §482).

distributions to the shareholder if the purported loan is a capital contribution or as capital contributions if the purported loan is a distribution. No additional interest is imputed if the purported loan is interest free or bears interest at a rate below the arm's length rate. Similarly, if a purported credit sale of property between controlled taxpayers is actually a lease, interest and principal payments on the indebtedness are recharacterized as rent.

4. *Relationship with other interest imputation rules.* Indebtedness between controlled taxpayers may be subject to interest imputation rules in addition to those of §482. For example, portions of the deferred payments under an installment sale of property may be characterized by §1274 or §483 as original issue discount (OID) or unstated interest unless the installment obligation bears interest at a rate at least equal to the AFR.[17] Also, when a loan between shareholder and corporation is interest free or bears interest at a rate below the AFR, interest is imputed at the AFR under §7872.[18] Section 482 is coordinated with these other interest imputation rules by the following steps:[19]

a. Scrutinize the transaction to determine whether the purported indebtedness is bona fide.

b. If there is bona fide indebtedness, apply §§483, 1274, and 7872 to determine the interest on the indebtedness (including OID and unstated interest) apart from §482.

c. If interest on the debt, as adjusted by §§483, 1274, or 7872, is not at an arm's length rate, adjust interest further under §482.

d. Test the principal amount remaining after these steps under the other rules of the §482 regulations (e.g., the rules for sales of property).

To illustrate rule *a*, assume an individual loans $20,000 to her wholly owned corporation, but an examination of the facts reveals that the $20,000 is in substance a capital contribution.[20] Because there is no bona fide indebtedness, none of the interest rules, including §482, applies. If the note bears interest, interest payments are treated as distributions, taxable as dividends to the extent of earnings and profits.

To illustrate rules *b* and *c*, assume a corporation, although not engaged in the business of lending money, loans $15,000 to a shareholder-employee for five years. The loan bears interest at the rate of 8 percent payable semiannually, but the AFR is 10 percent compounded semiannually.[21] Under §7872(b), the loan proceeds are deemed to include additional employee compensation to the borrower of $1,158, computed as the excess of the amount loaned ($15,000) over the present value of the payments under the note discounted at the AFR ($13,842).

---

[17] For §§483 and 1274, see supra ¶57.1.

[18] For §7872, see supra ¶58.1.

[19] Reg. §1.482-2(a)(3).

[20] Reg. §1.482-2(a)(4) Ex. 1.

[21] See Reg. §1.482-2(a)(4) Ex. 2.

The principal amount of the shareholder-employee's note is deemed to be $13,842, and the remaining $1,158 payable at maturity is OID. Because the yield equals the AFR, the loan falls within the §482 safe harbor, and no additional interest is imputed under §482. In contrast, if the amount loaned is only $9,000, §7872 may be inapplicable because of a de minimis exception applicable when the outstanding balance of loans between lender and borrower do not exceed $10,000.[22] However, in the latter case, interest is imputed under §482 if the corporation and the shareholder-employee are commonly controlled trades or businesses and all other requisites for the application of §482 are present.[23]

To illustrate the application of the foregoing rules to sales of property, assume X Corp. sells property to Y Corp., all of whose stock is owned by X's sole shareholder. The selling price is $2 million and is paid by X's five-year, level-payment note requiring semiannual payments. If the AFR is 12 percent and the note bears interest at the rate of 18 percent, neither §483 nor §1274 applies because the interest rate on the note exceeds the AFR.[24] However, the note is not within the §482 safe harbor because the interest rate (18 percent) exceeds 130 percent of the AFR (130 percent of 12 percent is 15.6 percent). If the IRS chooses to apply §482 in this case and the taxpayers fail to justify 18 percent as an arm's length interest rate, the selling price for the property is apparently deemed to be $2,110,127—the present value of the payments under the note discounted at 130 percent of the AFR. If $2,110,127 is not an arm's length price for the property, further adjustments are made under the §482 rules for sales of property.

Alternatively, assume the interest rate on X's note is 9 percent.[25] For notes in the principal amount of $2.8 million or less, §1274A(a) provides that the discount rate used in applying §483 or §1274 may not exceed 9 percent.[26] Additional interest thus is not imputed to X's note under §483 or §1274. However, the note falls outside the range of the §482 safe harbor. If the parties cannot show that 9 percent is an arm's length rate for this transaction, additional interest is imputed under §482 to bring the sum of stated and imputed interest up to the AFR of 12 percent. Section 482 is apparently applied in this case by leaving the stated purchase price of $2 million undisturbed and treating the parties as though the interest imputed under §482 was paid in addition to the actual payments under the note.

¶79.5 PERFORMANCE OF SERVICES

1. *Services for which arm's length charge is required.* A §482 allocation may be made if one member of a controlled group performs marketing, managerial,

---

[22] IRC §7872(c)(3), discussed supra ¶58.2.4 text accompanying notes 85–89 and 104.
[23] Reg. §1.482-2(a)(4) Ex. 3.
[24] See Reg. §1.482-2(a)(4) Ex. 4.
[25] See Reg. §1.482-2(a)(4) Ex. 5.
[26] See supra ¶57.3.2 text accompanying notes 11–24.

administrative, technical, or other services for another member, either without charge or for compensation not equal to an arm's length charge.[1] An allocation may be required whether the services are performed for the joint benefit of all members of the group or are performed by one member for the exclusive benefit of one other member.[2] Assume P Corp. undertakes sales promotion activities, some of which jointly benefit P and its subsidiary S and some of which are undertaken solely to promote S's products.[3] Unless P charges S an arm's length fee for the benefits to S from both categories of these activities, additional income to P and additional expense to S may be imputed under §482 as a charge for the benefits. The charge for the activities undertaken for the joint benefit of P and S must be "consistent with the relative benefits" of these activities.

The application of §482 to intercompany services is based on the benefits expected when the services are performed, and the allocation may not be defeated by showing that the expected benefits were not realized.[4] Generally, an arm's length charge is required if a service performed by a member of a controlled group relates "to the carrying on of an activity by another member or was intended to benefit another member, either in the member's overall operations or in its day-to-day activities." However, no charge is appropriate if the "probable" benefits to the other member are "so indirect or remote" that an unrelated person performing the services would not have been able to charge for them.

Assume X Corp. operates an international airline, and Y Corp., whose sole shareholder also owns all of X's stock, operates hotels in several cities served by the airline. X extensively advertises its services in newspapers and magazines. If X's advertisements picture Y's hotels and mention Y by name, an allocation may be made, even though the primary purpose of the advertisements is to promote X's airline services, because, if X and Y were unrelated, X would not mention Y in its advertisements without compensation.[5] On the other hand, if Y and its hotels are neither mentioned nor pictured in X's advertisements, no allocation is warranted because any benefit to Y from increased air traffic resulting from X's advertisements is so indirect that X could not charge Y for this benefit if X and Y were unrelated.[6]

---

[1] Reg. §1.482-2(b)(1). See United States Steel Corp. v. CIR, 617 F2d 942 (2d Cir. 1980) (no §482 allocation where taxpayer's shipping subsidiary charged taxpayer same rates it charged unrelated persons for same services); Bell v. CIR, 45 TCM (CCH) 97 (1982) (income reallocated to professional corporation, determined by comparison of prices charged unrelated persons by similar service corporations in community). See generally Mosteller, Comparability in the *U.S. Steel* Transfer Pricing Case, 55 Tax Notes 1251 (June 1, 1992). See also Chip & Safranek, The Brave New World of Insurance Transfer Pricing, 16 Tax Notes Int'l 1455 (May 4, 1998).

[2] Reg. §1.482-2(b)(2)(i).

[3] Reg. §1.482-2(b)(2)(i) Ex. 1.

[4] Reg. §1.482-2(b)(2)(i).

[5] Reg. §1.482-2(b)(2)(i) Ex. 2.

[6] Reg. §1.482-2(b)(2)(i) Ex. 3.

Also, no §482 allocation is made if a service performed by one member of the group "is merely a duplication" of an activity another member performs for itself.[7] Assume S Corp. has a staff of financial analysts who make an analysis of S's borrowing needs and conclude that S should obtain a $1 million loan from a particular bank. This recommendation is forwarded to S's parent P Corp., whose financial analysts review S's analysis to determine whether P should acquiesce in S's plans.[8] No charge for P's review may be imputed under §482 because the review duplicates S's analysis and is undertaken by P as part of its activities of overseeing its investment in S, not for the purpose of benefiting S. On the other hand, if S does not have personnel who can make an analysis of its borrowing needs, and financial analysts in P's employ make such an analysis, an arm's length charge must be made for this service since it is intended to benefit S and does not duplicate activities performed by S for itself.[9]

Moreover, if intercompany services are "merely ancillary and subsidiary" to an intercompany lease, license, or sale, the transaction is subject only to the rules for leases, licenses, or sales, and no separate allocation is made under the services rule.[10] Such ancillary and subsidiary services may include demonstrations and explanations of the use of the property, startup services, and work done under a guarantee given in connection with a startup. Similarly, if, in connection with the licensing of a secret process to a related entity, an employee of the licensor supervises the integration of the process into the licensee's manufacturing operations, these services are subsidiary to the license.

2. *Determining arm's length charge.* When a §482 allocation is made to reflect intercompany services, the allocation, which consists of additional income to the services performer and additional expense for the recipient of the services, generally equals the amount that would have been charged for the services if the two businesses were unrelated and dealing at arm's length.[11] However, if the services are not "an integral part of the business activity" of either the performer or the recipient of the services, this arm's length charge is deemed equal to the costs incurred in performing the services unless the taxpayer establishes a true arm's length price for the services. In these cases, in other words, a realistic sharing of costs may be substituted for the usual arm's length methodology. The underlying rationale seems to be that an enterprise's profits come primarily from its business activities and that cost sharing, without provision for profit, is not inappropriate for activities undertaken out of the regular course of business for the purpose of supporting the businesses of affiliates.

---

[7] Reg. §1.482-2(b)(2)(ii).

[8] Reg. §1.482-2(b)(2)(ii) Ex. 2.

[9] Reg. §1.482-2(b)(2)(ii) Ex. 1.

[10] Reg. §1.482-2(b)(8).

[11] Reg. §1.482-2(b)(3). See InverWorld, Inc. v. CIR, 73 TCM (CCH) 2777 (1997) (arm's length fee for services for parent corporation found to be fee charged unrelated clients for equivalent services); Yamaha Motor Corp. v. CIR, 63 TCM (CCH) 2176 (1992).

a. *Cost sharing.* When cost sharing is used, all costs that are "directly or indirectly related to the service performed" must be accounted for "on some reasonable basis."[12] Direct costs are "those identified specifically with a particular service,"[13] and indirect costs consist of other costs that "relate" to the direct costs.[14] Direct costs include compensation and travel expenses of employees and independent contractors performing the service and materials and supplies "directly consumed." Indirect costs include overhead of the department incurring the direct costs and an appropriate share of general and administrative costs, including the costs of supporting departments. However, the direct and indirect costs of a service do not include (1) interest expense unless incurred on borrowings "specifically for the benefit" of the recipient of the services, (2) expenses of stock issuance and shareholder relations, and (3) costs incurred in complying with government regulations that are imposed by the jurisdiction in which the services performer operates and are not "directly related to the service."[15]

Cost sharing may not be used unless the taxpayers maintain records from which the IRS can verify the application of these rules.[16] However, the IRS accepts a taxpayer's allocations of costs if the allocations are done by consistent methods and are "reasonable and in keeping with sound accounting practice."[17] A reasonable and sound accounting practice should reflect "all bases and factors," and must allocate the "full cost," not the "incremental cost."[18] For example, if the taxpayer leases a computer for use in an activity jointly benefiting the taxpayer and other members of its controlled group, rents and other costs of operating the computer must be allocated between the taxpayer and the other members, "even if the additional use of the machine for the benefit of the other members did not increase the cost to the taxpayer."

The taxpayer's allocations have added weight if they are also used in preparing statements or analyses for management, shareholders, creditors, or other outsiders.[19] Also, the IRS is more likely to defer to the taxpayer's allocations between domestic and foreign members of the group if the same methods are used in allocating costs among domestic members of the group.

b. *Cost sharing not allowed.* Cost sharing cannot be used in lieu of actual arm's length prices for intercompany services that are "an integral part of the business activity" of the entity performing or receiving the services.[20] The regulations identify four situations where services are considered an integral part of an entity's activities.

---

[12] Reg. §1.482-2(b)(4)(i).
[13] Reg. §1.482-2(b)(4)(ii).
[14] Reg. §1.482-2(b)(4)(iii).
[15] Reg. §1.482-2(b)(5).
[16] Reg. §1.482-2(b)(3).
[17] Reg. §1.482-2(b)(6)(i).
[18] Reg. §1.482-2(b)(6)(ii).
[19] Reg. §1.482-2(b)(6)(iii).
[20] Reg. §1.482-2(b)(7).

First, services are integral to the business of the performer or recipient of the services if it is "engaged in the trade or business of rendering similar services" to unrelated persons.[21] Assume *X* Corp., whose business is printing and mailing advertising material for unrelated persons, prepares and mails brochures advertising products of *Y* Corp., a manufacturing enterprise wholly owned by *X*'s sole shareholder.[22] The charge to *Y* for this service must be an actual arm's length price, not a price based on cost sharing, because the service is similar to services performed by *X* for unrelated persons in the ordinary course of its business. This rule applies even if *X*, which designs as well as prints and mails the brochure for *Y*, does not do designing on other printing and mailing projects.

Second, services are an integral part of the activities of the entity performing the services if the performance of services for related persons is "one of [the entity's] principal activities."[23] Whether such services are a principal activity usually depends on the facts and circumstances, including the time spent on performing the services, the regularity with which the services are performed, the capital invested in the services activity, and the risk of loss.[24] However, for services other than manufacturing, production, extraction, or construction, the performance of services for related persons is presumed not to be a principal activity if the costs incurred in performing the services are less than 25 percent of the entity's total costs for the taxable year.[25] In applying the 25 percent test, all entities organized under the laws of a particular country may, at the taxpayer's election, be treated as a single services performer if their income tax liability in that country is determined on a consolidated basis.[26] For example, if a domestic corporation and its domestic subsidiaries file consolidated returns for U.S. tax purposes, they may be treated as one entity in applying the 25 percent test to services performed by domestic members of the group for foreign subsidiaries.[27]

Third, services to a related person are integral if the entity performing the services is "peculiarly capable of rendering the services" and the services are a "principal element" of the recipient's operations.[28] The performer of the services is "peculiarly capable" if the value of the services "substantially" exceeds cost and the performer "makes use of a particularly advantageous situation or cir-

---

[21] Reg. §1.482-2(b)(7)(i).

[22] Reg. §1.482-2(b)(7)(v) Ex. 1.

[23] Reg. §1.482-2(b)(7)(ii)(A).

[24] See Reg. §1.482-2(b)(7)(v) Exs. 3, 7.

[25] See Reg. §1.482-2(b)(7)(ii)(B) (all direct and indirect costs of performing services for related persons, including costs of manufacturing, production, extraction, or construction activities, count as costs of services for related persons; total costs do not include inventory costs). For an illustration, see Reg. §1.482-2(b)(7)(v) Ex. 2. For the exclusion of manufacturing, production, extraction, and construction activities, see Reg. §1.482-2(b)(7)(v) Exs. 6, 8, 9.

[26] Reg. §1.482-2(b)(7)(ii)(C).

[27] See Reg. §1.482-2(b)(7)(v) Ex. 4.

[28] Reg. §1.482-2(b)(7)(iii).

cumstance such as by utilization of special skills and reputation, . . . an influential relationship with customers, or . . . its intangible property." Assume X Corp. is a finance company whose principal business is making automobile loans, and its sister corporation, Y, is an insurance agency that issues credit life insurance.[29] Although borrowers from X are not required to buy credit life insurance, X's employee's regularly suggest that such insurance be purchased from Y, and many customers follow this suggestion because obtaining insurance from other companies often delays the processing of the loan. The charge for X's services for Y must be an actual arm's length charge because the value of the services substantially exceeds cost and X utilizes an influential relationship with customers in performing the service.[30]

Fourth, services received from related persons are integral to the recipient's business if "a substantial amount" of these services is received during the taxable year.[31] The services are considered substantial if the costs allocated to the recipient under the cost sharing rule (excluding materials costs properly reflected in the recipient's inventory) would exceed 25 percent of its total costs. If the taxpayer establishes that total costs for the taxable year are abnormally low (e.g., because of the commencement or termination of an operation), the 25 percent test may be applied over a three-year period ending with the taxable year or, if later, the period consisting of the recipient's first three years.

¶79.6 USE OF TANGIBLE PROPERTY

If a member of a controlled group is allowed to use or occupy tangible property owned or leased by another member of the group without charge or for a charge not equal to an arm's length rental, a §482 allocation is required at an arm's length rate.[1] Generally, this arm's length rental is determined in light of all

---

[29] Reg. §1.482-2(b)(7) Ex. 10.

[30] For other illustrations, see Reg. §1.482-2(b)(7)(v) Exs. 11-13 (use of patented process in checking quality of related entity's products), Ex. 14 (manufacturing company not "peculiarly capable" in providing accounting services for related firm).

[31] Reg. §1.482-2(b)(7)(iv). See Reg. §1.482-2(b)(7)(v) Exs. 15, 16.

[1] Reg. §1.482-2(c)(1). See Central Bank of the South v. US, 834 F2d 990, 993 (11th Cir. 1987) (income allocated from lessee to related lessor equal to rents required by lease but not actually paid; taxpayer failed to show that uncontrolled lessor would not have insisted on payment; arm's length standard applies to "terms and conditions of payment as well as the monetary amount [of] the rental"); Procacci v. CIR, 94 TC 397 (1990) (arm's length rental for golf course was zero because operating expenses exceeded revenues; "any reasonably knowledgeable lessee would have realized that operating the golf course would have entailed substantial losses for a number of years [and] would [not] have agreed to pay any rent until after it had recouped its losses"); Cooper v. CIR, 64 TC 576 (1975); Bluefeld Caterer, Inc. v. CIR, 28 TCM (CCH) 315 (1969).

For leases made before May 9, 1986, if neither the owner nor the user was engaged in the business of renting property, the arm's length rent was deemed equal to (1) the sum

relevant factors, including "the period and location of the use, the owner's investment in the property or rent paid for the property, expenses of maintaining the property, the type of property involved, [and] its condition."[2]

Where one member of the group leases property from an unrelated person and subleases it to another member of the group, the arm's length rental under the sublease is deemed equal to the sum of the rents paid by the lessee-sublessor and any other expenses of the lessee-sublessor directly or indirectly "connected with the property," including maintenance, repair, utility, and management costs.[3] However, the taxpayer is given the opportunity to show that the arm's length rental for the sublease differs from the rents and expenses under the head lease. Also, the sublease rule does not apply if either sublessor or sublessee is regularly engaged in renting property of the same general type to unrelated persons.

¶79.7 SALES OF GOODS AND OTHER TRANSFERS OF TANGIBLE PROPERTY

¶79.7.1 Introductory

The regulations usually require a controlled sale of goods or other transfer of tangible property to be tested under §482 by one of five methods—the comparable uncontrolled price (CUP) method, the resale price method, the cost plus method, the comparable profits method, or the profit split method.[1] Under the CUP, resale price, and cost plus methods, which are described in this section, arm's length results are extracted from the prices charged by comparable uncontrolled sellers for comparable goods or from the gross profit margins of comparable uncontrolled buyer/resellers (under the resale price method) or comparable producers (under the cost plus method). The comparable profits and profit split methods, which may be applied for transfers of intangible property as well as for sales of goods, are described later in this chapter.[2] A method other than one of the five methods described in the regulations may be used for sales of goods if this method can be shown to be the best method under the circumstances.[3]

---

of depreciation, expenses, and a 3 percent return if the transferred property was owned by the transferor or (2) the deductions claimed by the transferor if it was a lessee rather than an owner. Reg. §1.482-2(c)(ii) (before amendment in 1988); Reg.§1.482-2(c)(2)(ii).

[2] Reg. §1.482-2(c)(2)(i). See Peck v. CIR, 904 F2d 525 (9th Cir. 1990) (for lease with fixed rental, arm's length rent is determined as of date lease is made).

[3] Reg. §1.482-2(c)(2)(iii).

[1] Reg. §1.482-3(a). See Levey, U.S. Distribution Companies Can Present Difficult Transfer Pricing Issues, 8 J. Int'l Tax'n 540 (1997).

[2] Infra ¶79.9 (comparable profits method), ¶79.10 (profit split method).

[3] Reg. §1.482-3(e), discussed infra ¶79.7.5.

Section 1059A, added in 1986, places an additional restriction on transfer prices for goods by stating that if "property is imported into the United States in a transaction (directly or indirectly) between related persons (within the meaning of section 482)," the transfer price used for income tax purposes cannot exceed the value at which the goods are declared for customs purposes.[4] According to the staff of the Joint Committee on Taxation:

> Congress understood that some importers could claim a transfer price for income tax purposes that was higher than would be consistent with the transfer price claimed for customs purposes. . . . Congress was particularly concerned that such practices between commonly controlled entities could improperly avoid U.S. tax or customs duties . . . . Congress was concerned only with establishing a limit on the price an importer could claim for income tax purposes. . . . [C]ustoms value (as appropriately adjusted) [thus] provides a ceiling on transfer price valuation for income tax purposes, [but] it does not provide a floor on that valuation.[5]

If intellectual property is used in producing or selling goods, the value added by this "embedded intangible" must be taken into account under all of the methods in evaluating the comparability of the taxpayer's transactions with those of uncontrolled taxpayers.[6] For example, because product comparability is very important under the CUP method, "trademarked" goods usually are not sufficiently comparable to "unbranded" goods to allow sales of unbranded goods to serve as uncontrolled comparables in applying the CUP method to controlled sales of trademarked goods.[7]

A sale of goods produced or sold with an embedded intangible is not treated as including a transfer of the intangible unless the controlled purchaser acquires "rights to exploit the intangible property" that go beyond "rights relating to the resale of the tangible property under normal commercial practices.[8] If the purchaser acquires no rights beyond those required for resale, the sale is tested solely under the rules for sales of goods. If the purchaser acquires rights to the intellectual property in addition to those necessary for resale, an arm's length con-

---

[4] See generally Reg. §1.1059A-1; Cody, Interaction of Customs and IRS Values: Recent Developments in Section 1059A, 20 J. Corp. Tax'n 394 (1993); Mavridis, Determining Income Tax Cost for Property Imported From Related Parties, 81 J. Tax'n 168 (1994); Singer & Linet, How Customs Valuations of Imported Goods Affect Related-Party Transactions, 67 J. Tax'n 346 (1987). See Brittingham v. CIR, 66 TC 373 (1976), aff'd, 598 F2d 1375 (5th Cir. 1979) (under prior law, taxpayer not bound by its customs declaration if declaration was shown to be erroneous).

[5] Staff of Joint Comm. on Tax'n, 99th Cong., 2d Sess., General Explanation of the Tax Reform Act of 1986 at 1062 (Comm. Print 1987).

[6] Reg. §1.482-3(f).

[7] See Reg. §1.482-8 Ex. 3 (rejecting CUP method, and instead applying resale price method, where goods in controlled and uncontrolled transactions were sold under different trade names).

[8] Id.

sideration may have to be determined separately for the sale of goods and the transfer of intangible rights, and the latter amount is governed by the rules for intangible property.[9] For example, if the sale of a machine "conveys the right to exploit a manufacturing process incorporated in the machine," an arm's length consideration for that right must be separately determined under the intangible property rules.

¶79.7.2   Comparable Uncontrolled Price (CUP) Method

Under the CUP method, the arm's length price of tangible property sold in a controlled transaction equals the price paid in a comparable uncontrolled transaction.[10] For example, if a foreign manufacturer sells a product to unrelated distributors in the United States for $100 per unit, but also has a U.S. subsidiary that distributes the product in competition with the unrelated distributors, the arm's length price under the CUP method for each item sold by the manufacturer to the U.S. subsidiary is $100.[11]

Under the best method rule, the CUP method is used only if it is determined to be the most reliable measure of arm's length results.[12] Whether a method is the most reliable measure depends primarily on the degree of comparability between the controlled and uncontrolled transactions and the quality of the data and assumptions underlying the method's application.[13] The CUP method is generally the best method if there are no differences between the controlled and uncontrolled transactions that would affect price or there are only "minor differences that have a definite and reasonably ascertainable effect on price and for which appropriate adjustments are made."[14] Assume P, a foreign manufacturer of toaster ovens, distributes the ovens in the United States through its subsidiary S, but it sells identical ovens to independent distributors in other countries in transactions not materially different from P's sales to S.[15] Because the products sold in the controlled and uncontrolled transactions are identical and the transactions do not differ materially, the CUP method is the best method.

The reliability of the method is diminished by any differences that are not minor and by minor differences for which reliable adjustments cannot be made, but in these circumstances, the method may still be the best method, depending on the reliability of other methods.[16] However, "material product differences for which reliable adjustments cannot be made" usually preclude the CUP method

---

[9] For the intangible property rules, see Reg. §1.482-4, discussed infra ¶79.8.
[10] Reg. §1.482-3(b)(1).
[11] See Reg. §1.482-3(b)(4) Ex. 1.
[12] Reg. §1.482-3(b)(2)(i).
[13] Reg. §1.482-1(c), discussed supra ¶79.3.3.
[14] Reg. §1.482-3(b)(2)(ii)(A).
[15] Reg. §1.482-8 Ex. 1.
[16] Reg. §1.482-3(b)(2)(ii)(A).

from providing a reliable measure. In the example, assume the toaster ovens that P sells to unrelated distributors in other countries are "of substantially higher quality" than those sold to S, but in addition to the toaster ovens purchased from P, S sells blenders purchased from unrelated suppliers.[17] Because of the product differences, the retail price method, applied using S's gross margin in the blender sales, may be a better method than the CUP method.

The comparability of controlled and uncontrolled transactions is determined under the comparability rules described elsewhere,[18] but the regulations elaborate on the application of these rules in this context. Generally, the most important comparability factor under the CUP method is "similarity of products."[19] For example, if a manufacturer sells a particular product to both controlled and uncontrolled distributors, the prices charged the uncontrolled distributor are probably the most reliable measure of arm's length prices for sales to the controlled distributors.[20] Even in the absence of identity of product, the CUP method may be the best method if the goods sold in controlled and uncontrolled transactions differ only in relatively minor ways for which price adjustments can reliably be made.[21] The CUP method is usually not the best method "if there are material product differences for which reliable adjustments cannot be made."[22]

Also, "because even minor differences in contractual terms or economic conditions could materially affect the amount charged in an uncontrolled transaction," either "close similarity" in these terms and conditions or adjustments to account for them are normally required.[23] The relevant contractual terms include the "scope and terms of warranties provided, sales or purchase volume, credit terms, [and] transport terms."[24] For example, if a manufacturer sells a particular product both to its distributing subsidiaries and to unrelated distributors, but the prices in the sales to the subsidiaries include delivery, whereas the sales to unrelated distributors are made F.O.B. the manufacturer's factory, adjustments must be made for the differing terms on transportation and insurance in transit.[25] However, because the transactions involve the same product and reliable adjustments can easily be made for transportation and insurance costs, the CUP method, applied using the sales to unrelated distributors as comparables, is likely to be the best method in this situation.

Relevant economic conditions include whether the transactions are at retail, wholesale, or some other level of the market, the "geographic" markets of the

---

[17] Reg. §1.482-8 Ex. 2.

[18] Reg. §1.482-1(d), discussed supra ¶79.3.4.

[19] Reg. §1.482-3(b)(2)(ii)(A).

[20] Reg. §1.482-3(b)(4) Ex. 1.

[21] Reg. §1.482-3(b)(4) Ex. 3.

[22] TD 8552, 1994-2 CB 93, 105.

[23] Reg. §1.482-3(b)(2)(ii)(A).

[24] Reg. §1.482-3(b)(2)(ii)(B)(2).

[25] Reg. §1.482-3(b)(4) Ex. 1.

transactions, when the transactions occur, and currency risks.[26] The regulations also require consideration of "alternatives realistically available to the buyer and seller."[27] As an illustration of the role of geographic markets, assume a foreign manufacturer distributes a particular product in the western portions of the United States through a U.S. subsidiary and in the remainder of the country through independent distributors.[28] The controlled and uncontrolled sales are comparable if the differences in geographic market either have no material effect on price or affect price in ways for which reliable adjustments can be made.

An especially important economic factor is whether "intangible property [is] associated with the sale."[29] For example, if a manufacturer distributes a particular product through both independent distributors and its own subsidiaries, attaching its valuable trademark to the goods sold to the subsidiaries but not to those sold to independent distributors, the sales to independent distributors are not likely to be comparable to the sales to the subsidiaries because the trademark's effect on price probably cannot be "reliably estimated."[30]

The CUP method is usually applied using data on particular transactions of particular uncontrolled taxpayers, but data from "public exchanges or quotation media" can sometimes be used instead.[31] For example, a domestic corporation purchasing crude oil from a foreign subsidiary might fix the price at the average of the prices for the same grade of oil published in a particular quotation medium for the five days preceding the date on which the subsidiary is to make delivery of the oil.[32] However, exchange or other publicly quoted prices may be used only if the following requirements are met:

1. "The data is widely and routinely used in the ordinary course of business in the industry to negotiate prices for uncontrolled sales,"
2. The data is used in setting prices in the controlled transactions in the same way it is used in the industry in transactions between unrelated persons, and
3. The price in the controlled transactions appropriately reflects "differences in product quality and quantity, contractual terms, transportation

---

[26] Reg. §§1.482-3(b)(2)(ii)(B)(3), (4), (5), (7).

[27] Reg. §1.482-3(b)(2)(ii)(B)(8).

[28] Reg. §1.482-3(b)(4) Ex. 4.

[29] Reg. §1.482-3(b)(2)(ii)(B)(6).

[30] Reg. §1.482-3(b)(4) Ex. 2. See Reg. §1.482-8 Ex. 3 (rejecting CUP method, and instead applying resale price method, where goods in controlled and uncontrolled transactions were sold under different trade names).

[31] Reg. §1.482-3(b)(5)(i). "Since these quoted prices are not themselves transactional prices, but may be averages based upon actual transactions, they do not qualify [for use under] the CUP method as that method is otherwise described in the regulations." TD 8552, supra note 22, at 105.

[32] Reg. §1.482-3(b)(5)(iii) Ex. 1.

costs, market conditions, risks borne, and other factors that affect the price that would be agreed to by uncontrolled taxpayers."[33]

Even if these requirements are satisfied, prices from public exchanges or quotation media "may not be appropriate under extraordinary market conditions."[34] In the example, the quoted prices for oil may not be a reliable basis for pricing the sale from subsidiary to parent if, shortly before arrangements are made for the sale, war breaks out in an oil-producing area, causing great instability in world oil prices.[35]

In many instances, the CUP method is applied using two or more uncontrolled comparables of equal reliability, in which case the comparables establish an arm's length range under rules described elsewhere.[36]

¶79.7.3 Resale Price Method

Under the resale price method, the arm's length price for a sale between controlled taxpayers is the price at which the goods are resold by the buyer to unrelated persons, less a gross profit comparable to that earned by a comparable uncontrolled distributor in comparable circumstances.[37] Assume a foreign manufacturing company sells goods to its U.S. subsidiary, which resells them to customers in the United States for $100 each.[38] If the comparable uncontrolled gross margin for the subsidiary's sales is 20 percent of sales, the arm's length price under the resale price method for the parent's sale to the subsidiary is $80—the subsidiary's resale price of $100, less 20 percent thereof.

The computations may be a bit more complex if the distributor purchases goods from both controlled and uncontrolled suppliers. Assume S, a U.S. subsidiary of foreign corporation P, has sales revenues of $1,000, and it reports a cost of goods sold of $800, consisting $600 for goods purchased from P and $200 for goods purchased from unrelated persons.[39] If the comparable uncontrolled gross margin is 25 percent, S's gross income is $250—25 percent of its sales revenues of $1,000. The gross income is subtracted from S's sales revenues, yielding a total cost of goods sold of $750, and from the latter amount is subtracted the $200 cost of goods purchased from unrelated persons. The remainder—$550—is the arm's length price for the goods purchased from P. Because the price paid to P—$600—exceeds the arm's length price, it is restated under §482 as $550.

---

[33] Reg. §1.482-3(b)(5)(i).

[34] Reg. §1.482-3(b)(5)(ii).

[35] Reg. §1.482-3(b)(5)(iii) Ex. 2.

[36] Reg. §1.482-1(e), discussed supra ¶79.3.5.

[37] Reg. §1.482-3(c)(2)(i). The provisions on the resale price method are "generally similar" to those of the 1968 regulations. TD 8552, supra note 22, at 106.

[38] Reg. §1.482-3(c)(4) Ex. 1.

[39] Reg. §1.482-3(c)(4) Ex. 2.

Because the resale price method "measures the value of [distribution] functions," it is most appropriate for entities that buy and resell goods without adding "substantial value" by "physically altering the goods."[40] For example, if a domestic corporation sells goods to a foreign subsidiary, the resale price method could be used if the subsidiary resells the goods without change to its customers, but not if the goods are materials and components that the subsidiary uses in its manufacturing operations. However, packaging, repackaging, labeling, and minor assembly are "ordinarily" not considered physical alterations.

The resale price method is usually inappropriate where the controlled buyer/reseller owns "intangible property," such as a trademark, that adds substantial value to the goods.[41] Assume S, a U.S. subsidiary of foreign corporation P, buys and resells in the United States goods produced by P in country X. S owns a trademark for the goods, developed by its own advertising and other promotional efforts, that allows it to command a price exceeding that for comparable unbranded goods. The resale price method, applied using the gross profit margins of U.S. sellers of the comparable unbranded goods, is not a reliable measure of an arm's length price for S's purchases from P because it would have the effect of allocating to P the price premium deriving from S's trademark.

The arm's length price under the resale price method is "the applicable resale price," less the "appropriate gross profit."[42] The applicable resale price usually is either the resale price of the particular item purchased in the controlled transaction or the price charged in "contemporaneous resales of the same property."[43] However, if the item is resold in another controlled transaction, the applicable resale price is the price at which the goods are eventually sold to unrelated persons or is the price in contemporaneous sales to unrelated persons. For example, if P sells goods to its subsidiary S1, which resells the goods to S2, another subsidiary of P, the applicable resale price is the price in S2's resales to unrelated persons, and the arm's length price for the sale from P to S1 is the resale price obtained by S2, less a gross profit margin reflecting the functions performed by both S1 and S2.[44]

The "appropriate gross profit" is the applicable resale price, multiplied by "the gross profit margin . . . earned in comparable uncontrolled transactions, . . . expressed as a percentage of total revenue derived from sales."[45] If the comparable uncontrolled transactions are made by "a sales agent that does not take title to goods or otherwise assume risks with respect to ownership of such goods," the

---

[40] Reg. §1.482-3(c)(1). See TD 8470, 1993-1 CB 90, 113 (resale price method "ordinarily" provides "an accurate measure of an arm's length result if the controlled taxpayer performs a distribution function and does not add substantial value to the goods that are distributed").

[41] Reg. §1.482-3(c)(1).

[42] Reg. §1.482-3(c)(2)(i).

[43] Reg. §1.482-3(c)(2)(ii).

[44] Reg. §1.482-3(c)(4) Ex. 3.

[45] Reg. §1.482-3(c)(2)(iii).

appropriate gross profit margin may be the sales agent's commission rate, expressed as a percentage of the uncontrolled sales price of the goods, adjusted for the differences in investment and risk.[46] "[P]revailing gross profit margins in the general industry" may not be used in applying the resale price method because, in the view of the authors of the regulations, "unadjusted industry average returns cannot independently establish an arm's length result."[47]

Under the best method rule, the resale price method is used only if, under the circumstances, it is the most reliable measure of arm's length results.[48] Whether a method is the most reliable measure depends primarily on the degree of comparability between the controlled and uncontrolled transactions used in applying the method and the quality of the data and assumptions underlying the method's application.[49]

Comparability is generally determined under rules described elsewhere,[50] but the regulations provide additional guidance on the application of these rules under the resale price method. The gross profit of a buyer/reseller is "compensation for the performance of resale functions" and includes "an operating profit . . . for the reseller's investment of capital and the assumption of risks."[51] Thus, under the resale price method, comparability "is particularly dependent on similarity of functions performed, risks borne, and contractual terms" unless adjustments can be made "to account for" material differences in these factors.

Uncontrolled transactions by the buyer/reseller in the controlled transaction are usually most comparable because "resales of property made by the same reseller" are typically more comparable than sales made by different resellers.[52] For example, if S resells toaster ovens purchased from its parent (P) and blenders purchased from an unrelated manufacturer, S's gross profit in resales of blenders likely provides a more reliable measure of arm's length prices for the goods purchased from P than the gross profit of other buyer/resellers.[53]

"[C]lose physical similarity" in products is less important under this method than under the CUP method.[54] For example, distributors of consumer durables might perform comparable distribution functions, even if the goods they sell are

---

[46] Reg. §1.482-3(c)(3)(ii)(D). Conversely, if the controlled distributor acts as a sales agent, rather than as buyer and seller, the gross profit margin in uncontrolled transactions of buyer/resellers may be the arm's length commission rate for the controlled distributor, although the commission rate is technically subject to the rules for services, rather than the rules for sales of goods.

[47] TD 8552, supra note 22, at 106.

[48] Reg. §1.482-3(c)(3)(i).

[49] Reg. §1.482-1(c), discussed supra ¶79.3.3.

[50] Reg. §1.482-1(d), discussed supra ¶79.3.4.

[51] Reg. §1.482-3(c)(3)(ii)(A).

[52] Id.

[53] See Reg. §1.482-8 Ex. 2.

[54] Reg. §1.482-3(c)(3)(ii)(B). However, "close product similarity will tend to improve the reliability of the result." TD 8552, supra note 22, at 106.

quite different, although "substantial differences in the products" may "indicate significant functional differences." Thus, uncontrolled comparables usually involve products of "the same general type (e.g., consumer electronics)."[55]

Comparability is also affected by "significant differences in the value" of the goods, particularly if these differences result from a trademark or other intellectual property.[56] Assume S Corp. is country X distributor of products manufactured by its U.S. parent, P Corp., which it resells with a valuable trademark owned by P. Five uncontrolled country X distributors of comparable products are identified.[57] If three of the uncontrolled distributors sell products bearing no brand name, whereas the other two sell products under brand names owned by the producers of those products, only the latter two distributors are comparable.

Moreover, "the reliability of profit measures based on gross profit may be adversely affected by factors that have less effect on prices," including "cost structures (as reflected, for example, in the age of plant and equipment), business experience (such as whether the business is in a start-up phase or is mature), or management efficiency (as indicated, for example, by expanding or contracting sales or executive compensation over time)."[58]

If the best available uncontrolled comparables differ from the controlled reseller, adjustments should be made for differences that might materially affect gross profit margins.[59] The regulations identify the following differences as possibly requiring adjustments:

1. "Inventory levels and turnover rates, and corresponding risks, including any price protection programs offered by the manufacturer."
2. "Contractual terms (e.g., scope and terms of warranties provided, sales or purchase volume, credit terms, transport terms)."
3. "Sales, marketing, [and] advertising programs and services (including promotional programs, rebates, and co-op advertising)."
4. "The level of the market (e.g., wholesale, retail, etc.)."
5. Currency risks.[60]

---

[55] See Reg. §1.482-8 Ex. 3 (applying resale price method to subsidiary selling toaster ovens manufactured by parent, using gross profit margins of uncontrolled distributors of toaster ovens, notwithstanding "significant differences," including brand names, between ovens sold in controlled and uncontrolled transactions).

[56] Reg. §1.482-3(c)(3)(ii)(B). See TD 8552, supra note 22, at 106 ("the reliability of the analysis [is] reduced if the uncontrolled taxpayer sells goods that are significantly more (or less) valuable than the goods in the controlled transaction or if either the uncontrolled taxpayer or the controlled taxpayer owns a trademark that is exploited in connection with the resale of the product").

[57] Reg. §1.482-3(c)(4) Ex. 7.

[58] Reg. §1.482-3(c)(3)(ii)(B).

[59] Reg. §1.482-3(c)(3)(ii)(C). For the general rules on adjustments, see Reg. §1.482-1(d)(2), discussed supra ¶79.3.4.

[60] Reg. §1.482-3(c)(3)(ii)(C).

Differences in "operating expenses associated with functions performed and risks assumed" should be considered in determining whether adjustments are necessary and, if so, in making the adjustments.[61] However, "the effect on gross profit of such differences is not necessarily equal to the differences in the amount of related operating expenses."

As under all of the methods, the reliability of the results under the resale price method depends on the "completeness and accuracy of the data used and the reliability of the assumptions made."[62] Assume domestic corporation's country X subsidiary performs functions similar to those of five uncontrolled distributors operating in country X, but it is not possible to determine whether the uncontrolled distributors provide warranties to their customers or to identify the payment terms in their sales.[63] The lack of information on warranties and payment terms diminishes the reliability of the uncontrolled comparables. However, if they are the most reliable data available, they may, after statistical enhancement (e.g., by the interquartile range), nevertheless be useable in establishing an arm's length range.

Similarity of accounting practices is especially important under the resale price method.[64] For example, material differences in "inventory and other cost accounting practices" may diminish the reliability of uncontrolled comparables unless reliable adjustments can be made for these differences. Similarly, the treatment of such items as "discounts, returns and allowances, rebates, transportation costs, insurance, and packaging" as part of the cost of goods sold or as operating expenses should either be the same in the controlled and uncontrolled transactions or be subject to reliable adjustment.[65]

The resale price method is often applied using two or more uncontrolled comparables of equal reliability, in which case the comparables establish an arm's length range under rules described elsewhere.[66] For example, if five uncontrolled distributors operating in foreign country X are comparable to S, a country X distribution subsidiary of P Corp., the gross profit margins of the uncontrolled distributors may comprise an arm's length range, and the prices that S paid to P are not subject to adjustment under §482 if S's gross profit margin is within that range.[67]

---

[61] Id.

[62] Reg. §1.482-3(c)(3)(iii)(A).

[63] Reg. §1.482-3(c)(4) Ex. 6.

[64] Reg. §1.482-3(c)(3)(iii)(B).

[65] See Reg. §1.482-3(c)(3)(iii)(B). See also Reg. §1.482-8 Ex. 3 (applying comparable profits method, rather than resale price method, because available data did not disclose how uncontrolled comparables allocated discounts, insurance, warranty costs, and supervisory, general, and administrative expenses between cost of goods sold and operating expenses).

[66] Reg. §1.482-3(c)(2)(iv). For arm's length ranges, see Reg. §1.482-1(e), discussed supra ¶79.3.5.

[67] Reg. §1.482-3(c)(4) Ex. 5.

¶79.7.4   Cost Plus Method

The arm's length price for a controlled sale under the cost plus method is the sum of the seller's cost of goods sold and a "gross profit markup" determined from comparable uncontrolled transactions.[68] The method is most often used to determine sales revenues of a manufacturer, assembler, or other producer of goods on sales to related persons. Assume foreign corporation S manufactures goods in country X at a cost of $1,000 and sells them to its parent (P), a domestic corporation that resells the goods in the United States. If a comparable manufacturer in country X sells goods in comparable transactions to unrelated buyers at a markup of 30 percent of cost, the arm's length price under the cost plus method for S' sales to P is $1,300—130 percent of S' cost of $1,000.

Under the cost plus method, the arm's length price for goods sold in a controlled transaction is the sum of the seller's "costs of producing the property" and an "appropriate gross profit."[69] The "appropriate gross profit" is product of the controlled seller's production costs and "the gross profit markup, expressed as a percentage of cost, earned in comparable uncontrolled transactions."[70]

Under the best method rule, the resale price method is used only if, under the circumstances, it is the most reliable measure of arm's length results.[71] Whether a method is the most reliable measure depends primarily on the degree of comparability between the controlled and uncontrolled transactions used in applying the method and the quality of the data and assumptions underlying the method's application.[72]

"A producer's gross profit provides compensation for the performance of the production functions . . . , including an operating profit for the producer's investment of capital and assumption of risks."[73] Controlled and uncontrolled transactions are therefore comparable for this purpose only if the manufacturing functions, capital investments, risks, and contract terms do not differ materially or reliable adjustments can be made for material differences. Ideally, the comparable uncontrolled transactions are transactions of the seller in the controlled transactions "because similar characteristics are more likely to be found among sales of property made by the same producer than among sales by other producers." For example, if foreign corporation S produces goods for sale both to its U.S. parent, P, and to unrelated buyers, the markup in the sales to unrelated buyers probably is the most reliable measure for determining arm's length results

---

[68] Reg. §1.482-3(d)(1). This method is "generally similar" to the cost plus method under the prior regulations. TD 8552, supra note 22, at 106.

[69] Reg. §1.482-3(d)(2)(i). Although this method is most often used in determining the income of producers, the term "costs of producing" includes the acquisition costs of goods purchased for resale. Reg. §1.482-3(d)(3)(iii)(B).

[70] Reg. §1.482-3(d)(2)(ii).

[71] Reg. §1.482-3(d)(3)(i).

[72] Reg. §1.482-1(c), discussed supra ¶79.3.3.

[73] Reg. §1.482-3(d)(3)(ii)(A).

in the sales to *P*. However, comparable uncontrolled transactions of other producers, including producers within the same controlled group, may be used if the seller in the controlled transactions makes no comparable uncontrolled sales.[74]

"[C]lose physical similarity" of the goods sold in the controlled and uncontrolled transactions is not essential, although it is "ordinarily . . . expected" that the goods will be "within the same product categories."[75] For example, although producers of a wide variety of components for consumer electronics might perform comparable manufacturing and assembly functions, producers of pharmaceuticals are not usually comparable to producers of apparel.

If the goods take additional value from intellectual property owned by the controlled producer (e.g., a patented invention used in producing the goods or a valuable trademark), the controlled transactions are not usually comparable to the production and sale of goods not benefiting from such property.[76] Moreover, the reliability of the comparison may be diminished if similar, but different intellectual property is used by the controlled and uncontrolled producers.

If possible, adjustments should be made for any differences between the controlled and uncontrolled transactions that materially affect gross profit margins.[77] Generally, adjustments are required for material differences in any of the following: (1) the complexity of manufacturing or assembly; (2) manufacturing, production, or process engineering; (3) procurement, purchasing, or inventory control; (4) testing function; (5) selling, general, or administrative expense; (6) currency risks; or (7) contract terms. Some of the relevant contract terms are provisions relating to warranties, sales or purchase volume, and credit and transport terms. Differences in operating expenses provide a hint of the presence of material differences in function, but the appropriate adjustment for these functional differences does "not necessarily" equal the differences in operating expenses.

Assume *S*, a foreign subsidiary of domestic corporation *P*, manufactures goods in country *X* under contract with *P* using materials provided by *P* on consignment. An otherwise comparable company manufactures comparable goods in country *X* from its own inventory of materials and sells them to unrelated buyers.[78] An adjustment must be made to the uncontrolled producer's gross margin to account for the fact that it maintains its own materials inventory, whereas *S* does not, unless this difference is shown to have no material effect on uncontrolled gross margins. If the effect of the difference on gross margins

---

[74] See Reg. §1.482-8 Ex. 5 (applying cost plus method to U.S. subsidiary manufacturing machine tool parts for sale to foreign parent, using gross profit markups of four U.S. companies manufacturing various types of machine tool parts for sale to unrelated persons).

[75] Reg. §1.482-3(d)(3)(ii)(B).

[76] Id.

[77] Reg. §1.482-3(d)(3)(ii)(C).

[78] See Reg. §1.482-3(d)(4) Ex. 3.

cannot be "reasonably ascertain[ed]," the reliability of results under the cost plus method is diminished.

As under all methods, the reliability of the results under the cost plus method depends on the quality and completeness of the underlying data and assumptions.[79] For example, the reliability of results derived from various uncontrolled comparables is diminished if the available data does not allow the IRS to determine the extent of the currency risks assumed by the uncontrolled taxpayers.[80]

Consistency of accounting treatment of items affecting gross profit margin is particularly important under this method.[81] For example, "differences in inventory and other cost accounting practices" can greatly affect the size of a business' gross profit markup, and the comparability of controlled and uncontrolled transactions is diminished by such differences unless reliable adjustments are made for them. It is also important that the classification of costs as part of the cost of goods sold or as operating expenses be the same in the controlled and uncontrolled transactions or that adjustments be made for any such differences. For example, if the taxpayer treats supervisory, general, and administrative costs as operating expenses, whereas uncontrolled comparables treat these costs as inventory costs, this accounting discrepancy diminishes the reliability of results under the cost plus method unless reliable adjustments can be made for the difference.[82]

If either the IRS or the taxpayer identifies two or more uncontrolled taxpayers of equal comparability but with different gross margins, these margins comprise an arm's length range, and any gross margin within the range is considered at arm's length.[83] Assume P, a domestic manufacturer of computer chips, sells chips to its foreign subsidiary; three other U.S. manufacturers sell computer chips to uncontrolled buyers at a gross margins that range from 10 to 12 percent.[84] If P's gross margin in the sales to the subsidiary is at least 10 percent but not more than 12 percent, the sales are considered to have been made at arm's length prices. In contrast, if P's gross margin in these sales is, for example, 8 percent, the sales are not at arm's length prices, and the prices are restated under §482 to yield a gross margin within the arm's length range.

¶79.7.5 Other Methods

A pricing method other than those described in the regulations, including a method devised by the taxpayer, may be used in testing whether controlled transactions are at arm's length if it satisfies the requirement of the best method rule: that

---

[79] Reg. §1.482-3(d)(3)(iii)(A).

[80] Reg. §1.482-3(d)(4) Ex. 4.

[81] Reg. §1.482-3(d)(3)(iii)(B).

[82] Reg. §1.482-3(d)(4) Ex. 2.

[83] Reg. §1.482-3(d)(2)(iii). For arm's length ranges, see Reg. §1.482-1(e)(2), discussed supra ¶79.3.5.

[84] See Reg. §1.482-3(d)(4) Ex. 1.

it provide the most reliable measure of arm's length results.[85] Such a method, referred to in the regulations as an "unspecified" method, "should take into account the general principle that uncontrolled taxpayers evaluate the terms of a transaction by considering the realistic alternatives to the transaction, and only enter into a particular transaction if none of the alternatives is preferable to it." An unspecified method should therefore be based on "information on the prices or profits that the controlled taxpayer could have realized by choosing a realistic alternative to the controlled transaction." For example, "a *bona fide* offer [may be] used to establish an arm's length price."[86] Assume a U.S. manufacturer distributes its goods in Canada through a Canadian subsidiary, but before entering the Canadian market received an offer from an unrelated distributor.[87] Depending on the circumstances, this offer may be a reliable indicator that an arm's length price for the sales to the subsidiary is no less than the price offered by the independent distributor.

However, unspecified methods need not be based on "potential transactions that did not occur. They should, in general, be based on actual transactions and other indicia derived from actual or potential market transactions."[88] An unspecified method based on "internal data" is less reliable than a method based on uncontrolled comparables.[89]

¶79.8 TRANSFERS OF INTANGIBLE PROPERTY

¶79.8.1 Introductory

Only one method—the comparable uncontrolled transaction (CUT) method—is provided specifically for licenses and other transfers of intangible property, but the comparable profits and profit split methods may also be used for such transfers.[1] Also, some other reasonable method may be devised for an intangible transfer if it can be shown to be the best method under the circumstances.[2]

The term "intangible" is defined for purposes of §482 to include all property having "substantial value independent of the services of any individual" that falls within any of the following six classes:

---

[85] Reg. §1.482-3(e)(1). For the best method rule, see supra ¶79.3.3.

[86] TD 8552, supra note 22, at 106.

[87] Reg. §1.482-3(e)(2) Ex.

[88] TD 8552, supra note 22, at 106.

[89] Reg. §1.482-3(e)(1).

[1] Reg. §1.482-4(a). For the comparable profits and profit split methods, see infra ¶¶79.9, 79.10. For economic analysis of the issues, see Grubert, Royalties, Dividends and R&D, 1994 Proc. 87th Ann. Conf. on Tax'n 13 (1995). See also Boykin, Transfer Pricing Policy Issues: Who Is the Developer? 12 Tax Notes Int'l 279 (Jan 22, 1995); Oosterhuis, International R&D and Technology Transfer Arrangements, 73 Taxes 905 (1995).

[2] Reg. §1.482-4(d), discussed infra ¶79.8.3.

1. Patents, inventions, formulae, processes, designs, patterns, or know-how.
2. Copyrights and literary, musical, or artistic compositions.
3. Trademarks, trade names, or brand names.
4. Franchises, licenses, or contracts.
5. Methods, programs, systems, procedures, campaigns, surveys, studies, forecasts, estimates, customer lists, or technical data.
6. Other similar items.[3]

The sixth category includes any property whose value derives "not from its physical attributes but from its intellectual content or other intangible properties."

In *Merck & Co. v. US*,[4] the IRS attempted under pre-1986 law to allocate royalty income to a parent corporation from a possessions subsidiary for the subsidiary's use of intangibles that the Claims Court essentially found to be nonexistent. The subsidiary produced a highly profitable pharmaceutical under a patent that had previously been transferred to the subsidiary by the parent tax-free under §351. The IRS nevertheless contended that if the corporations had dealt at arm's length, the subsidiary would have paid a royalty to the parent equal to 7 percent of sales for (1) the benefits flowing to the subsidiary from the parent's ongoing research and development work, (2) "continuing marketing programs," and (3) manufacturing intangibles not transferred to the subsidiary. However, the court found that the benefits from ongoing research and development were not adequately quantified by the IRS and that other intangibles allegedly furnished to the subsidiary were merely benefits flowing from the subsidiary's position as a member of the controlled group. According to the court, "organizational structure, without more, is not included in the concept of an enforceable property right that would support an arm's length license agreement."

The general standard for controlled transfers of intangibles is the same as for all controlled transactions: "[T]he standard to be applied in every case is that of a taxpayer dealing at arm's length with an uncontrolled taxpayer."[5] This standard is not necessarily satisfied by a royalty rate equal to the "prevailing" rate "within the same or similar industry" or the rate under an uncontrolled transfer that is not comparable to the controlled transfer.[6]

A controlled transfer of an intangible may be either a sale or other transfer of ownership or a license or other permission to use the intangible. The IRS normally respects the form chosen by the controlled taxpayers if it conforms to the economic substance of the transaction,[7] but this principle is limited in three ways. First, if the transferee "pays nominal or no consideration" and the transferor retains "a substantial interest in the property," the transfer is analyzed as

---

[3] Reg. §1.482-4(b).
[4] Merck & Co. v. US, 24 Cl. Ct. 73, 91-2 USTC ¶50,456 (1991).
[5] Reg. §1.482-1(b)(1).
[6] Reg. §1.482-4(f)(4).
[7] Reg. §1.482-1(f)(2)(ii)(A), discussed supra ¶79.3.8.

a license, regardless of the form in which it is cast in the parties' agreement, and the arm's length consideration for the transfer is "in the form of a royalty, unless a different form is demonstrably more appropriate."[8]

Second, even if the IRS respects the taxpayer's chosen form, alternatives to that form may be considered in assessing whether the consideration is at arm's length if persons dealing at arm's length would use one or more of the alternatives.[9] For example, in deciding whether a royalty is at arm's length, the IRS may consider the profits that would have been realized by the licensor if, instead of licensing the intangible, it had itself carried on the controlled licensee's activities (e.g., producing and selling goods under the licensed intangible).

Third, Congress added the following sentence to §482 in 1986: "In the case of any transfer (or license) of intangible property . . . , the income with respect to such transfer or license shall be commensurate with the income attributable to the intangible." The regulations construe the term "commensurate with income" to require periodic reexamination of, and possibly adjustments to, the consideration, even if the license or other agreement provides for no such adjustment.[10]

If a controlled sale of goods vests in the buyer rights to an intangible embedded in the goods and these rights exceed those needed to resell the goods, the transaction is treated as including both a sale of goods and an intangible transfer.[11] In this situation, the selling price must be split between the two elements of the transaction, with arm's length prices being determined for each element under the rules for sales of goods and intangibles transfers. This approach applies, for example, if a controlled purchaser of a machine is entitled to use "a manufacturing process incorporated in the machine."[12]

¶79.8.2 Comparable Uncontrolled Transaction (CUT) Method

Under the CUT method, the arm's length consideration for a controlled transfer of an intangible is "the amount charged in a comparable uncontrolled transaction."[13] This method is used only if, under the best method rule, it is determined to be the most reliable measure of arm's length results.[14] Whether a method is the best method depends primarily on the degree of comparability between the controlled and uncontrolled transactions used in applying the method and the quality of the data and assumptions underlying the method's application.[15]

---

[8] Reg. §1.482-4(f)(1).
[9] Reg. §1.482-1(d)(3)(iv).
[10] Reg. §1.482-4(f)(2), discussed infra ¶79.8.4.
[11] Reg. §§1.482-3(f); 1.482-4(e).
[12] Reg. §1.482-3(f).
[13] Reg. §1.482-4(c)(1).
[14] Reg. §1.482-4(c)(2)(i).
[15] Reg. §1.482-1(c), discussed supra ¶79.3.3.

If the intangible transferred in the controlled transaction was also transferred in an uncontrolled transaction "under the same or substantially the same circumstances," the CUT method, applied using the uncontrolled transfer as the comparable, is likely the best method.[16] The circumstances of controlled and uncontrolled transfers are "substantially the same" if "there are at most only minor differences that have a definite and reasonably ascertainable effect on the amount charged and for which appropriate adjustments are made." Assume U.S. pharmaceutical company P licenses a patented drug to an unrelated manufacturer for use in country Y and makes a substantially identical license to P's country X subsidiary.[17] The uncontrolled transfer to the country Y manufacturer is comparable to the license to the subsidiary if the markets for this particular drug in countries X and Y are substantially the same in terms of population, incidence of the disease or condition for which the drug is intended, legal protections of the patent, and other relevant factors.

If the same intangible has not been transferred in a substantially similar uncontrolled transaction, comparable transfers of comparable intangibles may be used in applying the CUT method, but the closeness of the comparison is examined carefully in determining whether this method is the best method under the circumstances.[18]

The comparability of controlled and uncontrolled transactions is determined under the comparability rules described elsewhere,[19] but the regulations elaborate on the application of these rules in this context. The most important factor under the CUT method is comparability of the intangibles involved in the controlled and uncontrolled transfers.[20] Two intangibles are considered comparable only if they are "used in connection with similar products or processes within the same general industry or market" and "have similar profit potential."[21] Assume a U.S. pharmaceutical company develops a new drug for migraine headaches, which is sufficiently superior to competing medications that it is expected to quickly dominate the worldwide market for migraine drugs. Some years previously, the company developed another migraine drug that enjoyed substantial success, but it was not significantly different from competing products in effectiveness and side effects and therefore never had the potential for dominating the market.[22] Given the differences in profit potential, the company's license to its Swiss sub-

---

[16] Reg. §1.482-4(c)(2)(ii).

[17] Reg. §§1.482-4(c)(4) Ex. 1, 1.482-8 Ex. 7.

[18] Reg. §1.482-4(c)(2)(ii).

[19] Reg. §1.482-1(d), discussed supra ¶79.3.4.

[20] Reg. §1.482-4(c)(2)(iii)(A).

[21] Reg. §1.482-4(c)(2)(iii)(B)(1). The stress on "profit potential" reflects "Congressional concern that royalty rates for 'high-profit' intangibles could 'be set on the basis of industry norms for transfers of much less profitable items.'" TD 8470, 1993-1 CB 90, 97, quoting Staff of Joint Comm. on Tax'n, 99th Cong., 2d Sess., General Explanation of the Tax Reform Act of 1986 at 1014 (Comm. Print 1987) [hereinafter 1986 Bluebook].

[22] Reg. §1.482-4(c)(4) Ex. 4.

sidiary of European rights to the earlier product is not likely to be comparable to a license of the new drug to the subsidiary, even if the licenses are made at similar stages in the drugs' development and the terms of the license agreements are the same.

Profit potential, which may consist of "prospective profits" or "costs to be saved," is "most reliably measured" as "the net present value of the benefits to be realized . . . through the use or subsequent transfer of the intangible," adjusted to reflect "the capital investment and start-up expenses required, the risks to be assumed, and other relevant considerations."[23] The importance of profit potential is greatest where potential profit or "the potential rate of return on investment necessary to exploit the intangible" is large. The reliability of a comparability analysis is reduced if "the profit potential attributable to the intangible [cannot clearly] be isolated from the profit attributable to other factors, such as functions performed and other resources employed."

Because the amounts charged in transfers of intangibles may be "materially" affected by "differences in contractual terms, or the economic conditions in which transactions take place," reliable results can be obtained under the CUT method only if the terms and conditions of the controlled and uncontrolled transfers are closely comparable or adjustments are made for material differences.[24] For example, if a U.S. pharmaceutical company licenses a patented drug to an unrelated manufacturer in country Y and to a wholly owned subsidiary in country X, the licenses are not comparable, even if their terms are identical, if the potential market for the drug is much greater in country Y because of a higher incidence of the disease the drug is intended to treat.[25]

The relevant terms and conditions include:

1. The extent of the rights granted by the transfer, including whether the rights are exclusive or nonexclusive and geographic or other limitations on the transferee's rights.
2. The stage of the intangible's development in the markets in which it is to be used, including whether needed government approvals or licenses have been obtained.
3. The transferee's rights to updates, revisions, or modifications of the intangible.
4. The intangible's uniqueness, and the period for which it will remain unique, including the extent and duration of the legal monopoly available to the transferee in the countries covered by the transfer.
5. If the transfer is of less than complete ownership, the duration of the license or agreement, and the extent of the transferee's rights on termination.

---

[23] Reg. §1.482-4(c)(2)(iii)(B)(*1*)(ii).
[24] Reg. §1.482-4(c)(2)(iii)(A).
[25] Reg. §1.482-4(c)(4) Ex. 2.

6. "Any economic and product liability risks to be assumed by the transferee."
7. "[A]ny collateral transactions or ongoing business relationships between the transferee and transferor."
8. "[A]ny ancillary or subsidiary services" to be performed by the transferor or transferee.[26]

As under all methods, the reliability of the results under the CUT method depends on the quality and completeness of the underlying data and assumptions.[27]

The CUT method is sometimes applied using two or more uncontrolled comparables of equal reliability, in which case the comparables establish an arm's length range under rules described elsewhere.[28] Assume the IRS, using data from documents filed with the Securities Exchange Commission, identifies 15 uncontrolled licenses that are similar to foreign corporation P's license of patented technology to S, its U.S. subsidiary.[29] The uncontrolled comparables, like P's license to S, are exclusive licenses for all of North America, involve products with similar levels of technology and similar markets, provide for continuing technical support and access to technical improvements, and are similar in age of technology and license duration. However, "unidentified material differences [likely] exist between the uncontrolled comparables and the controlled transaction." The comparables are therefore refined by a "statistical technique"—the "interquartile range." The four comparables with the lowest royalty rate and the four with the highest rate are excluded, and the seven remaining royalty rates make up the arm's length range. The royalty rate in the P-S license is deemed to be at arm's length if it falls within the range. If it does not, the royalty rate is restated under §482 at the median rate in the range.

¶79.8.3 Other Methods

A method other than the CUT, comparable profit, or profit split method can be used for a license or other transfer of an intangible if the method is shown to provide the most reliable measure, under the circumstances, of arm's length results.[30] The reliability of such a method, referred to as an "unspecified" method, depends on the completeness and accuracy of the data and assumptions used in applying it, "including any projections used." An unspecified method based on "internal data rather than uncontrolled comparables" is generally of a low grade of reliability.

---

[26] Reg. §1.482-4(c)(2)(iii)(B)(2).

[27] Reg. §1.482-4(c)(2)(iv).

[28] Reg. §1.482-4(c)(3). For arm's length ranges, see Reg. §1.482-1(e), discussed supra ¶79.3.5.

[29] Reg. §1.482-4(c)(4) Ex. 3.

[30] Reg. §1.482-4(d)(1).

An unspecified method should reflect "the general principle that uncontrolled taxpayers evaluate the terms of a transaction by considering the realistic alternatives to that transaction, and only enter into a particular transaction if none of the alternatives is preferable to it."[31] An unspecified method should therefore be based on "information on the prices or profits that the controlled taxpayer could have realized by choosing a realistic alternative to the controlled transaction." Assume domestic corporation P licenses S, its Netherlands subsidiary, to use a proprietary process for producing an industrial adhesive in manufacturing and selling the adhesive throughout Europe.[32] In evaluating whether the royalty provided by the license agreement is at arm's length, the IRS "may consider, subject to the best method rule . . . , [P's] alternative of producing and selling [the adhesive] itself." For example, if S pays a royalty of $100 per ton, P could produce and sell the adhesive in Europe at a cost of $300 per ton (including "a reasonable profit for [the] functions, risks and investments" of European operations), and if the European market price for the adhesive is $550, the IRS will conclude that the royalty is not at arm's length.

¶79.8.4 Commensurate With Income Standard

Section 482 requires that the consideration for an intangibles transfer between controlled taxpayers must be "commensurate with the income attributable to the intangible."[33] The staff of the Joint Committee on Taxation explained the reasons for this requirement as follows:

> The problems [with §482] have been particularly acute in the case of transfers of high-profit potential intangibles. Taxpayers may have transferred such intangibles to foreign related corporations or to possessions corporations at an early stage, for a relatively low royalty, and taken the position that it was not possible at the time of the transfers to predict the subsequent success of the product. Even in the case of a proven high-profit intangible, taxpayers frequently have taken the position that intercompany royalty rates may appropriately be set on the basis of industry norms for transfers of much less profitable items. . . .
>
> In many cases firms that develop high profit-potential intangibles tend to retain their rights or transfer them to related parties in which they retain an equity interest in order to maximize their profits. The transferor may well be looking in part to the value of its direct or indirect equity interest in the

---

[31] Id.

[32] Reg. §1.482-4(d)(2) Ex.

[33] Reg. §1.482-4(f)(2)(i). See generally Jacob, The New "Super-Royalty" Provisions of Internal Revenue Code 1986: A German Perspective, 27 European Tax'n 329 (1987); King, Is the Section 482 Periodic Adjustment Requirement Really Arm's Length? Evidence From Arm's Length Long-Term Contracts, 8 Tax Notes Int'l 1001 (1994); Levey & Ruchelman, Section 482—The Super Royalty Provisions Adopt the Commensurate Standard, 41 Tax Lawyer 611 (1988).

related party transferee as part of the value to be received for the transfer, rather than to "arm's length" factors. Industry norms for transfers to unrelated parties of less profitable intangibles frequently are not realistic comparables in these cases.

Transfers between related parties do not involve the same risks as transfers to unrelated parties. There is thus a powerful incentive to establish a relatively low royalty without adequate provisions for adjustment as the revenues of the intangible vary. There are extreme difficulties in determining whether the arm's length transfers between unrelated parties are comparable. Congress thus concluded that it is appropriate to assure that the division of income between related parties reasonably reflects the relative economic activities undertaken by each. Congress believed that payments made on a transfer of intangibles to a related [person] should be commensurate with the income attributable to the intangible. . . .

This requirement is established to fulfill the objective that the division of income between related parties reasonably reflect the relative economic activity undertaken by each.[34]

The commensurate with income rule is considered an application of the arm's length standard, not a repudiation of or deviation from it, because "looking at the income related to the intangible and splitting it according to relative economic contributions is consistent with what unrelated parties do."[35] Unrelated persons rarely make long-term licenses with no provision for royalty adjustments, particularly for intangibles with high profit potential.[36]

The commensurate with income standard applies "both to outright transfers of the ownership of the intangibles . . . and to licenses or other arrangements for the use of intangibles."[37] Although its principal target is transfers of high profit intangibles to low tax countries, the standard "applies to all related party trans-

---

[34] 1986 Bluebook, supra note 21, at 1015. See Notice 88-123, 1988-2 CB 458 ("the primary difficulty addressed by the legislation was the selective transfer of high profit intangibles to tax havens"). Notice 88-123 is entitled "A Study of Intercompany Pricing under Section 482 of the Code" and is sometimes referred to as the §482 White Paper. See generally Carlson, Fogarasi & Gordon, The Section 482 White Paper: Highlights and Implications, 41 Tax Notes 547 (1988); Fuller, The IRS Section 482 White Paper, 41 Tax Notes 655 (1988).

[35] Notice 88-123, 1988-2 CB 458, 472. See Reg. §1.482-4(f)(2)(i) (adjustments under commensurate with income rule "shall be consistent with the arm's length standard").

For applications of the arm's length standard under prior law, see Eli Lilly & Co. v. CIR, 856 F2d 855 (7th Cir. 1988) (profits from drug patent split between domestic corporation and its possessions corporation); Bausch & Lomb, Inc. v. CIR, 92 TC 525 (1989), aff'd, 933 F2d 1084 (2d Cir. 1991) (royalty rate redetermined for parent's license to foreign subsidiary of patents and other technology for making soft contact lenses); G.D. Searle & Co. v. CIR, 88 TC 252 (1987); Ciba-Geigy Corp. v. CIR, 85 TC 172 (1985) (acq.) (court relied on testimony of unrelated person as to what his company would have paid).

[36] Notice 88-123, 1988-2 CB 458, 476.

[37] 1986 Bluebook, supra note 21, at 1015.

fers of intangibles, both inbound and outbound, without quantitative or qualitative restrictions."[38]

Although the application of the arm's length standard normally depends on the facts existing when the parties make their contract, the commensurate with income standard is not so limited.

> Congress intended that consideration also be given to the actual profit experience realized as a consequence of the transfer. Thus, Congress intended to require that the payments made for the intangible be adjusted over time to reflect changes in the income attributable to the intangible. The [commensurate with income standard] is not intended to require annual adjustments when there are only minor variations in revenues. However, . . . adjustments will be required when there are major variations in the annual amounts of revenue attributable to the intangible.[39]

The arm's length method is thus applied to an intangibles transfer as though the parties' contract required a reopening of negotiations whenever revenues from the intangible significantly rise or fall.[40] An adjustment is required under the commensurate with income standard whenever "changes over time . . . create a substantial deviation from the parties' expectations at the time they entered into the contract," whether these changes are gradual or sudden.[41] When made, such an adjustment must "reflect substantial changes in the income stream attributable to the intangible as well as substantial changes in the economic activities performed, assets employed, and economic costs and risks borne by related entities."[42]

The commensurate with income standard applies whether the consideration for an intangible transfer is a periodic royalty or a noncontingent royalty or selling price that is payable in a single lump sum at the time of transfer.[43] Generally, the standard is applied to a lump sum by (1) converting the lump sum into a stream of periodic payments continuing over the life of the intangible (or, if shorter, the life of the agreement) and having a present value equal to the lump sum and (2) making a §482 adjustment for each year equal to the difference

---

[38] Notice 88-123, 1988-2 CB 458, 473.

[39] 1986 Bluebook, supra note 21, at 1016. See R.T. French Co. v. CIR, 60 TC 836 (1973) (under prior law, royalty rate could not be adjusted under §482 on basis of events occurring after royalty contract was made).

[40] See Notice 88-123, 1988-2 CB 458, 477 (commensurate with income standard derives "from a view that contractual arrangements between unrelated parties—particularly those involving high profit intangibles—are not entered into on a long term basis without some mechanism for adjusting the arrangement if the profitability of the intangible is significantly higher or lower than anticipated").

[41] Id. at 478.

[42] Id. at 477.

[43] Reg. §1.482-4(f)(5)(i). See Notice 88-123, 1988-2 CB 458, 479 ("a lump sum sale arrangement should . . . be treated as an open transaction to assure that the sale over time satisfies [the] commensurate with income standard").

between the arm's length royalty for that year, determined under the rules described below, and the imputed periodic payment under the parties' agreement.[44]

Whether the contract provides for a lump sum or a series of contingent payments, the periodic resettings of the consideration are based on "all relevant facts and circumstances throughout the period the intangible is used."[45] These circumstances include "the extent to which the transferee bears real risks with respect to its ability to make a profit from the intangible," but "primary weight" is given to "the profit or income stream generated by or associated with intangible property."[46] "[T]he functions performed, and the economic costs and risks assumed by each party to the transaction, [must be analyzed] so that the allocation of income from the use of the intangible will be made in accordance with the relative economic contributions and risk taking of the parties."[47] The commensurate with income standard is sometimes called a super royalty rule because, when applied to highly profitable intangibles, a very high royalty is often "required to appropriately reflect a relatively minor economic contribution by the transferee and achieve a proper allocation of income."[48]

A determination that the consideration for one year is at arm's length usually does not preclude an adjustment under §482 for a subsequent year.[49] An adjustment may be made for a subsequent year even if an earlier year for which no adjustment was made is closed by the statute of limitations. However, the regulations provide three safe harbors, described below, that, if applicable, preclude an adjustment for a latter year once the consideration has been determined to be at arm's length for an earlier year.

1. *CUT method applied with uncontrolled transfer of same intangible.* If the consideration in a controlled transfer of an intangible is at arm's length for "the first taxable year in which substantial periodic consideration was required to be paid," no adjustment may be made for any latter year, provided that:

    a. The intangible transferred in the controlled transaction was also transferred in an uncontrolled transaction "under substantially the same circumstances as those of the controlled transaction," and

    b. The consideration under the controlled transfer for that first taxable year was found to be at arm's length under the CUT method, applied using the

---

[44] Reg. §1.482-4(f)(5)(i). See Reg. §1.482-4(f)(5)(iii) Ex.

According to the regulations, present value is determined with "an appropriate discount rate." The IRS had earlier specified that present value be determined at "appropriate federal funds rate based on the anticipated life of the intangible." Notice 88-123, 1988-2 CB 458, 479. The term "appropriate federal funds rate" might refer to the applicable Federal rate (AFR) determined under §1274(d), discussed supra ¶57.2.

[45] Reg. §1.482-4(f)(2)(i).

[46] 1986 Bluebook, supra note 21, at 1016.

[47] Notice 88-123, 1988-2 CB 458, 472.

[48] Id. at 473.

[49] Reg. §1.482-4(f)(2)(i).

uncontrolled transfer as the comparable transaction.[50]

Assume U.S. pharmaceutical company P licenses a patented drug to an unrelated manufacturer for use in country Y and makes a substantially identical license of the patent to P's country X subsidiary.[51] A determination that the royalty in the controlled transaction is at arm's length for the first year precludes any adjustment under the commensurate with income rule for any subsequent year if (1) the license to the country Y manufacturer is made under substantially the same circumstances as the controlled license to the subsidiary and (2) the determination that the controlled royalty is at arm's length is made under the CUT method using the country Y license as the uncontrolled comparable.

2. *CUT method applied with uncontrolled transfer of different but comparable intangible.* No adjustment under the commensurate with income standard may be made for any year after the first year covered by the controlled transfer if all of the following requirements are met:

a. The controlled transfer is evidenced by a written agreement that provides a consideration for each year in the agreement's term and was in effect for the taxable year.

b. Under the CUT method, the consideration in this transfer was at arm's length "for the first taxable year in which substantial periodic consideration was required to be paid under the agreement."

c. The comparable uncontrolled transaction used in applying the CUT method was made by a written agreement.

d. The uncontrolled agreement does not allow a renegotiation or termination "in circumstances comparable to those of the controlled transaction in the taxable year" and contains no provisions for periodic changes in the consideration other than "specified, non-contingent, changes."

e. The controlled and uncontrolled agreements are "substantially similar" in duration and in the provisions for changing the amount of consideration.

f. Any provision of the controlled agreement limiting the "use of the intangible to a specified field or purpose" is "consistent with industry practice," and the uncontrolled transfer is comparably limited.

g. The functions performed by the controlled transferee have not substantially changed since the controlled agreement was made, except "by events that were not foreseeable."

h. The aggregate of the profits earned or cost savings realized by the controlled transferee "from the exploitation of the intangible" during the taxable years and all prior years is at least 80 percent and not more than 120 percent of the profits or cost savings "foreseeable" when the com-

---

[50] Reg. §1.482-4(f)(2)(ii)(A).
[51] Reg. §1.482-4(c)(4) Ex. 1.

parability of the controlled and uncontrolled transactions was established.[52]

3. *Consideration determined to be at arm's length under method other than CUT method.* If the controlled agreement is tested under a method other than the CUT method, periodic adjustments are barred only if all of the following conditions are met:

a. The controlled transfer is evidenced by a written agreement that provides a consideration for each year in the agreement's term and was in effect for the taxable year.

b. The consideration under this agreement is determined to be at arm's length for the first year "in which substantial periodic consideration was required to be paid."

c. This determination is supported by "relevant . . . documentation . . . prepared contemporaneously with the execution of the controlled agreement."

d. The "functions performed" by the controlled transferee have not substantially changed since the controlled agreement was made, except as required "by events that were not foreseeable."

e. The aggregate of the profits earned or cost savings realized by the controlled transferee "from the exploitation of the intangible" during the taxable years and all prior years is at least 80 percent and not more than 120 percent of the profits or cost savings "foreseeable" when the comparability of the controlled and uncontrolled transactions was established.[53]

4. *Modifications of rules 2 and 3.* The second and third of the foregoing sets of requirements are modified in two situations.

First, the last requirement of each set is waived if aggregate profits or cost savings are less than 80 percent or exceed 120 percent of the foreseeable profits or savings "due to extraordinary events that were beyond the control of the controlled taxpayers and that could not reasonably have been anticipated at the time the controlled agreement was [made]."[54] For example, the requirement would likely be waived where profits fall short of the 80 percent mark because of earthquake damage to the licensee's manufacturing facilities.[55]

Second, if either set of requirements is fully satisfied for each of the five successive years beginning with the first taxable year for which substantial periodic consideration is paid, no adjustment may be made under the commensu-

---

[52] Reg. §1.482-4(f)(2)(ii)(B).
[53] Reg. §1.482-4(f)(2)(ii)(C).
[54] Reg. §1.482-4(f)(2)(ii)(D).
[55] Reg. §1.482-4(f)(2)(iii) Ex. 3(iii).

rate with income standard for any subsequent year, even if one or more of the requirements is not satisfied for the subsequent year.[56]

¶79.8.5 Ownership of Intangibles

An arm's length consideration is required whenever "the owner of the rights to exploit an intangible" allows a controlled taxpayer to use these rights.[57] Identifying which member or members of a controlled group own a particular intangible is thus a crucial first step in applying §482.

Generally, the "legal owner of a right to exploit an intangible" is treated as the intangible's owner for purposes of §482.[58] "Legal ownership may be acquired by operation of law or by contract under which the legal owner transfers all or part of its rights to another."[59] An intangible "that is not legally protected" is deemed owned by its "developer."[60] The IRS may "impute an agreement to convey legal ownership" of an intangible if controlled taxpayers' conduct "indicates" that such an agreement exists in substance.[61]

An intangible may have more than one owner for this purpose.[62] For example, if the owner of an intangible licenses another person to use it exclusively "in a specified geographic area for a specified period of time," the licensor and the licensee are both treated as owners "with respect to their respective exploitation rights." Assume a foreign cheese manufacturer organizes a U.S. subsidiary to distribute its cheese in the United States under the parent's trademark, which is valuable elsewhere but is not known in the United States; parent and subsidiary enter into a long-term agreement entitling the subsidiary to the exclusive use of the trademark in the United States.[63] The parent and subsidiary are both treated as owners of the trademark. If the subsidiary makes large, unremibursed advertising and marketing expenditures to develop a market for the cheese, these expenditures are considered made for the subsidiary's own benefit, even though they may enhance the value of the trademark in the United States. Thus, the parent's failure to bear any portion of the expenditures is not cause for a §482 allocation.

Generally, if an intangible is developed jointly by two or more controlled taxpayers, one of the taxpayers is treated as developer and owner of the intangible, and the others as "assisters," unless the intangible is developed under a

---

[56] Reg. §1.482-4(f)(2)(ii)(E).

[57] Reg. §1.482-4(f)(3)(i). See Mentz & Carlisle, The Tax Ownership of Intangibles under the Arm's-Length Principle, 76 Tax Notes 453 (Oct. 27, 1997).

[58] Reg. §1.482-4(f)(3)(ii)(A).

[59] Reg. §1.482-4(f)(3)(ii)(A).

[60] Reg. §1.482-4(f)(3)(ii)(B).

[61] Reg. §1.482-4(f)(3)(ii)(A).

[62] Reg. §1.482-4(f)(3)(i).

[63] Reg. §1.482-4(f)(3)(iv) Ex. 4.

qualified cost-sharing arrangement.[64] In the absence of a cost sharing arrangement, if the developer-owner does not compensate the assisters at arm's length for their assistance, a §482 allocation may be made to provide this compensation.[65]

The developer-owner is the controlled taxpayer that "bore the largest portion of the direct and indirect costs of developing the intangible."[66] A "provision, without adequate compensation, of property or services likely to contribute substantially to developing the intangible" is treated as a contribution toward development costs, apparently in an amount equal to the fair market value of these rights and services. A controlled taxpayer is "presumed not to have borne" a development cost if, "before the success of the project is known," it obtains another person's agreement to reimburse it for the cost.[67] If the controlled taxpayer that bore the largest portion of the development costs cannot be identified, the developer-owner is determined from "all other facts and circumstances . . . , including the location of the development activities, the capability of each controlled taxpayer to carry on the project independently, the extent to which each controlled taxpayer controls the project, and the conduct of the controlled taxpayers."[68]

An assister's assistance may include "loans, services, or the use of tangible or intangible property."[69] For example, if one member of a controlled group allows another member, without compensation, to use laboratory equipment in developing an intangible, arm's length consideration from the latter member to the former is imputed under the §482 rules for intercompany uses of tangible property.[70] However, expenditures "of a routine nature" are not assistance if they are comparable to those "an unrelated party dealing at arm's length would be expected to incur under circumstances similar to those of the controlled taxpayer."[71] Assume a foreign producer of cheese organizes a U.S. subsidiary to sell the cheese in the United States under a trademark that is well known and valuable in other countries but is largely unknown in the United States. Substantial expenditures by the subsidiary for advertising and other marketing efforts will likely add value to the trademark. If the subsidiary is not reimbursed and acquires no long-term rights to the trademark, its expenditures thus benefit the foreign parent. However, if the expenditures are "comparable" to those incurred by independent distributors in the "U.S. cheese industry," no reim-

---

[64] Reg. §1.482-4(f)(3)(ii)(B). For qualified cost sharing arrangements, see infra ¶79.8.6.

[65] Reg. §1.482-4(f)(3)(i).

[66] Reg. §1.482-4(f)(3)(ii)(B).

[67] Reg. §1.482-4(f)(3)(ii)(B).

[68] Reg. §1.482-4(f)(3)(ii)(B).

[69] Reg. §1.482-4(f)(3)(iii).

[70] Reg. §1.482-4(f)(3)(iv) Ex. 1. For the rules on leases of tangible property, see supra ¶79.6.

[71] Reg. §1.482-4(f)(3)(iii).

bursement from the parent is imputed under §482.[72] In contrast, if the subsidiary spends "significantly" more than the unreimbursed expenditures an independent distributor would make under the circumstances, the subsidiary is treated as performing a service for the parent, and arm's length compensation for this service is imputed in an amount equal to the excess of the subsidiary's expenditures over those that an independent distributor would have made without reimbursement.[73]

¶79.8.6 Cost-Sharing Arrangements

Controlled taxpayers jointly developing an intangible can avoid the foregoing rules on intangible ownership by making a "qualified cost-sharing arrangement."[74] The participants in such an arrangement share the costs incurred by all of them in one or more research and development projects and are treated as jointly owning any intangible resulting from the projects. During the course of the project, the participants make payments to each other to adjust their costs for the project to prearranged proportions. For example, if a parent corporation performs the research activities under a cost-sharing arrangement with a subsidiary by which parent and subsidiary have agreed that the costs of the research should be borne 70 percent by the parent and 30 percent by the subsidiary, the subsidiary reimburses the parent for 30 percent of the parent's costs for the activities. Generally, the IRS adjusts the payments under a cost-sharing arrangement only to the extent necessary to bring the participants' shares of the costs in line with the benefits they reasonably expect to realize from the project. Since the participants are joint owners of any intangible developed under the arrangement (referred to as a covered intangible), each participant can generally utilize the intangible in its business without paying royalties or other compensation for this use.

---

[72] Reg. §1.482-4(f)(3)(iv) Ex. 2.

[73] Reg. §1.482-4(f)(3)(iv) Ex. 3.

[74] Reg. §1.482-7. See Carlson, Godshaw, Gordon, Hamada, Murphy & Leong, An Analysis of the Final Cost-Sharing Regulations, 70 Tax Notes 757 (Feb. 5, 1996); Carvey & Picciano, Final Regs. Clarify Cost Sharing of R & D Expenditures, Tax Adviser 27 (Jan. 1997); Dolan, Final Cost-Sharing Regulations, 25 Tax Mgmt. Int'l J. 147 (1996); Schnorberger, The Taxation of R & D Cost Sharing: An Economic Approach, 25 Intertax 415 (1997); Wood, Share and Share Alike—Final Cost-Sharing Regulations and Planning Considerations, 12 Tax Notes Int'l 421 (Feb. 5, 1996).

As described here, the regulations on cost-sharing arrangements are generally effective for taxable years beginning after 1995. Reg. §1.482-7(k). However, a cost-sharing arrangement complying with the requirements of prior temporary regulations (Reg. §1.482-7T) is treated as qualified for taxable years beginning during 1996 if the arrangement existed before 1996 and is amended by the end of 1996 to conform to the final regulations. Reg. §1.482-7(l).

In applying the cost-sharing rules, like all other aspects of the §482 regulations, the members of a affiliated group of corporations filing a consolidated return are collectively treated as one taxpayer.[75]

1. *Qualified cost-sharing arrangements.* A cost-sharing arrangement is "an agreement under which the parties agree to share the costs of development of one or more intangibles in proportion to their shares of reasonably anticipated benefits from their individual exploitation of the interests in the intangibles assigned to them under the arrangement."[76] Although the IRS can apply the cost-sharing rules to any arrangement that is "in substance" a cost-sharing arrangement, a taxpayer can utilize the rules only for "qualified" arrangements.[77] A cost-sharing arrangement is qualified if it satisfies all of the following requirements:

a. The arrangement must have two or more participants.

b. It must provide "a method to calculate each controlled participant's share of intangible development costs, based on factors that can reasonably be expected to reflect that participant's share of anticipated benefits."

c. It must provide for "adjustments" to these shares "to account for changes in economic conditions, the business operations and practices of the participants, and the ongoing development of intangibles under the arrangement."

d. It must be set out in a writing that is "contemporaneous with the formation (and any revision) of the cost-sharing arrangement."[78]

The writing must, among other things, describe the scope of the research contemplated under the arrangement and each participant's interest in any intangible resulting from the research. A intangible resulting from the research is referred to as a "covered intangible."

2. *Eligible participants.* The participants in a cost-sharing arrangement may include both controlled and uncontrolled persons.[79] However, a controlled person's participation is recognized only if it "reasonably anticipates that it will derive benefits from the use of the covered intangibles" and "substantially complies" with an accounting requirement and various "administrative" requirements.[80] A "trade or business" is "a specific unified group of activities that

---

[75] Reg. §1.482-7(c)(5).

[76] Reg. §1.482-7(a).

[77] Reg. §1.482-7(a)(1).

[78] Reg. §1.482-7(b).

[79] Reg. §1.482-7(c)(1).

[80] Reg. §1.482-7(c)(1). The accounting requirement is that the controlled participants must account consistently for their costs and benefits and must do currency translations on a consistent basis. Reg. §1.482-7(i). The administrative requirements are that the participant must maintain various documents and, if it is a U.S. taxpayer, must attach to its U.S. income tax return a statement indicating that it is a participant in a cost sharing arrangement and identifying the other participants in the arrangement. Reg. §1.482-7(j).

constitute (or could constitute) an independent economic enterprise carried on for profit," usually including "every operation which forms a part of, or a step in, a process by which an enterprise may earn income or profit."[81] A trade or business is actively conducted if the controlled participant "carries out substantial managerial and operational activities."[82]

Assume domestic corporation DC enters into a cost-sharing agreement with its foreign parent corporation with respect to research to be conducted by the parent in a foreign country on processes for making widgets. The agreement vests DC with ownership of U.S. rights to the results of the research and reserves to the parent the rights in the remainder of the world. If DC does not produce widgets, but only imports and sells widgets produced by its parent in foreign countries, its participation in the agreement is not accepted for U.S. tax purposes because it does not use the intangible.[83] In contrast, DC is deemed to use the intangible in the active conduct of a trade or business if it contracts to have widgets produced by an unrelated person in the United States, owns the materials and work in progress while the goods are being produced by the contract manufacturer, bears all risks of loss, and exercises substantial managerial and operational control over the activities of the contract manufacturer.[84]

Regardless of actual use, a controlled participant is deemed not to use or reasonably expect to use a covered intangible in the active conduct of its trade or business if "a principal purpose" for its participation in the cost-sharing arrangement is "to obtain the intangible for transfer or license to" another person, whether controlled or uncontrolled.[85] For example, if DC did not manufacture widgets but instead licensed unrelated persons to use its technology in producing widgets, it could not be a participant in a qualified cost-sharing arrangement covering widget research.

However, this rule does not disqualify all controlled persons who intend to transfer or license the results of the research. Assume corporation C enters into a cost-sharing agreement with two other members of its controlled group to do research for the development of a new technology. The agreement gives C exclusive rights to use the technology throughout Europe.[86] If C intends to use the technology to produce and sell goods in most countries of Europe, but intends to license the technology to unrelated persons for use in a particular European country considered too remote from C's operations, the active business use requirement is satisfied, notwithstanding the intention to license, because the license is "relatively insignificant in comparison to the overall purpose of exploiting the European market."

---

[81] Reg. §1.482-7(c)(2)(i), incorporating the definition of Reg. §1.367(a)-2T(b)(2).
[82] Reg. §1.482-7(c)(2)(ii).
[83] Reg. §1.482-7(c)(2)(iii) Ex. 1.
[84] Reg. §1.482-7(c)(2)(ii) Ex. 2.
[85] Reg. §1.482-7(c)(3)(i).
[86] Reg. §1.482-7(c)(3)(ii) Ex.

3. *Participant's cost shares.* A qualified cost-sharing arrangement must, among other things, provide for the calculation of each participant's share of "intangible development costs."[87] This share consists of "all of the costs incurred by that participant related to the intangible development area," including cost-sharing payments to other participants, less cost-sharing payments received by the participant.[88] Assume domestic corporation *DC* and its foreign subsidiary (*FS*) make a cost-sharing agreement under which they agree to share the costs of a research project in the proportions 40 percent to *DC* and 60 percent to *FS*; for a particular year these costs consist of operating expenses of 100x incurred by *DC* and 100x by *FS*.[89] *FS* must make a payment to *DC* under the agreement for the year of 20x (excess of 60 percent of total costs of 200x over 100x of costs incurred by *FS*). *DC*'s deduction under §174 for the year is 80x (100x incurred less 20x of reimbursement), and *FS*'s R & D costs for the year are 120x (sum of 100x and 20x).

The costs "related to the intangible development area" include operating expenses (apart from depreciation and amortization) and arm's length charges for the use of tangible property that any participant makes "available to the qualified cost-sharing arrangement."[90] Assume *DC*'s contribution under the agreement consist of 5x of cash operating costs and the use of a building owned by *DC* and made available to the cost-sharing arrangement. The fair use value of the building for the year is 95x.[91] Current costs under the agreement include the use value of the building and thus are 100x for each participant, as in the original example. *DC*'s §174 deduction is the sum of 5x and its deductions related to the building, less the reimbursement from *FS*. If *DC*'s costs attributable to the building are less than 20x, the §174 deduction is zero, and the excess is rental income. Assume *DC*'s only deduction related to the building is depreciation of 7x. The reimbursement of 20x reduces the §174 costs from 12x (sum of 5x and 7x) to zero, and 8x of the reimbursement is rental income. *FS*'s R & D costs are 120x, as before. No charge for the use of intangible property made available to the cost-sharing arrangement can be included as an intangible development cost.[92]

Intangible development costs must be shared among the participants in a way that "can reasonably be expected to reflect [each] participant's share of anticipated benefits" in the form of "additional income generated or costs saved

---

[87] Reg. §1.482-7(b)(2).

[88] Reg. §§1.482-7(d)(1), (h)(1).

[89] Reg. §1.482-7(h)(2) Ex. 1.

[90] See Reg. §1.482-7(d)(2) Ex. 2 (IRS may require that intangible development costs include costs of field testing of device developed by research under cost-sharing arrangement).

If tangible property is supplied by a controlled participant, the charges to the cost-sharing arrangement for the use of the property are subject to adjustment under §482. Reg. §1.482-2(c), discussed supra ¶79.6.

[91] Reg. §1.482-7(h)(2) Ex. 2.

[92] For the treatment of intangibles that a participant makes available to the arrangement, see Reg. §1.482-7(g)(2), discussed infra text accompanying note 111.

by the use of covered intangibles."[93] The "reasonably anticipated benefits are the aggregate benefits that [the participant] reasonably anticipates that it will derive from covered intangibles."[94]

Cost allocations under a cost-sharing arrangement are evaluated annually by comparing each controlled participant's share of intangible development costs for the year to "its share of reasonably anticipated benefits."[95] The participant's share of the costs and the reasonably anticipated benefits are expressed as percentages of the aggregate costs and benefits (exclusive of the costs and benefits of uncontrolled participants in the arrangement).[96]

Reasonably anticipated benefits must be estimated by the most "reliable" means available.[97] Anticipated benefits must be estimated on a consistent basis for all controlled participants and, absent a change in circumstances, from year to year.[98] Anticipated benefits can be estimated directly as the income or cost savings expected from the covered intangibles[99] or indirectly by using bases "that reasonably can be assumed to be related to income generated or costs saved." Examples of indirect bases are units used, produced, or sold, sales, and operating profit.[100] Whether the estimate should be direct or indirect and, if indirect, the

---

[93] Reg. §§1.482-7(b)(2),(e)(1).

[94] Reg. §1.482-7(e)(2).

[95] Reg. §1.482-7(f)(1).

[96] Reg. §§1.482-7(f)(2), (3)(i).

[97] Reg. §1.482-7(f)(3)(i) (estimate's reliability depends "largely on the completeness and accuracy of the data, the soundness of the assumptions, and the relative effects of particular deficiencies in data or assumptions on the different estimates").

[98] Reg. §1.482-7(f)(3)(ii).

[99] Reg. §1.482-7(f)(3)(iii)(E) Ex. 7 (research on development of materials for training new employees allocated based on number of new employees and relative compensation levels).

[100] Reg. §1.482-7(f)(3)(iii). Units used, produced, or sold is most likely to be reliable where the intangibles are expected to be "exploited by the controlled participants in the use, production or sale of substantially uniform items under similar economic conditions." Reg. §1.482-7(f)(3)(iii)(A). See Reg. §1.482-7(f)(3)(iii)(E) Ex. 1. The number of units may be weighted if, for example, the covered intangible is being developed to reduce the required amount of a particular input and the usage of that input per unit of output varies among the controlled participants. Reg. §1.482-7(f)(3)(iii)(E) Ex. 2.

Sales is most likely to be a reliable measure only if the controlled participants operate at the same level of the market (e.g., manufacturing or distribution) and "the costs of exploiting covered intangibles are not substantial relative to the revenues generated"—if, for example, the principal benefit is expected to be an increase in revenues (e.g., by "a price premium") without substantially affecting costs. Reg. §1.482-7(f)(3)(iii)(B). See Reg. §1.482-7(f)(3)(iii)(E) Ex. 6 (where one controlled participant distributes to consumers and other sells to independent distributors, sales is not reliable basis "unless adjustments are made to account for the difference in market levels").

Operating profits is likely to be a reliable basis for estimation if "covered intangibles are integral to the activity that generates the profit and the activity could not be carriedon or would generate little profit without use of those intangibles." Reg. §1.482-

appropriate indirect basis depends on relative reliability in the circumstances, given the available data and assumptions.

The estimates must also reliably reflect expectations about the future, including "the time period between the inception of the research and development and the receipt of benefits, . . . the time over which benefits will be received, and . . . the benefits anticipated for each year in which it is anticipated that the intangible will generate benefits."[101] Discounts to present value are required if these factors vary from one controlled participant to another.[102] The reliability of projections may be judged, at least in part, by comparing them to the benefits actually realized by the participants over time.[103] Also, if the taxpayer used an unreliable basis for allocation, the most reliable of projections will not save the allocations from adjustment.

4. *Section 482 adjustments.* Generally, the IRS may make adjustments under §482 "with respect to a qualified cost-sharing arrangement" only to make each participant's share of the costs under the arrangement "equal to its share of reasonably anticipated benefits attributable to such development."[104] Any reallocation of costs under §482 is made for the year in which the costs are deductible

---

7(f)(3)(iii)(C). See Reg. §1.482-7(f)(3)(iii)(E) Ex. 4 (operating profits found to be most reliable measure for pharmaceutical).

Other indirect bases are acceptable only if "there is expected to be a reasonably identifiable relationship between the basis of measurement used and additional income generated or costs saved by the use of covered intangibles." Reg. §1.482-7(f)(3)(iii)(D).

[101] Reg. §1.482-7(f)(3)(iv)(A). See Reg. §§1.482-7(f)(3)(iv)(D) Exs. 2, 3 (present sales found to be reliable basis for projecting future benefits where market shares of domestic parent and foreign subsidiary are stable and products under development are not expected to produce unusual profits for either, but not where foreign subsidiary's market share is rapidly expanding because of business failure of competitor).

[102] See Reg. §1.482-7(f)(3)(iv)(D) Ex. 1 (research on new car model, which will probably be introduced by domestic subsidiary one year after it is introduced by foreign parent; discount to present value required), Reg. §1.482-7(f)(3)(iv)(D) Ex. 10 (discount rate must reflect risk of venture).

[103] Reg. §1.482-7(f)(3)(iv)(B). Projections normally are not disturbed if they diverge from actual results by not more than 20 percent or if the divergence results from "an extraordinary event, beyond the control of the participants," that "could not reasonably have been anticipated at the time that costs were shared." See Reg. §1.482-7(f)(3)(iv)(D) Ex. 5 (projection that parent and subsidiary would have equal sales not disturbed where actual total sales were split between them 42 percent and 58 percent), §1.482-7(f)(3)(iv)(D) Ex. 7 (projection of 60 percent/40 percent; actual results of 50 percent/50 percent; IRS may find that actual results are more reliable because, although actual results are within 20 percent of projection for one participant (participant projected to have 60 percent), they are not for other participant (participant projected to have 40 percent)).

Normally, all foreign controlled participants are lumped together in comparing the projected benefits with actual benefits. However, the IRS may adjust the relative cost shares of foreign participants "if the variation between actual and projected benefits has the effect of substantially reducing U.S. tax." Reg. §1.482-7(f)(3)(iv)(C). See Reg. §§1.482-7(f)(3)(iv)(D) Exs. 8, 9.

[104] Reg. §1.482-7(a)(2).

under §174.[105] When a reallocation increases the amount of a cost-sharing payment between controlled taxpayers, the IRS may make additional adjustments in the nature of interest to reflect the delay in the payment of the increased amount.[106]

Also, if a controlled taxpayer provides "assistance" in the development of an intangible (e.g., loans, services, or the use of property, tangible or intangible) but does not qualify as a controlled participant in a cost-sharing arrangement, it must be compensated at arm's length for this assistance.[107] This compensation is treated as a cost of the arrangement, which must be allocated among the qualified participants in the arrangement like all other costs of the arrangement. Any intangibles resulting from the research is deemed owned by the qualified participants.

Assume domestic corporation *DC*, its foreign operating subsidiary (*FS*), and its foreign research subsidiary (*RS*) enter into a cost sharing arrangement to develop manufacturing intangibles. The agreement assigns North American rights to the results of the research to *DC*, European and African rights to *FS*, and Asian rights to *RS*.[108] *DC* and *FS* intend to use these rights to improve the manufacture products that they presently produce and sell. *RS* has no manufacturing operations and intends to license the rights in Asia. Under the cost-sharing agreement, the parties share the costs of the research in the proportions 40 percent by *DC*, 20 percent by *FS*, and 40 percent by RS. However, *RS* is not a qualified participant in the arrangement because it will not use the rights in the active conduct of a trade or business. The IRS may therefore make adjustments under §482 allocating to *RS*compensation from*DC* and *FS* for the last 40 percent of its costs (allocating the burden of this compensation between *DC* and *FS* in the two-thirds/one-third ratio suggested by their agreement). *DC* and *FS* are considered the owners of worldwide rights. Once the research generates results, additional compensation in the nature of royalties may be allocated from *RS* to *DC* and *FS* to reflect *RS*' use of the Asian rights, which are actually owned by *RS* but are treated for purposes of §482 as owned by *DC* and *FS*.

5. *Ownership of covered intangibles.* Generally, an intangible covered by a cost-sharing arrangement is considered owned in the proportions specified by the agreement among the participants. If the agreement does not specify the participant's interests, the intangibles are deemed owned in proportion to their shares of the costs under the arrangement.[109]

Also, the percentage interests in covered intangibles are determined by the substance of the arrangement, rather than its terms, if "a controlled participant

---

[105] Reg. §1.482-7(f)(4).

[106] The time-value-of-money adjustment must be "consistent with" §1.482-2(a), discussed supra ¶79.4.

[107] Reg. §1.482-7(c)(4)(i).

[108] Reg. §1.482-7(c)(4)(ii) Ex.

[109] Reg. §1.482-7(g)(6). If cost shares varied over the arrangement's term, costs are discounted to present value as of the date that the first costs were incurred.

bears costs of intangible development that over a period of years are consistently and materially greater or lesser than its share of reasonably anticipated benefits."[110] In this case, the IRS may, for example, treat the intangible as owned in the proportions that the costs were borne, and each controlled participant whose anticipated benefits are less than its share of the costs is entitled to compensation at arm's length for the excess use of the intangibles by the other participants.

6. *Use of preexisting intangibles.* If a controlled participant owns an interest in a preexisting intangible that is made available to other controlled participants "for purposes of research in the intangible development area" covered by a qualified cost-sharing arrangement, the latter must make a "buy-in payment" to the former.[111] The payment due from each of the latter must equal the arm's length compensation for the use of the intangible, multiplied by the participant's percentage share of the reasonably anticipated benefits from the research. If two or more controlled participants supply preexisting intangibles, the various payments among participants under this rule are netted against each other.

7. *Transfers of interests in covered intangibles.* If a controlled participant joins a cost-sharing arrangement after costs have been incurred, it must make an arm's length payment to one or more of the existing participants to compensate for the interest it acquires in the work in progress.[112] Assume four members of a controlled group enter into a cost-sharing arrangement for a long-term research project and, in the tenth year of the project, a fifth member of the group joins the arrangement, agreeing to pay a share of future costs in exchange for rights to the covered intangibles in a portion of the territory previously assigned to one of the other participants.[113] That other participant must receive a payment from the new participant equal to the value of the other participant's rights under the covered intangibles in the surrendered territory.

Conversely, if a controlled participant "transfers, abandons, or otherwise relinquishes an interest under the arrangement," it must receive arm's length compensation from the other participants for the interests in covered intangibles that pass to the latter.[114] This rule might apply if, for example, a parent corporation and its subsidiaries make a cost-sharing agreement for the development of a manufacturing process and, on completion of the research, one of the subsidiaries ceases manufacturing and becomes a distributor of goods produced by the parent.[115] If the relinquishing participant ever uses a covered intangible, it must compensate the other participants for this use.

---

[110] Reg. §1.482-7(g)(5).

[111] Reg. §1.482-7(g)(2).

[112] Reg. §1.482-7(g)(3).

[113] Reg. §1.482-7(g)(8) Ex. 1.

[114] Reg. §1.482-7(g)(4).

[115] Reg. §1.482-7(g)(8) Ex. 2.

8. *Collateral effects of cost-sharing arrangements.* A cost-sharing arrangement is not treated as a partnership subject to subchapter K of the Code.[116]

Also, a foreign corporation participating in a cost-sharing arrangement is not considered engaged in business in the United States merely because work under the arrangement is done in the United States by another participant in the arrangement.[117] For example, if a domestic parent corporation enters into a cost-sharing agreement with a foreign subsidiary with respect to research work done by the parent in the United States, the subsidiary's participation in the arrangement is not treated as engaging in business in the United States.

¶79.9 COMPARABLE PROFITS METHOD

The comparable profits method can be used in appropriate cases for testing and, if necessary, adjusting the prices charged in controlled transfers of tangible or intangible property.[1] Under this method, the operating profits reported by one party to a controlled transaction are compared with operating profits computed using "objective measures of profitability (profit level indicators) derived from uncontrolled taxpayers that engage in similar business activities."[2] If this comparison reveals that the reported profits deviate from those that would have resulted at arm's length, the arm's length consideration for the controlled transactions is the price that yields the arm's length profits. The comparable profits method "relies on the general principle that similarly situated taxpayers will tend to earn similar returns over a reasonable period of time."[3]

In promulgating the regulations on the comparable profits method (CPM), the Treasury commented:

> Given adequate data, methods that determine an arm's length price (*e.g.*, the CUP method) or gross margin (*e.g.*, the resale price method) generally achieve a higher degree of comparability than the CPM. Because the degree of comparability, including the extent and reliability of adjustments, determines the relative reliability of the result under the best method

---

[116] Reg. §1.482-7(a)(1). For subchapter K, see infra chs. 85-87.

[117] Reg. §1.482-7(a)(1).

[1] Reg. §§1.482-3(a)(4), 1.482-4(a)(2).

[2] Reg. §1.482-5(a). See generally Organisation for Economic Cooperation and Development, Transfer Pricing Guidelines for Multinational Enterprises and Tax Administrations ch. III (1995); Culbertson, A Rose by Any Other Name: Smelling the Flowers at the OECD's (Last) Resort, 11 Tax Notes Int'l 371 (Aug. 7, 1995). This method is similar to the Basic Arm's Length Return Method (BALRM) proposed by the IRS in A Study of Intercompany Pricing (White Paper) issued in 1988 and published as Notice 88-123, 1988-2 CB 458. See Horst, Profit Split Methods, 60 Tax Notes 335, 337-38 (1993).

[3] TD 8552, 1994-2 CB 93, 109.

rule, the results of these methods will be selected unless the data necessary to apply them is relatively incomplete or unreliable. In this regard the CPM generally would be considered a method of last resort.[4]

Assume a U.S. manufacturer distributes its goods in foreign country X through a subsidiary incorporated in that country. The subsidiary's net income might be computed under the comparable profits method by (1) determining the ratio of operating profit to sales of comparable uncontrolled distributors, (2) computing the subsidiary's operating profit as the product of that rate and the subsidiary's sales revenues, and (3) setting the arm's length price for the parent's sales to the subsidiary at the amount yielding the operating profit so computed. Assume the subsidiary has sales revenues of $1,000, and $150 of operating expenses. If the comparable parties' ratio of operating profit to sales is 4 percent, the subsidiary's operating profit under the comparable profits method is $40 (4 percent of $1,000), and the arm's length price for the parent's sales to the subsidiary is $810—the sales revenues ($1,000), less the sum of the subsidiary's operating expenses ($150) and operating profit ($40).

The comparable profits method may also be used in testing controlled transfers of intellectual property. Assume a U.S. company licenses valuable patents to a foreign subsidiary, which uses the patents in manufacturing goods that it sells to other subsidiaries of the parent.[5] The royalties paid by the manufacturing subsidiary to the parent might be tested by comparing the gross profits reported by the subsidiary to those of companies engaged in similar manufacturing operations, based, for example, on their rates of return on capital employed. If this comparison reveals that the subsidiary's operating profits are not at arm's length, the royalties are adjusted under §482 to be the amount that produces an arm's length operating profit for the subsidiary.[6]

The basic approach of the comparable profits method is to calculate the "operating profit that the tested party would have earned on related party transactions if its profit level indicator were equal to that of an uncontrolled comparable (comparable operating profit)."[7] The four crucial concepts in the quoted

---

[4] Id.

[5] Reg. §1.482-5(e) Ex. 4.

[6] Alternatively, the prices paid by the other subsidiaries for the goods produced by the manufacturing subsidiary might be tested by this method. However, the method cannot be applied to both transfers. For example, if the subsidiary's operating profits are determined not to be at arm's length, the comparable profits method does not indicate whether the deviation from arm's length was the royalties paid or the prices received. Even if the subsidiary's operating profits are at arm's length, this may be only because the royalties and the prices for the goods both deviate from arm's length in opposite directions. Thus, either the royalties or the prices for the goods must be determined by another method, so that determination can be used in applying the comparable profits method to the other. Since more methods are provided for sales of goods, the comparable profits method is probably most often reserved for the intangibles transfer.

[7] Reg. §1.482-5(b)(1).

words—"operating profit," "tested party," "profit level indicator," and "comparable operating profit"—are discussed below. The ensuing discussion also describes detailed comments in the regulations on the application under this method of the general requirements of comparability and reliability.

1. *Operating profit.* Under the comparable profits method, the operating profits reported by the tested party are compared with operating profits that can be inferred from a profit level indicator. "Operating profit" is sales revenues, less the cost of goods sold and operating expenses.[8] "Operating expenses" consist of all expenses not included in the cost of goods sold, except interest, income taxes, and "other expenses not related to the operation of the relevant business activity."[9] The costs of advertising, marketing, sales, warehousing and distribution, and administration, including a reasonable allowance for depreciation and amortization, are usually operating expenses. According to the regulations:

> Operating profit includes all income derived from the business activity being evaluated by the comparable profits method, but does not include interest and dividends, income derived from activities not being tested by this method, or extraordinary gains and losses that do not relate to the continuing operations of the tested party.[10]

"Reported operating profit" is the tested party's operating profit, as "reflected on a timely filed U.S. income tax return."[11] If the tested party does not file a U.S. income tax return for the year, its operating profit is "reflected" in a U.S. return if the controlled transactions affect the U.S. taxable income of any member of the controlled group. Assume the tested party is a foreign subsidiary of a domestic corporation, and its business is assembly of computers that it sells to the parent. The foreign subsidiary's operating profit is "reflected" in the parent's U.S. return because the parent's purchase of the computers from the subsidiary affects the parent's cost of goods sold, an item in the calculation of its U.S. taxable income. If the profit level indicator is taken from the financial statements, rather than the tax returns, of the comparable parties, the tested party's reported operating profit may be adjusted for differences between its financial statements and tax returns. The reported operating profit is also adjusted to include other §482 determinations that have already been finally determined.

2. *Tested party.* The first step in applying the comparable profits method is to identify one of the parties to the controlled transactions as the "tested party." This person is the participant in the controlled transactions whose operating profits from the transactions "can be verified using the most reliable data and requiring the fewest and most reliable adjustments, and for which reliable data

---

[8] Reg. §§1.482-5(d)(2), (4). "Sales revenues" are receipts from sales of goods and services, determined by accounting principles and conventions "accepted in the trade or industry," less returns and allowances. Reg. §1.482-5(d)(1).

[9] Reg. §1.482-5(d)(3).

[10] Reg. §1.482-5(d)(4).

[11] Reg. §1.482-5(d)(5).

regarding uncontrolled comparables can be located."[12] The tested party is usually "the least complex of the controlled taxpayers" since locating comparable situations is generally much easier for simple operations than for complex operations. Also, because copyrights, patents, and other intellectual property are, by nature, unique and blur profit comparisons, the tested party typically does "not own valuable intangible property or unique assets that distinguish it from potential uncontrolled comparables."[13] For example, if a foreign manufacturer distributes its products in the United States through a U.S. subsidiary, functioning as a wholesale distributor, the tested party is likely the subsidiary because a sales company is usually less complex and uses fewer intangibles than a manufacturing company.[14]

3. *Profit level indicator.* The comparison of operating profits that is the heart of the comparable profits method is done by applying a profit level indicator extracted from uncontrolled comparables to financial data of the tested party. "Profit level indicators are ratios that measure the relationships between profits and costs incurred or resources employed."[15] Examples are the rate of return on capital and the ratios of profit to costs or sales revenue. The appropriateness of a particular indicator in a particular case depends on whether it "is likely to produce a reliable measure of the income that the tested party would have earned had it dealt with controlled taxpayers at arm's length, taking into account all of the facts and circumstances." This depends, in turn, such things as "the nature of the activities of the tested party [and] the reliability of the available data with respect to uncontrolled comparables." The regulations elaborate on two types of ratios—rates of return and financial ratios—but do not rule out other indicators.

a. *Rate of return.* "The rate of return on capital employed is the ratio of operating profit to operating assets."[16] The tested party's "operating assets" consist of all assets used in the "relevant business activity," including both fixed assets (e.g., plant and equipment) and current assets (e.g., cash, cash equivalents, accounts receivable, and inventories).[17] Investments in subsidiaries, "excess cash," and "portfolio investments" are not operating assets. Operating assets may be valued at either book value or fair market value, but the same valuation

---

[12] Reg. §1.482-5(b)(2)(i).

[13] See Reg. §1.482-8 Ex. 9 (applying comparable profits method using as tested party foreign subsidiary manufacturing compact disks under technology, supplied by U.S. parent, that allows disks to be produced at much lower cost than under competing technology). However, because it is "possibl[e] that a comparable uncontrolled taxpayer with such intangibles might be found," the regulations do not "rule out" the use of a tested party whose income derives in material part from valuable intangibles. TD 8552, supra note 3, at 110.

[14] Reg. §1.482-5(e) Ex. 1.

[15] Reg. §1.482-5(b)(4).

[16] Reg. §1.482-5(b)(4)(i).

[17] Reg. §1.482-5(d)(6).

basis must be used for both the tested party and the comparable parties, and consistency from year to year is required. Regardless of valuation basis, operating assets must be reflected at the average of their values at the beginning and end of the taxable year, appropriately adjusted if "substantial fluctuations in the value of operating assets during the year make this an inaccurate measure of the average value over the year." According to the regulations, "it may be necessary to take into account recent acquisitions, leased assets, intangibles, currency fluctuations, and other items that may not be explicitly recorded in the financial statements of the tested party or the uncontrolled comparable."

The reliability of rate of return as a profit level indicator generally depends on three factors.[18] The first is the importance of the role played by operating assets "in generating operating profits for both the tested party and the uncontrolled comparable." For example, if a tested party manufactures goods under patents held by its parent corporation and resells the goods to other affiliates of the parent, rate of return might be the most reliable profit level indicator because operating assets are likely the most important factor in the generation of the tested party's profits and its investment risks are not unusual.[19] The second factor is the similarity of the "composition" of the assets of the tested and comparable parties.[20] Third, the reliability of this profit level indicator is diminished by any "difficulties in properly valuing operating assets."

b. *Financial ratios.* The regulations give two examples of financial ratios that are reliable in some cases—the ratio of operating profits to sales revenues and the ratio of gross profit to operating expenses.[21] Financial ratios are generally reliable indicators of arm's length results only if the functions performed by the tested party and the uncontrolled comparables are identical or, at least, very similar. "Since functional differences generally have a greater effect on the relationship between profit and costs or sales revenue than the relationship between profit and operating assets, financial ratios are more sensitive to functional differences than the rate of return on capital employed." Also, the reliability of the ratio of gross profit to operating expenses depends on the extent of the similarity of the "composition" of the operating expenses of the tested and uncontrolled parties.

c. *Other profit level indicators.* Other profit level indicators may also be used if they are "objective measures of profitability derived from operations of uncontrolled taxpayers engaged in similar business activities under similar circumstances" and are not derived from "internal data."[22] Other indicators, like the indicators described in the regulations, may be used only if they provide

---

[18] Reg. §1.482-5(b)(4)(i).
[19] See Reg. §1.482-5(e) Ex. 4.
[20] Reg. §1.482-5(b)(4)(i).
[21] Reg. §1.482-5(b)(4)(ii).
[22] Reg. §1.482-5(b)(4)(iii).

"reliable measures of the income that the tested party would have earned had it dealt with controlled taxpayers at arm's length."

d. *Requirements for all indicators.* Profit level indicators should be derived from data from a "sufficient number of years . . . to reasonably measure returns that accrue to uncontrolled comparables."[23] Usually, the taxable year and the two preceding years are the minimum. The profit level indicators are applied to the tested party over the same period. For example, if the comparable profits method is applied with a profit level indicator determined over the three years consisting of the taxable year and the preceding two years and if the tested party's average operating profit for those years is in line with that inferred from the profit level indicator, no §482 adjustment is made, even if the tested party's operating profit for the taxable year differs substantially from the inferred profit.[24]

However, if the tested party's average operating profit for these years is determined not to be at arm's length, §482 adjustments are determined year by year, without regard to the resulting multiyear average.[25] Moreover, in applying §482 in subsequent years, the tested party's average operating profits are based on reported operating profits, not operating profits after the comparable profits method has been applied in the earlier years, unless the adjustments for the earlier years have been "finally determined."[26] For example, if the comparable profits method is applied in a simultaneous audit of two successive years, §482 adjustments for the first year are not reflected in the average of operating profits used in applying the method to the second year.

4. *Comparable operating profit.* The comparable profits method is based on a comparison of the tested party's reported operating profit with the comparable operating profit. The comparable operating profit is determined by "applying a profit level indicator to the financial data related to the tested party's most narrowly identifiable business activity for which data is available (relevant business activity)."[27] For example, if the tested party manufactures goods using patents and know-how licensed from its corporate parent and the profit level indicator is the rate of return, the comparable operating profit is the product of the rate of return of the uncontrolled comparables and the value of the tested party's assets used in the manufacturing operations.

---

[23] Reg. §1.482-5(b)(4). See TD 8552, supra note 3, at 110 ("Comparison of multiple year averages may provide a more accurate reflection of a taxpayer's transfer pricing practices over a period than an analysis based on a single year and reduces the effect of short-term variations in operating profit that may be unrelated to transfer pricing").

[24] Reg. §1.482-5(e) Ex. 1.

[25] Reg. §1.482-5(e) Ex. 2.

[26] Reg. §§1.482-1(f)(2)(iii)(D), 1.482-5(e) Ex. 3. However, all §482 adjustments made under methods other than the comparable profits method, including adjustments for the taxable year and all earlier years, are reflected in the reported operating profit. Reg. §1.482-5(b)(2)(ii).

[27] Reg. §1.482-5(b)(1).

If possible, the profit level indicator should be applied "solely to the tested party's financial data" on the controlled transactions.[28] The reliability of the comparable profits method is usually reduced if the profit level indicator can be applied only with financial data on a broader group of transactions.[29] For example, if the tested party assembles appliances from components purchased from both controlled and uncontrolled persons, the comparable profits method might not be reliable because no available profit level indicator can be applied solely to data on the controlled transactions (controlled purchases of components).

5. *Comparability and reliability.* Under the best method rule, the comparable profits method may be used only if it is "the most reliable measure" of arm's length results.[30] The reliability of the method depends on "the degree of comparability between the tested party and the uncontrolled taxpayer."[31] The regulations contain two examples, involving a U.S. subsidiary manufacturing machine tool parts for sale to a foreign parent, comparing the cost plus and comparable profits methods under the best method rule. In the examples, the IRS is able to ascertain the gross profit markups of four U.S. companies manufacturing various types of machine tool parts for sale to unrelated persons. The cost plus method is found to be less "susceptible to any unidentified differences," and therefore the best method, if there is a "close functional similarity" between the controlled and uncontrolled transactions and the available data allows reliable adjustments to be made for any accounting differences.[32] On the other hand, if the controlled and uncontrolled transactions differ "significant[ly]" in the nature of the parts produced and the complexity of the manufacturing processes, these functional differences might have material effects on gross profit margins for which reliable adjustments cannot be made, in which case the comparable profits method might be the best method.[33]

Some factors that might affect comparability in particular cases are "the relevant lines of business, the product or service markets involved, the asset composition employed (including the nature and quantity of tangible assets, intangible assets and working capital), the size and scope of operations, and the stage in a business or product cycle."[34]

Since operating profits are "a return for the investment of resources and assumption of risks," comparability under this method "is particularly dependent on resources employed and risks assumed."[35] For example, if the tested party and an uncontrolled party have similar operations, but one assumes a

---

[28] Id.

[29] Reg. §1.482-5(c)(3)(iii).

[30] Reg. §1.482-5(c)(1). For the best method rule, see Reg. §1.482-1(c), discussed supra ¶79.3.3.

[31] Reg. §1.482-5(c)(2)(i).

[32] Reg. §1.482-8 Ex. 5.

[33] Reg. §1.482-8 Ex. 6.

[34] Reg. §1.482-5(c)(2)(i).

[35] Reg. §1.482-5(c)(2)(ii).

substantial business risk that the other does not bear, a profit level indicator derived from this uncontrolled party is not likely to be reliable.

The "functions performed" must also be considered "because resources and risks usually are directly related to functions performed."[36] However, a lesser functional comparability is required under this method than under the resale price or cost plus method. Moreover, because "operating profit usually is less sensitive than gross profit to product differences," product similarity is less important under the comparable profits method than under the resale price or cost plus method.[37] For example, if the tested party distributes goods produced by its parent corporation and all similar products are also sold through distributors controlled by the manufacturers, the comparable profits method, applied with profit level indicators taken from "the same industry segment," might provide the most reliable results because the lack of product similarity with uncontrolled comparables may preclude use of the CUP, resale price, and cost plus methods.[38]

On the other hand, some factors may be more important under the comparable profits method than under other methods.

> For example, operating profit may be affected by varying cost structures (as reflected, for example, in the age of plant and equipment), differences in business experience (such as whether the business is in a start-up phase or is mature), or differences in management efficiency (as indicated, for example, by objective evidence such as expanding or contracting sales or executive compensation over time).[39]

"Determining whether such differences exist may be difficult in some cases."[40]

Adjustments should be made for differences between the tested and comparable parties that "materially affect the profits determined under the relevant profit level indicator."[41] For example, it is sometimes appropriate to adjust an uncontrolled comparable's assets "to achieve greater comparability," in which case the comparable's operating profits must also be adjusted before a profit level indicator is computed. Assume the tested party is a U.S. company that manufactures goods and sells them to its parent corporation. The prices for the goods are tested under the comparable profits method, using rate of return as the profit level indicator.[42] If the tested party has substantially smaller accounts receivable than the uncontrolled comparables, the comparable profits method is likely not the best method unless reliable adjustments are made for this difference. The

---

[36] Id.

[37] Reg. §1.482-5(c)(2)(iii).

[38] Reg. §1.482-5(e) Ex. 1.

[39] Reg. §1.482-5(c)(2)(iii).

[40] TD 8552, supra note 3, at 110.

[41] Reg. §1.482-5(c)(2)(iv). For the adjustment rules, see Reg. §1.482-1(d)(2), discussed supra ¶79.3.4.

[42] Reg. §1.482-5(e) Ex. 5.

appropriate adjustments are (1) eliminating accounts receivable from the operating assets of the tested party and the uncontrolled comparables and (2) reducing reported operating profits (of both the tested party and the uncontrolled comparables) by imputed interest on the accounts receivable. The imputed interest should be at a rate appropriate for short-term instruments. Conversely, if the accounts payable of the tested and comparable parties differ materially, operating profits of all parties should usually be reduced by an imputed interest charge on the payables.[43]

As under all methods, the reliability of a particular application of the comparable profits method depends on the quality of the data and the soundness of the assumptions used.[44] Consistency in accounting methods between the tested and comparable parties is also important, except as to matters that do not materially affect operating profits. For example, differences in inventory and cost accounting practices can impair the reliability of the method if "reliable adjustments" cannot be made for these differences. However, a lack of information on how the uncontrolled comparables allocate costs between cost of goods sold and operating expenses does not rule out use of the comparable profits method, even though this allocation determines when the costs are charged against operating profits.[45]

Moreover, the reliability of profit level indicators and operating profit comparisons is affected by allocations of costs, income, and assets between the activities including the controlled transactions and other activities.[46] These allocations must be based on either "factual relationships" or a "reasonable allocation formula." Without "direct allocations," the comparable profits method may be less reliable than other methods requiring fewer allocations.

6. *Arm's length ranges.* As under all other methods, reported results are found to be at arm's length if they fall within an arm's length range constructed with data from several uncontrolled comparables.[47] For example, if data from 10 uncontrolled comparables establish an arm's length range of ratios of sales to operating profit from 3.8 to 6.7 percent, the uncontrolled transactions are considered at arm's length unless the tested party's reported operating profit is less than 3.8 percent of sales revenues or more than 6.7 percent.[48] Under the comparable profits method, the range must consist of "comparable operating profits

---

[43] Reg. §1.482-5(c)(2)(iv). See Reg. §1.482-5(e) Ex. 6.

[44] Reg. §1.482-5(c)(3)(i).

[45] But see Reg. §1.482-8 Ex. 3 (applying comparable profits method, even though available data did not disclose how uncontrolled comparables allocated discounts, insurance, warranty costs, and supervisory, general, and administrative expenses between cost of goods sold and operating expenses).

[46] Reg. §1.482-5(c)(3)(iii).

[47] For the rules on arm's length ranges, see Reg. §1.482-1(e)(2), discussed supra ¶79.3.5.

[48] Reg. §1.482-5(e) Ex. 1.

derived from a single profit level indicator."[49] For example, ratios of operating profit to sales for some uncontrolled comparables, and rates of return on capital employed for other comparables, cannot be combined in a single arm's length range.

If the reported results fall outside the arm's length range, they are adjusted under §482, usually at the median of the results in the range. Assume the comparable profits method is applied with the ratio of operating profits to sales, and the arm's length range is comprised of the ratios of 10 uncontrolled comparables, ranging from 0.5 to 7.4 percent.[50] If the tested party reported a loss for the year, its operating profits are adjusted to be at the median of the arm's length range. For example, if the fifth and sixth companies among the uncontrolled comparables had operating profits to sales ratios of 2.8 percent and 2.9 percent, the tested party's operating profits are restated as 2.85 percent of its sales.

¶79.10 PROFIT SPLIT METHOD

The profit split method tests "whether the allocation of the combined operating profit or loss attributable to one or more controlled transactions is at arm's length."[1] The "basic approach" of this method is "to estimate an arm's length return by comparing the relative economic contributions that the parties make to the success of a venture, and dividing the returns from that venture between them on the basis of the relative value of such contributions."[2] The relative values of the controlled taxpayers' contributions depend on "the functions performed, risks assumed, and resources employed."[3] The objective is to achieve an allocation of the combined operating profit "that would result from an arrangement between uncontrolled taxpayers, each performing functions similar to those of the various controlled taxpayers engaged in the relevant business activity." The Treasury has referred to the profit split method as a method "of last resort" because it is usually applied "either wholly or in part [with] internal data rather than data derived from uncontrolled taxpayers."[4]

The combined operating profit allocated under this method must be that of "the most narrowly identifiable business activity of the controlled taxpayers for which data is available that includes the controlled transaction (relevant business activity)."[5] The reliability of the method, and thus the possibility that it may be the best method, is usually highest when the method is applied using "financial

---

[49] Reg. §1.482-5(b)(3).

[50] Reg. §1.482-5(e) Ex. 2.

[1] Reg. §1.482-6(a).

[2] TD 8552, 1994-2 CB 93, 110.

[3] Reg. §1.482-6(b).

[4] TD 8552, supra note 2, at 110, 111.

[5] Reg. §1.482-6(a).

data that is related solely to the controlled transactions."[6] For example, if the relevant business activity is the production of goods assembled from components, some of which are purchased from controlled suppliers and some of which are purchased from uncontrolled suppliers, the profit split method may not yield reliable results because "it may not be possible to apply the method solely to financial data related to the controlled transaction."[7]

When this method is used, the operating profit allocated to a particular member of a controlled group may exceed the group's combined operating profit from the transactions.[8] That is, for any year, the allocation of the combined operating profit may consist of profits to some of the controlled taxpayers and losses to others.

The profit split method must be applied with one of two allocation methods—the comparable profit split or the residual profit split,[9] which are described below.

1. *Comparable profit split.* Under the comparable profit split, the combined operating profit of the controlled taxpayers is allocated among them in proportions inferred from a "comparable profit split . . . derived from the combined operating profit of uncontrolled taxpayers whose transactions and activities are similar to those of the controlled taxpayers in the relevant business activity."[10] Under the best method rule, the comparable profit split, like any other method, may be used only if it is the most reliable measure of arm's length results.[11]

Whether particular uncontrolled taxpayers are comparable is determined under the general rules for comparability;[12] however, the regulations provide the following guidance on the application of these rules under the comparable profit split method.

a. Since operating profits are "a return for the investment of resources and assumption of risks," comparability under this method "is particularly dependent on resources employed and risks assumed."[13] For example, if a controlled taxpayer and an uncontrolled party have similar operations, but one assumes a substantial business risk that the other does not bear, a profit split derived from this uncontrolled party is not likely to be reliable.

b. The "functions performed" must also be considered "because resources

---

[6] Reg. §§1.482-6(c)(2)(ii)(C)(1), (3)(ii)(C)(1).

[7] Reg. §1.482-6(c)(2)(ii)(C)(1).

[8] Reg. §1.482-6(b).

[9] Reg. §1.482-6(c)(1).

[10] Reg. §1.482-6(c)(2)(i).

[11] Reg. §1.482-6(c)(2)(ii)(A). For the best method rule, see Reg. §1.482-1(c), discussed supra ¶79.3.3.

[12] Reg. §1.482-6(c)(2)(ii)(B)(1). For the comparability rules, see Reg. §1.482-1(c), discussed supra ¶79.3.4.

[13] Reg. §§1.482-5(c)(2)(ii), 1.482-6(c)(2)(ii)(B)(1).

and risks usually are directly related to functions performed."[14] However, a lesser functional comparability is required under this method than under the resale price or cost plus method.

c. Product similarity is also less important under the comparable profit split than under the resale price or cost plus method because "operating profit usually is less sensitive than gross profit to product differences."[15]

d. The contracts among the controlled taxpayers must be comparable to those among the uncontrolled taxpayers "because the contractual terms of the relationship among the participants in the relevant business activity will be a principal determinant of the allocation of functions and risks among them."[16]

e. The comparable profit split may not be used if the combined operating profit of the uncontrolled taxpayers, expressed as a percentage of "the combined assets," is "significantly" different from that of the controlled taxpayers.[17]

As under all methods, the reliability of the results under the comparable profit split depends on "the quality of the data and assumptions used."[18] For example, although adjustments should be made for any differences between the controlled and uncontrolled taxpayers "that would materially affect the division of operating profit,"[19] the reliability of the comparable profit split depends on the soundness of the data and assumptions underlying the adjustments.[20]

A particularly important factor under the comparable profit split is "the reliability of the allocation of costs, income, and assets between the relevant business activity and the participants' other activities."[21] This allocation may be made by a "reasonable allocation formula" if "direct" allocations "based on factual relationships" are not possible. However, when formulas are used, "fewer allocations of costs, income, and assets" are likely to yield more reliable results than applications of the method requiring more such allocations.

Another important factor is "consistency between the controlled and uncontrolled taxpayers in accounting practices that materially affect the items that determine the amount and allocation of operating profit."[22] For example, if the controlled and uncontrolled taxpayers have different inventory and cost accounting practices, the comparable profit split is unlikely to be the best method unless

---

[14] Id.

[15] Reg. §§1.482-5(c)(2)(iii), 1.482-6(c)(2)(ii)(B)(*1*).

[16] Reg. §1.482-6(c)(2)(ii)(A)(*1*).

[17] Reg. §1.482-6(c)(2)(ii)(B)(*1*).

[18] Reg. §1.482-6(c)(2)(ii)(C).

[19] Reg. §1.482-6(c)(2)(ii)(B)(2).

[20] Reg. §1.482-1(d)(2).

[21] Reg. §1.482-6(c)(2)(ii)(C)(*1*).

[22] Reg. §1.482-6(c)(2)(ii)(C)(2).

reliable adjustments can be made for the accounting differences. Consistency in accounting practices among the controlled taxpayers is also important.

All other things being equal, the comparable profit split is most reliable if it is applied to all of the controlled taxpayers and least reliable if applied to only one of them.[23] However, a comparable profit split for only one controlled taxpayer may be the best method if the data and assumptions available for applying the method to that taxpayer are more sound than those available for applying the method to other members of the controlled group.

2. *Residual profit split.* The residual profit split method consists of two steps—allocating to each controlled taxpayer a market return on its "routine contributions" to the relevant business activity and allocating any remainder of the combined operating profit among the controlled taxpayers in proportion to their nonroutine contributions.[24] According to the regulations, each controlled taxpayer's contributions are identified by a "functional analysis" that considers "the functions performed, risks assumed, and resources employed."[25] However, the details of this method make it clear that "contributions" are assets and liabilities.

A contribution is routine if "contributions of the same or a similar kind [are] made by uncontrolled taxpayers involved in similar business activities for which it is possible to identify market returns."[26] Tangible property and services are usually routine, and intangibles can also be routine if services or property of the same type "are generally owned by uncontrolled taxpayers engaged in similar activities." However, an intangible is routine only if it is sufficiently similar to property owned by uncontrolled taxpayers to allow a reliable value to be established for the property.

The profit allocated to each controlled taxpayer in the first step of the residual profit split is the product of the taxpayer's routine contributions and a market rate of return. The market rates of return are those "achieved by uncontrolled taxpayers engaged in similar activities."[27]

In most cases, any combined operating profit not allocated in the first step is attributable to "valuable intangible property" that is not "similar" to that "owned by the uncontrolled taxpayers from which the market returns are derived."[28] In these cases, this portion of the combined operating profit—the "residual profit"—is "divided among the controlled taxpayers based upon the relative value of their contributions of intangible property to the relevant business activity," exclusive of any intangible property taken into account in the first step.

Ideally, this division should be based on fair market values. However, since these intangibles are, by definition, not "routine," fair market values usually

---

[23] Reg. §1.482-6(c)(2)(ii)(D).

[24] Reg. §1.482-6(c)(3)(i).

[25] Reg. §1.482-6(c)(3)(i)(A).

[26] Reg. §1.482-6(c)(3)(i)(A).

[27] Id.

[28] Reg. §1.482-6(c)(3)(i)(B).

cannot be reliably established.[29] The regulations therefore allow relative values to be "estimated" as "the capitalized cost of developing the intangibles and all related improvements and updates, less an appropriate amount of amortization based on the useful life of each intangible."[30] Moreover, in lieu of capitalizing the actual costs of each intangible, the relative amounts of expenditures "in recent years may be used to estimate the relative value of intangible contributions" if "the intangible development expenditures of the parties are relatively constant over time and the useful life of the intangible property of all parties is approximately the same." However, if an intangible is used both in the relevant business activity and other activities, its value must be "appropriate[ly]" allocated between the activities.

The residual profit split, like any other method, may be used only if, in the circumstances, it is the best method.[31] It is the best method only if, taking into account the "comparability and quality of data and assumptions," it provides the most reliable measure of arm's length results.[32]

Generally, comparability, and hence reliability, are reduced if, in the second step of the profit split, internal data—capitalization of development costs or expenditures in recent years—are used instead of "market benchmarks."[33] Development costs may not be a good surrogate for market value, the process of capitalizing development costs may require relatively arbitrary allocations among business activities, and useful life can usually only be estimated. Thus, if internal data is used, the reliability of the residual profit split declines "as the amount of the residual profit allocated pursuant to the second step increases."[34] However, although the residual profit split is "generally . . . considered a method of last resort," it may be the best method, even though applied with internal data, if "the data necessary to apply [other methods are] relatively incomplete or unreliable."

The reliability of the results under the residual profit split depends importantly on the soundness of the data and assumptions used.[35] Other important factors are the reliability of any allocations of costs, income, or assets and accounting consistency between and among the controlled and uncontrolled tax-

---

[29] TD 8552, supra note 2, at 111.

[30] Reg. §1.482-6(c)(3)(i)(B).

[31] For the best method rule, see Reg. §1.482-1(c), discussed supra ¶79.3.3.

[32] Reg. §1.482-6(c)(3)(ii)(A).

[33] Reg. §§1.482-6(c)(3)(ii)(B), (C)(3), (D). See TD 8552, supra note 2, at 111 (methods "based on the results of transactions between uncontrolled taxpayers are generally . . . more reliable than methods (such as the residual profit split) that only rely on such transactions in part").

[34] TD 8552, supra note 2, at 111.

[35] Reg. §1.482-6(c)(3)(ii)(C)(3).

payers.[36] Reliability is generally considered greater if the residual profit split is applied to all controlled taxpayers, rather than just one or some of them.[37] "[T]he analysis of both parties to the controlled transaction under this method may, to some extent, mitigate the reliability concerns attributable to the use of internal data in allocating the residual profit."[38]

The regulations provide the following example illustrating the residual profit split.[39] Assume P, a domestic corporation, manufactures and sells products for police use in the United States. It develops a bulletproof material, Nulon, for use in protective clothing and headgear, and it obtains a patent for this material. P licenses its European subsidiary, S, to manufacture and sell Nulon in Europe. S has developed markets in Europe for several of P's products, which it has also adapted for military use and sold to European governments under brand names that S has developed and owns. For year 1, P has no direct expenses allocable to the license to S, S's revenues from Nulon sales are $500, and S has operating expenses allocable to these sales, apart from royalties, of $300.

The IRS uses the residual profit split to determine an arm's length royalty for the license from P to S. In the first step, it determines that the operating assets used by S in the Nulon sales are worth $200, and, from "a sample of European companies performing functions similar to those of" S, it concludes that 10 percent is a market return on S's operating assets. From S's operating profit from the Nulon sales of $200 (revenues of $500, less operating expenses of $300), $20 is therefore allocated as a market return on the operating assets (10 percent of $200).

In the second step, the IRS determines that the fair market values of the intangibles cannot be determined, and it thus estimates the relative values of the intangibles from year 1 expenditures for research, development, and marketing. P's research and development expenditures on protective gear relate to the P group's worldwide activities in this field of business. The IRS thus allocates these expenditures to worldwide sales, and by comparing year 1 expenditures with worldwide sales for year 1, it determines that the contribution to gross profit made by P's intangibles is 20 percent of sales. In contrast, S's research, development, and marketing expenditures relate solely to European sales, and, by comparing these expenditures for year 1 with S's year 1 sales, the IRS determines that S's intangibles contribute 40 percent of sales. S's operating profits, before royalties but after subtracting the market return on operating assets, is thus allocated one-third ($.20/$.60) to P's patent and two-thirds ($.40/$.60) to S's intangibles. The arm's length royalty to P under the patent license is thus $60 (one third of the excess of $200 over $20).

---

[36] Reg. §§1.482-6(c)(3)(ii)(C)(*1*), (2). The allocation and consistency requirements are described more fully in connection with the comparable profit split. Reg. §§1.482-6(c)(2)(ii)(C)(*1*), (2), discussed supra text accompanying notes 21, 22.

[37] Reg. §1.482-6(c)(3)(ii)(D).

[38] TD 8552, supra note 2, at 111.

[39] Reg. §1.482-6(c)(3)(iii) Ex. For another example, see Reg. §1.482-8 Ex. 8.

¶79.11 CHARACTER AND COLLATERAL EFFECTS OF ADJUSTMENTS

When applicable, §482 authorizes the IRS "to distribute, apportion, or allocate gross income, deductions, credits, or allowances" among related organizations, trades, or businesses. For years, the power of the IRS to "create income where none is realized" was ardently debated, but this power is now widely conceded.[1] For example, the IRS can impose an arm's length price on an intercompany sale of goods even though the result is a profit to the seller before the related buyer has sold the goods to an outsider. Similarly, a profit can be forced on the seller even if the buyer disposes of the goods at a loss or in a nonrecognition transaction. The miracle of income without gain, which occurs every day in transactions between unrelated parties, is an inevitable consequence of the arm's length standard imposed by the §482 regulations.

Another battle ending with a victory for the IRS concerned its right to allocate the group's entire income to a single member, even though the statutory language—"distribute, apportion, or allocate"—implies a division.[2] Since the entire amount could be imputed to a single member in appropriate cases by applying assignment of income principles, a similar allocation of the whole hog under §482 will not bring the world to an end. Similarly, the statutory reference to "gross income" could be construed to imply that taxable income cannot be allocated. However, because this interpretation could readily be sidestepped by allocating the ingredients of taxable income (gross income and deductions), the courts have approved the more direct remedy of allocating the group's net income among its members.[3]

These expansive features of §482 are counterbalanced by three protaxpayer features of the regulations and IRS procedures thereunder:

1. *Correlative adjustments.* The regulations establish a "correlative adjustment" procedure, under which adjustments increasing the income of a member of the controlled group ("primary allocation") are accompanied by appropriate correlative adjustments to the income of the related party if U.S. tax liability would be affected by the change, currently or in a later year.[4] For example, if a

---

[1] Reg. §1.482-1(f)(1)(ii) (§482 allocation possible even if income anticipated from controlled transactions is never realized or is realized during later period); Latham Park Manor, Inc. v. CIR, 69 TC 199, 215-16 (1977), aff'd without published opinion, 618 F2d 100 (4th Cir. 1980) and cases there cited; Aladdin Indus., Inc. v. CIR, 41 TCM (CCH) 1515 (1981). See generally King & Dinur, Tax Court Gives In on Creation-of-Income Issue Under 482; What Decision Means, 48 J. Tax'n 66 (1978).

[2] See Your Host, Inc. v. CIR, 58 TC 10, 24 (1972), aff'd, 489 F2d 957 (2d Cir. 1973), and cases there cited.

[3] See Hamburgers York Road, Inc. v. CIR, 41 TC 821, 834 (1964) (acq.), and cases there cited.

[4] Reg. §1.482-1(g)(2)(i). See OTM Corp. v. US, 572 F2d 1046 (5th Cir.), cert. denied, 439 US 1002 (1978) (taxpayer cannot force IRS to invoke §482 and make correlative adjustments instead of disallowing excessive deductions under §162); Continental Equi-

parent provides services without charge to a subsidiary and the primary adjustment is an increase in the parent's gross income equal to an arm's length charge for the services, the correlative adjustment is a deduction for the subsidiary if payment for the services would qualify for deduction or an increase in the basis of the subsidiary's property if payment would be a capital expenditure.[5]

Section 482 itself does not explicitly allow, let alone require, these offsetting adjustments in the taxpayer's favor. They are obviously appropriate, however, and their inherent fairness may increase the willingness of courts to enforce IRS action under §482.

Once a primary allocation has been made, the IRS must provide to the taxpayer affected by the allocation a written statement of the amount and "nature" of the correlative allocation.[6] The correlative allocation must be "reflected" in the U.S. tax records of all affected entities, whether or not the allocation changes the U.S. tax liability of any person for any open year. For example, if a §482 adjustment increases the interest income of a domestic corporation on a below-market loan to a foreign subsidiary, the correlative allocation (an increase in interest expense) must be made in the subsidiary's records, even if the subsidiary is not a U.S. taxpayer, because the allocation affects the subsidiary's earnings and profits and thus may subsequently affect a shareholder's dividend income.[7] The primary allocation is considered made on the date of a "final determination" of tax liability that reflects the allocation (e.g., an assessment following the taxpayer's signing of a Form 870 or a final Tax Court decision).[8]

2. *Payments.* Allocations under §482 impute income to taxpayers receiving less than an arm's length consideration in a transaction with a related taxpayer, and the correlative adjustment procedure allows the latter to deduct the imputed amount or add it to the basis of its property when appropriate. Under Revenue Procedure 65-17, the imputed amount can be paid (or reflected on the books of the related taxpayers by accounts payable and receivable) without additional tax consequences, substantially as though the price had conformed at the outset to an arm's length standard, provided tax avoidance was not one of the principal purposes of the transaction and certain procedural requirements are satisfied.[9]

---

ties, Inc. v. CIR, 551 F2d 74 (5th Cir. 1977) (correlative adjustment procedure does not require payment of refund otherwise barred by statute of limitations); Fegan v. CIR, 71 TC 791 (1979) (time when correlative adjustments are required).

[5] See Reg. §1.482-1(g)(2)(iv) Ex. 2.

[6] Reg. §1.482-1(g)(2)(ii). See InverWorld, Inc v. CIR, 71 TCM (CCH) 3231 (1996), reconsideration denied, 73 TCM (CCH) 2777 (1997) (correlative adjustment denied because it would have taken form of deduction for foreign corporation that filed no return and §882(c)(2) denies deductions to foreign corporations not filing timely, true, and accurate returns).

[7] Reg. §1.482-1(g)(2)(iv) Ex. 3.

[8] Reg. §1.482-1(g)(2)(iii).

[9] Rev. Proc. 65-17, 1965-1 CB 833. See Rev. Proc. 72-53, 1972-2 CB 833 (same as to adjustments under §61 if they could have been made under §482); Rev. Rul. 82-80, 1982-1 CB 89 (application of Rev. Proc. 65-17). See also Rev. Proc. 91-24, 1991-1 CB 542

The regulations require "appropriate adjustments . . . to conform a taxpayer's accounts to reflect allocations made under section 482," which can consist of accounts receivable and payable under Revenue Procedure 65-17.[10]

3. *Setoffs.* Taxpayers can also avoid or mitigate a proposed adjustment by establishing that they participated in other transactions not at arm's length that, if taken into account, result in a setoff against the proposed allocation.[11] The regulations illustrate this tit-for-tat gambit by describing a parent-subsidiary relationship in which the parent bills the subsidiary $125,000 for services worth $100,000 but also permits the subsidiary to use without charge equipment with a rental value of $25,000. Since $125,000 is a fair charge for the package, no distortion of income results, and an adjustment under §482 is ordinarily not warranted.[12]

However, if the setoff has the effect of changing the character or source of income or deductions in "a manner" that affects the U.S. tax liability of any person, adjustments are "made to reflect the correct amount of each category of income or deductions."[13] In the example, the setoff defense has the collateral effect of recharacterizing the parent's income of $125,000 as $100,000 from the performance of services and $25,000 of rental income. If, for example, the rental income is personal holding company income, but the services income is not, the recharacterization might subject *P* to the personal holding company tax.[14] Appropriate adjustments are also made if the setoff in any way "distort[s] taxable income."

A setoff is made only if the taxpayer

("in situations involving a country with which the United States has an income tax convention in force [containing] a mutual agreement procedure article," Rev. Proc. 65-17 applies only if taxpayer requests assistance under mutual agreement procedure in connection with §482 adjustment); Announcement 95-9, 1995-7 IRB 57 (proposing restatement of Rev. Proc. 91-24).

See Cappuccilli v. CIR, 668 F2d 138 (2d Cir. 1981), cert. denied, 459 US 822 (1982) (where requirements of Rev. Proc. 65-17 are not followed, no bad debt deduction if taxpayer to whom income is imputed under §482 does not actually receive it; deduction would duplicate correlative deduction under §482 given to related taxpayer); Eisenberg v. CIR, 78 TC 336 (1982) (same). The *Cappuccilli* and *Eisenberg* cases should not be read to deny a bad debt deduction if an account receivable is established on thetaxpayer's books under Revenue Procedure 65-17 and the taxpayer seeks collection as aggressively as an arm's length creditor would have under the circumstances.

[10] Reg. §1.482-1(g)(3).

[11] Reg. §1.482-1(g)(4)(i). The setoff must arise from transactions between the same two controlled taxpayers. The 1993 regulations allowed setoffs for transactions between one of the controlled taxpayers and a third controlled taxpayer. However, objections to the latter provision were raised by treaty partners, and the final regulations, "in accordance with the practice of most treaty partners, [permit] set-offs . . . only for transactions between the same two controlled taxpayers that were parties to the transactions giving rise to the original allocation." TD 8552, 1994-2 CB 93, 104.

[12] Reg. §1.482-1(g)(4)(iii) Ex 1.

[13] Reg. §1.482-1(g)(4)(i).

[14] Reg. §1.482-1(g)(4)(iii) Ex 2.

a. Shows that the transaction on which the setoff is based was not at arm's length,

b. Establishes the "appropriate" arm's length charge for the transaction,

c. "Documents" all correlative adjustments resulting from the setoff, and

d. Notifies the IRS of the basis of the setoff within 30 days after the IRS presents an examination report to the taxpayer or, if earlier, within 30 days after a notice of deficiency is issued.[15]

¶79.12 RELATIONSHIP OF §482 TO OTHER TAX-AVOIDANCE PROVISIONS AND DOCTRINES

1. *Assignment of income doctrine.* Section 482 has much in common with the more pervasive assignment of income doctrine, and adjustments sometimes rest on both grounds, but each has areas of application that are beyond the reach of the other. For example, the results in two leading assignment of income cases—*Helvering v. Clifford* and *Helvering v. Horst*—could not have been reached under §482 because neither case involved two "organizations, trades, or businesses," a prerequisite to the invocation of §482.[1] The assignment of income doctrine is also applicable when earned income is assigned to charities, even though §482 does not apply because the assignor and assignee are not under common ownership or control.[2] On the other hand, bargain sales of property and the gratuitous rendition of services do not ordinarily bring the assignment of income doctrine into play, although they are standard grist for §482's mill.

2. *Substance over form.* Because the principle that substance controls over form has no clearly identifiable limits, this protean doctrine may encompass all of §482 in the sense that any adjustment sanctioned by §482 could instead rest on the principle that substance controls in applying the federal income tax to business arrangements. Indeed, allocations under §482 have been judicially described as the substitution of substance for form.[3] On the other hand, the substance over form principle embraces transactions that are beyond the reach of §482 because, for example, the parties are not under common ownership or control or are not "organizations, trades, or businesses."

3. *Section 269.* Section 269 allows the IRS to disallow deductions, credits, and other tax allowances if control of a corporation is acquired for the principal

---

[15] Reg. §1.482-1(g)(4)(ii).

[1] For Helvering v. Clifford, 309 US 331 (1940), and Helvering v. Horst, 311 US 112 (1940), see infra ¶80.2.1 and supra ¶75.3.3. As defined by §1.482-1(I)(1), the term "organization" includes sole proprietorships, but individuals are pointedly omitted.

[2] See, e.g., Rev. Rul. 71, 1953-1 CB 18.

[3] Simon J. Murphy Co. v. CIR, 231 F2d 639, 644 (6th Cir. 1956). See Stewart v. CIR, 714 F2d 977 (9th Cir. 1983) (substance over form doctrine and §482 overlap to such extent that IRS switch at trial from §482 to substance over form doctrine could not have surprised or prejudiced taxpayer). For the substance over form doctrine, see supra ¶4.3.3.

purpose of avoiding federal income taxes and certain other conditions are satisfied.[4] Section 269 is more sweeping than §482 because it permits the total disallowance of tax benefits, not merely their reallocation between two or more related parties. On the other hand, §269 is triggered only by a tax-avoidance purpose, while §482 can apply even if there is an inadvertent distortion of income. Moreover, §269 defines "control" in a much more restricted fashion than §482 and applies only to corporate tax allowances, whereas §482 also applies to sole proprietorships, partnerships, and other unincorporated enterprises.

4. *Section 446(b).* If the taxpayer's accounting method does not "clearly reflect income," §446(b) permits the IRS to compute taxable income by a method that remedies this defect.[5] Because §§446(b) and 482 are both aimed at practices that do not clearly reflect income, they can overlap. For example, if a manufacturer consistently bills its products to a sales subsidiary at cost, the practice can be viewed both as an erroneous accounting method subject to correction under §446(b) and as a failure to deal on an arm's length basis as required by the regulations under §482. Each provision also has its own turf. Section 482 applies to isolated transactions whose treatment by the taxpayer is not a "method of accounting" within the meaning of §446(b), while §446(b) requires taxpayers to use a proper accounting method whether or not their transactions are conducted with related taxpayers.

5. *Other provisions.* Because §482 is concerned with distortions of income, it necessarily incorporates by reference all provisions governing the computation of true taxable income. Given this relationship, some §482 adjustments could rest solely on the governing substantive provisions. For example, if a parent pays an excessive amount to a subsidiary for services, the excess would not be deductible under §162 even if §482 were repealed. Similarly, the parent's deduction of salaries and other expenses properly attributable to the business of a subsidiary can be disallowed under §162 without reference to §482.

The disallowance of deductions under §162 and other provisions on the ground that the item is properly allocable to a related person is often accompanied by an offsetting adjustment to the latter's income or basis or gives rise to a refund claim if the IRS does not make the adjustment on its own initiative. The correlative adjustment procedure established by the regulations under §482, however, is a handy bureaucratic foundation for the offset.[6]

Although deductions that are reallocated under §482 can ordinarily be disallowed under a substantive provision like §162, the definition of gross income in §61 does not usually require taxpayers to report income that they cannot and do not receive. For this reason, §482 vests the IRS with broad authority to allocate income to an unwilling taxpayer—a power that is not granted by any

---

[4] See infra ¶95.5.3.

[5] See infra ¶105.1.6.

[6] See OTM Corp. v. US, 572 F2d 1046 (5th Cir.), cert. denied, 439 US 1002 (1978).

other provision, except in such special circumstances as an anticipatory assignment of earned income.

¶79.13 ALLOCATIONS AFFECTING PERSONAL SERVICE CORPORATIONS

Beginning in the 1970s, many partners and shareholders in professional partnerships and corporations separately incorporated their partnership interests and shareholdings. Assume three lawyers—A, B, and C—each form a professional corporation, and the three professional corporations form a partnership. Each lawyer becomes an employee of her corporation, and each corporation provide the services of its shareholder to the partnership. The partnership carries on the practice of law.

The principal advantage of these separate incorporations was that they were thought to give greater flexibility in developing qualified pension and profit sharing plans. For example, A's corporation could adopt a plan covering A and suiting her special wishes, even if B's and C's corporations adopted very different plans or no plans at all. Arguably, employees of the partnership other than A, B, and C did not have to be covered by any plan of the partnership or the partner-corporations, thus avoiding the nondiscrimination requirements of the qualified plan rules.[1] Section 269A was enacted in 1982 to curb this practice by allowing the IRS to reallocate corporate income to the shareholders of the corporations.[2] Such an allocation saps the substance from the employment relationship, which is the backbone of the plan.[3]

Section 269A applies if (1) "substantially all of the services of a professional service corporation are performed for . . . 1 other corporation [or] partnership" and (2) the professional service corporation is formed or availed of for the primary purpose of evading tax by reducing the income of the "employee-owner"

---

[1] For the nondiscrimination rules, see supra ¶¶61.3.3, 61.4.1.

[2] The IRS had no luck attacking these schemes through the courts. See Keller v. CIR, 77 TC 1014 (1981), aff'd, 723 F2d 58 (10th Cir. 1983) (upholding validity of professional corporation organized by physician to take his place as general partner in partnership engaged in practice of clinical pathology).

[3] The legislative history mentions two other evasive tactics that could be attacked under §269A—obtaining the benefit of the corporate surtax exemption and adopting a taxable year having the effect of deferring tax. Staff of Joint Comm. on Tax'n, 97th Cong., 2d Sess., General Explanation of the Revenue Provisions of the Tax Equity and Fiscal Responsibility Act of 1982 at 326 (Comm. Print 1982). The Code was subsequently amended, however, to bar most personal service corporations from utilizing the surtax exemption and require such corporations to either account by the calendar year or make payments compensating the Treasury for any tax deferral resulting from the use of any other taxable year. IRC §§11(b)(2), 441(i), 444. See infra ¶105.1.2 for the taxable year requirements.

or securing the benefit of a deduction that would not otherwise be available.[4] Under a safe harbor that would be established by regulations proposed by the Treasury, a corporation would be considered free of tax avoidance purpose if, for each 12-month period, (1) the taxes paid by the corporation and the employee-owner are at least 90 percent of the taxes that would have been imposed had the services been performed by the employee-owner directly rather than through the corporation or (2) the tax reduction resulting from the corporate structure does not exceed $2,500.[5] Establishing a lack of tax avoidance purpose, however, only exempts the corporation and employee-owner from the reallocation rule of §269A. It does not immunize them from reallocations under other provisions, such as §482 or the assignment of income doctrine.[6]

The term "professional service corporation" refers to a corporation whose primary business is the performance of personal services that are "substantially performed by employee-owners."[7] The term "employee-owner" includes any employee who, on any day during the taxable year, owns, actually or constructively, 10 percent or more of the corporation's stock.[8] Constructive ownership is determined under §318.[9] For example, if A transfers all of her stock to her children or if the children rather than A are the original shareholders of A Corp., A is constructive owner of the stock and thus is an owner-employee of the corporation.

Section 269A likely applies in the example. The corporations of A, B, and C are professional service corporations because they perform personal services through their shareholders. Each of the shareholders is an employee-owner. And, the principal purpose for the corporations undoubtedly is to shelter the owner-employees from tax by obtaining deductions for contributions to employer plans that would not be qualified if adopted directly by the partnership.

When §269A applies, the IRS may allocate income, deductions, and credits between the corporation and its employee-owners in any way it considers necessary to reflect income clearly or frustrate evasion of tax.[10] In the example, the IRS might allocate each corporation's distributive share of partnership income directly to the shareholders. If this is done, the qualified plans collapse because

---

[4] IRC §269A(a). See Prop. Reg. §1.269A-1(a) ("[s]uch purpose is evidenced when use of the corporation either reduces the income of any employee-owner, or secures for any employee-owner one or more tax benefits which would not otherwise be available"), §1.269A-1(b)(4) ("not otherwise available" includes "any tax benefit that would not be available to an employee-owner had such employee-owner performed the personal services in an individual capacity").

[5] Prop. Reg. §1.269A-1(c).

[6] Prop. Reg. §1.269A-1(f).

[7] IRC §269A(b)(1).

[8] IRC §269A(b)(2).

[9] For §318, see infra ¶93.1.7.

[10] The operative language of §269A is borrowed from §482, discussed supra ¶79.1.

the corporation's role as intermediary between shareholder and partnership—which is the base on which the plans are built—disappears.

Section 269A's bark is worse than its bite, but the reason for this is little comfort to those seeking tax reduction through personal service corporations: Congress has enacted so many provisions curbing the tax benefits once enjoyed by these corporations that there is little left for §269A to bite.

¶79.14 ADVANCE PRICING AGREEMENTS

The IRS has promulgated procedures for advance rulings on intercompany prices, called advance pricing agreements (APAs).[1] An APA is an agreement between a taxpayer and the IRS specifying "transfer pricing methodologies" (TPMs) to be used by the taxpayer in allocating items among two or more controlled persons.[2] The TPM is an "application to the taxpayer's specific facts and circumstances of the best method . . . , as agreed pursuant to negotiations between the Service and the taxpayer." The APA procedures are intended "to be a flexible problem-solving process, based on cooperative and principled negotiations between taxpayers and the Service."[3] Their "central goals" are "prompt and fair resolution of APA requests and renewals, in keeping with the demands of the multinational economic environment."[4] A taxpayer making an APA with the IRS must submit annual reports to the IRS for use in administering the agreement.[5]

The taxpayer invokes the procedures by filing a request proposing one or more TPMs and providing data showing that the TPMs are the best method for

---

[1] Rev. Proc. 96-53, 1996-2 CB 375 (generally effective for requests received after 1996). These procedures were initially provided by Rev. Proc. 91-22, 1991-1 CB 526, superseded by Rev. Proc. 96-53, supra. See Announcement 96-124, 1996-49 IRB 22 (summarizing differences between Rev. Procs. 96-53 and 91-22); Birnkrant & Cole, Final Version of IRS Procedure Alters the Advance Pricing Agreement Process, 86 J. Tax'n 240 (1997); Patton & Wood, Rev. Proc. 96-53: Continuous Quality Improvement of the APA Process, 26 Tax Mgmt. Int'l J. 80 (1997). See generally Ernst & Young, Transfer Pricing: Risk Reduction and Advance Pricing Agreements, 11 Tax Notes Int'l 293 (July 31, 1995); Fallon, Advance Pricing Agreements, 75 Taxes 304 (1997); Olson, Boykin & Schwartz, Advance Pricing Agreements: The Role of the Economic Study, 63 Tax Notes 1755 (1994); Schwartz, Olson & Boykin, APAs: Successfully Reaching Agreement, 66 Tax Notes 1181 (Feb. 20, 1995); Schwartz, Olson & Felgran, Advance Pricing Agreements: Starting the Process, 65 Tax Notes 235 (Oct. 10, 1994); Schwartz, Olson & Boykin, Working With the APA Process, 63 Tax Notes 1359 (1994). See also Calderòn, Safe Harbor for Multinational Enterprises Operating in Spain: The New Spanish APA Procedure, 14 Tax Notes Int'l 1355 (Oct. 27, 1997).

[2] Rev. Proc. 96-53, 1996-2 CB 375, §1. For more on the legal effect of an APA, see id. §10 ("an APA is a binding agreement between the taxpayer and the Service").

[3] Id. §3.01.

[4] Id. §3.08.

[5] Id. §11.01. For other aspects of the administration of an APA, see id. §§11.02-11.09.

specified transactions between the taxpayer and specified affiliates (businesses or entities commonly controlled with the taxpayer, such as subsidiaries).[6] The request must usually illustrate the TPMs by applying them to the parties' tax and financial data for the three preceding years.[7] "By entering into an APA, the taxpayer agrees to do a great deal of work that would normally be done by the IRS during an audit,"[8] but the process probably also gives the taxpayer greater control over the terms on which the transfer price is determined. A user fee of $25,000 must usually accompany the request, but the fee is reduced to as little as $5,000 if the taxpayer's gross income is less than $1 billion.[9]

An APA request must usually include pricing information on "closely comparable uncontrolled transactions."[10] If such data is not available, "the taxpayer must identify any transactions it believes may be comparable, but for which reliable data is unavailable." If such transactions cannot be identified, the request must include, "to the extent possible, . . . relevant pricing data from uncontrolled transactions that are similar, even though not closely comparable, and propose adjustments to account for differences between such uncontrolled transactions and [the taxpayer's] operations." An APA can sometimes be obtained, even if "no comparable uncontrolled transactions can be identified." The taxpayer can be required to pay for an independent expert, acceptable to the IRS as well as the taxpayer, to review the taxpayer's request.[11]

The IRS will hold a "prefiling conference" with a taxpayer contemplating making an APA request.[12] Such conferences, which can be held without disclosing the taxpayer's identity, are highly recommended by practitioners with experience under the APA procedures as a means of identifying more clearly the data and documentation the IRS will require in processing the request.[13]

In appropriate cases, agreements with competent authorities of countries having income tax treaties with the United States may be made in conjunction with the APA.[14] Also, the IRS may make a transfer pricing agreement with a foreign competent authority in connection with an APA filed with that competent authority. Bilateral and multilateral APAs seem to be the norm in the

---

[6] Id. §2. For a complete itemization of the required content of an APA request, see id. §5. For the IRS' procedures in processing a request, see id. §6.

[7] Id. §5.02.

[8] McLennan, Responses to Section 482 Litigation: Advance Pricing Agreements or Arbitration? 54 Tax Notes 431, 436 (1992).

[9] Rev. Proc. 96-53, 1996-2 CB 375, §5.14.

[10] Id. §3.03.

[11] Id. §9.

[12] Id. §4.

[13] Turro, Transfer Pricing: Apple Computer Readies for APA Replay, 56 Tax Notes 694 (1992).

[14] Rev. Proc. 96-53, 1996-2 CB 375, §7.01. See id. §3.02 (IRS' "initial negotiating position" in competent authority negotiations is its "opinion, based on consultation with the taxpayer, of the best method").

developing APA practice.[15] The taxpayer is not likely to be a direct participant in competent authority negotiations, but the APA request may be withdrawn if the taxpayer is not satisfied with any resulting agreement. If competent authority negotiations do not result in an agreement satisfactory to the taxpayer, an APA between the taxpayer and the IRS may nevertheless be made, but either party is free to withdraw in this situation. If an agreement with foreign competent authorities is made, it typically includes an information exchange agreement covering future events affecting the APA.

The IRS "intends that the APA process [have] flexibility to address the needs of particular taxpayers," and it may, by agreement with the taxpayer, "adopt special procedures, including simplified procedures, that depart from those" described above.[16] The IRS has elaborated on how it might short-cut the process for a "small business taxpayer" (SBT)—a U.S. taxpayer with "total gross income" (sum of gross income, cost of goods sold, and interest excluded from gross income by §103) of less than $100 million for its last taxable year.[17] "To address the concern that the perceived costs to secure an APA are high in proportion to the size of the transactions involved, the special procedures focus on simplifying the APA process for SBT transactions."[18] These procedures include the following:

1. An SBT may, before paying a user fee, have a prefiling conference with the IRS "to determine as early as possible the best method for the SBT's proposed covered transactions."[19] Although the SBT must, at least 60 days before the conference, provide a "detailed description of the underlying facts and the proposed TPM," the records maintained by the taxpayer to avoid the substantial valuation misstatement penalty may satisfy this requirement.

2. At the prefiling conference, the parties will try to agree upon a "case management plan with the objective of concluding" proceedings with the IRS within six months after the APA request is filed.

3. The IRS may waive some of the items normally required in an APA request, including, in appropriate cases, the economic analysis of general industry pricing practices and markets functions, the description of research efforts to identify independent comparables, the detailed explanation of adjustments to independent comparables, and the proposed contents of annual reports to be filed during the APA's term.

---

[15] See id. §7.07 ("bilateral and multilateral APAs generally are preferable," and taxpayer "must show sufficient justification for a unilateral APA"); Turro, supra note 13 (as of August 1992, only one of 10 APAs completed or near completion is unilateral).

[16] Rev. Proc. 96-53, 1996-2 CB 375, §3.09.

[17] Notice 98-10, 1998-6 IRB 9; Rev. Proc. 96-53, 1996-2 CB 375, §5.14(7). See Patton & Wood, Fast Track for Small Fry—IRS Proposes Simplified APA Procedures for Small Business Taxpayers, 27 Tax Mgmt. Int'l J. 190 (1998).

[18] Notice 98-10, 1998-6 IRB 9, 10.

[19] Notice 98-10, 1998-6 IRB 9, 10.

4. To minimize travel, meetings may be conducted by teleconference.
5. The IRS will "reasonably assist" the taxpayer in selecting, evaluating, and adjusting comparables.
6. The initial term of the APA will be three years.
7. The IRS has developed a model APA, which may be used by a small business taxpayer as its proposed draft APA.[20]

Information submitted with an APA request is generally protected by the confidentiality requirements of §6103.[21] It may enjoy additional protection under trade secret and related laws and confidentiality provisions of treaties, and the APA, when issued, is not released to the public. This assurance has given rise to two conflicting fears. On the one hand, some fear that the IRS might not be successful in resisting disclosure of proprietary or sensitive information if disclosure is sought in a Freedom of Information suit; on the other hand, some have wondered whether nondisclosure of APAs might lead to the creation of a private body of law, known only to the IRS and practitioners involved in the making of APAs. Section 6103 should be adequate to assuage the former fear, and the IRS has addressed the latter fear by issuing revenue rulings or procedures airing significant issues arising in the APA process. For example, the IRS has issued a Notice describing APAs issued to several taxpayers engaged in "global trading"—functionally fully integrated operations in the global trading of commodities and derivative financial products.[22]

Although APAs are generally prospective in effect, a TPM adopted in an APA may be "used for resolving" issues for prior years for which the facts, law, and available records are consistent with the situation when the APA is issued.[23] The taxpayer can request a "rollback," which is a mutual agreement to apply the TPM of the APA "to resolve transfer pricing issues for years prior to the earliest year covered by the APA."[24] Even if a rollback is not requested, the IRS may, "under regularly applicable procedures," apply the TPM to earlier years.[25] An

---

[20] Notice 98-10, 1998-6 IRB 9, 11.

[21] Rev. Proc. 96-53, 1996-2 CB 375, §12.

[22] Notice 94-40, 1994-1 CB 351. A distinctive feature of these APAs is that they provide for profits from global trading to be allocated among countries by a "profit split method," based on such factors as the relative values of the assets of each "trading location," the "risk associated with a trading location," and "the extent of the activity of each trading location." The methodology is reminiscent of apportionment formulae used under state income tax laws. See Reich, U.S. Federal Income Taxation of U.S. Branches of Foreign Banks: Selected Issues and Perspectives, 2 Fla. Tax Rev. 1, 25–30 (1994); Snyder, Note, Taxation of Global Trading Operations: Use of Advance Pricing Agreements and Profit-Split Methodology, 48 Tax Lawyer 1057 (1995). See also Organisation for Economic Cooperation & Development, Taxation of Global Trading of Financial Instruments: A Discussion Draft (OECD 1997), reprinted in 14 Tax Notes Int'l 597 (Feb. 17, 1997).

[23] Rev. Proc. 96-53, 1996-2 CB 375, §3.06.

[24] Rev. Proc. 96-53, 1996-2 CB 375, §8.01.

[25] Rev. Proc. 96-53, 1996-2 CB 375, §3.06.

APA request does not "put into abeyance any examination or other enforcement proceeding," but various IRS personnel attempt to "coordinate their activities" to avoid duplicative information requests, "enhance the efficiency" of IRS operations, and "reduce overall taxpayer compliance burdens."[26]

¶79.15 ACCURACY-RELATED PENALTY

¶79.15.1 Generally

A 20 percent penalty is imposed under §6662 if a §482 adjustment discloses a "substantial valuation misstatement."[1] A substantial valuation misstatement exists if either

1. The consideration reflected in the return for a transaction between related persons is 200 percent or more, or 50 percent or less, of the amount ultimately determined to be correct under §482, or
2. The "net section 482 transfer price adjustment" for the taxable year exceeds the lesser of $5 million or 10 percent of the taxpayer's gross receipts.[2]

The penalty is referred to as the "transactional penalty" when imposed because of a misstatement of the former kind and as the "net adjustment penalty" in the latter situation.[3]

---

[26] Rev. Proc. 96-53, 1996-2 CB 375, §3.07.

[1] For §6662 generally, see infra ¶114.4. See generally Culbertson, Speaking Softly and Carrying a Big Shtick: The Interplay Between Substantive and Penalty Rules in the U.S. Transfer Pricing Regulations, 11 Tax Notes Int'l 1509 (Dec. 4, 1995); Hannes, Carney & Salch, Handling Controversy and Planning Effectively Under the Final IRS Transfer Pricing Penalty Regulations, 12 Tax Notes Int'l 671 (Feb. 26, 1996); Warner, Final Transfer Pricing Penalty Regulations: Regs. §1.6662-6, 25 Tax Mgmt. Int'l J. 505 (1996).

The IRS has established a Transfer Pricing Penalty Oversight Committee for the purpose of ensuring national uniformity in the application of this penalty. The Committee reviews every proposed assertion of the penalty and collects information from IRS district offices on cases where §482 adjustments exceed the penalty threshold but the penalty is not assessed. The review is an internal IRS procedure, and it is not possible for taxpayers to appear or otherwise argue their cases before the Committee. Announcement 96-16, 1996-13 IRB 22.

[2] IRC §6662(e)(1)(B) (applicable for taxable years ending after November 5, 1990). For regulations under these rules, see TD 8656, 1996-1 CB 329; Reg. §1.6662-6(g) (regulations are generally effective as of February 9, 1996, but taxpayers may elect to apply them for all taxable years beginning after 1993. The regulations were preceded by temporary regulations that were generally effective for taxable years beginning after 1993. TD 8519, 1994-1 CB 298, amended by TD 8551, 1994-2 CB 279.

[3] Reg. §1.6662-6(a)(1). For taxable years beginning before 1994, the net adjustment penalty applies only if the net section 482 transfer price adjustment exceeds $10 million.

The penalty rate is doubled to 40 percent for a "gross valuation misstatement," which arises if either (1) the transfer price reported in the taxpayer's return for a transaction between related persons is 400 percent or more, or 25 percent or less, of the amount ultimately determined to be correct under §482 or (2) the net section 482 transfer price adjustment for the taxable year exceeds the lesser of $20 million or 20 percent of the taxpayer's gross receipts.[4]

These rules, which were enacted in 1990 and amended in 1993, apply when an adjustment is made under §482 to the "price for any property or services (or for the use of property)," a phrase that Congress intended to be "broadly interpreted to encompass consideration of all kinds that may be adjusted by the IRS under section 482, including but not limited to purchase prices, fees for services, royalties, interest, and rents."[5] According to the Treasury, the rules are intended to "encourage . . . a taxpayer engaged in related party transactions to prepare a factual and economic analysis based on reasonably available related party and third party market data that substantiates the price chosen, and to maintain appropriate documentation of that analysis," thereby "ensur[ing] that the transfer price a taxpayer reports on its income tax return is determined in a manner consistent with the arm's length standard."[6]

The existence of a substantial valuation misstatement is determined by comparing the correct treatment of related party (controlled) transactions, as finally determined under §482, with the treatment reported on the taxpayer's return, not the actual terms of those transactions or the terms initially reported on the taxpayer's books.[7] Any change in the reported results made by an amended return is considered part of the reported results if the amended return is filed before the IRS "has contacted the taxpayer regarding the corresponding original return."

In order to avoid double counting, changes in net operating loss, capital loss, and other carryovers to the taxable year are ignored in applying the penalty rules.[8] Assume X Corp. reports a net operating loss for year 1 of $3 million, which is carried as a NOL deduction to year 2; on audit, X's taxable income for year 1 is increased by $6 million (from negative $3 million to positive $3 million). Since this increase exceeds the lesser of $5 million or 10 percent of gross receipts, the net adjustment penalty applies for year 1. The audit adjustment affects tax liability for both year 1 and year 2 because it creates positive taxable income for year 1 and has the effect of eliminating the NOL deduction for year 2, thereby increasing taxable income for that year by $3 million. However, because the increase in taxable income for year 2 is included in the net section 482 adjustment

---

[4] Reg. §§1.6662-6(b)(2),(c)(3).

[5] H.R. Rep. No. 964, 101st Cong., 2d Sess. 1075 (Conf. Rep. 1990).

[6] TD 8519, supra note 2, at 299.

[7] Reg. §1.6662-6(a)(2).

[8] IRC §6662(e)(3)(A); Reg. §§1.6662-6(c)(1), 1.6662-6(e).

for year 1, it is excluded in computing the net adjustment for year 2. The net section 482 adjustment for year 2 thus consists solely of any increases in taxable income that may result from adjustments to transfer prices for transactions reported on the year 2 return; the denial of the net operating loss carryover deduction for year 2 has no effect on the application of the penalty for that year.

¶79.15.2 Transactional Penalty—Reasonable Cause and Good Faith

The accuracy-related penalty is excused with respect to any portion of an understatement of tax if there is "reasonable cause" for this portion and the taxpayer acted in "good faith."[9] The regulations provide two special rules for applying the reasonable cause and good faith standards in cases involving the transactional penalty.

First, if the taxpayer relied on professional advice in determining a transfer price, "whether the professional is an employee of, or related to, the taxpayer is not determinative in evaluating whether the taxpayer reasonably relied in good faith on advice."[10] However, the regulations seemingly do not rule out the taxpayer's relationship with the professional advisor as a factor affecting the good faith issue.

Second, under rules described below,[11] various §482 adjustments are excluded in applying the net adjustment penalty. For example, an adjustment correcting a reasonable, but erroneous application of a transfer pricing method delineated in the regulations is excluded. A transfer price covered by one of these exclusions is deemed, for purposes of the transactional penalty, to be reasonable and in good faith.[12]

¶79.15.3 Net Adjustment Penalty—Generally

The net adjustment penalty applies if the "net section 482 transfer price adjustment" exceeds the lesser of $5 million or 10 percent of gross receipts, and there is a gross valuation misstatement, resulting in a doubling of the penalty, if the net section 482 adjustment exceeds the lesser of $20 million or 20 percent of gross receipts.[13] The net section 482 transfer price adjustment for any year is the sum of all increases in taxable income resulting from §482 adjustments (with some exceptions described below),[14] less any decreases in taxable income result-

---

[9] IRC §6664(b); Reg. §1.6664-4.
[10] Reg. §1.6662-6(b)(3).
[11] Infra ¶79.15.4.
[12] Reg. §1.6662-6(b)(3).
[13] Reg. §§1.6662-6(c)(2), (3).
[14] For the exceptions, see infra ¶79.15.4.

ing from collateral adjustments.[15] Increases in taxable income covered by the transactional penalty are included in determining whether the net adjustment threshold is exceeded,[16] but coordination rules are provided to ensure that a single increase in taxable income is not penalized twice.[17]

Assume the IRS makes three adjustments under §482: (1) a $2 million increase in royalty payments included in gross income; (2) an increase in taxable income of $2.5 million resulting from adjustments to the selling prices of goods sold to a related buyer; and (3) an $2 million increase resulting from adjustments to the prices paid for goods purchased from a related person.[18] The net section 482 adjustment is $6 million (sum of $2 million, $2.5 million, and $2 million). Since it exceeds $5 million, it is a substantial valuation misstatement, regardless of the taxpayer's gross receipts.

In determining whether the net section 482 adjustment exceeds 10 or 20 percent of gross receipts, the taxpayer's "gross receipts" consist of the receipts properly recognized under the taxpayer's method of accounting, determined after all §482 adjustments, including "total sales (net of returns and allowances)," "all amounts received for services," investment income, and income "from incidental or outside sources."[19] Gross receipts are not diminished by costs of goods sold, but the proceeds of sales of capital assets and of depreciable and real property used in a trade or business are reduced by the property's adjusted basis.

If an affiliated group of corporations files a consolidated return, the net section 482 adjustment is determined as though all members of the group were one corporation. Assume the IRS makes §482 adjustments to the taxable incomes of three members of an affiliated group—A Corp. ($2 million increase), B Corp. ($1 million increase), and C Corp. ($1.5 million increase).[20] The three increases are aggregated as a net section 482 adjustment of $4.5, but since this amount is less than $5 million, the net adjustment is a substantial valuation misstatement only if it exceeds 10 percent of the gross receipts of the affiliated group (including the gross receipts of members for whom no §482 adjustments are made). It is not relevant whether the adjustment for a particular corporation is more or less than 10 percent of its gross receipts.

---

[15] IRC §6662(e)(3)(A); Reg. §1.6662-6(c)(1). See Reg. §1.6662-6(d)(5) (if regular tax is computed from amount other than taxable income, that amount is substituted for "taxable income" for purposes of these rules). For collateral adjustments, see supra ¶79.4.

[16] Reg. §1.6662-6(c)(1).

[17] If the net adjustment penalty applies at the 20 percent rate, but the net section 482 adjustment includes items subject to the transactional penalty at 40 percent, these items are penalized at 40 percent, and the remainder of the net adjustment is penalized at 20 percent. Reg. §1.6662-6(f)(1). In any other case, the net adjustment penalty applies to the entire net adjustment, and the transactional penalty is ignored. Reg. §§1.6662-6(f)(1), (2).

[18] Reg. §1.6662-6(c)(7) Ex. 1.

[19] Reg. §§1.448-1T(f)(2)(iv), 1.6662-6(c)(5).

[20] Reg. §1.6662-6(c)(7) Ex. 5.

¶79.15.4 Items Excluded From Net Adjustment Penalty

In three situations, increases in taxable income resulting from §482 adjustments are excluded from the net section 482 adjustment.[21] The exclusions apply, subject to many limitations described below, to adjustments to (1) prices determined by reasonable (but erroneous) applications of pricing methods provided by the regulations, (2) prices reasonably (but erroneously) determined under other reasonable methods, and (3) the terms of transactions solely between foreign corporations. The reasonable cause exception to the accuracy-related penalty applies to a net section 482 adjustment only if the adjustment is excluded by one of these rules.[22]

Assume the taxable income of X Corp., whose gross receipts are $75 million, is increased by three §482 adjustments of $9 million, $2 million, and $9 million. The transfer prices adjusted by the two $9 million adjustments were determined by X under methods specified in the §482 regulations, and X demonstrates that it met all of the requirements of the first of the three exceptions described below.[23] The net section 482 adjustment is $2 million, which is less than both $5 million and 10 percent of X's gross receipts of $75 million. X is therefore not subject to the net adjustment penalty for the year. However, the transactional penalty may apply if the $2 million increase resulted from an adjustment to a reported transfer price that is more than 200 percent or less than 50 percent of the transfer price ultimately established to be correct.

1. *Use of pricing methods of regulations.* An increase in taxable income resulting from a redetermination under §482 is excluded from the net section 482 adjustment if each of the three requirements described below is met.[24]

First, the transfer price used in reporting the transactions in the taxpayer's returns must have been determined "in accordance with a specific pricing method set forth in the [§482] regulations."[25] This requirement is satisfied if the method is "described" in the §482 regulations and applies "to transactions of the type under review."[26]

---

[21] Reg. §1.6662-6(d)(1).

[22] Reg. §§1.6662-6(c)(6), 1.6664-4(d).

[23] Reg. §1.6662-6(d)(6) Exs. 1, 2.

[24] IRC §6662(e)(3)(B)(i); Reg. §1.6662-6(d)(2)(i). These rules apply for taxable years beginning after 1993. For earlier years, an adjustment to a particular price is excluded in applying the threshold if the taxpayer shows that it had "reasonable cause" for the price reflected on the return and "acted in good faith with respect to such price." IRC §6662(e)(3)(B)(i) (before amendment in 1993). The quoted words were intended to incorporate "the same standard of reasonable cause and good faith" that apply generally under the accuracy-related penalty. H.R. Rep. No. 964, supra note 5, at 1076. For the reasonable cause defense, see infra ¶114.4.7.

[25] IRC §6662(e)(3)(B)(i)(I).

[26] Reg. §1.6662-6(d)(2)(i). A "bona fide cost-sharing arrangement" can meet this requirement.

Second, the taxpayer's use of the method, although erroneous, must be "reasonable."[27] This requirement is met only if both the selection and the application of the method are reasonable—that is, if the taxpayer "reasonably concluded" that the method satisfied the "best method" rule of the §482 regulations, which requires that the method must provide a more reliable measure of arm's length results than any other method described in the regulations.[28] The taxpayer must have "made a reasonable effort to evaluate the potential applicability of the other ... methods [described in the regulations]."[29] The extent of this effort "generally will depend on the nature of the available data."

Whether the taxpayer was reasonable in concluding that the chosen method was the best method depends on all the facts,[30] including (1) the experience and knowledge of the taxpayer and other members of the controlled group that includes the taxpayer,[31] (2) the extent of the taxpayer's search for relevant data,[32] (3) the quality of the available data, (4) whether the taxpayer analyzed the data

---

[27] IRC §6662(e)(3)(B)(i)(I); Reg. §1.6662-6(d)(2)(ii).

[28] For the best method rule, see supra ¶79.3.3.

[29] Reg. §1.6662-6(d)(2)(ii). In response to complaints that the required comparison with other methods is overly burdensome, the Treasury has stated:

> The comparison to be done under the best method rule will not necessarily entail a through analysis under every potentially applicable method. The nature of the available data will often indicate either that a particular method should be the most reliable or that certain other specified methods would be clearly unreliable. Indeed, in some cases it might be reasonable to conclude that a particular method is likely to be the most reliable with virtually no consideration of other potentially applicable methods. For example, if the comparable uncontrolled price method can be applied based upon a closely comparable uncontrolled transaction, it normally would be unnecessary to give any serious consideration to the other methods. Whether more extensive consideration could be needed in other cases will depend on the facts and circumstances.

TD 8656, supra note 2, at 10.

[30] Reg. §1.6662-6(d)(2)(ii).

[31] See TD 8656, supra note 2, at 11 ("The purpose of this factor is to consider the experience and knowledge of all the parties that are likely to be involved in the pricing of the controlled transactions").

[32] The taxpayer must make "a reasonably thorough search for the data necessary to determine which method should be selected and how it should be applied." Reg. §1.6662-6(d)(2)(ii)(B). In determining how thorough a reasonable search must be, the expense of search efforts may be compared with the likely effects of additional data on taxable income. "[A]s the amount of taxable income potentially at stake declines (either because of low dollar amounts of the controlled transactions or because of low variability in results that are expected under the facts and circumstances), the need to continue to search for data also decreases." TD 8656, supra note 2, at 11.

Compare Reg. §1.6662-6(d)(2)(ii)(B) ("the taxpayer is not required to search for relevant data after the end of the taxable year," but it "must maintain as a principal document ... any relevant data it obtains after the end of the taxable year but before the return is filed") with H.R. Rep. No. 213, 103d Cong., 1st Sess. 649 (Conf. Rep. 1993) ("the application of any method [is] not considered reasonable if the taxpayer became

reasonably,[33] (5) whether, in applying the method, the taxpayer fulfilled all requirements of the regulations, (6) whether, if the taxpayer uses an arm's length range, the choice of uncontrolled comparables was reasonable, and (7) the relative sizes of the §482 adjustment and the transactions being adjusted. Reasonable reliance on professional analyses or studies, whether done by employees or outsiders, supports a finding of reasonableness if the taxpayer disclosed all relevant information to the persons doing the study and the study is "objective, thorough, and well reasoned."[34] It may also be reasonable to follow methodology developed in an Advance Pricing Agreement for a prior year or "specifically approved" in an IRS audit for an earlier year.

Third, the taxpayer must have "documentation," most of which must exist when the return was filed, that sets forth how the taxpayer applied the method and "establish[es]" the reasonableness of the taxpayer's selection and application of the method, and the taxpayer must provide the documentation to the IRS within 30 days after the IRS requests it.[35] The emphasis on contemporaneous documentation is explained by the IRS as follows:

> The experience of [IRS] international examiners has been that the majority of taxpayers are unable to provide an explanation of how their intercompany pricing was established. This may account in large part for the fact that in many cases international examiners' access to a corporation's transfer pricing information is delayed or denied. Moreover, experience has been that many taxpayers do not rely upon any form of comparables or other contemporaneous information either in planning or in defending intercompany transactions. Thus, the taxpayer, not having structured the transaction with any comparable in mind, seeks to defend its position by finding whatever transaction or method gives rise to a result that most closely approximates the controlled transaction result initially reported. Thus, the lack of contemporaneous documentation of how a controlled transaction result was determined increases the time spent and expense incurred by both the taxpayer and the Service in determining whether that result was arm's length.[36]

The regulations divide the required documentation into two categories—principal documents and background documents. The principal documents "should accurately and completely describe the [taxpayer's] basic

---

aware prior to filing its tax return that such application more likely than not did not lead to an arm's length result").

[33] See TD 8519, supra note 2, at 298 ("unrelated parties analyze the value of property or services prior to selling or buying such property or services in the open market").

[34] Reg. §1.6662-6(d)(2)(ii).

[35] Reg. §1.6662-6(d)(2)(iii)(A) (IRS may "excuse a minor or inadvertent failure to provide required documents, but only if the taxpayer has made a good faith effort to comply, and the taxpayer promptly remedies the failure when it becomes known"). See Durst, Transfer Pricing Documentation and APAs in the Era of Worldwide Transfer Pricing Scrutiny—Some Practice Points, 27 Tax Mgmt. Int'l J. 131 (1998); Ernst & Young 1995 Transfer Pricing Documentation Survey, 72 Tax Notes 1025 (Aug. 19, 1996).

[36] INTL-21-91, 1993-1 CB 846, proposing §§1.6662-5(e), (j).

transfer analysis" and must include the following: an overview of the taxpayer's business and organizational structure; documents "explicitly required" by the §482 regulations; a description of the method chosen; an explanation of the reason the method was selected; a description of other methods considered and an explanation of the reason they were not chosen; a description of the controlled transactions; a description of any comparables used in applying the method; an explanation of any economic analysis and projections relied on in developing the method; and a description of any relevant data obtained by the taxpayer after the close of the taxable year.[37] The background documents provide support for the "assumptions, conclusions, and positions contained in the principal documents."[38] The principal documents must also include a "general index" of the principal and background documents, and a description of the system for "cataloguing and accessing those documents."[39]

2. *Reasonable applications of other reasonable methods.* Even if the taxpayer did not use a pricing method described in the §482 regulations, an increase in taxable income resulting from a redetermination of a transfer price is excluded from the net section 482 adjustment if all of the requirements described below are met.[40]

First, the taxpayer must establish that none of the pricing methods described in the regulations "was likely to result in a price that would clearly reflect income" and that the taxpayer used a pricing method that "was likely to result in a price that would clearly reflect income."[41] If the transaction is of a type for which the §482 regulations specify pricing methods, these requirements are satisfied only if

the taxpayer reasonably concludes, given the available data, that none of the specified methods was likely to provide a reliable measure of an arm's length result, and that it selected and applied an unspecified method in a way that would likely provide a reliable measure of an arm's length result.[42]

If the transaction is of a type for which no pricing method is prescribed by the regulations, the taxpayer must reasonably conclude that its chosen method and its application of the method satisfy the best method requirement.[43] Whether the taxpayer's conclusion was reasonable depends on the factors described above in connection with the rules for taxpayers using methods specified in the regulations.[44]

---

[37] Reg. §1.6662-6(d)(2)(iii)(B).

[38] Reg. §1.6662-6(d)(2)(iii)(C).

[39] Reg. §1.6662-6(d)(2)(iii)(B)(10).

[40] IRC §6662(e)(3)(B)(ii) (applicable for taxable years beginning after 1993); Reg. §1.6662-6(d)(3)(i).

[41] IRC §6662(e)(3)(B)(ii)(I).

[42] Reg. §1.6662-6(d)(3)(ii)(B).

[43] Reg. §1.6662-6(d)(3)(ii)(C). See H.R. Rep. No. 213, supra note 32, at 650.

[44] Reg. §1.6662-6(d)(2)(ii), discussed supra text accompanying notes 30–34.

Second, when the return is filed, the taxpayer must have "documentation" that states how the taxpayer's price was determined and "establish[es]" that the taxpayer's method was likely to result in a price satisfying the first requirement described in the preceding paragraph.[45] This documentation, which must consist of principal and background documents, as described above in connection with the rules for taxpayers using methods specified in the §482 regulations,[46] must be provided to the IRS within 30 days after the IRS requests it. Also, for each year the method is used, the taxpayer must also include with its "timely filed" return a statement disclosing the method.

3. *Transactions among foreign corporations.* A §482 adjustment that is "attributable" to a transaction "solely between foreign corporations" is wholly excluded in applying the dollar threshold unless the transaction affects U.S. source income or income effectively connected with a trade or business carried on in the United States.[47] Assume a §482 adjustment is made to a royalty paid by one controlled foreign corporation (CFC) to another CFC, and as a consequence, the subpart F income includable in a U.S. shareholder's gross income is increased.[48] The royalty adjustment is excluded from the shareholder's net §482 adjustment if it does not affect either CFC's U.S. source income or income effectively connected with U.S. business.

4. *Setoffs for unrelated items.* A special rule applies if (1) some but not all §482 adjustments to a taxpayer's return are excluded under the foregoing rules and (2) a setoff is allowed for unrelated transactions that the taxpayer neglected, to its disadvantage, to report at arm's length prices.[49] The rule apportions the setoff between the included and excluded §482 adjustments in applying the dollar threshold. Assume the IRS makes §482 adjustments increasing taxable income by $9 million for one category of items and $6 million for another category, but it allows a $5 million offset for an overstatement of taxable income resulting from another category of items that the taxpayer did not report on an arm's length basis. The $9 million adjustment is excluded from the net §482 adjustment, but the $6 million adjustment is included. The $5 million offset is apportioned between the positive adjustments—$3 million ($9/$15) to the $9 adjustment and $2 million to the $6 million adjustment. The net section 482 adjustment is thus $4 million ($6 million included adjustment, less $2 million of the offset).

---

[45] Reg. §1.6662-6(d)(3)(iii).

[46] Reg. §1.6662-6(d)(2)(iii), discussed supra text accompanying notes 35-39.

[47] IRC §6662(e)(3)(B)(iii); Reg. §1.6662-6(d)(4). For taxable years beginning before 1994, this rule is found in §6662(e)(3)(B)(ii).

[48] H.R. Rep. No. 964, supra note 5, at 1076. See Reg. §1.6662-6(d)(6) Ex. 3 (similar example involving CFC's payment of interest to another CFC).

[49] Reg. §1.6662-6(c)(4).

Specially Treated Taxpayers

¶134.1 INTRODUCTORY

The gift, estate, and generation-skipping transfer taxes apply to all property transferred by gift or at death, regardless of the property's geographic situs, if the donor or decedent is "a citizen or resident of the United States" at the time of the gift or at death.[1] The taxes have a much more limited application if the donor or decedent is a "nonresident not a citizen of the United States."[2] Briefly summa-

---

[1] E.g. IRC §2001(a).

[2] IRC §§2101(a), 2501(a)(2). See generally 2 Schoenblum, Multistate and Multinational Estate Planning, Ch. 20 (Little, Brown 1982); Newton, International Estate Planning, Ch. 4 (Shepard's/McGraw Hill 1981). For background, see Blum, U.S. Transfer Taxation of Nonresident Aliens: Too Much or Too Little? 14 U. Pa. J. Int'l Bus. L. 469 (1994); Schneider, Aliens and the United States Estate and Gift Taxes, 35 Taxes 281

rized, the special rules for the taxation of nonresident aliens, residents of U.S. possessions, and citizens expatriating themselves to avoid taxes are as follows:

1. Nonresident aliens are subject to the gift tax only on gifts of real or tangible personal property situated within the United States, but these gifts are taxed at the rates applicable to citizens and resident aliens and without a unified credit.[3]

2. The estates of nonresident aliens are subject to the estate tax only with respect to property situated in the United States, including some intangibles, at the same rates as apply to the estates of citizens and resident aliens and with a unified credit of $13,000.[4]

3. Gifts and bequests by nonresident aliens to their spouses qualify for the marital deduction, but often only if the spouse is a U.S. citizen; the election to treat a gift as made one half by the donor and one half by the donor's spouse is not available if the donor is a nonresident alien.[5]

4. If a transfer by a nonresident alien is subject to gift or estate tax, a generation-skipping transfer resulting from the gift or bequest is subject to the generation-skipping transfer tax.[6]

5. The foregoing rules are altered in certain respects for donors and decedents who are citizens of or domiciled in countries with which the United States has made wealth transfer tax treaties.[7]

6. A U.S. citizen who resides in and is a citizen of a U.S. possession (e.g., Puerto Rico or the U.S. Virgin Islands) is treated as a nonresident alien if U.S. citizenship was acquired solely by reason of being a citizen of the possession or by birth or residence therein.[8]

7. Former citizens who reside abroad are classified as nonresident aliens for gift and estate tax purposes, but special rules apply if the loss of citizenship was principally motivated by a desire to avoid U.S. taxes and oc-

---

(1957); Wurzel, Nonresident Aliens and Federal Estate Tax: A Legislative Problem, 40 Colum. L. Rev. 52 (1940). See also Ferguson, Nonresident Alien Estates, 1990, 13 Stat Income Bull. 77 (Summer 1993) (143 estate tax returns were filed for nonresident aliens dying during 1990, reporting U.S. gross estates of approximately $80.7 million and U.S. estate tax liabilities, after credits, of approximately $20.5 million, including $6.9 million paid by estates of 11 Japanese decedents and $7.9 million paid by estates of five Venezuelan estates).

[3] See infra ¶134.2.2.

[4] See infra ¶¶134.2.3, 134.2.4, 134.2.5. Also, the deferral privilege granted by §6166, relating to certain closely held business interests, is not available to the estates of nonresident aliens. For §6166, see infra ¶137.5.

[5] See infra ¶134.2.2 (gifts), ¶134.2.4 (bequests).

[6] See infra ¶134.2.6.

[7] See infra ¶134.2.7.

[8] See infra ¶134.3.

curred within 10 years before the making of a gift or the individual's death.[9]

¶134.2 NONRESIDENT ALIENS

¶134.2.1 "Nonresident Alien"

The statutes use the terms "citizen or resident of the United States" and "nonresident not a citizen of the United States" without defining them.[1] Citizenship is determined under §1 of the Fourteenth Amendment ("all persons born or naturalized in the United States, and subject to the jurisdiction thereof" are citizens of the United States and of the state of residence) and by a vast body of nontax statutory and case law, an analysis of which is beyond the scope of this work.[2] The terms "resident" and "nonresident," however, have been the subject of extensive analysis in various tax regulations, rulings, and cases. For estate tax purposes, the starting point is the following definitions provided by the regulations:

A "resident" decedent is a decedent who, at the time of his death, had his domicile in the United States. The term "United States," as used in the Estate Tax Regulations, includes only the States and the District of Columbia. ... A person acquires a domicile in a place by living there, for even a brief period of time, with no definite present intention of later removing therefrom. Residence without the requisite intention to remain indefinitely will not suffice to constitute domicile, nor will intention to change domicile effect such a change unless accompanied by actual removal. ... A "nonresident" decedent is a decedent who, at the time of his death, had his domicile outside the United States under the principles set forth [above].[3]

The gift tax regulations are substantially identical, except that a donor's domicile is determined as of the time of the gift, rather than at death.[4]

The emphasis on domicile in the gift and estate tax regulations contrasts with tests applied for income tax purposes, which look to more objective factors,

---

[9] See infra ¶134.4.

[1] IRC §§2001(a), 2101(a), 2501(a)(2).

[2] See generally Gordon & Mailman, Immigration Law and Procedure, chs. 11–15 (Matthew Bender rev. ed. 1992); Schoenblum, Multistate and Multinational Estate Planning §§9.11.1, 20.02 (Little, Brown 1982). For dual citizenship, see Vriniotis' Est. v. CIR, 79 TC 298 (1982) (estate of decedent who was citizen of both United States and Greece at death taxed under rules for citizens).

[3] Reg. §§20.0-1(b)(1),(2). See Farmers' Loan & Trust Co. v. US, 60 F2d 618, 619 (SDNY 1932) ("the residence referred to in the statute imposing the estate tax is synonymous with domicile").

[4] Reg §25.2501-1(b).

including whether an alien is classified as a permanent resident of the United States under the immigration laws and, if not, the number of days on which the individual has been present in the United States.[5] The policy underlying the distinction may be that the gift and estate taxes, being concerned with the transmission of personal wealth over the lifetime of the donor-decedent, should be based on the relatively stable factor of domicile, while the income tax, being imposed year by year, can more properly be geared to the place where the taxpayer happens to be during a particular year. It has also been suggested that the estate tax regulations naturally gravitated to the concept of domicile because residence "is ordinarily used as the equivalent of domicile in statutes relating to probate, administration, and succession taxes" and because "the incidence of estate and succession taxes has historically been determined by domicile and situs, and not by the fact of actual residence."[6]

A 1980 ruling, although addressed to a specialized problem (the estate tax status of a person who entered the United States illegally but remained here for life), summarizes the generally accepted principles governing the issue of domicile:

> The requirements for acquiring a domicile are (1) legal capacity to do so; (2) physical presence; and (3) a current intention to make a home in the place. . . . Legal capacity to acquire a domicile of choice has been found to exist even when people are subject to transfer to another domicile at the direction of others. . . . Therefore, the fact that the decedent was subject to deportation does not render the decedent legally incapable of acquiring a domicile.
>
> Because the decedent was physically present in this country at the date of death, the decedent would have been domiciled in the United States if the decedent had a current intention to make the United States a home. However, once a person has established a domicile in one place, it is presumed to continue in that place until it is shown to have been changed. . . . The presumption can be rebutted upon facts showing an intention to remain in the United States for an indefinite period or on a permanent basis. . . . Some of the factors used in determining such requisite intention are home ownership, local community ties and living with one's family in the claimed domicile. . . .
>
> In the present case, the fact that the decedent lived in the United States for a long time with the decedent's family and that the decedent established strong community ties indicates an absence of any fixed intention of returning to the native country.
>
> The purchase of property located in a person's native country is not sufficient to conclude that the decedent was not domiciled in the United States, especially since the location of an investment is not indicative of

---

[5] IRC §7701(b), discussed supra ¶65.2.

[6] Bowring v. Bowers, 24 F2d 918, 921 (2d Cir.), cert. denied, 277 US 608 (1928) (taxpayer subject to income tax on basis of residence, despite long-established foreign domicile).

domicile. .... The facts in the present case thus indicate that the decedent intended to remain in the United States indefinitely.[7]

In a few cases, courts have held or strongly intimidated that an alien was a resident of the United States for income tax purposes but domiciled abroad for estate tax purposes.[8] Such a differential diagnosis is rarely required, however, because the objective facts determining whether an alien is a resident of the United States usually indicate that the individual is also domiciled here (or vice versa), particularly since "no factor is likely to be accorded as great a weight in determining an individual's domicile than where he lives."[9] The "intention" to establish or change one's domicile "must be judged by all the circumstances by which it is made manifest," and "conduct is no less, and often more, significant than statements."[10]

Neither resident nor nonresident status is uniformly advantageous for an alien. The situs rules often exempt transfers by nonresident aliens from gift or estate tax, but if the transfer is taxable, the resulting liability can exceed the tax that would be imposed on a similar transfer by a citizen or resident alien because citizens and residents qualify for a unified credit that exempts $600,000 from tax, while nonresident aliens have no unified credit under the gift tax and an estate tax credit that exempts only $60,000 from tax.

¶134.2.2 Gift Tax

Under §2501(a)(1), the gift tax reaches "the transfer of property by gift ... by any individual, resident or nonresident." However, for nonresident aliens, this broad principle is qualified by two exceptions: (1) §2501(a)(2), stating that the tax shall not apply to transfers of intangible property by a nonresident alien, and (2) §2511(a), stating that the tax applies to transfers by nonresident aliens only

---

[7] Rev. Rul. 80-209, 1980-2 CB 248, 249.

[8] Bowring v. Bowers, supra note 6; Nienhuys' Est. v. CIR, 17 TC 1149, 1159-61 (1952) (acq.). See Fifth Ave. Bank v. CIR, 36 BTA 534 (1937) (U.S. citizen, resident abroad, held domiciled in United States under prior law making domicile relevant in determining deductibility of certain administration expenses). See generally Reese & Green, That Elusive Word, "Residence," 6 Vand. L. Rev. 561 (1953).

[9] Schoenblum, supra note 1, at §8.02.

[10] Rodiek v. CIR, 33 BTA 1020, 1032-33 (1936) (nonacq.), aff'd on other issues sub nom. Rodiek v. Helvering, 87 F2d 328 (2d Cir. 1937) (taxpayer overcame presumption created by IRS finding of U.S. residence). Compare US v. Hellé, 38-2 USTC ¶9376 (D. Hawaii 1934) (not officially reported) (taxpayer failed to overcome IRS determination of nonresidence). See Khan's Est. v. CIR, 75 TCM (CCH) 1597 (1998) (alien holding U.S. greencard was domiciled in United States, even though his wife resided in their home country, he lived in United States for relatively short time, and he returned to home country for last years of his life, because he held substantial assets in United States and had sold most of his property in home country and because family had long history of immigration to United States).

if the property is "situated within the United States."[11] Nonresident aliens thus are subject to gift tax only on transfers of real or tangible personal property situated in the United States at the time of the gift.[12] Intangible property has been exempted since 1954, regardless of where situated, because pre-1954 efforts to tax gifts of intangibles could be "easily avoided if the donor merely moves the property from the United States to a foreign country and makes the gift there."[13] Moreover, when the tax was so avoided, the donee often kept the property abroad, thereby reducing the depository business of U.S. financial institutions.

The effectiveness of even the residual gift tax is open to question. Since ostensibly taxable property can usually be converted by incorporation into shares of a corporation, which can be transferred without gift tax liability, gift taxes are likely to be paid only by ill-advised foreign donors. Transfers to controlled corporations on the eve of a gift may prove ineffective if the issue is litigated,[14] but even the most blatant evasions may escape IRS attention unless a nervous or unusually conscientious domestic donee or financial institution is involved.

The $10,000 annual per-donee exclusion under §2503(b) is allowed to non-resident alien donors on the same basis as to U.S. citizens and residents.[15] A nonresident alien donor is also entitled to the marital deduction on the same terms as a citizen or resident, but these terms usually deny the deduction if the spouse is not a U.S. citizen.[16] In this context, the marital deduction is therefore allowed only in the relatively unusual case of a nonresident alien making a gift of

---

[11] Special rules apply to nonresident aliens who were formerly U.S. citizens. IRC §§2501(a)(3), 2511(b), discussed infra ¶134.4.

[12] Reg. §25.2511-1(b).

[13] S. Rep. No. 1622, 83d Cong., 2d Sess. 126 (1954). See Rohmer v. CIR, 21 TC 1099, 1104 (1954) (acq.) (gift of British author's manuscript and contract rights with U.S. publisher subject to tax under pre-1954 law because they were situated in United States when transferred); Wodehouse v. CIR, 19 TC 487 (1952) (acq.) (situs of British author's manuscript, not yet copyrighted in United States, was France, where it was located when transferred).

The exemption of gifts of intangibles did not originally apply to nonresident aliens engaged in business in the United States, but it was extended to them in 1966. See Reg. §25.2511-1(b)(2).

[14] See De Goldschmidt-Rothschild v. CIR, 168 F2d 975 (2d Cir. 1948) (conversion of stock and bonds of domestic corporations into Treasury notes solely to make tax-exempt gifts disregarded). See also Fillman v. US, 355 F2d 632 (Ct. Cl. 1966) (foreign corporations held shares of domestic corporations only as nominees for decedent, not as beneficial owners; held, shares included in gross estate).

For income tax purposes, a nonresident alien must usually recognize gain on a disposition of a "United States real property interest." IRC §897, discussed supra ¶66.4. However, a transfer of U.S. real property to a domestic corporation in exchange for stock is excepted from this rule if the exchange is within the nonrecognition rule of §351(a) and at least one half of the corporation's assets consist of U.S. real property. See supra ¶66.4.5. An incorporation exchange of U.S. real property for stock of a foreign corporation is not covered by this exception.

[15] See supra ¶124.1.

[16] IRC §2523(i), discussed supra ¶123.3.4.

U.S. property to a spouse who is a U.S. citizen. Moreover, the split-gift election of §2513, permitting a married person's gifts to third persons to be treated as though made one half by each spouse, is allowed only if both husband and wife are citizens or residents of the United States when the gift is made.[17]

Charitable contributions by nonresident aliens are deductible under §2522(b), which is similar to the rules applicable to charitable gifts of citizens and residents, except that (1) gifts to charitable, educational, religious, and similar corporations qualify only if the donee is a domestic corporation, (2) gifts to trusts, community chests, funds, foundations, and fraternal societies qualify only if the gift is to be used within the United States for charitable or other qualifying purposes, and (3) gifts to veterans groups qualify only if the donee is organized in the United States or a possession thereof.[18] For a determined donor, these restrictions are not a serious barrier to foreign largesse because a gift to a domestic charitable organization qualifies even if it engages in foreign charitable activities.

The gift tax on nonresident alien donors is imposed under the unified rate schedule of §2001(c), which also applies to citizens and residents.[19] However, the unified credit is not allowed to a nonresident alien,[20] and relatively small taxable gifts can therefore generate surprisingly high taxes. Assume a nonresident alien makes a gift to her spouse, who is also a nonresident alien, of a farm located in Minnesota that is worth $70,000. A $10,000 per-donee exclusion is allowed, but the marital deduction is not because the spouse is not a citizen. The taxable gift is $60,000 ($70,000, less $10,000), and if the donor has made no prior taxable gifts, the tax is $13,000.

¶134.2.3 Estate Tax—Gross Estate

The gross estate of a nonresident alien decedent is determined in two steps. First, the "entire gross estate" is assembled in the same way as the gross estate of a citizen or resident alien. It includes property owned at death, property transferred during life subject to reserved interests and powers described in §§2036–2038, the proceeds of insurance on the decedent's life in which the decedent had incidents of ownership within the meaning of §2042, and so forth, if and to the extent the property would be included in the gross estate of a citizen or resident alien decedent under §§2031–2044.[21] In making these determinations,

---

[17] For §2513, see supra ¶123.5.

[18] See IRC §7701(a)(4) (corporation is domestic if organized under laws of United States, one of its states, or District of Columbia), discussed supra ¶¶65.3.1, 65.3.2. For the charitable deduction under §2522(a) for donors who are citizens or residents of the United States, see supra ¶121.8.

[19] See supra ¶132.2.

[20] IRC §2505(a).

[21] Reg. §20.2103-1.

the situs of the property is immaterial. Second, the portion of the worldwide gross estate that is "situated" in the United States is determined.[22] The situs of property is ascertained at the time of death, except for property transferred during life and included in the gross estate under §§2035–2038, which is treated as situated within the United States if it had a U.S. situs either when transferred or at the time of the decedent's death.[23]

The first step can sometimes be omitted. The gross estate is limited to property with a U.S. situs, and the amount of the worldwide gross estate is relevant only under §2106(a)(2), which restricts deductions for expenses, claims, and mortgages to the otherwise deductible amount, multiplied by the ratio of the U.S. gross estate to the "entire gross estate." The regulations provide that property situated outside the United States need not be disclosed on the return unless deductions are claimed, the information is requested by the IRS, or the estate is subject to §2107, relating to tax-motivated expatriates.[24]

Although the phrase "situated in the United States" is crucial in determining the estate tax liability of nonresident aliens, neither the Code nor the regulations supply a comprehensive definition. There are, instead, several statutory provisions dealing with particular categories of assets, which reflect no unifying concept or principle and which must be augmented by ad hoc decisions about the situs of assets not covered by any statutory rule.

In an early estate tax case, the Supreme Court held that the value of securities issued by foreign corporations could be included in the gross estate of a nonresident alien, merely because the securities were physically present in the United States.[25] The Court recognized that the securities might be taxed by other

---

[22] IRC §2103. The "United States" consists of the 50 states and the District of Columbia. IRC §7701(a)(9); Reg. §20.0-1(b)(1).

[23] Reg. §20.2104-1(b). The situs of property brought into the gross estate under §§2035–2038 is determined under the estate tax situs rules, both as of the time of the gift and at death. Section 2501(a)(2), exempting transfers of intangible property by nonresident aliens from the gift tax, has no effect in this context. For example, if intangible property was transferred in trust during life, subject to a reserved right to income for life, the property is included in the U.S. gross estate under §2036 if, under the estate tax rules, it was situated in the United States at the time of the transfer. This is so regardless of the situs of the trust assets at the time of death and even though the gift of the remainder was not a taxable gift.

[24] Reg. §20.2103-1. See IRC §2106(b) (deductions other than marital deduction disallowed if executor fails to report property situated outside United States in estate tax return). For the deductions allowed to estates of nonresident aliens, see infra ¶134.2.4. For §2107, see infra ¶134.4.

The statute and regulations require disclosure of worldwide assets as a condition of the charitable deduction. IRC §2106(b); Reg. §20.2106-1(b). However, the rules for determining the charitable deduction make no reference to the decedent's foreign assets, and the estate tax form seemingly dispenses with this clear but unjustifiable requirement of the statute and regulations. Form 706NA (rev. May 1990).

[25] Burnet v. Brooks, 288 US 378 (1933). See Wurzel, Nonresident Aliens and Federal Estate Tax: A Legislative Problem, 40 Colum. L. Rev. 52 (1940).

countries on the basis of the decedent's citizenship or domicile, but it refused to find a remedy for multiple taxation in either the Constitution or in U.S. obligations under international law, observing that this was a matter for international negotiations rather than judicial action. Although the securities in the case before the Court would not be included in a nonresident alien's gross estate under current law, this is the effect of legislation,[26] and the courts continue to leave the problem of multiple taxation to Congress and the diplomatic arena.

1. *Real property.* Real property is "situated in the United States" if it is physically located in one of the states or the District of Columbia.[27] For many years, real property situated outside the United States was exempt from federal estate tax even if owned by a citizen,[28] and several of the most important cases in this area—classifying long-term leases of real estate and nonrecourse mortgages on land as real property—concerned this exemption.[29] Although the exemption was repealed in 1962, the principles established by these cases seem applicable in determining the situs of property of nonresident alien decedents.

2. *Tangible personal property.* Tangible personal property is also assigned to the place where it is located.[30] This physical location rule apparently applies to coins and currency.[31]

However, in *Delaney v. Murchie,* a case involving jewelry and other personal effects in the possession of a nonresident alien who died in the United States while on a trip from Canada to the Bahamas, the Court of Appeals for the First Circuit refused to construe the statutory term "situated" to mean "mere physical presence at a given place on the tax day," holding instead that the concept of situs as applied to chattels "involves some degree of permanence, an established abid-

---

[26] IRC §§2104(a), (c), discussed infra text accompanying notes 36-49.

[27] Reg. §20.2104-1(a)(1). See Reg. §20.0-1(b)(1) ("United States" includes only states and District of Columbia); §20.2105-1(a)(1) (real property located outside United States is not situated in United States).

[28] Reg. §20.2031-1(a) (second sentence) (gross estate of decedent dying before October 17, 1962 does not include real property situated outside United States). See Reg. §20.2103-1 (foreign real property not included in "entire gross estate" of nonresident alien who died before October 17, 1962).

[29] Fair v. CIR, 91 F2d 218 (3d Cir. 1937) (Cuban "hipotecas" on land, equivalent to mortgages without accompanying bond or personal obligation, classified by Cuban law as "immovables," were real property situated outside United States); de Perigny's Est. v. CIR, 9 TC 782 (1947) (nonacq.) (same for 99-year leases of Kenya land, convertible at lessee's option to 999-year leases; legislative exemption manifested acceptance of "almost universally established principle of estate taxation that real property should be subject to death duties only in the country where situated").

[30] Reg. §20.2104-1(a)(2) (tangible personal property located in United States), §20.2105-1(a)(2) (tangible personal property located outside United States).

[31] See Reg. §20.2104-1(a)(7) (last sentence) (currency not "debt obligation" within meaning of §2104(c)); Blodgett v. Silberman, 277 US 1 (1928) (coins and currency are tangible personal property for state inheritance tax purposes); Rev. Rul. 55-143, 1955-1 CB 465 (if held in safe-deposit box, money is not "deposited" with bank within meaning of prior law).

ing place or home base for the chattel, analogous to the notion of domicil as applied to the person."[32] The court said that "mere transitory presence" might be sufficient to establish a chattel's situs "for the purpose of giving the state jurisdiction to deal with the article as a menace to health, or perhaps to administer the property for the benefit of local creditors of a nonresident decedent, but the same transitory presence might not establish its situs in the state for the purpose of the imposition of an estate tax."[33]

The same idea underlies a statutory exception providing that works of art owned by a nonresident alien do not have a U.S. situs for federal estate tax purposes if they were imported into the United States solely for exhibition, were loaned for this purpose to a "public gallery or museum" whose "net earnings" do not inure "to the benefit of any private stockholder or individual," and were, when the decedent died, on exhibition or "en route to or from exhibition" in the public gallery or museum.[34] Given *Delaney v. Murchie*, the provision was probably not necessary to protect objects that are loaned only for temporary exhibition here. However, the statutory rule has no time limit,[35] and it eliminates other possible doubts about the scope of *Delaney v. Murchie*.

3. *Corporate stock.* Under §2104(a), stock "owned and held by" a nonresident alien is "property within the United States" if issued by a domestic corporation.[36] Shares of a foreign corporation are not situated in the United States, even if the certificates, corporate headquarters, and business assets are located in the United States and all business activities are conducted here.[37] However, in

---

[32] Delaney v. Murchie, 177 F2d 444, 448 (1st Cir. 1949). See Rev. Rul. 187, 1953-2 CB 291 (personal property used by duly accredited foreign envoys in conduct of official business not subject to federal estate tax; contra for investment and real property situated here; same for United Nations personnel covered by U.S.-U.N. agreement).

[33] Delaney v. Murchie, supra note 32, at 447.

[34] IRC §2105(c). The inurement test is borrowed from §501(c)(3). See supra ¶100.4. For the origin of §2105(c), see Coughlin, "Mystery Billionaire," Life (Nov. 27, 1980), p. 81 (works of art lent by Calouste Gulbenkian, when 80 years old, to National Gallery of Art).

[35] See City Bank Farmers Trust Co. v. Schnader, 293 US 112, 120 (1934) (paintings on loan of indefinite duration to Pennsylvania museum acquired taxable situs there for state inheritance tax purposes, despite owner's continued residence in New York; Pennsylvania location was "not merely transient, transitory, or temporary").

[36] See S. Rep. No. 1622, 83d Cong., 2d Sess. 125-26, 476-77 (1954); Reg. §20.2104-1(a)(5) (stock of domestic corporation is situated in United States, "irrespective of the location of the certificates"); Lockie's Est. v. CIR, 21 TC 64 (1953) (acq.) (nonresident alien decedent died after instructing broker to buy shares of domestic corporation but before so-called trade date; held, stock excluded from gross estate because decedent did not own it at death).

A corporation is domestic if it is organized under the laws of the United States, one of the states, or the District of Columbia. IRC §7701(a)(4), discussed supra ¶65.3 text accompanying notes 1-15.

[37] Reg. §20.2105-1(f) (location of certificates not relevant). See Shenton v. US, 53 F2d 249 (SDNY 1931) (warrants to purchase stock of foreign corporation not includable

cases of sham (e.g., a deathbed transfer of the shares of a domestic corporation to a foreign personal holding company), the decedent might be treated as owner of a foreign corporation's assets, not its stock.[38]

Although §2104(a) refers only to stock "owned and held" by a nonresident alien, presumably at death, the meager statutory language is properly construed by the regulations to confer a foreign situs on all shares of foreign corporations, without regard to the reason for their inclusion in the worldwide gross estate.[39] Thus, stock of a foreign corporation transferred during life subject to a reserved power to alter the donee's beneficial enjoyment is protected by §2104(a), even though it is not "owned and held" by the decedent at death.

4. *Debt obligations.* Generally, debt obligations are situated in the United States if the obligor is a United States person (a U.S. citizen or resident, domestic corporation, or domestic partnership) or the government of the United States, a state, the District of Columbia, or a political subdivision thereof.[40] A deposit with a U.S. branch of a foreign corporation has a U.S. situs if the branch is engaged in a commercial banking business.[41] Although the issue is not explicitly addressed in the statutes, the regulations make it clear that obligations of other obligors have a foreign situs.[42]

These basic rules, however, are virtually eclipsed by exceptions. Most importantly, an obligation of a U.S. debtor is not situated in the United States if interest received under the instrument immediately before death would have been exempted from income tax under §871(h)(1), which provides that "portfolio interest" is exempt from the withholding tax imposed by §871(a)(1) on various

---

in nonresident alien's estate even though documents were in custody of New York banking firm; court treated stock warrants as tantamount to stock, but only arguendo).

[38] See Fillman v. US, 355 F2d 632 (Ct. Cl. 1966) (foreign corporations held shares of domestic corporations only as nominees for decedent, not as beneficial owners; held, shares included in gross estate); Lemons, Olson & Marsden, Using Foreign Corporations to Avoid U.S. Estate Tax On U.S. Residences—With a Canadian Emphasis, 52 Tax Notes 947 (1991) (discussing delicate balance needed to have U.S. residence of Canadian individual treated as asset of foreign corporation owned by individual and simultaneously avoid Canadian tax on disguised dividend from shareholder use of corporate asset); Mene, Estate Planning for Nonresident Aliens, 59 Taxes 617, 628-29 (1981).

[39] Reg. §20.2105-1(f) ("shares of stock issued by a corporation which is not a domestic corporation" are situated outside United States).

[40] IRC §§2104(c), 7701(a)(30). For debts with two or more obligors, see Reg. §20.2104-1(a)(7) (apportion debt, taking into account rights of contribution among obligors and other relevant facts and circumstances).

Unlike prior law, the present situs rules do not take account of the location of the documents evidencing the debt. See Reg. §20.2104-1(a)(3) (decedents dying before Nov. 14, 1966); Rev. Rul. 66-236, 1966-2 CB 442, declared obsolete by Rev. Rul. 74-623, 1974-2 CB 406 (convertible debentures of domestic corporation are written evidences of debt, included in gross estate under prior law only if physically situated in the United States when decedent died).

[41] IRC §2104(c) (second sentence); Reg. §20.2104-1(a)(8).

[42] Reg. §20.2105-1(e).

nonbusiness income of nonresident aliens.[43] Generally, the portfolio interest exemption covers all interest on obligations of U.S. debtors, except certain unregistered (bearer) instruments and instruments held by a person owning at least 10 percent of the stock or other equity interests of the issuing entity.[44] The exemption cannot apply, however, if the interest is effectively connected with a business of the taxpayer in the United States.

Although most interest on bank deposits is portfolio interest, deposits are also covered by another exception. Deposits with a person carrying on a banking business (including savings institutions chartered under federal or state law) and deposits held by an insurance company under an agreement to pay interest thereon do not have a U.S. situs, even if the bank or insurance company is organized under domestic law and does business only in the United States, provided that interest on the deposits, if received immediately before death, would not have been effectively connected with the conduct of a trade or business of the decedent in the United States.[45] This exemption reflects a long-established

---

[43] IRC §2105(b)(3).

[44] See supra ¶66.2.2 text accompanying notes 22–61.

Also, contingent interest received is not portfolio interest. IRC §871(h)(4). If any part of an interest payment received on the date of the decedent's death would not have been portfolio interest because of the contingent interest rule, at least a proportionate part of the obligation is treated as property located in the United States. IRC §2105(b), as amended by Pub. L. No. 103-66, §13237(b), 107 Stat. 312 (1993) (applicable to estates of decedents dying after 1993).

The IRS has ruled privately that a noninterest-bearing obligation of a U.S. obligor with a term of 183 days or less is includable in the gross estate of a nonresident alien decedent. Although §871(a)(1) generally taxes original issue discount (OID) and the exemption for "portfolio interest" generally applies to OID, §871(g)(1)(B)(i) defines the term "original issue discount obligation" for purposes of §871 to exclude an obligation payable within 183 days of original issue. Thus, discount on such a bond, although not taxable under §871(a)(1), is not portfolio interest, and the exclusion of §2105(b)(3), which applies only if interest on the obligation would be exempted by the portfolio rules, is inapplicable. See Gilberti, Short-Term Debt Obligations Exempt From U.S. Income Tax But Not from U.S. Estate Tax: TAM 9422001, 23 Tax Mgmt. Int'l J. 446 (1994).

[45] IRC §2105(b)(1). See Rosenblum v. Anglim, 135 F2d 512 (9th Cir. 1943) (person receiving deposits solely from decedent was not carrying on banking business); Worthington's Est. v. CIR, 18 TC 796 (1952) (acq.) (decedent's share of cash on deposit in account of estate of decedent's grandfather; decedent had "direct and enforceable claim" to funds which were therefore funds on deposit for her use and benefit); Rev. Rul. 82-193, 1982-2 CB 219 (exemption only applies to "general deposits"—funds paid to bank, to depositor's general credit, that must be repaid on depositor's order or demand—excluding "specific deposits"—amounts "transferred to a bank for a specific purpose, not contemplating a credit or general account, [that] may not be commingled with the general funds of the bank"); Rev. Rul. 65-245, 1965-2 CB 379 (credit balance in nonresident alien decedent's trading account with domestic brokerage firm not "bank deposit"; decedent had no "specific claim against a specific banker"); Rev. Rul. 55-143, 1955-1 CB 465 (funds in bank safe-deposit box are not "moneys deposited").

The regulations limit this provision to decedents dying after Nov. 13, 1966 and before Jan. 1, 1976. Reg. §20.2105-1(i). However, the time limit was repealed in 1976

policy of encouraging nonresident aliens to use American banks as depositories for their funds by assuring them that the funds will not be taxed "merely because technically present in this country."[46]

The portfolio and deposit exemptions apply only if interest on the obligation or deposit was not effectively connected with a U.S. business of the decedent. In contrast, deposits with a foreign branch of a domestic corporation or partnership are not situated in the United States, whether or not connected with a business of the decedent in the United States, if the branch is engaged in a commercial banking business.[47] Similarly, an obligation of a domestic corporation does not have a U.S. situs if the corporation has one or more active businesses in foreign countries that accounted for at least 80 percent of its gross income during the preceding three years.[48] Obligations of domestic corporations issued pursuant to specified provisions of the pre-1976 Interest Equalization Tax are also exempted.[49]

5. *Life insurance.* In contrast to the complex rules governing debt instruments, §2105(a) promulgates a rule of startling simplicity for amounts receivable as life insurance on the life of a nonresident alien: They do not have a U.S. situs, regardless of the insurer's place of incorporation or business location.[50] This exemption is restricted to insurance on the decedent's life, presumably in recognition of the fact that the amount included in the gross estate in respect of policies on the life of anyone else is not governed by §2042, relating to amounts "receivable . . . as insurance," but by such other provisions as §2033 and §§2036-2038, which reach the value of the policy rather than the amount payable at death. Insurance on the life of a person other than the decedent apparently has a U.S. situs if the insurer is a U.S. resident or a domestic corporation.[51]

(Pub. L. No. 94-455, §1041, 90 Stat. 1520, reprinted in 1976-3 (vol. 1) CB 1, 110), and the regulations have not been updated to reflect this change.

[46] Swan's Est. v. CIR, 247 F2d 144, 148 (2d Cir. 1957).

[47] IRC §2105(b)(2); Reg. §20.2105-1(j) (exception applies whether deposit is denominated in U.S. or foreign currency).

[48] IRC §2104(c) (last sentence), incorporating 80-20 rule of §§861(a)(1)(A) and (c), discussed supra ¶70.2 text accompanying notes 7-15.

[49] IRC §2104(c) (last sentence); Reg. §20.2105-1(m).

The regulations also exempt obligations of the United States issued before March 1, 1941. Reg. §20.2105-1(d). This portion of the regulations is an anachronism because no pre-1941 obligations are still outstanding. Staff of Joint Comm. on Tax'n, 94th Cong., 2d Sess., General Explanation of the Tax Reform Act of 1976 (Comm. Print), reprinted in 1976-3 (vol. 2) CB 509. See Worthington's Est. v. CIR, 18 TC 796, 802-04 (1952) (acq.) (Federal Land Bank bonds are not obligations of "United States").

[50] IRC §2105(a); Reg. §20.2105-1(g).

[51] See Reg. §20.2104-1(a)(4) ("intangible personal property the written evidence of which is not treated as being the property itself" is situated in United States "if it is issued by or enforceable against a resident of the United States or a domestic corporation or governmental unit"); Reg. §20.2105-1(e) (such intangibles, if issued by anyone else, are not situated in United States); Riccio v. US, 71-2 USTC ¶12,801 (DPR 1971) (not officially reported) (insurance life of third person of which decedent was beneficiary was not

6. *Beneficial interests in trusts.* The situs of beneficial interests in trusts is determined by reference to the underlying assets.[52] For example, a nonresident alien's beneficial interest in a trust whose assets consist of certificates of deposit in a U.S. bank is not situated in the United States because the certificates, if held directly by the decedent, would not have had a U.S. situs.[53]

7. *Partnership interests.* The situs of a nonresident alien's interest in a partnership has received surprisingly little attention. In a 1955 ruling, the IRS held that partnership interests are situated "where the partnership business is carried on."[54] Although the ruling involved the meaning of "situs" as used in an estate tax convention between the United States and the United Kingdom, the IRS cited both British and U.S. cases in reaching its conclusion, and it held that state court decisions under which the location of the partnership assets is controlling "cannot be regarded as the Federal rule." An earlier federal court of appeals decision, however, held that the situs of the underlying assets was controlling in determining the situs of an interest in a Cuban entity terminating on decedent's death.[55]

8. *Other intangibles.* Sections 2104 and 2105 are silent on the situs of other intangibles, such as contract rights, patents, copyrights, goodwill, and franchises. According to the regulations, intangible property not covered by any other rule is situated in the United States if (1) the written evidence of the property is not treated "as being the property itself" and (2) the intangible "is issued by or enforceable against" a resident of the United States or a domestic corporation or

---

covered by §2105(a), but was intangible personal property, written evidence of which is not treated as being property itself).

[52] CIR v. Nevius, 76 F2d 109 (2d Cir.), cert. denied, 298 US 591 (1935) (nonresident alien's interest as donee of power of appointment over testamentary trust established by husband, also nonresident alien, with British trustee, held subject to estate tax to extent of trust's shares of U.S. corporations); Rev. Rul. 55-163, 1955-1 CB 674 (participating units of common trust fund operated under New York law, held by revocable trust established by nonresident alien decedent, have situs in United States).

This approach does not apply to interests in so-called business trusts that are classified as corporations for federal tax purposes. See IRC §7701(a)(3); Reg. §301.7701-2(a)(3), discussed supra ¶90.1.3. Under the rule for corporate stock, an interest in such a trust has a U.S. situs if the trust is organized under the laws of the United States, one of the states, or the District of Columbia.

[53] IRC §2105(b)(1) (bank deposit not within United States, regardless of bank's location, if interest was not effectively connected with U.S. business of decedent), discussed supra text accompanying notes 45–46; Rev. Rul. 82-193, 1982-2 CB 219 (reversionary interest in trust holding certificates of deposit issued by U.S. bank; "the deposit . . . retains its character as a general deposit and [decedent's] reversionary interest in the trust will be considered property situated outside the United States").

[54] Rev. Rul. 55-701, 1955-2 CB 836. See Rev. Proc. 98-7, 1998-1 CB —, at §4.01(21) (IRS ordinarily will not rule on "whether a partnership interest is intangible property for purposes of section 2501(a)(2)," which exempts transfers of intangibles by nonresident aliens from gift tax).

[55] Sanchez v. Bowers, 70 F2d 715 (2d Cir. 1934).

governmental unit.[56] A parallel provision assigns a foreign situs to similar items issued by or enforceable against foreign persons.[57]

The situs of intangibles evidenced by documents that are "treated as the property itself" is left ambiguous by the regulations, but presumably they are situated where the documents are located.[58] The regulations give no examples of intangibles evidenced by documents "treated as the property itself." The term is a contradiction; if the tangible "written evidence" is "the property itself," the property is tangible, not intangible. Presumably, the term is intended to cover situations where the benefits of ownership of the intangible cannot be enjoyed without possessing the written evidence. Bearer bonds are the classic example of such property, but they are not subject to this catchall rule because the statutes deal explicitly with debt obligations. Perhaps, lottery tickets and bearer stock rights or warrants are covered by the rule. Currency is apparently another example.[59] If so, U.S. dollars stuffed in the decedent's mattress in Panama City have a foreign situs, but Deutsche Marks kept in a vault in New York are situated in the United States.

The regulations provide no help in ascertaining the situs of rights that are not "issued by or enforceable against" anyone, such as goodwill. The situs of such items must be determined on a case-by-case basis, presumably by determining whether they are more closely related to the United States or to a foreign country.

¶134.2.4 Estate Tax Deductions

The taxable estate of a nonresident alien is determined by subtracting the deductions allowed by §2106 from the portion of the entire gross estate that is situated in the United States. Deductions are allowed under the deduction rules that apply to the estates of citizens and resident aliens, except as explained below.

1. *Expenses, losses, indebtedness, and taxes.* Deductions for funeral and administration expenses, claims against the estate, mortgages on property included in the gross estate, and casualty losses are initially determined under §§2053 and 2054 in the same way as they are for the estate of a citizen or resident

---

[56] Reg. §20.2104-1(a)(4). See Riccio v. US, 71-2 USTC ¶12,801 (DPR 1971) (not officially reported) (regulation applied to policy of insurance owned by decedent on life of another person).

[57] Reg. §20.2105-1(e). See Bickford-Smith v. US, 80 F. Supp. 660 (Ct. Cl. 1948) (following British government's seizure of decedent's stock in U.S. corporations, decedent did not "own" stock; claim against British government not included in gross estate, presumably because it was intangible claim against foreign obligor).

[58] See Rev. Rul. 66-236, 1966-2 CB 442, declared obsolete by Rev. Rul. 74-623, 1974-2 CB 406 (convertible debentures issued by domestic corporations excluded unless physically situated in United States).

[59] See Reg. §20.2104-1(a)(7) (last sentence) (currency is not covered by situs rules for debt obligations).

alien.[60] However, the aggregate amount (computed on a worldwide basis) is deductible only to the extent ratably allocable to the portion of the worldwide gross estate that is included in the U.S. gross estate.[61] The deduction is calculated as the worldwide amount, multiplied by a fraction whose numerator is the gross estate situated in the United States and whose denominator is the "entire gross estate." For example, if the deductions under §§2053 and 2054 total $200,000, the entire gross estate is $1 million, the gross estate situated in the United States is $600,000, the deductible amount is $120,000 ($200,000 times $600,000/$1,000,000).

The deduction mechanics operate on a purely pro rata basis, regardless of the extent to which U.S. and foreign assets or activities of the estate are responsible for the deductible items.[62] In the example, the deduction is $120,000, even if the worldwide amount consists of funeral expenses of $5,000 (incurred wholly in a foreign country), administration expenses of $5,000 attributable to the U.S. assets, and $190,000 of administration expenses and casualty losses attributable to the foreign assets.

Charitable pledges are deductible as a claim against the estate if the payment would have been deductible as a charitable contribution under §2106(a)(2), described immediately below, had the pledge been a bequest.[63] Although the statutory language might be construed to subject contributions pursuant to pledges to the apportionment rule, the regulations relieve them of this burden.[64]

2. *Charitable contributions.* Under §2106(a)(2), the estate of a nonresident alien is allowed a deduction for charitable bequests and other transfers, computed in the same manner as the deduction allowed by §2055 for citizen decedents,[65] except:

a. Bequests to or for the use of charitable, educational, religious, and other qualified corporations are deductible only if the donee is a domestic corporation.

b. Bequests to trustees and fraternal societies are deductible only if the gift is to be used "within the United States."[66]

c. Bequests to veterans' organizations, which are deductible under certain circumstances by the estates of resident decedents, are never deductible under §2106.

---

[60] For §§2053 and 2054, see ch. 131.

[61] IRC §2106(a)(1).

[62] Reg. §20.2106-2(a)(2) (immaterial whether amounts to be deducted were incurred or expended within or without United States).

[63] For the deductibility of charitable pledges by the estates of citizens or resident aliens, see supra ¶130.3.4.

[64] Reg. §20.2106-2(a)(1).

[65] For §2055, see ch. 130.

[66] See McAllister's Est. v. CIR, 54 TC 1407, 1415-16 (1970) (acq.) (bequest to Canadian foundation to be used for benefit of Canadian students attending Michigan College of Mining and Technology qualified for deduction; Michigan "wound up with the money").

Although only domestic charitable corporations qualify as donees, there is no geographical restriction on their use of the contributions. By contrast, contributions to a foreign trust or fraternal society are deductible if the contribution is to be used within the United States.

Subject to these limitations, charitable contributions are deductible in full, without regard to the amount of foreign property included in the worldwide estate or used to finance the contributions.[67]

3. *Marital deduction.* The marital deduction is allowed "with respect to property situated in the United States at the time of the decedent's death [in an amount determined] under the principles of section 2056," which governs the marital deduction for estates of citizens and residents.[68] For example, if a nonresident alien dies owning a condominium apartment in Florida, which she bequeaths to her surviving spouse, the apartment is included in the U.S. gross estate, but the estate may be entitled to a marital deduction in an equal amount. However, if the surviving spouse is not a U.S. citizen, the deduction is allowed only if the bequest is to a "qualified domestic trust" or the spouse places the property in such a trust soon after the decedent dies.[69] The purpose and effect of a qualified domestic trust is to ensure that the property will be subjected to the estate tax when it is withdrawn from the trust during the surviving spouse's lifetime or at the spouse's death if it remains in the trust until then.

Before the foregoing rules were enacted in 1988, the marital deduction was never allowed to the estate of a nonresident alien, possibly because the premise underlying the marital deduction—postponement of the estate tax until the surviving spouse dies—was unrealistic from an enforcement perspective when applied to nonresident aliens. However, the deduction was denied even if the surviving spouse was a U.S. citizen or the assets were included in the surviving spouse's gross estate for some other reason (e.g., the property remained in the United States until the second spouse died). The present rules do a better job of ensuring that the marital deduction does not open a means for passing the property from the marital unit to the next generation free of all gift or estate taxes, while providing a route to avoid subjecting the property to tax in the estates of both spouses.

Community property is included in the gross estate only to the extent of the decedent's interest therein.[70] As a result, only one half of the property is included

---

[67] For whether disclosure of foreign-situs property is a condition to a deduction for charitable contributions, see supra note 24.

[68] IRC §2106(a)(3) (applicable to estates of nonresident alien decedents dying after November 11, 1988).

[69] IRC §2056(d), discussed supra ¶129.2.5.

[70] See Lepoutre's Est. v. CIR, 62 TC 84 (1974) (decedent had one half interest in community property as result of antenuptial agreement under French law); Vandenhoeck's Est. v. CIR, 4 TC 125 (1944) (nonresident alien's estate included only one half

in the estate of the first spouse to die, even if neither spouse is a U.S. citizen. The rules therefore carry forward the pre-1948 distinction between the common law and community property systems, which was sharply reduced for citizens and resident aliens when Congress authorized the marital deduction.[71]

¶134.2.5 Computation of Estate Tax and Credits

The tax computation for estates of nonresident aliens closely resembles that used for the estates of U.S. citizens and residents.[72] The tax is the excess of (1) a tentative tax under the §2001(c) unified rate schedule on the sum of the taxable estate and the decedent's adjusted taxable gifts, over (2) a tax on the adjusted taxable gifts alone.[73] The term "adjusted taxable gifts" refers to the sum of all taxable gifts made by the decedent after 1976, exclusive of taxable gifts included in the gross estate.[74]

A unified credit of $13,000 is allowed.[75] It exempts from tax the first $60,000 of the taxable estate, as contrasted to the $600,000 exempted by the unified credit allowed to the estates of citizens and residents.[76] No unified credit is allowed to a nonresident alien in determining gift taxes, and the entire $13,000 credit is thus

---

community property interest in shares of U.S. corporations; "quantum" of ownership determined by French law, where decedent was domiciled); Rev. Rul. 72-443, 1972-2 CB 531 (decedent's estate includes only one half interest in real property located in noncommunity property state but purchased with Norwegian community funds because state recognizes vested interest of surviving spouse in property under Norwegian law).

[71] See supra ¶129.1.

[72] See supra ¶132.3.

[73] IRC §2101(b) (applicable to estates of decedents dying after November 10, 1988). Before 1988, the estates of nonresident aliens were taxed under a special rate schedule at rates ranging from 6 percent on the first $100,000 of taxable estate to 30 percent of the excess over $2 million. IRC §2101(d) (repealed in 1988).

Section 2108 authorizes the President to subject the estates of nonresident aliens to tax at the rates prevailing before 1967 and to impose certain other tax burdens as a retaliatory measure if the alien's country of residence imposes more burdensome estate taxes on U.S. citizens who are not residents of that country. This authority has apparently never been exercised. See generally Ross, United States Taxation of Aliens and Foreign Corporations: The Foreign Investors Tax Act of 1966 and Related Developments, 22 Tax L. Rev. 277, 352-54 (1967). For a parallel income tax provision, see §896, discussed supra ¶66.8.

[74] IRC §2101(c)(1).

[75] IRC §2102(c)(1). See H.R. Rep. No. 1104, 100th Cong., 2d Sess. 116 (Conf. Rep.), reprinted in 1988-3 CB 473, 606 (credit does not depend on proportion of worldwide estate included in U.S. gross estate because Congress wanted "to eliminate the need to determine the nonresident alien's worldwide estate in order to calculate the unified credit").

[76] During the period 1977-1988, the unified credit was $3,600, but its effect—to exempt $60,000—was the same because the estates of nonresident aliens were then taxed at lower rates.

available at death, regardless of whether the decedent made U.S. gifts.[77] The credit is in effect an estate tax, rather than unified, credit.

The credits under §2012 (gift taxes on pre-1977 gifts included in the gross estate) and §2013 (estate tax on estate of earlier decedent from whom decedent received property) are allowed on the same basis as they are to the estates of U.S. citizens and residents.[78] The credit under §2014 for foreign death taxes is not allowed.[79] The §2014 credit, which is allowed only if property is both situated within the foreign country imposing the tax and subject to the U.S. estate tax, is premised on the policy that the responsibility for alleviating international double taxation rests with the decedent's country of citizenship or residence.

The credit under §2011 for state death taxes is allowed, but it is subject to an additional limitation. State taxes are creditable up to the ceiling prescribed by §2011(b) only if all property included in the U.S. gross estate is subject to state death taxes; if any portion of the gross estate is not taxed by any state, the maximum credit is the §2011(b) amount, multiplied by a fraction whose numerator is the property included in the federal gross estate that is subject to state death taxes and whose denominator is the federal gross estate.[80] This limitation was enacted in 1966 to prevent states imposing so-called pick-up taxes, designed to absorb the credit allowed by §2011, from getting a disproportionate share of the federal tax.[81] Assume a nonresident alien's taxable estate consists of a ski lodge (worth $40,000) located in a state imposing a pick-up tax, and shares of a domestic corporation (worth $1,060,000), situated within the United States for federal estate tax purposes but not subject to death taxes in any state. The ceiling under the table given in §2011(b) is $38,800, but because only $40,000 of the taxable estate is subject to state death taxes, the special limitation restricts the credit to $1,411 ($38,800 times $40,000/$1,100,000).

To illustrate the overall computational mechanism, assume a nonresident alien decedent's U.S. gross estate consists of a farm in Minnesota that is worth $1.1 million on the estate tax valuation date; $100,000 of expenses, claims, mortgages, and losses are deductible under §§2053 and 2054 and allocated to the U.S. gross estate, no marital or charitable deduction is allowed, and Minnesota imposes an inheritance tax of $50,000. The taxable estate is $1 million (gross estate of $1.1 million, less deductions of $100,000). If the decedent made no U.S. gifts,

---

[77] If the decedent was formerly a U.S. citizen or resident and claimed any portion of the unified credit on a gift tax return reporting a gift made during the period of citizenship or residence, the unified credit allowed at death is reduced by the credit claimed for gift tax purposes. IRC §2102(c)(3)(B).

[78] IRC §2102(a). See supra ¶132.5 (credit for pre-1977 gift taxes), ¶132.6 (credit for federal estate tax on prior transfers).

[79] For §2014, see supra ¶132.7.

[80] IRC §2102(b). For examples illustrating this limitation, see Reg. §20.2102-1(b)(2). For the credit for state death taxes, see supra ¶132.4.

[81] S. Rep. No. 1707, 89th Cong., 2d Sess. (1966), reprinted in 1966-2 CB 1055, 1094-95.

the tentative tax is $345,800. The unified credit is $13,000, and the credit for state death taxes is $33,200 (lesser of $50,000 of tax paid or maximum credit under §2011(b) of $33,200). The final tax is $299,600 (tentative tax of $345,800, less credits of $13,000 and $33,200).

The computations for nonresident aliens who made U.S. taxable gifts are somewhat less complicated than those for estates of U.S. citizens and residents. Assume the decedent in the example made U.S. taxable gifts of $500,000. If none of the taxable gifts is included in the gross estate, the tentative tax is $400,000 (tax on sum of $1 million and $500,000, less tax on $500,000). The unified credit is $13,000, as in the preceding example, and the credit for state death taxes is also unchanged because the taxable estate has not changed.

As applied to the estates of decedents who made lifetime gifts that are drawn into the gross estate, the simplicity of these procedures masks an unfairness. Assume the decedent's only U.S. gift was a transfer to her children of the Minnesota farm, subject to a retained life estate; the remainder was worth $250,000 at the time of the gift. The farm is included in the gross estate under §2036 at its value on the estate tax valuation date ($1.1 million). Because all taxable gifts are included in the gross estate, adjusted taxable gifts is zero ($250,000 taxable gifts, less $250,000 included in gross estate). The tentative tax is $345,800 (tax under §2001(c) on sum of $1 million and zero, less tax on zero). The credits are $13,000 and $33,200, as in the original example, and the final tax is $299,600. The final estate tax is the same as in the original example, and no credit is given for the tax imposed on the gift of the remainder. The decedent is thus subject to gift and estate taxes on $1,250,000 with respect to the Minnesota farm, whose value may never have exceeded $1 million.[82]

¶134.2.6 Tax on Generation-Skipping Transfers

The generation-skipping transfer (GST) tax applies to three types of transfers:

1. A direct skip, which is an outright gift or bequest to a "skip person" (an individual who is two or more generations younger than the donor or decedent, such as a grandchild or great-grandchild) or a transfer to a trust whose beneficiaries are all skip persons.[83]

---

[82] This anomaly has existed since 1976. The House version of §2101(b) permitted the "gift taxes payable" on post-1976 gifts to be subtracted in computing the estate tax liability of nonresident aliens, but this proposal was changed in conference to an "offset" computed under the estate tax rate schedule for taxable gifts not included in the gross estate. Compare H.R. Rep. No. 1380, 94th Cong., 2d Sess. 14–15 (Conf. Rep.), reprinted in 1976-3 (vol. 3) CB 735, 748–49, with S. Rep. No. 1236, 94th Cong., 2d Sess. 608, reprinted in 1976-3 (vol. 3) CB 807, 958. The failure to provide a similar offset for taxable gifts included in the gross estate may have been inadvertent.

[83] IRC §2612(c), discussed supra ¶133.2.5.

2. A taxable termination, which occurs on the expiration or termination of an interest in a trust if all persons having an interest in the trust immediately thereafter are skip persons.[84]

3. A taxable distribution, which is a distribution from a trust to a skip person.[85]

Generally, every GST is taxed at a flat rate equal to the highest estate tax rate (55 percent), but an exemption insulates up to $1 million in transfers by each transferor from the GST tax.[86]

The basic policy underlying the GST tax is that gratuitous transfers of property should be subject to a transfer tax once for each generation and that the GST tax should apply whenever the beneficial ownership of property passes to a new generation without having been subject to an estate or gift tax at the level of the next oldest generation. For example, if property is transferred in trust to pay the income to the grantor's child for life, with the remainder to the grantor's grandchild, the transfer in trust is subject to the gift or estate tax, but the shift of the possessory interest from the child to the grandchild on the child's death is not; however, the expiration of the child's interest is a taxable termination, and a GST tax is therefore imposed at the child's death. Similarly, if property is bequeathed to a child who immediately gives the property to a grandchild, the bequest is subject to the estate tax, and the gift is subject to the gift tax; if property is bequeathed to a grandchild (a direct skip), the gift tax disappears, but a GST tax is imposed instead.

The GST tax does not explicitly distinguish between resident and nonresident transferors. However, it is a tax in addition to the gift and estate taxes, and it usually applies only to transfers that are or were subject to the gift or estate tax.[87] Assume a nonresident alien bequeaths Blackacre to her son for life, remainder to her grandchildren. For purposes of the GST tax, the bequest is treated as a transfer in trust,[88] and a taxable termination will occur when the son dies because, with the expiration of the son's life estate, skip persons (the grandchildren) will be sole owners of the property. However, the GST tax applies to this taxable termination only if the estate tax applied to the original bequest. For example, if Blackacre is a farm in Minnesota, the property's situs is in the United States, the estate tax applies to the bequest, and the expiration of the son's life estate triggers a GST tax. In contrast, if Blackacre is a meadow in England, the bequest is not subject to the estate tax because the property is not situated in the United States, and the termination of the son's life estate therefore is not subject to the GST tax.

---

[84] IRC §2612(a), discussed supra ¶133.2.6.
[85] IRC §2612(b), discussed supra ¶133.2.7.
[86] See supra ¶133.3.
[87] Reg. §26.2652-1(a)(1). See supra ¶133.2.2.
[88] See supra ¶133.2.12.

The regulations elaborate on the application of the GST tax to transfers by nonresident aliens as follows:

1. *Direct skip.* The GST tax applies to a direct skip only if the transfer is subject to a gift or estate tax.[89] For example, if a nonresident alien transfers Minnesota farmland to her grandson by gift, the transfer is subject to the gift tax because the property is located in the United States, and the transfer is also subject to the GST tax because the grandson is a skip person.[90]

2. *Taxable distributions and terminations.* The GST tax applies to a taxable distribution or taxable termination only "to the extent that the initial transfer of property to the trust by a NRA transferor, whether during life or at death, was subject to the Federal estate or gift tax."[91] For example, if a nonresident alien bequeaths Minnesota farmland in trust to pay the income to the decedent's child for life and to distribute the corpus to the decedent's grandchildren on the child's death, a taxable termination will occur on the child's death, and the GST tax will then apply to the value of the trust, even if the trustee sells the land during the child's lifetime and, at the child's death, the trust corpus consists entirely of property located outside the United States.

3. *Transfers in trust only partially subject to U.S. transfer trust.* If a nonresident alien's transfer in trust is only partially subject to the gift or estate tax (e.g., because only part of the property is situated in the United States), the GST tax applies to a fractional portion of the trust.[92] The fraction is (1) the excess of the value of the property transferred in trust over the sum of the "nontax portion" and the GST exemption allocated to the transfer, divided by (2) the value of the property. The property's value is the fair market value at the time of the transfer in trust, less any gift or estate tax on the transfer that is paid from the trust and any allowable charitable deduction.[93] The nontax portion is the value, at the time of the transfer in trust, of the property that is not subject to the gift or estate tax.[94] The fraction is generally determined at the time of the transfer subject to the gift or estate tax, but it must be recomputed if additional GST exemption is subsequently allocated to the trust.[95]

Assume a nonresident alien decedent bequeaths property in trust, consisting of stock of a publicly traded Delaware corporation worth $100 on the estate tax valuation date and bonds of various publicly traded corporations worth $400; the bonds are not included in the U.S. gross estate because interest on them is

---

[89] Reg. §26.2663-2(b)(1). See Neumann's Est. v. CIR, 106 TC No. 10 (1996) (although §2663(2) directs Treasury to promulgate regulations on application of GST tax to transfers by nonresident aliens, tax on direct skips was self executing and thus applied to transfers before issuance of regulations).

[90] Reg. §26.2663-2(d) Ex. 1.

[91] Reg. §26.2663-2(b)(2).

[92] Reg. §26.2663-2(b)(1).

[93] Reg. §26.2642-1(c).

[94] Reg. §26.2663-2(c)(2).

[95] See Reg. §26.2663-2(d) Ex. 4.

portfolio interest.[96] If $50 of GST exemption is allocated to the trust, the fraction is 0.1. The numerator is $50—the estate tax value of the trust property ($500), less the sum of the value of the nontaxable bonds ($400) and the GST exemption ($50), and the denominator is $500. If, for example, the trust is for the benefit of the decedent's child for life, remainder to the decedent's grandchildren, the GST tax will apply to one tenth of the value of the trust as it exists at the time of the taxable termination that will occur on the child's death.[97]

¶134.2.7 Tax Treaties

The gift, estate, and generation-skipping tax liability of a nonresident alien may be affected by a tax convention between the United States and the country of which the individual is a citizen or domiciliary.[98] Generalizations about treaties are perilous because the treaties vary. Even when two or more treaties employ identical language, the meaning of particular phrases may be affected by an interpretation peculiar to a particular treaty contained in a contemporaneous memorandum of understanding between the parties, a representation by the State Department when the treaty was proposed to the Senate for ratification, or a Senate reservation that accompanied ratification.

1. *Taxes covered.* Most treaties cover only the federal estate tax, but more recent treaties also apply to the federal gift tax, and treaties adopted after 1976 often include the generation-skipping tax as well.[99]

2. *Situs treaties.* Treaties adopted during the first 20 years or so after World War II generally allowed each country to apply its own laws in determining questions of citizenship and domicile, but sought to avoid double taxation by prescribing uniform rules to determine the situs of property and assigning ex-

---

[96] See Reg. §26.2663-2(d) Ex. 2.

[97] See Reg. §26.2663-2(d) Ex. 5.

[98] The United States has death tax treaties with the following countries: Australia, Austria, Canada (effective only for estates of persons dying before 1995), Denmark, Finland, France, Germany, Greece, Ireland, Italy, Japan, the Netherlands, Norway, South Africa, Sweden, Switzerland, and the United Kingdom. Gift tax treaties are in force with Australia, Austria, Denmark, France, Germany, Japan, Sweden, and the United Kingdom. IRS Pub. No. 448, Federal Estate and Gift Taxes 26, 39 (Rev. Aug. 1992); Fogarasi, Gordon, Venuti & Renfroe, Current Status of U.S. Tax Treaties, 25 Tax Mgmt. Int'l J. 523 (1996).See Kanter, The United States Estate Tax Treaty Program, 9 Tax L. Rev. 401 (1954).

Tax treaties do not affect a nonresident alien's liability for state or local gift or death taxes.

[99] For example, the treaty with Germany, which was concluded in 1980, covers the U.S. estate, gift, and GST taxes. Estate, Inheritance, and Gift Tax Convention, Dec. 3, 1980, United States-Germany, art. 2(1)(a) [hereinafter U.S.-Germany Treaty]. See PS-73-88, 1993-1 CB 867 (treaty provisions referring to 1976 version of generation-skipping transfer tax also apply to 1986 version of tax).

clusive taxing authority to the country of the situs. For a nonresident alien, the situs rules of such a treaty supersede any conflicting U.S. situs rules.

These treaties often entitle a nonresident alien to a specific exemption in an amount bearing the same ratio to the exemption that the value of the taxable property bears to the value of the property that would be subject to U.S. tax if the nonresident was domiciled here. However, the statutory specific exemption was replaced in 1976 with the unified credit, which, by statute, is $192,800 for the estates of citizens and residents and $13,000 for the estates of nonresident aliens. In *Burghardt's Estate v. CIR*, the Tax Court held that the term "specific exemption" was used in our treaty with Italy "merely to describe the mechanism whereby small estates are excluded from the scope of the United States estate tax" and that it encompasses the unified credit allowed for citizens and resident aliens.[100] The court rejected the IRS' contention that the unified credit for estates of nonresident aliens, which shields $60,000 of the taxable estate against tax, has the same practical effect as the pre-1977 $60,000 specific exemption and therefore fully satisfies treaty provisions referring to the specific exemption.[101] Section 2102(c)(3)(A), enacted in 1988, provides that "to the extent required under any treaty obligation of the United States," the unified credit equals $192,800, multiplied by the ratio of the U.S. gross estate to the entire gross estate. The legislative history indicates that this provision was intended to codify the holding in Burghardt's Estate.[102]

3. *Domicile treaties.* More recent gift and estate tax treaties have focused on the domicile rules of the signatory countries. These treaties assign a single fiscal domicile to persons who are claimed by both countries as domiciled therein and grant primary taxing authority to the designated country. A typical example is the treaty with Germany (concluded in 1980), under which the domicile of a donor or decedent is first determined under the internal laws of each country.[103] For this purpose, a donor or decedent is considered domiciled in the United States if the individual is a U.S. citizen or a U.S. resident under the U.S. rules. If a donor or decedent is domiciled in both countries, according to their separate rules, the individual is usually assigned a domicile in just one of countries by a series of tie-breaking rules. However, a donor or decedent who is a citizen of one

---

[100] Burghardt's Est. v. CIR, 80 TC 705 (1983), aff'd without opinion, 734 F2d 3 (3d Cir. 1984). See Mudry v. US, 11 Cl. Ct. 207, 86-2 USTC ¶13,706 (1986) (same under similar provision in treaty with Switzerland).

[101] Rev. Rul. 81-303, 1981-2 CB 255, revoked by Rev. Rul. 90-101, 1990-2 CB 315.

[102] H.R. Rep. No. 795, 100th Cong., 2d Sess. 594 (1988). See Rev. Rul. 90-101, supra note 101 (estate tax conventions with Australia, Finland, Greece, Italy, Japan, and Norway contain provisions similar to those in Italian and Swiss treaties construed in *Burghardt's Est.* and *Mudry*, and these provisions are similarly construed). See also Arnaud's Est. v. CIR, 90 TC 649 (1988) (although French treaty allows estate of French resident a marital deduction computed as if decedent were U.S. resident and although this requires that tentative tax be calculated by rates for U.S. decedents, unified credit is that for nonresident decedents under §2102(c), not credit for resident decedents).

[103] U.S.-Germany Treaty, supra note 99, at art. 4.

of the countries is considered domiciled in that country, even if the other country also claims the individual as a domiciliary and would win out under the tie-breaking rules, unless the individual is a citizen of both countries or has been domiciled in the noncitizenship country for more than five years.

Under the treaty with Germany, once the donor or decedent has been assigned a domicile in just one of the countries, that country has the right to tax the individual's worldwide gifts or estate. The nondomiciliary country may tax a narrow range of property considered situated in that country, including only "immovable" (real) property in the country, assets of a permanent establishment (fixed place of business) of the decedent in the country, and partnership interests (but only in part if the partnership holds assets other than real property and assets of a permanent establishment located in the taxing country).[104] The nondomiciliary country must allow certain deductions, but these deductions are essentially those allowed by statue under U.S. law.[105]

The treaty allows the United States to impose the gift and estate taxes on the worldwide gifts and estates of U.S. citizens, even if the treaty assigns the individual a domicile in Germany.[106] However, when the United States exercises this authority, it must allow credit for the German tax against the U.S. gift or estate tax, and the credit must include the German tax on property not situated in Germany under either the U.S. or treaty situs rules.[107]

¶134.3 U.S. CITIZENS RESIDENT IN U.S. POSSESSIONS

Sections 2208 and 2501(b) state that a U.S. citizen who resides in and is a citizen of a U.S. possession is treated as a citizen of the United States for estate and gift tax purposes unless the individual acquired U.S. citizenship solely by reason of being a citizen of the possession or by birth or residence therein.[1] These provisions seemingly announce a self-evident, though curiously limited proposition because, generally, all U.S. citizens, regardless of place of residence or the source of citizenship, are "citizens" as that term is used in the Code. In 1948, however, the Tax Court held that in the absence of a "clear expression" of congressional intention to impose the federal estate tax on U.S. citizens who were also citizens and residents of Puerto Rico, the historic policy of not treating

---

[104] Id. at arts. 5-9.

[105] Id. at art. 10. The application of the deduction rules may, however, be modified somewhat. For example, administration expenses and debts are allowed under the treaty to the extent specifically traceable to the property being taxed, whereas the statutory deduction is for a ratable share of all otherwise deductible items.

[106] Id. at art. 11(1)(a).

[107] Id. at art. 11(2)(b).

[1] The U.S. possessions are American Samoa, Guam, the Northern Mariana Islands, Puerto Rico, and the U.S. Virgin Islands. See supra ¶67.1. For the income tax rules applicable to citizens and residents of U.S. possessions, see supra ¶¶67.3, 67.4, 67.5.

Puerto Rico "as a source of revenue for Federal uses elsewhere" was controlling.[2] The same principle was applied in 1955 to a U.S. citizen who was a citizen and resident of the Virgin Islands at death.[3]

The resulting opportunity to escape both taxation and cold winters by moving to a U.S. possession was terminated in 1958 by the enactment of §§2208 and 2501(b). Under present law, "a United States citizen who moves from the United States to one of the possessions will continue to be treated for estate and gift tax purposes in the same manner in which he would have been treated if he had remained in the United States."[4] In short, the flag follows the citizen, and the Code follows the flag. The 1958 changes, however, apply only to persons who acquired U.S. citizenship "completely independently of their connections with the possessions"; the status of persons whose U.S. citizenship was a by-product of their connection with a U.S. possession was left open for further study.

In 1960, Congress concluded that persons with derivative U.S. citizenship should be treated as nonresident aliens for estate and gift tax purposes.[5] This legislative decision is embodied in §2209 (estate tax) and §2501(c) (gift tax), which apply to residents of a U.S. possession who acquired U.S. citizenship solely by reason of being a citizen of the possession or by birth or residence therein.[6] Donors qualifying under §2501(c), like nonresident aliens generally, are subject to the federal gift tax only on gifts of real property and tangible personal property located in one of the states of the United States or the District of Columbia.[7] Similarly, the estates of decedents qualifying under §2209 are subject to the estate tax only on property situated in the United States under the situs rules applicable to the estate taxation of nonresident aliens.[8] However, for estate tax purposes, the estate of a decedent subject to §2209 is entitled to a unified credit equal to the greater of (1) $13,000 (the unified credit usually allowed for estates of nonresi-

---

[2] Smallwood's Est. v. Cir, 11 TC 740, 741 (1948) (estate tax not imposed on person who was U.S. citizen by birth and citizen and domiciliary of Puerto Rico at death).

[3] Fairchild's Est. v. CIR, 24 TC 408 (1955) (acq.).

[4] Conf. Rep. No. 2632, 85th Cong., 2d Sess. 41, reprinted in 1958-3 CB 1188, 1228.

[5] See generally S. Rep. No. 1767, 86th Cong., 2d Sess., reprinted in 1960-2 CB 829, 832-34; Segall, Kelley, & McConnell, Estate Planning Comes to Puerto Rico, 55 ABAJ 464 (1969). For derivative citizenship resulting from birth or residence in a U.S. possession, see Gordon & Mailman, Immigration Law and Procedure §12.6 (Matthew Bender rev. ed. 1992).

[6] See Reg. §20.2209-1 Exs. 1-5; §25.2501-1(d) Exs. 1-5; Rev. Rul. 74-25, 1974-1 CB 284 (§2209 applies to person who was resident of one possession but acquired U.S. citizenship solely by reason of birth in another possession). The regulations construe the term "resident" as referring to domicile. Reg. §§20.2209-1, 25.2501-1(d). The term is similarly construed for other estate and gift purposes. See supra ¶134.2.1.

Section 2209 eliminates the exemption from federal estate tax mandated by CIR v. Rivera's Est., 214 F2d 60 (2d Cir. 1954) (estate of Puerto Rican resident and citizen with derivative U.S. citizenship not subject to federal estate tax).

[7] See supra ¶134.2.2.

[8] See supra ¶134.2.3.

dent aliens) or (2) $46,800 multiplied by a fraction whose numerator is the federal gross estate and whose denominator is the worldwide gross estate.[9]

¶134.4 TAX-MOTIVATED EXPATRIATION

Americans who give up U.S. citizenship and establish a foreign domicile become nonresident aliens for purposes of the U.S. gift and estate taxes, but the usual rules for nonresident alien donors and decedents are modified if the expatriation was tax-motivated.[1] The modifications are most significant under the gift tax, where a tax-motivated expatriate loses the benefit of the usual exemption of gifts of intangible property. The principal estate tax modification is that the gross estate includes all or part of the value of stock of a foreign corporation that owns U.S. property.

1. *Alien donors and decedents subject to modifications.* The modifications apply to a nonresident alien donor or decedent if the individual lost U.S. citizenship during the 10 years preceding the gift or the date of death and avoidance of federal income, gift, estate, or generation-skipping taxes was one of the principal purposes for the loss of citizenship. Two procedural buttresses are provided.[2] If the IRS establishes that it is reasonable to believe that the individual's loss of citizenship would result in a "substantial reduction" in gift or estate taxes, the taxpayer has the burden of proving that tax avoidance was not one of the principal purposes of the loss of citizenship.[3] Also, a former citizen is treated as having a principal purpose to avoid U.S. tax, regardless of actual motivation for loss of citizenship, if (1) the person's average annual net income tax exceeded $100,000 over the five taxable years ending before the loss of citizenship or (2) the person's net worth is at least $500,000 when citizenship is lost.[4]

The modifications also apply to an alien who has never been a U.S. citizen but was once a lawful permanent resident of the United States. Specifically, an alien is treated as a former citizen for purposes of the modifying rules in two situations: (1) where the individual ceases to be a lawful permanent resident of the United States and was a lawful permanent resident for at least eight of the fifteen years ending with the year in which residence is relinquished, and (2) where the individual becomes a resident of a country having a tax treaty with the United States, does not waive treaty benefits allowable to residents of that country, and was a lawful permanent resident for at least eight years during the

---

[9] IRC §2102(c)(2).

[1] IRC §§2107, 2501(a)(3). See Notice 97-19, 1997-10 IRB 40 (guidance on 1996 amendments to §§2107 and 2501(a)(3)). For parallel income tax rules, see supra ¶65.4.

[2] IRC §§2107(a), 2501(a)(3)(A).

[3] IRC §§2107(d), 2501(a)(4).

[4] IRC §2107(d) (before amendment in 1996), §2501(a)(3)(A) (before amendment in 1996).

15-year period ending with the year in which residence in the treaty country begins.[5] An alien caught by this rule is treated as having lost citizenship when lawful permanent residence in the U.S. ends or residence in the treaty country begins. Whether avoiding U.S. taxes was a principal purpose of this constructive loss of citizenship is determined by the same rules that apply to actual losses of citizenship. For example, if an alien giving up lawful permanent residence had average annual U.S. tax liability of more than $100,000 over the preceding five years and then had a net worth of at least $500,000, the constructive loss of citizenship is deemed tax-motivated, regardless of actual purpose.[6]

2. *Gift tax modifications.* If a donor lost citizenship (actually or constructively) during the 10 years preceding the gift and is found to have done so to avoid U.S. taxes, the donor is denied the benefit of the rule under which a gift of intangible property by a nonresident alien is usually exempted from the gift tax.[7] However, whether the property is tangible or intangible, taxable gifts are restricted to property situated in the United States.[8] The situs of property is determined under rules resembling those used in applying the estate tax to nonresident aliens.[9] Stock of a domestic corporation, as well as real and tangible personal property located in the United States, is considered situated in the United States and is therefore subject to gift tax if given during the tainted 10-year period by a tax-motivated expatriate. Also, debt instruments issued by U.S. obligors (including deposits in U.S. banks) have a U.S. situs for this purpose, even though they are not usually considered situated in the United States when held by other nonresident aliens.[10] The gift tax resulting from the expatriate rules may be offset by credit for foreign gift taxes on the same gift.[11]

However, a tax-motivated expatriate is not taxed on gifts of property situated outside the United States. An individual who renounces citizenship for the purpose of avoiding gift taxes thus succeeds in this objective, even if gifts are made during the ensuing 10 years, so long as the donor takes care to shift the situs of property outside the United States before giving it away (e.g., by selling

---

[5] IRC §877(e) (applicable to aliens who, after February 5, 1996, cease being U.S. residents or acquire residence in a treaty country). An alien ceases being a lawful permanent resident of the United States only if the right of permanent residence is revoked or is administratively or judicially determined to be abandoned. IRC §§877(e)(1), 7701(b)(6)(B). For purposes of the eight of fifteen test, treated as a lawful U.S. resident for any year for which he or she is entitled to treaty benefits as a resident of a treaty country.

[6] IRC §877(a)(2). A former citizen may exempted from this irrebuttable presumption if, for example, he or she was born a dual citizen. IRC §877(c), discussed supra text accompanying note 4. This exemption is not available to lawful permanent resident aliens or former lawful permanent residents. IRC §877(e)(3)(C).

[7] IRC §2501(a)(3)(A).

[8] IRC §2511(a).

[9] IRC §2511(b); Reg. §25.2511-3(b). For the estate tax situs rules, see supra ¶134.2.3.

[10] IRC §2511(b)(2); Reg. §25.2511-3(b)(4).

[11] IRC §2501(a)(3)(D) (effective for persons losing citizenship after February 5, 1996).

U.S. securities, depositing the proceeds in an account in a foreign bank, and writing a check to the donee from this account). However, a sale of U.S. property within 10 years of a tax-motivated expatriation subjects the taxpayer to U.S. income tax on gain realized in the sale.[12] Thus, a donor making a gift within the tainted 10-year period can easily avoid the gift tax or the income tax, but usually not both.[13]

3. *Estate tax modifications.* If a tax-motivated expatriate dies within 10 years after losing citizenship, the estate tax is imposed only on property situated in the United States, just as for the estates of other nonresident aliens, but with one modification.[14] The decedent's shareholdings in a foreign corporation are included in the U.S. gross estate, in whole or in part, if the decedent (1) owned at least 10 percent of the voting corporation's stock, actually or indirectly through other foreign corporations, and (2) owned more than 50 percent (by vote or value) of the stock actually, indirectly, or constructively through family members and related entities.[15] The amount included in the gross estate is the value of the stock owned actually or indirectly, multiplied by a fraction whose numerator is the value of the corporation's assets situated in the United States and whose denominator is the value of the corporation's worldwide assets. For purposes of this rule, the decedent is deemed to own at death any stock included in the gross estate under §§2035-2038.

Assume a nonresident alien decedent was sole shareholder of *X* Corp., a foreign corporation whose only assets are a portfolio of publicly traded stocks of domestic corporations. Because stock issued by a foreign corporation is generally considered not situated in the United States, regardless of the location of the corporation's business or assets, the *X* stock is not included in the U.S. gross estate unless the rules for tax-motivated expatriations apply. However, if the decedent lost U.S. citizenship for a tax-avoidance purpose during the 10 years preceding death, the *X* stock is included in the gross estate because the decedent satisfied the 10 percent and 50 percent ownership tests and the corporation's assets consist solely of property situated in the United States (stock of domestic corporations). In contrast, assume *X*'s assets consisted of stock and bonds of domestic corporations. Portfolio debt instruments of domestic corporation are deemed not situated in the United States,[16] and because only part of *X*'s assets have a U.S. situs, only part of the *X* stock is included in the gross estate under the rules for tax-motivated expatriates.

---

[12] IRC §877, discussed supra ¶65.4.

[13] With respect to tangible personal property located in the United States at the time of the expatriation, it is apparently possible to avoid both taxes by removing the property from the United States before making the gift. However, the Treasury may, by regulations, treat the removal as a taxable sale for income tax purposes. IRC §877(d)(2)(E).

[14] IRC §2107(a)(1).

[15] IRC §2107(b). For indirect and constructive ownership of stock, see §§958(a), (b), discussed supra ¶68.2.2 text accompanying notes 23-32.

[16] See supra ¶134.2.3 text accompanying notes 40-49.

The tax computation for the estate of an expatriate is generally the same as for other nonresident aliens. The tax is determined under the unified rate schedule of §2001(c).[17] A unified credit of $13,000 is allowed, and other credits are allowed subject to the same restrictions that apply to nonresident aliens' estates generally.[18] Also, a credit is allowed for foreign death taxes on property that is included in the gross estate solely because of the rules for expatriates.[19]

---

[17] IRC §2107(a).

[18] IRC §2107(c).

[19] IRC §2107(c)(2). The credit for taxes paid to a particular foreign country may not exceed the lesser of (1) the foreign death tax ratably allocable to property included in the gross estate solely because of the expatriate rules or (2) that property's proportionate share of the increase in U.S. estate tax resulting from the expatriate rules.

Table of Cases

[References are to paragraphs (¶) and notes (n.).]

[References are to paragraphs (¶) and notes (n.).]

[References are to paragraphs (¶) and notes (n.).]

[References are to paragraphs (¶) and notes (n.).]

[References are to paragraphs (¶) and notes (n.).]

[References are to paragraphs (¶) and notes (n.)]

Table of IRC Sections

[References are to paragraphs (¶) and notes (n.).]

[References are to paragraphs (¶) and notes (n.).]

[References are to paragraphs (¶) and notes (n.).]

[References are to paragraphs (¶) and notes (n.).]

[References are to paragraphs (¶) and notes (n.).]

[References are to paragraphs (¶) and notes (n.).]

[References are to paragraphs (¶) and notes (n.).]

[References are to paragraphs (¶) and notes (n.).]

[References are to paragraphs (¶) and notes (n.).]

TABLE OF IRC SECTIONS

[References are to paragraphs (¶) and notes (n.).]

[References are to paragraphs (¶) and notes (n.).]

[References are to paragraphs (¶) and notes (n.).]

[References are to paragraphs (¶) and notes (n.).]

[References are to paragraphs (¶) and notes (n.).]

[References are to paragraphs (¶) and notes (n.).]

[References are to paragraphs (¶) and notes (n.).]

[References are to paragraphs (¶) and notes (n.).]

[References are to paragraphs (¶) and notes (n.).]

[References are to paragraphs (¶) and notes (n.).]

[References are to paragraphs (¶) and notes (n.).]

[References are to paragraphs (¶) and notes (n.).]

[References are to paragraphs (¶) and notes (n.).]

Index

[References are to paragraphs (¶).]